Lecture Notes in Computer Science 11749

More information about this series at http://www.springer.com/series/7409

David Lamas · Fernando Loizides ·
Lennart Nacke · Helen Petrie ·
Marco Winckler · Panayiotis Zaphiris (Eds.)

Human-Computer Interaction – INTERACT 2019

17th IFIP TC 13 International Conference
Paphos, Cyprus, September 2–6, 2019
Proceedings, Part IV

 Springer

Editors
David Lamas
Tallinn University
Tartu, Estonia

Lennart Nacke
University of Waterloo
Waterloo, ON, Canada

Marco Winckler
Nice Sophia Antipolis University
Sophia Antipolis, France

Fernando Loizides
Cardiff University
Cardiff, UK

Helen Petrie
University of York
York, UK

Panayiotis Zaphiris
Cyprus University of Technology
Limassol, Cyprus

ISSN 0302-9743 ISSN 1611-3349 (electronic)
Lecture Notes in Computer Science
ISBN 978-3-030-29389-5 ISBN 978-3-030-29390-1 (eBook)
https://doi.org/10.1007/978-3-030-29390-1

LNCS Sublibrary: SL3 – Information Systems and Applications, incl. Internet/Web, and HCI

This Springer imprint is published by the registered company Springer Nature Switzerland AG
The registered company address is: Gewerbestrasse 11, 6330 Cham, Switzerland

Foreword

The 17th IFIP TC13 International Conference on Human-Computer Interaction, INTERACT 2019, took place during September 2–6, 2019, in Paphos, Cyprus. This conference was held at the Coral Beach Hotel & Resort. The conference was co-sponsored by the Cyprus University of Technology and Tallinn University, in cooperation with ACM and ACM SIGCHI.

The International Federation for Information Processing (IFIP) was created in 1960 under the auspices of UNESCO. The Technical Committee 13 (TC13) of the IFIP aims at developing the science and technology of human-computer interaction (HCI). TC13 has representatives from 32 countries, 2 international organizations, apart from 14 expert members and observers. TC13 started the series of INTERACT conferences in 1984. These conferences have been an important showcase for researchers and practitioners in the field of HCI. Situated under the open, inclusive umbrella of the IFIP, INTERACT has been a truly international in its spirit and has attracted researchers from several countries and cultures. The venues of the INTERACT conferences over the years bear a testimony to this inclusiveness.

INTERACT 2019 continued the INTERACT conscious efforts to lower barriers that prevent people from developing countries to participate in conferences. Thinkers and optimists believe that all regions of the world can achieve human development goals. Information and communication technologies (ICTs) can support this process and empower people to achieve their full potential. Today ICT products have many new users and many new uses, but also present new challenges and provide new opportunities. It is no surprise that HCI researchers are showing great interest in these emergent users. INTERACT 2019 provided a platform to explore these challenges and opportunities, but also made it easier for people from developing countries to participate.

Furthermore, hosting INTERACT 2019 in a small country with a small HCI community presented an opportunity to expose the local industry and academia to the concepts of HCI and user-centered design. The rich history and culture of the island of Cyprus provided a strong networking atmosphere and collaboration opportunities.

Students represent the future of our community. They bring in new energy, enthusiasm, and fresh ideas. However, it is often hard for students to participate in international conferences. INTERACT 2019 made special efforts to bring students to the conference. The conference had low registration costs, and thanks to our sponsors, we could provide several travel grants.

Finally, great research is the heart of a good conference. Like its predecessors, INTERACT 2019 aimed to bring together high-quality research. As a multidisciplinary field, HCI requires interaction and discussion among diverse people with different interests and backgrounds. The beginners and the experienced, theoreticians and practitioners, and people from diverse disciplines and different countries gathered together in Paphos to learn from each other and to contribute to each other's growth.

We thank all the authors who chose INTERACT 2019 as the venue to publish their research.

We received a total of 669 submissions distributed in 2 peer reviewed tracks, 4 curated tracks, and 4 juried tracks. Of these, the following contributions were accepted:

- 111 Full Papers (peer reviewed)
- 55 Short Papers (peer reviewed)
- 7 Industry Case Studies (curated)
- 3 Courses (curated)
- 9 Demonstrations (curated)
- 18 Interactive Posters (juried)
- 2 Panels (curated)
- 9 Workshops (juried)
- 1 Field Trips (juried)
- 17 Doctoral Consortium (juried)

The acceptance rate for contributions received in the peer-reviewed tracks was 29% for full papers and 28% for short papers. In addition to full papers and short papers, the present proceedings feature contributions accepted in the form of industry case studies, courses, demonstrations, interactive posters, panels, and description of accepted workshops. The contributions submitted to workshops were published in adjunct proceedings.

INTERACT 2019 innovated the reviewing process with the introduction of sub-committees. Each subcommittee had a chair and set of associated chairs who were in charge of coordinating the reviewing process with the help of expert reviewers. Hereafter we list the ten subcommittees of INTERACT 2019:

- Accessibility and Assistive Technologies
- Design for Business and Safety/Critical Interactive Systems
- Design of Interactive Entertainment Systems
- HCI Education and Curriculum
- Information Visualization
- Interaction Design for Culture and Development
- Interactive Systems Technologies and Engineering
- Methodologies for User-Centred Design
- Social Interaction and Mobile HCI
- Understanding Human Aspects of HCI

The final decision on acceptance or rejection of full papers was taken in a Program Committee meeting held in London, United Kingdom in March 2019. The full papers chairs, the subcommittee chairs, and the associate chairs participated in this meeting. The meeting discussed a consistent set of criteria to deal with inevitable differences among the large number of reviewers. The final decisions on other tracks were made by the corresponding track chairs and reviewers, often after electronic meetings and discussions.

INTERACT 2019 was made possible by the persistent efforts across several months by 10 subcommittees chairs, 62 associated chairs, 28 track chairs, and 510 reviewers. We thank them all.

September 2019   Panayiotis Zaphiris
David Lamas

IFIP TC13 (http://ifip-tc13.org/)

Established in 1989, the International Federation for Information Processing Technical Committee on Human–Computer Interaction (IFIP TC 13) is an international committee of 32 member national societies and 10 Working Groups, representing specialists of the various disciplines contributing to the field of human-computer interaction. This includes (among others) human factors, ergonomics, cognitive science, computer science, and design. INTERACT is its flagship conference of IFIP TC 13, staged biennially in different countries around the world. The first INTERACT conference was held in 1984 running triennially and became a biennial event in 1993.

IFIP TC 13 aims to develop the science, technology, and societal aspects of HCI by encouraging empirical research; promoting the use of knowledge and methods from the human sciences in design and evaluation of computer systems; promoting a better understanding of the relation between formal design methods and system usability and acceptability; developing guidelines, models, and methods by which designers may provide better human-oriented computer systems; and, cooperating with other groups, inside and outside IFIP, to promote user-orientation and humanization in systems design. Thus, TC 13 seeks to improve interactions between people and computers, to encourage the growth of HCI research and its practice in industry and to disseminate these benefits worldwide.

The main orientation is to place the users at the center of the development process. Areas of study include: the problems people face when interacting with computers; the impact of technology deployment on people in individual and organizational contexts; the determinants of utility, usability, acceptability, learnability, and user experience; the appropriate allocation of tasks between computers and users especially in the case of automation; modeling the user, their tasks, and the interactive system to aid better system design; and harmonizing the computer to user characteristics and needs.

While the scope is thus set wide, with a tendency toward general principles rather than particular systems, it is recognized that progress will only be achieved through both general studies to advance theoretical understanding and specific studies on practical issues (e.g., interface design standards, software system resilience, documentation, training material, appropriateness of alternative interaction technologies, design guidelines, the problems of integrating interactive systems to match system needs, and organizational practices, etc.).

In 2015, TC13 approved the creation of a Steering Committee (SC) for the INTERACT conference. The SC is now in place, chaired by Anirudha Joshi and is responsible for:

- Promoting and maintaining the INTERACT conference as the premiere venue for researchers and practitioners interested in the topics of the conference (this requires a refinement of the topics above)
- Ensuring the highest quality for the contents of the event

- Setting up the bidding process to handle the future INTERACT conferences (decision is made up at TC 13 level)
- Providing advice to the current and future chairs and organizers of the INTERACT conference
- Providing data, tools, and documents about previous conferences to the future conference organizers
- Selecting the reviewing system to be used throughout the conference (as this impacts the entire set of reviewers)
- Resolving general issues involved with the INTERACT conference
- Capitalizing history (good and bad practices)

In 1999, TC 13 initiated a special IFIP Award, the Brian Shackel Award, for the most outstanding contribution in the form of a refereed paper submitted to and delivered at each INTERACT. The award draws attention to the need for a comprehensive human-centered approach in the design and use of information technology in which the human and social implications have been taken into account. In 2007, IFIP TC 13 launched an Accessibility Award to recognize an outstanding contribution in HCI with international impact dedicated to the field of accessibility for disabled users. In 2013, IFIP TC 13 launched the Interaction Design for International Development (IDID) Award that recognizes the most outstanding contribution to the application of interactive systems for social and economic development of people in developing countries. Since the process to decide the award takes place after papers are sent to the publisher for publication, the awards are not identified in the proceedings.

This year a special agreement has been made with the *International Journal of Behaviour and Information Technology* (published by Taylor and Francis) with Panos Markopoulos as editor in chief. In this agreement, authors of BIT whose papers are within the field of HCI are offered the opportunity to present their work at the INTERACT conference. Reciprocally, a selection of papers submitted and accepted for presentation at INTERACT are offered the opportunity to extend their contribution to be published in BIT.

IFIP TC 13 also recognizes pioneers in the area of HCI. An IFIP TC 13 pioneer is one who, through active participation in IFIP Technical Committees or related IFIP groups, has made outstanding contributions to the educational, theoretical, technical, commercial, or professional aspects of analysis, design, construction, evaluation, and use of interactive systems. IFIP TC 13 pioneers are appointed annually and awards are handed over at the INTERACT conference.

IFIP TC 13 stimulates working events and activities through its Working Groups (WGs). Working Groups consist of HCI experts from many countries, who seek to expand knowledge and find solutions to HCI issues and concerns within their domains. The list of Working Groups and their area of interest is given below.

WG13.1 (Education in HCI and HCI Curricula) aims to improve HCI education at all levels of higher education, coordinate and unite efforts to develop HCI curricula, and promote HCI teaching.

WG13.2 (Methodology for User-Centered System Design) aims to foster research, dissemination of information and good practice in the methodical application of HCI to software engineering.

WG13.3 (HCI and Disability) aims to make HCI designers aware of the needs of people with disabilities and encourage the development of information systems and tools permitting adaptation of interfaces to specific users.

WG13.4 (also WG2.7) (User Interface Engineering) investigates the nature, concepts, and construction of user interfaces for software systems, using a framework for reasoning about interactive systems and an engineering model for developing user interfaces.

WG 13.5 (Human Error, Resilience, Reliability, Safety and System Development) seeks a framework for studying human factors relating to systems failure, develops leading-edge techniques in hazard analysis and safety engineering of computer-based systems, and guides international accreditation activities for safety-critical systems.

WG13.6 (Human-Work Interaction Design) aims at establishing relationships between extensive empirical work-domain studies and HCI design. It will promote the use of knowledge, concepts, methods, and techniques that enable user studies to procure a better apprehension of the complex interplay between individual, social, and organizational contexts and thereby a better understanding of how and why people work in the ways that they do.

WG13.7 (Human–Computer Interaction and Visualization) aims to establish a study and research program that will combine both scientific work and practical applications in the fields of HCI and Visualization. It integrates several additional aspects of further research areas, such as scientific visualization, data mining, information design, computer graphics, cognition sciences, perception theory, or psychology, into this approach.

WG13.8 (Interaction Design and International Development) is currently working to reformulate its aims and scope.

WG13.9 (Interaction Design and Children) aims to support practitioners, regulators, and researchers to develop the study of interaction design and children across international contexts.

WG13.10 (Human-Centered Technology for Sustainability) aims to promote research, design, development, evaluation, and deployment of human-centered technology to encourage sustainable use of resources in various domains.

New Working Groups are formed as areas of significance in HCI arise. Further information is available on the IFIP TC13 website: http://ifip-tc13.org/.

IFIP TC13 Members

Officers

Chair

Philippe Palanque, France

Vice-chair for Awards

Paula Kotze, South Africa

Vice-chair for Communications

Helen Petrie, UK

Vice-chair for Growth and Reach Out INTERACT Steering Committee Chair

Jan Gulliksen, Sweden

Vice-chair for Working Groups

Simone D. J. Barbosa, Brazil

Treasurer

Virpi Roto, Finland

Secretary

Marco Winckler, France

INTERACT Steering Committee Chair

Anirudha Joshi

Country Representatives

Australia
Henry B. L. Duh
Australian Computer Society

Austria
Geraldine Fitzpatrick
Austrian Computer Society

Belgium
Bruno Dumas
Interuniversity Micro-Electronics Center
(IMEC)

Brazil
Milene Selbach Silveira
Brazilian Computer Society (SBC)

Bulgaria
Stoyan Georgiev Dentchev
Bulgarian Academy of Sciences

Canada
Lu Xiao
Canadian Information Processing Society

Croatia
Andrina Granic
Croatian Information Technology
Association (CITA)

Cyprus
Panayiotis Zaphiris
Cyprus Computer Society

Czech Republic
Zdeněk Míkovec
Czech Society for Cybernetics
and Informatics

Finland
Virpi Roto
Finnish Information Processing
   Association

France
Philippe Palanque
Société informatique de France (SIF)

Germany
Tom Gross
Gesellschaft fur Informatik e.V.

Hungary
Cecilia Sik Lanyi
John V. Neumann Computer Society

India
Anirudha Joshi
Computer Society of India (CSI)

Ireland
Liam J. Bannon
Irish Computer Society

Italy
Fabio Paternò
Italian Computer Society

Japan
Yoshifumi Kitamura
Information Processing Society of Japan

The Netherlands
Regina Bernhaupt
Nederlands Genootschap voor
   Informatica

New Zealand
Mark Apperley
New Zealand Computer Society

Norway
Frode Eika Sandnes
Norwegian Computer Society

Poland
Marcin Sikorski
Poland Academy of Sciences

Portugal
Pedro Campos
Associacão Portuguesa para o
   Desenvolvimento da Sociedade da
   Informação (APDSI)

Serbia
Aleksandar Jevremovic
Informatics Association of Serbia

Singapore
Shengdong Zhao
Singapore Computer Society

Slovakia
Wanda Benešová
The Slovak Society for Computer
   Science

Slovenia
Matjaž Debevc
The Slovenian Computer Society
   Informatika

South Africa
Janet L. Wesson and Paula Kotze
The Computer Society of South Africa

Sweden
Jan Gulliksen
Swedish Interdisciplinary Society for
   Human-Computer Interaction
Swedish Computer Society

Switzerland
Denis Lalanne
Swiss Federation for Information
   Processing

Tunisia
Mona Laroussi
Ecole Supérieure des Communications
   De Tunis (SUP'COM)

UK
José Abdelnour Nocera
British Computer Society (BCS)

UAE
Ghassan Al-Qaimari
UAE Computer Society

International Association Members

ACM
Gerrit van der Veer
Association for Computing Machinery
(ACM)

CLEI
Jaime Sánchez
Centro Latinoamericano de Estudios en
Informatica

Expert Members

Carmelo Ardito, Italy
Orwa, Kenya
David Lamas, Estonia
Dorian Gorgan, Romania
Eunice Sari, Australia/Indonesia
Fernando Loizides, UK/Cyprus
Ivan Burmistrov, Russia

Julio Abascal, Spain
Kaveh Bazargan, Iran
Marta Kristin Larusdottir, Iceland
Nikolaos Avouris, Greece
Peter Forbrig, Germany
Torkil Clemmensen, Denmark
Zhengjie Liu, China

Working Group Chairpersons

WG 13.1 (Education in HCI and HCI Curricula)

Konrad Baumann, Austria

WG 13.2 (Methodologies for User-Centered System Design)

Regina Bernhaupt, The Netherlands

WG 13.3 (HCI and Disability)

Helen Petrie, UK

WG 13.4/2.7 (User Interface Engineering)

José Creissac Campos, Portugal

WG 13.5 (Human Error, Resilience, Reliability, Safety and System Development)

Chris Johnson, UK

WG13.6 (Human-Work Interaction Design)

Barbara Rita Barricelli, Italy

WG13.7 (HCI and Visualization)

Peter Dannenmann, Germany

WG 13.8 (Interaction Design and International Development)

José Adbelnour Nocera, UK

WG 13.9 (Interaction Design and Children)

Janet Read, UK

WG 13.10 (Human-Centred Technology for Sustainability)

Masood Masoodian, Finland

Conference Organizing Committee

General Conference Chairs

David Lamas, Estonia
Panayiotis Zaphiris, Cyprus

Technical Program Chairs

Fernando Loizides, UK
Marco Winckler, France

Full Papers Co-chairs

Helen Petrie, UK
Lennart Nacke, Canada

Short Papers Co-chairs

Evangelos Karapanos, Cyprus
Jim CS Ang, UK

Interactive Posters Co-chairs

Carmelo Ardito, Italy
Zhengjie Liu, China

Panels Co-chairs

Darelle van Greunen, South Africa
Jahna Otterbacher, Cyprus

Demonstrations and Installations Co-chairs

Giuseppe Desolda, Italy
Vaso Constantinou, Cyprus

Courses Co-chairs

Parisa Eslambolchilar, UK
Regina Bernhaupt, The Netherlands

Workshops Co-chairs

Antigoni Parmaxi, Cyprus
Jose Abdelnour Nocera, UK

Doctoral Consortium Co-chairs

Andri Ioannou, Cyprus
Nikolaos Avouris, Greece

Student Design Consortium Co-chairs

Andreas Papallas, Cyprus
Eva Korae, Cyprus

Field Trips Chairs

Andreas Papallas, Cyprus
Anirudha Joshi, India
Panayiotis Zaphiris, Cyprus

Industry Case Studies Co-chairs

Aimilia Tzanavari, USA
Panagiotis Germanakos, Germany

Proceedings Chairs

Fernando Loizides, UK
Marco Winckler, France

Sponsorship Chair

Andreas Papallas, Cyprus

Student Volunteers Chair

Vaso Constantinou, Cyprus

Web and Social Media Chair

Aekaterini Mavri, Cyprus

Program Committee

Sub-committee Chairs

Elisa Mekler, Switzerland
Fabio Paterno, Italy
Gerhard Weber, Germany
Jan Gulliksen, Sweden
Jo Lumsden, UK

Laurence Nigay, France
Nikolaos Avouris, Greece
Philippe Palanque, France
Regina Bernhaupt, The Netherlands
Torkil Clemmensen, Denmark

Associated Chairs

Adrian Bussone, UK
Anirudha Joshi, India
Antonio Piccinno, Italy
Bridget Kane, Sweden
Bruno Dumas, Belgium
Carla Maria Dal Sasso Freitas, Brazil
Célia Martinie, France
Chi Vi, UK
Christine Bauer, Austria
Daniel Buzzo, UK
Daniela Trevisan, Brazil
Davide Spano, Italy
Denis Lalanne, Switzerland
Dhaval Vyas, Australia
Dorian Gorgan, Romania
Effie Law, UK
Elisa Mekler, Switzerland
Fabio Paterno, Italy
Frank Steinicke, Germany
Frode Eika Sandnes, Norway
Gavin Sim, UK
Gerhard Weber, Germany
Giuseppe Desolda, Italy
Jan Gulliksen, Sweden
Jan Stage, Denmark
Jan Van den Bergh, Belgium
Janet Wesson, South Africa
Jenny Darzentas, Greece
Jo Lumsden, UK
Jolanta Mizera-Pietraszko, Poland
Jose Abdelnour Nocera, UK

José Creissac Campos, Portugal
Katrina Attwood, UK
Kaveh Bazargan, Iran
Kibum Kim, South Korea
Laurence Nigay, France
Luis Teixeira, Portugal
Lynne Coventry, UK
Marcin Sikorski, Poland
Margarita Anastassova, France
Marta Laursdottir, Iceland
Matistella Matera, Italy
Nervo Verdezoto, UK
Nikolaos Avouris, Greece
Özge Subasi, Austria
Patrick Langdon, UK
Paula Kotze, South Africa
Pedro Campos, Portugal
Peter Forbrig, Germany
Peter Johnson, UK
Philippe Palanque, France
Regina Bernhaupt, The Netherlands
Sayan Sarcar, Japan
Simone Barbosa, Brazil
Simone Stumpf, UK
Stefania Castellani, France
Tom Gross, Germany
Torkil Clemmensen, Denmark
Valentin Schwind, Germany
Virpi Roto, Finland
Yoshifumi Kitamura, Japan
Zdenek Mikovec, Czech Republic

Reviewers

Adalberto Simeone, Belgium
Aditya Nittala, Germany
Adriana Vivacqua, Brazil
Aekaterini Mavri, Cyprus
Agneta Eriksson, Finland
Aidan Slingsby, UK
Aku Visuri, Finland
Alaa Alkhafaji, UK
Alasdair King, UK
Alberto Boem, Japan
Alberto Raposo, Brazil
Albrecht Schmidt, Germany
Aleksander Bai, Norway
Alessio Malizia, UK
Alexander Wachtel, Germany
Alexandra Covaci, UK
Alexandra Mendes, Portugal
Alexandre Canny, France
Ali Rizvi, Canada
Ali Soyoof, Iran
Alisa Burova, Finland
Alistair Edwards, UK
Alla Vovk, UK
Amina Bouraoui, Tunisia
Ana Cristina Garcia, Brazil
Ana Paula Afonso, Portugal
Ana Serrano, Spain
Anders Lundström, Sweden
Anderson Maciel, Brazil
Andre Suslik Spritzer, Brazil
André Zenner, Germany
Andrea Marrella, Italy
Andreas Sonderegger, Switzerland
Andrew Jian-lan Cen, Canada
Andrew MacQuarrie, UK
Andrew McNeill, UK
Andrey Krekhov, Germany
Andrii Matviienko, Germany
Andy Dearden, UK
Angus Forbes, USA
Anind Dey, USA
Anja Exler, Germany
Anke Dittmar, Germany

Anna Bramwell-Dicks, UK
Anna Feit, Switzerland
Anna-Lena Mueller, Germany
Annette Lamb, USA
Anthony Giannoumis, Norway
Antigoni Parmaxi, Cyprus
Antonio Gonzalez-Torres, Costa Rica
Antonio Piccinno, Italy
Arash Mahnan, USA
Arindam Dey, Australia
Aristides Mairena, Canada
Arjun Srinivasan, USA
Arminda Lopes, Portugal
Asam Almohamed, Australia
Ashkan Pourkand, USA
Asim Evren Yantac, Turkey
Aurélien Tabard, France
Aykut Coşkun, Turkey
Barbara Barricelli, Italy
Bastian Dewitz, Germany
Beiyu Lin, USA
Ben Morrison, UK
Benedict Gaster, UK
Benedikt Loepp, Germany
Benjamin Gorman, UK
Benjamin Weyers, Germany
Bernd Ploderer, Australia
Bineeth Kuriakose, Norway
Bosetti Bosetti, France
Brady Redfearn, USA
Brendan Cassidy, UK
Brendan Spillane, Ireland
Brian Freiter, Canada
Brianna Tomlinson, USA
Bruno Dumas, Belgium
Burak Merdenyan, UK
Cagatay Goncu, Australia
Cagri Tanriover, USA
Carlos Silva, Portugal
Carmen Santoro, Italy
Cecile Boulard, France
Célia Martinie, France
Chaolun Xia, USA

Charlotte Magnusson, Sweden
Chee Siang Ang, UK
Chelsea Kelling, Finland
Chloe Eghtebas, Germany
Christian Sturm, Germany
Christina Schneegass, Germany
Christina Vasiliou, UK
Christophe Kolski, France
Christopher Johnson, UK
Christopher Lueg, Switzerland
Christopher Power, UK
Christos Mousas, USA
Cinzia Cappiello, Italy
Clarisse Sieckenius de Souza, Brazil
Claudio Jung, Brazil
Clauirton Siebra, Brazil
Cléber Corrêa, Brazil
Clodis Boscarioli, Brazil
Cornelia Murko, Austria
CRI Putjorn, Thailand
Cristina Gena, Italy
Cynara Justine, India
Daisuke Sato, Japan
Damien Mac Namara, Ireland
Dan Fitton, UK
Daniel Lopes, Portugal
Daniel Mallinson, USA
Daniel Orwa Ochieng, Kenya
Daniel Ziegler, Germany
Daniela Fogli, Italy
Danula Hettiachchi, Australia
Dario Bertero, Japan
David Navarre, France
David Zendle, UK
Davy Vanacken, Belgium
Debaleena Chattopadhyay, USA
Deepak Akkil, Finland
Dejin Zhao, USA
Demetrios Lambropoulos, USA
Denis Berdjag, France
Dennis Wolf, Germany
Deqing Sun, USA
Dhaval Vyas, Australia
Dimitra Anastasiou, Luxembourg
Diogo Cabral, Portugal
Dmitrijs Dmitrenko, UK

Donal Rice, Ireland
Dorian Gorgan, Romania
Dorothé Smit, Austria
Dragan Ahmetovic, Italy
Ebtisam Alabdulqader, UK
Ee Xion Tan, Malaysia
Elena Not, Italy
Elizabeth Buie, UK
Elizabeth Shaw, Australia
Emad Aghayi, USA
Emma Nicol, UK
Emmanuel Pietriga, France
Englye Lim, Malaysia
Eric Barboni, France
Éric Céret, France
Erica Halverson, USA
Eva Cerezo, Spain
Evangelos Karapanos, Cyprus
Fabien Ringeval, France
Fabio Morreale, New Zealand
Fausto Medola, Brazil
Federico Botella, Spain
Felipe Soares da Costa, Denmark
Filippo Sanfilippo, Norway
Florence Lehnert, Luxembourg
Florian Daniel, Italy
Florian Güldenpfennig, Austria
Florian Heller, Belgium
Florian Weidner, Germany
Francesca Pulina, Italy
Francesco Ferrise, Italy
Francisco Nunes, Portugal
François Bérard, France
Frank Nack, The Netherlands
Frederica Gonçalves, Portugal
Frode Eika Sandnes, Norway
Gabriel Turcu, Romania
Ganesh Bhutkar, India
George Raptis, Greece
Gerd Berget, Norway
Gerhard Weber, Germany
Gerrit Meixner, Germany
Gianfranco Modoni, Italy
Giulio Mori, Italy
Giuseppe Desolda, Italy
Giuseppe Santucci, Italy

Goh Wei, Malaysia
Guilherme Bertolaccini, Brazil
Guilherme Guerino, Brazil
Günter Wallner, Austria
Gustavo Tondello, Canada
Hatice Kose, Turkey
Heidi Hartikainen, Finland
Heike Winschiers-Theophilus, Namibia
Heiko Müller, Finland
Hsin-Jou Lin, USA
Hua Guo, USA
Hugo Paredes, Portugal
Huy Viet Le, Germany
Hyunyoung Kim, France
Ian Brooks, UK
Ilaria Renna, France
Ilya Makarov, Russia
Ilya Musabirov, Russia
Ilyena Hirskyj-Douglas, Finland
Ioanna Iacovides, UK
Ioannis Doumanis, UK
Isabel Manssour, Brazil
Isabel Siqueira da Silva, Brazil
Isabela Gasparini, Brazil
Isidoros Perikos, Greece
Iyubanit Rodríguez, Costa Rica
Jaakko Hakulinen, Finland
James Eagan, France
James Nicholson, UK
Jan Derboven, Belgium
Jan Plötner, Germany
Jana Jost, Germany
Janet Read, UK
Janki Dodiya, Germany
Jason Shuo Zhang, USA
Jayden Khakurel, Denmark
Jayesh Doolani, USA
Ji-hye Lee, Finland
Jingjie Zheng, Canada
Jo Herstad, Norway
João Guerreiro, USA
Joe Cutting, UK
Johanna Hall, UK
Johanna Renny Octavia, Belgium
Johannes Kunkel, Germany
John Mundoz, USA

John Rooksby, UK
Jolanta Mizera-Pietraszko, Poland
Jonas Oppenlaender, Finland
Jonggi Hong, USA
Jonna Häkkilä, Finland
Jörg Cassens, Germany
Jorge Cardoso, Portugal
Jorge Goncalves, Australia
José Coelho, Portugal
Joseph O'Hagan, UK
Judith Borghouts, UK
Judy Bowen, New Zealand
Juliana Jansen Ferreira, Brazil
Julie Doyle, Ireland
Julie Williamson, UK
Juliette Rambourg, USA
Jürgen Ziegler, Germany
Karen Renaud, UK
Karin Coninx, Belgium
Karina Arrambide, Canada
Kasper Rodil, Denmark
Katelynn Kapalo, USA
Katharina Werner, Austria
Kati Alha, Finland
Katrin Wolf, Germany
Katta Spiel, Austria
Kellie Vella, Australia
Kening Zhu, China
Kent Lyons, USA
Kevin Cheng, China
Kevin El Haddad, Belgium
Kiemute Oyibo, Canada
Kirsi Halttu, Finland
Kirsten Ellis, Australia
Kirsten Ribu, Norway
Konstanti Chrysanthi, Cyprus
Kris Luyten, Belgium
Kurtis Danyluk, Canada
Kyle Johnsen, USA
Lachlan Mackinnon, UK
Lara Piccolo, UK
Lars Lischke, The Netherlands
Lars Rune Christensen, Denmark
Leigh Clark, Ireland
Lene Nielsen, Denmark
Lilian Motti Ader, Ireland

Liliane Machado, Brazil
Lilit Hakobyan, UK
Lisandro Granville, Brazil
Lonni Besançon, Sweden
Loredana Verardi, Italy
Lorisa Dubuc, UK
Lorna McKnight, UK
Loukas Konstantinou, Cyprus
Luciana Cardoso de Castro Salgado, Brazil
Luciana Nedel, Brazil
Lucio Davide Spano, Italy
Ludmila Musalova, UK
Ludvig Eblaus, Sweden
Luigi De Russis, Italy
Luis Leiva, Finland
Lynette Gerido, USA
Mads Andersen, Denmark
Mads Bødker, Denmark
Maher Abujelala, USA
Maliheh Ghajargar, Sweden
Malin Wik, Sweden
Malte Ressin, UK
Mandy Korzetz, Germany
Manjiri Joshi, India
Manuel J. Fonseca, Portugal
Marc Kurz, Austria
Marcelo Penha, Brazil
Marcelo Pimenta, Brazil
Márcio Pinho, Brazil
Marco Gillies, UK
Marco Manca, Italy
Marcos Baez, Italy
Marcos Serrano, France
Margarita Anastassova, France
María Laura Ramírez Galleguillos, Turkey
Maria Rosa Lorini, South Africa
Marian Cristian Mihaescu, Romania
Marianela Ciolfi Felice, France
Marion Koelle, Germany
Marios Constantinides, UK
Maristella Matera, Italy
Marius Koller, Germany
Mark Billinghurst, Australia
Mark Carman, Italy

Marko Tkalcic, Italy
Martin Feick, Germany
Martin Tomitsch, Australia
Mary Barreto, Portugal
Massimo Zancanaro, Italy
Matthew Horton, UK
Matthias Heintz, UK
Mauricio Pamplona Segundo, Brazil
Max Bernhagen, Germany
Max Birk, The Netherlands
Mehdi Ammi, France
Mehdi Boukallel, France
Meinald Thielsch, Germany
Melissa Densmore, South Africa
Meraj Ahmed Khan, USA
Michael Burch, The Netherlands
Michael Craven, UK
Michael McGuffin, Canada
Michael Nees, USA
Michael Rohs, Germany
Michela Assale, Italy
Michelle Annett, Canada
Mike Just, UK
Mikko Rajanen, Finland
Milene Silveira, Brazil
Miriam Begnum, Norway
Mirjam Augstein, Austria
Mirko Gelsomini, Italy
Muhammad Haziq Lim Abdullah, Malaysia
Muhammad Shoaib, Pakistan
Nadine Vigouroux, France
Natasa Rebernik, Spain
Naveed Ahmed, UAE
Netta Iivari, Finland
Nick Chozos, UK
Nico Herbig, Germany
Niels Henze, Germany
Niels van Berkel, UK
Nikola Banovic, USA
Nikolaos Avouris, Greece
Nimesha Ranasinghe, USA
Nis Bornoe, Denmark
Nitish Devadiga, USA
Obed Brew, UK
Ofir Sadka, Canada

Takuji Narumi, Japan
Tanja Walsh, UK
Ted Selker, USA
Terje Gjøsæter, Norway
Tetsuya Watanabe, Japan
Thierry Dutoit, Belgium
Thilina Halloluwa, Australia
Thomas Kirks, Germany
Thomas Neumayr, Austria
Thomas Olsson, Finland
Thomas Prinz, Germany
Thorsten Strufe, Germany
Tifanie Bouchara, France
Tilman Dingler, Australia
Tim Claudius Stratmann, Germany
Timo Partala, Finland
Toan Nguyen, USA
Tomi Heimonen, USA
Tommaso Turchi, UK
Tommy Dang, USA
Troy Nachtigall, The Netherlands
Uran Oh, South Korea
Val Mitchell, UK
Vanessa Cesário, Portugal
Vanessa Wan Sze Cheng, Australia
Venkatesh Rajamanickam, India
Verena Fuchsberger, Austria
Verity McIntosh, UK
Victor Adriel de Jesus Oliveira, Austria

Victor Kaptelinin, Sweden
Vincenzo Deufemia, Italy
Vinoth Pandian Sermuga Pandian,
    Germany
Vishal Sharma, USA
Vit Rusnak, Czech Republic
Vita Santa Barletta, Italy
Vito Gentile, Italy
Vung Pham, USA
Walter Correia, Brazil
Weiqin Chen, Norway
William Delamare, Japan
Xiaoyi Zhang, USA
Xiying Wang, USA
Yann Laurillau, France
Yann Savoye, UK
Yannis Dimitriadis, Spain
Yiannis Georgiou, Cyprus
Yichen Lu, Finland
Ying Zhu, USA
Yong Ming Kow, SAR China
Young-Ho Kim, South Korea
Yue Jiang, USA
Yu-Tzu Lin, Denmark
Z Toups, USA
Zdeněk Míkovec, Czech Republic
Zhanna Sarsenbayeva, Australia
Zhihang Dong, USA
Zhisheng Yan, USA

Sponsors and Partners

Sponsors

 Research Centre on **Interactive** Media
RISE | **Smart** Systems and **Emerging** Technologies

 Springer

Partners

 ifip

International Federation for Information Processing

 Cyprus
University of
Technology

 TALLINN UNIVERSITY

 In-Cooperation

In-cooperation with ACM

 SIGCHI

In-cooperation with SIGCHI

Contents – Part IV

Users' Emotions, Feelings and Perception

Virtual and Augmented Reality I

Virtual and Augmented Reality II

Wearable and Tangible Interaction

Courses

Demonstrations and Installations

Industry Case Studies

Interactive Posters

User Modelling and User Studies

An Analysis of (Non-)Use Practices and Decisions of Internet of Things

Radhika Garg$^{(\boxtimes)}$

School of Information Studies, Syracuse University, Syracuse, USA
rgarg01@syr.edu

Abstract. Recent market reports have suggested that adoption of the Internet of Things (IoT) does not always lead to long-term use. This paper aims to advance an understanding of the sociological process of the (non-)use of the IoT. To this end, we present results from a mixed-methods study that analyzed survey data from 834 IoT users in the U.S. Many of our participants treated these devices as co-actors for achieving their goals and continued to use them because they had developed a routine or because the devices influenced their social interactions and identity. Participants limited their use of a device when they did not feel in control, when the device failed to understand their intent, or when they did not understand the device's behavior. We also found that excessive information offered by, disappointment due to, and the complexity of the devices led to their abandonment. Lastly, we discuss the implications of our results for understanding technology (non-)use and provide design recommendations.

Keywords: Use · Non-use · Topic modeling · Smart devices ·
Internet of Things · Smart speakers · Wearables · Smart thermostat ·
Smart locks

1 Introduction

A definition provided by Lazar et al. refers to smart devices as the *"devices that automatically sense data about users or their environment, assist them in automating their spaces or activities, or help the users in gaining knowledge about themselves"* [33]. These smart devices are collectively referred to as Internet-of-Things (IoT) [15]. The IoT therefore comprises a range of devices that play the roles of collector (e.g., wearables or activity trackers), an actor (e.g., smart thermostat, smart assistant), and a creator (e.g., futuristic robots) [14]. News media and researchers have suggested that both the adoption and abandonment of IoT devices is rampant. For example, researchers have found that about a third of activity tracking device owners in the United States stopped using their devices within the first six months of their purchase [34,38]. Another consumer report on IoT adoption suggests that users think these smart devices are "gimmicky"

© IFIP International Federation for Information Processing 2019
Published by Springer Nature Switzerland AG 2019
D. Lamas et al. (Eds.): INTERACT 2019, LNCS 11749, pp. 3–24, 2019.
https://doi.org/10.1007/978-3-030-29390-1_1

and not very functional [8]. Specifically, users of smart speakers use a variety of voice assistants' applications a few times, but abandon them afterwards [11]. This implies that such users face multiple barriers that either prevent them from engaging in the long-term use of IoT devices or lead to systematic limited use.

A recent movement in the HCI community advocates the study of non-use of technology along with its use. Wyatt [52] broadly clustered non-users into four categories – *resisters*, *rejectors*, the *excluded*, and the *expelled* – based on those who used a technology but abandoned it (rejectors and the expelled) and those who never used a technology (resisters and the excluded). Most related to our work is the category that Wyatt term as rejectors, who stop using a technology voluntarily, perhaps because they find it boring, expensive or if they find perfectly adequate alternative technology. Other researchers have noted that abandonment is "neither a singular moment nor a linear path" [10] and that a strict binary distinction between use and non-use can conceal more than it reveals [5]. While abandonment and the long-term use of wearables have been extensively studied (e.g., [19,33,37]), the same is not true in regards to other IoT devices (e.g., smart assistants, thermostats). Therefore, to fill this gap, the aim of this paper is to understand users' motivations, preferences, and justifications for choosing to use or not use the IoT in various forms and degrees. We framed our work around the following research questions:

RQ1: Why do some users continue to use their IoT devices over the long term, while others systematically limit their use or abandon the devices completely? RQ2: How do the reasons for using or not using differ (or not) for different types of IoT devices?

To build on the literature, disentangle monolithic perceptions of use and non-use with respect to IoT, and understand how the reasons for using different IoT devices overlap or not, we conducted a survey through Amazon Mechanical Turk (AMT), which consisted of several multiple-choice and open-ended questions aimed at understanding user practices and preferences in regard to IoT (non-) use. In the end, we collected responses from 834 participants. To analyze the open-ended survey responses, we adopted a mixed-methods approach, combining computational topic modeling [9] and qualitative reading, which helped us to identify users' reasons for using, not using, or limiting their use of IoT devices. This paper makes two main contributions:

First, the study provides empirical evidence about user preferences that influence decisions regarding the (non-)use of heterogeneous smart devices, as opposed to related literature that investigated user preferences associated only with activity trackers or wearables. Specifically, our findings reveal user practices and experiences with IoT devices, many of which have not been reported or have been under-reported. Our participants treated these devices as collaborative actors in achieving human-defined goals, and the participants continued to use them due to their social influences, the social interaction enabled by these devices, and habit formation. Conversely, the failure to understand a device's behavior, a device's inability to understand the user's intent, or the feeling of not being in control of the device led to limited or selective use, and various information concerns, disappointments, and the complexity of devices led to their abandonment.

Second, we discuss the implications of our findings for the theory of technology (non-)use. To this end, we discuss the relevance of considering "selective users" in the design process and provide design guidelines, with the aim of better supporting use of the IoT.

2 Related Work

Many researchers believe that the effects of technologies are less a function of the technologies themselves than of how they are *used* by people [18]. Smart device users form a heterogeneous group in terms of not only their usage patterns, but also their preferences and requirements. Recent work in HCI and related areas has highlighted the importance of studying this variation in users through the lens of technology (e.g., social media, mobile phones, wearables) non-use [2,52,53]. Satchell and Dourish [46] further argued for examining use and non-use as aspects of a single, broader continuum, particularly as digital technologies increasingly become cultural objects. Several prior studies have identified a number of practices and motivations for technology non-use, such as Kline's exploration of user resistance [30], and non-use practices with respect to the Internet [51], computers [48], and social media [4,10,27]. Examples of other studies that have specifically argued against making strict binary distinctions include a study by Schoenebeck, which examined intentional short-term breaks in the use of Twitter [47], and a study by Lampe et al., which differentiated among heavy, light, and non-users of Facebook [32].

Lazar et al. reported that 80% of devices that were purchased by the participants for use in their study were abandoned after two weeks [33]. Shih et al. provided 26 undergraduate students with activity trackers, and 75% of them stopped using the device within the first four weeks [49]. Other researchers have observed that people abandon a device when there is a misfit between the device and the participant's self-conception, when the data collected by the device are not useful, and when too much effort is required to use the device [33,43]. Lazar et al. found that when users evaluate the data provided by wearable devices as irrelevant and not actionable, the devices become frustrating or time-consuming and ultimately not worth the time investment [33]. However, these findings are based on devices that were provided to the participants after their recruitment for the study. This must have affected their choices, preferences, and (non-)use decisions.

Other studies focused on participants who adopted health-related tracking devices of their own volition, and identified several reasons behind their abandonment. For example, Clawson et al. investigated the rationale for why people abandon health-tracking technologies, by analyzing 1,600 advertisements for the resale of such technologies posted on Craigslist, an online marketplace [16]. They argue that in many cases, abandonment did not necessarily reflect individuals' dissatisfaction with the technology; that is, people may have been selling their devices because they achieved their goals or their life circumstances changed. Through a survey of 193 participants, Epstein et al. found that the cost of collecting, the cost of sharing the data, discomfort with the information revealed, data quality concerns, the lack of something new to learn, and changes in life circumstances led to the abandonment of self-tracking devices [19]. Harrison et al. identified poor device accuracy and aesthetics as reasons for abandonment, and discussed implications and workarounds to help overcome barriers to long-term use [28]. Rantakari et al. presented a study on people's preferences with respect to wearable devices, based on an online survey of 84 participants [43]. The findings show that 27% of the participants stopped using their devices within a month for one or many of the reasons listed above. However, in contrast, the highest-rated features of these devices were found to be their comfort and long battery lifetime. Patel and Ann O'Kane while examining technology use and non-use in the context of the gym use, showed that fitness informatics adopters pursued varied practices related to distraction, the appropriation of technology into their routines, and information needs [41].

Finally, another set of studies has focused on understanding the reasons underlying the long-term use of wearables [22,29,37]. For example, Frtiz et al. [22] indicated that long-term (between 3 and 54 months) users rely on activity trackers to motivate them to achieve a consistent level of activity. Similar findings emerged in a longitudinal study on the use of activity trackers, conducted with 34 patients recovering from myocardial infarctions [37]. Only a few studies discuss the challenges [54] or smart voice assistants [35], and they do not specifically discuss users' (non-)use practices and decisions.

Overall, previous research has primarily examined the (non-)use practices of social media and wearables. Furthermore, prior work has mostly examined these practices in regard to a particular device, rather than comparing how these practices vary across different devices. To fill these gaps, this study contributes to an understanding of the reasons that influence individuals' decisions to use or not use the IoT, and of how the reasons for using different devices overlap, if at all.

3   Methodology

We conducted an online survey with 834 IoT users from the U.S. in order to understand their reasons and preferences for (not-)using IoT devices. The data were collected between November 2017 and January 2018. The study was approved by our Institutional Review Board (IRB).

3.1   Survey Design and Data Collection

To identify people who had previously used IoT devices and the kinds of devices they had used, and to determine the reliability of users' experiences, the participants first completed a one-minute screener survey. The selection of participants who had adopted device(s) of their own volition helped us to identify the exact reasons for continued use, and benefits that faded away with time. In the screener survey, every participant was shown five scenarios to identify devices they had past experience with:

Scenario 1: A device for self-**security** purposes that collects your personal data (e.g., location) to be shared with trusted friends and family in case of emergency.

Scenario 2: A device that can be used during activities to collect your personal data (e.g., heart rate) or to keep track of or improve your **health and well-being**.

Scenario 3: A device that can be used to collect data (e.g., number of steps taken during the day) for personal **informatics/logging** purposes.

Scenario 4: A device that is part of your **connected and automated home** to notify you about the conditions of the objects to which the device is connected (e.g., for opening the garage or the main doors of your house), or to remotely control objects (e.g., lights, thermostats)?

These scenarios were designed to help participants gain a clear understanding of a situations in which a smart devices are used and thereby to remind them of their own devices. Four scenarios were selected (purposeful sampling [40]) to reveal variations and patterns in the challenges and dynamics of using IoT in day-to-day living. This increased the capability of generalizing our results to other devices. Based on the responses to the screener survey, each of the participants answered questions in the main survey with respect to only one of the above-mentioned scenarios. In connection with each scenario, two types of questions were presented to the participants.

The first category consisted of factual questions that included Likert scale questions and yes-or-no questions. Some of these were developed based on the most relevant factors, identified in prior research [16, 22, 33, 37, 39, 50] that examined people's attitudes and experiences toward using or not using tracking devices and wearables. For instance, to determine their level of *relatedness with the device*, we asked participants when they started using the device. We also asked them how *important* the task was that device helped them fulfill, and to what *extent* the device helped them to *achieve their purpose*. The survey also included question on whether they had any *privacy concerns* about using these devices, and how *relevant privacy* was to the way they used a device. The answers to Likert-scale questions were based on a five-point scale; for instance, with respect to the importance of the task, the scale ranged from 5 = "Extremely Important" to 1 = "Not Important At All."

The second category consisted of questions that were aimed at exploring experiences with IoT devices and the reasons for using them (completely or partially) or abandoning them. To this end, we adapted the method proposed by [42], who used a survey to elicit stories about issues related to computer security. The participants were asked to share a story about how and why they systematically limited/restricted their use, stopped using a smart device, or still used their device regularly. We emphasized at the outset of the main survey that

Table 1. Additional demographic breakdown of the 834 participants. The numbers in parentheses show the U.S. average, based on data from the 2015 census.

Education level (in %)	Annual income (in %)	Race/Ethnicity (in %)
No high school, 0.4 (10.9)	<$15K, 2.9 (11.6)	White, 60 (72.4)
High school, 6.1 (28.8)	$15K - $34K, 25.8 (20.5)	African American, 15 (12.6)
Associate's, 37.7 (10)	$35k - $74K, 41.3 (29.4)	Hispanic or Latino, 12 (16.3, of any race)
Bachelors, 42 (48.7)	$75K -$149, 24.5 (26.2)	Pacific Islander, 7 (0.2)
Professional, 11.9 (1.5)	$150K - $199K, 3.7 (6.2)	Asian, 4 (4.8)
No answer, 1.8	>$200K, 0.2 (6.1)	Native American, 2 (0.9)
	No answer, 1.6	

detailed responses to the open-ended questions would help with our analysis. While we did not specify how much detail was required, we informed participants about the possibility of earning an extra bonus for detailed responses, in addition to the standard compensation for finishing the survey. Lastly, to avoid priming the participants' responses in any way, we deliberately did not explain the terms "systematic limited use," "continued use," or "stopped use" throughout the study. Towards the end of the survey, we also collected the respondents' demographics, such as gender, age, and annual income.

3.2   Pilot Study

To assess the comprehensibility of these questions, we piloted the survey protocol with 20 graduate students in October 2017. The pilot results suggested that the students understood the questions, although most of them did not understand which devices qualified as smart devices or as part of the IoT. For instance, many of them asked if laptops are considered part of Internet of Things, as they support Internet connectivity and are capable of collecting personal information. We then revised the survey based on the feedback from the pilot study to include the definition of the IoT mentioned in the previous section.

3.3   Participants

The participants recruited through AMT had completed at least 1,000 tasks, with an approval rate of above 95%. Our survey was completed by 900 AMT workers from the U.S. We then checked each response to make sure it was meaningful. This led to the removal of 66 participants, and responses of 834 participants were included in our analysis. The average age of the participants was 36.47 years (min: 18, max: 74), which is very close to the US average of 37.9. Of the participants, 56.5% were female, 42.9% were male, and 0.6 percent declined to report their gender. Table 1 summarizes additional demographic information of our participants, along with corresponding US national averages.

We note our participants do not represent the entire population of IoT users. But, our study adds substantial knowledge to the existing literature as our sample composed of a large number of non-technical respondents who had adopted different types of smart devices voluntarily. We also note that all the devices that our participants listed for Scenarios 2 and 3 were identical. Therefore, we combined the respondents' answers for these two scenarios for the purposes of the analysis. The different types of devices that the participants owned for each of the scenario are listed below. The numbers in brackets represent the number of people who are continuing to use their device/ who have limited use of their device/ who have abandoned their device with respect to respective scenario.

Security (81/55/119): Security cameras, smart locks, baby monitors, GPS trackers

Health and well-being, informatics/logging (85/68/113): Activity trackers, smart watches, heart-rate monitors

Connected home (88/106/128): Smart thermostats, smart blinds, smart doorbells, smart locks, smoke alarm detectors, door sensors, smart speakers, smart plugs, smart light-sensing systems.

3.4   Content Analysis

While statistical information regarding responses to the yes-or-no and Likert scale questions is provided below, this paper primarily focuses on an analysis of the open-ended responses. This is driven by the aim to identify practices of, and reasons for, (not-)using the devices to various degrees. On an average each participant wrote around 175 words (total of approx. 1,50,000 words). Therefore, motivated by advocacy in recent work [6,7,12,13,26] for combining topic modeling [9] and qualitative reading to analyze free-text survey questions, this study used the Latent Dirichlet allocation (LDA) model [43], the most commonly used topic model in HCI and related communities, along with close inductive qualitative reading, to identify the underlying themes and label "topics" identified by the model.

Specifically, LDA is an unsupervised computational approach in which documents (in context of our study, the responses to open-ended questions) are represented as random mixtures of latent topics, where each "topic" is characterized by a distribution of words [9] that summarizes the main themes in the documents. A lexical word may occur in several topics with a different probability, however, with a different set of neighboring words in each topic. Therefore, LDA is based on automatic detection of the likelihood of term co-occurrence. Before identifying topics, each survey response was preprocessed to remove stop-words, such as prepositions and conjunctions. Since we wanted to identify reasons for, and practices of using or not using devices, we did not remove common pronouns (e.g., *I, it*) and a few determiners (e.g., possessives, demonstratives, quantifiers). As LDA is an approximating algorithm, we followed the approach proposed by Baumer et al. [7] to find stable topics and generated 10 independent topic modeling solutions, each consisting of 5 topics. The number of topics was chosen after manually increasing the number of topics from 2 to 30. We then manually examined each topic and the top 100 words most likely to occur across the solutions and excluded topics that exhibited more than a 50% variation in word distribution across solutions. This enabled us to identify topics that were distributions of identical words with small variations resulting from random initializations. The upper bound for the number of topics and the threshold for variation in word distribution per topic were chosen based on the limits suggested in the literature on topic modeling (e.g., [9, 26]).

As noted by Baumer et al. [7], algorithmic approaches such as topic modeling complement rather than replace the methods of grounded theory [23]. Therefore, while topic modeling provided empirical evidence in terms of the words that were most likely to occur in a topic, inductive analysis helped us to identify the links between these words, and their contexts, to understand the reasons for device use, limited use, and abandonment in our survey responses. Previous research (e.g., [6, 12, 26]) has also suggested that the top words within these topics can be considered equivalent to the "codes" that are otherwise assigned by human researchers using open coding [23]. However, identification of such codes or topics computationally neglects the syntactic and semantic knowledge of human coders. Therefore, the responses categorized within each topic (based on the topic's proportion, which indicated the topic's relevance in the response) were then carefully read to include the linguistic and contextual knowledge of the human coders use to identify the reasons for (non-)use.

Qualitative reading served three purposes. First, even though proportions of topics within each response differed substantially, the qualitative reading of all the responses ensured that each response was associated only with the topic that was present in the highest proportion. For example, the percentages of Topic 1 (the most frequently occurring topic) and Topic 2 (the second most frequently occurring topic) were 92% and 8%, respectively. A qualitative reading of this response corroborated that it belonged only to Topic 1. Second, through an inductive reading of the responses and the top 20 words of each topic as identified by LDA, relationships between codes or words emerged. These relationships were then used as the labels or themes of the corresponding LDA topics. Finally, qualitative analysis enabled a detailed and fine-grained analysis to identify subtopics within each of the topics that emerged with LDA.

Overall, our process was analogous to open coding, which fractures the data into categories (top words within each topic in context of our analysis), and then axial coding, which puts the data back together by making connections between these categories (the labels of the topics in context of our analysis) [23]. Depending on the participants' current status of use, limited use, or non-use of their devices, they gave their reasons for either continuing, limiting, or abandoning use. Also, our purpose was to identify separately the underlying reasons for use, limited use, and non-use. Therefore, we applied the above-mentioned procedure thrice; once on the textual corpus to determine reasons for use, next to determine reasons for limited use, and finally explanations for non-use. This process was also analogous to qualitative coding, where codes for reasons for use, limited use, and non-use would be developed separately.

Table 2. Distribution of responses to multiple-choice questions for different categories of (non-)users

Factor	Number of Current Users, Limited Users, Non-Users per Likert-Scale value
Duration	<6 months: 77, 67, and 93; 6 months–1 year: 64, 58, and 97; 1–2 years: 58, 42, 72, >2 years: 55, 51, and 98
Relevance of Privacy to Current State of Use	Extremely Important: 10, 39, 18; Very Important: 22, 20, 31; Neither Important or Unimportant: 117, 73, 177; Slightly Important: 40, 42, 71; Not Important: 65, 44, 73
Importance of Task for which Device was Adopted	Extremely Important: 78, 66, 41; Very Important: 75; 53, 35; Neither Important or Unimportant: 31, 31, 36; Slightly Important: 41, 36, 170; Not Important: 29, 32, 78
Extent to which Device Fulfills the Task	Extremely Helpful: 76, 41, 76; Very Helpful: 79, 31, 68; Neither Helpful or Unhelpful: 44, 49, 26; Slightly Helpful: 22, 66, 44; Not Helpful: 33, 31, 146

In the next section, we discuss the stable topics that were identified, their underlying theme(s) (obtained by establishing connections between top words by reading the responses within each topic), the breakdown of each topic's applicability to the different scenarios or categories of IoT devices, and the highest-ranking responses (based on the percentages of the corresponding topic in the responses) for every scenario.

4 Findings

Our analysis revealed that the IoT users developed various technology-oriented individual, collaborative, and social practices that affected their decisions to use or not use IoT devices in various forms and to various degrees. It also revealed not only that several participants used same types of devices in multiple scenarios, but also that their reasons for (not-)using different devices overlapped in many cases. Statistical information relevant to the multiple-choice questions is provided in Table 2.

4.1 Why Did the Participants Use Devices?

Topic modeling and qualitative analysis identified the following three stable topics associated with the reasons for continued use. These topics, along with the highest-ranking response corresponding to each device, are as follows:

Topic: Collaborative Support

Top 20 words: *monitor, together, track, other, senses, helps, itself, him, allow, does, me, her, supports, manages, us, it, ensures, partner, benefit, our*

This topic refers to the collaborative relationships that people develop with their devices to achieve their own goals, and the collaborative activities that these devices enable. The topic was found to be in the highest proportion in the responses of 72 current users. These 72 responses comprised 27, 19, and 26 responses to the scenarios of *security, health and informatics*, and *connected home*, respectively.

Over the past decade, several researchers in the HCI and CSCW communities have studied the collaborative practices that emerge from the use of personal trackers [17,20,44]. Atzori et al. recently pointed out that, with the IoT, many more objects and spaces have entered the realm of connectivity, thereby making possible cooperation among these devices to accomplish a particular task [3]. In contrast, our findings suggest that these devices are not currently perceived as objects cooperating with one another to complete a task; rather, devices act like, and are treated as, collaborative actors that work with or for users to achieve a human-defined goal. Participants' responses suggest that when their collaborative experience(s) with the device is/(are) positive and successful, the result is continued use. For example, participants wrote: *Smart sock for monitoring heart rate and oxygen levels of my kid during sleep helps me achieve so much. The device is like my extension as it allows me to constantly track the vitals when I cant be with my kid and other things that I could not do myself* (P325, Security), and *It [activity tracker] helps me like a partner in reaching the goals faster by tracking my steps by ensuring that I know how much I have walked. It does the tracking, I do the walking* (P123, Health and Informatics).

Thirty participants also mentioned that the ability to asynchronously collaborate with family members through a device for various activities (e.g., maintaining music or to-do lists, sharing calendars) and/or the ability to provide temporary access to others by configuring different access levels also contributed to their continued use. For example, participants observed: *My Google home brings so much benefit to me. Me and my husband make our common to-do list on Google home, when I go to shopping I know what my husband has added remotely. Same is true for calendar access and so many other things* (P712, Connected Home), and *When my mother visits I can give her partial access to Nest so that it learns her whereabouts and preferences but at the same time she can not change any settings. This saves me lot of time and energy to manually accommodate my mother's preferences* (P801, Connected Home).

Topic: Social Interaction and Influence

Top 20 words: *us, friend, together, people, like, fun, they, other, feel, family, group, flaunt, I, challenge, argue, enjoy, know, affect, personal, someone*

This topic was found to be in highest proportion in 91 responses – 31, 25, 35 survey responses with respect to the scenarios of *security, health and informatics*, and *connected home* respectively. Goffman [24] discusses how people tend to create impressions of themselves that are publicly visible. Forty eight responses suggested that people continue to use the IoT because it influences the way they are viewed or perceived by others. For example, participants responded *I flaunt my automated security systems and smart door locks each time friends, family or someone else come over. They feel I am rich, and I like that* (P756, Security), and *All of my friends have smart assistant. If I stop using mine they will feel I am not able to keep up with the changing times* (P345, Connected Home).

For 17 other participants, even though these devices became a source of contention with their significant others due to their having different preferences, they continued to use them for their utility. For example, P589 explained: *Sometimes I have argued with my husband over setting the boundaries of geofencing that I can set for the GPS tracker of my kid. However, the potential of knowing where our daughter is, reduces anxiety for us, and hence I continue using it despite a constant difference of opinions* (Security).

Fifteen participants indicated that the increased interactions that some of these devices enabled with their strong and weak social ties motivated their continued use. Strong social ties consist of blood ties, as well as friendship ties that are equivalent to family ties, and weak ties consist of affiliations such as friends of friends or friends of family [25,31,36]. Through participation in online groups that were supported by various activity trackers, people not only communicated with their strong ties, but also extended their links through recommendations and transitively created weak ties. For example, P843 wrote: *I do not see my family and friends that often. But through the Fitbit groups I can keep track of who is doing what from health point of view. If someone who desperately need to work out fails to do so, I can remind them about it* (Health and informatics).

Finally, while their devices motivated many of the participants to achieve their goals through reminders and notifications, for 11 participants these devices provided a platform whereby they competed with people in their network of close or weak ties. For example, community groups within Fitbit,[1] enabled them to discuss with, track the progress of, or compete with other people in the group. For example, P834 further explained, *In other cases when my friends are doing physical activities, the competition and challenge makes me workout even more to achieve my own goal* (Health and informatics).

Therefore, even though the focus of the study was on individuals' (non-)use of IoT, this topic illustrates that IoT devices have a greater social impact that extends beyond one-to-one relationships, and these relationships in turn influence an individual's use of these devices.

Topic: Developed Routine

Top 20 words: *goal, me, habit, use, do, I, my, long, always, time, reach, achieve, able, target, money, convenience, routine, myself, it, continue, help*

Previous work has reported that people try to integrate a wearable device into their life only when the device is not obtrusive or uncomfortable [33]. Responses for this topic were often from people who had been using a device for more than a year and had developed a routine for using it. A total of 91 responses – 23,

---

[1] Fitbit Community Groups: https://blog.fitbit.com/fitbit-community-announcem ent/.

41, 27 responses related to the scenarios of *security, health and informatics*, and *connected home* respectively – were categorized under this topic.

In contrast to previous work, the analysis of these responses indicated that the underlying reasons related to habit formation can be quiet varied and include factors such as the associated economic benefit users get from enrolling in rewards programs offered by various device manufacturers and their partners (e.g., the Rush Hour program for the Nest thermostat, the incentive program for Fitbit Health) (21 responses), convenience (11 responses), a higher probability of achieving goals with the help of the device (23 responses), intentional use arising from the fact that it was already purchased or was received as a gift (20 responses), and development of a compulsive habit of unconsciously using the device (16 responses). Interestingly, all these reasons were prevalent in responses to all three scenarios.

Examples reflecting these factors include this by P842: *During my initial use of the device I lost 30 lbs because I was able to log my food intake via the Fitbit app. I can see the difference in my lifestyle when I do not use it, so I will continue to use it till I reach my goal, and afterwards to maintain my healthy routine. I have now found myself wearing the Fitbit just absent mindedly too, it has become such a habit* (Health and informatics), this by P391 *The convenience of the device [smart lock] made me used to it. I don't have to carry my keys all the time. Now I use it always and can not do without it* (Connected Home), and these by P219 and P97 *I am enrolled in Rush Hour program of Nest so now I just use it habitually* (Security) and *I had bought [GPS tracker] for my kids a long time ago. Now my kid is in a habit of wearing it. So without me reminding him, he always wears it* (Security).

4.2   Why Did the Participants Limit Their Use of Devices?

For the corpus consisting of participants' reasons for limited use, two stable topics emerged. The reasons related to restricting the duration of use, engaging in occasional use, or using only specific application(s) on a device.

Topic: Understanding and Controlling the Capabilities of a Device
Top 20 words: *not, ability, allow, let, help, can, do, change, becomes, useful, modify, I, unable, my, understand, myself, adapt, need, decide, itself*

This topic consisted of 55, 34, and 52 responses to the scenarios for *security, health and informatics*, and *connected home*.

The responses indicated that a vague understanding of a device's capabilities not only reduced use, but also constrained participants in terms of their ability to successfully control or predict the capabilities of the device. For example, with respect to a GPS tracker, P100 said: *I find it tough to trust trackers for my children or pets. It's useful sometimes, but if connectivity is poor I do not know if it tries to send emergency notifications to me. Its unclear to me how soon after loosing connectivity it tries to connect back* (Security), and fuelled by the fear of smart assistant listening in a private space, P643 explained: *We are not sure if it really listens our conversation all the time or not. But to be on a safer side we always keep it on a mute mode. So the need of physically tapping it to unmute the device before giving any command has reduced our use* (Connected Home).

Furthermore, participants' also limited their use of a device due to doubts or disappointment in regard to its learnability and automatic adaptability. For instance, participants were disappointed with smart speakers, because the speakers could not base their responses on previous user interactions, and the users had to state their commands in a specific style (e.g., using simple words, not concatenating commands). For example, P710 said, *It [smart assistant] has a hard time adapting to my accent and the way I give commands. I am not even sure if the device is trying to learn it or not. Therefore, the only time smart assistant is useful is when I am next to it and I have 10 min to spare for a simple command* (Connected Home). Similarly, in the case of smart thermostats, not being able to precisely identify how and whether factors such as anomalous and manual temperature changes or occupancy levels in the room influenced the thermostat's learning led participants to not trust or use more sophisticated functionalities such as Auto-Schedule, Airwave, or Auto-Away. Similar concerns were reported with respect to wearables as well. For example, P329 wrote, *Without knowing the relevant parameters it is difficult to believe various scores such as cardio fitness score that it [activity tracker] generates for me. For example, I do not wear it all the time so that means score can be incorrect. So the device is good to count number of steps, but nothing fancy* (Health and Informatics).

Overall, such experiences led users to blame themselves for not being technically adept; for employing an economy of interaction, such as limiting the words used while giving a command to a smart speaker; for avoiding the complex capabilities of devices such as thermostats, wearables, or speakers; or for using only features that they understood and believed the device could perform successfully.

Topic: Devices' Inability to Understand Users' Intents and Contexts

Top 20 words: *understand, know, not, prefer, believe, kid, unclear, result, it, feel, difficult, try, want, tell, his, think, hard, my, aware, child*

This topic consisted of 34 responses to the scenario for *health and informatics* and 54 responses to the scenario for *connected home*. The analysis revealed that factors such as a device's inability to understand a user's changing behavior and contexts, and dissonance between the user's expectations and the pragmatics of a device, led users to stop using or relying on certain features of devices. For example, with respect to smart speakers, P334 said, *I feel it does not understand my context. If me and my wife start talking in middle of placing an order, it will start saying: sorry I don't understand that. As it can not learn that I always order after discussing with my wife, I do not use purchasing functionality anymore* (Connected Home), and with respect to activity trackers, P20 said *If I am walking or biking on a bumpy trail, I know I will get extra steps. Sometimes when I am walking too slow and arms are not moving fast enough, I know I will get a few steps less in my logs. So most of the times when I go for a bumpy trail I don't trust on the logs* (Health and Informatics).

Twenty of the participants specifically reduced their smart speaker use around children because of fears about the speakers' impact on children's social development skills, and their use of smart assistants for fear they might play inappropriate content when children were around. P210 said, *I have reduced the use of Google home infront of my children. There is no way I can make it understand that kids are around. I fear it might one day misinterpret me and start playing explicit content* (Connected Home). Along similar lines, P186 explained, *I do not want my children to feel everything is achievable by just giving a command. We reduced our use because our 6 year old used to get irritated when not being understood by the speaker, which is not acceptable to us* (Connected Home).

4.3   Why Did the Participants Stop Using Devices?

For the corpus comprising participants' reasons for non-use, the three following stable topics emerged:

Topic: Disappointment
Top 20 words: *never, lost, nervous, nothing, stress, goal, not, purpose, motivation, sad, me, work, fail, worry, achieve, myself, made, don't, it, help*

The negative emotions seen in this topic's top words (e.g., *sad, stress, nervous*) as seen in this topic's top words, and the subsequent reading of 128 responses that had this topic in the highest proportion suggest that disappointment is the primary reason for cessation of use. Even though feelings of disappointment were evident in the 60, 22, and 56 responses corresponding to the scenarios for *security, health and informatics*, and *connected home*, respectively, the reasons of the let down for each category of devices were different.

In regards to devices associated with the scenarios of *security* and *connected home*, users felt disappointed when the devices failed to serve any purpose. P440 explained: *The lock would only work if it had good Internet connectivity. The worry of it failing to secure the home and fulfilling its purpose due to any reason made me stop using it* (Security). Forty participants also perceived these devices as trivial and banal, which gradually led to their abandonment. For example, P333 said: *My Google home was fun in the beginning. But there is not much you can do with it, like a phone has so much purpose. It is mere waste of time* (Connected Home).

Devices belonging to *health and informatics* were abandoned as they demotivated the users through reminders about their failures or unattained goals. P208 explained, *The device keeping track of my activities did not help me achieve my goal rather it made me sad. Earlier the reminders used to trigger me to work. But then I started to become nervous of them coming and then it caused stress and sadness that my group members are getting fit but I am not. It started demotivating me by reminding me about my failures and then slowly I lost the motivation to use it* (Health and Informatics).

Topic: Information Concerns

Top 20 words: *much, privacy, many, too, distract, information, excessive, private, share, not, data, does, me, alter, allow, my, need, monitor, lot, disturb*

A total of 115 responses, comprising 24, 39, and 52 survey answers to the scenarios for *security, health and informatics,* and *connected home*), respectively, listed information concern(s) as the reason for abandonment.

Thirty-nine of these responses indicated that too much information annoyed the participants, distracting them from focusing on the task at hand or other important daily activities, and sometimes even affected their productivity. For example, one respondent remarked, *Every time getting a notification when something was ordered through my smart assistant or if somebody called my kid was annoying. I also think it was constantly collecting my information* (P250, Connected Home); another said, *It [activity tracker] used to distract me multiple times in a day while being at work or with family* (P1, Health and Informatics).

Thirty-seven responses suggested that not trusting the ways sensors worked rendered the devices less useful for participants. Participants explained, *I am not sure if the sensor was capable enough to save my energy cost* (P499, Connected Home), and *The fact that device gives better results on dominant wrist made me skeptical of its overall accuracy* (P222, Health and Informatics).

Another 17 participants mentioned the inability to customize information or learning behavior of a device as their reason for abandoning these devices. For example, P66 said, *The smart lock that I had did not allow me to customize my schedule. Also, as my schedule was getting stored on the Internet, there were high chances of it getting leaked* (Security).

Furthermore, the analysis of the respondents' answers to multiple-choice questions revealed that 301 (36.09%) of our participants reported privacy issues to be relevant to their decision to forgo use. A total of 140 (46.5%) of the participants reported privacy issues to be *extremely important* or *very important* to the way they used a device. However, only 22 participants highlighted data ownership and misuse of data by device manufacturers as the sole reason for abandonment. For example, P56 explained, *I am not sure how my location data and my temperature preferences are being used by Nest. They might be misusing the data by selling it for certain benefits* (Connected Home). Overall, even though privacy concerns of IoT are well documented (e.g., [39]) and may participants mentioned it being relevant to the decision of use, only few (22) of the participants in our study mentioned privacy as the sole reason for abandonment.

Topic: Overload of Features and Devices

Top 20 words: *money, cost, upgrade, maintain, it, much, like, looks, hate, annoy, feature, many, high, extra, difficult, dependent, less, function, not, manage*

The scenarios for *security, health and informatics,* and *connected home* drew 35, 52, and 30 responses on this topic, respectively.

In addition to issues over device aesthetics, comfort, and high frequency of maintenance, as found by other studies (e.g., [33,49]), the participants in our study also stopped using a device because it became too complicated to use due to an overload of features or because the cost of maintaining or owning it was too high. For example, one respondent said, *I stopped using the iWatch because*

I really didn't need all the extra features. Phone functions in a similar fashion, but is much less obtrusive, and I almost always have my phone on me anyway (P811, Health and Informatics); another observed, *The security device that we installed was difficult to maintain and I started to hate it after a while. It's costs so much money to maintain such high end devices* (P111, Security).

Twenty out of 117 responses also attributed abandoning the devices to negative consequences related to productivity and an overdependence on technology. Participants explained, *At some point I realized I am constantly using or checking one device or another. It kept me from doing other important tasks. So I got rid of my activity tracker as I was constantly checking my activity stats* (P542, Health and Informatics), and *I realized it was getting ridiculous that even for a simple task like switching on a light I was giving commands. I did not want to be so dependent on technology* (P777, Connected Home).

5   Discussion and Design Implications

The goal of this study was to identify reasons and practices that lead to the (non-) use of a variety of IoT devices adopted voluntarily by the participants. Previous research (e.g., [33,49]) has explored use or non-use only with respect to wearables such as activity trackers. To the author's best knowledge, this is the first study to empirically investigate reasons for the use, limited use, or abandonment of various IoT devices that are used for *security, health and informatics/logging,* and *connected home*. This section discusses our contribution to the literature on the (non-)use of technology and associated design implications for the future of the IoT.

Value of Considering Selective Users

In the past, HCI researchers have argued that the role of non-users is important and valuable in designing successful technologies (e.g., [46,52]). Our findings provide empirical evidence for the existence of *selective users*, who limit or restrict the use of their devices of their own volition. This highlights the value of further refining the categories of (non-)users, resisters, rejecters, the excluded, and the expelled [52] to include *selective users*. The participants who had limited their use of IoT devices either felt a lack of control while using them or did not understand devices' behavior. Therefore, disenfranchisement for a user can arise not only from technical and economic constraints [46], but also from conceptual barriers, such as limited knowledge of a device's capabilities and questions about what it means to take a particular action when the device is sensing. This calls for transparent designs that make a device's capabilities, functionalities, and processes easily observable and understood by users. Furthermore, a device's autonomy can add to its convenience for some users, but for others it can prove to be a barrier to continued use. For the latter group of users, devices that exercised a high level of control scored low on perceived ease of use and usefulness.

In order to cater to the different needs and preferences of users, future IoT devices need to balance end-user control with automation to match each user's preferred degree of interaction. Such a hybrid approach would enable users to decide if they want to opt out of "intelligent features" or willingly relinquish (some) control to avail themselves of a more automated version of a feature or device. Some devices and manufacturers (e.g., "mute button" on a smart speaker gives users control over whether the device can actively listen for the wake command) Further, we do not recommend abandoning autonomous devices; instead, we believe that devices with autonomy should aim to increase users' understanding of how their systems learn and makes decisions. For example, devices can visualize and point out (un)successful actions, making users aware of the unforeseen outcomes that may result from their decisions.

Devices that Integrate into Daily Activities

Previous research has noted that *lagging resistance*, a sense of wanting to quit but not deciding to do so just yet, to be the most prevalent phenomenon amongst users [4]. The responses of our participants, however, suggested that they make well-reasoned and lucid decisions to forgo the use of devices or to systematically limit their use of certain functionalities.

The non-users of IoT devices within this work resonate with the *rejectors* [52], as they first used the devices of their own volition, but did not continue to do so. Several previous studies (e.g., [33]) have suggested that an established routine is essential for people to not reject the technology. The participants in our study who regularly used their devices indicated economic incentives associated with a device's use, convenience, or a device's emotional relevance in their life as their reasons for routine use. Participants who used devices other than wearables, such as smart thermostats or plugs, also developed a habit of use because the devices did not have to be deliberately used or worn. In other words, a device's ability to work independently after installation to achieve human-defined goals led to its becoming an integral part of its owner's life. This suggests that users are more likely to continue using devices that are minimally obtrusive, do not require extra work, and fit easily into their daily routine.

The designers of future IoT devices should examine ways in which devices can blend into users' existing routines without adding to users' workloads or responsibilities, or can work independently to achieve human-defined goal(s). In other words, future designs need to integrate more context sensing capabilities so that devices do "not force users to adapt" [1] and support continuous, yet unobtrusive engagement.

Devices' Enabling Social Interaction and Support

Previous research has pointed out the influence of network structure – consisting of strong social ties, such as friends and family, and weak social ties, such as friends of friends – on the adoption of technology. However, our findings draw attention to the influence networks of strong and weak ties have on the continued use of IoT devices. Our results further resonate with Self Determination Theory and Social Comparison Theory. While the former emphasizes the innate role of social relatedness (the will to interact and connect with others) in self-motivation [45], the latter suggests that people alter their behavior based on how others perceive them [21]. For the participants in the study, the ways they were evaluated or viewed by others and the ability to connect with their network of strong or weak ties affected their decisions on whether or not to continue use.

We recommend leveraging the inclination of users to connect with others as an opportunity to help users develop suitable conceptual or mental models as they incorporate new smart devices into their daily lives. In other words, new IoT devices can support online platforms or topic-specific groups where users can discuss the challenges and benefits of using such devices. A few devices, such as Fitbit and Nest Thermostat, already provide online and public troubleshooting communities, but we believe the ability to connect with friends through private groups will enable users to learn from the experiences of others (strong ties) and collaboratively understand how a new device operates. Such groups can also promote reflection on one's failures and help users to develop strategies that accommodate the changing nature of their preferences and needs.

6   Limitations and Future Work

This research involves some limitations that should be addressed in subsequent studies. First, this study analyzed only self-reported data from the participants' past recollections of (non)-use. This may be inaccurate to varying degrees. Therefore, further work may expand on finding hidden motivations by evaluating actual usage logs for different types of IoT devices. Usage logs would also enable dynamic analysis, which can uncover other nuanced patterns pertaining to how use and non-use change with time. Second, our participants were all U.S. IoT users, and the Amazon Mechanical Turk population is not entirely representative of U.S. residents in general (as seen in Table 1). One advantage of such a population is that our sample was composed of a large number of non-technical respondents who had adopted different types of smart devices voluntarily, which is an improvement over other studies of the users of smart devices. However, since there is a large number of non-U.S. IoT users, our results may address only part of the phenomenon. Therefore, future studies might investigate how users of different backgrounds use or abandon IoT devices. Finally, in the course of this study, we also found that many of these devices were co-owned by members of a family. Therefore, another promising direction for future work could be to explore how people make decisions about (non-)use in a shared context.

7   Conclusions

In this paper, we have explored the key preferences and practices that affect decisions about whether or not to use IoT devices, through an empirical study of 834 users who had previously and voluntarily adopted various types of IoT devices. To analyze the data, we adopted a mixed-method approach consisting of topic modeling and the inductive qualitative analysis of responses under each topic. We found that the possibility of treating IoT devices as co-actors, the social influences of these devices, and habit formation led to the continued use of IoT devices. However, if the devices disappointed the users, demotivated them with negative notifications, distracted them from important activities, or were too complex, the participants abandoned them. While we discuss several design implications of our findings, we also advocate including the category of *selective users*, who intentionally use devices only to a limited extent, in the taxonomy of non-users. The participants of our study limited their use of IoT devices specifically when they felt a lack of control over the devices, when the devices failed to understand their intent, or when they did not understand the device's behavior. These findings have implications for the design of future IoT devices, which need to meet the needs of users more closely, thereby enabling long-term use.

Acknowledgement. The author would like to thank the survey respondents for sharing their insights and would also like to gratefully acknowledge the efforts of the entire research team with the analysis of data.

References

1. Ackerman, M.S.: The intellectual challenge of CSCW: the gap between social requirements and technical feasibility. Hum.-Comput. Interact. **15**(2), 179–203 (2000)
2. Ames, M.G.: Managing mobile multitasking: the culture of iPhones on Stanford campus. In: Proceedings of the 2013 Conference on Computer Supported Cooperative Work, pp. 1487–1498. ACM (2013)
3. Atzori, L., Iera, A., Morabito, G.: The internet of things: a survey. Comput. Netw. **54**(15), 2787–2805 (2010)
4. Baumer, E.P., et al.: Limiting, leaving, and (re) lapsing: an exploration of Facebook non-use practices and experiences. In: Proceedings of the SIGCHI Conference on Human Factors in Computing Systems, pp. 3257–3266. ACM (2013)
5. Baumer, E.P., Burrell, J., Ames, M.G., Brubaker, J.R., Dourish, P.: On the importance and implications of studying technology non-use. Interactions **22**(2), 52–56 (2015)
6. Baumer, E.P., Guha, S., Quan, E., Mimno, D., Gay, G.K.: Missing photos, suffering withdrawal, or finding freedom? How experiences of social media non-use influence the likelihood of reversion. Soc. Media+ Soc. **1**(2) (2015). https://doi.org/10.1177/2056305115614851
7. Baumer, E.P., Mimno, D., Guha, S., Quan, E., Gay, G.K.: Comparing grounded theory and topic modeling: extreme divergence or unlikely convergence? J. Assoc. Inf. Sci. Technol. **68**(6), 1397–1410 (2017)
8. Black, M., Dana, K., Gaskins, K., Gaynier, C., Lemieux, A., McKinley, K.: The internet of things: can it find a foothold with mainstream audiences today. Technical report, The Nielsen Company (2014)
9. Blei, D.M., Ng, A.Y., Jordan, M.I.: Latent Dirichlet allocation. J. Mach. Learn. Res. **3**(Jan), 993–1022 (2003)
10. Brubaker, J.R., Ananny, M., Crawford, K.: Departing glances: a sociotechnical account of 'leaving' Grindr. New Med. Soc. **18**(3), 373–390 (2016)

11. Business Insider Intelligence: Many people still see smart home voice assistants as a novelty (2017). https://www.businessinsider.com/voice-assistants-novelty-2017-1. Accessed Jan 2018
12. Chancellor, S., Lin, Z., Goodman, E.L., Zerwas, S., De Choudhury, M.: Quantifying and predicting mental illness severity in online pro-eating disorder communities. In: Proceedings of the 19th ACM Conference on Computer-Supported Cooperative Work & Social Computing, pp. 1171–1184. ACM (2016)
13. Chen, F., Chiu, P., Lim, S.: Topic modeling of document metadata for visualizing collaborations over time. In: Proceedings of the 21st International Conference on Intelligent User Interfaces, pp. 108–117. ACM (2016)
14. Cila, N., Smit, I., Giaccardi, E., Kröse, B.: Products as agents: metaphors for designing the products of the IoT age. In: Proceedings of the 2017 CHI Conference on Human Factors in Computing Systems, pp. 448–459. ACM (2017)
15. Clark, M., Newman, M.W., Dutta, P.: Devices and data and agents, oh my: how smart home abstractions prime end-user mental models. In: Proceedings of the ACM on Interactive, Mobile, Wearable and Ubiquitous Technologies, vol. 1, no. 3, p. 44 (2017)
16. Clawson, J., Pater, J.A., Miller, A.D., Mynatt, E.D., Mamykina, L.: No longer wearing: investigating the abandonment of personal health-tracking technologies on craigslist. In: Proceedings of the 2015 ACM International Joint Conference on Pervasive and Ubiquitous Computing, pp. 647–658. ACM (2015)
17. Consolvo, S., et al.: Activity sensing in the wild: a field trial of ubifit garden. In: Proceedings of the SIGCHI Conference on Human Factors in Computing Systems, pp. 1797–1806. ACM (2008)
18. DeSanctis, G., Poole, M.S.: Capturing the complexity in advanced technology use: adaptive structuration theory. Organ. Sci. 5(2), 121–147 (1994)
19. Epstein, D.A., Caraway, M., Johnston, C., Ping, A., Fogarty, J., Munson, S.A.: Beyond abandonment to next steps: understanding and designing for life after personal informatics tool use. In: Proceedings of the 2016 CHI Conference on Human Factors in Computing Systems, pp. 1109–1113. ACM (2016)
20. Epstein, D.A., Jacobson, B.H., Bales, E., McDonald, D.W., Munson, S.A.: From nobody cares to way to go!: a design framework for social sharing in personal informatics. In: Proceedings of the 18th ACM Conference on Computer Supported Cooperative Work & Social Computing, pp. 1622–1636. ACM (2015)
21. Festinger, L.: A theory of social comparison processes. Hum. Relat. 7(2), 117–140 (1954)
22. Fritz, T., Huang, E.M., Murphy, G.C., Zimmermann, T.: Persuasive technology in the real world: a study of long-term use of activity sensing devices for fitness. In: Proceedings of the SIGCHI Conference on Human Factors in Computing Systems, pp. 487–496. ACM (2014)
23. Glaser, B.G., Strauss, A.L.: The Discovery of Grounded Theory: Strategies for Qualitative Theory. Aldine Transaction, New Brunswick (1967)
24. Goffman, E.: The Presentation of Self in Everyday Life (1959). Garden City, NY (2002)
25. Granovetter, M.S.: The strength of weak ties. In: Social Networks, pp. 347–367. Elsevier (1977)
26. Guha, S., Baumer, E.P., Gay, G.K.: Regrets, I've had a few: when regretful experiences do (and don't) compel users to leave Facebook. In: Proceedings of the 2018 ACM Conference on Supporting Groupwork, pp. 166–177. ACM (2018)
27. Hargittai, E.: Whose space? Differences among users and non-users of social network sites. J. Comput.-Med. Commun. 13(1), 276–297 (2007)

28. Harrison, D., Marshall, P., Bianchi-Berthouze, N., Bird, J.: Activity tracking: barriers, workarounds and customisation. In: Proceedings of the 2015 ACM International Joint Conference on Pervasive and Ubiquitous Computing, pp. 617–621. ACM (2015)
29. Jarrahi, M.H., Gafinowitz, N., Shin, G.: Activity trackers, prior motivation, and perceived informational and motivational affordances. Pers. Ubiquitous Comput. **22**, 433–448 (2018)
30. Kline, R.: Resisting consumer technology in rural America: the telephone and electrification. In: How Users Matter: The Co-construction of Users and Technology, pp. 51–66 (2003)
31. Krackhardt, D., Nohria, N., Eccles, B.: The strength of strong ties. In: Networksin the Knowledge Economy, p. 82 (2003)
32. Lampe, C., Vitak, J., Ellison, N.: Users and nonusers: interactions between levels of adoption and social capital. In: Proceedings of the 2013 Conference on Computer Supported Cooperative Work, pp. 809–820. ACM (2013)
33. Lazar, A., Koehler, C., Tanenbaum, J., Nguyen, D.H.: Why we use and abandon smart devices. In: Proceedings of the 2015 ACM International Joint Conference on Pervasive and Ubiquitous Computing, pp. 635–646. ACM (2015)
34. Ledger, D., McCaffrey, D.: Inside wearables: how the science of human behavior change offers the secret to long-term engagement. Endeavour Partners **200**(93), 1 (2014)
35. Luger, E., Sellen, A.: Like having a really bad PA: the gulf between user expectation and experience of conversational agents. In: Proceedings of the 2016 CHI Conference on Human Factors in Computing Systems, pp. 5286–5297. ACM (2016)
36. Marsden, P.V., Campbell, K.E.: Measuring tie strength. Soc. Forces **63**(2), 482–501 (1984)
37. Meyer, J., et al.: Exploring longitudinal use of activity trackers. In: 2016 IEEE International Conference on Healthcare Informatics (ICHI), pp. 198–206. IEEE (2016)
38. Meyer, J., Wasmann, M., Heuten, W., El Ali, A., Boll, S.C.: Identification and classification of usage patterns in long-term activity tracking. In: Proceedings of the 2017 CHI Conference on Human Factors in Computing Systems, pp. 667–678. ACM (2017)
39. Naeini, P.E., et al.: Privacy expectations and preferences in an IoT world. In: Symposium on Usable Privacy and Security (SOUPS) (2017)
40. Palinkas, L.A., Horwitz, S.M., Green, C.A., Wisdom, J.P., Duan, N., Hoagwood, K.: Purposeful sampling for qualitative data collection and analysis in mixed method implementation research. Adm. Policy Ment. Health Ment. Health Serv. Res. **42**(5), 533–544 (2015)
41. Patel, M., O'Kane, A.A.: Contextual influences on the use and non-use of digital technology while exercising at the gym. In: Proceedings of the 33rd Annual ACM Conference on Human Factors in Computing Systems, pp. 2923–2932. ACM (2015)
42. Rader, E., Wash, R., Brooks, B.: Stories as informal lessons about security. In: Proceedings of the Eighth Symposium on Usable Privacy and Security, p. 6. ACM (2012)
43. Rantakari, J., Inget, V., Colley, A., Häkkilä, J.: Charting design preferences on wellness wearables. In: Proceedings of the 7th Augmented Human International Conference 2016, p. 28. ACM (2016)
44. Rooksby, J., Rost, M., Morrison, A., Chalmers, M.C.: Personal tracking as lived informatics. In: Proceedings of the 32nd Annual ACM Conference on Human Factors in Computing Systems, pp. 1163–1172. ACM (2014)

45. Ryan, R.M., Patrick, H., Deci, E.L., Williams, G.C.: Facilitating health behaviour change and its maintenance: interventions based on self-determination theory. Eur. Health Psychol. **10**(1), 2–5 (2008)
46. Satchell, C., Dourish, P.: Beyond the user: use and non-use in HCI. In: Proceedings of the 21st Annual Conference of the Australian Computer-Human Interaction Special Interest Group: Design: Open 24/7, pp. 9–16. ACM (2009)
47. Schoenebeck, S.Y.: Giving up Twitter for lent: how and why we take breaks from social media. In: Proceedings of the SIGCHI Conference on Human Factors in Computing Systems, pp. 773–782. ACM (2014)
48. Selwyn, N.: Digital division or digital decision? A study of non-users and low-users of computers. Poetics **34**(4–5), 273–292 (2006)
49. Shih, P.C., Han, K., Poole, E.S., Rosson, M.B., Carroll, J.M.: Use and adoption challenges of wearable activity trackers. In: IConference 2015 Proceedings (2015)
50. Stringer, M., Fitzpatrick, G., Harris, E.: Lessons for the future: experiences with the installation and use of today's domestic sensors and technologies. In: Fishkin, K.P., Schiele, B., Nixon, P., Quigley, A. (eds.) Pervasive 2006. LNCS, vol. 3968, pp. 383–399. Springer, Heidelberg (2006). https://doi.org/10.1007/11748625_24
51. Wyatt, S., Thomas, G., Terranova, T.: They came, they surfed, they went back to the beach: conceptualizing. In: Virtual Society, pp. 23–40 (2002)
52. Wyatt, S.M., Oudshoorn, N., Pinch, T.: Non-users also matter: the construction of users and non-users of the internet. In: Now Users Matter: The Co-construction of Users and Technology, pp. 67–79 (2003)
53. Wyche, S.P., Schoenebeck, S.Y., Forte, A.: Facebook is a luxury: an exploratory study of social media use in rural Kenya. In: Proceedings of the 2013 Conference on Computer Supported Cooperative Work, pp. 33–44. ACM (2013)
54. Yang, R., Newman, M.W.: Learning from a learning thermostat: lessons for intelligent systems for the home. In: Proceedings of the 2013 ACM International Joint Conference on Pervasive and Ubiquitous Computing, pp. 93–102. ACM (2013)

Analysis of Utilization in the Message Card Production by Use of Fusion Character of Handwriting and Typeface

Mikako Sasaki[✉], Junki Saito, and Satoshi Nakamura

Meiji University, 4-21-1, Nakano-ku, Tokyo, Japan
cs192018@meiji.ac.jp

Abstract. Many Japanese people hope to receive handwritten messages from others even though they have resistance to handwrite messages for them. In previous studies, we have revealed that fusion character with handwriting and typeface could reduce the resistance toward handwriting. However, the system used in the previous studies did not allow users to change the type of typeface and the fusion rate, so it was not clear how our fusion method can be utilized. In this paper, we implemented a prototype system to create message cards with a fusion method which enables users to control the fusion rate and to select the typeface. Then, we conducted experiments on whether writers change the way to use the system according to their relationship with the reader or the effect of the message card's design. The results of the experiments revealed that the writer changed the way to use the system depending on card designs and their relationship with the reader.

Keywords: Handwriting · Typeface · Fusion character · Message card · Analysis

1 Introduction

In Japan, people often have opportunities to write messages at scenes such as their friends' birthdays and weddings, farewell at school and workplace, and seasonal greetings. Here, they can type letters easily with computers or smartphones and create message cards. However, many Japanese people think it is desirable to create such message cards with their handwriting especially when they want to convey their feelings more strongly since handwriting can express the warmth and personality of the writer. In fact, according to a public opinion poll by Japanese Agency for Cultural Affairs [1], 90% of Japanese people answered they preferred cards such as New Year's cards to be handwritten rather than to be typed.

In the past, Zitnick et al. [2] and Niino et al. [3] conducted researches on how to help writers produce beautiful handwriting. However, most Japanese people still have resistance to handwriting messages themselves. Zebra Corporation [4] found that 90%

Electronic supplementary material The online version of this chapter (https://doi.org/10.1007/978-3-030-29390-1_2) contains supplementary material, which is available to authorized users.

© IFIP International Federation for Information Processing 2019
Published by Springer Nature Switzerland AG 2019
D. Lamas et al. (Eds.): INTERACT 2019, LNCS 11749, pp. 25–33, 2019.
https://doi.org/10.1007/978-3-030-29390-1_2

of Japanese people are aware that they are bad at handwriting. In fact, according to the Zebra survey, more than half of Japanese people have a negative impression on their own handwriting.

To solve these problems, Saito et al. [5] proposed a method to fuse handwriting and typeface easily to design texts in comics. Then, we applied this method for generating message cards and conducted an experimental test on whether the fusion character of handwriting and typeface can reduce resistance and shame toward one's handwriting [6]. The results of the experiments revealed that fusion character of handwriting and typeface could reduce resistance to one's handwriting, while it keeps characteristics of handwriting in that it expresses warmth and personality of the writer. In addition, we found that both the writers and the readers had a positive impression of the fusion character, and the usefulness of the fusion characters for messages cards was verified. However, this previous study of ours did not allow users to change the type of typeface and the fusion rate when they generated a message card. In addition, the experiments were conducted only for the situation where the writer and the reader are close friends. Thus, it was not clear whether message cards with fusion characters are useful for such situations as they are written to the writer's boss, teacher, or small children. In addition, Kato et al. [7, 8] conducted a study that focused on the emotions between the writer and the reader in communication. However, they did not reveal how the differences in the relationship between the writer and the reader in communication were influenced by the fusion of handwriting and typeface. Furthermore, Cross et al. [9] suggested the system of online educational videos that dynamically changes from handwriting to typeface. However, they have not suggested the system using a character that has advantages of handwriting and typeface on digital devices.

In this paper, we implement a system to create message cards with fusion characters with which users can change the type of typeface and the fusion rate. Then, we reveal how the utilization of the system is changed according to the relationship between the writer and the reader and the difference in card designs. Specifically, we examine changes in typeface selection and fusion rate due to difference in types of the reader (i.e. superior, close friends or children) and differences in card designs.

The contributions of this paper are as follows.

- We realized a prototype system to create message cards with fusion character.
- We clarified that the writers changed their usage behavior of the system in response to their relationship with the reader and the card design.

2   Message Card with Fusion Character

2.1   Method to Generate Fusion Character of Handwriting and Typeface

We used Saito et al.'s method [5] to generate fusion characters. This method represents type characters as a numerical formula that parameterizes "t" by performing Fourier series expansion to change the character's core and thickness. It also uses the weighted average of the typed character's numerical formula and the handwriting's numerical formula. The generation of the character at the fusion ratio between handwriting and type character of 0.0 (handwriting) – 1.0 (type character) at intervals of 0.2 using this method is given in Fig. 1. Moreover, handwriting is emphasized close to 0.0, and the typeface is emphasized close to 1.0.

Also, we set the fusion ratios of the core and the thickness separately this time. Here, the core is a portion of the character's skeleton.

0.0(Handwriting)   0.2   0.4   0.6   0.8   1.0(Typeface)

Fig. 1. Japanese character "あ" of the fusion ratio between handwriting and type character at intervals of 0.2 between 0.0 and 1.0.

2.2 Prototype System

We implemented a prototype system of message card with fusion character of handwriting and typeface (see Fig. 2) based on the algorithm of Subsect. 2.1.

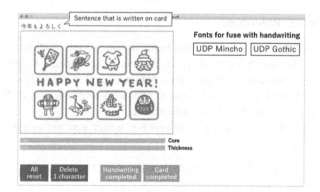

Fig. 2. Prototype system

First, a user presets the design and the content of the message. Then, they handwrite a sentence that is presented at the upper left of the screen on the message card. They can freely adjust the position and the size of the character and handwriting direction. Moreover, they can delete a character by pressing "Delete one character" button and delete all characters by pressing "All reset" button.

When they finish writing the specified sentence, they press the button of "Handwriting completed," and then they can select the type of typeface that is going to be fused with their handwriting at the upper right of the screen. In the system, we prepared two fonts for fusion with the handwriting: "BIZ UDP Mincho" and "BIZ UDP Gothic," both of which were generated by Morisawa [10] (Fig. 3). It is possible for the users to create their favorite fusion character by pressing the button of the type of typeface that is to be fused with their handwriting, and adjusting the fusion ratio of "core wire" and "thickness" with the slider at the bottom of the message card, the left side of the screen. The value of the slider is from 0% to 100%, in which handwriting is more emphasized when it is adjusted closer to 0% and the typeface is more emphasized as it is adjusted closer to 100%. Furthermore, because the fusion characters are generated in real time, it is possible for the users to see the change of the characters by changing the slider's value.

BIZ UDP Mincho BIZ UDP Gothic

Fig. 3. The typeface used in the experiment

3 Usage Experiment of the System

As mentioned in Sect. 2, we carried out experiments on how the creation behavior was changed in the use of the system to create message cards in response to the relationship between the writer and the reader and the card designs when the type of typeface and the fusion ratio can be adjusted freely.

3.1 Experimental Procedure

To analyze the differences of the creating behavior due to the relationship between the writer and the reader and the card designs, we asked participants to create a message card by using our prototype system with a tablet PC. The input device was Surface Book (Microsoft Corporation), and New Year's card was selected as the card to be created since Japanese people often handwrite it.

First, to clarify the relationship between the writer and the reader, we set three relationships as follows.

- The reader is a child who is younger than the writer.
- The reader is the writer's close friend.
- The reader is a boss or teacher who is older than the writer.

As for the sentence to be written, we selected "kotoshi mo yoroshiku" which is a common phrase used in New Year's card in Japanese and could be translated as "thank you in advance for this year." In the experiments, the expressions of the sentence end were changed in response to the relationships since Japanese people change the expressions of the phrase according to their relationship with the reader (e.g., Japanese people use the polite expression for elder readers).

In addition, we assumed that the usage behavior of the system would change more by using the card designs suitable for the relationship between the writer and the reader. For this reason, the experimental participants were divided into two groups of ten people. We asked the participants in one of the groups to use the same card design [11]

(Fig. 4) for all types of relationship, and we asked the participants in the other group to use different card [12–14] designs (Fig. 4) in response to the relationship. The participants were asked to create message cards in the order of ones for a younger person, one for a close friend and one for an older person, and to press the button of "Card complete" after they finished creating the message card. While the user is creating the message card, we kept record of the user's usage behavior such as working hours, the type of typeface fused with handwriting, the fusion ratio of the core wire and the thickness, the image of the message card before typeface was fused with handwriting, and the image of the completed message card.

In addition, after each of the message cards was completed, the participants were asked about the message card that they created and the utilization of the system. The participants of the same card design group were ten people (six males, four females), and the participants of the different card design group were ten people (four males, six females).

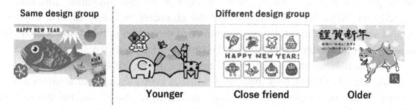

Fig. 4. Templates of the message card that we used in the experiment.

3.2 Results

The graphs in Fig. 5 summarized the mean of the ratio of the core wire and the thickness for every three types of relationships.

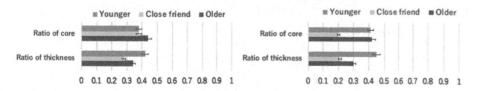

Fig. 5. Mean of the ratio of the core and thickness when the card was completed. Left: Group of the same design, Right: Group of the different design

From Fig. 5, it can be seen that, for the message cards with the same design, the mean of the ratio of the core wire and the thickness at the time when the message card was completed was equal regardless of the relationships between the writer and the reader. Also, we performed an analysis of variance in the ratio of the core wire and the thickness but did not find significant statistical differences.

It can also be seen in Fig. 5 that the mean of the ratio of the core wire and the thickness at the time when the message card was completed for the message cards with different designs had the lowest value on the occasion where the relationship between the writer and the reader was close friends. Also, we performed an analysis of variance for the ratio of the core wire and the thickness and found the only significant statistical difference for the ratio of the core wire in the different design ($p < 0.05$). Then, we performed an independent t-test for the ratio of the core wire and the thickness between the groups for the same relationship but did not find any significant statistical differences.

As for the type of typeface fused with handwriting, it was observed that Gothic was often used for younger readers, and Mincho was often used for older readers. The difference was particularly striking for message cards with different designs.

Figure 6 shows the results of the questionnaire on what the participants cared the most about when creating the message cards. As shown in Fig. 6, the participants answered that they cared "Fusion ratio" the most on the occasion when the reader is younger than the writer. On the occasion when the reader is a close friend to the writer, two participants selected "Other" as their answer to the question, and they both commented that they cared about whether the character is funny or not. One of the participants selected "Other" for the occasions that the reader is the writer's close friend or younger than the writer, and explained that they tried to make sure the character is easy to read and matches the card design when creating a card for a younger reader and tried to make the characters look beautiful while it keeps some characteristics of their handwriting since the original handwriting looked ugly. Note that for the occasions where the reader is an older person than the writer, many participants from both groups selected items about handwriting such as "Politeness of handwriting" and "Shape of handwriting," and "Balance of character" as their answer to the question.

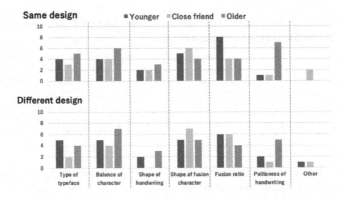

Fig. 6. What was emphasized when creating?

Also, the results of the questionnaire reported that fifteen participants answered that they want to use the system in the future. This means that 75% of the participants were thinking about using the system in the future.

Figures 7 and 8 respectively show examples of cards created with the same design and with the different designs. They show that the fusion ratio of handwriting and typeface and the type of typeface were different in response to the writer's relationship with the reader. Also, although the three cards in Fig. 7 and in Fig. 8 were created by a different person respectively, the writing direction and the thickness of the fusion character were changed in response to the relationships.

Fig. 7. Example of products with the same design

Fig. 8. Example of products with different design

3.3 Discussion

The experimental results revealed that the usage behavior of the system was changed in response to the relationship between the writer and the reader. The difference of the types of the typeface in response to the relationship was particularly remarkable, and we found that the writers tend to change the type of typeface in response to their relationship with the reader, as they use Gothic for the younger, and Mincho for the older.

In Fig. 5, there are significant statistical differences in the ratio of the core in the different design. From this result, the difference in the relationship affects the shape of the character. However, there was no significant statistical difference in the ratio of the core wire and the thickness between the groups in the same relationships. This result shows that it was not the card design but the relationship between the writer and the reader that influenced the fusion ratio.

In addition, we found that the difference in the card design also changed the usage behavior of the system. Specifically, the type of typeface fused with handwriting was changed for the cards with the same design in response to the relationship, but the difference of the type of typeface appeared more in the cards with the different designs. For this reason, we assumed that the writer was influenced by the characteristics of the characters originally written in the message card, and consciously changed the type of typeface fused with handwriting. Therefore, when our prototype system is realized as a service to create message cards, it should have a function of the automatic recommendation of the types of the typeface to be fused with handwriting in response to the relationship with the reader.

In the results of the questionnaire, we observed that participants in the different card design group had more difficulty in creating their ideal message cards compared to the participants in the same designs. This might be because the card designs were more formal for the different card design group, so it was difficult for many of them to create message cards that match the formal designs. Then, it needs to be examined in the future experiments whether this problem can be solved by preparing appropriate fonts for the designs or there is no way to solve it.

In addition, we showed from the record of the users' usage behavior through the experiments and the results of the questionnaire that the mean of the ratio of thickness was the highest and the fusion ratio was the most cared about during the creation when the reader is younger than the writer. This would suggest that the writers might have tried to make the card easy to read since the card receiver was assumed not only to be younger than the writer but also to be small children. In addition, when the relationship between the writer and the reader was close friends, the creation time of the message card was the shortest and it was observed that two of the participants cared the most about whether the characters look funny on not when creating. These might suggest that the writers strongly wanted to create message cards with less editing since the writer and the reader know each other very well.

Further, when the reader is older than the writer, the number of times when handwriting was rewritten was the largest and points related to handwriting were the most cared about when creating the message cards. In addition, the average creation time was the largest for this relationship. These results imply that the writers wanted to create their message cards for an older reader with beautiful characters, which made them write the message carefully.

4   Conclusion and Future Work

In this paper, we implemented a prototype system which enables users to create message cards with the fusion method and conducted an experimental test to investigate how the utilization of the system to create message cards is changed when there are differences in the relationship between the writer and the reader and the card design. Then, we clarified that the writers changed the type of typeface fused with handwriting in response to the relationship and were influenced by the card designs.

In the future, we will update the system so that handwriting can be fused with more variety of typeface because only two fonts were available in the experiment of the current study. By doing so, we will utilize not only existing fonts but also typeface generating by using the method of Zhu et al. [15] and Lin et al. [16].

In addition, it was pointed out in the questionnaire on the utilization of the system that the size of character differed depending on a character so that we will improve the system for this point. Moreover, we will allow the utilization of the system on the smartphone by making it an application or a service. Also, we will develop the system so that people can use fusion characters not only for message cards but also for other things such as lyrics on music videos, cartoon captions, text illustrations or movie subtitles.

Acknowledgments. This work was supported in part by JST ACCEL Grant Number JPMJAC1602.

References

1. The Agency for Cultural Affairs: The Public Opinion Poll on Japanese/ http://www.bunka. go.jp/tokei_hakusho_shuppan/tokeichosa/kokugo_yoronchosa/pdf/h26_chosa_kekka.pdf. Accessed 04 May 2019
2. Zitnick, C.L.: Handwriting beautification using token means. In: ACM Special Interest Group on Computer Graphics and Interactive Techniques (SIGGRAPH 2013), vol. 32, Anaheim (2013)
3. Niino, S., Hagiwara, N., Nakamura, S., Suzuki, M., Komatsu, T.: Analysis of average hand-drawing and its application. In: Chisik, Y., Holopainen, J., Khaled, R., Luis Silva, J., Alexandra Silva, P. (eds.) INTETAIN 2017. LNICST, vol. 215, pp. 34–48. Springer, Cham (2018). https://doi.org/10.1007/978-3-319-73062-2_3
4. Zebra Corporation: Attitude Survey on the Handwriting. http://www.zebra.co.jp/press/news/2014/0918.html. Accessed 04 May 2019
5. Saito, J., Nakamura, S.: Fontender: interactive Japanese text design with dynamic font fusion method for comics. In: Kompatsiaris, I., Huet, B., Mezaris, V., Gurrin, C., Cheng, W.-H., Vrochidis, S. (eds.) MMM 2019. LNCS, vol. 11296, pp. 554–559. Springer, Cham (2019). https://doi.org/10.1007/978-3-030-05716-9_45
6. Sasaki, M., Saito, J., Nakamura, S.: Improving visibility and reducing resistance of writers to fusion of handwritten and type characters. In: Egi, H., Yuizono, T., Baloian, N., Yoshino, T., Ichimura, S., Rodrigues, A. (eds.) CollabTech 2018. LNCS, vol. 11000, pp. 185–199. Springer, Cham (2018). https://doi.org/10.1007/978-3-319-98743-9_15
7. Kato, Y., Kato, S., Akahori, K.: Effects of emotional cues transmitted in e-mail communication on the emotions experienced by senders and receivers. Comput. Hum. Behav. **23**(4), 1894–1905 (2007)
8. Kato, Y., Kato, S., Akahori, K.: Influences of self-disclosure and styles of writing messages in e-mails of recipients' emotional aspects: a case study focusing on female university students. J. Sci. Educ. Jpn. **30**(4), 216–228 (2006)
9. Cross, A., Bayyapunedi, M., Cutrell, E., Agarwal, A., Thies, W.: TypeRighting: combining the benefits of handwriting and typeface in online educational videos. In: SIGCHI Conference on Human Factors in Computing Systems (CHI 2013), Paris (2013)
10. Morisawa: MORISAWA BIZ+. http://bizplus.morisawa.co.jp/. Accessed 05 Apr 2019
11. Brother at your side. https://online.brother.co.jp/ot/dl/Contents/nenga/nenga_casual/nengaj oucd_h0063/. Accessed 05 Apr 2019
12. Brother at your side. https://online.brother.co.jp/ot/dl/Contents/nenga/nenga_character/animalnenga_02/. Accessed 05 Apr 2019
13. Brother at your side. https://online.brother.co.jp/ot/dl/Contents/nenga/nenga_casual/etone ngajoucd_h0011/. Accessed 05 Apr 2019
14. Brother at your side. https://online.brother.co.jp/ot/dl/Contents/nenga/nenga_basic/etoneng ajoubd_h0010/. Accessed 05 Apr 2019
15. Zhu, X., Jin, L.: Calligraphic beautification of handwritten Chinese characters: a patternized approach to handwriting transfiguration. Semantic Scholar (2008)
16. Lin, J.-W., Hong, C.-Y., Chang, R.-I., Wang, Y.-C., Lin, S.-Y., Ho, J.-M.: Complete font generation of Chinese characters in personal handwriting style. In: 34th Computing and Communications Conference (IPCCC2015), Nanijing (2015)

Communicating User Insights
with Travel Mindsets and Experience
Personas in Intra-city Bus Context

Elina Hildén[✉] and Kaisa Väänänen

Tampere University, Korkeakoulunkatu 6, 33720 Tampere, Finland
elina.hilden@tuni.fi

Abstract. Design of attractive services for the bus travel context is important because of the aim to increase the usage of sustainable travel modes of public transportation. In bus travel, both user experience of the digital services and the broader service design context of the public transportation need to be addressed. Experience-Driven Design (EDD) can be used to take the passengers' needs and experiences in the core of the design process. This paper presents a qualitative diary and interview study on bus travel experience with 20 passengers in two major cities in Finland. The aim of this study was to identify and communicate frequent bus passengers' needs, experiences, values and activities as user insights to support experience-driven service design in the public transportation context. Based on the data analysis, we derived ten *Travel Mindsets*: *Abstracted, Efficient, Enjoyer, In-control, Isolation, Observer, Off-line, Relaxed, Sensitive,* and *Social*. To communicate the study findings on bus passengers' travel experience, *Travel Experience Personas* were created. The personas include primary and secondary travel mindsets, specific needs related to bus travel, insights on mobile device usage, and target user experience (UX) goals that could enhance the personas' travel experience. We also discuss how the personas can be used as a communicative design tool that supports EDD of novel services in the bus context.

Keywords: Experience-Driven Design · User experience (UX) ·
Travel experience · Bus · Design tool · UX goal · Persona · Mindset

1 Introduction

Bus as a vehicle is an interesting context to study, since both user experience of the digital services and the broader service design context of the public transportation need to be addressed. As in many other fields, taking users in the center of the design process has become topical also in the context of public transportation; to make public transportation a more appealing option to a wide audience, its services need to be developed with the passengers' needs and experiences in mind [8, 9]. One way to make public transportation more appealing is to enhance the services related to the travel activities. For instance, bus passengers are opportune targets to be entertained during their journeys [8]. Research [e.g. 2, 8, 17] shows that there is a need for additional services beyond travel information in the bus context. Existing studies focus on travel behavior

© IFIP International Federation for Information Processing 2019
Published by Springer Nature Switzerland AG 2019
D. Lamas et al. (Eds.): INTERACT 2019, LNCS 11749, pp. 34–52, 2019.
https://doi.org/10.1007/978-3-030-29390-1_3

[34], trip satisfaction [e.g. 9, 33], and travel experience [e.g. 2, 8]. These studies present mostly quantitative research efforts that cover the topic of improving the bus travel experience from the usability and efficiency perspectives. In order to create empathic understanding of passengers' needs, motivations and experiences, more qualitative research is needed.

In this study, we utilized Experience-Driven Design (EDD) approach to study and communicate bus passengers' needs. This paper presents findings from a qualitative field study on bus passengers' travel experience and proposes a way to communicate the findings as a design tool in form of Personas [4]. We utilized interviews and a diary method, inspired by the cultural probes [11] to collect insights of passengers' bus journeys. The study was conducted with altogether 20 participants, all frequent bus users, in two major Finnish cities: Tampere, and Helsinki region, during the spring and summer of 2017.

This study is part of a three-year research project *Living Lab Bus* that aims to develop a digital service ecosystem around modern electric buses in intra-city travel. One outcome of the research project is a developer portal for software developers to design and test digital services for bus travel. The aim of this study was to discover passengers' needs, and to gain understanding of bus travel experience, in order to derive useful insights which could be turned into visual format that the software developers and designers could utilize in the design process. Hence, our research question was: *What kind of travel mindsets do frequent bus passengers have?* We answer this question by analyzing the data and presenting ten *travel mindsets* derived from our study findings. These mindsets represent the central academic findings of the paper by contributing to the knowledge of intra-city bus passengers' travel experience.

To communicate our study findings – the found ten travel mindsets – in visual and tangible format, we created *Travel Experience Personas*. The personas as communicative design tool provide holistic understanding of the varying passenger needs to help the ideation and evaluation of new bus travel related services. Hence, the *Travel Experience Personas*, their travel mindsets and target UX goals enable the formulation of empathic understanding of bus passengers' varying needs.

This paper is organized as follows: next, we review related work on Bus Travel Experience, as well as EDD and Personas. Then we present our qualitative field study on bus travel experience. In the following section, we introduce the analysed findings structured as ten travel mindsets, after which, we present the visual and communicative Travel Experience Personas that can be utilized as a design tool in the development of travel related services. Finally, in the Discussion section, we address ways on how this communicative design tool can support the design of novel traveling services in the bus context.

2   Related Work

We present related work on Bus Travel Experience, Experience Driven Design (EDD), and Personas as tools for communicating user insights.

2.1 Bus Travel Experience

Trip satisfaction [e.g. 9, 33] and travel behavior [e.g. 34] are widely studied in the transportation literature, whereas travel experience has been left with relatively little focus [2, 3]. The aspects of travel have been studied across different travel modes. Passengers' traveling behaviour and experience is changing with the mix of transport modes and the services offered in them [34].

Bus is an interesting service context to study, since it contains services both in the physical realm, i.e. the actual transportation system, and in the digital sphere, i.e. the digital services in the bus, bus stops and on the passengers' mobile devices. According to Carreira et al. [2], travel experience in the context of public transportation is a result of the holistic view of the transportation service, including the different experience components: the customer's affective, cognitive, physical and social responses to the service. Their qualitative study investigated mid-distance bus journeys (intercity transportation), focusing on experience factors such as social environment, service interface, retail atmosphere, assortment, price, and retail brand (ibid.). In turn, Foth et al. [8] studied micro activities (social, entertainment, observational, travel, and routine) performed by passengers during commute, and how these activities impact the bus travel experience.

Other studies show that people spend their travel time listening to music and using social media applications in addition to reading newspapers and books or simply relaxing [23]. Several studies have been conducted to evaluate how certain services support the travel experience, these include traveller information systems [e.g. 7, 38]; games that for instance support social interaction [e.g. 25], communicate community information [e.g. 28], or simply entertain passengers with simple games [e.g. 21].

Research Gap

As seen above, several studies exist, ranging from trail experience [e.g. 27, 35] to air travel experience [e.g. 22]. Bus travel experience has also been studied, but for instance Carreira et al. [2, 3] focus on mid-distance intercity transportation, which has different characteristics to short-distance intra-city bus travel (for instance the vehicle itself, the length and purpose of the trip). Transportation literature is mostly presenting qualitative studies focusing on the efficiency and usability aspects of the travel. Studies that would investigate the travel experience from the aspects of service design and experience driven design are scarce in academic literature.

During the past three years, we have studied intra-city bus travel experience by conducting several qualitative studies that involve bus passengers in Finland. These studies include a preliminary interview study [16], collaborative ideation workshops by which we developed bus-specific design tool "Context Cards" [17], and this diary and interview study that was conducted in Helsinki and Tampere. Our aim has been to form holistic understanding of intra-city bus passengers' travel experience and communicate our study findings further to designers and developers working in the public transportation context. Hence, we have developed a *Travel Experience Toolkit* that consists of different tools that can be utilized in different phases of the design process to bring the user perspective to the centre of the design. A concept of this toolkit [19] consisted of preliminary personas, Context Cards [18], and a Passenger Journey Map. In addition to these tools, we have also created a *Bus Travel Experience Model* [20] that presents the elements impacting the intra-city bus travel experience: *Passenger* and their own mood and values, *Context* including social, temporal, task and physical context; *System* of public transportation and the *System* of digital services on the mobile device. Travel mindsets and experience personas enhance the existing tools by providing deep insights on specific user groups and their needs, and thus help designers and developers to serve the whole range of bus passengers.

2.2 Experience-Driven Design

Experience is a complex fabric of actions, feelings, and thoughts [15], whereas user experience (UX) refers to an individual's range of perceptions, interpretations of the individual's perceptions, and the emotions that result during an encounter with a system [30]. User experience consists of both pragmatic and hedonic attributes [12]. Pragmatic attributes refer to the product's, service's or system's functional usability, whereas the hedonic attributes relate to the emotional and non-instrumental needs of the user (ibid.).

The field of UX focuses on studying and evaluating the experiences that people have through the use of a system and designing better products or services that could enhance the user experience.

Experience-Driven Design is an approach that puts the user – their needs and experiences as a starting point of the design process [e.g. 6, 14]. The studied user needs are formulated into target experiences that are used to guide the design [6]. These target experiences can also be called *UX goals* [36]. Since experience is always subjective, it is not guaranteed that the targeted experience is evoked or the set UX goals fulfilled [14]. Thus, one can only design *for* certain experiences. Defined UX goals can be used as inspiration and target for the design [6, 14]. UX goals can have multiple purposes in design and development processes: according to Väätäjä et al. [37] a good UX goal provides focus and framing for design, it functions as a source for inspiration, ideation and innovation, and supports communication amongst different stakeholders. UX goals should be measurable in terms of experience, and therefore they can be utilized to support the evaluation of the product, service or system.

In this paper, EDD is utilized in the persona creation, to communicate the user needs and target UX goals.

2.3 Personas as a Tool to Communicate User Insights

In design field, 'personas' is a tool used to present and communicate user insights in order to support design team in gaining empathic understanding of the people they are designing for [e.g. 4, 5], and thus keeping the users' needs and characteristics at the forefront of the design process [10]. According to Cooper [5] personas provide a structural way of thinking and communicating users' behavior, goals, motivations, and the way they think. Personas are strongly based on research, and hence they differ a lot from archetypes or stereotypes, which often are only assumptions rather than factual data [5]. Personas communicate the ranges of users' behavior and thus, the tool does not seek to establish "an average user" but the variety of behaviors within the identified ranges [5]. In order to be effective design tool, personas must be based on research of not only the users, but also the usage context [5].

If utilized correctly, personas can help design team to make better decisions [1] and determine what the product should be [5]. Personas also enable communication with different stakeholders [5, 29] by providing a common language to support discussion and decision making [1, 5]. Cooper et al. [5] state that personas can also be utilized in measuring the effectiveness of the design choices by testing them on a persona in a similar way of testing with real users (however, this does not replace the need to test with real users, but rather provides a powerful "reality-check tool" for problem solving).

3 Methodology

To gain deep insights about passengers' bus travel experience, a qualitative field study approach was selected. Twenty participants were chosen for a three-week study that included a self-documentation period of bus trips using a diaries and semi-structured interviews in the end of the field period.

3.1 Study Context

The study was run in two cities in Finland. In Helsinki region, the public transportation is multimodal, which means that the passengers have access to bus, commuter train, tram, metro, and a commuter ferry with one travel card. The Greater Helsinki has over 1,4 million inhabitants, whereas Tampere, including the neighbouring municipalities has close to half a million inhabitants. The city of Tampere was chosen for our study because of its public transportation infrastructure is limited to buses and thus, focusing on studying the travel experience of buses was straightforward. Figure 1 shows interior of the intra-city bus in this study. In both cities, the public transportation could be described as a functioning and well-planned system. Still there is a general need to develop the attractiveness of the public transportation services.

Fig. 1. Examples of typical bus interior in Tampere.

3.2 Participants

Ten regular bus passengers were recruited for the study in both cities, providing us with twenty participants in total. Since the study aimed at gaining insights also on electric buses, the participants had to be passengers of the specific bus lines with electric buses. In order to incorporate different viewpoints to bus travel experience, participants of different age, gender and background were recruited through advertisement in local electric buses and in social media in Tampere, and flyers distributed by local transportation provider's workers in Helsinki. The selected participants – 16 females and four males – ranged from young students to senior citizens, with average age of 41,8 (range 21–72). While the participants included both men and women, the overrepresentation of women in the sample reflects the widely observed gender difference in travel mode use [31]. The participants included a wide variety of occupations: students, unemployed, workers, freelancers, pensioners and people on parental leave. All participants of this study were frequent bus users: 19 use public transportation at least four times a week, where one uses city buses 2–3 times a week.

3.3 Self-documentation with Bus Travel Diaries

For this study, we chose two complementary qualitative methods: diaries and interviews. The diary we designed for the main method of data collection is inspired by cultural probes [11]. Diary as a long-term self-documentation tool is a practical way to enrich the conventional qualitative methods, such as in-depth interviews and field observation [26].

The data collection in our study consisted of a three-week self-documentation period with a paper-based *Bus Travel Diary* (see Fig. 2 for visual representation). The participants were asked to fill in the diary of altogether nine journeys each. The questions focused on three main themes: Attributes of travel experience, Impact of the bus environment, and Activities during the trip – to gain holistic understanding of the bus travel, and the elements of travel experience. Among other things, the diary asked about the participants' feelings during the bus trip: *stressed, social, confident, awkward, relaxed, luxurious, annoyed, worried,* and *"other"* – based on the previous work by Hildén et al. [16]. The diary also included a reflection page of the documentation period that focused on the elements of bus travel that had biggest impact on the participant's travel experience. Data was received from 177 bus trips (one participant documented only six trips instead of nine).

Fig. 2. Bus Travel Diary consisted of both open-end and multiple-choice questions. We included visual elements to make it more appealing for the participants to fill.

3.4 Reflective In-Depth, Semi-structured Interviews

Semi-structured, in-depth interviews were used to collect additional deep, reflective insights of the bus travel experience. After the three-week self-documentation period, the participants were interviewed in groups of 2–4 people. Eight interview sessions were organized (four sessions in each city): one session with four participants, two sessions with three participants, and five pair interview sessions. The sessions lasted 1–2 h. The interviews were video and voice recorded for transcription and analysis.

The interview themes were closely related to the topics in the *Bus Travel Diary*. The themes were: General questions of the diary study; Questions regarding electric buses; General questions regarding travel experience, with questions regarding traveling by bus and the elements impacting the experience most; Questions regarding activities during the bus ride and the use of digital services focusing on activities people conduct during bus travel, their mobile service usage and the preferred content on the bus screens.

3.5 Analysis

The interviews and Bus Travel Diaries were transcribed. Insights related to passengers' *activities, values, needs,* and *feelings and experiences* were thematically coded and analysed [13]. 440 direct citations from the interviews were highlighted, making an average 22 citations per participant (range 13–36). In addition to the insights derived from the interview data the Bus Travel Diary data was utilized: the diary consisted in total of 81 open-end questions and 54 multiple-choice questions. Similarly, to the interviews, relevant diary answers were highlighted. We analyzed the highlighted insights of each participant separately in Excel and formulated user profile type of descriptions of each participant.

The travel mindsets were derived from the interview and diary insights from different participants who had experienced a specific travel mindset. The personas, on the other hand, were created by combining the participants with similar insights. This led us finally having ten *Travel Experience Personas* – one being the "main representative" of each travel mindset. Each travel experience persona is based on 1–5 participants in the data set. Each persona has one *primary mindset* that reflects the usual travel experience of that persona. Additionally, each persona has 1–4 *secondary mindsets* that are caused by special situations in the travel context, such as someone exceptionally traveling with small children.

4 Findings – Travel Mindsets

This section addresses our research question: *What kind of travel mindsets do frequent bus passengers have?* The findings of our study, i.e. the ten travel mindsets are presented below. The insights behind the mindsets were derived from our qualitative study that combined a three-week self-documenting period with Bus Travel Diaries, and in-depth, semi-structured interviews. The ten travel mindsets were utilized as building blocks to create the *Travel Experience Personas* presented in the Sect. 5.

4.1   Ten Travel Mindsets

Based on the data analysis, we defined ten travel mindsets. These describe the high-level categories that emerged from the passengers' travel experiences we traced from the diary and interview data. Thus, the travel mindsets presented here, include the passengers' varying actions, feelings, needs and experiences that have an impact on the passenger when traveling by intra-city buses. The travel mindsets are (in alphabetical order): *Abstracted, Efficient, Enjoyer, In-control, Isolation, Observer, Off-line, Relaxed, Sensitive,* and *Social*. Section 4.2 summarizes the pragmatic and hedonic traveler needs related to these mindsets.

Abstracted
This travel mindset includes insights from people who often feel forgetful and absent-minded. These people have to put extra effort to stay in focus in both familiar and unfamiliar routes. This mindset can be stressful and it even causes passengers to miss their stop: *"Even on a route that is fairly familiar to me, it sometimes suddenly strikes me that I have no clue where we are. It's like 'did I miss the stop again'"* (female, 33). The attention might be focused on the mobile device or being social with fellow passengers: *"I have to stay highly alert the whole journey, because if I start interacting with my mobile phone I forget to follow the route and then I don't know where I am anymore"* (female, 55). Abstractedness does not seem to be related to the length of the journey, passengers are simply too distracted to pay attention whether it is about choosing the right bus line or getting off at the right stop. *"Sometimes I might take a completely wrong bus"* (female, 55). **One participant was identified having this as a main mindset, and two as a secondary mindset.**

Efficient

People having *efficient* travel mindset often optimize their travels so that they can utilize the time in most efficient manner, including the time spent on the vehicle and at the bus stop: *"Even if the waiting time would only be 5 min, I usually check if there's faster options"* (male, 22). *Efficient*-minded people also utilise the travel time to "get things done", whether it is checking emails or planning the grocery shopping for the week. One participant makes use of the travel time by using dating apps: *"I use the time I spend in the bus swiping on Tinder"* (female, 32). Whereas one participant (female, 35) reported in her diary tasks such as book keeping, grocery planning, and studying languages. For some participants the commute was seen as a part of the workday, and hence, they were conducting work related activities during the journey. These included for instance reading work email and checking the day's agenda from the calendar. Some participants were even worried that they do not utilize the bus travel efficiently enough: *"Lately I've been thinking if the time I spend on traveling is actually used in the most efficient way"* (female, 21). **Two participants were identified having this as a main mindset, and three as a secondary mindset.**

Enjoyer

The *enjoyers* are often elderly people who get to travel without being in a hurry. They tend to travel outside the rush hours making the bus journeys more pleasant and enjoyable experiences: *"I love the fact that I can just sit and look back on the old times"* (male, 61). People having this *enjoyer* mindset might spend their travel time on socializing with fellow passengers or simply enjoying the view: *"I enjoy looking at the scenery and making notions of the nature's different seasons"* (male, 68). Even though feeling *stressed* was often mentioned in the diaries, bus context can still result opposite feelings: *"Sometimes I sit in the bus knowing that I will be late from work. In those moments, I tell myself that there is nothing I can do about it, and I might as well just sit and enjoy the moment"* (female, 48). **Two participants were identified having this as a main mindset, and three as a secondary mindset.**

In-control

People traveling with this mindset are often parents traveling with their kids. Based on the findings, we could see that parents' travel experience is often directly proportional to the behavior of the child. Key factors to successful bus travel are: avoiding the rush hours – *"Around 4 p.m. it is tricky to fit one person in, let alone the whole flock with a stroller"* (female, 33); and being well prepared – *"I always pack snacks, just in case... cookies, banana, chips etc. Snacks help if there's a scene"* (female, 33). It also helps if you can choose less crowded bus routes and avoid having to change. After fitting in to the bus (having space for the stroller), the second most important thing is to get seats for the kids: *"It makes things a lot easier if there is space for all of us in the quartet (two seat rows facing each other), or if at least I get space for the kids to sit next to each other. The worst is when you have to stand, or scatter the kids around the vehicle"* (female, 35). For the participants traveling with kids, bus was sometimes considered a more convenient choice compared to private vehicles: *"With a double stroller, it is easier to take the bus. Otherwise you have to first fold the stroller, then pack it into the car with all the other stuff and then – once you have reached your destination, unpack everything"* (female, 33). People traveling with kids, hence, having an *in-control* mindset, report activities that are very different to what they would do if travelling solo. Instead of spending time on one's mobile device, you observe the surroundings: *"We look outside and try to spot something extraordinary, like yellow cars or pretty flowers"* (female, 48). Traveling with kids also includes some social aspects, like being social with your own kids or bonding with the other parents taking the same bus. **Two participants were identified having this as a main mindset, and two as a secondary mindset.**

Isolation

In general, most participants preferred having their personal space in the bus. *"Usually I'm more like 'please don't notice me' so that the others wouldn't start a conversation"* (female, 42). Also, as one participant said: *"Most of the time I just want to be quiet and stay in my own bubble. The occasions are rare when I actually want to be social"* (female, 27). Participants stated that listening to music and immersing oneself with the mobile phone are good ways to isolate oneself from the others, and hence they do that to communicate the willingness to be alone: *"By putting headphones on, you usually get to be left alone. I often do that to prevent any kind of interaction with the fellow passengers"* (male, 22). **Two participants were identified having this as a main mindset, and three as a secondary mindset.**

Observer

People whose travel mindset is *observer* tend to pay more attention to the physical and social context of the bus than others. Observers notice the running people trying to catch the bus and sympathize their struggle, but also the relief when they can actually make it. *Observer*-minded people usually choose a seat that lets them carry out the observing activity: according to our *observer*-minded participants, the best seats are the rear-facing seats in the quartet: *"I often choose a seat facing the back, because in my opinion it's fun to observe what happens in the bus"* (female, 55), or the front seats: *"I find the front seat the best for relaxing, because the other people are hidden behind me. I'm also very curious person and from the front I see all the people who enter the bus"* (female, 32). In order to be able to see out and enjoy the scenery, the *observer*-minded people appreciate *"not having the windows covered with advertisements (or other visualizations) that would block the view"* (female, 72). **One participant was identified having this as a main mindset, and six as a secondary mindset.**

Off-line

People traveling with the *off-line* mindset do not use mobile devices at all or use them rarely when traveling. For some, the reasons were to have screen-free time, for example if work is heavily digital: *"I have to use my mobile phone at work all the time and that's why I choose not to do that anymore in the bus"* (female, 50). For others, the reasons were more social *"I like to see the people and the scenery. I rather interact with the fellow passengers than with my mobile device"* (female, 32). Some reported to suffer from poor eyesight and hence using a mobile phone was seen both unpleasant and impractical during bus journeys. Thus, these passengers rely more on the selection of on-board digital services showcased on the public screens. **Two participants were identified having this as a main mindset, and four as a secondary mindset.**

Relaxed

Many participants described the bus ride experience "automatic", allowing them to relax. For some, bus journeys were considered personal quality time. *"It takes half an hour for me to get to work and during that time I've learned to 'reset' myself completely"* (female, 50). Participants stated that they usually just sit quietly and zone out: *"On my way to work I might just close my eyes and relax"* (female, 27). Participants wishing to have *relaxed* travel experience, reported to use mobile devices for passive activities, such as audio content: *"I usually put on a radio-show, but for the rest of the journey the phone is in my pocket"* (female, 34). In order to get to the *relaxed* mindset, direct routes are preferred without having to change the vehicle: *"When I go home from work I choose the direct bus route. I use the time to recover by listening to meditation recordings. Having to change the vehicle would mean that my exercise would be interrupted."* (female, 32). Silent, noise-free bus rides were considered to improve the *relaxed* travel experience significantly. Hence, most were giving praises to the modern electric buses: *"The electric bus is so silent that it really increases my travel comfort, I somehow felt really calm in the bus"* (female, 25). *Five participants were identified having this as a main mindset, and six as a secondary mindset.*

Sensitive

These people include not only people having a sensitive mindset but also people suffering from physical illnesses or condition such as asthma, migraine, menopause, and motion sickness. Sensitive people get easily disturbed by noise, strong smells and odors and too high temperature. As one participant described: *"I guess I'm sensitive to smells and noise. Also, if the sun is shining and the heating is on I might start feeling really sick. Then I rather get off in half way, wait for the next bus or even walk to my destination."* (female, 42). For some people, the crowded buses in general were unpleasant and stressful experiences: *"I become anxious in a crowded bus. I might start panicking if the crowd blocks my way out"* (female, 35). Key factors to successful bus journeys were mentioned to be having good air conditioning including heating, cooling and air flow. Also choosing a seat from the front of the bus was stated to be a good way to minimize or prevent the feeling of nausea. The smooth ride provided by the electric buses was also experienced to lessen the motion sickness: *"It felt much smoother that when riding the old-fashioned ones. I didn't get as easily sick as I usually do"* (female, 29). One way to feel better is occupy the thoughts with using mobile phone *"I use my phone as a way to get rest from the irritants. When the heat gets overwhelming it helps if I can immerse myself to some content, no matter what it is"* (female, 48). *Two participants were identified having this as a main mindset, and three as a secondary mindset.*

Social

Even though feeling *unsocial* was often mentioned by the participants, some people reported to enjoy the social interaction with fellow passengers: *"It's so lovely if a neighbour or other acquaintance happens to be in the same bus! Unfortunately, the trips often run too short, since there should be enough time for us both to exchange the news."* (male, 68). Having *social* mindset is not limited to just familiar people – as one participant described: *"It's maybe even better if you have a good chat with a stranger!"* (male, 68). It seems that if you prefer to be social, the quartet (two seat rows facing each other) is the place to be: *"If you sit in the quartet, you often end up finding topics to discuss about"* (female, 50). **One participant was identified having this as a main mindset, and seven as a secondary mindset.**

4.2 Summary of Specific Needs Related to the Travel Mindsets

Table 1 presents the specific needs – pragmatic and hedonic attributes – of the ten travel mindsets. The travel mindsets are put in a rough order starting (from top to bottom) from the pragmatic mindsets to more hedonic ones.

Table 1. Travel mindsets and their specific travel related needs. (H) stands for hedonic need, (P) for pragmatic need, and (P/H) for need that is both pragmatic and hedonic.

Mindset	Most relevant bus travel related needs
Sensitive	Air condition (P), smooth ride (P), avoiding strong smells (P), avoiding noise (P), avoiding crowded vehicles (P)
In-control	Room for stroller (P), getting seats (P), entertainment for kids (P/H),
Efficient	Being on time (P), reliable journey planners (P), getting a seat (P)
Abstracted	Limiting the distractions (P), clear journey information (P)
Off-line	On-board information (P), getting a seat (P)
Observer	Getting a seat (P), clean and clear windows (H)
Isolation	Being left alone (H), active mobile entertainment (H), getting a seat (P)
Relaxed	Silence (P), getting a seat (P), passive mobile entertainment (H)
Social	Getting a seat (P), having someone to talk to (H)
Enjoyer	Avoiding rush hours (P/H), getting a seat (P/H)

5 Travel Experience Personas

Based on the travel mindsets, ten *Travel Experience Personas* were created. During the past decade, personas have become a well-lauded method [10], which is widely utilized for instance in interaction design [29] and service design [32].

These personas are based on the bus passengers' primary needs and preferred travel experience. In addition to the primary travel mindset describing the persona, each have secondary travel mindsets that are caused by abnormal travel contexts. For instance, if a passenger usually traveling with their kids travels alone, or if a passenger usually isolating oneself from the surroundings travels with a group of friends.

The personas in our study were created to describe different types of regular bus passengers, including their habits and needs related to bus travel and mobile device usage, as well as the specific elements that impact their travel experience the most. These personas help service developers to understand the varying needs and habits people have regarding bus travel and mobile device usage while traveling. The personas are: *Alba Abstracted, Edward Enjoyer, Emma Efficient, Ingrid In-control, Isac Isolation, Olga Observer, Olivia Off-line, Rachel Relaxed, Serena Sensitive,* and *Sophia Social.* Figure 3. presents the *Travel Experience Personas*, their additional travel mindsets and the UX goals we derived based on the study findings.

Alba Abstracted, 55-year old worker

Enjoys using public transportation, but still makes clumsy mistakes if she doesn't stay alert. Loves to socialize, play games and simply get deep in her thoughts. Gets stressed when having to focus on staying alert not to miss her stop.

TRAVELS BY BUS: Daily, prefers to walk short distance journeys **USES MOBILE DEVICE:** Sometimes. Would like to use more, but has to limit the usage to have more focus on the route **NEEDS RELATED TO BUS JOURNEYS:** Limiting the distractions, clear travel information **SECONDARY MINDSETS:** Social

UX GOALS: Competence, feeling of being in control, stimulation

Emma Efficient, 29-year-old student and entrepreneur

Effective utilization of bus trips makes the otherwise extremely busy days easier. Suitable tasks to conduct in the bus are for example, reading and answering to e-mails, making shopping lists and studying languages.

TRAVELS BY BUS: All trips, mostly to university or to work **USES MOBILE DEVICE:** All the time. Digital tasks vary depending on the length of the journey **NEEDS RELATED TO BUS JOURNEYS:** Avoiding noise, getting a seat, being on time, avoiding disruptions from fellow passengers **SECONDARY MINDSETS:** Relaxed, isolation, social

UX GOALS: Completion, efficiency

Edward Enjoyer, 68-year-old pensioner

Bus journeys are one of the essential parts of the everyday social activities. It's nice to be surrounded with people and occasionally have conversations. The best trips are the ones shared with an old friend!

TRAVELS BY BUS: Daily – shopping and leisure trips **USES MOBILE DEVICE:** Occasionally, mostly text messages, calls and camera. **NEEDS RELATED TO BUS JOURNEYS:** Getting a seat, avoiding rush hours, on-board travel information, smooth ride, being social with the driver and fellow passengers **SECONDARY MINDSETS:** Social

UX GOALS: Discovery, connectedness, sociability

Ingrid In-charge, 34-year old mother on parental leave

Every bus ride is an adventure when traveling with a toddler and a four-year old. The ride is succesfull if the kids behave well. Secret mom powers include knowing the least crowded bus lines and having endless supply of snacks.

TRAVELS BY BUS: Almost daily, mostly outside rush hours **USES MOBILE DEVICE:** Very little. Checks the journey information or messages only if needed. Sometimes allows the kids to play games or watch videos **NEEDS RELATED TO BUS JOURNEYS:** Room for stroller, getting seats for everyone, being on time, entertainment for kids **SECONDARY MINDSETS:** Relaxed, isolation, social

UX GOALS: Feeling of being in control, safety, trust, nurture

Fig. 3. Visual representation of the Travel Experience Personas, including their travel related needs, insights on mobile device usage, secondary travel mindsets and target UX goals.

Isac Isolation, 23-year-old student

Hopes to be left alone when traveling. Isolates himself from the fellow passengers by immersing into the mobile phone. Social only via smartphone or when traveling with friends.

TRAVELS BY BUS: Everywhere, mainly to school **USES MOBILE DEVICE:** Constantly – uses mobile phone to communicate with friends, listen to music and for various types of entertainment **NEEDS RELATED TO BUS JOURNEYS:** Being left alone, USB charging for mobile phones **SECONDARY MINDSETS:** Social

UX GOALS: Captivation, connectedness, feeling of being in control, relaxation

Olga Observer, 70-year old pensioner

Spends the bus journeys observing fellow passengers and the scenery. Enjoys being around people, but doesn't like to socialize with strangers. Prefers the front seat where she can hear the radio and see people entering the vehicle.

TRAVELS BY BUS: Almost daily, mostly shopping and leisure trips **USES MOBILE DEVICE:** Does not use mobile device during bus trips, actually often leaves it home **NEEDS RELATED TO BUS JOURNEYS:** Getting a seat next to doors, where she can observe people and also exit the vehicle easily **SECONDARY MINDSETS:** Enjoyer, social

UX GOALS: Discovery, exploration, sympathy

Olivia Off-line, 50-year-old office worker

Bus journeys are free of mobile device usage. Enough time is spent staring at a screen at work, and besides, she's not even wearing her reading glasses. Bus rides offer perfect 20 minute relaxation before and after the busy day at work.

TRAVELS BY BUS: Daily to work **USES MOBILE DEVICE:** Does not use mobile phone during bus trips **NEEDS RELATED TO BUS JOURNEYS:** On-board travel information, the service attitude of the driver, being on schedule, choosing an environmentally friendly travel mode **SECONDARY MINDSETS:** Social, observer

UX GOALS: Fellowship, serenity

Rachel Relaxed, 35-year-old worker and mother of small kids

Bus journeys are private quality time when she is able to relax and have time for herself. She puts headphones on, presses play and zones out. Of course, this change when she has the kids with her.

TRAVELS BY BUS: Daily to work **USES MOBILE DEVICE:** Constantly, but mostly for passive entertainment (music, audio books). **NEEDS RELATED TO BUS JOURNEYS:** Avoiding noise, getting a seat, being on time, avoiding disruptive behaviour of fellow passengers. **SECONDARY MINDSETS:** Isolation, social

UX GOALS: Serenity, relaxation

Fig. 3. (*continued*)

Serena Sensitive, 47-year old worker

Suffers from asthma and menopause, which is why bus rides vary from having relaxing quality time to complete nightmares. Strong odours, heat and poor air quality irritate her.

TRAVELS BY BUS: Everywhere, mainly to work **USES MOBILE DEVICE:** Most of the time, since it's one of the rare occasions when she has the time. Social media, news, and messaging. **NEEDS RELATED TO BUS JOURNEYS:** Air condition, smooth ride, avoiding strong smells, noise and crowded vehicles **SECONDARY MINDSETS:** Social, relaxed, In-charge, Isolation

UX GOALS: Serenity, feeling of being in control

Sofia Social, 42-year old worker and dog owner

Bus journeys are great opportunities to chat with fellow passengers. When traveling with the dog, it's very easy to start discussions - even with the unsocial ones. Suffers from migraine which sometimes strikes in the bus.

TRAVELS BY BUS: Everywhere **USES MOBILE DEVICE:** Sometimes, but prefers to socialize with fellow passengers **NEEDS RELATED TO BUS JOURNEYS:** Getting a seat from the quartet ("social area"), on-board travel information, finding someone to chat with **SECONDARY MINDSETS:** Sensitive, off-line

UX GOALS: Relatedness, connectedness, discovery, curiosity

Fig. 3. (*continued*)

6   Discussion

The aim of our study was to discover regular bus passengers' needs, and gain understanding of intra-city bus travel experience. Our motivation was two-fold: Firstly, to provide academic contributions by covering the research gap in short distance bus travel experience literature; existing studies focus on travel behavior [34], trip satisfaction [e.g. 9, 33], and travel experience [e.g. 2, 8] presenting mostly quantitative research efforts that cover the topic from the usability and efficiency perspectives. We wanted to tackle this research gap with insights of the varying travel mindsets. The ten travel mindsets: *Abstracted, Efficient, Enjoyer, In-control, Isolation, Observer, Off-line, Relaxed, Sensitive,* and *Social*, provided an answer to our research question *What kind of travel mindsets do frequent bus passengers have?*

Secondly, our aim was to create a design tool would make a practical contribution. Hence, we derived *Travel Experience Personas* that communicated our study findings in visual and tangible format. The personas as communicative design tool provide holistic understanding of the varying passenger needs to help the ideation and evaluation of new bus travel related services. The novelty of our personas in comparison to earlier work on personas is that they include secondary travel mindsets and UX goals. Hence, the Travel Experience Personas enable creation of empathic understanding of the regular bus passengers' varying needs.

One of our aims has been to conduct research on passengers' needs and travel experience and to provide human-centered insights in the forms of design tools in the *Living Lab Bus* developer portal. We believe that both the travel mindsets and the Travel Experience Personas provide valuable insights to designers and software developers utilizing this platform when developing digital services for the bus travel context. However, in today's world, user insights are needed by several stakeholders. Hence, in the context of our study they are not only the developers and designers, but also for instance the public transportation providers. Thus, the personas serve as a communication tool for transferring the research insights forward in a compact, meaningful and tangible format.

Personas as a design tool have been criticized for instance by Friess [10], of being resource-expensive tool for design development. This is true also in our study. However, we believe that in our case this is efficient and optimal way of transferring our gained and collected user insights forward to other stakeholders, who do not have the time and recourses to conduct similar studies. Personas have also been criticized of being statistically insignificant [24], which means that we would need a quantitative study to reveal the distribution and popularity of the travel mindsets and experience personas.

In conclusion: While the mindsets are the synthesis of the findings, personas are the practical tool to communicate these findings. The personas could be utilized by a wide range of stakeholders: software developers, experience designers, public transportation service providers and even bus companies in their service design. The personas can be utilized to gain insights of the wide variety of bus passengers' needs and experiences. They could also be combined with quantitative surveys utilized often in the transportation field. The usage of these personas will provide in-depth understanding of varying travel needs and UX goals that can be utilized to guide the design of bus traveling services.

6.1   Limitations and Future Work

The study was limited in the number of participants that represent only the public transportation users of the cities of Helsinki and Tampere. While both men and women were included, the overrepresentation of women in the sample reflects the widely observed gender difference in travel mode use [31]. The Travel Experience Personas include only two males and hence, they are in line with the gender distribution of our study participants.

Personas are based on the sample of 20 study participants, entailing rich qualitative insights. We started to see saturation of the data in the last third of the analysis. Additional personas and insights might emerge if the study would be conducted in a different city context. The travel mindsets and experience personas do not cover the full range of bus passenger, since our focus was on regular bus users, hence some travel mindsets might be missing. Also, one might claim that the travel mindsets are overlapping, for instance the enjoyer, observer, and social seem to have similar characteristics and travel related needs. So far, we have not been able to test these Travel Experience Personas. However, the preliminary personas were evaluated with software developers, and the findings show that the tool is seen valuable [19].

Even though the study was only limited to two Finnish cities, we believe that the found ten travel mindsets can be seen widely applicable to similar kinds of cities. Of course, there are cultural differences between different countries but because certain human characteristics are human (e.g. efficiency and sociability) we believe that similar mindsets can be valid also in other types of cultural contexts. Personas may differ more, because the traveller behaviour that they encapsulate is probably more contextual. Naturally, to make the mindsets and personas valid "universally", similar studies would need to be run in different types of countries and cities.

In the future work, we are planning to evaluate our study findings – the then travel mindsets with a quantitative survey study. We are eager to see how well the found mindsets map out to a large sample of bus passengers. We are also going to evaluate the Travel Experience Persona design tool with relevant stakeholders to see how well we succeeded to communicate the relevant insights and support the empathic understanding of bus passengers' needs and travel experience.

7 Conclusion

In this paper, we presented a qualitative diary and interview study on intra-city bus travel experience with 20 passengers. The aim of this study was to identify and communicate frequent bus passengers' needs, experiences, values and activities as *user insights* to support experience-driven service design in the public transportation context. Based on the data analysis, we derived ten travel mindsets: *Abstracted, Efficient, Enjoyer, In-control, Isolation, Observer, Off-line, Relaxed, Sensitive,* and *Social*. To communicate the study findings on bus passengers' travel experience, *Travel Experience Personas* were created. The personas include primary and secondary travel mindsets, specific needs related to bus travel, insights on mobile device usage and target user experience (UX) goals that could enhance the personas' travel experience. Thus, our findings – the ten travel mindsets, and the derived Travel Experience Personas can be utilized as communicative design tool to support EDD of novel services in the bus context.

Acknowledgments. We thank Business Finland and fellow researchers in Living Lab Bus project.

References

1. Adlin, T., Pruitt, J.: The Essential Personal Lifecycle: Your Guide to Building and Using Personas. Morgan Kaufmann, Burlington (2010)
2. Carreira, R., Patrício, L., Jorge, R.N., Magee, C., Van Eikema Hommes, Q.: Towards a holistic approach to the travel experience: a qualitative study of bus transportation. Transp. Policy **25**, 233–243 (2013)
3. Carreira, R., Patrício, L., Jorge, R.N., Magee, C.: Understanding the travel experience and its impact on attitudes, emotions and loyalty towards the transportation provider–a quantitative study with mid-distance bus trips. Transp. Policy **31**, 35–46 (2014)
4. Cooper, A.: The Inmates are Running the Asylum. Sams, Indianapolis (1999)

5. Cooper, A., Reimann, R., Cronin, D., Noessel, C.: About Face: The Essentials of Interaction Design. Wiley, Hoboken (2014)
6. Desmet, P., Schifferstein, R. (eds.): A Collection of 35 Experience-Driven Design Projects. Eleven International Publishing, The Hague (2012)
7. Ferris, B., Watkins, K., Borning, A.: OneBusAway: results from providing real-time arrival information for public transit. In: Proceedings of the SIGCHI Conference on Human Factors in Computing Systems, pp. 1807–1816. ACM (2010)
8. Foth, M., Schroeter, R., Ti, J.: Opportunities of public transport experience enhancements with mobile services and urban screens. Int. J. Ambient Comput. Intell. (IJACI) 5(1), 1–18 (2013)
9. Friman, M., Fellesson, M.: Service supply and customer satisfaction in public transportation: the quality paradox. J. Publ. Transp. 12(4), 4 (2009)
10. Friess, E.: Personas and decision making in the design process: an ethnographic case study. In: Proceedings of the SIGCHI Conference on Human Factors in Computing Systems, pp. 1209–1218. ACM (2012)
11. Gaver, B., Dunne, T., Pacenti, E.: Design: Cultural Probes. Interactions 6(1), 21–29 (1999)
12. Hassenzahl, M.: Hedonic, emotional, and experiential perspectives on product quality. In: Ghaoui, C. (ed.) Encyclopedia of Human Computer Interaction, pp. 266–272. Idea Group Reference, Hershey (2006)
13. Guest, G., MacQueen, K.M., Namey, E.E.: Applied Thematic Analysis. Sage, Thousands Oaks (2011)
14. Hassenzahl, M.: Experience Design, Technology for All the Right Reasons. Morgan & Claypool, San Rafael (2010)
15. Hassenzahl, M.: User experience and experience design. In: Soegaard, M., Dam, R.F. (eds.) The Encyclopedia of Human-Computer Interaction, 2nd edn. The Interaction Design Foundation, Aarhus (2014)
16. Hildén, E., Ojala, J., Väänänen, K.: User needs and expectations for future traveling services in buses. In: Proceedings of NordiCHI 2016. ACM (2016)
17. Hildén, E., Ojala, J., Väänänen, K.: A co-design study of digital service ideas in the bus context. In: Bernhaupt, R., Dalvi, G., Joshi, A., Balkrishan, D.K., O'Neill, J., Winckler, M. (eds.) INTERACT 2017. LNCS, vol. 10513, pp. 295–312. Springer, Cham (2017). https://doi.org/10.1007/978-3-319-67744-6_20
18. Hildén, E., Ojala, J., Väänänen, K.: Development of context cards: a bus-specific ideation tool for co-design workshops. In: Proceedings of the 21st International Academic Mindtrek Conference, pp. 137–146. ACM (2017)
19. Hildén, E., Väänänen, K., Chistov, P.: Travel experience toolkit: bus-specific tools for digital service design. In: Proceedings of the 17th International Conference on Mobile and Ubiquitous Multimedia, pp. 193–197. ACM (2018)
20. Hildén, E., Väänänen, K., Syrman, S.: Modeling bus travel experience to guide the design of digital services for the bus context. In: Proceedings of the 22nd International Academic Mindtrek Conference, pp. 143–152. ACM (2018)
21. Kostiainen, J., Jokinen, J-P., Pantic, N., Marko, F., Bylund, G.: Hackathons for innovation: case Living Lab Bus and passenger game Bussig in Junction 2017. In: 25th ITS World Congress, Copenhagen, Denmark, 17–21 September 2018
22. Le Bel, J.L.: Beyond the friendly skies: an integrative framework for managing the air travel experience. Manag. Serv. Qual.: Int. J. 15(5), 437–451 (2005)
23. Lyon, G., Urry, J.: Travel time use in the information age. Transp. Res. Part A: Policy Pract. 39(2–3), 257–276 (2015)

24. McGinn, J.J., Kotamraju, N.: Data-driven persona development. In: Proceedings of the SIGCHI Conference on Human Factors in Computing Systems, pp. 1521–1524. ACM (2008)

25. Müller, J., et al.: Honeypot: a socializing app to promote train commuters' wellbeing. In: Proceedings of the 17th International Conference on Mobile and Ubiquitous Multimedia, pp. 103–108. ACM (2018)

26. Nyblom, Å.: Making plans or "just thinking about the trip"? Understanding people's travel planning in practice. J. Transp. Geogr. **35**, 30–39 (2014)

27. Oliveira, L., Bradley, C., Birrell, S., Tinworth, N., Davies, A., Cain, R.: Using passenger personas to design technological innovation for the rail industry. In: Kováčiková, T., Buzna, Ľ., Pourhashem, G., Lugano, G., Cornet, Y., Lugano, N. (eds.) INTSYS 2017. LNICST, vol. 222, pp. 67–75. Springer, Cham (2018). https://doi.org/10.1007/978-3-319-93710-6_8

28. Pang, C., Pan, R., Neustaedter, C., Hennessy, K.: City explorer: the design and evaluation of a location-based community information system. In 2019 CHI Conference on Human Factors in Computing Systems Proceedings (CHI 2019). ACM (2019)

29. Pruitt, J., Grudin, J.: Personas: practice and theory. In: Proceedings of the 2003 Conference on Designing for User Experiences, pp. 1–15. ACM (2003)

30. Roto, V., Law, E.L.-C., Vermeeren, A.P.O.S., Hoonhout, J. (eds.): UX White Paper – Bringing Clarity to the Concept of User Experience. Outcome of Dagstuhl Seminar on Demarcating User Experience, Germany (2011). http://allaboutux.org/uxwhitepaper

31. Scheiner, J., Holz-Rau, C.: Gendered travel mode choice: a focus on car deficient households. J. Transp. Geogr. **24**, 250–261 (2012)

32. Segelström, F., Holmlid, S.: Visualizations as tools for research: service designers on visualizations, no. 3. Nordes (2009)

33. St-Louis, E., van Lierop, D., El-Geneidy, A.: The happy commuter: a comparison of commuter satisfaction across modes. Transp. Res. Part F: Traffic Psychol. Behav. **26**, 160–170 (2014)

34. Van Audenhove, F.J., Korniichuk, O., Dauby, L., Pourbaix, J.: The future of urban mobility 2.0: imperatives to shape extended mobility ecosystems of tomorrow. Arthur D. Little (2014)

35. van Hagen, M., Bron, P.: Enhancing the experience of the train journey: changing the focus from satisfaction to emotional experience of customers. Transp. Res. Procedia **1**(1), 253–263 (2014)

36. Varsaluoma, J.: Approaches to improve user experience in product development: UX goals, long-term evaluations and usage data logging, vol. 1585. Tampere University of Technology. Publication (2018)

37. Väätäjä, H., Savioja, P., Roto, V., Olsson, T., Varsaluoma, J.: User experience goals as a guiding light in design and development – early findings. In: INTERACT 2015 Adjunct proceedings, pp. 521–527. University of Bamberg Press (2015)

38. Watkins, K.E., Ferris, B., Borning, A., Rutherford, G.S., Layton, D.: Where Is My Bus? Impact of mobile real-time information on the perceived and actual wait time of transit riders. Transp. Res. Part A: Policy Pract. **45**(8), 839–848 (2011)

Effects of Age-Related Cognitive Decline on Elderly User Interactions with Voice-Based Dialogue Systems

Masatomo Kobayashi[1]($\boxtimes$), Akihiro Kosugi[1], Hironobu Takagi[1],
Miyuki Nemoto[2], Kiyotaka Nemoto[2], Tetsuaki Arai[2],
and Yasunori Yamada[1]

[1] IBM Research, Tokyo 103–8510, Japan
mstm@jp.ibm.com
[2] University of Tsukuba, Tsukuba 305–8577, Japan

Abstract. Cognitive functioning that affects user behaviors is an important factor to consider when designing interactive systems for the elderly, including emerging voice-based dialogue systems such as smart speakers and voice assistants. Previous studies have investigated the interaction behaviors of dementia patients with voice-based dialogue systems, but the extent to which age-related cognitive decline in the non-demented elderly influences the user experiences of modern voice-based dialogue systems remains uninvestigated. In this work, we conducted an empirical study in which 40 healthy elderly participants performed tasks on a voice-based dialogue system. Analysis showed that cognitive scores assessed by neuropsychological tests were significantly related to vocal characteristics, such as pauses and hesitations, as well as to behavioral differences in error-handing situations, such as when the system failed to recognize the user's intent. On the basis of the results, we discuss design implications towards the tailored design of voice-based dialogue systems for ordinary older adults with age-related cognitive decline.

Keywords: Voice-based interactions · Smart speakers · Voice assistants · Aging · Age-related cognitive decline

1 Introduction

Voice-based dialogue systems show good potential to help older adults maintain their independent living. Typical examples of such systems include smart speakers and voice assistants, such as Amazon Alexa and Google Home, Apple Siri, and Microsoft Cortana [1]. Older adults can use these systems for a variety of life support services such as asking about the time or weather, accessing healthcare applications [2], and strengthening social connections [3]. Other examples are companion agents or robots for eldercare purposes, which verbally communicate with older adults to provide assistance for daily living through medication reminders and home automations [4–6]. The use of voice-based natural interfaces is expected to enable older adults to easily access the system—even those who were excluded from traditional desktop or mobile technologies due to their limited literacy on information technologies or age-related decline of

© IFIP International Federation for Information Processing 2019
Published by Springer Nature Switzerland AG 2019
D. Lamas et al. (Eds.): INTERACT 2019, LNCS 11749, pp. 53–74, 2019.
https://doi.org/10.1007/978-3-030-29390-1_4

vision and motor abilities. In addition, previous studies have shown that voice input could be the most preferable input modality for older adults [7], and that the listening ability of older adults was comparable to that of younger adults when they are not visually impaired [8].

At the same time, special consideration of the user's cognitive functioning needs to be taken when designing voice-based dialogue systems for older adults. One study that analyzed human-human conversations revealed a significant difference between people with dementia and healthy controls in the appearance of breakdowns in communication, such as lack of uptake/continuation, where ignorance and interruptions occur [9]. Similar behaviors were found in human-robot conversations between people with Alzheimer's disease (AD) and a companion robot [10]. Studies on speech analysis have revealed associations between people's cognitive abilities and their linguistic and vocal characteristics. For example, we now know that linguistic features such as vocabulary richness may decrease in the conversations of people with AD [11, 12]. A difference in vocal features such as pauses and hesitations can be a sign of progress in AD and mild cognitive impairment (MCI) [13, 14]. These linguistic and vocal characteristics may reduce the quality of user experiences of voice-based dialogue systems due to resultant failure in automatic speech recognition (ASR) or conversation management engines.

As the studies above have investigated the conversational characteristics of people with MCI, AD, and other types of dementia, little is known about the effects of age-related cognitive decline in non-demented older adults, even though a large volume of older adults who may benefit from voice-based dialogue systems belongs to this cohort. A few exceptions include the studies on the MATCH corpus [15], a rich annotated dataset for the interactions of younger and older adults with a voice-based dialogue system, which also provides cognitive scores for each participant. However, no analysis has been conducted on vocal features, and no effect of cognitive measures on the completion of tasks has been reported in [15]. Further investigation is required to determine how age-related cognitive decline in ordinary older adults affects their interaction behaviors, which may lead to a failure in tasks, and whether there is any need for special considerations when designing voice-based dialogue interfaces for this cohort.

In this work, we conducted an empirical study to investigate the effect of age-related cognitive decline on the user experiences of modern voice-based dialogue systems, in which 40 non-demented older adults aged 60 or above were involved. The participants had cognitive scores assessed by standard neuropsychological tests to examine the relationship between their age-related cognitive decline and behavioral characteristics in interactions with a voice-based dialogue interface. We used a Wizard-of-Oz (WOz) interface [16] to perform three task scenarios that contain typical dialog patterns including error handling situations, which commonly appear in modern voice-based dialogue systems such as smart speakers and voice assistants. We analyzed the relationships between participants' cognitive scores and conversational characteristics from the perspectives of vocal features such as pauses and hesitations as well as rephrasing and correcting behaviors in error handling situations. Then we investigated the implications of our study towards tailored designs of voice-based dialogue systems for older adults who may have age-related cognitive decline.

The contributions of this work include: (i) providing the first empirical results investigating how age-related cognitive decline in ordinary older adults influences interaction characteristics on a voice-based dialogue system; (ii) identifying significant associations between cognitive scores and vocal features as well as error handling behaviors that may affect the user experience of voice-based dialogue systems; and (iii) presenting points for design consideration for voice-based dialogue systems for older adults who may be experiencing age-related cognitive decline.

2 Related Work

2.1 Screen- and Voice-Based Interactive Systems for the Elderly

Aging inevitably involves multiple declines in sensory, perceptual, motor, and cognitive abilities. A combination of accessibility considerations is therefore required, which has led to extensive studies on interface designs for the aged population. For example, elderly interactions on screen-based visual interfaces such as mobile touchscreens have been investigated from the perspectives of target selections, text entry, and gesture-based interactions [17]. Kobayashi et al. [18] studied typical touchscreen operations with ordinary older adults and introduced design implications for the population. Wacharamanotham et al. [19] tested the "swabbing" technique as an assistive input method for people with tremor. For text entry on a touchscreen, Nicolau and Jorge [20] conducted a detailed investigation on the relationship between users' tremor profiles and their text entry performance on mobile and tablet devices. On top of gesture analysis studies, Sato et al. [21] proposed an intelligent help system that automatically provides novice older users with context-aware instructions on gesture interactions. For traditional desktop interfaces, ability-based adaptation techniques have been proposed [22]. Gajos et al. [23] used their SUPPLE system to automatically generate customized interfaces based on users' ability profiles. Trewin et al. [24] introduced the Steady Clicks technique to assist with clicking actions for people with motor impairments, while Wobbrock et al. [25] proposed the Angle Mouse technique to assist them with mouse cursor movement. Sato et al. [26] reported that additional voice-based feedback could improve older users' subjective performance on a visual user interface. These studies on aging and screen-based visual interfaces motivated us to investigate aging and voice-based dialogue interfaces and to discuss prospective design adaptation for older adults.

The voice-based dialogue system is a promising style of interaction for older adults, given their performance on voice-based interactions. Smith and Chaparro [7] showed that voice input is the most effective and preferable input modality for older adults. Bragg et al. [8] reported that the listening speed of sighted older adults is comparable to that of sighted younger adults. Note that studies have also indicated challenges related to ASR for older adults with cognitive disorders. Weiner et al. [27] showed that the accuracy of ASR decreased not only for people with AD but also for those with age-related cognitive decline. Rudzicz [28] indicated that older adults with higher cognitive scores experienced fewer ASR errors, although the trend was not statistically significant. Zajicek [29] pointed out that "errors and error recovery represent the primary usability problem for speech systems". Even though there might be a challenge in terms of ASR accuracy, many studies have proposed and investigated voice-based dialogue agents and robots [30], some of them for ordinary older adults and others for those with dementia. Granata et al. [31] tested both voice and graphical input modalities for an eldercare robot for people with cognitive disorders and found there is a need for adaptation of vocabulary and the design of image icons. Wolters et al. [5] conducted focus group studies with people with dementia, caregivers, and older adults without a diagnosis of dementia, suggesting that voice-based dialogue systems should be able to adapt to diverse paths of cognitive aging. As for non-demented older adults, an example is Portet et al.'s work [4], in which a WOz study was conducted to investigate their acceptance of voice command interactions in a smart house environment. Ziman and Walsh [32] studied elderly perception of voice-based and traditional keyboard-based interfaces and reported that the voice-based interface was easier to learn and use, even though the keyboard-based interface was more preferred. Our study aims to provide design implications for these kinds of voice-based dialogue systems for older adults who may have age-related cognitive decline.

2.2 Corpus Analysis on Elderly Interactions with Conversational Systems

There have been some studies that built a corpus for research on the conversational interactions of older adults. The MATCH corpus [15] is a multi-modal dataset that involved both older and younger adults who interacted with nine different spoken dialogue systems. The task scenario used in the data collection phase was "appointment scheduling" as a relevant task for older adults. A unique aspect of this corpus is that it contains information about the users' cognitive abilities and detailed usability assessments of each dialogue system, in addition to utterances and transcripts with annotations. The findings from initial analyses suggested that there was no effect of any of the cognitive measures on task completion. This corpus allows analyses of the conversational characteristics of older adults. For example, it was found that older users more frequently used "social" words and phrases such as "thank you". Vipperla et al. [33] used the MATCH corpus to build language and acoustic models to improve ASR accuracy for older adults' speech. Bost and Moore [34] performed studies using the MATCH corpus as well; they used regression models and showed that users with higher cognitive scores had shorter dialogues while users with shorter dialogues were more satisfied with the dialogue system. Jasmin-CGN [35] is another corpus of multi-generational human-machine conversational interactions. Even though it does not contain information about the users' cognitive abilities, its conversation scenario covers simulated ASR errors. LAST MINUTE [36] is also a multi-modal corpus of younger and older users' interactions with a voice-based dialogue system and contains transcripts, videos, and responses to psychometric questionnaires. A study on the LAST MINUTE corpus [37] reported that discourse particles (a type of hesitation) increased in critical situations in human-computer conversations where, for example, the system's behavior was not understandable for the user. The CADENCE corpus [38], which involved older adults with a diagnosis of dementia or MCI, contains transcribed spoken interactions between a voice-based dialogue system and older users accompanied with detailed information about users' cognitive abilities; its aim is to support research on inclusive voice interfaces. The conversation data in the corpora above were collected using the WOz method, suggesting that this method is an appropriate way to collect conversation data for controlled empirical analyses.

Studies have also investigated the conversational characteristics of people with dementia. Watson [9] used data from human-human conversations between ten people with AD and ten without to analyze types of breakdowns in conversations (i.e., trouble indicating patterns) and to identify the relevant repair strategies. Rudzicz et al. [10] used a similar approach to analyze human-robot conversations between ten older adults with AD and a voice-based dialogue system and found that older adults with AD were very likely to simply ignore the robot. Rudzicz et al. [39] and Chinaei et al. [40] built a computational model that aimed to exploit linguistic and acoustic features to detect a breakdown in conversations. In contrast to these previous studies that investigated the conversations of older adults with AD, our focus in the present study is interactions between non-demented older adults who may have age-related cognitive decline and a voice-based dialogue system in simulated typical application scenarios with a modern smart speaker or voice assistant.

2.3 Language Dysfunctions Due to Cognitive Impairments

How cognitive functioning changes speech characteristics has mainly been investigated in patients, especially dementia patients. While the most typical symptom of dementia is memory impairment due to shrinkage of the medial temporal lobe [41, 42], both retrospective analysis and prospective cohort studies have shown that language dysfunctions prevail even from the presymptomatic period [43, 44]. Such clinical symptoms that can precede dementia (including AD) are considered to be a mild cognitive impairment (MCI) [45]. The concept of MCI has been used to identify an intermediate stage of cognitive impairment that is often, but not always, a transitional phase from cognitive changes in normal aging to those typically found in dementia [45]. People with MCI typically exhibit less severe symptomology of cognitive impairment than that seen in dementia. Many computation studies have aimed to automatically capture such gradual changes in cognitive functioning by investigating the difference of speech features, namely, acoustic, prosodic, and linguistic features, among healthy older adults and MCI and AD patients [14, 46–48]. They mainly investigated speech data during neuropsychological tests and medical interviews. For example, the impairment of short-term memory often makes normal conversation difficult due to language dysfunctions such as difficulties with word-finding and word-retrieving [49, 50]. These language dysfunctions have been measured as pauses and fillers (non-words and short phrases like "umm" or "uh") [45, 51]. In fact, some studies have shown that patients with AD and MCI use more pauses in spontaneous speech, and on average use longer pauses than healthy controls [14, 52]. Such speech changes seem likely to influence the user experience with an interactive system. For this reason, we should investigate whether and how such features occur and influence the user experience even in non-demented older adults with different levels of cognitive functioning.

In addition, many studies have demonstrated the ways in which text features significantly change over the course of cognitive impairment [12, 53]. Among them, numerous studies investigated the difference of information content in description tasks [54, 55] and found that individuals with MCI and AD tend to produce descriptions with lower information content than healthy controls in both verbal and written picture descriptions tasks [56, 57]. Our interest is whether such decline in information content can be observed in older adults with age-related cognitive decline during the use of a voice-based interaction system. If so, such decline might influence whether the system can understand the user requirements because the impact of misrecognized words might be more significant. Therefore, we decided to investigate the speech features described in the above that would change according to the level of cognitive functioning and influence the interaction with a voice-based system.

3 Research Hypotheses

As stated in the introduction, we particularly focused on vocal features such as pauses and hesitations as well as error handling behaviors such as rephrasing and correcting during the analysis. We hypothesized three behavioral characteristics of older adults with age-related cognitive decline, as follows.

H1. *Pauses, hesitations, and other disfluency features increase with cognitive decline* —this is a hypothesis regarding vocal features. We assumed that the disfluency found in vocal feature analysis on people with MCI and dementia could also appear in non-demented older adults with age-related cognitive decline. We chose pauses, hesitations, and delays as commonly used features in the previous vocal feature analysis studies such as [14]. An additional feature, interruptions, was also included, as inspired by [58] and based on our preliminary observations on elderly conversations.

The appearance of these features would cause speech recognition errors due to inappropriate segmentation of speech segments where, for instance, a long pause could be misinterpreted as a sentence delimiter. We also assumed that the occurrence of these vocal features would increase in cognitively demanding contexts such as in error handling situations and when responding to open-ended questions.

H2. *The failure in rephrasing increases with cognitive decline*—this is a hypothesis for error handling features. A voice-based dialogue system often fails to interpret the user's intention in a response, which could happen either because of speech recognition errors or inappropriate wording by the user. In these cases, the user is required to rephrase or simply repeat the response. We assumed that cognitive decline would affect interaction behaviors in this situation because slightly more complex cognitive functions are required, such as lexical access to perform appropriate rephrasing.

H3. *The failure in correcting increases with cognitive decline*—this is also a hypothesis for error handling features. A voice-based dialogue system often incorrectly recognizes the user's input (e.g., "thirteen" vs. "thirty"), which is mainly caused by speech recognition errors. In these cases, the user needs to notice the misrecognition when confirmed by the system and ask for a correction. We assumed that cognitive decline would affect interaction behaviors in this situation because more complex cognitive functions are required, such as paying attention to notice the misrecognition and then to perform the appropriate correction.

The second and third hypotheses were inspired by [29], which emphasized the importance of error handling in speech systems, and [35], which presented a corpus including simulated errors.

4   Method

4.1   Task Scenarios

Three task scenarios were prepared to simulate typical application scenarios on modern smart speakers and voice assistants, as well as to simulate ASR error conditions. The scenarios consisted of information retrieval (asking for tomorrow's weather), shopping online (booking a movie ticket), and personal schedule management (creating a calendar event) as representative scenarios on a voice-based dialogue system that would help older adults to live active, independent lives. In every scenario, participants started the task by speaking a wake word. The tasks were ordered to start with a simple scenario and then advance to more complicated ones:

1. *Ask for tomorrow's weather*: This is a single round-trip dialogue. The participant simply makes a request once to complete the task (Fig. 1).
2. *Book a movie ticket*: This scenario is a multiple turn dialogue. Once the participant asks the system to purchase tickets for a movie, the system asks what kind of movie the participant wants, the date, the show time, the number of tickets, and payment information.
3. *Create a calendar event*: This scenario is a multiple turn dialogue. The participant adds an event (watching a movie) that has been booked in the previous task. They are asked the date, time, title of the event, and when to set a notification alarm. This scenario purposely includes error handing situations. Specifically, the system verbalizes an error message indicating that it could not catch what the participant said, or it gives the wrong confirmation.

The questions presented by the system during the tasks were categorized as follows (Fig. 2):

- *Open-ended*: Participants respond with a free sentence to answer the question.
- *Multiple options*: Participants choose one from the options stated in the question.
- *Prepared input*: Participants respond with the information (e.g., passcode) specified by the experimenter.
- *Confirmation*: Participants need to accept or reject what the system has stated.

P: Kasuga-san?
S: Hello, how may I help you?
P: What will the weather be like tomorrow in this city?
S: It will be rainy tomorrow in this city.

Fig. 1. An example exchange between a participant (P) and the system (S) in "Ask tomorrow's weather" task. "Kasuga-san?" was the wake word starting the session.

(Open-ended)
S: What movie would you like to watch?
P: I'd like to watch a comedy.

(Multiple options)
S: When would you like to set the alarm? You can set it for 5 minutes, 10 minutes..., or 2 hours before the event.
P: Please set the alarm for 10 minutes before the event.

(Handling with recognition error)
S: How may I help you?
P: Please add a calendar event of going to a movie.
S: *Sorry, I couldn't catch you. Could you repeat the request again?*
P: Well, could you add an event please?

(Handling error confirmation)
S: What time will that event be?
P: It will be at 10:30.
S: *OK. The event is scheduled for 10:00.*
P: No, please set it for 10:30

Fig. 2. Examples of questions by types. System utterance in italics is an intentional error.

4.2 Apparatus

We took a Wizard-of-Oz (WOz) approach so that we could conduct quantitative analyses with a limited number of trials by controlling the content of the conversations. In particular, we wanted to control the appearance of error handling situations, where the participants had to perform appropriate responses such as rephrasing and correcting, assuming that such a cognitively demanding situation would lead to more differences in behavioral characteristics. With the WOz method, we could avoid unfavorable results due to environmental disturbances such as room noise.

The system consisted of a tablet (iPad Air2) as the front-end terminal for the participants and a laptop as the controller for the experimenter. Participants sat down in front of the tablet and talked with the system through the tablet to perform the tasks (Fig. 3). The tablet showed a screen indicating whether it was speaking or listening. To record the participants' voices, we used two microphones, a throat microphone

(NANZU SH-12iK) and a lavalier microphone (SONY ECM-CS3), in addition to the embedded microphone in the tablet. All the microphones were set up to record in raw format with the sampling rate of 44.1 kHz.

The iPad's default Siri Female voice was chosen for the vocal type of speech. The speed rate was set to 85% of the normal speed of the voice. The vocal type and speed rate were determined through informal preliminary trials, in which three cognitive-healthy older adults aged 60s–80s (1 male, 2 females) tried earlier versions of the experimental interface and were asked their preferences on the voice type and speed. Even though literature suggests that low-pitch male voices are more preferable for the elderly than female voices [59], we chose the female voice for three reasons: (i) a female voice is commonly set as the default in many voice-based dialogue systems; (ii) for the language we used, the quality of voice synthesis is much better for the default voice; and (iii) the participants in the preliminary trials preferred the female voice.

The experimenter simulated the conversation management engine through a browser-based controller interface that included buttons listing what the tablet would speak along with the scenarios. During the experimental session, the experimenter listened to the participants and determined what and when the system should speak next by clicking one of the buttons. The sentences were scripted in advance and the experimenter tried to mimic the behavior of typical conversation management engines as closely as possible.

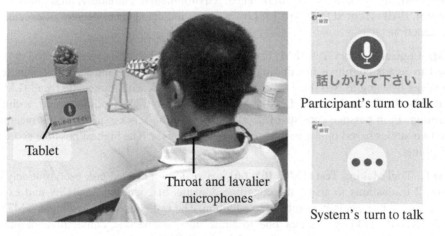

Tablet

Throat and lavalier microphones

話しかけて下さい

Participant's turn to talk

System's turn to talk

Fig. 3. Overview of experimental setup.

4.3 Participants

Forty older adults (20 female, age: 61–79, average = 69.85, SD = 4.7) in good health were invited. Participants were hired through a local recruiting company, and none of them were diagnosed as having dementia. The criteria for recruiting were "older than 60 without any serious diseases or disabilities including neurodegenerative diseases such as dementia". All participants had a perfect score on the Barthel Index of

Activities of Daily Living [60], indicating they did not need any assistance in their everyday lives. Even though 18 of the 40 participants stated that they had experience with voice-based interfaces such as voice-based text entry and single-turn dialogue, none of them had used multi-turn dialogue systems. This study was conducted under the approval of the local ethics committee.

4.4 Cognitive Measures

We collected cognitive measures of neuropsychological assessments that are typically used for clinically evaluating the cognitive functioning of older adults. Four different scales were used to quantitatively capture different aspects of cognitive functioning. These assessments were administered by clinical psychologists.

MMSE. Min-Mental State Examination (MMSE) [61] is used as a screening measure of global cognitive functioning. This test provides a composite score based on the assessment of multiple cognitive domains: orientation for place and time, memory and attention, language skills, and visuospatial abilities. The highest possible score is 30 points, and lower scores indicate greater degrees of general cognitive dysfunction. A score of 26 or above is typically considered normal.

FAB. Frontal Assessment Battery (FAB) [62] is designed to assess executive functions that are thought to be under the control of the frontal lobes. This test includes a brief battery of six neuropsychological tasks: conceptualization, mental flexibility, motor programming, sensitivity to interference, environmental autonomy, and inhibitory control. FAB is scored from 0 to 18. Lower scores indicate greater degrees of executive dysfunction.

LM. Logical Memory Test (LM) from the Revised Wechsler Memory Scale [63, 64] is used to assess cognitive functioning associated with memory and learning. This test involves listening to two short paragraph-length passages with immediate recall (LM1) and 30-min delayed recall (LM2). A delayed recall trial is administered without warning. Each passage consists of 25 elements, and the score is taken as the mean of the two stories based on the number of correct responses. The highest possible score is 25 points.

TMT. Trail Making Test (TMT) [65, 66] is a visuomotor timed task used routinely in clinical evaluations to assess the cognitive domains of cognitive flexibility and executive function, especially as related to attention. The test consists of two parts: TMT-A and TMT-B. TMT-A requires one to draw lines connecting consecutive numbers randomly distributed in space (i.e., 1-2-3...). TMT-B is similar, but instead of just linking numbers, participants are required to draw lines connecting numbers and letters alternately in their respective sequence (i.e., 1-A-2-B-3-C...).

4.5 Procedure

Participants went through an orientation session to help them understand what a voice-based interface is and how conversation through it should proceed. The orientation included: (i) explanation of the purpose, where participants were asked to test the voice-based dialogue system and then to share their impressions and suggestions; (ii) run-through practice with a simple scenario, where participants went through a practice session starting with a "wake word"; and (iii) confirmation if the volume of the tablet voice was high enough.

Then the participants proceeded to the main tasks, which they worked through in the same order described in Sect. 4.1. In each task, participants were provided with a printout containing the information required to proceed with the questions, such as the date of the reservation and the number of tickets, for which they would be asked during the session. After the tasks, we conducted a short interview with participants to uncover any difficulties they experienced throughout the experiment and points they felt were useful. Each experimental session took approximately 30 min per person.

4.6 Vocal Features

The following categories of vocal features were extracted from the recorded voices of participants by a semi-automatic process without any manual annotations. Each feature was averaged among all questions and four groups categorized by question types. Table 1 shows the full list of features.

Pause. The average length of silent sections in participants' speech. The silent section was defined as a section with a volume level below a certain threshold and lasting for a certain period, where the thresholds were manually determined by the experimenter before analyzing the collected data, so that the resulting "pause" segments were as consistent with human-perceived pause segments as possible. Specifically, the threshold of the volume level was set to 48 dB, and intervals that last longer than 500 ms were counted. We measured the total length of the pause sections in the responses for each question.

Hesitation. This feature counted how often the "hesitation" attribute applied in the result from ASR (Watson Speech-To-Text). The ASR feeds "hesitation" in the result for the period when participants uttered fillers or spoke unclearly or in a smaller voice. We counted the occurrence of hesitations in a response and divided the count by the length of the recognized text of the response for each question.

Delay. The average length of the silent section before the participants' speech after the system's question. The same conditions used for "pause" were used for the "delay" section, but it was only labeled as "delay" when the silent section was detected at the beginning of the speech. We measured the length of the section for each question.

Interruption. The average number of participants' interruptions while the system was speaking. Segments when the system was speaking were clipped from the sound recorded with the throat microphone. The throat microphone does not record the sound of open-air, so the sections of above a certain volume level in the clipped segment means the period of participants' interruption. We counted the number of occurrences of the sections for each question.

4.7   Error Handling Features

Participant responses in the simulated error situations were evaluated on the following aspects.

Failure in Rephrasing. A label of how the participant responded in the "handling with recognition error" case of the scenario example (Fig. 2). In the normal case, participants asked to create a calendar event in both trials (2nd and 4th line). However, when the request was rejected in the first trial with error, they sometimes rephrased differently, e.g., "I'm going to a movie", which is a request with insufficient information to be determined correctly. The interaction was labelled "failure" unless the contents of both the first and second trials of making a request included all the necessary keywords for the request.

Failure in Correcting. A label indicating if the participant accepted a confirmation of the wrong value in the "handling with error confirmation" case in the scenario example (Fig. 2). For example, if the participant replied "well done, thanks" in the 4th line of example dialogue, the value was labelled "failure".

As each error case was executed once in the "create a calendar event" task for each participant, both of the error handing features take a binary value.

4.8   ASR Error Feature

Given that previous studies have repeatedly reported the challenges related to ASR errors in voice-based dialogue systems, we examined it with an up-to-date ASR engine (Watson Speech-To-Text as of September 2018) with neither custom language nor acoustic models.

ASR Error Rate. This feature counted how often the ASR mis-transcribes the participant's utterance. We compared a sentence automatically transcribed by ASR with one manually transcribed by the experimenter (ground truth) to check how often the utterance of a participant was misrecognized. We counted the occurrence of different categorematic words between the automatic and manual transcriptions. This information was gathered for five questions whose responses were mostly the same among the participants, such as making the initial request or asking for confirmation. Then we divided the total occurrence of different words by the total count of categorematic words appearing in the ground truth text as the average ASR error rate over five questions.

Table 1. List of features used in the analysis.

Name	Category	Source	Value
Pause-All		All questions	
Pause-O		Open-ended questions	
Pause-M	Pause	Multiple options questions	Average length
Pause-P		Prepared input questions	
Pause-C		Confirmation questions	
Hesitation-All		All questions	
Hesitation-O		Open-ended questions	
Hesitation-M	Hesitation	Multiple options questions	Average rate
Hesitation-P		Prepared input questions	
Hesitation-C		Confirmation questions	
Delay-All		All questions	
Delay-O		Open-ended questions	
Delay-M	Delay	Multiple options questions	Average length
Delay-P		Prepared input questions	
Delay-C		Confirmation questions	
Interruption-All		All questions	
Interruption-O		Open-ended questions	
Interruption-M	Interruption	Multiple options questions	Average rate
Interruption-P		Prepared input questions	
Interruption-C		Confirmation questions	
F-Rephrasing	Failure in rephrasing	"Handling with recognition error" question	Binary
F-Correcting	Failure in correcting	"Handling error confirmation" question	Binary
E-ASR	ASR error rate	5 questions normally answered similarly	Average rate

4.9 Statistical Analysis

We investigated the association between cognitive scores and behavioral features by using a linear regression model with age and gender as covariates. We examined deviations of variables from normality with their skewness statistics. A log-transform was applied to variables whose skewness statistics were more than twice the standard error to normalize their distribution. In this study, we set the significance level to 0.05.

5   Results

All 40 participants went through all the task scenarios. We collected 1,040 utterances in total. One participant got upset after the "handling error confirmation" turn in the "create a calendar event" task. We excluded the values that followed this from the results. Another participant could not understand the request to state the title of the event in "create a calendar event". We excluded the value of that question and a subsequent one asking for more details of the title. In total, four open-ended questions and one confirmation question were excluded. Figure 4 shows an overview of the extracted vocal features. For error handling features, 12 and eight out of the 40 participants were labeled as "failure" in rephrasing and correcting, respectively. The median of the ASR error rate was 9.7% (interquartile range: 0.7%–17.1%).

The participants did not have any difficulty in hearing synthesized voices, seeing the tablet screen, and talking with the experimenters. The MMSE scores ranged between 25 and 30 (mean = 28, SD = 1.5).

We investigated the relationship between cognitive scores and behavioral features by using a linear regression model controlling for age and gender information, as shown in Table 2. Of the 23 behavioral features, we found statistically significant associations between MMSE scores and the following five features: Pause-O, Hesitation-All, Hesitation-O, F-Rephrasing, and F-Correcting. We also found significant associations between FAB, LM1, or LM2 and the following features: F-Rephrasing for FAB, Interruption-C for LM1, and Interruption-C and E-ASR for LM2. As for the TMT-A and TMT-B assessments, we used the number of errors and the time needed to complete the task. Results showed significant associations between the number of errors with Pause-P and F-Rephrasing for TMT-A and F-Correcting for TMT-B. We also found that time for the tasks was significantly related to Delay-O and F-Correcting for TMT-B, while no significant associations were found for TMT-A.

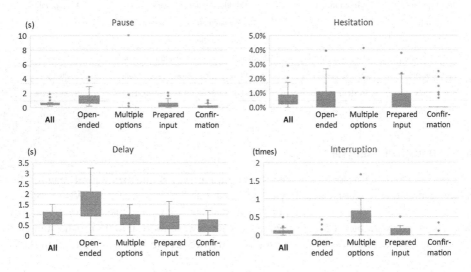

Fig. 4. Overall distribution of vocal features. The lines and boxes represent medians and interquartile ranges (IQR), respectively. The whiskers extend to most extreme data points up to 1.5 times the IQR. The dots represent outliers.

Table 2. Linear regression analysis on cognitive scores.

MMSE

Feature	β	95% CI		p Value
Pause-O	-0.5078	-1.0006	-0.0150	0.0438
Hesitation-All	-0.7045	-1.1807	-0.2284	0.0049
Hesitation-O	-0.6155	-1.0771	-0.1540	0.0104
F-Rephrasing	0.7044	0.2809	1.1280	0.0018
F-Correcting	1.1955	0.0154	2.3756	0.0472

FAB

Feature	β	95% CI		p Value
F-Rephrasing	0.7635	0.0783	1.4486	0.0300

LM1

Feature	β	95% CI		p Value
Interruption-C	1.5022	0.4406	2.5639	0.0068

LM2

Feature	β	95% CI		p Value
Interruption-C	1.5008	0.4417	2.5600	0.0068
E-ASR	-1.2822	-2.3612	-0.2033	0.0212

TMT-A (errors)

Feature	β	95% CI		p Value
Pause-P	-0.2375	-0.3845	-0.0905	0.0023
F-Rephrasing	-0.1710	-0.3280	-0.0140	0.0336

TMT-B (errors)

Feature	β	95% CI		p Value
F-Correcting	-1.7976	-3.5930	-0.0021	0.0497

TMT-A (time)

Feature	β	95% CI	p Value
		n.s.	

TMT-B (time)

Feature	β	95% CI		p Value
Start-O	13.4064	4.5527	22.2601	0.0041
F-Correcting	-28.1818	-51.0682	-5.2953	0.0172

β: standardized coefficients, F-Rephrasing and
F-Correcting took nominal value

6 Discussion

In this section, we discuss the implications of the experimental results, aiming to extend the general design guidelines for voice-based dialogue systems (e.g., [67–69]) by clarifying special consideration points for older users. The analysis of behavioral features should provide useful insights for the design of senior-friendly voice-based interactions. We first examine each hypothesis on the basis of the regression analysis results and then summarize some takeaways.

H1. *Pauses, hesitations, and other disfluency features increase with cognitive decline* —was partially confirmed. The regression analysis identified significant negative associations of MMSE scores with Pause-O and Hesitation-O. This result indicates that participants who had higher cognitive scores tended to exhibit fewer pauses or hesitations, particularly when responding to an open-ended question. As MMSE is known to assess multiple cognitive domains, this seems to indicate a general relationship between cognitive functioning and the appearance of pauses and hesitations. This trend has been repeatedly reported in studies on people with MCI or dementia (e.g., [14]). Our result suggests that the same trend appears for age-related cognitive decline in non-demented older adults when they interact with a voice-based dialogue system.

Most of the pauses and hesitations appeared in response to "open-ended" questions. This is not a surprising result because this type of question requires the participants to articulate their thoughts, confirming the findings in previous studies on spontaneous speech (e.g., [14]). In the median case, the values were roughly 1 s for Pause-O and 0.5% for Hesitation-O, which would not have any serious negative effect on user experience. However, in the worst case, Pause-O was longer than 4 s and Hesitation-O was roughly 4%. This would lead to turn-taking errors because, in a typical voice-based dialogue system, a long pause indicates the end of a response. The adaptation of the sentence segmentation criteria based on the user's cognitive scores and the type of the question could be effective to combat this. Also, the use of the acoustic model of ASR adapted to this trend would alleviate the problem, as suggested in previous work [33].

Interestingly, there was a significant positive correlation between both LM scores and Interruption-C. This result is opposite to our assumption. In short, the participants who had higher cognitive scores made more interruptions. A possible explanation is that healthy older adults with less age-related cognitive decline prefer faster conversations, and the 85% speech rate used in the experimental system was too slow for them. For interruptions, almost all of this type of behavior happened during "multiple options" questions. This seems to be a flaw in the dialogue design. In line with the design guidelines for developing applications on a commercial smart speaker [67], the typical "multiple options" question in our experimental system consisted of two sentences: (i) clearly presenting available options and (ii) clearly asking the user to make a choice. However, many participants started responding before the system finished the second sentence. It seems that, once they received the list of available options, participants wanted to answer as soon as possible. The system could avoid this type of conversation breakdown simply by accepting pre-emptive responses.

The ASR error rate was significantly higher for those who had lower cognitive (LM-2) scores, which confirmed the finding in [27, 28]. The accuracy of ASR is another critical aspect that could strongly affect user experience with a voice-based dialogue system. In the median case, the ASR error rate was lower than 10%. This is a much better value than the ASR accuracy reported in previous studies (e.g., [33]), and it seems to stem from the recent advances in ASR technology. This result indicates that the ASR accuracy itself could be less critical than ever, at least for those with less age-related cognitive decline, unless it comes in conjunction with other issues such as turn-taking errors and inappropriate wording on the part of the user. On the other hand, the ASR accuracy would still be relevant for those with cognitive decline or in confusing situations. Specifically, as stated below, participants tended to exhibit poor performance in an error handling situation. ASR errors in this situation would inhibit recovery from the error state, and have a serious negative impact on the user experience.

H2. *The failure in rephrasing increases with cognitive decline*—was confirmed. The regression analysis found that participants whose request lacked the necessary keywords at least in either the first or second trial during an error handling situation had significantly lower scores for MMSE and FAB. This result suggests that rephrasing requires executive functions. Interestingly, among the 12 participants who were not labeled as "success", seven failed only in the second trial. Even though they provided sufficient keywords at first, they incorrectly paraphrased their request after they received the error message. This change implies that reduction of information content [54] in the user's utterance could be observed in non-demented older adults particularly in an error handling situation. We prepared the error message (Fig. 2) as specified in the design guidelines [67], but it might be confusing to older adults with age-related cognitive decline. The error message should be designed more carefully. A personalized or context-based error message would probably be more effective.

H3. *The failure in correcting increases with cognitive decline*—was also confirmed. The regression analysis found that participants who failed to correct the system's recognition error had significantly lower MMSE scores as well as a larger amount of time and errors for TMT-B. This result suggests that older adults with lower attention ability tend to ignore the system's misrecognition, which makes "confirmation" questions ineffective. To address this challenge, the system could exploit a screen to allow users to visually review the recognition result. The use of social networks might be another solution, where the system would ask the user's close relatives to double-check a response, as long as the conversation does not contain privacy-sensitive contents. There is a trade-off between the potential solutions for H1 and H3. Specifically, open-ended questions in a dialogue design could be replaced with a series of closed questions to reduce the occurrence of pauses and hesitations, but that would increase the number of questions for confirmation and lead to more "failure in correcting" errors.

In summary, our analysis suggests that the language and behavioral dysfunctions reported in previous studies on neuropathological cognitive impairments could also occur in a broader range of older users—particularly in cognitively demanding situations such as when handling errors. Special considerations are needed to provide a better voice-based interaction experience for older users with age-related cognitive decline, which include:

Avoid Misrecognitions of the End of a Response. Older users with age-related cognitive decline tended to exhibit more pauses and hesitations. The system should allow users to keep talking intermittently. Note that the pauses and hesitations are more likely to appear in a response to an open-ended question, even though existing guidelines recommend the use of open-ended questions. A dynamic adaptation of thresholds [70] might be useful for this purpose.

Accept Pre-emptive Responses. Older users with a higher cognitive score tended to respond to the system in a pre-emptive manner, at least in the present study. Developers of voice-based dialogue systems should keep in mind that users could face different issues even if they have better cognitive functioning.

Provide Personalized, Context-Based Error Messages. Ageneral "could not catch it" message seemed to be ineffective for older users with age-related cognitive decline. The system should take into account the details of the situation and the user's cognitive profile and provide an instructive message that clearly tells the user how to recover from the error state. For example, it would be helpful if the system could indicate whether "rephrasing" or "repeating" is needed.

Assist with Confirmation. Older users with age-related cognitive decline, particularly those with lower attention ability, tended to incorrectly accept the response from the system. The system should help the user recognize its own mistake, for example, by providing screen-based visual confirmations in conjunction with voice-based ones.

These points have not been structurally emphasized in the design of senior-friendly dialogue interfaces, even though they have been shown to be relevant to older users' experience with voice-based dialogue interactions. Given the increase of aged people and the growing use of voice-based dialogue systems, these considerations will only become more critical.

7 Conclusion and Limitations

In this work, we presented the first empirical results of an investigation into how age-related cognitive decline in non-demented, ordinary older adults influenced behavioral characteristics (i.e., vocal and error handling features) in the use of a voice-based dialogue system. Our analysis on the collected human-machine conversations identified significant associations between the behavioral features and cognitive scores measured by standard assessment tools such as MMSE and LM. The results showed that differences in vocal features such as pauses and hesitations, which have been found in studies on language dysfunction related to MCI and AD, also appeared in typical voice-based dialogue interactions of a broader range of older adults with age-related cognitive decline. We then discussed the potential impact of the identified behavioral characteristics on the user experience of voice-based dialogue systems and presented points for design consideration as workarounds on prospective issues.

The main limitation of this work is the limited size of samples. Even though the number of participants is comparable to those in previous corpus studies such as [15], the collected data cover only a small portion of the diverse nature of cognitive aging. In particular, our investigation on error handling behaviors depends on a small number of question-response pairs observed during two pieces of controlled error handling situations. While this was intentional—i.e., these experimental conversation scenarios were specifically designed to examine realistic error handling behaviors—further samples are needed to quantitatively assess the result. Another potential limitation is the lack of comparison with younger people or people with MCI or dementia, even though this was also intentional as our investigation focused on the variance of age-related cognitive decline among non-demented older adults. To confirm or extend our findings, further controlled studies and large-scale wild studies will be needed. Also, the design consideration points presented in the previous section need to be implemented and evaluated with the target population.

The uniqueness of our study is that it highlighted variations in cognitive scores among healthy older adults, and then showed significant associations between the cognitive scores and interaction characteristics with a voice-based dialogue system, particularly in cognitively demanding error handling situations. We believe that our findings can provide voice-based dialogue interface designers with empirical evidence, which could not be directly supported by previous studies in different contexts.

Acknowledgements. We thank all of the participants in the experiment.

References

1. López, G., Quesada, L., Guerrero, L.A.: Alexa vs Siri vs Cortana vs Google Assistant: a comparison of speech-based natural user interfaces. In: Nunes, I. (ed.) International Conference on Applied Human Factors and Ergonomics, pp. 241–250. Springer, Heidelberg (2017). https://doi.org/10.1007/978-3-319-60366-7_23
2. Ma, M., Skubic, M., Ai, K., Hubbard, J.: July. Angel-echo: a personalized Health care application. In: Proceedings of the Second IEEE/ACM International Conference on Connected Health: Applications, Systems and Engineering Technologies, pp. 258–259. IEEE Press (2017)
3. Reis, A., Paulino, D., Paredes, H., Barroso, J.: Using intelligent personal assistants to strengthen the elderlies' social bonds. In: Antona, M., Stephanidis, C. (eds.) UAHCI 2017. LNCS, vol. 10279, pp. 593–602. Springer, Cham (2017). https://doi.org/10.1007/978-3-319-58700-4_48
4. Portet, F., Vacher, M., Golanski, C., Roux, C., Meillon, B.: Design and evaluation of a smart home voice interface for the elderly: acceptability and objection aspects. Pers. Ubiquit. Comput. 17(1), 127–144 (2013)
5. Wolters, M.K., Kelly, F., Kilgour, J.: Designing a spoken dialogue interface to an intelligent cognitive assistant for people with dementia. Health Inform. J. 22(4), 854–866 (2016)
6. Russo, A., et al.: Dialogue Systems and Conversational Agents for Patients with Dementia: the human-robot interaction. Rejuvenation Res. 22, 109–120 (2018)
7. Smith, A.L., Chaparro, B.S.: Smartphone text input method performance, usability, and preference with younger and older adults. Hum. Factors 57(6), 1015–1028 (2015)
8. Bragg, D., Bennett, C., Reinecke, K., Ladner, R.: A large inclusive study of human listening rates. In: Proceedings of the 2018 CHI Conference on Human Factors in Computing Systems, p. 444. ACM (2018)
9. Watson, C.M.: An analysis of trouble and repair in the natural conversations of people with dementia of the Alzheimer's type. Aphasiology 13(3), 195–218 (1999)
10. Rudzicz, F., Wang, R., Begum, M., Mihailidis, A.: Speech interaction with personal assistive robots supporting aging at home for individuals with Alzheimer's disease. ACM Trans. Access. Comput. (TACCESS) 7(2), 6 (2015)
11. Bucks, R.S., Singh, S., Cuerden, J.M., Wilcock, G.K.: Analysis of spontaneous, conversational speech in dementia of Alzheimer type: evaluation of an objective technique for analysing lexical performance. Aphasiology 14(1), 71–91 (2000)
12. Khodabakhsh, A., Yesil, F., Guner, E., Demiroglu, C.: Evaluation of linguistic and prosodic features for detection of Alzheimer's disease in Turkish conversational speech. EURASIP J. Audio Speech Music. Process. 2015(1), 9 (2015)
13. Hoffmann, I., Nemeth, D., Dye, C.D., Pákáski, M., Irinyi, T., Kálmán, J.: Temporal parameters of spontaneous speech in Alzheimer's disease. Int. J. Speech-Lang. Pathol. 12(1), 29–34 (2010)
14. König, A., et al.: Automatic speech analysis for the assessment of patients with predementia and Alzheimer's disease. Alzheimer's Dement.: Diagn., Assess. Dis. Monit. 1(1), 112–124 (2015)
15. Georgila, K., Wolters, M., Moore, J.D., Logie, R.H.: The MATCH corpus: a corpus of older and younger users' interactions with spoken dialogue systems. Lang. Resour. Eval. 44(3), 221–261 (2010)
16. Salber, D., Coutaz, J.: A wizard of Oz platform for the study of multimodal systems. In: INTERACT 1993 and CHI 1993 Conference Companion on Human Factors in Computing Systems, pp. 95–96. ACM, April 1993

17. Motti, L.G., Vigouroux, N., Gorce, P.: Interaction techniques for older adults using touchscreen devices: a literature review. In: Proceedings of the 25th Conference on l'Interaction Homme-Machine, p. 125. ACM, November 2013

18. Kobayashi, M., Hiyama, A., Miura, T., Asakawa, C., Hirose, M., Ifukube, T.: Elderly user evaluation of mobile touchscreen interactions. In: Campos, P., Graham, N., Jorge, J., Nunes, N., Palanque, P., Winckler, M. (eds.) INTERACT 2011. LNCS, vol. 6946, pp. 83–99. Springer, Heidelberg (2011). https://doi.org/10.1007/978-3-642-23774-4_9

19. Wacharamanotham, C., Hurtmanns, J., Mertens, A., Kronenbuerger, M., Schlick, C., Borchers, J.: Evaluating swabbing: a touchscreen input method for elderly users with tremor. In: Proceedings of the SIGCHI Conference on Human Factors in Computing Systems, pp. 623–626, ACM 2011

20. Nicolau, H., Jorge, J.: Elderly text-entry performance on touchscreens. In: Proceedings of the 14th International ACM SIGACCESS Conference on Computers and Accessibility, pp. 127–134. ACM, October 2012

21. Sato, D., Morimura, T., Katsuki, T., Toyota, Y., Kato, T., Takagi, H.: Automated help system for novice older users from touchscreen gestures. In: 2016 23rd International Conference on Pattern Recognition (ICPR), pp. 3073–3078. IEEE, December 2016

22. Wobbrock, J.O., Kane, S.K., Gajos, K.Z., Harada, S., Froehlich, J.: Ability-based design: concept, principles and examples. ACM Trans. Access. Comput. (TACCESS) 3(3), 9 (2011)

23. Gajos, K.Z., Weld, D.S., Wobbrock, J.O.: Automatically generating personalized user interfaces with Supple (2010)

24. Trewin, S., Keates, S., Moffatt, K.: Developing steady clicks:: a method of cursor assistance for people with motor impairments. In: Proceedings of the 8th International ACM SIGACCESS Conference on Computers and Accessibility, pp. 26–33. ACM (2006)

25. Wobbrock, J.O., Fogarty, J., Liu, S.Y.S., Kimuro, S., Harada, S.: The angle mouse: target-agnostic dynamic gain adjustment based on angular deviation. In: Proceedings of the SIGCHI Conference on Human Factors in Computing Systems, pp. 1401–1410. ACM, April 2009

26. Sato, D., Kobayashi, M., Takagi, H., Asakawa, C., Tanaka, J.: How voice augmentation supports elderly web users. In: The proceedings of the 13th International ACM SIGACCESS Conference on Computers and Accessibility, pp. 155–162. ACM, October 2011

27. Weiner, J., Engelbart, M., Schultz, T.: Manual and automatic transcriptions in dementia detection from speech. Proc. Interspeech 2017, 3117–3121 (2017)

28. Rudzicz, F., Wang, R., Begum, M., Mihailidis, A.: Speech recognition in Alzheimer's disease with personal assistive robots. In: Proceedings of the 5th Workshop on Speech and Language Processing for Assistive Technologies, pp. 20–28 (2014)

29. Zajicek, M.: Aspects of HCI research for older people. Univ. Access Inf. Soc. 5(3), 279–286 (2006)

30. Ienca, M., Fabrice, J., Elger, B., Caon, M., Pappagallo, A.S., Kressig, R.W., Wangmo, T.: Intelligent assistive technology for Alzheimer's disease and other dementias: a systematic review. J. Alzheimers Dis. 56(4), 1301–1340 (2017)

31. Granata, C., Chetouani, M., Tapus, A., Bidaud, P., Dupourqué, V.: September. Voice and graphical-based interfaces for interaction with a robot dedicated to elderly and people with cognitive disorders. In: 2010 IEEE RO-MAN, pp. 785–790. IEEE (2010)

32. Ziman, R., Walsh, G.: Factors affecting seniors' perceptions of voice-enabled user interfaces. In: Extended Abstracts of the 2018 CHI Conference on Human Factors in Computing Systems, CHI EA 2018, 6 p. (2018)

33. Vipperla, R., Wolters, M., Georgila, K., Renals, S.: Speech input from older users in smart environments: challenges and perspectives. In: Stephanidis, C. (ed.) UAHCI 2009. LNCS, vol. 5615, pp. 117–126. Springer, Heidelberg (2009). https://doi.org/10.1007/978-3-642-02710-9_14

34. Bost, J., Moore, J.D.: An analysis of older users' interactions with spoken dialogue systems. In: LREC, pp. 1176–1181 (2014)

35. Cucchiarini, C., Hamme, H.V., Herwijnen, O.V., Smits, F.: Jasmin-CGN: extension of the spoken Dutch corpus with speech of elderly people, children and non-natives in the human-machine interaction modality (2006)

36. Rösner, D.F., Frommer, J., Friesen, R., Haase, M., Lange, J., Otto, M.: LAST MINUTE: a multimodal corpus of speech-based user-companion interactions. In: LREC, pp. 2559–2566, May 2012

37. Rösner, D., et al.: The LAST MINUTE Corpus as a Research Resource: From Signal Processing to Behavioral Analyses in User-Companion Interactions. In Companion Technology (pp. 277–299). Springer, Cham 2017

38. Wolters, M.K., Kilgour, J., MacPherson, S.E., Dzikovska, M., Moore, J.D.: The CADENCE corpus: a new resource for inclusive voice interface design. In: Proceedings of the 33rd Annual ACM Conference on Human Factors in Computing Systems, pp. 3963–3966. ACM, April 2015

39. Rudzicz, F., Chan Currie, L., Danks, A., Mehta, T., Zhao, S.: Automatically identifying trouble-indicating speech behaviors in Alzheimer's disease. In: Proceedings of the 16th International ACM SIGACCESS Conference on Computers & Accessibility, pp. 241–242. ACM, October 2014

40. Chinaei, H., Currie, L.C., Danks, A., Lin, H., Mehta, T., Rudzicz, F.: Identifying and avoiding confusion in dialogue with people with Alzheimer's disease. Comput. Linguist. **43** (2), 377–406 (2017)

41. Kirshner, H.S.: Primary progressive aphasia and Alzheimer's disease: brief history, recent evidence. Curr. Neurol. Neurosci. Rep. **12**(6), 709–714 (2012)

42. MacKay, D.G., James, L.E., Hadley, C.B.: Amnesic HM's performance on the language competence test: parallel deficits in memory and sentence production. J. Clin. Exp. Neuropsychol. **30**(3), 280–300 (2008)

43. Van Velzen, M., Garrard, P.: From hindsight to insight–retrospective analysis of language written by a renowned Alzheimer's patient. Interdisc. Sci. Rev. **33**(4), 278–286 (2008)

44. Oulhaj, A., Wilcock, G.K., Smith, A.D., de Jager, C.A.: Predicting the time of conversion to MCI in the elderly role of verbal expression and learning. Neurology **73**(18), 1436–1442 (2009)

45. Petersen, R.C., Caracciolo, B., Brayne, C., Gauthier, S., Jelic, V., Fratiglioni, L.: Mild cognitive impairment: a concept in evolution. J. Intern. Med. **275**(3), 214–228 (2014)

46. Mueller, K.D., et al.: Verbal fluency and early memory decline: results from the Wisconsin registry for Alzheimer's prevention. Arch. Clin. Neuropsychol. **30**(5), 448–457 (2015)

47. Bertola, L., et al.: Graph analysis of verbal fluency test discriminate between patients with Alzheimer's disease, mild cognitive impairment and normal elderly controls. Front. Aging Neurosci. **6**, 185 (2014)

48. Lundholm, K.F., Fraser, K., Kokkinakis, D.: Automated syntactic analysis of language abilities in persons with mild and subjective cognitive impairment. Stud. Health Technol. Inform. **247**, 705–709 (2018)

49. Henry, J.D., Crawford, J.R., Phillips, L.H.: Verbal fluency performance in dementia of the Alzheimer's type: a meta-analysis. Neuropsychologia **42**(9), 1212–1222 (2004)

50. Kavé, G., Goral, M.: Word retrieval in connected speech in Alzheimer's disease: a review with meta-analyses. Aphasiology **32**(1), 4–26 (2018)

51. Lunsford, R., Heeman, P.A.: Using linguistic indicators of difficulty to identify mild cognitive impairment. In: Sixteenth Annual Conference of the International Speech Communication Association (2015)
52. Toth, L., et al.: A speech recognition-based solution for the automatic detection of mild cognitive impairment from spontaneous speech. Curr. Alzheimer Res. **15**(2), 130–138 (2018)
53. Ahmed, S., de Jager, C.A., Haigh, A.M., Garrard, P.: Semantic processing in connected speech at a uniformly early stage of autopsy-confirmed Alzheimer's disease. Neuropsychology **27**(1), 79 (2013)
54. Fraser, K.C., Meltzer, J.A., Rudzicz, F.: Linguistic features identify Alzheimer's disease in narrative speech. J. Alzheimers Dis. **49**(2), 407–422 (2016)
55. Sajjadi, S.A., Patterson, K., Tomek, M., Nestor, P.J.: Abnormalities of connected speech in semantic dementia vs Alzheimer's disease. Aphasiology **26**(6), 847–866 (2012)
56. Croisile, B., Ska, B., Brabant, M.J., Duchene, A., Lepage, Y., Aimard, G., Trillet, M.: Comparative study of oral and written picture description in patients with Alzheimer's disease. Brain Lang. **53**(1), 1–19 (1996)
57. Ahmed, S., Haigh, A.M.F., de Jager, C.A., Garrard, P.: Connected speech as a marker of disease progression in autopsy-proven Alzheimer's disease. Brain **136**(12), 3727–3737 (2013)
58. Natale, M., Entin, E., Jaffe, J.: Vocal interruptions in dyadic communication as a function of speech and social anxiety. J. Pers. Soc. Psychol. **37**(6), 865 (1979)
59. Brewer, R., Garcia, R.C., Schwaba, T., Gergle, D., Piper, A.M.: Exploring traditional phones as an e-mail interface for older adults. TACCESS **8**(2), 6 (2016)
60. Barthel Activities of Daily Living (ADL) Index: Occasional paper (Royal College of General Practitioners) (59), 24 (1993)
61. Folstein, M.F., Folstein, S.E., McHugh, P.R.: "Mini-mental state": a practical method for grading the cognitive state of patients for the clinician. J. Psychiatr. Res. **12**(3), 189–198 (1975)
62. Dubois, B., Slachevsky, A., Litvan, I., Pillon, B.F.A.B.: The FAB: a frontal assessment battery at bedside. Neurology **55**(11), 1621–1626 (2000)
63. Wechsler, D.: A standardized memory scale for clinical use. J. Psychol. **19**(1), 87–95 (1945)
64. Wechsler, D.: WMS-R: Wechsler memory scale-revised: manual. Psychological Corporation (1984)
65. Reitan, R.M.: Validity of the trail making test as an indicator of organic brain damage. Percept. Mot. Skills **8**(3), 271–276 (1958)
66. Stuss, D.T., Levine, B.: Adult clinical neuropsychology: lessons from studies of the frontal lobes. Annu. Rev. Psychol. **53**(1), 401–433 (2002)
67. Alexa Design Guide. https://developer.amazon.com/docs/alexa-design/intro.html. Accessed 25 Jan 2019
68. Conversation Design. https://designguidelines.withgoogle.com/conversation/conversation-design/. Accessed 25 Jan 2019
69. Cortana design guidelines. https://docs.microsoft.com/en-us/cortana/voice-commands/voice command-design-guidelines. Accessed 25 Jan 2019
70. Raux, A., Eskenazi, M.: Optimizing endpointing thresholds using dialogue features in a spoken dialogue system. In: Proceedings of the 9th SIGdial Workshop on Discourse and Dialogue (SIGdial 2008), pp. 1–10 (2008)

GDI as an Alternative Guiding Interaction Style for Occasional Users

Antonio L. Carrillo$^{(\boxtimes)}$ and Juan A. Falgueras

Department of Computer Sciences, University of Málaga,
Teatinos, 29071 Málaga, Spain
alcarrillo@uma.es

Abstract. It is usually taken for granted that *Direct Manipulation* is the best interaction style for inexperienced or non-expert users; moreover, this style of interaction is generally considered the best for almost every situation and user. The recent shifts in technology that we all are currently experiencing have given rise to a great deal of new kinds of users performing specific tasks in a variety of scenarios. In this paper, we focus on users who access a system occasionally, infrequently, or in an unplanned way; i.e., users who do not want or cannot afford a learning curve. We show that for them, *Direct Manipulation* is not always the most suitable style of interaction. We assess the advantages of guiding this kind of users, in particular through the guided interaction framework known as *Goal Driven Interaction*. GDI can be viewed as a superset of wizards providing support far beyond a few steps through dialogs. Indeed, GDI is an interaction style with characteristics of its own. We report a complete user test that backs up previous hypotheses. The analysis of empirical data proves that *GDI* is more time-efficient than *DM, requiring* fewer moderator assistances for the users. Post-test questionnaires confirmed that participants had a strong preference for *GDI*.

Keywords: Interaction design process and methods · Interaction paradigms · Empirical studies in interaction design · Interfaces for occasional users

1 Introduction

Interaction Style is a classic topic discussed in the mainstream HCI literature, e.g. [14, 43]. There are two main general approaches to interact with computers: the conversational world and the model world, corresponding to sequential and freely accessible dialogues, respectively. The former includes Question and Answer dialogues, Command Line interfaces, Menu-based interaction, Form Fill-in data entry, Natural Language, etcetera; text is therefore the primary tool for interaction between the user and the system in this model. The other general approach, the model world, makes use of graphics and metaphors [8] as well as tools like Windows, Icons, Menus and Pointer (WIMP), to assist the user with asynchronous and free management of objects on the screen. The Direct Manipulation (DM) [18, 42, 43] of interactive elements makes this general approach even more familiar and intuitive. Ideally, the users see and predict the behavior of well-known objects through metaphors. They then follow their natural

© IFIP International Federation for Information Processing 2019
Published by Springer Nature Switzerland AG 2019
D. Lamas et al. (Eds.): INTERACT 2019, LNCS 11749, pp. 75–96, 2019.
https://doi.org/10.1007/978-3-030-29390-1_5

intuition to manipulate them, receiving immediate feedback: "You don't notice the computer because you think of yourself as doing the task, not as using the computer", Norman [35]. However, DM-WIMP interfaces still require time to become acquainted with them. In particular, Stasko stated: "...Although GUI and WIMP interfaces are a big step past line-oriented terminals, they still have a learning curve and they can be awkward to use".

Whatever the case may be, the success of the DM approach has eclipsed the others. These interfaces are typically assumed to be the best solution for every possible scenario, task and user. However, the massive expansion of technology has caused the appearance of new scenarios of use in addition to quite different tasks and users for them. This requires revisiting the most appropriate approach for each case. The success of the interaction depends basically upon its suitability for the final user. There are many differences between how experts and novices perceive and use software applications [13]. On the one hand, experts have the best possible mental model thanks to their experience. As opposed to novices, they require less guidance and help. On the other hand, novices are users with little or no knowledge about the system. They initially have a deficient understanding about the possibilities of the application and have to focus on how to deal with the interface [28]. To gain expertise they follow a learning curve that is usually traversed through study and repeated use of the application. Moran [28] argued that for novices learning to use the interface is more important than being able to accomplish the task: "Learning is, of course, paramount for the novice whereas the time it takes to do a task is secondary". Interestingly, there are situations where learnability is not as important as the time elapsed in the interaction. For example, purchasing a train ticket in a self-service machine when the train is on the verge of departing. The aim here is to accomplish the transaction as quickly as possible. In such cases, learning how to use the application is not as relevant as just getting it done. Achieving the goal, i.e., getting the ticket in your hand, becomes the priority, while learning during the interaction – an action that may not even be repeated at all in the future – becomes secondary ("[the user] does not have any ambition to master the system and may prefer to be led by the hand to accomplish...") [46]. Then, some problems arise when a system is occasionally accessed and the user does not want or cannot afford a learning curve.

At least three arguments support an explicit design of systems for these occasional users: advances in UIs, new scenarios of use, and a more ambitious inclusive design. Firstly, the evolution of Graphical User Interface (GUI) [30, 43] and the correct inclusion of multi-touch systems [5, 36, 40] have brought about new kinds of devices and new ways of interaction. Secondly, the ubiquity and the permanent on-line interconnection of mobile devices have burst into unexplored contexts of use, e.g. shopping centres, leisure facilities, museums, airports... [11, 15, 41]. These technologies have facilitated new scenarios of use where human-computer interaction (HCI) is on the move, using technology as a mean to accomplish an immediate goal. Thirdly, this increase in the heterogeneity and number of occasional users is also driven by the incorporation of the principles of Accessibility [1, 29, 47], Usability [32, 33] and Inclusive Design [12, 39].

In summary, there is a wider spectrum of users able to perform not only planned but also occasional activities. This new scenario demands simplicity, immediacy and no previous knowledge, just like when buying a transport ticket in a self-service machine, visiting a new city, designing or furnishing a room, or using an audio-guide mobile app during the visit to a museum or archaeological site. Our aim is to check with real users which kind of interface – either guided or non-guided – they prefer. The selected guided interaction style, namely Goal Driven Interaction (GDI), is introduced in Sect. 2. We compare a GDI-guided standard application for furnishing kitchens with its non-guided counterpart. In Sect. 3 we present our experiment, and in Sect. 4 we discuss the results.

2 Goals Driven Interaction

Goals Driven Interaction (GDI) [9] is conceived as a human-computer interaction style especially suitable for occasional users, that is, users who do not want or cannot afford a learning curve. This means that even if the user dealt previously with the same or analogous technology, there are a number of factors that make it unwise to rely on the user's memory recall or implicit visual recognition as the main mechanisms to learn how to use the interface. Some of those factors could be the time elapsed since the last interaction, the difficulties users experience on learning, and, in many cases, their lack of interest [17]. It is recommended to assume that the user will have to cope with an unknown interface, with no requirement upon previous knowledge to use it. The corresponding style of interaction will be of conversational and sequential nature, even sacrificing the possibility of performing tasks in parallel as well as other typical advantages of pure DM interfaces. This does not prevent the user from deciding among alternatives. The objective here is to guide the user, step by step, in a hierarchical way along the whole interaction. Thus, hierarchically organized objectives and sub-objectives will be clearly presented to the user one at a time. The goals, once achieved, are left behind. Nevertheless, the user will have the possibility to return to past goals, via cancellation, whenever it is possible to do so. The user will be strictly guided on the "what to do" and the "how to do it," one step at a time. This strategy constrains the freedom of the DM in a similar way to processes guided by wizards [4, 27, 45, 48]. In some sense, GDI could be viewed as a layer over pure DM, making it a kind of assisted interaction, adding control over DM: it allows the user to touch, move or briefly interact with graphic objects, but only when the guide allows for it. It could also be viewed as a super-set of wizards. Standard DM transfers the control to the user whereas GDI guides them.

The fundamentals of GDI trace back to the work of [31] devoted to the mechanisms of human reasoning for problems resolution. Their vision (as in GDI) was based on breaking up the main or general goal into a hierarchical tree of sub-goals. The branches of that tree can have different lengths depending on the degree of fragmentation in sub-goals. The leaves of the tree are elementary actions or final goals that do not require further explanations nor decomposition. Based on this work, Card, Moran and Newell [6, 7] developed one of the most important cognitive models, the Human Processing Model, whose initial paradigm consisted in conceiving the interaction as a problem resolution task. They described a psychological model of humans comprising three interactive systems: perceptive, motor and cognitive. Each one would have its own memory and its own processor. This vision of the user as an information processing system permits the description of all the activities (both physical and mental) that take part in a task. This in turn gave origin to a family of methods for modelling, specifying and evaluating a user interface: the GOMS models [20–22]. A GOMS (Goals, Operators, Methods, and Selection rules) model is a description of the knowledge a user must have in order to carry out tasks and thereby goals on a device; it is a representation of the "how to do it". The aim of GDI is to preclude the user from having to devote time to acquire that knowledge. The user will not need to look anything up in any user manual, or help system, nor think about anything except navigating through the proposed steps. We only expect from the user to know the goal to achieve.

There are many versions derived from the original GOMS. In particular, Kieras [24, 25] contributed with the idea of a structured natural language, namely NGOMSL (Natural GOMS Language). These methodologies themselves are framed in a larger set of techniques enabling a hierarchical task analysis. The main goal of these techniques is the decomposition of a complex task in sub-tasks, so that the resolution method can be followed step by step. For instance, HTA [2], TAG [38], TKS [23], or the more recent CTT [37], that also includes the possibility of expressing the concurrency of the tasks. None of them were oriented to readiness but to formalization and have been discarded for our methodology. In contrast, NGOMSL presents a wide and detailed literature, as well as practical construction methods, e.g. [24, 25], that can be broadly applied. But above all, the most interesting feature of GDI is their closeness to the user's natural language: any user can read and follow it, as a recipe. NGOMSL can be used to specify GDI interfaces but it could not qualify to model some situations and aspects of GDI. To overcome this issue the authors have extended and adapted NGOMSL, for instance by including the possibility of cancelling goals. This extended version can be used as a source specification language [9].

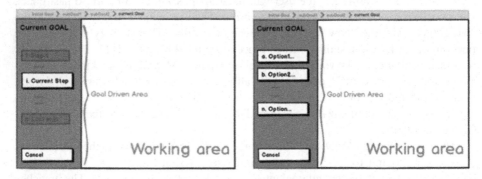

Fig. 1. Proposed layout of a *GDI interface*, when offering a *method* (on the left) or a *selection* (on the right)

From the specification obtained applying our extension of NGOMSL is possible, after an easy compilation process, to obtain the corresponding guide of the final GDI interface, which composes the Goal Driven Area. GDA is what explicitly guides the user through the hierarchy of goals (Fig. 1). This area becomes the substitute for the typical menus and toolbars used in standard MD-WIMP, not necessary for these guided interfaces. GDA will always show the method or the selection that allows the user to accomplish the current goal. If this goal requires the user to make a selection, GDA shows the different excluding options (alternatives) that compose that selection, so that the user can choose one of them. In case the goal must be accomplished following a specific method, GDA will offer the sequence of steps that compose this method. The interface underlines the current step, which could imply the initiation of a new subgoal (and then another method or selection), or the realization of an elementary action (without methods nor selections).

3   GDI vs Standard DM Interfaces: A Comparative Study

At the beginning of the previous section, we explained that GDI was proposed as a way to help occasional users who do not want or cannot afford a learning curve for specific goals. Our aim has been to test this postulate with real users. To that end, a comparative study between guided and non-guided interaction has been conducted. This empirical analysis gave us objective measurements and subjective opinions. We wanted to test 2 objectively measurable hypothesis, related to time and errors, and a third subjective hypothesis, related to satisfaction.

For non-computer experts, occasional users:

- (H1) they proceed quicker with GDI than with standard DM,
- (H2) they make fewer errors with GDI than with standard DM,
- (H3) they prefer GDI to standard DM.

As can be seen, the 3 pillars of usability are covered: efficiency (H1), effectivity (H2), and satisfaction (H3).

A first approach to this study was presented in [10] as "work in progress". However, that work could only show what appeared to be a trend, since it had very few participants, and lacked analysis, discussion and statistical study about the significance of the results.

3.1   Participants

The study involved twenty volunteer participants (n = 20), a number that meets the criteria of [3, 26, 34, 44]. There were 12 females and 8 males. Their ages ranged from 10 to 52 years, with a mean age of 44 years. All subjects were unaware of the final aim of the research. They had not participated in previous usability studies nor had they received any incentives to participate in the experiment. Each participant had to use two different versions of the same application (the two types of interfaces to be compared), following a *counterbalanced* strategy (as we will explain later).

Table 1 summarizes the main data and characteristics of the participants, collected by means of a Background Questionnaire.

Table 1. Overview of the main data and characteristics of the participants, collected by means of the *Background Questionnaire*: *Gender* (**G**), *Age* (**A**), ***Computer Expertise*** (**CE**), *Previously Used Software* (**PUS**) [options: Internet, Email, Word Processor, Spread_sheet, Multimedia, Accounting & management, Databases, social Networks, Others], *Kitchen Design Software Knowledge* (**KDSK**), *Tablets and Smartphones Expertise* (**TSE**), *Task Domain Knowledge* (**TDK**), *Academic Studies Level* (**ASL**) ranged from 0 to 3 [0: No studies; 1: Primary school; 2: Secondary school; 3: University], and *Other Relevant Knowledge* (**ORK**). The *Computer Expertise* (**CE**) of each participant was checked and validated in accordance with these items.

#	CE	PUS	KDSK	TSE	TDK	ASL	ORK
	[0..5]	[I, E, W, S, M, A, D, N, O]		[0..4]	[0..4]	[0..3]	
1	0		No	1	3	1	
2	0		No	1	3	1	
3	0	I	No	1	3	1	
4	0	I	No	2	1	0	
5	1	I, E	No	2	3	1	
6	1	I, M	No	2	3	2	
7	1	I, M, O	No	2	2	1	Occasional use of IKEA kitchen design app
8	2	I, E, W, S, M, A (forgotten)	No	2	3	2	Forgotten computer courses
9	2	I, E, W, M, N, O	No	2	3	1	
10	2	I, E, W, M, O	No	2	3	1	Medical software
11	2	I, E, W, M, O	No	2	3	3	Medical software
12	2	I, E, W, S, M, O (forgotten)	No	2	3	1	Pantograph. Forgotten computer courses
13	2	I, E, W, M, A, N, O	No	2	2	1	Photoshop
14	3	I, E, W, S, M, A, D	No	2	3	2	
15	3	I, E, W, S, M, A, D, O	No	2	2	3	Veterinary software
16	3	I, E, W, M, O	No	2	3	1	AutoCAD and Presto user
17	3	I, E, W, S, M, A, D, O	No	1	3	2	Forgotten computer courses
18	3	I, E, W, S, M, A, D, O	No	2	3	2	
19	3	I, E, W, S, M, A, O	Kitchens	3	4	2	Photoshop. Kitchen design professional
20	3	I, E, W, S, M, O	Kitchens	2	4	1	Kitchen design professional

To do the recruiting and screening of the participants, the primary requirement was no previous experience with similar applications to those tested in this study. Only two exceptions were intentionally included: two participants were professionals at the task domain. Both of them had this task as part of their daily activity using similar commercial direct manipulation software packages. The other screening criterion was to discard computer expert users, as reflected in Table 1: no participant had a self-graded Computer Expertise greater than 3 on a 5–point scale. This parameter is subjective. To confirm these self-assigned values, we also asked several complementary questions: PUS, KDSK, TSE, TDK, ASL, and ORK (see Table 1). A complementary study with Eye Tracker was conducted for two of the participants. See Sect. 3.6.4 for details.

3.2   Materials and Tasks

Although other applications could be plausible, we chose for our study a familiar domain, i.e. kitchen furniture. This scenario comprises three development stages: designing, furnishing and final adjustments of a kitchen. Some of the involved tasks require extensive object manipulation, usually implemented with standard DM interfaces. These characteristics could lead us to think that this is an application especially suitable for a classic DM interaction style, making it particularly challenging for our study.

We developed two versions of the same application (in Java language), one with a GDI interface and the other with a classic DM interface (Fig. 2). Both share most of the code except for the sections in which the user interfaces are involved. Both offer the same functionality and allow the user to achieve the same goals. The DM version is inspired by the desktop version offered by IKEA [19]. Figure 2 depicts a sub-task per row for each of the stages the user goes through. The left column corresponds to the DM interface whereas the right column is related to the GDI interface. The DM interface is a plain standard WIMP application. The user first introduces the shape and the dimensions of the kitchen and then furnishes it. To this end, the user has to pick elements and position them inside the boundaries following the canonical DM way, i.e. with undo/re-do, tool-tips for buttons, right-click pop-up menus, etc.

Regarding the three screenshots on the right column for the GDI interface, note that the user is presented with a list of actions to be read and followed. Each action is atomically performed by short DM interactions in the Working Area. The user cannot continue until the previous action is completed, as we explained in Sect. 2.

- A screencast of a participant using GDI can be watched in https://youtu.be/4owtCVMuqc4
- A screencast of a participant using DM is shown in https://youtu.be/QeafXLlsXzY
- The source code for both applications is available in https://github.com/juanfal/ADICO

Each participant was given a single piece of paper containing the information shown below. It briefly described the application scenario along with the three groups of tasks chosen for the test:

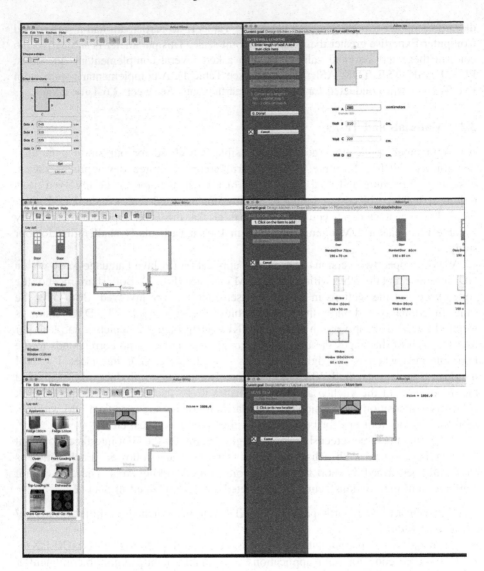

Fig. 2. Screenshots of the tested interfaces: (a) On the left, the DM interface; (b) On the right, the development of the same task using the GDI interface. The first pair of screenshots is related to the process of entering the dimensions of the kitchen walls. In the second pair the user is selecting and adding a window. In the third pair, the user is moving furniture around.

Imagine yourself arriving at a kitchen furniture shop. All employees are busy. However, a computer is available for you to specify your preferences for your kitchen: shape, dimensions, the furniture you want to buy and where you would particularly like to place it, make further adjustments, etc. To save time, you decide to use this system.

Task 1: Specifying how your kitchen is

Suppose that you bring a sketch (as the figure below) with the shape of your kitchen, the dimensions of the walls, doors and windows, and the location of all of them:

- Door 190 (high) x 70 (width) cm
- Window 100 (high) x 110 (width) cm

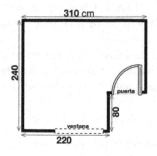

Task 2: Choosing furniture

Suppose the furniture you want to buy is listed below.

Choose and place the pieces as shown in the figure below:

1- Kitchen corner (80 cm wide)
2- Hob with Oven included
3- Showcase (80 cm, with 2 doors)
4- Metal extractor hood
5- Dishwasher

Write down the budget:
___(euros)

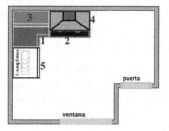

Task 3: Retouching and ordering

- Place the dishwasher next to the hob.
- A family is going to give you a metal extractor hood, therefore remove ours.
- Observe the kitchen in 3D.
- Look and see the detailed kitchen budget and note down the number of chosen items: ____ and the final budget: ____ (euros)
- If you think there is something important to be done (before commissioning the kitchen), do so.
- Commission the kitchen (to confirm with a kitchen seller)

3.3   Study Design

Our study used a Within-Subjects Design with one independent variable, namely the type of interaction. This independent variable has two levels: a GDI interaction and a classic DM interaction.

This Within-Subjects Design or Repeated Measures Design was necessary since we wanted each participant experienced both styles of interaction. It was important that both treatment groups exactly included the same participants. We wanted them to compare both interfaces expressing their preferences, and not to worry about personal characteristics that could bias our results.

On the other hand, in order to mitigate the potential transfer-of-learning effect caused by testing one type of interface prior to the other, a counterbalanced strategy was applied alternating the order among users. Half of the participants started with GDI, while the other half started with DM.

3.4   Measurements

3.4.1   Quantitative Measurements: Time on Task and Number of Errors

The first empirical data to be considered in this study is *time on task*. In this sense, we will denote as T_{t1}, T_{t2}, and T_{t3}, the time, in seconds, that participants spent on each of the three groups of tasks, respectively. These tasks were labelled in the task sheet (Sect. 3.2) as "Task 1: Specifying how your kitchen is," "Task 2: Choosing furniture" and "Task 3: Retouching and ordering," respectively. TT will be the total time, i.e. the sum of T_{t1}, T_{t2}, and T_{t3}.

The analysis of *types of errors* is an important and necessary complement to the timing analysis. If severe errors occurred (without the assistance of the moderator), then the time on task would be highly affected, or even worse, could prevent the user from completing the task.

Three degrees of errors have been considered, namely *slight*, *moderate*, and *severe*:

- The *severe or* blocking error took place when the user was stuck with something in the interface, preventing them from finishing the task. The moderator always assisted users with severe mistakes in order to have them finishing all the tasks and collect the corresponding user data.
- *Moderate* errors corresponded to non-blocking mistakes – not necessarily detected by the user – that could alter the outcome. In some cases, these issues could require warnings from the moderator.
- Finally, *slight* errors could not be categorised as actual errors because the user could resolve them without any moderator assistance, yet perhaps spending a bit more than the typically expected time.

Table 2 displays the concrete list of errors detected during the tests including, among other things, the type of interface and the task in which they occurred.

3.4.2   Subjective Measurements

We present two sets of subjective data in this paper, collected from two types of questionnaires. The first set is composed of two identical post-test questionnaires that participants filled immediately after finishing with each interface. These post-test questionnaires ask the participant seven questions (Q_i). All Q_i questions, except for Q_5, are scored with a numerical value (Table 7). The SUS (System Usability Scale) standard questionnaire was our first choice to use as the post-test questionnaire, but finally we decided to substitute its very generic questions for others more concrete and relevant for our study.

Table 2. Overview of the *Errors* (**S**: *Slight*/**M**: *Moderate*/**S**: *Severe*) specifying the interface (DM/GDI) and the tasks involved.

Type	Interface	#Task	Incidence description	Effect	Assistance
Slight (S)	DM	1	UNDO was confused with CLEAR when wanting to remove an item like a door (the user thought the system had failed because the item was not deleted)		
S	DM	1	The user accepted the default shape of the room; later he was aware of it and changed it		
S	DM	1	Window dimensions were confused with its distance to the walls	Put the proper window by chance	
S	DM	2 & 3	Tried to change the position of a door/window, while another operation (the placement of another door/window) was being in progress		
Moderate (M)	GDI	1	Not consciously placing a window, believing it did not matter	Consciously leaves an incomplete task (though not decisive for a correct final result)	
M	GDI	2	Instead of moving a piece of furniture (because this option was not found), deleted it and put another one at the targeted location	Inadequate procedure	
M	GDI	3	The user could not see the kitchen in 3D	Consciously leaves an incomplete task (though not decisive for a correct final result)	
M	DM	1	Entered the measurements in the default kitchen shape (without choose the correct shape), and did not realize below	Wrong final result, unconsciously	Warning
M	DM	1	The participant was unable to change the shape of the default kitchen, so he decided to start again	Inadequate procedure	

(continued)

Table 2. (*continued*)

Type	Interface	#Task	Incidence description	Effect	Assistance
M	DM	2 & 3	UNDO was confused with CLEAR (wanting to remove a cabinet), throughout the experiment	Persistent misinterpretation of an interaction (Inadequate procedure)	
M	DM	2 & 3	Learnt not to DRAG to move furniture –> Choose delete and put it back at the targeted location	Inadequate procedure	
M	DM	3	Chosen wrong furniture (high corner instead of low)	Wrong final result, unconsciously	Warning
M	DM	3	Oblivious to the only sub-task is not explicitly stated: "choose the common elements (granite, wood and handles)"	Wrong final result, unconsciously	Warning
Looking (L)	GDI	3	With everything done, the user would choose "design a plan" (which implies starting again) instead of the "order kitchen" option, so intend to start again	It would enlarge the experiment time without limit	Help
L	DM	2	Does not learn to SCROLL (necessary to choose the desired furniture)	Blocking	Help
L	DM	2	Does not learn to DRAG (needed for "placing" the furniture)	Blocking	Help
L	DM	2 & 3	Does not learn to DELETE furniture	Blocking	Help
L	DM	3	Does not learn to DRAG (necessary to relocate furniture)	Blocking	Help
L	DM	3	Does not learn to DELETE furniture –> Try to start again	It would enlarge the experiment time without limit	Help

These questions are:

- Q_1: "Do you consider that the application has helped you in knowing *what to do* in each moment?"
- Q_2: "Do you consider that the application has helped you in knowing *how* to do it? (what you needed to do)"
- Q_3: "What was *harder?* (1) knowing *what* to do, (2) knowing *how* to get it done, (0) both easy, or (3) both hard". The scores were chosen according to a range between the best and the worst-case scenarios.
- Q_4: "Would you like to have had a more complete help system inside the application interface?"
- Q_5: "Choose (multiple choice) types of periodicity of use you consider the application is appropriate for - Just once, - Very rarely (once a year), - Once a month, - Daily"
- Q_6: "Would you use a similar application for the design of your next kitchen?"
- Q_7: "To summarize, grade how easy the application is to use"

The second set of data comes from one unique and final comparative questionnaire that participants filled at the very end, once they had used both interfaces. This questionnaire makes them directly compare both interaction styles through the next eight questions (C_i):

- C_1: "With which interface is it easier to know what to do in each moment?"
- C_2: "With which interface is it easier to know how to do it?"
- C_3: "Which interface should include more help systems?"
- C_4: "Which interface is *easier to use* and requires *less training?*"
- C_5: "Which interface lets you work *quicker?*"
- C_6: "Which interface would you recommend to a *computer professional* for an *occasional use?*"
- C_7: "Which interface would you recommend to a *kitchen design professional* for a *daily use?*"
- C_8: "Which interface would you choose for furnishing your kitchen?"

3.5   Study Procedure

The estimated time per user (including questionnaires) ranged from 45 to 75 min. The tests were performed individually in an interference-free environment, except for the presence of the moderator. A common laptop computer was used for all the tests. This facilitated their relocation and was less intimidating and more familiar to users than any other bigger equipment. Mouse and keyboard were the input devices. The whole process of interaction was recorded from both the computer screen and the device microphone for further analysis when necessary.

Prior to the main study, a pilot experiment was carried out. It involved a group of 4 participants. This experiment allowed us to fine-tune the test procedure, the time span, and the descriptions of each task and questionnaire.

The procedure for the study followed the next steps:

1. All participants signed an informed consent and were briefed about the fact that the tests were taken voluntarily, being free to leave at any time without any justification.
2. The users read the *moderator script* to ensure that each participant received the same information about the type of test, the purpose of the study, and the testing process. This document also clarified that these tests were not intended to make any personal or psychological assessment, but were exclusively conducted for the evaluation of the involved computer interfaces. Then, the moderator answered any participant questions or concerns, if any.
3. The participants filled out a preliminary *background questionnaire* in order to collect user characteristics, such as age, gender, computer skills, previous software knowledge, task domain knowledge, etc. This helped to check whether the participants met the screening criteria (described in Sect. 3.1)
4. The users received a single-sheet document briefly describing the three groups of tasks to perform (detailed in Sect. 3.2).
5. As mentioned above, in order to implement a *counterbalanced* strategy, each participant was asked to use both versions of the application (alternating the order after each user). The so-called *Thinking Aloud* technique was also applied, but in a relaxed way. The participants were not forced to explain what they were doing any time, but they were free to express themselves. The moderator tried either not to interfere at all, or to intervene only in some non-blocking situations and always in the few critical or blocking situations that took place. Specific, the moderator couldn't answer any questions, and the users were allowed to express what they were thinking. The moderator tried not to interfere except with: (a) "severe errors", (b) some "moderate errors", and (c) to redirect a test. The concrete errors related to (a) and (b) and the type of assistance provided for each of them are shown in Table 2. In the last case, (c), the moderator intervened diverting a test if the user was lasting too long on it, or if they were overwhelmed not knowing how to do something. In some of these cases, we insisted we were evaluating the interface, not themselves.
   Every error was systematically noted down and categorised as part of the data collection. For every user and for each type of interface, the time the participant spent on achieving each task was written down as well. The whole process of interaction was recorded with a computer screen and voice recording software for further re-examination when necessary. In this sense, all the measurements were checked (and corrected, in necessary case) according to a thoroughly analysis of the screen recordings.
6. At the end of the use of each interface, but before moving on to the other, the participants filled out the corresponding *post-test questionnaire* (detailed in Sect. 3.4.2) on subjective and specific usability points about the interaction they have just experienced. This questionnaire covered important aspects for the final evaluation.
7. Finally, the participants filled out the *comparative questionnaire* (detailed in Sect. 3.4.2) for comparison of both styles of interaction, requiring them to directly express their preferences.

3.6   Results

On the one hand, we have repeated measures designs with two conditions in our experiments because the same participant uses both types of interfaces. On the other hand, the data are not normally distributed, and then do not meet the requirements for parametric tests. Thus, to verify the significance of the results, the most appropriate statistical method is a non-parametric Wilcoxon paired-sample test, also known as Wilcoxon signed-rank test [49].

We next present the results in the following order: first, in Sect. 3.6.1, the quantitative performance measurements through the time on tasks and the number of errors; second, in Sect. 3.6.2, the subjective data about each interface; and, third, in Sect. 3.6.3, the personal preferences. Finally, in Sect. 3.6.4, we elaborate on the Eye Tracker experiment.

A comprehensive document including all the tables can be downloaded from http:// bit.ly/2my1rYg.

3.6.1   Quantitative Empirical Measurements: Time on Task and Number of Errors

Tables 3 and 4 display the main statistics regarding *time on task* (T_{t1}, T_{t2}, T_{t3}, and T_T) and *number of errors* (slight, moderate, and severe), respectively.

Table 3. Statistics regarding *Time on task.*

Time on task (seconds)								
	TASK 1: "Designing the kitchen" T_{t1}		TASK 2: "Furnishing the kitchen" T_{t2}		TASK 3: "Retouching and ordering" T_{t3}		TOTAL T_T	
	DM	GDI	DM	GDI	DM	GDI	DM	GDI
Min	122	120	103	136	120	105	510	429
1st Qu.	181	150	175	206	283	147	754	525
Median	**305**	**193**	**238**	**251**	**393**	**203**	**880**	**678**
3rd Qu.	410	335	524	311	516	253	1374	836
Max	1023	512	1108	560	1075	491	2591	1431
Mean	**360**	**242**	**363**	**276**	**436**	**214**	**1160**	**732**
σ	236	124	276	110	219	99	605	288

The corresponding Wilcoxon tests (Table 5) for T_{t1}, T_{t3} and especially for T_T, revealed significant differences ($p < 0.01$) in favor of GDI, namely lower time intervals using GDI than using DM. Only the test for T_{t2}, a task consisting of repetitive operations, showed no significant difference between the two ways of interaction. Therefore, we may partially accept H1.

Table 4. Statistics regarding *number of Errors*.

Number of errors								
	Slight		Moderate		Severe		Total	
	DM	GDI	DM	GDI	DM	GDI	DM	GDI
Min	0	0	0	0	0	0	0	0
1st Qu.	0	0	1	0	0	0	1	0
Median	**0**	**0**	**2**	**0**	**0**	**0**	**3**	**0**
3rd Qu.	1	0	2	0	1	0	3	0.2
Max	2	1	3	1	3	1	7	1
Mean	**0.55**	**0.05**	**1.55**	**0.15**	**0.6**	**0.05**	**2.7**	**0.25**
σ	0.69	0.22	0.94	0.37	0.99	0.22	1.78	0.44

Concerning errors, the results of the *Wilcoxon* tests (Table 5) for the number of slight, moderate and severe errors produce significant differences ($p < 0.02$) in favor of GDI: DM presents a significant increase in the number of errors when compared with GDI. Therefore, we can accept H2.

Table 5. Results of the Wilcoxon tests on *Time on tasks* and *number of Errors*.

Time on task	p-value	−W	Type of test	#Errors	p-value	W	Type of test
T_{t1}	0.00250	180.5	one-tailed	E_{slight}	0.00750	50.5	one-tailed
T_{t2}	0.29430	134.0	two-tailed	$E_{moderate}$	0.00019	136.0	one-tailed
T_{t3}	0.00007	207.5	one-tailed	E_{severe}	0.01800	33.0	one-tailed
T_T	**0.00001**	204.0	one-tailed	E_{Total}	**0.00009**	171.0	one-tailed

Table 6 highlights how evident these results are by pointing out some relevant percentages: first, in accordance with T_T, 95% of users finished earlier using GDI than using the DM interface; second, 91% of the errors occurred under DM interaction versus only 9% under GDI.

Table 6. Some relevant results related to *Time on tasks* and *number of Errors*.

Interaction style	% earlier finishing	% Errors		
		Slight	Moderate	Severe
DM	5	92	91	92
GDI	95	8	9	8

3.6.2 Subjective Results from Post-tests Questionnaires

In Sect. 3.4.2 we remarked that the subjective post-test questionnaire used in this experiment included seven questions (Qi) for the participants. They answered them as soon as they finished the tasks with each type of interface.

Table 7 shows some statistics summarizing the scores of each Q_i, except for Q_5 (not answered with a numerical value). According to the corresponding Wilcoxon paired-sample tests, the result for each Q_i, except for Q_5, exhibits significant differences (p < 0.001) in the scores in favor of GDI. Therefore, we can accept H3.

Regarding Q_5, 80% of the participants considered that the DM interface is less appropriate for one-time or occasional use. Unexpectedly, 100% of the participants, including the two professionals at the task domain, considered GDI appropriate not only for occasional use but also for frequent use. Consequently, as far as these opinions are concerned, they did not find the use of guiding obtrusive.

Table 7. Statistics regarding the *post-test questionnaire* answers Q_i.

Q_i	Description	Scale	Mean		σ		Median		1st Qu.		3st Qu.	
			DM	GDI	DM	GDI	DM	GDI	DM	GDI	DM	GDI
Q_1	"Do you consider that the application has helped you in knowing what to do in each step?"	[1–7]	**3.25**	**6.30**	1.37	0.80	**3**	**6**	2	6	4.25	7
Q_2	"Do you consider that the application has helped you in knowing how to do it? (what you needed to do)"	[1–7]	**3.15**	**6.15**	1.26	0.58	**2**	**6**	3	6	4	6.25
Q_3	"What was *harder?* [1] knowing *what* to do, [2] knowing *how* to get it done, [0] both easy, or [3] both hard" The scores were chosen according to a range between the best and the worst-case scenarios"	[0–3]	**2.00**	**0**	0.51	0	**2**	**0**	2	0	2	0
Q_4	"Would you like to have had a more complete *help* system inside the application interface?"	[1–7]	**3.25**	**1.45**	1.20	0.94	**2**	**1**	3.5	1.45	4	2
Q_5	"Choose (multiple choice) types of *periodicity* of use you consider the application is appropriate for [A] Just once, - [B] Very rarely (once a year), - [C] Once a month, - [D] Daily"	Multiple choice	C +D	A +B +C +D								
Q_6	"Would you *use* a similar application for the design of your next kitchen?"	[1–5]	**3.20**	**4.65**	1.96	0.58	**2**	**4**	3	5	4	5
Q_7	"Do you consider that the application has helped you in knowing what to do in each step?"	[1–7]	**3.90**	**6.20**	1.25	0.61	**3**	**6**	4	6	5	7

3.6.3   Results from the Comparative Questionnaire: the User Preference

Regarding the final questionnaire composed of eight Ci comparative questions, Table 8 shows the percentage of participants preferring one way of interaction over the other. 100% of participants were clearly in favor of GDI. This might not be surprising among unskilled users, but it is remarkable in the case of kitchen designers, who are used to more completed and sophisticated DM interfaces.

We next quote some samples of the opinions expressed by the participants:

- "... [GDI interface] liked me a lot for its reliance explaining it all... the other system [DM] leaves you sort of lost",
- "It doesn't matter you don't know about it, the system [GDI] tells you all along what's next",
- "I like it more the other [GDI], it's much easier; this one [DM] doesn't tell you what you have to do, you have to know it, the other guides you"

Table 8. Results of the *Comparative Questionnaire* answers. Percentage (%) of participants preferring one interaction style to the other one.

C_i	Description	DM	GDI
C_1	"With which interface is it easier to know *what* to do in each moment?"	0	100
C_2	"With which interface is it easier to know *how* to do it? (what you needed to do) in each moment?"	0	100
C_3	"Which interface should include *more help* systems?"	100	0
C_4	"Which interface is *easier to use* and requires *less training*?"	0	100
C_5	"Which interface lets you work *quicker*?"	5	95
C_6	"Which interface would you recommend for a *computer professional occasional use*?"	10	90
C_7	"Which interface would you recommend for a *kitchen design professional daily use*?"	25	75
C_8	"Which interface would you *choose* for furnishing your kitchen?"	0	100

3.6.4   Results from a Short Eye Tracker Analysis

Aside from the main study, we conducted a quick and simple eye tracking experiment only for two participants randomly chosen. We did not try to draw important conclusions here but simply to know the most frequent screen regions the users were looking at with each type of interface. The algorithm k-means was executed using the statistical package R, searching for hot regions manifested through point clustering. The optimum value of k for the k-means was obtained using the elbow method. This algorithm helps to automatically find, through iterative evaluation, the optimum number of clusters for a cloud of points (see, for example, [16]). This analysis showed many more points and a larger number of clusters for the DM than for the GDI type of interface. The larger number of points logically corresponds with longer time periods spent whereas the double number of clusters (12 versus 6) is associated with higher complexity. This simply reinforced our study, but as no relevant conclusions could be drawn, it was not extended to more users. The experiment results have not been included in the final numerical analysis.

4 Discussion and Conclusions

The recent shift in technology has brought about many new kinds of users who use systems occasionally in more scenarios. These are mostly users who do not want or cannot afford a learning curve. There have been many attempts to help them while they are interacting with the system. Agents, floating help windows, tooltips, direct video demonstrations, etc., have shown us the necessity of guiding the user. These help systems are ways to support the DM appealing style, but inevitably add an extra layer of supporting material over the basic direct manipulation.

We propose GDI as the basis for a completely different approach: do not expect the user to understand and use a metaphor but guide them throughout the whole process. The help system is part of the interaction; it is integrated in the interface. The user will be closely guided on the "what to do" and the "how to do," one step at a time, always according to their current goal. Consequently, these users do not have much freedom of action. They do not need to be familiar with graphical widgets or think what the next command should be. No previous knowledge is required, shortening significantly the learning curve, if any.

To support the previous assertions the authors have developed a real interface for each type of interaction. Then they have made occasional users choose which one they consider the best.

It was necessary to decide what kind of application could be appropriate for the study. The premises were: first, being an application suitable for an occasional use. Second, being an application for a widespread domain, valid for all ages, genders, and domain knowledge. And third, being an application that normally uses direct manipulation with different kinds of tasks. As a previous step, we verified that there are no interfaces other than classic DM interfaces available for kitchen design. This is a task mostly performed on an occasional basis. The design of a kitchen is a fairly open and well-known task that requires a lot of interactive objects for the user to manipulate.

When comparing both types of interfaces, three hypotheses, H1, H2, and H3, were established. The second hypothesis refers to the number of errors. It seemed natural to expect that guiding the users would prevent them from making mistakes, needing fewer moderator assistances. The obtained results have totally proven this hypothesis: for occasional use, users who are not computer experts make fewer errors using GDI than using DM.

Our first hypothesis refers to timing: non-expert occasional users proceed quicker with GDI than with standard DM. H1 may seem counterintuitive: following a sequence of steps seems to be slower than directly manipulate elements. However, the analysis of the collected data shows that GDI is more time-efficient than DM. The only task for which there was no significant difference was the repetitive Task 2.

The last hypothesis H3 has been first indirectly demonstrated from the answers of users in the *post-test questionnaires*, and then directly demonstrated from the final *comparative questionnaires*. These answers highlighted the fact that all the participants had a strong preference for GDI. For example, according to C_4, 100% of them consider that GDI is easier to use and requires less training than DM. The answers to the questions Q_1 to Q_4 and C_1 to C_3 showed the users felt guided on the "what to do" and the "how to do," which is one of the main goals of a GDI interface.

Regarding Q_5, being a question about the prospect of using both types of interfaces in the future, we should not take it but as an indication of satisfaction and never should it be taken as an accurate prediction. Still, it was unexpected to find that all participants, professionals included, considered GDI appropriate not only for occasional but for frequent use. Moreover, 80% of the participants considered that the DM interface is appropriate neither for one-time nor occasional use.

Domain professional users provided additional unexpected results: first, they managed to do the job sooner and with fewer errors with GDI; second, they showed a preference for that style. This preference could arise from the lower quality of our DM application compared to the commercial ones. But this must have been the case for both of our interfaces, not only for the DM one. In any case, the professional users did say that our DM interface had a close resemblance to commercial ones. This feedback from professionals referred only to the way they had worked with GDI. They did not consider necessary to allude to the quality of our DM version.

One of the limitations of GDI is its unsuitability for creative users or applications with many concurrent functionalities. GDI is not appropriate for users who interact creatively with applications, in such a way that the own interaction notably inspires and influences the final result. For example, a graphics editor could not be suitable for its use with a guided interface. Other examples could be spreadsheet, word processor or powerful video editing applications.

On the other hand, the specificity of the goals in less creative tasks is of utmost importance when it comes to guiding the interaction. Booking a room in a hotel, choosing a seat for our theatre performance, or applying specific transformations to a batch of files, are some examples where GDI is definitely appropriate.

We do not try here to diminish the huge importance DM interfaces have been having for decades and will have in the future. What we show here is only that an integrated guiding system as GDI is generally a better option for users who do not want or cannot afford a learning curve, offering an alternative for designers and developers of interactive systems that have occasional users as their main target users.

References

1. Americans with Disabilities. Act of 1990 incorporating the changes made by the ADA Amendments Act of 2008. http://www.ada.gov/pubs/adastatute08.pdf. Accessed 01 Aug 2015
2. Annett, J., Duncan, K.D.: Task analysis and training design. Occup. Psychol. **41**, 211–221 (1967)
3. Barnum, C.M.: Usability Testing Essentials: Ready, Set...Test!. Morgan Kaufmann Publishers, Burlington (2011)
4. Bollaert, J.: Crafting a wizard. In: IBM Developer Works. http://www.ibm.com/developerworks/library/us-wizard. Accessed 30 May 2015
5. Buxton, B.: Multi-touch systems that I have known and loved. Microsoft Res. **56**, 1–11 (2007)

6. Card, S., Moran, T., Newell, A.: Computer text-editing: an information processing analysis for a routine cognitive skill. Cogn. Psychol. **12**, 32–74 (1980)
7. Card, S., Moran, T., Newell, A.: The Psychology of Human-Computer Interaction. Erlbaum, Hillsdale (1983)
8. Carroll, J.M., Thomas, J.C.: Metaphor and the cognitive representation of computing systems. IEEE Trans. Syst. Man Cybern. **12**, 107–116 (1982)
9. Carrillo, A.L., Falgueras, J., Guevara, A.: A notation for goal driven interfaces specification. In: Navarro-Prieto, R., Vidal, J. (eds.) HCI Related Papers of Interacción, 337–344. Springer, Dordrecht (2006). https://doi.org/10.1007/1-4020-4205-1_28
10. Carrillo, A.L., Falgueras, J.: Goal driven interaction vs. direct manipulation, an empirical comparison. In: Proceedings of the XVI International Conference on Human Computer Interaction (Interacción 2015). ACM, New York, Article 24, 4 p. (2015)
11. Charland, A., Leroux, B.: Mobile application development: web vs native. Commun. ACM **54**(5), 49–53 (2011)
12. Clarkson, J., Coleman, R. (eds.): Special Issue: Inclusive design. Appl. Ergon., part B, January **46**, 233–324 (2015)
13. Coe, M.: Human Factors for Technical Communicators. Wiley, New York (1996)
14. Dix, A., Finlay, J., Abowd, G., Beale, R.: Human-Computer Interaction, 3rd edn. (Chapter 3). Pearson Education. Prentice Hall (2004)
15. Gong, J., Tarasewich, P.: Guidelines for handheld mobile device interface design. In: Proceedings of DSI 2004 Annual Meeting, pp. 3751–3756 (2004)
16. Gorakala, S.K., Usuelli, M.: Building a Recommendation System with R, pp. 15–18. Packt Publishing Ldt., Birmingham (2015)
17. Hollnagel, E., Woods, D.: Joint Cognitive Systems: Foundations of Cognitive Systems Engineering. CRC Press, Boca Raton (2005)
18. Hutchins, E.L., Hollan, J.D., Norman, D.A.: Direct manipulation interfaces. In: Norman, D. A., Draper, S.W. (eds.) User-Centered System Design, pp. 87–124. Erlbaum, Hillsdale (1986)
19. IKEA. http://kitchenplanner.ikea.com/US/UI/Pages/VPUI.htm. Accessed 06 Feb 2015
20. John, B.E., Kieras, D.E.: The GOMS family of analysis techniques: Tools for design and evaluation. Carnegie Mellon University School of Computer Science Technical Report No. CMU-CS-94-181. Also appears as the Human-Computer Interaction Institute Technical report No. CMU-HCII-94-106 (1994)
21. John, B.E., Kieras, D.E.: The GOMS family of user interface analysis techniques: Comparison and contrast. ACM Trans. Comput.-Hum. Interact. **3**(4), 320–351 (1996)
22. John B.E., Kieras, D.E.: Using GOMS for user interface design and analysis: which technique? ACM Trans. Comput.-Hum. Interact. **3**(4), 287–319 (1996b)
23. Johnson, P.: Task knowledge structures. In: Diaper, D. (ed.) Task Analysis in Human Computer Interaction. Ellis Horwood (1989)
24. Kieras, D.: A guide to GOMS model usability. Evaluation Using NGOMSL. In: Helander, M., Landauer, T., (eds.) The Handbook of Human-Computer Interaction, 2nd edn., pp 733–766. North-Holland, Amsterdam (1997)
25. Kieras, D.: Task analysis and the design of functionality. In: Tucher, A. (ed.) The computer Science and Engineering Handbook, pp. 1401–1423. CRC Inc., Boca Raton (1997)
26. Loranger, H.: Checklist for Planning Usability Studies. NN/g Nielsen Norman Group (2016). www.nngroup.com/articles/usability-test-checklist
27. Microsoft. Wizards. https://msdn.microsoft.com/en-us/library/windows/desktop/dn742503 (v=vs.85).aspx. Accessed 28 May 2015
28. Moran, T.P.: An applied psychology of the user. Comput. Surv. **13**, 1–11 (1981)

29. Mueller, J.P.: Accessibility for Everybody: Understanding the Section 508 Accessibility Requirements. Apress (2003)
30. Myers, B., Hudson, S.E., Pausch, R.: Past, present, and future of user interface software tools. ACM Trans. Comput.-Hum. Interact. (TOCHI) **7**(1), 3–28 (2000)
31. Newell, A., Simon, H.: Human Problem Solving. Prentice-Hall, Upper Saddle River (1972)
32. Nielsen, J.: Usability Engineering. United States of America. Academic Press, San Diego (1993)
33. Nielsen, J., Budiu, R.: Mobile Usability. New Riders, Indianapolis (2012)
34. Nielsen, J.: Quantitative Studies: How Many Users to Test? NN/g Nielsen Norman Group. www.nngroup.com/articles/quantitative-studies-how-many-users/. Accessed 17 Nov 2015
35. Norman, D.A.: The Design of Everyday Things. Basic Books Inc., New York (2002)
36. Norman, D.A.: Natural user interfaces are not natural interactions. Interactions **17**(3), 6–10 (2010)
37. Paternò, F.: ConcurTaskTrees: an engineered notation for task models. In: Diaper, D., Stanton, N. (eds.) The Handbook of Task Analysis for Human-Computer Interaction, Chapter 24, pp. 483–503. Lawrence Erlbaum Associates, Mahwah (2003)
38. Payne, S.J., Green, T.R.G.: Task action grammar: recent developments. In: Diaper, D. (ed.) Approaches to Task Analysis. Cambridge University Press (1990)
39. Savidis, A., Stephanidis, C.: Unified user interface design: designing universally accessible interactions. Interact. Comput. **16**(2), 243–270 (2004)
40. Selker, T.: Touching the future. Commun. ACM **51**(12), 14–16 (2008)
41. Sharples, M.: The design of personal mobile technologies for lifelong learning. Comput. Educ. **34**(3), 177–193 (2000)
42. Shneiderman, B.: Direct manipulation: a step beyond programming languages. IEEE Comput. **16**(8), 57–69 (1983)
43. Shneiderman, B., Plaisant, C., Cohen, M., Jacobs, S., Elmqvist, N., Diakopoulos, N.: Designing the User Interface: Strategies for Effective Human-Computer Interaction, 6th edn. Pearson, London (2016)
44. Sova, D.H., Nielsen, J.: How to Recruit Participants for Usability Studies. NN/g Nielsen Norman Group. www.nngroup.com/reports/how-to-recruit-participants-usability-studies. Accessed 28 Oct 2017
45. Tidwell, J.: Designing Interfaces: Patterns for Effective Interaction Design. O'Reilly Media Inc., Sebastopol (2011)
46. Turoff, M.: The design and evaluation of interactive systems. Section 1.4.3: "User Roles and Types". http://web.njit.edu/∼turoff/coursenotes/IS732/book/tablecon.htm. Accessed 23 May 2014
47. US Rehabilitation Act Amendments Section 508 (1998). http://www.section508.gov/. Accessed 01 Oct 2015
48. Wickham, D.P., Pupons, D., Mayhew, D.L., Stoll, T., Toley III, K.J., Rouiller, S.: Designing Effective Wizards: A Multidisciplinary Approach. Prentice Hall, Upper Saddle River (2002)
49. Wilcoxon, F.: Individual comparisons by ranking methods. Biometrics **1**, 80–83 (1945)

User Experience

A Novel Method to Build and Validate
an Affective State Prediction Model
from Touch-Typing

Subrata Tikadar[(⊠)] and Samit Bhattacharya

Indian Institute of Technology Guwahati, Guwahati, India
subratatikadar@gmail.com, samit3k@gmail.com

Abstract. Affective systems are supposed to improve user satisfaction and hence usability by identifying and complementing the affective state of a user at the time of interaction. The first and most important challenge for building such systems is to identify the affective state in a systematic way. This is generally done based on computational models. Building such models requires affective data. In spite of the extensive growth in this research area, there are a number of challenges in affect induction method for collecting the affective data as well as for building models for real-time prediction of affective states. In this article, we have reported a novel method for inducing particular affective states to unobtrusively collect the affective data as well as a minimalist model to predict the affective states of a user from her/his typing pattern on a touchscreen of a smartphone. The prediction accuracy for our model was 86.60%. The method for inducing the specific affective states and the model to predict these states are validated through empirical studies comprising EEG signals of twenty two participants.

Keywords: Affective state · Emotion induction method · Mobile-HCI · Smartphone interaction · Touchscreen keyboard · Typing pattern · Unobtrusive approach · Valence and arousal

1 Introduction

A system that is able to identify and/or complement the affective states of its users at the time of interaction can be termed as affective system [29]. The first and the most challenging step to build such systems is to identify the affective states in real-time. The challenges are more if the target systems are small and mobile, compared to that of large static systems. This is because small mobile systems may not always allow additional expensive hardware and/or probes for supporting services. Otherwise, the mobility and affordability of the devices (probably the two of the most important reasons for them being popular) might be affected. Extensive research has been going on since last decade for addressing the challenges [30]. Nevertheless, issues still persist. The issues include erroneous and fake data in the existing methods of inducing affect and emotion together with the way of collecting the affective data, and complex model to identify the states in real-time. Additionally, in most of the cases neither the induction methods nor the model

© IFIP International Federation for Information Processing 2019
Published by Springer Nature Switzerland AG 2019
D. Lamas et al. (Eds.): INTERACT 2019, LNCS 11749, pp. 99–119, 2019.
https://doi.org/10.1007/978-3-030-29390-1_6

to identify the states are systematically validated. Researchers depend on users' feedback for this purposes, which is not always reliable [31].

Our contribution in this research area is twofold. The first contribution is proposing a novel method for inducing specific affective states to unobtrusively collect the affective data. We have proposed a gaming approach for this. We have developed an android game having multiple stimulants for affect and emotion. The game is able to induce specific affective states, as well as to collect and label the affective data. The data collection and labeling are done without making the users aware of it. This helps to reduce the inaccuracy and imitation in affective data. Our second contribution is proposing a minimalist model to identify the affective states of the users from their typing pattern on touchscreen keyboard of smartphones. Taking the lowest number of input features from users' typing pattern, the model is able to classify a user into any of the four states with high accuracy: *positive-high, positive-low, negative-high, and negative-low*. The states have been chosen based on the circumplex model of emotion [32, 34], where positive and negative specify the level of valence whereas high and low indicate the level of arousal.

We have ascertained the efficiency of our proposed method and model through controlled empirical studies. We have used EEG (electroencephalogram) data of twenty two participants for these purposes. Additionally, we have also tested whether our model works for other applications (social network and instant messaging apps) where typing data is available, not restricted to the special purpose game application developed by us.

The rest of the article is organized as follows. In Sect. 2, we have presented the literature review for identifying related works of existing methods for inducing affects and emotions, as well as of existing models to identify users' affective states from users' typing pattern. We have also highlighted the importance and novelty of our proposed method and model in this section. Section 3 presents the proposed approach where the method for inducing specific affective states, and the model for identifying the states are described in detail. In Sect. 4, we discussed about the variation of the model, and strength and limitations of our approach with future scope. Section 5 concludes the article.

2   Literature Review

2.1   Literature Review for Existing Works to Induce Affects and Emotions

Affective data are required to build and train models for automatic identification of the affective states in real-time. Collection of the affective data from 'natural source' is cumbersome and most of the time is infeasible [8, 9]. Affective data from natural source means the corresponding affective states are stimulated naturally, not induced in laboratory setting. For example, someone has got a mail with an extremely bad/good news and s/he is typing for replying the mail. In this case, the typing data can be considered as affective data from natural source. Moreover, the way of labeling these naturalistic data may involve inaccuracy. The data are labeled by either observation or feedback based method. Inaccuracy in observation based methods occurs due to the fact that feeling and perceiving the affective states are not the same [19]. At the same time, the user-feedback method for labeling the data may sometimes be unreliable because human beings may not always be able to report their own exact affective state of a particular moment [19]. Furthermore, limited types of affective data (e.g., speech, image) can be collected from natural sources, which are copyrighted most of the time [10]. As a result, particular affects and emotions are induced in laboratory setting to collect and label the data [14, 28, 31]. It can be noted that although the terms "affect", "emotion", "mood", and "personality traits" are sometimes used interchangeably by the researchers, they are not the same. They are distinguished based on the duration, intensity, cause, and other aspects [2]. In this work, we have worked with the Circumplex model [32, 34] of emotional states. The states in this model can generally be termed as 'affective states'.

Existing methods for inducing affective states include affective music and film, hypnosis, making unnecessary delay, stressful interview, sudden attack, surprise exam, threat of painful electric shock, and unsolvable puzzle and game [14, 28, 31, 39].

The methods are not free from issues like involvement of fake and inaccurate data. In case of inducing emotion through affective film and music, the participants may be aware of the fact that they are being induced. As a result, they may not behave naturally [31]. There is a chance of imitation in emotion and thereby resulting in fake data collection. If a decision is taken based on the fake affective state, the decision may be wrong. Moreover, when the participants are aware of the fact that they are being induced, some additional affects and emotions (anxiety, fear, hesitation, hostility, and nervousness) are induced with the intended specific affect and emotion to be induced [31]. The additional affects and emotion may be incorporated in the attack and threat methods as well. Furthermore, most of the existing methods for inducing emotion together with the collection of affective data consider participants' feedback for labeling the data. For the data labeling, the participants are first induced with some specific affective states. After that, they are given some tasks to be completed, through which the affective data can be collected. The participants are asked to report their states for labeling the collected data afterwards (sometimes beforehand the task-execution), as it is not possible for them to execute the tasks and give feedback at exactly the same time. The affective states at the time of induction, task execution, and taking feedback may not be the same. This is because of the fact that affects and emotions stays for very short duration (e.g., emotion stays in facial expression up to five seconds) [2, 28]. As a result, data may be wrongly labeled, and consequently inaccuracy in the affective data occurs.

We therefore propose a novel method, following a gaming approach, to induce specific affective states. Our method neither directly/indirectly informs the participants that they are getting induced nor considers participants' feedback for collecting and labeling the data. It is expected that the proposed method addresses the challenges in existing methods of inducing affects and emotion for collecting the affective data.

2.2   Literature Review for Existing Works to Identify Affects and Emotions

Literature contains many works to identify humans' affective states. The states can be identified from facial expression [12, 15, 22], gestures and posture [3, 4, 20], speech and voice [26, 33], physiological signals (like EBR, EEG, EMG, GSR, HR) [17, 18, 36] and multimodal inputs [18, 22] (where more than one input modalities are considered). Although the works are substantial, these are not free from issues. For instance, identifying affective states from facial expression involves expensive computation like computer vision and image processing, fixed camera position to capture the facial image, and proper lighting conditions. These constraints may not be satisfied everywhere, particularly in the context of mobile environment. Moreover, facial expression may not always be real (e.g., sometimes we smile for the sake of formalities, although we are not actually happy at that moment). The issues may also exist in case of identifying affective states from humans' gestures and postures. There may be some complications in the method of identifying the affective states form speech and voice as well. One of the major complications is surrounding noise, particularly in the mobile environment. Moreover, the accuracy of identifying affects and emotions depends on the corpus used for training the models developed in this method. Furthermore, the languages and geographical locations are two additional obstacles for the lack of accuracy in real-time emotion identification through this method. This is because of the fact that a particular word may be pronounced differently based on the ethnicities of the speakers. Although the physiological signals and multimodal based methods identify users' affective states with high accuracy, there are some difficulties to apply these for real-time identification of the states. These methods requires involvement of additional and highly expensive sensors and/or probes to sense the signals, which is not acceptable and affordable in mobile environment, particularly in the context of smartphones. Moreover, no user is expected to be comfortable and willing to wear these additional sensors and probes at the time of interaction with the mobile device. Researchers are therefore looking for alternative input for identifying affect and emotion so that the concept of affective computing can be practically applied. The use of interaction behavior can be a good alternative.

Interaction behavior may include haptic behavior, device handling patterns, touch patterns, and typing patterns. The advantages of considering the behavioral inputs include inexpensive computation and hardware setting. However, choosing the appropriate behavioral input is difficult. The inputs for identifying affect and emotion may vary based on the environments and applications. For instance, identifying emotion from mouse clicking pattern [43] may not be applicable for the context of smartphone interaction. Existing models for identifying emotion from users' typing pattern on physical keyboard [13, 21, 40] also may not be suitable in case of smartphone interaction as typing pattern on physical keyboard and smartphone's keyboard are not the same (we use almost all the fingers of our two hands while typing on physical keyboard whereas generally only two thumbs for typing on touchscreen keyboard of the smartphone). Literature contains few works where users' affect and emotion have been identified from touch patterns on touchscreen (e.g., [5, 35, 38]). Although these are suitable for smartphone interaction, we cannot always assume that all the interactions are performed through touches. Considering typing pattern on touchscreen of smartphone may be one of the useful inputs in this context. Although the typing on smartphone keyboard is performed through touch, the touch pattern while typing on the keyboard and the pattern while touching on any place of the screen for touch interactions may not be the same. For example, differences in frequency of touches may be observed in these two different scenario.

Lee et al. [23, 24] used virtual keystroke data to identify the affective state of the users. Although their approach is suitable in the context smartphone interaction, we identified few limitations in their work including data collection and feature selection. The participants were emotionally induced by "International Affective Picture System (IAPS)" before the actual data collection. The affective state may change within the period of emotion-induction and data collection because emotions remains for very short duration [2, 28]. Secondly, users were asked to indicate their affective states after finishing the typing by posting 'smilies'/self-assessment manikin (SAM). This alone can change the affective state of the users. The approach, hence, is not unobtrusive in true sense. Moreover, some of the input features used in their model ('special symbol frequency', 'erased text length', and 'backspace key press frequency') are unnecessary and/or inappropriate for the current context. We therefore propose a model with minimum number of appropriate features.

3 Proposed Approach

Taking users' typing pattern on touchscreen keyboard of a smartphone as input, our proposed model classifies the affective state of a user into any of the following four categories:

- Positive-High,
- Positive-Low,
- Negative-High, and
- Negative-Low.

Here, positive and negative specify the valence level whereas high and low indicate the level of arousal. We chose these affective states based on the Circumplex model of affective states [32, 34], where continuous states are discretized based on the level of arousal and valence. The reason behind choosing the Circumplex model of emotion is its vast application areas [11, 39]. Moreover, identifying affective states based on the Circumplex model is most suitable for some specific applications. For instance, identifying the affective states of a student in the classroom should be in the form of valence and arousal for its better utilization [42].

The novel game for inducing these specific affective states, data collection through the game, building the minimalist model with these data, and the study for validating the induction method as well as the model is described in detail in this section.

3.1   Method for Inducing the Specific Affective States

We designed a special purpose android typing game for inducing the specific affective states without the knowledge of the users, as well as for labelling and collecting data without any user feedback. The approach was expected to induce the states minimizing the imitation in emotion (as it was done without users' knowledge), and result in labeled data minimizing the inaccuracy (as the method was unobtrusive).

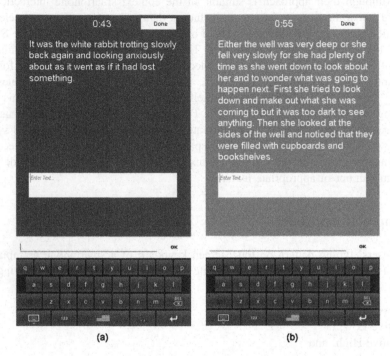

Fig. 1.   Snapshots of two modes of the game interface; (a) fascinating mode, and (b) dull mode

Game Description. The game had two modes: *fascinating* mode and *dull* mode. While playing the game, a player had to play two fascinating modes and two dull modes. In the fascinating modes s/he had to type a small paragraph (of 110–120 characters – possible to type for a normal person) whereas in the dull mode s/he had to type a long paragraph (of approximately 350–400 characters – might be impossible to type for a normal person) within the time limit of sixty seconds. Lengths of the paragraphs were decided based on the work of [21, 25], and [27]. Based on the correctness and speed, the score was displayed on the screen in the fascinating modes (players were informed that rewards will be given as per the score). For the correctness of typing, we used a string matching algorithm. The algorithm compares each of the character of the typed text with each of the character of the given paragraph. The typing was considered to be accurate when both the texts match exactly. Erased characters and backspace key were not considered for string matching. The score was displayed in the fascinating modes only. In the dull modes, the players were informed that they would be rewarded if and only if they could complete the typing task within the time limit. Two affective colors were kept as background colors in the two modes of the game to aid the induction method. Background color for the fascinating mode was kept blue whereas that of the dull mode was kept red [1, 37]. Figure 1 shows the snapshots of the two modes of the game: (a) when a user was playing fascinating mode, and (b) when a user was playing dull mode.

It was expected that the multiple stimulants of the fascinating mode (ease and possibility of typing a short paragraph, keenness of earning a maximum reward, and the blue color in background) were able to induce positive emotions to the players. The emotions here were assumed to be of positive valence. On the other hand, stimulants used in dull mode (asking for completing an impossible typing job, practically no reward, and the red color in background) were expected to induce negative emotions to the players. The emotions here were assumed to be of negative valence.

All along during the gameplay, background music were played as additional stimulants for the induction method. Music capable of inducing positive valence with high arousal (Tchaikovsky's "Mazurka from Swan Lake Ballet") was kept in one fascinating mode and music capable of inducing positive valence with low arousal (Gluck's "Orpheus and Eurydice") was kept in another fascinating mode. Similarly, music capable of negative valance with high arousal (Mussorgsky's "Night on Bald Mountain") was kept in one dull mode and music capable of negative valence with low arousal (Marcello's "Adagio from Oboe Concerto in D minor") was kept in another dull mode. In between the fascinating and dull mode, we kept a neutral music (Kraftwerk's "Pocket Calculator") to neutralize the induced emotion. We chose affective music based on [6, 39]. For example, Västfjäll [39] has mentioned that a music having major-mode, fast-tempo, medium-pitch, firm-rhythm, dissonance-harmony, and high-loudness has the capability to make one excited. They have also mentioned a list of music pieces responsible for positive, neutral, and negative states specifying high and low arousal.

The modes were placed randomly to avoid bias. In between the two modes score and reward details were shown to neutralize the affects. Music capable of inducing neutral affect were also kept for this. Transitions of the music in between different modes were done smoothly (the volume of the music was reduced) to avoid the feeling of jerk. The players were aware of neither the strategy for the induction mechanism nor the modes of the game.

Validating the Purpose of the Game. We assumed that our special purpose typing game was able to induce the four specific affective states (positive-high, positive low, negative-high, and negative-low) to the users while playing the game, as we kept such stimulants. However, it was required to validate whether the game was really able to induce these states. For this, we used EEG signal of the players. We captured the EEG signals by Emotiv EPOC+[1] (a 14-channel wireless EEG headset: AF3, F7, F3, FC5, T7, P7, O1, O2, P8, T8, FC6, F4, F8, and AF4; the device collects the signals with the sample rate of 2048 per second – filtered and downsampled to 128 SPS/ 256 SPS, user

---

[1] https://www.emotiv.com/epoc/.

configured; the response frequency (bandwidth) of the device is 0.16 to 43 Hz.). EEG signals were processed by EmotivPRO[2] software, which was able to analyze the raw EEG and derive six affective states ('stress', 'engagement', 'interest (valence)', 'excitement (arousal)', 'focus', and 'relaxation (meditation)') from the raw signals in real-time. However, for this particular study, we were interested in only the two states (valence and arousal) among the six affective states. Although an earlier study [7] verified the reliability of a previous model of the device for capturing EEG (EPOC), we conducted a pilot study to establish the ground truth for the affective states before validating our induction method through these.

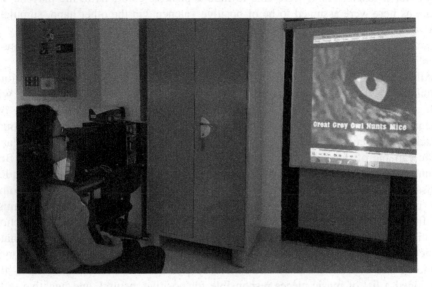

Fig. 2. Pilot Study to establish the ground truth of affective states

Pilot Study for Establishing the Ground Truth of Emotion. Ten students (five males and five females, mean age of 24.7 with SD = 3.37) took part in the study. To establish the ground truth for the identified affective states by the EmotivPRO, we asked each of the ten participants to wear the EPOC+ headset (Fig. 2) which was connected with the EmotivPRO software running on a laptop computer. After recording the baseline emotion, the participants were shown two videos having the elements of inducing arousal and valence emotion (one video to check two levels of arousal i.e., high and low arousal, and another to check two levels of valence i.e., positive and negative valence). The works including [39] and [6] helped us to select the videos having emotion inducing element. We downloaded the videos from YouTube. Following are the lists of audio-visual used for this experiment (Table 1).

---

[2] https://www.emotiv.com/emotivpro/.

Table 1. List of audio-visual used in the pilot study

Name of the audio-visual	Link (URL)	Used to examine
High Arousal Music Playlist	https://www.youtube.com/watch?v=WHUo4pZLAAA	Arousal levels
The Best Of Eagle Attacks 2018 - Most Amazing Moments Of Wild Animal Fights! Wild Discovery Animals	https://www.youtube.com/watch?v=RB4RCOe-ZEw	Arousal levels
World most Shocking Video that made the whole world cry!	https://www.youtube.com/watch?v=QJxwE7mdGns	Arousal levels
14 Strange Ways of Life the Ancient Egyptians Practiced	https://www.youtube.com/watch?v=GiMbVa6XzTw	Valence levels
What Will Happen to Humans Before 2050?	https://www.youtube.com/watch?v=Cip3LmqQ7Y0	Valence levels
25 True Facts That Will Shock You	https://www.youtube.com/watch?v=HChCEGR_0lg	Valence levels

We showed the videos partially (for a maximum two minutes) on a large projector screen with amplified sound. Short videos were shown because we have observed that participants were unable to report their affective states if these were asked few minutes later. This proves that the obtrusive approaches to collect emotional data may have incorrect information. The affective states (arousal and valence) were recorded by EmotivPRO while the participants were watching the videos. After the completion of each video, we told them about their affective states (valence and arousal i.e., interest and excitement) at different points of the video (after every ten seconds) and asked them to report on their agreement with the output by EMotivPRO. We replayed the videos for them to recall their affective state at the time of watching the particular instances of the videos. We compared the affective states reported by the participants and the affective state identified by EmotivPRO, and found the similarity of 92.08%. Thus, we considered the afffective state identified by the EmotivPRO as the ground truth of the users' affective state.

Validating the Induction Method. Considering the affective states identified by the EmotivPRO as ground truth, we conducted a validation study with ten different volunteers (five male and five female, mean age of 25.3 years with SD = 3.94). In the study, the participants were asked to wear the EPOC+ headset which was connected to the EmotivPRO software installed on a laptop computer. We then asked the participants to play the special purpose game we developed. We observed that the players' interest (valence) was higher in the fascinating mode and lower in dull mode. As the EmotivPRO does not show the valence in negative scale (it shows both the arousal and valence in a 100 point scale ranging from 0 to 100 with a scale division of 10), we considered the higher reading (51–100) of valence as positive valence and lower reading (0–50) of valence as negative valence. We observed that negative valence was shown while the players played the dull mode, and positive valence was shown at the time of playing fascinating mode. These indicate that the game is capable of inducing two required levels of valence. We also observed that the arousal was high in one fascinating

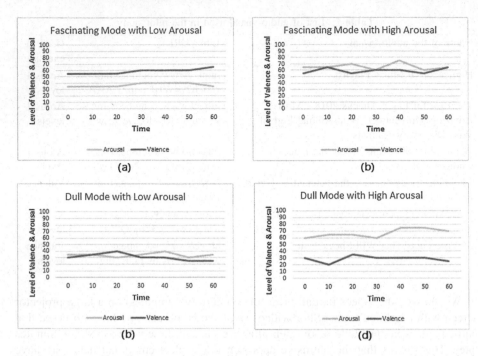

Fig. 3. Four specific affective states induced to a particular participant by our proposed method (identified from EEG signals by EmotivPRO)

mode and the same was low in another fascinating mode. As expected, similar observations for arousal were made in the dull modes as well (arousal was observed high in one dull mode, whereas the same was observed in another dull mode). This was because we kept such stimulants in the particular modes (the music capable of eliciting high arousal in one fascinating and dull mode, and the music capable of eliciting low arousal in another fascinating and dull mode). Figure 3 contains the level of arousal and valence of fascinating and dull mode of a particular participant (identified by EmotivPRO): Fig. 3(a) when the participant was playing one of the fascinating modes where music capable of eliciting low arousal was there; Fig. 3(b) when the participant was playing another fascinating mode of the game where music capable of eliciting high arousal was there; Fig. 3(c) when the participant was playing one of the dull modes where music capable of eliciting low arousal was there; and Fig. 3(d) when the player was playing another dull mode where music capable of eliciting high arousal was there. If we observe closely, we can see that fascinating mode of the game is able to induce positive valence whereas dull mode is able to induce negative valence. We have considered valence ≤ 50 (shown by EmotivPRO) as negative, as discussed earlier. Keeping the valance level fixed, it is possible to induce two different level of arousal by changing the additional stimulant (affective music). This means, through our game it is possible to induce four specific affective states to a participant: positive-high, positive-low, negative-high, and negative-low. Similar observations were made for other nine participants as well. The observations validate the fact that the gaming approach with multiple stimulants, proposed by us, is able to induce the four specific affective states.

3.2   Building the Minimalist Model

Data Collection Through the Game. The special purpose game application we developed is able to induce specific affective states. At the same time, it can store the typing data (all the key-press details) after labelling these as per the induced affective states. However, it was required to know what exact typing data should be collected for building a model for identifying affective states. Initially, we considered the following seven as input features for our proposed model as they seem to have some relations with affect and emotion [23, 24].

1. *Typing speed*: Number of characters typed per second.
2. *Backspace key press frequency*: Number of backspace key presses per second.
3. *Special symbol frequency*: Number of special symbols (for instance, emojis, smileys, astrological symbol) typed per second.
4. *Max text length*: Maximum number of characters typed without pressing the 'del' key for a second.
5. *Erased text length*: Number of characters erased in a second.
6. *Touch count*: Total number of key presses (including 'del' key) per second.
7. *Device shake frequency*: Number of times the device's position in space changed above an acceptable level of displacement (above a threshold value) per second.

However, 'Special symbol frequency' was discarded as it may not be available and/or not important in case of some applications. For instance, unlike chat application, it may not be required to exchange emotion with friends while taking class note. Moreover, if we take special symbol, for instance 'emojis', the approach will not remain unobtrusive as it seems to be one kind of user feedback (users themselves report their states through the emojis). One can hide her/his actual emotion while exchanging emotion using 'emojis'. There is a chance of collecting fake affective data, in this case. The 'Erased text length' has also been discarded because in case of android keyboard, multiple characters can be deleted with a single backspace key press.

We, therefore collected the typing data for the remaining five features: typing speed, backspace key press frequency, max text length, touch count, and device shake frequency. Among these five features, we required a threshold value for the 'device shake frequency'. Otherwise, it was difficult to determine how much 'displacement' of the device could be considered as a shake. The absolute shake value is obtained when a trigger[3] is detected. The trigger refers to automatic detection of the displacement of the device. The android version we worked on (Marshmallow 6.0.1), checks for a trigger every 0.02 s. The absolute shake value is calculated as the scalar displacement in terms of the x, y and z coordinates of the accelerometer sensor following the Eq. (1).

$$displacement = \sqrt{x^2 + y^2 + z^2} \tag{1}$$

For determining the shake threshold, we conducted an experiment with another set of ten participants (five male and five female, mean age of 25.1 years with SD = 3.14).

---

[3] https://developer.android.com/reference/android/hardware/TriggerEvent.html.

All the participants were asked to play the same game application twice per level. Once they were asked to type the target text, keeping the device as still as possible. A Second time, the users were allowed to handle the device as they usually do it while typing. Figure 4 represents the plots obtained corresponding to low and high shake.

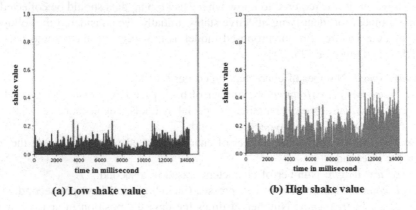

(a) Low shake value   (b) High shake value

Fig. 4. Low and high shake value

It clearly indicates that the shake values in the usual typing occasion are much higher than the same in the first occasion where the device was kept still as much as possible while typing. This indicates that the data can be naturally clustered into two separate groups. Therefore, we calculated the shake threshold as the mean of the two cluster centers. Cluster centers were decided by taking the means of the shake values in the individual clusters. The threshold value was found to be 0.04. We did not require any threshold value to record the data for the other four features.

We collected the data from thirty three participants for further analysis to build the minimalist model. Data was collected by using a smartphone (having 5.5 inches screen, 'Android Marshmallow' OS, 2.5 GHz quad-core processor, and 3 GB RAM) where the game we developed was installed.

Selection Strategy and Details of the Participants for Data Collection. We wrote a formal mail to all of the students in our institute for voluntarily participating in the data collection experiment. On arrival, we asked a set of questions to the students to know their current health condition as well as the history of their health for selecting them as participants. We did not collect data from the students who were in severe medical condition (e.g., serious headache, shortness of breath), who consumed any intoxicating substance in last three hours, or did not sleep well in last night for at least six hours [7]. Some of the volunteers could not participate due to their finger sizes (were relatively large compared to the size of the keys). This was because we wanted to avoid the 'fat finger' problem. We followed the same strategy to select the participants for every study mentioned in this paper. Once selected, each participant was asked to sign a 'participant consent form' which was signed by one of the authors (as experimenter) as well. We selected thirty three participants for the data collection. Among the thirty three participant seventeen were male and sixteen were female. The mean age of the participants was 24.19 with SD = 2.91. Although the participation was voluntary, we offered some packaged food at the end of the study to thank the volunteers.

Data Analysis. We analyzed the collected data (a) to minimize and finalize the number of features, (b) to decide the appropriate time slice for which the final set of selected features should be taken together before applying the classifier and (c) to decide the classifiers to be used. The detail analyses are described below.

(a) *Feature Reduction.* We used the Principle Component Analysis (PCA) to identify the number of features which could be rejected. We plotted a graph for cumulative proportion of variance against the number of features (Fig. 5).

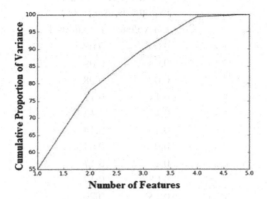

Fig. 5. Result after applying PCA

It was observed that the curve became almost parallel to the x axis after four features. Hence, we decided that one among the five features could be rejected. Therefore, our final set of features could be of size four. We applied the 'f-regression technique' to identify the feature which could be discarded among the five features. The f-regression technique calculates the correlation between two variables. It selects the features one by one, which has a high correlation with the output variable (valence and arousal level, in our case), and at the same time very less dependency with the already selected features. We observed that except for 'backspace key press frequency', all the other four features: 'typing speed', 'touch count', 'max text length' and 'device shake frequency' had high correlation with valence and arousal level. Thus backspace key press frequency was rejected from the final set of features.

(b) *Identification of Appropriate Time Slice.* We also identified the appropriate time slice for which all the features should be taken together before applying the classifier. We empirically found out the appropriate time slice by statistically testing the following hypothesis for each time slice from one second to ten seconds.

The null hypothesis corresponding to each feature was:

"For feature X; the mean of feature values of X for low arousal is same as the mean of feature values X for high arousal".

Hence, the alternative hypothesis for each feature was:

"For feature X; the mean of feature values of X for low arousal is different from the mean of feature values X for high arousal"

Table 2. Hypothesis testing for different time slices

Time slice	Minimum significance level to reject all null hypothesis using t-test	
	For valence	For arousal
1 s	0.09	0.08
2 s	0.08	0.09
3 s	0.08	0.08
4 s	0.14	0.13
5 s	0.13	0.15
6 s	0.16	0.14
7 s	0.04	0.04
8 s	0.16	0.17
9 s	0.08	0.12
10 s	0.18	0.20

We applied the t-test for each feature for all the time slices to find out the appropriate time slice for which the hypothesis for all remaining features were rejected. In the similar way, the statistical test was done for valence as well. The results are presented as follows (Table 2).

The result above showed that the window size of 7 s had the minimum required significance level ($P < 0.05$) to reject all null-hypothesis. Moreover, it was the only window size for which null hypothesis for all the features got rejected. We therefor chose 7 s as an interval, i.e., in each seven second our model should predict the affective stated based on the four features. We used the t-test also to verify whether rejection of the backspace key frequency feature was justified or not. The null hypothesis for backspace key frequency could not be rejected even for a significance level as high as 0.80. This implies that our decision to remove the particular feature was justified.

(c) *Choice of the Classifiers.* As our intension was to classify the users' states based on two levels of binary classifications (first for valence and then for arousal), the state-of-art binary classifier Support Vector Machine (SVM) with linear kernel could be chosen as one of the classifiers. We chose multilevel SVM for the classification. We assumed that all the four affective states identified by our predictive model were almost equally probable. This was because we trained our model with such type of data where data about all the four emotional sates were equally distributed. At the same time, the size of the data set was small. Therefore, Naïve Bayes classifier was also a good choice for the classification. It also tends to avoid the problem of over-fitting. We, therefore explored both the SVM and Naïve Bayes classifiers.

Results. The model was trained by approximately 80% (data of twenty six participants) of total data (data of thirty three participants). Remaining data (data of seven participants) were used for testing. We did not do this in a simple manner because in that case the model could not learn anything from the set of data used only for testing. Hence, we have applied cross validation technique (CV). We followed Leave-One-Subject-Out cross-validation (LOSOCV) technique for training and testing the model. We chose this particular CV because Hammerla and Plötz [16] have argued that this CV is best applicable for the classifiers we chose. They have also argued that LOSOCV is best for the type of experiment we conducted. In LOSOCV, instead of random division, dataset is divided participant wise for the cross validation. The classification accuracy found after applying the two classifiers are shown in Table 3. We observed that the Naïve Bayes gave the highest average classification accuracy of 86.60%. The phrase 'average classification accuracy' denotes the summation of accuracy in each trial divided by the number of trials (five in our case – as we made five trials to cover the data of all the participants). It may be noted that although the Naïve Bayes gave higher average accuracy, the SVM also gave high accuracy. Moreover, the classification accuracy in case of the SVM is comparatively more stable. Therefore, we can claim that both the classifiers are equally likely to become candidates for our model.

Table 3. Affective states prediction accuracy

Trials	Percentage of accuracy	
	Naïve Bayes	SVM
1	92.02	86.50
2	88.27	83.89
3	78.54	85.28
4	89.96	75.72
5	84.23	84.68
Average percentage of accuracy	**86.60**	**83.21**

Validating the Model. Other than testing the model with collected data, we conducted a separate validation study. For this we used EEG data of a different group of twelve participants (six male and six female, mean age of 24.67 years with SD = 2.53).

The participants were asked to play the same game application we developed. Data was recorded as before. However, this time they wore the EPOC+ headset at the time of playing the game. The EPOC+ was connected with EmotivPRO software installed on a laptop computer through a dedicated Bluetooth dongle. The clocks of the laptop and the smartphone where the game was installed were synchronized before conducting the experiment. We recorded the valence and arousal identified by the EmotivPRO when the participants were playing the game.

After the experiment, using the collected feature value, we predicted the affective states using our model and compared these with the affective states identified by the EmotivPRO. We found 88.05% similarities for this. The high similarity validates the fact that our model is able to predict users' affective state into any of the specific four circumplex state with high accuracy.

Testing the Generalizability of the Model. We also wanted to test whether our model works for other applications where typing data is available as the input for interactions, not just restricted to the game application we have developed. Thus, we could validate the generalizability of the model. We conducted an additional study with a different set of ten participants (five male and five female, mean age of 24.9 years with SD = 1.85) for this. The participants were asked to wear the EPOC+ and access their favorite instant messaging service (IMS, e.g., WhatsApp, Facebook Messenger) and social networking (SNS e.g., Facebook, Twitter) apps for ten minutes each. In case of IMS, they were instructed to chat with their friends/relatives whereas for SNS, they were instructed to write some comments on some shared image/video by their friends/relatives. All the participants chose Facebook as SNS and WhatsApp as IMS as they have accounts in these. The EmotivPRO recorded the valence and arousal while the participants were performing the tasks. The typing data were collected by a background app written by us. We compared the four specific affective states predicted by our model (with Naïve Bayes classifier) and the same identified by the EmotivPRO. States predicted by our model and predicted by the EmotivPRO at each instant (after every 7 s) is compared. In 87.90% cases, the predictions were the same. This indicate that our model can be applied in other application areas where interactions involve touch-typing data.

4   Discussion

4.1   Variation in the Model

We further extended our research making slight variation in the model based on particular research argument and target application area.

Variation with Meaningless Text. Epp et al. [13] argued that the classifier works best in this type of model when we use simple English words with simple structure of sentence avoiding complex linguistic features. Complex linguistic features in sentences introduce memory biases. In our work, we tested the model using text from children's novel "Alice in Wonderland" (Fig. 1) which was also used by Epp et al. [13]. To determine the correlation between the feature used and arousal level after completely removing the linguistic features from the text we made a variation in the model. We used text with meaningless words generated randomly. The following is an example of randomly generated meaningless text.

"fffff sssss eeeee ccccc bbbbb kkkkk lllll pppppp aaaaa zzzzz vvvvv nnnnn rrrrr yyyyy qqqqq mmmmm jjjjj ooooo ttttt uuuuu".

This was done for removing the linguistic features completely to remove memory biasness. After performing hypothesis testing on this data, we observed that the null hypothesis for all the features other than the 'backspace key press frequency' were rejected for a significance level as low as 0.01. This concludes that the correlation between the features (used in the model) and arousal level increases when linguistic features are removed. We, therefore, suggest to avoid complex linguistic features in this kind of experiment.

Variation without 'Device shake frequency' Feature. In some application, sometimes it is possible that the input devices are stable (e.g., 'smart' classroom with smartphone/tablet for each student fixed on the desk [41]). Moreover, sometimes user may put their device on the table/desk/bed for typing. 'Device shake frequency' is insignificant in these scenarios. Therefore, we wanted to make another variation of the model where device shake frequency was not considered. Through this variation, we examined the performance of the model. Following observation was made (Table 4).

Table 4. Accuracy of prediction with and without considering 'device shake frequency' feature

Classifier used	Average accuracy considering 'device shake frequency' (%)	Average accuracy without considering 'device shake frequency' (%)
Naïve Bayes	86.60	82.46
SVM	83.21	80.25

Although accuracy reduces slightly without considering 'Device shake frequency' feature, still the accuracy is high. However, we advise to consider the device shake frequency feature for additional accuracy.

4.2   Strength, Limitation, and Future Scope

Following our approach, it is possible to build models for predicting users' affect and emotion without taking any user feedback. The data collection method is purely unobtrusive, which helps to reduce the inaccuracy in emotional data. We have built a model following the approach which can predict the specific affective states of the users of small handheld touchscreen devices without their knowledge. This minimizes the imitation in emotion. Moreover, no extra hardware and sensors are required to capture the emotional data in our model. Only typing patterns and dynamics are sufficient to identify the users' affective states. We claim our model to be ubiquitous as the affective states are identified without the knowledge of the user by a device which stays always with the user, and it does not matter where the user is. The number of features to be used in the model has been minimized by excluding the unnecessary and application specific features used by earlier works ([23, 24]). This makes the model simple, generalized, and inexpensive in terms of computation. This in turn increases the adaptability of the model in various applications. Most of the related works (e.g., Lee et al. [23, 24]) were validated based on the users' feedback which may not be always reliable [31]. Our additional validation studies (consist of EEG signals of the participants) demonstrate that our proposed affect induction method is really able to induce the intended specific affective states. These studies also validate that our proposed minimalist model of affection is really able to predict users' affective states with high accuracy.

Despite the novelty and strengths of the proposed approach, there are some limitations and scopes for future work. Our model fits best in some specific application area (e.g., in education [42]), as it is able to detect only the four affective states based on the Circumplex model. However, it may be required to identify the affective states of a user more specifically as per the requirement of various other application areas. For instance, in movie making and promotion industry, it may be required to distinguish 'anger' from 'fear' where both of them are in 'negative-high' state. Our model, in its current state is unable to predict user's state with such distinction. In the future, we intend to refine the model which can identify the users' affect and emotion in a comprehensive way. We conducted a preliminary study for testing the generalizability of the model and observed that the model works (with high accuracy) for two other applications (SNS and IMS) where it is possible to get touch-typing input. The model can therefore be applied in these applications. If applied, the users of these applications will be able to know the affective states (in terms of the level of arousal and valence) of their friends and/or the followers while chatting and/or commenting on some posts. These can be made optional as well as mandatory, as per the requirements. The affective states exchanged in these applications by conventional methods (i.e., through emojis, stickers, GIFs), may not always be true because sometimes the users may intentionally hide their actual states. Nevertheless, an extensive study is required to identify more number of real-time applications where the model can be applied. Further research is also required for developing techniques to complement the identified affective states as well as its effects on users. We want to work on these as well. In future, we also intend to work on applying the model for building affective interactive system like affective classroom.

5 Conclusion

A novel method for inducing specific affective states has been proposed to minimize the inaccuracy and imitation in affective data. We have built a special purpose android game for this. It has been shown that the game is really able to induce the affective states without the knowledge of the users, and collect the affective data without any feedback from them. This in turn reduces the inaccuracy and imitation. We have also built a minimalist model for identifying the affective states of the users of small handheld mobile devices like smartphone from typing pattern on touchscreen. We reduced the unnecessary and application specific features used in earlier works to make the model simple and minimal so the applicability and adaptability increase. It has been shown that the model is really able to predict the specific affective states of the users with high accuracy. We want to work on refining the model, and applying the model to develop affective systems in future.

Acknowledgements. We are thankful to all the volunteers who participated in the empirical studies. We also sincerely acknowledge the contribution of Kshitiz Agarwal, Tarun Sharma, and Yash Mehta in this work. We also thank all the reviewers and the shepherd for their constructive suggestions in improving the quality of the manuscript.

References

1. Bartram, L., Patra, A., Stone, M.: Affective color in visualization. In: Proceedings of the 2017 CHI Conference on Human Factors in Computing Systems (CHI 2017), pp. 1364–1374. ACM, Denver (2017)
2. Beedie, C.J., Terry, P.C., Lane, A.M.: Distinctions between emotion and mood. Cogn. Emot. **19**(6), 847–878 (2005)
3. Bianchi-Berthouze, N., Kleinsmith, A.: A categorical approach to affective gesture recognition. Conn. Sci. **16**(1), 259–269 (2004)
4. Camurri, A., Lagerlöf, I., Volpe, G.: Recognizing emotion from dance movement: comparison of spectator recognition and automated techniques. Int. J. Hum Comput. Stud. **59**(1–2), 213–225 (2003)
5. Ciman, M., Wac, K., Gaggi, O.: iSenseStress: assessing stress through human-smartphone interaction analysis. In: Proceedings of the 9th International Conference on Pervasive Computing Technologies for Healthcare, ICST (Institute for Computer Sciences, Social-Informatics and Telecommunications Engineering), pp. 84–91. ACM & IEEE, Istanbul (2015)
6. Collier, G.L.: Beyond valence and activity in the emotional connotations of music. Psychol. Music **35**(1), 110–131 (2007)
7. Debener, S., et al.: How about taking a low-cost, small, and wireless EEG for a walk? Psychophysiology **49**(11), 1617–1621 (2012)
8. Devillers, L. et al.: Real life emotions in French and English TV video clips: an integrated annotation protocol combining continuous and discrete approaches. In: LREC 2006, pp. 1105–1110, Genoa (2006)
9. Douglas-Cowie, E., et al.: Emotional speech: towards a new generation of databases. Speech Commun. **40**(1–2), 33–60 (2003)
10. Douglas-Cowie, E., et al.: The HUMAINE database: addressing the collection and annotation of naturalistic and induced emotional data. In: Paiva, A.C.R., Prada, R., Picard, R. W. (eds.) ACII 2007. LNCS, vol. 4738, pp. 488–500. Springer, Heidelberg (2007). https://doi.org/10.1007/978-3-540-74889-2_43
11. Eerola, T., Vuoskoski, J.K.: A comparison of the discrete and dimensional models of emotion in music. Psychol. Music **39**(1), 18–49 (2011)
12. Ekman, P., Sorenson, E.R., Friesen, W.V.: Pan-cultural elements in facial displays of emotion. Science **164**(3875), 86–88 (1969)
13. Epp, C., Lippold, M., Mandryk, R.L.: Identifying emotional states using keystroke dynamics. In: Proceedings of the SIGCHI Conference on Human Factors in Computing Systems, pp. 715–724. ACM, Vancouver (2011)

14. Gaffary, Y., et al.: Gestural and postural reactions to stressful event: design of a haptic stressful stimulus. In: 2015 International Conference on Affective Computing and Intelligent Interaction (ACII), pp. 988–992. IEEE, Xi'an (2015)

15. Gratch, J., et al.: Felt emotion and social context determine the intensity of smiles in a competitive video game. In: 2013 10th IEEE International Conference and Workshops on Automatic Face and Gesture Recognition (FG), pp. 1–8. IEEE, Shanghai (2013)

16. Hammerla, N.Y., Plötz, T.: Let's (not) stick together: pairwise similarity biases cross-validation in activity recognition. In: Proceedings of the 2015 ACM International Joint Conference on Pervasive and Ubiquitous Computing, pp. 1041–1051 ACM, Osaka (2015)

17. Hazlett, R.L.: Measuring emotional valence during interactive experiences: boys at video game play. In Proceedings of the SIGCHI Conference on Human Factors in Computing Systems (CHI 2006), pp. 1023–1026. ACM, Montréal (2006)

18. Healey, J., Picard, R.W.: Detecting stress during real-world driving tasks using physiological sensors. IEEE Trans. Intell. Transp. Syst. **6**(2), 156–166 (2005)

19. Gabrielsson, A.: Emotion perceived and emotion felt: same or different? Music Sci. **5** (1_suppl), 123–147 (2001)

20. Glowinski, D., et al.: Toward a minimal representation of affective gestures. IEEE Trans. Affect. Comput. **2**(2), 106–118 (2011)

21. Khanna, P., Sasikumar, M.: Recognising emotions from keyboard stroke pattern. Int. J. Comput. Appl. **11**(9), 1–5 (2010)

22. Lang, P.J., et al.: Looking at pictures: affective, facial, visceral, and behavioral reactions. Psychophysiology **30**(3), 261–273 (1993)

23. Lee, H., et al.: Towards unobtrusive emotion recognition for affective social communication. In: 2012 IEEE Consumer Communications and Networking Conference (CCNC), pp. 260–264. IEEE, Las Vegas (2012)

24. Lee, P.M., Tsui, W.H., Hsiao, T.C.: The influence of emotion on keyboard typing: an experimental study using visual stimuli. Biomed. Eng. Online **13**(1), 81–92 (2014)

25. Lim, Y.M., Ayesh, A., Stacey, M.: The effects of typing demand on emotional stress, mouse and keystroke behaviours. In: Arai, K., Kapoor, S., Bhatia, R. (eds.) Intelligent Systems in Science and Information 2014. SCI, vol. 591, pp. 209–225. Springer, Cham (2015). https://doi.org/10.1007/978-3-319-14654-6_13

26. Murray, I.R., Arnott, J.L.: Toward the simulation of emotion in synthetic speech: a review of the literature on human vocal emotion. J. Acoust. Soc. Am. **93**(2), 1097–1108 (1993)

27. Nahin, A.N.H., et al.: Identifying emotion by keystroke dynamics and text pattern analysis. Behav. Inf. Technol. **33**(9), 987–996 (2014)

28. Philippot, P.: Inducing and assessing differentiated emotion-feeling states in the laboratory. Cogn. Emot. **7**(2), 171–193 (1993)

29. Picard, R.W.: Affective Computing, 1st edn. MIT Press, Cambridge (1997)

30. Politou, E., Alepis, E., Patsakis, C.: A survey on mobile affective computing. Comput. Sci. Rev. **25**(1), 79–100 (2017)

31. Polivy, J.: On the induction of emotion in the laboratory: discrete moods or multiple affect states? J. Pers. Soc. Psychol. **41**(4), 803–817 (1981)

32. Posner, J., Russell, J.A., Peterson, B.S.: The circumplex model of affect: an integrative approach to affective neuroscience, cognitive development, and psychopathology. Dev. Psychopathol. **17**(3), 715–734 (2005)

33. Rao, K.S., et al.: Emotion recognition from speech. Int. J. Comput. Sci. Inf. Technol. **3**(2), 3603–3607 (2012)

34. Russell, J.A.: A circumplex model of affect. J. Pers. Soc. Psychol. **39**(6), 1161–1178 (1980)

35. Sano, A., Picard, R.W.: Stress recognition using wearable sensors and mobile phones. In: 2013 Humaine Association Conference on Affective Computing and Intelligent Interaction (ACII), pp. 671–676. IEEE, Geneva (2013)
36. Schmidt, L.A., Trainor, L.J.: Frontal brain electrical activity (EEG) distinguishes valence and intensity of musical emotions. Cogn. Emot. **15**(4), 487–500 (2001)
37. Sokolova, M.V., Fernández-Caballero, A.: A review on the role of color and light in affective computing. Appl. Sci. **5**(3), 275–293 (2015)
38. Tikadar, S., Kazipeta, S., Ganji, C., Bhattacharya, S.: A minimalist approach for identifying affective states for mobile interaction design. In: Bernhaupt, R., Dalvi, G., Joshi, A., Balkrishan, Devanuj K., O'Neill, J., Winckler, M. (eds.) INTERACT 2017. LNCS, vol. 10513, pp. 3–12. Springer, Cham (2017). https://doi.org/10.1007/978-3-319-67744-6_1
39. Västfjäll, D.: Emotion induction through music: a review of the musical mood induction procedure. Music. Sci. **5**(1_suppl), 173–211 (2001)
40. Vizer, L.M., Zhou, L., Sears, A.: Automated stress detection using keystroke and linguistic features: an exploratory study. Int. J. Hum. Comput. Stud. **67**(10), 870–886 (2009)
41. Whitehill, J., et al.: The faces of engagement: automatic recognition of student engagement from facial expressions. IEEE Trans. Affect. Comput. **5**(1), 86–98 (2014)
42. Woolf, B., et al.: Affect-aware tutors: recognising and responding to student affect. Int. J. Learn. Technol. **4**(3–4), 129–164 (2009)
43. Zimmermann, P., et al.: Affective computing—a rationale for measuring mood with mouse and keyboard. Int. J. Occup. Saf. Ergon. **9**(4), 539–551 (2003)

Acceptability of Persuasive Prompts to Induce Behavioral Change in People Suffering from Depression

Rabiah Arshad[✉], Murtaza Ali Baig, Marium Tariq, and Suleman Shahid

Lahore University of Management Sciences, Lahore, Pakistan
{18100285,16030014,18020160,suleman.shahid}@lums.edu.pk

Abstract. In recent years, there has been a growing concern regarding the increased occurrence of mental health disorders amongst the population worldwide and its debilitating effects on not only the individual suffering from it but also on the economy. Depression, being the most prevalent mental illness, urges the need to test different methodologies to try and tackle the issue. One such method is the adoption of persuasive behavioral change models in prompts for mHealth applications to assist in 'prompting' the user to adopt healthier behaviors. However, the acceptability of such persuasive prompts along with the selection of behavioral change models most suitable for people suffering through depression is unknown. In this work, we present the results of a cross-sectional acceptability study that tested the acceptability of persuasive prompts through two types of users: ones suffering from depression and ones without any depressive symptoms. In a study with 29 individuals without depression and 21 individuals with depression, we observed the differences between the results of both types of users and were able to show that not only were the prompts accepted by both users, but they have the potential to induce behavioral change.

Keywords: Depression · Mental health · Persuasion · Prompt · Persuasive technology · mHealth

1 Introduction

Depression is one of the most common mental disorders in the world. It is associated with impairment in daily functioning, significant losses of quality of life in patients and their relatives, loss of years due to disability, including increased mortality rates and enormous economic costs [18]. The World Health Organization (WHO) has declared that worldwide, over 300 million people belonging to different age groups suffer from depression. Studies conducted by WHO revealed that a significantly large proportion of people with mental health disorders do not receive treatment [1,4]. These barriers to treatment exist in forms of adherence difficulties, hesitance to open up to psychologists especially in cases of face-to-face counseling, lack of awareness, high treatment costs and social stigma that

© IFIP International Federation for Information Processing 2019
Published by Springer Nature Switzerland AG 2019
D. Lamas et al. (Eds.): INTERACT 2019, LNCS 11749, pp. 120–139, 2019.
https://doi.org/10.1007/978-3-030-29390-1_7

is attached to therapy [23]. Mental health patients, especially in underdeveloped countries such as Pakistan, are stigmatized in such a way that not only does it disrupt their daily functioning, but it also hinders their integration into society [16]. The aforementioned issues faced by mental health patients, who mostly tend to be similar across the globe, have led to an exponential growth in the field of Human-Computer Interaction (HCI). Through this, designers and researchers explore ways to improve access to, and engagement with, therapeutic treatment [35]. Modern-day approaches to detect and treat depression and other mental illnesses comprise of availing the benefits of pervasive technology.

Recently, some notable developments in the field have been made; ranging from self-help therapies, such as computerized Cognitive Behavioral Therapy (CBT) programs [12], to designs that supplement traditional psychotherapy programs [35]. It is important to note that these non-conventional approaches to therapy are not invented to replace psychologists but merely to provide a small boost to patients who are initially reluctant to see a therapist due to the aforementioned hesitancies. Mobile-health (mHealth) possesses several advantages consisting of constant and easier access to therapy, the benefit of feasibility, impartiality of mental health resources, immediate and instant support, and anonymity [30]. It is also widely agreed upon that technology-based approaches could specifically be suitable for engaging adolescents who may be more accepting of and comfortable with using technology to seek help and treatment over traditional routes such as visiting a therapist [6]. Lastly, mHealth applications reduce the barriers of face-to-face counseling, including the stigma or "embarrassment" of discussing one's mental health problems [15]. For these reasons, mobile health provides its users with a particularly powerful and ubiquitous platform for delivering mental health interventions. However, while mobile health applications are becoming more common, there is not enough research being done regarding the content of the applications. Hence, the primary motivation behind this study is bridging the gap between the determination of which interventions mHealth applications should contain and how they should be presented.

1.1 Persuasive Technology for the Improvement of Mental Health

Alteration of an individual's lifestyle is considered to be one of the primary factors that could prevent the onset of various mental health disorders such as depression and anxiety. It is also widely acknowledged that lifestyle modification could be beneficial in reducing the present symptoms of a range of mental health disorders, including depression. Lifestyle interventions may include factors like regular exercise, improving one's diet, getting proper sleep, and avoiding substance intake such as alcohol.

While the adoption of healthy habits became our intervention of choice, we opted for persuasive prompts as the tool of intervention. By persuasive prompts, we mean messages shown to the user on mobile application screens during the interaction between human and computer. These messages try to persuade the user to perform particular tasks or try to embed an idea into the user's mind. Dennison et al. suggested that tools which monitor or track behavior alone may be insufficient in the absence of some advice or intervention to help patients adopt behavior modifications [10]. Since our persuasive prompts are targeting people with depression, it was of the utmost importance for us to take care when developing our messages by consulting psychiatrists and using behavior change models and message diversification techniques. This allowed us to ensure a variety of choice while catering to the sensitive nature of our user group.

We mapped persuasive prompts onto two persuasive models, namely the Fogg Behavior Model (FBM) and the Theory of Reasoned Action Model (TRA). FBM shows that three elements must converge at the same moment for a behavior to occur: Motivation, Ability, and Trigger. That is, in order to perform a certain behavior, all three of the aforementioned factors should co-exist; there needs to be sufficient level of motivation, the individual must have the ability to carry out that behavior and lastly, the person should be triggered to perform that behavior [13]. When a behavior does not occur, at least one of these three elements is absent from the equation.

Theory of Reasoned Action is used to predict how individuals will behave based on their pre-existing attitudes and behavioral intentions. According to Icek Ajzen, individuals first perceive a behavior as either positive or negative combined with how the society would perceive that same behavior, before intending to engage in it [2]. An individual's decision to engage in a behavior is based on the outcomes the individual expects as a result of performing the behavior. According to the theory, the intention to perform a certain behavior precedes the actual behavior. Put simply, TRA first tries to gauge an individual's attitude and intentions before trying to persuade them to do something.

1.2   A Study of Acceptability Using User-Centered Design Principles

The aim of this study is to test the acceptability of persuasive prompts in inducing behavioral change in people with depression. The Acceptability model evaluates a system on four factors. The first factor is utility, which matches the needs of the user with the functionalities of the system. The second factor is usability, which is if the functionalities are utilizable. The third factor is likability, i.e., the affect of the system on the user. The fourth and final factor is cost, which includes both financial and social costs of the system [19]. When it comes to mHealth applications, McCallum et al. defined acceptability as users' subjective preferences and experiences [27]. Due to the sensitive nature of our study and the fact that it was set in a country like Pakistan where the stigma attached to depression is still very high, it was essential to first test if persuasive prompts are even accepted as an intervention for people suffering through depression based on their preferences and experiences.

The principles of User-Centered Design (UCD) would best enable us to carry an acceptability study as they are based on an explicit understanding of the user [14]. The persuasive prompts were designed keeping the user's capabilities and limitations in mind. The user's then evaluated the prompts and based on their selection, particular prompts were then incorporated in an mHealth application.

2   Related Works

Addressing issues like depression through technology requires a multi-disciplinary review. For this study, we have tried to cover most of the relevant aspects while reviewing the related works.

2.1   Effects of Lifestyle Change on Mental Health

Derman et al. sheds light on the basic lifestyle modifications which should be considered and incorporated when planning out a treatment and management program for patients with mental health issues, particularly depression. The authors opt for a holistic approach and recommend using a combination of physical training, nutritional interventions and psychosocial interventions alongside anti-depressant medications as all these components are quite essential in patient management. Evidence shows that short term psychological treatments (duration of up to 3 months) can be as effective as anti-depressant medication in mild to moderate depression. Therefore, pairing physical activity with psychological treatments (CBT for instance) can have optimal results in terms of achieving improved mental health [11].

Al-Eisa et al. establishes a relationship between physical activity and psychological factors such as insomnia, depression and attention span of an individual. Physical activity was inversely related to insomnia, mood disturbance and depression. It was observed that activity of any type and degree seemed to have positive effects on depressive symptoms. As depression and insomnia influence attention span, physical activity reduces distraction and attention shifting [3].

A study was conducted by Chekroud et al. aimed to examine the association between exercise and mental health burden and to understand the impact of elements like type of exercise, its frequency, duration or intensity. The results showed that while keeping all other socio-economic factors constant, individuals who engaged in some sort of physical activity had about 1.5 fewer days of poor mental health in a particular month than individuals who did not [9]. Similarly, the results of a study by Meyer et al. showed that exercise had a significant impact on the participants' depressive mood 10 and 30 min following the exercise irrespective of the intensity. As a result, it was suggested that physical activity should be employed as a symptom management tool in order to improve depressive mood and symptoms [28].

A study by Schlarb et al. examined the prevalence of sleep disturbances and mental strain in students from two European countries, Luxembourg and Germany. Students from Germany and Luxembourg Universities reported high level of mental stress and heightened sleep disturbances, elevating to a clinical level such as anxiety issues, attention deficit/hyperactivity problems, and depressive problems. The results indicate that poor sleep quality is significantly associated with diminished mental health in students from both the countries. Schlarb et al. recommends specialized intervention programs to be introduced and implemented to enhance the students' mental and physical well being [34].

A Finnish diabetes prevention study was conducted during a 36-month randomized clinical trial to assess the effect of intervention on depressive symptoms. The treatment group received individualized counseling aimed at reducing weight and increasing physical activity. The results showed that successful implementation of lifestyle modifications, such as reduction in body weight, resulted in an even greater reduction of depressive symptoms and a positive mood change, regardless of the intensity of treatment [33].

A longitudinal study with a 5 year dietary intervention program observed changes in emotions, particularly negative emotions, among participants of a cholesterol lowering study. It was seen that the changes and improvements in diet were related to reduction in depressive symptoms, hostility/aggression and lower cholesterol levels [37].

2.2   Persuasive Technology as a Tool for Intervention

Along with persuasive prompts, Behavior Change Support System (BCSS) is another persuasive tool designed to bring about a desirable change in people's behaviors by providing comprehensive support through employing a combination of carefully selected and integrated software features. Two domains where BCSS is most commonly used are Health and Energy. In the health domain, people are encouraged to change their behaviors or lifestyles for the better, such as incorporating exercise into their daily routines or by eating healthier. For BCSS to be effective, there needs to exist some level of motivation to begin with. BCSS brings in the element of rehearsal as a software feature to educate users and improve their self-confidence in tackling well-being issues. Researches also incorporated email-based reminders in the system. The aim of the reminders was also to prompt participants to rehearse mindfulness and other experiential exercises included in the treatment program [17].

Zang [38] conducted an experiment testing the perspective associated with an e-coaching application, BeActive!, to promote physical exercise at work. E-coaching is a persuasive mechanism aimed at encouraging sustainable positive behavioral change. The paper studies factors that could make exercise seem more appealing to its users. Choice modeling was the model employed for the study. A comparison with the Fogg Behavior Model suggested that while Fogg points out the three factors that would result in a change in behavior, it is not as simple as it seems; there exists a competing effect. When having to choose between two or more options, the change in behavior would depend on the option that is preferred at that point in time, given a specific context and the behaviors involved. Option attractiveness was tweaked through a mechanism known as choice modeling; users' decision to exercise more was dependent on whether there was a trade-off involved with respect to their productivity of the main task, and whether it was socially awkward for them to engage in that activity. An interesting insight showed how adding one extreme option (doing jumping jacks) can nudge people to perceive even a moderate activity (walking) in a positive light.

Lentferink studied the effectiveness of e-technologies in behavioral change, establishing that the impact is dependent on how well the design fits the end users' and its stakeholders' values and requirements [24]. Workers found the self-tracking mechanism to be particularly useful as it helped them gain awareness about the probable stressors as well as their current state of emotions, which ultimately helped them deal with their negative emotions. Moreover, it was observed that reminding the user in real-time about negative emotions enables the provision of just-in-time suggestions [29]. Just-in-time suggestions provide the individual with the necessary resources that allow him/her to deal with the negative emotions right at the very beginning, when it is most needed and also effective [26].

Persuasive Technology to Support Chronic Health Conditions by Zechmann [36] was a study intended to investigate the perceived effectiveness of 17 persuasive strategies. Of the lot, the ones considered to be most persuasive were personalization, reminder, commitment, self-monitoring, rewards and customization. The author also stresses upon the difference between perceived persuasiveness and individual susceptibility to persuasion.

2.3   User-Centered Design

It is necessary to follow the key principles of User-Centered Design (UCD) practices for designing impactful mental health applications [14]. Thus, it was very important for us to understand the existing work done in technology for mental illness, particularly depression, using UCD. The key principles of UCD include user focus, active user involvement in design, evolutionary system development, prototyping, and usability evaluation. Based on these principles a framework has been developed by researchers for persuasive healthcare systems, named as, Patient-Clinician-Designer (PCD) Framework.

The PCD framework accounts for the perspectives of all three stake holders when designing a persuasive mental health app, the patient, the clinician and the designer. The framework also helps in overcoming the challenges of designing a mental health system. It accommodates complex symptoms of mental illness, supports uncertain treatment processes, maintains a high-degree of sensitivity to the seriousness of the disease and mental stigma associated with it [26]. MONARCA, a mobile application, is built using the PCD framework and is used for monitoring patients with bi-polar disorder [7]. Similarly, prompts for inhibiting behavior change can also be designed using PCD by taking into account the perspective of the stakeholders.

Since prompt design plays a central role in the process of behavior modification and habit formation, Kuo et al. conducted a study to test different design features for habit formation and behavior change [22]. The study employed daily challenges to induce habit formation of a healthy lifestyle. In this study 139 participants were recruited for a 20 day field trial. A mobile application was used to provide daily behavioral prompts, thus, supplying users with healthy and sustainable lifestyle challenges. The study provided the following design implications for mobile phone interventions focused on habit formation:

- It is feasible to have daily prompts for behavior formation since 79.1% of the participants were in favor of daily challenges
- Daily prompts with reminders can produce positive outcomes in terms of habit formation
- Diversity and repetition of the content used in prompts matter.

3   Methodology

A structured meta-analysis was carried out and one of the research objectives of the analysis was to analyze the need and current availability of mHealth applications for depression monitoring, awareness and behavioral intervention of depression. For this purpose, we tested a total of 100 free mHealth applications. The meta-analysis is a separate study on its own, however, observations made in the analysis were used as part of the preliminary research for the current study. We observed that a simple interface with basic user guidelines along with a more personalized user experience proves to have a high usability rating. It was seen that the number of prompts shown to the user is vital for effective intervention. Although research remains inconclusive about the ideal number of behavioral prompts to be delivered in an intervention, it is suggested that daily prompts along with reminder(s) are able to bring about significant positive outcomes [22]. With the meta-analysis, we were able to identify the potential of mHealth applications for depression along with observing a major gap in current mHealth applications in terms of the usage of specific behavioral prompts as an intervention technique. Patel et al. argues that self-tracking in itself is not sufficient, and that personalized suggestions should also be a part of the strategy as it would help bridge the gap between awareness and actual behavioral change [32].

3.1   Persuasive Prompts

To create our persuasive prompts, we mapped the Fogg Behavior Model (FBM) and Theory of Reasoned Action Model (TRA) on to 10 different behaviors resulting in 20 prompts. We then further divided each of the 20 prompts into Self-Diverse and Target-Diverse messages, giving us a total of 40 prompts with 4 variations of each behavior. The 4 variations are namely FBM using Self-Diverse messages, FBM using Target-Diverse messages, TRA using Self-Diverse messages, and TRA using Target-Diverse messages.

Self-Diverse(SD) and Target-Diverse(TD) are message diversification strategies [20] which we used to generate trigger messages to better understand which types of triggers would be more effective in inducing behavior change in a person with depression. SD uses concepts cognitively close to the message's recipient while TD uses concepts cognitively close to the targeted action.

For example, a SD message would persuade the user to be more active by mentioning how exercise(target concept) can benefit the user (the self), while a TD message would focus on a specific component of the target concept, such as walking (target action) and how it can benefit the user. SD/TD did influence the design of the persuasive prompts; they provided tools of diversification, i.e., they allowed us to make each message unique. However, the persuasive models, FBM and TRA, were the main tools in the design of the prompts. They provided the basis for the flow of the prompts along with the tone used in each message. Furthermore, text, images, audios and videos were collectively combined in the completion of the prompts.

Figure 1 shows a sample of the first variation; FBM using SD messages along with a sample of the second variation FBM using TD messages.

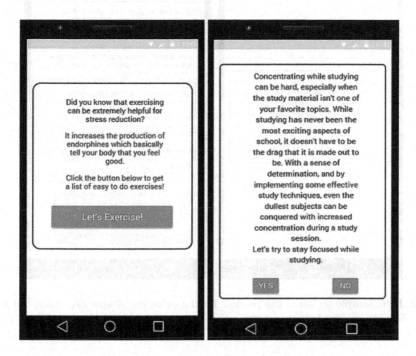

Fig. 1. Left: Sample screen of the prompt for the behavior 'exercise' using FBM-SD Right: Sample screen of the prompt for the behavior 'concentration' using FBM-TD.

The left screen is one of the screens for the prompt persuading the user to incorporate exercise in their daily routine. This particular prompt is using FBM which requires motivation, ability and trigger. The screen in the figure is handling motivation. It is establishing the idea that exercise is a good habit and has positive results giving the user a reason to exercise. Along with FBM the prompt also incorporates SD messaging by focusing on one benefit of exercising and relaying that to the user. The right screen is one of the screens for the prompts persuading the user to adopt concentration techniques when they are unable to focus. Again, this prompt is using FBM to induce the particular behavioral change by first motivating the user to do so. However, in this prompt we use TD messaging by focusing on concentration in a particular scenario, namely studying, rather than generally discussing the benefits of concentration. We chose studying as our target behavior given that our target group was university students who spend most of their time studying. Figure 2 shows a sample of the third variation, TRA using SD messages and a sample of the fourth variation, TRA using TD messages.

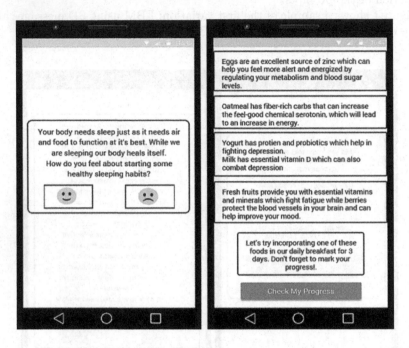

Fig. 2. Left: Sample screen of the prompt for the behavior 'sleep more' using TRA-SD Right: Sample screen of the prompt for the behavior 'eat healthy' using TRA-TD.

The left screen is the first screen for the prompt persuading the user to start healthy sleeping habits. As this particular prompt is using TRA, we first need to know if the user perceives the behavior as positive or negative. If the user selects the happy face, implying a positive attitude, the next screen will reinforce that positive attitude and give suggestions on how they can improve their sleeping pattern. If the user selects the sad face, implying a negative attitude, the next screen will try to inverse that emotion by instilling positive aspects of the behavior. Furthermore, as we are using SD messaging, the focus of the prompt is on the benefits of sleeping. The right screen is the last screen for the prompt persuading the user to start healthy eating habits. For the TD version we chose eating breakfast as our target behavior. This screen is suggesting healthier food options that can be incorporated into an individuals daily breakfast. Furthermore, this screen will only be shown if the user has a positive attitude towards the behavior 'eat healthy'.

Table 1. Major category of symptoms according to DSM-5 and ICD-10

Category	DSM-5	ICD-10
Mood		Clearly abnormal depressive mood
Interest	Markedly diminished interest or pleasure in all or almost all activities	Marked loss of interest or ability to enjoy activities that were previously pleasurable
Appetite and weight	Significant weight loss or gain, or increase or decrease in appetite	Changes of appetite (decrease or increase), with the corresponding weight change
Sleep	Sleep problems	Sleep alterations of any kind
Psychomotor agitation	Psychomotor agitation or retardation	Changes of psychomotor activity, with agitation or inhibition
Psychomotor retardation	Psychomotor agitation or retardation	Changes of psychomotor activity, with agitation or inhibition
Fatigue	Fatigue or loss of energy	Lack of vitality or increase of fatigability
Guilt and self-esteem	Feelings of guilt, worthlessness, negative self-appraisal	Disproportionate self-reproaches and feelings of excessive guilt or inadequacy; loss of confidence and self-esteem and feelings of inferiority
Concentration	Diminished concentration or indecisiveness	Complaints about or decrease of the ability to concentrate and think, accompanied by a lack of decision and vacillation
Suicide	Recurrent thoughts of death and suicidal ideation	Recurrent thoughts of death or suicide or any suicidal behavior
Anxiety	Anxiety	Anxiety
Alcohol and substance use	Substance abuse	Excessive consumption of alcohol
Histrionic behavior	Histrionic behavior	Histrionic behavior

Choice of Behaviors: The 10 behaviors are mapped on the major symptoms of depression as categorized by DSM-5 (Diagnostic and Statistical Manual of Mental Disorders) [5] and ICD-11 (International Statistical Classification of Diseases and Related Health Problems) [31] (Table 1). The behaviors were chosen to be the most effective in combating a majority of the major symptoms of depression. Namely, these are exercise, relax, sleep less, eat healthy, hydrate, sleep more, call someone, concentrate, self-worth and abstain from substance abuse.

3.2 Mobile Application-System of Intervention

A mobile e-coaching application was specifically developed for this study. The application uses persuasive prompts to persuade the user to adopt behaviors proven to improve mental health. To select the appropriate and most effective persuasive prompts, we conducted a cross-sectional study through which we obtained the preferred persuasive prompt for each behavior. These prompts were then integrated into the application. For this study, the application was simply used as a tool to present the messages (prompts). However, in the future the prompts themselves are to be part of an mHealth application, hence, the usability of the application was also tested in this study.

3.3 Participants and Study Design

We conducted two cross-sectional studies. 50 participants were recruited to join the first study and were divided into two groups. To obtain our sample of participants we used opportunity sampling i.e., we used people from the target population available at the time of the study and those willing to take part. All 50 participants met the recruitment criteria that they had to be students going to an educational institute of higher education between the ages of 18 and 25. Each individual was made to take a PHQ-9 test. PHQ-9 is a self-reporting tool consisting of nine questions. It is used for screening, monitoring, diagnosing, and measuring the severity of an individuals depression [21]. Group 1 (G1) included 21 participants and had the added criteria of either being clinically diagnosed as depressed or having a large number of symptoms of depression (high PHQ-9 score) as verified by a doctor. Group 2 (G2) included 29 individuals and had the added criteria of not being clinically diagnosed as depressed and showing a low number of symptoms of depression (low PHQ-9 score) as verified by a doctor. The objective of the first study was to determine which behavior change model (Fogg Behavior Model/Theory of Reasoned Action Model) was more effective in triggering behavior change in the context of depression and anxiety and to test the acceptability of the persuasive prompts. Participants from group 2 further went on to take part in the second study which was a user acceptability study of our mobile application.

Given the sensitive nature of our research, we took extra care in ensuring an ethical testing environment. Each participant was made to sign a consent form regarding their willful participation in the study along with an assurance of their privacy and anonymity. The study took place in a private setting where the user was not afraid of unwanted visitors. Furthermore, each participant was unaware of the other participants taking part in the study as we used code names assigned to each individual rather than their real names. The testing sessions were scheduled with a substantial amount of extra time before and after each session to prevent the participants from crossing paths.

3.4 First Study: Persuasive Prompts

The acceptability of the persuasive prompts was tested by both group 1 and group 2. Along with the acceptability of prompts, the participants also selected which behavior change model (FBM/TRA) they preferred and which trigger mechanism (Target-Diverse/Self-Diverse) they favored to trigger the behavior change. Each behavior was divided into 4 prompts; for the scope of this study, we will only focus on the preference of the behavior change models, hence, a participant who chose the FBM-SD version of a behavior was equivalent to a participant who chose the FBM-TD version of the same behavior. Furthermore, the ten behaviors were divided into 3 categories (Fig. 3) with each participant being randomly assigned one category.

The categories were created in such a way that each one had a difficult behavior, a moderate behavior and an easy behavior. The difficulty level was based on the time taken to navigate through the prompts for each behavior. For group 2, ten individuals were assigned to each category 1 and 2, while nine individuals were assigned to category 3. For group 1, each category had the same

Category	Total Group1 (G1) Participants	Total Group2 (G2) Participants	Behaviour	Persuasive Model	G1	G2
Category-1	7	10	Exercise	BFM	0	7
				TRA	7	3
			Sleep Less	BFM	1	7
				TRA	6	3
			Relax	BFM	1	5
				TRA	6	5
Category-2	7	10	Eat Healthy	BFM	1	10
				TRA	6	0
			Hydrate	BFM	1	10
				TRA	6	0
			Sleep More	BFM	0	7
				TRA	7	3
Category-3	7	9	Concentration	BFM	5	7
				TRA	2	2
			Calling Someone	BFM	5	8
				TRA	2	1
			Self-Worth	BFM	2	2
				TRA	5	7
			Substance Abuse	BFM	3	5
				TRA	4	4

Fig. 3. Figure with tabular representation of participant division and preferred model results for each behavior)

number of assigned individuals, i.e, seven. For each behavior in their category, the participants scored the acceptability of the selected prompt on a Likert scale from 1–5 which contributed to our quantitative data and also, through an informal interview, further elaborated why they chose their preferred prompt; this contributed to our qualitative data [25].

3.5   Second Study: Mobile Application

21 participants from group 1 further took part in the usability and accept-ability of the mobile application. The final persuasive prompts selected by the participants in the first study were integrated into the application and the indi-viduals from group 1 were again invited into a secluded lab setting to reassure confidentiality. Each participant was first given a 10 min demonstration of the application after which they had an opportunity to test it for themselves. Each user was given two tasks: (1) Navigate to the 'Information' section. (2) Navigate through the prompts. While the participant was using the application, an infor-mal conversation took place between the tester and the testee. This allowed the testee to become more comfortable in the given scenario which further resulted in vital extensive feedback which contributed to our qualitative data. After the users completed their tasks, they were given a System of Usability Scale (SUS) form to fill [8]. The SUS score contributed to our quantitative data.

4   Results

4.1   First Study: Persuasive Prompts

Results showed a clear difference in preference for prompts between group 1 and group 2. Overall, group 2 (without depression) preferred FBM over TRA as they believed that it is more effective to be directly given a challenge rather than being asked if a challenge is desired or not. For TRA, most of the participants from group 2 felt that if an individual needs motivation to complete a task, you must motivate them without taking their preference into consideration. They claimed it was obvious the user would not be willing to do a challenge which is why they need that push that FBM offers. While on the other hand participants from group 1 (with depression) preferred TRA over FBM. They claimed that TRA takes a kinder approach by giving importance to the user's preferences. FBM's direct approach might appear over-burdening and even harsh when someone with depression is at a low point. The following graphs represents the behavior-wise break down of the preference of participants from group 1 and group 2 respectively (Figs. 4 and 5):

A total number of 70 ratings from 21 participants of Group 1 on the Likert scale from 1–5 for all the prompts have shown a significant difference in means for the choices of FBM and TRA. The mean score for FBM is 2.94 and for TRA is 3.66 and the results are significant ($p < 0.01$, $t = -5.1884$). Similarly, a total number of 116 ratings from 29 participants of Group 2 on the Likert scale

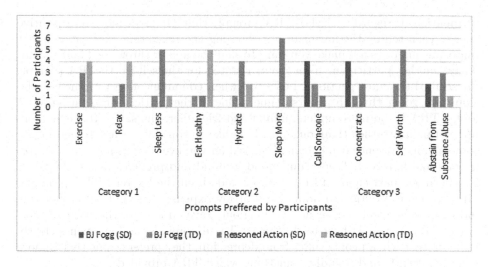

Fig. 4. Prompts preferred by group 1 (high depressive symptoms)

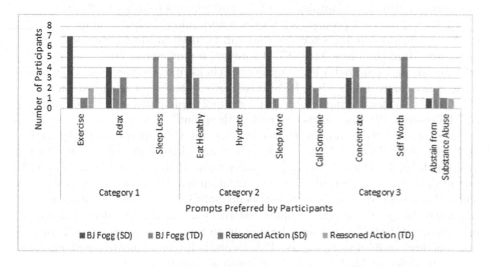

Fig. 5. Prompts preferred by group 2 (low or no depressive symptoms)

from 1–5 for all the prompts have shown a significant difference in means for the choices of FBM and TRA in favor of FBM. The mean score for FBM is 3.75 and for TRA is 2.54 and the results are significant ($p < 0.01$, $t = 5.02$).

There is a substantial difference in opinion between the participants of group 1 and group 2, which clearly shows that depression affects the perception of users about persuasion and behavior change. Participants of group 2 preferred FBM which persuades users with a direct message, straight away telling the user what to do. While group 1 preferred TRA which they found 'friendlier' and it provided them 'freedom of choice'. For example, participant-13 (group

1) mentioned, regarding Relax-TRA prompt, that "It gives more of a positive energy than telling the harms of not choosing the relaxation exercise. It is not imposing and does not make you want to shut the app or throw the phone". Similarly, another participant from group 1 stated for the self-worth-TRA prompt, "It seemed the most gentle and effective when communicating to someone who would be going through a harsh time". One of the participants from group 1 found TRA to be more understanding and friendlier, she said, "It seems more understanding rather than bugging. It is like if you don't want something or someone, its presence is not being imposed on you even if it is good for you like friends and family. It keeps your mood in mind and provides personal space." Furthermore, participant-4 from group 2 said about the Exercise-TRA prompts, "It gave me the option to do as I feel at my expense. It didn't seem offensive, didn't make me feel bad for not working out, gave an idea of what type of exercises to do as well as how to do them." These opinions and comments clearly indicate that when people suffer from depression, they prefer a tone that is more generous, gentle and friendly, something which TRA provided.

On the other hand, group 2 participants preferred the straight to the point prompts of FBM. For example, one of the participants from group 2 commented about their preferred prompt for Exercise and said, "It has a simpler layout, to the point and calming exercises that can be used in most situations". Similarly, regarding the Sleep More-FBM prompt, a participant said, "It had more information and required a lesser number of clicks, more to the point than other screens and more interactive. It addressed my problem of insomnia directly". On another instance, a participant from group 2 commented about the Hydrate-FBM Prompts, "It was interactive and to the point".

In general, both groups unanimously thought the prompts are informative and have great potential to inhibit behavioral change in users. They found prompts helpful and encouraging, e.g., participant-19 from group 1 gave a remark about the self-worth prompt, "It comforts an individual when they're down and when the existence of one's own self seems pointless and he/she thinks he/she can never be good enough". Finally, referring to the Eat Healthy Prompt, a participant stated, "I can relate the prompt to my daily routine where I usually take one kind of food more or less. This screen helped to educate me about roles played by different kinds of food in maintaining my health".

4.2 Second Study: Mobile Application

19 out of 21 participants from group 1 took part in a second study where they reviewed and tested the android application. These participants were asked to explore all the different screen flows of the application and provide feedback about its usability and acceptability.

Usability and Acceptability of the Application Overall participants were satisfied with the usability of the application and the average SUS score of the overall application (including prompts) was 87.9 %. According to our observation and the feedback of the participants, the design and flow of the application is user friendly. Almost all the users successfully completed all of the tasks given to them without getting stuck at any point. Only two participants found it difficult to navigate back to the main menu once they reached the last screen of one of the vertical flows. The reason for this could be that the application itself was android, while both participants were iPhone users. One of them (Participant 13) said, "I use an iPhone may be that is the reason I am unable to navigate back properly". Participant 3 commented about the usability of the application by saying, "The design is easy to understand, and the formatting of the content is quite good." In general, the feedback about the acceptability of the application was encouraging. All the participants said they would use the application and would also refer this application to others for use if available. They thought that the persuasive messages were conveyed through the prompts quite naturally not causing any discomfort. Participant 18 commented, "The persuasive prompts, and screening features of the application are really good, these features will help a lot in gauging the mental state of the user and also help in behavior change."

5   Discussion

5.1   Use of Persuasive Prompts for Behavior Change Based on Persuasive Models

Persuasive models are followed by mental professionals around the world to help people understand their mental situation and adopt changes accordingly. One of the main research objectives of this study was to identify if such models can be used with technology to create awareness and induce behavior change in people suffering from depressive symptoms. The results of our study show that there is high potential in the effectiveness of persuasive prompts to induce behavior change. However, it is also important to note that constricting ourselves to one model might not be the most adequate route to take; it can clearly be seen that different people prefer different models. While our results for group 1 clearly point in the direction of TRA, a few participants did prefer FBM. For group 2, majority of the sample selected FBM; however some did lean towards TRA. Furthermore, the clear difference in both groups allows us to better understand which models have what type of effect on a mental state. People who have depression prefer the gentler TRA model, while people who do not have depression and just want to get things done prefer the more aggressive FBM. This gives us further motivation to map the effects of a large number of persuasive models against different levels of depression.

From our visits to different psychiatrists, one common theme we observed was the use of kindness and encouragement when talking to a patient suffering from depression. For someone going through depression, something as simple as remembering to drink water can be difficult. Most of our participants that were clinically diagnosed with depression informed us that they do not have the motivation to get things done making it extremely difficult to get through a day and it is not just the lack of motivation, but also lack of wanting to be motivated. The use of persuasive prompts in a mobile application provides an effective medium through which encouragement and kindness can be a constant part of an individual's routine. The main focus of persuasive behavior change models is to provide encouragement in the form of motivation and to give reminders to ease the pressure of having to constantly remember what to do. This further strengthens the importance of not just mental health applications, but applications that are using persuasive models to help their users.

Preference of TRA by Patients with Depression: Majority of our users that suffered through depression anonymously chose TRA as their preferred model. This is a vital contribution of our paper as it provides more insight into what factors have a larger impact in intervention for depression patients. Through qualitative analysis and user feedback we were able to reflect on why TRA was preferred. As mentioned before, the prompts based on this model were of a softer tone, keeping in account the preferences of the users. Participants felt that their input was valued but at the same time they also felt that the prompts provided the required push to motivate them. They stated that the fact that even after the 'sad face' was chosen, the prompt still didn't give up on the user, rather it gently tried to change their mind, provided motivation to try the task. As a result of this, users were ultimately able to carry out the desired task which normally they would not be able to do. Patel et al. also makes a similar recommendation, the paper advises the practitioners to involve the patient extensively when planning out a treatment or intervention program for them as it would help the patient in making well informed choices with respect to their lifestyle to promote physical health and mental wellbeing [32].

General Implications of the Study: From the findings, we observed that there is potential for persuasive prompts to act as a viable intervention to encourage behavior change in people suffering with depression. If an individual with depressive symptoms who strongly suffers from the lack of motivation to carry out different tasks, can find the motivation to perform certain tasks assigned to them by a mobile application due to the nature of the prompts being shown, implies that the persuasive prompts have potential beyond the scope of this study. As lack of motivation is faced by individuals with and without depression, persuasive prompts can even be extended to daily use and not just be restricted to people with mental health issues. For instance, they can also be used by an individual who does not seem to have depressive symptoms, yet lacks motivation to reach the goals they have set for themselves. It is important to note that individuals who do not generally suffer from this problem would be further encouraged by either of the models.

5.2   Usability and Acceptability of an mHealth Application for Depression

As mentioned before, in a country like Pakistan a lack of awareness regarding mental health has resulted in people not even knowing if they are suffering from depression or anxiety. Furthermore, the stigma attached to this topic makes it more difficult for them to accept help from any source. In such a scenario, the biggest challenge is to identify if people would accept the general idea of mental health intervention and deem it appropriate in their setting. Our study has shown that mental health interventions for behavioral change are not only acceptable but welcomed by the younger generations of Pakistan. Most participants that took part in our study felt that the application has the potential to change the behavior of the user. They also took a keen interest in the study and provided feedback on how the features and design can be enhanced further to have a better impact. Majority of the participants were also comfortable with the content used in the prompts. Participants showed no signs of anger or discomfort while using the application and encouraged the idea of such interventions. Regarding the usability of the application, the SUS score of 87.9 and the qualitative feedback clearly shows that the application was simple, well designed and easy to use.

6 Conclusion

In this paper, we presented the results of the acceptability of the use of persuasive prompts to encourage behavioral change in people suffering from depression. We show that the use of persuasive models in an mHealth application can influence behavioral change and such models are acceptable. Furthermore, there was a distinct preference division between both user groups with regard to the preferred model. The Theory of Reasoned Action Model was preferred by users with depression, while users not showing symptoms of depression preferred the Fogg Behavioral Model. Future directions for this work include studying the long-term effects of persuasive prompts through mHealth applications and confirm their ability to induce behavioral change.

References

1. Mental disorders. https://www.who.int/en/news-room/fact-sheets/detail/mental-disorders. Accessed 06 Mar 2019
2. Ajzen, I., Fishbein, M.: Understanding attitudes and predicting social behaviour (1980)
3. Al-Eisa, E., Buragadda, S., Melam, G.R.: Association between physical activity and psychological status among Saudi female students. BMC Psychiatry 14(1), 238 (2014)
4. Andrade, L.H., et al.: Barriers to mental health treatment: results from the who world mental health surveys. Psychol. Med. 44(6), 1303–1317 (2014)
5. Association, A.P., et al.: Diagnostic and Statistical Manual of Mental Disorders (DSM-5®). American Psychiatric Publishing (2013)
6. Bakker, D., Kazantzis, N., Rickwood, D., Rickard, N.: Mental health smartphone apps: review and evidence-based recommendations for future developments. JMIR Ment. Health 3(1), e7 (2016)

7. Bardram, J.E., Frost, M., Szántó, K., Marcu, G.: The MONARCA self-assessment system: a persuasive personal monitoring system for bipolar patients. In: Proceedings of the 2nd ACM SIGHIT International Health Informatics Symposium, pp. 21–30. ACM (2012)
8. Brooke, J., et al.: SUS-a quick and dirty usability scale. Usability Eval. Ind. 189(194), 4–7 (1996)
9. Chekroud, S.R., et al.: Association between physical exercise and mental health in 1 · 2 million individuals in the USA between 2011 and 2015: a cross-sectional study. Lancet Psychiatry 5(9), 739–746 (2018)
10. Dennison, L., Morrison, L., Conway, G., Yardley, L.: Opportunities and challenges for smartphone applications in supporting health behavior change: qualitative study. J. Med. Internet Res. 15(4), e86 (2013)
11. Derman, E.W., Whitesman, S., Dreyer, M., Patel, D., Nossel, C., Schwellnus, M.: Healthy lifestyle interventions in general practice: Part 12: lifestyle and depression. S. Afr. Family Pract. 52(4), 271–275 (2010)
12. Doherty, G., Coyle, D., Sharry, J.: Engagement with online mental health interventions: an exploratory clinical study of a treatment for depression. In: Proceedings of the SIGCHI Conference on Human Factors in Computing Systems, pp. 1421–1430. ACM (2012)
13. Fogg, B.J.: A behavior model for persuasive design. In: Proceedings of the 4th international Conference on Persuasive Technology, p. 40. ACM (2009)
14. Gulliksen, J., Göransson, B., Boivie, I., Blomkvist, S., Persson, J., Cajander, Å.: Key principles for user-centred systems design. Behav. Inf. Technol. 22(6), 397–409 (2003)
15. Gulliver, A., Griffiths, K.M., Christensen, H.: Perceived barriers and facilitators to mental health help-seeking in young people: a systematic review. BMC Psychiatry 10(1), 113 (2010)
16. Kapungwe, A., et al.: Mental illness-stigma and discrimination in Zambia. Afr. J. Psychiatry 13(3) (2010)
17. Kelders, S.M., Kulyk, O.A., van Gemert-Pijnen, L., Oinas-Kukkonen, H.: Selecting effective persuasive strategies in behavior change support systems. In: BCSS@ PERSUASIVE, pp. 1–6 (2015)
18. Kessler, R.C.: The costs of depression. Psychiatr. Clin. 35(1), 1–14 (2012)
19. Kim, H.C.: Acceptability engineering: the study of user acceptance of innovative technologies. J. Appl. Res. Technol. 13(2), 230–237 (2015)
20. Kocielnik, R., Hsieh, G.: Send me a different message: utilizing cognitive space to create engaging message triggers. In: Proceedings of the 2017 ACM Conference on Computer Supported Cooperative Work and Social Computing, pp. 2193–2207. ACM (2017)
21. Kroenke, K., Spitzer, R.L., Williams, J.B.: The PHQ-9: validity of a brief depression severity measure. J. Gen. Intern. Med. 16(9), 606–613 (2001)
22. Kuo, P.Y.P., Horn, M.S.: Daily challenges for sustainable lifestyles: design implications from a mobile intervention study. In: Proceedings of the 2017 ACM International Joint Conference on Pervasive and Ubiquitous Computing and Proceedings of the 2017 ACM International Symposium on Wearable Computers, pp. 635–641. ACM (2017)
23. Langrial, S., Oinas-Kukkonen, H., Lappalainen, P., Lappalainen, R.: Rehearsing to control depressive symptoms through a behavior change support system. In: CHI 2013 Extended Abstracts on Human Factors in Computing Systems, pp. 385–390. ACM (2013)

24. Lentferink, A., Polstra, L., de Groot, M., Oldenhuis, H., Velthuijsen, H., van Gemert-Pijnen, L.: The values of self-tracking and persuasive eCoaching according to employees and human resource advisors for a workplace stress management application: a qualitative study. In: Ham, J., Karapanos, E., Morita, P.P., Burns, C.M. (eds.) PERSUASIVE 2018. LNCS, vol. 10809, pp. 160–171. Springer, Cham (2018). https://doi.org/10.1007/978-3-319-78978-1_13

25. Likert, R.: A technique for the measurement of attitudes. Archives of psychology (1932)

26. Marcu, G., Bardram, J.E., Gabrielli, S.: A framework for overcoming challenges in designing persuasive monitoring and feedback systems for mental illness. In: 2011 5th International Conference on Pervasive Computing Technologies for Healthcare (PervasiveHealth) and Workshops, pp. 1–8. IEEE (2011)

27. McCallum, C., Rooksby, J., Gray, C.M.: Evaluating the impact of physical activity apps and wearables: interdisciplinary review. JMIR mHealth uHealth 6(3), e58 (2018)

28. Meyer, J.D., Koltyn, K.F., Stegner, A.J., Kim, J.S., Cook, D.B.: Influence of exercise intensity for improving depressed mood in depression: a dose-response study. Behav. Ther. 47(4), 527–537 (2016)

29. Nahum-Shani, I., Hekler, E.B., Spruijt-Metz, D.: Building health behavior models to guide the development of just-in-time adaptive interventions: a pragmatic framework. Health Psychol. 34(S), 1209 (2015)

30. Olff, M.: Mobile mental health: a challenging research agenda. Eur. J. Psychotraumatology 6(1), 27882 (2015)

31. Organization, W.H., et al.: International classification of diseases, 11th revision (icd-11) (2018). Recuperado de http://www.who.int/classifications/icd/en

32. Patel, M.S., Asch, D.A., Volpp, K.G.: Wearable devices as facilitators, not drivers, of health behavior change. JAMA 313(5), 459–460 (2015)

33. Ruusunen, A., et al.: How does lifestyle intervention affect depressive symptoms? Results from the Finnish Diabetes Prevention Study. Diabet. Med. 29(7), e126–e132 (2012)

34. Schlarb, A.A., Claßen, M., Grünwald, J., Vögele, C.: Sleep disturbances and mental strain in university students: results from an online survey in Luxembourg and Germany. Int. J. Ment. Health Syst. 11(1), 24 (2017)

35. Thieme, A., et al.: Challenges for designing new technology for health and wellbeing in a complex mental healthcare context. In: Proceedings of the 2016 CHI Conference on Human Factors in Computing Systems, pp. 2136–2149. ACM (2016)

36. Wais-Zechmann, B., Gattol, V., Neureiter, K., Orji, R., Tscheligi, M.: Persuasive technology to support chronic health conditions: investigating the optimal persuasive strategies for persons with COPD. In: Ham, J., Karapanos, E., Morita, P.P., Burns, C.M. (eds.) PERSUASIVE 2018. LNCS, vol. 10809, pp. 255–266. Springer, Cham (2018). https://doi.org/10.1007/978-3-319-78978-1_21

37. Weidner, G., Connor, S.L., Hollis, J.F., Connor, W.E.: Improvements in hostility and depression in relation to dietary change and cholesterol lowering: the family heart study. Ann. Intern. Med. 117(10), 820–823 (1992)

38. Zhang, C., Starczewski, A.P., Lakens, D., IJsselsteijn, W.A.: A decision-making perspective on coaching behavior change: a field experiment on promoting exercise at work. In: Ham, J., Karapanos, E., Morita, P.P., Burns, C.M. (eds.) PERSUASIVE 2018. LNCS, vol. 10809, pp. 87–98. Springer, Cham (2018). https://doi.org/10.1007/978-3-319-78978-1_7

The UX Construct – Does the Usage Context Influence the Outcome of User Experience Evaluations?

Andreas Sonderegger[1]([⊠]), Andreas Uebelbacher[2], and Jürgen Sauer[3]

[1] EPFL+ECAL Lab, EPFL Lausanne, Lausanne, Switzerland
andreas.sonderegger@epfl.ch
[2] Access for All, Zürich, Switzerland
[3] Department of Psychology, University of Fribourg, Fribourg, Switzerland

Abstract. How are different measures of user experience (UX) related to each other? And does it differ if a technological device is used for work or leisure with regard to UX? In the present study, the influence of context factors (i.e. usage domain) on the outcomes of UX tests is examined. Using a 2×2 experimental design, in addition to usage domain (work vs. leisure), system usability was manipulated (normal vs. delayed response time). Sixty participants completed various tasks with a mobile internet application. Performance indicators and subjective indicators of UX were recorded (e.g. emotion, perceived usability, and task load). Interestingly, results indicated little evidence for an influence of usage context on UX. System usability showed the expected effects on performance and on user emotion, whereas no influence on perceived usability was observed. In addition, the correlations between the different measures of UX were rather low, indicating that it is advisable to assess UX by distinct dimensions. Implications of these results for practice and research are discussed.

Keywords: User experience · UX · UX test · UX measures ·
System response time · Usage domain · Perceived usability · User performance

1 Introduction

There is a long tradition in psychology to conceive behaviour as being highly dependent on context [1]. This also applies to the field of human-computer interaction (HCI), where context is considered one of the main determinants of user behaviour when operating interactive systems [2]. The importance of the concept is reiterated by the fact that it is also part of ISO FDIS 9241-210, which defines context as covering users, tasks and equipment, and the specific social and physical environment in which a product is used [3]. In this regard, a product's usability can only be evaluated taking into account the context in which the product will be used [4]. In other words, a system that may be usable in one context may not be in another. Context factors however play not only an important role in the evaluation of usability of a system but may influence the entire experience of a user. User experience (UX) can be considered an extension of the usability construct, which has a focus on user cognition and performance, by adopting a more holistic approach focusing on user emotions and considering the

© IFIP International Federation for Information Processing 2019
Published by Springer Nature Switzerland AG 2019
D. Lamas et al. (Eds.): INTERACT 2019, LNCS 11749, pp. 140–157, 2019.
https://doi.org/10.1007/978-3-030-29390-1_8

experience of a user interacting with an interface in its entirety. The assumption of such a holistic approach to the construct suggests to individually assess and report the various facets of experience in UX evaluations.

While users, tasks and equipment are routinely specified in UX studies, the environmental aspects of context are rarely considered in practice and research [5, 6]. However, empirical work has provided evidence that a number of context factors might influence the outcomes of UX tests, such as lab vs. field set-up [7], observer presence [8, 9], or the use of electronic recording equipment [10]. One important characteristic of the usage environment which received little attention in previous research is the influence of the usage domains of leisure and work context on outcomes of UX evaluations.

2   Current State of Research

2.1   The UX Construct

Up into the 1980s, most people experienced interactive technology almost exclusively in the workplace [11]. Since then, information technology became an integral part of our daily lives and increasingly pervades all societal activities (e.g. personal computers have reached people's homes, and mobile phones have become mobile computing devices). Today, the pervasiveness of interactive technology in all areas of people's lives, including leisure, is a reality [12]. In this process, the distinction between technology for work and technology for leisure use has become increasingly fuzzy, as devices often cannot be described anymore as clearly being one or the other. Many of today's technical devices are dual-domain products [13], as they can equally be used in a work context as in a leisure context (e.g. mobile phones and laptops).

Since research in HCI traditionally concentrated on interactive technology in the work domain, the discipline was primarily performance oriented, with the goal to provide highly usable interfaces to increase efficiency at work [14]. This is reflected in the usability definition of the International Standardisation Organisation (ISO), which describes the concept in terms of efficiency and effectiveness (and satisfaction) with which a user can accomplish certain tasks with a system [3]. As a result of a recent shift in the domain towards a less functional and more experiential approach, the notion of UX has gained an increased interest in research and practice. Despite its popularity, the term UX is often criticised for being ill defined and elusive [1, 15]. While some theorists adopted a rather holistic approach describing UX as the totality of actions, sensations, thinking, feelings and meaning-making of a person in a specific situational context [e.g. 16, 17], others attempted to be more concise and focus on emotions or affective states when UX is described [e.g. 18–20]. This piece of research follows a holistic view defining UX as an umbrella construct which encompasses the entire experiential space of person interacting with a system. In this respect, UX enlarges the mere functional concept of usability (e.g. effectiveness, efficiency, subjective appraisal) by explicitly encompassing a broad range of other experiential components (c.f. Fig. 1). This holistic view of UX implies however the difficulty of a meaningful and effective assessment of the construct. This is because it might be rather complicated to measure *everything* a user experiences when interacting with a system. Furthermore, the holistic view of UX makes it difficult to estimate one exact UX score since it is not clear how measures of affective sates are to be combined with indicators of performance and evaluations of satisfaction and workload. In this regard, we suggest to define the most relevant experiential facets or dimensions for each UX evaluation individually based on the specific needs and requirements of the project. These facets or dimensions should then be assessed and reported individually (as suggested to some extent by [21] in their UX scale, see also [6, 15, 22]).

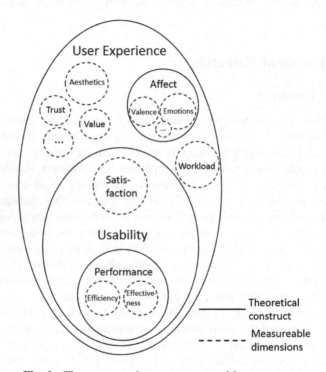

Fig. 1. The user experience construct and its components

2.2 Work vs. Leisure Domain

As a result of the shift from usability to UX, research in HCI has started to increasingly evaluate leisure-oriented technology, such as portable digital audio players [23] or video games [24]. For dual-domain products, however, both domains are equally relevant and different requirements may result from these contexts, which might need to be considered during product evaluation. In order to identify the domain-specific requirements, the differences between work and leisure need to be analysed. There is one previous study that empirically compared work and leisure domains but found little differences between them [13]. However, this may be due to the fact that in addition to usage domain, product aesthetics was manipulated as a second factor. It was assumed that aesthetics would play a more important role in a leisure context than at work but this was not confirmed. Since system usability is a more direct determinant of effectiveness and efficiency of use than aesthetics, its influence in different usage domains is worth examining.

In addition to the lack of empirical research in that field, there have also been difficulties in establishing a clear theoretical distinction between work and leisure so that no widely accepted definition of the concepts has yet been proposed. Three approaches to distinguish between the two domains have been discussed [25]. (a) The purely time-based or 'residual' definition of leisure is most commonly used. According to this approach, leisure is when people do not do paid or unpaid work, do not complete personal chores, and do not fulfil obligations. (b) An activity-based approach distinguishes between work and leisure by means of specific behaviours people show in each domain. (c) The third approach conceives work and leisure by the attitudes people have towards their activities. Beatty and Torbert [25] argue that the third approach is considered to be most promising to distinguish leisure from other domains, and there is also some empirical evidence in support of this approach. Several studies confirmed that people described work in terms of goal-directed and performance-oriented behaviour and connected with external rewards while leisure was associated with intrinsic satisfaction, enjoyment, novelty and relaxation [26, 27].

The distinction between work and leisure domain according to this third approach allows for a more precise definition of domain-specific requirements for interactive technology. Since users perceive a work context as more goal- and performance-oriented than a leisure context, usability (e.g. effectiveness and efficiency of task completion) might be perceived by users as a more important requirement in a work than in a leisure context.

2.3 Response Time as a Facet of System Usability

One aspect of system usability which previous research has shown to be directly relevant for various outcome variables is system response time (SRT). SRT is defined as the time it takes from a user input to the moment the system starts to display the response [28]. Although delayed SRT are less of a problem with today's much increased processing power, delays may still be a problem in human-computer interaction [29, 30].

Negative effects of SRT delays have been shown at several levels. First, there is evidence that response time delays have a negative effect on user satisfaction with a system [31–34]. Systems with delayed responses are generally perceived as being less usable and more strenuous to operate, which also extends to web pages with long download times being judged to be less interesting [35]. Second, user performance has been shown to be impaired by SRT delays [28, 29, 36, 37]. Third, system delays have resulted in impaired psychophysiological well-being, increased anxiety, frustration and stress, and were even found to reduce job satisfaction [31, 38–41].

Various moderators of the effects of system response delays have been identified in the context of internet usage, such as webpage properties [42] user expectations [43], and processing information displays such as progress bars [44]. For example, users were less willing to accept download delays when websites were highly graphical compared to plain text documents [42]. It also emerged that information about the duration of the download had a positive effect on user evaluation [43], and progress bars as delay indicators performed best in terms of user preference and acceptability of the waiting time [44]. To our knowledge, only one study has researched SRT in a work context [31]. Conducting a field study in a large telephone circuit utility observing professionals in their work domain, the authors reported that increased SRT not only impaired performance but also system evaluation and even job satisfaction. To our knowledge, no study investigated SRT delays in a leisure context so far.

2.4   The Present Study

The main goal of the present study was to investigate the requirements that result from the two domains of work and leisure with respect to UX design and evaluation. For this purpose, a UX test was conducted in which the two domains of work and leisure were experimentally modelled. The two types of testing context were created by a combination of various experimental manipulations such as lab design (office vs. living room), task wording (work related vs. leisure related) and a priming task which directed participants' attention towards their own work or leisure activities, respectively. As a second independent variable, system usability was manipulated through SRT delays.

As a test system, an internet site was specifically set up for the experiment, which was designed to offer realistic tasks for both contexts. Care was taken that the tasks for the two experimental conditions were comparable in terms of mental demands but only differed in type of context. The tasks used were information search tasks that required navigating through various levels of a menu hierarchy.

Typical measures for UX evaluation were recorded. Task performance was assessed by task completion rate, page inspection time, and efficiency of task completion. Self-report data was collected for emotion, task load and perceived usability.

Our hypotheses were as follows: (a) Test participants in the work context perform better and report higher perceived task demands than those in the leisure context, since the work context is perceived as more goal- and performance-oriented. (b) Performance is lower when working in the condition with low usability compared to working with high usability. (c) Perceived usability of the system and emotional reactions are less positive in the low usability condition, since the reduced system usability is reflected in participants' evaluation and emotion. (d) At work, low usability causes a stronger decrease in perceived usability and in emotion than in the leisure context, since the negative impact of system delay on performance is perceived as more relevant in the goal- and performance-oriented work context.

3   Method

3.1   Participants

The sample of the experiment consisted of 60 participants, aged between 19 and 44 years ($M = 22.6$ yrs; $SD = 3.3$), the majority of which were female (60.3%). Participants were recruited among students at the University of Fribourg (Switzerland), and it was made sure that none of them had previous usage experience with the specific mobile phone model employed in the experiment. To motivate participants to take part in the study, they could enter a prize draw (worth 50 $).

3.2 Experimental Design

A 2 × 2 between-subjects design was used to investigate the two independent variables usage domain and usability. Usage domain was varied at two levels (work vs. leisure context), and so was usability (high vs. delayed system response time).

3.3 Measures and Instruments

Performance
The following three measures of user performance were recorded: (a) task completion rate (percentage of successfully completed tasks); (b) page inspection time (time a user stays on a page); (c) efficiency of task completion (minimum number of interactions needed for task completion divided by actual number of interactions). Participants were allowed to work on each task for a maximum of 5 min, after which a task was recorded as failed and participants moved on to the next task. All analyses of performance data took into account the shorter overall time participants had available in the delay condition (i.e. delay time was deducted from task completion time).

Affective State
The PANAS scale ('Positive and Negative Affect Schedule' [45]) was used to measure short-term changes in affective states before and after task completion. The scale allows the assessment of two independent dimensions of affect: positive and negative affect. It was shown to have good psychometric properties (Cronbach's $\alpha = 0.84$). The scale uses 20 adjectives to describe different affective states (e.g. 'interested', 'exciting', 'strong'), for which the intensity is rated on a 5-point Likert scale ('very slightly or not at all', 'a little', 'moderately', 'quite a bit', 'extremely').

Task Load
To assess task load the well-established NASA task load index (TLX) was used [46]. It measures the six dimensions of task load: mental demands, physical demands, temporal demands, performance, effort and frustration. In the subsequent analysis, each dimension was given the same weight. Based on our data, psychometric properties were shown to be satisfactory for the translated scale (Cronbach's $\alpha = 0.72$).

Perceived Usability
Perceived usability of the test system was measured by two instruments. First, we used a 100 mm visual analogue scale to measure an overall evaluation of perceived usability ('This website is usable') [8]. The use of one-item scales to evaluate technical systems was found to be appropriate, as other work has shown [e.g. 47]. Second, the PSSUQ ('Post Study System Usability Questionnaire') [48] was applied, which was slightly modified to be relevant for the test system in question (the term 'system' was replaced by 'software' to make sure only the software and not the device was judged). The scale consists of 19 items and uses a 7-point Likert scale (ranging from 'strongly agree' to

'strongly disagree'). The questionnaire was developed for usage in usability tests in a lab setting, and the author [48] reports very good psychometric properties (Cronbach's $\alpha > 0.90$).

Previous Mobile Phone Experience

Previous mobile phone experience was assessed by a visual analogue scale on which participants reported an intermediate self-rated mobile phone experience of 5.0 on a scale ranging from 0 to 10 (labelled 'not experienced' and 'very experienced'). They indicated using their devices 12.6 times on average during a day. Mobile phone experience and daily usage were used as covariates in the analysis.

3.4   Materials: Mobile Phone, Server and Software

The test device was a Motorola Android smartphone. The web application was running on a server software XAMPP. In the delay condition, a PHP script was running on the server and generated a random system response delay of between 0 s and 3 s (1.3 s on average) whenever a new page was requested. These system delays were chosen based on pre-tests which showed that changing intervals were perceived as more disturbing than constant (and hence predictable) ones. In addition, the pilot tests have shown that latencies of more than 4 s were not considered realistic. A server log recorded the pages viewed, the time at which the page was accessed, the duration during which the page was displayed and the size of the delay.

The web application used for task completion was specifically set up for the experiment. It consisted of a tourist guide for a large European city containing a hierarchical navigation system, offering a number of categories at each level and detailed pages at the deepest level. Navigation options were 'return to the previous page', 'return directly to the home page', or selecting one of the displayed categories. Scrolling was necessary for some of the pages, which had a larger number of categories than the screen could display. Category labels were deliberately named such that it was not always obvious in which the target page would be found so that a trial and error approach to target search became necessary (e.g. a specific Asian restaurant was located under the category 'Japanese', while other categories available included 'Asian', 'Chinese', 'German', 'Greek', 'Indonesian', and 'Italian'). A message on the target page stated clearly that the task had been solved and requested that the user directly went back to the home page.

3.5   Procedure

Participants were randomly assigned to one of the four testing conditions. The testing sessions were conducted in a usability laboratory at the University of Fribourg. The experimental manipulation of the usage domain consisted of three factors: laboratory set up, task wording and priming task. With regard to the *laboratory set up* for the leisure condition, the lab was set up like a living room, containing a sofa (on which the participant was seated), wooden furniture with travel books, a (switched off) TV set, plants on the window sill, and pictures on the wall. In the work condition, the laboratory contained several desks, a (switched off) computer, a desk lamp, some folders and typical office stationery (stapler, etc.). The *tasks* used in this study were the same in all experimental groups with regard to the interactions they required to be accomplished successfully. Tasks differed however with regard to the framing that was used, with work-specific context presented in the work condition (e.g. plan a meeting in a café with colleagues to discuss a work-related assignment) and leisure-context (e.g. plan a get-together to meet with friends in a café) for the leisure condition. For the *priming task* in the work condition, participants were asked to imagine that they would be working the following two days and to think about what they would have to do during these days. A similar instruction was given in the condition simulating the leisure context.

The experimenter described the purpose of the experiment as testing the usability of a web application for smartphones, giving an overview of the experimental procedure. Participants filled in the PANAS and the questionnaire measuring previous mobile phone experience. The experimenter presented the test device, showed all functions of the web application and explained how to operate it (e.g. choosing categories, home, back, scrolling). Participants completed a practice trial to become familiar with the web application. They were given the opportunity to ask questions, and then instructions about the usage context were provided and participants were asked to start the introspection phase. After one minute of introspection for putting oneself into a specific work or leisure situation, the experimenter informed the participants about the first task. They had five minutes for each task, but were not informed about this time constraint. If the task was not completed after five minutes, the experimenter thanked them and presented them the next task. After the last task, the participants completed the PANAS a second time, then the NASA-TLX, the subjective usability questionnaires (one-item scale and PSSUQ), and finally the manipulation check. The participants were debriefed and could leave their e-mail address to take part in the draw. The duration of a testing session was about 45 min.

3.6 Manipulation Check

The manipulation check consisted of a visual analogue scale (0–100; ranging from 'rather leisure-oriented' to 'rather work-oriented'), on which participants judged the situation in which they completed the tasks. Results confirmed a significant impact of the context manipulation, as participants indicated to have experienced the situation significantly more work-related in the work context condition ($M = 56.4$; $SD = 2.2$), compared to the leisure context condition ($M = 27.7$; $SD = 2.4$; $t(58) = 4.82$; $p < 0.001$, Cohen's $d = 1.24$).

4 Results

Self-reported mobile phone experience, daily mobile usage and gender were entered as covariates into the analysis in order to control for their influence. However, the analysis showed that none of the covariates had a significant influence on the reported findings. Therefore, results of the data analysis without covariates are reported.

4.1   User Performance

Task Completion Rate

Data analysis showed significant differences in the number of completed tasks as a function of the usability manipulation (see Table 1). When operating the system with a delayed response, participants solved significantly fewer tasks ($M = 83.3\%$) than when response time was not delayed ($M = 93.3\%$; $F = 5.28$; $df = 1$, 56; $p < 0.05$; $\eta^2_{partial} = .086$). Testing context (work vs. leisure) had no effect and there was no interaction between usability and testing context (both $F < 1$).

Task Completion Time

Overall task completion time differed significantly with regard to the usability manipulation (see Table 1). When operating the system with a delayed response, participants took longer to complete the tasks (corrected by the delay time) than when response time was not delayed ($M_{delayed} = 526.7$, $SD = 145.4$; $M_{undelayed} = 397$, $SD = 126.5$; $F = 13$; $df = 1$, 56; $p < 0.05$; $\eta^2_{partial} = .19$). Testing context (work vs. leisure) had no effect and there was no interaction between usability and testing context (both $F < 1$).

Page Inspection Time

As the data in Table 1 indicates, participants in the delay condition stayed significantly longer on a page ($M = 5.84$ s) than those working with a non-delayed system ($M = 5.33$ s). This difference was statistically significant ($F = 4.46$; $df = 1$, 56; $p < 0.05$; $\eta^2_{partial} = .188$). With regard to the other independent factors, there was neither a significant effect of testing context ($F < 1$) nor an interaction ($F < 1$).

Efficiency of Task Completion

An important indicator of user efficiency is determined by the calculation of the ratio of the actual number of user inputs and the optimal number of user inputs. The data in Table 1 indicate overall a medium level of efficiency of about $M = 0.4$. This efficiency index shows that 40% of the user inputs contributed towards task completion, whereas the remaining inputs did not directly lead to the task goal or were part of a less direct path towards task completion. This indicates that the tasks were reasonably difficult to solve. As the data in Table 1 suggests, there was little difference between conditions, which was confirmed by analysis of variance (all $F < 1$).

4.2   Subjective Ratings

Affective State

For the analysis of the emotional state of the user as a consequence of using the product, a comparison was made between the baseline measurement (i.e. prior to task completion) and a second measurement taken after task completion. This analysis revealed a change in positive affect as a function of SRT. While participants reported an increase in positive affect after task completion when working with a non-delayed system ($M = 0.12$), lower positive affect was reported when working with a delayed system ($M = -0.17$; $F = 4.67$; $df = 1$, 56; $p < 0.05$; $\eta^2_{partial} = .077$). Regarding the changes in negative affect, no significant difference was found ($F < 1$). As the data in

Table 1 shows, testing context had no effect on the change of positive affect levels and there was no interaction either (both $F < 1$). Equally, there was no effect on the change of negative affect ($F = 2.98$; $df = 1, 56$; $p > 0.05$; $\eta^2_{partial} = .051$), nor was there an interaction ($F < 1$).

Task Load

The data for the overall NASA-TLX score are presented in Table 1. While this indicates overall a low task load score, there was generally very little difference between experimental conditions. This was confirmed by analysis of variance, which revealed neither a main effect for the two independent factors nor an interaction between them (all $F < 1$). To evaluate whether any differences could be found at the single item level, a separate analysis of the NASA-TLX items was carried out. Also, this analysis did not show any significant effect.

Perceived Usability

The data for perceived usability, as measured by the PSSUQ, are presented in Table 1. Interestingly, the expected effect of SRT did not affect subjective usability evaluations, with ratings being nearly identical in both conditions ($F < 1$). Usability ratings appeared to be higher in the work domain than in the leisure domain but this difference failed to reach significance ($F = 2.01$; $df = 1, 52$; $p > 0.05$). No interaction between the two factors was found ($F < 1$). An additional analysis examined the PSSUQ

Table 1. Measures of user performance, affective state, task load, and perceived usability as a function of usage domain and usability.

	Leisure context		Work context		
	No delay Mean (SD)	Delayed Mean (SD)	No delay Mean (SD)	Delayed Mean (SD)	Overall Mean (SD)
Task completion rate (%)	96.4 (9.1)	82.8 (21.8)	90.6 (15.5)	83.9 (18.6)	88.3 (17.5)
Task completion time (s)	395.9 (96.5)	534 (168.7)	397.9 (151.2)	518.3 (119.2)	461.8 (150.1)
Page inspection time (s)	5.34 (1.04)	5.93 (1.19)	5.32 (0.75)	5.73 (0.54)	5.58 (0.94)
Efficiency of task completion	0.41 (0.08)	0.39 (0.15)	0.39 (0.13)	0.38 (0.12)	0.39 (0.12)
Affective state (1–5)					
Positive affect (Δ: pre-post)	0.09 (0.42)	−0.15 (0.48)	0.14 (0.56)	−0.20 (0.59)	−0.03 (0.53)
Negative affect (Δ: pre-post)	−0.29 (2.23)	−1.31 (2.50)	0.44 (3.05)	0.21 (2.08)	−0.25 (2.55)
Task load (1–20)	8.3 (1.5)	7.4 (2.7)	8.0 (3.0)	7.8 (3.0)	7.8 (2.6)
Perceived usability (1–7)	4.7 (0.88)	4.5 (1.33)	4.9 (1.02)	5.0 (0.86)	4.8 (1.03)

Δ: all values represent changes from baseline (pre) to task completion phase (post); a positive value denotes an increase.

subscales separately but revealed the same pattern of results as for the overall scale. Finally, results for the one-item usability scale indicated an overall rating of $M = 52.2$ with little differences between the four experimental conditions (all $F < 1$), herewith confirming the results pattern found for the PSSUQ.

4.3   Correlational Analysis of Data

In addition to the comparisons between experimental conditions using analyses of variance, the size of correlations between variables may provide further insights for a better understanding of the UX construct and the interplay of its different components. This point has notably been addressed by Hornbæk and Law [49] arguing that studies in this domain should report such correlations in order to facilitate interpretation and comparison of outcomes.

Interestingly, correlation coefficients (see Table 2) indicate in general rather low correlations between the different UX measures. Significant relationships were found for the different measures of objective performance, whereas performance indicators showed only small correlations with evaluation of perceived usability and task load. In contrast, subjective evaluation of task load was negatively correlated with perceived usability. Furthermore, negative affect showed significant links with perceived task load and task completion rate (c.f. Table 2).

Table 2. Correlations between different UX measures (N = 60).

	Task completion time (s)	Efficiency of task completion	Task load	Perceived usability	Positive affect	Negative affect
Task completion rate (%)	−.38**	.12	−.23	.16	.14	−.29*
Task completion time (s)		−.72**	.19	−.08	−.17	.18
Efficiency of task completion			−.09	.13	.24	-.11
Task load				−.26*	−.05	.36**
Perceived usability					.24	−.25
Positive affect						.03

* Correlation is significant at the 0.05 level (2-tailed).
** Correlation is significant at the 0.01 level (2-tailed).

5   Discussion

The aim of the study was to investigate the influence of usage domain on the outcomes of user experience evaluations and whether any such influence would be mediated by poor system usability in the form of SRT delays. The findings showed that, contrary to expectations, usage domain did not have the expected impact, with none of the measures showing differences between domains. In contrast, system response time showed the expected effects on performance and on user emotion whereas, surprisingly, no influence on perceived usability was observed.

Given that context of use has been considered an important determinant of usability [4] and that the two domains of work and leisure have been associated with different perceptions and behaviour [26], we expected that testing a product in one domain would produce differences in usability test results compared to the other domain. The manipulation check showed very clearly that participants perceived the leisure domain differently from the work domain. Despite this successful manipulation of context (involving different usability lab set-ups, domain-specific task instructions, and a priming task), there were no differences in usability test results, neither for performance nor for subjective measures. Although it is important to interpret non-significant results with caution [50], the publication and discussion of such findings is still very important [51–53].

A possible interpretation of this nil-result might be that there is no need for practitioners to test dual-domain products in both usage domains. The domains of work and leisure may not require specific consideration in test set-ups, as long as the relevant use cases are covered in the test. The absence of an interaction between usage domain and system usability strengthens this argument, suggesting that even under conditions of impaired system usability the work domain provides test results that are no different from the leisure domain. One previous study comparing work and leisure domains also found little difference between these two application domains [13]. However, in that study the usability of the technical device was not manipulated. Taken together, this study and the present work provide first evidence that across a range of conditions (i.e. different levels of product aesthetics and of product usability) the influence of usage domains appears to be of smaller magnitude than expected. The results support Lindroth and Nilsson's [54] claim that environmental aspects of usage context are generally not an important issue in usability testing as long as stationary technology usage is concerned (which was the case in the present study as the smartphone was operated like a desktop device). While Lindroth and Nilsson did not empirically test their proposition, the present work provides first empirical evidence to support it. Additional research (i.e. replication studies) corroborating these results are required however, in order to be able to interpret such nil-results as arguments for practitioners to refrain from considering usage context in UX evaluation.

While these nil-results do not allow us (yet) to make such a decisive statement with regard to the context-dependency of UX evaluation outcomes, the findings have some implications for researchers and practitioners interested in the domain dependence of UX evaluation. The results of this study indicate that the manipulation of the usage context (as suggested in this piece of research) did not show the expected effect.

Although the successful manipulation check indicated that a distinction was made by participants in this study, this manipulation showed no influence on UX measures. This may raise some concerns with regard to the extent to which motivational processes associated with the usage context could be appropriately reproduced in the lab. However, it has to be noted that this problem would affect all lab-based UX assessment, independently of the domain. In addition, previous research has shown that lab-based testing often provides similar results compared to conducting tests in the field [55]. In this context, the sample recruited for this study needs to be considered as a limitation since the work context of students may not be fully transferable to salary workers. Therefore it might be worthwhile to address this research question with an additional user sample. Nonetheless do these results provide a strong argument for the need for additional field-based research addressing the influence of usage-context in UX assessment, preferably by making a direct comparison with lab-based data.

While usage domain had little impact on the results of usability testing, a number of effects of poor system usability were found, confirming several of our research hypotheses. First, it emerged that poor system usability had the hypothesised negative effect on task performance. When SRT was delayed, task completion rate was lower and participants spent more time on a page, compared to participants working with a system without delays. These findings are consistent with an extensive body of research showing a negative impact of delayed system response on performance [e.g. 31, 37]. One explanation for this effect is that users adapt their speed of task completion to SRT and work faster when the system responds more promptly [56]. An alternative explanation for longer page inspection times under delayed SRT could be that participants adjusted their strategy, moving from a trial and error approach to a more reflective one, thus reducing the number of delayed system responses. Previous work has shown that even short SRT delays made participants consider their actions more carefully [38, 57].

Second, poor usability had a negative effect on participants' affective state, consistent with our hypothesis. When working with a delayed system, participants showed a stronger reduction in positive affect than when working with a non-delayed system. This finding is consistent with an extensive body of research, showing negative effects of delayed SRT on various aspects of affective states, such as frustration, anxiety, stress and impatience [e.g. 38–40]. The present study adds to these findings by showing that such effects on emotion may occur, even if such SRT delays are short.

Third, although poor system usability had a negative effect on performance and affected participants' emotional state, no such effects were found for perceived usability. This observation is of particular interest since other work found a substantial positive association between performance and preference [58]. While users generally provide a more positive evaluation when systems are more usable, Nielsen and Levy [58] also cited some cases in their meta-analysis, in which users preferred systems, with which they performed worse. These systems, however, had rather short SRT delays and performance impairments did not reach critical levels. The magnitude of the delay in our study might have been below that critical level and therefore did not have an effect on perceived usability. An alternative explanation for the observed finding is that participants did perceive such delays but the SRT delay was not associated with the application but with the server from which the pages were downloaded. Similar observations were made in other work where users of internet-based software attributed the cause of delayed response to internet connection rather than the software itself [59]. Overall, although we employed rather short SRT delays, most of our hypotheses were confirmed, which highlights the importance of paying attention to even short delays during system design as it may affect performance and user emotion.

The correlational analysis of the different measures of the UX construct revealed in general rather low correlations. Objective performance measures, subjective evaluations of usability and affective states as important aspects describing an experience episode seem to be rather independent dimensions and hence should be assessed and reported separately when UX is the scope of measurement. Hence, a combination into a single UX-score seems not to be useful. These findings are in line with results of previous studies indicating that measures of user performance often have only a weak link to subjective measures of usability [49, 57, see also 60]. Radar charts might represent a useful and easy to understand way to display results of a holistic UX evaluation consisting of different dimensions or facets. Results of this study could represented as suggested in Fig. 2 with regard to the evaluation of the two different versions of the prototype.

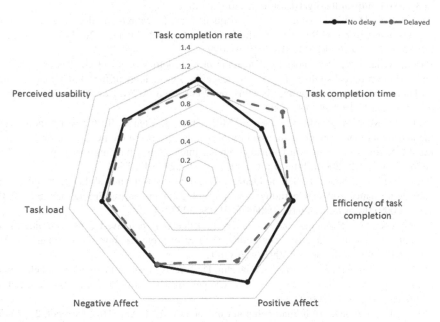

Fig. 2. Presentation of the results of UX evaluations of the two versions of the mobile app as radar diagram

The findings presented have several implications for research and practice. First, the findings provide first evidence that results of a usability test can be transferred between the work and the leisure domain. This would facilitate usability testing of dual-domain products for practitioners since several testing contexts would not have to be covered so that they only need to ensure that the relevant tasks are included in the test set-up. Second, practitioners and researchers interested in context-dependent UX evaluation should address this issue in field-based research. Third, even rather short delays in SRT can have an effect on performance as well as on user emotion, suggesting that careful consideration should be given to SRT in product design and evaluation.

References

1. Law, E., Roto, V., Vermeeren, A.P.O.S., Kort, J., Hassenzahl, M.: Towards a shared definition of user experience. In: CHI 2008, Extended Abstracts on Human Factors in Computing Systems, pp. 2395–2398. ACM, New York (2008). https://doi.org/10.1145/1358628.1358693
2. Bevan, N., Macleod, M.: Usability measurement in context. Behav. Inf. Technol. **13**, 132–145 (1994). https://doi.org/10.1080/01449299408914592
3. ISO 9241-210:2010: Ergonomics of human-system interaction – Part 210: human-centred design for interactive systems (2010). http://www.iso.org/cms/render/live/en/sites/isoorg/contents/data/standard/05/20/52075.html
4. Maguire, M.: Context of use within usability activities. Int. J. Hum.-Comput. Stud. **55**, 453–483 (2001). https://doi.org/10.1006/ijhc.2001.0486
5. Alonso-Ríos, D., Vázquez-García, A., Mosqueira-Rey, E., Moret-Bonillo, V.: A context-of-use taxonomy for usability studies. Int. J. Hum.-Comput. Interact. **26**, 941–970 (2010). https://doi.org/10.1080/10447318.2010.502099
6. Bargas-Avila, J.A., Hornbaek, K.: Old wine in new bottles or novel challenges: a critical analysis of empirical studies of user experience. In: Proceedings of the SIGCHI Conference on Human Factors in Computing Systems, pp. 2689–2698. ACM, New York (2011). https://doi.org/10.1145/1978942.1979336
7. Nielsen, C.M., Overgaard, M., Pedersen, M.B., Stage, J., Stenild, S.: It's worth the hassle!: the added value of evaluating the usability of mobile systems in the field. In: Proceedings of the 4th Nordic Conference on Human-computer Interaction: Changing Roles, pp. 272–280. ACM, New York (2006). https://doi.org/10.1145/1182475.1182504
8. Sonderegger, A., Sauer, J.: The influence of laboratory set-up in usability tests: effects on user performance, subjective ratings and physiological measures. Ergonomics **52**, 1350–1361 (2009). https://doi.org/10.1080/00140130903067797
9. Uebelbacher, A., Sonderegger, A., Sauer, J.: Effects of perceived prototype fidelity in usability testing under different conditions of observer presence. Interact. Comput. **25**, 91–101 (2013). https://doi.org/10.1093/iwc/iws002
10. Harris, E., Weinberg, J., Thomas, S., Gaeslin, D.: Effects of social facilitation and electronic monitoring on usability testing. In: Proceedings of Usability Professionals Association Conference, pp. 1–8 (2005)
11. Grudin, J.: Three faces of human-computer interaction. IEEE Ann. Hist. Comput. **27**, 46–62 (2005). https://doi.org/10.1109/MAHC.2005.67
12. den Buurman, R.: User-centred design of smart products. Ergonomics **40**, 1159–1169 (1997). https://doi.org/10.1080/001401397187676
13. Sonderegger, A., Uebelbacher, A., Pugliese, M., Sauer, J.: The influence of aesthetics in usability testing: the case of dual-domain products. In: Proceedings of the SIGCHI Conference on Human Factors in Computing Systems, pp. 21–30. ACM, New York (2014). https://doi.org/10.1145/2556288.2557419

14. Carroll, J.M.: Community computing as human-computer interaction. Behav. Inf. Technol. **20**, 307–314 (2001). https://doi.org/10.1080/01449290110078941
15. Tractinsky, N.: The usability construct: a dead end? Hum.-Comput. Interact. **33**, 131–177 (2018). https://doi.org/10.1080/07370024.2017.1298038
16. Forlizzi, J., Battarbee, K.: Understanding experience in interactive systems. In: Proceedings of the 5th Conference on Designing Interactive Systems: Processes, Practices, Methods, and Techniques, pp. 261–268. ACM, New York (2004). https://doi.org/10.1145/1013115. 1013152
17. Wright, P., McCarthy, J., Meekison, L.: Making sense of experience. In: Blythe, M.A., Overbeeke, K., Monk, A.F., Wright, P.C. (eds.) Funology, vol. 3, pp. 43–53. Springer, Dordrecht (2003). https://doi.org/10.1007/1-4020-2967-5_5
18. Desmet, P., Hekkert, P.: Framework of product experience. Int. J. Des. **1**(1), 57–66 (2007)
19. Hassenzahl, M.: User experience (UX): towards an experiential perspective on product quality. In: Proceedings of the 20th Conference on L'Interaction Homme-Machine, pp. 11–15. ACM, New York (2008). https://doi.org/10.1145/1512714.1512717
20. Law, E.L.-C., van Schaik, P., Roto, V.: Attitudes towards user experience (UX) measurement. Int. J. Hum.-Comput. Stud. **72**, 526–541 (2014)
21. Minge, M., Thüring, M., Wagner, I., Kuhr, C.V.: The meCUE questionnaire: a modular tool for measuring user experience. In: Soares, M., Falcão, C., Ahram, T.Z. (eds.) Advances in Ergonomics Modeling, Usability & Special Populations, vol. 486, pp. 115–128. Springer, Cham (2017). https://doi.org/10.1007/978-3-319-41685-4_11
22. Bevan, N.: Classifying and selecting UX and usability measures. In: International Workshop on Meaningful Measures: Valid Useful User Experience Measurement. pp. 13–18, Institute of Research in Informatics of Toulouse (IRIT), Toulouse, France (2008)
23. Thüring, M., Mahlke, S.: Usability, aesthetics and emotions in human–technology interaction. Int. J. Psychol. **42**, 253–264 (2007). https://doi.org/10.1080/00207590701396 674
24. Mandryk, R.L., Inkpen, K.M., Calvert, T.W.: Using psychophysiological techniques to measure user experience with entertainment technologies. Behav. Inf. Technol. **25**, 141–158 (2006). https://doi.org/10.1080/01449290500331156
25. Beatty, J.E., Torbert, W.R.: The false duality of work and leisure. J. Manag. Inq. **12**, 239–252 (2003). https://doi.org/10.1177/1056492603256340
26. Rheinberg, F., Manig, Y., Kliegl, R., Engeser, S., Vollmeyer, R.: Flow bei der Arbeit, doch Glück in der Freizeit. Zeitschrift für Arbeits- und Organisationspsychologie A&O. **51**, 105–115 (2007). https://doi.org/10.1026/0932-4089.51.3.105
27. Tinsley, H.E., Hinson, J.A., Tinsley, D.J., Holt, M.S.: Attributes of leisure and work experiences. J. Couns. Psychol. **40**, 447–455 (1993). https://doi.org/10.1037/0022-0167.40. 4.447
28. Shneiderman, B.: Response time and display rate in human performance with computers. ACM Comput. Surv. (CSUR) **16**, 265–285 (1984)
29. Szameitat, A.J., Rummel, J., Szameitat, D.P., Sterr, A.: Behavioral and emotional consequences of brief delays in human–computer interaction. Int. J. Hum.-Comput. Stud. **67**, 561–570 (2009). https://doi.org/10.1016/j.ijhcs.2009.02.004
30. Roto, V., Oulasvirta, A.: Need for non-visual feedback with long response times in mobile HCI. In: Special Interest Tracks and Posters of the 14th International Conference on World Wide Web, pp. 775–781. ACM, New York (2005). https://doi.org/10.1145/1062745. 1062747
31. Barber, R.E., Lucas Jr., H.C.: System Response Time, Operator Productivity and Job Satisfaction. Social Science Research Network, Rochester (1983)

32. Dellaert, B.G.C., Kahn, B.E.: How tolerable is delay?: Consumers' evaluations of internet web sites after waiting. J. Interact. Mark. **13**, 41–54 (1999). https://doi.org/10.1002/(SICI) 1520-6653(199924)13:1%3c41:AID-DIR4%3e3.0.CO;2-S

33. Hoxmeier, J.A., DiCesare, C.: System response time and user satisfaction: an experimental study of browser-based applications. In: AMCIS 2000 Proceedings, pp. 140–145 (2000)

34. Rushinek, A., Rushinek, S.F.: What makes users happy? Commun. ACM **29**, 594–598 (1986). https://doi.org/10.1145/6138.6140

35. Ramsay, J., Barbesi, A., Preece, J.: A psychological investigation of long retrieval times on the World Wide Web. Interact. Comput. **10**, 77–86 (1998). https://doi.org/10.1016/S0953-5438(97)00019-2

36. Butler, T.W.: Computer response time and user performance. In: Proceedings of the SIGCHI Conference on Human Factors in Computing Systems, pp. 58–62. ACM, New York (1983). https://doi.org/10.1145/800045.801581

37. Galletta, D.F., Henry, R., McCoy, S., Polak, P.: Web site delays: how tolerant are users? J. Assoc. Inf. Syst. **5**, 1 (2004)

38. Guynes, J.L.: Impact of system response time on state anxiety. Commun. ACM **31**, 342–347 (1988). https://doi.org/10.1145/42392.42402

39. Polkosky, M.D., Lewis, J.R.: Effect of auditory waiting cues on time estimation in speech recognition telephony applications. Int. J. Hum.-Comput. Interact. **14**, 423–446 (2002). https://doi.org/10.1080/10447318.2002.9669128

40. Selvidge, P.R., Chaparro, B.S., Bender, G.T.: The world wide wait: effects of delays on user performance. Int. J. Ind. Ergon. **29**, 15–20 (2002). https://doi.org/10.1016/S0169-8141(01)00045-2

41. Trimmel, M., Meixner-Pendleton, M., Haring, S.: Stress response caused by system response time when searching for information on the Internet. Hum. Factors **45**, 615–622 (2003). https://doi.org/10.1518/hfes.45.4.615.27084

42. Jacko, J.A., Sears, A., Borella, M.S.: The effect of network delay and media on user perceptions of web resources. Behav. Inf. Technol. **19**, 427–439 (2000). https://doi.org/10.1080/014492900750052688

43. Hui, M.K., Tse, D.K.: What to tell consumers in waits of different lengths: an integrative model of service evaluation. J. Mark. **60**, 81–90 (1996). https://doi.org/10.1177/002224299606000206

44. Branaghan, R.J., Sanchez, C.A.: Feedback preferences and impressions of waiting. Hum. Factors **51**, 528–538 (2009). https://doi.org/10.1177/0018720809345684

45. Watson, D., Clark, L.A., Tellegen, A.: Development and validation of brief measures of positive and negative affect: the PANAS scales. J. Pers. Soc. Psychol. **54**, 1063–1070 (1988). https://doi.org/10.1037/0022-3514.54.6.1063

46. Hart, S.G., Staveland, L.E.: Development of NASA-TLX (Task Load Index): results of empirical and theoretical research. In: Meshkati, P.A.H. (ed.) Advances in Psychology, pp. 139–183, North-Holland (1988)

47. Christophersen, T., Konradt, U.: Reliability, validity, and sensitivity of a single-item measure of online store usability. Int. J. Hum.-Comput. Stud. **69**, 269–280 (2011). https://doi.org/10.1016/j.ijhcs.2010.10.005

48. Lewis, J.R.: IBM computer usability satisfaction questionnaires: psychometric evaluation and instructions for use. Int. J. Hum.-Comput. Interact. **7**, 57–78 (1995). https://doi.org/10.1080/10447319509526110

49. Hornbæk, K., Law, E.L.-C.: Meta-analysis of correlations among usability measures. In: Proceedings of the SIGCHI Conference on Human Factors in Computing Systems, pp. 617–626. ACM, New York (2007). https://doi.org/10.1145/1240624.1240722

50. Altman, D.G., Bland, J.M.: Statistics notes: absence of evidence is not evidence of absence. BMJ **311**, 485 (1995). https://doi.org/10.1136/bmj.311.7003.485
51. Chalmers, L.: Underreporting research is scientific misconduct. JAMA **263**, 1405–1408 (1990). https://doi.org/10.1001/jama.1990.03440100121018
52. Fanelli, D.: Do pressures to publish increase scientists' bias? An empirical support from us states data. PLoS ONE **5**, e10271 (2010). https://doi.org/10.1371/journal.pone.0010271
53. Stern, J.M., Simes, R.J.: Publication bias: evidence of delayed publication in a cohort study of clinical research projects. BMJ **315**, 640–645 (1997). https://doi.org/10.1136/bmj.315.7109.640
54. Lindroth, T., Nilsson, S., Rasmussen, P.: Mobile usability—rigour meets relevance when usability goes mobile. In: Bjørnestad, S., Moe, R.E., Mørch, A.I., Opdahl, A.L. (eds.) Proceedings of the 24th Information Systems Research Seminar in Scandinavia (IRIS 24), pp. 641–654. IRIS Association, Ulvik (2001)
55. Kjeldskov, J., Stage, J.: New techniques for usability evaluation of mobile systems. Int. J. Hum.-Comput. Stud. **60**, 599–620 (2004). https://doi.org/10.1016/j.ijhcs.2003.11.001
56. Boucsein, W.: Forty years of research on system response times – what did we learn from it? In: Schlick, C.M. (ed.) Industrial Engineering and Ergonomics, pp. 575–593. Springer, Berlin Heidelberg (2009). https://doi.org/10.1007/978-3-642-01293-8_42
57. Teal, S.L., Rudnicky, A.I.: A performance model of system delay and user strategy selection. In: Proceedings of the SIGCHI Conference on Human Factors in Computing Systems, pp. 295–305. ACM, New York (1992). https://doi.org/10.1145/142750.142818
58. Nielsen, J., Levy, J.: Measuring usability: preference vs. performance. Commun. ACM **37**, 66–75 (1994). https://doi.org/10.1145/175276.175282
59. Rose, G.M., Meuter, M.L., Curran, J.M.: On-line waiting: the role of download time and other important predictors on attitude toward e-retailers. Psychol. Mark. **22**, 127–151 (2005). https://doi.org/10.1002/mar.20051
60. Sonderegger, A., Sauer, J.: The role of non-visual aesthetics in consumer product evaluation. Int. J. Hum.-Comput. Stud. **84**, 19–32 (2015). https://doi.org/10.1016/j.ijhcs.2015.05.011

User Experience of Driver State Visualizations: A Look at Demographics and Personalities

Michael Braun[1,2]($\boxtimes$), Ronee Chadowitz[1], and Florian Alt[2,3]

[1] BMW Group Research, New Technologies, Innovations, Munich, Germany
{michael.bf.braun,ronee.chadowitz}@bmw.de
[2] LMU Munich, Munich, Germany
[3] Bundeswehr University, Munich, Germany
florian.alt@unibw.de

Abstract. Driver state detection is an emerging topic for automotive user interfaces. Motivated by the trend of self-tracking, one crucial question within this field is how or whether detected states should be displayed. In this work we investigate the impact of demographics and personality traits on the user experience of driver state visualizations. 328 participants experienced three concepts visualizing their current state in a publicly installed driving simulator. Driver age, experience, and personality traits were shown to have impact on visualization preferences. While a continuous display was generally preferred, older respondents and drivers with little experience favored a system with less visual elements. Extroverted participants were more open towards interventions. Our findings lead us to believe that, while users are generally open to driver state detection, its visualization should be adapted to age, driving experience, and personality. This work is meant to support professionals and researchers designing affective in-car information systems.

Keywords: Affective computing · Emotion detection · Demographics · Personality · Driver state visualization · Automotive user interfaces

1 Introduction

Human-computer interaction has been experiencing a trend of personal data analytics in recent years: fitness trackers, smart watches, and wearables allow consumers to monitor themselves during sports, to track sleep patterns, to watch their calories, and much more. This phenomenon is widely known as the quantified self movement [11]. The technology behind this trend, namely pattern recognition through machine learning, can also be applied to other data sources. In automotive research, this has been happening for some time in the form of fatigue detection from steering and video data [13,33] or the deduction of cognitive load from pupil diameters [37]. Driver states on an emotional level have also been

© IFIP International Federation for Information Processing 2019
Published by Springer Nature Switzerland AG 2019
D. Lamas et al. (Eds.): INTERACT 2019, LNCS 11749, pp. 158–176, 2019.
https://doi.org/10.1007/978-3-030-29390-1_9

extracted from physiological data, speech recordings, and facial images [23,38]. Detecting driver states in real-time might be one of the big upcoming topics in future cars, as it enables personalized and affective interfaces [17]. At the same time, it is yet unclear whether this state should be communicated to the driver, and if personalization can help promoting acceptance of such new features. In our vision, user-aware automotive UIs can inform the driver if they show signs of hazardous affective states and ultimately increase road safety by raising awareness for the impacts of the driver state on driving performance.

We designed three approaches for the graphical representation of driver states based on successful examples from previous work in the automotive and other domains. They were evaluated in a public driving simulator experiment (N = 328). We report insights on the participants' user experience and emotional facial expressions, analyzed by age groups, personality traits, and driving experience.

According to our core findings, we can see that older and inexperienced drivers are in favor of reduced graphical representations as they fear distraction. Users with high scores in neuroticism like a continuous display of their driver state, while drivers with high scores in extraversion rather prefer notifications in case their state could threaten safe driving. We also show that a constant display of the driver state in a GUI works more efficiently in reducing negative states than visual notifications. This work is meant as a foundation for practitioners and researchers working on user state displays in the automotive context and other multi-task environments.

2   Background and Related Work

The idea of visualizing information on user states has been long established by computer gaming and in recent years also found its way into everyday life through step counters or fitness trackers. We introduce this concept into an automotive environment. In this process we have to consider the challenges and opportunities automotive user interfaces bring to the table.

2.1   Affective Automotive User Interfaces

Cars are the perfect environment to detect the user's state, as everything happens in a confined, easily observable space. In-vehicle applications can also consult information collected from their environment sensing systems to understand a situation's larger context. An example of this was shown in an early approach for an integrated driver safety and wellness system presented by Coughlin et al. [13]. They propose a sequence framework built on the three steps: "detect, display, alert". Especially while driving, the user should not be distracted or strained with visual load, which can be achieved through a mix of continuous display and proactive interventions [22,27].

A detection of the driver state, for example on an emotional level, can be realized using image-video processing techniques and speech analysis [26]. This approach can also be combined with physiological data [21]. Thirunavukkarasu et al. have shown a prototype for an in-car HMI which detects emotions and synchronizes the data with information from an on-board diagnosis (OBD) interface in order to trigger interventions [48]. We take up from their work with an approach of classification with camera-based detection of facial action coding units [16,30] as previously demonstrated by, for example, Abdic et al. [1].

Emotional states can be related to critical behavior behind the wheel: not only anger, but also sadness has been connected to poorer driving performance [6, 24]. Several approaches for automotive UIs have worked with this knowledge, enhancing driving safety by adapting the UI to the driver's emotional state [34] or increasing interactivity by mirroring the driver's emotions in natural language interfaces [35]. Apart from these reactive approaches, prophylaxis of negative states could also be interesting to investigate. We can learn from experiments in other domains, for example, Tsujita and Rekimoto's smart home appliance which achieved positive influences on emotions by making users smile [49], or we consider gamification approaches in automotive environments, which try to bring joy and driver safety together by focusing the driver's attention to the driving task in a playful manner [43,46]. One current challenge in automotive research is bringing user experience and safety together, as measures to make the driver more aware of their current state might raise reactance when users feel patronized by the system [9].

2.2   Visualizing the User State

Visual interfaces are the most regulated information channels in the automotive domain as they can demand visual resources and thus distract the driver from events on the road [39]. To avoid dangerous interactions in situations with increased workload, in-car information systems should make use of mostly static visualizations and ideally include the driving context into the timing of notifications [47]. In current in-car systems, a limited number of notifications are used to communicate the car's states (low fuel level, speed limits, etc.), which we need to adapt to when designing interventions based on the driver sate.

Related work on driver state visualization is scarce, which is why we also looked at concepts from other domains. We especially searched for ways to make drivers aware of their current state and, if possible, induce positive change. This is based on work by Choe et al., who describe the promotion of self-reflection and the support of self-experimentation as the primary goals for the design of supporting systems [11]. Fan et al. provide guidelines for quantified-self visualizations, which suggest the use of graphs or abstract geometry, preferably placed within an interaction space of daily usage (like the car) [18]. This approach was used for our concept *Quantified Self*. A second concept (*Gamification*) was inspired by the idea of gamification, meaning the introduction of game elements to motivate users towards a specific behavior, as demonstrated by Steinberger et al. with a gamified speedometer to encourage safer driving [45]. Our third concept *Notification* is based on notification systems, which are used to nudge users into a change of behavior [14] or improve wellbeing through text interventions [25].

2.3 Personalization of User Interfaces

Automotive UIs are currently developed with little personalization features, although recent work suggests that an adaptation to user-specific characteristics, can increase personal reference and with it improve user experience and trust [4,5,41]. One widespread framework to classify such personality features is the big five inventory, also called OCEAN model due to the initials of its categories openness, conscientiousness, extraversion, agreeableness, and neuroticism [20,31]. Chen and Donmez analyzed personality and driving data from 525 drivers and found that young drivers are rather influenced by normative behavior, while drivers over the age of 30 show interactions with their associated big five classifications [10]. They see higher risk-taking attitudes in drivers with high extraversion and low conscientiousness ratings, and increased fearfulness in drivers with high neuroticism. Arthur and Graziano looked at traffic accidents and found that high conscientiousness predicted less crashes [2]. Benfield et al. found aggressive driving to correlate with low scores in openness, agreeableness, and conscientiousness [3]. If we consider this framework for the evaluation of driver state visualizations, we might experience preferences for different systems by different personalities, which may also prove to positively modulate driving behavior.

3 Focus Group: Attitudes Towards Driver State Detection

Despite the possibilities we see in driver state detection, we experienced mixed feedback and skepticism towards such concepts when talking to potential users in preparation for this study. We had the impression that users were afraid of being spied on by their cars, and similar fears have been identified in a survey by Schmidt and Braunger [40]. To understand where these notions come from, we conducted two focus groups with experienced drivers (>10.000 km per year). The groups consisted of 24 participants from the US and 21 from Germany, as these are the two main vehicle markets we had access to. 25 of the participants were women, 20 men. All described themselves as generally open towards digital innovations. All participants used a smartphone daily. 8 owned a smartwatch, 14 regularly used a fitness tracker of whom 12 belong to the US sample.

The goal of the focus groups was to get an impression of how users receive the idea of user state detection in the car. Generally speaking, one third of the participants stated that they would agree to share personal data to use digital services, another third would agree only under certain conditions. US participants were more open towards data usage than Germans.

When confronted with the idea of an in-vehicle information system which can detect and act upon the driver's or passengers' emotions through sensors, both groups expressed curiosity. However, German users often described it as an "invasion of privacy" while US participants stated things like "I love this technology" and it could be a "good and handy offer". General privacy concerns

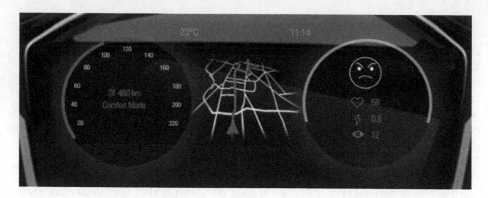

Fig. 1. Our prototype of an affective interface showed driver state data in the instrument cluster. Focus group participants (US and Germany) expressed general curiosity and potential for improving driver safety, but also concerns regarding paternalism.

and the fear of being patronized were stated as negative implications. On the other hand, an improvement of driver safety and enhanced smart suggestions were perceived positively.

Participants were then shown a prototype of an ordinary automotive UI with a speedometer and navigation, which we enhanced with visualizations of physiological features and emotion detection (Fig. 1). This design is well known from fitness tracking apps and was proposed as a potential UI to indicate driver state. The visual prototype received more positive feedback than the verbalized ideas, as it was perceived as simple and intuitive to interpret.

3.1 Focus Group Insights

The feedback from this focus group was condensed into four key learnings using thematic analysis [8]. We incorporated these take-aways into the proposed concepts and used them to guide our main study.

Show, Don't Tell. When asked to evaluate an idea, the visual concept received more positive feedback than a textual description. Since a participant's understanding of a concept profits from seeing a concrete application, we strive to keep theoretical input at a minimum.

Respect Cultural Diversity. Participants from different cultures showed diverging concerns. Germans are more aware of data privacy, Americans were immediately keen to use the system. Different demographics might bring new insights and participants' needs may adapt (cf. GDPR in the EU/CSL in China).

Beware of Patronism. User concerns about a feeling of being patronized should be taken seriously. 35 users stated to only want information or suggestions. Only 5 would accept a system trying to influence the driver subconsciously.

Fig. 2. Concept *Notification*: a minimalistic background animation combined with text notifications in case of negative user valence.

Emphasize Safety Features. Participants often mentioned the advantages of driver state detection in case of a medical emergency and on long, tiring rides. Users are aware of the dangers on the road and might be more open to new technologies when they are seen in connection to safety improvements.

4   System Design

Based on the focus group, we designed three interface prototypes to be tested with a larger sample of participants. As a main requirement, each concept should be easy to use from the start, without further explanations. This way we make sure to gather feedback on the idea itself and not the technology behind it.

Participants should experience the prototype in a driving context, thus we have to embed the driver state visualizations into a realistic dashboard design and adhere to standards for in-car UIs, meaning the display should only require minimal active attention while driving. The concepts should also avoid appearing manipulative or patronizing. The ideas for each concept come from related work, which we have illuminated closer in Sect. 2.2.

4.1   Concept Notification

Concept *Notification* implements interventions to positively influence the driver without constant driver state display. In case the lower threshold for detected driver valence is reached, a text message meant to cheer up the driver is displayed (see Fig. 2). This message stays on the screen for at least 3 s to prevent fidgetiness and only fades out as the detected valence levels rise. The main idea of concept *Notification* is to reduce visual load and to only interact with the driver in form of interventions when they are in a negative state.

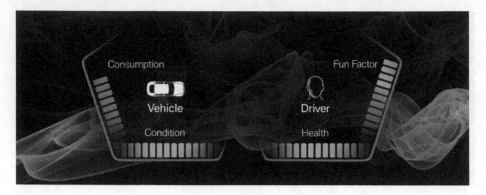

Fig. 3. Concept *Gamification* displays current stats of car and driver in an interactive way. The general idea is to involve the driver and make their ride more fun.

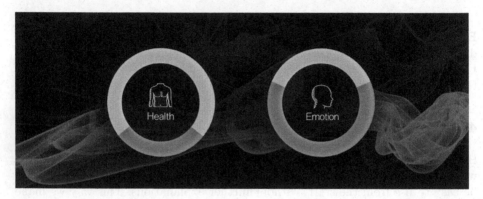

Fig. 4. Concept *Quantified Self* visualizes user vitality and emotion data in circular diagrams. Users can see at one glance whether their condition is classified as positive (green), neutral (blue), or negative (red). (Color figure online)

4.2 Concept Gamification

Concept *Gamification* consists of four scales, representing car status, fuel consumption, driver health, and driver fun levels (Fig. 3). The inspiration was taken from computer games, where players have health levels they can directly influence through power-ups. In our prototype, users could keep consumption low by driving responsibly or increase their personal fun factor by smiling. Fun levels decreased over time if no positive expressions were detected. The general idea stems from approaches of increasing driver engagement through gamification [45] and the notion that the act of smiling itself makes people feel happier [49]. In our prototype the values for driver health was simulated with random positive values as we did not collect health data during the experiment.

4.3   Concept Quantified Self

Concept *Quantified Self* is borrowed from the visualization style know from fitness tracking apps. This display variant follows the idea of a quantified self, allowing the user to experiment on themselves through behavioral changes with an intended outcome of self-improvement [11,42]. Two circular diagrams display the vital and emotional states of the drivers, which are color coded to allow quick information extraction (Fig. 4). When a dangerous driver state is detected, the outline turns red, which we refer to as intervention in the experiment. Here, again, we simulated driver health values, as we did not collect health data.

4.4   Prototype Implementation

The system was built using the *Affdex SDK* [32] which analyzes facial images to estimate an emotional user state. We process a live video feed of the driver's face and then classify the driver state conditional to the resulting metrics: measurements exceeding anger values of 60 (out of 100) or falling below a valence of -50 (from -100 to 100) triggered interventions in concepts *Notification* and *Quantified Self*. Users were classified as happy when joy was above 60 or when a smile was detected. Additionally, in concept *Quantified Self* the valence values were transferred one-to-one to the fill percentage of the ring. In each session only one, single, visualization concept was experienced by each user.

5   Deployment Study: Driver State Visualization

The described concepts were tested in a publicly accessible driving simulator deployed close to a busy shopping street in Nuremberg, Germany. We chose Germany over the US as German participants in our focus group were more critical towards the concept of driver state detection. Nuremberg was selected as the city has no direct connection to the automotive industry, so we expected a more generalizable sample than in other cities. In order to minimize bias effects, all company affiliations and characteristic design features were also concealed.

5.1   Methodology

The unique setting in a public space allowed us to open participation for all passers-by, providing us with a much more diverse participant sample than a standard lab test would allow for. The test ran for three months, Monday through Saturday, from 10 am to 6 pm, during which close to 800 user sessions were logged. We modeled the public simulator setup according to best practices from related work, e.g. sturdy hardware, easy setup for the user, and short, concise explanations for every single step within the process [7].

Each participant experienced one visualization approach assigned randomly, resulting in a between-subject design. As additional independent variables we queried user demographics (gender, age, driving experience) and personality

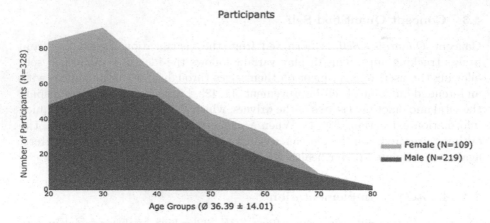

Fig. 5. A total of 109 women and 219 men with a mean age of 36 years finished the experiment with evaluable data.

traits (BFI-20 Big Five Inventory [15]). The dependent variables were attractiveness, design quality, and usability, assessed using the user experience questionnaire (UEQ [29]), and emotion recognition data based on facial features from a frontal video feed.

5.2 Demographics

During a period of 12 weeks, 798 sessions were logged, of which 328 contained complete and valid measurements and no exclusion criteria (e.g. too young to drive, intoxication, unserious behavior). For an overview of age and gender distributions, see Fig. 5. When asked about driving experience, 6.4% of included participants stated they never drive themselves, 12.5% drive once a month, 13.1% once a week, 26.1% every other day and 41.8% identified themselves as daily drivers. Of the final subset, 33.8% of participants experienced the concepts *Notification* and *Gamification* and 32.4% experienced the concept *Quantified Self*.

5.3 Apparatus

The study was conducted in a white label seating box situated at a research booth at Fraunhofer JOSEPH'S in Nuremberg [19]. The concepts were shown on a curved wide screen display above the steering wheel. (Figure 6) A camera on top of the screen provided a live video stream for facial expression analysis. The simulation was controlled by the driver using a steering wheel and pedals. Participants were provided step by step instructions on a tablet placed in the center console. We provided general information on our research and explained the technology behind the prototype on a nearby information screen. Staff assured smooth operations by answering questions. Participation was possible without personal on-boarding.

Fig. 6. Publicly deployed medium fidelity driving simulation showing a participant experiencing the concept *Gamification*, displayed above the steering wheel.

5.4 Procedure

Participants were welcomed by a starting screen and introduced to the setting and tasks. They were presented questions on their demographics, driving experience and exclusion criteria (for example, alcohol consumption, legal driving age). The main task consisted of following a white car on a highway with moderate traffic, the secondary task was assessing the UI on the dashboard screen.

After completing the ride, which took about 5 min, users were presented two questionnaires; a UEQ questionnaire to rate the user experience of the driver state visualization [29] and the BFI-20 short version of the Big Five Inventory to classify the participant's personality [15]. We also logged the output of the emotion detection system to see whether interventions had an effect on participants. After the ride, participants were asked to rate the idea of driver state visualizations as negative, neutral, or positive and explain their decisions.

5.5 Limitations

The driving simulator experiment was conducted without further restrictions on participation and a rather short experiment duration. This is attributed to the public study design, which in return allowed for a larger sample than traditional driving studies. Furthermore, although we take into account cultural particularities, our focus group does not reflect input from China as the third big market. This is simply due to a lack of access. We can, however, expect an open attitude from Chinese users, as they are generally appreciative of new technology [28].

6   Results

We collected UEQ ratings on the tested visualization concepts, emotion recognition data from the Affdex SDK and an estimation of participants' personality characteristics provided by the BFI-20 questionnaire. The personality characteristics and demographic data were combined and used to create participant subsets in order to understand if they experienced and evaluated concepts differently. Results with $p < 0.05$ are reported as statistically significant.

6.1   Subjective Feedback

Participants gave us an estimation on how they perceived the concept of driver state detection in the car. 12% said they would not like to use a system like the one exhibited. They voiced concerns regarding paternalism or data protection issues. 28% reacted indifferent, one of them said they liked the idea for special groups like novice drivers or to test for intoxication but they would not accept it for themselves. A majority of 60% rated the idea as positive. Feedback included the wish for the detection of fatigue or health-related conditions and an optional annexation of control through the car if the driver was found incapable. Other ideas were music selection according to the driver's mood or windshield filters when increased pupil sensitivity is detected.

Looking back at our initial focus groups, we expected the feedback to be more narrow-minded. The hands-on presentation might have convinced participants who would have disliked theoretical concepts. We also see that younger users within this group were more open to the driver state detection than older users. There were no differences between genders.

6.2   Concept Ratings

We first analyzed the UEQ data without differentiation between user subsets with an analysis of variance and pairwise comparisons for each concept rating (see Table 1). The data distribution fulfils requirements for parametric tests. Concept *Quantified Self* was generally liked by the entirety of participants. Concept *Gamification* and *Quantified Self* were rated significantly more attractive than concept *Notification* ($p < 0.01$), while concept *Quantified Self* also had significantly higher ratings in novelty than *Gamification* ($p < 0.05$). Feedback on the design quality shows a tendency towards a slight disregard for concept *Gamification*.

This general look at the data suggests that the quantified-self approach of concepts *Quantified Self* could be a good first step towards displaying driver states in the car. If we however look at sub-groups within the user sample, we can generate further insights on the opportunities of personalization.

Demographic Influences. Our dataset contains demographic information on the subjects, which we used to create subsets based on gender, age, and driving

Table 1. When we look at the entirety of participants, concept *Notification* is perceived significantly less attractive than the other tested concepts and concept *Gamification* received the noticeably worst ratings in Design Quality. Only concept *Quantified Self* scored well in all dimensions of the UEQ.

	Notification		Gamification		Quantified self	
	Mean	SD	Mean	SD	Mean	SD
Attractiveness	**2.66**	1.13	3.05	1.06	3.04	1.15
Design quality	3.18	1.00	**2.93**	1.04	3.23	0.97
Usability	3.23	0.84	3.27	0.78	3.35	0.83

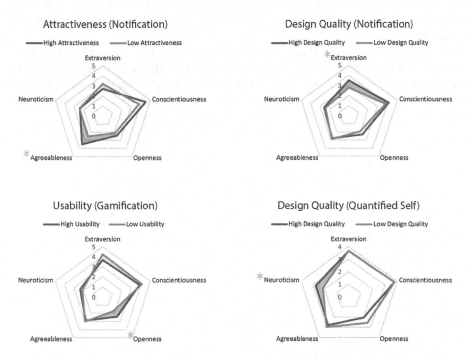

Fig. 7. UEQ ratings visualized by corresponding user personality traits.

experience. This deep dive into demographics was only possible due to our public setup, as it allowed us to include a high number of participants with diverse backgrounds. We discovered no gender differences but age played a role in the UEQ ratings: young drivers (aged 17–24) preferred the gamified concept, while older drivers (age groups 55–64 and 65+) favored concept *Notification*. This can be explained with preferences of younger drivers for gamification due to understimulation [44] and an increased sensitivity for visual load in older drivers [36].

Driving experience also had an effect on ratings as inactive drivers preferred the visually less demanding concept *Notification*, while experienced drivers have balanced ratings for all three concepts.

Personality Preferences. Each user took a personality test which led to a personality placement in the five dimensions extraversion, conscientiousness, openness, agreeableness, and neuroticism. We did an analysis of the interplay between UEQ ratings and personality traits for each concept and found high variances in answers on attractiveness and dependability from participants with high values in neuroticism and openness. High openness also led to higher variances in perspicuity. Other groups were generally comparable in ratings. It is noticeable that extremes in neuroticism, extraversion, and openness show greater variances than other categories which makes us think that these are the most important traits when it comes to the personalization of driver state visualizations. We can also see that users with high agreeableness tend to rate all concepts rather well and might therefore be a less ideal demographic to chose from when conducting evaluations.

It is interesting to see that concept *Notification*, which gives proactive feedback and behaves thus rather extroverted, was rated higher by extroverted users, while concept *Quantified Self* achieved better ratings from participants with high neuroticism. This makes sense since an emotionally reactive person may also be more receptive to the constant display of their state (see Fig. 7).

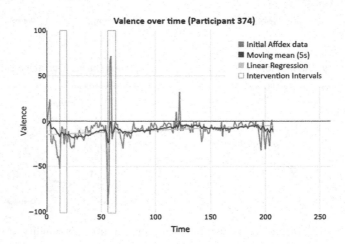

Fig. 8. An exemplary view of emotion recognition data for detected valence values of one user: moving mean smoothing is used to visualize trends, linear regression shows the overall slope to categorize positive or negative development. Intervention frames display how this user was twice alerted due to low valence and e.g. in the second instance instantly started smiling.

6.3   Emotion Detection

We analyzed the data provided by the Affdex SDK for emotion detection with a focus on time intervals after interventions performed by the system. Concepts

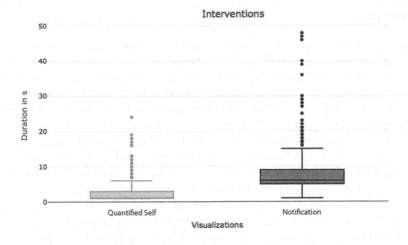

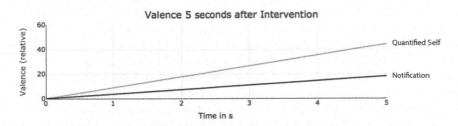

Fig. 9. Interventions during the concepts *Quantified Self* (495 instances) and *Notification* (442 instances). Concept *Quantified Self* worked more effectively in inducing positive valence through interventions.

Quantified Self and *Notification* performed different actions when the detected valence of the user fell below a threshold of −50 (from −100 to 100). In concept *Notification*, a written message appeared which was designed to bring the driver into a more positive state and only disappeared when an improvement was measured. Concept *Quantified Self* constantly displayed the valence values and switched to an alerting red color scheme when the value was less than the threshold. Figure 8 shows exemplary valence data of a user performing a ride with concept *Notification*: they experienced two interventions of 6 and 7 s duration and both led to a brief improvement. In the second intervention they actively reacted with a smile as we can see from the high valence values.

We analyzed the development of valence values after each of the total of 937 interventions in our dataset and see significantly better performance in concept *Quantified Self* than in concept *Notification* (see Fig. 9). Interventions in concept *Notification* also took significantly longer ($t^{(611.43)} = -16.527, p < 0.001$), supposedly because the written text was harder to process than the abstract representation of concept *Quantified Self*.

7   Discussion

In this paper we present three different approaches to visualizing driver states. Participants in our study were rather open towards the idea of user state detection in the car (only 12% opposed) with seniors being more sceptical than young drivers. Some users also expressed issues concerning privacy or data protection.

Concept *Quantified Self*, which incorporates quantified-self visualizations, is generally more preferred than *Notification* and *Gamification*. The gamified approach *Gamification*, however, scores well with the subset of young drivers (cf. related literature [45]). Older and unpracticed drivers prefer the more subtle concept *Notification*. This shows that users are actually aware of the dangers visual distraction poses on driving. We think a system with real-time cognitive load measurement could recognize available resources and select the appropriate means to visualize information, e.g. an interaction-free visualization in demanding situations and a more involving approach when the driver is bored [44].

Participants with extreme ratings on the big five scales of openness, extraversion, and neuroticism showed the most diverging UEQ ratings. Extroverted users preferred proactive behavior, which resembles an extroverted agent. Neurotic users liked a constant display of their state, possibly because they see this as a way to get feedback on their condition, motivated through higher emotional reactiveness. Users with high agreeableness scores liked all approaches, which was to be expected in a way, and suggests that we do not need to focus our future work on this character trait. Conscientiousness scores also did not have any influence on UX ratings. We however know from related work that this dimension is connected with driving performance, hence still important.

According to the analyzed valence data from image-based emotion detection we found that concept *Quantified Self* works faster and is more effective in decreasing negative emotions than concept *Notification* (concept *Gamification* did not utilize interventions). We see this as an important finding of our study, as current fatigue warning systems work with notifications. We see potential in defining a dedicated area within the in-vehicle UI to display the driver state to keep the driver always in the loop.

8   Conclusion and Future Work

We investigated user preferences on driver state visualization in the car. We conducted a focus group and evaluated three proposed GUIs in a public driving simulator study. The findings lead us to believe there is no one-fits-all solution to driver state visualizations. We propose that interfaces should adapt to age, driving experience, and personality. When testing with users, the personality dimensions openness, extraversion, and neuroticism should be at the focus of attention. We are also aware that personality is a highly complex field to explore.

The main contribution of our focus group and study are a high acceptance of driver state detection within our broad user sample, as well as the positive influences a constant display can have on the driver's affective state. We hope this affirms other researchers to keep working on user-aware interfaces.

This field offers plenty of directions for future work. One interesting question that emerged while we were working on this project, is whether users will accept such a system in long-term usage or if we will see an abandonment after habitual usage, as was reported for fitness trackers [12]. Furthermore, cultural differences for personalization might play an important role and should be investigated. Therefore, we would like to motivate future research on the long-term usage of user-aware in-vehicle UIs and try to transfer these research questions into culturally different markets.

References

1. Abdić, I., Fridman, L., McDuff, D., Marchi, E., Reimer, B., Schuller, B.: Driver frustration detection from audio and video in the wild. In: Proceedings of the 25th International Joint Conference on Artificial Intelligence, IJCAI 2016, pp. 1354–1360. AAAI Press, New York (2016).https://doi.org/10.1007/978-3-319-46073-4
2. Arthur, W., Graziano, W.G.: The five-factor model, conscientiousness, and driving accident involvement. J. Pers. **64**(3), 593–618 (1996). https://doi.org/10.1111/j.1467-6494.1996.tb00523.x
3. Benfield, J.A., Szlemko, W.J., Bell, P.A.: Driver personality and anthropomorphic attributions of vehicle personality relate to reported aggressive driving tendencies. Pers. Individ. Differ. **42**(2), 247–258 (2007). https://doi.org/10.1016/j.paid.2006.06.016
4. Blom, J.: Personalization: a taxonomy. In: CHI 2000 Extended Abstracts on Human Factors in Computing Systems, CHI EA 2000, pp. 313–314. ACM, New York (2000). https://doi.org/10.1145/633292.633483
5. Braun, M., Mainz, A., Chadowitz, R., Pfleging, B., Alt, F.: At your service: designing voice assistant personalities to improve automotive user interfaces. In: Proceedings of the 2019 CHI Conference on Human Factors in Computing Systems, CHI 2019. ACM, New York (2019). https://doi.org/10.1145/3290605.3300270
6. Braun, M., Pfleging, B., Alt, F.: A survey to understand emotional situations on the road and what they mean for affective automotive UIs. Multimodal Technol. Interact. **2**(4), 75 (2018). https://doi.org/10.3390/mti2040075
7. Braun, M., Roider, F., Alt, F., Gross, T.: Automotive research in the public space: towards deployment-based prototypes for real users. In: Proceedings of the 10th International Conference on Automotive User Interfaces and Interactive Vehicular Applications, AutomotiveUI 2018, pp. 181–185. ACM, New York (2018). https://doi.org/10.1145/3239092.3265964
8. Braun, V., Clarke, V.: Using thematic analysis in psychology. Qual. Res. Psychol. **3**(2), 77–101 (2006). https://doi.org/10.1191/1478088706qp063oa
9. Brehm, S.S., Brehm, J.W.: Psychological Reactance: A Theory of Freedom and Control. Academic Press (2013)
10. Chen, H.Y.W., Donmez, B.: What drives technology-based distractions? A structural equation model on social-psychological factors of technology-based driver distraction engagement. Accid. Anal. Prev. **91**, 166–174 (2016). https://doi.org/10.1016/j.aap.2015.08.015
11. Choe, E.K., Lee, N.B., Lee, B., Pratt, W., Kientz, J.A.: Understanding quantified-selfers' practices in collecting and exploring personal data. In: Proceedings of the SIGCHI Conference on Human Factors in Computing Systems, CHI 2014, pp. 1143–1152. ACM, New York (2014). https://doi.org/10.1145/2556288.2557372

12. Clawson, J., Pater, J.A., Miller, A.D., Mynatt, E.D., Mamykina, L.: No longer wearing: investigating the abandonment of personal health-tracking technologies on craigslist. In: Proceedings of the 2015 ACM International Joint Conference on Pervasive and Ubiquitous Computing, UbiComp 2015, pp. 647–658. ACM, New York (2015). https://doi.org/10.1145/2750858.2807554
13. Coughlin, J.F., Reimer, B., Mehler, B.: Monitoring, managing, and motivating driver safety and well-being. IEEE Pervasive Comput. **10**(3), 14–21 (2011). https://doi.org/10.1109/MPRV.2011.54
14. Czerwinski, M., Gilad-Bachrach, R., Iqbal, S., Mark, G.: Challenges for designing notifications for affective computing systems. In: Proceedings of the 2016 ACM International Joint Conference on Pervasive and Ubiquitous Computing: Adjunct, UbiComp 2016, pp. 1554–1559. ACM, New York (2016). https://doi.org/10.1145/2968219.2968548
15. Danner, D., et al.: Die deutsche version des big five inventory 2 (BFI-2). Technical report, Zusammenstellung sozialwissenschaftlicher Items und Skalen (2016). https://doi.org/10.6102/zis247
16. Ekman, P., Rosenberg, E.L.: What the Face Reveals: Basic and Applied Studies of Spontaneous Expression Using the Facial Action Coding System (FACS). Oxford University Press, Oxford (1997)
17. Eyben, F., et al.: Emotion on the road: necessity, acceptance, and feasibility of affective computing in the Car. Adv. Hum.-Comp. Int. **2010**, 5:1–5:17 (2010). https://doi.org/10.1155/2010/263593
18. Fan, C., Forlizzi, J., Dey, A.K.: A spark of activity: exploring informative art as visualization for physical activity. In: Proceedings of the 2012 ACM Conference on Ubiquitous Computing, UbiComp 2012, pp. 81–84. ACM, New York (2012). https://doi.org/10.1145/2370216.2370229
19. Fraunhofer-Arbeitsgruppe für Supply Chain Services SCS des Fraunhofer-Instituts für Integrierte Schaltungen IIS: Josephs service manufaktur - megatrends (2018). http://www.josephs-service-manufaktur.de/besucher/vorherige-themenwelten/themenwelt-megatrends/. Accessed 16 Apr 2018
20. Goldberg, L.R.: The structure of phenotypic personality traits. Am. Psychol. **48**(1), 26 (1993)
21. Hassib, M., Pfeiffer, M., Schneegass, S., Rohs, M., Alt, F.: Emotion actuator: embodied emotional feedback through electroencephalography and electrical muscle stimulation. In: Proceedings of the 2017 CHI Conference on Human Factors in Computing Systems, CHI 2017, pp. 6133–6146. ACM, New York (2017). https://doi.org/10.1145/3025453.3025953
22. Häuslschmid, R., Klaus, C., Butz, A.: Presenting information on the driver's demand on a head-up display. In: Bernhaupt, R., Dalvi, G., Joshi, A., Balkrishan, D.K., O'Neill, J., Winckler, M. (eds.) INTERACT 2017. LNCS, vol. 10514, pp. 245–262. Springer, Cham (2017). https://doi.org/10.1007/978-3-319-67684-5_15
23. Hoch, S., Althoff, F., McGlaun, G., Rigoll, G.: Bimodal fusion of emotional data in an automotive environment. In: 2005 Proceedings of IEEE International Conference on Acoustics, Speech, and Signal Processing (ICASSP 2005), Philadelphia, PA, USA, vol. 2, pp. ii/1085-ii/1088. IEEE, March 2005. https://doi.org/10.1109/ICASSP.2005.1415597
24. Jeon, M.: Don't cry while you're driving: sad driving is as bad as angry driving. Int. J. Hum.-Comput. Interact. **32**(10), 777–790 (2016). https://doi.org/10.1080/10447318.2016.1198524

25. Jeong, S., Breazeal, C.L.: Improving smartphone users' affect and wellbeing with personalized positive psychology interventions. In: Proceedings of the Fourth International Conference on Human Agent Interaction, HAI 2016, pp. 131–137. ACM, New York (2016). https://doi.org/10.1145/2974804.2974831

26. Katsis, C.D., Rigas, G., Goletsis, Y., Fotiadis, D.I.: Emotion recognition in Car industry, chapter 20, pp. 515–544. Wiley-Blackwell (2015). https://doi.org/10.1002/9781118910566.ch20

27. Kushlev, K., Proulx, J., Dunn, E.W.: "Silence your phones": smartphone notifications increase inattention and hyperactivity symptoms. In: Proceedings of the 2016 CHI Conference on Human Factors in Computing Systems, CHI 2016, pp. 1011–1020. ACM, New York (2016). https://doi.org/10.1145/2858036.2858359

28. Lachner, F., von Saucken, C., Mueller, F., Lindemann, U.: Cross-cultural user experience design helping product designers to consider cultural differences. In: Rau, P.L.P. (ed.) CCD 2015. LNCS, vol. 9180, pp. 58–70. Springer, Cham (2015). https://doi.org/10.1007/978-3-319-20907-4_6

29. Laugwitz, B., Schrepp, M., Held, T.: Konstruktion eines fragebogens zur messung der user experience von softwareprodukten. In: Heinecke, A.M., Paul, H. (eds.) Mensch und Computer 2006: Mensch und Computer im Strukturwandel, pp. 125–134. Oldenbourg Verlag, München (2006)

30. Lien, J.J., Kanade, T., Cohn, J.F., Li, C.C.: Automated facial expression recognition based on FACS action units. In: Proceedings Third IEEE International Conference on Automatic Face and Gesture Recognition, pp. 390–395, April 1998. https://doi.org/10.1109/AFGR.1998.670980

31. McCrae, R.R., Costa Jr., P.T.: A five-factor theory of personality. In: Handbook of Personality: Theory and Research, vol. 3, pp. 159–181. Guilford Press, New York (2008)

32. McDuff, D., Mahmoud, A., Mavadati, M., Amr, M., Turcot, J., Kaliouby, R.E.: AFFDEX SDK: a cross-platform real-time multi-face expression recognition toolkit. In: Proceedings of the 2016 CHI Conference Extended Abstracts on Human Factors in Computing Systems, CHI EA 2016, pp. 3723–3726. ACM, New York (2016). https://doi.org/10.1145/2851581.2890247

33. Melnicuk, V., Birrell, S., Crundall, E., Jennings, P.: Towards hybrid driver state monitoring: review, future perspectives and the role of consumer electronics. In: 2016 IEEE Intelligent Vehicles Symposium (IV), Gothenburg, Sweden, pp. 1392–1397. IEEE, June 2016. https://doi.org/10.1109/IVS.2016.7535572

34. Nasoz, F., Lisetti, C.L., Vasilakos, A.V.: Affectively intelligent and adaptive Car interfaces. Inf. Sci. 180(20), 3817–3836 (2010). https://doi.org/10.1016/j.ins.2010.06.034

35. Nass, C., et al.: Improving automotive safety by pairing driver emotion and car voice emotion. In: CHI 2005 Extended Abstracts on Human Factors in Computing Systems, CHI EA 2005, pp. 1973–1976. ACM, New York (2005). https://doi.org/10.1145/1056808.1057070

36. Owsley, C., Ball, K., Sloane, M., Roenker, D.L., Bruni, J.: Visual/cognitive correlates of vehicle crashes in older drivers. Psychol. Aging 6, 403–415 (1991). https://doi.org/10.1037//0882-7974.6.3.403

37. Pfleging, B., Fekety, D.K., Schmidt, A., Kun, A.L.: A model relating pupil diameter to mental workload and lighting conditions. In: Proceedings of the SIGCHI Conference on Human Factors in Computing Systems, CHI 2016. ACM, New York, May 2016. https://doi.org/10.1145/2858036.2858117

38. Riener, A., Ferscha, A., Aly, M.: Heart on the road: HRV analysis for monitoring a driver's affective state. In: Proceedings of the 1st International Conference on Automotive User Interfaces and Interactive Vehicular Applications, AutomotiveUI 2009, pp. 99–106. ACM, New York (2009). https://doi.org/10.1145/1620509.1620529

39. Riener, A., Jeon, M., Alvarez, I., Frison, A.K.: Driver in the loop: best practices in automotive sensing and feedback mechanisms. In: Meixner, G., Müller, C. (eds.) Automotive User Interfaces. HIS, pp. 295–323. Springer, Cham (2017). https://doi.org/10.1007/978-3-319-49448-7_11

40. Schmidt, M., Braunger, P.: A survey on different means of personalized dialog output for an adaptive personal assistant. In: Adjunct Publication of the 26th Conference on User Modeling, Adaptation and Personalization, UMAP 2018, pp. 75–81. ACM, New York (2018). https://doi.org/10.1145/3213586.3226198

41. Schneider, H., Schauer, K., Stachl, C., Butz, A.: Your data, your vis: personalizing personal data visualizations. In: Bernhaupt, R., Dalvi, G., Joshi, A., K. Balkrishan, D., O'Neill, J., Winckler, M. (eds.) INTERACT 2017. LNCS, vol. 10515, pp. 374–392. Springer, Cham (2017). https://doi.org/10.1007/978-3-319-67687-6_25

42. schraefel, m.c., Churchill, E.F.: Wellth creation: using computer science to support proactive health. Computer **47**(11), 70–72 (2014). https://doi.org/10.1109/MC.2014.339

43. Schroeter, R., Rakotonirainy, A., Foth, M.: The social Car: new interactive vehicular applications derived from social media and urban informatics. In: Proceedings of the 4th International Conference on Automotive User Interfaces and Interactive Vehicular Applications, AutomotiveUI 2012, pp. 107–110. ACM, New York (2012). https://doi.org/10.1145/2390256.2390273

44. Steinberger, F., Moeller, A., Schroeter, R.: The antecedents, experience, and coping strategies of driver boredom in young adult males. J. Saf. Res. **59**, 69–82 (2016). https://doi.org/10.1016/j.jsr.2016.10.007

45. Steinberger, F., Proppe, P., Schroeter, R., Alt, F.: CoastMaster: an ambient speedometer to gamify safe driving. In: Proceedings of the 8th International Conference on Automotive User Interfaces and Interactive Vehicular Applications, Automotive'UI 2016, pp. 83–90. ACM, New York (2016). https://doi.org/10.1145/3003715.3005412

46. Steinberger, F., Schroeter, R., Lindner, V., Fitz-Walter, Z., Hall, J., Johnson, D.: Zombies on the road: a holistic design approach to balancing gamification and safe driving. In: Proceedings of the 7th International Conference on Automotive User Interfaces and Interactive Vehicular Applications, AutomotiveUI 2015, pp. 320–327. ACM, New York (2015). https://doi.org/10.1145/2799250.2799260

47. Tchankue, P., Wesson, J., Vogts, D.: The impact of an adaptive user interface on reducing driver distraction. In: Proceedings of the 3rd International Conference on Automotive User Interfaces and Interactive Vehicular Applications, AutomotiveUI 2011, pp. 87–94. ACM, New York (2011). https://doi.org/10.1145/2381416.2381430

48. Thirunavukkarasu, G.S., Abdi, H., Mohajer, N.: A smart HMI for driving safety using emotion prediction of EEG signals. In: 2016 IEEE International Conference on Systems, Man, and Cybernetics (SMC), pp. 004148–004153, October 2016. https://doi.org/10.1109/SMC.2016.7844882

49. Tsujita, H., Rekimoto, J.: Smiling makes us happier: enhancing positive mood and communication with smile-encouraging digital appliances. In: Proceedings of the 13th International Conference on Ubiquitous Computing, UbiComp 2011, pp. 1–10. ACM, New York (2011). https://doi.org/10.1145/2030112.2030114

Users' Emotions, Feelings and Perception

As Light as Your Scent: Effects of Smell and Sound on Body Image Perception

Giada Brianza[1](✉)(iD), Ana Tajadura-Jiménez[2,3](✉)(iD),
Emanuela Maggioni[1](✉)(iD), Dario Pittera[1](✉)(iD),
Nadia Bianchi-Berthouze[3](✉)(iD), and Marianna Obrist[1](✉)(iD)

[1] SCHI Lab, Creative Technology Research Group,
School of Engineering and Informatics, University of Sussex, Brighton, UK
{G.Brianza,E.Maggioni,D.Pittera,M.Obrist}@sussex.ac.uk
[2] DEI Interactive Systems Group, Computer Science Department,
Universidad Carlos III de Madrid, Madrid, Spain
atajadur@inf.uc3m.es
[3] UCLIC, University College of London, London, UK
n.berthouze@ucl.ac.uk

Abstract. How people mentally represent their body appearance (i.e., body image perception - BIP) does not always match their actual body. BIP distortions can lead to a detriment in physical and emotional health. Recent works in HCI have shown that technology can be used to change people's BIP through visual, tactile, proprioceptive, and auditory stimulation. This paper investigates, for the first time, the effect of olfactory stimuli, by looking at a possible enhancement of a known auditory effect on BIP. We present two studies building on emerging knowledge in the field of crossmodal correspondences. First, we explored the correspondences between scents and body shapes. Then, we investigated the impact of combined scents and sounds on one's own BIP. Our results show that scent stimuli can be used to make participants feel lighter or heavier (i.e., using lemon or vanilla) and to enhance the effect of sound on perceived body lightness. We discuss how these findings can inform future research and design directions to overcome body misperception and create novel augmented and embodied experiences.

Keywords: Body image perception · Smell · Sound ·
Crossmodal correspondence · Scent · Emotions

1 Introduction

A negative body perception or misconception can cause an elevated risk of eating disorders, isolation, and mental disease [16,29,34]. Such distortions of one's

Electronic supplementary material The online version of this chapter (https://doi.org/10.1007/978-3-030-29390-1_10) contains supplementary material, which is available to authorized users.

© IFIP International Federation for Information Processing 2019
Published by Springer Nature Switzerland AG 2019
D. Lamas et al. (Eds.): INTERACT 2019, LNCS 11749, pp. 179–202, 2019.
https://doi.org/10.1007/978-3-030-29390-1_10

Fig. 1. Graphical representation of the concept of BIP, which refers to the picture we have in our mind of the shape, size, and form of our body.

own body image affect one's way of interacting with others and with the environment, negatively impacting one's emotional state [29,57]. Thus, being able to manipulate this perception through technology can open up the opportunity for novel and more effective therapies for people with body perception disorders, and allow for new design explorations of virtual body augmentation [1,37]. Research in neuroscience [20,56] has shown that our brain holds several mental models of one's own body appearance, known as body perceptions, necessary for successful interactions with the environment. These studies have demonstrated that these body perceptions are continuously updated in response to sensory inputs received from outside and inside the body [21]. Our study suggests an opportunity to design sensory feedback oriented toward changing one's BIP.

In this paper, we investigate for the first time how olfactory feedback can be used and combined with auditory feedback to change a person's BIP. The influence of multisensory feedback on body perception has been investigated since the early 1990s [47]. Of all the human senses, vision, touch, and proprioception are the ones most studied with respect to their impact on BIP [1,27,38], with audition recently joining the effort [46,50]. Many studies have exploited visual-tactile stimulations to induce body illusions, in which the participant can embody an avatar with a different appearance (e.g., different weight [40], body mass index [39], body shape [37], skin colour [38]). Sound, in particular, has been used to manipulate the perception of one's body appearance and weight [50]. However, an important sense that has been largely unexplored from a BIP perspective is that of smell, which is surprising given the ubiquity of smell (i.e., scents surround us even if we are not aware of them [33]).

While the effects of smell on BIP have not been investigated, we see a growing interest in the integration of the sense of smell in the design of technology [13] and in several emerging HCI studies [12,22,25]. These emerging efforts are prompted by the proliferation of scent-delivery systems and interfaces (e.g., [12,13,23,30,36]) that enable the scientific investigation of the role of smell in various contexts. We contribute to this emerging research and design space by investigating the effect of different scent stimuli on a person's BIP. We particularly draw upon the rich knowledge generated in multisensory perception research and crossmodal correspondences [11,49]. We investigate the relationships between scent and body shape, and furthermore the relationship between scent, sound, and BIP.

In summary, our work offers contributions on three levels: (i) insights into the relationship between smell & BIP, (ii) the integration of scent & sound to change BIP, and (iii) implications regarding the ability to modify our BIP through multisensory stimuli.

2   Related Work

In this section, we discuss related works that have explored the concept of BIP, the use of technology and sensory feedback to change BIP, and the unknown effect of scents based on crossmodal correspondences research.

2.1   Body Image Perception (BIP)

Our brain holds at least three types of mental body representations: body image, body schema, and peripersonal space. With the last term, we refer to the space surrounding our body, where the body can grab and manipulate objects, integrating visual, motile, and proprioceptive feedback [20]. The second term, body schema, refers to the representation of the different parts of the body in space [21]. The first and relevant term for our work, body image, defines how we picture our body [43], or in other words, how we perceive what our body looks like. The term "body image" was coined in 1935 by Slade [47], who defined it as *"the picture we have in our minds of the size, shape and form of our bodies, and our feelings concerning these characteristics and our constituent body parts"* (Fig. 1). This definition specifies two relevant components: body size estimation (as a perceptual task) and feelings towards the body (i.e., tactile, visceral, sensorial, postural, and emotional experience) [47]. More recently, studies have shown that our BIP is continuously updated according to the feedback received from our actions or to the action exerted on our body (e.g., the role of visual, tactile and proprioceptive cues to induce embodiment) [21,28,43]. There are many studies in neuroscience and HCI that have used these findings to investigate embodiment and body perception in virtual reality (i.e., VR) [48]. However, there is no research on the concept of BIP and its perceptual modulation through the sense of smell. Before we highlight the potential around smell, we review relevant research on the change of BIP through sensory stimulation.

2.2   Changing BIP Through Vision, Touch, and Sound

The perception people have of their BIP does not always match with reality. According to Garner and Garfinkel [16], there are two types of BIP distortion: (i) perceptual (i.e., body size distortion: a misperception of one's own size and shape), and (ii) cognitive (i.e., body dissatisfaction: feeling uncomfortable with one's own body).

Nowadays, as a result of technological progress, the concept of body misperception can be widely studied and reproduced by carefully designing sensory feedback that changes BIP [24,37,41]. Visual, tactile, and proprioceptive are the stimuli most used to change and modulate BIP [9]. In addition, Tajadura-Jiménez et al. [52,54,55] showed that it is possible to induce body illusions through sound stimuli. These studies showed that people's perception of the length of their limbs (arms [54], legs [52], fingers [55]) can be altered by modifying the sound feedback that those limbs make as they are moved in the environment. Most relevant for our work, Tajadura-Jiménez et al. [50,51] showed that changing the sound frequency of participants' footsteps could make participants feel lighter or heavier. They built a device able to change the perceived sound of a participant's footsteps in real time [50]. Shifting the frequency spectra of the footstep's sound was found to alter the perceived body weight. More specifically, shifting the sound of the footsteps to lower frequencies resulted in the perception of a heavier body, while shifting the sound to higher frequencies resulted in the perception of a lighter body. The results showed that the induced changes in BIP also caused changes in walking behaviour. The same device was used with patients affected by complex regional pain syndrome who suffer from strong BIP distortions [51]. The above studies show how controlled manipulation of sensory stimuli contributes to changes in a person's BIP. Such knowledge does not yet exist for the sense of smell.

2.3   The Unknown Effect of Smell on BIP

The sense of smell has not yet been studied in relation to BIP. This could be because of its invisibility and dissociation from any specific action performed by the body. To date, the only sensory feedback that has been demonstrated to influence BIP is associated with an action performed by or on the body, or a representation of it (e.g., the movement of our hands [55], the sound of our footsteps [50]). With respect to our sense of smell, we are possibly less aware of our own scent (due to olfactory adaptation [8]) and what an action may smell like. Given the immediacy and ubiquity of smell and its importance for our daily life and emotional well-being, including its unknown effect on BIP, we deem it worthwhile to investigate in order to open up future research and design directions.

Several studies have investigated multisensory associations between smell and other modalities [29], adding new knowledge to crossmodal correspondence research. This research provides evidence for an association between scents and visual feedback during grasping movements. For example, some research has shown that participants opened their fingers wider when the scent evoked large objects (e.g., an orange), compared to a scent evoking smaller-sized objects (e.g., an almond) [5,6]. Other research has shown an association between scents and colours (e.g., between strawberry scent and red colours, or spearmint scent and turquoise [2,10,35,42]). Similarly, some scents have been shown to be associated with the classical "Bouba-Kiki" paradigm [19,44], where the sound of "Bouba" is associated with a rounded shape (i.e., visual) and "Kiki" is associated with a spiky shape. Hanson-Vaux et al. [19] found that lemon and pepper were associated with spiky shapes, while raspberry and vanilla with rounded ones.

Furthermore, multisensory associations have also been reported between sound and the sense of smell, which are more integrated into the perception than is commonly assumed. This was pre-figured in 1857 by Piesse [18], who wrote: *"Scents, like sounds, appear to influence the olfactory nerve"*. Later, Grimshaw and Walther-Hansen [18] proved that sound can influence our ability to interiorise scents, and they built an olfactory device that produces scents instead of sound waves, called a "Smeller". Visually similar to an organ, the "Smeller" could play "smellodies" instead of melodies [18]. It was shown, also, that different scents were matched with different sound pitches, such as fruity scents with high- pitched sounds [2,11]. These results point to a subconscious semantic correspondence between smell and sound. In our work, we used this existing but under-exploited association between smell and sound.

3   Exploration of Combined Smell and Sound on BIP

Based on the research on sensory stimuli and BIP, we explored the unknown effect of smell on users' BIP. We did this through two user studies. As previously done for other types of feedback, we first ran Study 1 to investigate if there is an association between scent stimuli and the body through the crossmodal correspondence between scent and shapes (building on the "Bouba-Kiki" paradigm described above). We presented a body silhouette (Fig. 2b) as a representation of the body shape while perceiving a scent.

Following the confirmatory results from Study 1, in Study 2 we examined the multisensory impact of combined scents and sound on BIP, following the findings from prior work on BIP adaptation [2,11] and inspired by the idea that *"what is essential in the sensuous-perceptible is not that which separates the senses from one another, but that which (...) unites them among themselves"* (Von Hornbostel, The Unity of the Senses, 1927/1950, p. 214) [49,51]. We exploit this unification of the senses to investigate the multisensory effects on BIP through combining two devices: first, a scent-delivery device that allows full control over scent delivery [50]; second, a device that is able to change the sound of users' footsteps in real time, similar to that described in [12]. In the following section, we describe each of the two studies in detail.

4   Study 1: Scents and Body Shape Associations

The first user study aimed to validate scent-shape associations reported in prior work [19,49] and establish an understanding of scent and body shape associations. More specifically, we investigated whether thin and thick body silhouettes (Fig. 2b) are perceptually linked with different scents.

4.1   Experimental Design

Based on prior work on crossmodal correspondences between scents and shapes [19], we selected vanilla and lemon scents. Both scents are described as pleasant scents and are correlated with rounded and spiky shapes respectively (building on the "Bouba-Kiki" paradigm [19,49]). We added an unpleasant scent (i.e., civet - a pungent animal scent) because it has been found that pleasantness and unpleasantness are respectively associated with curved and spiky shapes [44]. More importantly, the unpleasant scent was used to remove the confound of valence on the perception of body shapes. In addition, we used water as a neutral olfactory stimulus (i.e., there is nothing like air as a neutral scent). To represent visually the shape of the body, we used 2D body silhouettes (www.makehuman. en) (Fig. 2b). We also captured possible relationships between the selected scents and sounds (i.e., low- and high-pitched sounds), with two audio tracks played and other crossmodal correspondences (i.e., pleasantness and temperature using the two pairs of words pleasant-unpleasant and cold-hot) to achieve a more comprehensive overview of the topic.

Overall, the experiment followed a within-participant design and was composed of four blocks (one for each scent and the neutral condition) of 10 trials each. The experimental blocks were presented in a randomised order.

4.2   Setup and Procedure

The study took place in a quiet room. An information sheet and a consent form were provided to the participants upon their arrival. Participants sat in front of a desk with a computer screen while wearing headphones. We delivered the olfactory stimuli through a 3D-printed nozzle (diameter 3.5 cm) that was positioned at 1 m distance from the participant. Throughout the study, participants were asked to rest their chin on a chinrest to keep the distance consistent between participants (details in Fig. 2(a). The scent-delivery device used (described in [12]) allows full control over scent delivery and regulates its exact timing: as previously tested with respect to scent lingering, the residual effect of released scent is no longer perceived after 10 s using 1 Bar pressure (we delivered scents every 24 s at 1 Bar pressure). The device is composed of 4 electrovalves (4 mm Solenoid/Spring pneumatic valve) that regulate the air passage (on-off) from a tank of compressed air. The tank (70 l/s, maximum pressure of 8 Bar) supplies airflow through 4 mm plastic pipes linked through electrovalves and which open into four small glass bottles that contain 2.5 ml of three undiluted natural essential oils (lemon, vanilla, and civet) and the same amount of water (neutral condition). Before each of the four blocks, participants were informed of the upcoming delivery. After that, they were asked to rate the perceived scent using a Visual Analogue Scale (VAS, measures used below). The study lasted 30 min and was approved by the University Ethics Committee.

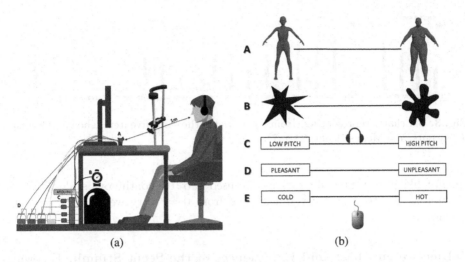

(a)   (b)

Fig. 2. (a) Setup Study 1. A: nozzle to deliver scents (positioned 1 m distance); B: tank of compressed air; C: electrovalves; D: glass bottles to contain essential oils and water. During the experiment participants rested their heads on a chinrest. (b) VAS capturing participants' responses on five main items, with A representing the body silhouettes.

4.3 Measures Used

To capture participants' feedback on the associations, we used two questionnaires (i.e., the VAS, post association task questionnaire) and some open feedback questions. To rate all the measurements, we used continuous scales from 0 to 1. Participants were asked to enter the answers by moving the mouse to the desired point on the scale. The distance from the beginning of the scale to the point was computed and used as a score (i.e., a number with two decimals).

Scent Association Task with Visual Analogue Scale (VAS). We gathered participants' feedback on five pairs of scent associations and attributes (Fig. 2b): (A) thin vs thick body silhouettes; (B) spiky vs rounded shapes [19]; (C) low vs high pitch [59]; (D) pleasantness vs unpleasantness [44]; (E) cold vs hot [60]. The VAS was presented on a screen. All the attributes (Fig. 2b) were randomised and presented in a counterbalanced order. Every participant was exposed to ten trials, half of the trials with the order of anchors left-right and the other half with the reversed order, right-left.

Post Association Task Questionnaire. After completing all the VAS for each scent condition, participants filled in a post association task questionnaire. This questionnaire focused on the emotions elicited by the scent stimuli and the liking and perceived intensity of the scent. To capture the emotional effect we used Self-Assessment Manikins (SAM) to rate valence, arousal, and dominance

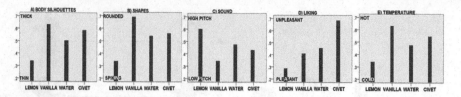

Fig. 3. Bar charts representing (from left to right) the same five items shown in Fig. 2b. X = scents, Y = Means (from .2 to .7).

[4]. For liking and intensity ratings, we used two 0–1 continuous scales (from 0 = "not at all" to 1 = "very much" and from 0 = "very weak" to 1 = "very strong").

Subjective Feedback and Experiences of the Scent Stimuli. Following the post task questionnaire, we delivered each scent one more time and asked participants to label the scent typing its name, if recognised, alongside any other descriptors they could think of.

4.4   Participants

An a priori statistical power analysis was performed for sample size estimation in G*Power, using a repeated measures ANOVA with 40 trials (10 VAS items × 4 scents). A power of 0.95, an α level of 0.05, and a medium effect size (f = 0.25, $\eta p2$ = 0.06) require a sample size of approximately twelve participants. We recruited fourteen people to take part in the study (ten males, Mage = 29.64, SD = ±5.26). They had normal or corrected-to-normal vision and hearing and no olfactory impairments (e.g., allergies, cold).

4.5   Results

Here we present the results of the analyses of the VAS scores and the post association task questionnaire, alongside participants' subjective responses on elicited emotions, liking, and perceived intensity of the scents. We opted for the use of one-way repeated measures multivariate analysis of variance (MANOVA) due to the within-participant study design and because it allows exploration of the factor interactions across dependent variables. Furthermore, MANOVA is quite robust to moderate deviations from normality [31].

Scent Association Results Based on the VAS. We ran a MANOVA, with one independent factor (scent) at four levels (lemon, vanilla, civet, and water). The results shown in Fig. 3 report a significant difference for all the attributes based on different scents (F(15, 132.908) = 4.64, p < .001, Wilk's λ = 0.313, ηp^2 = .35). As shown in Fig. 3, results illustrate a significant effect of scent on body silhouettes ($(F(3,52) = 10.688$ $p < .001$ $\eta p^2 = .381$); pairwise comparisons with Bonferroni correction showed significant differences ($p < .05$) between lemon and vanilla, and lemon and civet scent conditions. With respect to shapes, we found a significant effect for scent ($F(3,52) = 11.210$ $p < .001$ $\eta p^2 = .393$); pairwise comparisons with Bonferroni correction showed significant differences ($p < .05$) between lemon and vanilla, lemon and water, and lemon and civet scent conditions. Moreover, concerning sound, a significant effect was found ($F(3,52) = 5.605$ $p = .002$ $\eta p^2 = .244$); pairwise comparisons with Bonferroni correction showed significant differences ($p < .05$) between lemon and vanilla, and lemon and civet scent conditions. Also for liking, we found a significant difference ($F(3,52) = 11.417$, $p < .001$, $\eta p^2 = .347$); pairwise comparisons with Bonferroni correction showed significant differences ($p < .05$) between lemon and civet, vanilla and civet, and water and civet scent conditions. Finally, a significant effect on temperature was shown ($F(3,52) = 6.495$, $p = .001$ $\eta p^2 = .273$); pairwise comparisons with Bonferroni correction showed significant differences ($p < .05$) between lemon and vanilla, and lemon and civet scent conditions.

In summary, the results suggest that lemon is associated with thin silhouettes, spiky shapes, high-pitched sounds, and coldness. Vanilla is associated with thick silhouettes, rounded shapes, low-pitched sounds, and warmth. Civet is associated with thick silhouettes, rounded shapes, low-pitched sounds, and warmth. Moreover, as expected, both lemon and vanilla were considered pleasant (Fig. 3). In the following section, we report additional analyses on participants' emotional responses.

Post Association Task Questionnaire Data. It is known that smell and emotion are strongly correlated. Hence, we present the analysis of the emotional responses in detail. We ran a MANOVA with one independent factor (scent) at four levels (lemon, vanilla, civet, and water) for valence, dominance, and arousal.

The results report a significant difference for all the dimensions based on different scents ($F(15, 132.908) = 4.64$, $p < .001$, Wilk's $\lambda = 0.335$, $\eta p^2 = .30$).

Results showed a significant effect of scent on valence ($F(3,52) = 9.632$, $p < .001$, $\eta p^2 = .357$). Further comparison tests with Bonferroni correction showed a significant difference between lemon and water ($p = .021$), lemon and civet ($p = .001$), and vanilla and civet ($p = .005$). With respect to arousal, we found a significant effect for scent ($F(3,52) = 8.240$, $p < .001$, $\eta p^2 = .322$); comparison tests with Bonferroni correction showed a statistical difference between lemon and water ($p < .001$). Concerning dominance, the results did not show any significant difference. Overall, these results indicate that both lemon and vanilla scents were perceived positive (resp., M = .0.72, SD = ±0.18; M = 0.60 SD = ±0.24). Civet was rated as negative (M = 0.35, SD = ±0.19). Furthermore, lemon and civet were much more arousing than vanilla and water (resp.; M = 0.69, SD = ±0.21; M = 0.66, SD = ±0.17; M = 0.47, SD = ±0.21; M = 0.32, SD = ±0.29).

Liking, Perceived Intensity, and Subjective Feedback. We ran a MANOVA on the ratings in the post-association questionnaire, with one factor (scent) at four levels (lemon, vanilla, civet, and water).

Results showed a significant effect of scents on liking ($F(3,52) = 9.628$, $p < .001$, $\eta p^2 = .357$). Further comparison tests with Bonferroni correction showed a significant difference between vanilla and civet ($p = .011$), lemon and civet ($p < .001$), and lemon and water ($p = .022$). We also found a main effect of scents on the perceived intensity ratings ($F(3,52) = 11.022$, $p < .001$, $\eta p^2 = .389$). Further comparison tests with Bonferroni correction showed significant differences between lemon and water ($p < .001$), vanilla and water ($p = .023$), and civet and water ($p < .001$). These effects illustrate high liking levels for lemon and vanilla scents and low liking levels for civet (resp., $M = 0.72$, $SD = \pm0.19$; $M = 0.57$, $SD = \pm0.25$; $M = 0.32$, $SD = \pm0.22$). Moreover, lemon and civet were perceived more intensely than water (resp., $M = 0.68$, $SD = \pm0.18$; $M = 0.67$, $SD = \pm0.17$; $M = 0.25$, $SD = \pm0.26$), while vanilla did not differ significantly from the other scent conditions ($M = 0.51$, $SD = \pm0.28$). In addition, based on the qualitative feedback at the end of the study, despite intersubjective differences, we observed a partial recognition of the scents; in fact, 8/14 participants recognised lemon, 7/14 recognised vanilla or something sweet (e.g., chocolate), 12/14 said air or nothing, and 7/14 described civet as negative (e.g., fertiliser, rubbish).

5   Study 2: Scent-Sound Effect on BIP

Having established a scent-body shape association in Study 1, we further investigated the effect of scents on BIP in Study 2. As a person's BIP is continuously updated through multisensorial signals [47], we integrated scent with sound stimuli to investigate the multisensory effect on BIP. This is based on the established associations between scents and sounds in prior work [2,11,18]. Moreover, as discussed, prior work within HCI has demonstrated that sounds modulated through a novel device can change a person's perceived body weight [50]. Hence, building on this cross-disciplinary research, we investigated for the first time the multisensory effects on BIP by combining two stimuli: olfactory and auditory.

5.1   Experimental Design

We combined two devices. We used a shoe-based device built similarly to the one used by Tajadura-Jiménez et al. [50]. This device consists of a pair of strap sandals with a stiff rubber sole able to elicit clear and distinctive footstep sounds. Each sandal was equipped with a microphone (Core Sound) that captured the walking sound (Fig. 4a). Both microphones were connected to a small stereo preamplifier (SP-24B) which was connected to an equaliser (Behringer FBQ800) that changed the sound spectra. The resulting sound was played back to participants via headphones. We integrated this device with the scent-delivery device used in Study 1. This time participants were standing; hence, we adjusted the scent-output nozzle for the specific setup (details in Setup & Procedure below and Fig. 4a). We were particularly interested in exploring the interaction between scent and sound, and whether scent could increase or affect the sound-driven BIP modulation found by Tajadura-Jiménez et al. [50]. We based our investigation on the existing interactions between olfactory and auditory modalities, which are in general congruently associated with the same types of shapes [7,11,49].

Based on the Study 1 results, we selected lemon and vanilla scents, respectively associated with thin and thick body shapes, and water as a neutral condition. Building on prior work [50,51], we used three sound conditions: (i) a frequency condition in which the frequency of the footstep sounds in the range 1–4 kHz was amplified by 12 dB and those in the range 83–250 Hz were attenuated by 12 dB; (ii) a low frequency condition in which the frequency components in the range 83–250 Hz were amplified by 12 dB and those above 1 kHz were attenuated by 12 dB; (iii) a control condition (no sound manipulation) where participants were provided with their natural footstep sounds equally amplified across frequency bands to study if scents have an impact on BIP when there is no manipulation of the frequency of the produced sounds. We hypothesised that participants would feel thinner and lighter when smelling lemon, and thicker and heavier when smelling vanilla, compared to the neutral water condition. Moreover, we expected that when combining a high-pitched sound with a lemon scent participants would feel even thinner and lighter compared with the sound-only condition. Similarly, when combining a low-pitched sound condition with a vanilla scent, participants were expected to feel even thicker and heavier compared with the sound-only condition.

Overall, this study had a within-participant design with three blocks (one for each scent and the neutral condition) of three trials each (one for each sound condition). The blocks and conditions were presented in a randomised order.

5.2 Setup and Procedure

The study took place in a quiet room. An information sheet was provided to the participants upon their arrival, containing the details of the experiment (e.g., tasks, devices, measures). They were also asked to sign a consent form. Afterwards, participants were asked to adjust the size of a 3D avatar using a body visualisation tool (www.bodyvisualizer.com) (details in Methods used below and Fig. 4b). Thereafter, the researcher assisted participants with putting on the shoe-based device, the backpack (containing the wires and the amplifier), and a pair of sensors to track their gait (Fig. 4a). Participants were then asked to move onto a wooden board and to walk on the spot without wearing the headphones, just to familiarise themselves with the device and setup. When they felt comfortable, they were asked to put on the headphones and follow the instructions. Participants were instructed to start and stop walking on the spot by vocal commands (following the procedure in [50]). The walking lasted one minute, during which a scent was delivered three times (i.e., $t1 = 0$ s, $t2 = 24$ s, $t3 = 48$ s). In other words, the scent was delivered at the start and then every 24 s

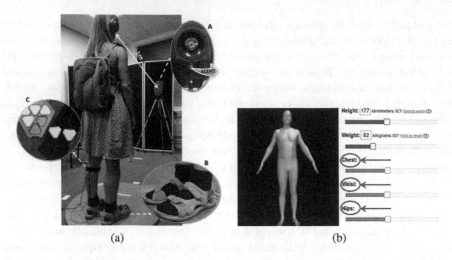

(a)   (b)

Fig. 4. (a) Setup Study 2. A: nozzle to deliver scents on a tripod (positioned 1 m distance); B: shoe-based device; C: motion-capture sensors. During the experiment, participants walked on the spot and received scent & sound stimuli. (b) 3D body avatar. Real height and weight were typed and kept fixed. Participants were asked to change chest, waist, and hips measures after each trial. The starting points of the sliders were always set in the middle to prevent any bias. The entire body was automatically scaled by the software in function of the manipulation of the parameters.

(accounting for 6 s scent lingering time + 18 s pause). We used the same scent-delivery device as in Study 1. However, in this study the nozzle was mounted onto an adjustable tripod at 1 m distance to adapt the delivery of the scent to the participants' height (Fig. 4a).

After the walking phase, participants were asked to use the body visualisation tool (i.e., the 3D body avatar, see Fig. 4b) to review the chest, waist, and hip measurements. Finally, they were asked to complete a short questionnaire about their emotions (SAM) and perceived body behaviour (details in Methods Used below). This procedure was repeated for each of the three blocks. After completing each block, participants were asked to rate the scent based on the perceived intensity and liking. At the end, they were provided with a Debriefing Sheet with more details about the study, contact information, and a sign-up option to receive further details (e.g., publication of the results). The study lasted 45 min and was approved by the University Ethics Committee.

5.3   Methods Used

To capture participants' responses on the scent-sound feedback while walking, we used a combination of subjective and objective measures. To rate body feelings, we used continuous scales from 0 to 1. Participants were asked to enter the answers by moving the mouse to the desired point on the scale. The distance from the beginning of the scale to the point was computed and used as a score (i.e., a number with two decimals).

Body Feelings. To measure the BIP, we needed an adjustable body visualisation tool that went beyond the static use of the body silhouettes from Study 1. Hence, we used a 3D body avatar (Fig. 4b) before and after each walking phase. The researcher chose the gender and fixed height and weight, according to the real ones, without any possibility of later changes. Participants, instead, were able to increase or decrease chest, waist, and hips by matching visually the part of the body in the silhouette to their perceived body. The entire body was automatically scaled by the software in function of the manipulation of a selected parameter. The numerical values associated with the sliders were hidden.

In our study, we only focused on chest, waist, and hips according to the literature on BIP disease, which recognises them as critical regions [15] for the allocentric perception people have of their body. We collected additional feedback on participants' BIP (following questions used in prior work: [32,50,55]). We asked them to rate their level of agreement using continuous scales from 0-"strongly disagree" to 1-"strongly agree" for: (i) sense of agency regarding the footsteps, (ii) vividness of the experience and (iii) feet localization. We inserted this task to ensure they had recognised the amplified sound as their own footstep, as a prerequisite for bodily illusion to take place. We also asked participants to assess their perceived walking speed (slow vs. quick), body weight (light vs. heavy), body strength (weak vs. strong), and body straightness (stooped/hunched vs. straight), as additional information about the BIP, using a continuous scale from 0 to 1.

Post Body Feelings Questionnaire. As in Study 1, we measured participants' emotional responses on three dimensions (i.e., valence, dominance, and arousal) by using the self-assessment manikins (SAM) [4]. Additionally, we asked participants to rate their liking and perceived intensity of the scents used (respectively from 0-"not at all" to 1-"very much" and from 0-"very weak" to 1-"very strong").

Behavioural Changes (Gait Sensors). Following the approach in prior work [50], we also asked participants to fit two wearable motion-capture sensors (www.wearnotch.com) on the left calf and thigh to collect the position data to quantify the maximum foot lifting elevation, acceleration, gait speed, and number of footsteps in each condition.

5.4   Participants

An a priori statistical power analysis was performed for sample size estimation in G*Power, using a repeated measures ANOVA with nine trials (three sound conditions × three scents). A power of 0.95, an α level of 0.05, a medium effect size (f = 0.25, ηp2 = 0.06), requires a sample size of approximately twenty-two participants. We recruited twenty-two participants to take part in this study (fifteen males, nine females, Mage = 27.96, SD = ±6.08). They reported having normal or corrected-to-normal vision and audition, with no olfactory impairments (e.g., allergies, cold, flu). Out of the twenty-two participants in Study 2, eight participated also in Study 1. However, Study 1 & 2 are focused on different aspects, and in Study 2 there is no effect of experience.

5.5   Results

Here, we present the results of the body feelings questionnaire, alongside the participants' subjective responses on elicited emotions, liking, and perceived intensity of the scents. We used a MANOVA due to the within-participant design and because it allows exploration of the factor interactions across dependent variables. Furthermore, MANOVA is quite robust to moderate deviations from normality [31]. For the gait data, we used a repeated measures ANOVA since the dependent variables were calculated based on the same data and were interconnected.

Body Feelings Data. Concerning the 3D body visualiser (Fig. 4b) data, we ran a one-way repeated measure MANOVA, with 3 × 3 factors (scent and sound), for each variable (hips, waist, and chest). As extra testing, we calculated the difference between the baseline condition, recorded before the beginning of the experiment, and all the others, recorded after each trial. We did not find any significant effects.

For the questionnaire items on the body feelings, we ran a one-way repeated measure MANOVA, at 3 × 3 factors (scent and sound). The results report a significant main effect of scents (F(28,352) = 1.63, p = 0.25, Wilk's λ = 0.784, ηp^2 = .115). However, there are no main effect of audio (F(28,352) = .356, p = .999, Wilk's λ = 0.946, ηp^2 = .028) and no interaction (F(56,686.78) = .507, p = .999, Wilk's λ = .854, ηp^2 = .039).

These results were obtained despite the fact that, according to Fig. 5, participants agreed that the sounds they heard were produced by their own body (sense of agency) and they did not find the experience more vivid or surprising than normal (vividness and surprise). The reason to test these items was to make sure people felt all the conditions similarly and, since the means of the variables for each condition do not differ significantly, we can say that the setup worked. Furthermore, we found no effect of sound or scent or their interaction on the level of confidence participants reported when localising their feet. Figure 5 also provides an overview of the additional items relevant to the BIP. The results showed a main effect of scent on straightness (F(2,189) = 5.071, p = .007, ηp^2 = .051), and further comparison tests with Bonferroni correction showed a significant difference between vanilla and lemon (p = .005).

Results showed a main effect of scent on weight (F(2,189) = 3.645, p = .028, ηp^2 = .037), and further comparison tests with Bonferroni correction showed

Scales	WATER_CONT	WATER_HIGH	WATER_LOW	LEMON_CONT	LEMON_HIGH	LEMON_LOW	VANILLA_CONT	VANILLA_HIGH	VANILLA_LOW
AROUSAL	0.45 (0.20)	0.45 (0.21)	0.46 (0.19)	0.52 (0.21)	0.52 (0.20)	0.57 (0.17)	0.46 (0.18)	0.49 (0.17)	0.45 (0.17)
VALENCE*	0.56 (0.14)	0.57 (0.17)	0.58 (0.15)	0.67 (0.19)	0.63 (0.20)	0.60 (0.19)	0.51 (0.21)	0.57 (0.17)	0.56 (0.19)
DOMINANCE*	0.53 (0.19)	0.49 (0.20)	0.53 (0.22)	0.58 (0.16)	0.59 (0.14)	0.58 (0.16)	0.49 (0.19)	0.49 (0.17)	0.48 (0.18)
SPEED	0.43 (0.24)	0.48 (0.23)	0.42 (0.22)	0.50 (0.18)	0.50 (0.26)	0.49 (0.21)	0.43 (0.25)	0.42 (0.26)	0.43 (0.23)
WEIGHT*	0.54 (0.22)	0.51 (0.23)	0.52 (0.26)	0.50 (0.23)	0.48 (0.23)	0.59 (0.23)	0.58 (0.24)	0.56 (0.23)	0.62 (0.28)
STRAIGHTNESS*	0.42 (0.22)	0.45 (0.17)	0.47 (0.23)	0.54 (0.22)	0.50 (0.23)	0.55 (0.25)	0.40 (0.21)	0.39 (0.23)	0.43 (0.26)
STRENGTH	0.52 (0.21)	0.53 (0.18)	0.51 (0.22)	0.53 (0.16)	0.49 (0.20)	0.56 (0.18)	0.45 (0.19)	0.48 (0.16)	0.53 (0.20)
AGENCY	0.77 (0.27)	0.69 (0.30)	0.75 (0.21)	0.75 (0.25)	0.74 (0.25)	0.74 (0.26)	0.68 (0.32)	0.70 (0.27)	0.72 (0.31)
VIVIDNESS	0.48 (0.28)	0.48 (0.23)	0.45 (0.29)	0.45 (0.30)	0.40 (0.27)	0.48 (0.28)	0.44 (0.28)	0.46 (0.26)	0.44 (0.27)
FEET LOCALIZATION	0.67 (0.23)	0.66 (0.25)	0.65 (0.26)	0.68 (0.21)	0.59 (0.28)	0.66 (0.23)	0.64 (0.26)	0.69 (0.21)	0.65 (0.24)
SURPRISE	0.45 (0.27)	0.37 (0.23)	0.35 (0.25)	0.44 (0.29)	0.46 (0.30)	0.48 (0.29)	0.42 (0.28)	0.35 (0.26)	0.41 (0.28)

Fig. 5. Means (SD) for SAM and body feelings questionnaire data (continuous 0–1 scales). *= significant mean differences.

a significant difference between vanilla and lemon (p = .030). No main effect of sound and no interaction effects were found for both factors. Further, no significant effects of sound and scent were found for the strength and speed self-reported variables.

Overall, these results indicate that the lemon scent, as we hypothesised, is associated with the feeling of lightness and standing straight; the vanilla scent, instead, is associated with heaviness and being stooped.

Post Body Feelings Questionnaire. After each walking phase, we measured participants' emotional feelings through the three SAM scales. To rate each of the three dimensions we used a 0–1 continuous scale, and participants had to move the slider to the desired point on the scale. We normalised our data with the LOG-transformation and ran a one-way repeated measures MANOVA, with 3×3 factors (scent and sound).

As demonstrated in Fig. 5, results showed a significant effect of scents on valence $(F(2,189) = 6.126$, p = .003, $\eta p^2 = .061)$, and further comparison tests with Bonferroni correction showed a significant difference between lemon and vanilla (p = .002). No main effect of sound or interactions were shown. A significant main effect of scent on dominance was also shown $(F(2,189) = 5.063$, p = .007, $\eta p^2 = .051)$, and further comparison tests with Bonferroni correction showed a significant difference between lemon and vanilla (p = .007). No main effect of sound or interactions were shown. A trend of scent on arousal was also shown $(F(2,189) = 2.945$, p = .055, $\eta p^2 = .030)$, and further comparison tests with Bonferroni correction showed a trend between lemon and vanilla (p = 0.114) and lemon and water (p = .108). Overall, these results indicate that lemon caused participants to feel more positive compared to vanilla and water. Furthermore, lemon conveyed a stronger feeling of control (p = .005) and was more arousing than vanilla (trend).

Gait Sensors Data. For the gait data, we calculated the elevation angle, average of steps, lift velocity and acceleration, inter-step interval, and the number of steps/minutes. We used one-way repeated measure ANOVAs, with 3×3 factors (scent and sound).

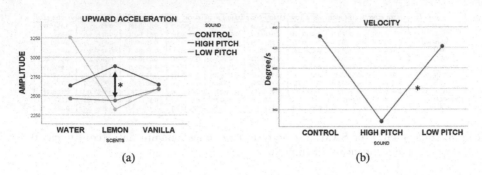

Fig. 6. (a) Line chart scent-sound interaction effect on acceleration. X = scents, Y = Means. (b) Line chart main effect of sound on velocity. X = sound, Y = Means.

The results of the tests of within-subject contrasts showed a significant main effect of sound on velocity (F(1,18) = 4.673, p = .044, ηp^2 = .206), and further comparison tests showed a significant difference between the high frequency and low frequency condition (p = .004) (Fig. 6b). A significant quadratic main effect of sound on acceleration was also shown (F(1,18) = 6.790, p = .018, ηp^2 = .274), and further comparison tests showed a significant difference between the high frequency and low frequency condition (p = .042) (Fig. 6a). We did not find any significant main effect of scent. However, we found a significant interaction effect between sound and scent for acceleration (i.e., increased acceleration was detected during the high frequency condition and when smelling the lemon scent) (F(1,19) = 5.381, p = .032, ηp^2 = .221).

Overall, these results show an increase in velocity and acceleration in the high frequency condition compared to the low frequency condition (i.e., participants walked faster in the high frequency condition) (Fig. 6a and b). There is also an interaction between lemon scent and sound (p = .032): when smelling the lemon scent instead of vanilla participants walked faster during the high frequency condition and slower during the low frequency condition (Fig. 6a).

Liking, Perceived Intensity and Subjective Feedback. Using the ratings from the post association questionnaire, we ran a one-way multivariate ANOVA, with one factor (scent) with three levels (lemon, vanilla, and water).

Results suggest a significant effect of scents on liking (F(2,69) = 10.595, p < .001, ηp^2 = .235). Further comparison tests showed a significant difference between lemon and water (p < .001) and lemon and vanilla (p = .001). We also found a main effect of scent on the perceived intensity ratings (F(2,69) = 49.126, p < .001, ηp^2 = .587). Further comparison tests showed significant differences between lemon and water (p < .001), water and vanilla (p < .001), and lemon and vanilla (p = .002). These effects illustrate a liking for lemon scent (M = 0.72, SD = ±0.25) and neutral judgements for water and vanilla scent (resp., M = 0.41, SD = ±0.25; M = 0.44, SD = ±0.28). Moreover, as expected, lemon and vanilla were perceived more intensely than water (resp., $M = 0.75$, $SD = \pm 0.15$; $M = 0.51$, $SD = \pm 0.29$; $M = 0.10$, $SD = \pm 0.22$).

Finally, based on the qualitative feedback and, despite intersubjective differences, we observed a good understanding of the scents; 21/24 participants recognised lemon, 12/24 recognised vanilla or something sweet (e.g., flower), and 23/24 said air or nothing.

6   Discussion

We showed for the first time an association between scents and BIP, and a combined interaction between scents and sounds.

In Study 1 we investigated the existence of scent and body shape associations using 2D body silhouettes (Fig. 2b). We used a VAS to test the relationship between lemon and vanilla, previously associated with spiky and rounded shapes [19,45,49], and thin and thick body silhouettes. As both scents were known to be pleasant (positive valence), we added civet as an unpleasant scent (negative valence) to remove the confound of valence. Our results confirmed the association of lemon with thin silhouettes and vanilla with thick ones. These findings contribute new knowledge to the field of crossmodal correspondences for smell. For the first time, our work focused on the body and how we picture ourselves using a simple body silhouette visualisation.

To deepen this line of research, in Study 2 we used an adjustable 3D body visualiser (Fig. 4b) and a questionnaire about body feelings to capture changes on BIP based on the combined scent-sound stimulation. We found, through the questionnaire, that the scent of lemon results in feeling lighter, while the scent of vanilla makes participants feel heavier. When combined with the sounds of a participant's footsteps, which were modified as in [50] to make participants perceive their body as heavier or lighter, the results showed that the highly arousing scent of lemon enhances the effect of high-pitch sounds related to perceiving one's body as lighter. We observed also that, captured in the self-report questionnaires, participants tended to feel as if they were walking with a straighter posture when smelling lemon than when smelling vanilla.

Implicit Effect of Scent-Sound Stimulation on Gait. While our study results are based on self-report data, we also captured data on participants' gaits using sensors attached to participants' left calves and left thighs. Based on prior work [50], we expected that shifting the pitch of walking footstep sounds would modulate the gait of participants making them adopt a behaviour consistent with having a lighter/heavier body. We hypothesised that the addition of a lemon scent would result in feeling lighter when combined with high-pitched sounds. This would also result in an increased velocity and acceleration of gait. For the vanilla scent, we assumed an association with a feeling of heaviness when combined with low-pitched sounds. This would also result in a decreased velocity and deceleration of gait. Results from Study 2 support these assumptions (i.e., lemon & high pitch are linked with faster gait), despite the explicit walking speed questionnaire showing a significant effect only for scents.

We found an interesting interaction between sound & scents: participants walked faster when smelling lemon than vanilla. The results support the literature that emphasises the multisensory concept of BIP and underlines the importance of unified sensory stimulation [49]. Based on our findings, it seems that sound has a stronger effect on unconscious behaviour (i.e., an action we do not think about) based on the gait data results, whilst scent had a stronger effect on conscious behaviour (i.e., actions we are aware of) based on questionnaire results. This hypothesis might show the novelty of the scent stimulation, which can be consciously processed and reflected in the responses.

Emotional Link to Scent Stimuli and Scent-Sound Interaction. We captured participants' emotional reactions after each trial. Although the emotional effect of scent and its relation to the perceived body image was not a key focus of our work, the emotional link to scent stimuli and to scent-sound interaction is important to consider in HCI and experience design. We found that the interaction between scents and sound had an emotion-modulation effect. In other words, we explain the fact that lemon scent enhanced the acceleration of gait during the high pitch condition and the deceleration of gait in the low-pitch condition (Fig. 6a) by referring to the concept of dominance (tested through SAM). A heavy feeling is often linked to a sense of strength that could be associated with high levels of dominance and arousal. Based on this assumption, it is possible that the lemon scent, being arousing, may have enhanced the feeling of lightness during the high pitched sound condition, and, at the same time, enhanced the dominance level during the low pitched sound condition. These findings might also be explained by the unequal gender sample (i.e., we tested more male than female participants) and the possible association between the feeling of heaviness, strength, and dominance typical of males. A. Tajadura-Jiménez's work [53], found that the effect of sound interacted with participant's actual body weight and masculinity/femininity aspirations, the effect of the high pitch condition was enhanced on people reporting a wish to be more feminine, and the effect of the low pitch condition was enhanced on people reporting a wish to be more masculine. Hence, it would be interesting to investigate how personality characteristics could affect BIP and how smell can have an impact.

Overall, our work opens up a range of future research and design endeavours, ranging from integrating scent and scent-sound stimulation in the therapy of body misperception diseases (e.g., anorexia), and to the creation of novel augmented and embodied experiences (e.g., in VR). Below we discuss the implications of our findings for HCI, highlighting the opportunities for future work.

6.1 Usage Scenarios

Based on our findings, we now explore possible design opportunities. We present three possible scenarios for the use of multisensory stimuli in the context of BIP.

Scenario 1: One possible scenario is linked to the creation of more embodied interaction experiences in VR, designing accurate environments to remove ambient distractors (e.g., focusing on a mirror in VR) to avoid possible objectification of olfactory stimuli in VR. Based on our findings, it would be interesting to study if we can enhance gaming experiences and facilitate embodiment in VR (e.g., [1,38,40]) by adding scents and modulating the auditory feedback. We see an opportunity to expand on efforts related to the creation and investigation of body illusions in VR, which can be exploited not only for entertainment scenarios but also for training people with distorted BIP (see Scenario 3) (e.g., body illusion in VR for clinical aims [1,38]).

Scenario 2: Another usage scenario is linked to interactive clothes and wearable technology. In fact, the world of fashion is expanding its boundaries by exploiting multisensory feedback with different purposes. Examples include TapTap (a wearable system that records touch and play back for emotional therapy) [3], and Scarfy (a scarf-based device which detects the way it is tied and can deliver information through shape-change and vibration) [58]. Looking beyond HCI, we see contemporary artists experimenting with olfactory interaction. As an example, Jenny Tiollotson designed an interactive scent outfit (www.escent. ai/smartsecondskin), a smart second skin dress that mimics the body's circulation system and emits a selection of scents depending on a person's mood. Our idea is to use scents not only to manipulate emotional states, and to produce relaxing or activating effects, but also, from our study results, to enhance people's self-confidence in their appearance and recalibrate distorted feelings of body weight.

Scenario 3: As mentioned at the beginning, the way people perceive their own body does not always match their actual appearance. BIP distortions are prominent in relation to eating disorders (e.g., anorexia, bulimia) and chronic pain. In fact, as the National Association of Anorexia Nervosa and Associated Disorders (ANAD) reports, at least 30 million people of all ages and genders suffer from an eating disorder in the U.S (Le Grange, D., 2012) and eating disorders have the highest mortality rate of any mental illness (Smink, F. E.,2012). One of the reasons for the increasing number of reported cases of eating disorders in the last ten years is the "distorted" body representations in our society (e.g., best exemplified by skinny fashion models) [29]. We see an opportunity to use our work as an inspiration to explore design interventions in therapies for patients with eating disorders, but also generically for those with BIP disorders. Moreover, by being able to influence self-esteem, our findings could be applied to mitigate against sedentary lifestyles -one of the main causes of obesity- which affect one quarter of the adult population and more than 80% of school-going adolescents across the world [14,26]. In fact, the advantages that the sense of smell and sound provide are their ease of use, their subtlety in everyday life, and their mobility (i.e., ubiquitous settings).

6.2   Limitations and Future Work

Although we can envision several implications of our work, we also need to acknowledge some limitations. Firstly, the group of participants was limited to healthy individuals. Considering our Scenario 3, it is important to extend these findings to a clinical sample with body misperception. In order to achieve this aim, we must take into account the cumbersomeness of our scent delivery system and undertake future work on more flexible and convenient devices and measurements. Additionally, since our subject sample did not allow us to test gender differences, it would be interesting to test if they exist, given the media pressure on women regarding body size [2]. It would also be interesting to explore the sense of heaviness as a sense of strength, as some people may want to feel stronger, and thus then heavier, rather than lighter. Our results suggest a possible effect of this type as already suggested in [50]. Secondly, although we combined self-report and sensor data, the insights are limited as BIP is a very complex concept. Capturing more parameters and carrying out repeated measures in different sessions could increase the confidence in the results found. We are also convinced that qualitative data can contribute to the understanding of BIP and the effects of sensory stimuli. We achieved an initial glimpse of the value of qualitative data in both studies (i.e., qualitative feedback). However, we want to expand on this by applying a psycho-phenomenological or think-aloud approach in future studies, previously used in HCI [60] to help people in verbalising their subjective experiences and understand individual differences. Thirdly, we tested only a small set of scents. This choice was based on literature on crossmodal correspondences [19, 49]. However, we could expand our study by adding different scents with similar characteristics of valence and arousal, such as pepper instead of lemon and lavender instead of vanilla [19]. Finally, it would be interesting to explore the use of scents linked to the human body (e.g., sweat [17]).

7   Conclusion

We investigated if and how the sense of smell and its combination with sound can impact BIP. We presented novel insights into the effect of lemon scent on the feeling of lightness, and vanilla scent on heaviness. This effects were further modulated through high- and low-pitched sounds. Most interestingly, we found that each modality contributed to the modulation of BIP in either more conscious behaviour (self-reports through smell) or unconscious behaviour (tracked through sound). Even more interesting is the interaction between smell and sound showing that arousing scents enhanced the effect of sound by making people feel lighter when hearing a high-pitched sound and possibly stronger when hearing a low-pitched sound. This interaction could be affected by how people would like themselves to be. Hence, the results point to a complex interaction between the modalities and emotional factors triggered by scents and people's desires in relation to their body. Finally, we discussed our findings in the context of HCI and present three usage scenarios where our work could make a difference in the short-, medium-, and long-term (e.g., creation of new embodied experience in VR, integration with wearable and sensor technologies, interventions in therapies for people with eating disorders).

Acknowledgements. This project has been funded by the European Research Council (ERC) under the EU's Horizon 2020 research and innovation program under Grant No.: 638605. Ana Tajadura-Jiménez was supported by Grants No.: RYC-2014-15421, PSI2016-79004-R (MAGIC SHOES; AEI/FEDER, UE), Ministerio de Economía, Industria y Competitividad of Spain. We would like to thank all participants for taking part in our experiments.

References

1. Banakou, D., Groten, R., Slater, M.: Illusory ownership of a virtual child body causes overestimation of object sizes and implicit attitude changes. Natl. Acad. Sci. U. S. A. **110**(31), 12846–51 (2013)
2. Belkin, K., Martin, R., Kemp, S.E., Gilbert, A.N.: Auditory pitch as a perceptual analogue to odor quality. Psychol. Sci. **8**(4), 340–342 (1997)
3. Bonanni, L., Lieberman, J., Vaucelle, C., Zuckerman, O.: TapTap : a haptic wearable for asynchronous distributed touch therapy. In: CHI 2016, pp. 1–7 (2006)
4. Bradley, M.M., Lang, P.J.: Measuring emotion: the self-assessment manikin and the semantic differential. J. Behav. Ther. Exp. Psychiatry **25**(1), 49–59 (1994)
5. Castiello, U., Zucco, G.M., Parma, V., Ansuini, C., Tirindelli, R.: Cross-modal interactions between olfaction and vision when grasping. Chem. Senses **31**(7), 665–671 (2006)
6. Chen, K., Zhou, B., Chen, S., He, S., Zhou, W.: Olfaction spontaneously highlights visual saliency map. Proc. R. Soc. **280**, 20131729 (2013)
7. Crisinel, A.S., Jacquier, C., Deroy, O., Spence, C.: Composing with cross-modal correspondences: music and odors in concert. Chemosens. Percept. **6**(1), 45–52 (2013)
8. Dalton, P.: Psychophysical and behavioral characteristics of olfactory adaptation. Chem. Senses **25**(4), 487–492 (2000)
9. De Vignemont, F., Ehrsson, H.H., Haggard, P.: Bodily illusions modulate tactile perception. Curr. Biol. **15**(14), 1286–1290 (2005)
10. Dematte, M.L.: Cross-modal interactions between olfaction and touch. Chem. Senses **31**(4), 291–300 (2006)
11. Deroy, O., Crisinel, A.S., Spence, C.: Crossmodal correspondences between odors and contingent features: odors, musical notes, and geometrical shapes. Psychon. Bull. Rev. **20**(5), 878–896 (2013)
12. Dmitrenko, D., Maggioni, E., Obrist, M.: OSpace: towards a systematic exploration of olfactory interaction spaces, pp. 171–180. ACM, New York (2017)
13. Dobbelstein, D., Herrdum, S., Rukzio, E.: InScent: a wearable olfactory display as an amplification for mobile notifications. In: International Symposium on Wearable Computers: ISWC 2017, pp. 130–137 (2017)
14. Ebrahim, S., Garcia, J., Sujudi, A., Atrash, H.: Globalisation of behavioral risks needs faster diffusion of interventions. Prev. Chronic Dis. **4**(2), A32 (2007)
15. Espeset, E.M.S., Nordbø, R.H.S., Gulliksen, K.S., Geller, J., Holte, A.: The concept of body image disturbance in anorexia nervosa: an empirical inquiry utilizing patients' subjective experiences. Eat. Disord. **0266**, 175–193 (2011)

16. Garner, D.M., Garfinkel, P.E.: Body image in Anorexia Nervosa: measurement, theory and clinical implications. Int. J. Psychiatry Med. **11**(3), 263–284 (1982)
17. Granqvist, P., et al.: The scent of security: odor ofromantic partner alters subjective discomfort and autonomic stress responsesin an adult attachment-dependent manner. Physiol. Behav. **198**, 144–150 (2018)
18. Grimshaw, M., Walther-Hansen, M.: The sound of the smell of my shoes. In: Proceedings of the Audio Mostly 2015 on Interaction With Sound - AM 2015, pp. 1–8 (2015)
19. Hanson-Vaux, G., Crisinel, A.S., Spence, C.: Smelling shapes: crossmodal correspondences between odors and shapes. Chem. Senses **38**(2), 161–166 (2013)
20. Holmes, N.P., Spence, C.: The body schema and multisensory representation(s) of peripersonal space. Cogn. Process. **5**(2), 94–105 (2004)
21. Iriki, A.M., Maravita, A.: Tools for the body (schema). Trends Cogn. Sci. **8**(2), 79–86 (2004)
22. Jezler, O., Gatti, E., Gilardi, M., Obrist, M.: Scented material: changing features of physical creations based on odors. In: Proceedings of the 2016 CHI Conference Extended Abstracts on Human Factors in Computing Systems, pp. 1677–1683 (2016)
23. Kakutani, Y., et al.: Taste of breath: the temporal order of taste and smell synchronized with breathing as a determinant for taste and olfactory integration. Sci. Rep. **7**(1), 1–4 (2017)
24. Keizer, A., Van Elburg, A., Helms, R., Dijkerman, H.C.: A virtual reality full body illusion improves body image disturbance in Anorexia Nervosa. PLoS ONE **11**(10), 1–21 (2016)
25. Kim, S.J., Shin, D.H.: The effects of ambient scent on hedonic experience on online shopping. In: Proceedings of the 11th International Conference on Ubiquitous Information Management and Communication - IMCOM 2017, pp. 1–5 (2017)
26. Ko, S.U., Stenholm, S., Ferrucci, L.: Characteristic gait patterns in older adults with obesity-results from the Baltimore longitudinal study of aging. J. Biomech. **43**(6), 1104–1110 (2010)
27. Kokkinara, E., Slater, M.: Measuring the effects through time of the influence of visuomotor and visuotactile synchronous stimulation on a virtual body ownership illusion. Perception **43**(1), 43–58 (2014)
28. Lackner, J.R.: Some proprioceptive influence on the perceptual representation of body shape and orientation. Brain **111**, 281–297 (1988)
29. Levine, M.P., Murnen, S.K.: "Everybody knows that mass media are/are not a cause of eating disorders": a critical review of evidence for a causal link between media, negative body image, and disordered eating in females. J. Soc. Clin. Psychol. **28**(1), 9–42 (2009)
30. Lundström, J.N., Gordon, A.R., Alden, E.C., Boesveldt, S., Albrecht, J.: Methods for building an inexpensive computer-controlled olfactometer for temporally-precise experiments. Int. J. Psychophysiol. **78**(2), 179–189 (2010)
31. McDonald, J.: Handbook of Biological Statistics. Sparky House Publishing, Baltimore (2014)
32. Menzer, F., Brooks, A., Halje, P., Faller, C., Vetterli, M., Blanke, O.: Feeling in control of your footsteps: conscious gait monitoring and the auditory consequences of footsteps. Cogn. Neurosci. **1**(3), 184–192 (2010)
33. Moessnang, C., et al.: The scent of salience - is there olfactory-trigeminal conditioning in humans? NeuroImage **77**, 93–104 (2013)

34. Mölbert, S.C., et al.: Investigating body image disturbance in anorexia nervosa using novel biometric figure rating scales: a pilot study. Eur. Eat. Disord. Rev. **25**(6), 607–612 (2017)
35. Morrot, G., Brochet, F., Dubourdieu, D.: The color of odors. Brain Lang. **79**(2), 309–320 (2001)
36. Narumi, T., Nishizaka, S., Kajinami, T., Tanikawa, T., Hirose, M.: Augmented reality flavors: gustatory display based on edible marker and cross-modal interaction. In: Proceedings of the SIGCHI Conference on Human Factors in Computing Systems, pp. 93–102 (2011)
37. Normand, J.M., Giannopoulos, E., Spanlang, B., Slater, M.: Multisensory stimulation can induce an illusion of larger belly size in immersive virtual reality. PLoS ONE **6**(1), e16128 (2011)
38. Peck, T.C., Seinfeld, S., Aglioti, S.M., Slater, M.: Putting yourself in the skin of a black avatar reduces implicit racial bias. Conscious. Cogn. **22**(3), 779–787 (2013)
39. Piryankova, I.V., Stefanucci, J.K., Romero, J., De La Rosa, S., Black, M.J., Mohler, B.J.: Can I recognize my body's weight? The influence of shape and texture on the perception of self. ACM Trans. Appl. Percept. **11**(3), 1–18 (2014)
40. Piryankova, I.V., et al.: Owning an overweight or underweight body: distinguishing the physical, experienced and virtual body. PLoS ONE **9**(8), e103428 (2014)
41. Preston, C., Ehrsson, H.H.: Illusory obesity triggers body dissatisfaction responses in the insula and anterior cingulate cortex. Cereb. Cortex **26**(12), 4450–4460 (2016)
42. Schifferstein, H.N., Tanudjaja, I.: Visualising fragrances through colours: the mediating role of emotions. Perception **33**(10), 1249–1266 (2004)
43. Schilder, P.: The Image and Appearance of the Human Body, vol. 145 (1951)
44. Seo, H.S., et al.: Cross-modal integration between odors and abstract symbols. Neuroscience **478**(3), 175–178 (2010)
45. Shukla, A.: The Kiki-Bouba paradigm: where senses meet and greet. Indian J. Ment. Health **3**, 240–252 (2016)
46. Singh, A., et al.: Motivating people with chronic pain to do physical activity: opportunities for technology design. In: SIGCHI Conference on Human Factors in Computing Systems, pp. 2803–2812 (2014)
47. Slade, P.D.: What is body image? Behav. Res. Ther. **32**(5), 497–502 (1994)
48. Slater, M., Spanlang, B., Sanchez-Vives, M.V., Blanke, O.: First person experience of body transfer in virtual reality. PLoS ONE **5**(5), 1–9 (2010)
49. Spence, C.: Crossmodal correspondences: a tutorial review. Atten. Percept. Psychophys. **73**(4), 971–995 (2011)
50. Tajadura-Jiménez, A., Basia, M., Deroy, O., Fairhurst, M., Marquardt, N., Bianchi-berthouze, N.: As light as your footsteps: altering walking sounds to change perceived body weight, emotional state and gait. CHI 2015, pp. 2943–2952 (2015)
51. Tajadura-Jiménez, A., Cohen, H., Bianchi-Berthouze, N.: Bodily sensory inputs and anomalous bodily experiences in complex regional pain syndrome: evaluation of the potential effects of sound feedback. Front. Hum. Neurosci. **11**(July), 1–16 (2017)
52. Tajadura-Jiménez, A., et al.: Audio-tactile cues from an object's fall change estimates of one's body height. PLoS ONE **13**(6), 1–20 (2018)
53. Tajadura-Jiménez, A., Newbold, J., Rick, P., Bianchi-Berthouze, N.: As light as you aspire to be: changing body perception with sound to support physical activity. In: CHI 2019 (2019)
54. Tajadura-Jiménez, A., Tsakiris, M., Marquardt, T., Bianchi-Berthouze, N.: Action sounds update the mental representation of arm dimension: contributions of kinaesthesia and agency. Front. Psychol. **6**, 1–18 (2015)

55. Tajadura-Jiménez, A., Väljamäe, A., Toshima, I., Kimura, T., Tsakiris, M., Kitagawa, N.: Action sounds recalibrate perceived tactile distance. Curr. Biol. **22**(13), R516–R517 (2012)
56. Tsakiris, M.: My body in the brain: a neurocognitive model of body-ownership. Neuropsychologia **48**(3), 703–712 (2010)
57. Vannucci, A., Ohannessian, C.M.C.: Body image dissatisfaction and anxiety trajectories during adolescence. J. Clin. Child Adolesc. Psychol. **47**, 1–11 (2018)
58. Von Radziewsky, L., Krüger, A., Löchtefeld, M.: Scarfy: augmenting human fashion behaviour with self-actuated clothes. In: Ninth International Conference on Tangible, Embedded, and Embodied Interaction, pp. 313–316 (2015)
59. Wesson, D.W., Wilson, D.A.: Smelling sounds: olfactory-auditory sensory convergence in the olfactory tubercle. J. Neurosci. **30**(8), 3013–3021 (2010)
60. Wnuk, E., de Valk, J.M., Huisman, J.L., Majid, A.: Hot and cold smells: odor-temperature associations across cultures. Front. Psychol. **8**(AUG), 1–7 (2017)

Experiencing Materialized Reading: Individuals' Encounters with Books

Verena Fuchsberger[✉] and Thomas Meneweger

Center for Human-Computer Interaction, University of Salzburg, Salzburg, Austria
{verena.fuchsberger,thomas.meneweger}@sbg.ac.at
http://hci.sbg.ac.at

Abstract. In the past few years, the materials of which objects are made of have increasingly gained attention, particularly in relation to the design and usage of computational objects. Different kinds of materialities have been investigated, discussed, and attentively designed. In order to contribute knowledge on how the materiality of things influences how individuals experience (im-)material artefacts, this paper presents an inquiry into two independent debates on Twitter about whether or not consuming alternative material representations of books (audiobooks or ebooks) "count as" reading. Our findings indicate that experiential aspects of the material instantiations of books are of high relevance and that individuals show strong emotional and reflective responses about them. We discuss several aspects of materialized reading and conclude by detailing how the findings may influence (research on) the design of future books.

Keywords: Materiality · Experience · Reading · Books · E-Books · Audiobooks

1 Introduction

Books and associated individuals' practices have been widely studied over the past centuries in diverse research communities. There is thorough research on what people read and the effects it has on them (e.g., [40]), how they read (e.g., [30]), how they learn to read (e.g., [44]), how books are created and crafted (e.g., [35]), etc. In the realm of Human-Computer Interaction (HCI), it is of specific interest how people interact with interactive instantiations of digital books (*e-books*), and how they are accessed. E-book readers and screen reading have been investigated to understand what practices are associated with these forms of reading (e.g., [18]), and to create artifacts and interactions that facilitate such practices (e.g., [52]).

In this paper, we pursue the question of what "reading a book" may mean for individuals when different (im-)material instantiations of books are available to access them. We position this research within the scientific discourse around materiality in HCI and Interaction Design. We do so to emphareize the experiential consequences of different material instantiations of the same content. We

D. Lamas et al. (Eds.): INTERACT 2019, LNCS 11749, pp. 203–224, 2019.
https://doi.org/10.1007/978-3-030-29390-1_11

complement existing work that focuses on the differences of digital and physical books (mainly e-books as opposed to printed books, e.g., [19]) by including a further instantiation, namely audiobooks, and by investigating people's debates (on Twitter) about these different formats. These debates were triggered by asking whether or not listening to audiobooks or reading electronically count as reading; though we do not aim to find an answer of what counts as reading, the respective discussions are highly informative to better understand how the materiality of books influences individuals' experiences, perceptions, and opinions.

Although HCI might primarily be interested in the future of digital books, we also include non-digital books into our research for three reasons. First, reading physical books or listening to audiobooks allows us to extrapolate individuals' preferences and practices around reading that may be of value for future interactive books as well. Second, all formats of books are interactive in their specific ways; researching how individuals interact with them (whether they are physical or digital, material or immaterial) may reveal issues and potentials for future interactions. And finally, there is a reciprocal interaction between the evolution of different formats, e.g., not only do physical books inspire the design of ebook readers – ebook readers also influence the advancement of physical books. For instance, Dresang explored non-linear reading [13] to create books with characteristics of digital media; the publisher Dutton recently released mini books, which are cell phone-sized books with pages "as thin as onion skin". They can be read with one hand, the text flows horizontally and one can flip pages upward, "like swiping a smartphone", "hoping that younger readers from a generation that grew up with the internet and smartphones might be receptive to the concept of a miniature flipbook." [1] Furthermore, individuals' skills and preferences may change, showing the increasing entanglement between physical and digital reading and reading practices that provide challenges for HCI and Interaction Design:

> This is going to sound incredibly lazy, like someone who gets in their car to drive a few blocks rather than walk, but the physicality of the book, having to hold it open then lift and turn each page, was a lot more exhausting than I remembered. All of that holding and lifting and turning distracted me from the act of reading, took me out of the story if you will. A few pages into it I gave up, logged in to Amazon, and bought the Kindle book. [46]

In order to inspire discussions around individuals' (materialized) reading experiences, we engage with qualitative material by analyzing two independent Twitter threads that address this topic, being interested in the range of things people would associate with "reading", i.e., different experiences, meanings, opinions, or concerns. The respective research question for the study at hand was, consequently, what "reading a book" may mean for individuals when different (im-)material instantiations of books are available. After summarizing the related work, the study and its finding in the following, we provide a discussion and depict implications for (research on) the design of future books.

2   Related Work

The work at hand is positioned within HCI's and Interaction Design's scientific discourse around materiality in the design and usage of interactive objects, and, in particular, it is focusing on reading as an interactive practice. Consequently, what follows is a summary of related work on materiality and reading. Of specific interest is related work that addresses the intersection of (interactions with) physical and digital books, which is mainly to be found in discourses around tangible interactions and interaction design for children.

2.1   Materiality

Design materials and materiality have received increasing attention in HCI and Interaction Design in the previous years (e.g., [5,16,47]). Materiality may be considered "a holistic paradigm of feeling and sensing the material, which allows also subtle peculiarities of materials to be recognized and used in design" [16, p. 2858]. Thus, the way how interactions are materialized is decisive for designing and experiencing them.

In regards to the design of interactive artifacts, design materials can be understood in various ways; material things, such as leather [43] or concrete [45], immaterial things, such as light [50] or radio [5], as well as digital materials, such as code [20], play a crucial role, as they only together result in interactive things. Consequently, Interaction Design may be understood as the practice of imagining and designing interaction through material manifestations [48]. Doing so requires material sensitivity, "i.e. an ability to carefully consider how different materials could be brought together in the design of an interactive system." [48, p. 203] An emphasis on materials, considered as critical in design processes is not new. In his 1992 article about "designing as a reflective conversation with the materials of a design situation", Donald Schön accentuated the influential role of the material [38].

When it comes to experiencing different materialities in interactive objects, it is increasingly recognized that the social world is heavily characterized by material aspects. "Sociomateriality", the term used to emphasize this, refers to social practices that shape the materiality of a technology as well as its effect; materiality is present in all phenomena that are considered social [27]. In the realm of HCI, the important role of materials in humans' experience with (interactive) systems has been evidenced often times. For instance, in an earlier work, we investigated workers' experiences in an industrial setting through an ethnographic study [15]. Thereby, we found that depending on whether electronic or physical materials were interacted with, experiences weere different in such a context. This results in consequences for Interaction Design in this domain, such as taking into account subtle qualities that (invisibly) influence workers' routines. Overall, new materials and combinations of analogue and digital materials are promising to "enable new experiences of computational power" [47].

In order to further the understanding and articulation of situated experiences of materials that eventually supports design, Giaccardi and Karana [17] defined a framework of materials experience. This framework is of particular relevance for the work at hand, since it is based on Interaction Design and HCI's emerging practice-orientation and, consequently, proposes a dynamic relationship between people, materials, and practices. Materials are characterized by properties (e.g., computational properties) and embodiments through which properties can be experienced and performed (e.g., physical or temporal form). People are characterized by different competences and values; practices are situated ways of doing. Furthermore, they suggest to distinguish four experiential levels that materials are experienced on: The sensorial level defines how materials' properties impact human senses; the interpretive level denotes how individuals interpret and judge materials; the affective level is characterized by emotions that result in affective dispositions towards the embodiment of a material; the performative level indicates humans' performances that they establish around material objects, which are influenced by perceptions, meanings, and affects.

> The unfolding of performances into unique and peculiar ways of doing, and their assimilation into practices, are both mediated and affected by the material character of such performances. [17, p. 2451]

In this understanding, materials may not just have a functional or aesthetic role (i.e., sensorial, interpretive, affective level), but also be active in unfolding or transforming practice (i.e., performative level), "when performances are rooted in the unique properties of the material" [17, p. 2454].

Given this notion that materials are important, if not decisive, for how practices develop and transform, it can be assumed that the same is true for how books are materialized – humans might develop practices for reading that are inherently shaped by the format of the book, the interaction that it enables, and the constraints it involves. In the following, we provide an overview of existing research on reading from an HCI and Interaction Design viewpoint and how it already incorporates questions about the book's materiality and individuals' material experiences, and we depict the gaps that are still to be filled within the state of the art.

2.2   Reading Experience

In HCI and Interaction design, different aspects of reading have been investigated in the past years, many focusing on the intersections between the physical and the digital world. For instance, Wu et al. [51] suggested a system that would allow readers to access digital content through fingertip interactions on physical books. Similarly, Bailey et al. [4] designed a way to turn digital pages through actually turning physical pages. Burstyn [8] presented the gbook, a two-page e-book reader, which recognizes page-flipping motions for page navigation. Yoshino et al. [53] created a UI system for public spaces that mimics look, feel, and usability of traditional books; Pillias et al. go even further back in history and revamp the antique scroll by exploring digital rolls as reading surfaces [31]. Kim et al. implemented a paper-book metaphor for flipping pages on a tablet [23].

Explorations of how physical materials can coincide with computation in order "to construct devices that look, feel, and function very differently from the boxes [the usual form of computational devices] we have become accustomed to" [32, p. 127] are also increasingly described in relation to books, such as Qi and Buechley's exploration of computationally-enhanced pop-up books [32], or Zhao et al.'s design of a "paper-book based interactive reading system" that supports information revisiting processes through a combination of page flipping as in a "real" book complemented with electronic functions such as keyword searching [54]. Dunser and colleagues investigated a combination of paper and on-screen elements as instructional media for children, finding that the tangible input devices triggered physical interaction "too well", when children transferred physical world affordances to 3D elements [14].

Others focused on improving reading on screens, such as how to optimize skim reading [26], how students would make use of e-book readers [41], whether dual-display e-book readers would be beneficial, for instance, in case of multi-document interactions [9], or how to best interact with materially flexible e-book readers [49]. Yoo et al. [52] experimented with humans' interactions with "living" books by capturing the readers' head shake as a sign of not understanding the words and providing vocabulary hints, or capturing when the reader comes closer, interpreted as curiosity, leading to display additional text for the reader. Raffle and colleagues created an e-book as a shared interaction for grandparents and their grandchildren in long-distance relationships, which resulted in remarkably longer sessions in comparison to typical video chats [33]. Nonetheless, there are also concerns about the effects of different material manifestations of books. For instance, Revelle and Bowman found that when children interacted with e-books, even if these had limited interactive features, there was less parent-child conversation about the book content than if they had interacted with paper books [34].

Another strand of research focuses on how to provide reading experiences for people with impairments, such as visual impairments. For instance, Thomas and Rufus investigated parameters of laterotactile Braille reading [42]; Stangl et al. explored how to improve the technical and human processes required for 3D printed textile picture books as a means to support parents and teachers of children with visual impairments, who have emergent literacy needs [39]. However, haptics supplementing narratives are not only favourable for people with impairments, but also recommended, for instance, for children's e-books [10].

Though rarely in form of audiobooks, sound in regards to books has also been discussed in HCI and Interaction Design. For instance, Colombo and Landoni investigated how children would experience e-books and found that read-aloud narrations in enhanced e-books had a particularly positive effect on children's experience [11]. The engaging effect of sound was also evidenced by Knoche et al., whose findings indicated that such interactive elements would trigger longer spontaneous utterances in children [24]. Another way to consider sound in books has been suggested by Back et al. in form a "personal interactive reading experience that combines the look and feel of a real book – a beautiful cover, paper pages and printed images and text – with the rich, evocative quality of a movie soundtrack" [3, p. 202], which was designed "with the idea that form affects meaning, and in fact is inextricable from it" [2, p. 28].

As this overview of related works shows, findings are available on various levels, from reading practices with different forms of books to experiments with novel forms of materialized reading. However, there are several research gaps that are yet to be filled. While there is HCI and Interaction Design research on children and their perception of (e-)books, we lack a substantive discussion of reading experiences in other readers beyond experiments with novel interaction formats. Recent research starts to contribute to this discussion, such as studies on the affordances of physical and digital books and how individuals value and use them over time [19]. It focuses on how people used and felt towards them as "objects": people display and re-use books differently than e-books, e.g., the visibility of physical books reinforces ownership with physical books in contrast to e-books [19].

Furthermore, Hupfeld et al. have, by means of diary studies, intensively investigated people's practices with e-books, finding, among others, that people would choose printed books if the books mattered to them while digital books were rather seen as transitory. Further, e-books were not considered to replace physical books [22]. Additionally, Hupfeld et al. interviewed people about their temporal, spatial, material, and social practices with books, demonstrating that books are more than reading devices, such as placing books around them for comfort or augmenting them to create traces. While e-readers seem to be valued primarily as reading devices, individuals' relationships with physical books seemed intensely emotional – a finding that may impact the design of e-reading technologies [21].

While our work is inspired by the aforementioned related work, it is driven by a question that extends beyond the opposition of physical books and e-books in that it asks how individuals experience, have opinions and concerns, or create meaning with different forms of materialized reading, including physical books, e-books and e-book readers, audiobooks, etc. It aims to reveal reading qualities rather than to focus on specific aspects by trying to understand the experienced commonalities and differences of materialized reading.

The timeliness of this research is furthermore evidenced by the Stavanger Declaration on the Future of Reading [12], which has been released in January 2019. This document, an outcome of the European research initiative E-READ[1], was published by over a hundred scientists who had researched the impact of digitization on reading practices (understood as how well individuals' comprehend or remember written text when using print versus digital materials) over a period of four years. Among others, they found that

> Digital text offers excellent opportunities to tailor text presentation to an individual's preferences and needs. Benefits for comprehension and motivation have been demonstrated where the digital reading environment was

---

[1] Evolution of Reading in the Age of Digitisation, see http://ereadcost.eu.

carefully designed with the reader in mind; [...] Our embodied cognition (i.e. that how and what we learn, know, and can do depends on features of the entire physical body) may contribute to differences between reading on paper and on screen in terms of comprehension and retention. This factor is underestimated by readers, educators and even researchers. [12, p. 1f]

One of their concluding recommendations is directed to educators, reading experts, psychologists, and technologists, who "should partner to develop digital tools (and related software) that incorporate insights from research about the processing of digital and printed formats, including the role of embodied cognition, for reading practices" [12, p. 2]. The research at hand aims to contribute through inquiring into materialized reading practices that translate into design recommendations.

3 Method

The research goal of the study was to shed light on individuals' experiences with and reflections on different forms of accessing books in order to inspire discussions around the design of future interactive books. The respective research question for the study at hand was, consequently, what "reading a book" may mean for individuals when different (im-)material instantiations of books are available.

One of the researchers involved came across a Twitter thread (see thread 1 below), a thread that perfectly matched the aforementioned research interest as it asked people to respond to a poll about whether or not listening to audiobooks would count as reading. This thread contained a reference to another similar one, with a similar number of statements, but with an additional focus on e-book readers (see thread 2 below). The material was considered relevant, as it was assumed that individuals would describe their perspectives, without us as researchers intervening.

3.1 Data

The first Twitter thread was following a poll of an account of a radio show (a show focusing on arts, literature, film, etc.), asking "If you've listened to an audiobook, can you say you've read the book?" The poll resulted in 69% saying "Yes, absolutely", while the other 31 % said "No, it's not the same". However, it was not this quantitative data that we were interested in, but the reactions from individuals to this poll. The thread consisted of 331 individual tweets, whereof nine were excluded from the analysis due to their irrelevant content (being an argument of two individuals on their respective attitudes).

The second Twitter thread was referred to in the first one by a book blogger. This thread was started by the blogger's tweet, stating "Audiobooks count as reading and ereaders are as good as paperbacks". This thread consisted of 329 individual tweets, whereof five were excluded from the analysis since they were either incomprehensible or without any content (such as references to people without any statement).

One limitation with this material is based on the formulation of the starting statements of both threads. Certainly, they impact how people answer, how they debate and contend, and what they focus on. While the first thread opposes books to audiobooks, the second one equals e-book readers and physical books, and both are phrased as a provocation in order to (successfully) trigger reactions by playing with the word "reading". This needs to be kept in mind when interpreting the subsequent findings, especially when it comes to discussions of semantics.

Another limitation is that we do not know much about the socio-cultural backgrounds of the people contributing to the two Twitter threads. From their Twitter profiles, we know that most of them indicated Europe or Northern America, and a few Australia, Africa, or Asia as their location. About half of the contributors indicated their profession, with a majority of professions related to books (writers, book bloggers, editors, etc.) and arts (artists, musicians, etc.). Further professions ranged from retired nurses and soldiers to scientists, students, journalists, etc. Many profiles revealed interests in books or reading (along coffee, dogs, or politics), which is not surprising given the topic of the Twitter threads. We also know that they are English speaking. However, the availability and inferability of this socio-demographic data is limited. Consequently, we refrain from relating them to specific findings. We also need to acknowledge that the contributors seem to share many characteristics (such as a passion for reading and books), meaning that the findings are specific to this group of individuals and cannot be generalized beyond the sample.

3.2 Ethical Considerations

Certainly, there are specific conditions associated with research that relies on data extracted from Twitter in regards to ethical considerations. Therefore, we consulted the "Ethics Guidelines for Internet-mediated Research" [7], wherein a main aspect of whether to use such data freely is the difference between public and private data. Public maybe "perhaps best thought of as 'readily accessible by anyone' " [7, p. 7], which we consider applicable to the two aforementioned Twitter threads because (a) they can be considered public, since they were collected from a public radio show's thread that was the basis for a subsequent public radio show, and a book blogger's thread that was referred to in the radio show's thread; (b) it can be assumed that individuals posting to these threads were aware that their contributions are public. In cases of sensitive information (e.g., about disabilities) we do not use any quotes that would draw attention to a particular person.

We also refrain from backtracking contributors (e.g., regarding socio demographic characteristics), since we do not want to invade someone's privacy. While this limits the interpretability of the findings, as they cannot be socio-culturally contextualized, they are nonetheless relevant for our research as we are interested in the qualitative range of opinions and experiences, rather than in quantitative, generalizable correlations or predictions. We also decided not to publish the names of and links to the two threads to retain anonymity as far as possible.

3.3   Data Collection and Analysis

We collected the research material by copying and pasting it from Twitter to an Microsoft Excel spreadsheet instead of collecting it via an API given the small number of tweets and the possibility to prepare the data at the same time (e.g., examine appropriateness). We (two HCI researchers) then familiarized ourselves with the material and excluded what was irrelevant. We engaged with the qualitative, subjective material in order to inform and inspire discussions around the materiality of reading. Methodologically, we followed thematic analysis [6] by going through the material several times to identify themes. After merging some identified themes as they occurred to be highly related, five themes remained that we eventually labelled as "meanings", "norms and values", "inter-individual needs and preferences", "the reader and the book", and "situatedness". In the following, we describe the themes in detail and add quotes to complement the abstracted material with individual thoughts. We refrain from adding any (individual or socio-cultural) information to these quotes for the aforementioned reasons. As mentioned earlier, we did not quantify the results as we are aiming to unfold qualitative issues around reading experiences; furthermore, given the non-representative nature of our data, any quantification would potentially be misleading.

4   Results

4.1   Meanings of Materialized *reading*

Given the trigger questions of both threads, it is not surprising that much of the discussion centered around terminology. Whether "reading" is to be understood literally or not was one major debate, with some people arguing that the meaning of the word may change or evolve alongside developments of different materializations of books, while others persisted on a narrow meaning that would include written representation only, i.e., visual perception would be essential for reading a book. However, there were further notions in between those contrasting two that included or excluded different sensory perceptions, such as reading via Braille being fine, but listening not. Furthermore, the boundaries were discussed if listening would count as reading, such as whether plays or films would be "valid" forms of books as well – with many people agreeing that, if text is adapted or cut, it is not reading any more.

People suggested a variety of alternative terms to overcome the opposition of "reading" and "listening". Many alternative terms concern the act of reading or listening, such as "getting the stories", "going through a book", "consuming an author's ideas", "accessing a story", "completing a book", "consuming words", "absorbing" or "processing information", etc. Some of them already entail experiential allusions, such as "encountering stories", "engaging with a narrative", "learning information", etc. Others discussed what it means to "have read a book", i.e., after having completed reading or listening: knowing a book, appreciating it, comprehending it: *I know how well I listened. So I know if I read* or not. (thread 1)*

Similarly: *If you ask me what book I read last, you want to know if I consumed the content not how I did so, so I'm going to say I finished Anthony Bourdain's "Kitchen Confidential" yesterday. If you ask me the format of the book though, I'll say audiobook and Bourdain was the narrator. (thread 2)*

While there were several mentions that the activity of "consuming" would need to be characterized literally (listen as opposed to read), it seemed to be fine to talk about having read the book after completion, independent from the material manifestation. Overall, audiobooks and e-books were mentioned to nicely complement reading physical books; sometimes, even consuming the same book in different formats was considered to have an added value.

4.2   Norms and Values of Materialized *reading*

The question of whether or not audiobooks and e-readers would count as reading resulted in many normative statements (concerning mainly what is better, what is proper reading) as well as to discussions about the benefits and downsides of each format. Among others, people were considered "snobbery" if they disregarded alternative manifestations to physical books as reading. Some referred to audiobooks and e-books as "real", "legitimate", or "valid" ways of reading, and audiobooks or story tapes were considered to be an (performance) art form on their own: *Audiobooks are however very valuable for their own unique aspects: listening to well crafted words. (thread 2)*

Celebrating reading independent from the formats was regarded as important. Furthermore, the impact of literature was valued over the format. Another subthread discussed the bounding box of listening – would listening prevent from learning grammar and orthography, or even prevent from acquiring proper reading skills? Would it need to support skill development anyways? What about learning pronunciation? Would reading and listening at the same time be cheating? One mentioned to feel guilt when having listened to an audiobook, but said to have read the book, another one indicated to feel unfaithful: *All reading is good BUT..I just can't get into e-books..I'd feel like I'm being unfaithful to printed matter.. "you've been around so long..." (thread 2)*

Would listening to audiobooks while doing something else (see details on what activities audiobooks accompany below) allow to immerse oneself, to create meaning? Overall, meaningfulness was discussed intensively, which seemed to be a major value in reading, similar to bed time stories that were mentioned to contribute to developing reading skills and interest in reading in children.

In terms of efforts of reading, audiobooks and physical books/e-books were assessed similarly, since all of them require time and attention. Some were arguing that listening would require less effort – leading to a discussion whether or not it would be less valuable then: *I wonder if it's a repressed protestant work ethic which makes us imagine that consuming the audiobook rates lower than reading. (thread 1)*

It seemed to be very important though, that the audiobooks are not abridged, which is easier today than it was in the past, since cassettes required to cut text to fit their length.

4.3   Inter-individual Material *reading* Needs and Preferences

People seemed to acknowledge that the ways and formats of reading are highly influenced by individual needs and preferences. There is no 'proper' reading, but a variety of approaches (see section above). They argued over whether or not the experience of books in different material manifestations would be akin to each other or not; children's books were often referred to: would reading out the book to children mean that the children had read the book? *Yes! Our youngest son learned a love* [sic] *of stories by having professionals read him books at bed time (audio books.) So he started school with excellent listening skills and the ability to follow a story. He learned the best stories are in books, and that motivated him to read.(thread 1)*

Furthermore, the imagery that was created through reading or listening was discussed; some considered physical books to facilitate the creation of an own world better than audiobooks, while others reported that audiobooks would result in rich imaginative worlds. There was also disagreement of whether books or audiobooks would provide more detail or lead to increased involvement, or whether recollection was facilitated. However, there seemed to be agreement that those experiences would differ for individuals.

The triggering questions as whether or not audiobooks and e-books count as reading led to intensive discussions about individual accessibility needs as a result from impairments. If individuals are not able to handle a physical book for any reason, would they never have "read" a book? Many conditions were mentioned that would prevent people from reading a physical book, ranging from visual impairments (low sight, double vision, glaucoma, blindness) to dyslexia, fatigue, attention difficulties, aphantasia, autism, arthritis, chronic pain, multiple sklerosis, travel sickness, and illiteracy. Audiobooks were considered to be helpful: *Some ppl can not access books in written form whether due to visual impairment or learning difficulty. Audiobook versions are their way of reading a book and a lifeline to many. (thread 1)*

For instance, fidgeting in case of attention deficit disorders, or providing the correct tone and thereby supporting understanding the content, emotions, or sarcastic tones were mentioned to be particularly beneficial (expect for people with aphantasia, for whom this would not be helpful). E-book readers were specifically valued for their low weight, since they would allow holding them, as opposed to physical books, which would be painful to hold in case of arthritis, for instance.

4.4   The *reader* Engaging with the (im-)material Book

One of the major things that seemed to matter to the readers was their relationship with the author of the book. Physical books were considered to be experienced as intended by the author, resulting in a "direct" conversation between the reader and the author, whereby the reader creates his own interpretation *All I'll say is that when you read a book, you create the voices in your had* [sic]. *You add the context, the inferences, the tone etc. You become part of it. In audio books you're hearing someone else's interpretation. Maybe that's an arguement* [sic] *over enjoyment rather than better/worse. (thread 1)*

Own interpretations would be less relevant in audiobooks because the third person, the narrator, might alter the experience through her/his performance, substituting one's own interpretation with someone else's. It, thus, would remain unclear whether the author reaches the audience as intended, whether the book is authentic. *I think there's a difference between reading as practise and consuming an author's ideas in audio. I love audiobook, the tone is set for you as author intended, but reading allows more active participation in the creative process; more resistance, debate, tension, subversion. (thread 1)*

Others considered it differently: *[...] I've connected w/ the words, the characters, the story as closely when reading an audiobook as I have reading* [sic] *a physical book. Reading a physical book is not somehow magically "more authentic" than reading audio. (thread 1)*

Some considered books to be more authentic than audiobooks, while others indicated that listening would be very authentic given that stories were passed on verbally in the past. The narrator might even improve the experience, e.g., the narrator's voice sounding better than one's own, or audiobooks might provide different readers or voices, similar to a play. Audiobooks, furthermore, would have advantages since they allow to speed up or help with pronunciation. They may also slow down, since they preset the pace. However, revisiting specific places in a book differs (rewinding, finding the right spot, etc.), and footnotes and references are missing. Physical books were valued due to several advantages over audiobooks, for instance, they provide a specific smell, they are tangible, they allow to physically turn pages, and they can be arranged in form of a library. They allow a dynamic reading experience, and the experience after finishing it seems to feel more complete than with other formats. E-books, however, may be tailored to personal needs and situations (fonts and font size, contrast, lights), and they provide immediate access to books: *Never wanted an ereader until I got one. Finish a book? You have 10 to choose from right away. Read a review of a book that sounds interesting, 2 clicks and it's waiting for you whenever you need it. Love it! (thread 2)*

However, they often imitate the feel of a book, though they lack qualities that physical books have, such as the possibility to have them signed by the author. Also, some have low screen resolutions and bad scrolling modes, which affect the experience.

4.5   Situated Materialized *reading*

In particular in regards to audiobooks, the possibility of doing things in parallel was mentioned several times. Audiobooks were described as particularly beneficial for time consuming activities, with low (mental) workload. They may accompany driving (e.g., commuting, bringing kids), doing sports, housework (e.g., cleaning, cooking, doing the dishes), crafting (e.g., knitting), watching and walking the baby, and they are valuable in case of sleeplessness. A lack of time (e.g., due to work, due to parental obligations) was indicated as one reason for turning to audiobooks, others were boredom, tiredness, work conditions (e.g., being a lorry driver, or working all day with a screen and aiming for a break for the eyes), aiming for a larger "output" (finishing more books) that audiobooks would allow. The possibility to listen together was considered specifically valuable, resulting in a shared, social activity. However, audiobooks would not meet requirements for textbook reading, such as skipping and re-reading. E-book readers were preferred for their mobility advantages (e.g., on holidays, on planes, while camping): *Since becoming a student mine* [e-book reader] *lives in my handbag, if I'm waiting for anything I can get it out and do some revision even if it's just 10 mins. It's also great for camping. (thread 2)*

E-book readers were also considered to be particularly useful at night due to included light. Physical books were not discussed too much in regards to their situated potentials and problems, except for mentioning that they do not need to be charged.

5   (Inter-)disciplinary Positioning of Findings

The difficulty associated with the aforementioned findings is that they affect various (intersections of) disciplines. For instance, findings related to how imagery is created while reading or listening to books may be positioned within linguistics, developmental and cognitive psychology, cultural studies, etc. While a discussion that connects the different disciplines would be desirable, it is beyond the possibilities of this paper. Thus, we focus our discussion on those findings that may have an immediate implication for HCI and Interaction Design research, but integrate related work from other disciplines where possible. In particular, we aim to strengthen the relation between audiobooks and HCI, which seems to be somehow deprived in our field. Thus, we take a glimpse at "audionarratology", "an umbrella term for narrative approaches that take into view forms and functions of sound and their relation to narrative structure." [29, p. 8] Therein, text experience [25] is a relevant notion, i.e., how individuals experience narratives; among others, we address this in the following discussion.

6   Discussions and Implications

In regards to the specific notion of materiality of reading artifacts, which this paper started from, we now revisit the earlier described framework of materials experience [17]. Considering the four experiential levels that materials are experienced on, there had been many statements in the findings that affect the sensory level. The diverse statements regarding sensory qualities that books, e-book readers, and audiobooks have, underline that the very question of whether audio is a valid form of reading matters to individuals; based on the findings we might assume that the form of sensory input does make a difference for individuals. On an interpretative level, especially norms and values associated with reading were vividly discussed, including the notion of elitism or inclusiveness of reading. Further, there were also statements belonging to the affective level that denoted affective dispositions towards the material embodiment of books, such as different experiences in regards to immersion, likings, or aversions.

Finally, it seems that reading is a highly performative activity, i.e., happing on the level of humans' performances, which they establish around material objects that are influenced by perceptions, meanings, and affects. Performative reading activities ranged from spatially, temporally, or socially situated reading that are influenced by (and, at the same time influence) the material manifestations of the book.

Giaccardi and Karana furthermore talk about materials experience patterns (different material experiences for different individuals, i.e., a "situational whole"). These patterns can be active or broken; the latter only fulfil a functional or aesthetic role, in the former, materials play "an active role in the unfolding and transformation of practice" [17, p. 2451]. In our findings, we find both active and broken patterns. For instance, the notion that physical books can be displayed in form of a library may be considered an active pattern, since the very material configuration of the physical book allows to do so: the paper in the specific format, book binding and cover is self-standing, it can lean against a bookshelf or another book, etc. In contrast, in regards to displaying books in form of a library, patterns in e-book readers may be considered broken, since the material reality is not resulting in a specific "performance" (here: organizing one's library). In contrast, practices of searching for something within the book may form an active pattern in e-books, but not in physical books.

Implication #1: In order to take the materials serious in the design of future books may mean to deliberately explore active material experience patterns to create novel and rich reading experiences. Therefore, radical material explorations are needed that go beyond the known text-material relationships in physical books, e-book readers, and audiobooks.

On one hand, our findings support existing research on reading in that we also found that physical books have values that e-books or audiobooks don't have, such as providing the possibility to arrange them in libraries (e.g., [19]), or that the form factor of e-book readers (e.g., lightweight, mobile) influences how and when they are used (e.g., [22]). On the other hand, our findings also add to the existing body of research. For instance, while there is a huge body of knowledge around reading practices and experiences with physical books and e-book readers, there is surprisingly little engagement with audiobooks in HCI and Interaction Design research. Though one could argue that research on audio players of different kinds would include audiobooks, it might be important to consider audiobooks as a material manifestation of reading and, as such, include it into research on reading and (interactive) reading experiences.

Apparently, e-book readers are hardly researched independent from their content, i.e., fiction or non-fiction texts (e.g., [4]) or pictures (e.g., [36]), while HCI research on audio players hardly seems to focus on texts. This, however, would be highly important; our findings unveil that people highly value audiobooks next to physical books or e-book readers. Furthermore, the content defines how people interact with the particular material manifestation. For instance, in her work on text experience, Kuzmičová discusses differences in people's desire to go back in reading or listening to grasp details; in contrast to academic reading, narrative reception is characterized by a fluency of experience, meaning "that recipients prefer trying to catch up with a narrative before taking the radical step of rereading or re-listening" [25, p. 229]. This may have serious implications for the design of audio players that may not focus on optimizing rewind or forward features, but on immersion, e.g., through providing additional details via additional sensory information. Consequently, if we consider audio as a design material, we might be able to overcome the current use of audio as an add-on to "enhanced books", which seems to be the prevalent form of auditive components (e.g., [24]).

Implication #2: Audio might be considered a design material as much as visual text or computation, to enrich text experiences for individuals. More specifically, audionarratology, (i.e., forms and functions of sound and their relation to narrative structure [29]) may be the material to start from.

Much of the experiments in HCI and Interaction Design regarding computational books are rooted in the idea that mimicking physical books would support ease of interaction, such as allowing to turn pages in e-book readers just as in physical books(e.g., [4,8,23]). However, our inquiry also showed that people value physical books, e-book readers, and audiobooks for different reasons and in different situations. Thus, creating different options that do not aim to replace, but complement each other, would be beneficial. Qi and Buechley's suggestion to design artifacts that function differently than what we are accustomed to [32] might provide guidance here, though not only affecting the function, but also the form and interaction gestalt (i.e., the composition of interaction qualities [28]) of future books. When considering that the readers (or listeners) develop a distinguishable relationship to the author of the book depending on how the text is materialized, it is imperative to reflect these substantial differences in the design of future artifacts.

Implication #3: Research and design need to envision different alternatives for reading that go beyond translations from one into another material. Novel materialized reading options should be created instead of computational artifacts replacing physical books through mimicking them as much as possible.

In particular, the situatedness of reading seems to be highly related to the experience of different (material) manifestations. Our inquiry revealed that the qualities of the manifestations facilitate, constrain or afford specific use practices, which supports the aforementioned notion of socio-materiality. However, it may be considered the other way round as well, when the environment that one aims to read or listen in affords a specific material manifestation:

> [A]dults with developed reading skills and relatively solid reading habits rarely ask themselves whether they want to read a narrative or listen to one instead. Rather, they choose between the two media based on their instantaneous situation and the type of reception it affords. [25, p. 220]

Based on our findings it may be assumed that there are many instances were the material manifestation is chosen to fit the environment, rather than creating an environment that fits the material manifestation of reading (i.e., rather using an e-book reader at night instead of turning on the light in the room to be able to read a physical book).

Implication #4: In order to facilitate individuals' reading, HCI and Interaction Design research may deliberately focus on both the affordances of the technology and the affordances of the reading environment, and, in particular, on their intersections and dynamic nature; designing for reading may also mean to design the (interactive) reading environment and situations rather than just the interactive book.

Finally, the many examples in the research material, which relate to accessibility, remind us to rethink the relation between reading and the reader's body and mind. Though the differently materialized forms of books already provide various possibilities for different bodily or mental needs and preferences, we have not yet developed sufficient, satisfying options. For instance, Schilhab et al. [37] explain how

> We all outsource otherwise fragile and costly mental processes to the environment as we integrate the materiality of the text in our memory. The materiality of the printed book makes it a stable environment in the same sense as the familiar rooms. [37]

In contrast, when individuals read digitally, solid external crutches that are formed by different sensory processes are almost absent. Thus, "[t]he unfolding meaning attribution to the text occurs without much material anchoring." [37]. And the same might apply to audiobooks as well. As mentioned earlier, the Stavanger Declaration on the Future of Reading also emphasized the necessity to focus on embodied cognition in (novel forms of) reading [12]. Our inquiry supports this notion in that it points to issues of individuals' bodily experiences (e.g., the pace of listening or reading, bodily capabilities and impairments, or the tangibility of books); it becomes apparent that the body, the mind, the material, and the environment play together. We have argued earlier that we need additional options (rather than replacements) for reading, but this is actually not enough.

Implication #5: The body-book relationship is a matter of accessibility, which not only means that there should be some access, but that alternatives for rich experiential accesses become avaiable. Furthermore, there are much more complex relationships (body-mind-material, body-mind-material-experience-text, body-mind-material-experience-text-author, etc.) that need exploration and, eventually, fitting designs. In order to reach this, research and design may need to focus on multi-sensory, materially-rich devices and environments.

7   Conclusion

This work was motivated by the observation that there are various material manifestations of reading (what we call *materialized reading*) that evolve, influence, and inspire each other – independent from whether they are physical, computational, or auditive. Positioned within the scientific discourse in HCI and Interaction Design around materiality, i.e., the material qualities of interactive artifacts that affect how individuals experience them, we addressed the question of how the materiality of books influences individuals' experiences, perceptions, and opinions, and what we can learn from respective findings for the design of future books. We therefore engaged with qualitative, subjective material in form of two discussions on Twitter in order to inform and inspire discussions around the materiality of reading. We found five themes to be central: meanings of reading, norms and values of reading, inter-individual reading needs and preferences, the reader engaging with the [audio/physical/e-]book, and situated reading. Our findings expand the existing body of HCI research, among others, by focusing not only on physical books in contrast to e-book readers, but by including audio-books as another material manifestation of *reading*. For instance, we found that the intermediary role of narrators in audiobooks is a powerful one, in that it can change (improve or diminish) the individuals' experience or interpretation by interfering "the conversation between readers and authors". We also saw people engaging in discussions around accessibility, a topic that is of high relevance in regards to the materiality of books.

Overall, the findings urge us to continue to research and design for rich reading experiences that are inherently influenced by the (interactive) material manifestations not only of the texts, but also of the reading environments. As our study was a qualitative inquiry with limited insights on people's socio-demographic, socio-cultural, or motivational background, we refrained from establishing any inferences. These will be necessary and worthwhile research directions to take in the future.

Through our work, we contribute recommendations for research on and design of future books: Our (most evident) recommendation for HCI and Interaction Design research and practice is to take the materials serious in the design of future (interactive) books; hereby, we specifically aim to draw attention to audio (and, in particular, audionarratology) as a neglected design material, going beyond adding sound, but considering it an inherent sensorial quality in the experience of texts. Additionally, we suggest to put efforts into envisioning different – novel – alternatives for reading that not just mimic the qualities of a physical book in an e-book reader. Eventually, we hope to see alternatives for rich experiential reading evolving that address the complexity of the relationships between body, mind, material, and text.

Acknowledgements. We gratefully acknowledge the financial support by the Austrian Science Fund (FWF): I 3580-N33.

References

1. Alter, A.: Tiny books fit in one hand. will they change the way we read? (2018). https://www.nytimes.com/2018/10/29/business/mini-books-pocket-john-green.html?smtyp=cur&smid=tw-nytimes
2. Back, M., Cohen, J., Gold, R., Harrison, S., Minneman, S.: Listen reader: an electronically augmented paper-based book. In: Proceedings of the SIGCHI Conference on Human Factors in Computing Systems, CHI 2001, pp. 23–29. ACM, New York (2001). https://doi.org/10.1145/365024.365031
3. Back, M., Gold, R., Kirsch, D.: The sit book: audio as affective imagery for interactive storybooks. In: CHI 1999 Extended Abstracts on Human Factors in Computing Systems, CHI EA 1999, pp. 202–203. ACM, New York (1999). https://doi.org/10.1145/632716.632843
4. Bailey, G., Sahoo, D., Jones, M.: Paper for E-paper: towards paper like tangible experience using e-paper. In: Proceedings of the 2017 ACM International Conference on Interactive Surfaces and Spaces, ISS 2017, pp. 446–449. ACM, New York (2017). https://doi.org/10.1145/3132272.3132298
5. Belenguer, J.S., Lundén, M., Laaksolhati, J., Sundström, P.: Immaterial materials: designing with radio. In: Proceedings of the Sixth International Conference on Tangible, Embedded and Embodied Interaction, TEI 2012, pp. 205–212. ACM, New York (2012). https://doi.org/10.1145/2148131.2148177
6. Braun, V., Clarke, V.: Using thematic analysis in psychology. Qual. Res. Psychol. **3**(2), 77–101 (2006). https://doi.org/10.1191/1478088706qp063oa
7. British Psychological Society: Ethics guidelines for internet-mediated research. Leicester (2017). https://www.bps.org.uk/news-and-policy/ethics-guidelines-internet-mediated-research-2017
8. Burstyn, J., Herriotts, M.A.: gBook: an E-book reader with physical document navigation techniques. In: CHI 2010 Extended Abstracts on Human Factors in Computing Systems, CHI EA 2010, pp. 4369–4374. ACM, New York (2010). https://doi.org/10.1145/1753846.1754155
9. Chen, N., Guimbretiere, F., Dixon, M., Lewis, C., Agrawala, M.: Navigation techniques for dual-display e-book readers. In: Proceedings of the SIGCHI Conference on Human Factors in Computing Systems, CHI 2008, pp. 1779–1788. ACM, New York (2008). https://doi.org/10.1145/1357054.1357331
10. Cingel, D., Blackwell, C., Connell, S., Piper, A.M.: Augmenting children's tablet-based reading experiences with variable friction Haptic feedback. In: Proceedings of the 14th International Conference on Interaction Design and Children, IDC 2015, pp. 295–298. ACM, New York (2015). https://doi.org/10.1145/2771839.2771900

11. Colombo, L., Landoni, M.: A diary study of children's user experience with EBooks using flow theory as framework. In: Proceedings of the 2014 Conference on Interaction Design and Children, IDC 2014, pp. 135–144. ACM, New York (2014). https://doi.org/10.1145/2593968.2593978

12. COST E-READ: Cost E-read stavanger declaration concerning the future of reading (2019). http://ereadcost.eu/wp-content/uploads/2019/01/StavangerDeclaration.pdf

13. Dresang, E.T., Kotrla, B.: Radical change theory and synergistic reading for digital age youth. J. Aesthetic Educ. **43**(2), 92–107 (2009)

14. Dünser, A., Hornecker, E.: Lessons from an AR book study. In: Proceedings of the 1st International Conference on Tangible and Embedded Interaction, TEI 2007, pp. 179–182. ACM, New York (2007). https://doi.org/10.1145/1226969.1227006

15. Fuchsberger, V., Murer, M., Meneweger, T., Tscheligi, M.: Capturing the in-between of interactive artifacts and users: a materiality-centered approach. In: Proceedings of the 8th Nordic Conference on Human-Computer Interaction, NordiCHI 2014, pp. 451–460. ACM, New York (2014). https://doi.org/10.1145/2639189.2639219

16. Fuchsberger, V., Murer, M., Tscheligi, M.: Materials, materiality, and media. In: Proceedings of the SIGCHI Conference on Human Factors in Computing Systems, CHI 2013, pp. 2853–2862. ACM, New York (2013). https://doi.org/10.1145/2470654.2481395

17. Giaccardi, E., Karana, E.: Foundations of materials experience: an approach for HCI. In: Proceedings of the 33rd Annual ACM Conference on Human Factors in Computing Systems, CHI 2015, pp. 2447–2456. ACM, New York (2015). https://doi.org/10.1145/2702123.2702337

18. Gruning, J.: Paper books, digital books: how the medium of an object affects its use. In: Proceedings of the 2016 CHI Conference Extended Abstracts on Human Factors in Computing Systems, CHI EA 2016, pp. 208–212. ACM, New York (2016). https://doi.org/10.1145/2851581.2859015

19. Gruning, J.: Displaying invisible objects: why people rarely re-read E-books. In: Proceedings of the 2018 CHI Conference on Human Factors in Computing Systems, CHI 2018, pp. 139:1–139:12. ACM, New York (2018). https://doi.org/10.1145/3173574.3173713

20. Hansen, N.B., Nørgård, R.T., Halskov, K.: Crafting code at the demo-scene. In: Proceedings of the 2014 Conference on Designing Interactive Systems, DIS 2014, pp. 35–38. ACM, New York (2014). https://doi.org/10.1145/2598510.2598526

21. Hupfeld, A., Rodden, T.: Books as a social technology. In: Proceedings of the 17th ACM Conference on Computer Supported Cooperative Work & Social Computing, CSCW 2014, pp. 639–651. ACM, New York (2014). https://doi.org/10.1145/2531602.2531647

22. Hupfeld, A., Sellen, A., O'Hara, K., Rodden, T.: Leisure-based reading and the place of E-books in everyday life. In: Kotzé, P., Marsden, G., Lindgaard, G., Wesson, J., Winckler, M. (eds.) INTERACT 2013. LNCS, vol. 8118, pp. 1–18. Springer, Heidelberg (2013). https://doi.org/10.1007/978-3-642-40480-1_1

23. Kim, S., Kim, J., Lee, S.: Bezel-flipper: Design of a light-weight flipping interface for e-books. In: CHI 2013 Extended Abstracts on Human Factors in Computing Systems, CHI EA 2013, pp. 1719–1724. ACM, New York (2013)

24. Knoche, H., Ammitzbøll Rasmussen, N., Boldreel, K., Ostergaard Olesen, J.L., Etzerodt Salling Pedersen, A.: Do interactions speak louder than words? Dialogic reading of an interactive Tabletbased Ebook with children between 16 months and three years of age. In: Proceedings of the 2014 Conference on Interaction Design and Children, IDC 2014, pp. 285–288. ACM, New York (2014). https://doi.org/10.1145/2593968.2610473

25. Kuzmičová, A.: Audiobooks and print narrative: similarities in text experience. Audionarratology: Interfaces Sound Narrat. **52**, 217 (2016)

26. Lee, B., Savisaari, O., Oulasvirta, A.: Spotlights: attention-optimized highlights for skim reading. In: Proceedings of the 2016 CHI Conference on Human Factors in Computing Systems, CHI 2016, pp. 5203–5214. ACM, New York (2016). https://doi.org/10.1145/2858036.2858299

27. Leonardi, P.M.: Materiality, sociomateriality, and socio-technical systems: what do these terms mean? How are they different? Do we need them. In: Materiality and Organizing Social Interaction in a Technological World, 25 (2012)

28. Lim, Y.k., Stolterman, E., Jung, H., Donaldson, J.: Interaction gestalt and the design of aesthetic interactions. In: Proceedings of DPPI 2007, DPPI 2007, pp. 239–254. ACM, New York (2007). https://doi.org/10.1145/1314161.1314183

29. Mildorf, J., Kinzel, T.: Audionarratology: prolegomena to a research paradigm exploring sound and narrative. Audionarratology: Interfaces Sound Narrat. **52**, 1 (2016)

30. O'Reilly, T., Feng, D.G., Sabatini, D.J., Wang, D.Z., Gorin, D.J.: How do people read the passages during a reading comprehension test? The effect of reading purpose on text processing behavior. Educ. Assess. **23**(4), 277–295 (2018). https://doi.org/10.1080/10627197.2018.1513787

31. Pillias, C., Hsu, S.H., Cubaud, P.: Reading with a digital roll. In: CHI 2013 Extended Abstracts on Human Factors in Computing Systems, CHI EA 2013, pp. 1377–1382. ACM, New York (2013). https://doi.org/10.1145/2468356.2468602

32. Qi, J., Buechley, L.: Electronic popables: exploring paper-based computing through an interactive pop-up book. In: Proceedings of the Fourth International Conference on Tangible, Embedded, and Embodied Interaction, TEI 2010, pp. 121–128. ACM, New York (2010). https://doi.org/10.1145/1709886.1709909

33. Raffle, H., et al.: Hello, is grandma there? Let's read! Storyvisit: family video chat and connected E-books. In: Proceedings of the SIGCHI Conference on Human Factors in Computing Systems, CHI 2011, pp. 1195–1204. ACM, New York (2011). https://doi.org/10.1145/1978942.1979121

34. Revelle, G., Bowman, J.: Parent-child dialogue with ebooks. In: Proceedings of the 2017 Conference on Interaction Design and Children, IDC 2017, pp. 346–351. ACM, New York (2017). https://doi.org/10.1145/3078072.3079753

35. Rosner, D.K., Perner-Wilson, H., Qi, J., Buechley, L.: Fine bookbinding meets electronics. In: Proceedings of the Fifth International Conference on Tangible, Embedded, and Embodied Interaction, TEI 2011, pp. 345–348. ACM, New York (2011). https://doi.org/10.1145/1935701.1935782

36. Sargeant, B., Mueller, F.F.: How far is up? Encouraging social interaction through children's book app design. In: CHI 2014 Extended Abstracts on Human Factors in Computing Systems, CHI EA 2014, pp. 483–486. ACM, New York (2014). https://doi.org/10.1145/2559206.2574784

37. Schilhab, T., Balling, G., Kuzmičová, A.: Decreasing materiality from print to screen reading. First Monday **23**(10) (2018). https://doi.org/10.5210/fm.v23i10.9435

38. Schön, D.: Designing as reflective conversation with the materials of a design situation. Knowl.-Based Syst. **5**(1), 3–14 (1992)
39. Stangl, A., Kim, J., Yeh, T.: 3D printed tactile picture books for children with visual impairments: a design probe. In: Proceedings of the 2014 Conference on Interaction Design and Children, IDC 2014, pp. 321–324. ACM, New York (2014). https://doi.org/10.1145/2593968.2610482
40. Stern, S.C., Robbins, B., Black, J.E., Barnes, J.L.: What you read and what you believe: genre exposure and beliefs about relationships. Psychol. Aesthet. Creat. Arts **18**, 1–12 (2018)
41. Thayer, A., Lee, C.P., Hwang, L.H., Sales, H., Sen, P., Dalal, N.: The imposition and superimposition of digital reading technology: the academic potential of e-readers. In: Proceedings of the SIGCHI Conference on Human Factors in Computing Systems, CHI 2011, pp. 2917–2926. ACM, New York (2011)
42. Thomas, A., Rufus, E.: Investigations on laterotactile braille reading. In: Bernhaupt, R., Dalvi, G., Joshi, A., Balkrishan, D.K., O'Neill, J., Winckler, M. (eds.) INTERACT 2017. LNCS, vol. 10513, pp. 196–204. Springer, Cham (2017). https://doi.org/10.1007/978-3-319-67744-6_13
43. Tsaknaki, V., Fernaeus, Y., Schaub, M.: Leather as a material for crafting interactive and physical artifacts. In: Proceedings of the 2014 Conference on Designing Interactive Systems, DIS 2014, pp. 5–14. ACM, New York (2014). https://doi.org/10.1145/2598510.2598574
44. Verhoeven, L., Reitsma, P., Siegel, L.: Cognitive and linguistic factors in reading acquisition. Read. Writ. **24**, 387–394 (2011)
45. Wang, Y., Liu, S., Lu, Y., Duan, J., Yao, C., Ying, F.: Designing with concrete for enhancing everyday interactions. In: Proceedings of the 2016 CHI Conference Extended Abstracts on Human Factors in Computing Systems, CHI EA 2016, pp. 1497–1502. ACM, New York (2016). https://doi.org/10.1145/2851581.2892372
46. White, K.: shift happened (2011). http://futureofthebook.org/blog/2011/03/23/shift_happened/
47. Wiberg, M.: Interaction, new materials & computing - beyond the disappearing computer, towards material interactions. Mater. Des. **90**, 1200–1206 (2016). https://doi.org/10.1016/j.matdes.2015.05.032
48. Wiberg, M.: Addressing IoT: towards material-centered interaction design. In: Kurosu, M. (ed.) HCI 2018. LNCS, vol. 10901, pp. 198–207. Springer, Cham (2018). https://doi.org/10.1007/978-3-319-91238-7_17
49. Wightman, D., Ginn, T., Vertegaal, R.: BendFlip: examining input techniques for electronic book readers with flexible form factors. In: Campos, P., Graham, N., Jorge, J., Nunes, N., Palanque, P., Winckler, M. (eds.) INTERACT 2011. LNCS, vol. 6948, pp. 117–133. Springer, Heidelberg (2011). https://doi.org/10.1007/978-3-642-23765-2_9
50. Windlin, C., Laaksolahti, J.: Unpacking visible light communication as a material for design. In: Proceedings of the 2017 CHI Conference on Human Factors in Computing Systems, CHI 2017, pp. 2019–2023. ACM, New York (2017). https://doi.org/10.1145/3025453.3025862
51. Wu, C.S.A., Robinson, S.J., Mazalek, A.: Turning a page on the digital annotation of physical books. In: Proceedings of the 2nd International Conference on Tangible and Embedded Interaction, TEI 2008, pp. 109–116. ACM, New York (2008). https://doi.org/10.1145/1347390.1347414

52. Yoo, S., Lakshminarayana, C., Basu, A.: Nellodee 1.0: a living book to enhance intimacy with head gestures and kinetic typography. In: Proceedings of the Eleventh International Conference on Tangible, Embedded, and Embodied Interaction, TEI 2017, pp. 517–520. ACM, New York (2017). https://doi.org/10.1145/3024969.3025086

53. Yoshino, K., Obata, K., Tokuhisa, S.: FLIPPIN': exploring a paper-based book UI design in a public space. In: Proceedings of the 2017 CHI Conference on Human Factors in Computing Systems, CHI 2017, pp. 1508–1517. ACM, New York (2017). https://doi.org/10.1145/3025453.3025981

54. Zhao, Y., Qin, Y., Liu, Y., Liu, S., Zhang, T., Shi, Y.: QOOK: enhancing information revisitation for active reading with a paper book. In: Proceedings of the 8th International Conference on Tangible, Embedded and Embodied Interaction, TEI 2014, pp. 125–132. ACM, New York (2013). https://doi.org/10.1145/2540930.2540977

"I Kept Browsing and Browsing, But Still Couldn't Find the One": Salient Factors and Challenges in Online Typeface Selection

Y. Wayne Wu[1(✉)], Michael Gilbert[2], and Elizabeth Churchill[3]

[1] University of Illinois at Urbana-Champaign, Champaign, IL 61801, USA
yuwu4@illinois.edu
[2] Google Inc., New York, NY 10011, USA
[3] Google Inc., Mountain View, CA 94043, USA

Abstract. Web fonts quickly gained popularity among practitioners. Despite their wide-spread usage and critical role in design, there is a lack of empirical research regarding how practitioners select web fonts and what problems they encounter in the process. To fill this knowledge gap, we took a mixed-method approach to examine the salient factors and common issues in the typeface selection process. To understand the landscape of the problem, we first analyzed adoption data for Google Fonts, a representative online fonts directory. Then, we interviewed practitioners regarding their experience selecting web fonts and the problems they encountered. Finally, we issued a follow-up survey to validate the qualitative findings. Our study uncovered how practitioners operationalized three salient factors—affordability, functionality, and personality—in the typeface selection process. Participants reported difficulty in finding typefaces that satisfy the functionality and personality needs. We discuss patterns that led to this difficulty and offered practical design guidelines that alleviated the identified issues.

Keywords: Typeface selection · Tools for design · Empirical study

1 Introduction

Typeface plays a critical role in design. In online environments, web fonts allow practitioners to deliver the ideal user experience perfectly as designed without burdening users with installing required fonts. Widely welcomed by platform designers, billions of users read web fonts every day [29]. Because of this popularity, the number of web typefaces has risen quickly in recent years. Google Fonts alone, one of the most popular font directories, offers nearly one thousand typefaces in various styles. However, this surge in web fonts makes typeface selection a more tedious process than it was a decade ago when there was only a handful to choose from. To make the matter worse, evaluating potential typeface candidates also takes time. An ideal typeface complements the graphics and text on a web page to fulfill a preset purpose. To find the typeface most suitable for their design needs, practitioners must browse through hundreds of potential candidates and scrutinize the subtle differences among them.

© IFIP International Federation for Information Processing 2019
Published by Springer Nature Switzerland AG 2019
D. Lamas et al. (Eds.): INTERACT 2019, LNCS 11749, pp. 225–234, 2019.
https://doi.org/10.1007/978-3-030-29390-1_12

Despite the popularity and the critical role typefaces play, empirical research regarding how practitioners select typefaces is scarce in the HCI community.

To fill this knowledge gap, we designed a mixed-method approach to study practitioners' experience in selecting web typefaces. Specifically, we identified salient factors and the obstacles practitioners frequently encounter in the selection process. Also, we sought to uncover patterns in the typeface adoption process, such as herding behaviors. In this work, Google Fonts serves as a reference point that helps us to understand the problem space. We interviewed practitioners regarding their general online design and typeface selection process. Participants use Google Fonts as a concrete example to describe the shortcomings of existing tools and desired functions. We followed up with a survey to validate the generalizability of the qualitative findings.

Our results show that three factors played vital roles in participants' typeface selection process: affordability, functionality, and personality. As typeface selection is a critical step in the broader design process, which includes many parts that influence each other dynamically, the requirement for each factor in typeface selection constantly changes based on business and design needs. Participants found it challenging to meet these ever-changing requirements and found the support from existing typeface selection tools insufficient. The survey results confirmed the qualitative findings. Participants also reported the functionality and personality requirements were significantly harder to satisfy than affordability.

In summary, our work makes three main contributions: (a) we reported how practitioners operationalized three salient factors in typeface selection process and validate the generalizability of the findings via a large-scale survey study; (b) we uncovered common difficulties practitioners face in the process; and (c) we offered practical design guidelines that addressed the identified problems.

2   Related Work

Prior work has identified the importance of typeface functionality and personality and proposed various ways to measure them. The functionality of a typeface usually depends on the display medium. Typefaces that read well on paper may be illegible on digital screens [1]. Recent technology advancement allowed users to read in new mediums, such as e-ink and augmented/virtual reality displays, but also raised new legibility challenges for typefaces [8, 27]. Even on the same medium, the legibility of a typeface may vary depending on screen resolution [4, 27], text layout [9, 24], text direction [16], font size and type [3, 16]. Moreover, practitioners also need to consider accessibility requirements from users with specific conditions, such as dyslexia [22, 23] and low vision [25]. While researchers have devised a set of standard test to evaluate a specific font within a given display environment [28], it is still time-consuming for practitioners to run these tests for all potential typeface candidates.

Typefaces have personalities reflected in their emotional connotations. Reading the same text rendered in different typefaces triggers different emotional reactions and influences the reading experience [5, 13, 18, 19]. Prior work shows users tend to reach a consensus about associations between specific typefaces and personality traits [15, 17].

At a high level, the design family of a typeface, e.g. serif, san serif, etc., also associates with the perceived personality of the typeface [26]. Accurately assigning emotional connotations for a large set of typefaces is more labor-intensive. O'Donovan et al. built a crowdsourcing system to facilitate this process [20]. However, there is still no widely accepted taxonomy for emotional connotations of typefaces in real-world settings. Furthermore, participants in our study expressed the need to connect the typeface personality with business needs; popular online platforms provide no support for this function. Prior research has also explored innovative ways to display fonts that convey emotional connotations, such as using animation in kinetic fonts [14]. While the participants in our study did not request this specific feature, many expressed the desire to modify existing fonts to meet their personality needs.

Researchers have explored how practitioners make design decisions in real-world settings. Prior research found that design firms invest a significant amount of resources in well-studied methods to facilitate decision-making, such as building user personas to inform design decisions [12]. However, real-world practices are occasionally disconnected from design theories. Prior work found that novice designers were frequently well versed on user-centric design theories, but in practice, they seldom relied on related theories to make design decisions [10] or had misconception regarding how users perceive specific fonts [2]. Instead, they often made decisions without referencing related user research data [11]. This disconnection may be caused by the fast-paced and limited-resource nature of the tech industry. In our study, we proposed platform design guidelines that could narrow this gap and make it easier for practitioners to follow related design theories while selecting fonts.

3   Study Background

To understand the landscape of the problem, we started our study by analyzing the adoption trends of Google Fonts. The analyses were conducted over the HTTP Archive datasets [30]. The archive collects traffic rank and external request data twice a month for the 500k most popular sites ranked by Amazon Alexa [31]. Sites with frequent requests sent to fonts.googleapis.com or fonts.gstatic.com were considered as adopters. Data for several dates were missing from the original HTTP Archive dataset and thus excluded from the analysis.

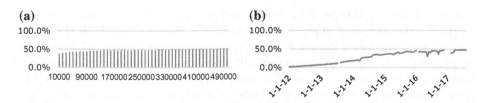

Fig. 1. a. (left) Google Fonts adoption rate (vertical axes) across Alexa rank ranges (horizontal axis); b. (right) Historical adoption rate trend.

Our results showed that web fonts were adopted pervasively across sites in different rank ranges. Figure 1a shows the percent of sites that adopted Google Fonts across Alexa ranks as of August 2017. It appeared that there was no strong association between the site rank and the likelihood of adoption. Approximately half of the sites adopted Google Fonts across rank ranges. Figure 1b shows the historical trend of the adoption rate, which grew steadily and reached 47.5% as of July 2017. As Google Fonts provided half of the fonts on the Internet, the problems we uncovered were representative and pervasive across tiers of web services.

4   Qualitative Interview

In this section, we report salient factors and noticeable patterns in typeface selection.

4.1   Methodology

We conducted interviews with 10 practitioners who had direct experience in selecting fonts for a public facing mobile app and/or website. We recruited a diverse set of participants to gain a comprehensive understanding of the typeface selection process. The 10 participants (4 females, 6 males) had different roles (4 designers, 3 design managers, 3 engineers with design experience), different experience levels (two years to three decades of experience), and worked in companies of different sizes (three worked for early-stage startups or in freelancing, four worked for companies with fewer than 100 employees, three worked for companies with more than 100 employees). Qualified participants were contacted via email and compensated $125 for the interview. Two authors conducted the interviews in English at a user research lab in San Francisco. A pilot study with two non-participant designers helped us to devise the interview script. During the sessions, participants answered questions regarding their experience with typeface selections and the issues they had encountered. We transcribed and analyzed the interviews in a grounded theory approach [6].

4.2   Results

We found a typeface was evaluated using three salient factors: affordability, functionality, and personality. As prior work has explored typeface functionality and personality, below we report only the novel findings that complement prior work.

Salient Factor #1 Affordability. While prior work rarely discusses the cost of a typeface in the context of online design, participants repeatedly emphasized the limitation of funds and how it influences their typeface selection. Premium typefaces would be excluded from consideration because of monetary cost. As one participant in a management role said: *"If we have a marketing budget that is unlimited, and my designer came to me and made a compelling case about a font selection. And that's something we have to pay for. Probably I'll give him what he wanted. But the mission for this company is to run as lean as possible, so we would never have this discussion."*

A typeface may also be unaffordable even it is free. Participants found some typefaces costly because of the amount of engineering required. One participant stated while the designers in her company disliked the in-use typeface, they lacked the engineering resources to update the outdated infrastructure to support modern web fonts. A company might also be reluctant to change fonts because it is too expensive to replace the existing ones. One participant said the official typeface for their company had been used for many years and changing it would require them to discard existing printed marketing materials, which they could not afford.

Salient Factor #2 Functionality. Participants emphasized that a functional typeface should be legible across different platforms. In addition, we also found participants strongly desired typefaces that were efficient in development cycles. A functional typeface should be rendered in the same way by design software (e.g., Photoshop or Sketch) as by the Internet browsers on the user end. Inconsistency between software environments often increased friction across functions. One engineer participant said: *"When [designers] pick bad ones [typefaces], they may look yucky in browser. I spent too much time explaining to designers the difference between [what you see in] Photoshop and what you see on screen and websites."*

While participants recognized the importance of typeface functionality, they often found it very time-consuming to evaluate the legibility of typeface candidates. The problem was more acute for small to medium size companies because of resource scarcity. The design team often did not have time to conduct rigorous evaluations. As a result, participants chose to blindly trust online typeface directories hoping the offered typefaces had already passed strict legibility tests.

Salient Factor #3 Personality. While understanding typefaces had different emotional connotations, participants often struggle to find the typeface that most suitable for the business needs and yet consistent with the product/brand image. One participant from a financial services company emphasized the importance of a "professional" typeface; another participant from a social community company preferred more "active" type-faces. Practitioners needed to adopt a design style associated with the public perception of their industry sector. On the other hand, practitioners also needed to differentiate themselves from their competitors. One participant said he intentionally avoided using the most popular typefaces to deliver a unique impression.

Even when participants knew exactly what impression they wanted to deliver, they still had a difficult time finding the ideal typeface. One participant said: *"When I'm looking for a particular font, you know what feeling you want the font to have. But I just spent so much time browsing and browsing, and still couldn't find the one."* Online directories provide common typeface categories (serif, sans serif, etc.) and filters (by thickness, width, etc.) to facilitate the search. However, as design trends and business needs shift constantly, it was still challenging to find the ideal typeface.

Weak Herding Behavior. One consideration at the outset of this research was to determine whether popular typeface choices would influence practitioners' typeface selection and to what degree platform designers should emphasize popular choices. Our results showed weak herding behavior in the selection process. Participants reported visiting various sources, such as blogs, newsletters, and magazines, to collect design examples. Later, they would incorporate elements gleaned from these sources into their design rather than directly mimicking the sources. Even design recommendations from trustworthy sources needed to be critically evaluated. One participant said: *"If a really good designer friend of mine shows me a design that makes no sense, I'll be like I know that person is a good designer, maybe there is something I don't know ... depending on the experience of the designer, I may put more thought in it."*

We found that participants would not blindly follow their peers or other design sources. They might take recommendations from trusted sources into consideration, but they still wanted to spend significant effort in searching for suitable typefaces.

Inability to Adjust Typefaces. After participants expressed frustration in finding the ideal typeface, they indicated their desires to "slightly tweak" the typefaces. Sometimes, participants could find a typeface that partially fulfilled their needs but was "just a little bit off." Existing tools for crafting typefaces were mainly designed for experienced typographers. Participants worried that their adjustments might lead to typeface quality issues, such as lowering the aesthetic value and legibility of the typeface. Practitioners with less experience in typefaces might benefit from a tool that supports a moderate amount of adjustment to typefaces without causing significant quality issues.

5   Survey Study

After the qualitative study, we ran a survey to gauge the generalizability of our findings.

5.1   Methodology

The survey included three parts. The first part focused on the salient factors in the typeface selection process. For each of the three salient factors, we devised two options covering different aspects of the factor based on the qualitative findings. The second part of the survey focused on herding behaviors. Two questions asked participants about their reactions to typefaces used by design leaders and popular online typefaces. The last part of the survey asked participants about their desire to modify typefaces and the extent to which they would like to do so.

We followed a strict process to recruit participants in Arts and Design professions from Amazon Mechanical Turk. Qualified participants must work as a design professional and have experiences selecting typefaces. We designed the survey in a way that participants had no incentive to misreport their background – all participants received payments regardless of responses; none was aware of the screening either. 37% of the collected responses (144/389) passed the screening and were used in the analysis. Among these, 41.6% had fewer than three years of design experience, 20.8% had more than three and fewer than five years, and 37.5% had more than five years of experience. 63.2% of the participants have made a typeface selection for at least once and the rest 36.8% have participated in such a process. All participants resided in the U.S.

5.2   Results

More than half the participants viewed personality as an important factor in the typeface selection process, and approximately half the participants viewed functionality as important (Table 1). Fewer participants selected affordability as an important salient factor; this might be caused by the bias in the participant pool towards design professionals. Although in a real-world setting, practitioners might only be able to use typefaces that fit the budget, they viewed the other two factors as being more important in the selection process. On a 5-point scale, participants reported spending significantly more effort searching for typefaces that met the functionality and personality requirements than they did for affordability.

Table 1. Ratio of participants who valued different salient factors. For the mean effort invested in the search, values (max = 5) with different superscripts are significantly different. Participants spent significantly more effort searching for functional and personal typefaces than for affordable ones.

Factor	Statement	Perc.	Effort (std.)
affordability	Engineering wise, it is very easy to implement the new typeface	20.1%	2.69^a (0.96)
	The typeface has a low price or comes free	29.2%	2.79^a (0.89)
functionality	The typeface is rendered the same across platforms and software	41.7%	3.33^b (1.07)
	The typeface reads well in different sizes and weights	48.6%	3.24^b (0.82)
personality	The typeface conveys a feeling that fits well with my design style	62.5%	3.41^b (0.99)
	The typeface has a consistent feel with the product/brand image	64.6%	3.42^b (0.97)

Consistent with the qualitative findings, few participants said they prefer to use typefaces used by design leaders (6.9%) or popular typefaces (9.0%). Significantly more participants said they tried to learn why a typeface was used by design leaders (36.1%) or why it was popular online (38.2%) and then selected typefaces using the same principles. A similar number of participants did not value typefaces used by design leaders (39.6%) or popular ones (34.0%) more than other typefaces. The rest of the participants had negative opinions about typefaces used by design leaders (17.2%) and popular ones (18.7%). Most participants would consider the typefaces recommended by design leaders and popular opinion, instead of blindly making the same selection. Overall, participants showed a weak herding behavior in the typeface selection process.

Most participants were interested in tools that allow them to create new typefaces (25.7%) and make changes to existing typefaces (68.7%). 28.5% expressed interests in making major changes, such as creating new characters; 30.6%, medium changes, such as revising part of a character and adjusting height/width; and 9.7%, minor changes, such as adjusting kerning and font weights. Only 5.6% of the participants said they had no interest. These results were consistent with our earlier qualitative findings.

6 Discussion and Recommendations

Our results showed practitioners often struggle to find typefaces that met the functionality and personality needs. Instead of imposing the burden on practitioners, online typeface directories could offer more legibility information to facilitate the search, such as recommended font sizes based on standard tests [28] or typefaces accessible to people with disabilities (e.g. dyslexia [21], low vision [25], etc.). In terms of costs, it is relatively inexpensive for platform designers to evaluate typefaces, especially when compared to the cost of creating new ones. Web font providers could also share font usage data to empower practitioners to make more informed decisions, such as the up-to-date distribution of screen sizes or display mediums.

Regarding typeface personality, platform designers should consider offering more up-to-date recommendations. Existing platforms, including Google Fonts, Font Squirrel, offer curated typeface collections based on style and personality [32]. Prior work has also explored using online crowds to label typeface personality [20]. Platforms offer the same static collections for years and rarely update them. However, our results showed practitioners often selected typefaces in response to the ever-changing design trends within the industry sector. Platform designers could provide more present font usage data in different industry sectors to empower practitioners. Alternatively, practitioners may benefit from context-aware typeface recommendations. Prior work has explored algorithms that recommend typefaces for image pairing [7]. As practitioners usually make service-wide typeface selections beyond the scope of one single image, future research could explore the possibility of recommending typeface pairings based on the content, image, together with other design elements.

Participants expressed strong interests in adjusting and creating typefaces when they couldn't find an ideal one. Platform designers may consider offering such features as a last resort for practitioners after an unfruitful search. On the other hand, while the interest was strong, participants worried misadjustment might reduce the typeface's legibility or aesthetic appeal. In recent years, some tools have started to support parametric typeface creation [33, 34]. However, such tools do not yet offer quality-checks for the typefaces created. Platform designers could offer ways to quickly assess the functionality and personality of a new typeface in an affordable way, such as using online crowds. Participants also expressed their desire to change an existing typeface. Future work could explore parametric ways to modify typefaces in addition to creating new ones.

7 Conclusion

Our research makes three contributions: (a) we provided empirical evidence regarding how practitioner operationalize salient factors in their typeface selection and validated the generalizability of our findings via a survey; (b) our mixed-method study uncovered the difficulties practitioners frequently encountered in this process; and (c) we offered practical design guidelines that alleviated the identified issues for platform designers. We envision a future where our findings help platform designers to improve the user experience of typeface browsing, to help practitioners make more informed typeface selections, and ultimately, to build a more functional and more personal Internet.

References

1. Ali, A.Z.M., Wahid, R., Samsudin, K., Idris, M.Z.: Reading on the computer screen: does font type has effects on web text readability? Int. Educ. Stud. **6**(3), 26–35 (2013). https://doi.org/10.5539/ies.v6n3p26
2. Bartram, D.: The perception of semantic quality in type: differences between designers and non-designers. Inf. Des. J. **3**(1), 38–50 (1982). https://doi.org/10.1075/idj.3.1.04bar
3. Beymer, D., Orton, P.Z., Russell, D.M.: An Eye Tracking Study of How Pictures Influence Online Reading, pp. 456–460. https://doi.org/10.1007/978-3-540-74800-7_41
4. Boyarski, D., Neuwirth, C., Forlizzi, J., Regli, S.H.: A study of fonts designed for screen display. In: Proceedings of the SIGCHI Conference on Human Factors in Computing Systems - CHI 1998, pp. 87–94 (1998). https://doi.org/10.1145/274644.274658
5. Candello, H., Pinhanez, C., Figueiredo, F.: Typefaces and the perception of humanness in natural language chatbots. In: Proceedings of the 2017 CHI Conference on Human Factors in Computing Systems - CHI 2017, pp. 3476–3487 (2017). https://doi.org/10.1145/3025453.3025919
6. Charmaz, K.: Constructing Grounded Theory: A Practical Guide Through Qualitative Analysis, 1st edn. SAGE Publications Inc., London (2006)
7. Choi, S., Aizawa, K., Sebe, N.: FontMatcher. In: Proceedings of the 2018 Conference on Human Information Interaction & Retrieval - IUI 2018, pp. 37–41 (2018). https://doi.org/10.1145/3172944.3173001
8. Di Donato, M., Fiorentino, M., Uva, A.E., Gattullo, M., Monno, G.: Text legibility for projected augmented reality on industrial workbenches. Comput. Ind. **70**, 70–78 (2015). https://doi.org/10.1016/j.compind.2015.02.008
9. Dyson, M.C.: How physical text layout affects reading from screen. Behav. Inf. Technol. **23**(6), 377–393 (2004). https://doi.org/10.1080/01449290410001715714
10. Friess, E.: Defending design decisions with usability evidence: a case study. In: CHI EA 2008 CHI 2008 Extended Abstracts on Human Factors in Computing Systems, p. 2009 (2008). https://doi.org/10.1145/1358628.1358631
11. Friess, E.: Designing from data: rhetorical appeals in support of design decisions. J. Bus. Tech. Commun. **24**(4), 1–42 (2010). https://doi.org/10.1177/1050651910371197
12. Friess, E.: Personas and decision making in the design process. In: Proceedings of 2012 ACM Annual Conference on Human Factors in Computing Systems - CHI 2012, p. 1209, May 2012. https://doi.org/10.1145/2207676.2208572
13. Larson, K., Hazlett, R.L., Chaparro, B.S., Picard, R.W.: Measuring the aesthetics of reading. In: Bryan-Kinns, N., Blanford, A., Curzon, P., Nigay, L. (eds.) People and Computers XX—Engage, pp. 41–56. Springer, London (2007). https://doi.org/10.1007/978-1-84628-664-3_4
14. Lee, J., Jun, S., Forlizzi, J., Hudson, S.E.: Using kinetic typography to convey emotion in text-based interpersonal communication. In: Proceedings of the 6th ACM Conference on Designing Interactive Systems - DIS 2006, p. 41 (2006). https://doi.org/10.1145/1142405.1142414
15. Li, Y., Suen, C.Y.: Typeface personality traits and their design characteristics. In: Proceedings of the 8th IAPR International Workshop on Document Analysis Systems - DAS 2010, pp. 231–238 (2010). https://doi.org/10.1145/1815330.1815360

16. Lin, H., Wu, F.-G., Cheng, Y.-Y.: Legibility and visual fatigue affected by text direction, screen size and character size on color LCD e-reader. Displays **34**(1), 49–58 (2013). https://doi.org/10.1016/j.displa.2012.11.006

17. Mackiewicz, J., Moeller, R.: Why people perceive typefaces to have different personalities. In: International Professional Communication Conference, 2004, Proceedings, IPCC 2004, pp. 304–313 (2005). https://doi.org/10.1109/IPCC.2004.1375315

18. Morrison, G.R.: Communicability of the emotional connotations of type. Educ. Commun. Technol. **34**(4), 235–244 (1986). https://doi.org/10.1007/BF02767404

19. Nakahata, S., Sakamoto, E., Oda, A., Kobata, N., Sato, S.: Effects of color of book cover and typeface of title and author name on gaze duration and choice behavior for books: evidence from an eye-tracking experiment. Proc. Assoc. Inf. Sci. Technol. **53**(1), 1–4 (2016). https://doi.org/10.1002/pra2.2016.14505301100

20. O'Donovan, P., Lībeks, J., Agarwala, A., Hertzmann, A.: Exploratory font selection using crowdsourced attributes. ACM Trans. Graph. **33**(4), 1–9 (2014). https://doi.org/10.1145/2601097.2601110

21. Rello, L., Baeza-Yates, R.: Good fonts for dyslexia. In: Proceedings of the 15th International ACM SIGACCESS Conference on Computers and Accessibility - ASSETS 2013, pp. 1–8 (2013). https://doi.org/10.1145/2513383.2513447

22. Rello, L., Baeza-Yates, R., Dempere-Marco, L., Saggion, H.: Frequent words improve readability and short words improve understandability for people with dyslexia. In: Kotzé, P., Marsden, G., Lindgaard, G., Wesson, J., Winckler, M. (eds.) INTERACT 2013. LNCS, vol. 8120, pp. 203–219. Springer, Heidelberg (2013). https://doi.org/10.1007/978-3-642-40498-6_15

23. Rello, L., Barbosa, S.D.J.: Do people with dyslexia need special reading software? In: Human-Computer Interaction – INTERACT 2013, Workshop on Rethinking Universal Accessibility: A Broader Approach Considering the Digital Gap (2013)

24. Rello, L., Pielot, M., Marcos, M.-C.: Make it big! In: Proceedings of the 2016 CHI Conference on Human Factors in Computing Systems - CHI 2016, pp. 3637–3648 (2016). https://doi.org/10.1145/2858036.2858204

25. Russell-Minda, E., et al.: The legibility of typefaces for readers with low vision: a research review. J. Vis. Impair. Blind. **101**(7), 402–415 (2007). https://doi.org/10.1177/0145482X0710100703

26. Shaikh, A.D., Chaparro, B.S., Fox, D.: Perception of fonts: perceived personality traits and uses. Usability News **8**(1), 1–6 (2006). https://doi.org/10.1103/PhysRevD.48.3160

27. Smith, B., Groenewold, T.D.: Developing a typeface for low resolution e-ink displays. In: Extended Abstracts of the 2018 CHI Conference on Human Factors in Computing Systems - CHI 2018, pp. 1–6 (2018). https://doi.org/10.1145/3170427.3180306

28. Vinot, J.-L., Athenes, S.: Legible, are you sure? In: Proceedings of the 2012 ACM Annual Conference on Human Factors in Computing Systems - CHI 2012, p. 2287 (2012). https://doi.org/10.1145/2207676.2208387

29. Analytics - Google Fonts. https://fonts.google.com/analytics. Accessed 7 Apr 2019

30. HTTP Archive. http://httparchive.org/. Accessed 7 Apr 2019

31. AWS—Alexa Web Information Service. https://aws.amazon.com/awis/. Accessed 7 Apr 2019

32. Featured Collections - Google Fonts. https://fonts.google.com/featured. Accessed 7 Apr 2019

33. Prototypo—Design custom fonts that perfectly fit your needs. https://www.prototypo.io/

34. Variable Fonts. https://v-fonts.com/. Accessed 7 Apr 2019

Integrating a Binaural Beat into the Soundscape for the Alleviation of Feelings

Noko Kuratomo, Yuichi Mashiba, Keiichi Zempo$^{(\boxtimes)}$, Koichi Mizutani, and Naoto Wakatsuki

University of Tsukuba, 1-1-1, Tennodai, Tsukuba, Ibaraki 305-8573, Japan
`zempo@iit.tsukuba.ac.jp`

Abstract. A binaural beat is the sound that makes beat in human brain by providing sounds of different frequencies to left and right ears. It has been reported that the brain wave of frequency difference is easily induced when we listen to it. In this study, it is verified whether brain waves can be induced if a binaural beat is provided in a living environment. In reproducing living environments, soundscape is used and binaural beat is integrated into it. Brain wave is measured and users' subjective assessment is conducted in experimental. As a result, the effect of binaural beat to the alleviation of feelings is verified. It has been clarified binaural beat has positive effects, even under negative condition.

Keywords: Binaural beat · User interface

1 Introduction

We live in a variety of environments and feel happy, relaxed, stressed and so on. Positive emotion is increased in nature [4], while negative emotion is increased in urban environments featuring sounds like car horns and ambulance sirens, as well as in situations in which we are confined, like while studying [5,6]. So, if emotion can be controlled to suit the situation, we can live with better conditions, *e.g.* amplifying positive emotions and alleviating negative emotions, as shown in Fig. 1.

It is known that human emotions are related to brain waves [11]. Brain wave activity is observed by measuring its frequency as electric signals. Brain wave signals include delta (0.1 to 3.5 Hz), theta (3.5 to 7.5 Hz), alpha (7.5 to 13 Hz), beta(13 to 30 Hz), and gamma(30 to 50 Hz) [12]. The conditions connected to these brain wave types are shown in Table 1.

It is reported that the brain wave condition is induced by external stimuli [1]. When a flash is used as a stimulus, there is a possibility of giving users become acute symptoms based on photosensitivity [2,3,8]. On the other hand, it is hard to induce the desired condition by the sound since the ranges are different between brain waves and audible frequencies. Therefore, a binaural beat is proposed as a method of changing emotions.

© IFIP International Federation for Information Processing 2019
Published by Springer Nature Switzerland AG 2019
D. Lamas et al. (Eds.): INTERACT 2019, LNCS 11749, pp. 235–242, 2019.
https://doi.org/10.1007/978-3-030-29390-1_13

Fig. 1. Construction of a binaural beat and its assumed effect under negative emotion: If sounds of f are provided at the left ear and sounds of $f+x$ are provided at the right ear, a sound of x is recognized as a beat.

Table 1. Brain wave types and conditions [13]

Type	Frequency	Conditions
delta	0.1–3.5 Hz	Deep sleep
theta	3.5–7.5 Hz	Light sleep, creativity, insight
alpha	7.5–13 Hz	A calm and peaceful, yet alert state
beta	13–30 Hz	Thinking, focused state, intensity or anxiety
gamma	30–50 Hz	Perception, fear, consciousness

A binaural beat is a sound that makes a beat in the human brain by playing sounds of different frequencies in the left and right ears respectively. An image representing this concept is shown in Fig. 1. It is reported that a binaural beat can change the frequency of brain waves to a roughly desired state. For example, if sounds at 440 Hz are supplied to the left ear and sounds at 450 Hz supplied to the right ear, the frequency difference between ears is 10 Hz, so an alpha wave is induced in the listener's brain and the listener may feel relaxed [7]. The desired brain wave condition determines which audio signals should be input.

So far, most research about the effects of binaural beats investigates a binaural beat used alone [7, 10]. However, binaural beats should be applied to our daily life, and the effect of binaural beats on human brain wave activity in a real-life environment is still not clear.

Sound plays an important role in our living environment, which affects feelings. Sound environments created by nature and social activity are generally called soundscapes. Soundscapes are classified into six main types by Murray Schafer's soundscape taxonomy, shown in Table 2 [13]. Therefore, this soundscape taxonomy is able to be used for reproducing daily life in terms of sound.

Table 2. Sounds of the environment categories [9]

Category	Soundscape
Natural sounds	Birds, chickens, rain, sea shore
Human sounds	Laughing, whispering, shouting, talking, coughing
Sounds and society	Parties, concerts, grocery stores
Mechanical sounds	Engines, cars, air conditioners
Quiet and silence	Wild space, silent forest
Sound as indicators	Clocks, doorbells, sirens

The purpose of this paper is to investigate a method to use a binaural beat to adapt oneself to a condition needed in a particular environment. When the integrated sound of the soundscape and the binaural beat is provided, the condition variable of the listener's brain wave is observed and examined.

2   The Intention of a Binaural Beat Display

To know how to control emotions by listening to a binaural beat in daily life, it is necessary to research how binaural beats affect brain activities in various environments. Users perceive a binaural beat as a beat made by two pure sounds. For example, when a stereo sound having a frequency difference corresponding to an alpha wave is input, a sound of that frequency is recognized as a beat. That is, to induce a desired brain wave condition, the signal which should be input is specified according to Table 1.

In experiments, daily environments are reproduced by using environmental sounds. Whether emotions change is analyzed through brain wave measurements and subjective assessment when binaural beats are integrated into soundscapes, e.g., distracting places or annoying scenes.

3   Experiment

3.1   Binaural Sound Signals

To verify the possibility of inducing feelings, three kinds of binaural beat corresponding to three kinds of brain waves are prepared. The frequency difference of the sound is set at 5, 12, and 23 Hz corresponding to theta, alpha, and beta waves, respectively. In this experiment, we set a sine wave of 440 Hz as the standard, which is provided to the left ear. Tuned up sine signals at 445, 452, and 463 Hz were provided to participants' right ears.

Soundscapes are classified into six types by Murray Schafer's soundscape taxonomy [9]. From this taxonomy, we prepared four kinds of the environmental sounds as outside stimuli to affect human feelings: sea, forest, shopping mall and ambulance siren.

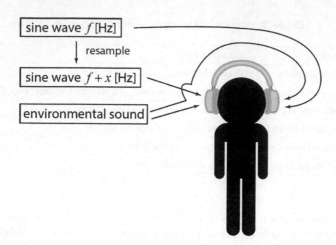

Fig. 2. The sound algorithm used in the experiment, containing a binaural beat integrated into environmental sound.

The sound algorithm is shown in Fig. 2. We set the ratio of the binaural beat to the soundscape to 1:9. A total of 12 kinds of experimental stimuli is prepared by integrating the three binaural beats into four soundscapes.

3.2   Measurement Equipment

Participants wear three electrodes to measure brain waves and headphones to listen to the sound. Two electrodes are attached at the back of the head and one is at the earlobe. A photo of the experiment is shown in Fig. 3. We analyze the measured brain wave with the Fourier spectrum and examine the strength of each frequency component. For brain wave analysis, we use the data processing module developed by the Brain Function Research Center.

3.3   Experimental Protocol

During the experiment, participants closed their eyes and moved as little as possible in order to minimize the influence of eye movements on brain wave measurement. The measurement time is 180 s per set. The flow of these experiments is shown in Fig. 4.

Sixteen sets (12 integrated sounds and four environment-only sounds) of experiments are carried out. Besides brain waves, participants assess the soundscape subjectively on two scales: upset to relax and uncomfortable to comfortable. There are seven assessment values, which are shown in Fig. 5. Participants consist of 10 people (average age: 23, 7 men and 3 women) with good hearing.

This experiment was reviewed and approved by the ethics committee of the organization to which we belong.

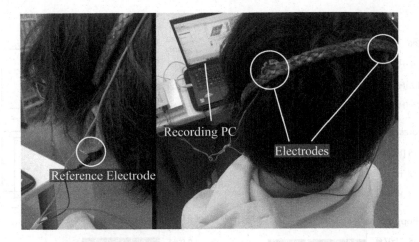

Fig. 3. Equipment for measuring brain waves

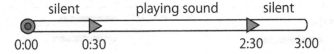

Fig. 4. Flow of experiment

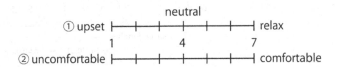

Fig. 5. Participant assessment axis

4   Results and Discussion

Figure 6 shows results in two ways: as a fluctuation of brain waves and as a participants' subjective assessments. The fluctuation of brain waves measured during the period from 60 to 120 s is analyzed, where the brain wave is stable. We measure the ratio of participants whose brain waves fluctuate as intended when the each sound is provided, compared to when listening to an environment-only sound. That is, it counts if the component of the theta wave increased when an integrated sound at 5 Hz frequency difference was provided. The same is true for both the alpha wave and 12 Hz frequency difference, the beta wave and 23 Hz frequency difference. In Fig. 6, the environmental sounds used in the experiment are sorted into (a)–(d). From this figure, the following findings arise.

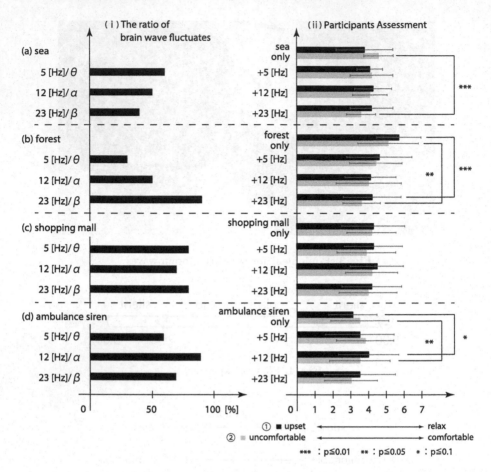

Fig. 6. Experiment Results – (i) shows the ratio of brain wave fluctuates and (ii) shows participants' assessment average and its standard deviation.

(1) According to (b)-(ii), most participants relaxed when in an environment of forest sound only. However, they became somewhat upset when sounds at a 23 Hz frequency difference were provided. As shown in (b)-(i), nine participants' beta waves increased. Therefore, the beta wave is likely induced in relaxed conditions.

(2) According to (d)-(ii), the ambulance siren makes participants feel upset and uncomfortable. Conversely, the subjective assessment improves when sounds at a 12 Hz frequency difference are provided. The ratio of brain waves in which the alpha wave increased is higher than others ((d)-(i)). It is clear that sounds at a 12 Hz frequency difference can alleviate distressing emotions.

These results can be also seen in the p-value in Fig. 6 (the p-value is calculated by a one-sided test only in cases in which the brain wave fluctuated as intended).

However, it is hard to detect an improvement when participants are in a relaxed environment, and vice versa.

5   Conclusion

This study's purpose is to research whether emotions can be controlled by listening to a binaural beat in daily life. In the experiment, we investigated how a binaural beat integrated into the soundscape affects brain activities by measuring brain waves and collecting subjective assessments. In result, the effect of binaural beat integrated into soundscape to the alleviation of feelings is verified. It has been clarified binaural beat has positive effects, even under negative condition.

From now on, it is necessary to conduct experiments focusing on alleviating of feelings to more people. As areas for further study, the effects of a binaural beat on a person performing simple work should be investigated, and the possibility of applying a binaural beat to many situations in which someone may feel stressed.

References

1. Adrian, E.D., Matthews, B.H.: The berger rhythm: potential changes from the occipital lobes in man. Brain **57**(4), 355–385 (1934)
2. Enoki, H., Akiyama, T., Hattori, J., Oka, E.: Photosensitive fits elicited by tv animation: an electroencephalographic study. Pediatr. Int. **40**(6), 626–630 (1998)
3. Fylan, F., Harding, G.: The effect of television frame rate on EEG abnormalities in photosensitive and pattern-sensitive epilepsy. Epilepsia **38**(10), 1124–1131 (1997)
4. Hartig, T., Evans, G.W., Jamner, L.D., Davis, D.S., Gärling, T.: Tracking restoration in natural and urban field settings. J. Environ. Psychol. **23**(2), 109–123 (2003)
5. Ishikawa, T., Tatsumoto, M., Maki, K., Mitsui, M., Hasegawa, H., Hirata, K.: Identification of everyday sounds perceived as noise by migraine patients. Int. Med. 2206–2218 (2019)
6. Jena, S.K., Misra, A.K., Mohanty, A., et al.: Effect of examination stress on blood sugar in medical students. CHRISMED J. Health Res. **3**(4), 268 (2016)
7. Puzi, N.M., Jailani, R., Norhazman, H., Zaini, N.M.: Alpha and beta brainwave characteristics to binaural beat treatment. In: 2013 IEEE 9th International Colloquium on Signal Processing and its Applications, pp. 344–348. IEEE (2013)
8. Ricci, S., Vigevano, F., Manfredi, M., Trenité, D.G.K.N.: Epilepsy provoked by television and video games, safety of 100-Hz screens. Neurology **50**(3), 790–793 (1998)
9. Schafer, R.M.: The Soundscape: Our Sonic Environment and the Tuning of the World. Simon and Schuster, New York City (1993)
10. Settapat, S., Ohkura, M.: An alpha-wave-based binaural beat sound control system using fuzzy logic and autoregressive forecasting model. In: 2008 SICE Annual Conference, pp. 109–114. IEEE (2008)
11. Stastny, J., Sovka, P., Stancak, A.: EEG signal classification. In: 2001 Conference Proceedings of the 23rd Annual International Conference of the IEEE Engineering in Medicine and Biology Society, vol. 2, pp. 2020–2023. IEEE (2001)

12. Trivedi, P., Bhargava, N.: Effect of left and right hemisphere of brain in both eye open and close state on minimum power values and frequency of alpha wave activity. Brain **6**(2), 170–174 (2017)
13. Zaini, N., Omar, H., Latip, M.F.A.: Semantic-based Bayesian network to determine correlation between binaural-beats features and entrainment effects. In: 2011 IEEE International Conference on Computer Applications and Industrial Electronics (ICCAIE), pp. 574–579. IEEE (2011)

What Is Beautiful Continues to Be Good

People Images and Algorithmic Inferences on Physical Attractiveness

Maria Matsangidou[1]([⊠])[ID] and Jahna Otterbacher[1,2][ID]

[1] Research Centre on Interactive Media,
Smart Systems and Emerging Technologies (RISE), Nicosia, Cyprus
{m.matsangidou, j.otterbacher}@rise.org.cy
[2] Cyprus Center for Algorithmic Transparency,
Open University of Cyprus, Nicosia, Cyprus

Abstract. Image recognition algorithms that automatically tag or moderate content are crucial in many applications but are increasingly opaque. Given transparency concerns, we focus on understanding how algorithms tag people images and their inferences on *attractiveness*. Theoretically, attractiveness has an evolutionary basis, guiding mating behaviors, although it also drives social behaviors. We test image-tagging APIs as to whether they encode biases surrounding attractiveness. We use the Chicago Face Database, containing images of diverse individuals, along with subjective norming data and objective facial measurements. The algorithms encode biases surrounding attractiveness, perpetuating the stereotype that "what is beautiful is good." Furthermore, women are often misinterpreted as men. We discuss the algorithms' reductionist nature, and their potential to infringe on users' autonomy and well-being, as well as the ethical and legal considerations for developers. Future services should monitor algorithms' behaviors given their prevalence in the information ecosystem and influence on media.

Keywords: Algorithmic bias · Attractiveness · Image recognition · Stereotyping

1 Introduction

Image recognition is one of the success stories of modern machine learning and has become an indispensable tool in our information ecosystem. Beyond its early applications in more restricted domains such as military (e.g., satellite imagery), security and surveillance, or medical imaging, image recognition is an increasingly common component in consumer information services. We have become accustomed to seamlessly organizing and/or searching collections of images in real time - even those that lack descriptive metadata. Similarly, the technology has become essential in fields such as interactive marketing and campaigning, where professionals must learn about and engage target audiences, who increasingly communicate and share in a visual manner.

Underpinning the widespread "democratization" of image recognition is that it has enjoyed rapid technical progress in recent years. Krizhevsky and colleagues [34] first

© The Author(s) 2019
D. Lamas et al. (Eds.): INTERACT 2019, LNCS 11749, pp. 243–264, 2019.
https://doi.org/10.1007/978-3-030-29390-1_14

introduced the use of deep learning for image classification, in the context of the ImageNet Challenge.[1] This work represented a significant breakthrough, improving classification accuracy by over 50% as compared to previous state-of-the-art algorithms. Since then, continual progress has been made, e.g., in terms of simplifying the approach [49] and managing the required computational resources [55].

Nevertheless, along with the rapid uptake of image recognition, there have been high-profile incidents highlighting its potential to produce socially offensive – even discriminatory – results. For instance, a software engineer and Google Photos user discovered in 2015 that the app had labeled his photos with the tag "gorillas." Google apologized for the racial blunder, and engineers vowed to find a solution. However, more than three years later, only "awkward workarounds," such as removing offensive tags from the database, have been introduced.[2] Similarly, in late 2017, it was widely reported that Apple had offered refunds to Asian users of its new iPhone X, as its Face ID technology could not reliably distinguish Asian faces. The incident drew criticism in the press, with some questioning whether the technology could be considered racist.[3]

Given the rise of a visual culture that dominates interpersonal and professional exchanges in networked information systems, it is crucial that we achieve a better understanding of the biases of image recognition systems. The number of cognitive services (provided through APIs) for image processing and understanding has grown dramatically in recent years. Without a doubt, this development has fueled creativity and innovation, by providing developers with tools to enhance the capabilities of their software. However, as illustrated in the above cases, the social biases in the underlying algorithms carry over to applications developed.

Currently, we consider whether tagging algorithms make inferences on *physical attractiveness*. There are findings suggesting that online and social media are projections of the idealized self [13] and that the practice of uploading pictures of one's self represents a significant component of self-worthiness [52]. At the same time, some researchers have argued that the media culture's focus on physical appearance and users' repeated exposure to this is correlated to increased body image disturbance [41]. This was further supported by a recent study [5] suggesting that individuals with attractive profile photos in dating websites, are viewed more favorably and with positive qualities.

The role of physical appearance in human interaction cannot be denied; it is the first personal characteristic that is observable to others in social interactions. These obvious characteristics are perceived by others and in response, shape ideas and beliefs, usually based on cultural stereotypes. Figure 1 presents three images from the Chicago Face Database (CFD) as well as the respective demographic information, subjective ratings and physical measures provided in the CFD [38]. In the last row, the output of four tagging algorithms is shown. As illustrated, while tagging algorithms are not designed

---

[1] http://www.image-net.org/challenges/LSVRC/.

[2] https://www.wired.com/story/when-it-comes-to-gorillas-google-photos-remains-blind/.

[3] https://www.newsweek.com/iphone-x-racist-apple-refunds-device-cant-tell-chinese-people-apart-woman-751263.

to be discriminatory, they often output descriptive tags that reflect prevalent conceptions and even stereotypes concerning attractiveness. For instance, the woman on the left, who CFD judges found to be the most attractive and feminine of the three persons (see "Attractive" score), is described with tags such as "cute" and "smile," while the others are described more neutrally. Furthermore, the less attractive woman is described as a man. The question is to what extent this happens systematically.

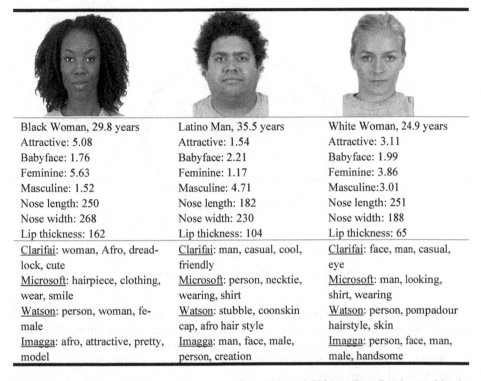

Black Woman, 29.8 years	Latino Man, 35.5 years	White Woman, 24.9 years
Attractive: 5.08	Attractive: 1.54	Attractive: 3.11
Babyface: 1.76	Babyface: 2.21	Babyface: 1.99
Feminine: 5.63	Feminine: 1.17	Feminine: 3.86
Masculine: 1.52	Masculine: 4.71	Masculine:3.01
Nose length: 250	Nose length: 182	Nose length: 251
Nose width: 268	Nose width: 230	Nose width: 188
Lip thickness: 162	Lip thickness: 104	Lip thickness: 65
Clarifai: woman, Afro, dreadlock, cute	Clarifai: man, casual, cool, friendly	Clarifai: face, man, casual, eye
Microsoft: hairpiece, clothing, wear, smile	Microsoft: person, necktie, wearing, shirt	Microsoft: man, looking, shirt, wearing
Watson: person, woman, female	Watson: stubble, coonskin cap, afro hair style	Watson: person, pompadour hairstyle, skin
Imagga: afro, attractive, pretty, model	Imagga: man, face, male, person, creation	Imagga: person, face, man, male, handsome

Fig. 1. Example people images with tags from four APIs and Chicago Face Database subjective ratings/physical measures.

We approach the study of "algorithmic attractiveness" through the theoretical lens of *evolutionary social psychology*. This reductionist approach attempts to explain why certain physical characteristics are correlated to human judgments of attractiveness, from an evolutionary perspective (i.e., explaining sexual selection) [12]. As early as 1972, Dion and colleagues [19] discovered a commonly held belief: "what is beautiful is good". This led researchers to describe a stereotype, that attractive people are often perceived as having positive qualities. Many researchers have validated this finding and have suggested that the stereotype is applied across various social contexts [21].

While these theories are not without controversy, we find the evolutionary perceptive particularly interesting in light of algorithmic biases. While people use dynamic and non-physical characteristics when judging attractiveness, algorithms may make subjective judgments based on one static image. These reductionist judgments, an "algorithmic attractiveness," carry over into applications in our information ecosystem (e.g., image search engines, dating apps, social media) as illustrated in Fig. 2. From media effects theories (e.g., cultivation theory [26], social learning theory [6]) we know that with repeated exposure to media images (and judgments on those images) we come to accept these depictions as reality. Thus, there is a real danger of exacerbating the bias; whoever is deemed to be "beautiful and good" will continue to be perceived as such.

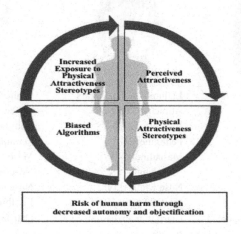

Fig. 2. Conceptual model of bias perpetuation.

In light of the need for greater algorithmic transparency and accountability [18], and the growing influence of image recognition technology in the information landscape, we test popular tagging algorithms to answer three research questions:

(RQ1) Do the algorithms exhibit evidence of evolutionary biases with respect to human physical attractiveness?

(RQ2) Do the taggers perpetuate the stereotype that attractive people are "good," having positive social qualities?

(RQ3) Do the algorithms infer gender accurately when tagging images of men and women of different races?

2   Related Work

We provide a review of evolutionary social psychology theory that provides an explanation for the human biases surrounding physical attractiveness. In addition, we explain the potential for social consequences – the so-called "physical attractiveness stereotype." Finally, having seen that gender and physical attractiveness are closely related, we briefly review recent work on gender-based biases in image recognition algorithms.

2.1 Evolutionary Roots of Physical Attractiveness

Interpersonal relationships are essential for healthy development. However, subjective differences occur when it comes to choosing/rejecting another person. *Physical appearance* plays a key role in the development of interpersonal attraction, the positive attitudes or evaluations a person holds for another [3, 30]. Walster and colleges provided an influential example in the early 60s [58]. In their study, they matched individuals based on personality, intelligence, social skills, and physical attractiveness. Results revealed that only attractiveness mattered in terms of partners liking one another.

Evolutionary theory has long been used to explain the above. As Darwin [16] claimed, sexual selection of the preferable mate is influenced by aesthetic beauty. In humans, research suggests that heterosexual men tend to select a partner based on physical attractiveness, more so than women. This is because of reproductive value, the extent to which individuals of a given age and sex will contribute to the ancestry of future generations [22]. As a result, men show a particular interest in women of high fertility. In women, reproductive value typically peaks in the mid-teens and declines with age [56]. Therefore, women's physical attractiveness is usually associated with youthful characteristics, such as smooth skin, good muscle tone, lustrous hair, a small waste-to-hip ratio, and babylike features such as big eyes, a small nose and chin, and full lips [10, 11, 14, 50, 53, 54, 60].

Physical appearance is less important for heterosexual women. Women are believed to be concerned with the external resources a man can provide, such as his earning capacity, ambition, and industriousness [10]. This is because male parental investment tends to be less than female parental investment. Specifically, a copulation that requires minimal male investment can produce a 9-month investment by the woman that is substantial in terms of time, energy, resources, and foreclosed alternatives. Therefore, women tend to select men who can provide them with the resources necessary to raise their child [57, 60]. These characteristics might be inferred from a man's physical appearance and behaviors; favorable traits include being tall, displaying dominant behavior, having an athletic body, big cheekbones, a long and wide chin, and wearing fashionable clothing that suggests high social status [11].

RQ1 asks whether there is evidence of evolutionary biases in the tags output by algorithms to describe input person images. As will be explained, the dataset we use provides human (subjective) ratings on a large set of people images, as well as physical facial measurements; therefore, we will compare human and algorithmic attractiveness judgments on the depicted persons, in relation to the above-described findings.

2.2 Physical Attractiveness Stereotype

The physical attractiveness stereotype ("what is beautiful is good") is the tendency to assume that people who are attractive also possess socially desirable traits [19, 42]. A convincing example was given by a study where a photo of either a "beautiful" or an "unattractive" woman was given to a heterosexual man, along with biographical information [51]. Men tended to be positively biased toward a "beautiful" woman, who was perceived as being a sociable, poised, humorous, and skilled person. This was in stark contrast to the perceptions expressed by men who were given an "unattractive" woman's picture. "Unattractive" women were expected to be unsociable, awkward, serious, and socially inept. In a follow-up analysis, a blind telephone call between the man and the depicted woman was facilitated. The expectations of the men had a dramatic impact on their behavior. Specifically, the men who spoke with an "attractive woman" exhibited a response and tone of voice evaluated as warm and accepting. However, those who spoke with an "unattractive" woman used a less inviting tone [51].

Many studies have highlighted the tendency to believe that "what is beautiful is good" [19, 35, 42]. Furthermore, research has shown that several stereotypes link personality types to a physically attractive or unattractive appearance. Specifically, individuals in casual acquaintances invariably assume that an attractive person is more sincere, noble and honest, which usually results in pro-social behavior towards the attractive person in comparison to a non-attractive person [19, 21]. However, these stereotypes are not consistent worldwide. Cultural differences may affect the perception of beauty stereotype. Research has shown that the content of an attractive stereotype depends on cultural values [59] and is changing over time [31].

To answer **RQ2**, we will examine the extent to which humans and tagging algorithms tend to associate depicted persons deemed to be physically attractive with more positive traits/words, as compared to images of less attractive individuals.

2.3   Gender and Image Recognition

Most research to date on social biases in image recognition has come from outside HCI and has focused on technical solutions for specific gender biases. For instance, Zhao and colleagues [62] documented gender-based activity biases (e.g., associating verbs such as cooking/driving with women/men) in image labels in the MS-COCO dataset [37]. They introduced techniques for constraining the corpus that mitigate the bias resulting in models trained on the data.

Looking more specifically at face recognition in images, Klare and colleagues [33] warned that certain demographic groups (in particular, people of color, women, and young people ages 18 to 30) were systematically more prone to recognition errors. They offered solutions for biometric systems used primarily in intelligence and law enforcement contexts. Introna and Wood's results [32] confirms these observations. More recent work [36] applied deep learning (convolutional neural networks (CNNs)) to age and gender recognition. They noted that while CNNs have brought about remarkable improvements in other image recognition tasks, "accurately estimating the age and gender in unconstrained settings...remains unsolved."

In addition, the recent work by Buolamwini and Gebru [8] found not only that gender classification accuracy in popular image recognition algorithms is correlated to skin color, but also that common training data sets for image recognition algorithms tend to over-/under-represent people with light/dark skin tones. Furthermore, computer vision researchers are taking seriously the issue of diversity in people image processing, as evidenced by new initiatives such as the InclusiveFaceNet [46].

To address **RQ3**, we consider the extent to which image recognition algorithms produce tags that imply gender and examine the accuracy of the implied gender.

3 Methodology

3.1 Image Recognition Algorithms

We study four-image recognition APIs – Clarifai, Microsoft Cognitive Services' Computer Vision, IBM Watson Visual Recognition and the Imagga Auto-Tagger. All are easy-to-use; we made minimal modifications to their Python code examples to upload and process images. While three of the companies offer specific models for face recognition, we experiment with the general tagging models. First, tagging algorithms are more broadly used in information services and applications (e.g., image sharing sites, e-commerce sites) to organize and/or moderate content across domains. Face recognition algorithms infer specific, but more limited, attributes (e.g., age, gender) whereas more general tools often make additional inferences about the depicted individual and who he or she is (e.g., doctor, model), often using subjective tags (e.g., attractive, fine-looking). Finally, face recognition algorithms are less mature and, as mentioned previously, not yet very accurate. Next, we provide descriptions of each tagger. As proprietary tools, none provides a specific explanation of how the tags for an input image are chosen (i.e., they are opaque to the user/developer). As these services are updated over time, it is important to note that the data was collected in July – August 2018.

Clarifai[4] describes its technology as a "proprietary, state-of-the-art neural network architecture." For a given image, it returns up to 20 descriptive concept tags, along with probabilities. The company does not provide access to the full set of tags; we used the general model, which "recognizes over 11,000 different concepts." Microsoft's Computer Vision API[5] analyzes images in various ways, including content-based tagging as well as categorization. We use the tagging function, which selects from over 2,000 tags to provide a description for an image. The Watson Visual Recognition API[6] "uses deep learning algorithms" to analyze an input image. Its default model returns the most relevant classes "from thousands of general tags." Finally, Imagga's tagger[7] combines "state-of-the-art machine learning approaches" with "semantic processing" to "refine the quality of the suggested tags[8]." Like Clarifai, the tag set is undefined; however, Imagga returns all associated tags with a confidence score (i.e., probability). Following Imagga's suggested best practices, we retain all tags with a score greater than 0.30.

---

[4] https://clarifai.com/technology.

[5] https://docs.microsoft.com/en-us/azure/cognitive-services/computer-vision/home#tagging-images.

[6] https://www.ibm.com/watson/developercloud/visual-recognition/api/v3/curl.html?curl#introduction.

[7] https://docs.imagga.com.

[8] https://imagga.com/technology/auto-tagging.html.

3.2 Person Images: The Chicago Face Database (CFD)

The CFD [38] is a free resource[9] consisting of 597 high-resolution, standardized images of diverse individuals between the ages of 18 and 40 years (see Table 1). It is designed to facilitate research on a range of psychological phenomena (e.g., stereotyping and prejudice, interpersonal attraction). Therefore, it provides extensive data about the depicted individuals (see Fig. 1 for examples). The database includes both subjective norming data and objective physical measurements (e.g., nose length/width), on the pictures.[10] At least 30 independent judges, balanced by race and gender, evaluated each CFD image.[11] The questions for the subjective norming data were posed as follows: "Now, consider the person pictured above and rate him/her with respect to other people of the same race and gender. For example, if the person was Asian and male, consider this person on the following traits relative to other Asian males in the United States. - **Attractive** (1–7 Likert, 1 = Not at all; 7 = Extremely)". Fifteen additional traits were evaluated, including Babyface, Dominant, Trustworthy, Feminine, and Masculine.

For our purposes, a significant benefit of using the CFD is that the individuals are depicted in a similar, neutral manner; if we were to evaluate images of people collected "in the wild", we would have images from a variety of contexts with varying qualities. In other words, using the CFD enables us to study the behavior of the tagging algorithms in a controlled manner.

Table 1. Mean/median attractiveness of depicted individuals.

	Asian	Black	Latino/a	White
Women	N = 57; 3.64/3.62	N = 104; 3.33/3.15	N = 56; 3.81/3.56	N = 90; 3.45/3.39
Men	N = 52; 2.85/2.85	N = 93; 3.17/3.12	N = 52; 2.94/2.90	N = 93; 2.96/2.96

3.3 Producing and Analyzing Image Tags

The CFD images were uploaded as input to each API. Table 2 summarizes the total number of tags output by each algorithm, the unique tags used and the most frequently used tags by each algorithm. For all taggers other than Imagga, we do not observe subjective tags concerning physical appearance amongst the most common tags. However, it is interesting to note the frequent use of tags that are interpretive in nature; for instance, Watson often labels people as being "actors" whereas both Microsoft and Watson frequently interpret the age group of depicted persons (e.g., "young," "adult"). Imagga's behavior clearly deviates from the other taggers, in that three of its most frequent tags refer to appearance/attractiveness.

---

[9] http://faculty.chicagobooth.edu/bernd.wittenbrink/cfd/index.html.

[10] Physical measurements are reported in pixels (i.e., are measured from photos).

[11] See [38] for additional details. Scores by individual judges are not provided; the CFD contains the mean scores over all judges.

Table 2. Tags generated by the APIs across 597 images.

	Clarifai	Microsoft	Watson	Imagga
Total	11,940	12,137	3,668	6,772
Unique	95	74	72	54
10 most frequent	Portrait, one, people, isolated, casual, looking, look, eye, man, face	White, shirt, wearing, standing, posing, young, black, smiling, glasses, looking	Person, light brown color, people, ash grey, coal black, face, stubble, adult person, actor, woman	Portrait, face, person, handsome, man, male, beard, adult, attractive, model

We post-processed the output tags using the Linguistic Inquiry and Wordcount (LIWC) tool [45]. LIWC is a collection of lexicons representing psychologically meaningful concepts. Its output is the percentage of input words that map onto a given lexicon. We used four concepts: female/male references, and positive/negative emotion.

Table 3 provides summary statistics for the use of tags related to these concepts. We observe that all four taggers use words that reflect gender (e.g., man/boy/grandfather vs. woman/girl/grandmother). While all taggers produce subjective words as tags, only Clarifai uses tags with negative emotional valence (e.g., isolated, pensive, sad).

Finally, we created a custom LIWC lexicon with words associated with physical attractiveness. Three native English speakers were presented with the combined list of unique tags used by the four algorithms (a total of 220 tags). They worked independently and were instructed to indicate which of the words could be used to describe a person's physical appearance in a positive manner. This yielded a list of 15 tags: *attractive, casual, cute, elegant, fashionable, fine-looking, glamour, masculinity, model, pretty, sexy, smile, smiling, trendy, handsome.* There was full agreement on 13 of the 15 tags; two of three judges suggested "casual" and "masculinity." As shown in Table 3, the Watson tagger did not use any tags indicating physical attractiveness. In addition, on average, the Microsoft tagger output fewer "attractiveness" tags as compared to Clarifai and Imagga.

Table 3. Mean/median percentages (%) of tags reflecting LIWC concepts.

	Clarifai	Microsoft	Watson	Imagga
Total tags	20.00/20	20.33/20	11.31/11	11.69/12
Female ref.	2.49/0	1.56/0	5.02/0	.01/0
Male ref.	4.66/4.75	4.26/4.76	2.47/0	17.73/21.43
Positive	14.0/14.3	4.58/4.76	.31/0	11.14/9.09
Negative	7.52/9.5	N/A	N/A	N/A
Attractiveness	14.9/15	4.58/4.76	N/A	18.49/16.67

3.4   Detecting Biases in Tag Usage

To summarize our approach, the output descriptive tags were interpreted by LIWC through its lexicons. LIWC scores were used in order to understand the extent to which each algorithmic tagger used gender-related words when describing a given image, or whether word-tags conveying positive or negative sentiment were used. Likewise, our custom dictionary allowed us to determine when tags referred to a depicted individual's physical attractiveness. As will be described in Sect. 4, we used appropriate statistical analyses to then compare the taggers' descriptions of a given image to those assigned manually by CFD judges (i.e., subjective norming data described in Sect. 3.2). In addition, we evaluated the taggers' outputs for systematic differences as a function of the depicted individuals' race and gender, to explore the tendency for tagging bias.

4   Results

We examined the perceived attractiveness of the individuals depicted in the CFD, by humans and tagging algorithms. Based on theory, perceived attractiveness as well as the stereotypes surrounding attractiveness, differ considerably by gender. Therefore, analyses are conducted separately for the images of men and women, and/or control for gender. Finally, we considered whether the algorithms make correct inferences on the depicted person's gender.

Table 4 summarizes the variables examined in the analysis. In some cases, for a CFD variable, there is no corresponding equivalent in the algorithmic output. Other times, such as in the case of gender, there is an equivalent, but it is measured differently. For clarity, in the tables below, we indicate in the top row the origin of the variables being analyzed (i.e., CFD or algorithmic output).

Table 4. Summary of variables examined and (type).

	CFD	Algorithmic output
Gender	Self-reported (nominal)	Use of gendered tags (continuous)
Age	Self-reported (continuous)	N/A
Race	Self-reported (nominal)	N/A
Physical characteristics	Facial measurements (continuous)	N/A
Attractiveness	Human-rated (ordinal)	Use of attractiveness tags (continuous)
Other subjective (e.g., Trustworthy)	Human-rated (ordinal)	Use of positive/negative emotion tags (continuous)

4.1   Evolutionary Biases and Physical Attractiveness

4.1.1   Human Judgments

We examined whether the CFD scores on physical attractiveness are consist with the evolutionary social psychology findings. Gender is highly correlated to physical attractiveness. Over all images, judges associate attractiveness with femininity

($r = .899, p < .0001$). However, for images of men, attractiveness is strongly related to masculinity ($r = .324, p < .0001$), which is negatively correlated to women's attractiveness ($r = −.682, p < .0001$). Similarly, men's attractiveness is positively correlated to being perceived as "Dominant" ($r = .159, p < .0001$), where the reverse is true of women's attractiveness ($r = −.219, p < .0001$). For both genders, "Babyface" features and perceived youthfulness (-age) are correlated to attractiveness in the same manner. The Pearson correlation analyses are presented in Table 5.

Table 5. Correlation between perceived attractiveness and youthful characteristics by gender in the CFD[a].

CFD Gender						
CFD judgments	Men			Women		
	1	2	3	1	2	3
1. Attractive	–	$-.24^{***}$	$.18^{***}$	–	$-.32^{***}$	$.22^{***}$
2. Age		–	$-.68^{***}$		–	$-.69^{***}$
3. Babyface			–			–

[a]We use the following conventions for statistical significance in tables: $*p < .05$, $**p < .01$, $***p < .001$.

4.1.2 Algorithmic Judgments

Next, we assessed if algorithms encode evolutionary biases. In parallel to the observation that CFD judges generally associate femininity with attractiveness, Table 6 examines correlations between algorithms' use of gendered tags and attractiveness tags. Clarifai and Imagga behavior is in line with CFD judgments. For both algorithms, there is a negative association between the use of masculine and attractiveness tags, while feminine and attractiveness tags are positively associated in Clarifai output.

Table 6. Correlations between algorithms' use of "attractiveness" tags and gendered tags.

	Gendered tags	
	Female	Male
Clarifai	$.32^{***}$	$-.28^{***}$
Microsoft	.05	−.04
Watson	N/A	N/A
Imagga	.06	$-.45^{***}$

While Table 6 examined correlations of two characteristics of algorithmic output, Table 7 examines correlations between the algorithms' use of attractiveness tags and three CFD characteristics. We observe a significant correlation between Clarifai and Imagga's use of "attractiveness" tags, and the human judgments on attractiveness. These two algorithms exhibit the evolutionary biases discussed, with a positive correlation between indicators of youthfulness and attractiveness. The Microsoft tagger shows a reverse trend. However, it may be the case that its tags do not cover a broad enough range of words to capture the human notion of attractiveness; there is a positive, but insignificant, correlation between the CFD Attractiveness and attractiveness tags.

Since Clarifai and Imagga exhibited the most interesting behavior, a more in-depth analysis was carried out on them to see which static, physical characteristics correlate to the use of attractiveness tags. A separate Pearson correlation was conducted for images of men and women, in terms of their physical facial measurements in the CFD and the two algorithms' use of "attractiveness" tags (Table 8). The analysis revealed a strong positive correlation for men between attractiveness and having a wide chin. Both genders revealed a positive correlation between attractiveness and luminance; once again, this feature can be considered a signal of youth.

Table 7. Correlations between algorithms' use of "attractiveness" tags and CFD Attractiveness.

CFD judgments			
Algorithmic attractiveness tags	Attractiveness	Babyface	Age
Clarifai	$.25^{***}$	.06	$-.18^{***}$
Microsoft	.05	$-.12^{**}$	$.11^{**}$
Watson	N/A	N/A	N/A
Imagga	$.32^{***}$	$.11^{***}$	$-.17^{***}$

Finally, a strong positive correlation was observed between attractiveness and nose length for women. This result, along with the negative correlation between women's attractiveness and nose width and shape highlights the relationship between the existence of a small nose and the perception of attractiveness. We should also point out that for both genders, attractive appearance is correlated with petite facial characteristics, such as light lips, small eyes.

In conclusion, we observe that both humans (i.e., CFD judges) and algorithms (particularly Clarifai and Imagga), associate femininity, as well as particular static facial features with attractiveness. Furthermore, there is a strong correlation between CFD indicators of attractiveness and the use of attractiveness tags by algorithms.

4.2   Social Stereotyping and Physical Attractiveness

We examined whether the attractiveness stereotype is reflected in the CFD judgments, and next, whether this is true for the algorithms as well. Table 9 details the correlations between perceived attractiveness and the other subjective attributes rated by CFD judges. The first six attributes refer to perceived emotional states of the persons whereas as the last two are perceived character traits. There is a clear correlation between the perception of attractiveness and positive emotions/traits, for men and women.

Table 8. Correlations between facial measurements and algorithms' use of attractiveness tags.

Static, physical facial measurements from CFD

		1	2	3	4	5	6	7	8	9	10	11	12
Men	1.Attractive (Clarifai)_	-	.49***	-.24***	.10	-.23***	-.24***	-.26***	.03	-.01	.01	-.23***	.17***
	Attractive (Imagga)		.38***	-.32***	.12*	-.30***	-.17**	-.14**	.01	-.04	.03	-.07	.12*
	2.Luminance		-	-.58***	.32**	-.60***	-.58***	-.60***	-.06	-.04	-.06	-.47***	.37***
	3.Nose Width			-	-.16**	.75***	.58***	.54***	-.05	-.14*	-.14*	.16***	-.28***
	4.Nose Length				-	-.76***	-.19***	-.29***	.32***	.23***	.19***	-.32***	-.12*
	5.Nose shape					-	.51***	.55***	-.24***	-.24***	-.21***	.31***	-.10
	6.Lip Thickness						-	.97***	.15*	.07	.05	.19***	-.51***
	7.Lip Fullness							-	.10	.05	.09	.23***	-.50***
	8.Eye Height								-	.89***	.93***	.00	-.18***
	9.Eye Width									-	.07	-.23**	-.00
	10.Eye Shape										-	-.03	-.21***
	11.Eye Size											-	-.13*
	12.Chin Length												-
Women	1. Attractive (Clarifai)	-	.40***	-.24***	.20***	-.31***	-.16***	-.22***	.02	-.18***	-.06	-.05	-.11
	Attractive (Imagga)		.32***	-.06	.18**	-.17**	-.05	-.07	-.01	-.01	.01	-.02	-.01
	2.Luminance		-	-.52***	.31***	-.57***	-.49***	-.57***	.01	-.31***	.02	-.07	.35***
	3.Nose Width			-	-.04	.71***	.60***	.49***	-.05	-.17**	-.20***		-.32***
	4.Nose Length				-	-.72***	-.05	-.24***	.42***	-.43***	.29***	.17***	-.21***
	5.Nose shape					-	.43***	.50***	-.32***	.32***	-.32***	-.26***	-.05
	6.Lip Thickness						-	.94***	.04	-.01	-.06	-.08	-.54***
	7.Lip Fullness							-	-.02	.12*	-.04	.02	-.52***
	8.Eye Height								-	-.05	.87***	.89***	-.23***
	9.Eye Width									-	.04	.31***	-.07
	10.Eye Shape										-	.87***	-.23***
	11.Eye Size											-	-.19***
	12.Chin Length												-

Table 9. Correlation between Attractiveness and other subjective attributes in the CFD.

CFD subjective norming	Men	Women
	CFD gender	
Afraid	-.99	-.25***
Angry	-.27***	-.35***
Disgusted	-.26***	-.37***
Happy	.45***	.48***
Sad	-.28***	-.43***
Surprised	.04	.03
Threatening	-.23***	-.40***
Trustworthy	.55***	.59***

We do not always have equivalent variables in the CFD and the algorithmic output. Therefore, to examine whether algorithms perpetuate the stereotype that "what is beautiful is good," we considered the use of LIWC positive emotion words in tags, as a function of the known (CFD) characteristics of the images. Images were divided into two groups (MA/more attractive, LA/less attractive), separated at the median CFD score (3.1 out of 7). Table 10 presents an ANOVA for each algorithm, in which attractiveness (MA vs. LA), gender (M/W) and race (W, B, L, A) are used to explain variance in the use of positive tags. For significant effects, effect size (η^2) is in parentheses.

Table 10. ANOVA to explain variance in the use of positive emotion tags.

CFD characteristics (demographic information and attractiveness rating)								
	Attractive (A)	Gender (G)	Race (R)	A * G	A *R	G * R	A * G * R	Sig. Diff.
Clarifai	6.08* (.0006)	24.26*** (.04)	4.93** (.02)	4.17* (.006)	.38	3.91** (.02)	1.85	A: MA > LA G: W > M R: A, W > B G * R: AW > BW, BM, WM WW > AM, BW, LM, WM
Microsoft	5.05* (.006)	.065	3.16* (.02)	.02	1.38	1.18	.72	A: MA > LA R: W > L
Watson	6.327* (.004)	9.71** (.02)	6.54*** (.03)	1.15	2.28	.77	.70	A: MA > LA G: W > M R: W > L L > B
Imagga	5.526* (.003)	31.76*** (.01)	16.00*** (.03)	6.45* (.001)	.88	4.19** (.004)	.18	A: MA > LA G: W > M R: A > W B > L, W

The right-most column reports significant differences according to the Tukey Honestly Significant Differences test. All three taggers tend to use more positive words when describing more versus less attractive individuals. However, while the main effect on "attractiveness" is statistically significant, its size is very small. It appears to be the case that the depicted person's gender and race play a greater role in explaining the use of positive tags. Clarifai and Watson describe women more positively than men. Clarifai describes images of Blacks less positively than images of Asians and Whites, while Watson favors Latinos/as over Blacks, but Whites over Latinos/as. The Microsoft tagger, which shows no significant main effect on gender, favors Whites over Latinos/as.

4.3   Gender (Mis)Inference

Although the tagging algorithms studied do not directly perform gender recognition, they do output tags that imply gender. We considered the use of male/female reference words per the LIWC scores. Table 11 shows the percent of images for which a gender is implied (% Gendered). In particular, we assume that when an algorithm uses tags of only one gender, and not the other, that the depicted person's gender is implied. This is the case in 80% of the images processed by Clarifai and Imagga, whereas Microsoft and Watson-produced tags imply gender in almost half of the images. Implied gender was compared against the gender recorded in the CFD; precision appears in parentheses. As previously mentioned, the Imagga algorithm used female reference tags only in the case of one woman; its strategy appears to be to use only male reference words.

Table 11. Use of gendered tags (per LIWC) and precision on implied genders.

Algorithmically implied gender					
	% Gendered	Male only	Female only	Male & Female	No gendered tags
Clarifai	80%	358 (.81)	122 (1.00)	117	0
Microsoft	42%	245 (.53)	5 (1.00)	178	169
Watson	44%	141 (.86)	124 (.97)	0	329
Imagga	78%	465 (.61)	1 (1.00)	0	131

The algorithms rarely tag images of men with feminine references (i.e., there is high precision when implying that someone is a woman). Only three images of men were implied to be women, and only by Watson. In contrast, images of women were often tagged incorrectly (i.e., lower precision for inferring that someone is a man). Table 12 breaks down the gender inference accuracy by the depicted person's race. Cases of "no gendered tags" are considered errors. The results of the Chi-Square Test of Independence suggest that there is a relationship between race and correct inference of gender, for all algorithms other than Imagga. For these three algorithms, there is lower accuracy on implied gender for images of Blacks, as compared to Asians, Latino/as, and White.

Table 12. Proportion of correctly implied genders, by person's self-reported race in the CFD.

Race reported in the CFD						
	Overall accuracy	Asian (n = 109)	Black (n = 197)	Latino/a (n = 108)	White (n = 183)	χ^2
Clarifai	.69	.75	.59	.76	.72	14.35**
Microsoft	.23	.28	.10	.26	.31	29.34***
Watson	.41	.44	.31	.49	.45	12.96**
Imagga	.47	.47	.47	.47	.48	.09

5   Discussion and Implications

5.1   Discussion

Consumer information services, including social media, have grown to rely on computer vision applications, such as taggers that automatically infer the content of an input image. However, the technology is increasingly opaque. Burrell [9] describes three types of opacity, and the taggers we study exhibit all three. First, the algorithms are proprietary, and their owners provide little explanation as to how they make inferences about images or even the set of all possible tags (e.g., Clarifai, Imagga). In addition, because all are based on deep learning, it may be technically infeasible to provide meaningful explanations and, even if they were provided, few people are positioned to understand an explanation (technical illiteracy). In short, algorithmic processes like image taggers have become "power brokers" [18]; they are delegated many everyday tasks (e.g., analyzing images on social media, to facilitate our sharing and retrieval) and operate largely autonomously, without the need for human intervention or oversight [61]. Furthermore, there is a tendency for people to perceive them as objective [27, 44] or even to be unaware of their presence or use in the system [20].

As our current results demonstrate, image tagging algorithms are certainly *not objective* when processing images depicting people. While we found no evidence that they output tags conveying negative judgments on physical appearance, positive tags such as "attractive," "sexy," and "fine-looking" were used by three algorithms in our study; only Watson did not output such descriptive tags. This is already of concern, as developers (i.e., those who incorporate APIs into their work) and end users (i.e., those whose images get processed by the APIs in the context of a system they use) might not expect an algorithm designed for tagging image content, to produce such subjective tags. Even more telling is that persons with certain physical characteristics were more likely to be labeled as attractive than others; in particular, the Clarifai and Imagga algorithms' use of such tags was strongly correlated to human judgements of attractiveness.

Furthermore, all four algorithms associated images of more attractive people (as rated by humans), with tags conveying positive emotional sentiment, as compared to less attractive people, thus reinforcing the physical attractive stereotype, "beautiful is good." Even when the depicted person's race and gender were controlled, physical attractiveness was still related to the use of more positive tags. The significant effects on the race and gender of the depicted person, in terms of explaining the use of positive emotion tags, is also of concern. Specifically, Clarifai, Microsft and Watson tended to label images of whites with more positive tags in comparison to other racial groups, while Clarifai, Watson and Imagga favored images of women over men.

As explained, the theoretical underpinnings of our study are drawn from evolutionary social psychology. These theories are *reductionist* in nature – they rather coldly attempt to explain interpersonal attraction as being a function of our reproductive impulses. Thus, it is worrying to observe correlations between "algorithmic attractiveness" and what would be predicted by theory. In a similar vein, Hamidi and colleagues [29] described automatic gender recognition (AGR) algorithms, which extract specific features from the input media in order to infer a person's gender, as being more about "gender reductionism" rather than recognition. They interviewed transgender individuals and found that the impact of being misgendered by a machine was often even more painful than being misrecognized by a fellow human. One reason cited was the perception that if algorithms misrecognizes them, this would solidify existing standards in society.

As depicted in Fig. 2, we fear that this reductionism could also influence standards of physical attractiveness and related stereotypes. As mentioned, while offline, people use other dynamic, non-physical cues in attractiveness judgments, image tagging algorithms do not. Algorithms objectify static people images with tags such as "sexy" or "fine-looking." Given the widespread use of these algorithms in our information ecosystem, algorithmic attractiveness is likely to influence applications such as image search or dating applications, resulting in increased circulation of people images with certain physical characteristics over others, and could lead to an increased stereotypical idea of the idealized self. Research on online and social media has shown that the online content that is uploaded by the users can enhance and produce a stereotypical idea of perfectionism [13] that in many cases leads to narcissistic personality traits [15, 28, 39].

In addition, there is some evidence suggesting that media stereotypes have a central role in creating and exacerbating body dissatisfaction. Constant exposure to "attractive" pictures in media enhances comparisons between the self and the depicted ideal attractive prototype, which in return creates dissatisfaction and 'shame' [25, 41, 48]. In some cases, the exposure has significant negative results for mental health such as the development of eating disorders since the user shapes projections of the media idealized self [2, 7, 43]. One can conclude that the continuous online exposure to attractive images that are tagged by algorithms with positive attributes may increase these stereotypical ideas of idealization with serious threats to users' mental health.

With specific reference to gender mis-inference, it is worth noting again that certain applications of AGR are not yet mature; as detailed in the review of related work, AGR from images is an extremely difficult task. Although general image tagging algorithms are not meant to perform AGR, our study demonstrated that many output tags do imply a depicted person's gender. On our dataset, algorithms were much more likely to mis-imply that women were men, but not vice versa. The application of these algorithms, whether specifically designed for AGR or a general image-tagging tool, in digital spaces, might negatively impact users' sense of *human autonomy* [24].

Being labelled mistakenly as a man, like the right-most woman in Fig. 1, or not being tagged as "attractive," when images of one's friends have been associated with such words, could be a painful experience for users, many of whom carefully craft a desired self-presentation [4]. Indeed, the prevalence of algorithms in social spaces has complicated self-presentation [17], and research has shown that users desire a greater ability to manage how algorithms profile them [1]. In short, our results suggest that the use of image tagging algorithms in social spaces, where users share people images, can pose a danger for users who may already suffer from having a negative self-image.

5.2   Implications for Developers

Third party developers increasingly rely on image tagging APIs to facilitate capabilities such as image search and retrieval or recommendations for tags. However, the opaque nature of these tools presents a concrete challenge; any inherent biases in the tagging algorithms will be carried downstream into the interactive media developed on these. Beyond the ethical dimensions of cases such as those described in Sect. 1, there are also emerging legal concerns related to algorithmic bias and discrimination. In particular, the EU's new General Data Protection Regulation - GDPR, will affect the routine use of machine learning algorithms in a number of ways.

For instance, Article 4 of the GDPR defines profiling as "any form of automated processing of personal data consisting of the use of personal data to evaluate certain aspects relating to a natural person[12]." Developers will need to be increasingly sensitive to the potential of their media to inadvertently treat certain groups of users unfairly and will need to implement appropriate measures as to prevent discriminatory effects. In summary, developers – both those who provide and/or consume "cognitive services" such as image tagging algorithms - will need to be increasingly mindful of the quality of their output. Because of the lack of transparency in cognitive services may have multiple sources (economic, technical) future work should consider the design of independent services that will monitor them for unintended biases, enabling developers to make an informed choice as to which tools they use.

5.3   Limitations of the Study

We used a theoretical lens that was reductionist in nature. This was intentional, as to highlight the reductionist nature of the algorithms. However, it should be noted that the dataset we used, the CFD, also has some limiting characteristics. People depicted in the images are labeled strictly according to binary gender, and their respective races are reported as a discrete characteristic (i.e., there are no biracial people images). Gender was also treated as a binary construct in the APIs we examined. Nonetheless, the current study offered us the opportunity to compare the behavior of the tagging algorithms in a more controlled setting, which would not be possible if we had used images collected in the wild. In future work, we intend to expand the study in terms of both the datasets evaluated, and the algorithms tested. It is also true that algorithms are updated from time-to-time, by the owners of the cognitive services; therefore, it should be noted the temporal nature and the constant updating of the machine learning driving the API's propose another limitation for the study. In future work we shall improve the study with the newest versions of the APIs to process the images.

6   Conclusion

This work has contributed to the ongoing conversation in HCI surrounding AI technologies, which are flawed from a social justice perspective, but are also becoming intimately interwoven into our complex information ecosystem. In their work on race and chatbots, Schlesinger and colleagues [47] emphasized that "neat solutions" are not necessarily expected. Our findings on algorithmic attractiveness and image tagging brings us to a similar conclusion. We have highlighted another dimension upon which algorithms might lead to discrimination and harm and have demonstrated that image tagging algorithms should not be considered objective when it comes to their interpretation of people images. But what can be done? Researchers are calling for a

---

[12] https://gdpr-info.eu/art-4-gdpr/.

paradigm shift; *Diversity Computing* [23] could lead to the development of algorithms that mimic the ways in which humans learn and change their perspectives. Until such techniques are feasible, HCI researchers and practitioners must continue to scrutinize the opaque tools that tend to reflect our own biases and irrationalities.

Acknowledgements. This project has received funding from the European Union's Horizon 2020 research and innovation programme under grant agreement No 739578 complemented by the Government of the Republic of Cyprus through the Directorate General for European Programmes, Coordination and Development. This research has been also funded by the European Union's Horizon 2020 research and innovation programme under grant agreement No 810105.

References

1. Alvarado, O., Waern, A.: Towards algorithmic experience: initial efforts for social media contexts. In: Proceedings of the 2018 CHI Conference on Human Factors in Computing Systems (CHI 2018), pp. 286–298. ACM, New York (2018)
2. Agras, W.S., Kirkley, B.G.: Bulimia: theories of etiology. In: Handbook of Eating Disorders, pp. 367–378 (1986)
3. Aron, A., Lewandowski, G.W., Mashek, Jr., D., Aron, E.N.: The self-expansion model of motivation and cognition in close relationships. In: The Oxford Handbook of Close Relationships, pp. 90–115 (2013)
4. Birnholtz, J., Fitzpatrick, C., Handel, M., Brubaker, J.R.: Identity, identification and identifiability: the language of self-presentation on a location-based mobile dating app. In: Proceedings of the 16th International Conference on Human-Computer Interaction with Mobile Devices & Services (MobileHCI 2014), pp. 3–12 (2014)
5. Brand, R.J., Bonatsos, A., D'Orazio, R., DeShong, H.: What is beautiful is good, even online: Correlations between photo attractiveness and text attractiveness in men's online dating profiles. Comput. Hum. Behav. 28(1), 166–170 (2012)
6. Brown, J.D.: Mass media influences on sexuality. J. Sex Res. 39(1), 42–45 (2002)
7. Brownell, K.D.: Personal responsibility and control over our bodies: when expectation exceeds reality. Health Psychol. 10(5), 303–310 (1991)
8. Buolamwini, J., Gebru, T.: Gender shades: intersectional accuracy disparities in commercial gender classification. In: Conference on Fairness, Accountability and Transparency, pp. 77–91 (2018)
9. Burrell, J.: How the machine "thinks": understanding opacity in machine learning algorithms. Big Data Soc. 3, 1–12 (2016)
10. Buss, D.M.: Sex differences in human mate preferences: evolutionary hypotheses tested in 37 cultures. Behav. Brain Sci. 12(1), 1–14 (1989)
11. Buss, D.M.: The Evolution of Desire. Basic Books, New York City (1994)
12. Buss, D.M., Kenrick, D.T.: Evolutionary social psychology. In: Gilbert, D.T., Fiske, S.T., Lindzey, G. (eds.) The Handbook of Social Psychology, pp. 982–1026. McGraw-Hill, New York, NY, US (1998)
13. Chua, T.H.H., Chang, L.: Follow me and like my beautiful selfies: Singapore teenage girls' engagement in self-presentation and peer comparison on social media. Comput. Hum. Behav. 55, 190–197 (2016)
14. Cunningham, M.R.: Measuring the physical in physical attractiveness: quasi-experiments on the sociobiology of female facial beauty. J. Pers. Soc. Psychol. 50(5), 925–935 (1986)

15. Davenport, S.W., Bergman, S.M., Bergman, J.Z., Fearrington, M.E.: Twitter versus Facebook: exploring the role of narcissism in the motives and usage of different social media platforms. Comput. Hum. Behav. **32**, 212–220 (2014)
16. Darwin, C.: The Descent of Man, and Selection in Relation to Sex. John Murray, London (1871)
17. DeVito, M.A., Birnholtz, J., Hancock, J.T., French, M., Liu, S.: How people form folk theories of social media feeds and what it means for how we study self-presentation. In: Proceedings of the 2018 CHI Conference on Human Factors in Computing Systems (CHI 2018), Paper 120 (2018)
18. Diakopoulos, N.: Accountability in algorithmic decision making. Commun. ACM **59**(2), 56–62 (2016)
19. Dion, K., Berscheid, E., Walster, E.: What is beautiful is good. J. Pers. Soc. Psychol. **24**(3), 285–290 (1972)
20. Eslami, M., et al.: "I always assumed that I wasn't really that close to [her]": reasoning about invisible algorithms in news feeds. In: Proceedings of the 33rd Annua 17
21. Feingold, A.: Good-looking people are not what we think. Psychol. Bull. **111**(2), 304–341 (1992)
22. Fisher, R.A.: The Genetical Theory of Natural Selection. Clarendon Press, Oxford (1930)
23. Fletcher-Watson, S., De Jaegher, H., van Dijk, J., Frauenberger, C., Magnée, M., Ye, J.: Diversity computing. Interactions **25**(5), 28–33 (2018)
24. Friedman, B.: Value-sensitive design. Interactions **3**(6), 16–23 (1996)
25. Garner, D.M., Garfinkel, P.E.: Socio-cultural factors in the development of anorexia nervosa. Psychol. Med. **10**(4), 647–656 (1980)
26. Gerbner, G., Gross, L., Morgan, M., Signorielli, N., Shanahan, J.: Growing up with television: Cultivation processes. Media Eff.: Adv. Theor. Res. **2**, 43–67 (2002)
27. Gillespie, T.: The relevance of algorithms. In: Gillespie, T., Boczkowski, P., Foot, K. (eds.) Media Technologies: Essays on Communication, Materiality and Society, pp. 167–193. MIT Press, Cambridge (2014)
28. große Deters, F., Mehl, M.R., Eid, M.: Narcissistic power poster? On the relationship between narcissism and status updating activity on Facebook. J. Res. Pers. **53**, 165–174 (2014)
29. Hamidi, F., Scheuerman, M.K., Branham, S.M.: Gender recognition or gender reductionism? The social implications of embedded gender recognition systems. In: Proceedings of the 2018 CHI Conference on Human Factors in Computing Systems (CHI 2018). ACM (2018)
30. Hatfield, E., Rapson, R.L.: Love, Sex, and Intimacy: Their Psychology, Biology, and History. HarperCollins College Publishers, New York (1993)
31. Hatfield, E., Sprecher, S.: Mirror, Mirror: The Importance of Looks in Everyday Life. SUNY Press, Albany (1986)
32. Introna, L., Wood, D.: Picturing algorithmic surveillance: the politics of facial recognition systems. Surveill. Soc. **2**, 177–198 (2004)
33. Klare, B.F., Burge, M.J., Klontz, J.C., Bruegge, R.W.V., Jain, A.K.: Face recognition performance: role of demographic information. IEEE Trans. Inf. Forensics Secur. **7**(6), 1789–1801 (2012)
34. Krizhevsky, A., Sutskever, I., Hinton, G.E.: Imagenet classification with deep convolutional neural networks. In: Advances in Neural Information Processing Systems (NIPS), pp. 1097–1105 (2012)
35. Langlois, J.H.: From the eye of the beholder to behavioral reality: development of social behaviors and social relations as a function of physical attractiveness. In: Physical Appearance, Stigma, and Social Behavior: The Ontario Symposium, vol. 3, pp. 23–51. Lawrence Erlbaum (1986)

36. Levi, G., Hassner, T.: Age and gender classification using convolutional neural networks. In: Proceedings of the IEEE Conference on Computer Vision and Pattern Recognition Workshops (2015)

37. Lin, T.Y., et al.: Microsoft COCO: common objects in context. In: Fleet, D., Pajdla, T., Schiele, B., Tuytelaars, T. (eds.) Computer Vision – ECCV 2014. Lecture Notes in Computer Science, vol. 8693, pp. 740–755. Springer, Cham (2014). https://doi.org/10.1007/978-3-319-10602-1_48

38. Ma, D.S., Correll, J., Wittenbrink, B.: The Chicago face database: a free stimulus set of faces and norming data. Behav. Res. Methods **47**(4), 1122–1135 (2015)

39. McKinney, B.C., Kelly, L., Duran, R.L.: Narcissism or openness? College students' use of Facebook and Twitter. Commun. Res. Rep. **29**(2), 108–118 (2012)

40. McLellan, B., McKelvie, S.J.: Effects of age and gender on perceived facial attractiveness. Can. J. Behav. Sci. **25**(1), 135–143 (1993)

41. Meier, E.P., Gray, J.: Facebook photo activity associated with body image disturbance in adolescent girls. Cyberpsychology Behav. Soc. Netw. **17**(4), 199–206 (2014)

42. Miller, A.G.: Role of physical attractiveness in impression formation. Psychon. Sci. **19**(4), 241–243 (1970)

43. Morris, A., Cooper, T., Cooper, P.J.: The changing shape of female fashion models. Int. J. Eat. Disord. **8**(5), 593–596 (1989)

44. O'Neil, C.: Weapons of Math Destruction: How Big Data Increases Inequality and Threatens Democracy. Crown Random House, New York City (2016)

45. Pennebaker, J.W., Boyd, R.L., Jordan, K., Blackburn, K.: The development and psychometric properties of LIWC2015 (2015). https://utexasir.tdl.org/bitstream/handle/2152/31333/LIWC2015_LanguageManual.pdf'sequence=3

46. Ryu, H.J., Adam, H., Mitchell, M.: Inclusivefacenet: improving face attribute detection with race and gender diversity. In: ICML 2018 FATML Workshop, Stockholm, Sweden (2017)

47. Schlesinger, A., O'Hara, K.P., Taylor, A.S.: Let's talk about race: identity, chatbots, and AI. In: Proceedings of the 2018 CHI Conference on Human Factors in Computing Systems (CHI 2018). ACM, New York (2018)

48. Silberstein, L.R., Striegel-Moore, R.H., Rodin, J.: Feeling fat: a woman's shame. In: Lewis, H.B. (ed.) The Role of Shame in Symptom Formation, pp. 89–108. Lawrence Erlbaum Associates, Inc., Hillsdale (1987)

49. Simonyan, K., Zisserman, A.: Very deep convolutional networks for large-scale image recognition. arXiv preprint arXiv:1409.1556 (2014)

50. Singh, D.: Adaptive significance of female physical attractiveness: role of waist-to-hip ratio. J. Pers. Soc. Psychol. **65**(2), 293–307 (1993)

51. Snyder, M., Tanke, E.D., Berscheid, E.: Social perception and interpersonal behavior: on the self-fulfilling nature of social stereotypes. J. Pers. Soc. Psychol. **35**(9), 656–672 (1977)

52. Stefanone, M.A., Lackaff, D., Rosen, D.: Contingencies of self-worth and social-netwoking-site behavior. Cyberpsychology Behav. Soc. Netw. **14**(1–2), 41–49 (2011)

53. Stroebe, W., Insko, C.A., Thompson, V.D., Layton, B.D.: Effects of physical attractiveness, attitude similarity, and sex on various aspects o interpersonal attraction. J. Pers. Soc. Psychol. **18**(1), 79–91 (1971)

54. Symons, D.: The Evolution of Human Sexuality. Oxford University Press, Oxford (1979)

55. Szegedy, C., et al.: Going deeper with convolutions. In: Proceedings of the IEEE Conference on Computer Vision and Pattern Recognition, pp. 1–9 (2015)

56. Thornhill, R., Alcock, J.: The Evolution of Insect Mating Systems. Harvard University Press, Cambridge (1983)

57. Trivers, R.L.: Parental investment and sexual selection. In: Campbell, B. (ed.) Sexual Selection and the Descent of Man. Aldine (1972)

58. Walster, E., Aronson, V., Abrahams, D., Rottman, L.: Importance of physical attractiveness in dating behavior. J. Pers. Soc. Psychol. **4**(5), 508–516 (1966)
59. Wheeler, L., Kim, Y.: What is beautiful is culturally good: the physical attractiveness stereotype has different content in collectivistic cultures. Pers. Soc. Psychol. Bull. **23**(8), 795–800 (1997)
60. Williams, G.C.: Pleiotropy, natural selection and the evolution of senescence. Evolution **11**, 398–411 (1957)
61. Wilson, M.: Algorithms (and the) everyday. Inf. Commun. Soc. **20**(1), 137–150 (2017)
62. Zhao, J., Wang, T., Yatskar, M., Ordonez, V., Chang, K.W.: Men also like shopping: reducing gender bias amplification using corpus-level constraints. In: Proceedings of the 2017 Conference on Empirical Methods in Natural Language Processing, Copenhagen, Denmark, 7–11, 20 September, pp. 2979–2989 (2017)

Virtual and Augmented Reality I

Design and Evaluation of Three Interaction Models for Manipulating Internet of Things (IoT) Devices in Virtual Reality

Günter Alce$^{(\boxtimes)}$, Eva-Maria Ternblad, and Mattias Wallergård

Lund University, Lund, Sweden
Gunter.Alce@design.lth.se

Abstract. More and more things are getting connected to the internet, including lights, speakers, and refrigerators. These connected things are an example of what a smart home system that is part of the Internet of Things (IoT) can incorporate. IoT enables advanced services by interconnecting physical and virtual things. But, building interactive prototypes for smart home systems can be difficult and costly, since it involves a number of different devices and systems with varying technological readiness level. Virtual reality (VR) is a technology that can create computer-generated environments and has been used as a design tool in many different domains, such as architecture, city planning, and industrial design. However, the focus has traditionally been on visualizing design proposals rather than letting the intended users directly interact with them. Recently, we have seen an intensified development of VR headsets such as HTC Vive and Oculus Rift. These headsets come with relatively well-developed hand controllers, which can be used to interact with the virtual environment. This opens up opportunities to develop and evaluate interactive virtual smart home systems.

This paper presents three interaction models developed and evaluated using the new generation of VR technology. The interaction models were then compared in a user study with 18 participants. Some statistically significant differences and subjective preferences could be observed in the quantitative and qualitative data respectively.

The main contribution of this paper is to elucidate knowledge about using VR as a prototyping tool to explore IoT interaction. Moreover, this study implies that you can collect and analyze data for statistical analysis using VR.

Keywords: Virtual Reality · Internet of Things · Method · Interaction

1 Introduction

Virtual reality (VR) has been used as a design tool in many different domains, such as architecture, city planning, and industrial design [1]. However, the focus has traditionally been on visualizing design proposals for the users rather than letting them directly interact with them. The main problem has been the maturity of VR technology; it has been either too expensive or difficult to build VR applications that allow for immersive embodied interaction.

© IFIP International Federation for Information Processing 2019
Published by Springer Nature Switzerland AG 2019
D. Lamas et al. (Eds.): INTERACT 2019, LNCS 11749, pp. 267–286, 2019.
https://doi.org/10.1007/978-3-030-29390-1_15

This has changed with the latest generation of commercial VR hardware (e.g. HTC Vive and Oculus Rift) which comes with tracking of headset and hand controllers in sub-millimeter precision. Moreover, they allow the user to walk around and interact with the virtual environment (VE) in a relatively realistic manner.

A general benefit of using a VE to build prototypes of interactive systems is that it allows researchers to test complex systems or hardware that does not actually exist in a controlled manner. A smart home system is an example of a complex system, which is difficult to develop and test [2, 3]. The complexity of a smart home system increases since more and more things are being connected to the Internet, including lights, dishwasher and refrigerator. Everything that has a unique id and is sending data over a network can be considered as part of the Internet of Things (IoT) [4].

Several smart home frameworks are currently being developed, with an application running on a mobile device that can control things in a smart home. Examples of such frameworks are the Samsung SmartThings [5], the Apple HomeKit [6] and Google Weave [7]. However, having yet another application to control things is perhaps not the best solution and does not utilize the potential of IoT interaction in a smart home environment. Building interaction prototypes with these applications can be difficult and costly, since it involves a number of different devices and systems with varying technological readiness level [3]. In particular, it is difficult to achieve prototypes that offer an integrated user experience and show the full potential of IoT interaction concepts. The ideal prototyping methodology would offer high-fidelity at a relatively low cost and the ability to simulate a wide range of IoT use cases.

This paper presents three interaction models, which were developed and evaluated in a controlled experiment, using the new generation of VR technology such as HTC Vive [8] together with the game engine Unity [9].

The main contribution of this paper is to elucidate knowledge about the method of using VR as a prototyping tool to explore IoT interaction for a smart home environment.

2 Related Work

Using VR as a prototyping method is an area that has been well studied. This section reviews previous related research in using VR as a prototyping method including earlier user experiments and evaluation methods.

2.1 Using VR to Simulate Smart Home Systems

A number of researchers have been using different simulation tools to prototype smart home systems. The main argument of using simulation to prototype IoT environments is to reduce development time and cost [2]. There are many different smart home simulators with a variety of fidelity. SHSim [2] is built on a dynamic mechanism that allows the user to configure the system and test different use cases. Other examples of smart home simulators are UbiWise [10] that can show a close-up view of virtual devices, TATUS [11] that can simulate adaptive systems, UbiReal [12] that have functions to facilitate deployment of virtual devices, and Furfaro et al. [13] which tried to illustrate how VEs can be a valuable tool to assess security properties. However, these tools are desktop based tools that mainly focus on the installation and configuration of a smart home system and lack embodied user interaction.

Other simulation tools take in account context awareness and some user interaction such as Nguyen et al. [14] proposed Interactive SmartHome Simulator (ISS) that models the relationship between the environment and other factors and simulates the behavior of an intelligent house. CASS [15] is a context-aware tool which can generate the context information associated with virtual sensors. Armac and Retkowitz [16] proposed eHomeSimulator, that can be used to simulate multiple environments with different spatial structures. Hu et al. [17] proposed a web-based tool to check the home status and control devices with a 3D interface. However, the focus of this work is more on a system level and hence they do not offer high fidelity user interaction with IoT devices.

2.2   Using VR for Interaction

There are several examples of research attempts to develop immersive VR user interaction in different domains. For example, Bowman and Wingrave [18] used VR to design various types of menu systems to be used within the VE i.e. 3D graphical user interface. de Sá and Zachmann [19] investigated the steps needed to apply VR in maintenance processes in the car industry. In the paper, they present several interaction paradigms e.g. how to assemble the front door of a car, and other functionalities, which a VR system needs to support. The results from their study show the users being very optimistic of how VR can improve the overall maintenance process. Alce et al. [20] used VR for simulating IoT interaction with glasses-based AR. This had the advantage of creating a realistic experience in terms of AR display resolution and tracking. However, it might be hard for the user to discriminate the augmented stimuli from the VE and it can be difficult to interact with the simulated environment in an easy and realistic manner. Furthermore, the movements of the user are restricted by the range of the VR tracking system, which makes some use cases difficult or impossible to simulate. More recently, Ens et al. [21], introduced Ivy which is a spatially situated visual programming tool using immersive VR. Ivy allows users to link smart objects, insert logic constructs and visualize real-time data flows between real-world sensors and actuators. However, Ivy focus on how to configure a smart home system and not on how users can discover and control with the IoT devices.

2.3   Using VR with Wizard of Oz Method

Wizard of Oz (WOZ) is a well-known method where a human operates undeveloped components of a technical system. Above all, the WOZ method has been widely used in the field of human-computer interaction to explore design concepts. Carter et al. [22] state that WOZ prototypes are excellent for early lab studies but do not scale to longitudinal deployment because of the labor commitment for human-in-the-loop systems. Recently Gombac et al. [23] used WOZ for prototyping multimodal interfaces in VR. They compared voice and mid-air gesture interface while interacting with a computer system. WOZ is often used for voice interaction and one of the interaction model presented in this study used WOZ to simulate voice interaction together with head-gaze.

In summary, over the past 20 years, researchers have developed a range of different VR simulators to prototype different systems. User studies show the benefits of VR as a prototyping tool regarding simulation to save time and cost. However, it seems that there has been little research on using VR to prototype IoT interaction. The described approaches have their merits in the view of using VR as a prototyping tool but lack exploring user interaction models, which can be a problem if it is discovered late in the project when the smart home system is put into operation. VR facilitates the development of IoT applications since it is cheaper and easier to add a myriad of virtual devices compared to real devices [3]. Therefore, we have focused on utilizing the new VR hardware such as HTC Vive as a prototyping tool for immersive embodied VR IoT interaction.

3   Building the Prototype

One of the main goals with the presented work was to design and test a set of embodied IoT interaction models by exploring the possibilities and technical advantages with the VR environment. This prototyping method implicates that relatively futuristic models can be explored, and technical obstacles can be avoided in favor of human preferences, natural behavior, and cognitive capacities. Consequently, the process of designing the prototype was performed in an iterative approach, starting with user preferences and a wider concept of IoT interaction, followed by exploring and testing implementation possibilities in VR until the final prototype was developed and evaluated.

3.1   Low-Fidelity Interaction and User Observations

For choosing appropriate types and modes of interaction, six participants (one male and five women) were recruited within the project members' social network. The participants were between 17 to 52 years old, had different backgrounds and different experiences concerning smart home systems. Each session last about 15 min.

The participants were invited to a real but small living room, where they were told to imagine a variety of day-to-day objects as being hyper-intelligent and connected to the Internet. They were then asked to freely "interact" with these objects with the use of their own bodies and modalities, without any help from devices, remote controls or traditional interfaces. During the test a concurrent think-aloud protocol (CTA) was utilized. CTA is a common procedure within the field of usability testing that is considered to be both reliable and cost efficient [24, 25]. Being well aware of that the question about whether CTA affects user performance or not has been debated over several years [26, 27] we concluded that the benefits from this method outweighed the disadvantages. Asking the participants to share their ideas and thoughts with us made it possible to retain valuable tacit information.

After the introduction, the participants were asked to interact with four devices:

- **TV**, turning it on/off, change channel, increase volume
- **Light bulbs**, turning on/off and changing the luminance
- **Music player**, to turn it on/off, select favorite song and increase the volume
- **Coffee machine**, start the coffee machine which is not in the room.

Although the interaction was completely imaginary and performed without any type of feedback, this highly explorative test lead to very useful findings, making it possible to select a limited sample of plausible and testable types of IoT-interaction. Interestingly, the participants showed similar preferences concerning the choice of interaction modalities including voice commands and gestures. However, their personal expressions of precise manipulations of hand gestures and verbal utterances had a larger variation (see Fig. 1a–d). One participant would use voice for all interaction except for selecting a device which pointing was preferred. Four participants used pointing with finger, one used open hand and one used the fist and wanted to turn/on/off by opening the fist (see Fig. 1c and d). The same participant would also like to be able to increase and decrease the volume or the luminance of the light bulbs depending on how much the fist was open, so fully open hand would be max volume or luminance while half open would be half volume or luminance depending on which device was selected.

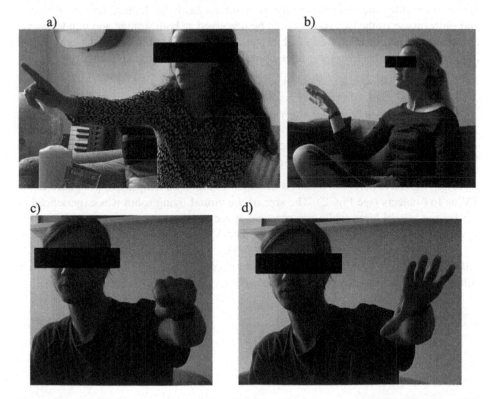

Fig. 1. (a) Pointing to start (b) swiping gesture (c) close lights or TV (d) Open lights or TV.

After discussing, retrying and analyzing these outcomes a set of interaction types were chosen and categorized according to Ledo et al.'s [28] four different stages of interaction: Discover, Select, View status and Control. This classification helps to identify necessary components that have to be fulfilled in an IoT environment. Finally, after subsequent low-fidelity testing, the following interaction patterns were decided to advance into the stage of VR prototyping and implementation:

1. To discover objects: Raise one hand
2. To select objects: Point with your hand; or head-gaze; or proximity (walk towards an object)
3. To view the status of objects: Feedback from the objects themselves and/or through a virtual smartwatch device
4. To control objects: Point and click; or head-gaze and voice; or simple hand movements.

3.2   VR Implementation

The interaction with the IoT objects was decided to take place within a realistic but sparsely furnished virtual living room. Moreover, for making it possible to study and evaluate IoT-interaction in relation to traditional object manipulation such as the use of switches for turning on/off lamps, this interaction type was added. Since the difference between selecting and controlling objects could not easily be defined, and since a strict and uniform use of the two stages could be perceived as both strange and unnecessarily complicated for several of the IoT objects, these two stages of interaction were merged into one. Finally, the following interaction models were implemented:

1. To discover objects: Raise one hand
2. To view the status of objects: Feedback from the objects themselves and/or through a virtual smartwatch device showing the status of the object
3. To select and control objects: Point and click; head-gaze together with voice; and physical manipulation (the participant had to walk to the wall and press on the switches in which they got haptic feedback)

The virtual living room consisted of four wall-mounted lamps, two pot plants and a TV as IoT objects (see Fig. 2). The size of the virtual living room was experienced as ten by ten meters large while the physical space were nine square meters due to the limited tracking space of the VR system. The VE was implemented with Unity ver. 5.5.0f3, and the VR hardware was an HTC Vive with resolution 2160×1200 (1080×1200 per eye) and >90 frames per second frame rate, rendering the user a sufficient realistic experience without delays or visual discomfort.

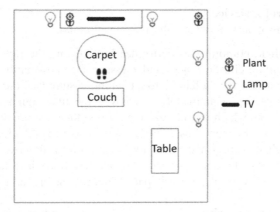

Fig. 2. A drawing of the virtual living room with four wall-mounted lamps, two pot plants and a TV as IoT-objects.

Discover Devices

To discover IoT objects, the user had to raise the right hand above the head (see Fig. 3a). Since the gesture is common and natural, it was presumed to be used with ease and expertise. As long as the participant's hand remained above the head, all IoT objects replied by casting a beam of yellow light, indicating their belonging to the IoT-family and showing that they were ready to be used and controlled accordingly.

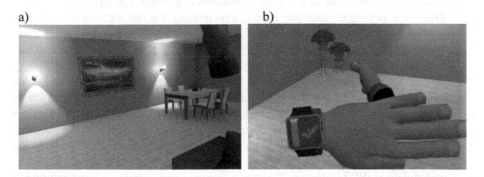

Fig. 3. (a) IoT objects could be discovered by rising the hand. (b) Looking at feedback from one of the pot plants.

View Status

In the prototype, some of the objects (such as the TV and the lamps) changed and revealed their status themselves when the participant was controlling them i.e. turning them on/off. Another way to see the status of the IoT objects was through the virtual smartwatch situated on the participant's left wrist (see Fig. 3b).

Select and Control a Device

To select and control an IoT device, the participant could:

(a) **Point and click**, pointing was performed by directing the right or the left-hand control towards a chosen object and pressing a control button. This command animated the active virtual hand into a pointing gesture (see Fig. 3b) and used an invisible ray-casting technique (i.e. removed the line segment attached to the participant's hand which would have represented the direction of the ray) towards the actual object. For the chosen object to be activated, the direction of the ray-cast (although invisible) had to hit the item within a defined area, equal to or slightly larger than the object's virtual boundaries. Since, it is not easy to select a small object distant from the participant without a visible ray-cast neither in VR nor in reality.

(b) **Head-gaze together with voice**, the participant could also use head-gaze and voice for activating IoT devices. The reason for merging these communicative tools is mainly due to their nature. First, to use gaze as a single behavioral pattern for selecting or controlling objects would not be easy. The human eye is almost never still, blending longer fixations and saccades into complex patterns [27], and it is quite possible to show an interest in an object without wanting to interact with it. Secondly, voice interaction in general is unable to discover what you can interact with and is unable to make all possible actions visible to the user. You could perhaps ask a "virtual voice assistant", but you might have trouble remembering what was listed and what the different devices were called. Moreover, as pointed out by Norman and Nielsen [29], user interfaces built on gestures and speech interaction lack several fundamental principles of interaction design. These are principles that are completely independent of technology, such as visibility (affordances or signifiers), feedback, consistency, non-destructed operation (undo), discoverability, scalability and reliability [29]. This is, of course, less of a problem in a familiar home environment, where the user knows what devices and services are available, and where they are located. However, in an un-known environment, such as a new workplace, it could be difficult for a user to discover nearby devices and their capabilities. Hence, we decided to use head-gaze together with voice for turning on and off objects, making the head direction the selecting part and the voice the controlling part. However, since the used VR equipment does not support eye tracking or voice control, this interaction model was simulated with a WOZ solution. We chose identical and extremely easy commands for all implemented smart objects, namely "ON" for turning objects on and "OFF" for turning objects off. One of the test leaders were acting as a wizard and used predefined keys on the computer to turn on and off each virtual device in the virtual living room. For example, the "1" key was used to alternate between turning on and off the TV. The Wizard could follow what the test person was looking at on the computer display and could hear the test person during the whole test session. Prior the test session the wizard trained to avoid mistakes during the real test.

(c) **Traditional switch buttons,** switch buttons mounted on the virtual wall also controlled the four light bulbs in our VR-prototype. The vibration from the hand controller gave haptic feedback when the participant pressed the button. This implementation made it possible to compare traditional and futuristic ways of interaction even though it is important to point out the fact that all interactions were virtual.

4 Experiment

A comparative evaluation was conducted in a VR laboratory environment to compare the proposed interaction models: (a) point and click; (b) head-gaze together with voice; and (c) traditional switch button for selecting and controlling IoT devices. Both quantitative and qualitative data were collected. The purpose of this test was mainly to explore the participants' preferences and to identify possible differences between the interaction models in regard to physical or cognitive load. At the same time, we wanted to gather valuable information concerning participants' immersion and feel of reality.

As dependent variables, we used NASA TLX values, and individual ratings for the interaction patterns. The two main null hypothesizes was that neither the NASA TLX values nor the individual ratings would differ in regard to the type of interaction model. We also decided to analyze qualitative data concerning any stated difficulties with certain types of interaction and comments on feedback, and to measure user presence with the use of a standard questionnaire.

4.1 Setup

The evaluation was conducted in a VR laboratory environment with audio and video recording facilities. One single session involved one participant and two test leaders, where one was in charge of the HTC Vive equipment and one guided the participants through the test and performed interviews (see Fig. 4). All test sessions were recorded.

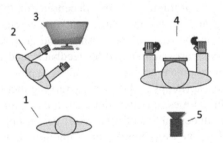

Fig. 4. The experiment setup. (1) test leader (introducing), (2) test leader (HTC Vive equipment, (3) computer running the HTC Vive, (4) test participant, (5) camera.

4.2 Participants

18 participants were recruited by notifications on Facebook and through advertisements on public billboards at university faculties and cafés. The participants consisted of twelve males and six females, between 19 and 51 years old ($M = 25.1$) and from various backgrounds (although 12 of them were students at the University). Nine of them had previous experience of VR while nine of them had none.

4.3 Procedure

All participants were given a brief introduction to the project and its purpose. Next, all participants filled in a short questionnaire together with informed consent regarding their participation and the use of collected data. Thereafter they were introduced to the HTC Vive where they performed a quick training session in a very basic and minimalistic VE. The purpose of this exercise was for the participants to get familiarized with the fictive world and the virtual interactive patterns of pressing buttons and pointing at objects (see Fig. 5).

Fig. 5. Pointing is exercised by aiming at virtual cubes and spheres in a minimalistic environment.

After one or two rounds of training (mainly depending on the participants' capacity of successfully pointing at objects), the participants were sent into the virtual living room. Here they were introduced to the raising-hand-gesture for discovering IoT devices as well as to the smartwatch device for feedback, and they were asked to get familiarized with the environment and talk about their experience. Subsequently, they interacted with all of the four lamps in the room by turning them on and off from left to right. This was done three times, one time for each interaction model.

In an attempt to understand and describe the users' perceived workload NASA TLX was used as an assessment tool. Although, it is normally reported in writing we let the participants respond orally. Moreover, we simplified the NASA TLX scales, the scores were calculated out of 10 instead of 100. NASA TLX is commonly used to evaluate perceived workload for a specific task. It consists of two parts. The first part is referred to as raw TLX (RTLX) and consists of six subscales (Mental Demand, Physical Demand, Temporal Demand, Performance, Effort, and Frustration) to measure the total workload. The second part of the NASA TLX creates an individual weighting of the subscales by letting the subjects compare them pairwise based on their perceived importance. However, as reported by Hart [30], using the second part of the NASA TLX might actually decrease experimental validity. For this reason, it was not used in this experiment.

To make the physical effort equal in all interaction models, each one of the scenarios were initiated by directing the participant to a specific starting point marked on the virtual carpet by two-foot prints (see Fig. 2). To avoid sequential effects, the order of the interactive types were balanced to obtain all possible orders (see Table 1).

Table 1. The Interactive types were balanced accordingly.

Test Person	1st Interaction	2nd Interaction	3rd Interaction
1, 7, 13	Switchers	Pointing	Gaze & Voice
2, 8, 14	Pointing	Gaze & Voice	Switches
3, 9, 15	Gaze & Voice	Switches	Pointing
4, 10, 16	Switches	Gaze & Voice	Pointing
5, 11, 17	Pointing	Switches	Gaze & Voice
6, 12, 18	Gaze & Voice	Pointing	Switches

After this, the participants were allowed to interact with all smart objects in the room, choosing one or several interactive patterns of their own liking. They were also asked to verbally report the visual feedback from the smartwatch. The VR-session ended with a short interview regarding the subject's individual interactive preferences, perceived difficulties under the test and his or her general VR experience. The questions asked during the interview:

1. If you got to rank your interaction methods. Which one was the best, the worst and the one between them?
2. What did you experience as hardest in the entire test?
3. What did you experience as easiest in the entire test?
4. Was there any moment that surprised you?
5. Do you have any comments on the VR environment?
6. Do you have any comments on the test itself?

Finally, the participants filled in the Slater-Usoh-Steed Presence Questionnaire (SUSPQ), which is a common tool for measuring the presence a user experiences in a VE [31], and received coffee and cake as a reward for participating. Each session last about 30 min. The whole procedure of the test session is visualized in a block diagram (see Fig. 6).

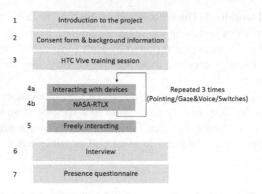

1	Introduction to the project
2	Consent form & background information
3	HTC Vive training session
4a	Interacting with devices
4b	NASA-RTLX
5	Freely interacting
6	Interview
7	Presence questionnaire

Repeated 3 times (Pointing/Gaze&Voice/Switches)

Fig. 6. Test session procedure.

4.4 Result

The measurements were successful and all participants performed all moments without incidents or major problems. The training session was generally performed twice (six participants did it only once) and eight of the participants needed to exercise the pointing gesture with the help of additional instructions and tips. The most common problem in this session was to point at a distant object, and two of the participants had to practice with a visible ray-casting technique, i.e. a line segment that would extend out to touch the virtual object being pointed to. The visible directed ray-cast helped to learn how to correctly hold and direct the hand controller for a successful hit.

The interaction model "Raise-hand gesture" was used for discoverability of IoT devices, and half (nine) of the participants were able to locate and identify all of the smart devices quickly and without errors. Some users mistook the loudspeakers for IoT objects, while others missed the pot plants or lamps. However, the gleam of light from the objects was correctly interpreted, and the raise-hand gesture was easily remembered. At the end of the test, all participants except for one recalled the gesture without any further instructions.

Cognitive and physical load

The overall RTLX scores generated relatively low average values (see Table 2), and a one-way ANOVA for dependent measures showed a significant relation: $F(2, 51) = 3.40$, $p = .041$. Multiple pairwise-comparison showed significant difference between the reported RTLX_Point and RTLX_gaze_voice with an adjusted p-value of $p = 0.034$ (see Fig. 7).

Table 2. The RTLX scores for the different interaction models. Means and standard deviations.

	RTLX_button	RTLX_point	RTLX_gaze_voice
Mean	12.28	14.39	8.50
SD	5.65	10.02	3.01

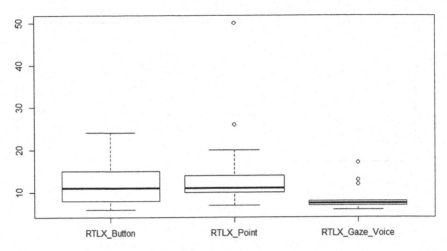

Fig. 7. The RTLX scores illustrated in a boxplot.

Preference

When it comes to the individual rankings, the differences between the interaction models were similar to the perceived workload, the same interaction type were preferred as the one which was perceived as the lowest workload (head-gaze and voice) (see Table 3). A one-way ANOVA for dependent measures showed a significant relation between the reported "ranked interaction-value" (RINT-value) and the corresponding interactive pattern: $F(2, 51) = 7.4$, $p = .001$. Multiple pairwise-comparison showed significant difference between RINT_gaze_voice and RINT_button with an adjusted p-value of $p = .001$. Moreover, it was close to the margin of statistical significance between RINT_Point and RINT_gaze_voice with an adjusted p-value of $p = .072$. The interaction type with voice and head-gaze were preferred prior to the traditional pressing on switch buttons (see Fig. 8). However, in the free interaction phase, the main part of the participants (11 of 18) actually used pointing as their main model of interaction, even though this was not always easily performed. Six of these 11 participants also ranked pointing as their primary choice, while five of them stated head-gaze and voice as their main preference. This inconsistency indicates a curiosity for testing new or challenging interaction models. The result equally implicates a need for complementary evaluation methods when prototyping unfamiliar IoT-environments.

Table 3. Order of priority (values of 1, 2 or 3) for the different interaction models. Means and standard deviations (note that high values correspond to high rankings, and vice versa).

	RINT_button	RINT_point	RINT_gaze_voice
Mean	1.6	1.9	2.5
SD	0.62	0.80	0.79

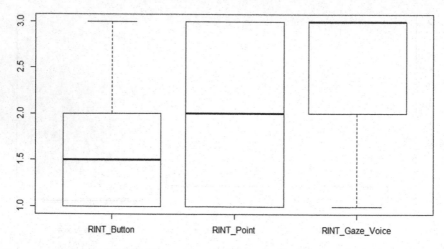

Fig. 8. Preferred interaction models in the free interaction phase.

Presence

The results obtained from the SUSPQ present a total mean value of $M = 5.4$ ($SD = .98$). Since the maximum value is 7 for all of the 6 questions, this has to be considered as relatively high rating (the actual usefulness and validity of the SUSPQ measure has, however, been a subject for discussion [31]. To analyze if the user experience could depend on the previous use of VR equipment, the group of participants was divided into VR novices (completely novice and with no experience of VR) and VR veterans (with at least one experience of virtual worlds). The resulting mean values were $M = 6.0$ ($SD = .87$) and $M = 4.9$ ($SD = .78$) respectively (see Fig. 9).

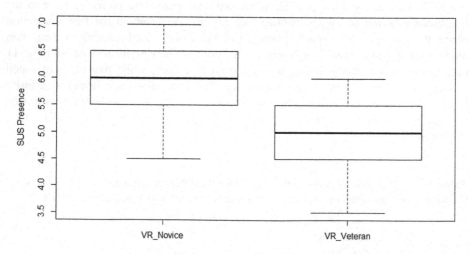

Fig. 9. SUSPQ for different users.

A T-test verified that this difference between the groups were significant: $t(8) = 2.49$, $p = .038$.

Qualitative findings

On the question, "What did you experience as hardest in the entire test?" The majority of the participants replied "To point at distant objects." Other responses referred to feedback or interactive possibilities in general (see Table 4). The easiest aspect of the test was, according to nine of the participants, to use head-gaze and voice as interaction pattern (not surprisingly since this never failed due to the WOZ-solution). For other responses regarding this question, see Table 5.

Table 4. Responses regarding difficulties in the test.

What did you experience as hardest in the entire test?	Number of participants
Point at distant objects	10
Match switch buttons to lamps	3
Understand interactive possibilities	2
Notice feedback from smartwatch	1
Understand depth	1
Nothing (everything was easy)	1

Table 5. Responses regarding what was easy in the test.

What did you experience as easiest in the entire test?	Number of participants
To use head-gaze and voice as interactive pattern	10
Everything was quite easy	3
Point at TV or lamps	2
To use the switches for turning on lamps	2
Hands-up-gesture	1

The feedback from the smartwatch was generally quite well understood, although several of the participants forgot to look at the watch when interacting with the pot plants. One reason for this could be the lack of feedback from the plants themselves. Since these did not confirm the interactive gesture by changing their visible state (similar to the TV and lamps), several participants got confused and interpreted their interaction as unsuccessful. Another consideration is that the participants did not expect the plants to be smart at all, and seven participants named the smartness and feedback from the pot plants as the least expected element during the test (see Table 6). On the question, "Was there any moment that surprised you?" some participants replied that traditional interaction with switches and haptic feedback was not expected, while other expressed their astonishment over the successful interaction in general.

Table 6. Responses regarding surprising moments.

Surprising moments	Number of participants
The smartness of the flowers	4
The haptic feedback from the wall switches	3
That the interaction actually worked	2
Nothing was surprising	2
Smartwatch feedback	2
The test environment	2
No feedback when pointing correctly	1
Being able to use "normal switches	1
Turning on the TV	1

5 Discussion

As a whole, VR could be considered as an interesting and valuable tool for prototyping and evaluating IoT-interaction, mainly due to the immersive user experience and the possibility of evaluating non-existing interaction technologies with good ecological validity.

5.1 Comparative Study

Overall, the RTLX scores of all three-interaction models were relatively low. The perceived workload of the head-gaze and voice had the lowest score and was significantly lower than the point and click. One can argue that it is not fair to compare head-gaze and voice with the other two interaction models. Since it was based on a WOZ solution. However, the commands was really simple "Turn on/off" and most of the available voice assistants such as Siri and Google Assistance can handle much more advanced commands and the participants were not aware that a human was operating the specific interaction model.

Usability evaluation in VR requires the participant to step out of the VE to answer questionnaires, or have the questionnaire available in the VE. If the virtual environment is equipped with sound effects it could of course also be hard to instruct or talk to the user during interaction. The experiences drawn from this study were that is was possible to state the NASA TLX questions orally during the virtual interaction. Moreover, statistically significant differences could be observed regarding the preferred interaction model, which was the same as the one having the lowest perceived workload i.e. head-gaze and voice. However, in order to evaluate and investigate users' cognitive workload, the experiment would have benefited of having eye tracking integrated in the HMD. Zagerman et al. [32], for example, "encourage the use of eye tracking measurements to investigate users' cognitive load while interacting with a system." The fact that several manufacturers of eye tracking equipment, e.g. Tobii and SMI, currently are integrating their products in popular VR systems.

One of the major advantages with VR as an interactive environment is the fictive but realistic setting, and many users in our test did not only experience relatively high presence but also quickly accepted the hand controls as replacements for their own hands. However, current VR systems only allows relatively coarse hand gestures without the variation and nuance offered by finger gestures e.g. pinch to zoom.

5.2   VR Limitations

As have been mentioned earlier, the physical space obtainable for the user was very limited in relation to the virtual space in the prototype. Even though the size of this area (9 m^2) partly depended on practicalities in the VR laboratory environment, the discrepancies between these two spaces are one of the limitations with current room-scale VR systems. Not only could it be hard to simulate large IoT-environments, such as warehouses, parks, squares or entire buildings, it equally complicates the testing of spaces with a lot of objects. If virtual objects cannot be reached or explored from different angles, they risk concealing each other, which in turn hinders interaction. To facilitate for the user to explore a larger area, it would therefore be necessary to introduce some sort of locomotion technique. Today, the two most common locomotion techniques for VR headsets are "teleportation" and "trackpad-based locomotion." Both have their pros and cons and the locomotion technique of choice should therefore depend on the specific IoT use case. However, it is important to note that adding an artificial locomotion upon the room-scale tracking potentially could give rise to higher cognitive load due to a less natural user interface. Higher cognitive load in turn might impair the user's performance and render a task more difficult than it would have been in real life. An alternative to using locomotion techniques could be to exploit new VR locomotion hardware, such as the Cyberith Virtualizer [33], which facilitates walking in place locomotion.

5.3   VR as a Prototyping Tool

Results from a similar study by Alce et al. [20] suggested that using VR as a tool for IoT interaction has potential but that "several challenges remain before meaningful data can be produced in controlled experiments." Tracking was identified as one such challenge: the 3DOF tracking of the Oculus Rift DK1 used in that study limited the usefulness of the method. However, the HTC Vive with its sub-millimeter precision and 6DOF tracking constitutes a huge step in the right direction, which could be observed in this study. For example, in Alce et al. [20] study the authors were not able to find any statistically significant differences between the evaluated interaction concepts while in this study we could. However, this should be compared with similar IoT interactions in with physical prototypes to provide more evidence of using VR for prototype IoT interactions.

One can ask, why not use augmented reality (AR) glasses, which combines virtual and real objects such as Microsoft HoloLens or Magic Leap to evaluate prototypes? Alce et al. [34] developed three basic AR interaction models that focused on similar aspects as this paper, discovering and selecting devices. However, the current AR glasses comes with even more limitations, for instance, the field of view is very small compared with VR headsets, the interaction is very limited, and you need to track and detect things in order to make e.g. plants smart. The VR headsets are more mature in these cases, but the vast development of AR glasses will solve some of the limitations in the near future.

Finally, when evaluating prototypes in VR, it is important to remember the discrepancy between real and virtual interaction. Obviously, it is the virtual interaction that is evaluated, and the transfer of this to reality will most certainly not be perfect. Furthermore, if the users are not immersed enough, it could very well be that similarities between interactions are enhanced (that is to say, all interactions in the virtual environment feel equally awkward or strange), whereupon any differences become concealed and unnoticed.

6   Conclusion

This paper used VR to prototype IoT interaction in a smart home environment. Three IoT interaction concepts were compared in a controlled experiment. The results showed that statistically significant differences and subjective preferences could be observed. The participants preferred the combination of head-gaze and voice. Additionally, this study implies that VR has the potential to become a useful prototyping tool to explore IoT interaction for a smart home environment.

References

1. Davies, R.C.: Applications of systems design using virtual environments. In: Stanney, K.M. (ed.) Handbook of Virtual Environments - Design, Implementation, and Applications, pp. 1079–1100. Lawrence Erlbaum Associates Publishers, Mahwah (2002)
2. Lei, Z., Yue, S., Yu, C., Yuanchun, S.: SHSim: an OSGI-based smart home simulator. In: 2010 3rd IEEE International Conference on Ubi-Media Computing (U-Media), pp. 87–90. IEEE (2010)
3. Seo, D.W., Kim, H., Kim, J.S., Lee, J.Y.: Hybrid reality-based user experience and evaluation of a context-aware smart home. Comput. Ind. **76**, 11–23 (2016)
4. Rogers, Y., Sharp, H., Preece, J.: Interaction Design - Beyond Human-Computer Interaction, 3rd edn. Wiley, Hoboken (2011)
5. Samsung SmartThings. https://www.smartthings.com/. Accessed 15 Jan 2019
6. Apple HomeKit. https://www.apple.com/ios/home/. Accessed 15 Jan 2019
7. Weave. https://openweave.io/. Accessed 15 Jan 2019
8. HTC Vive. https://www.vive.com/eu/. Accessed 15 Jan 2019
9. Unity Technologies. http://unity3d.com/. Accessed 25 Aug 2017
10. Barton, J.J., Vijayaraghavan, V.: UBIWISE, a simulator for ubiquitous computing systems design. Hewlett-Packard Laboratories Palo Alto, â AI HPL-2003-93 (2003)
11. O'Neill, E., Klepal, M., Lewis, D., O'Donnell, T., O'Sullivan, D., Pesch, D.: A testbed for evaluating human interaction with ubiquitous computing environments. In: First International Conference on IEEE Testbeds and Research Infrastructures for the Development of Networks and Communities, Tridentcom 2005, pp. 60–69. IEEE (2005)
12. Nishikawa, H., et al.: UbiREAL: realistic smartspace simulator for systematic testing. In: Dourish, P., Friday, A. (eds.) UbiComp 2006. LNCS, vol. 4206, pp. 459–476. Springer, Heidelberg (2006). https://doi.org/10.1007/11853565_27

13. Furfaro, A., Argento, L., Parise, A., Piccolo, A.: Using virtual environments for the assessment of cybersecurity issues in IoT scenarios. Simul. Modell. Pract. Theor. **73**, 43–54 (2017)
14. Van Nguyen, T., Nguyen, H., Choi, D.: Development of a context aware virtual smart home simulator. arXiv Preprint arXiv:1007.1274 (2010)
15. Park, J., Moon, M., Hwang, S., Yeom, K.: CASS: a context-aware simulation system for smart home. In: 2007 5th ACIS International Conference on IEEE Software Engineering Research, Management & Applications, SERA 2007, pp. 461–467. IEEE (2007)
16. Armac, I., Retkowitz, D.: Simulation of smart environments. In: IEEE International Conference on Pervasive Services, pp. 322–331. IEEE (2007)
17. Hu, W., Zhou, H., Lin, C., Chen, X., Chen, Z., Lu, Y.: Design of web-based smart home with 3D virtural reality interface. In: 2012 UKACC International Conference on IEEE Control (CONTROL), pp. 223–228. IEEE (2012)
18. Bowman, D.A., Wingrave, C.A.: Design and evaluation of menu systems for immersive virtual environments. In: Proceedings of the Virtual Reality 2001 Conference (VR 2001), pp. 149–156. IEEE (2001)
19. de Sá, A.G., Zachmann, G.: Integrating virtual reality for virtual prototyping. In: Proceedings of DETC 1998, Atlanta, Georgia, pp. 1–12 (1998)
20. Alce, G., Hermodsson, K., Wallergård, M., Thern, L., Hadzovic, T.: A prototyping method to simulate wearable augmented reality interaction in a virtual environment-a pilot study. Int. J. Virt. Worlds Hum. Comput. Interact. **3**, 18–28 (2015)
21. Ens, B., Anderson, F., Grossman, T., Annett, M., Irani, P., Fitzmaurice, G.: Ivy: exploring spatially situated visual programming for authoring and understanding intelligent environments. In: Proceedings of the 43rd Graphics Interface Conference, pp. 156–162. Canadian Human-Computer Communications Society (2017)
22. Carter, S., Mankoff, J., Klemmer, S., Matthews, T.: Exiting the cleanroom: on ecological validity and ubiquitous computing. Hum.-Comput. Interact. **23**(1), 47–99 (2008)
23. Gombac, B., Zemljak, M., Širol, P., Deželjin, D., Copic Pucihar, K., Kljun, M.: Wizard of Oz experiment for Prototyping Multimodal Interfaces in Virtual Reality (2016)
24. Barnum, C.M.: Usability Testing Essentials: Ready, Set... Test! Elsevier, Amsterdam (2010)
25. Nielsen, J., Pernice, K.: How to Conduct Eyetracking Studies. Nielsen Norman Group, Fremont (2009)
26. Hertzum, M., Hansen, K.D., Andersen, H.H.K.: Scrutinising usability evaluation: does thinking aloud affect behaviour and mental workload? Behav. Inf. Technol. **28**(2), 165–181 (2009)
27. Holmqvist, K., Nyström, M., Andersson, R., Dewhurst, R., Jarodzka, H., de Weijer, J.: Eye Tracking: A Comprehensive Guide to Methods and Measures. OUP, Oxford (2011)
28. Ledo, D., Greenberg, S., Marquardt, N., Boring, S.: Proxemic-aware controls: designing remote controls for ubiquitous computing ecologies. In: Proceedings of the 17th International Conference on Human-Computer Interaction with Mobile Devices and Services, pp. 187–198. ACM (2015)
29. Norman, D.A., Nielsen, J.: Gestural interfaces: a step backward in usability. Interactions **17**(5), 46–49 (2010)
30. Hart, S.: NASA-task load index (NASA-TLX); 20 years later. In: Proceedings of the Human Factors and Ergonomics Society Annual Meeting (2006). http://pro.sagepub.com/content/50/9/904.short. Accessed 15 Jan 2019
31. Usoh, M., Catena, E., Arman, S., Slater, M.: Using presence questionnaires in reality. Presence: Teleoperators Virtual Environ. **9**(5), 497–503 (2000)

32. Zagermann, J., Pfeil, U., Reiterer, H.: Measuring cognitive load using eye tracking technology in visual computing. In: Proceedings of the Sixth Workshop on Beyond Time and Errors on Novel Evaluation Methods for Visualization, pp. 78–85. ACM (2016)
33. Cyberith Virtualizer. https://www.cyberith.com/. Accessed 30 Nov 2017
34. Alce, G., Roszko, M., Edlund, H., Olsson, S., Svedberg, J., Wallergård, M.: [POSTER] AR as a user interface for the internet of things—comparing three interaction models. In: 2017 IEEE International Symposium on Mixed and Augmented Reality (ISMAR-Adjunct), pp. 81–86. IEEE (2017)

Head Mounted Display Interaction Evaluation: Manipulating Virtual Objects in Augmented Reality

Maite Frutos-Pascual$^{(\boxtimes)}$, Chris Creed, and Ian Williams

DMT Lab, School of Computing and Digital Technology,
Birmingham City University, Birmingham, UK
`maite.frutos@bcu.ac.uk`

Abstract. Augmented Reality (AR) is getting close to real use cases, which is driving the creation of innovative applications and the unprecedented growth of Head-Mounted Display (HMD) devices in consumer availability. However, at present there is a lack of guidelines, common form factors and standard interaction paradigms between devices, which has resulted in each HMD manufacturer creating their own specifications. This paper presents the first experimental evaluation of two AR HMDs evaluating their interaction paradigms, namely we used the HoloLens v1 (metaphoric interaction) and Meta2 (isomorphic interaction). We report on precision, interactivity and usability metrics in an object manipulation task-based user study. 20 participants took part in this study and significant differences were found between interaction paradigms for translation tasks, where the isomorphic mapped interaction outperformed the metaphoric mapped interaction in both time to completion and accuracy, while the contrary was found for the resize task. From an interaction perspective, the isomorphic mapped interaction (using the Meta2) was perceived as more natural and usable with a significantly higher usability score and a significantly lower task-load index. However, when task accuracy and time to completion is key mixed interaction paradigms need to be considered.

Keywords: Augmented Reality · Hand interaction ·
Natural interaction

1 Introduction

Augmented Reality (AR) is defined as an interactive technology that incorporates virtual objects into the real world [30]. AR is now maturing and getting close to real use cases [35], this leading to the creation of innovative applications [38] and the unprecedented growth of Head-Mounted Display (HMD) devices and consumer availability. Similarly, User Interfaces are rapidly evolving beyond traditional desktop and mobile environments. Technologies such as AR, tangible

© IFIP International Federation for Information Processing 2019
Published by Springer Nature Switzerland AG 2019
D. Lamas et al. (Eds.): INTERACT 2019, LNCS 11749, pp. 287–308, 2019.
https://doi.org/10.1007/978-3-030-29390-1_16

interfaces and immersive displays currently offer more natural ways of interaction, leveraging user interaction capabilities with the real world [7].

This timely combination of hardware availability and technology advances has led to the incorporation of AR in real application cases outside laboratory environments, leading it to been dubbed as one of the key technologies in the Industry 4.0 revolution [27,33]. Its current use-cases have expanded beyond to health-care [24], education [3], and tourism [54], among others. This growth of AR applications outside traditional Human Computer Interaction (HCI) research environments implies that technology is currently being used outside laboratory environments. As such, there is an urgent need to understand how people naturally interact with immersive systems to make sure AR can reach its full potential. However, these emerging technologies currently have no established design guidelines, interaction metaphors or form factors [21], which has resulted in each HMD manufacturer creating their own.

This lack of guidelines and standard interaction paradigms is evident when analysing two of the most current AR HMDs enabling freehand interaction, that is without wearables or controllers, applications and research, namely the Microsoft HoloLens v1[1] and Meta's Meta2[2] HMDs. Both devices currently offer direct freehand interaction [20], however each supports different interaction paradigms and form factors that may have an effect on their perceived usability (i.e. the position of AR objects, the headset Field Of View (FOV) and also the recommended user interaction space). In terms of the inherent interaction paradigms, the Microsoft HoloLens v1 offer a head/gaze and tap based interaction paradigm (see Fig. 1(b)) which is a restricted form of gesture interaction [29] that could be labelled as a metaphoric mapping interaction [37], as it is similar to single mouse clicks on a desktop. The Meta2 offers a spatially co-located interaction [29] where users can manually (see Fig. 1(d)) or bi-manually (see Fig. 1(e)) interact with virtual objects and it is somewhat comparable to manipulating objects in real life, thus it was labelled as isomorphic mapping interaction, defined as a one-to-one literal spatial relation between actions and system effects [37]. These interaction paradigms offer a distinctive natural interaction, one based on remote manipulation of objects akin to current PC interaction paradigms (metaphoric) while the other mimics real world tasks, enabling a physical manipulation (isomorphic).

While both interaction paradigms and device form factors offer viable interaction methods [29], usability, interactivity and precision of these two devices for task-based AR scenarios has not been fully addressed before. Therefore no formal studies have aimed to evaluate a user's response to these devices and their inherent interaction paradigms in AR. Research in this area can help identifying users' real needs and expectations before designing application concepts [8]. We present the first study evaluating two commercially available AR devices and their inherent interaction paradigms for AR object manipulation. These paradigms are applied following the stringent design considerations of the com-

---

[1] https://www.microsoft.com/en-us/hololens, *(12th of December 2018)*.
[2] https://www.metavision.com/ *(12th of December 2018)*.

peting devices. We evaluate these on the users' ability to manipulate virtual objects. We measured effectiveness, efficiency and user satisfaction for each condition and task.

Finally we present our findings and considerations, thus enabling future AR developers and UX designers to determine which is the most suitable device and interaction paradigm to fit their interaction and user experience needs.

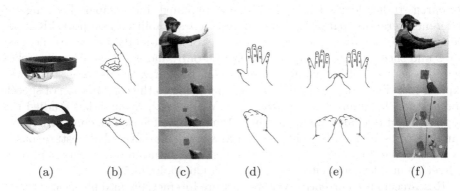

(a)   (b)   (c)   (d)   (e)   (f)

Fig. 1. Microsoft HoloLens v1 (a) supports metaphoric interaction via the head/gaze and tap (b) (c). Meta2 (a) supports a isomorphic interaction in both Manual (d) (f) and BiManual configurations (e) (f).

2 Related Work

The accessibility of consumer AR systems is growing and the adoption of AR systems into application domains is becoming commonplace [14]. With the recent advances in consumer hardware and the integration of on-board sensor technology, interactive AR applications in healthcare [15,18], education [13] and industry [19] are now possible. This advanced hardware is driving the integration of AR into the workplace with many industries keen on applying AR into their work-flow processes [22]. Now naive users have the possibility to use AR systems that contain plausible realistic environments and also facilitate direct real-time interaction between themselves and the virtual objects in ways that were not easily possible previously.

2.1 Commercial Devices

Commercial head-mounted see-through AR solutions offer new platforms for AR developers, designers and industry applications through facilitating an increased ease of development. However they all differ in their fundamental hardware configurations (e.g tethering, tracking and physical dimensions) and conversely offer different paradigms interaction with AR content (e.g. metamorphic as with the

HoloLens, isomorphic as with the Meta2 and the use of hand-held controllers as in the Magic Leap One). As new devices become available in the near future, it is crucial to understand user's response to available devices and form factors, so new cross-device interaction standards can be established.

2.2   Interaction Approaches

Research studies focused around AR have explored and compared a range of different interaction paradigms to examine their suitability to support AR experiences. Lee *et al.* [34] compared the usability of multi-modal interfaces (i.e. gestures and speech recognition) against speech-only, and gesture-only approaches (across a series of object manipulation tasks). Similarly, the use of gestures was explored for direct physical grasping in comparison to the combination of speech and gestures for indirect interactions [41]. While much research has studied the application of freehand interaction in AR, most have focused on comparing freehand gestures alone [45]. This work has shown that overall a gesture based interaction paradigm can offer ease of access and naturalness to users, and does deliver an intuitive and effective interaction [26, 36, 40, 43, 52].

Researchers are currently evolving gesture interactions into physical interactions, thus, completely mimicking the interaction performed in the real world, into AR environments [46, 49]. The work of Al-Kalbani *et al.* [4] and [5] have sought to understand the complex nature of the human grasp for freehand interaction and defined the problems associated with grasping objects in AR, Ciodota *et al.* [15] evaluated the application of grasps in AR and also Swan *et al.* [51] evaluated the problems associated with representing and reaching the true located space of augmented objects.

While different input combination approaches have been explored in the literature, together with different gesture based interactions and the impact of physical interactions alone. There has since been limited research focused on evaluating the problems and benefits to compare different interaction paradigms inherent to off-the-shelf commercial devices.

3   Methods

An experiment was conducted that analysed two commercially available AR devices with their underlying interaction paradigms. We used a within participants design. As this study focuses on the comparison of two off-the-shelf AR HMDs, we used the interaction paradigms recommended by each device manufacturer and their stringent environment configuration as deemed to be the most suitable and stable way of interfacing with the hardware. As this study focuses on the evaluation of devices form factors, design guidelines and interaction metaphors on perceived usability of naive participants, the use of configurations outside the recommended guidelines in [1, 2] were not included in this study.

3.1   Conditions

Two different interaction paradigms were studied in this work. Interaction paradigms outlined in this section are the recommended for optimal object manipulation by the device manufacturers [1,2]. Both conditions facilitate direct freehand interaction between the user and the AR content. However, they offer a different interaction approach that may become apparent when interacting virtual objects in an AR environment. Tasks described in Subsect. 3.4 were performed in each of these conditions. There is no current knowledge of which interaction paradigm is preferred for object manipulation in AR environments.

- **Metaphoric mapped interaction** *(using the HoloLens v1)*. Following Macaranas *et al.* definition, this is defined as the mental models generated from repeated patterns in everyday experiences [37]. Microsoft HoloLens v1 hand interaction paradigm replicates the most classic input paradigm in computer systems, the point and click interaction using the mouse. Head gaze control is used for targeting virtual objects (commonly referred to as *holograms*) in the 3D space and tap gesture interaction is for acting on specific selected virtual objects (i.e. similar to mouse clicks) [2]. This offers a remote interaction paradigm, enabling users to access any virtual object in the interaction space remotely.
- **Isomorphic mapped interaction** *(using the Meta2)*. This interaction is defined as the one-to-one literal spatial relations between input actions and their resulting system effects [37]. Meta2 offers this level of interaction, requiring the user to be physically placed in the location of the virtual object to be able to access it and trigger the interaction. This creates a spatial equivalence between the virtual environment and user's actions which is akin to manipulating virtual objects as if they were real objects [29,42].

3.2   Apparatus

We built a custom experimental framework for the HoloLens v1 and Meta2 using Unity 2017.3, Windows Holographic platform[3] and the Mixed Reality Toolkit[4] for the HoloLens v1, and Meta2 SDK 2.7[5] for the Meta2. C# was used as scripting language.

- **Microsoft HoloLens v1.** The HoloLens v1 is a wireless, optical see-through stereographic AR HMD with a 30 × 17 Field of View (FOV). The device has built-in integrated Inertial Measurement Uni sensor, a depth camera, four environment understanding cameras, HD video camera enabling Mixed Reality capture and four microphones. It supports voice input, gesture recognition and head/gaze positioning tracking. It weights 579 g, as per its specification description.

---

[3] https://developer.microsoft.com/windows/mixed-reality, *(12th of December 2018)*.
[4] https://github.com/Microsoft/MixedRealityToolkit-Unity, *(12th of December 2018)*.
[5] https://devcenter.metavision.com/, *(12th of December 2018)*.

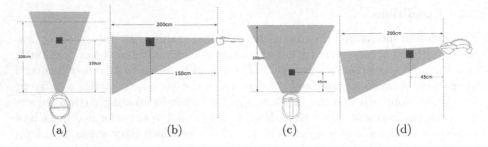

(a)   (b)   (c)   (d)

Fig. 2. Microsoft HoloLens v1 - interaction space configuration. (a) Top view with the object displayed 150 cm away from the user standing position. (b) Side view with the interactive virtual object displayed 150 cm away and in the horizon line of the device. **Meta Meta2** - interaction space configuration. (c) Top view with the object displayed 45 cm away from the user standing position. (d) Side view with the interactive virtual object displayed 45 cm away and 10° below the horizon line of the device.

- **Meta's Meta2.** The Meta2 is a tethered, optical see-through stereographic AR HMD with a 90° FOV. The device has built-in hand interaction and positional tracking sensors, a 720p front-facing RGB camera, four surround speakers and three microphones. It natively supports hand tracking and head/gaze positioning tracking. It weights 500 g, as per its specification description.

3.3   Origin Position

Interactive virtual objects were always presented at the initial origin position. This position was selected to comply with device manufacturers' recommendations as displayed in Fig. 2.

- **Metaphoric mapped interaction** *(using the HoloLens v1)*: Interactive virtual objects and targets for this condition were placed within the preferred interacting area as reported in the *HoloLens v1 Development Guidelines - Holograms* [2]. The initial position of the interactive virtual object was at the device's horizon line and 150 cm away from the device, as reported in Figs. 2(a) and (b) and in alignment with manufacturer's hologram placement guidelines [2].
- **Isomorphic mapped interaction** *(using the Meta2)*: The interactive virtual object and targets were placed within the preferred interacting area as reported in the *Meta2 User Interface Guidelines and Ergonomics* [1]. The initial position of the interactive virtual object was 10° below the device's horizon line and 45 cm away from it, within arm reach, as reported in Figs. 2(c) and (d) and in alignment with their guidelines about the optimal interaction space [1].

Different origin positions were used to comply with manufacturers' recommendations and devices form factors; being the Meta2 a tethered device that enable co-located interaction, manufacturer's guidelines recommend virtual objects to be placed within arm reach [1] while the Microsoft HoloLens v1 guidelines recommend a remote interaction, with the virtual objects to be placed between 1.25 m and 5 m away, with the ideal interaction space being 1+ m away [2].

3.4 Tasks

Tasks were selected based on the survey presented in [42], where Piumsomboom *et al.* categorised the most common AR interaction tasks into 6 categories. This study analysed a subset of tasks extracted from the Transform category complemented by an additional move in depth (z axis) task.

For each task the user is presented with an interactive object (a cube) and a target object. The target object represents the different task attributes (i.e. position for move tasks, size for re-size task and rotation orientation for the rotate task). Target objects were not interactive and they were displayed as virtual outlined objects using different colour and texture to avoid confusion. Each task was comprised of four different targets appearing one after the other in random order. The interactive object resets to its original position, rotation and size after every target.

- **Move Tasks.** Participants were asked to move a virtual interactive cube in the 3D space to match the position of a target. Three different move tasks were performed:
  - **Short distance.** In this tasks targets appeared within the Field of View (FOV) of the devices. Table 1 shows the specific position of the targets while Fig. 3(a) displays a graphical representation of their spatial distribution.
  - **Long distance.** Targets appeared spatially distant to the interactive object initial position for both conditions in Sect. 3.1. These targets will appear outside the initial FOV of the devices. Table 1 shows the specific position of the targets while Fig. 3(a) displays a graphical representation of their spatial distribution.
  - **Depth (z axis).** Depth perception and estimation is a long-standing research field in Augmented Reality literature, with a well known set of perception issues and estimation problems defined and studied [16, 28, 31, 32, 44, 48, 50]. We considered relevant to extend Piumsomboom *et al.* [42] move task category with an additional movement solely in z (depth). This tasks is formed by four targets that appeared one after the other spatially distributed in the interaction space, with two of them rendering virtually close to the user initial standing position and the other two further away, as described in Table 1 and Fig. 3(b).

- **Resize Task.** Participants were asked to uniformly resize a virtual interactive cube in the 3D space to match the size of a target. The task was to grow or shrink a 10 cm width × 10 cm height × 10 cm depth virtual cube to different target sizes. Target size distribution is shown in Fig. 4 and target sizes are reported in Table 1.

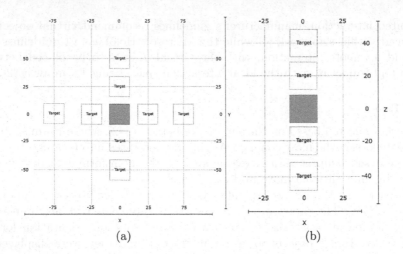

Fig. 3. Spatial distribution of targets for move tasks. (a) shows target distribution for tasks move short (inner targets) and move long (outer targets). (b) displays targets for move depth task. Targets are shown as distance from the origin in cm. The interactive virtual object initial position is represented as a dark gray square in (a) and (b).

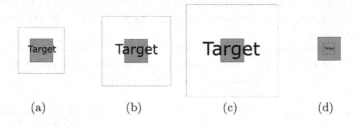

| (a) | (b) | (c) | (d) |

Fig. 4. Resize targets for the interactive object (gray square). Fig. 5(a) Target1 in Table 1; Fig. 5(b) Target2 in Table 1; Fig. 5(c) is Target3 in Table 1 and Fig. 5(d) is Target4 in Table 1.

– **Rotate Task.** Participants were asked to rotate a virtual cube in the 3D space to match the rotation of a target. Target distribution is displayed in Fig. 5 and specific target rotation values are reported in Table 1; covering roll (x axis rotation), pitch (y axis rotation) and yaw (z axis rotation) as described by [42] and a combination of the three (x, y and z axis rotation).

3.5   Environment

Participants performed the test in a controlled environment under laboratory conditions. A clear room layout was used. Interactive space dimensions were 270 cm by 180 cm. The test room was lit by a 2700k (*warm white*) fluorescent with controlled external light source. Task initial position was marked on the floor and participants were free to move around the space to complete the target tasks.

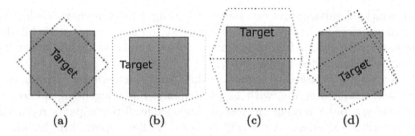

Fig. 5. Rotate targets for the interactive object (gray square). (a) Target1 in Table 1; (b) Target2 in Table 1; (c) is Target3 in Table 1 and (d) is Target4 in Table 1.

Table 1. Target distribution per tasks. Targets are displayed as distance away from the initial position for move tasks. Positions refer to distance from the origin [in cm] in x, y z. Targets are displayed as target size [in cm] for resize task. The same target resize options were displayed in both conditions. Original size of the interactive object was *(10*cm $\times$ *10*cm $\times$ *10*cm*)*. The same target rotation options were displayed in both interaction conditions. Rotation displayed per axis (x, y, z) in degrees. Initial rotation of the interactive object was $(0°, 0°, 0°)$.

Move - Short distance [in cm]			
Target1	Target2	Target3	Target4
(25, 0, 0)	*(−25, 0, 0)*	*(0, 25, 0)*	*(0, −25, 0)*
Move - Long distance [in cm]			
Target1	Target2	Target3	Target4
(75, 0, 0)	*(−75, 0, 0)*	*(0, 50, 0)*	*(0, −50, 0)*
Move - Depth [in cm]			
Target1	Target2	Target3	Target4
(0, 0, −40)	*(0, 0, −20)*	*(0, 0, 20)*	*(0, 0, 40)*
Resize [in cm]			
Target1	Target2	Target3	Target4
(2×) 20 × 20 × 20	*(3x)* 30 × 30 × 30	*(4×)* 40×40 × 40	*(0.5×)* 5 × 5 × 5
Rotate [in degrees]			
Target1	Target2	Target3	Target4
$(45°, 0°, 0°)$	$(0°, 45°, 0°)$	$(0°, 0°, 45°)$	$(45°, 45°, 45°)$

3.6 Participants

20 right-handed participants (5 female, 15 male) from a population of university students and staff members were recruited to take part in this study. Participants' mean age was 28.05 (SD: 9.78).

All participants performed the tasks described in Sect. 3.4 in both conditions. Participants completed a standardised consent form and were not compensated.

Visual acuity of participants was measured using a Snellen chart, each participant was also required to pass an Ishihara test to exclude for colour blindness.
Participants with colour blindness and/or visual acuity of <0.80 (where 20/20
is 1.0) were not included in this study.

Participants were asked to self-assess their level of experience with Mixed and
Augmented reality systems, with 12 participants reporting being *novices* with
the technology and 8 having an *average* knowledge. 6 participants reported on
having previous experience with HMDs, notably they reported on having used
Virtual Reality headsets (i.e. Oculus Rift, Samsung Gear or Google Cardboard).
None of the participants had any previous substantial experience with HMDs in
Augmented Reality.

3.7   Protocol

A within participants test protocol design was used. Participants were counterbalanced across the two interaction paradigms; half of the participants (10)
started the tests with the metaphoric mapped interaction using the Microsoft
HoloLens v1 and the other half (10) started with the isomorphic mapped interaction approach using the Meta2.

(a) **Pre-test.** Prior to the test, participants were given a written informed con-
    sent where the test protocol and main aim of the study was described. Addi-
    tionally, participants filled in a pre-test questionnaire inquiring about their
    background level of experience with AR systems and their previous use of
    HMDs (if any).
(b) **Calibration.** Before each test, the test coordinator followed manufacturers'
    guidelines to help participants fitting the devices in the most suitable and
    comfortable way. For the Meta2, the additional headset calibration process
    was launched as per the manufacturer's recommendation.
(c) **Training.** Participants underwent initial hand interaction and task training
    with both devices.
    – **Hand Interaction training:** Participants were trained with the inter-
      action paradigm inherent to the device. For this, the standard built-in
      gesture/hand interaction training application provided by the devices'
      manufacturers were used. For the HoloLens v1, the Microsoft *Learn Ges-
      ture App* was used to help users understand the interaction paradigm.
      For the Meta2, the *Hand Training App* provided with the Meta2 2.5
      Beta SDK was used to help users understand the isomorphic interaction
      required for this condition.
    – **Task training:** Once participants were comfortable with the device and
      the hand tracking, recognition and interaction system, they were asked to
      undergo specific task-related training. This task training was the same for
      both conditions in Sect. 3.1. Participants were trained in a representative
      version of tasks in Sect. 3.4: move, rotate and resize, one after the other
      in this order.

(d) **Test.** Once participants were comfortable with the interaction paradigm, the hand recognition system and user interface, participants were presented with the main experimental task. Tasks reported in Sect. 3.4 were loaded in random counterbalanced order, as with the different targets in each task. Participants were free to move around the interaction space. In between tasks and targets, they were asked to get back to the starting position, marked clearly on the floor.

(e) **Post-test.** After each of the conditions were completed, participants were asked to fill in the NASA TLX [23], the System Usability Scale (SUS) [11] and a post-test questionnaire asking about their experience with the device and their opinion on device specifics (FOV, tracking accuracy, hand tracking accuracy, preferred interaction).

3.8 Metrics

Following Piumsomboon *et al.* [41] definitions, we define the interactivity as the users' ability to interact with the virtual objects and the precision as the level of control the user has when interacting. An example measure of precision would be how accurately the user can rotate or move an object to match a target, while we reported on interactivity as the perceived usability of the system.

– **Precision metrics.** Precision metrics were defined as follows: *time to completion* as the time it took to complete the task and *accuracy* as the difference between the target and the interactive object at the end of the task. For move tasks, the accuracy is measured as the euclidean distance between the target and the interactive object at the end of the task; for resize it was the difference between the target scale and the interactive object scale at the end of the task; for rotation it was the difference between the total rotation of all angles between the target cube and the interactive object. Angles were normalised to a ($45°$) degree range due to the nature of the interactive object being a cube with the same colour surfaces.

– **Interaction metrics.** Interaction metrics were defined as the subjective metrics obtained from users using observation, NASA TLX [23], the System Usability Scale (SUS) [11] and a post-test questionnaire.

3.9 Hypotheses

Following the methodology defined in this paper, we propose the hypotheses listed below:

– **Hypothesis H_1.** The interaction paradigm within the device conditions (see Sect. 3.1) has no effect on time to completion for tasks in Sect. 3.4.
  - *Alternative hypothesis AH_1.* The interaction paradigm within the device conditions used has an effect on time to completion for tasks in Sect. 3.4.
– **Hypothesis H_2:** The interaction paradigm within the device conditions (see Sect. 3.1) has no effect on accuracy for every task reported in Sect. 3.4.

- *Alternative hypothesis AH_2.* The interaction paradigm within the device conditions has an effect on accuracy for every task reported in Sect. 3.4.
- **Hypothesis H_3:** The interaction paradigm within the device conditions (see Sect. 3.1) has no effect on the interaction metrics; especially in *(a)* NASA-TLX and *(b)* SUS
  - *Alternative hypothesis AH_3.* The interaction paradigm within the device conditions has no effect on the interaction metrics reported in metrics; especially in *(a)* NASA-TLX and *(b)* SUS

3.10   Statistical Analysis

The Shapiro-Wilk [47] normality test found the data to be non-parametric and not normally distributed. We test for significance between the two conditions described in Sect. 3.1 for the metrics shown in Sect. 3.8 using a non parametric Wilcoxon signed-rank test [53] with an alpha of 5%.

4   Results

4.1   Precision Metrics

- **Move - Short distance**
  - *Time To Completion.* A statistically significant difference in completion time was found between the two interaction conditions in Sect. 3.1 ($Z = 1.10 \times 10^3, p < 0.05$). Hypothesis H_1 was rejected for this task. Therefore we accepted alternative hypothesis AH_1. Time to completion for this task is displayed in Fig. 6(a).
  - *Accuracy:* A statistically significant difference was found when comparing the average euclidean distance between conditions ($Z = 1.15 \times 10^3, p < 0.05$). Hypothesis H_2 was rejected for this task. Therefore, we accepted the alternative hypothesis AH_2. Overall accuracy and time to completion per task are displayed in Table 2.
- **Move - Long distance**
  - *Time to Completion.* A statistically significant difference in completion time was found between the two interaction conditions in Sect. 3.1 ($Z = 1.07 \times 10^3, p < 0.05$). Hypothesis H_1 was rejected for this task. Therefore we accepted alternative hypothesis AH_1. Time to completion for this task is displayed in Fig. 6(b).
  - *Accuracy.* A statistically significant difference was found when comparing the average euclidean distance between conditions in Sect. 3.1 ($Z = 1.13 \times 10^3, p < 0.05$). Hypothesis H_2 was rejected for this task. Therefore we accepted alternative hypothesis AH_2 for this task. Overall accuracy and time to completion per task are reported in Table 2.

- **Move - Depth**
  - *Time to Completion.* A statistically significant difference in completion time was found between the two conditions in Sect. 3.1 ($Z = 1.12 \times 10^3, p < 0.05$). Hypothesis H_1 was rejected for this task. Therefore we accepted alternative hypothesis AH_1. Time to completion for this task is displayed in Fig. 6(c).
  - *Accuracy.* A statistically significant difference was found when comparing the average euclidean distance between conditions ($Z = 1.13 \times 10^3, p < 0.05$). Hypothesis H_2 was rejected for this task. Therefore we accepted alternative hypothesis AH_2 for this task. Overall accuracy and time to completion per task are presented in Table 2.
- **Resize**
  - *Time to Completion.* A statistically significant difference in completion time was found between the two interaction conditions in Sect. 3.1 ($Z = 1.14 \times 10^3, p < 0.05$). Therefore, hypothesis H_1 was rejected for this task and alternative hypothesis AH_1 was accepted. Time to completion for this task is displayed in Fig. 6(d).
  - *Accuracy.* A statistically significant difference was found when comparing the average scale differences between conditions ($Z = 1.14 \times 10^3, p < 0.05$). Therefore, hypothesis H_2 was rejected for this task, and the alternative hypothesis AH_2 was accepted. Overall accuracy and time to completion per task are displayed in Table 2.
- **Rotate**
  - *Time to Complete.* No significant differences were found in completion time between the two interaction conditions in Sect. 3.1. Therefore, hypothesis H_1 was accepted for this task. Time to completion for this task is displayed in Fig. 6(e).
  - *Accuracy.* No significant differences were found when comparing the average angle difference in (x, y, z) between conditions in Sect. 3.1. Therefore, hypothesis H_2 was accepted. Overall accuracy and time to completion per task are displayed in Table 2.

4.2   Interaction Metrics

- **NASA-TLX.** The metaphoric mapped interaction using the HoloLens v1 condition obtained an average NASA-TLX score of 60.18 (SD = 17.74) while the isomorphic mapped interaction condition using the Meta2 scored a 44.61 (SD = 16.80). The metaphoric mapped interaction paradigm using the HoloLens v1 was perceived to have a significantly higher workload, with significant differences found between conditions ($Z = 15.0, p < 0.05$). Consequently, we rejected H_3 for NASA-TLX metric and accepted the alternative hypothesis that the interaction paradigms within the device conditions had an effect on the perceived workload.
- **System Usability Scale (SUS).** Metaphoric mapped interaction condition using the HoloLens v1 obtained an average SUS score of 55.12 (SD = 21.32) while the isomorphic mapped interaction group using the Meta2

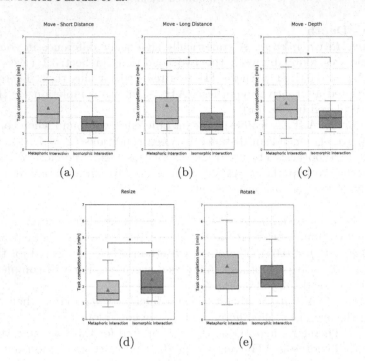

Fig. 6. Completion time per task: (a) Move - Short distance task; (b) Move - Long distance task; (c) Move - Depth task; (d) Resize task; (e) Rotate task.

scored a 67.25 (SD = 16.52). Scores can be labelled as just acceptable for the HoloLens v1 condition and 'OK' for the Meta2 interaction group [9]. Significant differences were found between conditions when comparing these scores ($Z = 41.5, p < 0.05$). Consequently, we rejected **H3** for SUS, accepting the alternative hypothesis that the interaction paradigm within the device conditions used had an effect on perceived usability.

– **Post-Questionnaire.** Participants were asked to complete a post-test questionnaire to gain a better understanding of their preferred interaction paradigm. They were asked to rate the performance of each of the devices (Microsoft HoloLens v1 and Meta's Meta2), in terms of their perceived FOV, hand recognition, tracking accuracy and preferred interaction method.

  • **Ease of Use:** Participants were asked to rate the ease of use of both devices using a Likert scale from 1 (Very difficult) to 7 (Very easy). The average score for the HoloLens v1 was 4.2 (SD: 1.75) and for the Meta2 5.18 (SD: 1.37). No significant differences were found between conditions.

  • **Field of View (FOV):** Participants were asked to rate the FOV of each device and if they noted any tracking differences. FOV was rated using a Likert scale ranging from 1 (very narrow) to 7 (very wide). The HoloLens v1 scored a 3.45 (SD: 1.35) while the Meta2 received a rating of 4.25 (SD: 1.60). Additionally, 16 participants out of 20 reported on noticing FOV

Table 2. Overall accuracy and time to completion per task and device interaction paradigm. Time to completion is reported in [min] while accuracy is reported in [cm] for move and resize tasks and in degrees for rotate task. *(* denotes statistical significance between conditions and bold face the best result)*

	Time to completion		Accuracy	
	Metaphoric	*Isomorphic*	*Metaphoric*	*Isomorphic*
Move-Short	2.58 min*	**1.75 min***	14.01 cm*	**6.86 cm***
	(SD: 1.58 min)	**(SD: 0.73 min)**	(SD: 31.32 cm)	**(SD: 2.18 cm)**
Move-Long	2.72 min*	**1.97 min***	18.85 cm*	**6.57 cm***
	(SD: 1.84 min)	**(SD: 1.05 min)**	(SD: 47.14 cm)	**(SD: 1.48 cm)**
Move-Depth	2.88 min*	**2.03 min***	19.86 cm*	**6.85 cm***
	(SD: 1.70 min)	**(SD: 0.94 min)**	(SD: 39.00 cm)	**(SD: 2.06 cm)**
Resize	**1.79 min***	2.44 min*	**4.12 cm***	13.67 cm*
	(SD: 0.79 min)	(SD: 1.33 min)	**(SD: 9.60 cm)**	(SD: 12.42 cm)
Rotate	**3.28 min**	3.32 min	**28.09°**	33.33°
	(SD: 1.96 min)	(SD: 2.35 min)	**(SD: 41.99°)**	(SD: 51.25°)

differences between devices; of those 16, 10 agreed that the Meta2 had a wider FOV, which matched the specifications of the device. No significant differences were found between conditions.

- **Hand tracking accuracy:** Participants were asked to rate the hand tracking accuracy of the device with a Likert scale ranging from 1 (very inaccurate) to 7 (Really accurate). Both devices scored similar results, with the HoloLens v1 scoring a 4.5 (SD 1.5) out of 7 and the Meta2 a 4.15 (SD: 1.15).18 out of the 20 participants reported on noticing tracking differences between devices; 12 of those stated that the HoloLens v1 had a more stable tracking. No significant differences were found between conditions.

- **Movement:** Despite the Meta2 being a tethered device, none of the participants reported feeling their movement or interaction constrained by this in any way. However, for larger interaction spaces this needs to be considered as a limitation.

- **Preferred interaction method:** When asked to select their preferred general interaction method, 18 participants chose the Meta2 while the remaining 2 selected the HoloLens v1. When asked in task by task basis, participants reported the following:
  * *Move tasks (long, short and depth):* 17 participants (85%) preferred the isomorphic mapped interaction paradigm, while 2 (10%) selected the metaphoric mapped paradigm and 1 (5%) reported no preference.
  * *Resize task:* 11 participants (55%) preferred the isomorphic mapped interaction paradigm, while 7 (35%) selected the metaphoric mapped paradigm and 2 (10%) reported no preference.
  * *Rotate task:* 13 participants (65%) preferred the isomorphic mapped interaction paradigm, while 7 (25%) selected the metaphoric mapped paradigm and 2 (10%) reported no preference.

- **Observations and feedback.** Twelve participants (60%) reported fatigue or pain during the metaphoric mapped interaction condition while 8 (40%) reported it during the isomorphic mapped interaction condition.
  - **Metaphoric mapped paradigm** *(using the HoloLens v1)*: Five participants reported arm tiredness and ache during the interaction. One participant reported "hard to control objects in the distance but smoother interaction" while another said "the inability to get closer to the objects using the HoloLens v1 did limit my accuracy in the tasks".
  - **Isomorphic mapped interaction paradigm** *(using the Meta2)*: None reported arm fatigue or pain in this condition. One participant reported on this interaction being "fun and intuitive, finding easier with the moving aspect to move objects below me more than above", another said "The interaction felt natural and intuitive. The resize was the most difficult as sometimes the tracking of the hands was less accurate." while a third one reported on "the headset being too heavy and having issues with the tracking".

5 Discussion

This study was designed to compare the interaction paradigms and design form factors beneath the two most current, as of the writing of this paper, commercial wearable AR solutions for freehand interaction, namely the Microsoft's HoloLens v1 and the Meta's Meta2. Therefore we presented a formal study to evaluate naive users' response to these devices in a task-based scenario for object manipulation in AR.

As highlighted by Gabbard *et al.* [21], it is important to understand the fundamental perceptual and cognitive factors for new technologies that alter the way humans perceive the world as in immersive technologies (Virtual Reality (VR), AR and Mixed Reality (MR)). Previous research has found promising possibilities for natural interaction in AR applications [12,17,42], and while both interaction paradigms had proven to offer a viable interaction method [29], the usability, interactivity and precision of these two devices for object manipulation has not been fully addressed before. We started by exploring and analysing precision metrics, namely time to completion and accuracy. Considering solely these metrics, a compromise between devices' interaction paradigms and spatial considerations need to be considered to optimise task precision and accuracy. Results suggested that the isomorphic mapped interaction paradigm, with all the design considerations associated, was helpful with tasks that required the movement and position of the virtual objects in specific locations in the space (as with move tasks reported in Sect. 3.4). This may be linked to the way we manipulate real world objects, as people move (translate) objects around with their hands, placing them in positions where they are physically optimal for each task [25]. However, the metaphoric mapped paradigm using the HoloLens v1 was significantly more accurate and it took significantly shorter time for the uniform resize manipulation task. This may be linked again to users past experience performing shape scale transformations on desktop environments rather than in reality where this form of object scale manipulation is not commonly feasible. Finally the rotation task presented no significant differences between conditions showing consistency across both interaction paradigms. These results show the convenience of adopting a mixed methods interaction paradigm design for task manipulation in AR, enabling users to move objects around using an isomorphic spatial interaction while enabling a metaphoric gesture based interaction for transformation tasks (i.e. rotate and resize).

Reviewing interaction metrics, the metaphoric mapped *(using the HoloLens v1)* interaction condition was reported to have a significantly higher task load index than the isomorphic interaction paradigm *(using the Meta2)*; as reported in Sect. 4.2. This trend is maintained for the usability score obtained by the two conditions, where the isomorphic mapped interaction paradigm *(using the Meta2)* scored higher in usability according to the SUS results. Usability studies have been deemed helpful to identify design flaws in application concepts at earlier phases of the development of AR [8].

Participants were asked to report on their generally preferred interaction paradigm, where the isomorphic mapped interaction paradigm *(using the Meta2)* received 18 out of 20 votes. The close link between this interaction and real world object manipulations may have an impact on users feeling more confident, as prior experience is a leading contributor to intuitive use [10]. Considering the device form factors, they did not seem to have a determinant effect on the perceived usability, with no statistical differences reported in the post-test questionnaire.

In summary isomorphic mapped interaction *(using the Meta2)* was considered the most intuitive and natural interaction paradigm, with a nearly unnoticeable learning curve. However, when task accuracy and time to completion is key for successfully completing a task, mixed interaction paradigms need to be considered, enhancing these isomorphic interactions with more abstract gestures for certain transform manipulations, While a combination of paradigms may need to be considered, it is key to evolve current interactions to achieve a standardised approach that are device and technology independent.

5.1 Limitations and Generalisation

We explicitly limited our study to the tasks and conditions reported in this paper. The interaction conditions metaphoric mapped *(using the HoloLens v1)* and isomorphic mapped *(using the Meta2)* were selected as they were inherent and recommended, as of the writing of this paper, to the two commercial wearable AR solutions used.

The environment was adapted for each condition in Sect. 3.1 to comply with both manufacturers' recommendations. This paper presents a comparison study between both devices and interaction paradigms using their ideal environment guidelines for virtual object placement and interaction. Therefore, the use of interaction paradigms and spatial considerations different from the ones outlined in the guidelines [1, 2] were not included in this study.

This study focused around freehand interaction in Mixed Reality, thus, without the use of controllers or wearable devices. Therefore, other interaction metaphors and devices outside this definition were not considered. The overall preference for freehand natural interaction versus the use of hand-held controllers need to be further explored.

Studied tasks were limited to the transformation tasks reported by [42] to be the most common transform tasks used in the literature [6,39].

Participants had no previous substantial experience with the devices used in this study, as reported in Sect. 3.6, as we were interested in evaluating naive users' perspective. However, it is being previously explored that training may lead to further improvements in immersive AR systems, as people learn to coordinate perception and interaction [7]. However, this is out of the scope of the presented study and it was not explored.

6   Conclusion and Future Work

We have conducted a study comparing two different freehand AR HMDs and their interaction paradigms associated, namely metaphoric mapped interaction *(using the HoloLens v1)* and isomorphic mapped interaction *(using the Meta2)* in a task based interaction environment. We followed a within participants study design and we reported on interaction and precision metrics. Our results suggest that each device has specific strengths, specially from a precision point of view, with move deemed more accurate under the isomorphic mapped interaction paradigm *(using the Meta2)* and resize being more accurate under the metaphoric mapped condition *(using the HoloLens v1)*. From an interaction perspective, the isomorphic mapped interaction *(using the Meta2)* was perceived as more natural and usable with a higher usability score and a lower task-load index.

Further work needs to be done analysing described tasks in Sect. 3.4, i.e. evaluating non-uniform object manipulation (resize task) or alternative shaped objects, as these may lead to differences in accuracy and usability.

Tasks outside the transform category described by [42] were not explored, it may be interesting to further analyse browsing, editing and menu tasks in [42] as these tasks are commonly presented in recent literature [6,39].

Our findings have some interesting implications for the design and usage of specific AR devices and interaction paradigms for virtual object manipulation tasks. This study has shown that while isomorphic mapped interaction may feel more natural with participants, care must be taken to ensure that the correct interaction paradigm and device are being used, as for environments where accuracy is a requirement, a combination of both paradigms may be key. We also believe that more powerful tracking and visualization devices (i.e. with increased FOV, higher tracking accuracy, device ergonomics) may lead to novel or improved interaction, enhancing usability, comfort and accessibility of AR experiences in the near future.

References

1. Meta Meta2 User Interface Guidelines. http://devcenter.metavision.com/design/user-interface-guidelines-overview. Accessed 12th Dec 2018
2. Microsoft Hololens Interaction Design Guidelines. https://developer.microsoft.com/en-us/windows/mixed-reality/category/interaction_design. Accessed 12th Dec 2018
3. Akçayır, M., Akçayır, G.: Advantages and challenges associated with augmented reality for education: a systematic review of the literature. Educ. Res. Rev. **20**, 1–11 (2017)
4. Al-Kalbani, M., Williams, I., Frutos-Pascual, M.: Analysis of medium wrap free-hand virtual object grasping in exocentric mixed reality. In: 2016 IEEE International Symposium on Mixed and Augmented Reality (ISMAR), pp. 84–93. IEEE (2016)
5. Al-Kalbani, M., Williams, I., Frutos-Pascual, M.: Improving freehand placement for grasping virtual objects via dual view visual feedback in mixed reality. In: Proceedings of the 22nd ACM Conference on Virtual Reality Software and Technology, pp. 279–282. ACM (2016)
6. Alce, G., Roszko, M., Edlund, H., Olsson, S., Svedberg, J., Wallergård, M.: [POSTER] AR as a user interface for the Internet of Things comparing three interaction models. In: 2017 IEEE International Symposium on Mixed and Augmented Reality (ISMAR-Adjunct), pp. 81–86. IEEE (2017)
7. Bach, B., Sicat, R., Beyer, J., Cordeil, M., Pfister, H.: The hologram in my hand: how effective is interactive exploration of 3D visualizations in immersive tangible augmented reality? IEEE Trans. Vis. Comput. Graph. **24**(1), 457–467 (2018)
8. Bai, Z., Blackwell, A.F.: Analytic review of usability evaluation in ISMAR. Interact. Comput. **24**(6), 450–460 (2012)
9. Bangor, A., Kortum, P., Miller, J.: Determining what individual SUS scores mean: adding an adjective rating scale. J. Usability Stud. **4**(3), 114–123 (2009)
10. Blackler, A., Popovic, V.: Towards intuitive interaction theory (2015)
11. Brooke, J., et al.: SUS-A quick and dirty usability scale. Usability Eval. Ind. **189**(194), 4–7 (1996)
12. Buchmann, V., Violich, S., Billinghurst, M., Cockburn, A.: FingARtips: gesture based direct manipulation in augmented reality. In: Proceedings of the 2nd International Conference on Computer Graphics and Interactive Techniques in Australasia and South East Asia, pp. 212–221. ACM (2004)
13. Cascales, A., Laguna, I., Pérez-López, D., Perona, P., Contero, M.: An experience on natural sciences augmented reality contents for preschoolers. In: Shumaker, R. (ed.) VAMR 2013. LNCS, vol. 8022, pp. 103–112. Springer, Heidelberg (2013). https://doi.org/10.1007/978-3-642-39420-1_12
14. Chen, L., Day, T., Tang, W., John, N.: Recent developments and future challenges in medical mixed reality. In: 2017 IEEE International Symposium on Mixed and Augmented Reality, pp. 123–135. IEEE (2017)
15. Ciodota, M., Lukosch, S., Bank, P., Ouwehand, P.: Towards engaging upper extremity motor dysfunction assessment using augmented reality games. In: 2017 IEEE International Symposium on Mixed and Augmented Reality (ISMAR-Adjunct), pp. 275–278. IEEE (2017)
16. Diaz, C., Walker, M., Szafir, D.A., Szafir, D.: Designing for depth perceptions in augmented reality. In: 2017 IEEE International Symposium on Mixed and Augmented Reality (ISMAR), pp. 111–122. IEEE (2017)

17. Dingler, T., Funk, M., Alt, F.: Interaction proxemics: combining physical spaces for seamless gesture interaction. In: Proceedings of the 4th International Symposium on Pervasive Displays, pp. 107–114. ACM (2015)

18. Foronda, C., et al.: Virtually nursing: emerging technologies in nursing education. Nurse Educ. **42**(1), 14–17 (2017)

19. Funk, M., Kritzler, M., Michahelles, F.: HoloCollab: a shared virtual platform for physical assembly training using spatially-aware head-mounted displays. In: Proceedings of the Seventh International Conference on the Internet of Things, pp. 1–7. ACM (2017)

20. Furlan, R.: The future of augmented reality: Hololens-Microsoft's AR headset shines despite rough edges [Resources_Tools and Toys]. IEEE Spectr. **53**(6), 21 (2016)

21. Gabbard, J.L., Swan II, J.E.: Usability engineering for augmented reality: employing user-based studies to inform design. IEEE Trans. Vis. Comput. Graph. **14**(3), 513–525 (2008)

22. Gabriel, E., Jack, M., Mariangely, I.P., Anastacia, M., Winer, E.: Evaluating the Microsoft HoloLens through an augmented reality assembly application. In: Proceedings of SPIE, vol. 10197, p. 10197 (2017)

23. Hart, S.G., Staveland, L.E.: Development of NASA-TLX (Task Load Index): results of empirical and theoretical research. In: Advances in psychology, vol. 52, pp. 139–183. Elsevier (1988)

24. Herron, J.: Augmented reality in medical education and training. J. Electron. Resour. Med. Libr. **13**(2), 51–55 (2016)

25. Houde, S.: Iterative design of an interface for easy 3-D direct manipulation. In: Proceedings of the SIGCHI Conference on Human factors in Computing Systems, pp. 135–142. ACM (1992)

26. Jankowski, J., Hachet, M.: Advances in interaction with 3D environments. Comput. Graph. Forum **34**, 152–190 (2015)

27. Jetter, J., Eimecke, J., Rese, A.: Augmented reality tools for industrial applications: what are potential key performance indicators and who benefits? Comput. Hum. Behav. **87**, 18–33 (2018)

28. Jones, J.A., Swan II, J.E., Singh, G., Kolstad, E., Ellis, S.R.: The effects of virtual reality, augmented reality, and motion parallax on egocentric depth perception. In: Proceedings of the 5th Symposium on Applied Perception in Graphics and Visualization, pp. 9–14. ACM (2008)

29. Karam, M., Schraefel, M.C.: A taxonomy of gestures in human computer interactions. Technical report (2005)

30. Kim, K., Billinghurst, M., Bruder, G., Duh, H.B.L., Welch, G.F.: Revisiting trends in augmented reality research: a review of the 2nd decade of ISMAR (2008–2017). IEEE Trans. Vis. Comput. Graph. **24**(11), 2947–2962 (2018)

31. Kruijff, E., Swan, J.E., Feiner, S.: Perceptual issues in augmented reality revisited. In: 2010 9th IEEE International Symposium on Mixed and Augmented Reality (ISMAR), pp. 3–12. IEEE (2010)

32. Lampton, D.R., McDonald, D.P., Singer, M., Bliss, J.P.: Distance estimation in virtual environments. In: Proceedings of the Human Factors and Ergonomics Society Annual Meeting, vol. 39, pp. 1268–1272. SAGE Publications Sage CA, Los Angeles, CA (1995)

33. Lasi, H., Fettke, P., Kemper, H., Feld, T., Hoffmann, M.: Industry 4.0. Bus. Inf. Syst. Eng. **6**, 239–242 (2014)

34. Lee, M., Billinghurst, M., Baek, W., Green, R., Woo, W.: A usability study of multimodal input in an augmented reality environment. Virtual Reality **17**(4), 293–305 (2013)
35. Lee, S., Lee, B., Cho, J., Jang, C., Kim, J., Lee, B.: Analysis and implementation of hologram lenses for see-through head-mounted display. IEEE Photonics Technol. Lett. **29**(1), 82–85 (2017)
36. Lin, S., Cheng, H.F., Li, W., Huang, Z., Hui, P., Peylo, C.: Ubii: physical world interaction through augmented reality. IEEE Trans. Mob. Comput. **16**(3), 872–885 (2017)
37. Macaranas, A., Antle, A.N., Riecke, B.E.: What is intuitive interaction? Balancing users' performance and satisfaction with natural user interfaces. Interact. Comput. **27**(3), 357–370 (2015)
38. Moser, K.R., Swan, J.E.: Evaluation of hand and stylus based calibration for optical see-through head-mounted displays using leap motion. In: 2016 IEEE Virtual Reality (VR), pp. 233–234. IEEE (2016)
39. Nguyen, H., Ketchell, S., Engelke, U., Thomas, B., de Souza, P.: [POSTER] HoloBee: augmented reality based bee drift analysis. In: 2017 IEEE International Symposium on Mixed and Augmented Reality (ISMAR-Adjunct), pp. 87–92. IEEE (2017)
40. Ni, T., Bowman, D.A., North, C., McMahan, R.P.: Design and evaluation of freehand menu selection interfaces using tilt and pinch gestures. Int. J. Hum Comput Stud. **69**(9), 551–562 (2011)
41. Piumsomboon, T., Altimira, D., Kim, H., Clark, A., Lee, G., Billinghurst, M.: Grasp-Shell vs gesture-speech: a comparison of direct and indirect natural interaction techniques in augmented reality. In: 2014 IEEE International Symposium on Mixed and Augmented Reality (ISMAR), pp. 73–82. IEEE (2014)
42. Piumsomboon, T., Clark, A., Billinghurst, M., Cockburn, A.: User-defined gestures for augmented reality. In: CHI 2013 Extended Abstracts on Human Factors in Computing Systems, pp. 955–960. ACM (2013)
43. Ren, G., O'Neill, E.: 3D selection with freehand gesture. Comput. Graph. **37**(3), 101–120 (2013)
44. Rolland, J.P., Gibson, W., Ariely, D.: Towards quantifying depth and size perception in virtual environments. Presence: Teleop. Virt. Environ. **4**(1), 24–49 (1995)
45. Santos, B.S., Cardoso, J., Ferreira, B.Q., Ferreira, C., Dias, P.: Developing 3D freehand gesture-based interaction methods for virtual walkthroughs: using an iterative approach. In: Handbook of Research on Human-Computer Interfaces, Developments, and Applications, pp. 52–72. IGI Global (2016)
46. Sato, M., Suzuki, S., Ebihara, D., Kato, S., Ishigaki, S.: Pseudo-softness evaluation in grasping a virtual object with a bare hand. In: SIGGRAPH Posters, p. 40 (2016)
47. Shapiro, S.S., Wilk, M.B.: An analysis of variance test for normality (complete samples). Biometrika **52**(3/4), 591–611 (1965)
48. Singh, G., Swan II, J.E., Jones, J.A., Ellis, S.R.: Depth judgment measures and occluding surfaces in near-field augmented reality. In: Proceedings of the 7th Symposium on Applied Perception in Graphics and Visualization, pp. 149–156. ACM (2010)
49. Suzuki, S., Suzuki, H., Sato, M.: Grasping a virtual object with a bare hand. In: ACM SIGGRAPH 2014 Posters, p. 51. ACM (2014)
50. Swan, J.E., Jones, A., Kolstad, E., Livingston, M.A., Smallman, H.S.: Egocentric depth judgments in optical, see-through augmented reality. IEEE Trans. Vis. Comput. Graph. **13**(3), 429–442 (2007)

51. Swan, J.E., Singh, G., Ellis, S.R.: Matching and reaching depth judgments with real and augmented reality targets. IEEE Trans. Vis. Comput. Graph. **21**, 1289–1298 (2015)
52. Wachs, J.P., Kölsch, M., Stern, H., Edan, Y.: Vision-based hand-gesture applications. Commun. ACM **54**(2), 60–71 (2011)
53. Wilcoxon, F., Wilcox, R.A.: Some rapid approximate statistical procedures. Lederle Laboratories (1964)
54. Yung, R., Khoo-Lattimore, C.: New realities: a systematic literature review on virtual reality and augmented reality in tourism research. Curr. Issues Tour. 1–26 (2017)

On the Use of Persistent Spatial Points for Deploying Path Navigation in Augmented Reality: An Evaluation Study

Vasileios Bachras, George E. Raptis$^{(\boxtimes)}$ (ID), and Nikolaos M. Avouris (ID)

HCI Group, Interactive Technologies Lab,
Department of Electrical and Computer Engineering, University of Patras,
Rio Achaea, Western Greece, 26504 Patras, Greece
{ece8131,avouris}@upatras.gr, raptisg@upnet.gr

Abstract. People use various techniques and tools to perform spatial navigation tasks, such as asking a local person for instructions in order to reach a destination or creating a detailed route plan for their trip through technology-mediated tools. Novel technologies, such as augmented reality, have been introduced to improve the performance and enhance the experience of the end-users. To provide navigation experiences with improved accuracy and decent stability, the developers of such tools can use *persistent spatial points*, which are stationary points in the real world that an augmented-reality system should keep track of over time. However, the use of persistent spatial points can dramatically increase the development effort, as it requires additional and time-consuming actions to be made by the developers. In this paper, we investigate the use of persistent spatial points for navigation in an AR environment from a developer and an end-user perspective, aiming to understand the trade-off between the development effort, the user performance, and the user experience. We report an empirical study in which a software engineer developed two versions of an augmented-reality navigation application (one with persistent spatial points and one without) which were used by twenty-eight individuals to navigate. Our study results revealed a trade-off between the development effort, the user performance, and the user experience, which depends on the length of the navigation path. The shorter the path is, the less the need for persistent spatial points is, while, on the other hand, the longer the path is, the more critical it is to use persisting spatial points. Based on the results, we discuss ways of mitigating the development effort while maintaining high user performance and experience.

Keywords: Spatial navigation · Augmented reality ·
Persistent spatial points · Spatial anchors · Empirical study ·
User study · Evaluation · Microsoft HoloLens

© IFIP International Federation for Information Processing 2019
Published by Springer Nature Switzerland AG 2019
D. Lamas et al. (Eds.): INTERACT 2019, LNCS 11749, pp. 309–318, 2019.
https://doi.org/10.1007/978-3-030-29390-1_17

1   Introduction

People follow a wide range of different strategies, from traditional (e.g., asking other people about a route) to novel ones (e.g., use of new technologies), to navigate. To support users in navigation, several tools have been built, based on positioning and location-aware technologies. However, they suffer from limitations that are mainly due to the users' disengagement of the environment [7], such as orientation and navigability problems and inconsistencies. To overcome such limitations, novel technologies, such as augmented reality (AR), have been introduced. Such technologies aim to increase the level of accuracy and detail when demonstrating the navigation paths, and thus, improve the user performance and enhance the user experience [2,15,16,18].

Despite the fact that AR technology can be used to provide a more natural way of interaction when navigating, it introduces limitations, which are mainly related to spatial mapping and rendering, especially in outdoor conditions. To overcome such issues, *persistent spatial points* can be used in AR applications. Persistent spatial points represent important points, which "force" the virtual objects that augment the physical space to stay in specific real world positions across instances of the AR application. The use of such persistent points could enhance the user performance and experience, however, it can significantly complicate the development process and be a burden for the developers.

Hence, in this paper, we evaluate the use of persistent spatial points for navigation in an AR environment and we investigate the trade-off between the development effort, the user performance, and the user experience. We start with a discussion on the related work upon which we build our motivation. Then, we present a two-fold evaluation study; from the designer and the end-user perspective. Finally, we discuss the findings, the implications, and the limitations of the present work and conclude the paper.

2   Related Work

Use of Technology in Spatial Navigation. Many technologies and tools (e.g., Google Maps) have been used by people for spatial navigation. Such tools recommend a path to the user by considering varying factors such as identification of obstacles [5], accessibility issues [6], points of interest [8], emergent events [9], and diverse means and routes [17]. Novel technologies, such as AR, have been used to improve the user experience that was offered by conventional technologies, such as web and mobile applications. Such improvements can be achieved with various ways such as real-time detection of objects (e.g., obstacles) in the surroundings [2], use of virtual objects that guide the user through the recommended route [15] which are displayed in various formats and points (e.g., different height) on the display [16], real-time generation of the recommended path on the display [18], use of dynamic and real-time notification messages about not expected situations in the surroundings of the recommended path [13], and keeping aware the user of important events and situations [1], such as lights, estimated time, distance of alternative paths, etc.

Use of Persistent Spatial Points in AR Applications. Persistent spatial points have been used to improve accuracy by identifying the target objects clearly without ambiguity [10], improve the stability of the augmented objects [3], and avoid the misplacement (e.g., shifting away) of the augmented objects which can lead to the disconnection of the virtual experience with reality over time [12]. However, while the use of persistent spatial points improves the experience, it is not an automatic process, but a process that requires the developer to define the persistent points and anchor them to the real world, through spatial scanning and mapping, which may require time and repetitive adjustments to provide the desired outcome.

2.1 Motivation

From the discussion on the related work, it is evident that while AR has been used to enhance the user experience in navigation tasks and that while persistent spatial points have been used to overcome positioning problems of the augmented virtual objects, it has not been investigated, to the authors' knowledge, the trade-off between development effort, user performance, and user experience for navigation tasks. Therefore, in this paper, our research question is whether and how the use of persistent spatial points influences the development effort, user performance, and user experience in AR navigation.

3   User Study

3.1   Method

To answer our research question, we followed a two-step study approach. In step I, we investigated the overall effort of a software engineer for developing *HoloNav*, which is a spatial-navigation AR tool. In step II, we investigated the performance and experience of 28 individuals who used *HoloNav* to navigate through various paths in the city of Patras, Greece.

Tool. *HoloNav* is an AR navigation tool that guides the users to their destinations through auto-generated paths. It augments the physical space by presenting virtual arrows that guide the users through the path. *HoloNav* scans the area around the user and dynamically places the arrows about 50 cm above the ground without any action required from the user (Fig. 1). *HoloNav* supports both versions implied in the research question (i.e., with and without persistent spatial points).

Apparatus. *HoloNav* was developed for Microsoft HoloLens, which is a head-mounted display (HMD) device developed and manufactured by Microsoft. All participants used the same device, which was adjusted for each of them to best fit their head and not affect their experience. To implement the functionality of the persistent spatial points, the software engineer used the *spatial anchors* feature of Microsoft HoloLens.

Fig. 1. Virtual arrows augmented the physical space and guided the users to their destination.

Participants. We recruited 28 participants (12 females, 16 males) of varying age ($MIN = 19$, $MAX = 36$, $M = 26$, $SD = 5$). All participants had the same level of experience with navigation tools (they were familiar with geolocation and positioning technologies, such as GPS and Google Maps), HoloLens (none of them had ever used HoloLens or other HMD device), and use of AR systems to navigate (none of them had ever navigated with the assistance of an AR tool). Each participant used only one version of $HoloNav$, hence, they were allocated in either the $W - PSP$ or the $WO - PSP$ group. The participants of the $W - PSP$ group used the $HoloNav$ version that was built with persistent spatial points (i.e., spatial anchors), while the participants of the $WO - PSP$ group used the $HoloNav$ version that was not based on persistent spatial points. Aiming to create balanced groups (e.g., same size, equal distribution of age and gender), the allocation was based on the participants' demographic characteristics.

Paths. We designed three paths of varying length (short: 250 m, medium: 500 m, long: 1000 m) in a city area that all participants were familiar with. However, they were not aware of the final destination or the path prior to the study, as $HoloNav$ generated the paths and demonstrated them (one path each time) to the participants during the study. When the participant reached the destination of the first path, the second one was activated, and so on.

Metrics. To measure the development effort, we focused on (a) the time needed to create each version, (b) the actions and resources required to create each version, and (c) the application footprint. To measure the user performance, we used (a) the success rate and (b) the completion time. To measure the user experience, we used the NASA-TLX [4] and User Engagement Scale (UES) [11] tools. We also conducted an interview with each participant after the completion of the task to uncover hidden aspects regarding their experience.

Procedure. In step I, a software engineer (SE), who had intermediate experience in developing AR applications, created two versions of *HoloNav*: one with the persistent spatial points $(W - PSP)$ and one without $(WO - PSP)$. The SE developed *HoloNav* in his own working conditions (i.e., ecologically valid conditions). He was asked to keep track of the activities, resources, and the time needed to perform the necessary tasks, adopting an activity diary-log approach. Moreover, several semi-structured interviews were conducted during and after the development phase.

In step II, (a) we recruited the participants via posting flyers on bulletin boards at various places on the campus, and directly by contacting acquaintances of the research team; (b) each participant was given an overview of the study, and provided their consent; (c) each participant completed a demographics questionnaire and was allocated to a group (d) each participant undertook a tutorial in HoloLens to familiarize themselves with the technology; (e) each participant performed the activity using the allocated version of *HoloNav*; (f) each participant answered the questionnaires and had an interview.

3.2   Results

Development Effort. The SE spent approximately the same *time to create each version* for coding, as the only additional step for developing the $W - PSP$ version was to include the *spatial anchors* feature of Microsoft HoloLens. This was a quick procedure with minimum integration effort. In particular, the SE spent 48 man-hours to develop the $WO - PSP$ version and 56 man-hours to develop the $W - PSP$ version (8 of which were allocated for using the *spatial anchors* feature). However, considering that each persistent spatial point represents an important point in the world that the system should keep track of over time, the SE needed to perform *spatial rendering and mapping* tasks to ensure that anchored holograms will stay precisely in place. Hence, the SE navigated through the city and performed the aforementioned tasks by scanning the various important points, and thus, the total time spent to create the $W - PSP$ version increased. The SE spent 20 additional man-hours to develop the $W - PSP$ version. Overall, the SE spent 48 man-hours to create the $WO - PSP$ version and 76 man-hours to create the $W - PSP$ version. Hence, the use of persistent spatial points resulted in an increase of the total development time by more than 50%.

Likewise, the *actions and resources* required to develop each version were similar regarding the coding part, as the only additional step for the $W - PSP$ version was the use of the *spatial anchors* feature. However, the overall procedure of creating persistent spatial points included the commuting of the SE to the city, the navigation through the various paths, the scanning, mapping, and rendering of the important points, etc. Therefore, the additional actions and resources required for the creation of the $W - PSP$ version had a direct impact on the total creation time and increased the development effort, which highly depend on the size of the area that the navigation tool supports. The resulting assets can be re-used once the actions performed (e.g., the persistent spatial points remain stored in the device), saving time and development effort for future projects.

Regarding the *application footprint*, the total size depends on the number of the meshes, which in turn, depends on the desired accuracy and the covered area. The larger the area is, the more meshes are required, and thus, the bigger the file-size is. In our scenario, the filesize of $W - PSP$ version was 350 MB bigger than the filesize of $WO - PSP$ version, which was expected, as the $W - PSP$ stores spatial mapping meshes. Nonetheless, increasing the length and/or the number of the paths could lead to unrealistically large filesize, which might also affect the application performance, and thus, user experience and/or performance. Regarding the loading-time, it depends both on the application and on the technical characteristics of the device used. In our case, no differences between the two $HoloNav$ versions when using Microsoft HoloLens were revealed.

User Performance. All participants reached their destinations; hence, no difference was found on the *success rate* (i.e., *success_rate* = 1.00). Regarding the *completion time*, the independent-samples t-test (independent variable (IV): $HoloNav$ version; dependent variable (DV): completion time) revealed statistically marginal and significant differences for the medium and long paths respectively (Fig. 2). $WO - PSP$ users needed more time to reach their destination than $W - PSP$ users (medium path: $t = 2.023$, $p = .065$, $d = 1.012$; long path: $t = 3.016$, $p = .009$, $d = 1.151$). In the $WO - PSP$ version, the paths are not "anchored" with any spatial point of the real world, and there is an increased likelihood of "drifting", meaning that the arrows may shift away and the path will be misplaced. In short-distance paths, a light drifting was observed which did not influence the users, as they were aware of the path during the navigation and reached their destination without any problems. However, in middle- and in long-distance paths, the absence of stationary spatial points, which would serve as reference points, negatively affected the user performance in terms of completion time. The virtual arrows were often misplaced, and the users followed misleading paths which ended up to dead ends. Thus, they had to start over the process, and they spent more time for reaching the end point of the paths. The longer a path without persistent points was, the more likely it was for a virtual arrow to be misplaced and a misleading path to be generated. On the other hand, in the $W - PSP$ version, the paths were precisely located as they were based on stable and stationary reference points, and thus, the users performed well in all conditions (short-, middle-, and long-distance paths).

User Experience. According to the results of the NASA-TLX questionnaire, the $WO - PSP$ users put more effort than the $W - PSP$ users in accomplishing the navigation tasks (Fig. 2), which was a statistically significant difference (t-test with $HoloNav$ version as IV and effort dimension as DV: $t = 3.076$, $p = .005$,

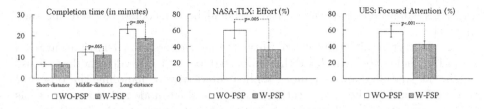

Fig. 2. Left: $WO-PSP$ users spent more time navigating in middle- and long-distance paths; middle: $W-PSP$ users put more effort in accomplishing the navigation tasks; right: $WO-PSP$ users had higher focused attention than the $W-PSP$ users.

$d = 1.158$). No difference was found for any of the other NASA-TLX dimensions. The discussion with the users revealed that the difference derived from the effort made by the $WO-PSP$ users to re-adjust their route by starting the navigation over when the arrows were misplaced, which was frequent in long-distance paths where there was an increased likelihood of poor accuracy or drifting.

Regarding the UES questionnaire, the analysis revealed that the $WO-PSP$ users had higher focused attention than the $W-PSP$ users (Fig. 2), which was a statistically significant difference (t-test with $HoloNav$ version as IV and focused-attention dimension as DV: $t = 4.173$, $p < .001$, $d = 1.568$). In particular, the $WO-PSP$ users mentioned that they lost track of time, lost track of the world around them, and they were absorbed in following the arrows. Considering that the path was not precisely located (e.g., it could be traversed through shops) the $WO-PSP$ users could not follow it "arrow-by-arrow", and thus, they had to pay attention to the direction of the arrows, and often, they had to guess the path when the arrows were not visible (e.g., inside buildings) or indistinguishable. The aforementioned condition was frequent in long-distance paths. Finally, an issue raised by the $W-PSP$ users was the "jittering" effect of the arrows, which was intense in long-distance paths. The users observed the arrows to be shaking in high frequency, which was a result of the high demand of spatial mapping in scenarios with increased amount of persistent spatial points.

4   Discussion

Our study results revealed that a trade-off between the development effort, the end-user performance, and the end-user experience when considering (or not) persistent spatial points in AR navigation. This trade-off depends on the length of the navigation paths. In short-distance paths, there is no need of including persisting spatial points that increase the development effort, because the user performance and user experience are comparably similar to the condition where persisting spatial points are used. However, as the length of the navigation path increases, it is critical for the developer to use persisting spatial points in order to ensure a high user performance and an enhanced user experience. But, as the length of the navigation path increases, the development effort also increases, and thus, smart and efficient solutions should be considered to overcome such limitations.

As a direct implication of our work, the developers of AR navigation tools should consider the length of the supported paths to decide whether to use persistent spatial points. A more sophisticated way of handling the observed trade-off would be the consideration of adaptive dual-mode AR navigation tools that activate the use of persistent points after determining the length of the path. Regarding the long-distance paths, the developers should consider releasing spatial points that are not needed, through dynamic allocation and prioritization techniques, to minimize the application footprint. For example, when a persistent point is active, the system will keep the points around it activated, while the others will remain deactivated. To mitigate the jittering and drifting effects, the augmented objects should form clusters that are dynamically rendered based on stationary reference points. To handle the trade-off, we could also investigate the minimum distance between the successive persistent spatial points, aiming to identify the minimum required number based on the length of the paths. Moreover, considering that the density of the points affected the rendering, as a future step we will experiment with density levels to provide additional insights about maximum area size for navigation and maximum density within the path.

To further decrease the development effort, we envisage the re-use of created persistent spatial points through an open and cloud-based repository. Through such a repository, the developers could upload and download spatial points, and thus, they contribute to collective generation of large and interconnected navigation paths and worlds, which can be used for the design of multi-user and collaborative navigation experiences. Cloud infrastructures could host persistent spatial points that would be dynamically available to the users, contributing to a realistic application footprint, an improved user performance, and an enhanced user experience while keeping the development effort minimum (e.g., a developer is not required to scan an area than had been scanned by another developer in the past) in varying distance conditions.

Regarding the limitations of our work, our sample size was relatively small, but, the statistical tests performed met the required assumptions. Another limitation is the fact that the end-users were familiar with the city, and as a future work, we will investigate scenarios with users unfamiliar with the city. Moreover, we will investigate the effect of other factors that influence user experience in AR settings, such as cognitive characteristics [14].

5 Conclusion

In this paper we evaluated the use of persistent spatial points in an AR navigation tool from a developer and an end-user perspective. We performed a two-fold empirical study with one software engineer, who created two versions of an AR navigation application (one with persistent spatial points and one without), and twenty-eight individuals who used the application to navigate. The analysis of the results revealed a trade-off between development effort, user performance, and user experience, which depends on the length of the navigation path. The shorter the path is, the less the need for persistent spatial points is, whilst, the longer the path is, the more critical it is to use persisting spatial points. The present study provides evidence on the importance of the trade-off between development effort and user experience, and is a starting point towards incorporating the new emerging technologies in everyday tasks.

References

1. Bark, K., Tran, C., Fujimura, K., Ng-Thow-Hing, V.: Personal Navi: benefits of an augmented reality navigational aid using a see-thru 3D volumetric HUD. In: Proceedings of the 6th International Conference on Automotive User Interfaces and Interactive Vehicular Applications, Automotive UI 2014, pp. 1:1–1:8. ACM, New York (2014). https://doi.org/10.1145/2667317.2667329
2. Cao, C., Li, Z., Zhou, P., Li, M.: Amateur: augmented reality based vehicle navigation system. Proc. ACM Interact. Mob. Wearable Ubiquit. Technol. **2**(4), 155:1–155:24 (2018). https://doi.org/10.1145/3287033
3. Chinara, C., Feingold, G., Shanbhag, A., Weiniger, K.: ARnold: a mixed reality short film using Microsoft HoloLens. In: SMPTE 2017 Annual Technical Conference and Exhibition, SMPTE, pp. 1–12 (2017). https://doi.org/10.5594/M001756
4. Hart, S.G., Staveland, L.E.: Development of NASA-TLX (Task Load Index): results of empirical and theoretical research. Adv. Psychol. **52**, 139–183 (1988). https://doi.org/10.1016/S0166-4115(08)62386-9
5. Holone, H., Misund, G., Tolsby, H., Kristoffersen, S.: Aspects of personal navigation with collaborative user feedback. In: Proceedings of the 5th Nordic Conference on Human-computer Interaction: Building Bridges, NordiCHI 2008, pp. 182–191. ACM, New York (2008). https://doi.org/10.1145/1463160.1463180
6. Kasemsuppakorn, P., Karimi, H.A.: Data requirements and a spatial database for personalized wheelchair navigation. In: Proceedings of the 2nd International Convention on Rehabilitation Engineering & Assistive Technology, iCREATe 2008, pp. 31–34, Singapore Therapeutic, Assistive & Rehabilitative Technologies (START) Centre, Kaki Bukit TechPark II, Singapore (2008). http://dl.acm.org/citation.cfm?id=1983222.1983232
7. Leshed, G., Velden, T., Rieger, O., Kot, B., Sengers, P.: In-car GPS navigation: engagement with and disengagement from the environment. In: Proceedings of the SIGCHI Conference on Human Factors in Computing Systems, CHI 2008, pp. 1675–1684. ACM, New York (2008). https://doi.org/10.1145/1357054.1357316
8. Li, Y., Su, H., Demiryurek, U., Zheng, B., Zeng, K., Shahabi, C.: PerNav: a route summarization framework for personalized navigation. In: Proceedings of the 2016 International Conference on Management of Data, SIGMOD 2016, pp. 2125–2128. ACM, New York (2016). https://doi.org/10.1145/2882903.2899384
9. Lin, A.Y., Kuehl, K., Schöning, J., Hecht, B.: Understanding "Death by GPS": a systematic study of catastrophic incidents associated with personal navigation technologies. In: Proceedings of the 2017 CHI Conference on Human Factors in Computing Systems, CHI 2017, pp. 1154–1166. ACM, New York (2017). https://doi.org/10.1145/3025453.3025737
10. Müller, J., Rädle, R., Reiterer, H.: Remote collaboration with mixed reality displays: how shared virtual landmarks facilitate spatial referencing. In: Proceedings of the 2017 CHI Conference on Human Factors in Computing Systems, CHI 2017, pp. 6481–6486. ACM, New York (2017). https://doi.org/10.1145/3025453.3025717

11. O'Brien, H.L., Cairns, P., Hall, M.: A practical approach to measuring user engagement with the refined user engagement scale (UES) and new UES short form. Int. J. Hum Comput Stud. **112**, 28–39 (2018). https://doi.org/10.1016/j.ijhcs.2018.01.004

12. Ong, S.: Using spatial mapping. In: Beginning Windows Mixed Reality Programming: For HoloLens and Mixed Reality Headsets, pp. 115–139. Apress, Berkeley, CA (2017). https://doi.org/10.1007/978-1-4842-2769-5_6

13. Palinko, O., et al.: Towards augmented reality navigation using affordable technology. In: Proceedings of the 5th International Conference on Automotive User Interfaces and Interactive Vehicular Applications, Automotive UI 2013, pp. 238–241. ACM, New York (2013). https://doi.org/10.1145/2516540.2516569

14. Raptis, G.E., Fidas, C., Avouris, N.M.: Effects of mixed-reality on players' behaviour and immersion in a cultural tourism game: a cognitive processing perspective. Int. J. Hum Comput Stud. **114**, 69–79 (2018). https://doi.org/10.1016/j.ijhcs.2018.02.003

15. Shirose, M., Hirose, M., Oku, K., Koide, M., Hirai, N.: Passage+: mobile content platform of an augmented reality and virtual objects. In: Proceedings of the 20th ACM International Conference on Multimedia, MM 2012, pp. 1497–1498. ACM, New York (2012). https://doi.org/10.1145/2393347.2396534

16. Tonnis, M., Klein, L., Klinker, G.: Perception thresholds for augmented reality navigation schemes in large distances. In: Proceedings of the 7th IEEE/ACM International Symposium on Mixed and Augmented Reality, ISMAR 2008, pp. 189–190. IEEE Computer Society, Washington, DC, USA (2008). https://doi.org/10.1109/ISMAR.2008.4637360

17. Vaittinen, T., Laakso, K., Itäranta, J.: Kuukkeli: Design and Evaluation of Location-based Service with Touch UI for Hikers. In: Proceedings of the 5th Nordic Conference on Human-computer Interaction: Building Bridges, NordiCHI 2008, pp. 373–382. ACM, New York (2008). https://doi.org/10.1145/1463160.1463201

18. Wen, J., Deneka, A., Helton, W., Billinghurst, M.: Really, it's for your own good...making augmented reality navigation tools harder to use. In: CHI 2014 Extended Abstracts on Human Factors in Computing Systems, CHI EA 2014, pp. 1297–1302. ACM, New York (2014). https://doi.org/10.1145/2559206.2581156

User Experience Guidelines for Designing HMD Extended Reality Applications

Steven Vi[1], Tiago Silva da Silva[1,2(✉)], and Frank Maurer[1]

[1] University of Calgary, 2500 University Dr NW, Calgary, AB, Canada
{stvi,fmaurer}@ucalgary.ca
[2] Federal University of São Paulo,
Av. Cesare Lattes, 1201, São José dos Campos, SP, Brazil
silvadasilva@unifesp.br

Abstract. With the rise of Extended Reality (XR) technologies, such as head mounted displays (HMD) for Virtual Reality (VR), Mixed Reality (MR), and Augmented Reality (AR), designers are presented with many unique challenges and opportunities when creating applications. Publications can be found from research and industry that offer insights and ideas surrounding user experience (UX) for XR applications. However, these publications often vary in format and content. Based on a thorough analysis of 68 different resources from research, industry, and 2D design, we present a set of eleven UX guidelines for designing XR applications. Our work serves as a reference to the literature for understanding what others have tried and discovered and provides an integrated set of guidelines. Furthermore, our guidelines offer guidance to a software developer to aid in the design of XR applications for HMD devices.

Keywords: Extended Reality · User experience · Design guidelines · Virtual Reality · Augmented Reality · Mixed Reality

1 Introduction

Recent developments in Extended Reality (XR) technologies, such as wearable Head Mounted Displays (HMD) for Virtual Reality (VR), Mixed Reality (MR), and Augmented Reality (AR), have yielded affordable hardware for experiencing immersive virtual environments in multidimensional space. 2D displays are limited to showing content on a screen, but XR applications can embed a user in his or her digital information, utilizing a 360-degree view, perceived depth, physical location, and movement tracking to expand what can be experienced in a digital application. Furthermore, continued development in this space has seen additional capabilities, such as haptics, spatial audio, hand tracking, improved sensors, etc., be continually added to XR platforms.

While XR provides increased potential for interacting with digital information, it is important to remember that these advancements require an expansion

© IFIP International Federation for Information Processing 2019
Published by Springer Nature Switzerland AG 2019
D. Lamas et al. (Eds.): INTERACT 2019, LNCS 11749, pp. 319–341, 2019.
https://doi.org/10.1007/978-3-030-29390-1_18

of our current understanding of UX design. Established patterns and guidelines are built around applications running on a 2D screen and do not address the potential additional considerations that come with spatial environments and interactions. As long as existing design lessons are not extended for the capabilities of XR, designers likely face barriers to unlock the full potential of these technologies.

Recent works from various communities, such as device manufactures, developer blogs, news sites, and academic sources, can be found that provide ideas around designing for XR platforms. These resources vary in content, in supporting evidence, and in format, such as first-hand experiences, proposed guidelines, speculative ideas, prototypes, etc. This provides a diverse wealth of information; however, it also makes it difficult to identify valid patterns that can be beneficial for designers.

Inspired by this work, we developed a set of UX guidelines for designing XR applications that aim at integrating various ideas from different XR and UX communities. We used an approach adapted from Rusu et al. [22] and Quinõnes et al. [21] to formulate, specify, correlate and refine a set of design guidelines. A total of 60 web resources, 1 peered reviewed paper, 1 book, 3 non-peered review academic sources, and 3 traditional UX sources, were analyzed and used to derive our guidelines. Our work is targeted towards aiding in the design of applications for wearable HMD XR devices, such as the Microsoft HoloLens, Magic Leap, Meta, HTC Vive, Oculus Rift, etc., that uses stereoscopic imaging, spatial audio, and head tracking to provide users with an immersive experience. This paper is not meant to present absolute rules, but rather to provide in a concise manner a reference for understanding what others have tried and discovered.

Our work makes three contributions. First, we provide a guided overview into the existing literature on UX for XR applications in academic research and in industry. Second, we propose a set of guidelines that are encompassing the body of work in a concise and structured manner. Third, based on our guidelines, we make statements about which topics have been emphasized, which topics are not well covered, and areas of opportunities for further research.

2   Background

2.1   Extended Reality

As the industries around these platforms develop, so does the terminology. Different definitions have been used in this field, but there have been distinct categories of technologies that have emerged in recent years. For the purpose of this paper, we will use the following terminology to classify Virtual Reality (VR), Augmented Reality (AR), Mixed Reality (MR), and Extended Reality (XR). VR allows users to be fully immersed in a computer-generated environment while the real world is occluded when the device is in use [14]. AR allows for information to be superimposed around a user without blinding them to their own physical surroundings [25]. Similar to AR, MR overlays information onto the real world, but also includes the capability to understand and use the environment around the user to show or hide part of the digital content [24]. Building off Milgram et al. [17] work on classifying the reality-virtuality continuum, we updated his terminology to define XR as technologies in which real world and virtual world objects are presented within a single display. As such, XR encompasses all the previously mentioned categories.

2.2 Guidelines

Consistent with Nielsen [18], design guidelines are well-known principles for user interface design which should be followed in the development project and that can also be used to evaluate the usability of a system. According to Endsley et al. [5], in user interface design, the term guideline is almost synonymous with heuristics, and can be used by both designers and evaluators. Certainly, the most well-known design guidelines/heuristics are the ten usability heuristics from Molich and Nielsen [20]. Like psychological heuristics, usability guidelines are often used as shortcuts when data from a formal user study is not available. Guidelines can be used across the stages of the design process, guiding small and large decisions and predicting success or failure of the usability in prototypes with varying levels of fidelity.

Several authors have stated that it is necessary to create new guidelines for evaluating specific applications, for example, in [16], the authors conclude that the existing usability guidelines were too general to be applicable for evaluating the usability of mobile map applications. Thus, it is necessary to develop a new set that evaluates the specific features of that domain.

2.3 Related Work

The most recent and relevant study for our purposes is [5]. Endsley et al. [5] aimed at providing practitioners with a set of AR heuristics. They developed their heuristics by making use of affinity diagrams, expert evaluations, feedback from active AR designers, and statistical analyses. According to these authors, the literature review revealed few validated, generalized AR heuristics in use. The authors used a set of 11 heuristics, including related fields, such as: [1, 4, 6, 8, 9, 12, 14, 15, 19]. Their affinity diagramming approach sought to leverage the existing heuristics in the AR space and generating themes for immersive AR interactions.

Wheeler Atkinson et al. [1] proposed the MHET (Multiple Heuristics Evaluation Table), which describes an approach to integrate existing approaches chosen by the authors in a single table. Their approach also sought to enhance these approaches by addressing existing gaps and providing concrete examples that illustrate the application of concepts. Although providing valuable insights, this work is not directly related to ours.

Dunser et al. [4] also investigated how general HCI guidelines may relate to the domain of AR application design. To do so, they combined some known user-centered design guidelines – [18, 27, 30, 34, 37] – with the demands of AR systems to identify issues that should be considered by AR interface researchers. According to the authors, this work was an initial attempt to fill the gap that existed in the area and the presented design guidelines were just a small overview and the guidelines given were rather general and had to be further refined.

Ko et al. [14] proposed the creation of usability guidelines for the development and evaluation of smartphone applications using AR technology. The authors developed these guidelines by analyzing existing research about heuristic evaluation methods, design guidelines for AR systems, guidelines for handheld mobile device interfaces, and usability guidelines for tangible user interfaces.

Kourouthanassis et al. [15] proposed a set of interaction design guidelines for the development of Mobile Augmented Reality (MAR) applications. According to the authors, the design recommendations adopt a user-centered perspective and, thus, they focus on the necessary actions to ensure high-quality MAR user experiences.

In addition to those mentioned above, we also identified non-peer reviewed studies, such as a master's thesis from Kalalahati [12], another master's thesis from Bloksa [2], and a bachelor degree project from Frojdman [7], that discuss research and guidelines related to XR applications.

The reviewed work present interesting, novel and useful approaches for the purpose of this paper, and our work ultimately builds on the ideas and information introduced by the literature. With that said, these works also highlight the limited academic research and the lack of real-world validation around this topic. Additionally, observations from other communities, such as XR device manufactures, news articles, and developer's blogs, has shown that there is a wealth of knowledge that was not being reflected in academic works. Even though not all of the information or ideas found were academically validated, they were concepts that developers were using to build and design XR applications. This suggest that non-academic sources provide additional insights and should be incorporated in the development of guidelines. Our eleven UX guidelines extend to include the wealth of insights from other communities in conjunction with academic work. As such, concepts that developers have used to build and design current XR applications are being reflected in our research that were not in prior works.

3   Research Method

Previous work in the creation of heuristics have stated the importance of using a formal process to develop an effective and efficient set of heuristics [21]. As such, we used an approach by Rusu et al. [22] and Quiñones et al. [21] as the bases for creating our set of proposed guidelines. The authors describe stages to be followed to formulate, specify, correlate and refine a new set of heuristics. These stages were adapted and applied to fit within the context of our situation and research goals.

3.1   Conducting Search for Resources

In the first stage, a search was conducted to obtain existing literature from different sources regarding design guidelines for XR applications. To achieve this, we defined a search string, following systematic literature reviews (SLR) recommendations [13], that was iteratively reworked to accurately reflect the scope of the research. The resulting search string was:

(heuristic OR principle OR guideline) AND ("virtual reality" OR "augmented reality" OR "mixed reality" OR immersive) AND (usability OR "user experience") AND (design). The search string was then applied to search title, abstract, and keywords in Scopus[1], a database containing a variety of peer-reviewed papers published in either conferences or journals, which resulted in 350 papers found. Each paper was screened by two researchers with a third providing feedback to exclude studies that are not relevant to our topic. The criteria we used was based on the abstract explicitly mentioning dealing with HCI guidelines, heuristics or guidelines for VR, AR or MR applications and, from the abstract, being able to deduce that the focus of the paper has relevance to the creation of HCI guidelines for HMD XR design and/or evaluation. Through this process, only one paper (Endsley et al. [5]) fit in our inclusion criteria.

To broaden our resources, we conducted a search to find different information sources, such as scientific articles, thesis, previous experiments, books, and websites [21] outside of peer-reviewed databases to include in our research. We started our search for resources throughout the internet by applying multiple variations of our initial search string on the Google search engine[2]. This search resulted in a large number of related resources. After a quick overview, using backward snowballing as a complement to SLRs [26], we selected resources which focused on providing information regarding UX design for different XR technologies. The collection process continued until the researchers found that the resources continually contained repeat ideas and that new concepts became difficult to come by. We ended up with an additional 60 web resources, 3 non-peer reviewed academic sources, and 1 book which brought our total to 65. The list of resources is likely not exhaustive due to limitations of the search engine/process, however, it represents a large range of resources from different communities.

3.2   Theme Extraction and Thematic Analysis

In order to extract themes from our collection of resources, we choose to conduct a thematic analysis, in which we iteratively grouped, labelled, discussed and re-labelled categories and guidelines that described and explained the various guidelines and recommendations. This process involved several meetings among the researchers.

According to Hawkins [10], researchers conducting thematic analysis look for recognizable reoccurring topics, ideas, or patterns – themes – occurring within the data that provide insight. When a researcher uncovers common themes throughout the data, those themes may indicate areas that help explain phenomena or point out areas of needed improvement. Therefore, information that

---

[1] https://www.scopus.com/.
[2] https://www.google.com/.

supports the theme is extracted directly from the data. As the analysis continues, the researcher revisits the data to ensure the understandings extracted within the data contribute to the research questions. A theme indicates a common line of understanding occurring within the data and may contribute explicit or implicit information. Themes may be overarching, providing a general idea under which subthemes exist and contribute to understanding [3].

It should be noted that we have used an Inductive – bottom-up – approach, in which, researchers choose to locate themes inductively, and build themes directly from the data under investigation. No prior theoretical frameworks specifically guided the research project. Therefore, any and all reoccurring themes within the data are under investigation as long as themes align with the goal of the project [10]. Thus, after the thematic analysis process, we ended up with our set of guidelines, containing eleven UX guidelines for XR.

3.3 Correlating Existing Work

After the creation of our initial set of UX guidelines, we correlated our findings with related works. In this step, our goals were to identify the existing heuristics and guidelines that were already addressed in our initial set of guidelines and discover new ideas that can be incorporated into our work [10]. There were two categories in which the resources we used fell under, academic research, found in our initial search, that proposed high level design guidelines surrounding XR applications, such as [2,4,5,7,12] and traditional UX heuristics and design guidelines such as: [11,20,23]. The motivation behind using traditional design principles came from the belief that these resources still provide valid and useful information for designing XR applications despite the differences in medium. In order to find relevancy, two authors separately read each related resource and compared their high-level ideas to our initial set of guidelines. Each was marked as relevant or not relevant to indicate if the ideas were addressed in our work. Afterward, the results were combined. Discrepancies were resolved by looking at the paper together and coming up with a consensus through discussion. In the end, 32 of the existing guidelines were identified as not related by our guidelines. For each of them, we discussed whether to discard, to incorporate with our existing guidelines, or create a new guideline based on the idea. This decision was based on importance, similarities to other guidelines, and whether or not they fit within our scope. For example, through this process, we identified ideas from [4,11,20,23] around error tolerance and prevention that were not being reflected in our work. Eventually, a new guideline was created to incorporate these concepts due to their perceived value and lack of parallels with other guidelines. Through this process, we used three new resources to correlate to traditional UX heuristics and design guidelines which brought our total used resources to 68.

3.4   Refining UX Guidelines

In addition to integrating new ideas, the correlation stage identified aspects that needed to be improved. For example, we were able to find ambiguous parts through the different interpretations and discrepancies among the researchers. Based on the insights and new ideas until this point, we refined our initial set of guidelines. This process involved several meetings among the researchers around regrouping, merging, rewording, and restructuring different aspects of our work. Additionally, based on the structure from [21], we organized our guidelines by providing a name, definition, and explanation with sub guidelines for each guideline. In the end, we had eleven guidelines.

4   UX Guidelines for Extended Reality Applications on HMD

In this section, we present eleven UX guidelines for developing XR applications. They are ordered based on their specificity to the context of HMD XR applications.

4.1   Organize the Spatial Environment to Maximize Efficiency

Definition. XR is inherently spatial. Use space as an organizational tool to create an environment that is comfortable to use and minimizes the amount of conscious thinking a user has to do to accomplish his or her goals [7, 27, 29–31, 40, 41, 48–50, 52–54, 57, 61, 66, 67, 71, 72, 74–77, 80, 81, 84].

Explanation. XR can leverage how humans interpret spatial information to free up working memory and create dynamic environments. With that said, it is easy to create uncomfortable experiences depending on how the elements are placed around the user. It is important that the environment is carefully designed to take advantage of the extra space while limiting physical movement for accomplishing a task.

Keep Visual and Physical Restrictions in Mind When Arranging Content. When positioning content, it is important to remember that users have physical limitations and a limited field of view. Place visual elements in areas where users' can comfortably view for long periods and interactive elements in areas where interaction is relaxed [7, 27, 29, 31, 40, 41, 48, 50, 52–54, 57, 66, 67, 74–76, 80, 81, 84].

Explore How Space Can Be Utilized. XR provides users with a larger area for placing and interacting with content. Depending on the context and type of application, designers should explore how the additional space can be used to avoid cluttering of objects and information. For example, the Windows Mixed Reality Home application in Fig. 1 lets users place apps and content in a virtual house similar to a 2D desktop. It showcases how a 3D environment can be used to spread out content to help with organization, multitasking, and visual appeal [37, 52, 53, 61, 71, 72].

Group Similar Objects to Make Them Easier to Find. Placing similar objects together can use attention chaining behaviour to conceptually link application features together. This can help users find digital objects and information more efficiently and effectively [30,53,71,77].

Fig. 1. The picture is of Windows Mixed reality home. The application lets users customize and place content throughout a 3D virtual house.

4.2   Create Flexible Interactions and Environments

Definition. Provide users with the capability to customize the application to their personal preferences and comforts. Build in options that cater to a range of users that take into account different experience levels and physical considerations [2,11,20,23,48,50,52,73].

Explanation. It is important to build in features that makes the XR application accessible to a wide range of individuals. By giving users some control over the physical placement of digital elements, they will have opportunities to improve the overall satisfaction and ease of use for themselves. This is even more important for XR as the users are exposed to more factors that affect the overall experience than 2D displays.

Build in Interactions for Both Inexperienced and Experienced Users. The applications should have options that cater to users of varying level of experiences. Create cues for interactions for novice users and options to accelerate actions for more advanced users [2,11,20,23].

Let Users Shape Their Environment to Optimize Their Workflow. Customization can be used to improve efficiency. Provide users with options to personalize the environment based on their preferences. For example, users can place frequently used content in their immediate line of sight and change them depending on the situation [50,52,73] (Fig. 2).

Fig. 2. Picture from Google's Tilt Brush VR application. Shows how the menu can be altered based on user preference by allowing parts to be grabbed and placed in different areas of the menu.

Let Users Define What it Means to Be Comfortable. Factors that affect comfort like personal boundaries, physical limitations, social considerations, brightness, etc. should be flexible. The designer should identify potential aspects of their application that could negatively impact the user and build in options to adjust them in the settings [48].

4.3   Prioritize User's Comfort

Definition. The XR application should keep the user safe by taking extra precautions to maintain the physical, physiological, and environmental comforts for the user throughout the experience.

Explanation. Being immersed in a 360-degree environment opens the user up to a lot of different factors that impact users' comfort. Avoid putting users in situations where potential distresses might arise and provide options for users to adjust settings related to comfort [27–29, 31, 33, 34, 36, 40–42, 44, 46–50, 52–54, 57, 59, 66, 67, 74–76, 80–84, 86].

Respect Users' Personal Space. People are both physically and mentally sensitive, especially around the head, to objects that are placed too close to them. Make sure objects are defaulted to a comfortable distance away from the user and allow them to dictate what happens within their personal space [27, 29, 42, 48, 50, 52, 53, 59, 66, 75].

Physiological Considerations. Due to the fact that XR provides users with an immersive experience, users might experience discomfort due to the disparity between what one feels and what one expects to feel. It is the designer responsibility to take extra precautions to reduce the chances of users experiencing motion sickness. Oculus[3] and google[4] have a set of additional guidelines for designers to help mitigate this effect [28,31,33,34,40,44,46–49,53,57,59,75,76,80,82,83,86].

Environment Comfort. Certain users can experience various discomforts in certain situation like heights, small spaces, etc. Provide options for users to change or adjust the environment if they are uncomfortable [36,40,47,50].

Be Mindful of Physically Draining Interactions. XR applications provide designers with the opportunity to create 3D interactions. Be cautious of the fact that 3D interactions can be physically exerting for users especially over long periods and repeated repetitions. Additionally, where content is placed also dictates the type of physical interactions that are required. For example, content placed outside a user's field of view requires them to turn their body or head to view or interact with the object [27,31,40,47–49,52,53,57,66,74,81,83] (Fig. 3).

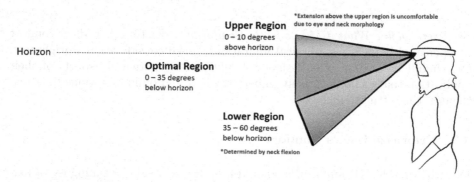

Fig. 3. Microsoft proposed allowable field of view determined by the range of motion of the neck. The picture was adapted from Microsoft blog on mixed reality comfort (https://docs.microsoft.com/en-us/windows/mixed-reality/comfort).

4.4 Keep It Simple: Do Not Overwhelm the User

Definition. The more there is, the less the user remembers. Create simple and relevant elements in an environment that do not distract the user from what is important.

Explanation. There is a fine line between enhancing an experience through additional information and overwhelming the user. XR provides more virtual space but the user still has a limit to how much information she can consume. Designers should focus on minimalism as irrelevant information competes for user attention [2,31,42,43,47,48,50,52,53,59,75–77].

---

[3] https://developer.oculus.com/design/latest/concepts/bp-locomotion/.
[4] https://designguidelines.withgoogle.com/cardboard/designing-for-google-cardboar
d/physiological-considerations.html.

Keep Tools and Information Ready, but not Distracting. Designers can provide a lot of information, but they should be implemented in a way that does not distract users when they do not require them. Provide users with the ability to hide, minimize, or turn off elements. Additionally, the element should be visually quiet while inactive as to not take the focus away from other tasks [2,31,43,48,50,52,53,77] (Fig. 4).

Don't Obscure the User's Vision with Virtual Elements. Minimize the density of information within a user's field of view and be wary of using persistent heads-up displays (HUD) that takes up a large portion of a user's view [42,47,52,53,59, 75,76].

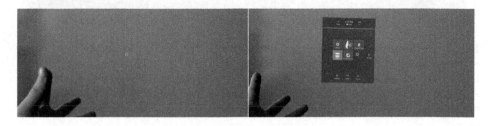

Fig. 4. Microsoft Hololens can toggle between showing and hiding the main menu through a bloom gesture.

4.5   Design Around Hardware Capabilities and Limitations

Definition. The way users interact and explore the environment will be greatly dependent on the system they are using. Always keep the capabilities of the hardware in mind when crafting XR experiences [27,28,50,83].

Explanation. Currently, there is a lack of standardization across XR devices. VR, AR, and MR offer different experiences that require different design considerations. Additionally, there is a lot of variety within these categories regarding input type, tracking limitations, device features set, etc. As such, it is important that designers understand the medium and build an experience that suits its capabilities.

Sensitive to the Capabilities of the Hardware. Applications should not include features that go beyond the limits of the hardware. The designer should be selective and choose features that comfortably stay within the capabilities of the system. For example, the Microsoft HoloLens has a field of view (FOV) of 35° while HTC Vive has a FOV of 110°. This difference affects how much content can be placed within a user's immediate line of sight. As such, the size and placement of visual elements should be adjusted based on the targeted system of the application [27,28,83] (Fig. 5).

Use the Strengths of the Medium. It is important that designers focus on features that highlight the strength of the given hardware in their application. Showing off the advantages of the system will minimize the impact hardware limitations have on UX [50].

Fig. 5. Picture showcase a range of different HMD XR product. From left to right: HP windows mixed reality headset with inside-out tracked controllers, Meta 2 with built-in hand tracking, Microsoft Hololens with gesture controls, HTV Vive with base station tracking. All these devices have differences that should be considered when designing for them.

4.6   Use Cues to Help Users Throughout Their Experience

Definition. Create signifying cues to help users to get started, provide additional information, guide user's attention, and simplify choice within the application [2,20,28,30–32,36–40,48–53,59,61,65,66,76,81–83,85].

Explanation. The expanded capabilities of XR also comes with the greater potential of users being overwhelmed or lost. Designers should take extra measures to make sure that they provide enough guidance throughout the applications to keep frustrations to a minimum.

Use Attention Directors to Help Users Discover What They Can Do and Where They Should Go. Provide the user with directional indicators to point them to important content in the application. This is especially vital for XR as the area in which content can be placed is much larger than traditional 2D application [28,30,36,39,40,49–53,59,65,76,81,82,85].

Simplify Choice. Use cues to explicitly inform users what they can do next especially if the steps are not obvious. This can help reduce hard cognitive thinking and ease frustrations throughout the experience. For example, Fig. 6 illustrates how The Lab uses a yellow arrow to explicitly inform the user of a possible action that she could take [30,32,37,38,48,49,52,61,66,83].

Do not Overload the User's Senses with Notifications. Be mindful of the fact that users can be easily overwhelmed by an excessive amount of information, especially in XR. When designing cues, not only think about delivering the information but also how it can be conveyed in an efficient and comfortable manner [2,52].

Use Cues to Integrate Help and Tutorials in the Experience. It is important that users have access to help when they need it. Instead of just providing external documentation, think about how different cues can be used to integrate help into the XR application to create a seamless experience [2,20].

Inform the Users of Actions That May Result in Errors. The best way to deal with an error is to prevent it from happening in the first place. Use cues to inform users of the potential dangers and consequences of an action before it is executed [20].

Fig. 6. Picture from Valve's The Lab: Robot Repair. Yellow cues are placed throughout the experience to inform the user of the actions that need to take place in order to progress. (Color figure online)

4.7   Create a Compelling XR Experience

Definition. XR allows users to be immersed in the virtual environment. Enhance their senses through visuals, audio, and narrative elements that captivate them in the experience [28,34,36,42–44,46,48–50,52,53,55,60,61,65,66,73–76,78–83].

Explanation. Users senses are more exposed when immersed in XR applications. This presents additional challenges for designers, but it also offers an opportunity to elevate the experience. Explore how aesthetic elements can be used to captivate the user and provide them with an application that they want to use continually.

Make the Experience Appealing. Add visual elements that make viewing and interacting with the application enjoyable [49,50,52,55,61,65,82,83].

Use Audio to Enhance the Experience. In the real world, sound plays an important role in how people interact and understand the space around them. Use spatial sound to help users feel situated, suggest spatial relationships through feedback, and create ambiences to immerse users in the virtual environment [34,36,42,44,46,48–50,52,53,61,62,66,73–76,79–82].

Make a Complete Experience. The more comprehensive the environment, the more it resonates. XR provides the tools for immersion, but it is up to the designers to build in details to maintain the feeling of being in an environment the user know is not completely real [28,35,42,49,50,60,61,79,80,82,83].

4.8   Build upon Real World Knowledge

Definition. Help users to understand how to use the application by designing the interactions, objects, and environments around existing knowledge of the real world [27,28,31,32,36,37,42,48–50,52,55,58,62–64,66,68–70,72,77,79].

Explanation. People have prebuilt mental models on how objects should behave based on prior real-world knowledge and experiences. XR designers can capitalize on these familiarities by using aspects of the real world as inspirations for designing virtual environments. This can help lessen cognitive load and educate users without being explicit.

Use Real-Life Inspiration to Create Affordances in Objects. Affordance refers to the properties of an object that informs the user how it should be interacted with and used. Build in virtual elements which reflect properties from real objects that hint at how users should use certain elements. For example, Fig. 7 shows how Weightless, a demo from Leap motion, used properties of a bowling ball to help inform users on the correct way to grasp certain objects in the application [27,31,36,37,48–50,52,55,58,63,66,68–70,72,77] (Fig. 8).

Pair Actions with Outcomes That Users Expect. Keep in mind that certain visual characteristics may affect users' expectation of how certain elements should behave. Make sure that virtual elements act in accordance with their characteristics and associated affordances [32,37,42,48,52,62,64,79].

Consider the Use of 3D (Volumetric) Representation. XR applications give designers the ability to create elements that can be explored and interacted with in 3D. This can be leveraged to better mimic and build upon real world objects [37,50,52].

Be Cautious of Simplified Interactions. Users' expectations for the detail of interactions may be higher in XR due to the increased associations with real experiences that comes with immersion. For example, a real screwdriver is a tool meant for screwing and unscrewing screws, but it has physical properties that allow it to do more than its original purpose. A virtual screwdriver may not

Fig. 7. Picture is based on leap motions' blog Interaction Sprints at Leap Motion: Exploring the Hand-Object Boundary and Designing Physical Interactions for Objects That Don't Exist. It shows the process of building real life affordances into the design of a grabbable object in their demo Weightless. (http://blog.leapmotion.com/interaction-sprint-exploring-the-hand-object-boundary/)

have additional interactions outside its intended purpose. It is important that designer build protections to deal with or inform the user of the limitations of the application [28].

4.9   Provide Feedback and Consistency

Definition. Use feedback to generalize perception of events and interactions. Additionally, feedback should be consistent such that users can build an understanding of what they can and cannot do within the application [27, 29, 34, 36, 37, 44, 45, 48–50, 52–56, 58, 63, 66, 74, 76, 79, 80, 83, 85].

Explanation. The more consistent feedback that is provided to the user, the better off they will be to make informed decisions. Due to the immersive nature of XR applications, the importance of feedback is amplified as users may have expectations on how certain aspect of the application should behave based on real-life experiences. For example, real objects have properties, like weight, hardness, size, etc., that governs how they behave. Despite having similar visual appearance, digital elements do not have guarantees that their behaviour will match that of real-world objects with similar properties. As such, it is important that developers build in consistent feedback to inform the user on how to interact with the application.

Use Feedback to Standardize Interactions States. Consider how elements in a digital environment should react to user interactions. All interactions should have distinct states that are conveyed through visual feedback. Furthermore, different states should have distinct properties that are consistent such that users can familiarize themselves and recognize them as they use the program [27, 29, 34, 36, 44, 45, 48–50, 52–55, 58, 66, 74, 76, 79, 80, 83, 85].

Use Feedback to Help Recognizes Errors and Unwanted States. Inform users of the results whenever an action is performed. For instance, the system should make it clear if an action is possible, whether an interaction was detected, if all requirements were met to perform a certain action, etc., such that users can alter their behaviour to learn from their interaction mistakes [54].

Design for Dynamic Exploration: Let the User Explore the Environment and Understand it Through Feedback. Provide users with enough information to learn how to use the application through using the application [37,48,52,55,56,58,63].

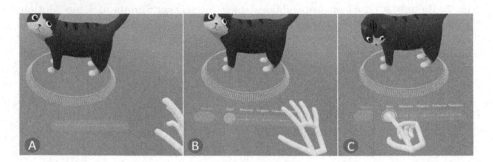

Fig. 8. Example of dynamic feedback from leap motion's Cat Explorer. A: Menu does not appear when the user's hand is far away B: Menu appears when the user brings their hands' closer C: The button light up when it is pressed.

4.10   Allow Users to Feel in Control of the Experience

Definition. The application should act and respond in a way that gives users the sense that they are in charge.

Explanation. Users are vulnerable when they are immersed in XR environments. It is important for the application to establish a feeling of trust with the user by making sure that they feel in control during the whole experience [7,11,20,23,29,37,47,48,50,52,53,76,83,85].

Don't Force Actions Without User's Permission. The application should never assume what a user wants to do. Make sure express permission is given by a user before performing actions with consequences [29,48,83,85].

Provide Exits for Users to Leave Unwanted States. Provide users with easy options to abandon certain actions or leave unwanted situations with minimal resistance and hassle from the application [7,11,20,23].

The Application Should Be "Honest". Make sure the behaviour of the system matches the user's expectations. Failure to achieve this will make the user feel like they are being deceived by the application [37,50,52].

Let Users Control Their Movements. For HMD XR applications, it is always important that the control of the virtual world camera stays with the user. This will help her or him feel in control and immersed in the experience [7,47,53,76].

4.11 Allow for Trial and Error

Definition. As much as possible, allow actions to be reversible and set up protections around potential mistakes made by users. This will help relieve user's anxiety and promote exploration of the application [4,11,20,23].

Explanation. XR designers have more opportunities to provide users with interactions that have a bigger impact on the experience. However, more control also equates to a larger possibility for mistakes. Furthermore, previous error tolerance techniques, such as dedicated back buttons or keyboard shortcuts, are not always meaningful in XR applications. It is important that designer builds in protections for when users' inevitably make errors.

Permit Easy Reversal of Actions. Provide users with clear options to deal with actions that they may want to undo such that can freely explore the application without worries [4,11,20,23].

5 Discussion

In this section, we overview several points of discussions that were identified through the creation of our UX guidelines.

Emphasis on VR Devices and Experiences. During our analysis of the literature, it was noticed that most of the resources found were based around VR experiences. This may be due to the differences in accessibility among XR devices. VR headsets, such as the HTC Vive, Oculus Rift, and the Window Mixed reality suite are cheaper on average and provide a larger range of options when compared to AR and MR devices. At the time of collecting the resources, many AR or MR manufactures, such as the Microsoft HoloLens and Magic Leap, only had developers/creators or business version of their devices available to the public. As such, the community around VR is larger and has had more time to explore the technology, which was reflected in the content of our resources. This trend suggests that there is an opportunity for further research around UX design practices specifically in the context of AR and MR.

Emphasis on Addressing Comfort. Our guidelines show that ideas around comfort were a common theme in previous works. In addition to the high occurrence, these guidelines were often more defined and consistent throughout the various resources. For example, [27,40,41,53,75,76,84] all explicitly discussed zones of comfort for XR based on human ergonomics. All these sources shared similarities concepts, and a few referenced each other. This pattern extends to the other sub guidelines under UX guideline 3 –Prioritize user's comfort–. This trend was not as prominent in other guidelines which suggest that comfort has been a common problem that designers faced when building applications for HMD XR devices. Further exploring user comfort within XR application may be a valuable area for future research to be conducted.

Few Developed XR Examples. While exploring the resources, we found relatively few XR examples that were given to support the concepts being conveyed. Instead, the literature would often borrow from other domains to further explain a concept. For example, [37] discusses how space can be used to amplify mental capabilities for spatial applications. Instead of showing an example in XR, the author references how chefs, carpenters and other experts constantly rearrange items to easily track the state of different tasks or to better notice properties signalling what to do next. From the lack of XR examples, it becomes apparent that there is a need for further work around applying these concepts in actual applications.

Opportunity for Evaluation, Validation and Empirical research. By opening up our search for resources to communities outside of academic sources, we drew upon ideas and concepts that were not academically validated. Additionally, as seen in Sect. 2, related academic literature showed limited work around validation and often express the need for further research in this area. This suggests that there are lots of opportunities for these concepts to be further explored to understand better if and how these ideas can help in the development of XR applications.

6   Limitations

While our work focused on creating a reference for understanding what others have tried and discovered, we acknowledge that our research only scratches the surfaces for what is needed to fully understand how to design XR applications. One of our primary limits is the lack of evaluation. As mentioned in the previous section, a majority of the resources that were used were not validated. Additionally, our research did not include studies to evaluate our UX guidelines. Future research building on our findings is required to further explore the concepts within our guidelines and understand their effectiveness for designers and developers.

7   Conclusion

Recent developments in XR has provided hardware that allows users to experience spatial environments and interactions. While initial searches for academic resources around XR design guidelines yielded limited results, a wealth of information can be found from different communities that provide insights into this topic. To further inform the design of XR applications, we conducted an analysis of 68 different resources to derive eleven UX design guidelines for HMD devices from various communities. We presented our findings by providing each guideline with a name, definition, and explanation with additional sub guidelines. Ultimately, our guidelines are not meant to provide absolute rules for designers to follow but serve as a reference to build off from and adapt based on their intended medium and situation. With our work, we aimed at providing a resource for understanding what others have tried and discovered such that future research can challenge, build off, and extend the ideas presented in this paper.

Acknowledgements. Grant #2017/23684-3, São Paulo Research Foundation (FAPESP), and NSERC Discovery Grant.

References

1. Wheeler Atkinson, B.F., Bennett, T.O., Bahr, G.S., Walwanis Nelson, M.M.: Development of a multiple heuristics evaluation table (MHET) to support software development and usability analysis. In: Stephanidis, C. (ed.) UAHCI 2007. LNCS, vol. 4554, pp. 563–572. Springer, Heidelberg (2007). https://doi.org/10.1007/978-3-540-73279-2_63
2. Bloksa, J.: Design guidelines for user interface for augmented reality. Master's thesis, Masaryk University - Faculty of Informatics (2017)
3. Braun, V., Clarke, V.: Using thematic analysis in psychology. Qual. Res. Psychol. **3**(2), 77–101 (2006)
4. Dünnser, A., Grasset, R., Seichter, H., Billinghurst, M.: Applying HCI principles to AR systems design, January 2007
5. Endsley, T.C., Sprehn, K.A., Brill, R.M., Ryan, K.J., Vincent, E.C., Martin, J.M.: Augmented reality design heuristics: designing for dynamicinteractions. Proc. Hum. Factors Ergon. Soc. Ann. Meet. **61**(1), 2100–2104 (2017). https://doi.org/10.1177/1541931213602007
6. Franklin, F., Breyer, F., Kelner, J.: Usability heuristics for collaborative augmented reality remote systems. In: 2014 XVI Symposium on Virtual and Augmented Reality, pp. 53–62, May 2014. https://doi.org/10.1109/SVR.2014.31
7. Fröjdman, S.: User experience guidelines for design of virtual reality graphical user interfaces (2016)
8. Furmanski, C., Azuma, R., Daily, M.: Augmented-reality visualizations guided by cognition: perceptual heuristics for combining visible and obscured information. In: Proceedings of the International Symposium on Mixed and Augmented Reality, pp. 215–320, October 2002. https://doi.org/10.1109/ISMAR.2002.1115091
9. Gong, J., Tarasewich, P.: Guidelines for handheld mobile device interface design, January 2004
10. Hawkins, J.M.: Thematic analysis. The SAGE encyclopedia of communication research methods, October 2018. https://doi.org/10.4135/9781483381411,http://methods.sagepub.com/reference/the-sage-encyclopedia-of-communication-research-methods
11. ISO: Ergonomie der mensch-system-interaktion - teil 110: Grundstze der dialoggestaltung (ISO 9241–110:2006); deutschefassung en iso 9241–110:2006, September 2008

12. Kalalahti, J.: Developing usability evaluation heuristics for augmented reality applications. Master's thesis, Lappeenranta University of Technology (2015)
13. Kitchenham, B., Charters, S.: Guidelines for performing systematic literature reviews in software engineering. Technical report EBSE 2007–001, Keele University and Durham University Joint Report (2007)
14. Ko, S.M., Chang, W.S., Ji, Y.G.: Usability principles for augmented reality applications in a smartphone environment. Int. J. Hum. Comput. Interact. **29**(8), 501–515 (2013). https://doi.org/10.1080/10447318.2012.722466
15. Kourouthanassis, P.E., Boletsis, C., Lekakos, G.: Demystifying the design of mobile augmented reality applications. Multimedia Tools Appl. **74**(3), 1045–1066 (2015). https://doi.org/10.1007/s11042-013-1710-7
16. Kuparinen, L., Silvennoinen, J., Isomäki, H.: Introducing usability heuristics for mobile map applications, August 2013
17. Milgram, P., Takemura, H., Utsumi, A., Kishino, F.: Augmented reality: a class of displays on the reality-virtuality continuum. In: Telemanipulator and Telepresence Technologies, vol. 2351, pp. 282–293. International Society for Optics and Photonics (1995)
18. Nielsen, J.: Usability Engineering. Academic Press, Cambridge (1993)
19. Nielsen, J.: Enhancing the explanatory power of usability heuristics. In: Proceedings of the SIGCHI Conference on Human Factors in Computing Systems, CHI 1994, pp. 152–158. ACM, New York (1994). https://doi.org/10.1145/191666.191729
20. Nielsen, J., Molich, R.: Heuristic evaluation of user interfaces. In: Proceedings of the SIGCHI Conference on Human Factors in Computing Systems, CHI 1990, pp. 249–256. ACM, New York (1990). https://doi.org/10.1145/97243.97281
21. Quiñones, D., Rusu, C., Rusu, V.: A methodology to develop usability/user experience heuristics. Comput. Stand. Interfaces **59**, 109–129 (2018). https://doi.org/10.1016/j.csi.2018.03.002. http://www.sciencedirect.com/science/article/pii/S09205 48917303860
22. Rusu, C., Roncagliolo, S., Rusu, V., Collazos, C.A.: A methodology to establish usability heuristics. In: ACHI 2011: The Fourth International Conference on Advances in Computer-Human Interactions (2011)
23. Shneiderman, B.: Designing the User Interface: Strategies for Effective Human-Computer Interaction, 3rd edn. Addison-Wesley Longman Publishing Co., Inc., Boston (1997)
24. de Souza e Silva, A., Sukto, D.M.: Digital Cityscapes: Merging Digital an Urban Playspaces. Peter Lang Publishing, Bern (2009)
25. Van Krevelen, R., Poelman, R.: A survey of augmented reality technologies, applications and limitations. Int. J. Virtual Reality **9**, 1 (2010). ISSN 1081-1451
26. Wohlin, C.: Guidelines for snowballing in systematic literature studies and a replication in software engineering. In: Proceedings of the 18th International Conference on Evaluation and Assessment in Software Engineering, EASE 2014, pp. 38:1–38:10. ACM, New York (2014). https://doi.org/10.1145/2601248.2601268

Web Resources

27. Alger, M.: VR interface design pre-visualisation methods. https://www.youtube.com/watch?v=id86HeV-Vb8&t=861s

28. The Art & Bussiness of Making Games: Making great VR: six lessons learned from I expect you to die. http://www.gamasutra.com/blogs/JesseSchell/20150626/247113/

29. Coding Artist: Learn react VR (Chapter 7—UI/UX principles for VR design). https://medium.com/coding-artist/learn-react-vr-chapter-7-ui-ux-principles-for-vr-design-9202ed2ac56d

30. Virtual Reality (VR)/Augmented Reality Spatial : Understanding spatial cognition makes VR better. https://medium.com/shopify-vr/understanding-spatial-cognition-makes-vr-better-bd29033dd980

31. Backchannel: Immersive design: Learning to let go of the screen. https://medium.com/backchannel/immersive-design-76499204d5f6

32. Beloola: 5 lessons I learned from designing the VRUI of Beloola. https://medium.com/beloola-all-our-news-updates/5-lessons-i-learned-from-designing-the-vrui-of-beloola-754f16062c0b

33. Robot Invader Blog: Comfortable VR movement in dead secret. http://robotinvader.com/blog/?p=493

34. Creative Bloq: The UX of VR. http://www.creativebloq.com/ux/the-user-experience-of-virtual-reality-31619635

35. Ching, T.C.: The concept of presence in virtual reality. https://medium.com/@choongchingteo/the-concept-of-presence-in-virtual-reality-6d4332dc1a9c

36. Collective UX: Design practices in virtual reality. https://medium.com/@jonathanravasz/design-practices-in-virtual-reality-f900f5935826

37. Collective UX: A room for understanding - the dawn of a new workspace. https://uxdesign.cc/a-room-for-understanding-593ef6f8c76e

38. Fast Company: Google's 3 rules for designing virtual reality. https://www.fastcodesign.com/3060315/googles-3-rules-for-designing-virtual-reality

39. Cronin, B.: Speculations on neuro-motivated design for VR - skeuomorphic vs flat is the wrong question: we need a new way forward. https://medium.com/@beaucronin/speculations-on-neuro-motivated-design-for-vr-3f26685c5c40

40. Google Design: From product design to virtual reality - personal experience and intro to VR. https://medium.com/google-design/from-product-design-to-virtual-reality-be46fa793e9b

41. Kickpush Design: Beyond virtual reality - first steps into the unknown. https://medium.com/kickpush-design/beyond-reality-first-steps-into-the-unknown-cbb19f039e51

42. Doolwind: Virtual reality development tips. http://www.doolwind.com/blog/virtual-reality-development-tips/

43. Virtual Machine Experiments: The storyteller's guide to the virtual reality audience. https://medium.com/stanford-d-school/the-storyteller-s-guide-to-the-virtual-reality-audience-19e92da57497

44. Google: Designing for Google cardboard. https://www.google.com/design/spec-vr/designing-for-google-cardboard/

45. Startup Grind: 4 things I learned designing user interfaces for VR at Disney. https://medium.com/startup-grind/4-things-i-learned-designing-user-interfaces-for-vr-cc08cac9e7ec

46. Block Interval: The fundamentals of user experience in virtual reality. http://www.blockinterval.com/project-updates/2015/10/15/user-experience-in-virtual-reality

47. Block Interval: Ten do's and don'ts to improve comfort in VR. http://www.blockinterval.com/project-updates/2015/10/16/ten-ways-to-improve-comfort-in-vr

48. Jaime, S.: UX + VR: 14 guidelines for creating great first experiences. https://medium.com/@oneStaci/https-medium-com-ux-vr-18-guidelines-51ef667c2c49
49. Jerald, J.: The VR Book: Human-Centered Design for Virtual Reality. Association for Computing Machinery and Morgan, Claypool (2016)
50. Leap Motion: Magic leap design guidelines. https://creator.magicleap.com/learn/guides/design-spatial-computing
51. Mahmood, B.: A quick guide to designing for augmented reality on mobile (part 2). https://medium.com/@goatsandbacon/a-quick-guide-to-designing-for-augmented-reality-on-mobile-part-2-fb76fe87dd41
52. Meta: Spatial interface design - meta augmented reality. https://devcenter.metavision.com/spatial-interface-design/
53. Microsoft: Design for mixed reality - microsoft docs. https://docs.microsoft.com/en-us/windows/mixed-reality/design
54. Leap Motion: Leap motion blog - 6 principles of leap motion interaction design. http://blog.leapmotion.com/6-principles-of-interaction-design/
55. Leap Motion: Leap motion blog - design sprints at leap motion: a playground of 3D user interfaces. http://blog.leapmotion.com/design-playground-3d-user-interfaces/
56. Leap Motion: Leap motion blog - designing cat explorer. http://blog.leapmotion.com/designing-cat-explorer/
57. Leap Motion: Leap motion blog - explorations: ergonomics and user safety. http://blog.leapmotion.com/ergonomics-vr-design/
58. Leap Motion: Leap motion blog - explorations: object interaction design. http://blog.leapmotion.com/designing-physical-interactions-for-objects-that-dont-exist/
59. Leap Motion: Leap motion blog - explorations: space and perspective. http://blog.leapmotion.com/space-and-perspective/
60. Leap Motion: Leap motion blog - explorations: storytelling and narrative. http://blog.leapmotion.com/art-storytelling-narrative-vr/
61. Leap Motion: Leap motion blog - from idea to demo: your VR development roadmap. https://medium.com/@LeapMotion/from-idea-to-demo-2f8f900afe8
62. Leap Motion: leap motion blog - how sound design can add texture to a virtual world. http://blog.leapmotion.com/explorations-vr-sound-design/
63. Leap Motion: Leap motion blog - interaction sprints at leap motion: exploring the hand-object boundary. http://blog.leapmotion.com/interaction-sprint-exploring-the-hand-object-boundary/
64. Leap Motion: Leap motion blog - reaching into 3D data, exploring cad designs, virtual meetings, and more. http://blog.leapmotion.com/reaching-3d-data-exploring-cad-designs-virtual-meetings/
65. Leap Motion: Leap motion blog - the design process behind itadakimasu!. http://blog.leapmotion.com/design-process-behind-itadakimasu/
66. Leap Motion: Leap motion blog - VR design guide. http://blog.leapmotion.com/vr-design-guide/
67. Leap Motion: Leap motion blog - VR interface design and the future of hybrid reality. http://blog.leapmotion.com/vr-interface-design-future-hybrid-reality/
68. Leap Motion: Leap motion blog - weightless remastered: building with the interaction engine. http://blog.leapmotion.com/weightless-remastered-building-interaction-engine/
69. Leap Motion: Leap motion blog - what do VR interfaces and teapots have in common?. http://blog.leapmotion.com/vr-interfaces-teapots-common/#more-5897

70. Leap Motion: Leap motion blog - what makes a spoon a spoon? Form and function in VR industrial design. http://blog.leapmotion.com/what-makes-a-spoon-a-spoon-form-and-function-in-vr-industrial-design/

71. Leap Motion: Leap motion blog - what would a truly 3D operating system look like?. http://blog.leapmotion.com/truly-3d-operating-system-look-like/

72. Leap Motion: Leap motion blog - world design: setting the stage. http://blog.leapmotion.com/world-design-setting-stage/

73. Leap Motion: New unity module for user interface input. http://blog.leapmotion.com/ui-input-module/

74. UXNess: UX & virtual reality - designing for interfaces without screens. http://www.uxness.in/2015/08/ux-virtual-reality.html

75. Oculus: VR best practices. https://developer.oculus.com/design/latest/concepts/book-bp/

76. Virtual Reality Pop: Practical VR: a design cheat sheet. https://medium.com/@hitsmachines/practical-vr-ce80427e8e9d

77. Virtual Reality Pop: Reducing cognitive load in VR - 6 ways to improve your VR UX. https://medium.com/@namegoeshere/reducing-cognitive-load-in-vr-d922ef8c6876

78. Punchcut: Design insights for virtual reality UX. https://medium.com/@Punchcut/design-insights-for-virtual-reality-ux-7ae41a0c5a1a

79. Rosenthal, L.: Virtual is reality again : interface vs interference design 2014 - VR-Facebook Oculus rift/3D design primer version 4.0 by cube3. https://medium.com/@LarryRosenthal/virtual-is-reality-again-interface-vs-interference-design-2014-6361e6f45b8c

80. Telepathy: You're the center of the universe: a UX guide to designing virtual reality experiences. http://www.dtelepathy.com/blog/philosophy/ux-guide-designing-virtual-reality-experiences

81. Unboring: Case study: deep linking - how to turn a 6 slides keynote into a WebVR experience. http://unboring.net/cases/deepLinking.html

82. USTWO: Designing for virtual reality. https://ustwo.com/blog/designing-for-virtual-reality-google-cardboard/

83. UXVR: The user experience of virtual reality - human-centered design principles for VR. https://medium.com/uxxr/the-user-experience-of-virtual-reality-c464762deb8e

84. VRUX: Lean best practices in designing UX for VR. https://lensreality.com/category/vrux/

85. West, T.: UX pointers for VR design. https://medium.com/@timoni/ux-pointers-for-vr-design-dd52b718e19

86. YVR: Don't teleport: Fly! - how to do it in VR without motion sickness. https://medium.com/yvr/dont-teleport-fly-b175a5c8fd73#.nx9b0gukm

Virtual and Augmented Reality II

Am I Moving Along a Curve? A Study on Bicycle Traveling-In-Place Techniques in Virtual Environments

Tanh Quang Tran[1,2]($\boxtimes$), Holger Regenbrecht[2], and Minh-Triet Tran[1]

[1] University of Science, VNUHCM, Ho Chi Minh City, Vietnam
tqtanh@selab.hcmus.edu.vn, tmtriet@fit.hcmus.edu.vn
[2] University of Otago, Dunedin, New Zealand
tanh.tran@postgrad.otago.ac.nz, holger.regenbrecht@otago.ac.nz

Abstract. There are many techniques for locomotion and navigation that can support the exploration of large virtual environments in a limited physical area. Previous studies focused on measuring curvature gains and bending gains applied to the walking direction in the real world. However, the effects of different moving techniques and their relationship with shapes and patterns of virtually moving paths have not been studied extensively before. In this study, we present our experimental results on how users perceive two different traveling-in-place techniques with different bending gains of moving paths using a hybrid electric bike simulator. Moreover, the impact of different factors including road textures, road widths, and road curve directions and their relationships with the techniques are investigated. Generally, users could travel along a curve without noticing with a point of subjective equality (PSE) at bending angle $\beta = 1.42°$, and a just-noticeable difference (JND) of $0.75°$ for a movement at around $20\,\text{km/h}$ during $5\,\text{s}$. In addition, movement technique, curve direction, and future travel path significantly affected how they perceived the curvature of their travel path.

Keywords: Curve perception · Locomotion · Virtual reality · Traveling-in-place · Human perception · Redirected walking

1 Introduction

Virtual reality (VR) is becoming more and more popular. It has been applied in many different fields and circumstances from research communities to users' daily activities. Modern VR systems can be operated in immersive desktop setups but also allow for natural walking movements within limited spaces of a couple of meters. However, if the virtual space is larger than the physical space, locomotion

Electronic supplementary material The online version of this chapter (https://doi.org/10.1007/978-3-030-29390-1_19) contains supplementary material, which is available to authorized users.

and traveling techniques have to be introduced. How to travel in large virtual environments is still a challenging task and subject to a lot of research.

Locomotion techniques can be classified into three categories: walking-in-place [27], natural walking (eg. redirected walking [20]), and using different virtual locomotion metaphors or mechanical systems (eg. teleportation [1] and treadmills [4]). In order to reorient users in virtual environments, different reorientation techniques were developed. One of the techniques is to use an external device, eg. a joystick while on a treadmill. However, such techniques are not very natural, can cause simulation sickness, and might reduce the users' sense of presence.

Actual 1:1 walking interfaces stimulate proprioceptive and vestibular cues more appropriately than other locomotion interfaces in virtual environments [19]. Unfortunately, they can't always be applied. If the real space is very small, walking-in-place and virtual locomotion metaphors are the most effective techniques. For very large spaces, users can travel at a higher speed with vehicle simulators. Many of those simulators have limited degrees of freedom when compared to their real-world counterparts. E.g., popular bike interfaces often lack the actual ability to turn (or lean) to change direction, a long enough straight path has to be provided for users to travel.

In this study, we focus on figuring out how to develop a locomotion interface for large virtual environments supporting two traveling-in-place techniques infinitely. In particular, we investigate to what extent travel path bends with different rotation gains are considered as curved in virtual environments. In addition, we compare the difference in perceiving the applied gains between *"pedaling"* and *"throttling"* techniques. The effects of road materials, road width, and road directions on perceiving the amount of degrees by which travel paths are bent, called *"curved-ness"* level, were also examined. Moreover, we explore how participants perceive the environment, make decisions, experience simulation sickness and a sense of presence.

This paper is structured as follows. Section 2 presents related work, Sect. 3 describes our experiment design and procedure. Section 4 present the experimental result. We discuss and conclude our study in Sect. 5.

2   Related Work

Users can change their position and orientation in virtual environments, while they are naturally walking and reorienting in the real world. However, the virtual environment is often larger in its extent or scaled compared to the users' physical area. There are locomotion techniques, called redirected walking, which were developed to address this problem. These techniques manipulate users' movement in the virtual world by relocating and reorienting continuous or discretely with subtle or obvious changes in the virtual environment [30]. This can lead users to perceive to be moving on a straight path, while their actual travel path in the real world is curved or bent.

To reorient users, different visual manipulation techniques (eg. rotation gains [20,28]) and other sensory effects [18] are applied. There are two different notions of curvature gains or rotations gains. The first notion is represented by radii, which is used to indicate the physical space required for a specific redirected walking technique. However, it was argued that radii do not scale in a linear way with how the manipulation is applied and should not be used to compare different gains [24]. On the other hand, the second notion refers to the amount of rotation angles applied on a particular walking distance and is usually presented in units of °/m; rotation gains measured as angle per meter can be converted to individual radii [24]. In different conditions, research groups found different thresholds of undetectable bending gains. Steinicke et al. [29] found a imperceptible bending gain could be up to 2.6 °/m. 4.9 °/m and 15.4 °/m have been found in studies by Grechkin et al. [7] and Langbehn et al. [10] respectively. In a revisited study, Rietzler et al. [24] figured out that users can virtually go straight ahead boundlessly in a 6 m × 6 m physical area. In addition, their real travel paths can be bent up to 20 °/m. In this study, we present rotation gains in both of these notions.

There are also studies investigating detection thresholds and effects of additional sensory feedback and specific tasks. Bruder et al. [3] studied redirected walking on cognitive tasks, while Matsumoto et al. [11] investigated the effects of negative haptic cues supporting users to walk infinitely and turn freely. Paludan et al. [17] found that the number of objects in the virtual environment scene did not perceptibly affect users on detecting rotation gains. In addition, there are studies examining rotation gains perception with the effect of audiovisual feedback by Nilsson et al. [15] and redirected driving with a wheelchair by Bruder et al. [2]. There is a study by Kim et al. on redirected jump in a micro gravity virtual environment with a cable-driven system [9]. They showed that users could leap up to virtual stairs in the virtual environment while they jumped on a flat floor in the their real world. To sum up, there are available reviews on redirected walking and natural walking in virtual environments [13,16]; however, traveling-in-place techniques have not been surveyed yet.

For walking-in-place techniques, users can move in the virtual environments by mimicking the movements of their body in the real world, while they do not change their physical position [5,27,35]. Besides these techniques, the movement of users is controlled or manipulated by mechanical systems or using external input devices, eg. joystick or wand, while their position in the real world is not actively changed. In order to reorient, users can directly rotate their physical body or head and their orientation in the real world is recorded and mapped to their virtual orientation [27,31,34]. In addition, their orientation can be applied with different rotation gains [21]. However, users can not always reorient their direction, especially when walking on a treadmill or performing locomotion in a one-way direction. Terziman et al. [32] revisited the walking-in-place procedure and present a novel technique, called "Shake-Your-Head". This technique can stimulate different locomotion postures which include forwarding, jumping and crawling, an turning dependent on the rotation of the head. Williams et al. [36] presented a walking-in-place technique using a Wii balance board. In this technique, data from an orientation sensor is used to orient users' direction in virtual environments. There were two different gesture inputs, namely wiping and tapping, for walking-in-place locomotion by Nilsson et al. [14]. Interactive portals which are placed by making ray-casting selections with a pointing device are used to reorient users in the virtual world [6]. In addition, they found that users can reach to their desirable position with only one reorientation. There are efforts on developing new walking-in-places walking-in-place techniques, mechanical supported locomotion, and walking metaphors to increase performance. However, it is reported that locomotion techniques which are natural and include users' physical manipulation induce higher sense of presence, reduce simulation sickness, and increase performance while reducing manipulation time [23,30,34].

Although, there is a wide extensive research effort on locomotion techniques in virtual environments. We could not find any study of bending detection on users moving on a curved path in virtual environments while they are traveling in a stationary position with a fixed straight ahead direction in the real world. In addition, the effects of additional factors such as textures and sizes of travel paths have not been studied before. In this study, we address these issues.

3   Experiment

3.1   Experiment Setup

We conducted an experiment in a laboratory environment using a hybrid bike simulator (Fig. 1). The simulator could be operated in both traveling-in-place techniques supported by a real electric bike. A 36V/350W power supply adapter was used to power the bike when participants performed *the "throttling" movement technique*. The movement speed of the simulator was calculated and recorded by a speedometer. This included a Hall sensor, and a magnet on the back flywheel and an Arduino Nano board. The simulator provided airflow by a fan attached at 90 cm from the head of the bike. The fan was powered by a 12 V/150 W motor with three slender plastic blades. The generated airflow could be perceived from participants' hip to their head and arms. In our experiment, the speed of airflow was stimulated and equal to the movement speed of the bike through a Unity3D and an Arduino Uno board.

Users see the virtual environment through a Dell Visor head-mounted display (HMD). This HMD supports inside-out tracking and comprises two 1440 × 1440 pixels resolution liquid crystal displays. The headset had a refresh rate at 90 Hz and can provide 105° field of view.

3.2   Experiment Design

In this study, we used the method of constant stimuli in Yes-No tasks. The experiment is mainly designed based on two traveling-in-place techniques and rotation gains. A multi-factorial 2 × 5 × 2 × 2 × 2 design was applied with two techniques for locomotion in virtual environments, five rotation gains, two curve directions, two road materials, and two road widths (independent variables).

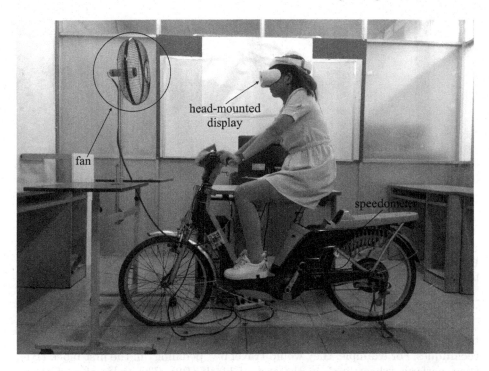

Fig. 1. Experiment Setup. Our experiment was conducted with a bike simulator. The simulator comprises of an electric bike with a head mounted display, a fan, and a speedometer.

- The *traveling-in-place technique* (movement technique) was how people traveled in the virtual environments when they did not change their position in the real world. In this study, we investigated two different techniques, namely *"pedaling"* and *"throttling"* as in a study of Tran et. al. [33]. For *"pedaling"*, users have to directly power their movement by cycling using their feet. Or, they can control their movement speed by hand twisting the throttle grip with the *"throttling"* technique. The speed of these movement techniques was higher than walking speed, so we named them traveling-in-place techniques.
- The *rotation gain* (β) was the level at which the moving path was curved. After pilot tests, there were five different gains chosen. We found 0.25, 0.5, 1, 1.75, and 2.5°, see Fig. 2. The gains were applied to the travel path in for five seconds with a movement speed 20 km/h and a path of 27.78 m in length.
- The *curve direction* was the direction towards which the travel path was curved: *"left"* or *"right"*.
- The *road material* was the pattern of the travel path. There were two different road appearances in our experiment. Either a paved road with a marked line (*"paved"*) or a dirt road without any markings (*"dirt"*).
- The *road width* was the horizontal size of the path. We considered two different road widths in our experiment: 2 m (*"small"*) and 4 m (*"large"*).

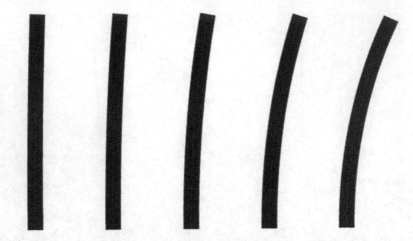

Fig. 2. Five different rotation gains applied to the travel path in our experiment. From left to right: β = 0.25, 0.5, 1, 1.75, and 2.5°, respectively.

The entire experiment was divided by the traveling-in-place techniques into two different blocks. For each block, participants would perform one of the two techniques. For example, they would travel by "pedaling" in the first block (B1), then perform "throttling" in the second block (B2). The order of performing traveling-in-place techniques was counter-balanced, whereas the representation order of rotation gain, curve direction, road material, and road width was randomized.

All participants did wear the aforementioned HMD while riding the bike and performing the experiment trial. They were requested to maintain their movement speed at around 20 km/h during trials. There were three main steps for each experiment trial. In the first step, each participant initially experienced a ride on a straight path for five seconds, then, traveled on a path which was curved by the rotation gains in the next step. In the final step, the participant was required to respond to the question: *"Did you perceive the recent path as curved?"*. If the participant perceived that they had recently traveled on a curved path, a "Yes" response was saved, otherwise, a "No" response was recorded. The travel path for this step (*"after trial path"*) could be *"straight"* or *"curved"* as the same rotation gain as the path in the second step. For this reason, the travel path in the last step was considered as an additional independent variable. After this step, a new trial started and the participant was requested to perform the same procedure. An illustration summarizing the travel paths for each experimental trial is shown in Fig. 3. In addition to the participants' responses, their real velocity during the experiment was recorded. The response and real velocity were examined as dependent variables in our experiment.

Participants performed forty ($5 \times 2 \times 2 \times 2$) combinations of 5 rotation gains, 2 curve directions, 2 road materials, and 2 road widths for each experiment block. For each combination, they were asked to decide each time for each type

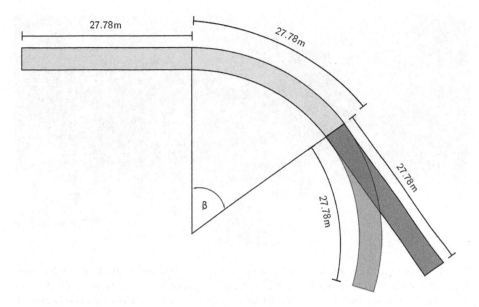

Fig. 3. Illustration of travel paths for the experiment trial. For each trial, participants would move on a 27.78 m straight path or be traveling at 20 km/h for 5 s, before riding on a 27.78 m curved path. After experiencing the bending path, they have another 5 s to travel at 20 km/h on either a curved or bent path.

after trial path if the path was perceived as curved. In total, each participant accomplished 80 (40 × 2) trials and responses for each block.

3.3   Participants and Experiment Procedure

There were thirty-two university students (22 male, 8 female, and 2 would not say) taking part in our experiment. They were from 18 to 22 year-old (M = 20.26, SD = 1.55). Seventeen participants frequently rode bikes, whereas twenty-eight often travel by motorcycles, electric bikes, scooters, or mopeds. Twenty-two volunteers reported that they had tried a head-mounted display and eight of them had experienced a ride in virtual environments. All participants had normal or corrected-to-normal vision and no participants reported any issue with their vestibular system. All volunteers were compensated for their participation.

When a participant arrived,they were randomly assigned to one of two groups. In the first group, participants performed block B1 before block B2. Otherwise, participants in the second group completed block B2 first, then block B1. After the assignment, they were presented with a document about experiment details and requirements. They were requested to carefully read the document and make their decision on whether to take part in our experiment. After agreement, they were asked to sign a consent form and were given a brief introduction document. The consent form included their agreements and responsibilities, while the introduction form was used to ascertain their experience with virtual

Fig. 4. Representation of our experiment virtual environment. In this virtual environment, users could see their traveling path, different types of trees, and the blue sky with clouds. In addition, their virtual avatar and a virtual bike corresponding to their current movement technique are also shown. However, their visible distance is not far in order to preventing them from guessing based on the shape of the path in the distance.

reality and real-world transport. They, then, were trained with two different traveling-in-place techniques, while encountering different road materials and widths. During the training session, they were instructed to get familiar with the virtual environment and to maintain their moving speed at around 20 km/h. After training, they took a break for 5 min before performing the experimental blocks.

For each experiment block, they were asked to perform 80 trials. Each trial had three different steps. Firstly, they had 5 s to experience locomotion on a straight road. They, then, moved on a curved path. This path was bent with one of the rotation gains. At the final step, they were traveling on a straight or curved path which was the same as in the previous step while responding to answer the question: "Did you perceive the recent path as curved?" (Fig. 5). If they agreed, they were instructed to select the virtual "YES" button by moving a small cursor in their view to that button and press a green button next to the left hand grip of the bike. Otherwise, they were asked to select "NO". It took about 20 min to perform one block. After finishing a block, they had a 5 min break and answered a collection of three questionnaires. These questionnaires included a Simulator Sickness Questionnaire (SSQ) [8], the Igroup Presence Questionnaire (IPQ) [22,25], and a feedback questionnaire in order to investigate how participants perceived the experiment and the traveled path as curved. The total time

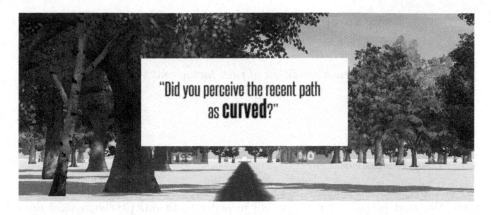

Fig. 5. Users had to make their decision after each experimental trial.

for our experiment was about 70 min. In summary, our experiment procedure is presented in Table 1.

Table 1. Experiment procedure.

Step	Time (min)
Instruction and informed consent	10
Training	5
Break	5
Experiment with the 1st block	20
Questionnaire and Break	5
Experiment with the 2nd block	20
Questionnaire	5

3.4 Hypotheses

For the experiment design, we would like to figure out detection thresholds of rotation gain at which users travel on curved paths, but perceiving as straight. That is to answer the question:

"To what extent are users unaware of a bend while traveling on a curved path?"

In addition, the contributions of movement techniques, road materials, road widths, road directions are also addressed. For these factors, we want to identify the difference between each condition of each factor and their impact on users' perception leading to two research questions:

"To what extent does each factor affect users' perception?"

and

"To what extent does each condition of each factor contribute to the perception of bends?".

4 Results

4.1 User Responses

All of participants' responses were analysed using MathWorks MATLAB and SAS. We used psignifit 4 toolbox [26] in order to fit our psychophysical data with a logistic function. All parameters for the fitting process were set free, while asymptotes were additionally assumed to be equal. The point of subjective equality (*PSE*) is the point participants randomly choose between "Yes" and "No" response and is set at 50% proportion of "Yes" responses (or threshold level at 0.5). In addition, the just-noticeable difference (*JND*) is the difference range of stimuli for participants to be detectable. The JND was calculated by half of the distance between threshold levels 0.75 and 0.25. Overall, we found *PSE* = 1.42 and *JND* = 0.75 with the fitted psychometric curve for the whole experiment presented in Fig. 6.

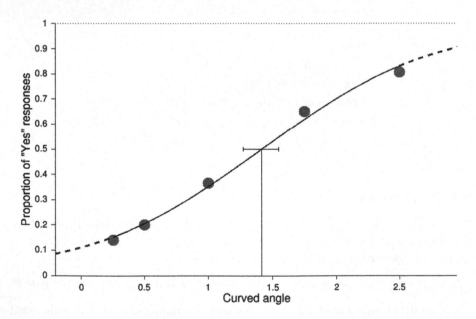

Fig. 6. The psychometric function fitted for the whole experiment psychophysical data with the point of subjective equality (PSE) indicated by the vertical central line with confidence intervals. Overall, the PSE is biased to 1.42.

The PSEs and JNDs for each condition of the independent variables are shown in Table 2. For the movement techniques, users could not discriminate whether the travel path was straight or curved when they traveled at around 20 km/h on 1.49°. In addition, the range of detectable stimuli for this technique is 0.82. On the other hand, the PSE and JND for "throttling" is biased to 1.35 and 0.5 respectively. The psychometric curves fitted for each movement technique is showed in Fig. 7.

Moreover, Fig. 8 presents the sigmoid functions fitted for the curve direction. The users could perceive the straight and curved path as identical when the bent angles are 1.52° and 1.26° for "left" and "right" respectively. The JNDs are 0.76 and 0.52 for these directions in the same order. In addition, if the rotation gains are set to 1.52° for *"dirt"* and 1.33° for *"paved"* road material, the participants would perceive a curved path as straight. The ranges of noticeable stimuli for these road materials are 0.48 and 0.65, respectively. The psychometric functions fitted for both *"dirt"* and *"paved"* are showed in Fig. 9.

The sigmoid functions fitted for the road width and after trial road variables are illustrated in Figs. 10 and 11 respectively. For the road width factor, the subjects cannot distinguish between the bent path with 1.35° and 1.49° and the straight path for *"small"* and *"large"* condition, respectively. Their discernible dimensions of stimuli are 0.7 and 0.74 For the after trial road, *"curved"* has the value of PSE at 1.25, whereas that of *"straight"* is at 1.55. The values of detectable stimuli ranges for these conditions are 0.47 and 0.79 respectively.

Table 2. PSE and JND for each condition of independent variables.

Factor	Condition	PSE	JND
Movement technique	Pedaling	1.46	0.82
	Throttling	1.35	0.5
Direction	Left	1.52	0.76
	Right	1.29	0.52
Road material	Dirt	1.52	0.48
	Paved	1.33	0.65
Road width	Small	1.35	0.7
	Large	1.49	0.74
After trial road	Curved	1.25	0.47
	Straight	1.55	0.79

In addition, PSEs and JNDs of each subject for each independent variables and the interactions between movement technique and the other independent variables were estimated. We conducted ANOVA analyses in order to find significant effects of the independent variables and their interactions.

The analysis of one-way interaction showed that there were significant effects of movement technique, curve direction, and road after trial ($p < .05$). Tukey

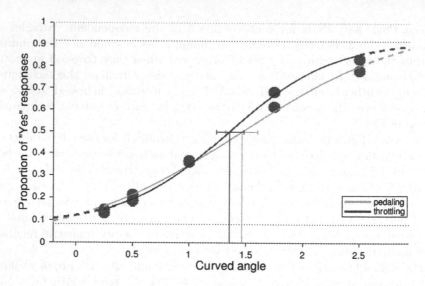

Fig. 7. The psychometric functions fitted for each condition of movement technique and the vertical central lines indicate their PSEs with confidence intervals. Overall, the PSEs are biased to 1.46 for "pedaling" and 1.35 for "throttling".

post-hoc tests were conducted for these variables. For movement technique, *"throttling"* had significantly higher PSE than *"pedaling"*. The PSE for *"right"* was significantly smaller than for *"left"* curve direction. With road after trial, *"straight"* had a significantly higher PSE value than *"curved"*. On the other hand, we could not observe any significant impact of the independent variables on the value of JND.

The two-way interaction analysis results showed significant effects for the interaction between movement technique and road after trial ($p < .05$). The Tukey post-hoc test showed that *"straight"* road after trial had significant higher PSE than *"curved"* for all of the movement technique. However, we did not observe any significant effects of movement technique and other independent variables on the PSEs and JNDs.

The relationship between participants' responses and their decision time was analyzed using Spearman's rank-order correlation. The result of this analysis showed that their association was monotonic. The relationship was weak and negative ($r_s = -0.11$, $p < .01$). Therefore, we can conclude that there was a weak correlation between users' decision time and their responses.

4.2   Questionnaires

All participant feedback on the questionnaires was examined using Friedman tests. We conducted Wilcoxon signed-rank tests as post-hoc tests for significant difference.

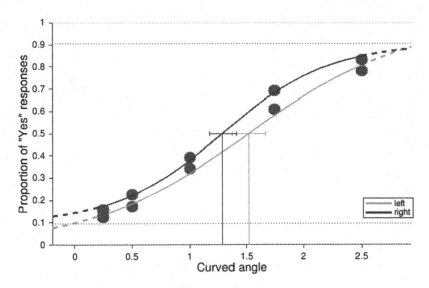

Fig. 8. The psychometric functions fitted for each condition of curve direction and the vertical central lines indicate their PSEs with confidence intervals. Overall, the PSEs are biased to 1.52 for "left" and 1.29 for "right".

Overall, we did not observe any significant difference between traveling-in-places in SSQ responses. Most participants reported none to slight symptoms for all of the conditions. In addition, there was also no significant difference in responses for components of the IPQ. All participants reported that they felt a sense of presence while performing our experiment. They paid attention on performing trials and made selection decisions carefully.

Participants' feedback showed that they felt the experiment trials were normal or easy to finish. In addition, they reported to perceive as traveling in the virtual environment (Fig. 4). Moreover, they used mainly the shape of the travel path ahead to judge whether their recent travel path was curved. For the paved pattern road, users used the line marker in the center of the road to decide, whereas the shape of the travel path was utilized for dirt road pattern.

5   Discussion and Conclusion

The results of our experiment showed that subjects could travel on a curved path while perceiving it as straight. In general, they cannot distinguish between a straight path and a curved path which is bent by $\beta = 1.42°$. In addition, we found that different conditions of independent variables have different values for PSEs. There was a significant difference in PSEs between the conditions. The PSE for "pedaling" was significantly smaller than "throttling". It was reported that participants had to put much effort on maintaining their moving speed at around 20 km/h. In addition, it was more difficult to keep the speed for "pedaling" than "throttling". In addition, the HMD moved more for "pedaling"

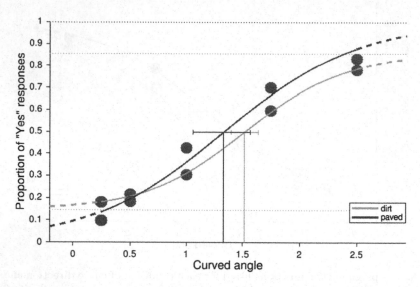

Fig. 9. The psychometric function fitted for each condition of road material and the vertical central lines indicate their PSEs with confidence intervals. Overall, the PSEs are biased to 1.52 for *"dirt"* and 1.33 for *"paved"*.

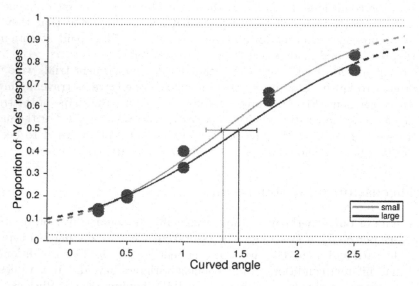

Fig. 10. The psychometric functions fitted for each condition of road width and the vertical central lines indicate their PSEs with confidence intervals. Overall, the PSEs are biased to 1.35 for *"small"* and 1.49 for *"large"*.

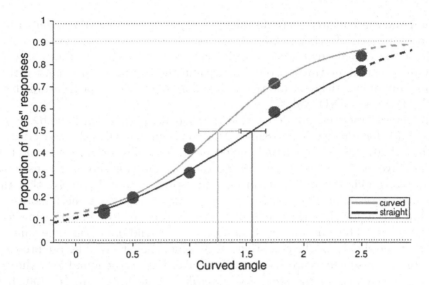

Fig. 11. The psychometric functions fitted for each condition of after trial road and the vertical central lines indicate their PSEs with confidence intervals. Overall, the PSEs are biased to 1.25 for *"curved"* and 1.55 for *"straight"*.

when the participants were performing the experiment. This could affect how the subjects focused on observing their travel path. This means that the more users paid attention on their travel path, the higher the chance that they perceived a curved travel path.

In addition, conditions of curve direction had significantly different PSEs. This outcome can be explained by participants' habits. The reason is that all of the recruited participants were from a country driving on the right hand side of the road. Although, participants were traveling in the middle of the travel path for the whole experiment, their habit on driving on the right could have led to lower PSE for the "right" curve direction. This means that they were focusing more on the right side of the road than the left side. We additionally observed that subjects probably judge their travel path as straight or curved based on their future travel path ahead. They reported that the changes in road shape were used as cues to perceive whether they were moving on a curved path. Our experiment showed similar results with the curved road after trial had significantly lower PSE than the straight one. Because there would be a straight travel path for the next trial after this travel path.

Although, there were significant differences in PSEs between some of the independent variables for participants' responses, the JNDs were not significant different between them. Conditions of the independent variables were changed; however the range of curved angles must be changed in order for participants to detect that they recently traveled on a curved path was consistent and not significantly different or affected by them. This means that the noticeable range of stimuli is identical for all of the participants. In addition, the subjects were careful and concentrated on performing our experiment. They did not suffer from severe symptoms of cyber-sickness even though they were traveling on a curved path in the virtual environment while they were stationary in the real world. Overall, users might travel around a circle in the virtual environment without having any serious sickness and the radius of the circle should be measured based on the PSEs and JNDs values.

In general, users cannot detect that their moving path which could be bent by up to $1.42°$ for a length of 27.78 m or $0.05°/m$ is curved when they are traveling at around 20 km/h in the virtual environment, regardless of different conditions of the travel path and the shape of the road ahead. This shows that users can travel along a circle with 1120.9 m in radius while they still perceive that they are traveling on a straight path. In general, we observe that the unnoticeable bending angles for all of the conditions of the factors are around $0.05°/m$ except for "*straight*". The gain for this condition is at around $0.06°/m$. The values of different thresholds for the conditions of the independent variables are presented in Table 2. These values are significantly smaller than those found for redirected walking techniques in the studies of Grechkin et al. ($4.9°/m$) [7], Langbehn et al. ($15.4°/m$) [10], Rietzler et al. ($20°/m$) [24], and Steinicke et al. ($2.6°/m$) [29]. The reason for this significant difference can be that the participants had to travel at a dramatically higher speed than walking speed in the virtual environment. This proves that users are more sensitive to travel on a bent path for higher movement speed as presented by Neth et al. [12]. In addition, the shape of the future travel path has a significant impact on how users perceive the "*curved-ness*" level of their moving path.

Unfortunately, the bike system does not have a resistant force for the flywheel. So, participants felt pedaling with this simulator be lighter than normal. As a result, they could reach to the speed of 20 km/h easier and faster with the system. In addition, this also made them hard to keep their moving velocity at baseline. Also, participants did not feel pleasant for a long travel with the bike because the bike seat was not soft and comfortable.

In conclusion, we present our experimental results on how users perceive two different traveling-in-place techniques with different bending angles of virtual moving paths. Moreover, we also investigated the impact of different factors including path textures, path widths, and bent directions, and the shape of future travel path and their relationships with the techniques. We observed that users could perceive their moving path as straight while they are traveling along a curve bent by up to $0.05°/m$ at around 20 km/h . In addition, the factors which include movement technique, curve direction, and after trial path significantly affected how they perceive the curvature of their moving path.

The results of our study can inform the development of new locomotion techniques in virtual environments, especially for seated and stationary users and contribute to the design of new virtual environments supporting infinite travel. In the future, we plan to investigate potential disorientation issues on users in navigation tasks while traveling on curved paths.

Acknowledgments. The authors would like to thank Thanh Dat Ngoc Tran and Tam Duy Nguyen for supporting the development of the bicycle system and the virtual environment. In addition, we would also like to thank Trung-Hieu Hoang and Mai-Khiem Tran for assisting in conducting users study. The authors would also like to thank our participants for taking part in the experiment. Finally, the authors also would like to thank the anonymous reviewers and the coordinator for their constructive comments and useful recommendations.

References

1. Bozgeyikli, E., Raij, A., Katkoori, S., Dubey, R.: Point & teleport locomotion technique for virtual reality. In: Proceedings of the 2016 Annual Symposium on Computer-Human Interaction in Play, CHI PLAY 2016, pp. 205–216. ACM, New York (2016). https://doi.org/10.1145/2967934.2968105

2. Bruder, G., Interrante, V., Phillips, L., Steinicke, F.: Redirecting walking and driving for natural navigation in immersive virtual environments. IEEE Trans. Visual. Comput. Graphics **18**(4), 538–545 (2012). https://doi.org/10.1109/TVCG.2012.55

3. Bruder, G., Lubos, P., Steinicke, F.: Cognitive resource demands of redirected walking. IEEE Trans. Visual. Comput. Graphics **21**(4), 539–544 (2015). https://doi.org/10.1109/TVCG.2015.2391864

4. Darken, R.P., Cockayne, W.R., Carmein, D.: The omni-directional treadmill: a locomotion device for virtual worlds. In: Proceedings of the 10th Annual ACM Symposium on User Interface Software and Technology, UIST 1997, pp. 213–221. ACM, New York (1997). https://doi.org/10.1145/263407.263550

5. Feasel, J., Whitton, M.C., Wendt, J.D.: LLCM-WIP: low-latency, continuous-motion walking-in-place. In: 2008 IEEE Symposium on 3D User Interfaces, pp. 97–104, March 2008. https://doi.org/10.1109/3DUI.2008.4476598

6. Freitag, S., Rausch, D., Kuhlen, T.: Reorientation in virtual environments using interactive portals. In: 2014 IEEE Symposium on 3D User Interfaces (3DUI), pp. 119–122, March 2014. https://doi.org/10.1109/3DUI.2014.6798852

7. Grechkin, T., Thomas, J., Azmandian, M., Bolas, M., Suma, E.: Revisiting detection thresholds for redirected walking: combining translation and curvature gains. In: Proceedings of the ACM Symposium on Applied Perception, SAP 2016, pp. 113–120. ACM, New York (2016). https://doi.org/10.1145/2931002.2931018

8. Kennedy, R.S., Lane, N.E., Berbaum, K.S., Lilienthal, M.G.: Simulator sickness questionnaire: an enhanced method for quantifying simulator sickness. Int. J. Aviat. Psychol. **3**(3), 203–220 (1993). https://doi.org/10.1207/s15327108ijap0303_3

9. Kim, M., Cho, S., Tran, T.Q., Kim, S., Kwon, O., Han, J.: Scaled jump in gravity-reduced virtual environments. IEEE Trans. Visual. Comput. Graphics **23**(4), 1360–1368 (2017). https://doi.org/10.1109/TVCG.2017.2657139

10. Langbehn, E., Lubos, P., Bruder, G., Steinicke, F.: Bending the curve: sensitivity to bending of curved paths and application in room-scale VR. IEEE Trans. Visual. Comput. Graphics **23**(4), 1389–1398 (2017). https://doi.org/10.1109/TVCG.2017.2657220

11. Matsumoto, K., Ban, Y., Narumi, T., Yanase, Y., Tanikawa, T., Hirose, M.: Unlimited corridor: redirected walking techniques using visuo haptic interaction. In: ACM SIGGRAPH 2016 Emerging Technologies, SIGGRAPH 2016, pp. 20:1–20:2. ACM, New York (2016). https://doi.org/10.1145/2929464.2929482

12. Neth, C.T., Souman, J.L., Engel, D., Kloos, U., Bulthoff, H.H., Mohler, B.J.: Velocity-dependent dynamic curvature gain for redirected walking. IEEE Trans. Visual. Comput. Graphics **18**(7), 1041–1052 (2012). https://doi.org/10.1109/TVCG.2011.275

13. Nilsson, N.C., et al.: 15 years of research on redirected walking in immersive virtual environments. IEEE Comput. Graphics Appl. **38**(2), 44–56 (2018). https://doi.org/10.1109/MCG.2018.111125628

14. Nilsson, N.C., Serafin, S., Laursen, M.H., Pedersen, K.S., Sikström, E., Nordahl, R.: Tapping-in-place: increasing the naturalness of immersive walking-in-place locomotion through novel gestural input. In: 2013 IEEE Symposium on 3D User Interfaces (3DUI), pp. 31–38, March 2013.https://doi.org/10.1109/3DUI.2013.6550193

15. Nilsson, N., Suma, E., Nordahl, R., Bolas, M., Serafin, S.: Estimation of detection thresholds for audiovisual rotation gains. In: IEEE Virtual Reality 2016, Greenville, SC, p. ID: A22. IEEE, March 2016. http://ieeevr.org/2016/posters/

16. Nilsson, N.C., Serafin, S., Steinicke, F., Nordahl, R.: Natural walking in virtual reality: a review. Comput. Entertain. **16**(2), 8:1–8:22 (2018). https://doi.org/10.1145/3180658

17. Paludan, A., et al.: Disguising rotational gain for redirected walking in virtual reality: effect of visual density. In: 2016 IEEE Virtual Reality (VR), pp. 259–260, March 2016. https://doi.org/10.1109/VR.2016.7504752

18. Peck, T.C., Whitton, M.C., Fuchs, H.: Evaluation of reorientation techniques for walking in large virtual environments. In: 2008 IEEE Virtual Reality Conference, pp. 121–127, March 2008. https://doi.org/10.1109/VR.2008.4480761

19. Peck, T.C., Fuchs, H., Whitton, M.C.: Improved redirection with distractors: a large-scale-real-walking locomotion interface and its effect on navigation in virtual environments. In: Proceedings of the 2010 IEEE Virtual Reality Conference, VR 2010, pp. 35–38. IEEE Computer Society, Washington, DC, USA (2010). https://doi.org/10.1109/VR.2010.5444816

20. Razzaque, S., Kohn, Z., Whitton, M.C.: Redirected walking. In: Eurographics 2001 - Short Presentations. Eurographics Association (2001). https://doi.org/10.2312/egs.20011036

21. Razzaque, S., Swapp, D., Slater, M., Whitton, M.C., Steed, A.: Redirected walking in place. In: Proceedings of the Workshop on Virtual Environments 2002, EGVE 2002, pp. 123–130. Eurographics Association, Aire-la-Ville, Switzerland, Switzerland (2002). http://dl.acm.org/citation.cfm?id=509709.509729

22. Regenbrecht, H.T., Schubert, T.W., Friedmann, F.: Measuring the sense of presence and its relations to fear of heights in virtual environments. Int. J. Hum.-Comput. Interact. **10**(3), 233–249 (1998). https://doi.org/10.1207/s15327590ijhc1003_2

23. Riecke, B.E., Bodenheimer, B., McNamara, T.P., Williams, B., Peng, P., Feuereissen, D.: Do we need to walk for effective virtual reality navigation? Physical rotations alone may suffice. In: Hölscher, C., Shipley, T.F., Olivetti Belardinelli, M., Bateman, J.A., Newcombe, N.S. (eds.) Spatial Cognition 2010. LNCS (LNAI), vol. 6222, pp. 234–247. Springer, Heidelberg (2010). https://doi.org/10.1007/978-3-642-14749-4_21

24. Rietzler, M., Gugenheimer, J., Hirzle, T., Deubzer, M., Langbehn, E., Rukzio, E.: Rethinking redirected walking: on the use of curvature gains beyond perceptual limitations and revisiting bending gains. In: 2018 Proceedings of the IEEE International Symposium for Mixed and Augmented Reality (2018, to appear)

25. Schubert, T., Friedmann, F., Regenbrecht, H.: The experience of presence: factor analytic insights. Presence: Teleoperators Virtual Environ. **10**(3), 266–281 (2001). https://doi.org/10.1162/105474601300343603
26. Schuett, H.H., Harmeling, S., Macke, J.H., Wichmann, F.A.: Painfree and accurate Bayesian estimation of psychometric functions for (potentially) overdispersed data. Vision Res. **122**, 105–123 (2016). https://doi.org/10.1016/j.visres.2016.02.002, http://www.sciencedirect.com/science/article/pii/S0042698916000390
27. Slater, M., Usoh, M., Steed, A.: Taking steps: the influence of a walking technique on presence in virtual reality. ACM Trans. Comput.-Hum. Interact. **2**(3), 201–219 (1995). https://doi.org/10.1145/210079.210084
28. Steinicke, F., Bruder, G., Jerald, J., Frenz, H., Lappe, M.: Analyses of human sensitivity to redirected walking. In: Proceedings of the 2008 ACM Symposium on Virtual Reality Software and Technology, VRST 2008, pp. 149–156. ACM, New York (2008). https://doi.org/10.1145/1450579.1450611
29. Steinicke, F., Bruder, G., Jerald, J., Frenz, H., Lappe, M.: Estimation of detection thresholds for redirected walking techniques. IEEE Trans. Visual. Comput. Graphics **16**(1), 17–27 (2010). https://doi.org/10.1109/TVCG.2009.62
30. Suma, E.A., Bruder, G., Steinicke, F., Krum, D.M., Bolas, M.: A taxonomy for deploying redirection techniques in immersive virtual environments. In: 2012 IEEE Virtual Reality Workshops (VRW), pp. 43–46, March 2012. https://doi.org/10.1109/VR.2012.6180877
31. Templeman, J.N., Denbrook, P.S., Sibert, L.E.: Virtual locomotion: walking in place through virtual environments. Presence **8**(6), 598–617 (1999). https://doi.org/10.1162/105474699566512
32. Terziman, L., Marchal, M., Emily, M., Multon, F., Arnaldi, B., Lécuyer, A.: Shake-your-head: revisiting walking-in-place for desktop virtual reality. In: Proceedings of the 17th ACM Symposium on Virtual Reality Software and Technology, VRST 2010, pp. 27–34. ACM, New York (2010). https://doi.org/10.1145/1889863.1889867
33. Tran, T.Q., Tran, T.D.N., Nguyen, T.D., Regenbrecht, H., Tran, M.T.: Can we perceive changes in our moving speed: a comparison between directly and indirectly powering the locomotion in virtual environments. In: Proceedings of the 24th ACM Symposium on Virtual Reality Software and Technology, VRST 2018, pp. 36:1–36:10. ACM, New York (2018). https://doi.org/10.1145/3281505.3281510
34. Usoh, M., et al.: Walking ≫ walking-in-place ≫ flying, in virtual environments. In: Proceedings of the 26th Annual Conference on Computer Graphics and Interactive Techniques, SIGGRAPH 1999, pp. 359–364. ACM Press/Addison-Wesley Publishing Co., New York (1999). https://doi.org/10.1145/311535.311589
35. Wendt, J.D., Whitton, M.C., Brooks, F.P.: GUD WIP: gait-understanding-driven walking-in-place. In: 2010 IEEE Virtual Reality Conference (VR), pp. 51–58, March 2010. https://doi.org/10.1109/VR.2010.5444812
36. Williams, B., Bailey, S., Narasimham, G., Li, M., Bodenheimer, B.: Evaluation of walking in place on a wii balance board to explore a virtual environment. ACM Trans. Appl. Percept. **8**(3), 19:1–19:14 (2011). https://doi.org/10.1145/2010325.2010329

Design and Evaluation of an Augmented Reality App for Learning Geometric Shapes in 3D

Pornpon Thamrongrat[(⊠)] and Effie Lai-Chong Law[(⊠)]

Department of Informatics, University of Leiecster, Leicester LE1 7RH, UK
{ptl71,lcl9}@leicester.ac.uk

Abstract. Augmented Reality (AR) is increasingly used as an educational tool in a range of domains with the goal of enhancing students' performance as well as their learning experience, thanks to the interactivity and visual appeal of AR objects. While some attempts, albeit limited, have been undertaken to prove these beneficial effects in learning 3D geometry, the results remain inconclusive and there are some methodological issues such as under-evaluation of user experience. With the aim to enrich the applied body of knowledge on this specific topic, we developed an AR application that allows its users to learn about cross-sectional shapes and variables in 3D geometry. We compared the AR-based approach with the traditional chalk-and-board approach by involving sixty 12–16 year-olds from two schools. The AR class showed a significantly stronger learning effect than the traditional class, especially for the more complex geometric concepts. The AR class found the application engaging, regardless of their level of knowledge gain, which bore no significant relation with their intention to use it. The methodological challenge for implementing control groups and the practical challenge for affordable emerging educational tools should be tackled in future research.

Keywords: Augmented Reality · Geometry · Education · UX · User engagement

1 Introduction

The rapid growth of computing technology enhances the use of software to support human activities in various fields such as education, health and entertainment. The rise of multimodal and multisensory interactions enabled by mobile devices, for instance accelerometer-based [1], camera-based [2], location-based [3], voice-based [4] and touch-based [5], leads to the development of a variety of specific applications.

In particular, Augmented Reality (AR) has attracted more and more research attention in different areas. AR is a technology used to create an enhanced real-time interactive experience by combining computer-generated 3D and real-world contents. Apart from visual images, some AR systems provide enhanced audio or haptic experiences [6]. Such enhanced experiences render AR a powerful tool in engaging customers in business [7], visitors in cultural heritage [8], players in games [9], and learners in education [10, 11], to name just a few examples of AR-enhanced human

© IFIP International Federation for Information Processing 2019
Published by Springer Nature Switzerland AG 2019
D. Lamas et al. (Eds.): INTERACT 2019, LNCS 11749, pp. 364–385, 2019.
https://doi.org/10.1007/978-3-030-29390-1_20

activities. The research study presented in this paper focuses on the application of AR in education.

In the domain of computer science, Yilmaz [12] studied teachers' and children's opinions on the educational effect of AR-based magic toys and found that the 3D virtual objects in the magic toys could make children more interested in learning. Furthermore, Fotouhi-Ghazvini and colleagues [13] proposed a mobile AR for adding a real sense of learning to a game for students, which could enhance their learning motivation. According to the study of Kysela and Štorková [14] on tourism education, using AR to provide tourists with experiences at cultural heritage sites by overlaying 3D virtual objects onto the real scene could serve as an attractive environment for studying history. These examples illustrate that the attractiveness and interactivity of AR can be used to support people to learn with enjoyment and effectiveness.

Geometry is an area of mathematics that involves studying a broad range of shapes such as pyramid, rectangular, cuboid and sphere. They are difficult to learn in 2D format, especially when they can be cut at any angle to produce various cross-sectional shapes. Indeed, the study of Adolphus [15] showed the difficulty in teaching and learning geometry, as the conventional instructional environment is not conducive to learning geometric concepts in 3D. Geometry is also relevant to learning chemistry with abstract concepts as well as concrete examples such as molecular structures, which are composed of three-dimensional spaces of atoms that are not easily understood in a classroom or a laboratory. To explain such shapes, people use general presentation software (e.g., PowerPoint) where, however, learners can only view passively the learning objects presented because they cannot interact with them [16]. In contrast, AR allows dynamic and interactive manipulations of 3D images [17] and thus can be useful for teaching geometry. Students can move, rotate, reflect, or stretch the images. Nonetheless, only a small number of research studies (e.g. [18–20]) have been conducted to investigate the effectiveness of learning geometric 3D shapes with AR, and they reached inconsistent conclusions. Furthermore, some methodological limitations were identified in the existing work on this specific topic. First, the lack of control group to assess the effect of learning geometric shapes with the conventional teaching approach as compared with an AR-based approach. Second, the evaluation of the AR application focused on the learning effect, but overlooked the user experience aspect.

Consequently, we have been motivated to collect more empirical data to address the main research question: *To what extent can AR-enabled 3D virtual objects make learning more effective and more engaging for students as compared with the traditional 2D approach?* The answer to this question is important for informing the design of this new learning technology, which should be usable, useful and desirable. Accordingly, we developed a dedicated AR-based application that can be beneficial to children of 12–16 years old to learn geometric shapes in 3D and assess its learning and experiential effects with this target group. Overall, the main contribution of this work is to enrich the relatively small applied body of knowledge on this specific topic from the methodological and practical aspects.

The rest of the paper is structured as follows: We first present the literature review in Sect. 2, followed by the outline of our methodological framework in Sect. 3. Then we report our empirical study and results in Sects. 4 and 5, respectively. In Sect. 6, we discuss three issues that we deliberated when planning and implementing our study. In Sect. 7, we conclude and draw implications for future research.

2   Literature Review

In this section we first provide an overview of AR in education, followed by a review on the existing technological approaches to learning geometric concepts. Then we outline the related work on user experience (UX) and user engagement (UE), especially the UE scale that we adopted for our empirical studies (Sect. 3).

2.1   AR in Education

One of the most essential functions of AR is the dual-presence of information where two information displays are overlaid on each other [21]. Wu and colleagues [22] reported that one of the common AR applications is education. Mayer [23] argued, based on the cognitive theory of multimedia learning, that AR comprising texts, 2D or 3D images could be used to improve learning because people tend to learn better from words and pictures combined together than from words alone. Sommerauer and Müller [24] examined the use of AR for education through conducting an experiment at a mathematics exhibition. Their experimental study was similar to that of Morrison and colleagues [21] in that both studies made a comparison between the use of AR and non-AR. While the results of Morrison and colleagues [21] were not conclusive, the results of Sommerauer and Müller [24] showed that museum visitors learned significantly better from the AR exhibition than from the non-AR one.

AR has also been applied to education in various domains such as cultural heritage [25] for which, however, no formal evaluation of the learning or experiential effect was performed. The study of Ibáñez and colleagues [26] showed that using AR was more effective in promoting students' knowledge of electromagnetic phenomena with a higher level of enjoyment as compared with using web-based applications. For learning astronomical phenomena, using AR with three markers - sun, earth and moon - could enhance the learners' perceptions of mobilization [27]. By using a new interaction method with a pico-projector as an AR system to enhance the digital display on static paper, teachers, students, and experts commented that AR was useful for learning [28]. Yang, Chu, and Yang [29] demonstrated the use of an inquiry-based AR learning system to learn about the properties of gas in a real-world context with 70 students of eleventh grade. It helped students to improve their learning performance on gas properties in terms of adjusting the parameters of pressure and temperature. In another research study [30], twenty computer science students took part in an experiment aimed to compare two educational approaches: an AR-based application and a non-AR approach to programming debugging. The results found that the AR application was more effective in increasing the students' computational thinking and learning outcomes when compared with the non-AR approach.

Overall, as indicated in the above literature review, in the last decade the use of AR for educational purposes has been expanded to a large range of domains, especially STEM. However, the research work is scattered over the broad range and the number of empirical studies per domain, say mathematics, is small. This makes it difficult to draw any conclusive claims on the learning effect of AR. Hence, it is necessary to conduct more systematic research to substantiate the applied body of knowledge on applying AR as an educational tool in general and as an enabler to understand geometric concepts in particular.

2.2   Learning Geometric Concepts

Study of geometry as a branch of mathematics has a long tradition and is highly relevant to other science subjects as well as to art. Traditionally, basic geometric shapes are drawn with pencil, paper, ruler and compass. In recent decades, computing technologies have played an ever-increasingly important role in education in general and in study of geometry in particular. Using 3D computer-aided design (CAD), such as AutoCAD^{TM}, Maya^{TM}, 3DStudio Max^{TM} and others, has become commonplace in teaching and learning geometric concepts in 3D. While such software applications can help create beautiful 3D shapes, they should also support the process of learning geometry (e.g., 3D shapes and geometric variables). Hence, their user interfaces should be easy to understand.

With computers having the built-in ability to record user activities, the related software was able to track how users created geometric shapes, to reproduce the process of construction with changes in parameters (e.g. size, coordinate, color) and to present the resulting shape instantly. Today, there are different proprietary software applications for dynamic two-dimensional geometry, and the most popular ones are Cinderella [31] and Euklid [32].

AR is the current technological advancement with strong potential for enhancing education in a broad range of domains [22], including geometry. In fact, AR is more than the combination of hardware, software and contextually relevant information [33]. Utilizing the power of the AR technology, especially its interactivity and visual appeal, can support people to learn 3D geometry with high effectiveness and efficiency, and positive learning experience.

2.3   User Experience and User Engagement

User experience (UX) and user engagement (UE) are very closely related concepts for designing interactive systems. UX puts emphasis on the experiential aspect of human-computer interaction, encompassing a broad range of emotional responses with engagement being one of the key qualities.

Norman [34] was one of the authors to use the word "User Experience" to describe a person's total experience with every aspect of a system. He argued that 'usability' was too narrow to show a holistic vision of human-computer interaction. UX as a study explores factors influencing the subjective experience humans have when interacting with technology. Moreover, Gegner and colleges [35] proposed that UX is a 'counter-movement to usability thinking' that focuses on pragmatic quality (cf. hedonic quality). While different definitions of UX exist (e.g. [36, 37]), researchers tended to agree that UX involves users' emotional, cognitive and behavioral responses before, during and after interacting with a system, product or service [38].

Like UX, the notion of user engagement (UE) has different definitions. Grounded in relevant theoretical frameworks, O'Brien [39] defined user engagement as "a quality of UX characterized by the depth of an actor's cognitive, temporal, affective and behavioural investment when interacting with a digital system". Apart from the definitional challenge, O'Brien and colleagues [39] tackled the issue of operationalising UE by developing a standardized UE scale based on their systematic literature review and on their own empirical work in a range of domains, including e-learning, e-commerce and gaming. Specifically, they adopted the attribute-based approach [39]. Deriving from Jacques's UE work on educational multimedia [40] and Webster and Ho's on presentation software [41], O'Brien and colleagues [39] identified a set of user-system attributes (e.g., attention, motivation, perception of control, curiosity, intrinsic interest) that constitute an engaging experience. The original UES consists of 31 items for six dimensions of engagement, and has been used in a variety of domains such as education, online news, and social network systems. Subsequently, O'Brien and colleges [39] validated a short form (UES-SF) where the number of items was reduced to 12 representing four dimensions of engagement: *focused attention (FA), perceived usability (PU), aesthetic appeal (AE),* and *reward (RW),* which are defined as follows:

- *FA: Focused attention,* feeling absorbed in the interaction and losing track of time.
- *PU: Perceived usability,* negative affect experienced as a result of the interaction and effort expended.
- *AE: Aesthetic appeal,* the attractiveness and visual appeal of the interface.
- *RW: Rewards,* the worthwhile and feeling interested in the experience.

The UES-SF was proved to have strong psychometric properties [39]; this characteristic together with its relevance to our research topic can well justify our choice of this instrument for our empirical study.

3 Methodology

In this section, we first present the methodological framework for the empirical studies of which details are reported in Sect. 4. Next, we describe the development of the AR application as the intervention for enhancing children's learning of 3D geometry.

3.1 Methodological Framework

As described in Introduction, this research aims to analyse the effectiveness of an AR application for supporting high school students to learn geometric shapes in 3D. The methodological framework is illustrated in Fig. 1. Accordingly, the empirical studies were conducted with students of 12–16 years old. The intervention was developed with the User-centered Design (UCD) approach [42], involving students and teachers, who were key stakeholders of the intervention, throughout the development process in order to understand their needs and preferences.

The phases of the UCD approach were implemented as follows (cf. Sect. 3.2):

(1) *Expert interview*: We conducted interviews with teachers to get input how they typically teach 3D geometry and what the learning objectives and outcomes are.
(2) *Specify the context of use*: To understand the context where the AR application would be used, we carried out in situ observations in classrooms to understand how children typically learn 3D geometry and also conducted interviews with some children to identify their preferences with regard to the alternative approach to learning geometry.
(3) *Specify requirements*: Based on (1) and (2), a set of requirements was derived to inform the development of the AR application.
(4) *Produce design solutions and evaluate them*: Early prototypes were designed and evaluated with the teachers and children. Feedback was obtained to improve the design.

For the experimental design, we employed the between-subject method. The two key independent variables (IVs) were *learning outcome* and *user experience*, which were evaluated with a domain-specific knowledge test (i.e. the pre-/post-test) on 3D geometry and the standardized UES-SF (Sect. 2.3), respectively. School children were recruited through their teachers whom the first author acquainted through his network. They were randomly allocated to two groups under different conditions. The impact of the learning approach typically used in classroom (Normal Class) was compared with that of the AR-based approach (AR Class). Post-intervention interviews with children were also conducted. This mixed-method approach is recommendable for triangulating the empirical data collected to draw valid conclusions [43].

3.2 Augmented Reality Application Design

With the user requirements gathered with the UCD approach (Sect. 3.1) and the results of the analysis of the learning content on 3D geometry, the AR application was developed. The tool Unity 3D [44] based on C# programming was used. 3D models are built by using Autodesk Maya and they can be displayed on a camera by using the Vuforia AR plug-in. In general, users interact with physical markers by putting them in front of a camera. The images are captured and processed by the AR system. After that, virtual 3D objects are overlaid onto the corresponding markers to be displayed on a computer screen. Users can view the resulting 3D objects and respond to feedback.

In accord with the UCD approach, a prototype design needs input from relevant stakeholders. Three teachers in secondary schools who have been teaching mathematics for about 5 years were interviewed on how what they typically teach 3D geometry in classroom. In addition, in situ observations of classroom teaching were made. It was found that the teachers rely on the use of chalk and board to draw 3D shapes when explaining the concepts to their students. Furthermore, ten students aged 12–16 years old were interviewed to share their opinions about learning 3D geometry. They commented that 3D shapes, particularly cross-sectional shapes, were difficult to understand in 2D form such as hand-drawn geometric shapes on cardboard. They were enthusiastic about an interactive application that can show them the shapes clearly. This student feedback resonated with what was shared by the teachers interviewed, who stated that the seven important geometric shapes - cone, cube, cuboid, cylinder, prism, pyramid and sphere - and their cross-sectional shapes were difficult for students to understand when they were taught with cardboard or paper. The teachers proposed the need of a tool that can display 3D models clearly and allow such 3D models to be zoomed, scrolled, scaled, moved or rotated, thereby enabling students to view the models from different perspectives. The AR application prototype was designed accordingly and was later checked with the teachers to invite further feedback. The AR application prototype was developed with a set of AR markers consisting of seven shapes with five angles for learning cross-sectional shapes and geometry variables (Figs. 2 and 3).

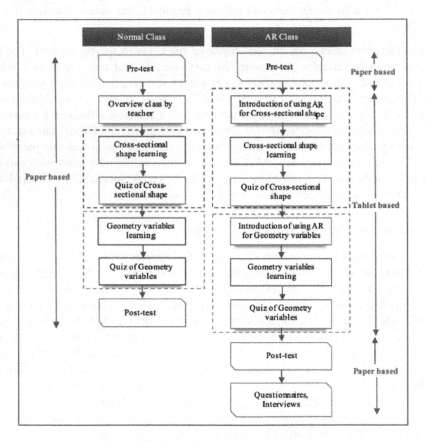

Fig. 1. The research methodology framework.

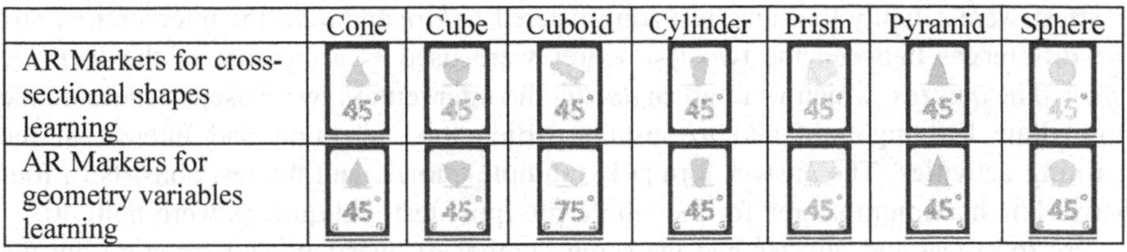

	Cone	Cube	Cuboid	Cylinder	Prism	Pyramid	Sphere
AR Markers for cross-sectional shapes learning	45°	45°	45°	45°	45°	45°	45°
AR Markers for geometry variables learning	45°	45°	75°	45°	45°	45°	45°

Fig. 2. AR Marker of seven geometric shapes.

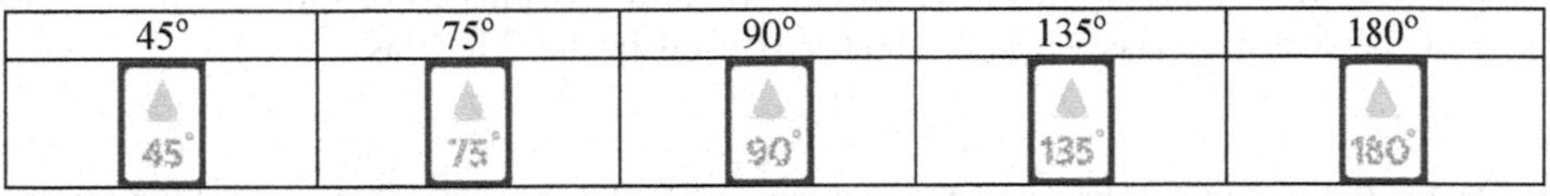

45°	75°	90°	135°	180°
45°	75°	90°	135°	180°

Fig. 3. AR Markers of Cone shape in five different angles.

Children can move and push the markers in front of the camera of a tablet, then the corresponding 3D geometric shapes are presented to enhance the learning process by enabling children to interact with the 3D digital objects displayed. Later on, children were given quizzes to assess their knowledge gain.

4 Empirical Study

4.1 Instruments

AR Application and Tablet. The AR application (Sect. 3.2) is installed in a tablet with the following technical specifications: Screen size: 8 inches; Operating system: Android 7.X Nougat; Processor: Octa Core; Resolution: 1920 × 1200; Memory: 128 GB. This is a quality device with a relatively high price (£250/$330). To ensure that the learning process and user experience would not be compromised by a less powerful tablet, we opted for this choice. However, the drawback was the small number of tablets we could afford to purchase with a limited budget for the study. As the AR Class would be taken on an individual basis, we estimated that the impact of having a small group of five instead of thirty children working on their own tablet at the same time could be marginal, especially if the AR application was meant to engage their attention in the tasks at hand. Nonetheless, we acknowledge that this may not be an ideal arrangement.

Pretest, Posttest and Quizzes. The domain-specific knowledge pretest/posttest and quizzes were constructed by the first author in collaboration with three math teachers, who were also interviewed for gathering requirements (Sect. 3.2). The pretest and posttest were actually the same test administered *before* and *after* the intervention, and the differences between the two test scores were used as a measure of the *learning effect*. The quizzes, which were given *during* the intervention, were used to measure the immediate learning gain and to sustain participants' attention and interest in the learning activities. The answer format is multiple-choice, and the test consists of four parts. The maximum scores for the whole pre-/post-test and quizzes were both 40.

Pre-/post-test and quizzes had the same number of questions and structure but the questions were different, though they were all related to the topics covered in the Normal/AR class (Table 1). There was no time limit to answer them. Paper was used for the pre-/post-test in both the Normal class and AR class. For quizzes, paper was used in the Normal class while a tablet was used in the AR Class.

Table 1. The structure of pre-/post-test and quizzes; Part A to D are of increasing complexity.

Parts	Number of questions	Description: the questions are about …
Part A	13	What the cross-sectional shapes are after the cutting
Part B	13	At which angle the shapes are cut
Part C	7	Geometric variables
Part D	7	Formulae with geometric variables

Questionnaires and Interviews. To evaluate the user experience of the AR application (Sect. 2.3), two research methods - questionnaire and interview – were employed. After interacting with the AR application, participants were asked to complete the questionnaire comprising the 12-item UES-SF [39] and 2 items on 'Intention to Use' [45] derived from the Technology Acceptance Model (TAM). Accordingly, an individual's behavioral intention to use a system is largely determined by the perceived usefulness and perceived ease of use [45]. After that, semi-structured interviews (group discussion) were conducted to collect further information about user experience. It took on average about ten minutes to complete both the questionnaire and interview.

4.2 Procedure

AR Class. It took place in a regular classroom where a group of children followed the given workflow (Table 2). The Class was taken on an individual basis when each participant interacted with the AR application on the tablet with a set of AR markers on his/her own. Participants were instructed not to discuss the tasks with their peers during or after the AR Class.

Table 2. The AR Class workflow

Tasks	Display screens	Descriptions
1 Pretest	Paper-based	It has four parts of questions: Part A, Part B, Part C and Part D
2 Introduction		The introduction is about how to use the AR application for learning cross-sectional shapes.
3 Cross- sectional shapes learning		This section is for children to learn cross-sectional shapes. Children need to put a marker in front of the tablet, which displays the 3D shape with the name of its cross-sectional shape. Children can press the cut button to view the cut.
4 Quiz on Cross-sectional shapes		Quiz of Part A: The question is about what is the cross-sectional shape after the cutting? When a child clicks one of answer buttons, the application will show the correct one.
		Example: The question about a rectangular shape and the answer is Square.
		Quiz of Part B: The question is about at which angle is the shape cut? When a child clicks one of answer buttons, the application will show the correct one.
		Example: The question is about a cross sectional shape of a rectangular shape and the answer is 45.
5 Introduction		The introduction is about how to use the AR application for learning geometry variables.
6 Geometry variables learning		This section is for children to learn cross sectional shapes. Children need to put the marker in front of the tablet, which then displays the 3D shape with its variables such as length, width and the name of its cross-sectional shape.

Tasks	Display screens	Descriptions
7 Quiz of Geometry variables		Quiz of Part C: The question is about geometry variables.
		Example: Which letters represent Radius? When a child clicks one of answer buttons, the application will show the correct one: the 2D plane and its variables.
		Quiz of Part D: The question is about calculation with the geometry variables.
		Example: Find the area of a circle, where area is Pi * Radius * Radius? When a child clicks one of answer buttons, the application will show the correct one.
8 Posttest	Paper-based	The children will take the posttest which has the same questions as the pretest.

Table 3. The Normal class workflow

	Tasks	Descriptions
1	Pretest	It has four parts on a piece of paper: Part A, Part B, Part C and Part D
2	Introduction	The teacher introduces the topic of cross-sectional shapes in 3D geometry
3	Cross-sectional shape learning	The teacher describes the seven shapes of 3D geometry and shows the 3D geometry cross-sectional shapes (45°, 75°, 90°, 135°, 180°) in 2D representations
4	Quiz on Cross-sectional shapes	The children take a quiz on cross-sectional shapes
5	Introduction	The teacher introduces the topic of 3D geometry variables
6	Geometry variables learning	The teacher shows the 3D geometry variables such as width, length and diameter in 2D representations
7	Quiz on geometry variables	The children take a quiz on 3D geometry variables
8	Posttest	The children take the posttest

Normal Class. It was delivered by a math teacher who was asked to follow the steps corresponding to those of the AR application (cf. Table 2). The teacher used chalk and board to draw the shapes, cross-sectional shapes, and variables of 3D geometry (Step 2, 3 & 5 in Table 3) and administered the quizzes (Step 5 & 7 in Table 3) in the way similar to the corresponding steps in Table 2. Participants were instructed not to discuss the tasks with their peers during the class.

4.3 Participants

The empirical study was approved by the Ethics Review Committee of the University of Leicester. Altogether 60 children aged 12 to 16 years were involved in the study, which took place in two secondary schools. All participations were voluntary and consented by the children and their parents/guardians and school authorities. The participants were divided into two groups: the Normal Class for the first school and the AR Class for the second school with 30 each. For the AR class, all participants (18 male, 12 female; average age: 14.07) were asked to carry out a set of tasks on an individual basis in a session that lasted about 30 min (Table 4). None of them had any AR experience before taking part in the study. For the Normal class (11 male, 19 female; average age: 14 years old), the teacher used the conventional approach (Sect. 4.2) and the class lasted about 45 min. The longer duration was attributed to the fact that the teacher needed time to draw the shapes by hand whereas the AR application retrieved and displayed the shapes instantly.

Table 4. The descriptive statistics the AR class.

Gender	AR class		
	Mean (minutes)	SD	N
Female	30.56	11.85	12
Male	29.72	7.74	18

4.4 Research Model and Hypotheses

The data collected in this study were to evaluate our research model (Fig. 4) and verify the six associated hypotheses (H). The key assumption underpinning the hypotheses is that the AR application can support children to learn 3D geometry more effectively and in a more engaging manner than the traditional chalk-and-board approach.

In addition, we hypothesize that the learner attributes, including *gender, prior knowledge,* and *age,* may influence the relations between the IV (i.e. learning approach) and two DVs (i.e. learning effect, user experience). Note that the participants' prior knowledge was assessed only by the pretest. However, as the learning

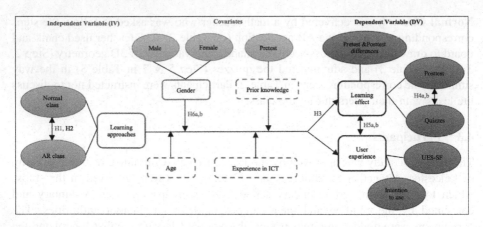

Fig. 4. The diagram of the research model with the hypotheses

effect was operationalized in terms of the differences between the posttest and pretest scores, we cannot evaluate the role of prior knowledge as a covariate. It could have been measured, for instance, by the participants' academic performance at school (e.g. math exam grades), but such data could not be made available to us. Furthermore, as the participating children were from the same year group, there was basically no difference in age, which cannot be verified as a co-variate in this context. Another covariate could be 'previous experience in computing technology'. Apart from asking the participants of the AR class if any of them had used AR (none of them put up their hand), we did not collect any other data in this regard. Hence, we cannot verify this co-variate.

- **H1:** Participants in the Normal Class have the same 3D geometry background knowledge level as those in the AR Class as measured by the pretest scores.
- **H2:** Participants in the Normal Class have the same 3D geometry knowledge level as those in the AR Class during the learning process as measured by the quiz scores.
- **H3:** Participants in the AR Class gain a significantly higher level of 3D geometry knowledge than those in the Normal Class, as measured by the *difference scores* (i.e. the discrepancy between the posttest and pretest scores).
- **H4a:** There is a significant correlation between the total quiz scores and posttest scores of the Normal Class.
- **H4b:** There is a significant correlation between the total quiz scores and posttest scores of the AR Class.
- **H5:** There is a significant correlation between the learning effect as measured by the difference scores and (a) user engagement as measured by the self-reported questionnaire; and (b) intention to use of the AR Class.

- **H6a:** There is a significant difference in the learning effect between two genders in the AR Class.
- **H6b:** There is a significant difference in the UES scores between two genders in the AR Class.

5 Results

5.1 Learning Effect

The Shapiro-Wilk test was applied to individual datasets to assess if they are normally distributed, and the result thereof informed the selection of appropriate parametric or non-parametric statistical methods for verifying each of the hypotheses. The statistical results from Pretest, Posttest and Quizzes are shown in Table 5.

Table 5. Results of Normal classroom and AR classroom.

Knowledge test	Class	Medium	Parts	Mean	SD.
Pretest	Normal class	Paper	A	8.37	1.56
			B	7.63	2.19
			C	4.67	1.12
			D	4.57	1.43
			Total	**25.23**	**2.73**
	AR class	Paper	A	8.60	1.25
			B	7.23	2.60
			C	5.13	1.04
			D	4.73	1.34
			Total	**25.70**	**3.79**
Quizzes	Normal class	Paper	A	10.60	1.40
			B	8.63	3.05
			C	5.23	1.19
			D	4.53	1.48
			Total	**29.00**	**5.17**
	AR class	Tablet	A	9.83	1.12
			B	9.87	1.76
			C	6.20	0.71
			D	6.07	0.69
			Total	**31.97**	**2.91**
Posttest	Normal class	Paper	A	9.67	1.58
			B	8.77	3.01
			C	5.47	1.33
			D	4.90	2.06
			Total	**28.80**	**5.72**
	AR class	Paper	A	8.97	1.25
			B	9.57	1.89
			C	6.07	0.91
			D	5.87	0.73
			Total	**30.47**	**3.07**

H1: To ensure that the children in the two experimental groups started with the same level of 3D geometry knowledge, a statistical analysis of their total pretest scores was carried out. The independent samples t-test was used to verify the significance of the difference between the two groups. The results showed that participants in the Normal Class had the same 3D geometry background knowledge level as those in AR Class as measured by the pretest scores ($t(58) = .55$, $p = 0.586$).

H2: The independent samples t-test was used to verify the significance of the difference between the two groups. The results (Table 6) showed that participants in the Normal Class did *not* have the same 3D geometry knowledge level *during* the learning process as those in the AR Class as measured by the *total* quiz scores ($t(58) = 2.74$, $p = 0.008$). However, when breaking it down into four parts, the two groups had the same 3D geometry knowledge level as measured by the quiz scores of Part B (t $(58) = 1.92$, $p = 0.06$). Interestingly, for Part A with the least difficult questions, the Normal Class performed significantly better than the AR Class whereas for Part C and Part D, the AR Class performed significantly better. The results suggest that the interactivity and visual-spatial representation enabled by AR can help children learn more complex geometric concepts.

Table 6. Independent sample test of the quiz scores of the Normal Class and AR class.

	t-test		
	t	*df*	*p*
Part A	−2.34*	58	0.023
Part B	1.92	58	0.060
Part C	3.80**	58	0.000
Part D	5.14**	58	0.000
Total	2.74**	58	0.008

*p < .05; **p < .01

H3: The independent samples t-test was used to verify the significance of the difference between the AR and Normal Class in terms of the difference scores (Posttest – Pretest). The results (Table 7) showed that there was no significant difference in the learning effect between the two groups ($t(58) = 1.04$, $p = 0.303$), although the AR Class had higher scores in Part B, C, and D.

These results were inconsistent with those of the quiz scores (H2), which showed that the AR Class could learn better. The contrast might be attributed to the fact that for the quizzes the AR Class used the same digital presentation medium whereas for the posttest the AR Class needed to shift from the digital tablet to paper. This might have impact on the children's perceptual and cognitive load. Indeed, some attempts have been undertaken to investigate the relation between the assessment medium and performance [46–48], though the findings are inconclusive.

Table 7. Independent sample test of the difference scores of the Normal Class and AR class.

	t-test		
	t	df	p
Part A	2.25	58	0.028
Part B	1.60	58	0.117
Part C	0.36	58	0.719
Part D	1.88	58	0.066
Total	1.04	58	0.303

H4a: The result showed that there was a significant correlation between the total quiz and posttest scores (N = 30, r_s = .468, $p < .01$). It implies that the higher the quiz scores, the higher the posttest scores the children in the Normal class would gain.

H4b: The result showed that there was a significant correlation between the total quiz and posttest scores (N = 30, r_s = .431, $p < .05$). It implies that the higher the quiz scores, the higher the posttest scores the children in the AR class would gain.

5.2   User Experience

As shown in Fig. 1, only the participants in the AR Class completed the questionnaires on the user experience of the AR application. Results are shown in Table 8.

Table 8. Results of the UES-SF and Intention to Use

	#	Statements	Mean (N = 30)
UES short form	FA-1	I lost myself in this experience	3.70
	FA-2	The time I spent using this AR just slipped away	4.10
	FA-3	I was absorbed in this experience	4.37
	PU-1	I felt frustrated while using this AR	2.03
	PU-2	I found this AR confusing to use	1.83
	PU-3	Using this AR was taxing	1.97
	AE-1	This AR was attractive	4.10
	AE-2	This AR was aesthetically appealing	4.07
	AE-3	This AR appealed to my senses	4.23
	RW-1	Using AR was worthwhile	4.60
	RW-2	My experience was rewarding	4.43
	RW-3	I felt interested in this experience	4.73
Intention to use	IU-1	Assuming I have access to this AR, I intend to use it	4.60
	IU-2	Given that I have access to this AR, I predict that I would use it	4.33

H5a: The results of Spearman's rank test showed no significant correlations between the difference scores and the average scores of Focused Attention, Perceived Usability, Aesthetic Appeal and Reward Factors (N = 30, r_s = −.246, −.005, −.019, −.114, respectively, p > .05).

H5b: The result of Spearman's rank test showed no significant correlation between the difference scores and Intention to Use (N = 30, r_s = 0.075, p > .05).

Overall, the above findings showed that the learning effect and user experience had no significant correlation. Nonetheless, the ratings of the four dimensions of UES-SF indicated that the AR application could engage its users in the learning activities (focused attention [FA] = 4.1) with good usability (perceived usability [PU] = 4.1, reversed), high attractiveness (aesthetic appeal [AE] = 4.1) and very high level of worthiness and interest (reward [RW] = 4.6). However, the level of engagement in interacting with the AR application bore no relation with the level of knowledge gain. Interestingly, the user experience also bore no relation with the intention to use, although it was rated very high with the mean of 4.5.

H6a: The independent samples t-test was used to verify the significance of the difference in the learning effect as measured by the difference scores between two genders in the AR Class (M_{male} = 4.61, SD_{male} = 3.10; M_{female} = 5.00, SD_{female} = 3.88). The results showed no significant difference between the male and female participants (t (28) = .304, p = 0.764).

H6b: The Mann-Whitney test was used to verify the significance of the differences in the UES-SF four dimensions between two genders. The results (Table 9) showed no significant difference in the perceived user engagement quality of the AR application between two genders.

Table 9. Mann-Whitney test of the UES-SF scores between male and female participants

UES-SF	Gender (Mean)		Mann-Whitney test results		
	Male	Female	U	Z	P
Focused attention	16.17	14.50	77.50	−1.45	.628
Perceived usability	15.92	14.88	98.50	−.57	.759
Aesthetic appeal	15.08	16.13	96.50	−.65	.759
Reward factors	14.19	17.46	89.00	−.99	.304

Interview/Group Discussion. The original plan was to conduct individual semi-structured interviews, but it was found practically challenging to do so, given the time constraint. Instead, a group discussion with the whole class was conducted with the first author being the moderator. We summarize some key comments shared.

First, participants stated that they could learn 3D geometry with the AR app in a way better than with the traditional approach using chalk and board and paper. It was because the geometric shapes were displayed in 3D, which could be seen much more clearly than they were in 2D.

Second, the visualization effect enabled by the AR app helped children better understand the geometric shapes, because they could be zoomed, scrolled, scaled and easy to view from different angles. The most interesting part was the use of the camera to display the images and 3D shapes with quizzes.

Third, all users intended to recommend the AR app to others. It was fun to use with playful interactions and, unlike the classroom teaching, cross-sectional shapes resulted from cutting could be observed instantly with precise measures, although some participants suggested that the app support a wider range of cutting angles.

6 Discussion

In this section we discuss three practical issues on which we have reflected when planning and implementing our empirical work. The issues – high costs of emerging technologies and organizational constraints for running field studies - are relevant for other researchers pursuing along this line of enquiry to consider.

6.1 Affordability of Digital Devices

Mobile touch devices like tablets can be used in education in many ways as shown by our AR app. Learners can benefit from their compactness, portability, interactivity and personalisation. Nonetheless, our study was constrained by the costs of such devices; the issue of affordability should be addressed, considering the risk of digital divide. While we cannot estimate the future costs for immersive technology and tablets, we anticipate that they will drop in about five years, given the trend of increasing usage[1]. The extent of cost reduction much depends on the pace of the growing market. Above all, educationalists need to take the equality into account when employing new technology to enhance teaching and learning.

6.2 Augmented Reality (AR) vs. Virtual Reality (VR)

In VR environments users can manipulate objects by moving, rotating and resizing them [49]. Virtual reality provides users with immersive experience as if they were in the physical world being mimicked, thanks to sensors (e.g. accelerometer) and instruments (e.g. camera) that support multimodal and multisensory interactions [50]. Although VR can be used as an integrated educational tool to make children more engaged, it demands extra infrastructure and equipment such as head-mounted display headsets and hand-held controllers, which are expensive. The use of VR may make the issue of affordability (Sect. 6.1) more acute, because schools normally do not have sufficient resources to buy extra equipment. Consequently, we pursue a more promising approach to learning with AR.

---

[1] https://www.statista.com/topics/3286/augmented-reality-ar/;/2532/virtual-reality-vr/;841/tablets/.

6.3 Longitudinal Study

The learning effect of an educational intervention should be long-lasting, and such effect can be evaluated with retention tests in the context of a longitudinal study [51]. Unfortunately, we were not able to implement it because we had only been given a short window of time to carry out our empirical work at the schools. In fact, getting cooperation from schools to support research study is challenging. The schools where we conducted our study could not accommodate our request to track the children's related progress in a longer-term. Outreach activities to promote benefits of getting involved in educational research may facilitate the realization of empirical work.

7 Conclusion

The results of this study showed that the AR Class performed better than the Normal class when the children were learning complex 3D geometry. Furthermore, the children had a high level of user engagement as indicated by the ratings of the four dimensions of the UES-SF, irrespective of the strength of the learning effect demonstrated. One encouraging finding was that the AR application could engage the children in the learning activities. However, there was no significant relation between the level of engagement in interacting with the AR application and the level of knowledge gain, which bore no relation with the intention to use the AR application in future either.

There are some limitations in our study. First, the sample size was relatively small because the challenge of recruiting schools to participate. Second, the number of tablets constrained the number of children who could take the AR Class at the same time. While this constraint should not affect the children's performance, as it was individual-based learning, it made the study much more time-consuming. A practical implication of this issue is how to contain the price of emerging technologies to make them affordable for their wide adoption as educational technology that can benefit a large number of children. Third, the target group of our study was secondary school children. It would be interesting to examine whether the results would be similar for children of different ages and with varied levels of prior experience in technology.

Overall, our study has demonstrated the potential of AR technology as an effective tool for learning complex geometric concepts. Based on our ongoing review of the burgeoning area of digital game-based learning [52], we are motivated to explore how the promise of AR for technology-enhanced learning tool will further be strengthened with the motivational power of gamification [53].

References

1. Browne, K., Anand, C.: An empirical evaluation of user interfaces for a mobile video game. Entertain. Comput. 3(1), 1–10 (2012)
2. Bucolo, S., Billinghurst, M., Sickinger, D.: Mobile maze: a comparison of camera based mobile game human interfaces. In: Proceedings of the 7th International Conference on Human Computer Interaction with Mobile Devices & Services, pp. 329–330. ACM (2005)

3. Puja, J.C., Parsons, D.: A location-based mobile game for business education. In: 11th IEEE International Conference on Advanced Learning Technologies (ICALT), pp. 42–44. IEEE (2011)
4. Zyda, M.J., Thukral, D., Ferrans, J.C., Engelsma, J., Hans, M.: Enabling a voice modality in mobile games through voicexml. In: Proceedings of the 2008 ACM SIGGRAPH Symposium on Video Games, pp. 14147. ACM (2008)
5. Hung, C.Y., Chang, T.W., Yu, P.T., Cheng, P.J.: The problem-solving skills and learning performance in learning multi-touch interactive jigsaw game using digital scaffolds. In: 2012 IEEE Fourth International Conference on Digital Game and Intelligent Toy Enhanced Learning (DIGITEL), pp. 33–38. IEEE (2012)
6. Wei, S., Ren, G., O'Neill, E.: Haptic and audio displays for augmented reality tourism applications. In: 2014 IEEE on Haptics Symposium (HAPTICS), pp. 485–488. IEEE (2014)
7. Scholz, J., Smith, A.N.: Augmented reality: designing immersive experiences that maximize consumer engagement. Bus. Horiz. 59(2), 149–161 (2016)
8. Pedersen, I., Gale, N., Mirza-Babaei, P., Reid, S.: More than meets the eye: the benefits of augmented reality and holographic displays for digital cultural heritage. J. Comput. Cultural Heritage (JOCCH) 10(2), 11 (2017)
9. Zsila, Á., et al.: An empirical study on the motivations underlying augmented reality games: the case of Pokémon Go during and after Pokémon fever. Personality Individ. Differ. 133, 56–66 (2018)
10. Bower, M., Howe, C., McCredie, N., Robinson, A., Grover, D.: Augmented Reality in education–cases, places and potentials. Educ. Media Int. 51(1), 1–15 (2014)
11. Chow, E.H., Thadani, D.R., Wong, E.Y., Pegrum, M.: Mobile technologies and augmented reality: early experiences in helping students learn about academic integrity and ethics. Int. J. Humanit. Soc. Sci. Educ. 2(7), 112–120 (2015)
12. Yilmaz, R.M.: Educational magic toys developed with augmented reality technology for early childhood education. Comput. Hum. Behav. 54, 240–248 (2016)
13. Fotouhi-Ghazvini, F., Earnshaw, R.A., Robison, D., Excell, P.S.: Designing augmented reality games for mobile learning using an instructional-motivational paradigm. In: 2009 International Conference on CyberWorlds, CW 2009, pp. 312–319. IEEE (2009)
14. Kysela, J., Štorková, P.: Using augmented reality as a médium for teaching history and tourism. Procedia-Soc. Behav. Sci. 174, 926–931 (2015)
15. Adolphus, T.: Problems of teaching and learning of geometry in secondary schools in Rivers State, Nigeria. Int. J. Emerg. Sci. 1(2), 143–152 (2011)
16. Irwansyah, F.S., Yusuf, Y.M., Farida, I., Ramdhani, M.A.: Augmented Reality (AR) technology on the android operating system in chemistry learning. In: IOP Conference Series: Materials Science and Engineering, vol. 288, no. 1, p. 012068. IOP Publishing (2018)
17. Krichenbauer, M., Yamamoto, G., Taketomi, T., Sandor, C., Kato, H.: Augmented reality vs virtual reality for 3D object manipulation. IEEE Trans. Visual. Comput. Graphics 24(2), 1038–1048 (2017)
18. Lin, H.C.K., Chen, M.C., Chang, C.K.: Assessing the effectiveness of learning solid geometry by using an augmented reality-assisted learning system. Interact. Learn. Environ. 23(6), 799–810 (2015)
19. Young, J.C., Santoso, H.B.: Preliminary study of JunoBlock: marker-based augmented reality for geometry educational tool. In: Abdullah, N., Wan Adnan, W.A., Foth, M. (eds.) i-USEr 2018. CCIS, vol. 886, pp. 219–230. Springer, Singapore (2018). https://doi.org/10.1007/978-981-13-1628-9_20
20. Liu, E., Li, Y., Cai, S., Li, X.: The effect of augmented reality in solid geometry class on students' learning performance and attitudes. In: Auer, M., Langmann, R. (eds.) Smart Industry & Smart Education. LNCS, vol. 47, pp. 549–558. Springer, Cham (2018). https://doi.org/10.1007/978-3-319-95678-7_61

21. Morrison, A., et al.: Collaborative use of mobile augmented reality with paper maps. Comput. Graph. **35**(4), 789–799 (2011)
22. Wu, H.K., Lee, S.W.Y., Chang, H.Y., Liang, J.C.: Current status, opportunities and challenges of augmented reality in education. Comput. Educ. **62**, 41–49 (2013)
23. Mayer, R.E.: Multimedia Learning, 2nd edn. Cambridge University Press, Cambridge (2009)
24. Sommerauer, P., Müller, O.: Augmented reality in informal learning environments: a field experiment in a mathematics exhibition. Comput. Educ. **79**, 59–68 (2014)
25. Ridel, B., Reuter, P., Laviole, J., Mellado, N., Couture, N., Granier, X.: The revealing flashlight: Interactive spatial augmented reality for detail exploration of cultural heritage artifacts. J. Comput. Cultural Heritage (JOCCH) **7**(2), 6 (2014)
26. Ibáñez, M.B., Di Serio, Á., Villarán, D., Kloos, C.D.: Experimenting with electromagnetism using augmented reality: impact on flow student experience and educational effectiveness. Comput. Educ. **71**, 1–13 (2014)
27. Fleck, S., Simon, G., Bastien, J.C.: [Poster] AIBLE: an inquiry-based augmented reality environment for teaching astronomical phenomena. In: 2014 IEEE International Symposium on Mixed and Augmented Reality-Media, Art, Social Science, Humanities and Design (ISMAR-MASH'D), pp. 65–66. IEEE (2014)
28. Kim, J., Seo, J., Han, T.D.: AR Lamp: interactions on projection-based augmented reality for interactive learning. In: Proceedings of the 19th International Conference on Intelligent User Interfaces, pp. 353–358. ACM (2014)
29. Yang, K.J., Chu, H.C., Yang, K.H.: Using the augmented reality technique to develop visualization Mindtools for chemical inquiry-based activities. In: 2015 IIAI 4th International Congress on Advanced Applied Informatics (IIAI-AAI), pp. 354–357. IEEE (2015)
30. Alrashidi, M., Gardner, M., Callaghan, V.: Evaluating the use of pedagogical virtual machine with augmented reality to support learning embedded computing activity. In: Proceedings of the 9th International Conference on Computer and Automation Engineering, pp. 44–50. ACM (2017)
31. Kortenkamp, U., Richter-Gebert, J.U.R.G.E.N.: The interactive geometry software Cinderella. In: Mathematical Software: Proceedings of the First International Congress of Mathematical Software, Beijing, China, 17–19 August 2002, vol. 1, p. 208. World Scientific (2002)
32. Mechling, R.: EUKLID DynaGeo von innen-ein Blick hinter die Kulissen (1999)
33. Holden, C.: The local games lab ABQ: homegrown augmented reality. TechTrends **58**(1), 42–48 (2014)
34. Norman, D., Miller, J., Henderson, A.: What you see, some of what's in the future, and how we go about doing it: HI at Apple Computer. In: Conference companion on Human Factors in Computing Systems, p. 155. ACM (1995)
35. Gegner, L., Runonen, M., Keinonen, T.: Oscillating between extremes: a framework for mapping differing views on user experience. In: Proceedings of the 2011 Conference on Designing Pleasurable Products and Interfaces, p. 57. ACM (2011)
36. Desmet, P.M.A., Hekkert, P.: Framework of product experience. Int. J. Des. **1**, 57–66 (2007)
37. Law, E., Roto, V., Hassenzahl, M., Vermeeren, A., Kort, J.: Understanding, scoping and defining UX: a survey approach. In: Proceedings of the ACM Conference on Human Factors in Computing Systems (CHI 2009), Boston, USA. ACM (2009). http://dx.doi.org/10.1145/1518701.1518813
38. Roto, V., Law, E., Vermeeren, A.P.O.S., Hoonhout, J.: User experience white paper-bringing clarity to the concept of user experience (2011)
39. O'Brien, H.L., Cairns, P., Hall, M.: A practical approach to measuring user engagement with the refined user engagement scale (UES) and new UES short form. Int. J. Hum.-Comput. Stud. **112**, 28–39 (2018)

40. Jacques, R.D.: The nature of engagement and its role in hypermedia evaluation and design. Doctoral dissertation, South Bank University (1996)
41. Webster, J., Ho, H.: Audience engagement in multimedia presentations. ACM SIGMIS database: DATABASE Adv. Inf. Syst. **28**(2), 63–77 (1997)
42. Jokela, T., Iivari, N., Matero, J., Karukka, M.: The standard of user-centered design and the standard definition of usability: analyzing ISO 13407 against ISO 9241–11. In: Proceedings of the Latin American conference on Human-Computer Interaction, pp. 53–60. ACM (2003)
43. Cohen, L., Manion, L., Morrison, K.: Research Methods in Education (2007)
44. Unity 3D website. https://unity3d.com/unity/
45. Venkatesh, V., Davis, F.D.: A theoretical extension of the technology acceptance model: four longitudinal field studies. Manag. Sci. **46**(2), 186–204 (2000)
46. Noyes, J.M., Garland, K.J.: Computer-vs. paper-based tasks: are they equivalent? Ergonomics **51**(9), 1352–1375 (2008)
47. Bayazit, A., Aşkar, P.: Performance and duration differences between online and paper–pencil tests. Asia Pacific Educ. Rev. **13**(2), 219–226 (2012)
48. Cheesman, M.J., Chunduri, P., Manchadi, M.L., Colthorpe, K., Matthews, B.: Student interaction with a computer tablet exam application replicating the traditional paper exam. Mobile Comput. **4**, 10–21 (2015)
49. Mendes, D., Caputo, F.M., Giachetti, A., Ferreira, A., Jorge, J.: A survey on 3D virtual object manipulation: from the desktop to immersive virtual environments. Comput. Graph. Forum **38**(1), 21–45 (2019)
50. Alshaer, A., Regenbrecht, H., O'Hare, D.: Immersion factors affecting perception and behaviour in a virtual reality power wheelchair simulator. Appl. Ergon. **58**, 1–12 (2017)
51. Ruiz-Ariza, A., Casuso, R.A., Suarez-Manzano, S., Martínez-López, E.J.: Effect of augmented reality game Pokémon GO on cognitive performance and emotional intelligence in adolescent young. Comput. Educ. **116**, 49–63 (2018)
52. All, A., Castellar, E.P.N., Van Looy, J.: Assessing the effectiveness of digital game-based learning: best practices. Comput. Educ. **92**, 90–103 (2016)
53. Kapp, K.M.: The Gamification of Learning and Instruction. Wiley, San Francisco (2012)

Enhance Engine Room Diagnostics Through Audio-Focused VR Simulation

Tychonas Michailidis[1]([✉]) [iD], Christopher Barlow[2], Gordon Meadow[3],
John Gouch[3], and Eshan Rajabally[4]

[1] Research, Innovation and Enterprise, Solent University, Southampton, UK
`tychonas.michailidis@solent.ac.uk`
[2] School of Media Arts and Technology, Solent University, Southampton, UK
[3] Warsash Maritime Academy, Solent University, Southampton, UK
[4] Central Technology, Rolls-Royce plc, Derby, UK

Abstract. A marine engineer's task is to maintain all systems in an operational state, to diagnose and rectify problems arising, and to understand what maintenance will be required to keep the vessel appropriately operational and safe. This capability is built upon the training and experience of the engineering crew, the information that can be gained by reading and interpreting engine room instrumentation, and the familiarity with the vessel and an in-situ *intuitive feel* for normal operation. In this paper, we examine how audio can enhance remote interaction and feedback information. We gathered real-world data from an engine room that allow us to create a realistic virtual engine room for testing. We carried out usability test on simulated failure scenarios where we look at how VR technology might enable engineers to experience immersive information from a remote location and allow them to diagnose and give feedback on the system. Our findings suggest that sound plays a vital role in identifying failures and could potentially be used in the operation of unmanned and autonomous vessels.

Keywords: Audio failures · Engine room · Diagnostics · VR · Feedback

1 Introduction

Marine engineers on board ship use a wide variety of multi-sensory feedback in addition to the system data [3]. This feedback includes sound, vibration, heat and smell. The sense of sound and vibration is an invaluable tool for initial detection of faults by engineers. Pumps, filters, generators, main engine and other moving parts in the engine room (ER) have a unique audio signature which changes over time when potential failure is imminent. Sounds may be caused by increased friction, insufficient lubrication or general component failure which result in changes of frequency, knocking sounds, whining, squeaking or

© IFIP International Federation for Information Processing 2019
Published by Springer Nature Switzerland AG 2019
D. Lamas et al. (Eds.): INTERACT 2019, LNCS 11749, pp. 386–394, 2019.
https://doi.org/10.1007/978-3-030-29390-1_21

arrhythmic sounds all of which have a distinctive sound quality [4]. Engineers are intuitively trained to accumulate this rich source of audio information, and it subconsciously becomes part of their diagnostics ritual and inspection. While it may not always allow an engineer to diagnose the cause of failure only by listening, it is particularly useful in identifying and narrowing down the source of a problem as well as confirming the validity of known data. Engineers commonly report not fully trusting the control data [3] due to regular false alarms from systems or 'wrong readings' from the sensors. Despite advances in monitoring and diagnostics technology, onboard engineers still rely on their intuitive feel and senses to assess system health or confirm control data before system failure is imminent. Engineers may use audio to identify if a piece of machinery failed to run; to identify the state of machinery/pipes; to access the *harshness* of a component through variations in sound level and pitch.

Due to excessive loudness within the ER (above 100 db), engineers are required to wear ear defenders. As a result, potential details of audio features are lost. Audio can play a significant role in providing a diagnostics tool otherwise unavailable in-situ for example, in the potential crewless vessel scenario. It is possible to isolate the audio of a component from background noise, and therefore focus more closely into audible failures. Within a VR environment, engineers can enhance audio information and their ability and have a clear sound source of information to support their diagnostics.

1.1 Real Word Challenges

The primary challenge of this project was to understand and measure how the engineering crew uses sensory feedback to characterise the state of the vessel while onboard, for both normal and abnormal conditions, and to assess the mechanisms by which this tacit information may be communicated and interpreted effectively to a remote location. Experimentation with artificial data, including a non-realistic visual representation of engine room, data from machinery (e.g. temperature and pressure), and audio, would have resulted in false readings and results. The ferry company Red Funnel[1] granted access to the team to collect data from the engine room of a Raptor Class ro-pax ferry that operates daily services between Southampton and Isle of White with a round-trip duration around two hours. We were able to get the schematics of machinery layout, photographs and audio recording of the ER ambience sound and the machinery as well as real data values from pressure and temperature of relevant components for developing the VR system. The simulated engine room is 1:1 ratio with the real engine room.

Computer simulations have the potential to immerse remote operators concerning the system in question. Maritime, military and aerospace industries have been using computer-simulated systems for operator training, including navigation and bridge systems [2]. Current VR systems have now become readily available to implement them in a wide range of industries apart from gaming,

---

[1] https://www.redfunnel.co.uk.

Fig. 1. Engine room of the Red Falcon, Red Funnel fleet

offering a low cost large-scale simulation. Their potential for the presentation of real-time data is already being explored [6]. Engineers on board ship use a wide variety of sensory feedback information in addition to the system data. However, sound, vibration, heat and smell, these are not commonly replicated effectively in simulations [5] (Fig. 1).

2   Methodology

Initial user requirements were assessed through a combination of interviews with stakeholders, engineers and literature review through a successive approximation method [1] enabling us to develop a basic VR simulation in Unreal Engine 4 using the HTC VIVE Pro HMD system. Feedback by a dedicated of five subject matter experts (SMEs) from Warsash Maritime Academy were employed to refine the simulation at each iteration of the development cycle as well as accessing how realistic were the simulated failure sounds created for each scenario. SMEs were invited to provide feedback on multiple iterations throughout the development stage.

2.1   Representation of Sound and Vibration

Our research was not only aiming to replicate the real-world experience into virtual space but also to offer some potential enhancement of audio feedback. In particular, we examined how audio features, that are being lost due to the high sound pressure levels within the ER (measured value of $106dBL_{Aeq,15}$ using the *NTi XL2 acoustic analyzer*), can enable engineers to diagnose current and potential issues and interact with.

The general background sound of the engine room was captured with a *Soundfield SPS200* placed in key positions. To capture airborne sound with maximum rejection of spill from other components we use the *Røde NTG2* shotgun microphone placed around 20 cm from the source. We also use the *Cold Gold*TM *electret* contact microphones to capture sound directly from different locations of each machinery. These microphones are 'electronic stethoscopes' in which the electret transducer is embedded in a silicone cup, allowing direct connection to a device while ensuring very high levels of rejection of spill. With the three different recording data, an operator from a remote location would be able to isolate and listen to specific components, as well as to the overall space, which would add to the capability of the system in terms of identification of mechanical problems. During interviews and discussions with engineers, they all point how experiencing vibrations as a whole or from individual components play a significant role in identifying failures. Sound and vibration are intrinsically linked to the performance and state of the machinery. To increase the level of impressiveness as part of the diagnostic feedback, it was important to include a representation of this vibration into the simulation. Several different options were considered; however, the majority of vibration based systems require the user to be seated. The *Subpak M2* is a body-worn bass transducer, which is designed to apply vibration directly from the audio signal to the back of the user. Therefore the user is mobile, which is an integral part of the VR experience.

2.2   System Failure Simulation

Mechanical failures such as cavitation of a pump, misfiring of the main engine and generator, single phasing of the compressor, air bleeds from the compressor, and damaged bearings or insufficient lubrication on several systems have particular sound characteristics. During our recording sessions, it was not feasible to disable active systems on the vessel or wait for a machinery failure to appear, and as a result, mechanical failure had to be simulated.

Recordings of similar system failures on isolated components were sourced through sound libraries and recordings from the engineering workshop. Sound files were combined ensuring that the simulated failure blended effectively with the original audio. The new sound was recognisably the same component, but with a characteristic of the sound associated with a particular mechanical failure. The SMEs who took part were asked to identify which sounds from engine room components were most accurately identified and which are the most accurate representations of particular mechanical failures to be used for the final simulator.

2.3   Server and User Interface

In order to test the ability of engineers to identify failures from a remote location, we had to be able to introduce failure scenarios into the VR system. A web interface hosted on a remote server was developed. The server enables the reproduction of real data and audio as if they are streamed from a real vessel into the remote location control centre. The server feeds data and audio control to the simulation in real time. Data for each component in the simulation including audio, and thus the felt vibrations, can be controlled to provide realistic representations of various levels of failure.

All critical components were modelled and receive simulated control data from the remote server. This enables the system administrator to set up varying scenarios, in which a combination of appropriate data values as well as audio and vibration signals are used across several components to represent a particular mechanical failure. As a result, a user can explore and identify virtual failures using familiar techniques as he/she might do normally in-situ. Handheld controllers allow the user to navigate around the ER, through a transport feature, and select components to examine within the engine room. When selecting a component, a virtual handheld display (Fig. 2), attached to one of the controllers, shows the available data from the conventional sensors. These are mainly pressure and temperature, ability to isolate the sound of the selected machinery, mute background sounds to listen to the component directly as well as the ability to scroll through a ten-hour time history of system performance, including audio, vibration and data for snapshots at hourly intervals.

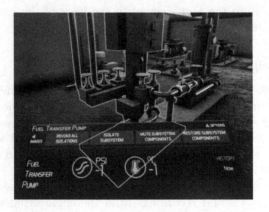

Fig. 2. Selected component outlined, virtual handheld display shown towards the bottom of the figure

3   User Testing

Seven marine engineers went through different simulate failure scenarios user with an average of 27 years of experience ranking between Chief Engineer and Second engineer. The usability test was undertaken using a blend of quantitative and qualitative methods in order to triangulate results. A set of performing tasks was aimed to determine the usability of the VR system for engineers with different levels and types of experience. Mainly to access how marine engineers were able to diagnose system failures using the simulation; examine to what extend audio feedback plays a role in enabling marine engineers to diagnose and predict early failures of components in remote monitoring situations.

The signal was spatialised using a binaural encoder and played simultaneously on a 4 channel (4.0) arrangement as well on the headset built-in headphones. This enabled users to choose to listen to either the loudspeaker based audio, or the headphone-based audio, and get spatial cues from each. Engineers were first familiarised with the system, without any simulated faults, in order to ensure that they were able to navigate around the virtual space and access the data and controls. After a period of familiarisation, each participant went through one of four simulated scenarios. Two scenarios involve simulated faults, and two had no fault. Simulations were presented in a randomised order. Participants were not told whether or not there would be faults present but were asked to undertake a system health check of the simulated ER as if they were undertaking a normal 'rounds check'. They were asked to assess whether or not they felt there was a potential system failure, or if the system was operating normally. If they felt failure was present, they were asked to state what was the likely problem and cause.

Participants were asked to 'think aloud' throughout the familiarisation as well as during the test so that a verbal record existed of their interaction with the system. The facilitator observed noted the user's behaviour, comments, and actions.

A post-test questionnaire took place providing feedback regarding Attractiveness, Perspicuity, Efficiency, Dependability, Stimulation, and Novelty of the system. A semi-structured interview followed aiming to gather further information and comments about their experience and functionality of the system. Interviews were audio recorded, transcribed and analysed using a *Qualitative data analysis* (QDA) method.

4   Results

The focus of the usability testing was primarily qualitative, as the primary aim was to ascertain whether engineers felt that the system had the potential for diagnostic use, whether the virtual environment and user interface were effective, their perception of the immersive elements, and what improvements or alternative uses they felt the system could have. All seven engineers were able to identify whether or not there was a system failure accurately, and also the location of the failure, even if the simulated failure was a low risk. Three participants accurately diagnosed the exact failure type, while the others identified a problem, but stated that they would need further investigation in order to identify the exact cause.

The overall response strongly focused on the immersive features, with 'sound' appearing in 22.8% of coded phrases, 'vibration' in 8.7% and 'immersion' in 5.8%. Within the features, 'sound' was by far the strongest theme. Participants focused on how sound and vibration enable them to be immersed and made the space familiar. Overall participants consider stimulation as 'Excellent' (Fig. 3) against the benchmark provided by the *User Experience Questionnaire (UEQ)*[2].

The use of vibrations was also a key theme as it was specifically identified in terms of improving the ability to diagnose failures in the simulation along with

---

[2] https://www.ueq-online.org.

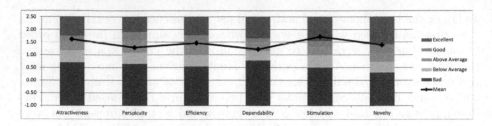

Fig. 3. UEQ results showing the mean values of different aspects of the questionnaire

the audio. One participant said that even though the vibration was limited it did give an edge. Another participant said that he couldn't hear changes of sound but could feel the vibration.

5   Discussion

The project focused on exploring how sound can be enhanced to compensate and even exceed the missing sensory information from a remote location. The simulation demonstrated that immersive audio and vibration feedback could aid towards remote operators in diagnosis of engine room failures. Engineers mentioned:

> *If the pressures are fine, the temperatures are fine, but the noise has changed you know something's up (P5). Even though you see the data...you are more convinced that something has gone wrong through sound rather than the data(P1).*

There were some negative statements regarding the fidelity of the system as the data values used for simulated machinery readings could be improved. These statements generally focused on technical aspects of implementation. For example, a machine which has been switched off in the simulation should retain data due to the heat at the sensors. In terms of user experience, the overall focus was on positive aspects. Users found the system to be generally easy to navigate and stated that they very quickly adapted to the simulation. Some concerns were raised regarding the use of the system when unfamiliar with the interface and controls, and the comfort of the system. From a usability perspective overall, the system was considered highly satisfactory. When analysing statements which expressed opinion, 74.9% of coded statements were 'positive' in focus. When questioned about the system potential for remote diagnosis through audio, all respondents gave overall positive feedback regarding the potential use. The ability to identify failures and the possible cause of the problem under time constrained circumstances on an unfamiliar vessel, suggests that the virtual environment and the integration of real-time immersive features offer significant potential for enhancing remote diagnostics. A key statement from several participants was that they did not listen for specific characteristics, but for change of audio.

Scrolling of historical data of any system was listed as a particularly positive feature. It allowed engineers to quickly identify changes in both audio/vibration and the data. Often the audio change would occur before a significant change in system's temperature or pressure. Engineers commented they were easily immersed in the space which resulted in becoming alert as if it was a real engine room. One engineer, when putting on the HMD to enter the simulation started talking louder even though the background sound levels remained the same. Due to high sound pressure levels, engineers need to talk loudly in order to communicate. The participant unconsciously spoke louder, feeling like he was in a real ER. When asked, after the session, why he spoke louder, he was unaware that he had done so.

6   Conclusion

This paper looks at how marine engineers can interact and diagnose failures from a remote location through audio. The potential of using VR systems with immersive audio and vibration enhances the diagnostic capabilities, particularly for remote operation of vessels at sea. Engine rooms are complex and active systems that change over time which are hard to replicate. Information like smell, heat and whole-body vibration proved to be impossible to reproduce precisely within the scope of this research. We recognise that due to excessive sounds in the ER vital information is often missed. Even though data from machinery can provide a good overview of the system they are not always reliable. As a result, the knowledge and experience of an engineer play an essential role in identifying failures including anticipating future failures.

We focused on exploring how sound qualities can be enhanced to compensate and even exceed the missing sensory information. The sound can be analysed and provide focused information to the operator in a remote location. The perception of sound experience in a virtual environment can be enhanced and refined to provide the best possible experience and information to the user. Our research showed that being able to control the volume, ability to filter out any unwanted surrounding noise, focus on a particular component, and the ten-hour audio history, engineers were able to understand failures and issues associated with the system failure. With the advances of sound techniques, live audio feed can be analysed and transmitted to a remote location providing a holistic view of the situation.

From the results presented above, we are confident that real-time feeds of sound as a diagnostic feature would be a significant benefit to remote operation and engine room diagnostics in the autonomous shipping industry, and this would benefit from further exploration and investigation. Engineers showed great interest in the 'time history' (from data and sound) as they could easily and quickly identify not only changes in the ER but also identify possible causes of failure. VR technology is a promising way forward in an immersive experience and possible development in monitoring and interaction in future autonomous shipping.

References

1. Allen, M.: Leaving ADDIE for SAM: An Agile Model for Designing the Best Learning Experiences. ASTD Press, Alexandria (2012)
2. Fachot, M.: Virtual reality is central to aviation and maritime training. IEC e-tech (2016). https://iecetech.org/issue/2016-04/Virtual-reality-is-central-to-aviation-and-maritime-training. Accessed 21 March 2019
3. Meadow, G., et al.: IMAGINE - Work Package 1. Technical report (unpublished). Rolls- Royce/Solent University (2017)
4. Kuschel, J., Ljungberg, F.: Decentralized remote diagnostics: a study of diagnostics in the marine industry. In: Fincher, S., Markopoulos, P., Moore, D., Ruddle, R. (eds.) People and Computers XVIII - Design for Life, pp. 211–226. Springer, London (2005). https://doi.org/10.1007/1-84628-062-1_14
5. Kilteni, K., Groten, R., Slater, M.: The sense of embodiment in virtual reality. Presence: Teleoperators Virtual Environ. **21**(4), 373–387 (2012)
6. Resch, B., Wichmann, A., Goell, N.: Usability in 4D AR: visualising multi-temporal real-time geo-data in augmented reality environments. iJIM **9**(4), 23–33 (2015)

Head-Controlled Menu in Mixed Reality with a HMD

Charles Bailly[1,2](✉), François Leitner[2](✉), and Laurence Nigay[1](✉)

[1] Univ. Grenoble Alpes, CNRS, Grenoble INP, LIG, 38000 Grenoble, France
{charles.bailly,laurence.nigay}@univ-grenoble-alpes.fr
[2] Aesculap SAS, 38130 Echirolles, France
{charles.bailly,francois.leitner}@bbraun.com

Abstract. We present a design-space and three new techniques for head-based interaction with menus in Mixed Reality (MR) with a Head-Mounted Display (HMD). Usual input modalities such as hand gestures and voice commands are not suitable in noisy MR contexts where the users have both hands occupied as in augmented surgery and machine maintenance. To address the two issues of noisy MR contexts and hand-free interaction, we systematically explore the design space of head-controlled menu interaction by considering two design factors: (1) head-controlled menu versus head-controlled cursor (2) virtual targets versus mixed targets anchored on physical objects. Based on the design space, we present three novel menu techniques that we compared with a baseline head-controlled cursor technique. Experimental results suggest that head-controlled menu and head-controlled cursor techniques offer similar performance. In addition, the study found that mixed targets do not impact ultimate user performance when users are trained enough, but improve the learning phase. When using virtual targets, users still progressed after the training phase by reducing their mean selection time by 0.84 s. When using mixed targets, the improvement was limited to 0.3 s.

Keywords: Mixed Reality · HMD · Menu technique

1 Introduction

Mixed Reality (MR) using a Head-Mounted Display (HMD) has a strong potential in several domains [6,38], including medicine, manufacturing and repair. Superimposing virtual content on a working environment allow users to visualize relevant data directly in place instead of relying on a distant screen. For instance, MR can replace manuals by superimposing instructions directly on the working environment to help technicians [36,52]. MR is also studied as a training tool for assembly tasks [41].

For augmented surgery, a HMD can be used: (1) to display medical information directly on the patient body [3,27,32] and/or (2) to display the Graphical

© IFIP International Federation for Information Processing 2019
Published by Springer Nature Switzerland AG 2019
D. Lamas et al. (Eds.): INTERACT 2019, LNCS 11749, pp. 395–415, 2019.
https://doi.org/10.1007/978-3-030-29390-1_22

User Interface (GUI) of the surgical system including medical images, menus and palettes. Surgical navigation systems like the OrthoPilot® [1] are interactive systems supporting surgeons during the entire workflow of the surgery (hence the term *navigation* systems). Issuing commands with such systems is usually done through 1-level menus currently displayed on a distant screen in the operating room. As a first step towards replacing the distant screen by using a HMD, this paper focuses on pointing to a menu in MR.

Existing interaction techniques for MR using a HMD are not always adapted to specific contexts of use as in augmented surgery and machine maintenance. Surgeons must follow strict sterility rules and often have both hands occupied by surgical tasks. The same applies for mechanical tasks: technicians need both hands to hold tools and perform their repair task while still needing to interact with the system. In addition, operation rooms and machine areas are both noisy and congested environments. Finally, surgeons and military mechanics both have a significant cognitive load because of the complexity and critical aspects of their tasks [11,19]. Such constraints limit the possible techniques for interacting with the system. New hand-free interaction techniques adapted to these specific contexts of use are needed. This work focuses on menu techniques for HMD-based MR that are adapted for these contexts of use.

The contribution of this work is the design and the evaluation of 3 head-based techniques for interacting with a menu in MR. These techniques are based on two design factors: (1) Head-controlled menu versus Head-controlled cursor and (2) virtual targets versus mixed targets. In the following, the augmented surgery scenario is taken as a running example. However, the techniques we designed target any context where users work with both hands occupied in a noisy and congested environment. In the rest of this paper we discuss background work, present the design space of head-based menu techniques in MR and describe the three designed techniques we developed. We then present the results of two conducted studies to compare the performance of the designed menu techniques. We conclude by discussing design implications for the menu techniques we have studied, and suggest potential future pathways for developing menu techniques in MR using a HMD.

2 Related Work

2.1 Interaction Techniques in MR

Gesture-Based Interaction: Gesture-based interaction is commonly used for HMD-based MR. Some approaches are based on specific gloves to allow direct hand manipulation of virtual objects as [10], while more recent approaches use bare hand gesture recognition systems [12,13,18]. However, adapting the gestural recognition system to specific environments like operating rooms requires significant effort [37]. Operation rooms are very bright environments and gestures from other surgical team members must not be interpreted as commands. Besides, gesture-based interaction requires one to use one or two hands. This is an issue for surgeons and mechanics, who need both hands to perform their technical tasks.

Direct Touch Interaction: For the same reasons as before, interaction based on tangibles or body direct touch is not adapted to augmented surgery or maintenance. In the case of surgery, strict sterility constraints prevent direct touch interaction on the body [5]. Furthermore, all objects in the operating field must be sterilized before the surgery. Introducing new tangibles to interact with menus as in [48] would increase this already long preparatory phase. As explained in Sect. 1, the lack of available space is also an issue. For instance, Henderson and Feiner [19] describe a prototype MR application to help military mechanics perform maintenance inside an armored vehicle turret, where available space is really limited.

Voice Control: When hands are not available for interacting, voice commands offer an alternative interaction technique [2,34]. However, ambient noise is a issue for voice recognition software [21,37]. The operating theatre is a noisy environment due to the medical equipment and oral communication between surgical team members. This also holds for machine rooms which often have noisy equipment. Besides, as pointed out by Mitrasinovic et al. [35], speaking slowly and distinctly is a luxury during a surgery since time is a critical factor. Therefore, voice commands are not suitable for our targeted application contexts.

2.2   Head-Based Interaction

Head-based gestures have been studied in the literature as a technique to interact with virtual content displayed on a HMD [33,50,51]. However, using a set of previously defined head-gestures may not be suitable in our application contexts. In [33], users have to perform different head gestures depending on the task. Having to learn and remember which gesture must be done for each type of command may increase the cognitive load of an already highly-focused user with busy hands (e.g. a surgeon, a technician). Moreover, head gestures also raise the issue of tiredness, especially for the case of surgeons performing more than one hour long operations. Finally, as for voice commands, head gestures must also be distinguished from unintentional inputs [50].

In addition to head gestures, head motion has also been explored as a technique for pointing tasks. Head motion is used to control a virtual cursor, in Virtual Reality (VR) [4,40] and in MR [29,39]. Jagacinski and Monk showed in 1985 that Fitt's Law is a good predictor of a head pointing task performance [25]. When compared to eye-gaze input, head-controlled cursor was found more comfortable to use and more accurate [26,29]. Comfort and accuracy are key factors, in particular for surgeons: comfort because operations can last more than one hour and a half; accuracy to avoid errors and feel in precise control. Cassell highlighted that the feeling of certitude and control are crucial in the operating room because surgeons have to take life-and death decisions [11]. Anything threatening the confidence surgeons have in the mastery of their tools and environment must be avoided [15].

Using the head as a technique for interacting with graphical widgets displayed on the HMD is therefore a promising approach that matches the requirements of our targeted contexts. As mentioned in Sect. 1, this paper focuses on head-based interaction with a menu.

3   Design Space for Head-Based Menu Techniques in MR

We used two factors to define the basis of a design space for head-based menu techniques. Our design rational is based on the specificities of MR with a HMD. In particular, the augmented Field Of View (FOV) is limited but directly controlled by the head.

3.1   Interaction Element Controlled by Head Movements

The first design factor is the element controlled by users when moving their head: a cursor or the menu itself. When using a HMD, the augmented FOV is directly linked to the head position. Therefore, any graphical element displayed at a fixed position on the HMD will move in the physical world frame of reference according to the head movements. The graphical element is fixed in the screen frame of reference and movable in the physical world frame of reference. When interacting with a menu, this principle leads to two solutions: moving the cursor or moving the menu. With a Head-Controlled Cursor (HCC), users aim at targets (i.e. menu items) that are fixed in the physical world frame of reference by orienting their head and aligning a cursor on the targets (see Fig. 1a and Sect. 2.2). HCC minimizes the visual intrusion on the HMD: the cross displayed at the center of the screen. This is a significant advantage since the augmented FOV is limited on current HMDs. Besides, HCC reproduces the same metaphor as in GUI using the mouse, and is therefore familiar to MR novice users.

Instead of moving a cursor to a menu item, the menu can be directly controlled with the head. When using a Head-Controlled Menu (HCM), the targeted menu item must be brought to a fixed location in the physical world frame of reference (i.e. a cursor position) in order to be selected (see Fig. 1b). To some extent, this approach is similar to the Toolglass technique [9]. The Toolglass is a transparent sheet with a set of tools (*i.e.* a palette) which can be controlled with a trackball. This palette can thus be superimposed onto the object of interest with one hand while the other hand control the mouse, allowing users to select both the command and its target at the same time. HCM and Toolglass share one idea: bringing what Beaudouin-Lafon [8] calls meta-instruments to a selection area (i.e. the cursor for a HCM and the object of interest for a Toolglass).

Of course, a Head-Controlled Menu implies a significant visual intrusion by displaying the menu at the center of the HMD, especially as compared to a Head-Controlled Cursor. During the critical phases of their work, surgeons and mechanics only focus on the complex gestures to be performed, and any visual intrusion may threaten the process. However, when interacting with the navigation system, these users are not performing such critical phases. Therefore, visual intrusion at these moments is less of an issue. Visual intrusion can also be mitigated by the fact that menus do not require permanent screen space.

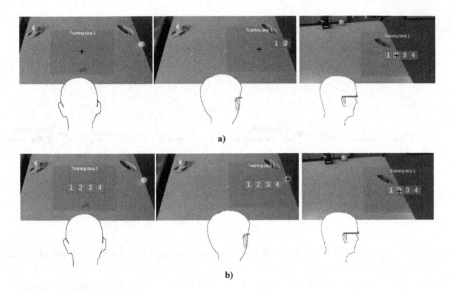

Fig. 1. (a) Head-Controlled Cursor: head-based movement of a cursor towards a menu. (b) Head-Controlled Menu: head-based movement of a menu towards a cursor

Menus are transient: they are closed immediately after the selection of an item and they appear on demand [7]. For instance, the system could display the menu only when users move their head away from the main area of interest in a given direction, or after a footswitch pedal press. These actions could be a trigger to indicate that the current goal is to interact with the system. One benefit of HCM is that right at the beginning of the selection users perceive the menu and are therefore aware of the currently available commands.

Head-Controlled Cursor (HCC) and Head-Controlled Menu (HCM) define the first axis of our design space, namely Controlled Interaction Element (see Fig. 2a).

3.2   Tangibility of the Target

Contrary to Virtual Reality where every visible element is virtual, MR opens more possibilities along the Reality-Virtuality Continuum. Interaction elements can either be physical, mixed or virtual. Physical and virtual elements are straightforward: physical objects are visible even without the HMD while virtual elements are only visible through the HMD. The tangible menu proposed by Ullmer et al. [47] is an example of a physical interaction element. Mixed elements are different since they have both a physical and a virtual component. These physical and virtual components can share the same position (in the case of augmented objects for instance), but can also be spatially disjoint.

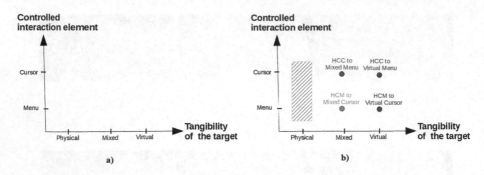

Fig. 2. (a) Design space for head-based interaction with a menu in MR with HMD. (b) The 4 studied interaction techniques located in the design space

Nonetheless, even when outside of the limited augmented FOV, mixed elements are still partially visible thanks to their physical component.

On the one hand, since we focus on head-based interaction with a menu, the interaction element controlled by head movements must be virtual. Attaching an object to the head just to be able to interact would me much more cumbersome. Thus, by moving the head, users control either a virtual cursor (Head-Controlled Cursor) or a virtual menu (Head-Controlled Menu). On the other hand, the target can belong to any position along the Reality-Virtuality Continuum. This aspect defines the second axis of our design space, which describes the tangibility of the target (see Fig. 2a). Our goal was to determine if materializing the graphical element brings any benefit to the user. We study if embodying the location of targets to make them visible in the peripheral vision even outside the augmented FOV is suitable or not. Using physical objects as anchors for virtual content is not new: Henze et al. mentioned this approach as future work in their study of visualization of off-screen objects in augmented maps [20]. However, this approach needs to be studied and evaluated. In particular, we are interested in studying if such physical anchors have an impact on learning the location of targets (in our case, menu items).

As detailed in Sect. 2, introducing new objects as anchors for virtual content in operation rooms is not suitable. However, some already present objects could be used as anchors. For instance, surgeons fix *rigid bodies* on the patient's body to allow a navigation system like the OrthoPilot® to get anatomical points of reference. Rigid bodies are metallic objects with infrared markers and are already part of the sterilization process. Therefore, they could be used as physical anchors for virtual targets. The same approach is applicable to others contexts like manufacturing and maintenance. Introducing new physical objects can be difficult, but objects already present in the environment could be detected and used.

4   Design and Implementation of Head-Based Menu Techniques

We extracted four menu techniques from the design space. Three of these techniques are new, and the fourth one is used as a baseline since it already exists in the literature.

4.1   Design of the Menu Techniques

The two-axes design space of Fig. 2a defines 6 types of menu techniques. However, we choose to study only 4 menu techniques by excluding the 2 techniques that involve a physical target (see Fig. 2b). We motivate the decision by the targeted contexts of use:

1. Pointing to a tangible menu is a very unlikely scenario in surgery or maintenance since it would mean introducing a new tangible in these specific environments. We thus eliminated the *Head-Controlled Cursor to Physical Menu* technique.
2. The other menu technique with a physical target, *Head-Controlled Menu to Physical Cursor*, would be easier to design and implement than a complete tangible menu. However, since we exclude the first type of menu technique involving a physical target, we do not consider *Head-Controlled Menu to Physical Cursor* in this study. We thus keep the entire Physical target category (hatched area in Fig. 2b) for a later study.

Among the 4 remaining menu techniques, we particularly focus on the 2 techniques with a Head-Controlled Menu (HCM) as there are the most innovative ones. The *Head-Controlled Cursor to Virtual Menu* already exists in the literature [25,30] and in some VR headsets like the first version of the Oculus Rift. This technique is used as a baseline. However, the influence of pointing to a *Mixed* menu instead of a *Virtual* menu still needs to be studied (*HCC to Mixed Menu* technique).

As a first exploration of the design space, we consider a simple one-level menu. The menu techniques can be used in several contexts, like surgery, machine maintenance and repair. We thus did not adapt the menu to a specific group of users. Environmental conditions can also be different from one context to another: surgery rooms are very bright environments, which is not the case for the mechanics working on vehicles in [19] for instance. Therefore, since we do not aim to recreate specific ecological conditions, we choose to consider a simple menu design as shown in Fig. 1. A one-level horizontal menu is used and each menu item is labeled with a number.

4.2   Implementation of the Menu Techniques

The 4 menu techniques were developed with the Epson Moverio BT-300, running on Android 5.1. We chose this HMD because of its light weight (70 g for the headset). Machine maintenance and surgery are physically and mentally tiring tasks, so minimizing the weight of the HMD was a determinant factor of choice. To be able to track the position of the HMD, we fixed three passive markers on it. The markers were tracked by a set of four Flex3 cameras monitored by the *Tracking Tools* software (version 2.3.1). This software was executing on a nearby laptop. The position of the MR glasses (and thus the participant's head orientation) was sent to the HMD through Wifi thanks to a custom Python script. The screen of the HMD was then updated according to where the participant was facing.

To validate a selection, dwell time is a classical approach to validate the selection of a target, and was often used for eye-gaze selection [24,44]. However, it was also criticized by several authors because this methods slows down the interaction in order to avoid errors and it requires significant concentration from the user [46]. Since both of these limitations would have a significant impact for the case of our targeted scenarios, we chose another approach using a pedal like in [17]. To validate a target, a 2-pedals Steute orthopedic footswitch was used as this device is commonly used by surgeons for validation in the operating room. This technique corresponds to the first foot interaction style identified by Rovers et al.: a simple toggle action [42]. In the following section, we describe the experimental studies we conducted to compare the 4 implemented menu techniques.

5   Study 1

This first experimental study had two goals. Our first goal was to compare the Head-Controlled Cursor (HCC) and Head-Controlled Menu (HCM) approaches. Since HCC is more similar to well-known WIMP interaction than HCM, we expected participants to prefer and perform better with HCC (**H1**). Our second goal was to evaluate the benefits of physically anchoring virtual targets using physical objects. The resulting *Mixed targets* have a physical component (the anchor) visible even outside of the augmented FOV. We hypothesized that *Mixed targets* would have a positive impact on the menu interaction for two reasons: (1) it may facilitate learning target locations; (2) it could change how participants are planning their head movements, leading to better performance (**H2**).

5.1   Participants

Twelve participants (3 female, 9 male) from 22 to 39 years old ($sd = 5.3$) were recruited for this study. As reported in our preliminary questionnaire, they were all novices in Mixed Reality. Participants had normal or corrected-to normal vision, and could use glasses in addition to the HMD if necessary.

5.2   Setup

The goal of our setup was to recreate the conditions of a general scenario when users have both hands occupied. To do so, we were inspired by a generic augmented surgery scenario. However, we did not try to recreate ecological conditions as it is beyond the scope of this study. Participants stood behind a grey squared table (81 cm long, 73 cm high) representing the working area. They were asked to hold two light plastic bones to keep both hands occupied. Physical anchors for the 2 *Mixed targets* conditions were represented by orange ping-pong balls to be sure they were clearly visible on the grey table in terms of size (diameter: 3.7 cm) and color (see Fig. 3).

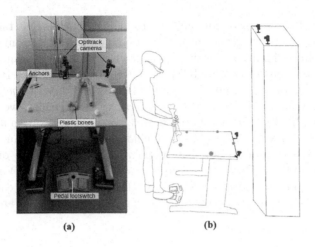

(a)   (b)

Fig. 3. (a) Annotated experimental setup. (b) A participant's pose during the experiment

5.3 Task

Participants were told they had to quickly and accurately select an item from a virtual menu using their head. They had to hold the plastic bones with both hands and keep them in a given position. A supervisor payed attention to be sure they maintained a correct pose during the entire experiment. This was done to ensure they could not use their hands to interact. A one-level horizontal menu with four 100 * 100 pixel items was used (see Fig. 1). Such a one-level menu with four items corresponds to the main menu of the OrthoPilot® navigation system [1]. This system from the Aesculap company guides surgeons during orthopaedic operations of the knee or ankle.

Similarly to the study performed by Louis and Berard [31], we chose to keep a small number of five targets to allow participants to quickly memorize the different target locations. We wanted to be sure that participants had prior knowledge of target locations to avoid exploration phases during trials. This was motivated by the fact that surgeons and mechanics cannot afford wasting time searching for targets while performing their main tasks.

Target Positions: Inspired by the approach adopted by Guillon et al. [16], we applied a modified version of the ISO 9241-9 pointing task [23]. As stated before, five targets are placed on the operating table and form a circular shape. We asked participants to go back to the center of this circle (which was also the center of the table) to start a new pointing task. To be sure they were correctly placed, they were asked to align a small circle displayed on the HMD with a small circle at the center of the table. When correctly oriented the circle displayed on the HMD became green, and participants could validate in order to get the next target.

The order of targets was randomized. To identify the current target, a green arrow pointing to the target location was displayed at the bottom of the HMD (see Fig. 1). This guidance arrow disappeared when the target menu (in the HCC case) or the target cursor (in the HCM case) became visible on the HMD. All targets were outside of the initial augmented FOV. With *Mixed targets* conditions, physical anchors were visible in the peripheral vision. Besides, we chose to set the Index of Difficulty (ID) of all targets to 3.2 to have tasks with a comparable difficulty to the tasks in the study by Guillon et al. [15]. The authors studied target expansion techniques for distant pointing in the context of augmented surgery with the OrthoPilot® [1]. The ID was computed using Wingrave's and Bowman's formulation of Fitts' law [49]. An ID of 3.2 is relatively easy according to the range of ID values between 2 and 8 suggested by Soukoreff and Mackenzie [45].

Selection: When the mobile part of the interaction was correctly positioned, the targeted menu item was highlighted with a green color (see Fig. 1). To validate the selection, participants used a footswitch similar to what surgeons currently use in the operating room as a validation device. If the selection was correct, the target disappeared and the participant was asked to go back to the initial position. When correctly positioned, participants had to click again to start a new trial. If an error was made during a trial, the participant had to continue with the current target until he finally reached it.

5.4   Study Design

The experiment was divided into 4 blocks of 30 trials each, one block per Technique. The order of blocks was counterbalanced using a Latin-square design. The menu item which had to be selected (item number 2) was the same for the entire experiment to keep the same index of difficulty for each target. Therefore, we had 4 menu techniques (2 *Controlled interaction element* × 2 *Tangibility of target* design options) × 5 target positions × 6 repetitions, leading to 120 trials per participant.

Before each block, a corresponding training session was conducted. Training trials were identical to real trials, but nothing was recorded except the total training time. At the beginning of the experiment, we explained to participants that they had to learn the position of the five targets around the operating table, and that these targets would remain the same during the entire experiment. Participants were asked to train with the current menu technique until (1) they knew the five target locations and (2) they felt efficient and comfortable with it. A minimum of 12 training trials was imposed.

We observed during our pilot study that some participants experienced eye tiredness after doing more than 60 consecutive trials. Therefore, between each block of 30 trials, participants were encouraged to take a break. After the break, participants were given a questionnaire to collect their feedback about the menu technique they just experienced. A final questionnaire was also given at the end of the experiment to obtain feedback about the comparison of all techniques.

5.5   Measures

For each trial, the time to perform the valid selection and the number of errors made by participants were recorded. When a mistake was made, the distance between the current position and the target center was recorded as well. Hereafter, this distance will be called *error distance*. Moreover the head trajectory was also recorded to be able to compare it to the ideal one. To do so, the head position was saved every 100 ms during trials. The goal was to better understand the participant's performance and discriminate movement phases. Qualitative feedback was divided in two kinds of questionnaire. First, participants were given a questionnaire based on a 7-degrees Likert scale after each block. The questions were about subjective performance (speed, accuracy) and subjective comfort (easy to understand, physical and cognitive loads). Then, at the end of the experiment, a global questionnaire asked participants to rank the 4 menu techniques according to the same criteria (subjective performance and comfort). Tiredness, perceived utility of mixed targets and preferences were also discussed during semi-structured interviews.

5.6   Results

For analysis, we used a repeated-measures ANOVA (with $\alpha = 0.05$). Post hoc tests were conducted with pairwise t-tests and Bonferroni corrections. Following the guidelines by Dragicevic [14], a log transform was applied to the data when it was relevant (i.e. for the case of positive skewness in time measurements). When using ANOVA was not appropriate, we used a Friedman test instead followed by a Wilcoxon post-hoc test with Bonferonni corrections. 13 trials (0.9% of the 1440 total trials) were removed from the analysis because of lag due to tracking system (*e.g.* hair partially masking the tracked markers of the HMD) or because participants had to adjust the HMD on their head in the middle of a trial.

Target Selection Time: Considering the entire experiment, results are largely inconclusive concerning the differences between the four techniques in terms of target selection time ($F(3, 33) = 0.11$, $p = 0.95$), as shown in Fig. 4a. The mean selection time was close to 3.5 s for all menu techniques. No difference was found between the HCC and HCM techniques. However, we observed a different tendency when comparing the first 10 trials of each block with the 20

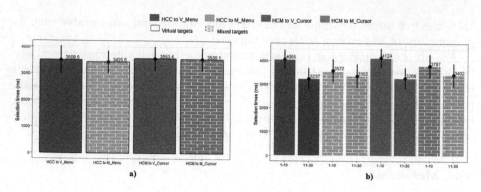

Fig. 4. (a): Study1: Target selection times for the four menu techniques. (b): Study1: Comparing selection times within each block: the 10 first trials versus the 20 last trials. Error bars are 95% CI

remaining trials (Fig. 4b). In this case, we found good evidence of differences between techniques with virtual targets and techniques with mixed targets. The evidence was strong for *HCM to Virtual Cursor* ($p = 0.01$) and *HCC, to Virtual Menu* ($p = 0.02$). In comparison, we did not find evidence for *HCM to Mixed Cursor* ($p = 0.66$) and no evidence at all for *HCC to Mixed Menu* ($p = 1$). When using virtual targets, participants still progressed after the training phase by reducing their mean selection time by 0.84 s. When using mixed targets, the improvement was limited to 0.3 s. Besides, participants' training times were similar for all techniques (no differences found, $p = 0.48$). Participants thus still progressed significantly during trials when using the two techniques with virtual targets. In order to counter-balance this learning effect, we also checked if the performances were the same once the learning curve was stabilized for all techniques. To do so, we analyzed only the 20 last trials. Once again, we found no evidence of difference between techniques ($F(3,33) = 0.2$, $p = 0.91$).

Errors: Similarly to selection time, results are inconclusive about the 4 techniques in terms of error. More precisely, the mean number of errors ($\chi^2 = 2.9$, $p = 0.41$) and mean error distances ($F(3,33) = 1.73$, $p = 0.18$) did not highlight any evidence of difference between techniques (Fig. 5). In both cases, the discrepancies between participants also prevented us from drawing any conclusion. We observed similar results when comparing the beginning and the end of each trial block. No difference was found between the 10 first trials and the 20 last trials for both the number of errors ($\chi^2 = 1.9$, $p = 0.2$) and error distances ($F(7,77) = 0.9$, $p = 0.51$).

Qualitative Feedback: Based on the global questionnaire at the end of the experiment, *HCM to Virtual Cursor* was ranked first (globally preferred). Most participants preferred using the Head-Controlled Menu rather than using the Head-Controlled Cursor. 8 participants over 12 reported preferring Head-

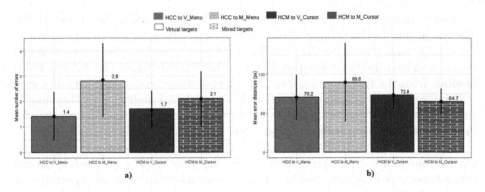

Fig. 5. (a): Study1: Mean error number for the four menu techniques. (b): Study1: Mean error distance for the four menu techniques. Error bars are 95% CI

controlled menu techniques because they felt it was easier, quicker and/or more precise. Figure 6 presents an overview of the main qualitative results for each technique.

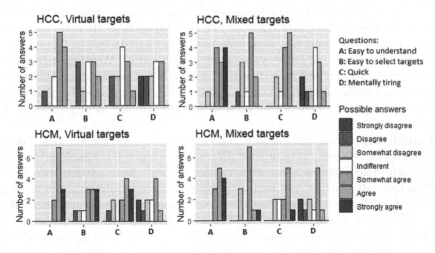

Fig. 6. Study1: Qualitative feedback collected from participants

Interestingly, Participant 12 explicitly mentioned the benefit of seeing the menu from the start: *"I preferred moving the menu with the head (HCM) because you already see it and just search the cross. The two others (HCC) are like twice the effort because first you search the menu, then the item"*. Participant 11 also pointed out that there were less moving elements on screen with HCM (since the menu was fixed at the center of the screen), thus he found HCM less confusing. The 4 participants who preferred HCC techniques gave the same type of reasons: they found HCC easier to use, quicker or felt more in control. Participant 3 also reported being more familiar with the HCC condition.

Five participants did not perceive the difference between HCC and HCM. They said during the training that it was exactly the same (for instance, doing *HCC to Virtual Menu* after *HCM to Virtual Cursor*), and needed several training steps to understand the difference. For the other 7 participants, the difference was obvious from the first training step. At the end of the trials, 2 participants were still unsure of the difference between HCC and HCM techniques. They finally captured the difference during the final questionnaire thanks to the reminder drawings representing each technique that were given with the questionnaire.

Opinions about mixed targets and their physical anchors were more diverse. On the one hand, 4 participants declared that they were really useful. On the other hand, 2 participants disliked them. Three other participants reported that they used anchors at the beginning to learn target locations, but not afterwards since they already knew where the targets were positioned. Interestingly, the last 3 participants reported that they found anchors useful, but that the superposition of anchor and targets created visual discomfort.

6   Discussion

All the menu techniques lead to similar performances in terms of target selection time, number of errors and error distances. This result is in contradiction with H1 since we thought HCC techniques would be faster than their HCM counterparts. Moreover, the HCM condition was preferred by most participants. These results highlight the potential of HCM when using simple menus. We purposely chose a simple one-level menu design, with only 4 items to be close to the existing main menu of the OrthoPilot® navigation system [1]. As commented by Participant 10, our current results may not be valid with more complex menus with multiple levels.

Partially supporting H2, marking the location of virtual targets with physical objects impacted the learning process. Participants reached optimal performance faster with mixed targets than with virtual targets. Since participants had to confirm they felt ready before each trial block and that training times were not statistically different, it seems that more repetitions were necessary with virtual targets to reach optimal performance. Further study is required to determine the influence of mixed targets on the different phases of the learning process. Scarr et al. proposed in 2011 a framework of interface expertise [43]. This framework characterizes the evolution of user performance from novice to expert mode, and can be applied to menus [7]. A valuable research question would then be to evaluate to which extent mixed targets impact the *initial performance* and *extended learnability* phases of the user performance [43].

However, it is important to note that once participants were trained enough, physical anchors did not improve performance, which is in contradiction with H2. This performance may be explained by the fact that participants perfectly knew the target locations. Thus, anchors were not useful anymore. This explanation is supported by the feedback of 3 participants.

The visual discomfort reported by some other participants may also have an influence on the performance when using mixed targets. This visual discomfort origin may be due to a vergence-accommodation conflict, a well-known issue with stereo displays [28]. This conflict occurs when the eyes converge on an object (i.e. the physical anchor), but the eyes' lenses accommodate at a different depth (i.e. the depth of the HMD screen where the virtual target is displayed). Vergence-accommodation conflicts have a negative impact on performance and increase visual fatigue [22]. The 3 participants who reported visual discomfort all declared feeling visual fatigue at the end of the experiment. We conducted a second experiment to further study this issue.

7   Study 2

The goal of this second study is to focus on the visual discomfort that was reported by some participants in Study 1. To do so, we designed and implemented alternative versions of the two menu techniques with mixed targets that suppress this visual discomfort. We then compared the 2 new menu techniques with the two menu techniques of Study 1 with virtual targets. The goal was to evaluate if these new menu techniques with mixed targets allow participants to outperform the menu techniques with virtual targets because the visual discomfort was suppressed. The experimental protocol of this second study was similar to the one of the first study. Only the differences between the two protocols are reported in this section. 9 participants (5 female, 4 male) from 20 to 30 years old ($sd = 3.3$) were recruited for this second study.

7.1   Alternative Menu Techniques: Design Rational

When using mixed targets, the users have to focus first on the virtual green arrow to know which target has to be selected, then on the physical anchor, and finally back on virtual elements when the menu appeared. This forces additional eyes accommodation and potentially creates vergence-accommodation conflicts. Moreover, since both the menu and the cursor are partially transparent, it is still possible to perceive the real world behind them, which could disturb the users. When no physical anchor is used, the users can only focus on virtual elements and ignore the real world features.

To address this issue, we propose to progressively mask the real world. The closer the users are to the target, the more opaque the background color of the augmented FOV will become, as illustrated in Fig. 7. The opacity change starts as soon as the target appears in the augmented FOV. Thus, when the users have reached the virtual target, they can no longer perceive any real world feature in the augmented FOV and can fully focus on virtual elements. The goal of this design is to eliminate both the required eye focus transitions and the disturbance from real world features. Conceptually, it corresponds to a progressive transition from a Mixed Reality (MR) mode to a Virtual Reality (VR) mode. However, users are still conscious of their physical environment since the real world remains visible in their peripheral vision. The separation with the physical environment is thus limited in time (only when close to the target) and space

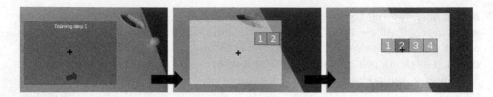

Fig. 7. New menu techniques: Progressive change in the background opacity illustrated with the *HCC to Mixed Menu* technique

(only in the augmented FOV). The concept of these new techniques can also be seen as a shift in the design space from a mixed target to a virtual one (Fig. 2a). A particularly interesting aspect of this shift is that it happens during the interaction. Users begin with a mixed target to be able to see the target location in the peripheral vision. Then, when they no longer need the guidance of the physical anchor, they switch to a virtual target to limit vergence-accommodation conflicts.

We hypothesized the following: masking the real world at the end of the pointing task would help participants by minimizing vergence-accommodation conflicts. Thus, menu techniques with change in opacity will outperform menu techniques without physical anchor (**H3**).

7.2   Results

Selection Time: As shown in Fig. 8, results for target selection times for the 4 techniques were inconclusive (F(3,24) = 0.35, $p = 0.81$). Applying the same analysis process as for Study 1, we checked if participants reached optimal performance after the training phase. Like in Study 1, we compared each pair of the 8 conditions (4 techniques divided in two parts each, 10 first trials and 20 last trials). However, we only found a weak evidence of difference (F(7,56) = 1.8, $p = 0.11$). When running a post-hoc test, the sole identified tendency was between <the 20 last trials of *HCC with Mixed targets*> and <the 10 first trials of *HCM with Virtual targets*>, which is not relevant for comparison. However, the tendency for *HCM to Virtual Cursor* seems different from Study 1, where user improvement during trials was clearly observed. Besides, target selection times for the two HCM techniques seem a bit higher than for Study 1 (around 3.9 s instead of 3.5 s).

Errors: Similarly to Study 1, we did not find any evidence of difference between techniques when focusing on errors. Both the mean number of errors ($\chi^2 = 9.7$, $p = 0.2$) and mean error distances (F(3,24) = 0.46, $p = 0.72$) were similar for all techniques.

Qualitative Feedback: 6 of the 9 participants perceived the change in background opacity as an additional feedback for pointing. They reported that this

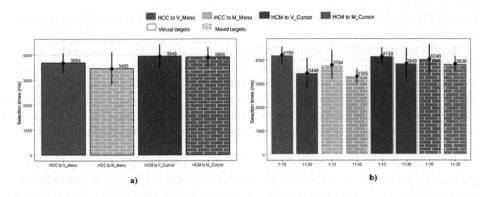

Fig. 8. (a): Study2: Target selection times for the four menu techniques. (b): Study2: Comparing target selection times within each block: the 10 first trials versus the 20 last trials. Error bars are 95% CI

change helped them to adjust their speed when they got close to the target. Interestingly, this was the only benefit reported by the participants: none of them mentioned the change in the nature of the target from a mixed to a purely virtual target. The 3 other participants were more skeptical about the impact of the change in opacity and felt neutral about it. Mixed targets were judged less useful than the change in opacity. 5 participants reported than physical anchors could be useful at the beginning to learn the location of targets. They reported that after a while they did not use the physical anchors anymore. Only 2 participants found anchors really helpful during the whole experiment, and the last 2 participants disliked them. However, no participant reported any visual discomfort.

H3 does not seem to be supported by the results. By masking the real world and therefore minimizing the visual discomfort reported in Study 1, we wanted to improve the performance of the menu techniques with mixed targets. However we did not find evidence of such an improvement. A possible explanation is that participants perfectly knew the positions of the virtual targets and did not consider physical anchors anymore. Vergence-accommodation conflicts then disappeared since participants did not focus on the physical anchors and results suggest equivalent performance between virtual and mixed targets.

8   Lessons Learned and Future Work

This paper contributes to interaction with a menu displayed on a HMD without using hands or voice control. We establish a design space by identifying two factors: the element controlled by the user (Head-Controlled Cursor or Head-Controlled Menu) and the presence (or absence) of physical anchors at the location of the virtual targets (i.e. mixed targets). Based on the design space, we designed and evaluated three head-based techniques. In the following, we first discuss the lessons learned from the two experimental studies and then the future research axes.

In the first study, Head-Controlled Cursor (HCC) and Head-Controlled Menu (HCM) have similar performances, but HCM was preferred by most participants. While causing a significant visual intrusion, HCM allows users to directly see the menu items. This was possible thanks to a simple menu design where all menu items were visible on screen from the beginning of the task. This opens new perspectives on head-based techniques beyond moving a cursor displayed at the center of the HMD.

The first study also highlighted that mixed targets did not improve performance. To evaluate if the visual discomfort reported by some participants was related to the simultaneous visual perception of the virtual and physical components of mixed targets (i.e. vergence-accommodation conflicts), we conducted a second study with alternate menu techniques. However, temporarily masking the real-world did not impact performance. A possible explanation of the absence of effect of physical anchors is that after enough repetitions participants perfectly knew the virtual target positions. In this case, participants did not need to focus on physical anchors anymore, thus eliminating the vergence-accommodation conflicts and their impact on performance. However, we do not conclude that physically anchoring virtual targets is not useful. Our first study provided good evidence that mixed targets allowed participants to reach optimal performance faster than virtual targets. Such a result raises several follow-up research questions about the choice of physical anchors, their design and their precise impact on the different phases of the learning process [7]. Furthermore, we also plan to conduct a study in which the users will not know in advance the positions of the targets. The goal is to experimentally study the extension of the limited FOV of the HMD by relying on physical anchors.

The menu techniques were designed to be used in several possible contexts, and we purposely evaluated the techniques in a non-ecological lab setting. This is an unavoidable step to first explore the design choices. Our on-going work focuses on the augmented surgery scenario. So far, we have implemented the three techniques into the classical surgery workflow of the OrthoPilot® [1] system as part of an established partnership with the Aesculap company. We collected promising informal feedback from Aesculap engineers who have a deep knowledge of the operation workflow and of surgeons needs. Our next step is to conduct experimental studies with surgeons in pseudo ecological conditions, namely the demonstration room of Aesculap.

References

1. Aesculap: Orthopilot®navigation system. https://www.bbraun.com/en/products-and-therapies/orthopaedic-joint-replacement/orthopilot.html/orthopilot.html
2. Allaf, M.E., et al.: Laparoscopic visual field. Surg. Endosc. **12**(12), 1415–1418 (1998)
3. Andersen, D., et al.: Virtual annotations of the surgical field through an augmented reality transparent display. Vis. Comput. **32**(11), 1481–1498 (2016)

4. Atienza, R., Blonna, R., Saludares, M.I., Casimiro, J., Fuentes, V.: Interaction techniques using head gaze for virtual reality. In: 2016 IEEE Region 10 Symposium (TENSYMP), pp. 110–114, May 2016
5. Azai, T., Ogawa, S., Otsuki, M., Shibata, F., Kimura, A.: Selection and manipulation methods for a menu widget on the human forearm. In: Proceedings of the 2017 CHI Conference Extended Abstracts on Human Factors in Computing Systems, CHI EA 2017, pp. 357–360. ACM, New York (2017)
6. Azuma, R.T.: A survey of augmented reality. Presence: Teleoperators Virtual Environ. **6**(4), 355–385 (1997)
7. Bailly, G., Lecolinet, E., Nigay, L.: Visual menu techniques. ACM Comput. Surv. (CSUR) **49**(4), 60 (2017)
8. Beaudouin-Lafon, M.: Instrumental interaction: an interaction model for designing post-WIMP user interfaces. In: Proceedings of the SIGCHI Conference on Human Factors in Computing Systems, CHI 2000, pp. 446–453. ACM, New York (2000)
9. Bier, E.A., et al.: Toolglass and magic lenses: the see-through interface. In: Conference Companion on Human Factors in Computing Systems, CHI 1994, pp. 445–446. ACM, New York (1994)
10. Buchmann, V., Violich, S., Billinghurst, M., Cockburn, A.: FingARtips: gesture based direct manipulation in augmented reality. In: Proceedings of the 2nd International Conference on Computer Graphics and Interactive Techniques in Australasia and South East Asia, GRAPHITE 2004, pp. 212–221. ACM, New York (2004)
11. Cassell, J.: On control, certitude, and the paranoia of surgeons. Cult. Med. Psychiatry **11**(2), 229–249 (1987)
12. Colaço, A., Kirmani, A., Yang, H.S., Gong, N.W., Schmandt, C., Goyal, V.K.: Mime: compact, low power 3d gesture sensing for interaction with head mounted displays. In: Proceedings of the 26th Annual ACM Symposium on User Interface Software and Technology, UIST 2013, pp. 227–236. ACM, New York (2013)
13. Datcu, D., Lukosch, S.: Free-hands interaction in augmented reality. In: Proceedings of the 1st Symposium on Spatial User Interaction, SUI 2013, pp. 33–40. ACM, New York (2013)
14. Dragicevic, P.: Fair statistical communication in HCI. In: Robertson, J., Kaptein, M. (eds.) Modern Statistical Methods for HCI. HIS, pp. 291–330. Springer, Cham (2016)
15. Guillon, M., Leitner, F., Nigay, L.: Static Voronoi-based target expansion technique for distant pointing. In: Proceedings of the 2014 International Working Conference on Advanced Visual Interfaces, AVI 2014, pp. 41–48. ACM, New York (2014)
16. Guillon, M., Leitner, F., Nigay, L.: Target expansion lens: it is not the more visual feedback the better! In: Proceedings of the International Working Conference on Advanced Visual Interfaces, AVI 2016, pp. 52–59. ACM, New York (2016)
17. Hatscher, B., Luz, M., Nacke, L.E., Elkmann, N., Müller, V., Hansen, C.: Gaze-Tap: towards hands-free interaction in the operating room. In: Proceedings of the 19th ACM International Conference on Multimodal Interaction, pp. 243–251. ACM (2017)
18. He, Z., Yang, X.: Hand-based interaction for object manipulation with augmented reality glasses. In: Proceedings of the 13th ACM SIGGRAPH International Conference on Virtual-Reality Continuum and Its Applications in Industry, VRCAI 2014, pp. 227–230. ACM, New York (2014)
19. Henderson, S.J., Feiner, S.: Evaluating the benefits of augmented reality for task localization in maintenance of an armored personnel carrier turret (2009)

20. Henze, N., Boll, S.: Evaluation of an off-screen visualization for magic lens and dynamic peephole interfaces. In: Proceedings of the 12th International Conference on Human Computer Interaction with Mobile Devices and Services, MobileHCI 2010, pp. 191–194. ACM, New York (2010)

21. Hirsch, H.G., Pearce, D.: The aurora experimental framework for the performance evaluation of speech recognition systems under noisy conditions. In: ASR2000-Automatic Speech Recognition: Challenges for the new Millenium ISCA Tutorial and Research Workshop (ITRW) (2000)

22. Hoffman, D.M., Girshick, A.R., Akeley, K., Banks, M.S.: Vergence-accommodation conflicts hinder visual performance and cause visual fatigue. J. Vis. **8**(3), 33 (2008)

23. Ergonomic requirements for office work with visual display terminals (VDTs) - Part 9. Standard, International Organization for Standardization (2000)

24. Jacob, R.J.: What you look at is what you get: eye movement-based interaction techniques. In: Proceedings of the SIGCHI Conference on Human Factors in Computing Systems, pp. 11–18. ACM (1990)

25. Jagacinski, R.J., Monk, D.L.: Fitts' law in two dimensions with hand and head movements movements. J. Mot. Behav. **17**(1), 77–95 (1985)

26. Jalaliniya, S., Mardanbeigi, D., Pederson, T., Hansen, D.W.: Head and eye movement as pointing modalities for eyewear computers. In: 2014 11th International Conference on Wearable and Implantable Body Sensor Networks Workshops (BSN Workshops), pp. 50–53. IEEE (2014)

27. Katic, D., et al.: Context-aware augmented reality in laparoscopic surgery. Comput. Med. Imaging Graph. **37**(2), 174–182 (2013)

28. Kruijff, E., Swan, J.E., Feiner, S.: Perceptual issues in augmented reality revisited. In: 2010 IEEE International Symposium on Mixed and Augmented Reality, pp. 3–12, October 2010

29. Kytö, M., Ens, B., Piumsomboon, T., Lee, G.A., Billinghurst, M.: Pinpointing: precise head- and eye-based target selection for augmented reality. In: Proceedings of the 2018 CHI Conference on Human Factors in Computing Systems, CHI 2018, pp. 81:1–81:14. ACM, New York (2018)

30. Lin, M.L., Radwin, R.G., Vanderheiden, G.C.: Gain effects on performance using a head-controlled computer input device. Ergonomics **35**(2), 159–175 (1992)

31. Louis, T., Berard, F.: Superiority of a handheld perspective-coupled display in isomorphic docking performances. In: Proceedings of the 2017 ACM International Conference on Interactive Surfaces and Spaces, pp. 72–81. ACM, New York (2017)

32. Mahmoud, N., et al.: On-patient see-through augmented reality based on visual SLAM. Int. J. Comput. Assist. Radiol. Surg. **12**(1), 1–11 (2017)

33. Mardanbegi, D., Hansen, D.W., Pederson, T.: Eye-based head gestures. In: Proceedings of the Symposium on Eye Tracking Research and Applications, pp. 139–146. ACM (2012)

34. Mentis, H.M., et al.: Voice or gesture in the operating room. In: Proceedings of the 33rd Annual ACM Conference Extended Abstracts on Human Factors in Computing Systems, CHI EA 2015, pp. 773–780. ACM, New York (2015)

35. Mitrasinovic, S., et al.: Clinical and surgical applications of smart glasses. Technol. Health Care **23**(4), 381–401 (2015)

36. Neumann, U., Majoros, A.: Cognitive, performance, and systems issues for augmented reality applications in manufacturing and maintenance. In: Proceedings of IEEE 1998 Virtual Reality Annual International Symposium, pp. 4–11. IEEE (1998)

37. O'Hara, K., et al.: Touchless interaction in surgery. Commun. ACM **57**(1), 70–77 (2014)

38. Ong, S., Yuan, M., Nee, A.: Augmented reality applications in manufacturing: a survey. Int. J. Prod. Res. **46**(10), 2707–2742 (2008)
39. Özacar, K., Hincapié-Ramos, J.D., Takashima, K., Kitamura, Y.: 3D selection techniques for mobile augmented reality head-mounted displays. Interact. Comput. **29**(4), 579–591 (2016)
40. Qian, Y.Y., Teather, R.J.: The eyes don't have it: an empirical comparison of head-based and eye-based selection in virtual reality. In: Proceedings of the 5th Symposium on Spatial User Interaction, SUI 2017, pp. 91–98. ACM, New York (2017)
41. Reiners, D., Stricker, D., Klinker, G., Müller, S.: Augmented reality for construction tasks: Doorlock assembly. In: Proceedings of IEEE and ACM IWAR 1998, no. 1, pp. 31–46 (1998)
42. Rovers, A., Van Essen, H.: Guidelines for haptic interpersonal communication applications: an exploration of foot interaction styles. Virtual Reality **9**(2–3), 177–191 (2006)
43. Scarr, J., Cockburn, A., Gutwin, C., Quinn, P.: Dips and ceilings: understanding and supporting transitions to expertise in user interfaces. In: Proceedings of the SIGCHI Conference on Human Factors in Computing Systems, pp. 2741–2750. ACM (2011)
44. Sibert, L.E., Jacob, R.J.: Evaluation of eye gaze interaction. In: Proceedings of the SIGCHI Conference on Human Factors in Computing Systems, pp. 281–288. ACM (2000)
45. Soukoreff, R.W., MacKenzie, I.S.: Towards a standard for pointing device evaluation, perspectives on 27 years of Fitts' law research in HCI. Int. J. Hum.-Comput. Stud. **61**(6), 751–789 (2004). Fitts' law 50 years later: applications and contributions from human-computer interaction
46. Špakov, O., Majaranta, P.: Enhanced gaze interaction using simple head gestures. In: Proceedings of the 2012 ACM Conference on Ubiquitous Computing, pp. 705–710. ACM (2012)
47. Ullmer, B., et al.: Tangible menus and interaction trays: core tangibles for common physical/digital activities. In: Proceedings of the 2nd International Conference on Tangible and Embedded Interaction, TEI 2008, pp. 209–212. ACM (2008)
48. White, S., Feng, D., Feiner, S.: Interaction and presentation techniques for shake menus in tangible augmented reality. In: Proceedings of the 2009 8th IEEE International Symposium on Mixed and Augmented Reality, ISMAR 2009, pp. 39–48. IEEE Computer Society, Washington, DC, USA (2009)
49. Wingrave, C., Bowman, D.: Baseline factors for raycasting selection. In: Proceedings of HCI International. Citeseer (2005)
50. Yan, Y., Yu, C., Yi, X., Shi, Y.: HeadGesture: hands-free input approach leveraging head movements for HMD devices. In: Proceedings of ACM Interactive, Mobile, Wearable and Ubiquitous Technologies, vol. 2, no. 4, pp. 198:1–198:23, December 2018
51. Yi, S., Qin, Z., Novak, E., Yin, Y., Li, Q.: GlassGesture: exploring head gesture interface of smart glasses. In: IEEE INFOCOM 2016-The 35th Annual IEEE International Conference on Computer Communications, pp. 1–9. IEEE (2016)
52. Yuan, M., Ong, S., Nee, A.: Augmented reality for assembly guidance using a virtual interactive tool. Int. J. Prod. Res. **46**(7), 1745–1767 (2008)

VR Interaction Modalities for the Evaluation of Technical Device Prototypes

Patrick Harms[✉] [iD]

Institute of Computer Science, University of Goettingen, Göttingen, Germany
patrick.harms@cs.uni-goettingen.de

Abstract. Virtual Reality (VR) systems have reached the consumer market which offers new application areas. In our paper, we examine to what extent current VR technology can be used to perform local or remote usability tests for technical devices, e.g., coffee machines. For this, we put virtual prototypes of the technical devices into VR and let users interact with them. We implemented four interaction modalities that are suitable for low-level smartphone-based VR systems up to high fidelity, tethered systems with room-scale tracking. The modalities range from a simple gaze pointer to interaction with virtual hands. Our case study and its counter evaluation show that we are able to detect usability issues of technical devices based on their virtual prototypes in VR. However, the quality of the results depends on the matching between the task, the technical device, the prototype level, and the interaction modality.

Keywords: Virtual Reality · Usability · Usability testing · Virtual prototype · Device assessment · Interaction pattern

1 Introduction

Virtual Reality (VR) is of interest for performing usability evaluations of technical device prototypes. In this area, a virtual prototype of a technical device, e.g., a coffee machine, is put into VR. Then potential users of this device are asked to interact with it in VR. The problems that the users have when interacting with the device may be an indicator of usability issues of the device. This basic idea was already proposed and done with former generations of VR systems, e.g., [4]. These former technologies had a lower quality than those today and interacting with them was not always easy. Through this, former VR systems may have influenced the usability test and it was not always clear if an issue stems from the virtual device prototype or from the VR system.

Because of the improvement of their quality, we think it is worth evaluating if the current state-of-the-art VR systems serve better for usability evaluations of technical device prototypes. In addition, as VR devices are also affordable by consumers, it is worth to consider performing these usability tests in a remote

D. Lamas et al. (Eds.): INTERACT 2019, LNCS 11749, pp. 416–435, 2019.
https://doi.org/10.1007/978-3-030-29390-1_23

fashion as it is already done for websites and mobile apps [22,23]. This means, users perform the tests separated in space and/or time from the evaluator while using their own technical setup. This setup may differ from user to user and from simple smartphone/cardboard VR to high fidelity, tethered systems with room-scale tracking. Hence, it is important to use interaction modalities that are easy to use by the user, match the users' technical setup, and serve the purpose of usability evaluations for technical device prototypes. As a first step in this direction, we focus in this paper on the following research question:

RQ 1: To what extent can different types of current consumer VR systems and corresponding interaction modes be used for interacting with virtual representations of technical devices in VR?

To answer this question, we implemented four established interaction modes and checked whether they are applicable for interacting with virtual device prototypes. Each mode can be implemented with a different technical level of consumer VR systems. As our goal is to use VR for usability evaluations of technical device prototypes in VR, we also consider the following research question:

RQ 2: How and to what extent can different types of current consumer VR systems be used for usability evaluations of technical device prototypes in VR?

This second question is especially important as even the best mode for virtual prototype interaction in VR (RQ 1) would be worthless if it does not allow to detect usability problems of the virtual prototype in a usability engineering scenario (RQ 2). We executed a case study with 85 participants to answer both questions. We evaluated the interaction modes and used them in a usability evaluation scenario for virtual prototypes of two different technical devices.

The paper is structured as follows. First we introduce the main terminology in Sect. 2 and provide an overview of related work in Sect. 3. We describe the interaction modes in Sect. 4. Our case study description in Sect. 5 covers details on its execution, our findings, and a discussion of the results including potential threats to validity. We conclude the paper in Sect. 6.

2   Foundations

In this section, we introduce the terminology used in this paper, such as usability, VR, and VR system.

Usability is the matching between user groups, their tasks, the context of task execution, and a product, e.g., hardware or software. If this is given, then users can perform their tasks with *effectiveness, efficiency* and *satisfaction* [1]. In addition, a high usability can increase the *learnability* for a system and decrease the number of *errors* users make [19]. To assess and improve the usability of a product, a diverse set of methods can be applied which is referred to as *usability engineering* [19]. Examples for such methods are *usability tests* [25]. Here, potential users of a product are asked to utilize a prototype or a final product for predefined and realistic tasks. During that, an evaluator observes the users and takes notes of the users' issues. Afterwards, the issues are analysed to identify potential for improvements. For a better analysis, the test sessions can be recorded, e.g., using video cameras or by logging the users' interactions. In addition, it is possible to determine the users' thoughts and opinions by, e.g., asking them to think aloud during the test, by interviewing them, or by letting them fill in questionnaires after the test [11].

VR is a technique in which the user's senses are triggered by a *VR system* to pretend that the user is in another world, a *virtual world* [8]. The technical level of a VR system is called *immersion*. With an increasing immersion, usually the users feeling of being in the virtual world, the *presence*, increases. A term related to immersion and presence is *interaction fidelity*. It considers the similarity of the users physical actions for real world tasks compared to his or her actions to fulfill the same tasks in VR. A high fidelity means that the performed actions in the real world are very similar to the ones necessary to complete a task in the virtual world [3]. A high fidelity can increase the learnability for VR.

State-of-the-art consumer VR systems differ in their technical setup. For our work, we divide them into four categories according to their immersion and interaction fidelity. We list those categories with their basic characteristics and examples in Table 1. VR systems of Category 1, such as Google Cardboard [30], are smartphone-based. They only track the users head orientation and do not provide controllers. Hence, their immersion and interaction fidelity are rather rudimentary. Category 2 VR systems extend category 1 by the use of hand-held controllers providing buttons. An example is Oculus Go [20]. These VR systems track orientation movements of the controller and react on the usage of the controller buttons for allowing users to interact with objects in VR. Category 3 VR systems provide a room-scale tracking for headsets and controllers. This means, they do not only track their orientation but also their movement in space. All orientation changes and movements of the head set and the controllers are transferred to movements in the VR. This allows users to move freely, restricted only by the boundaries of the physical world. This also applies to virtual representations of the controllers that are usually shown in VR on this level. Overall, this

Table 1. VR system categories and examples.

Characteristic	Category 1	Category 2	Category 3	Category 4
Head-mounted display	Yes	Yes	Yes	Yes
Head tracking	Orientation	Orientation	Orientation, movement	Orientation, movement
Controller	None	Orientation	Orientation, movement	None
User tracking	None	None	None	Yes
Example	Google Cardboard [30]	Oculus Go [20]	HTC Vive [6]	HTC Vive [6] with Leap Motion [18]

level allows users to approach and touch virtual objects with the controllers. An example for a category 3 VR system is the HTC Vive [6]. Category 4 is characterized by its possibility to display parts of the users body in VR. These virtual body parts are used for interacting with the VR instead of a controller. For this, additional tracking systems are required. An example for such a tracking system is the Leap Motion [18]. It captures the users hands and their movements and transfers them into a digital hand model in VR. With such a system, a rather high immersion and interaction fidelity can be accomplished.

Interaction with VR concerns mainly the *selection* and *manipulation* of virtual objects [14]. With a selection, users identify the object in VR for further interaction. With the manipulation, they change an object's position, orientation, scale, or other features. In our work, we further divide the manipulation of objects into the two actions *grab* and *use*. Grabbing an object means the same as in real world, i.e., selecting and moving it. Using refers to objects that cannot be moved but manipulated otherwise, like fixed buttons that can be pressed. Objects on which grab or use actions can be performed are called *tangible objects*.

Virtual worlds may incorporate *snap drop zones*. A snap drop zone is an area that detects objects in a defined proximity. If an object comes close to the snap drop zone, it is moved to a predefined position and locked there.

3   Related Work

The idea of using VR and Augmented Reality (AR) for usability evaluations of product prototypes is not new. There were attempts to assess a wheelchair-mounted robot manipulator [7], a microwave oven and a washing machine [4], as well as a phone [16]. Also the automotive sector utilizes virtual prototyping and evaluation [24]. While many of the studies focus on larger machinery, only few studies focus on consumer product usability [9] as we do.

The existing studies utilize a wide range of VR technologies from simple 2D screens [15] via 3D video walls [5] to Cave Automatic Virtual Environments (CAVEs) [26]. For interaction, the studies use, e.g., the Wizard of Oz technique [29], tracked objects [21], or special tracked gloves [4]. To the best of our knowledge, there are no studies focusing on current state-of-the-art consumer VR systems as done in our work. In addition, the related work does not consider performing remote usability testing on the side of the end user as we do. Furthermore, none of the existing studies had a test sample as large as ours.

The existing studies showed that with their corresponding technical setup, diverse problems are introduced. For example, test participants have problems in perceiving depth in a CAVE or request for haptic feedback [17]. Also tracked gloves can be problematic when trying to perform usability evaluations with many participants as they need to be put on and off again [17]. Such issues can have a strong influence on the evaluation results [27]. In our work, we analyze if similar issues arise with the current state-of-the-art consumer VR systems or if the typical interaction concepts, although being not fully immersive, are anyway sufficient for usability evaluations of technical device prototypes.

A similar study as ours was executed by Holderied [13]. In her student project, the author asked participants to use a virtual coffee machine and evaluated its usability as well as four different interaction modes. In addition, she had a control group of seven participants which used the real world exemplar of the coffee machine. In our work, we analyze two devices and, due to our case study setup, also assess learning effects. In addition, our interaction modes are different and base on what was learned in the study of Holderied. The former study, furthermore, did not evaluate a hand mode as we do, used a less efficient highlighting of the tangible objects, and utilized other and less intuitive controller buttons.

4   Interaction Modes

We intend to use VR for usability evaluations of technical devices prototypes. In these evaluations, end users shall interact with the virtual devices while using their own VR systems to allow for a potential remote usability evaluation. As the VR system category per user may differ, we implemented four different interaction modes, one for each of the VR systems categories mentioned in Table 1. The modes are extensions and improvements of the interaction modes defined by Holderied [13] as referenced in the related work (Sect. 3). In this chapter, we describe these interaction modes in a generic way to allow for an implementation with different concrete VR systems. The descriptions follow the same pattern in which we mention the modes name, the aimed VR system category, how the selection, grabbing and using of objects works, and further important details such as the highlighting of tangible objects for user feedback.

4.1   Interaction Mode 1: Gaze Mode

VR System Category: Category 1.

Object Selection: Looking at objects, i.e., positioning a cross hair in the view center on them.

Object Grabbing: After selection, leave the cross hair on the object for a defined period of time. Afterwards, the object becomes attached to the cross hair and can be moved by rotating the head. The object can only be released in close proximity to snap drop zones.

Object Usage: After selection, leave the cross hair on the object for a defined period of time.

Further Details: If the cross hair is positioned on a tangible object, the object's color changes to a highlighting color. If the cross hair stays on the object, the color blurs to a second highlighting color. After a predefined time, the color blur ends and the object is manipulated, i.e., grabbed or used.

4.2   Interaction Mode 2: Laser Mode

VR System Category: Category 2.

Object Selection: Pointing a virtual laser beam on the object using the orientation tracked controller.

Object Grabbing: After selection, press and hold a button on the controller. The object stays attached to the tip of the virtual laser beam. To release the object, the controller button must be released.

Object Usage: After selection, press a button on the controller.

Further Details: When the laser beam points on a tangible object, the object's color changes to a highlight color. If the controller has a virtual representation in VR, a tooltip next to the required button can be displayed indicating the possible action. An example for this is shown in Fig. 1a. This figure contains a virtual representation of an HTC Vive controller emitting the virtual laser beam. The tooltip is shown if the user points on a tangible object. We change the tooltip text while grabbing an object to indicate how the object can be released.

4.3   Interaction Mode 3: Controller Mode

VR System Category: Category 3.

Object Selection: Colliding the virtual representation of the room-scale tracked controller with the object (see object usage for further details).

Object Grabbing: After selection, press and hold a button on the controller. The object stays attached to the virtual representation of the controller. To release the object, the controller button must be released.

Object Usage: For object usage, colliding the controller with the object may be problematic in case the object is small. Hence, object usage in this mode is similar to the laser mode. The object selection is done using a virtual laser beam. In contrast to the laser mode, the beam in this mode must first be enabled. For this, the users use a second, pressure sensitive button on the controller. With a slight pressure on this button, the laser beam is enabled. To use an object, the users point the laser beam on the object and then fully press the button.

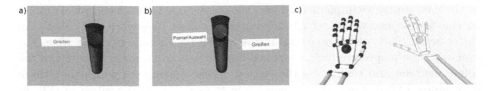

Fig. 1. Screenshots of HTC Vive based example implementations of three of our interaction modes: a) laser mode with controller attached tooltips, b) controller mode with tooltips, c) hand mode.

Further Details: The mechanism for object usage can also be used for object grabbing. We implemented this for the purpose of consistency. We implemented a color highlighting if an object is selected using the laser beam as in the laser mode. Also in this mode, tooltips can be used to describe the controller buttons functionality. An example for this implemented with an HTC Vive controller is shown in Fig. 1b. As multiple buttons are used in this mode, the tooltips should become partly transparent to indicate which button is pressed. In addition, they should change their caption depending on what can be triggered with the buttons (use or grab) in a certain situation.

4.4 Interaction Mode 4: Hand Mode

VR System Category: Category 4.

Object Selection: Touching an object with the virtual representations of the user's hand(s).

Object Grabbing: Closing the hand(s) around the virtual object.

Object Usage: Touching an object with the virtual representations of the user's hand(s).

Further Details: In this mode, users see virtual representations of their hands as shown in Fig. 1c. Every hand and finger movement is transferred to this virtual hand model. If a grabbable object is touched with a virtual hand, its color changes to a highlight color. If a usable object is approached, its color changes already on close proximity of the virtual hand.

5 Case Study

To answer our research questions, we performed a case study. In this case study, we asked users to interact with two virtual technical devices in VR, a coffee machine and a copier. In the following subsections, we describe the technical setup of the case study, the execution, and our findings. Furthermore, we discuss the results and identify threats to the validity of our analyses.

5.1 Technical Setup

In the case study, we implemented two VR scenes, one for each technical device. In the first scene, we asked users to brew a coffee. Therefore, we call it the *coffee scene*. The coffee scene contains a cup and a virtual coffee machine. For executing the respective task, users need to put the cup under the outlet of the coffee machine and then press the button on the machine of which they think it produces coffee. This setup is similar to the case study described in [13]. In the second scene, our participants were asked to copy a sheet of paper. Hence, we call it the *copy scene*. The scene contains a copier and a sheet of paper lying

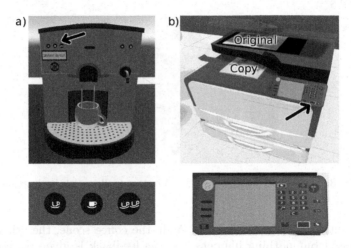

Fig. 2. Screenshots of both VR scenes of our case study including enlargements of the three coffee machine buttons that brew coffee and the interaction pad of the copier.

next to it on a table. In this scene, the participants need to open the copier top, put the paper on the copier screen, and close the copier. Then they need to push the button on the copier which to their opinion creates the copy. Screenshots of both scenes are shown in the upper parts of Fig. 2 (a: coffee scene, b: copy scene). In both scenes, the cup and the paper have already been put in place. The arrows mark the correct buttons to use for the respective tasks. In the copy scene, there is an additional sheet of paper being an already created copy.

We decided for this scene setup as it covers typical actions for interacting with technical devices. This includes moving parts of the device, moving utility objects, and pressing buttons. For both scenes, we implemented our four interaction modes. For moving the cup, the copier top, and the paper, we used the mode specific grab action, for pushing a button on the virtual device, the mode specific use action.

The scenes were created using Unity 3D [28]. The virtual devices were modeled using Blender [10]. They are based on a real coffee machine and a real copier. The functionality of the virtual devices was implemented as provided by the real devices. For the coffee machine, the three buttons on the top left produce coffee (enlarged in bottom part of Fig. 2a). Per button, there is a different type of coffee produced, being light coffee for the left button, strong coffee for the center button, and two light coffees for the right button. The functionality of these three buttons was implemented so that coffee flows into the cup if one of the buttons is pressed. The other buttons on the coffee machine can be pressed, but no functionality is triggered and no other feedback is given. The display of the coffee machine shows "Gerät bereit" which is German for "Device Ready".

The functionality of the virtual copier was also partially implemented. The copy button is the large one on the bottom right of the interaction pad (enlarged in the bottom part of Fig. 2b). When pressed, a copy of the paper is created at

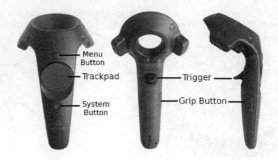

Fig. 3. Different views on an HTC Vive controller with its buttons.

the copier outlet as shown in Fig. 2b. As in the coffee scene, the other buttons can be pressed but nothing happens, and no feedback is given. In contrast to the coffee machine, the copier's display is empty and does not show anything.

In both scenes, the destination of the objects to move, i.e., the cup and the paper, are defined by snap drop zones. In the coffee scene, the coffee buttons work no matter if the cup is put into the snap drop zone. In the copy scene, the copy button only works if the paper is snapped correctly in the snap drop zone.

As VR system, we utilized an HTC Vive [6]. It comes with a head-mounted display and two controllers all being tracked at room scale. A visualization of a controller is shown in Fig. 3. A controller has multiple buttons of which only some are of relevance for our case study. Those are the trigger button at the lower side of the controller and the trackpad on the upper side. The trigger button is pressure sensitive. We used the trackpad as a simple click button. In addition to the Vive, we used a Leap Motion [18]. This device is a small hand tracker. It can be attached to the headset of the Vive so that the tracking of the hands is performed from the head of the user. Both devices allowed us to implement the four categories of VR systems and our interaction modes as follows:

- **Gaze mode:** Usage of Vive headset only (category 1 VR system).
- **Laser mode:** Usage of Vive headset and one controller (category 2 VR system); grab and use action are performed with the trigger button on the controller.
- **Controller mode:** Usage of Vive headset and one controller (category 3 VR system); as pressure sensitive button required for this mode, the trigger button is used; as click button the trackpad is used.
- **Hand mode:** Usage of Vive headset and the Leap motion (category 4 VR system).

For both scenes, we had a concept for resetting them. This helped to overcome unexpected situations. For the gaze mode, a reset was possible by restarting the scene. For the laser and the controller mode, we put a reset functionality on the grip button of the controller (see Fig. 3). For the hand mode, we put a large red push button on the rear side of the scene.

5.2 Usability Test Setup

Using the technical setup we performed usability tests of the coffee machine and the copier in VR. For this we recruited test participants and asked them to use the virtual devices. All participant sessions consisted of the following steps:

1. Welcome and introduction
2. Usage of first device
3. Interview on interaction mode
4. Usage of second device
5. Interview on device usage
6. Discharge

During the usage of the devices and the interviews, we took notes of the issues the participants had as well as of any statements they made with respect to the VR system, the interaction mode, and the virtual technical device. Through this, we ensured to cover both our research questions, i.e., if the interaction modes can be used for interacting with technical device prototypes (RQ 1) and if usability defects of the technical devices are found (RQ 2).

Each participant used both, the coffee and the copy scene, but only one of our four interaction modes (Sect. 4). This means, our case study had a between-subject-design considering the interactions modes. The case study design allowed us to measure, how the participants can learn and apply a certain interaction mode. For identifying learning effects, we flipped the order of the scenes between participants. This means, half of the participants first used the coffee scene and then the copier scene, whereas the other half used the scenes in opposite order.

The welcome and introduction (step 1) included asking for demographic information, describing the case study setup, and what data is acquired. Then, we let the participants put on the VR headset. Initially, they were in the center of a virtual sports stadium, a default scene provided by the Vive. For the laser and controller mode, we gave a brief introduction into the controller usage. This started with showing the controller in front of the participants. We then asked the participants to take the controller into their hand as well as feel and try out the important buttons. For the controller mode, we gave the additional hint that the trigger button is pressure sensitive. For the gaze and the hand mode, we gave no additional introduction.

Afterwards, we started the first scene (step 2) and asked the participants to perform the respective task. If they were unsure how to proceed, we gave them a mode specific hint. For example, for the gaze mode, we asked them to look around hoping that an accidental highlighting in this mode caused the participants to detect the gaze pointer. If a participant required any additional help, e.g., a repeated description of the controller buttons, we took a note.

After the task in the first scene was completed, we asked the participants to put down the VR headset. Then we interviewed them on their experience with the interaction mode (step 3). For this, we used four guiding statements and the participants had to assess whether they agreed to a statement or not. We also took notes of any additional comment. The guiding statements were

– I appreciate this type of interaction with a VR.
– I found the interaction with the VR unnecessarily complex.
– I would imagine that most people would learn this interaction very quickly.
– I found the interaction very cumbersome.

Then, we asked the participants to put on the headset again and started the second scene (step 4). In addition, we mentioned the scene-specific task. We gave no further help regarding the interaction to see whether the participants learned the interaction mode after the first scene. Only for few participants, we had to provide additional mode specific help in the second scene. After the task in the second scene was completed, we again asked the participants to put down the VR headset for the second interview (step 5). Here we also used four guiding statements to which the participants had to agree or disagree. These statements were as follows and focused on the technical device only:

– I thought the device was easy to use.
– I found the device unnecessarily complex.
– I would imagine that most people would learn to use this device very quickly.
– I found the device very cumbersome to use.

Again, we took notes of any additional comments of our participants. Finally, we asked our participants to provide us with any further feedback that came to their minds. Then we thanked for their participation and closed the test (step 6).

For the solving of the tasks in both VR scenes, the participants had to press one of the correct buttons on the devices. If they initially tried one or more wrong buttons, we gave them a hint to try other buttons. If a participant required a reset for the scene for some reason, we instantly mentioned that this is possible, and either performed it by restarting the scene or by describing to the participant how the reset can be triggered.

During the usage of the VR scenes, we recorded the screen of the computer, i.e., what the participant saw and did in the scenes. In addition, both scenes were equipped with a logging mechanism. Through this, we additionally got technical recordings of which controller buttons were used, the orientation and movements of the user's head, and the actions relevant for our case study, i.e., grabbing and using an object. The individual user actions were logged together with a time stamp in the order in which they occurred.

5.3 Execution and Data Analysis

We executed the case study in two separate sessions in June 2017. The first session was done at a central location between multiple lecture halls at our university. The second session took place at a shopping mall. Overall, we had 85 test participants (46 students, 22 employed, 11 pupils, 3 retired, 1 unemployed, 2 unknown). 23 participants used the gaze mode, 21 the laser mode, 21 the controller mode, and 20 the hand mode.

We did not do a specific participant screening. This allowed us to assess whether our interaction modes can be used by a broad variety of different user groups. This is of major importance for our overall goal of allowing for usability evaluations of technical device prototypes in VR. The reason is that also for such evaluations a broad variety of test persons may need to be recruited.

A majority of 65 participants had no experience with VR and 14 only heard about it. None of our participants considered him- or herself a VR expert. 45 participants first used the coffee scene and 40 first used the copy scene. The logging of actions and the recording of the screen did not work for the first participant (gaze mode, coffee scene first) resulting in one recording less.

As we were at central locations, we had to ensure that our participants were not biased by observing other participants. This is important for correctly measuring if there is a learning effect between the interaction in the first and the second scene. For this, we did not project anything of what the participants saw during a test to a larger screen. We also informed new audience that if they wanted to participate, they must not look at our computer screen. In addition, if participants had observed previous test participants, we informed them that their own sessions will be different and that their observations will be of no help or relevance. We also ensured that subsequent participants used different interaction modes.

All participants were introduced and observed by the same two evaluators. The evaluators split their tasks. The first evaluator did the introduction and the interviews of the participants and ensured that the participants were physically safe while interacting with the scenes. The other evaluator started the VR scenes and took the notes. For test and data consistency, these roles stayed the same for all test sessions.

After the case study execution, we performed a data post-processing and analysis. This included a card-sorting for grouping the detected usability issues. For this, both evaluators were asked separately to define categories of user issues and statements and to assign the notes to these categories. The categories of both evaluators were then matched to each other and harmonized. Through an analysis of the screen casts and the log files, we determined additional data, such as the duration of individual actions of the participants.

5.4 Findings

From the case study data, we derive different types of usability issues. Some issues concern the interaction in general and occurred for both scenes (*general issues*). Other issues are specific to an interaction mode (*mode issues*) or to one of the virtual prototypes (*device issues*). In addition, we took note of other user comments. All issues and comments as well as our duration measurements are listed in the following.

General Issues: Table 2 shows an overview of the general issues and their number for each interaction mode as well as in total. In the first row the table also lists the number of participants that used a certain interaction mode for better reference. The most prominent issue (29 times) concerns the participants' need for a more detailed help of how to interact with the VR. For the controller mode

(18 times), this includes a second demonstration of the two pressure points of the trigger button. Another problem is that the cup or the paper fell down unwillingly. This happened 21 times, most often for the hand mode (12 times). 19 participants stood too far away from the technical device to be able to interact properly, 12 of them using the gaze mode. It was difficult for some participants to use the snap drop zones correctly. In total, 15 struggled to understand the concept of this feature and tried to place the object exactly without letting this be taken over by the snap drop zones.

Mode Issues: 7 participants using the gaze mode did not look long enough at a tangible object to trigger an action, 3 did not recognize the cross hair, and 2 grabbed an object unintentionally. With the controller mode, the participant had two possibilities to grab an object: 14 grabbed it by touching it with the controller, the other ones used the laser. 8 participants of this mode tried to trigger the use action by touching a button with the controller. For the laser mode, 1 participant would have liked to have the controller tooltips in the field of view and another did not see them initially. With the hand mode, 6 participants had difficulties to grab an object and 4 mentioned that the hardware needs improvement for this mode, especially due to tracking and grabbing problems.

Device Issues: For the coffee machine, 38 participants initially tried to use a wrong button (19 the buttons below the display, 17 the buttons on the top right, and 2 the display itself). When the participants used one of the three correct buttons, 56 used the middle one (strong coffee), 17 the left (light coffee), and 7 the right (two light coffees). The other five participants pressed several buttons at once (hand mode). For the copier, the most prominent issue was that 35 participants did not open it before trying to place the paper. Furthermore, 28 participants initially pressed a wrong button (16 the top left, 10 the top right, and 2 the button left of the actual copy button). 12 participants placed the paper incorrectly at first. 8 put it into the paper tray and 4 on the paper spawn zone. 5 participants already knew our printer model. 4 participants asked if the paper needed to be turned to be copied.

Table 2. General issues with the total and mode specific number of occurrences.

	Gaze	Laser	Controller	Hand	Total
Number of participants	23	21	21	20	85
Genera issues					
Detailed help	-	9	18	2	29
Object detached	5	4	-	12	21
Too far away	12	4	3	-	19
Snap Drop Zone	5	2	4	4	15
Reset	-	-	1	12	13
Mode unintuitive	2	1	-	-	3

Table 3. Additional comments of at least two participants of the case study.

Issue	Number
Icons diffuse	29
One button for task would be sufficient	7
Easy to learn	7
Icons partially unclear	6
Easier for younger people	5
Prefer to see own body	3
Prefer to use hands (did not use hand mode)	3
Problems with concept of VR	3
Icons too small	2
Haptic feedback missing	2
Easier for technically skilled people	2
Does not like VR	2
Copier more difficult than coffee machine	2

Additional Comments: The additional comments of the participants are listed in Table 3. Most prominently, 29 participants said that they had difficulties in seeing the icons of the coffee machine or copier properly because they seemed to be diffuse. For 6 participants, the meaning of the icons was unclear even though they could see them sharply. 2 participants mentioned this for the coffee machine, 2 for the copier, and 2 for both devices. 7 claimed that, for the given task, only one button would suffice and the other ones were distracting. 7 participants stated that the interaction was easy to learn, in contrast to 5 other participants who said that the interaction would be easier for younger people.

Time Measurements: For analyzing the performance and learnability of the different modes and scenes, we measured the duration of the interaction. For this, we divided the tasks into two phases. The first phase starts when the participants intentionally touched a tangible object and ends when the cup or paper are placed correctly. This starts the second phase which ends with the task completion, i.e., when the participant pressed the correct button on the technical device. The first phase of the copy scene includes the opening of the copier, the second phase includes its closing. The resulting mean durations in seconds for each interaction mode distributed on the VR scenes and the corresponding phases are listed in Table 4 in the columns called *total*.

The values show, that for all interaction modes, the first phase was completed faster with the coffee machine than with the copier (total values). For the coffee machine, the participants of the controller mode were fastest (6.8 s), the participants of the hand mode slowest (19.4 s). For the copy scene, the gaze mode participants finished fastest (24.9 s) while the hand mode participants were slowest (56.8 s). The second phase was about equally quick to accomplish in both scenes. In contrast to the first phase, the hand mode participants were fastest (20.1 s coffee scene, 12.5 s copy scene) and the controller participants slowest (34.2 s coffee scene, 30.1 s copy scene). These differences are significant. We performed a pairwise two-sided Wilcoxon test [31] for every column in Table 4 with a Hochberg p-value adjustment [12]. We rejected the null hypothesis, that durations are equal, if the p-value is below 0.005 [2].

Table 4 also shows differences of the durations between completing the task and phases depending on whether a scene was the first or the second scene to use by the participants. These values are shown in the columns named *first* and *second* in the respective parts of the table. From the values, we can see that for the coffee scene, the participants were always faster in all aspects (phases or complete duration) when they used the scene as the second one, i.e., they used the copier scene first. This is also independent of the concrete interaction mode. For the copier scene, this is only the case for the controller and the leap mode. In the other modes, the participants using the scene as the second one were not necessarily faster. According to our Wilcoxon test, only the differences between the hand and the gaze mode, and the hand and the controller mode for phase two in column *second* for the copier are significant.

5.5 Counter Evaluation

As mentioned, our virtual devices were based on real technical devices. To be able to evaluate, whether we correctly identify usability issues of these devices in VR, we also performed usability evaluations of the real devices. These evaluations were structured as the second phase of the VR evaluations described above. This means, we asked the participants to use the device for the same task as in VR. In the meantime, we observed them and took notes of comments and issues. Afterwards, we interviewed them using the same guiding statements as for the device assessment in VR. The test participants we recruited for this evaluation were different from those using our VR scenes.

We had 10 participants for the coffee machine evaluation. 9 of them had misconceptions or verbalized an unsureness about the three buttons for brewing the coffee. 7 participants used the middle button. 2 of them explicitly mentioned that the icon on this button looks like a full cup matching the goal of their task.

Table 4. Mean durations for the individual phases and overall usage of the coffee and the copy scene in seconds.

Mode	Coffee scene								Copy scene							
	Phase 1			Phase 2			Complete		Phase 1			Phase 2			Complete	
	First	Second	Total	First	Second	Total	First	Second	First	Second	Total	First	Second	Total	First	Second
Gaze	13.9	10.8	12.7	23.9	19.8	22.3	37.8	30.6	24.4	25.1	24.9	24.4	26.7	25.8	48.9	51.9
Laser	21.1	8.6	15.1	26.4	15.1	21.0	47.5	23.7	46.1	27.7	36.5	19.7	19.8	19.8	65.8	47.6
Controller	8.9	4.9	6.8	43.4	25.9	34.2	52.3	30.8	45.1	32.8	39.2	34.9	24.9	30.1	80.0	57.7
Hand	24.4	14.3	19.4	21.0	19.1	20.1	45.4	33.4	63.8	49.8	56.8	16.3	8.7	12.5	80.1	58.5

These results are similar to a counter evaluation for the same device described by Holderied [13].

Also for the copier, we had 10 participants. 3 mentioned an unsureness about the copy button, but used it correctly. 2 users used the input tray, the others opened the top and put the paper there.

5.6 Discussion

Based on our results, we answer our research questions. RQ 1 asks to what extent current consumer VR systems and corresponding interaction modes can be used for interacting with virtual prototypes of technical devices in VR. Our results show that all but one participants were able to accomplish all given tasks. Hence, we conclude:

> *The identified four categories of consumer VR systems and corresponding interaction modes can all be used for interacting with virtual prototypes of technical devices.*

But there are differences between the interaction modes resulting in different user efficiency. The values below one minute for task completion seem, at least for us, in an acceptable range for all interaction modes considering the application area of usability testing. But due to different results for phase 1 and phase 2 of the scenes and also our list of interaction mode specific user issues, we derive that for grabbing and using objects, different interaction modes work best. This means in detail:

> *Using buttons works best with the hand mode.*
> *Grabbing objects is easiest with the controller mode.*

For the usage of VR for usability evaluations of technical device, it is also important that users can easily learn the interaction modes. For assessing this learnability, we compared the different times the participants needed using a certain scene either as first or as second scene. The reduced time that the users needed with a specific mode when used in the second scene indicates that:

> *The learnability of all interaction modes is generally high.*

This applies although the interaction times within the VR were relatively short. For the laser and the controller mode, the learnability was strongest. The gaze mode instead does not show an efficiency improvement. However, it has a low error rate except for virtually standing too far away. This can be derived from the mode specific issues we detected. Hence, we derive:

> *The initial position of test participants in VR when using the gaze mode must be tested and selected with care.*

The required resets and the number of detached objects let us conclude that the hand mode needs improvement for actions like grabbing. In contrast, the need for a more detailed help is highest for the controller mode. This also indicates that an initial understanding of the controller itself, especially with multiple pressure points of a button, is difficult.

Based on our results, we also provide answers for RQ 2 focusing on the applicability of current consumer VR systems for usability evaluations of technical device prototypes. Our results show that independent of the interaction modes:

> *It is possible to detect real usability issues of the technical devices using virtual prototypes in VR.*

For example, we found that for brewing coffee, most users used the button for a strong coffee. This result correlates with the findings of our counter evaluation and the ones in [13]. A similar problem was detected for the copier. For some participants, it was unclear which button triggers the copy function. Considering our setup, we also conclude that:

> *For the virtual prototypes, all affordances related to an evaluated user tasks must be implemented.*

This stems from the fact that some participants tried to put the paper in the tray on the copier top instead of opening the copier. This means, they tried to use an affordance for which we did not provide an implementation. Hence, if a technical device has multiple affordances for the same task, all of them must be simulated. In contrast, we also saw that neither displays of devices need to show anything nor additional functionality needs to be implemented. We derive this from the fact that the virtual copier did not show anything on its display but only one user asked if the copier needed to be switched on.

From the study, we can also draw conclusions considering the differences between local and remote usability evaluation. In local usability evaluation, the evaluators can support the participants. Hence, the challenges for the participants to interact with the VR can be a bit higher. For remote evaluation, the evaluators are separated from the participants. Hence, the VR systems and interaction modes in this scenario should be as simple as possible and easy to learn. Our results show, that this is given best for the gaze and the laser mode. Hence, we propose:

> *For remote usability evaluations, use the gaze or the laser mode.*
> *For local usability evaluations, use the controller or hand mode.*

This would also match the fact that the corresponding VR system categories for remote usability evaluation would be less complex and cheaper than for local evaluations reducing the overall burden for test participation. Our participants partially mentioned problems with a diffuse view leading to a bad recognition of icons on buttons. Hence, when performing usability tests with current consumer VR systems, it needs to be considered that:

The resolution of the VR system may influence the evaluation results negatively.

Finally, considering the technical setup of the VR scenes and the snap drop zones, we conclude that:

Snap drop zones must be implemented as realistic as possible.

Otherwise, users may become distracted as partially happened in our study. The evaluators of usability tests also need to keep in mind that technical issues like an overheating of the VR system or tracking problems may occur. We did not observe typical VR issues as cyber sickness [8]. But this may be caused by the relatively short usage times.

5.7   Threats to Validity

The validity of our case study may have been affected by several threats. For example, due to the setup of our VR area, some participants may have watched the interaction of their predecessors and might have experienced a learning effect, even though they used another interaction mode and although we actively tried to prevent this. Since we executed one of our sessions in the university, half of our participants were students and, therefore, our test sample might be too homogeneous. On top of that, many potential participants in the mall did not want to join the case study for different reasons like being afraid or having heard bad things about VR. So we might have missed a relevant user group. Furthermore, we still had only a small number of participants per mode and first scene combination.

During the case study, many participants seemed rather impressed by VR. Our demographic data also shows that 65 of our participants did not have any previous experience with VR. This may have positively influenced their assessment of our interaction modes or the virtual technical devices.

During the case study, the same two evaluators were responsible for executing the whole case study. This might have caused an evaluator effect. Furthermore, we did not switch off the room scale tracking of the HTC Vive for the gaze and the laser mode although the envisaged VR systems categories for these modes only provide orientation tracking for the head set. We did this to allow for position corrections of the participant during the evaluation. But this may have influenced the results for these two modes.

6   Conclusion and Outlook

In our work, we assessed how state-of-the-art consumer VR technology can be used for performing usability testing based on virtual prototypes of technical devices. For this, we first identified four different categories of consumer VR systems. Then we implemented one interaction mode per category and tested in a large case study if they can be used for interacting with the virtual technical devices. Overall, we found that a gaze mode and a laser mode currently work best. In addition, a mode where users can use their real hands for interaction has quite some potential as long as the required tracking techniques improve. We also showed that usability issues of technical devices can be found by using VR. In addition, we uncovered some issues that may occur when performing this type of usability evaluation, such as difficulties in correctly seeing details of the technical devices.

For future research, similar case studies should be executed with other VR systems and further user groups to have an enhanced validation of our results. In these evaluations, a first study with remote usability evaluation should be performed. This would include recording and analyzing the VR usage without creating screen casts. For this, our already used logging mechanism may be an option. The logged actions may be used for replaying the VR usage. In addition, we will consider how our hand-based interaction can be improved so that it becomes an option for our intended scenarios, as it seems to be most intuitive but technically challenging.

7   Replication Kit

All the data we recorded in the case study, the performed statistical tests, as well as the VR scenes have been published in a replication kit available at https://doi.org/10.5281/zenodo.894173.

References

1. ISO 9241–11: Ergonomic requirements for office work with visual display terminals (VDTs) - Part 11: Guidance on usability (ISO 9241–11:1998) (1998)
2. Benjamin, D.J., et al.: Redefine statistical significance. Nat. Hum. Behav. **2**, 6 (2017)
3. Bowman, D.A., McMahan, R.P., Ragan, E.D.: Questioning naturalism in 3D user interfaces. Commun. ACM **55**(9), 78–88 (2012)
4. Bruno, F., Muzzupappa, M.: Product interface design: a participatory approach based on virtual reality. Int. J. Hum Comput Stud. **68**(5), 254–269 (2010)
5. Carulli, M., Bordegoni, M., Cugini, U.: An approach for capturing the voice of the customer based on virtual prototyping. J. Intell. Manuf. **24**(5), 887–903 (2013)
6. HTC Corporation: Vive (2017). https://www.vive.com/. Accessed September 2017
7. Di Gironimo, G., Matrone, G., Tarallo, A., Trotta, M., Lanzotti, A.: A virtual reality approach for usability assessment: case study on a wheelchair-mounted robot manipulator. Eng. Comput. **29**(3), 359–373 (2013)
8. Dörner, R., Broll, W., Grimm, P., Jung, B. (eds.): Virtual und Augmented Reality (VR/AR): Grundlagen und Methoden der Virtuellen und Augmentierten Realität. Springer, Heidelberg (2013). https://doi.org/10.1007/978-3-642-28903-3
9. Falcão, C.S., Soares, M.M.: Application of virtual reality technologies in consumer product usability. In: Marcus, A. (ed.) DUXU 2013. LNCS, vol. 8015, pp. 342–351. Springer, Heidelberg (2013). https://doi.org/10.1007/978-3-642-39253-5_37
10. Blender Foundation: Blender (2017).https://www.blender.org/.Accessed September 2017
11. Hegner, M.: Methoden zur Evaluation von Software. Arbeitsbericht. IZ, InformationsZentrum Sozialwiss (2003)

12. Hochberg, Y.: A sharper Bonferroni procedure for multiple tests of significance. Biometrika **75**, 800–802 (1988)
13. Holderied, H.: Evaluation of interaction concepts in virtual reality. In: Eibl, M., Gaedke, M. (eds.) INFORMATIK 2017. LNI, pp. 2511–2523. Gesellschaft für Informatik, Bonn (2017)
14. Jerald, J.: The VR Book: Human-Centered Design for Virtual Reality. Association for Computing Machinery. Morgan & Claypool, New York (2016)
15. Kanai, S., Higuchi, T., Kikuta, Y.: 3D digital prototyping and usability enhancement of information appliances based on usixml. Int. J. Interact. Des. Manuf. (IJIDeM) **3**(3), 201–222 (2009)
16. Kuutti, K., et al.: Virtual prototypes in usability testing. In: Proceedings of the 34th Annual Hawaii International Conference on System Sciences, 7 pp., January 2001
17. Lawson, G., Salanitri, D., Waterfield, B.: Future directions for the development of virtual reality within an automotive manufacturer. Appl. Ergon. **53**, 323–330 (2016). Transport in the 21st Century: The Application of Human Factors to Future User Needs
18. Inc. Leap Motion. Unity (2017). https://developer.leapmotion.com/unity/. Accessed September 2017
19. Nielsen, J.: Usability Engineering. Morgan Kaufmann Publishers Inc., San Francisco (1993)
20. Oculus: Oculus go (2018). https://www.oculus.com/go/. Accessed September 2018
21. Park, H., Moon, H.C., Lee, J.Y.: Tangible augmented prototyping of digital handheld products. Comput. Ind. **60**(2), 114–125 (2009)
22. Paternò, F.: Tools for remote web usability evaluation. In: HCI International 2003. Proceedings of the 10th International Conference on Human-Computer Interaction, vol. 1, pp. 828–832. Erlbaum (2003). Accessed September 2017
23. Paternò, F., Russino, A., Santoro, C.: Remote evaluation of mobile applications. In: Winckler, M., Johnson, H., Palanque, P. (eds.) TAMODIA 2007. LNCS, vol. 4849, pp. 155–169. Springer, Heidelberg (2007). https://doi.org/10.1007/978-3-540-77222-4_13
24. Reich, D., Buchholz, C., Stark, R.: Methods to validate automotive user interfaces within immersive driving environments. In: Meixner, G., Müller, C. (eds.) Automotive User Interfaces. HIS, pp. 429–454. Springer, Cham (2017). https://doi.org/10.1007/978-3-319-49448-7_16
25. Richter, M., Flückiger, M.D.: Usability Engineering kompakt: Benutzbare Software gezielt entwickeln. IT Kompakt. Springer, Heidelberg (2013). https://doi.org/10.1007/978-3-642-34832-7
26. Sutcliffe, A., Gault, B., Fernando, T., Tan, K.: Investigating interaction in cave virtual environments. ACM Trans. Comput.-Hum. Interact. **13**(2), 235–267 (2006)
27. Sutcliffe, A., Gault, B., Maiden, N.: ISRE: immersive scenario-based requirements engineering with virtual prototypes. Requirements Eng. **10**(2), 95–111 (2005)
28. Unity Technologies: Unity 3D (2017). https://unity3d.com/. Accessed September 2017
29. Verlinden, J., Van Den Esker, W., Wind, L., Horváth, I.: Qualitative comparison of virtual and augmented prototyping of handheld products. In: Marjanovic, D. (ed.) DS 32: Proceedings of DESIGN 2004, the 8th International Design Conference, Dubrovnik, Croatia, pp. 533–538 (2004)
30. Google VR: Google cardboard (2017). https://vr.google.com/cardboard/. Accessed September 2017
31. Wilcoxon, F.: Individual comparisons by ranking methods. Biomet. Bull. **1**(6), 80–83 (1945)

Wearable and Tangible Interaction

Combining Tablets with Smartphones for Data Analytics

Gary Perelman[1,2(✉)], Marcos Serrano[2], Christophe Bortolaso[1],
Celia Picard[1], Mustapha Derras[1], and Emmanuel Dubois[2]

[1] Berger-Levrault, 31670 Labège, France
{gary.perelman,christophe.bortolaso,celia.picard,
mustapha.derras}@Berger-Levrault.fr
[2] University of Toulouse III, 31062 Toulouse Cdx9, France
{gary.perelman,marcos.serrano,emmanuel.dubois}@irit.fr

Abstract. While ubiquitous data analytics is a promising approach, analyzing spreadsheets data on tablets is a tedious task due to the limited display size and touch vocabulary. In this paper, we present the design and evaluation of novel interaction techniques relying on the combination of a tablet, holding the data, and a smartphone, used as a mediator between the user and the tablet. To this end, we propose to use stacking gestures, i.e. laying one edge of a smartphone on the tablet screen. Stacking is a cheap, easy to implement and effective way of employing always-available smartphones to improve data analysis on tablets, by augmenting the input vocabulary and extending the display surface. We first explore stacking gestures to delimitate the possible interaction vocabulary and present the manufacturing of a conductive smartphone case. Then, we propose novel stacking-based techniques to perform spreadsheet data analysis, i.e. pivot table creation and manipulation. We evaluate our stacking techniques against touch interaction as provided by current mobile spreadsheet apps. Our studies reveal that some of our interaction techniques perform 30% faster than touch for creating pivot tables.

Keywords: Mobile interaction · Stacking gestures · Data manipulation ·
Multimodality · Interaction with small displays

1 Introduction

Ubiquitous data analytics [9] consists in embedding the analytical process into the environment to make sense of data anywhere and anytime. This type of analytical process is of growing importance as mobile devices and particularly tablets become a professional computing platform [2]. To facilitate data analysis, users usually transform raw data into tables or graphical visualizations such as charts or scatter plots. One of the best-known solution to rapidly generate these data visualizations is pivot table [20, 25], a type of table that combines data by applying a so-called "summary function"

Electronic supplementary material The online version of this chapter (https://doi.org/10.1007/978-3-030-29390-1_24) contains supplementary material, which is available to authorized users.

D. Lamas et al. (Eds.): INTERACT 2019, LNCS 11749, pp. 439–460, 2019.
https://doi.org/10.1007/978-3-030-29390-1_24

such as sorting, averaging or summing. Numerous mobile apps (e.g. Excel [10], QlikView [30], QlikSense [29], Tableau mobile [35]) and web-based systems (Voyager [41]) provide this tool. However, interaction with pivot tables on tablets is still difficult: the small display size (inducing multiple pans and views switching) and, most of all, the limitations of touch interaction (i.e. gestures mostly bound to navigation in the data space) fail at providing a convenient solution to create and adjust pivot tables for data analysis on tablets. Our work thus seeks to broaden the interaction possibilities for data analytics on tablets, by extending the currently available interaction capabilities.

To address this problem, previous approaches explored the use of multi-touch [1, 17, 39] and pen based [21, 27] interaction to extend input degrees of freedom (DoF). However, these approaches do not extend the limited display size of mobile devices. Besides, users have to learn a new multitouch vocabulary, and only active pens can be differentiated from finger touch. Instead, we propose to use an always-available device, the smartphone [32], as a tangible interactor with the tablet, and to employ stacking gestures, i.e. bringing one edge of the smartphone in contact with the tablet screen containing the spreadsheet application. The smartphone constitutes a mediator (as defined in [5]) between the user and the tablet by providing a set of additional tools. The interest is threefold: (1) our stacking gestures do not impede the use of regular touch interaction; (2) touch vocabulary, devoted to navigate data, is augmented with stacking gestures, dedicated to manipulate data; and (3) the initial display area is extended with a second screen, which allows to separate multiple visualizations, such as data spreadsheets, graphs or pivot tables.

In this work, we investigate a concrete use case that illustrates the need of real users (local elected officials) in terms of ubiquitous data analytics. It highlights the need for a novel solution to rapidly generate pivot tables on tablets and lead to the definition of a usage scenario. Then, we explore the comfort and technical feasibility of stacking gestures. Based on these studies, we design and evaluate stacking-based techniques for the two steps of data analysis on spreadsheets (see Fig. 1): first, the selection of a data cell range (required prior to any data manipulation) and second the pivot table creation (a task representative of the data analytics domain [20, 21]). We evaluate these techniques in two different user studies and compare them to the regular touch interactions.

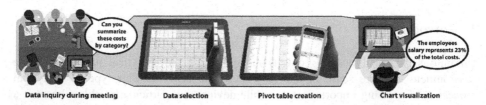

Fig. 1. Usage scenario: during a meeting, Jessica uses her smartphone and our stacking-based techniques to rapidly (1) select the data on the tablet, and (2) create a pivot table to generate a chart.

Our contributions are (1) the analysis of the physical and technological feasibility of stacking-based interaction techniques (ITs); (2) the design and evaluation of stacking-based ITs for data selection in spreadsheets on tablets; (3) the design and evaluation of stacking-based ITs to create pivot tables that summarize the previous data.

2 Use Case: Ubiquitous Analytics for Local Authorities

As part of a collaboration with a company developing software solutions for the public administration and local authorities, we conducted a set of semi-guided interviews to analyze the needs of their end-users in terms of interaction techniques for mobile contexts. We focused on one of their most important users, i.e. local elected officials (such as mayors or heads of district authorities). These users rely on a wide variety of mobile devices and they regularly need to access community data (budgets, demography) outside of their desktop environment (e.g. council meetings).

2.1 Interview Protocol and Results

The semi-guided interview focused on the working environment and the main tasks performed by the elected officials. To preserve the form of a free discussion, the questions served only to drive or refocus the discussion. These interviews were conducted with eight elected officials (all men). Their respective communities are composed of 563 to 466.297 habitants and 14 to 69 elected members. The interviewees were familiar with desktop computers as well as conventional mobile devices (7.5 on a scale of 1 to 10). All of them use office suites (spreadsheets and presentation programs). The interview lasted on average 66 min per participant.

Among all the tasks carried out by elected officials, many require the exploration and manipulation of graphical representations of data through charts (budget management, demographic analysis, etc.). For this purpose, elected officials use software such as Microsoft Excel or QlikView [10, 30] in a fixed environment. Although their job requires ubiquitous data analysis, several elected officials reported the lack of suitable and easy to use tools to perform this task on mobile devices: *"We use a pre-made dashboard in council meetings. If the pre-made charts are not sufficient, the meeting is adjourned so we can make new ones on a [desktop] computer"*. As this requirement was the most frequent outcome of the interviews, we developed with the participants a usage scenario in which elected officials need to perform data analysis on a mobile device.

2.2 Usage Scenario

Before a council meeting, Jessica, an elected official, performs a data analysis on the current year's city budget, sorted by districts (Fig. 1). Equipped with her professional tablet only, the presentation of her analysis during the council meeting raises questions from other officials concerning the increase of costs for this year. To answer these questions, she needs to perform a new analysis by separating the types of costs for each district, for instance the employees' salary, the outsourcing cost and the materials cost.

She uses a pivot table [10] to quickly produce a cross-analysis summary, from which a graphical representation is rapidly generated. To this end, she performs a two-step process: (1) select the spreadsheet dataset corresponding to the city budget; (2) create the pivot table by affecting the "district" variable to the table rows, the "types of costs" variable to the table columns, and defining the summary function (e.g. in this case the "average" function, to calculate the average cost of material for each district). While this process is easy and rapid on desktop interfaces, selecting the data on the spreadsheet and configuring the pivot table requires multiple touch manipulations that are quite tedious on tablets (see State of the art section for a detailed description).

This scenario serves as a basis for our work and illustrates the need for a set of interaction techniques to facilitate the use of pivot tables on tablets. Beyond the context of elected officials, such interaction techniques would also be relevant in many other contexts such as building inspection reports, budget meetings, employee's management, resource management during crisis, etc. Our approach is to employ an always-available device, the smartphone, as an interactor to facilitate interaction with spreadsheets on tablets. We designed and experimentally compared different stacking-based techniques for each of the two steps of pivot table creation: data selection (study 1) and pivot table creation (study 2).

3 State of the Art

In this section, we first summarize the limitations of regular touch interaction with spreadsheets on tablets. Then we review existing approaches for overcoming these limitations by extending input/output interaction capabilities.

3.1 Spreadsheets on Tablets: Current Touch Approaches

Interacting with spreadsheets on tablets usually relies on the direct mapping of a touch gesture (swipe, pinch/spread, tap, double tap) to a specific task (pan, zoom in/out, selection of a single cell, edition) [9, 12]. Any other task requires a combination of these fundamental touch gestures. For example, to select a range of cells (see Fig. 2) (1) the user taps to select a cell, (2) taps on the selected cell anchor, and (3) drags the finger to extend the selected range. Using touch gestures for such a frequent and common task is quite tedious due to the length of the process and the small size of cell anchors. And yet, it is usually followed by even more complex tasks (i.e. filter, generate and configure a chart, calculate sums, etc.): to activate those tasks, the user relies on shortcuts on the title bar, or a menu bar on the top-right corner with dropdown menus, making the overall interaction even longer.

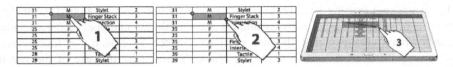

Fig. 2. Cells selection: tap on a cell (1), select the anchor (2) and drag to extend the selection (3)

As mobile screen size is limited, displaying icons or menus for the numerous commands results in occlusions; not displaying them results in long browsing through the multiple menus and commands available before reaching the appropriate functionality. To cope with these issues, the following section discusses interaction techniques that have been proposed to extend the classical mobile device input and output interaction capabilities.

3.2 Extending Interaction Capabilities on Tablets

Multimodal Interaction for Tablets. Multi-touch gestures based on chords [1, 37, 39], consecutive taps [16, 17] or bimanual interaction [11] have been explored to extend the touch vocabulary. Using speech in combination with a tactile device for querying a data set [36] also extends input possibilities. Mid-air interaction techniques located around the device [2, 15] have been considered to organize menus or to manipulate the app data (e.g. manipulate a 3D object). In these approaches, tablet output capabilities are not extended and may even be reduced to provide a dedicated feedback for supporting the use and memorization of these modalities.

Combining pen+touch for spreadsheets manipulation on tablets has also been explored to enhance the access to multiple features (edit a cell, copy-paste data, navigate in a sheet and format/color a cell) [27] and for creating meaningful charts faster and easier through the manipulation of pivot tables [21]. Nonetheless, these two approaches require a dedicated pen device (to differentiate it from of a finger touch), and parallel viewing of raw data and graphical rendering is still limited.

Tangible UIs such as MagGetz [19] propose to manipulate several interactors which can be bound to specific actions like controlling a slider or pushing an app button. Tangible interaction usually requires dedicated objects that have to be carried on, and may be less convenient in a mobile context.

Multi-display Interaction Around Tablets. Compared to the previous approaches, multi-display interaction has the advantage of extending at the same time input and output. Combining tablets allows for example to distribute visualization views on multiple devices, while extending input capabilities through the use of the various touchscreens and the spatial awareness of each other [23, 43]. A less cumbersome alternative consists in exploring how to take advantage of the smartphone position and movement around a tablet. It has been used for example to explore a graphical representation displayed on the tablet as in Thaddeus [42] or to trigger actions (pie-menu selection, drawing tool activation) as in BATMAN [28]. However, these approaches rely on external sensing systems to track the smartphone position around the tablet, which constrains the use of such techniques outside lab (i.e. equipped) environments. Authors have also explored the use of a smartwatch to extend the touchscreen vocabulary [8]. However its benefits are counterbalanced by the size of the watch screen, restricting its role to being a complementary device [18], used mostly for providing feedback or command shortcuts.

Multi-display Stacking. Multi-display stacking, i.e. when one display (called support) detects the presence of another device (called interactor), offers the advantage of not requiring any external sensor. For example, in THAW [24], the computer screen displays a specific pattern which can be detected by the smartphone screen. This pattern allows the smartphone to track its position with regards to the computer screen. An embedded IMU is used to detect its orientation. As a result, the smartphone can be used as a magic lens or directly as a tangible object on the application. In Phonetouch [33, 34], a smartphone corner stack can be detected by a tactile table using a combination of sensors (smartphone accelerometers and touch interaction on the table). In this case, the smartphone is used to transfer data between the smartphone and the tablet, to display private feedback, or as a tangible interaction tool. In ACTUI [26] the smartphone is equipped with a copper shell (with a specific pattern on its edge). The tablet screen can then detect and track the smartphone position and orientation. In this case, the smartphone is used to explore the third dimension of a 2D model displayed on the tablet screen. Our approach is based on a similar technical tracking solution.

These works provide concrete technological solutions to facilitate the detection of stacking gestures. They also propose specific usage scenarios taking advantage of the stacking properties in terms of (1) additional screen and (2) extended interaction vocabulary. In this paper we explore in a more systematic manner the design space of stacking gestures. We also propose and evaluate a new set of stacking techniques for data analysis on tablets.

4   Stacking Gestures: Comfort and Technical Feasibility

As a first step in our work on how to use stacking to facilitate data analysis on tablets, we conducted an exploratory study of stacking gestures. We first identified the dimensions of stacking gestures, and then conducted a preliminary study that aims to discard uncomfortable gestures. Based on this analysis we developed a running prototype.

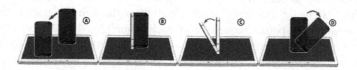

Fig. 3. Stacking physical gestures: (A) translation, (B) flat rotation, (C) tilt, and (D) corner rotation

4.1 Stacking Gestures Dimensions

In our context, stacking consists in bringing a smartphone in contact with a tablet screen, which detects it. Three major aspects characterize stacking gestures:

- Stacked surface: corresponds to the edge or corner of the smartphone detected by the tablet. Although the front and rear faces of the smartphone could also be stacked, they would occlude an important part of the tablet screen.
- Holding hand: describes which hand holds the smartphone. Given our usage scenario (cf. Sect. 2.2), the user holds the smartphone with the dominant hand, as a tangible and tactile interactor, while the tablet lays on a table. Touch gestures on the tablet and smartphone screens can be performed with the non-dominant hand. We leave the study of stacking gestures on a handheld tablet while standing up for future work.
- Types of gestures: defines the possible user input gestures. With the smartphone, the user can stack (i.e. lay a smartphone edge/corner on the tablet screen) and unstack (i.e. lift up the smartphone). Once stacked, four physical manipulations are possible (see Fig. 3): translation of the smartphone on the tablet screen (A); flat rotation of the smartphone on the tablet screen (B); tilt of the smartphone around the stacked edge, which stays in contact with the tablet screen (C); and corner rotation of the smartphone (D). Finally, touch gestures (tap, drag or pinch/spread) may be used on both devices. As a result, once stacked, the user can perform a set of touch, physical or compound (i.e. physical then touch) gestures.

4.2 Preliminary Study on Stacking Gestures Comfort

Stacking requires the user to hold a smartphone and move it on the tablet screen. As this may seem unnatural at first, we decided to assess the comfort of stacking gestures through a preliminary study and discard the most uncomfortable ones. We used a 10.5″ Samsung Galaxy tab S tablet and a 5″ Galaxy S4 smartphone (both devices were switched off). Six participants (age = 26.4, SD = 1.67, 2 females) performed a set of stacks in different orientations (e.g. portrait or landscape mode, screen facing the user or partially rotated) followed by a touch, physical or compound (physical then touch) gesture. The participants rated the comfort of each gesture using a 5-points Likert scale. Touch gestures on the smartphone were performed in two different ways: with the hand holding the smartphone or with the other hand (bi-manually). We did not study touch gestures on the tablet, as they are independent from the stacking gesture.

Regarding all touch gestures (unimanual and bimanual), tap and drag gestures were largely considered comfortable (95.83% and 87.5% respectively rated 3 or above). Pinch/spread were overall deemed uncomfortable (rated 1 or 2), especially when performed with one hand (in 47.9% of the trials). Concerning physical gestures, results reveal that the Translation gesture was deemed comfortable (rated 3 or above) in 87.8% of the trials. All the other physical gestures revealed some level of discomfort. Indeed, rotation was found uncomfortable (rated 1 or 2 in 37.5% of the trials) in some orientations. Tilting around a corner was deemed uncomfortable in 29.2% of the trials. The compound gestures were considered uncomfortable (rated 1 or 2) in 38.9% on the trials, especially when a pinch/spread was required (rated 1 or 2 in 69.8% of these trials).

Based on these results we decided to use only Translation gestures and Tap/Drag touch input (unimanual and bimanual), as these were deemed comfortable. Results also revealed that the smartphone should be in portrait mode: this means that only the bottom edge of the smartphone is stacked.

4.3   Stacking Prototype Implementation

To implement these translation gestures, we needed a prototype capable of detecting the smartphone bottom edge position, orientation and translation on the tablet screen. To create this prototype, we used a similar approach to CapStones and CapTUI [3, 7]. We 3D-printed a smartphone case and covered its back with copper foil (0.1 mm thickness), extended through three copper strips on every edge of the device (Fig. 4 - Left). The tablet detects these three strips (5–6 mm width) as three simultaneous touch events and generates a stack event. We choose to use three strips to detect the orientation of the smartphone on the tablet screen because there is no common touch gesture requiring three simultaneous aligned touch points: hence, our stacking implementation does not impede regular touch interaction. By controlling the relative distance between these strips, we can create a unique pattern for each smartphone edge thus allowing the tablet to recognize which edge of the smartphone is stacked. We also engineered a metallic version of the case with the same patterns on each side (Fig. 4 - Right).

To detect this pattern, we implemented an algorithm in Java on the Android platform. We use the specific distance and alignment of the three detected copper strips to identify the associated edge. Our algorithm detects the smartphone stack as soon as the copper strips are detected on the tablet screen. Our algorithm also handles situations where the smartphone is partially out of the tablet screen: in these cases, we estimate the outside points' position using the known distance between them.

Fig. 4. Two versions of the conductive case: a 3D printed version with copper strips (left) and a market-ready metallic version with strips already integrated on the edges (right). These were designed and engineered in collaboration with the technical college Renée Bonnet in Toulouse.

5   Study 1: Cell Range Selection

Cell range selection is a fundamental task for data analysis as it is required for creating a pivot table, and prior to most of the other spreadsheet commands. A cell range selection defines the range of cells to which a command or function applies.

5.1   Design of Stacking-Based Interaction Techniques for Cells Selection

Selecting a cell range requires two actions, to select the beginning and end of the cell range. Based on a user centered process, we designed three stacking-based techniques to select a cell range, illustrating the combination of two design considerations: number of hands involved (one or two hands), and number of stacking gestures (one or two gestures):

- *"Intersection"* combines two successive stacking gestures with the dominant hand. To select a range of cells using the *Intersection* technique (Fig. 5 – Left), the user simply selects a range of rows and then a range of columns: the intersection between the set of selected rows and columns defines the range of selected cells. These two steps are independent and can be performed in any order. To select columns or rows, the user first stacks the smartphone respectively with a vertical orientation (90° ± 25°) or horizontal orientation (0° ± 25°, Fig. 5 – Left). In both cases, translating the smartphone extends the selected range of rows/columns. To modify a column/row selection, the user can stack again on the first or last selected column/row and translate the smartphone to adjust the selection edge.
- *"Stack-and-Drag"* uses only one stacking gesture and only the dominant hand. It is based on a stylus metaphor: when stacking the smartphone, the center of the smartphone edge acts as a pointer on the tablet. This pointer is represented by a red dot displayed on the tablet screen 1 cm in front of the smartphone (in the middle of the edge) to prevent occlusion issues (Fig. 5 – Center). To select the cell range, the user stacks the smartphone on the tablet screen. Translating the smartphone extends the current cell range selection (Fig. 5 – Center). To adjust the selection, the user can stack again the smartphone on the top-left or bottom-right cell and translate the smartphone.
- *"Finger Stack"* combines a finger-touch with the non-dominant hand and a stacking gesture with the dominant hand. Finger Stack consists in defining the top-left corner of the cell range with a finger touch and the bottom-right corner with the smartphone stack (Fig. 5 – Right). The bottom-right corner is selected using the center of the smartphone edge with the help of the red dot feedback, as in the Stack-and-Drag technique. The selection of the two corner cells can be adjusted with a finger drag and/or smartphone translation gesture. To modify the selection, a touch or stack respectively on the top-left corner or bottom-right corner, allows dragging the selected corner.

A fourth technique based on using two hands and two stack gestures would generate more than two actions, which is not necessary here. For the three proposed techniques, if the desired cell range exceeds the screen limits, the smartphone can be dragged close to the screen edges to trigger a rate-based scroll. The center of the contact edge is used to trigger the scroll mechanism.

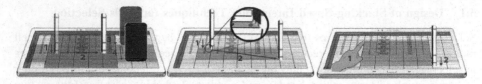

Fig. 5. Intersection (left), Stack-and-Drag (center) and Finger Stack (right) selection techniques. (Color figure online)

Each of the three techniques offers different advantages for cell range selection. Intersection is based on two simple gestures that do not require a precise pointing on a single cell, which is usually small. Stack-and-Drag is similar to a mouse-based selection on desktop spreadsheets but avoids the need to accurately select the tiny anchor on the corner of a selected cell. Finger Stack offers the advantage of a direct selection (a simple touch and stack) without any smartphone translation. We decided to confront these advantages in a controlled study and to compare them with touch interaction.

We found no mobile spreadsheet app providing the required API and software tools to integrate custom interaction techniques and stacking gestures recognition. Therefore, we developed a new spreadsheet app that conforms exactly to the Google Spreadsheet app [12] in terms of interface layout, touch interaction, and cell size (284 × 53 px). We also integrated our three interaction techniques and stacking gestures recognition. The techniques are demonstrated in the adjunct video.

In this study, we compare the performance of the three stacking-based techniques against a baseline, the touch interaction, for a cell range selection task.

5.2   Experimental Protocol

Task. The participants were asked to select different cell ranges as quickly as possible with each of the four proposed interaction techniques. To limit experimental biases, we deactivated pan/zoom actions as they could have affected the cell range selection strategy with all the techniques. The scroll action was available during a selection.

To represent the diversity of cell ranges, we considered seven categories: complete rows, complete columns, 1 × M (one column, M rows), N × 1 (N columns, one row) and 3 forms of N × M (visual square, horizontal and vertical rectangle). The values for N were 1, 2, 4 or 9 columns, and 1, 7, 13, or 33 rows for M. These values were chosen with regards to the difference between the cells' height and width. The origin of the cell range was always the cell D6. We evaluated two conditions for each range: one where the range was totally within the screen (i.e. no scroll required) and one where the range exceeded the screen limits (i.e. scroll required).

Each trial corresponded to one range selection and was carried out as follows. A first panel, displayed on the tablet screen, showed the information of the range to select in multiple formats (textual, cell headers and schematic image Fig. 6 – Left). When ready, the user touched a button on the tablet to start the trial and display the spreadsheet. The headers associated with the targeted cell range were red colored. After cell selection, for the selected cells within the targeted range, the headers turned green. Otherwise, they turned yellow (Fig. 6 – Middle), thus highlighting a mistake. Once the target range was correctly selected, an automatic validation of the trial was triggered after 500 ms.

Fig. 6. Main screen of the app (left), incorrect selection (middle) and correct selection (right). (Color figure online)

Design. Our study followed a 4 * 7 * 2 within-subjects design with Interaction technique (Tactile, Intersection, Stack-and-Drag and Finger Stack), Cell range (the seven types described previously) and Scroll (with or without) as factors. The study was divided into four blocks, each block corresponding to one interaction technique (IT). The order of blocks was counterbalanced across participants by means of a 4 × 4 Latin square.

For each block, participants had to perform 14 training trials (half of them with scroll), then 42 range selections (14 conditions × 3 repetitions). The order of trials within a block was randomized. Participants could take a break between each trial and block. We collected a total of 4 IT × 42 trials (7 ranges × 2 scroll conditions × 3 repetitions) × 12 participants = 2016 selections.

Apparatus, Participants and Collected Data. We used a Samsung Galaxy Tab S (Android 5.1, octa-core 1.9 GHz and 1.3 GHz) with a 10.5″ display (2560 × 1600 px), and a Samsung Galaxy S4 (Android 5.1, quad-core 1.9 GHz) with a 5″ display (1920 × 1080 px). The smartphone was equipped with our conductive case and the tablet was equipped with a plastic screen protection. Our spreadsheet app was installed on the tablet. The user was sitting, holding the smartphone with his/her dominant hand, and the tablet laid on the table in front of him/her.

We recruited 12 participants (5 females), aged 27.7 years on average (SD = 4.7). Six of them had been involved in the preliminary study. They were all right-handed and familiar with mobile devices (7.5 on a 0–9 scale) and desktop spreadsheets (7.0). Only one subject was familiar with spreadsheets on tablets (7.0, compared with 2.1 for the others). The experiment lasted one hour on average.

We measured the time to perform each trial, from the button press to the automatic validation. At the end of each block, we asked the participants to fill a SUS questionnaire [4] and we collected informal feedbacks. Participants were also asked to rate (like/dislike) the interaction techniques on a 7-points Likert scale.

5.3   Results

We chose to rely on estimation techniques with 95% confidence intervals and ratio analysis as recommended by the APA [38]. Ratio is an intra-subject measurement that expresses the effect size (pair-wise comparison) and is computed between each of the geometric means. All CIs are 95% BCa bootstrap confidence interval. For the reader more used to interpret the p-values, a parallel might be drawn with results obtained through the estimation technique and CIs reports (see Fig. 3 in [22]). Scripts used to compute the geometric mean and CIs were used in [40] and are available online [14].

Selection Time. The results on selection time show a clear difference between the four interaction techniques. Indeed, *Finger Stack* and *Intersection* required clearly less time (resp. 6.35 s, CI [5.79, 6.93] and 6.54 s, CI [6.02, 7.3]) than *Tactile* (7.64 s CI [6.87, 8.94]) and *Stack-and-Drag* (8.27 s, CI [7.3, 9.46]) (Fig. 7 - left). The intra subject analysis based on the time ratio (Fig. 7 - right) confirms this finding and establishes that trials with *Tactile* took 19.9% more time than with *Finger Stack* (ratio = 1.199 and no intersection of the 95% CI with the value 1.0) and 16.1% more time than with *Intersection* (ratio = 1.161, no intersection with 1.0).

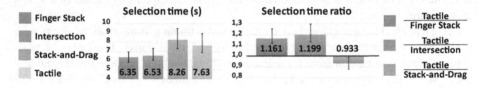

Fig. 7. Mean selection time in s (left) and ratio (right) regarding *Tactile* (95% CI).

This result holds when considering the different cells range categories individually. When analyzing the impact of the Scroll factor (cells range categories involving N = 9 and/or M = 33), results show that when scrolling is required, trials take on average 64% CI [58.8, 69.5] more time for every technique, with no difference among techniques. Thus, our scrolling mechanism did not negatively impact completion time.

Usability and User Preference. The analysis of the SUS questionnaires clearly establishes a better usability score for *Tactile* and *Intersection* techniques, (resp. 85.8, CI [78.3, 91.3] and 82.1, CI [73.5, 87.3]) than for *Finger Stack* (68.3, CI [58.1, 76.9]) and *Stack-and-Drag* (52.7, CI [36.7, 63.1]). The general rating of the techniques confirms these results with 11 participants out of 12 who liked (5 and above on a 7-points Likert Scale) Tactile, 10 who liked Intersection, 8 Finger Stack and 5 Stack-and-Drag.

Informal comments reported by the participants are in line with these analyses. Indeed, the Tactile interaction has been described as: "Intuitive, coherent with classical touch gestures" (8/12). However, users found that it is "difficult to aim at the right cell" (10/12). The Intersection technique was qualified as "Simple to use because the dimensions are clearly separated" (9/12). The Finger Stack technique was described as "Practical because the selection is almost immediate" (12/12). The Stack-and-Drag technique is considered "Difficult to manipulate because it is hard to aim the correct cell with the red dot [smartphone pointer]" (9/12).

Conclusion. The results show that the *Tactile* interaction takes on average 19.9% more time than *Finger Stack* and 16.1% more time than *Intersection* to correctly select a range of data. These results remain valid when performing a scroll. In terms of usability, the stacking-based technique *Intersection* obtains a SUS score similar to the one obtained for the baseline technique *Tactile*, using touch interaction only, a score which is higher than for the other techniques. In addition, participants reported very enthusiastic comments about the *Intersection* technique.

Given these results, we only consider the *Intersection* and *Tactile* (as baseline) techniques on the subsequent part of our work on stacking-based techniques for pivot table creation and manipulation.

6 Study 2: Pivot Table Creation

After validating the initial and necessary step of selecting a cell range, we focus on the remaining actions needed to create and manipulate a pivot table to support ubiquitous data analysis. In Excel on a Microsoft Surface tablet, after selecting the desired data (step 1) and pressing on the right menu/sub-menu to insert the pivot table, the app activates a wizard. The wizard is displayed on the right side of the screen, on a secondary tab or on the tab containing the data. The wizard presents the headers of the selected rows and four shelves, representing the four components of a pivot table (Row, Column, Value and Filter [25] – see Fig. 8-C). Each column header can then be dragged and dropped (step 2) on one of the four wizard's shelves. A touch on the elements in the Value shelf allows changing the summary function using a pop-up window. To filter the elements, a touch on the pivot table opens a specific pop-up. To improve the interaction with pivot table on tablets we designed a set of stacking-based interaction techniques.

6.1 Design of Stacking-Based Interaction Techniques for Pivot-Tables

We adopted a user-centered process to design three different stacking-based techniques for controlling a pivot-table creation and edition. These three designs differ in terms of manipulation type:

- **"Dual-Screen Touch"**, is based solely on the use of touch interaction on the tablet and on the smartphone. With this technique, a first touch on a column header displayed on the tablet selects the column. Then, the user can insert this data into the wizard by touching a wizard's shelves on the smartphone (Fig. 8 – A-Top). The data can then be dragged and dropped between the multiple shelves of the wizard. A touch on the elements allows filtering and changing the summary function. A long press on an element removes it from the shelf.
- **"Stack-and-Touch"** combines touch interaction on the smartphone screen with stacking on the tablet. This technique is based on stacking the smartphone on the desired column to select it (as in the *Intersection* technique). After selecting the

column, the interaction is the same as with the *Dual-Screen Touch* technique, i.e. touch on a wizard's shelves on the smartphone (Fig. 8 – A-Bottom).

- *"Stack-and-Translate"* is based on stacking only. When stacking the smartphone on the desired column, the wizard is temporarily replicated on the tablet screen (in addition to the smartphone screen) directly under the stacking position (Fig. 8 – B). To insert a data column into the wizard, the user translates the smartphone in the direction of the desired wizard shelf. Then, the wizard on the tablet screen disappears to prevent occlusions.

The smartphone always displays the pivot table wizard, while the tablet displays the data cells. The initial cell range selection (step 1) is performed using the Intersection technique with the smartphone in the dominant hand (best technique in study 1).

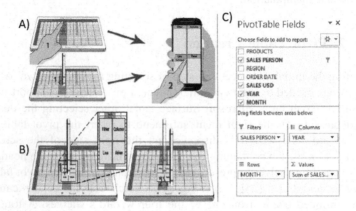

Fig. 8. Selecting cells (step 1) and affecting them to one Pivot-Table wizard shelf (step 2) using Dual-Screen Touch (A-Top), Stack-and-Touch (A-Bottom), Stack-and-Translate technique (B). The pivot-table wizard as displayed in Excel on the MS-Surface (C).

We modified our spreadsheet app running on the tactile tablet to integrate a pivot table wizard displayed on the tablet screen (for the baseline technique): our app strictly conforms to the Excel application on a MS-Surface (tactile interaction, structure and size). In addition, we further extended our app so that the lower part of the same pivot table wizard could be displayed on the smartphone screen (for the stacking-based techniques) and we integrated our three interaction techniques. The techniques are demonstrated in the adjunct video.

To assess the performance of our interaction techniques to create a pivot table, we compared them to the regular touch interaction.

6.2   Experimental Protocol

Task. The experimental task involved two consecutive steps: selecting a range of cells and then creating one pivot table. Given that results of the first experiment were similar for the different cells range categories, for each trial, participants first had to select a single form of cells range made of 50 rows × 12 columns. The same feedback than in the first study was provided during this step. An automatic validation occurred once the appropriate cells range was selected.

After the selection, participants had to open the pivot table wizard using a menu bar button, on the top-left corner of the tablet for the Tactile technique, and on the smartphone for the stacking-based techniques. Then, they had to fill the shelves of the pivot table wizard according to the given instructions. Each trial consisted in filling one (Value), two (Value and Row), three (Value, Row and Column) or four (Value, Row, Column and Filter) shelves of the wizard with one element. In some trials participants also had to modify the summary function (Sum, Number, Mean).

Participants were asked to complete the task as fast and accurately as possible. The task instructions were displayed on the tablet screen before each trial and on a secondary computer screen during the trial. The instructions consisted of a pivot table wizard already filled with the required elements and configured with a specific summary function. A touch button allowed the user to start the trial. Once the wizard was correctly filled, an automatic validation was triggered after 500 ms.

We used the same dataset as in [21], consisting in movie attributes (e.g. genre, MPAA rating), budget, total gross and review ratings. We trimmed the dataset to 200 rows and 12 columns as in [21].

Design. Our study followed a 4 * 4 * 2 within-subjects design with Interaction technique (Tactile, Dual-Screen Touch, Stack-and-Touch, Stack-and-Translate), Number of wizard's Shelves to modify (one, two, three or four) and Summary Function (yes or no) as factors. The study was divided into 4 blocks, each block corresponding to one technique. The order of blocks was counterbalanced across participants by means of a 4 × 4 Latin square.

For each block, participants could perform training trials until they felt ready. Then they performed 24 pivot table creations (8 conditions performed 3 times). The order of trials was randomized. Participants could take a break between each trial and each block. In total, we collected 4 ITs × 8 configurations × 3 repetitions × 12 participants = 1152 trials.

Apparatus, Participants and Collected Data. We used the same tablet and smartphone than in the previous study. We upgraded both devices to Android 7.1 to run our pivot table code (which required Java 8). We also used a computer screen (16", 1366 × 768 pixels) to permanently display the instructions during a trial.

We recruited 12 participants (7 females), aged 31.7 years on average (SD = 6.8). Participants were all students of the local university's computer science department. Two of them took part in study 1, limited to the selection phase (step 1). They were all right-handed and familiar with mobile devices (7.8 on a 0–9 scale), desktop spreadsheets (6.5) and pivot tables (6.3). The experiment lasted 78 min on average.

For each trial, we measured the total completion time, as well as selection and wizard filling times. We logged selection errors (i.e. selecting an incorrect cell range) and assignation errors (i.e. assigning an item to the wrong pivot table shelf or assigning the wrong summary function). At the end of each block, we asked the participants to fill a SUS questionnaire and we collected informal feedbacks. They were also asked to rate their general appreciation of the interaction technique on a 7-points Likert scale.

6.3   Results

The overall interaction is divided into two steps: selection and assignation. Therefore, we report the quantitative measures (time, error) for each step separately.

Selection Time (Step 1). The results confirm the first experiment measures: on average, selecting the cell range requires more time with the *Tactile* technique (10.6 s CI [10.2, 10.9]) than with our stacking techniques (9.2 s CI [8.6, 9.7] (Fig. 9 - Left). The intra subject analysis based on the time ratio confirms this finding and establishes that it took on average 14.8% more time (ratio = 1.148 no intersection with 1.0, Fig. 9 - Right) with *Tactile* than with our stacking-based technique.

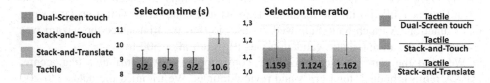

Fig. 9. Mean selection time in s (left) and ratio (right) regarding *Tactile* (95% CI).

Assignation Time (Step 2 and 3). Results strongly establish that assignation (i.e. filling the pivot table wizard shelves with the corresponding elements, Fig. 10) with *Stack-and-Translate* requires less time (7.3 s, CI [6.9, 7.9]) than with the three other techniques. Results also establish that *Dual-Screen Touch* (8.3 s, CI [7.8, 8.9]) and *Stack-and-Touch* (8.7 s, CI [8.3, 9.1]) are similar in terms of assignation time, while *Tactile* (9.5 s, CI [9.0, 10.0]) requires clearly more time than the three other. These results remain valid for each number of shelves tested (i.e. the techniques relative performance is equivalent for each number of shelves condition). The intra subject analysis based on the time ratio confirms this finding and establishes that it took on average 30.1% more time (ratio = 1.301 no intersection with 1.0) with *Tactile* than with *Stack-and-Translate*.

When modifying the summary function of the Value shelf (for instance Sum instead of Mean), assignation time required with the *Tactile* technique increases by 42.6% CI [32.7, 54.4] whereas it only increases by 14.2% CI [8.6, 21.3] on average for our 3 techniques (individual details in Fig. 11a). We can explain these results by the fact that it is harder to reach the configuration buttons on the tablet when using *Tactile* than those displayed on the smartphone when using stacking-based techniques.

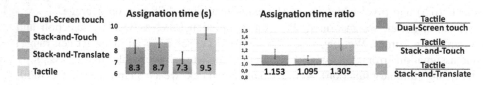

Fig. 10. Mean assignation time in s (left) and ratio (right) regarding *Tactile* (95% CI).

Errors. Given the experimental protocol, there was no possible selection error. Regarding assignment errors, i.e. a column affected to a wrong shelf of the wizard (Fig. 11b), it seems that less errors occurred with *Stack-and-Translate* (8.3% of trials contained at least one error CI [5.6, 11.5]) and *Stack-and-Touch* (9.4% of trials CI [6.6, 12.5]) than with *Tactile* (14.9% of trials CI [11.1, 18.1]) and *Dual-Screen Touch* (13.5% of trials CI [10.4, 19.1]). With the *Tactile* technique, in order to affect a column to one shelf of the wizard, the user selects an item with a finger touch in the list of column headers displayed on the upper part of the wizard, as in the Excel application. With the other techniques, the user selects the column through a stacking gesture. We believe that with touch based interaction, the accuracy required to select the item on the list of columns is responsible for the increase of error during the assignment phase.

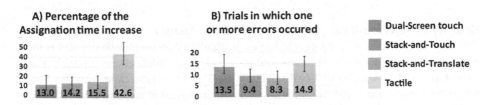

Fig. 11. (A) Percentage of the assignation time increase (95% CI) when modifying the summary function is requested (versus not). (B) Percentage of the trials in which at least one assignation error occurred (95% CI).

Usability and Users Preference. The SUS questionnaires establish a better usability score for *Stack-and-Translate* (90.4, CI [76.9, 95.4]) and *Dual-Screen Touch* (80.8, CI [73.3, 87.9]), than *Tactile* (70.2, CI [63.3, 75.0]) and *Stack-and-Touch* (73.1, CI [68.5, 76.0]). The general rating of the techniques, collected using a 7-points Likert scale, confirms these results with 11 participants out of 12 who liked (5 and above) *Stack-and-Translate*, 10 who liked *Dual-Screen touch*, 9 *Stack-and-Touch* and 7 *Tactile*.

Informal participants comments are in line with these analyses. Stack-and-Translate was described as "very simple and very fast" (9/12). The Dual-Screen Touch technique was qualified as "simple and easy to learn" (11/12) although "clicking on the column header is not convenient; I'd like to click on any of the column cells" (9/12). The Stack-and-Touch technique was described as "simpler because the menu on the smartphone is clearer than on the tablet" (7/12). The Tactile technique was considered "really disturbing: [...] I can drag it but I often fail to place correctly" (8/12).

Conclusion. The results from this study first confirm that, even when combined with another task, a cell range selection requires on average 15% more time with the *Tactile* technique than with the stacking-based techniques, as established in the first experiment. They also establish that filling a pivot table wizard (step 2) with the *Stack-and-Translate* technique requires less time than the other techniques (7.3 s against 8.3 s for *Dual-Screen Touch*, 8.7 s for *Stack-and-Touch* and 9.5 s for *Tactile*): using the regular *Tactile* technique to create a pivot-table requires up to 30% more time than using the *Stack-and-Translate* technique.

In addition, *Stack-and-Translate* and *Dual-Screen Touch* obtain better SUS scores than the other techniques, including the *Tactile* one, and subjective ratings of the techniques largely confirm the positive opinion of the participants towards the *Stack-and-Translate* technique. When the task (selection + assignation) becomes more complex because the summary function need to be modified after the assignation (i.e. opening the menu "function" and selecting a different summary function – such as Sum), stacking-based techniques performed even better than the *Tactile* technique: it thus seems that the added display space on the smartphone allows an easy access to more features. These results thus demonstrate the advantages of stacking-based techniques over traditional touch interaction for creating pivot tables.

7 Discussion and Future Work

Benefits of Stacking-Based Interaction for Data Analysis. Our two studies reveal that the use of stacking-based interaction to manipulate data on mobile devices is more efficient than the current touch interaction provided on spreadsheet apps on tablets. In a first step we demonstrated that cell selection requires 15% more time with the *Tactile* interaction than with a stacking-based technique; in a second step we established that cell selection and assignation to the pivot table wizard requires on average up to 22% more time with the *Tactile* technique than with one of the stacking-based techniques. Finally, among stacking-based techniques, the one based only on stacking input (*Stack-and-Translate* – 7.3 s) requires less time than those using touch only (*Dual-Screen Touch* – 8.3 s) or a combination of touch and stacking (*Stack-and-Touch* – 8.7 s).

The physical manipulation of the smartphone allows direct manipulation of the data without interfering with the regular touch gestures, and shortens the interaction path. Furthermore, the use of the smartphone screen to display the pivot table wizard was found convenient and useful (see users' informal comments). Overall, stacking-based interaction seems well suited to facilitate ubiquitous data analysis on tablets.

Speed Trade-Off for Picking the Smartphone. Using our stacking-based approach for data analysis initially requires picking up the smartphone and setting it on the tablet, which could raise a speed trade-off for picking the smartphone. However during a lengthy data analysis (municipal councils last on average 2 h), once the smartphone has been positioned, it will only continue to be used, and thus accrue further benefits compared to regular touch interaction. This justifies the trade-off for using the smartphone as the main interactor on the dominant hand: in such conditions our techniques are up to 19.9% and 30.1% faster than touch respectively for cell range selection and pivot table wizard configuration.

Future Work. In the future, we plan to incorporate in our application further features of pivot table such as the ordering or filtering of elements on the wizard and switching between the pivot table visualizations (chart vs. table representations). These two visualizations could be available on the smartphone screen using a left/right swipe gesture. Once these features will be integrated to our application, we plan to compare our solution to an advanced tactile technique (e.g. based on three-fingers touch). Then we will run a longitudinal study with our targeted users, i.e. elected officers, in a concrete context.

Furthermore, we hope to exploit the whole potential of stacking gestures. While in our initial exploration we unveiled a large stacking vocabulary, made of different types of gestures (physical or touch), we only used a subset of them in our spreadsheet interactions. Enlarging even more the interaction vocabulary with mobile device through stacking should unveil current limitations in other usages. Stacking-based interaction could be valuable for setting up spreadsheet graphs, could be used in overview-detail contexts [31] or to transfer data between devices in a multi-device environment [6, 13].

Regarding long-term usage of stacking-based techniques, since both the tablet and the smartphone are most often laying on the table, we do not expect much fatigue. We did not get any comments on fatigue during our tests that lasted an hour. However, future studies should evaluate this concern.

8   Conclusion

In this paper, we presented different stacking-based techniques to facilitate ubiquitous data analysis on tablets. We explored the available stacking gestures to discard the most uncomfortable ones. Based on these results, we designed a conductive case that allows the detection of the smartphone on the tablet screen. We then proposed stacking-based techniques with the final goal to support data analysis using pivot tables in a two-step approach: first, performing a cell range selection and then creating a pivot table from the previous cell range. We showed that stacking-based techniques are faster than regular touch interaction for cell range selection. Furthermore, we also showed that using the smartphone as a tangible interactor with a complementary touchscreen extends the interaction capabilities of a mobile device in terms in input (stacking-based interaction) and output (complementary screen): in particular, it speeds-up the pivot table creation and manipulation, and is more usable than regular touch interaction.

References

1. Banovic, N., Li, F.C.Y., Dearman, D., Yatani, K., Truong, K.N.: Design of unimanual multi-finger pie menu interaction. In: Proceedings of the ACM International Conference on Interactive Tabletops and Surfaces (ITS 2011), pp. 120–129. ACM, New York (2011). https://doi.org/10.1145/2076354.2076378
2. Baudisch, P., Holz, C.: My new PC is a mobile phone. XRDS: Cross-roads 16(4), 36–41 (2010)
3. Blagojevic, R., Plimmer, B.: CapTUI: geometric drawing with tangibles on a capacitive multi-touch display. In: Kotzé, P., Marsden, G., Lindgaard, G., Wesson, J., Winckler, M. (eds.) INTERACT 2013. LNCS, vol. 8117, pp. 511–528. Springer, Heidelberg (2013). https://doi.org/10.1007/978-3-642-40483-2_37
4. Brooke, J.: SUS - A quick and dirty usability scale. Usability Eval. Ind. 189(194), 4–7 (1996)

5. Brudy, F., Houben, S., Marquardt, N., Rogers, Y.: CurationSpace: cross-device content curation using instrumental interaction. In: Proceedings of the ACM Conference on Interactive Surfaces and Spaces, pp. 159–168. ACM (2016). https://doi.org/10.1145/2992154.2992175

6. Chen, N., Guimbretière, F., Sellen, A.: Graduate student use of a multi-slate reading system. In: Proceedings of the SIGCHI Conference on Human Factors in Computing Systems (CHI 2013), pp. 1799–1808. ACM, New York (2013). https://doi.org/10.1145/2470654.2466237

7. Chan, L., Müller, S., Roudaut, A., Baudisch, P.: CapStones and ZebraWidgets: sensing stacks of building blocks, dials and sliders on capacitive touch screens. In: Proceedings of the SIGCHI Conference on Human Factors in Computing Systems (CHI 2012), pp. 2189–2192. ACM, New York (2012). https://doi.org/10.1145/2207676.2208371

8. Chen, X.A., Grossman, T., Wigdor, D.J., Fitzmaurice, G.: Duet: exploring joint interactions on a smart phone and a smart watch. In: Proceedings of the SIGCHI Conference on Human Factors in Computing Systems (CHI 2014), pp. 159–168. ACM, New York (2014). https://doi.org/10.1145/2556288.2556955

9. Elmqvist, N., Irani, P.: Ubiquitous analytics: interacting with big data anywhere, anytime. Computer **46**(4), 86–89 (2013)

10. Excel on Android: https://play.google.com/store/apps/details?id=com.microsoft.office.excel&hl=fr. Accessed 20 Sept 2018

11. Goguey, A., Casiez, G., Pietrzak, T., Vogel, D., Roussel, N.: Adoiraccourcix: multi-touch command selection using finger identification. In: Proceedings of the 26th Conference on l'Interaction Homme-Machine (IHM 2014), pp. 28–37. ACM, New York (2014). https://doi.org/10.1145/2670444.2670446

12. Google Spreadsheet on Android. https://play.google.com/store/apps/details?id=com.google.android.apps.docs.editors.sheets&hl=fr. Accessed 18 Sept 2017

13. Hamilton, P., Wigdor, D.J., Conductor: enabling and understanding cross-device interaction. In: Proceedings of the SIGCHI Conference on Human Factors in Computing Systems (CHI 2014), pp. 2773–2782. ACM, New York (2014). https://doi.org/10.1145/2556288.2557170

14. INRIA - AVIZ Group: R Macros for data analysis. www.aviz.fr/reliefshearing

15. Hasan, K., Ahlström, D., Irani, P.: Ad-binning: leveraging around device space for storing, browsing and retrieving mobile device content. In: Proceedings of the SIGCHI Conference on Human Factors in Computing Systems (CHI 2013), pp. 899–908. ACM, New York (2013). https://doi.org/10.1145/2470654.2466115

16. Heo, S., Gu, J., Lee, G.: Expanding touch input vocabulary by using consecutive distant taps. In: Proceedings of the SIGCHI Conference on Human Factors in Computing Systems (CHI 2014), pp. 2597–2606. ACM, New York (2014). https://doi.org/10.1145/2556288.2557234

17. Heo, S., Jung, J., Lee, G.: MelodicTap: fingering hotkey for touch tablets. In: Proceedings of the 28th Australian Conference on Computer-Human Interaction (OzCHI 2016), pp. 396–400. ACM, New York (2016). https://doi.org/10.1145/3010915.3010993

18. Horak, T., Badam, S.K., Elmqvist, N., Dachselt, R.: When David meets Goliath: combining smartwatches with a large vertical display for visual data exploration. In: Proceedings of the 2018 CHI Conference on Human Factors in Computing Systems, p. 19. ACM, April 2018

19. Hwang, S., Ahn, M., Wohn, K.: MagGetz: customizable passive tangible controllers on and around conventional mobile devices. In: Proceedings of the 26th Annual ACM Symposium on User Interface Software and Technology (UIST 2013), pp. 411–416. ACM, New York (2013). https://doi.org/10.1145/2501988.2501991

20. Jelen, B., Alexander, M.: Pivot Table Data Crunching: Microsoft Excel 2010, 1st edn. Que Publishing Company, London (2010)

21. Jo, J., L'Yi, S., Lee, B., Seo, J.: TouchPivot: blending WIMP & post-WIMP interfaces for data exploration on tablet devices. In: Proceedings of the 2017 CHI Conference on Human Factors in Computing Systems (CHI 2017), pp. 2660–2671. ACM, New York (2017). https://doi.org/10.1145/3025453.3025752

22. Krzywinski, M., Altman, N.: points of significance: error bars. Nat. Methods **10**(10), 921–922 (2013)

23. Langner, R., Horak, T., Dachselt, R.: VisTiles: coordinating and combining co-located mobile devices for visual data exploration. IEEE Trans. Vis. Comput. Graph. **24**(1), 626–636 (2018)

24. Leigh, S., Schoessler, P., Heibeck, F., Maes, P., Ishii, H.: THAW: tangible interaction with see-through augmentation for smartphones on computer screens. In: Proceedings of the Ninth International Conference on Tangible, Embedded, and Embodied Interaction (TEI 2015), pp. 89–96. ACM, New York (2015). https://doi.org/10.1145/2677199.2680584

25. Microsoft Office Support: Create a PivotTable to Analyze Worksheet Data. https://support.office.com/en-gb/article/create-a-pivottable-to-analyze-worksheet-data-a9a84538-bfe9-40a9-a8e9-f99134456576Accessed 22 Sept 2019

26. Li, M., Kobbelt, L.: ACTUI: using commodity mobile devices to build active tangible user interfaces. In: Proceedings of the 17th International Conference on Human-Computer Interaction with Mobile Devices and Services Adjunct (MobileHCI 2015), pp. 592–597. ACM, New York (2015). https://doi.org/10.1145/2786567.2792895

27. Pfeuffer, K., Hinckley, K., Pahud, M., Buxton, B.: Thumb + pen interaction on tablets. In: Proceedings of the 2017 CHI Conference on Human Factors in Computing Systems (CHI 2017), pp. 3254–3266. ACM, New York (2017). https://doi.org/10.1145/3025453.3025567

28. Piazza, T., Fjeld, M., Ramos, G., Yantac, A.E., Zhao, S.: Holy smartphones and tablets, Batman!: mobile interaction's dynamic duo. In: Proceedings of the 11th Asia Pacific Conference on Computer Human Interaction (APCHI 2013), pp. 63–72. ACM, New York (2013). https://doi.org/10.1145/2525194.2525205

29. QlikSense. https://www.qlik.com/fr-fr/products/qlik-sense. Accessed 20 Sept 2018

30. QlikView. https://www.qlik.com/fr-fr/products/qlikview. Accessed 20 Sept 2018

31. Saidi, H., Serrano, M., Dubois, E.: Investigating the effects of splitting detailed views in Overview + Detail interfaces. In: Proceedings of the 18th International Conference on Human-Computer Interaction with Mobile Devices and Services (MobileHCI 2016), pp. 180–184. ACM, New York (2016). https://doi.org/10.1145/2935334.2935341

32. Santosa, S., Wigdor, D.: A field study of multi-device workflows in distributed workspaces. In: Proceedings of the 2013 ACM International Joint Conference on Pervasive and Ubiquitous Computing, Zurich, Switzerland, 08–12 September 2013. https://doi.org/10.1145/2493432.2493476

33. Schmidt, D., Chehimi, F., Rukzio, E., Gellersen, H.: PhoneTouch: a technique for direct phone interaction on surfaces. In: Proceedings of the 23rd Annual ACM Symposium on User Interface Software and Technology (UIST 2010), pp. 13–16. ACM, New York (2010). https://doi.org/10.1145/1866029.1866034

34. Schmidt, D., Seifert, J., Rukzio, E., Gellersen, H.: A cross-device interaction style for mobiles and surfaces. In: Proceedings of the Designing Interactive Systems Conference (DIS 2012), pp. 318–327. ACM, New York (2012). https://doi.org/10.1145/2317956.2318005

35. Tableau Software. https://www.tableau.com/fr-fr. Accessed 20 Sept 2018

36. Srinivasan, A., Lee, B., Stasko, J.: Facilitating spreadsheet manipulation on mobile devices leveraging speech. In: MobileVis 2018 Workshop at CHI 2018, Montreal, QC, Canada, 21 April 2018 (2018). https://mobilevis.github.io/

37. Uddin, Md.S., Gutwin, C.: Rapid command selection on multi-touch tablets with single-handed handmark menus. In: Proceedings of the 2016 ACM on Interactive Surfaces and Spaces (ISS 2016), pp. 205–214. ACM, New York (2016). https://doi.org/10.1145/2992154.2992172

38. VandenBos, G.R. (ed.): Publication Manual of the American Psychological Association, 6th edn. American Psychological Association, Washington, DC (2009). http://www.apastyle.org/manual/

39. Wagner, J., Lecolinet, E., Selker, T.: Multi-finger chords for hand-held tablets: recognizable and memorable. In: Proceedings of the SIGCHI Conference on Human Factors in Computing Systems (CHI 2014), pp. 2883–2892. ACM, New York (2014). https://doi.org/10.1145/2556288.2556958

40. Willett, W., Jenny, B., Isenberg, T., et al.: Lightweight relief shearing for enhanced terrain perception on interactive maps. In: Proceedings of the 33rd ACM Conference on Human Factors in Computing Systems (CHI 2015) (2015). https://doi.org/10.1145/2702123.2702172

41. Wongsuphasawat, K., Moritz, D., Anand, A., Mackinlay, J., Howe, B., Heer, J.: Voyager: exploratory analysis via faceted browsing of visualization recommendations. IEEE Trans. Visual. Comput. Graph. (TVCG) **22**(12), 649–658 (2016)

42. Woźniak, P., Lischke, L., Schmidt, B., Zhao, S., Fjeld, M.: Thaddeus: a dual device interaction space for exploring information visualisation. In: Proceedings of the 8th Nordic Conference on Human-Computer Interaction: Fun, Fast, Foundational (NordiCHI 2014), pp. 41–50. ACM, New York (2014). https://doi.org/10.1145/2639189.2639237

43. Wozniak, P., Goyal, N., Kucharski, P., Lischke, L., Mayer, S., Fjeld, M.: RAMPARTS: supporting sensemaking with spatially-aware mobile interactions. In: Proceedings of the 2016 CHI Conference on Human Factors in Computing Systems (CHI 2016), pp. 2447–2460. ACM, New York (2016). https://doi.org/10.1145/2858036.2858491

COMMONS: A Board Game for Enhancing Interdisciplinary Collaboration When Developing Health and Activity-Related Wearable Devices

Dennis Arts[1,2(✉)], Len Kromkamp[1], and Steven Vos[1,2]

[1] School of Sport Studies, Fontys University of Applied Sciences,
Eindhoven, The Netherlands
{d.arts,l.kromkamp}@fontys.nl
[2] Eindhoven University of Technology, Eindhoven, The Netherlands
s.vos@tue.nl

Abstract. Physical activity provides substantial health benefits yet physical inactivity is one of the most challenging problems of these days. Development in mHealth and eHealth applications, such as wearable technology, create vast opportunities but are still insufficiently used to promote sustainable physical activity. To enhance the development of such products, participation and cooperation of professionals with different knowledge and expertise is required. We developed a board game called COMMONS to enhance interdisciplinary collaboration in the design of health-related wearable technologies. In this paper we present the design process of COMMONS, results of the play sessions and discuss the future development of COMMONS and the possible implications within the field of Human-Computer Interaction.

Keywords: Interdisciplinary teams · Communication ·
Human-Computer Interaction · Board games · Physical activity

1 Introduction

There is ample evidence that being physically active provides substantial health benefits [1]. However, to stimulate people to be physically active is one of the most challenging problems of these days. Individual characteristics such as knowledge, social support and motivation but also modernization trends, and environmental and economic conditions influence physical activity [1, 2].

In recent years reducing physical inactivity and enhancing active lifestyles have been an ongoing topic in Human-Computer Interaction (HCI) and have increasingly become a field of application for low-cost technology, including mHealth and eHealth applications. In the past five years, the market of so-called wearables has grown exponentially, partly due to developments in IT and sensor technology [3, 4]. Developments in low-cost technologies have created vast opportunities for health improvement and facilitate behaviour change [5] but are still insufficiently used to promote sustainable physical activity [6]. One of the possible reasons for this would be that

D. Lamas et al. (Eds.): INTERACT 2019, LNCS 11749, pp. 461–470, 2019.
https://doi.org/10.1007/978-3-030-29390-1_25

engineers, when designing wearable devices for measuring and promoting physical activity (such as trackers), mainly focus on the technological aspects [7, 8]. This leads to technically ingenious products with advanced functions suitable for data collection. However, the impact of these wearable technologies on health is therefore also limited [9]. Moreover, wearables are often no longer used after just a few months [7, 9].

To prevent this, technological aspects will have to integrate with individual, social and environmental aspects. A personalized approach is absent in most consumer available wearables because limited non-technological expertise is consulted and the user is often not properly involved in the design process [7]. For example, the specific knowledge of various experts, such as behavioral scientists and human movement and health scientists, is often not mutually incorporated in the development of wearable devices [10]. Janssen et al. (2018) argue that designing health-related products for a heterogeneous group of people requires an interdisciplinary design approach [8]. To enhance the success of problem-solving the participation and cooperation of individuals with different knowledge and expertise is required [11]. Interdisciplinary research and development can transfer knowledge, insights and findings between disciplines [12]. Yet, a collaboration between disciplines is not straightforward and needs special attention. Although the need for interdisciplinary teams has increased, researchers and developers have become more specialized over the past years [12]. Given the speed of change, technological possibilities and different user needs during the research and development of wearable technology, there is often not enough time to build a stable, interdisciplinary team [11–13]. Often members of interdisciplinary teams have different ways of communicating, have different definitions for the same words per their expertise and might have a mental model in which they fully or partially disregard other disciplines as they perceive their expertise as the better one [11, 12, 14–16]. This leads to sub-optimal outcomes.

In this article we present COMMONS a tool developed to enhance interdisciplinary collaboration in the design of health-related wearable technologies. This board game approach provides a playful situation during which different experts can learn, in a safe environment, to share expertise, knowledge and skills. COMMONS brings them up to speed with each other's definitions, ways of thinking, and showing what's important to them. The goal is to facilitate an interdisciplinary team with the opportunity to progress through their design cycle earlier, more effective and more qualitative.

2   What's in a Game

In the last decennia, the use of game elements is becoming increasingly popular [17]. Simultaneously, there has been a resurgence of board games. Many new kinds of board games, with different mechanics, themes and gameplay, have been introduced and become popular [18]. Games have several general characteristics in common [19]. They are often a simulation of a real event or situation but have little real-life consequences (i.e. it is not real, it is play). Next, games usually have a location (board) and a duration of play. Players compete against each other or the game, individually or collaborating with other players. Further, games often require a certain amount of skills, be it physical or mental, and playing the game improves these skills. Moreover, games usually have an element of chance and a level of uncertainty. If it is obvious who will win at hand, it is no longer fun to play [19].

Serious games go beyond entertainment. They are developed to have a certain impact on behavioral, motivational or attitudinal outcomes which are widespread linked to learning outcomes [20, 21]. In the last decennia, the use of these kind of games is becoming increasingly popular [20]. Besides this we see that board games for entertainment use serious subjects more often in their design.

3 Design of a Board Game for Interdisciplinary Collaboration

Our aim was to develop a board game as a tool to enhance interdisciplinary collaboration in designing wearable technology. The game focuses on communication and value of skills and expertise with an output as a result. First, we identified interesting mechanics in existing games like Dixit (2008) and Codenames (2015) that we believe can achieve this goal in our board game design. We have not limited our research and development to these games, but they have provided us with a starting point for our iterations and user testing. In playtesting with the co-authors, we played Dixit and Codenames in a purpose-shifted setting in which the clues were focused around wearables (i.e. activity tracking devices). The authors have a background in different disciplines (i.e. human movement sciences, behavioral sciences and industrial design), and therefore value properties of activity tracking devices differently. By playing these games, we recognized we started to understand each other's expertise, and furthermore were trying to think like the other.

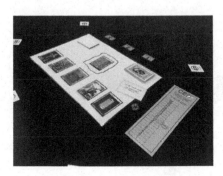

Fig. 1. Cooperation

Second, we developed a paper-prototype of two games with similar game characteristics as Dixit and Codenames. In a second playtesting we tested these games: Marketplace and Cooperation. We found that certain characteristics of the first developed game (Marketplace) were counterproductive to the goals of the game: improving communication, shifting mental models and valuing each other's knowledge and skills. Participants were playing tactical, to win the game, instead of cooperating. An important lesson was that players must collaborate to win the game.

In the second developed game (Cooperation, see Fig. 1) the intended objectives were approached. Within the game, players are part of a development team and must develop an activity tracker based on various features. Each round consists of discussing a card with a feature on it. Players jointly determine whether or not this feature is used in their activity tracker to be developed. When there is no consensus players have to roll a dice, and there is a disruptive element we call 'The CEO'. This disruptive element are cards with a command that change the state of the game. Important lessons that we learned were that players cannot have the exclusive right to reject a card and must be actively involved in taking a decision. Furthermore, since we are focusing on improving communication, we need to clearly define what is effective and what is not. Communication involves multiple facets such as frequency of communication between individuals, the context of what is communicated, the role of each within a team, and the aforementioned differences between experts. As such, measuring communication can be difficult [23].

We built the next iteration of the Cooperation game based on the acquired knowledge and experience gained from the previous steps. We call this game COM-MONS (see Fig. 2), which refers to shared resources in which each stakeholder has an equal interest [24]. Players of COMMONS are part of a development team, composed by a fictitious woman who calls herself 'Kairos'. The assignment for this team is to develop an activity tracker based on various features and focused on a persona. This persona consists of a description of a person's interests, motivation, character and goals in relation to physical activity. Each round consists of a player reading a card out loud with a feature (related to hardware, software, user experience design or behavioral change technique) on it. Players then have to vote according to the consent method. We incorporated this so every player is actively involved in the decision making. Consent means that a decision has been taken when none of the players present argue or predominantly object to taking the decision. Meaning: only when there's agreement, there's a decision. In this case a player presses the 'green' button if he wants the feature to be a part of the activity tracker, the 'blue' button if he gives consent (neutral) and the 'red' button if he has a predominant objection.

Fig. 2. COMMONS (Color figure online)

A result of the voting there are three options:

1. All players press green or blue and the card is accepted and will be placed on the board.
2. At least one player presses red, with the rest of the players pressing either red or blue and the feature has been rejected. The card goes onto the discard pile.

3. At least one player has voted green, with another voting red, resulting in no agreement and thus discussion.

When option 3 occurs, there is a minute to discuss the overriding objections. The players have to explain their arguments and discuss them with the others. A better understanding of each other's position arises and there may be a shift in one's view and choice. Then the second round of voting occurs and again the same three options are possible. If option 3 arises again the card will then be placed in the 'discussion box' and will not be placed on the board. When a card is placed on the board there are 5 positions in which the card can be placed. Position 1 is most important to the players, position 5 the least important. If a card is placed all other cards move one position. So, if a card is placed on number 4 this card shifts to number 5 and number 5 falls off the board and will be placed in the 'nice-to-have box'. The players have limited time to discuss the placement of the card. They must agree on the position of the card but if time runs out, a single player decides where the card will be placed. Because, at that moment, there is no proper consent, the dice must be rolled. 'Kairos' comes around when throwing a specific number of eyes. When this occurs, the players draw a 'Kairos card'. These cards contain a command that changes the state of the game (switch cards, taking back a card form the 'discussion box', etcetera). This game characteristic works disruptively and causes unpredictability. The only way players can deal with this is by working together.

By facilitating choice and discussion, participants are actively involved in the process and they have to share their point of view. Participants gain insight into each other's arguments, what is important to them and at the same time they are creating a mutual language and a set of definitions. Participants must compromise, and at the end of the game, they have created a joint solution.

4 Research Through Design Prototype

COMMONS is a research trough design prototype with elements for logging data (e.g. data on voting, time spent on voting and discussion, card positioning, etcetera) [25]. By logging data while playing we hope to gain insights into the dynamic process of choice, discussion and compromise between member of an interdisciplinary team while they work to accomplish common goals [26, 27]. We have set a number of variables that can give us information about these topics. To collect the intended data this prototype works with voting boxes, cards with RFID tags and RFID card readers in the board. The prototype registers rounds, time, votes, and card movements.

In Table 1 we give an overview of the data acquired based on a play session with four players with a different expertise. Player 1 has a background as movement scientist, player 2 is a UX designer, player 3 has a background in business and marketing and player 4 is an industrial designer. We developed 89 features, divided in four categories: (i) Hardware [15], (ii) Software [17], (iii) User Experience Design (9) and (iv) Behavioral Change Technique (BCT) (48). For this play session we selected 35 features (cards) and therefore 35 rounds. 9 features for Hardware, 7 features for software, 5 features for User Experience Design and 14 features for Behavioral Change Technique.

Table 1. Column A: round number, B: type of card, C, D, E, F: vote player 1, 2, 3 and 4, G: Consent or not, H: combination of votes; I, J, K, L: vote player 1, 2, 3 and 4 after discussion, N: combination of votes after discussion, O: card gets on the board, P: Round number card gets on the board, Q: Round number card gets off the board, R: Number of rounds the card is on the board, S: Is the card a feature of end solution, T: Highest position on the board

A	B	C	D	E	F	G	H	I	J	K	L	M	N	O	P	Q	R	S	T
1	BCT: Habit formation	1	1	1	1	Accepted	1						0	Yes	1	8	7	No	2
2	Software: Notification function	3	3	2	3	Rejected	12						0	No					
3	User Design: Supports scientific data	2	2	1	3	Discussion	6	3	3	2	2	Rejected	12	No					3
4	BCT: Social support (emotional)	1	2	1	1	Accepted	3						0	Yes	4	8	4	No	5
5	Hardware: Changeable straps	3	1	1	2	Discussion	7	2	2	1	2	Accepted	4	Yes	5	8	3	No	4
6	User Design: Adjustments in look & feel	1	2	1	2	Accepted	5						0	Yes	6	8	2	No	4
7	BCT: Focus on past success	1	1	1	1	Accepted	3						0	Yes	7	8	1	No	4
8	Hardware: Heartrate monitor	2	1	1	2	Discussion	8	1	2	1	3	Discussion	3	No					4
9	BCT: Discrepancy	1	1	1	1	Accepted	1						0	Yes	9	24	15	No	1
10	Hardware: Large battery life	1	1	1	1	Accepted	1						0	Yes	10	15	5	No	2
11	Software: Goalsetting adjustments	1	3	3	1	Discussion	7	2	2	2	2	Accepted	4	Yes	11	15	4	No	3
12	BCT: Feedback outcome	1	1	1	1	Accepted	1						0	Yes	12	35	23	Yes	1
13	Software: Coach guidance	2	3	1	2	Discussion	8	2	3	1	1	Discussion	7	No					
14	Hardware: Accelerometry	1	1	1	3	Discussion	10	1	1	1	1	Accepted	1	Yes	14	35	21	Yes	2
15	BCT: Goalsetting behaviour	1	2	1	2	Accepted	3						0	Yes	15	23	8	No	4
16	Hardware: GPS meter	2	3	3	3	Rejected	14						0	No					
17	Hardware: Large memory	3	3	3	3	Rejected	15						0	No					
18	Software: Goalsetting outcome	2	2	1	2	Accepted	4						0	Yes	18	20	2	No	5
19	Software: Playing music	3	3	3	3	Rejected	15						0	No					
20	BCT: Social reward	2	1	1	1	Accepted	3						0	Yes	20	28	8	No	3
21	Software: Programmed activities	3	1	3	3	Discussion	11	3	3	3	3	Rejected	15	No					
22	Hardware: Vibration function	3	3	3	3	Rejected	15						0	No					
23	BCT: Prompts/ Cue's	1	1	1	1	Accepted	1						0	Yes	23	35	12	Yes	3
24	Software: Exporting data	3	3	3	3	Rejected	15						0	No					
25	BCT: Commitment	2	1	2	2	Accepted	4						0	Yes	25	27	2	No	5
26	User Design: Help function	3	3	3	3	Rejected	15						0	No					
27	User Design: Intuitive	2	1	3	1	Discussion	6	1	1	1	1	Accepted	1	Yes	27	35	8	Yes	1
28	BCT: Reward approximation	2	1	1	1	Accepted	5						0	Yes	28	32	4	No	5
29	Hardware: Altimeter	3	3	3	3	Rejected	15						0	No					
30	BCT: Behavioral contract	3	3	3	3	Rejected	15						0	No					
31	Software: Adjust privacy level	2	1	3	2	Discussion	8	3	3	3	3	Rejected	15	No					
32	User Design: Feedback adjustments	1	1	2	1	Accepted	3						0	Yes	32	38	6	No	5
33	BCT: Emotional consequence	1	1	3	3	Discussion	11	3	2	2	2	Rejected	12	No					
34	Hardware: Colourscreen	3	3	3	3	Rejected	15						0	No					
35	BCT: Feedback behaviour	2	1	3	1	Discussion	7	2	1	2	1	Accepted	5	Yes	35	35	0	Yes	4

14 of the 35 features were directly accepted, 10 of the features were directly rejected and 11 of the features were the reason for discussion. These 11 features were discussed and after the second round of voting 5 features were accepted, 4 features rejected and 2 features were still reason for discussion. What stood out is the kind of property that is most accepted on the one hand and most discussed on the other hand. Eighty percent of the BCT features were directly accepted against none of the software features. 11 percent of the Hardware features were directly accepted compared to 40 percent for User Experience Design features. In the end solution there were 3 BCT features, 1 Hardware feature and 1 User Experience Design feature. When we look at the voting behaviour of the players (see Table 1), we see that there are notable differences between the players. Player 1 agrees on 11 of the 35 features to be a part of the activity tracker against 19, 15 and 12 for player 2, 3 and 4. The inter-player differences in disagreeing with a feature are smaller. Player 1 disagrees on 12 of the features compared to 13, 14 and 15 for player 2, 3 and 4. Player 3 stands out when voting after the discussion. In these cases, he agrees on 6 of the 11 features compared to 3, 3 and 4 for players 1, 2 and 4.

Features that were voted to be a part of the activity tracker were on average 7 rounds on the board. One of the BCT-related features 'Discrepancy' was on the board for 8 rounds but was not part of the final solution. Two other BCT-related features 'Goalsetting behaviour' and ' Social reward' were both on the board for 6 rounds but were also no longer on the board at the end of the game.

5   Discussion and Future Work

What we have learned so far is that COMMONS facilitates the conversation between different disciplines. Due to the structure the game offers, players are encouraged to talk about the content without having unproductive debates of expertise or loss of time by talking about a feature for too long. Researchers, designers and developers who work within HCI often work from a multidisciplinary point of view. COMMONS, and the ideas behind it, could be an addition to existing toolboxes and methodologies.

It is currently too early to draw conclusions from this data. Yet, it is striking that most 'software' features were directly rejected and were not part of the end solution. The background of the players might have played a role here. Also the voting behavior of player 2, 54% directly agree, and player 3, 55% agree after discussion, is notable. Although the features were divided proportionally over the rounds, in the second part of the game (round 19 to 35) the players rejected 7 features compared to 3 features in the first part of the game. Whether this is due to a better understanding of each other's position or a more common language is too early to conclude.

In the next research phase, we will make adjustments in game rules. For instance, the 'Kairos cards' must not be drawn too quickly but do have to be drawn more often and the commands must be less disruptive. For instance, players indicated that the command: 'remove all cards from the board' caused a depressed atmosphere. During the play session we experimented with longer discussion time and players indicated that they prefer this. This gave them more time to understand each other. We also saw that they shielded their voting boxes when pressing the voting button. Upon further inquiries, it turned out that players preferred to cast their votes anonymously after which the choices will be made public. This also prevents players from casting a vote based on a vote by another player. Furthermore, players pointed out that the cards must not contain too much information, because that blocks the possibility of discussion as the cards become too descriptive.

During the next iterations, the game is played with different kinds of groups. Participants will fill out a questionnaire that we have developed beforehand which contain questions relating to gaining insight in each other's point of view and arguments. This allows us to map these variables to our data. In addition, play sessions will be recorded on video to also collect information about the content and quality of the mutual conversations, arguments and discussions. The first testing was recorded and we are exploring the possibilities to measure the quality of the communication. We know from literature that communication is important within interdisciplinary teams. The National Academies of Science [28] states that "At the heart of interdisciplinarity is communication - the conversations, connections, and combinations that bring new insights to virtually every kind of scientist and engineer" (p. 19). Also certain communication processes are important for good quality communication: spending time together, discussing language differences and shared laughter [16]. We can gain insight into these processes through observation with targeted items.

Once these adjustments have been made, extensive testing will take place with players from different expertises. In addition, we are curious about the differences between teams that do know each other, and those who do not. We aim at five different teams that know each other and five teams that don't know each other. Given the context in which this game is developed (wearable technology related to physical activity), we want to question various areas of expertise related to this. This includes movement scientists, behavioral scientists, industrial designers, engineers, sport- and exercise coaches, and users of wearable technology.

Our goal is to facilitate an interdisciplinary team with a tool to enhance their progress through their design cycle earlier, more effective and with more quality. And perhaps, with more pleasure and fun as well.

Acknowledgement. This work is supported by the Netherlands Organization for Scientific Research (Grant 023.012.054).

References

1. Bauman, A., Bill, B., Cavill, N., Chandrasiri, O., Friedman, D., Martin, K., et al.: A technical package for increasing physical activity. World Heal Organ 2018 [Internet] (2018). http://apps.who.int/iris/bitstream/handle/10665/275415/9789241514804-eng.pdf?ua=1
2. Michie S, van Stralen MM, West R. The behaviour change wheel: A new method for characterising and designing behaviour change interventions. Implement Sci. [Internet] 6(1), 42 (2011). http://www.implementationscience.com/content/6/1/42
3. Middelweerd, A., Mollee, J.S., van der Wal, C.N., Brug, J., te Velde, S.J.: Apps to promote physical activity among adults: a review and content analysis. Int. J. Behav. Nutr. Phys. Act. 11, 9 (2014)

4. Vos, S.: Designerly Solutions for Vital People. University of Technology, Eindhoven (2016)
5. Hermsen, S., Frost, J., Renes, R.J., Kerkhof, P.: Using feedback through digital technology to disrupt and change habitual behavior: a critical review of current literature. Comput. Human Behav. [Internet]. **57**, 61–74 (2016). http://dx.doi.org/10.1016/j.chb.2015.12.023
6. Shih, P., Han, K., Poole, E.S., Rosson, M.B., Carroll, J.: Use and Adoption challenges of wearable activity trackers. iConference Proc. (1), 1–12 (2015)
7. Vos, S., Janssen, M., Goudsmit, J., Lauwerijssen, C., Brombacher, A.: From problem to solution: developing a personalized smartphone application for recreational runners following a three-step design approach. Procedia Eng. **147**, 799–805 (2016)
8. Janssen, M., van den Heuvel, R., Megens, C., Levy, P., Vos, S.: Analysis of the design and engineering-process towards a first prototype in the field of sports and vitality (Forthcomming)
9. Schoeppe, S., et al.: Efficacy of interventions that use apps to improve diet, physical activity and sedentary behaviour: a systematic review. Int. J. Behav. Nutr. Phys. Act. [Internet] **13**(1) (2016). http://dx.doi.org/10.1186/s12966-016-0454-y
10. Epstein, D.A., Kang, J.H., Pina, L.R., Fogarty, J., Munson, S.A.: Reconsidering the device in the drawer. In: Proceedings of the 2016 ACM International Joint Conference on Pervasive and Ubiquitous Computing - UbiComp 2016 [Internet], pp. 829–840 (2016). http://dl.acm.org/citation.cfm?doid=2971648.2971656
11. Moglen, G., et al.: How to avoid train wrecks when using science in environmental problem solving. Bioscience **52**(12), 1127 (2006)
12. Kostoff, R.N.: Overcoming Specialization. Bioscience **52**(10), 937 (2006)
13. Edmondson, A.C.: Organization & culture: teamwork on the fly. Harv. Bus. Rev. **90**(4), 72–80 (2012)
14. Blandford, A., Newhouse, N., Perski, O., Murray, E., Gibbs, J., Singh, A.: Seven lessons for interdisciplinary research on interactive digital health interventions. Digit Heal. **4**, 205520761877032 (2018)
15. McGloin, R., Wasserman, J.A., Boyan, A.: Model matching theory: a framework for examining the alignment between game mechanics and mental models. Media Commun. **6**(2), 126 (2018)
16. Thompson, J.: Building collective communication competence in Interdisciplinary research teams. J Appl Commun Res. **37**(3), 278–297 (2009)
17. Landers, Richard N., Armstrong, Michael B., Collmus, Andrew B.: How to use game elements to enhance learning: applications of the theory of gamified learning. In: Ma, M., Oikonomou, A. (eds.) Serious Games and Edutainment Applications, pp. 457–483. Springer, Cham (2017). https://doi.org/10.1007/978-3-319-51645-5_21
18. Booth, P.: Game Play: Paratextuality in Contemporary Board Games. Game Play: Paratextuality in Contemporary Board Games. 264 p. Bloomsbury Academic, London (2015)
19. Bartmann, N., et al.: Games and gamification. A litarature review. Durham (2018)
20. Landers, R.N.: Developing a Theory of Gamified Learning: Linking Serious Games and Gamification of Learning. Simul. Gaming **45**, 752–768 (2014)
21. Emmerich, K., Bockholt, M.: Serious games evaluation: processes, models, and concepts. In: Dörner, R., Göbel, S., Kickmeier-Rust, M., Masuch, M., Zweig, K. (eds.) Entertainment Computing and Serious Games. LNCS, vol. 9970, pp. 265–283. Springer, Cham (2016). https://doi.org/10.1007/978-3-319-46152-6_11
22. Game Play: Paratextuality in Contemporary Board Games. Game Play: Paratextuality in Contemporary Board Games (2015)

23. Anania, E.C., Keebler, J.R., Anglin, K.M., Kring, J.P.: Using the cooperative board game pandemic to study teamwork. In: Proceedings of the Human Factors and Ergonomics Society (2016)
24. Indiana University. Digital library of the commons [Internet] (2006). http://dlc.dlib.indiana.edu/dlc/contentguidelines. Accessed 3 Apr 2019
25. Lim, Y.K., Stolterman, E., Tenenberg, J.: The anatomy of prototypes: prototypes as filters, prototypes as manifestations of design ideas. ACM Trans. Comput. Interact. **15**, 7 (2008)
26. Salas, E., Shuffler, M.L., Thayer, A.L., Bedwell, W.L., Lazzara, E.H.: Understanding and improving teamwork in organizations: a scientifically based practical guide. Hum. Resource Manag. **54**, 599–622 (2015)
27. Wolters, E., Frens, J., Trotto, A., Hummels, C., Jaasma, P.: [X]Changing perspectives, pp. 259–269 (2017)
28. Sciences NA of, Engineering NA of, Medicine I of. A Vision of Interdisciplinary Research. In: Facilitating Interdisciplinary Research (2005)

On-Body Tangible Interaction: Using the Body to Support Tangible Manipulations for Immersive Environments

Houssem Saidi[1]($\boxtimes$), Marcos Serrano[1], Pourang Irani[2],
Christophe Hurter[3], and Emmanuel Dubois[1]

[1] IRIT, University of Toulouse, Toulouse, France
Houssem.saidi@irit.fr
[2] Department of Computer Science, University of Manitoba, Winnipeg, Canada
[3] ENAC, French Civil Aviation University, Toulouse, France

Abstract. Recent technological advances in immersive devices open up many opportunities for users to visualize data in their environments. However, current interactive solutions fail at providing a convenient approach to manipulate such complex immersive visualizations. In this article, we present a new approach to interact in these environments, that we call On-Body Tangible interaction (OBT): using the body to physically support the manipulation of an input device. The use of the body to support the interaction allows the user to move in his environment and avoid the inherent fatigue of mid-air interactions. In this paper, we explore the use of a rolling device, which fits well on-body interaction thanks to its form factor and offers enough degrees of freedom (DoF) for data manipulation. We first propose a new design space for OBT interactions, and specifically on the forearm. Then we validate the feasibility of such an approach through an experiment aimed at establishing the range, stability and comfort of gestures performed with the device on the forearm. Our results reveal that on-body tangible interaction on the forearm is stable and offers multiple DoFs with little fatigue. We illustrate the benefits of our approach through sample applications where OBT interactions are used to select and execute space-time cube operations.

Keywords: Immersive environment · On-body interaction · Tangible interaction

1 Introduction

Immersive systems such as the Hololens[1], MetaVision[2] or Moverio[3] allow the user to display data and visualizations directly on the physical world by attaching them to a fixed physical anchor; we hereafter refer to these as immersive visualizations.

---

[1] https://www.microsoft.com/en-us/hololens.

[2] http://www.metavision.com/.

[3] https://epson.com/moverio-augmented-reality.

Electronic supplementary material The online version of this chapter (https://doi.org/10.1007/978-3-030-29390-1_26) contains supplementary material, which is available to authorized users.

D. Lamas et al. (Eds.): INTERACT 2019, LNCS 11749, pp. 471–492, 2019.
https://doi.org/10.1007/978-3-030-29390-1_26

Immersive visualization offers a large set of advantages, such as spatialization of data, physical exploration of data, wide display area, etc. It thus constitutes a compelling alternative to visualizing multidimensional data on 2D displays. However, data exploration involves many tasks, such as filter, select, adjust or annotate the dataset, which are not entirely covered in existing solutions.

Indeed, a large interaction vocabulary is required and approaches based on mouse, touch and mid-air interaction fail to offer enough degrees of freedom (DoF) [17, 34, 39]; other solutions are often ambiguous and tiring (especially mid-air gestures [7, 34, 35]); finally many restrict the user's interaction to a defined place, usually a desktop, to use the input device (3D mouse or other [30]). The challenge then is to provide an interactive solution for immersive environments that preserves the freedom of movement of mid-air interaction and the DoFs of tangible interaction.

To this end, we propose to explore On-Body Tangible (OBT) interactions, i.e. a new approach using the body as a physical support for manipulating a tangible object to interact with immersive environments. This approach combines: (1) the use of a connected physical object, that offers multiple degrees of freedom and, (2) the use of the body to guide the physical manipulations of the tangible object and exploit the user's proprioception (i.e. sensing its own body parts). While the first aspect offers the multi-DoF of tangibles, the second aspect ensures that the solution can be used anywhere and can potentially contribute to reduce muscle fatigue, two inherent characteristics of mid-air interactions.

Our contribution is both conceptual and experimental. First, we propose a design space that encompasses the physical properties of the body (support) and the interactions that can be performed on it. Second, we validate the fundamental advantages of the OBT interactive approach (the feasibility of the gestures, their amplitudes, the comfort and fatigue related to the interaction) through a three-part experiment: the first part of the study focuses on on-body translations of the object, the second on rotations and the third evaluates rolls. Finally, we discuss the advantages and disadvantages of on-body tangible interactions, and we present two illustrative applications where on-body tangible interaction is used to select and execute space-time cube operations.

2   Related Work

This section synthesizes the main interaction solutions proposed for immersive environments, i.e. tactile, mid-air, tangible and on-body interactions.

2.1   Tactile Approaches

Whether the interaction is integrated directly on the immersive device itself [39], or deported to an external device (mobile device, interactive tabletop) [14, 31], different forms of tactile interaction have been applied to manipulate immersive visualizations [18, 20, 31, 32, 39]. However, Bergé's [7] and Besançon et al. [10] works established that tactile interaction is neither the most efficient, nor the preferred interaction modality for 3D data manipulation. Moreover, tactile interaction requires a dedicated surface [7], which can divert the attention of the user from the task to perform, and may constrain the movements if using fixed tactile display [30, 32].

2.2 Mid-Air Interactions

Mid-air interaction offers obvious advantages for immersive environments, such as unconstrained mobility, and are light and easy to perform [13, 38, 43, 51]. These advantages led to multiple developments, such as the interactive immersive experience proposed by Benko et al. [5] where users could employ mid-air gestures to interact with an augmented dome. Interestingly, authors evaluated the mid-air gestures and found that the proposed interaction was simple to perform but understanding how to perform it was not easy. Other well-known problems with mid-air interactions are fatigue [12], ambiguity when no appropriate feedback is provided [7] and discoverability, i.e. finding the right mid-air interaction for a given task/action [7].

2.3 Tangible Objects

Tangible interaction provides multiple degrees of freedom for interaction with immersive environments [1, 8, 50]. Its physicality suggests how to perform the interaction, minimizing the learning process. Used for the design of DNA (Deoxyribonucleic acid) components, tangible 3D input devices in immersive interface appear to be more satisfying than a 2D interface [41]: the direct 3D mappings between the 3D space and the tangible device manipulation facilitates the understanding. Besançon et al. [10] also established that tangible interactions perform better than its mouse and tactile counterparts, and that tangible's affordance limits the need for a learning phase. However, they pointed out that the mouse was more precise than tangibles used in mid-air. Interestingly, TUI (Tangible user interface) for have been tested in many different contexts such as interactive visualization of thin fiber structures [26], 3D visualization [15], exploration of volumetric data [25], etc.

Along the same lines, multi-DoF devices have been explored through the augmentation of a mouse in order to overcome the mere 2 degrees of freedom offered. The Rockin' Mouse [3] and the VideoMouse [23] are based on a semi-rounded shapes that allows tilting the device but do not totally support compound gestures. The Roly-Poly Mouse (RPM) [37] uses a completely rounded bottom. It has been shown to provide larger amplitude of movement than previous tilting devices and efficient in 3D contexts and Multi-Display Environments [40].

2.4 On-Body Interaction Techniques

As opposed to the previous solutions, on-body interactions have been scarcely used in immersive environments. Serrano et al. [42] explored hand-to-face gestures arguing that they are well suited for HWDs. Dobbelstein et al. [17] proposed the use of the belt as a tactile surface to interact with HWDs. Wang et al. [47] proposed PalmType, an interaction technique that enables users to type with their fingers on the palm to input text in smart-glasses. These works illustrate that on-body interaction techniques allow eyes-free interactions by exploiting the proprioception capabilities of users and do not divert their attention from the task at hand. However, the explored approaches offer a limited set of possible gestures, making it unsuitable for complex data visualization.

3   On-Body Tangible Interactions

In this section, we present a new interaction approach for immersive environments based on the use of the body to support tangible interactions. We detail the main requirements to interact with immersive environments, our choices of body parts and tangible objects to use, before presenting the design space.

3.1   Requirements for Immersive Environments

We illustrate the requirements for immersive environments through the specific case of immersive visualization. There are different types of immersive visualizations according to the data to visualize, which ranges from simple 3D objects to complex multidimensional data. All these immersive visualizations share a set of basic inter-action requirements:

- Unconstrained mobility (**R1**): it has been demonstrated that the spatial exploration of data allows for a better spatial understanding of the visualization [27]. The user can have an overview of the visualization from afar, a more detailed view by getting closer, as well as different views from different angles [27]. It is thus important that the interaction techniques do not constrain the mobility of the user.
- Multiple degrees of freedom (**R2**): the multidimensional nature of data in immersive systems requires enough degrees of freedom to tackle its manipulation [4] through multiple commands (filter, sort, annotate, highlight, clusterize, aggregate, etc.).
- Visual access (**R3**): the interaction techniques should not occult the data visual-ization. They should also allow the user to interact with data without diverting his attention from the visualization [27].
- Stability (**R4**): the interaction techniques should offer enough stability to properly tackle data visualization tasks in mobility.

While these requirements apply for immersive visualizations, they hold true for several other interaction environments, such as VR caves, augmented maintenance, gaming, etc. Therefore, the solution presented in this paper can be applied to such other interaction environments. We leave the investigation of these other environments for future work.

3.2   Combining Tangible and On-Body Interaction

After clarifying the requirements for immersive visualizations, we now describe and justify the properties of On-Body Tangible interaction: the tangible object used in the interaction, the body part used to support it and their combination.

Tangible Object. Among the plethora of existing tangible objects introduced in the literature, we decided to use a semi-spherical object. The rationale behind this choice is manifold. (1) It has been demonstrated [37] that such a form factor offers up to six degrees of freedom (R2), in the form of three types of manipulations (translations, rotations and rolls), facilitating the manipulation of multidimensional data [37]. (2) As opposed to other forms (that have flat surfaces), the contact of a rounded object with the interaction surface is minimal (i.e. a point), which will easily adapt to the outline of any part of the body. Other small sharp objects (such as a pen) have also a minimal contact point, but their sharpness is detrimental as they may hang onto the clothes or hurt on the skin. (3) As opposed to objects that includes flat surfaces, the manipulation of a round object remains continuous, does not interrupt the interaction flow and do not artificially promote the use and need of modes in the application. (4) The choice of a semi-spherical form rather than full spherical one is motivated by the fact that it is easier to hold [37].

Body-Parts Used to Support the Interaction. Many research works have focused on interaction on or with the body [9, 21, 28, 46, 49]. Arms and hands were the preferred body parts in most works. These body parts offer numerous advantages: they are easily accessible for interaction; they are in the user's field of vision and generate less social discomfort than other body parts [28, 45]. Karrer et al. experimentally identified the most appropriate region of the body to perform interaction with clothes [28]. Among their observations, the non-dominant arm as well as the hip are the preferred body-parts for interaction. Other parts of the body, such as the stomach and legs, have been rejected for social or personal reasons in the same study.

We decided to focus on the forearm of the non-dominant arm to support the interaction for several reasons. It is an always-available physical support that favors physical exploration of data and it does not constrain the movement of the user (R1). Thanks to the body's natural capacity to sense its own body parts (proprioception), the user can perform tangible interactions on the body without having to switch his attention from the data visualization to the interaction tool (R3). Using the forearm offers a large surface on which the tangible object can be laid, and it is effortlessly accessible by the dominant hand as opposed to the upper arm which needs a consequent effort to be touched by the dominant hand (R1, R2). Furthermore, its combination with a tangible object (which use can be extended to mid-air manipulations, as suggested by the Lift-Up option in [40]) does not constrain the user's movement (R1). Finally, several stable poses can be adopted with the forearm (R4), which increases the range of possibilities (R2) (Fig. 1).

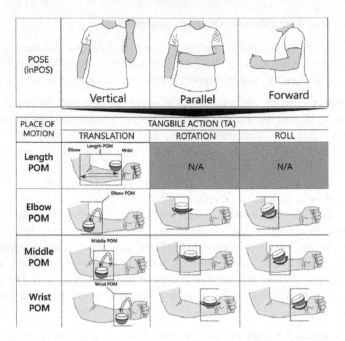

Fig. 1. Design Space for on-body tangible interaction on the forearm

3.3 Mapping the Input Interaction Space with the Data Visualization Space

While the user's gestures are performed in a 3D physical environment, they trigger actions in a 3D virtual environment. It is therefore important to choose the right frame of reference for the interaction. The frame of reference can be allocentric (external: it can be world-centered, data centered…) or egocentric (relative to the body). In an egocentric frame of reference, the output of a given manipulation is determined by how it is performed with regards to the body, and will have the same effect regardless of the body position and orientation in the world. In our approach, we adopt an egocentric frame of reference to allow the user to interact from anywhere with geographically anchored data in the physical world [33]. Indeed, previous research found that a lack of a logical relationship between the manipulated data's frame of reference and the user's frame of reference can affect performances negatively [36, 48].

3.4 Design Space for On-Body Tangible Interaction

Based on the main design properties of OBT interactions introduced above, we now present a design space describing the possible use of the forearm as interaction support. It is composed of 3 dimensions: The Pose, the Place of motion and the Tangible action.

Restricting interaction to the forearm –more socially acceptable, accessible and with a large interaction area– has the disadvantage of reducing the available interaction vocabulary. To address this limitation and increase the interaction vocabulary, we propose to consider the posture of the arm (Pose) as well as the use of sub-regions on the forearm (places of motion) and the tangible action (TA) that can be applied.

Pose (inPOS). The pose describes the position of the forearm with respect to the user's body. We identified three main poses for the forearm. In the Vertical pose, the forearm is vertical, the hand points upwards. In the Forward pose, the forearm is perpendicular to the shoulders. In the Parallel pose, the forearm is parallel to the shoulders (Fig. 1). We chose these three poses because they are the most comfortable poses, the most accessible with the non-dominant hand and they are significantly different from each other, facilitating their distinction by both the system and the user.

Place of Motion (POM). The Place of motion represents the surface of the forearm on which the tangible object can beused. We identified two types of places: the first one extends over the length of the forearm, from the elbow to the wrist (length POM); the second one, called width POM, divide the forearm into several sub-regions. The number of sub-regions was defined according to the following criteria: (1) the sub-regions have to be large enough to accommodate interaction with the tangible object (diameter = 8 cm); (2) the sub-regions have to be easily distinguishable. Applying these criteria, we divided the forearm in three sub-regions: close to the Elbow (Elbow POM), in the middle of the forearm (Middle POM) or close to the wrist (Wrist POM) (Fig. 1). This results into 12 different interaction supports (3 poses × 4 places), which increases the possibilities of interactions exploiting the proprioception of the user and contributes to avoid the fatigue of a mid-air usage.

Tangible Action (TA). It stands for the physical actions than can be performed with the tangible object. The round shape of the tangible object offers three physical manipulations: translation, roll and rotate. Rotations and rolls along the length of the forearm (Length POM) were not considered. Indeed, they are performed with the tangible object motionless, in the same spot, thus, rendering them too similar to rotations and rolls on one of the other three places of motion. The following experiments will analyze the benefits and limits of each of them separately.

4   Study: Translations, Rotation, Rolls on the Forearm

We present a three parts experiment in which we explore the feasibility and potential of on-body tangible interaction in the different configurations described above. We explore the potential along three aspects: (1) the maximum range of motion for each of the three physical manipulations; (2) the stability of the interaction; and (3) the width of places of motions

We define the range of motion (RoM) as the maximum comfortable amplitude of each Tangible Action (translation, rotation and roll) for each pair of Pose and Place of motion. Concretely, it represents (1) the maximum distance that can be covered with the tangible object when translating it; (2) the total amplitudes of clockwise and counterclockwise rotations; (3) the total amplitude of forward and backward rolls. The greater the range of motion, the greater the range of values that can be manipulated.

Stability concerns the forearm (i.e. is it steady enough) and the tangible object manipulation: in the first case, a stable support is required; in the second case, it is important to know if unexpected tangible actions occur while performing one specific tangible actions [37, 40].

Width of Place of Motions corresponds to the space of the forearm used by the users when performing a tangible action in this PoM. It is important to determine whether the PoMs are large enough to hold the interaction without overlapping.

4.1 Task

Our study was divided into three parts. During the first part, we asked participants to perform translations on the four different places of motion (PoM): the full length of the forearm (length POM), as well as on the Elbow, Middle and Wrist PoMs, as illustrated in Fig. 1. A trial is defined as a back-and-forth translation on the forearm. The starting points of the translations were chosen by the participants at the beginning of each trial. It was not necessary to control the starting points as each trial was composed by 10 consecutive gestures.

In the second and third part of the study, we examined rotations and rolls respectively. A rotation (resp. roll) trial consisted in a rotation (resp. roll) towards the wrist (clockwise) followed by a rotation towards the elbow (counterclockwise) and a return to the initial state. The participants were asked to perform the maximum comfortable rotation (resp. roll) in both directions (clockwise, counterclockwise). Rolls perpendicular to the forearm would be too difficult to distinguish from translation in the width of the forearm and were not considered in this experiment.

Participants were asked to manipulate the device with the dominant hand and to perform the gestures on the forearm of the non-dominant hand. The physical manipulations were performed for each *Pose* (Vertical, Parallel, Forward, see Fig. 1). The poses and places of motion were explained and illustrated to the participants at the beginning of the experiment. Participants were free to grasp the object as they wished. Finally, since the purpose of the experiment was to study the use of the tangible on the forearm, no feedback was provided to the participants.

4.2 Apparatus

The diameter of the rounded tangible object used for the experiment was 8 cm. In order to detect rotations and rolls of the tangible object, we used an IMU of X-io Technologies (x-IMU: 48 g, 57 mm × 38 mm × 21 mm). The IMU is composed of a triple-axis gyroscope, accelerometer and magnetometer, offering an angular precision of $1°$. The refresh rate of the sensors goes up to 512 Hz and we used Bluetooth to connect the IMU with the computer.

To locate the position of the tangible object and the body parts, we used an OptiTrack system composed of 12 cameras that track infrared reflective markers with a precision of 1 mm. The markers were carefully placed on the tangible object so that they do not influence the participant's grasp (Fig. 2). Additional infrared reflective markers were placed on the main joints of the arm/forearm (Fig. 2). The wrist, elbow of the non-dominant arm and the shoulders were also tracked.

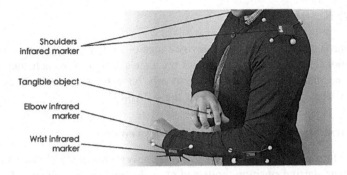

Shoulders
infrared marker

Tangible object

Elbow infrared
marker

Wrist infrared
marker

Fig. 2. Placement of the infrared tracking markers

4.3 Procedure

The first part of the study (on translations) follows a 3×4 within-subject design with the Pose (Forward, Parallel, Vertical) and the Place of Motion (Length, Elbow, Middle, Wrist) as factors. The second and third parts of the study (on rotation and roll respectively) followed a 3×3 within-subject design, with the same factors but without the Length Place of Motion (which is not in our design space, see Fig. 1).

The Pose factor is counterbalanced using a 3×3 Latin square. Each part of the study is composed of 3 blocks, each block corresponds to one Pose and consists of all the Places of motion in a random order. For each pair of Pose and Place of motion, participants had to do 3 repetitions of each trial (which is composed of 10 consecutive gestures). The participants could take a break between each repetition. Each part of the study lasted between 30 and 40 min. We collected 4320 trials in total for the translations study (360 trials per participant), 3240 trials for the rotation study (270 trials per participant) and 3240 trials for the rolls study (270 trials per participant).

4.4 Participants

We recruited 36 (12 participants for each of the 3 studies) (9 female), aged 26.0 on average (SD = 3.4). All the participants were right-handed. Most of the participants were students (PhD, MSc) from the computer science department of the local university; all other participants were familiar with electronic equipment.

4.5 Collected Data

We measured the circumference of the forearm near the elbow and the wrist for each participant as well as the inner and outer length of the forearm. Every 10 ms, we recorded the position, rotation and roll of the tangible object, as well as the position of the wrist, the elbow and the shoulders. To evaluate the physical fatigue, we asked participants to fill out a Borg scale [19] for each pair of (Pose, Place of motion).

5 Study: Results

We report the forearm stability; the device range of motion; the gestures overlapping, the unintentional device movements and the user's fatigue for each tangible action. Regarding the data analysis, we chose to rely on estimation techniques with 95% confidence intervals as recommended by the APA [44].

5.1 Forearm Stability: Elbow and Wrist Movements

To study the forearm stability, we analyzed the movements of the elbow and wrist with regards to their starting position, collected at the beginning of each trial. Results show that the elbow was relatively stable: the maximum movement observed, all directions included (along the X, Y and Z axis) and all physical manipulations included (Translations, Rotations, Rolls) did not exceed 1,7 cm on average. This result remain valid when considering each *Pose and Place of motion* independently. Taking into consideration these findings, we can say that the forearm is sufficiently stable to support tangible interactions.

5.2 Range of Motion

Translations. The *ROM* for translations along the forearm *was* computed by calculating the average distance covered by the tangible object for each group of 10 successive gestures. It was computed for each pair of *Pose and Place of motion*. As the size of the forearm differs from one participant to another, we standardized the collected data.

Participants exploited at least 93,6% of the forearm length when performing translation on the Length PoM (Vertical pose: 93,6% [87,1%; 99,8%]; Parallel pose: 101,8% [92,8%; 110,3%]; Forward pose: 98,6% [92,2%; 104,8%]). We observed that the translations performed in the Parallel pose extended to the hand, thus surpassing the wrist (explaining the values above 100% on Fig. 3A). The results do not reveal a difference of translation amplitudes between poses: overall, participants were able to exploit almost all the length of the forearm in the three conditions (see Fig. 3A).

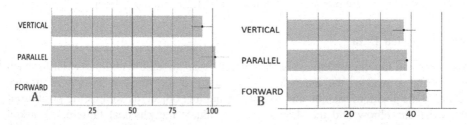

Fig. 3. (A) Translation amplitudes along the forearm in percentage of the forearm length (with 95%CIs); (B) Translation amplitudes around the forearm in percentage of the arm circumference (with 95%CIs)

The amplitude of translations performed around the forearm (Elbow, Middle and Wrist places of motion) represents the length of the arc covered by the movement of the object. The results are presented in the form of percentages of the forearm circumference and standardized for all participants. The biggest translation amplitudes were observed for the Forward pose, as illustrated in Fig. 3B (Vertical pose: 37,6% [34,0%; 41,5%]; Parallel pose: 38,6% [34,9%; 42,4%]; Forward pose: 45,2% [40,9%; 49,9%]). There was no significant difference between the places of motion.

Rotations. Regarding the rotations, we collected the maximum clockwise (CW) and counterclockwise (CCW) rotations. Overall, CW rotations among the 3 poses were slightly bigger (58° vs 50°) than CCW. This difference between CW and CCW amplitude is in line with those obtained with a device of similar form [37] (CW:73°, CCW:59°). The participants in our study used the "squeeze" hand posture [37] to grasp the object. The global amplitudes of rotations (CW + CWW) were clearly larger in the *Vertical* pose (Vertical pose: 138° [111°; 176°]; Parallel pose: 90° [74°%; 109°%]; Forward pose: 95° [82°; 107°]). We noticed that in this pose participants could move the arm holding the device to a greater extent than in the *Parallel* and *Forward* pose, hence resulting in larger rotations (Fig. 4A).

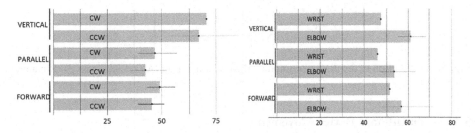

Fig. 4. (A) Rotations amplitudes in degrees (with 95%CIs); (B) Rolls amplitudes in degrees (with 95%CIs)

Rolls. We collected the maximum rolls towards the wrist and the elbow (Fig. 4B): (1) towards the wrist: The observed amplitudes ranged from 46° to 51° for rolls towards the wrist (Vertical pose: 48° [40°; 55°]; Parallel pose: 46° [40°%; 51°%]; Forward pose: 51° [43°; 61°]). (2) towards the elbow: The amplitude ranged from 53° to 61° for roll towards the elbow (Vertical pose: 61° [55°; 69°]; Parallel pose: 53° [47°%; 63°%]; Forward pose: 57° [48°; 72°]). Therefore, results tend to establish that rolls towards the elbow had bigger amplitudes for the 3 poses than rolls toward the wrist.

5.3   Gestures Overlapping

However, when refining this result through the analysis of the distribution of the device position, results show that the interaction on the *Elbow* and *Middle* overlaps over a third of the forearm (Fig. 5A); the overlap between interaction in the *Middle* and *Wrist* represents a fifth of the forearm. However, it clearly appears that the translations on the *Elbow* and *Wrist do never overlap*. Finally, despite the clear instruction that required participants to perform translation from the elbow to the wrist, we can observe that a fair number of translations were performed beyond the wrist position (i.e. on the hand). During **rotations**, participants used 23% of the forearm to perform rotations. The surface used was slightly smaller on the Elbow (21%) compared to the Middle and Wrist (23% & 24% respectively). A reason for that could be that interaction near the elbow are more restricted due to the upper arm. Similarly, to the translations results, we observed a large distribution of the exploited surfaces (Fig. 5B).As with translations and rotations, the exploited surfaces when performing **rolls** on the forearm Fig. 5C) were fairly small (Elbow POM: 19%, Middle POM: 21%, Wrist POM: 20%) but their dispersion was large enough for them to overlap.

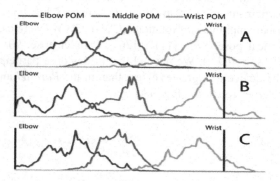

Fig. 5. Distribution of the device position on the forearm during (A) Translations, (B) Rotations, (C) Rolls

5.4 Unintentional Device Movements

As underlined in [21], rolls are the most probable unintentional manipulations that can occur during translations, which could lead to the activation of unwanted commands. This is particularly true in our case, since users perform translations over the circumference of the forearm, unlike the flat surface used in [21]. Therefore, we analyzed the stability of the device during interaction by looking at unintentional rolls during translations, similar to [21].

Rolls During Translations Along the Forearm (Length POM). Results show that on average, involuntary rolls during translations of the device did not exceed 12,6° [8,7°; 16,2°] for the *Forward* pose, 8.2° [6,5°; 11,2°] for the *Parallel* pose and 2.7° [1,9°; 4,2°] for the *Vertical* pose. The *Vertical* pose clearly triggers less involuntary rolls than the other poses. It also seems that the *Forward* pose is the most prone to unintentional rolls. These findings are in line with the results of the previous studies conducted on devices of similar form factors (12°) [37].

Rolls During Translations Around the Forearm. We wanted to know whether participants roll the device when translating it around the forearm (i.e. on the Elbow, Middle and Wrist). The results show that, for all poses, the translations around the forearm are systematically performed with a large roll of the device (at least 58°). This reveals that the tangible object was not maintained horizontally during translations around the forearm. The rolls were more important in the *Vertical* pose where the average roll was approximately 78°. This number decreases to 62° on average for the *Parallel* pose and 58° for the *Forward* pose. This observation remains valid for all *places of motion* taken separately (*Elbow, Middle and Wrist*).

5.5   Fatigue

Fatigue was measured using a 6–20 Borg scale [11]. The average Borg score obtained for the poses ranged from 'very light' for the Forward (9) and Parallel (10) pose, to 'light' for the Vertical pose (11). The pose does not appear to affect the fatigue scores and overall, participants did not consider tangible on-body interaction tiring. However, with an average of 13, rotations in the Vertical pose were found relatively tiring to perform ('somewhat hard'). It should also be noted that while participants had the opportunity to take breaks during the experiment between each group of 10 gestures, only one participant asked for a break.

6   Discussion

The findings presented above consolidate our hypothesis that on-body tangible interaction is a promising approach for use in immersive environments. It is stable, fatigue free, and offers a very rich set of interactions. Multiples actions, poses and places can be combined to best fit the user's set of tasks to perform, offering a wide input vocabulary to manipulate immersive environment.

The **forearm stability** did not diminish over time. The forearm position was steady for the entire study (all physical manipulations included), making this body part a reliable support for interaction. The interaction itself did not induce fatigue according to the users' feedback, even if the sessions took more than 30 min.

The **surfaces covered** while performing physical manipulations with the tangible object on the Elbow, Middle and Wrist POM were small enough (less than a fourth of the forearm at most) to consider three distinct regions of the forearm for interaction. However, the dispersion of these surfaces showed that they overlap (all physical manipulations included), making it difficult to employ more than 2 distinct regions of the forearm in practice. We want to point out that our experimental setup did not offer any feedback regarding the available places of motion. We believe that with a visual feedback showing the position of each region on the forearm in the immersive environment, the three regions would be more easily distinguishable. This hypothesis should be studied in a complementary study.

From the previous results, we can draw some **design suggestions** on how to use on-body tangible interaction for visualization tasks:

- The translations performed on the length POM were the most robust in terms of involuntary rotations and rolls (in line with previous results on desktop [37]). In terms of exploitable interaction surfaces, most (at least 73,7%) of the forearm sub-regions available for interaction was exploited to perform on-body tangible interactions. Due to their stability and large amplitudes, translations on the length POM can be used to control a large set of values, to have a substantial precision or a greater data coverage. For instance, they could be used to manipulate slider type controllers that require a certain degree of precision depending on the manipulated data. Their stability allows them to be used in compound gestures (in combination with a roll or a rotation) which can allow for the design of expert modes.

- Translations around the forearm (Elbow, Middle and Wrist POM) exploited at most half of the surface available for interaction. These gestures seem to be better adapted to controllers that do not require a large amplitude, i.e. "rate control" type input.
- The amplitudes observed for rolls (ranging from ranged from 46° to 51°) were slightly bigger than those reported for a similar device in [37] on a desktop context (40° on average), while rotations' amplitudes were smaller (66° on average). This shows that on-body tangible interaction offers similar interaction possibilities than its desktop counterpart.
- Rotations in the vertical pose were larger than the two other poses at the cost of an increased fatigue. Therefore, these gestures are prime candidates for short interactions, such as controlling menus (limited number of sub-items) or activate toggles (two modes, discrete two-state tasks).

Theoretically, our design space describes a vocabulary composed of 30 continuous interactions: 12 1D-Translation gestures (3 poses * 4 POM), 9 1D-Rotation gestures and 9 1D-Roll gestures (3 poses * 3 POM each). The three-part study conducted in this work showed that it is possible to perform all the translations and rotations identified in our design space. Thus, our approach interaction vocabulary offers a rich and large set of possibilities to carry data visualization tasks. However, it is necessary to choose the right mapping between the possible On-Body Tangible controls and the tasks, which raises several questions: What is the optimal mapping that allows the user to keep a good balance between exploiting a great number of the possible interactions and memorizing them? Is it better to allow the user to create his own mapping, or should a predefined mapping be proposed to him? Answering these questions is not possible without an evaluation of the two approaches, which is one of the perspectives of this work. In the following sections, we introduce both of these approaches through a usage scenario for controlling space-time cube operations, and by introducing a meta-UI developed to help users assign OBT interactions to tasks.

7   Illustrative Application

In this section, we present an illustrative use of OBT interaction in the context of space-time cube data visualization. It is firstly used to select the appropriate space-time cube operation (e.g. scale); Then it is used to execute the selected operation (e.g. adjust the scaling ratio). In the first case we illustrate how the operations can be assigned to OBT interactions in a predefined manner; In the second case we illustrate how OBT interactions can be dynamically assigned to different aspects of the operation execution.

7.1 Space-Time Cube Operations

Visualizing and interacting with spatio-temporal datasets is rather difficult, as illustrated by the continuous research dedicated to this topic. One of the reasons for this difficulty is the important number of operations that can be performed on these datasets as well as the complexity of these operations. Bach et al. [2] introduced a taxonomy of elementary space-time cube operations to organize them. Bach's taxonomy encompasses interactive operations that are relevant to all visualizations representing a combination of time (1D) and space (2D). The taxonomy is composed of four main groups of operations: extraction; flattening; geometry transformation and content transformation. As per Bach's descriptions [2]:

- Extraction: consists in selecting a subset of a space-time object (e.g., extracting a line or cut from a volume).
- Flattening: consists in aggregating a space-time object into a lower-dimensional space-time object (e.g., projecting a volume onto a surface).
- Geometry transformation: consists in transforming a space-time object spatially without change of content, i.e. without affecting the data presented.
- Content transformation: consists in changing the content of a space-time object without affecting its geometry.

In the following subsection, we demonstrate how our OBT interaction approach can be used to support the selection of one of these operations (Sect. 7.2) and we present a different use of OBT interaction to support their execution (Sect. 7.3).

7.2 Mapping of OBT Interactions to Elementary Space-Time Cube Operations

In this section, we illustrate how a predefined mapping can be built between a set of operations and the 30 available OBT interactions, to allow selecting one of the space-time cube operations.

Available OBT Interactions. We used the following subset of gestures from of our interaction vocabulary:

- The three main poses: Forward, Vertical and Parallel, each corresponding to one line on Fig. 6
- Each pose has three places of motion: Elbow, Middle and Wrist, each corresponding to one column in Fig. 6
- On each Place of motion, we decided to use discrete instead of continuous tangible actions and retained the following tangible actions:
  - 2 Translations: a translation can occur in two directions around the forearm (clockwise, counterclockwise) (red arrows in each cell of Fig. 6).
  - 4 Rolls: a roll can be performed in two directions (towards the hand or towards the elbow). In each direction, 2 thresholds have been defined so that a roll in each direction can be assigned to 2 different commands (green dots in each cell of Fig. 6).
- As a validation mechanism, we used a physical button positioned on top of the device.

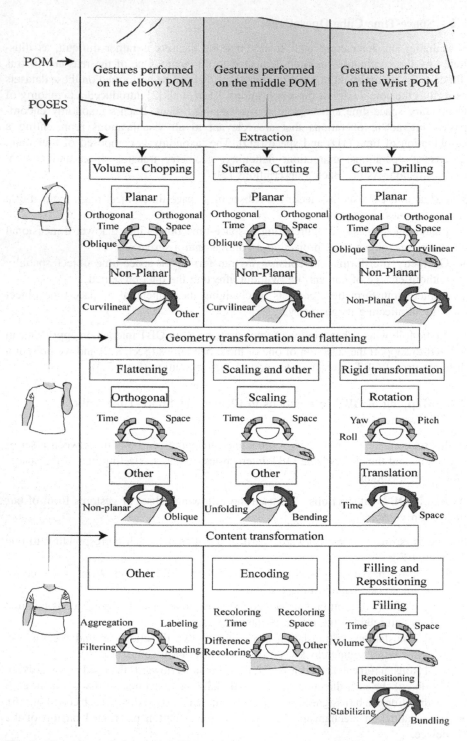

Fig. 6. Illustration of the use of OBT interaction for selecting space-time cube operations. (Color figure online)

A total of 54 commands can be selected with such vocabulary (6 per place of motion × 3 Places of Motion × 3 Poses).

Mapping Space Time Cube Operation to OBT Interactions. Bach's taxonomy [2] lists 4 groups of general operations. Each one contains several specific operations: *extraction* (16 operations); *flattening* (4 operations); *geometry transformation* (9 operations) and *content transformation* (13 operations). As the flattening operations are performed directly on the cube, we added them to the geometry transformation group (performed directly on the cube too). This resulted in a new group of operations that we called "Geometry transformation and flattening". Regrouping these operations resulted in 3 balanced groups of operations. We mapped each group of operations to a pose (see Fig. 6-POSES): (1) Extraction (group with the most tasks) is mapped to the forward pose (the most accessible pose); (2) Geometry transformation and flattening are mapped to the vertical pose; (3) Content transformation is mapped to the parallel pose. Next, we mapped each sub-group to a place of motion on the forearm (Fig. 6-POM), and finally, the specific operations to one of the possible tangible actions (translate or roll). As an example, to select the task Rotation pitch (Fig. 6), the user puts his forearm in the Vertical pose, places the tangible object on the wrist POM, and performs a small roll towards the hand before validating by pressing the button on the device. In this case, the mapping is predefined and appropriate feedback will have to be displayed to the user to confirm the selected operation. Of course, one important issue in this process is to adopt a coherent, easy to learn mapping. Alternatively, the choice of the mapping may be left to the user. In the next section we illustrate the use of a MetaUI to help the user establish himself the desired mapping between operations and OBT interactions.

7.3   A Meta UI Supporting User's Assignments of OBT Interaction to Operation

The use case in the previous section focused on the use of OBT interaction for the selection of space time cube operations. After the command is selected, the next step consists in applying a tangible action of the device (translation, roll or rotation) to control the execution of the space-time cube operation. To facilitate this second step, we implemented a tool (Fig. 7) that allows the user to quickly define his own mapping between the available OBT interactions and the operations to control.

The metaUI includes a mapping panel (Fig. 7A). Here the user chooses a pose, place of motion and gesture, and assigns to it a function i.e. controlling one aspect of the visualization operation selected (e.g. value of the operation filtering; starting time of the operation Volume-Chopping; …). The MetaUI also includes a simulation panel (Fig. 7B) that allows to simulate the defined mapping through a set of UI elements. The results of the simulated OBT interaction are applied directly to the visualization. This tool is demonstrated in the supplementary video.

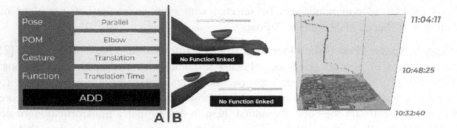

Fig. 7. Customization interface: (A) Defining the mapping between OBT interactions and visualization operations; (B) Simulating the defined mapping (control: B - left, effect: B - right).

8   Conclusion and Future Work

In this paper, we proposed, described and studied a new approach for interaction with immersive environments: on-body tangible interactions. This approach is based on the use of the forearm to support tangible interactions using a rounded object that offers multiple degrees of freedom. It takes advantage of the body's natural capacity to sense its own body parts (proprioception) without switching user's attention from the data and minimizing the fatigue. We proposed a design space describing the Pose and the Place of Motion of interaction. We conducted a study to confirm the stability of the forearm to support tangible interaction, to measure the range of motion of the physical manipulations and measure user fatigue. The results showed that on-body tangible interactions are a promising approach to interact with immersive environments since the interaction support (forearm) is stable, the tangible object combined with the different poses and places of motions offers a large number of degrees of freedom, and users found the approach comfortable. Finally, we illustrated the possible usage of this approach through a concrete illustrative application concerning the selection of spatio-temporal operations. This example was thought to demonstrate several ways of using OBT: with a predefined mapping or with a user defined mapping (i.e. with the Meta UI). Our hypothesis is that the user defined mapping will help to recall the commands and ultimately, improve data visualization exploration. However, further experiments need to be conducted to measure the impact and benefits of each approach.

The next step of this work consists in exploring the technological feasibility of our approach. As it is, the tangible object integrates an IMU to detect rolls and rotations autonomously, while the arm pose and the object translation are detected with a camera-based tracking system. This approach is robust and satisfied the objective of our work, i.e. evaluate the advantages of OBT interaction. To implement a viable technical solution, we plan to explore the use of a bracelet to detect the arm pose, and the use of the accelerometer of the IMU to detect the object translation.

Once we develop this integrated solution, we plan to investigate other relevant research questions, such as the performance (in terms of precision and time) or the memorization of OBT gestures. Indeed, while our current approach allows to map a very large number of commands, it increases the difficulty of learning them. To solve this limitation, one solution is to provide suitable feedforward and feedback mechanisms, which will help with both discoverability and recall of mappings. Moreover, the memorization of OBT gestures could also benefit from semantic and spatial aids of the body places considered in our design space, as demonstrated in previous work [19]. Finally, it will be interesting to explore the usage of this approach under different frames of reference: while the egocentric approach seems to better fit this type of interaction, the effects of using a world-centric reference should be evaluated in a controlled study.

Acknowledgments. This work is partially funded by the AP2 project grant AP2 ANR-15-CE23-0001.

References

1. Bach, B., Sicat, R., Beyer, J., Cordeil, M., Pfister, H.: The Hologram in my hand: how effective is interactive exploration of 3D visualizations in immersive tangible augmented reality? IEEE Trans. Vis. Comput. Graph. (TVCG) **24**, 457–467 (2018)
2. Bach, B., Dragicevic, P., Archambault, D., Hurter, C., Carpendale, S.: A descriptive framework for temporal data visualizations based on generalized space-time cubes. Comput. Graph. Forum **36**(6), 36–61 (2017). https://doi.org/10.1111/cgf.12804
3. Balakrishnan, R., Baudel, T., Kurtenbach, G., Fitzmaurice, G.: The Rockin'Mouse: integral 3D manipulation on a plane. In: Proceedings of the ACM SIGCHI Conference on Human factors in Computing Systems, pp. 311–318, Atlanta, Georgia, USA, 22–27 March 1997. https://doi.org/10.1145/258549.258778
4. Beaudouin-Lafon, M.: Instrumental interaction: an interaction model for designing post-WIMP user interfaces. In: Proceedings of the SIGCHI Conference on Human Factors in Computing Systems (CHI 2000), pp. 446–453. ACM, New York (2000). https://doi.org/10.1145/332040.332473
5. Benko, H., Wilson, A.D.: Multi-point interactions with immersive omnidirectional visualizations in a dome. In: ACM International Conference on Interactive Tabletops and Surfaces (ITS 2010), pp. 19–28. ACM, New York (2010). https://doi.org/10.1145/1936652.1936657
6. Benko, H., Izadi, S., Wilson, A.D., Cao, X., Rosenfeld, D., Hinckley, K.: Design and evaluation of interaction models for multi-touch mice. In: Proceedings of Graphics Interface 2010, 31 May–02 June 2010, Ottawa, Ontario, Canada (2010)
7. Bergé, L.-P., Serrano, M., Perelman, G., Dubois, E.: Exploring smartphone-based interaction with overview+detail interfaces on 3D public displays. In: Proceedings of the 16th International Conference on Human-Computer Interaction with Mobile Devices & Services (MobileHCI 2014), pp. 125–134. ACM, New York (2014). https://doi.org/10.1145/2628363.2628374
8. Bergé, L.-P., Dubois, E., Raynal, M.: Design and evaluation of an "Around the SmartPhone" technique for 3D manipulations on distant display. In: Proceedings of the 3rd ACM Symposium on Spatial User Interaction (SUI 2015), pp. 69–78. ACM, New York (2015). https://doi.org/10.1145/2788940.2788941
9. Bergstrom-Lehtovirta, J., Hornbæk, K., Boring, S.: It's a wrap: mapping on-skin input to off-skin displays. In: Proceedings of the 2018 CHI Conference on Human Factors in Computing Systems (CHI 2018), 11 p. ACM, New York, Paper 564 (2018). https://doi.org/10.1145/3173574.3174138

10. Besançon, L., Issartel, P., Ammi, M., Isenberg, T.: Mouse, tactile, and tangible input for 3D manipulation. In: Proceedings of the 2017 CHI Conference on Human Factors in Computing Systems (CHI 2017), pp. 4727–4740. ACM, New York (2017). https://doi.org/10.1145/3025453.3025863

11. Borg, G.: Borg's Perceived Exertion and Pain Scales, p. 104. Human Kinetics, Champaign (1998). viii

12. Burgess, R., et al.: Selection of large-scale 3D point cloud data using gesture recognition. In: Camarinha-Matos, L.M., Baldissera, T.A., Di Orio, G., Marques, F. (eds.) DoCEIS 2015. IAICT, vol. 450, pp. 188–195. Springer, Cham (2015). https://doi.org/10.1007/978-3-319-16766-4_20

13. Clarke, S., Dass, N., Chau, D.H.(Polo).: Naturalmotion: exploring gesture controls for visualizing time-evolving graphs. In: Proceedings of IEEE VIS (Poster Session) (2016)

14. Coffey, D., et al.: Interactive slice WIM: navigating and interrogating volume datasets using a multi-surface, multi-touch VR interface. IEEE Trans. Vis. Comput. Graph. **18**(10), 1614–1626 (2012). https://doi.org/10.1109/TVCG.2011.283

15. Cordeil, M., Bach, B., Li, Y., Wilson, E., Dwyer, T.: A design space for spatio-data coordination: tangible interaction devices for immersive information visualisation. In: Proceedings of the 10th IEEE Pacific Visualization Symposium (PacificVis) (2017)

16. Cordeil, M., Dwyer, T., Hurter, C.: Immersive solutions for future air traffic control and management. In: Proceedings of the 2016 ACM Companion on Interactive Surfaces and Spaces (ISS Companion 2016), pp. 25–31. ACM, New York (2016). https://doi.org/10.1145/3009939.3009944

17. Dobbelstein, D., Hock, P., Rukzio, E.: Belt: an unobtrusive touch input device for head-worn displays. In: Proceedings of the 33rd Annual ACM Conference on Human Factors in Computing Systems (CHI 2015), pp. 2135–2138. ACM, New York (2015). https://doi.org/10.1145/2702123.2702450

18. Giannopoulos, I., Komninos, A., Garofalakis, J.: Natural interaction with large map interfaces in VR. In: Proceedings of the 21st Pan-Hellenic Conference on Informatics (PCI 2017), Article no. 56, 6 p. ACM, New York (2017). https://doi.org/10.1145/3139367.3139424

19. Fruchard, B., Lecolinet, E., Chapuis, O.: Impact of semantic aids on command memorization for On-Body interaction and directional gestures. In: Proceedings of the International Working Conference on Advanced Visual Interfaces, AVI 2018 - International Conference on Advanced Visual Interfaces, Castiglione della Pescaia, Grosseto, Italy, May 2018. ACM, AVI 2018 (2018)

20. Hancock, M., Carpendale, S., Cockburn, A.: Shallow-depth 3D interaction: design and evaluation of one-, two- and three-touch techniques. In: Proceedings of the SIGCHI Conference on Human Factors in Computing Systems—CHI 2007, pp. 1147–1156. ACM Press (2007)

21. Harrison, C., Tan, D., Morris, D.: Skinput: appropriating the body as an input surface. In: Proceedings of the SIGCHI Conference on Human Factors in Computing Systems (CHI 2010), pp. 453–462. ACM, New York (2010). https://doi.org/10.1145/1753326.1753394

22. Hinckley, K., Wigdor, D., Input technologies and techniques. In: The HCI Handbook, 3rd edn. Taylor & Francis. Chap. 9

23. Hinckley, K., Sinclair, M., Hanson, E., Szeliski, R., Conway, M.: The VideoMouse: a camera-based multi-degree-of-freedom input device. In: Proceedings of the 12th annual ACM Symposium on User Interface Software and Technology, pp. 103–112, Asheville, North Carolina, USA, 07–10 November 1999. https://doi.org/10.1145/320719.322591]

24. Hurter, C., Tissoires, B., Conversy, S.: FromDaDy: spreading aircraft trajectories across views to support iterative queries. IEEE Trans. Vis. Comput. Graph. **15**(6), 1017–1024 (2009). https://doi.org/10.1109/tvcg.2009.145

25. Issartel, P., Guéniat, F., Ammi, M.: A portable interface for tangible exploration of volumetric data. In: Proceedings VRST, pp. 209–210. ACM, Edinburgh, Scotland (2014). https://doi.org/10.1145/2671015.2671130. ISBN 978-1-4503-3253-8

26. Jackson, B., et al.: A lightweight tangible 3D interface for interactive visualization of thin fiber structures. IEEE Trans. Vis. Comput. Graph. **19**(12), 2802–2809 (2013). http://doi.org/10.1109/TVCG.2013.121. http://ieeexplore.ieee.org/xpls/abs_all.jsp?arnumber=6651934

27. Jansen, Y., Dragicevic, P., Fekete, J.-D.: Tangible remote controllers for wall-size displays. In: Proceedings of the SIGCHI Conference on Human Factors in Computing Systems (CHI 2012), pp. 2865–2874. ACM, New York (2012). http://dx.doi.org/10.1145/2207676.2208691

28. Karrer, T., Wittenhagen, M., Lichtschlag, L., Heller, F., Borchers, J.: Pinstripe: eyes-free continuous input on interactive clothing. In: Proceedings of the SIGCHI Conference on Human Factors in Computing Systems (CHI 2011), pp. 1313–1322. ACM, New York (2011). https://doi.org/10.1145/1978942.1979137

29. Kim, J.-S., Gračanin, D., Matković, K., Quek, F.: Finger walking in place (FWIP): a traveling technique in virtual environments. In: Butz, A., Fisher, B., Krüger, A., Olivier, P., Christie, M. (eds.) SG 2008. LNCS, vol. 5166, pp. 58–69. Springer, Heidelberg (2008). https://doi.org/10.1007/978-3-540-85412-8_6

30. Klein, T., Guéniat, F., Pastur, L., Vernier, F., Isenberg, T.: A design study of direct-touch interaction for exploratory 3D scientific visualization. Comput. Graph. Forum **31**, 1225–1234 (2012)

31. Lopez, D., Oehlberg, L., Doger, C., Isenberg, T.: Towards an understanding of mobile touch navigation in a stereoscopic viewing environment for 3D data exploration. IEEE Trans. Vis. Comput. Graph. **22**(5), 1616–1629 (2016)

32. Lundström, C., et al.: Multi-touch table system for medical visualization: application to orthopedic surgery planning. IEEE Trans. Vis. Comput. Graph. **17**(12), (2011). https://doi.org/10.1109/TVCG.2011.224

33. Milgram, P., Colquhoun, H.: A taxonomy of real and virtual world display integration. Mixed Reality Merg. Real Virtual Worlds **1**, 1–26 (1999)

34. Miranda, B.P., Carneiro, N.J.S., dos Santos, C.G.R., de Freitas, A.A., Magalhães, J., Meiguins, B.S., et al.: Categorizing issues in mid-air InfoVis interaction. In: 2016 20th International Conference Information Visualisation (IV), pp. 242–246. IEEE (2016)

35. Ortega, M., Nigay, L.: AirMouse: finger gesture for 2D and 3D interaction. In: Gross, T., et al. (eds.) INTERACT 2009. LNCS, vol. 5727, pp. 214–227. Springer, Heidelberg (2009). https://doi.org/10.1007/978-3-642-03658-3_28

36. Parsons, L.M.: Inability to reason about an object's orientation using an axis and angle of rotation. J. Exp. Psychol. Hum. Percept. Perform. **21**(6), 1259–1277 (1995)

37. Perelman, G., Serrano, M., Raynal, M., Picard, C., Derras, M., Dubois, E.: The roly-poly mouse: designing a rolling input device unifying 2D and 3D interaction. In: Proceedings of the 33rd Annual ACM Conference on Human Factors in Computing Systems, Seoul, Republic of Korea, 18–23 April 2015. https://doi.org/10.1145/2702123.2702244]

38. Rautaray, S.S.: Real time hand gesture recognition system for dynamic applications. IJU Int. J. UbiComp **3**(1), 21–31 (2012)

39. Rudi, D., Giannopoulos, I., Kiefer, P., Peier, C., Raubal, M.: Interacting with maps on optical head-mounted displays. In: Proceedings of the 2016 Symposium on Spatial User Interaction (SUI 2016), pp. 3–12. ACM, New York (2016). https://doi.org/10.1145/2983310.2985747

40. Saidi, H., Serrano, M., Irani, P., Dubois, E.: TDome: a touch-enabled 6DOF interactive device for multi-display environments. In: Proceedings of the 2017 CHI Conference on Human Factors in Computing Systems (CHI 2017), pp. 5892–5904. ACM, New York (2017). https://doi.org/10.1145/3025453.3025661

41. Steven, S., Ishii, H., Schroder, P.: Immersive design of DNA molecules with a tangible interface. In: Proceedings of the Visualization, pp. 227–234. IEEE Computer Society, Los Alamitos (2004). https://doi.org/10.1109/VISUAL.2004.47

42. Serrano, M., Ens, B.M., Irani, P.P.: Exploring the use of hand-to-face input for interacting with head-worn displays. In: Proceedings of the SIGCHI Conference on Human Factors in Computing Systems (CHI 2014), pp. 3181–3190. ACM, New York (2014). https://doi.org/10.1145/2556288.2556984

43. Song, P., Goh, W.B., Fu, C.-W., Meng, Q., Heng, P.-A.: WYSIWYF: exploring and annotating volume data with a tangible handheld device. In: Proceedings of the SIGCHI Conference on Human Factors in Computing Systems (CHI 2011), pp. 1333–1342. ACM, New York (2011). https://doi.org/10.1145/1978942.1979140

44. VandenBos, G.R.(ed): Publication Manual of the American Psychological Association, 6th edn. American Psychological Association, Washington, D.C. (2009)

45. Vo, D.-B., Lecolinet, E., Guiard, Y.: Belly gestures: body centric gestures on the abdomen. In: Proceedings of the 8th Nordic Conference on Human-Computer Interaction: Fun, Fast, Foundational (NordiCHI 2014), pp. 687–696. ACM, New York (2014). https://doi.org/10.1145/2639189.2639210

46. Wagner, J., Nancel, M., Gustafson, S.G., Huot, S., Mackay, W.E.: Body-centric design space for multi-surface interaction. In Proceedings of the SIGCHI Conference on Human Factors in Computing Systems (CHI '13), pp. 1299–1308. ACM, New York (2013). https://doi.org/10.1145/2470654.2466170

47. Wang, C.-Y., Chu, W.-C., Chiu, P.-T., Hsiu, M.-C., Chiang, Y.-H., Chen, M.Y.: PalmType: using palms as keyboards for smart glasses. In: Proceedings of the SIGCHI Conference on Human-Computer Interaction with Mobile Devices and Services (MobileHCI 2015), pp. 153–160 (2015). http://dx.doi.org/10.1145/2785830.2785886

48. Ware, C., Arsenault, R.: Frames of reference in virtual object rotation. In: Proceedings of APGV 2004, pp. 135–141 (2004)

49. Wong, P.C., Zhu, K., Fu, H.: FingerT9: leveraging thumb-to-finger interaction for same-side-hand text entry on smartwatches. In: Proceedings of the 2018 CHI Conference on Human Factors in Computing Systems, p. 178. ACM, April 2018

50. Zhai, S., Milgram, P.: Quantifying coordination in multiple DOF movement and its application to evaluating 6 DOF input devices. In: Karat, C.-M., Lund, A., Coutaz, J., Karat, J. (eds.) Proceedings of the SIGCHI Conference on Human Factors in Computing Systems (CHI 1998), pp. 320–327. ACM Press/Addison-Wesley Publishing Co., New York, NY (1998). https://doi.org/10.1145/274644.274689

51. Zhu, K., Ma, X., Chen, H., Liang, M.: Tripartite effects: exploring users' mental model of mobile gestures under the influence of operation, handheld posture, and interaction space. Int. J. Hum.-Comput. Interact. 33(6), 443–459 (2017)

SplitSlider: A Tangible Interface to Input Uncertainty

Miriam Greis[1], Hyunyoung Kim[1,2(✉)], Andreas Korge[1],
Albrecht Schmidt[1], and Céline Coutrix[1,2]

[1] University of Stuttgart, Stuttgart, Germany
miriam.greis@codecentric.de,
{hyunyoung.kim, celine.coutrix}@imag.fr,
andi-korge@web.de, albrecht.schmidt@um.ifi.lmu.de
[2] Université Grenoble Alpes, CNRS, Grenoble, France

Abstract. Experiencing uncertainty is common when answering question-naires. E.g., users are not always sure to answer how often they use trains. Enabling users to input their uncertainty is thus important to increase the data's reliability and to make better decision based on the data. However, few inter-faces have been explored to support uncertain input, especially with TUIs. TUIs are more discoverable than GUIs and better support simultaneous input of multiple parameters. It motivates us to explore different TUI designs to input users' best estimate answer (value) and uncertainty. In this paper, we first generate 5 TUI designs that can input both value and uncertainty and build low-fidelity prototypes. We then conduct focus group interviews to evaluate the prototypes and implement the best design, *SplitSlider*, as a working prototype. A lab study with *SplitSlider* shows that one third of the participants (4/12) were able to discover the uncertainty input function without any explanation, and once explained, all of them could easily understand the concept and input uncertainty.

Keywords: Tangible user interface · Uncertainty · Input modality · Dial · Slider

1 Introduction

Inputting data into a system while being uncertain about it is a common task. For instance, in a usage survey at the train station, we might get asked about how often we take the train. If we do not take the train regularly, it is difficult to answer a precise value between like "daily" and "never". Our answer might rather be "between every 6 months and weekly, and most often every 2 months". Other examples range from satisfaction surveys in airports to availability inquiry or medical questionnaires, where we might hesitate between 54 kg and 56 kg to input our weight. Currently, respondents are forced to answer a single, precise value even when they are uncertain. However,

Electronic supplementary material The online version of this chapter (https://doi.org/10.1007/978-3-030-29390-1_27) contains supplementary material, which is available to authorized users.

allowing respondents to express their uncertainty about their answer enables the people who requested the questionnaire to have precise and reliable data. For example, intra-participant uncertainty can increase transparency and reliability of the data [22, 25], produce relevant results [2, 10] and help to make better decisions [15, 25], e.g., when designing a fidelity program for a company. Therefore, input mechanisms should allow expressing uncertainty together with the most probable input value.

However, there is a tradeoff between the usage simplicity and the ability to express the uncertainty. Interactions with questionnaires are recommended to be easy to use and discoverable while providing sufficient information [7]. Respondents often stay novices when responding to a survey, as they rarely answer to the exact same questionnaires twice. Hence survey companies either choose to offer a simple interface to encourage as many respondents as possible, or a more complex interface able to gather richer data from fewer participants but with the help of surveyors. Corresponding examples can be found in public transportation surveys, where clients are offered either happy/angry faces buttons in airports, or a surveyor approaching respondents with tablets and multiple questions. Allowing respondents to input uncertainty can increase data reliability, but it can also increase the survey's interface complexity and cost.

This motivates us to balance the simplicity and the ability to express the uncertainty. To achieve this goal, we explore Tangible User Interfaces (TUIs) as a way to offer users with a flexible compromise between simplicity and the ability to express the uncertainty. TUIs are a good candidate to offer a flexible compromise between simplicity and expressiveness, as they were found more discoverable than GUIs [14, 19] and better foster the simultaneous adjustments of parameters than GUIs, even more than multitouch GUIs [20]. TUIs are already used to answer questionnaires, e.g., VoxBox [9] and happy/angry faces tangible buttons in satisfaction surveys in airports [12]. However, these TUIs do not yet allow users to express their uncertainty about their answer.

To balance the simplicity and the ability to express the uncertainty, we explore the design of physical dials and sliders that can capture users' value and uncertainty on one device. We first use Morphees+ [17] features to design five controls based on standard tangible dials and sliders and that can input both value and uncertainty. We then present low-fidelity prototypes and conduct a focus group study to find design requirements for uncertain, tangible input. Following these findings, we present the most promising design: the *SplitSlider*. The *SplitSlider*'s thumb supports entering one value (1-thumb slider) and can be split to additionally enter a probability distribution (2- and 3-thumb slider). We implemented and evaluated a functional tangible prototype. The results of our study show that the use of *SplitSlider* as 1-thumb slider is discoverable. The use of *SplitSlider* as 3-thumb slider is not as discoverable as the 1-thumb mode, but after its explanation, it was found easy to use to express the uncertainty. *SplitSlider* allows users to choose on the fly between its discoverable use as a standard 1-thumb slider or the ability to express their uncertainty as a 3-thumb slider.

2 Related Work

In the following, we present related work addressing the communication of uncertainty, graphical interfaces supporting users to input uncertainty and tangible user interfaces (TUIs) that could support uncertain input.

2.1 Uncertainty and Its Communication

Uncertainty, as described by Pang et al. [23], includes statistical variations or spread, errors and differences, minimum and maximum range values, noise, or missing data. Studies show that decision-making is better supported by capturing, modeling, and visualizing uncertain data [2, 15, 22, 25]. For instance, communicating uncertainty can increase transparency and reliability of weather forecasts [22, 25].

Pang et al. [23] also name three steps of data processing in which uncertainty can be introduced: acquisition, transformation and visualization. In data acquisition, uncertainty is inevitable due to inexact measurements. During transformation, the original data can be altered by a human or an algorithm. Lastly, visualization may introduce uncertainty as it does not usually use the same media as the original data. We focus on the transformation step, where humans alter the data when answering questionnaires. We especially tackle the input of the possible spread of an input value.

Users answer questionnaires in many different ways. Among the most common methods, we find pen and paper, e.g., in trains, and computer systems. The interfaces to computer systems include TUIs, e.g., in airports with happy/angry buttons to give feedback about a service, or GUIs, e.g., to fill forms on the Web. Previous work proposed GUIs for users to express their uncertainty [10]. Among others, they compared 1-thumb, 2-thumb and 3-thumb sliders to input uncertain data:

- The 1-thumb slider allows users to input a probability distribution by moving the single thumb: users move the peak of the distribution, while the standard deviation, skew and kurtosis are fixed.
- The 2-thumb slider allows users to input a probability distribution by independently moving two thumbs: users move the minimum and maximum values, while the peak of the distribution stays in the middle of these two values.
- The 3-thumb slider allows users to input a probability distribution by independently moving three thumbs: users move the minimum, the maximum and the peak values of the distribution.

Our study focuses on gradual transition between certain and uncertain TUI inputs in questionnaire settings. We consider the discoverability of interactions and the compromise between ease of use and expressiveness.

The previous study did not evaluate the discoverability of each slider, as each slider was first explained to participants. The study rather focused on ease of use. Even though the graphical 3-thumb slider was experimentally found the best compromise between easiness and the ability to express uncertainty [10], it offers a *fixed* compromise between easiness and the ability to express uncertainty. Moving the three thumbs in sequence was found cumbersome by the participants, compared to the 1-thumb slider. In addition, the 1-thumb slider was better suited for users with little knowledge in statistics, while the 3-thumb slider was better suited for users with more expertise in statistics. We aim at supporting all levels of expertise in statistics.

To support all levels of expertise in statistics, we explore deformable TUIs that allow both certain and uncertain inputs. Instead of using the one-, two-, three- thumbed sliders, we suggest different deformation of both dials and sliders to learn the advantages and disadvantages of the interactions with them.

2.2   Communicating Input Uncertainty with TUIs

Even though TUIs have not explicitly addressed the problem of inputting uncertain data, prior work could be used for this purpose.

Coutrix et al. suggest a resizable tangible slider [5] to compromise between travel time of the thumb and input accuracy. The design could be also used to input uncertain continuous data. By interpreting the size of the slider as the certainty (smaller size means less precision and thus more uncertainty), this slider would be able to represent a Gaussian distribution (uncertainty $\approx$ standard deviation; value $\approx$ mean).

The Inflatable mouse [18] could be also used for uncertain input. The mouse has an elastic chamber, and users can squeeze it to zoom a map in/out or to change their scroll settings. For uncertain input, users could squeeze the mouse to express their certainty. The device can be used when users are inputting 2D data (e.g., X-Y coordinate values) with 1D uncertainty (same standard deviation in both dimensions).

In our work, we choose to systematically explore the design space of uncertain input TUIs from scratch, rather than starting from the previous work. By doing so, we consider more interactions than extending [5] and squeezing [18] only.

3   Design Exploration for Uncertain Input TUIs

To design deformable tangible input controls that allow the quantitative input of uncertainty, we generated variations of conventional continuous interfaces: dials and sliders. We keep their rotational or linear control to input value and added other modalities to input uncertainty. As an idea generation tool, we used the Morphees+ taxonomy [17]. The taxonomy describes all possible system-actuated shape-changes and manual deformations in a systematic way. The generated designs can express uncertainty in two ways: (1) all the dials and Expandable Slider (Figs. 1 and 2-left) can input uncertainty as an amount centered around the value (i.e., 0–100%), and (2) Split Slider (Fig. 2-right) can input a range of estimated values, independently of the central value. When the device was to input an amount of uncertainty, we mapped the larger surface or open space with more uncertainty and less pressure with more uncertainty for design coherency.

3.1   Dial-Based Designs

Dials are common TUIs for continuous variables. They can have bounded and unbounded input ranges depending on parameters and user needs. In this paper, we choose to use unbounded ranges to emphasis their difference with sliders, which have bounded input ranges. The usual interaction of turning dials changes the best estimate value (≈mean of a desired input). The extended interactions inspired by Morphees+ change uncertainties (≈standard deviation of a desired input, see Fig. 1).

Expandable Dial (Fig. 1-left) was driven by Morphees+' Area feature, which describes changes in area size on a surface. The dial's diameter can be increased or decreased, resulting in the area change at the top of the dial. The larger diameter the dial has, the more uncertainty the users are inputting. When the users are 100% sure (no uncertainty), they can decrease the diameter to the minimum.

Pinch Dial (Fig. 1-middle) includes an open space between the center and one side of the circumference of the dial. The open space can be closed or opened, making the dial looks as a full circle or a sector from the top of the dial. This is inspired by the Closure feature in Morphees+. A larger open space allows to input more uncertainty.

Pressure Dial (Fig. 1-right) can be pressed downwards in addition to the rotation, similarly to Button+ [26]. It was driven by the Strength feature of Morphees+, i.e. the force needed to move a control point to another position. The stronger the dial is pressed, the more certain the input is.

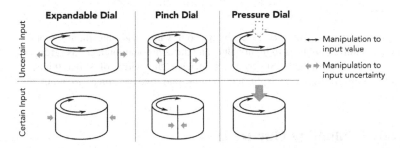

Fig. 1. The dial-based interfaces, enabling both value and uncertainty input. The usual rotation interactions are to input value and the extended inputs (grey arrows) are to input uncertainty. Expandable Dial: users increase the diameter to express more uncertainty. Pinch Dial: users increase the open space – between the center and one side of the circumference – for more uncertainty. Pressure Dial: users enter their uncertainty by adjusting the pressure at the top of the dial (less pressure = more uncertainty).

3.2 Slider-Based Designs

Sliders are widely used in both graphical and tangible user interfaces for ranged variables. The standard interaction of sliding the (central) thumb changes the best estimate value (≈mean of a desired input). The extended interactions inspired by Morphees+ change uncertainty (≈standard deviation of a desired input or range of a desired input).

Expandable Slider (Fig. 2-left) was inspired by Morphees+'s Area feature as was the Expandable Dial. It has one thumb that can be expanded along the slider axis to communicate uncertainty. The center of the thumb represents the best estimate value, and the size of the thumb represents the amount of uncertainty.

Split Slider (Fig. 2-right) was driven by Morphees+'s Modularity, which describes an object's ability to be split into multiple pieces. It has a thumb that can be split into two or three thumbs. In the one-thumb mode, it functions as a standard slider and can input a single, precise value. When the thumb is split into two, the two thumbs input a range of uncertainty, and the center of the range is the input value. When the thumb is split into three, the middle thumb inputs a value while the outer thumbs enter the range of uncertainty.

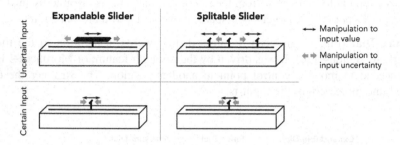

Fig. 2. The slider-based interfaces, enabling both value and uncertainty input. The usual interaction of sliding thumbs is to input value, and the additional interactions (grey arrows) are to input uncertainty. Expandable Slider: users increase the width of slider thumb to increase uncertainty. Split Slider: users split the thumbs into two or three, to input the range of uncertainty.

4   Study Evaluating Our Designs

In this section, we aim at learning design criteria for uncertain input TUIs. We first implement low-fidelity prototypes of the explored design. We then conduct a focus group study where the participants evaluate the low-fidelity prototypes.

4.1   Low-Fidelity Prototype Implementation

We implemented low-fidelity prototypes of all the design explorations, except for the pressure dial, where we used a consumer product [24] (Fig. 3d). We had six prototypes as we had two different prototypes for the Expandable Dial, one that could be stretched (Fig. 3a) and one that could be squeezed (Fig. 3b). Here we briefly describe how they are implemented, and how they work.

Expandable Dial: Stretching Design (Fig. 3a). We use a Hoberman mechanism [13] to create an expandable circular shape. The center of the mechanism is connected to a rotational axis for value input. At the external corners, there are concave disks where users put their fingers on. Users can slightly press them and stretch the fingers inwards or outwards for inputting uncertainty.

Expandable Dial: Squeezing Design (Fig. 3b). We use an aerospace design [11] to fold a paper sheet into a condensed shape. The tension of the paper keeps the dial expanded, and users squeeze it to change the diameter.

Pinch Dial (Fig. 3c). We create six equilateral prisms from a laser cutter and connect them into a hexagon, roughly resembling the round shape of a dial. They are held together with adhesive tape on the outer faces. We place a bent piece of plastic sheet between two prisms to act as a spring to open the dial. Users can close the dial by pinching the device.

Pressure Dial (Fig. 3d). We used a PowerMate Bluetooth [24] for the design. It has a spring inside to push the upper rotational part back up when pressed. The device has only two states of height – pressed and not-pressed.

Expandable Slider (Fig. 3e). We place a bent piece of plastic sheet between two thumbs of a laser-cut slider. The plastic sheet forced the thumbs to separate. Users can squeeze the thumbs for more certain input.

Split Slider (Fig. 3f). There are three thumbs on a laser-cut slider. The thumbs have grooves on them, and users can place a U-shaped plastic piece to combine two thumbs together. Hence, the number of thumbs can be changed between one (certain input), two (range of uncertainty), and three (e.g., range of uncertainty and median).

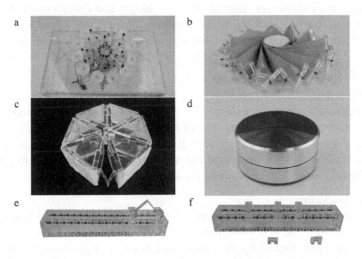

Fig. 3. Low-fidelity prototypes of the explored uncertain input dials/sliders designs. (A) Expandable Dial – Stretching Design (B) Expandable Dial – Squeezing Design, (C) Pinch Dial, (D) Pressure Dial, (E) Expandable Slider, (F) Split Slider.

4.2 Focus Group Study Design

To evaluate our design explorations, we conducted two focus group interviews. For this, we provided the low-fidelity prototypes for the explored designs.

Participants. We recruited twelve participants (10 male, 2 female) between 20 and 34 years old ($M = 24.92$, $SD = 3.65$) via personal invitations in order to have varying backgrounds such as social sciences and natural sciences. Their degrees ranged from A-level to M.Sc.

Task and Procedure. We had two participant groups. Each focus group interview lasted about 30 min. We took pictures and recorded the audio during the interviews.

The participants were asked to sign the consent form and provide their demographic information. The task aimed to evaluate the low-fidelity prototypes when inputting value and uncertainty. The participants were grouped in three pairs, and we introduced our prototypes to the participants. Each pair was assigned a scenario to work for, e.g., inputting an uncertain time. Then each pair was randomly given one of the low-fidelity prototypes, so that three prototypes were given in total. They were asked to write down advantages, disadvantages, improvements and suitability of their respective prototypes for their scenario. Each pair then presented their findings to the others. We then repeated this step with the remaining three prototypes.

4.3   Results

Design Requirements of Uncertain Input TUIs. Using thematic analysis [3], we identified preliminary requirements for designing tangible devices for uncertain input. The requirements confirm previous work for rotational and linear input [16]. It shows that the general purposes of the input interfaces are similar. However, introducing uncertain input to these devices revealed a new requirement that were not considered for dials and sliders and that we present here. There are in total seven requirements, which we grouped in four categories.

Fast Manipulation
R1 **Simultaneous input.** In general, the participants liked to input both value and uncertainty simultaneously as this allowed fast manipulation. For instance, they could change the diameter of both Expandable Dial prototypes while rotating them. However, they complained that the Pinch Dial was difficult to pinch when the opening is no longer between the thumbs and index fingers.

Precise Manipulation
R2 **Small intervals.** Dials were preferred for small intervals in value inputs, because they could have small control display gain. On the other hand, the input ranges of the sliders were limited by the slider sizes, hence a larger control display gain.
R3 **No interference between inputs.** Participants preferred not to have interference between the value and uncertainty inputs, i.e., sometimes they wanted to change either value or uncertainty and did not want to change the other by accident. E.g., when participants changed uncertainty (stretching or squeezing) with Expandable Dial, it could rotate the device slightly. When users grasped Pinch Dial, it applied some pressure on it, and it could cause unwanted change on uncertainty.
R4 **Easy finalization.** The participants needed to finalize the inputs easily. With all designs, users needed another input interface (e.g., button) to finalize their inputs

after changing value or uncertainty. It would require users either: to use another hand to press the button while the users are manipulating the devices, or to take off their hands from the devices and then press the button. We considered the second interaction was easier, as users do not have to keep the tension on the device (e.g., squeezing or pressing the devices) while pressing the button. It allows users to take off their hands from the devices and rest between manipulating the devices. For instance, with the Stretching Design of the Expandable Dial or Split Slider, the participants were able to take off their hands from it and then finalize their inputs.

Observable Uncertainty for Speed and Precision

R5 **Visual feedback.** The participants preferred explicit visual information on the amount of uncertainty. For instance, the participants liked that Split Slider's thumb intervals supported fast and precise interaction through clear visual feedback on the uncertainty.

R6 **Force feedback.** Participants also liked that Pinch Dial and Expandable Slider supported fast and eyes-free interaction through force feedback on uncertainty. The force feedback provided additional information on the visual feedback. The participants also mentioned that using more pressure for more certainty feels intuitive.

Supporting Statistical Knowledge

R7 **Supporting both experts and novices.** The participants liked that the Split Slider supported both novice and expert users through the input mode change between 1 and three thumbs. Novice users with limited knowledge of statistics could use the one- or two-thumb modes. Expert users could use the three-thumb mode, allowing input of probability distributions such as normal distribution.

Evaluation of the Designs. We evaluated the 5 designs based on the design requirements and user comments from the focus group study (see Table 1). The fulfillment of the requirements was sometimes dependent on implementations. For

Table 1. Evaluation of the designs based on the design requirements.

	Expandable Dial	Pinch Dial	Pressure Dial	Expandable Slider	Split Slider
R1. Simultaneous input	✓			✓	
R2. Small intervals	✓	✓	✓		
R3. No interference between inputs					✓
R4. Easy finalization	✓				✓
R5. Visual feedback				✓	✓
R6. Force feedback		✓	✓	✓	
R7. Supporting both experts and novices					✓

instance, the spring of the Pressure Dial was strong, and the participants complained that it is hard to keep the pressure while rotating it. In this case, we clarify that the advantages and disadvantages are related to the implementation methods and discuss other implementation methods that could fulfill the requirements and used for future implementations.

R1 **Simultaneous input.** The Expandable Dial and Expandable Slider fulfilled the requirement. The participants could change the diameter of the Expandable Dial and thumb size of the Expandable Slider while changing the value. Although the interactions of changing uncertainty with the Pinch Dial and the Expandable Dial – Squeezing Design (Fig. 3b) were both through squeezing, it was difficult for the participants to squeeze the Pinch Dial when the open space was not between the thumb of the index finger. With the Pressure Dial, it was not easy to adjust the level of the pressure on it while rotating. It could be improved by replacing the spring to a mechanism that allows a wider range of pressure such as memory foam. The Split Slider did not allow simultaneous input of value and uncertainty, because it had separate thumbs for them.

R2 **Small intervals.** The dial-based designs had boundless input. It allows inputting small intervals and thus users can enter precise values. The slider-based designs had bounded ranges and resulted inevitably in bigger intervals than the dial-based designs. This can be mitigated with a longer input axis for the slider.

R3 **No interference between inputs.** Only the Split Slider fulfilled this requirement, because it had separated thumbs. Both prototypes of the Expandable Dials could cause unwanted change in the value or uncertainty, when the users were changing uncertainty (stretching or squeezing), or value (rotating). It was the same with the Pinch Dial (squeezing and rotating), Pressure Dial (pressing and rotating) and Expandable Slider (squeezing and sliding).

R4 **Easy finalization.** The Expandable Dial – Stretching Design (Fig. 3a) could keep both the angle and the diameter even when the users took off their hands. The Split Slider thumbs stayed still when the users were not manipulating them. They allowed the users to rest their hands while finalizing the inputs (e.g., pressing another button for finalization). On the other hand, the prototypes with spring mechanisms – the Squeezing Design of the Expandable Dial, Pinch Dial, Pressure Dial, and Expandable Slider changed the amount of uncertainty to an initial amount when the users were not manipulating them. Hence the users needed to keep the tension on the device to preserve the wanted amount of uncertainty and would need another hand to press a button for finalization.

R5 **Visual feedback.** The slider-based designs could clearly show the relative amounts of uncertainty. The users could see the ranges of the possible input on the axis of the sliders. The users could see the uncertainty between the thumbs of the Expandable Slider or between the outer thumbs of the Split Slider. The users could see the amount of uncertainty relatively to the ranges. The boundless dials did not provide such clear visual feedback. For instance, it was not clear for the users whether Pinch Dial was 50% or 60% open.

R6 **Force feedback.** This requirement was mutually exclusive with the *R4, easy finalization of inputs*. The spring mechanisms of the Pinch Dial, Pressure Dial and

Expandable Slider could give force feedback but also caused unwanted movement when finalizing input.

R7 **Supporting both experts and novices.** The Split Slider was the only design that had two input modes for uncertainty: ranged input with 2-thumb mode and probabilistic distribution input with 3-thumb mode.

The evaluation shows that the Split Slider performs the best as an uncertain input TUI. It allowed no interference between the value and uncertainty input, and the finalization of the input was easy. It provided a clear visual feedback on the amount of uncertainty. The feature that the slider could have between one and three thumb(s) supported users with both limited and good knowledge of statistics. We decide to build a high-fidelity prototype of the Split Slider to evaluate its ability to capture uncertain input.

5 *SplitSlider*: A Tangible Slider for Uncertain Input

We implement *SplitSlider*, a tangible interface that allows both certain and uncertain input (Figs. 4 and 5). We use three off-the-shelf sliders as sensors (Bourns PSM 100 mm). They are placed next to each other in a box, with dimensions W168 × L68 × D52.5 mm. This gives an illusion that the device is a single slider with three thumbs. We use 3D-printed thumbs to cover the width of all the three sliders. We insert small magnets (Ø5 mm, height 2 mm, strength 520 g) on both sides of the thumbs to give haptic feedback on the (un)combination of the thumbs, and to hold the thumbs together.

The outer thumbs are slightly higher than the middle thumb. When the three thumbs are combined, they create a concave shape that most of slider thumbs have. Each thumb's long edges are cut in order to let users easily put fingers between combined thumbs and split them. Each thumb can travel around 88 mm. We use an Arduino UNO to connect the prototype to a computer.

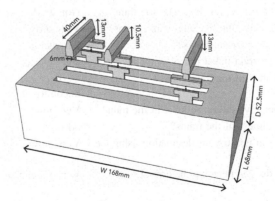

Fig. 4. The schematic of the *SplitSlider* device with dimensions.

Fig. 5. Working prototype of *SplitSlider*. Left: One-thumb mode to input a single value. Right: Separated thumbs for communicate both a value and a range of uncertainty.

6   Evaluation of the *SplitSlider*

The *SplitSlider* aims at balancing simplicity and ability to express the uncertainty. In order to measure how **discoverable** it is, we first asked participants to use it without being provided any explanation. Then, in a second phase, after having explained *SplitSlider* to participants, we measured its perceived **ease of use** and its **ability to express the participants' uncertainty**. Note that we decided to focus on the 1-thumb and 3-thumb modes only in this study to keep the study simple.

6.1   Study Design

We asked participants to use the working *SplitSlider* to answer public transportation survey questions (see Table 2). The questions were selected to have continuous and quantitative answers, which our interface accommodates.

Table 2. Questions used to evaluate the *SplitSlider*, with their respective min and max values.

Question	Min	Max
1. How often do you use the train?	Never	Daily
2. How full is the train in general?	Empty	Very crowded
3. How much do you like traveling with the train?	Not at all	Very much
4. How do you perceive the hygiene within trains?	Very dirty	Very Clean
5. How secure do you feel in trains?	At risk	Very safe
6. How do you find train ticket prices?	Very cheap	Very Expensive
7. How is the comfort of the train chairs?	Very uncomfortable	Very comfortable
8. How do you perceive the noise level in the train?	Very loud	Silent
9. How is the timeliness of the trains?	Always late	Always on time
10. How fast do you get to your destination using the train?	Very slowly	Very fast
11. How reliable do you perceive the arrival time displays?	Very unreliable	Very reliable
12. How modern do you find the trains?	Very old-fashioned	Very modern

As an independent variable, we had the two phases of the study: the phase before and the phase after the explanation of the prototype, to see if the use of the slider is discoverable and participants can use the uncertain input function without explanation. At the end of each phase, the participants filled in a *feedback questionnaire*, including a "Usability Metric for User Experience" (UMUX) questionnaire [8]. We used the same Likert scale for all these feedback questions, ranging from 1 (Strongly Disagree) to 7 (Strongly Agree). The participants then answered the Berlin Numeracy Test [4]. We did it at the end of the experiment not to bias the participants.

6.2 Participants

For the study, we recruited 12 participants (7 males, 5 females). Their ages ranged from 16 to 59 years (M = 35.25, SD = 16.09). None of them had seen or heard of the prototype prior to their participation. The participation was voluntary, and no compensation was given.

6.3 Apparatus

We implemented the software using C++ and openFrameworks. It showed a user interface that displays the questions for the user study and gives feedback of the device interpretation in a form of a gradient visualization on a distant screen (Fig. 6).

Fig. 6. (a) Experimental setup used by the participants. (b) Close-up of the distant visual feedback.

The slider was taped on the table to prevent it from moving. We placed a keyboard on the left side to use its spacebar to finalize the input on the prototype. A 1440 × 900px (∼287 × 180 mm) laptop was positioned approximately 50 cm behind the slider, displaying the questions of the *transportation survey* and a graphical representation of the participant's answer below the questions. The slider on the screen had 1000px width (∼199 mm), and 10 mm movement of a *SplitSlider* thumb moved a cursor on the screen around 114px (∼23 mm). One question was displayed at once. The *feedback questionnaire* was prepared on a separate laptop. The participants swapped between a block of public transportation survey and a block of feedback questionnaire. As advised in previous work [21], landmarks were not present on the slider's scale.

6.4   Tasks and Procedure

The participants signed a consent form and completed a demographic questionnaire. They were given a brief overview of the study procedure. The study was divided into two phases, and the participants answered six questions of the *transportation survey* per phase. The questions' order was pseudo-randomized. The study took around 30 min per participant.

- Phase 1: Participants used the prototype to answer the first six *transportation survey* questions. No explanation of the prototype was provided but they were asked to explore it. The three thumbs were combined at the beginning of the study. Afterwards, they filled in the *feedback questionnaire*.
- Prototype explanation: The instructor explained the operating mode of the prototype to the participants. This included deterministic input with the one-slider mode, the meaning of each individual thumb when split, and an example of how these options could be used.
- Phase 2: The participants answered the last six *transportation survey* questions with the prototype. Following the task, the participants filled in the identical *feedback questionnaire* that they already completed after Phase 1.

6.5   Results

The *SplitSlider* as a 3-thumb slider is not discoverable without explanation to most people. Only one third of the participants were able to discover the splitting function and used it to input uncertainty in Phase 1 (before explanation) (4/12, 33.3%, Fig. 7a). Among the other eight participants, only one managed to split the thumb into three at the last question of Phase 1, but he tried them for ~ 8 s and then put them back together to answer the question. In Phase 2 (after explanation), all participants used three thumbs to answer questions.

Although the questions were calling for similar amount of uncertainty in Phase 1 and in Phase 2, the participants expressed different amount of uncertainty in both phases. Figure 7b shows how much variance (i.e., uncertainty) was expressed in the two phases in a range of [0, 1000].

In Phase 1 the participants used the 3-thumb mode less than in Phase 2. Figure 7c shows how often the different thumb modes were used in the two phases. A chi-square test of independence showed that participants used the 3-thumb mode significantly more often after the explanation ($p < 0.001$), showing that the prototype is not self-explanatory.

The *SplitSlider* is easy to use, both in 1-thumb and 3-thumb modes. The median UMUX score was 87.5 (Q0 = 33.3, Q1 = 75, Q3 = 92.7, Q4 = 95.83, mean = 82.29) in the first phase, with a minor increase to 89.58 in the second phase (Q0 = 29.17, Q1 = 83.33, Q3 = 96.88, Q4 = 100, mean = 85.75, see Fig. 8). Both scores are interpreted as *excellent* [1], and there was no significant difference between the scores ($p = 0.366$). This shows that the *SplitSlider* was found easy to use, whether expressing uncertainty or not.

The major criticisms in the qualitative feedback were the lack of smoothness of the thumb movement and the too large minimum interval between the thumbs. Removing the magnets could solve the problem.

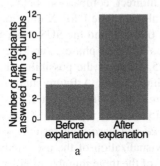
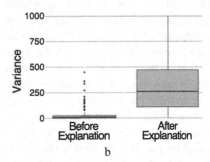

Fig. 7. Thumb usage of the *SplitSlider*, comparing Phase 1: before explanation and Phase 2: after explanation of the three thumbs. (a) Number of participants that answered the questionnaires with three thumbs in each phase. (b) Amount of variance the participants used to answer the questionnaire.

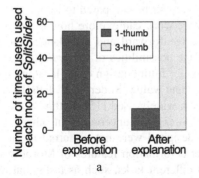
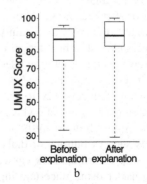

Fig. 8. (a) Counted usage of the 1-thumb and 3-thumb modes in Phase 1: before explanation and Phase 2: after explanation of the three thumbs. (b) UMUX scores comparing Phase 1: before explanation and Phase 2: after explanation of the three-thumb mode for uncertainty input.

7   Discussion and Future Work

The impact of the low fidelity of the prototypes on the results of a qualitative study should be further investigated. The aim of the first study was to find the design requirements and evaluate the low-fidelity prototypes, and we decided not to make obvious improvements, such as making the pressure of the Pressure Dial gradual to make the pressing interaction easy. Although the participants did not make any comments about the gradual pressing and the use of low-fidelity prototypes essential in HCI to evaluate the designs [6, 19], it would be interesting to explore if different prototypes would have resulted different design requirements.

The suggested design requirements are preliminary and should be evaluated. For example, R4 Easy finalization and R6 Force feedback were mutually exclusive, and we do not know which one is more important to novice or expert users. A future evaluation of the requirements can give priority to one over the other requirements.

The UMUX scores of the *SplitSlider* allow indirect comparison between the *SplitSlider* and its graphical counterpart by Greis et al. [10]. The UMUX questionnaire has strong correlation with SUS scores (higher than 0.8 [8]), and the SUS was used in [10]. The mean UMUX score of the *SplitSlider* was 85.75 in phase 2, and the mean SUS score of the graphical 3-thumb slider was 72.5. It shows the possibility that the SplitSlider may offer better usability than the graphical slider. A future study should investigate this comparison and explore different strengths of the two interfaces, such as discoverability, ease of use, accuracy and precision of user inputs.

The results of this work can be *improved*, *refined* and *used*. Our results could be *improved* by conducting further studies. First, the visualization of the user study was based on [21]. We chose not to mention the meaning of the three thumbs, in order to let users freely interpret them, and include users with limited statistical knowledge. We could have added minimum value, most probable value and maximum value to balance between confusion and simplicity.

Our results can be *refined* in three directions. First, future work can check if participants' answers to the transportation survey were accurate by interviewing them before or after the study. Second, the *SplitSlider* can be compared to future alternative techniques to express uncertainty. Third, future work can explore how to improve its discoverability. Further design cues such as feedforward and affordances should be explored to better invite the user to explore the possibilities of the *SplitSlider*.

Our results could be *used* as an inspiration for future design of TUIs supporting the expression of uncertainty together with the input value. Sliders and dials have each their own benefits and drawbacks and are both widely used [15]. Future work should further explore how to introduce the ability to express uncertainty in other common widgets such as buttons or dials. Our dials designed were not preferred in our focus group study. Further work can explore other deformation features of Morphees+ and also consider using uncertain input dials in different tasks, such as tasks that require more accuracy in value input (primary input through precise rotation [16]) and less accuracy in uncertainty input (secondary input).

8   Conclusion

In this paper, we aimed at balancing the simplicity and the ability to express the uncertainty. We explored the design of physical dials and sliders that can capture users' value and uncertainty on one device. We first used Morphees+ [17] features to design 5 controls that can input both value and uncertainty, which are based on standard tangible dials and sliders. We then presented low-fidelity prototypes and conducted a focus group study to find design requirements for uncertain, tangible input. Following these findings, we presented the most promising design: the *SplitSlider*. The *SplitSlider*'s thumb supports entering one value (1-thumb slider) and can be split to additionally enter a probability distribution (2- and 3-thumb slider). We implemented and evaluated a functional tangible prototype. The results of our study show that the use of the *SplitSlider* as 1-thumb slider is discoverable. The use of the *SplitSlider* as 3-thumb slider is not discoverable, but after explanation, it was found easy to use to express the uncertainty. The *SplitSlider* allows users to choose on the fly between its use as a standard 1-thumb slider or the ability to express their uncertainty as a 3-thumb slider. We envision that the *SplitSlider* to be the next standard TUI for uncertain input. In future work we are thus interested in its ability to accurately input uncertainty and compare it with traditional TUIs and other designs such as dial-based ones in different context.

References

1. Bangor, A., Kortum, P., Miller, J.: Determining what individual SUS scores mean: adding an adjective rating scale. J. Usability Stud. **4**(3), 114–123 (2009). http://dl.acm.org/citation.cfm?id=2835587.2835589
2. Boukhelifa, N., Duke, D.J.: Uncertainty visualization: why might it fail? In: CHI 2009 Extended Abstracts on Human Factors in Computing Systems (CHI EA 2009), pp. 4051–4056. ACM, New York (2009). http://dx.doi.org/10.1145/1520340.1520616
3. Braun, V., Clarke, V.: Using thematic analysis in psychology. Qual. Res. Psychol. **3**(2), 77–101 (2006). https://doi.org/10.1191/1478088706qp063oa
4. Cokely, E.T., Galesic, M., Schulz, E., Ghazal, S., Garcia-Retamero, R.: Measuring risk literacy: the Berlin numeracy test. In: Judgment and Decision Making, vol. 7, no.1, p. 25 (2012). (Cited on pp. 23, 39, 40)
5. Coutrix, C., Masclet, C.: Shape-change for zoomable TUIs: opportunities and limits of a resizable slider. In: Abascal, J., Barbosa, S., Fetter, M., Gross, T., Palanque, P., Winckler, M. (eds.) Human-Computer Interaction – INTERACT 2015. Lecture Notes in Computer Science, vol. 9296, pp. 349–366. Springer, Cham (2015). https://doi.org/10.1007/978-3-319-22701-6_27
6. Dow, S.P., Glassco, A., Kass, J., Schwarz, M., Schwartz, D.L., Klemmer, S.R.: Parallel prototyping leads to better design results, more divergence, and increased self-efficacy. ACM Trans. Comput.-Hum. Interact. **17**(4), 18–24 (2010). http://doi.org/10.1145/1879831.1879836
7. Fink, A.: How to Conduct Surveys: A Step-by-Step Guide. Sage Publications, Thousand Oaks (2015)
8. Finstad, K.: The usability metric for user experience. Interact. Comput. **22**(5), 323–327 (2010). ISSN 0953-5438. https://doi.org/10.1016/j.intcom.2010.04.004. (Cited on p. 40)
9. Golsteijn, C., Gallacher, S., Koeman, L., Wall, L., Andberg, S., Rogers, Y., et al.: VoxBox: a tangible machine that gathers opinions from the public at events. In: Proceedings of the Ninth International Conference on Tangible, Embedded, and Embodied Interaction (TEI 2015), pp. 201–208. ACM, New York (2015). https://doi.org/10.1145/2677199.2680588
10. Greis, M., Schuff, H., Kleiner, M., Henze, N., Schmidt, A.: Input controls for entering uncertain data: probability distribution sliders. Proc. ACM Hum.-Comput. Interact. **1**(1), Article 3, 17 p. (2017). http://dx.doi.org/10.1145/3095805
11. Guest, S.D., Pellegrino, S: Inextensional wrapping of flat membranes. In: Motro, R., Wester, T. (eds.) First International Conference on Structural Morphology, Montpellier, 7–11 September, pp. 203–215 (1992)
12. Happy or Not. https://www.happy-or-not.com/en/

13. Hoberman Associates, Inc. http://www.hoberman.com/index.html. Accessed 24 July 2018
14. Horn, M.S., Solovey, E.T., Crouser, R.J., Jacob R.J.K.: Comparing the use of tangible and graphical programming languages for informal science education. In: Proceedings of the SIGCHI Conference on Human Factors in Computing Systems (CHI 2009), pp. 975–984. ACM, New York (2009). https://doi.org/10.1145/1518701.1518851
15. Joslyn, S.L., LeClerc, J.E.: Uncertainty forecasts improve weather-related decisions and attenuate the effects of forecast error. J. Exp. Psychol.: Appl. 18(1), 126–140 (2012). https://doi.org/10.1037/a0025185
16. Kim, H., Coutrix. C., Roudaut, A.: KnobSlider: design of a shape-changing UI for parameter control. In: Proceedings of the 2018 CHI Conference on Human Factors in Computing Systems (CHI 2018), Paper 339, 13 p. ACM, New York (2018). https://doi.org/10.1145/3173574.3173913
17. Kim, H., Coutrix. C., Roudaut, A.: Morphees+: studying everyday reconfigurable objects for the design and taxonomy of reconfigurable UIs. In: Proceedings of the 2018 CHI Conference on Human Factors in Computing Systems (CHI 2018), Paper 619, 14 p. ACM, New York (2018). https://doi.org/10.1145/3173574.3174193
18. Kim, S., Kim, H., Lee, B., Nam, T., Lee, W.: Inflatable mouse: volume-adjustable mouse with air-pressure-sensitive input and haptic feedback. In: Proceedings of the SIGCHI Conference on Human Factors in Computing Systems (CHI 2008), pp. 211–224. ACM, New York (2008). http://dx.doi.org/10.1145/1357054.1357090
19. Lim, Y., Stolterman, E., Tenenberg, J.: The anatomy of prototypes: prototypes as filters, prototypes as manifestations of design ideas. Trans. Comput.-Hum. Interact. (TOCHI) 15(2), 1–27 (2008). https://doi.org/10.1145/1375761.1375762
20. Ma, J., Sindorf, L., Liao, I., Frazier, J.: Using a tangible versus a multi-touch graphical user interface to support data exploration at a museum exhibit. In: Proceedings of the Ninth International Conference on Tangible, Embedded, and Embodied Interaction (TEI 2015), pp. 33–40. ACM, New York (2015). https://doi.org/10.1145/2677199.2680555
21. Matejka, J., Glueck, M., Grossman, T., Fitzmaurice, G.:. The effect of visual appearance on the performance of continuous sliders and visual analogue scales. In: Proceedings of the 2016 CHI Conference on Human Factors in Computing Systems (CHI 2016), pp. 5421–5432. ACM, New York (2016). https://doi.org/10.1145/2858036.2858063
22. Morss, R.E., Demuth, J.L., Lazo, J.K.: Communicating uncertainty in weather forecasts: a survey of the U.S. public. Weather Forecast. 23(5), 974–991 (2008). http://dx.doi.org/10.1175/2008WAF2007088.1
23. Pang, A.T., Wittenbrink, C.M., Lodha, S.K.: Approaches to uncertainty visualization. Vis. Comput. 13(8), 370–390 (1997). https://doi.org/10.1007/s003710050111
24. Powermate Bluetooth. https://griffintechnology.com/us/powermate-bluetooth
25. Roulston, M.S., Bolton, G.E., Kleit, A.N., Sears-Collins, A.L.: A laboratory study of the benefits of including uncertainty information in weather forecasts. Weather Forecast. 21(1), 116–122 (2006). https://doi.org/10.1175/WAF887.1
26. Suh, J., Kim, W., Bianchi, A.: Button+: supporting user and context aware interaction through shape-changing interfaces. In: Proceedings of the Eleventh International Conference on Tangible, Embedded, and Embodied Interaction (TEI 2017), pp. 261–268. ACM, New York (2017). https://doi.org/10.1145/3024969.3024980

The Possibility of Personality Extraction Using Skeletal Information in Hip-Hop Dance by Human or Machine

Saeka Furuichi[✉], Kazuki Abe, and Satoshi Nakamura

Meiji University, Nakano 4-21-1, Nakano-ku, Tokyo, Japan
ev60533@meiji.ac.jp

Abstract. The same dance can give different impressions depending on the way the dancers convey their own emotions and personality through their interpretation of the dance. Beginner dancers who are teaching themselves often search for dance videos online that match their own personality in order to practice and mimic them, but it is not easy to find a dance that suits their own personality and skill level. In this work, we examined hip-hop dance to determine whether it is possible to identify one's own dance from skeleton information acquired by Kinect and whether it is possible to mechanically extract information representing the individuality of dance. Experimental results showed that rich experienced dancers could distinguish their own dances by only skeleton information, and it was also possible to distinguish from averaged skeletal information. Furthermore, we generated features from the skeletal information of dance and clarified that individual dance can be distinguished accurately by machine learning.

Keywords: Dance · Personality · Kinect · Skeleton · Random forest

1 Introduction

In Japan, interest in dance has been increasing, and dance has become mandatory in physical education classes in junior high school since 2012 as a means of improving the ability to express oneself and communicate. In addition, on video sharing websites such as *Nico Nico Douga*, dance videos uploaded by individuals are extremely popular. As the number of people who enjoy dancing increases, there has also been a huge demand for learning to dance well.

One way to improve dancing ability is to go to a dance class and learn from a skilled instructor. However, it has also become common for beginners to watch dance videos online and teach themselves, as a large number of dance videos are available on the Web. The advantages of learning from an instructor are that users can learn and practice choreography that matches their level and they can receive corrections or advice for elements to work on. In contrast, when teaching themselves, they need to

Electronic supplementary material The online version of this chapter (https://doi.org/10.1007/978-3-030-29390-1_28) contains supplementary material, which is available to authorized users.

© IFIP International Federation for Information Processing 2019
Published by Springer Nature Switzerland AG 2019
D. Lamas et al. (Eds.): INTERACT 2019, LNCS 11749, pp. 511–519, 2019.
https://doi.org/10.1007/978-3-030-29390-1_28

find appropriate choreographies themselves, which can be hard due to the difficulty of objectively grasping their own level. It is also somewhat complicated to search for dance videos at the right level from among the overwhelming number of videos on such sites.

Here, personality is one of the key elements of dance. In dance, personality leads to broadening the expression of dance and add uniqueness to one's own dance style. By developing personality, it is possible to dance in a way that is more attractive to the audience. In contrast, when personality is not clearly expressed in dance, even if the dancers have sufficient skill, their performances tend to be superficial and boring. Therefore, it is crucial that dancers develop their own personality.

Although many studies [1, 2] have focused on dance level, very few have focused on the personality of dance, and the specific elements of dance in which personality appears are not yet known. In our past work [3], we investigated whether dancers could distinguish their own dance based only on skeletal information on their movement. The results showed that dancers could subjectively determine their own dance to a certain extent, but the specific movements or features in which personality appeared were not clear. To investigate the personality, we have to clarify which features work most effectively when the system judges the personality mechanically by machine learning.

One way to observe the dancing movement of a person is to use skeletal information of the human body obtained by techniques such as motion capture. In this paper, we examine hip-hop dance to identify whether it is possible to extract personality in dance, specifically, by using approximate skeletal information obtained not from high-precision motion capture but from inexpensive depth cameras such as Kinect and methods that can obtain skeletal information from moving images such as OpenPose [4]. We use only skeletal information and avoid information that is not related to actual dancing, such as physique and appearance. Then, we conduct the experimental test by human and by machine learning techniques, and clarify the possibility to extract personality.

2   Related Work

To extract motion characteristics for hip-hop dance evaluation, Sato et al. [5] focused on hand waves and clarified that the constant propagation speed is the most important factor to feel smooth waving. Chan et al. [1] proposed a method of making an average dancer appear better by using images of the movements of a more skilled dancer. These studies have extensively analyzed the movements and features of dance, but the characteristics and personality of an individual's dancing style remain unclear. In this research, we investigate which elements of dance are related to the personality of dance.

There were several studies on dance education. Yonezawa et al. [6] studied changes in the attitudes of elementary and junior high school teachers who began to add dance to the curriculum, as well as the effects of this curriculum. Yamaguchi et al. [7] proposed a system to support dance education by generating sounds in real time according to the dance, thus supporting the creativity of beginner dancers. Nakamura et al. [8] demonstrated a device that uses vibration to tell the user when to start a dance action, and Yang et al. [9] used VR to show beginners the movements of dance experts and have conducted research to support dance improvement by imitating them. Fujimoto et al. [2] proposed a method for beginners to identify and improve their dance form by mapping their movements to those of more experienced dancers. The purpose of these studies is to support the creativity of dance, to improve individual movements, and to mimic the movements of dance experts. In addition to these studies, it is considered that clarifying the personality of dance will be helpful for improving dance skills and helping beginners make rich expressions that capture their personality. Therefore, in this research, we investigate the personality of dance and use it as a foothold to support dance advancement with personality.

Studies on dance videos have also been increasing as the release of individual dance videos has become more popular. Tsuchida et al. [10] proposed an interactive editing system for multi-view dance videos that can be used to easily create attractive dance videos without requiring video editing expertise. They also developed a new searching system [11] that utilizes the user's dance moves as a query to search for videos that include music appropriate for that style of dancing. However, the system does not take personality into consideration, as it is characterized by whether the choreography itself is similar. The purpose of our study is to clarify how these points are identified in order to consider personality.

On the other hand, researches using body motion data are widely conducted. Mousas [12] studied the structure of dance motions by hidden Markov model (HMMs) and developed a method to make dance motions natural on VR. Aristidou et al. [13] conducted a study on dance motions and emotions using Laban Movement Analysis (LMA) and classified dance motions related to emotions. In addition, Senecal et al. [14] analyzed behavior that expresses the emotion of performers and proposed a system for emotional behavior recognition. These studies investigate human movement, but do not take the performer's personality into account. The purpose of this research is to focus on the personality of the dance movement and to clarify whether there is a difference among people.

3 Dataset Construction for Dance Skeleton

In this research, we investigate whether information that expresses the personality of dance can be extracted from the skeletal information of dance. We worked with participants who have dance experience and constructed the skeletal information (dance skeleton dataset) of actual dance.

Skeletal information of the human body is extracted from dancing movement by using Kinect, a motion sensor device. The participants were 22 university students (seven males, 15 females) in a university dance club with dance experience ranging from five months to six years (average: 2.4 years). We asked them to dance about 15 s (seven bars) of specific choreography five times and used Kinect to extract skeletal information. The information obtained from Kinect was composed of the 15-point 3D coordinates shown in Fig. 1 (left).

The choreography used to construct the dataset is classified as hip-hop dance and is characterized by a large number of movements featuring the entire body, including raising the legs, squatting, turning, and hitting the chest. The participants practiced this choreography on a daily basis. The music used was Traila$ong's "Gravity".

We used a large space for the experiment and the participants danced in front of the Kinect. These participants all belong to the same dance club at Meiji University and had 1-h practice sessions twice a week for three weeks, so their dance performance during the data collection was sufficient. Each participant danced five times and then answered a brief questionnaire about their dance experience. There was a short break between each dance performance. In total, the dataset consisted of 110 items of data comprising five 15-s dance samples for each of the 22 participants.

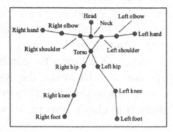 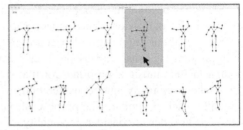

Fig. 1. (left) Fifteen points of skeletal information captured by Kinect. (right) Screenshot of the experiment system.

4   Dance Personality Estimation by Subjective Evaluation

In this paper, we investigate whether it is possible to distinguish one's own dance from the video of only the skeletal information. In addition, to clarify where the personality of the dance appears in the skeletal information, we administered interviews to determine the distinction. Here, participants were divided into two groups: 11 with little dance experience (average 1.0 year) and 11 with relatively rich dance experience (average 3.6 years). This was done because the manner of expressing personality differs depending on the level of dance experience.

In the experiment, as shown in Fig. 1 (right), we prepared a task in which participants were asked to select which dance they felt was their own from among dance images of several people presented as skeletal information only. Twelve different dance images were presented: 11 performed by the participants in that group and one from a member of the other group who had the most similar amount of dance experience. This was done to increase the number of participants which close to the dance level. For the selection of dance, participants were asked to rank the skeletons that they thought were similar to their own dance style from first to third place. The experiment was conducted five times for each item of skeletal information and average skeletal information, and the position of the skeleton dance on the screen was randomized each time. Scores were determined in accordance with the order provided by the participants, and the average score of each skeleton was considered. The score was 5 points for first place, 3 points for second place, and 1 point for third place.

The experimental result showed that among the participants with little dance experience, two out of the 11 participants gave their own dance of skeletal information the highest score and one out of 11 participants gave their own dance of average skeletal information the highest score. In addition, while there were few participants who could accurately identify their own dance, those who did not choose their own dance tended to choose one dancer (i.e., the same one) exclusively. On the other hand, among the participants with rich dance experience, five out of the 11 participants gave their own dance of skeletal information the highest score and six of the 11 gave their own dance of average skeletal information the highest score. This indicates that, compared to the dancers with little experience, these participants were able to identify their own dance with greater accuracy. Also, here too, participants who did not choose their own dance tended to choose one person exclusively.

After the experiments, we conducted an interview to precisely see which spot in the skeletal information was judged to be similar to one's own dance style. From the interview, we found that participants with rich experience tended to respond by designating the factors in detail. For example, seven out of the 11 participants with little experience stated simply that they moved specific body parts (e.g., arms, knees, and whole body), and six mentioned the shape of the hand (e.g., position and bending condition). In contrast, among the participants with rich experience, ten of the 11 made comments on the hand shape (e.g., the position and angle of the hand), and most of them explained they felt that their personality was likely to appear in the hand position. Six of the 11 stated that they used speed for parts on the outer side of the body (e.g., hands and feet) and whole body. Moreover, four of the five participants who had correctly identified their own dance in the skeletal information experiment commented about the characteristics of their own dance style.

The participants with rich experience provided more detail about their selection process and had a higher selection accuracy. From this, we can assume that they understood the features of their own dances more firmly. In particular, ten of the 11 mentioned hand shape, which indicates that their personality tends to appear in hand. Moreover, none of them mentioned movement, which was the most frequent response among the less experienced participants, so we can conclude that these experienced participants place more emphasis on individual form than on movement style.

5 Dance Personal Estimation with Machine Learning

In order to clarify whether the skeletal information can convey the personality of the dancer, we analyzed whether it is possible to distinguish the individuals with machine learning from the skeletal information obtained using Kinect. Here, we conducted an experiment to classify the dance for each individual by generating feature quantities based on the discrimination factors used by the participants obtained from the interview in the subjective evaluation experiment.

According to the responses to the interview in the subjective evaluation experiments, many participants relied on the shapes of their hands and feet to identify their own dance from others'. Therefore, for the dance in the constructed dataset, we calculated the joint angles of six places of the elbow, the shoulder, and the knee on the left and right for each frame based on the 3D skeletal coordinates of 15 points obtained by Kinect. Next, we generated a 6D vector by calculating the average of angles every second (30 frames). Here, since the dance samples in the dataset are less than 15 s long, these 6D vectors can be acquired for up to 14 s. We combined 84 dimensions of 14 s × 6 dimensions into one and generated them as angle features. At this time, as a countermeasure for noise, we did two approaches, linear interpolation from the frame before and after the defect frame, and smoothing by the method of exponential moving average.

We also generated feature values for motions in which the response was high among participants with little experience. Here, with regard to the 3D skeletal information of the chest and the 13 points of the left and right hands, elbows, hips, knees, and feet, the amount of spatial movement of each skeletal point in one second was acquired as a 13D vector. As with the angular features, the dance samples in the dataset are less than 15 s long, so these 13D vectors can be obtained for up to 14 s. We combined 182 dimensions of 14 s × 13 dimensions into one and generated them as movement features. For these two features, we compare the estimation accuracy when each feature is used.

We divided participants into two groups—those with little dance experience (the same individuals as in the experiment in Sect. 4) and those with rich experience—to determine how well dancers can be identified from skeletal information.

We used a random forest as the classifier algorithm. Three dances out of five were used as training data and the remaining two as test data. Each group includes 60 data of 12 persons × 5 times, and for the two dances used as test data, 36 data are training data, 24 data are test data, and 12-value classification learning is performed. In addition, since $_5C_2 = 10$ 10 combinations of training and test data can be made from data per person, we learned ten patterns each time and calculated the average accuracy rate and classification probability from the results.

	a's	b's	c's	d's	e's	f's	g's	h's	i's	j's	k's	l's
a	0.25	0.07	0.10	0.05	0.05	0.09	0.08	0.07	0.05	0.09	0.05	0.06
b	0.05	0.40	0.06	0.04	0.07	0.07	0.06	0.07	0.02	0.06	0.04	0.06
c	0.08	0.07	0.27	0.03	0.04	0.08	0.07	0.07	0.06	0.09	0.06	0.07
d	0.06	0.06	0.04	0.31	0.08	0.06	0.08	0.08	0.07	0.06	0.06	0.03
e	0.05	0.08	0.04	0.07	0.26	0.08	0.09	0.06	0.05	0.08	0.09	0.05
f	0.07	0.06	0.06	0.04	0.06	0.24	0.09	0.10	0.04	0.09	0.08	0.06
g	0.06	0.06	0.05	0.06	0.08	0.09	0.30	0.07	0.05	0.07	0.07	0.07
h	0.05	0.07	0.06	0.05	0.05	0.10	0.07	0.26	0.06	0.08	0.08	0.09
i	0.05	0.03	0.07	0.07	0.05	0.07	0.07	0.07	0.28	0.11	0.09	0.04
j	0.06	0.05	0.08	0.04	0.06	0.09	0.06	0.09	0.07	0.26	0.08	0.06
k	0.03	0.03	0.05	0.04	0.07	0.08	0.06	0.07	0.05	0.07	0.38	0.06
l	0.04	0.06	0.06	0.02	0.05	0.05	0.07	0.10	0.03	0.07	0.08	0.36

	A's	B's	C's	D's	E's	F's	G's	H's	I's	J's	K's	L's
A	0.26	0.04	0.04	0.14	0.09	0.05	0.04	0.08	0.09	0.08	0.05	0.03
B	0.03	0.37	0.07	0.04	0.04	0.07	0.06	0.05	0.05	0.06	0.09	0.06
C	0.04	0.07	0.32	0.04	0.04	0.05	0.09	0.03	0.06	0.10	0.08	0.08
D	0.14	0.04	0.05	0.24	0.10	0.05	0.05	0.08	0.10	0.08	0.05	0.03
E	0.08	0.04	0.04	0.09	0.37	0.08	0.03	0.07	0.08	0.07	0.04	0.02
F	0.05	0.07	0.05	0.05	0.08	0.34	0.03	0.05	0.08	0.09	0.09	0.03
G	0.04	0.07	0.09	0.04	0.03	0.05	0.24	0.06	0.06	0.09	0.09	0.15
H	0.09	0.07	0.03	0.09	0.08	0.06	0.05	0.26	0.10	0.08	0.06	0.03
I	0.08	0.05	0.06	0.09	0.08	0.07	0.05	0.11	0.18	0.10	0.08	0.05
J	0.08	0.05	0.08	0.07	0.07	0.08	0.07	0.07	0.09	0.20	0.08	0.06
K	0.05	0.09	0.08	0.04	0.04	0.08	0.07	0.06	0.08	0.09	0.25	0.08
L	0.03	0.08	0.10	0.03	0.03	0.04	0.16	0.05	0.06	0.08	0.10	0.25

Fig. 2. (left) The average classification probability of learning using angle features for participants with little experience. (right) The average classification probability of learning using angle features for participants with rich experience.

Figure 2 shows the classification probabilities when learning is performed using angle features. The columns in the table indicate the participants to be classified and the rows show each dance. For example, in the left table, when "a" in the column and "a's (dance)" in the row are selected, the classifier estimated the dance of participant "a", then it is determined that participant "a" has a probability of 0.25 on average. The total of the table row direction is 1.0. The classifier outputs the most probable of these classification probabilities as the estimation result. The stronger the background color is, the higher the classification probability of each participant is. According to the tables, in both groups, each participant's own dance had the highest classification probability. In addition, the average accuracy rate for ten iterations of learning was high: 99.1% for the group with little experience and 92.0% for the group with rich experience. From these results, we conclude that it is possible to distinguish individuals by machine learning, with joint angles as feature quantities. In addition, similar results were obtained with other classifications used movement amount of the skeleton point.

Table 1. The average classification accuracy by machine learning in each feature.

	Little experience	Rich experience
Angle feature	99.1%	92.0%
Movement feature	95.4%	89.5%

Table 1 shows the average classification accuracy in each experience group and by using each feature. From these results, we conclude that it is possible to distinguish individuals using machine learning, with joint angles as feature quantities.

Here, the random forest is ensemble learning that learns by a set of decision trees, and the importance of each feature vector can be evaluated by comparing each decision tree. We therefore measured which feature vector was effective for the features in each learning. Regarding angle features, we found that the angle of the left and right knees is a feature vector with relatively high importance for both groups. In addition, regarding the movement feature, the importance of the feature vectors in the upper body (such as the chest and right shoulder) tended to be high for both groups.

6 Discussion

Here, we discuss the personality of dance on the basis of the results of the subjective evaluation in Sect. 4 and the results of the machine learning in Sect. 5.

In the subjective evaluation, we observed a tendency to continuously select the movement of a specific participant, and it became clear that it was possible to find features subjectively from dances with only skeletal information. However, not many of the participants could correctly identify their own dance. Of course, it can be difficult to objectively grasp one's own dance in ordinary practice, even if you have rich experience in dance. On the other hand, in the experiment by machine learning, although learning was performed using two features (angle and movement amount), it was possible to discriminate dances with high accuracy regardless of the feature used. We conclude that there are many dancers who cannot recognize their own personality despite the existence of characteristics and movements that point to this personality, and that it should become easier to find the personality of one's own dance by using these characteristic features.

Next, we consider the position and elements of the body where personality tends to appear. In the subjective evaluation, most of the participants concentrated on the hands in the skeleton regardless of experience, and more than half judged the balance of the whole body. In addition, it became clear that the participants with less experience placed more emphasis on movement and the participants with more experience placed emphasis on the shape. On the other hand, in the experiment by machine learning, the learning by angle features emphasized the shape of the foot, and in the learning by movement amount features, the movement of the chest was emphasized. Two factors—the degree of bending of the foot and the movement of the chest (upper body)—are considered to correspond to the balance of the whole body emphasized in the subjective evaluation, because the ratio occupied in the video used for the subjective evaluation is large. On the other hand, with regard to the hand having the highest number of mentions from participants in the subjective evaluation, which was not emphasized in the experiments using machine learning, there is a possibility that personality appears in the direction and shape of their hand rather than its position. Therefore, by focusing on the state of hands, it is possible that the individuality can be further highlighted.

In order to make use of the results of this study, there are several challenges to be overcome in exploring dance videos for learning independently. In this research, we asked participants to dance to specific choreography, and we performed experiments from two points of view, namely, subjective evaluation and machine learning. However, when we actually explore dance videos, the dancers use different choreographies for each video. Therefore, it is necessary not only to be able to identify the person by comparing dances with the same choreography but also to be able to determine the individuality of the person in completely different choreography. It is therefore necessary to conduct additional experiments with a greater variety of choreography, and to clarify whether it is possible to identify the dancer in such cases. We also need to acquire personality and implement a mechanism to search for dance videos based on this.

7 Conclusion

In this paper, we investigated hip-hop dance to determine whether it is possible to extract personality in dance from skeletal information acquired by Kinect. In a subjective evaluation, we found that more experienced participants could distinguish their own dance from only the skeletal information, and they could also be judged from the average skeleton as well. We also found that the main points for judging dance differed depending on the level of experience: for example, less experienced participants tended to emphasize the way of movement and more experienced ones emphasized the hand shape. In dance estimation by machine learning using skeletal features, we found through learning and comparing with two features, namely, angle and movement amount, that it is possible to discriminate individuals with high accuracy using either of them. Overall, using the angle feature was more accurate, as it is close to the judgment criteria of the experienced participants.

In the future, we intend to clarify what constitutes personality in dance by extending these analyses and to further examine the application method of the extracted personality. We will also consider a method to search for dance videos that have completely different choreography but that match the personality of the user.

Acknowledgments. This work was supported in part by JST ACCEL Grant Number JPMJAC1602, Japan.

References

1. Chan, C., Ginosar, S., Zhou, T., Efros, A.A.: Everybody dance now. In: arXiv 2018, vol. 1, no. 1 (2018)
2. Fujimoto, M., Tsukamoto, M., Terada, T.: A dance training system that maps self-images onto an instruction video. In: The Fifth International Conference on Advances in Computer-Human Interactions (ACHI2012), pp. 309–314, Valencia (2012)
3. Saito, H., Maki, Y., Tsuchiya, S., Nakamura, S.: Can people sense their personalities only by watching the movements of their skeleton in street dancing performances? In: Kurosu, M. (ed.) HCI 2018. LNCS, vol. 10903, pp. 344–354. Springer, Cham (2018). https://doi.org/10.1007/978-3-319-91250-9_27
4. Cao, Z., Simon, T., Wei, S.E., Sheikh, Y.: Real time multi-person 2D pose estimation using part affinity fields. In: Computer Vision and Pattern Recognition (CVPR2017), Honolulu (2017)
5. Sato, N., Imura, S., Nunome, H., Ikegami, Y.: Motion characteristics in hip hop dance underlying subjective evaluation of the performance. In: The 30th Conference of the International Society of Biomechanics in Sports (ISBS2012), pp. 17–20, Melbourne (2012)
6. Yonezawa, M.: The investigations on the teachers' attitudes to dance in the face of scholastic requirement of dance in middle schools in Heisei 24 (2012) academic year. In: Studies in Humanities of Kanagawa University, vol. 178, pp. 53–80, Kanagawa (2012)
7. Yamaguchi, T., Kadone, H.: Supporting creative dance performance using a grasping-type musical interface. In: 2014 IEEE International Conference on Robotics and Biomimetics (ROBIO2014), Bali (2014)
8. Nakamura, A., Tabata, S., Ueda, T., Kiyofuji, S., Kuno, Y.: Dance training system with active vibro-devices and a mobile image display. In: 2005 IEEE/RSJ International Conference on Intelligent Robots and Systems (IROS 2005), Edmonton (2005)
9. Yang, U., Kim, G.: Implementation and evaluation of "Just Follow Me": an immersive, VR-based, motion-training system. Presence **11**(3), 304–323 (2002)
10. Tsuchida, S., Fukayama, S., Goto, M.: Automatic system for editing dance videos recorded using multiple cameras. In: Cheok, A.D., Inami, M., Romão, T. (eds.) ACE 2017. LNCS, vol. 10714, pp. 671–688. Springer, Cham (2018). https://doi.org/10.1007/978-3-319-76270-8_47
11. Tsuchida, S., Fukayama, S., Goto, M.: Query-by-dancing: a dance music retrieval system based on body-motion similarity. In: Kompatsiaris, I., Huet, B., Mezaris, V., Gurrin, C., Cheng, W.-H., Vrochidis, S. (eds.) MMM 2019. LNCS, vol. 11295, pp. 251–263. Springer, Cham (2019). https://doi.org/10.1007/978-3-030-05710-7_21
12. Mousas, C.: Performance-driven dance motion control of a virtual partner character, pp. 57–64 (2018)
13. Aristidou, A., Charalambous, P., Chrysanthou, Y.: Emotion analysis and classification: understanding the performers' emotions using the LMA entities. Comput. Graph. Forum **34**, 262–276 (2015)
14. Senecal, S., Cuel, L., Aristidou, A., Thalmann, N.: Continuous body emotion recognition system during theater performances. Comput. Anim. Virtual Worlds **27**, 311–320 (2016)

Courses

Introduction to Automation and to Its Potential for Interactive Systems Design

Philippe Palanque, Célia Martinie[(✉)], and Elodie Bouzékri

ICS-IRIT – Université Paul Sabatier Toulouse 3, Toulouse, France
{palanque, martinie, bouzekri}@irit.fr

Abstract. Automation is pervasive and polymorph but still usually not considered as a design option per se when designing interactive systems. This course takes a practical approach to introduce automation, its principles and how this can be used for the design of interactive systems. This one unit course introduces the automation from a Human Factors perspective (such as Levels of Automation) to highlight its foundations, its limitations and how recent research contributions demonstrate the high potential of automation as a design option for interaction and interactive systems designers. The course highlights success stories from various domains such as aviation, power plants and air traffic management. Beyond, it highlights limitations and failures from automotive, aviation (MCAS) and everyday life products (e.g. public spaces appliances). Course attendees will learn what is automation and how this high-level concept can be decomposed into practical elements that can be fruitfully used in interactive systems designs.

Keywords: Automation · Interaction design · Interactive systems design · Assessment of partly-autonomous systems

1 Introduction

While early approaches in automation were focusing on allocating basic functions to the best player (e.g. Fitts' approach Machine Are Better At – Men Are Better At) [5], this course focuses on the use of the concept of automation for interaction design and for interactive systems designs. The course promotes the point of view of automation as a design alternative resulting on the migration of actions previously performed by users to actions performed by a system. Current push in automation is towards fully autonomous systems (such as google cars) raising critical issues such as: how to make it possible to users to foresee future states of the automation, how to disengage automation or how to make sure that users are able to take over when automation fails …. When higher automation levels are considered, users' activity gets closer to supervision, which is a different interaction paradigm. Supervision activities are very different from directly performing activities and the migration of activities to the system might have severe consequences, in terms of overall performance of the couple (user, system), in terms of skilling (and especially deskilling) [9], in terms of errors related to the very nature of human behavior [8], in terms of training [4]… This course promotes **automation as a mean** and **not automation as a goal** and takes a practical approach to

D. Lamas et al. (Eds.): INTERACT 2019, LNCS 11749, pp. 523–526, 2019.
https://doi.org/10.1007/978-3-030-29390-1_29

introduce attendees to the principles, methods and tools for the design and the assessment of automation within the design of interactive systems.

2 Contribution and Benefit

This course intends to provide newcomers with background in automation. It provides an overview on how the recent advances in automation can be exploited to design and assess interactive systems. This course will also provide material for lecturers who want to include automation in their HCI courses. Finally, the course will provide examples from various domains including aviation, Air Traffic Management, Automotive highlighting both successes and failures of automation. Concrete examples and exercises will also be provided to support the application of the course elements to practical cases.

3 Learning Objectives

On completion of this tutorial, attendees will:
- Know the intrinsic and extrinsic characteristics of automation, [2, 5, 10]
- Be able to use AFAR paradigm (Allocation of Functions, Authority and Responsibility) [13] when designing and assessing interactive systems,
- Know many examples on how automation has been used in various domains such as automotive, aviation, Air Traffic Control, space domain … [11]
- Know and understand that automation is already pervasive in interactive systems and that the consequences are usually underestimated, [2]
- Have experience in analyzing an interactive systems focusing on the tasks users have to perform with it and how automation impacts user's work and activities,
- Know the danger and the benefits of more automation in interactive systems [12].

4 Description and Content

This course focuses on the foundations of automation and how this concept can be used while designing and assessing interactive systems
- Introduction to automation its basic principles and how this concept can be decomposed in components [10] …),
- Basic principles for describing user activity and tasks (hierarchical view on human activities, abstraction and refinement, temporal ordering, objects, information and knowledge … [6]) and also about human activity with a focus on automation [14],
- Overview of automation designs and how they are pervasive in interactive systems and interaction techniques as well as their desired properties (intelligibility, transparency [2], …)

- Overview of automation principles that are used and deployed in various domains as well as their intended objectives (enhance user, protect the user via safety or security nets, increase user comfort, entertain used, protect against automation …).
- List of design principles for the identification of users' activities that could be good candidates for task migration towards automation, authority sharing, impact of automation degradation on tasks performance) [7].
- Taking into account human errors [1] at design time as well as possible degradation of automation [3] to assess relevance of automation in a given context (identification of types, location and likelihood of human errors)

5 Presentation

Lecture with slides, demonstrations and practical exercises. The lecture will include demonstration of various partly-autonomous systems that will be used to apply the principles introduced in the course. Detailed examples will be presented on large case studies in various application domains such as Air Traffic Control, Aircraft cockpits and Space Ground Segments, we will demonstrate how to deal with complex work settings.

6 Audience and Prerequisite

This course is open to researchers, practitioners, educators and students of all experience levels. No specific skills or knowledge are required beyond a background in User Centered Design. Paper [14] should be read before attending the lecture.

References

1. Fahssi, R., Martinie, C., Palanque, P.: Enhanced task modelling for systematic identification and explicit representation of human errors. In: Abascal, J., Barbosa, S., Fetter, M., Gross, T., Palanque, P., Winckler, M. (eds.) INTERACT 2015. LNCS, vol. 9299, pp. 192–212. Springer, Cham (2015). https://doi.org/10.1007/978-3-319-22723-8_16
2. Bernhaupt, R., Cronel, M., Manciet, F., Martinie, C., Palanque, P.: Transparent automation for assessing and designing better interactions between operators and partly-autonomous interactive systems. In: ATACCS 2015. ACM DL (2015)
3. Fayollas, C., Martinie, C., Palanque, P., Deleris, Y., Fabre, J-C., Navarre, D.: An approach for assessing the impact of dependability on usability: application to interactive cockpits. In: IEEE European Dependable Computing Conference, pp. 198–209 (2014)
4. Martinie, C., Palanque, P., Navarre, D., Winckler, M., Poupart, R.: Model-based training: an approach supporting operability of critical interactive systems. In: ACM SIGCHI EICS, pp. 53–62 (2011)
5. Fitts, P.M.: Human engineering for an effective air navigation and traffic control system. National Research Council, Washington, DC (1951)

6. Martinie, C., Palanque, P., Ragosta, M., Fahssi, R.: Extending procedural task models by systematic explicit integration of objects, knowledge and information. In: European Conference on Cognitive Ergonomics, pp. 23–34. ACM DL (2013)
7. Martinie, C., Palanque, P., Barboni, E., Ragosta, M.: Task-model based assessment of automation levels: application to space ground segments. In: IEEE System Man and Cybernetics Conference, pp. 3267–3273 (2011)
8. Mackworth, N.H.: The breakdown of vigilance during prolonged visual search. Q. J. Exp. Psychol. 1, 6–21 (1948)
9. Cavestro, W.: Beyond the deskilling controversy. Comput. Integr. Manuf. Syst. 3(1), 38–46 (1990)
10. Palanque, P.: Engineering automations: from a human factor perspective to design, implementation and validation challenges. In: EICS, pp. 2:1–2:2 (2018)
11. Meschtscherjakov, A., et al.: Interacting with autonomous vehicles: learning from other domains. In: CHI Extended Abstracts. ACM DL (2018)
12. Palanque, P., Martinie, C., Fayollas, C.: Automation: danger or opportunity? Designing and assessing automation for interactive systems. Course, CHI Extended Abstracts (2018)
13. Bouzekri, E., Canny, A., Martinie, C., Palanque, P., Gris, C.: Using task descriptions with explicit representation of allocation of functions, authority and responsibility to design and assess automation. In: IFIP Working Conference on Human Work and Interaction Design, pp. 36–56 (2018)
14. Parasuraman, R., Sheridan, T.B., Wickens, C.D.: A model for types and levels of human interaction with automation. IEEE Trans. Syst. Man Cybern. Part A: Syst. Hum. 30(3), 286–297 (2000)

Introduction to Data Visualization

Simone Diniz Junqueira Barbosa$^{(\boxtimes)}$ ⓘ and Gabriel Diniz Junqueira Barbosa ⓘ

Pontifical Catholic University of Rio de Janeiro (PUC-Rio),
Rua Marques de Sao Vicente, 225, Gavea, Rio de Janeiro, RJ, Brazil
`simone@inf.puc-rio.br`, `gabrieldjb@gmail.com`

Abstract. The objective of this course is to provide students, young researchers, and practitioners without a formal education in data visualization with an introduction and overview of the field. In addition to introducing basic concepts, the course will present diverse visualizations for different kinds of data (*e.g.*, categorical, numeric, hierarchic, network, temporal, and spatial data); and for different kinds of visualization tasks and goals (*e.g.*, retrieve value, filter, compute derived value, find extremum, sort, determine range, characterize distribution, find anomalies, cluster, and correlate). We will also discuss the role of data stories to convey data-driven insights.

Keywords: Data visualization · Data types · Visualization tasks · Storytelling with data

1 Learning Objectives

In this course, students will learn how to produce data-driven visualizations for both exploration and communication purposes, given the types of data and visualization goals and tasks. By exploring real-world examples, they will learn to identify and avoid misleading visualizations. They will also learn how to convey their insights through data stories.

2 Content

The course material is divided into seven sections:

1. **Why visualize:** this section argues for the need to visualize data to improve understanding and communication. By integrating statistical data and visualizations, we show how we are able to improve the reader's understanding of the underlying information.
2. **Human perceptual system:** this section presents basic concepts of the human perceptual system and how they apply to visualization, such as visual variables – *e.g.*, color (hue, luminance, and saturation), size (length, height, width, area), shape, orientation, opacity, position – and Gestalt principles.

© IFIP International Federation for Information Processing 2019
Published by Springer Nature Switzerland AG 2019
D. Lamas et al. (Eds.): INTERACT 2019, LNCS 11749, pp. 527–529, 2019.
https://doi.org/10.1007/978-3-030-29390-1_30

3. **Types of data:** this section introduces different types of data, *e.g.*, categorical, numeric, hierarchic, network, temporal, and spatial data, illustrated through real-world examples.

4. **Basic charts:** this section describes widely used charts and some of their variations, *e.g.*, bar chart, line chart, histogram, dot plot, box plot, scatter plot, bubble plot, maps, trees, networks, and heat maps. We show good and bad examples, and discuss common mistakes and misleading visualizations.

5. **Visualization tasks:** this section describes how the set of suitable visualizations is determined by the combination of data types and visualization tasks – *e.g.*, retrieve value, filter, compute derived value, find extremum, sort, determine range, characterize distribution, find anomalies, cluster, and correlate [1]. As in some situations a single visualization is insufficient, we explore how visualizations may be combined to achieve an exploration or a communication goal.

6. **Interactivity in data visualization:** this section presents some interaction mechanisms for manipulating data visualizations, *e.g.*, filtering, zooming, brushing and linking. For high-volume data, complex data, or complex visualization tasks, interactivity is essential for proper understanding.

7. **Storytelling with data:** this section discusses how to tell stories by using visualizations within a narrative so as to communicate data-driven insights. As humans learn better through stories, data stories may create empathy and be more memorable than isolated data facts and visualizations.

For pedagogical reasons, these sections will not be presented in a strict sequence, *i.e.*, content from different sections may be intermingled.

3   Course Format

The course is formatted as a 3-h lecture split in two sessions, with several examples given throughout.

The examples will be explored in both top-down and bottom-up approaches: (i) by presenting students with visualization goals, we will explore how to produce data-driven visualizations to achieve them; and (ii) by presenting students with (well and poorly designed) visualizations, they will be provoked to reflect on their quality and consequences, as well as discuss alternative visualizations to achieve the same goal.

All slides, public data sets, and code (in R and Python) used in the course will be provided beforehand, as well as instructions on how to install the (open source) software necessary to run the examples.

4   Intended Audience

The intended audience is made up of students, young researchers, and professionals in information and communication technology-related fields who have not yet had a systematic exposure to data visualization. As an introductory course, it is not suitable for people with advanced knowledge of visualization concepts and techniques.

Programming knowledge of R and Python is not required, but students are encouraged to bring their own laptops to run the course examples throughout the sessions.

References

1. Amar, R., Eagan, J., Stasko, J.: Low-level components of analytic activity in information visualization. In: 2005 IEEE Symposium on Information Visualization, INFOVIS 2005, pp. 111–117, October 2005. https://doi.org/10.1109/INFVIS.2005.1532136
2. Berinato, S.: Good Charts: The HBR Guide to Making Smarter, More Persuasive Data Visualizations. Harvard Business Review Press, Boston (2016)
3. Bertin, J.: Semiology of Graphics: Diagrams, Networks, Maps, 1st edn. Esri Press, Redlands (2010)
4. Cairo, A.: The Functional Art: An Introduction to Information Graphics and Visualization, 1st edn. New Riders, Berkeley (2012)
5. Cairo, A.: The Truthful Art: Data, Charts, and Maps for Communication, 1 edn. New Riders (2016). Place of publication not identified
6. Card, S.K., Mackinlay, J.D., Shneiderman, B.: Readings in Information Visualization: Using Vision to Think. Morgan Kaufmann, Burlington (1999)
7. Few, S.: Now You See It: Simple Visualization Techniques for Quantitative Analysis, 1st edn. Analytics Press, Oakland (2009)
8. Few, S.: Information Dashboard Design: Displaying Data for At-a-Glance Monitoring, 2nd edn. Analytics Press, Burlingame (2013)
9. Kirk, A.: Data Visualisation: A Handbook for Data Driven Design, 1st edn. SAGE Publications Ltd., Los Angeles (2016)
10. Knaflic, C.N.: Storytelling with Data: A Data Visualization Guide for Business Professionals, 1st edn. Wiley, Hoboken (2015)
11. Munzner, T.: Visualization Analysis and Design, har/psc edn. CRC Press, Boca Raton (2014)
12. Steele, J., Iliinsky, N. (eds.): Beautiful Visualization: Looking at Data through the Eyes of Experts, 1st edn. O'Reilly Media, Sebastopol (2010)
13. Tufte, E.R.: Envisioning Information. Graphics Press, Cheshire (1990)
14. Tufte, E.R.: Visual Explanations: Images and Quantities, Evidence and Narrative. Graphics Press, Cheshire (1997)
15. Tufte, E.R.: The Visual Display of Quantitative Information, 2nd edn. Graphics Press, Cheshire (2001)
16. Tufte, E.R.: Beautiful Evidence. Graphics Press, Cheshire (2006)
17. Ware, C.: Information Visualization: Perception for Design, 3rd edn. Morgan Kaufmann, Waltham (2012)
18. Yau, N.: Visualize This: The FlowingData Guide to Design, Visualization, and Statistics, 1st edn. Wiley, Indianapolis (2011)
19. Yau, N.: Data Points: Visualization That Means Something, 1st edn. Wiley, Indianapolis (2013)

The Science Behind User Experience Design

Asad Ali Junaid[(⊠)]

Bangalore, India

Abstract. Planning and conducting User Experience (UX) activities in a structured and scientific manner has many advantages. It is important that UX Professionals understand the scientific basis of UX methods and leverage them to enhance the UX of the application being designed. It would also be easier for the UX designer to get a buy-in from the stakeholders if his design recommendations are based in scientific logic and whetted by supporting data. In this course, UX relevant social sciences based scientific concepts and methods will be presented to the audience in a way which is simple to understand and easily to assimilate.

Keywords: User Experience · Empirical Research · Scientific methods · UX · Experimental Design · Logic · Data collection and analysis · Data representation · Measuring user performance · Biases in research

1 Introduction

The underlying purpose of employing a scientific method in the User Experience profession is to make sure we, as User Experience (UX) Practitioners, have not been misled into thinking we have deduced something which is far from correct while making a design/process recommendation which in turn would adversely impact the application being built. In such situations, the credibility of the UX designer in an organization would be affected while the confidence of the stakeholders in the UX profession itself would erode.

Planning and conducting UX activities in a structured and scientific manner has many advantages. The primary end user would be the direct beneficiary – the application being built would be the designed and built for the user's ease-of-use while the stakeholders would also see the maximum returns on their investment in UX. The cost of development would also decrease drastically due to reduced rework when the primary end user has been thoroughly understood; screens have been logically designed and have been empirically tested by a UX designer.

2 Learning Objectives

It is important that UX Professionals understand the scientific basis of UX methods enough and leverage them for improving the UX of the application being designed. When the UX process and design recommendations are based on empirical evidence and irrefutable data, then they will be received well.

D. Lamas et al. (Eds.): INTERACT 2019, LNCS 11749, pp. 530–532, 2019.
https://doi.org/10.1007/978-3-030-29390-1_31

By learning how to scientifically conduct UX studies, methodically analyzing data collected during such studies and subsequently providing sound design recommendations, the UX Professional will not just increase his own credibility within the organization but he will be easily able to evangelize and implement UX processes with a fair degree of ease across the organization.

Based on a deeper understanding of UX relevant scientific concepts and processes, the UX Designer would be able to better plan and conduct UX activities such as strategizing UX approach for solving the specific design problem, planning for and setting timelines of UX deliverables, planning and conducting User Research, creating and validating Personas, Heuristic Analysis of existing applications, planning and conducting Usability Tests, analyzing data obtained from User Research and Usability Tests and subsequently designing or proposing re-designs of applications/products.

3   Course Content and Schedule

My intent is to present some UX relevant social science based scientific concepts and process to the audience in a way which is simple to understand and easily to assimilate. With the knowledge and expertise gained from this course, the UX Professional would be able to take their UX practice a notch higher and by making recommendations which are scientific, and data driven – in other words, recommendations which are credible and irrefutable. I will cover the essential fundamentals of the course in two 90-min sessions. The course content is detailed below:

- Origins and background of User Experience Design (30 min)
  - Introduce the audience to the principles of Human Factors and Human Computer Interaction which were precursors of the field of User Experience Design. This would enable the user to understand the origins and the scientific rationale behind some of the methods employed in UX Design
- Principles of Applied psychology in relevance to UX Design (90 min)
  - Introduce the audience to concepts of Cognitive Psychology, the Information Processing model, Memory, Sensation, Perception, Affordance and Attention in the contexts of Human Computer Interaction with specific examples.
- The concept of Empirical Research and takeaways for UX Design (40 min)
  - Introduce the concepts of Empirical Research, Hypothesis, Theory, Law, Experimental Design, Measuring Human Performance and Empirical Methods of Data collection & analysis.
- Data Science in the context of UX (20 min)
  - One of the goals Data Science is to communicate insights obtained from data gathering and analysis in the form of simple stories/visualizations that a layman can understand and come to conclusions on. Conducting UX activities in a structured and scientific manner yields plenty of data with invaluable insights hidden within it. When this data is cleaned up and visualized in a way which makes sense, deep awareness of end-user preferences and behaviors come to light. The last module focuses on Data Visualization Methods where insights obtained from analysis of data can be represented in a way which the stakeholders can easily derive meaning out of.

4 Background of Attendees

The course would be interest to

i. UX Practitioners who want to understand the scientific basis behind the profession and to also understand how to logically and scientifically base their arguments for the designs or design process they will be proposing to stakeholders coming from varied backgrounds.

ii. Project Managers who want to get insights on the decision-making process of UX practitioners and also to understand the importance of the scientific methodology behind some of the UX processes.

iii. Designers who are from a graphic design or content writing background and are not familiar with the core fundamentals and the empirical origins of the User Experience Profession

iv. The course would not be useful for someone who is well versed with the methodologies of social science research.

5 Presentation Format

A set of presentation decks will be used to deliver the course contents to the audience. I am envisioning a workshop model with mini assignments and experiments within the course content to enable the audience to grasp the core takeaways from the course.

6 Audience Size

Anything around or above 20 participants would be a good audience size.

Demonstrations and Installations

A Multitouch Drawing Application with Occlusion-Free Interaction Strategies

Yi Ren Tan[1], Hyowon Lee[1(✉)], Insuk Ko[1], Dongliang Zhang[2],
and Chunxiao Li[2]

[1] Singapore University of Technology and Design,
8 Somapah Road, Singapore 487372, Singapore
hlee@sutd.edu.sg
[2] Zhejiang University, Hangzhou 300058, Zhejiang, China

Abstract. Increasing number of desktop applications are becoming available
on smartphones and tablets today with multitouch capabilities, allowing the
users' fingers to perform sophisticated or fine-grained interactivities. However,
finger occlusion and imprecision continue to limit the performance of multitouch
interactions. Quite a few studies proposed the ways to address this issue, and
some of them are now used in commonly encountered situations such as text
editing. Many occlusion-avoiding techniques used today focus on initial target
acquisition step of touch interaction (e.g. accurately selecting an item or
touching a desired starting point in drawing a line), having possible consequences to any further intended action (e.g. dragging the selected item to a
different location or drawing a line on the canvas). In order to better understand
the influence of finger occlusion-free techniques on other parts of the overall
interactions, in this paper we report a full-fledged sketch app that incorporates
combinations of basic target acquisition features. As the app is a full-featured,
end-to-end tablet prototype, such usability issues can be more readily revealed
and discussed in the context of realistic drawing situations.

Keywords: Finger occlusion · Pointing precision · Multitouch interaction

1 Introduction

Multitouch platforms are becoming increasingly popular today due to their intuitive-
ness and convenience. However, such platforms continue to suffer from the problem of
finger occlusion, also known as "fat-finger problem", which refers to the difficulty of
selecting or manipulating small targets on a screen due to the relatively larger size of
the user's finger. Small targets tend to be hidden under the finger during interaction,
resulting in error and imprecision.

While stylus is a straightforward solution to imprecision and finger occlusion, it is
not without its own set of disadvantages. Stylus requires a stable surface to perform
well, and most styluses are inconvenient to carry along. Styluses can also introduce

Electronic supplementary material The online version of this chapter (https://doi.org/10.1007/
978-3-030-29390-1_32) contains supplementary material, which is available to authorized users.

D. Lamas et al. (Eds.): INTERACT 2019, LNCS 11749, pp. 535–539, 2019.
https://doi.org/10.1007/978-3-030-29390-1_32

other usability problems such as parallax error and pen/hand occlusion as addressed in previous studies (e.g. [1, 3]). In the context of applications that allow the user to draw lines and other visual sketches, the impact of finger occlusion becomes greater as the action of drawing often requires the finger to contact the display surface for longer durations and with much finer control.

A drawing action can be broken down into two distinct input steps: (1) accurately positioning of the initial point of selection (i.e. target acquisition), and (2) accurately dragging along the desired path of drawing. While past studies have attempted at solving occlusion and imprecision using various indirect pointing techniques (e.g. [2–5]), their main focus of attention and evaluation was on positioning the initial and/or end point of selection. Little is known about the performances of these techniques in accurately supporting any remaining interaction such as dragging along a path, having once accurately targeted a point.

A quick review of existing sketching-related apps today shows that most of them do not include any occlusion-free features. Top surface-based drawing apps such as Procreate[1] and Autodesk Sketchbook[2] are feature-rich and used by hobbyists as well as professionals. Yet, none of them have explicitly addressed the issue of finger occlusion on their user-interfaces. Most users either depend on a stylus for better accuracy, or frequently "undo" to redraw their inaccurate lines repeatedly.

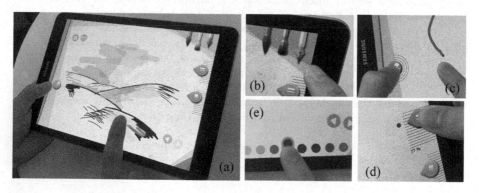

Fig. 1. (a) Drawing performed in the occlusion-free app; (b) Main drawing tools; (c) Activation button tapped with offset pointer; (d) Selecting brush thickness; (e) Selecting a colour. (Color figure online)

In this demonstration, we present a full-fledged tablet sketch app we developed (Fig. 1), incorporating some combinations of basic occlusion-free interaction strategies as integral features of the app. By implementing these occlusion-free features in a realistic sketch app, we aim to explore, reveal and better understand how some of the techniques for multitouch interaction can impact the usability when adopted in a real tablet app in the context of drawing tasks. We believe that the app, though in itself does

---

[1] Procreate: https://procreate.art/.

[2] Sketchbook: https://sketchbook.com/mobile.

not feature any novel occlusion-free techniques, very effectively raises a number of useful discussion points that help re-visit the concept, scope and value of finger occlusion-avoiding techniques thus far proposed and adopted, by placing some of the representative techniques in the context of realistic application situations.

2 Sketch Application Overview

The design of our sketching app aims to fulfill three key objectives. Firstly, in order to capture the full spectrum of use cases in actual drawing applications, we attempt to replicate essential drawing features found in commercial apps such as variety of brush types (Fig. 1(b)), controls for brush size and opacity (Fig. 1(e)), color palette (Fig. 1 (d)), canvas zoom/rotation/pan, as well as the undo/redo functions. It is not feasible to replicate every single feature we see in commercial apps such as layers, filters and image manipulation, so we decided to prioritize features that would directly impact the action of drawing on the canvas.

Secondly, all elements of the user interface were designed to be occlusion-free when interacting directly with a finger. We approached this using large finger-sized buttons that are easy to target and clear animated visual feedback that pops out around the point of touch to prevent information from being hidden under the finger (Fig. 1).

Thirdly, some of the occlusion-free target acquisition techniques are incorporated to support the actual drawing actions, further elaborated in the next section[3].

The app was developed in Unity game engine, and works on any tablet platforms. It was installed and tested on Samsung Galaxy Tab S2 tablet with 9.7-in. multitouch display with the resolution of 2048 px by 1536 px, a mid-range tablet device widely used as of today.

3 Occlusion-Free Strategies in the Application

When formulating our occlusion-free input strategies, we adopted a design space consisting of two factors: (1) Input Mapping and (2) Activation Method.

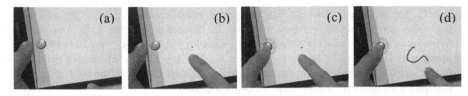

Fig. 2. Offset-UMM technique: (a) Activation button is featured to be pressed with non-dominant hand; (b) dominant hand now touches the surface, showing the offset pointer above the finger; (c) once targeting is satisfactory, the activation button is pressed; (d) draws while the button is kept pressed.

---

[3] A short video demonstrates the app in action: https://youtu.be/YYTWjidj4OM.

Input Mapping refers to how the cursor is positioned on the screen in relation to the point of contact of the finger. When we tap on a surface, the action of the cursor usually happens directly under our finger, causing the cursor action to be hidden. Through introducing an indirect input mapping to our system, we can position the cursor away from under the finger so the action of the cursor becomes visible again.

Activation Method refers to the gesture used to commit an action with the cursor. For example, on a desktop mouse input, the activation method is to press the left mouse button to commit an action. The usual way of committing an action on an interactive surface is to simply tap the finger on the display. This method is error-prone, as it forces the user to commit the action before the user can visually identify exactly where the cursor is. By introducing alternative activation methods, along with indirect input mapping, the accuracy of touch input may be significantly improved.

Combination of the two factors allows us to arrive at our primary occlusion-free strategy, the Offset-UMM technique. This technique uses an input mapping known as Offset and an activation method called UMM (User-Maintained Mode) interaction [6]. The Offset input mapping positions the cursor a short distance (e.g. 1.5 cm) vertically above the point of touch of the finger [2]. This prevents occlusion while keeping the cursor close to the finger so it is easy for the user to locate. However, the offset cursor only appears when the finger touches the screen (Figs. 2(a), (b)). In this strategy, the UMM interaction is used for activation where the line drawing is committed only when a dedicated, separate button is pressed and kept pressed (Figs. 2(c), (d)). Overall this strategy works well when both hands are available. Such bimanual use of UMM in interaction design has been shown to be a promising alternative interaction in a number of application scenarios [6]. In a similar fashion, three other occlusion-free strategies were formulated, using different input mappings and activation methods. While a usability testing was conducted and its detailed analysis is reported elsewhere [7], in this demonstration paper we mainly introduce the app that feature the 4 occlusion-free strategies as a demonstrator to encourage discussions on the usability of the techniques on the remaining interactivity when conducting a task.

References

1. Lee, D., Son, K., Lee, J., Bae, S.: PhantomPen: virtualization of pen head for digital drawing free from pen occlusion & visual parallax. In Proceedings of the 25th Annual ACM Symposium on User Interface Software and Technology (UIST 2012), pp. 331–340 (2012)
2. Matejka, J., Grossman, T., Lo, J., Fitzmaurice, G.: The design and evaluation of multi-finger mouse emulation techniques. In: Proceeding of the SIGCHI Conference on Human Factors in Computing Systems (CHI 2009), pp. 1073–1082 (2009)
3. Vogel, D., Balakrishnan, R.: Occlusion-aware interfaces. In: Proceedings of the SIGCHI Conference on Human Factors in Computing Systems (CHI 2010), pp. 263–272 (2010)
4. Roudaut, A., Huot, S., Lecolinet, E.: TapTap and MagStick: improving one-handed target acquisition on small touch-screens. In: Proceedings of the Working Conference on Advanced Visual Interfaces (AVI 2008), pp. 146–153 (2008)
5. Lai, J., Zhang, D.: ExtendedThumb: a motion-based virtual thumb for improving one-handed target acquisition on touch-screen mobile devices. In: CHI 2014 Extended Abstracts on Human Factors in Computing Systems (CHI EA 2014), pp. 1825–1830 (2014)

6. Fennedy, K., Lee, H., Ko, I., Tan, Y., Zhang, D., Li, C.: Augmenting user-maintained interaction through mode locking and reversing. In: 32nd British Computer Society Human Computer Interaction Conference (2018)
7. Lee, H., Ko, I., Tan, Y.R., Zhang, D., Li, C.: Usability impact of occlusion-free techniques on commonly-used multitouch actions. In: 5th International ACM in Cooperation HCI and UX Conference (CHIuXiD 2019) (2019)

CityCompass VR - A Collaborative Virtual Language Learning Environment

Pekka Kallioniemi$^{(\boxtimes)}$, Kimmo Ronkainen, Jussi Karhu,
Sumita Sharma, Jaakko Hakulinen, and Markku Turunen

Tampere University, Tampere, Finland
{pekka.kallioniemi, kimmo.ronkainen, jussi.karhu,
sumita.sharma, jaakko.hakulinen, markku.turunen}@tuni.fi

Abstract. CityCompass VR is a collaborative virtual language learning environment that utilizes interactive omnidirectional video (iODV) content. In the application, two remotely located users navigate through cityscapes in order to reach a common goal. One of the users takes the role of a tourist who needs to find a local attraction, and the other one acts as their guide. The users communicate in a foreign language with each other via headsets. The application is used with HMD device and uses a dwell-time, head-position based interaction.

Keywords: Collaborative virtual learning environments ·
Interactive omnidirectional videos · Language learning

1 Introduction

Technological leaps in both Virtual Reality (VR) technologies and recording and production of omnidirectional videos (ODV in short; also known as 360° videos) has enabled the creation of immersive and realistic virtual environments (VEs). These environments are typically explored with a head-mounted display (HMD) device or within a CAVE environment. Utilizing VEs in educational settings has been reported more active participation and higher interactivity among the students [6]. CityCompass VR is a collaborative virtual environment developed for language learning purposes. It utilizes iODV content and supports two remotely located, simultaneous users. It has been initially evaluated with 30 Spanish participants (mAge = 27.5) learning English as a secondary language [2]. More extensive evaluations have been planned in Finland and India for students of various ages and school levels, starting from elementary school.

2 CityCompass VR

CityCompass VR is a third evolutionary stage of the CityCompass application family. Its predecessors and their pedagogical potential have been evaluated and reported in several previous studies, e.g. [1, 2, 4 and 7]. These studies reported results regarding user experience, embodied interaction, cross-cultural collaboration and immersion. In the future, we want to expand our research on cross-cultural collaboration and also study the effects of immersion on the user's learning experience.

D. Lamas et al. (Eds.): INTERACT 2019, LNCS 11749, pp. 540–543, 2019.
https://doi.org/10.1007/978-3-030-29390-1_33

User Interface and Interaction. In CityCompass VR, the users can freely explore the ODV content by turning their head to the desired direction. The screen is divided into two viewports, thus creating the illusion of a stereoscopy and a sense of depth to the user. Both users have their own HMD (Fig. 1) devices and have their own individual views of the application (see Fig. 2).

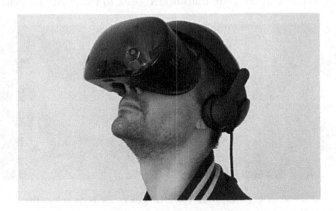

Fig. 1. HMD device with an integrated headset.

Fig. 2. Screenshot from the CityCompass VR application. The application is divided into two viewports.

The application has two types of user interface elements: *exits* and *hotspots*. Exits transition both users to the next scene, and hotspots provide contextual information about the environment. These interface elements are activated with a dwell-timer, i.e. the user has to focus on the desired element for pre-defined time in order to activate it.

Wayfinding Scenario. In CityCompass VR, two users collaborate and navigate through cityscapes in order to find a local tourist attraction. One of the users is the wayfinder, referred as a tourist, who is being guided by the other user, referred as a guide. In the application, the users have to transition from one scene to another through collaboration. Each scene has multiple exits, but only one of these takes the users closer to their goal. The tourist is the one who can transition between the scenes per the guide's instructions. The application also offers assistance for the guide. If the tourist activates a wrong exit, both users are taken to a dead-end scene. Dead end scenes are indicated with a red lock symbol at the center of the both user's viewports. Once the users activate a dead-end scene, their roles are reversed – now the user acting as a guide needs to find the correct route from given exits, and the tourist needs to guide them (see Fig. 3). After activating the correct exit, they are transitioned back to the previous scene.

Fig. 3. Dead end scene in CityCompass VR. The guide needs to select the correct exit from three options [2]. (Color figure online)

3   System Architecture

CityCompass VR was developed on Unity. Currently it supports Samsung Galaxy S7 and S8 smartphones together with Samsung Gear HMD device, but can also be ported for HTC Vive and for Oculus Go. It deploys a client-server architecture, and also has a separate view for the observer. This observer view is used on a laptop computer and it provides the researcher information regarding the progression of the wayfinding task and can also playback the audio from both clients. The ODV content used in CityCompass VR is 360° × 180°, and it has a field of view of 60°. In addition to the HMD device, both users wear a headset for communication purposes. For the application architecture, see Fig. 4.

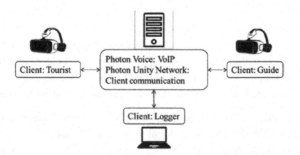

Fig. 4. CityCompass VR application architecture. The two clients are connected to each other via Photon Unity Network and communicate via Photon Voice VoIP service. All activity can be recorded by the logger client [2].

4   Conclusion and Future Work

This paper introduced CityCompass VR, a collaborative virtual language learning environment. In the application, two users collaborate and communicate with each other in order to reach a common goal. The application utilizes head-mounted display devices and interactive omnidirectional videos, which together create an immersive experience for the users. CityCompass VR is a promising tool for research purposes for various domains, including education and language learning. It is suitable for various age groups, starting from elementary school, and the application also has potential for cross-cultural studies (see for example [7]). For future, we are planning on adding several routes from around the world, including night time scenes. Our goal is also to provide a crowdsourcing platform where users can upload their own routes.

References

1. Kallioniemi, P., et al.: Evaluating landmark attraction model in collaborative wayfinding in virtual learning environments. In: Proceedings of the 12th International Conference on Mobile and Ubiquitous Multimedia, p. 33. ACM, December 2013
2. Kallioniemi, P., Keskinen, T., Hakulinen, J., Turunen, M., Karhu, J., Ronkainen, K.: Effect of gender on immersion in collaborative iODV applications. In: Proceedings of the 16th International Conference on Mobile and Ubiquitous Multimedia, pp. 199–207. ACM, November 2017
3. Kallioniemi, P., Mäkelä, V., Saarinen, S., Turunen, M., Winter, Y., Istudor, A.: User experience and immersion of interactive omnidirectional videos in CAVE systems and head-mounted displays. In: Bernhaupt, R., Dalvi, G., Joshi, A., KB, D., O'Neill, J., Winckler, M. (eds.) INTERACT 2017. LNCS, vol. 10516, pp. 299–318. Springer, Cham (2017). https://doi.org/10.1007/978-3-319-68059-0_20
4. Kallioniemi, P., Posti, L.P., Hakulinen, J., Turunen, M., Keskinen, T., Raisamo, R.: Berlin Kompass: multimodal gameful empowerment for foreign language learning. J. Educ. Technol. Syst. 43(4), 429–450 (2015)
5. Mikropoulos, T.A., Natsis, A.: Educational virtual environments: a ten-year review of empirical research (1999–2009). Comput. Educ. 56(3), 769–780 (2011)
6. Pantelidis, V.S.: Virtual reality in the classroom. Educ. Technol. 33(4), 23–27 (1993)
7. Sharma, S., Kallioniemi, P., Heimonen, T., Hakulinen, J., Turunen, M., Keskinen, T.: Overcoming socio-technical challenges for cross-cultural collaborative applications. In: Proceedings of the 17th ACM Conference on Interaction Design and Children, pp. 325–336. ACM, June 2018

GazeMotive: A Gaze-Based Motivation-Aware E-Learning Tool for Students with Learning Difficulties

Ruijie Wang[✉], Yuanchen Xu, and Liming Chen

De Montfort University, Leicester LE1 9BH, UK
ruijie.wang@my365.dmu.ac.uk

Abstract. We developed a gaze-based motivation-aware e-learning tool, a Windows desktop learning application, for students with learning difficulties that aims at motivation-enhanced learning by dynamically assessing and responding to students' motivational states based on the motivation model that we developed previously using rigorous methodologies including domain knowledge and empirical studies with participants with learning difficulties. The learning application uses an eye tracker to monitor a user's eye movements during the user's learning process, assesses the user's motivational states using the prediction models we developed before to output personalised feedback from a pedagogical agent in the system based on both the eye gaze features and user's self-input data for enhancing users' motivation and engagement in real-time. Our e-learning tool is an example of applying user modelling and personalisation to an e-learning environment targeting at users' learning motivation, producing great insight on how eye tracking can assist with students' learning motivation and engagement in e-learning environments.

Keywords: Eye tracking · Motivation assessment · Personalised feedback

1 Introduction

1.1 Background

Students' high level of motivation is fundamental for their learning success. Specifically, students with learning difficulties such as dyslexia can cause low levels of engagement with the education system or dropouts. Thanks to the advancement of assistive learning systems and user modelling techniques for personalised learning, different individual learning needs can be met by personalising learning environments based on user models. User modelling combined with mechanisms of personalisation is necessary to apply the user models to the real-world scenarios and tailor learning service and experience to different individuals' learning needs or mental states. Most of the research pertaining to personalized learning has focused on emotion and cognition of learners such as inducing more positive emotions or reattracting attention; in contrast, e-learning system designers have neglected to apply user modelling and personalized interventions that aims at improvements in exactly learners' motivational states. Therefore, we have developed inference rules based on our motivation model

© IFIP International Federation for Information Processing 2019
Published by Springer Nature Switzerland AG 2019
D. Lamas et al. (Eds.): INTERACT 2019, LNCS 11749, pp. 544–548, 2019.
https://doi.org/10.1007/978-3-030-29390-1_34

developed previously [1] to identify user's motivational states based on the data collected during a learning process including both self-reported data and eye gaze data that can be recorded automatically and finally enable the pedagogical agent to output personalised feedback to user to sustain and enhance motivation in real-time.

1.2 Motivation Assessment

Motivation is a multi-faceted concept, and we have developed a conceptual motivation model previously from domain knowledge and interviews as well as a multi-item questionnaire study [1, 2]. The model contains factors that determine the continued use intention in an e-learning environment from intrinsic motivation such as Self-efficacy, extrinsic motivation such as Visual Attractiveness, and mediators such as Reading Experience. Eye gaze data has shed light on human's various cognitive process including problem solving [3], and eye gaze features like pupil dilation has been used as indicators of emotional states [4]. In a previous experiment with students with learning difficulties [5], we have found that gaze features such as average pupil diameter and fixation number can play significant roles in assessing learners' motivation in e-learning context with a prediction accuracy up to 81.3%, which can be a good alternative to the approach using merely self-reported data to avoid the self-reported bias.

1.3 The Demonstration System

The demonstration system is a gaze-based learning application that assesses a learner's motivation related to the factors in our motivation model mentioned before based on the features computed from both the self-input data and real-time data from the Tobii eye tracker 4c. The system then uses personalization algorithms to generate personalised feedback based on the motivation assessment to address the corresponding motivational needs. Different motivational factors are assessed based on different gaze features with different parameters using the logistic regression models resulted from our previous study [5], starting from which, we have improved the prediction models by including only the gaze features that have significant prediction power. The system implemented some regression models to assess the corresponding motivational factors (e.g., Confirmed Fit and Reading Experience) purely based on gaze features. Other factors such as Attitudes Toward School and Self-efficacy were assessed based on self-reported data collected at the beginning of a learning process, as they involve intrinsic motivation that usually remains stable in a short-term period. The system also outputs personalised feedback at the stage of self-assessment quizzes based on both a user's answer and gaze data. Given that we have developed the motivation model and classification algorithms using rigorous approaches and have evaluated the relevant motivational strategies [5], we have confidence that the present system will yield motivation-enhanced learning experience and better learning performance over the long term by monitoring and incorporating eye tracking it into motivation assessment and providing personalised feedback to respond to different motivational states in real-time.

2 GazeMotive Walkthrough

GazeMotive was designed for two user groups, expert and learner. When a user logs on with a username and a password (see Fig. 1a), the system will redirect the user to either the expert interface or the learner interface. The expert interface allows an expert user to add or delete learning materials, page by page. The expert user can then input self-assessment quizzes after each lesson (see Fig. 1b). Any learning materials can be added to our system in front-end by expert users in picture format, and this demonstration system uses materials adapted from a free e-learning course [6], the frozen planet, as an example. We adopted 16–40pt Verdana dark fonts on light yellow background and visual elements like images according to the design principles for students with learning difficulties [7]. Our system assesses learners' motivational states from gaze features, some of which are computed based on AOIs (Areas of Interest), and different learning materials and pages have different AOIs, so expert users need to select one or more AOIs for each page by clicking on the points at the corners of the polygons to enable relevant gaze features to be computed, and an AOI can also be selected for review or deletion by the expert users (see Fig. 1c and d).

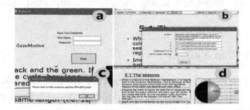

Fig. 1. Screenshots of expert interface showing an example of (a) login, (b) adding a quiz, (c) the process of adding an AOI, and (d) the AOIs added.

The learner interface is similar with the expert one, the main difference is the personalised feedback output from the system to user dependent on the motivational states detected by the system from eye-tracking data or self-reported data or a combination of both. During a learning process, a pedagogic agent representing a virtual tutor will output personalised feedback to address specific motivational needs. The feedback implemented in our system is in format of text and picture, and more diverse formats of feedback and interventions such as speech and animation can also be incorporated into the inference rules and implemented following our present work. Figure 2 shows two examples of personalised feedback based on real-time motivation assessment, in the learning stage (see Fig. 2a) and the quiz stage (see Fig. 2b), respectively.

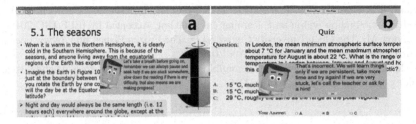

Fig. 2. Screenshots of user interface showing the examples of personalized feedback to provide motivational help (a) when the system detects a user to have negative reading experience from eye-tracking data in a learning page, and (b) when the user submits an incorrect answer to a quiz and is meanwhile detected from the eye-tracking data as having not put enough effort.

3 Conclusion

In this paper, we demonstrate how we have applied the motivation model and corresponding personalisation rules to real-world scenarios. The motivation model and classification algorithms were developed from our previous studies using interviews, a multi-item questionnaire and an experiment with target users. The inference rules and motivational strategies were adapted to our learning environment based on our motivation model. Our system uses eye tracking technology to assess motivational states by monitoring gaze features and self-input data during user's learning process, and this motivation-aware system demonstrated a way of applying the motivational strategies to dynamically respond to the motivational states detected based on our motivation model using gaze data instead of relying on obtrusive self-report data towards accurate real-time motivation assessment for enhanced motivation in an e-learning environment. In future, we will keep validating the models and algorithms to maximize the accuracy of motivation assessment and personalised feedback, as well as improving the interface design. Additionally, more dimensions of motivation and more diverse formats of feedback will be implemented using the logic that has been developed in the system.

References

1. Wang, R., Chen, L., Solheim, I., Schulz, T., Ayesh, A.: Conceptual motivation modeling for students with dyslexia for enhanced assistive learning. In: Proceedings of the 2017 ACM Workshop on Intelligent Interfaces for Ubiquitous and Smart Learning, SmartLearn 2017, pp. 11–18. ACM, Leicester (2017)
2. Wang, R., Chen, L., Solheim, I.: Modeling dyslexic students' motivation for enhanced learning in E-learning systems. Submitted to ACM TiiS
3. Poole, A., Ball, L.: Eye tracking in human-computer interaction and usability research: current status and future prospects. In: Encyclopedia of Human Computer Interaction, pp. 211–219 (2006)
4. Alghowinem, S., Alshehri, M., Goecke, R.: Exploring eye activity as an indication of emotional states using an eye-tracking sensor. In: Chen, L., Kapoor, S., Bhatia, R. (eds.) Intelligent Systems for Science and Information. Studies in Computational Intelligence, pp. 261–276. Springer, Cham (2014). https://doi.org/10.1007/978-3-319-04702-7_15

5. Wang, R., Chen, L., Ayesh, A., Shell, J., Solheim, I.: Gaze-based assessment of dyslexic students' motivation within an E-learning environment. Accepted by IEEE UIC 2019
6. Brandon, M.: The Open University Course S175: The Frozen Planet. http://www.open.ac.uk/courses/modules/s175. Accessed 08 Apr 2019
7. Dyslexic.com. https://www.dyslexic.com/blog/dyslexia-and-visual-stress-what-assistive-technology-can-help. Accessed 08 Apr 2019

Hybrid Wireless Sensor Networks: A Prototype

Alá Khalifeh[1]([⊠]), Novella Bartolini[2], Simone Silvestri[3],
Giancarlo Bongiovanni[2], Anwar Al-Assaf[4], Radi Alwardat[5],
and Samer Alhaj-Ali[5]

[1] German Jordanina University, Amman, Jordan
ala.khalifeh@gju.edu.jo
[2] Sapienza University of Rome, Rome, Italy
{novella,bongiovanni}@di.uniroma1.it
[3] University of Kentucky, Lexington, USA
silvestri@cs.uky.edu
[4] Arab Robotics and AI Organization, Amman, Jordan
Muaddi13@yahoo.com
[5] The King Abdullah II Design and Development Bureau (KADDB), Amman, Jordan
{ralwardat,shajali}@kaddb.mil.jo

Abstract. Wireless sensor networks (WSNs) are widely used to assist monitoring of an area of interest whenever manual monitoring by skilled personnel is not convenient if not prohibitive. In this paper, we propose a step ahead with respect to the current status of art, with the design and implementation of a novel networked architecture which integrates a set of static ground nodes, an Unmanned Ground Vehicle (UGV), and an Unmanned Aerial Vehicle (UAV) in a unique monitoring system. All these devices are equipped with sensors, a microcontroller and a wireless communication module such that they are capable of covering an AoI in the terrestrial and aerial dimension. In the proposed architecture, the mobile robot can inspect areas which have no fixed ground sensors, whereas sensors installed on the UAV cover the ground areas from above, ensuring wider coverage. Once data is collected by the ground sensors, it is sent via the UAV to a remote processing center, which elaborates the gathered data for decision making.

Keywords: Wireless sensor networks (WSN) ·
Unmanned Ground Vehicle (UGV) · Unmanned Aerial Vehicle (UAV) ·
Remote monitoring · Decision making

1 Introduction

Wireless sensor networks consist of a group of nodes deployed over an area of interest to monitor a variety of environmental features, depending on the appli-

This work is supported by NATO - North Atlantic Treaty Organization, under the SPS grant G4936 "SONiCS: Hybrid Sensor Network for Emergency Critical Scenarios.

© IFIP International Federation for Information Processing 2019
Published by Springer Nature Switzerland AG 2019
D. Lamas et al. (Eds.): INTERACT 2019, LNCS 11749, pp. 549–553, 2019.
https://doi.org/10.1007/978-3-030-29390-1_35

cation. As coverage and connectivity remain an issue for static sensor network deployments [1,2], and severely limit their applicability to small and safe areas of interest, we propose a novel monitoring architecture which encompasses the above limitations. Our monitoring system integrates static and mobile devices cooperating with each other to ensure a flexible and quickly deployable monitoring network, to be used in a wide range of operating settings, including health crop monitoring for agriculture as well as monitoring of critical scenarios for homeland security. For example, the proposed system can be used to monitor wildfires, or areas which have been exposed to chemical plumes, gas leakage, radiation or to an intentional attack with nuclear or chemical weapons, in case of war, which is dangerous to explore by humans, thus the proposed system provides safe, efficient and convenient way for remote sensing, that can be used by decision makers for assessing the safety of the monitored area of interests. In the literature, several network architectures have been proposed to achieve this purpose. The authors in [3] proposed to utilize UAVs in conjunction with static sensors on the ground to improve the quality of packet routing. Another work that utilizes UAVs to assist ground sensors is presented in [4], where UAVs are used to spray crops while adaptively planning their route based on the findings of the ground sensors. Some researchers modeled WSN networks that use both ground and aerial nodes as a three-dimensional network, focusing on the study of connectivity and coverage problems [5]. Unlike previous approaches, our network architecture utilizes both static and mobile terrestrial sensors, as well as aerial sensing vehicles, such that the three elements work collaboratively to provide comprehensive sensing and coverage of the area of interest, and efficient communications with the processing center. Differently from previous studies [6–8] mostly based on simulations, this work focuses on the actual implementation of such a network: in Sect. 2 we describe our monitoring architecture, while in Section 3 we conclude the discussion and outline future research directions.

2   WSN Architecture and Implementation

As shown in Fig. 1, the proposed monitoring network consists of three types of nodes: static nodes, an Unmanned Ground Vehicle (UGV) and an Unmanned Aerial Vehicle (UAV). The monitoring process consists of two main stages. In stage 1, sensed data are captured and stored by the static nodes, sent to the UGV node, which acts as a sink node, then transferred to the UAV node. After that, the data is transferred by the UAV to the remote data analysis and decision making center. Where responsible people who are observing the AoI will analyze the data and use it for decision making process.(e.g. declaring the AoI to be safe for humans or not.)

2.1   Static Nodes

Figure 1(a) shows static nodes to be deployed on the ground along the area of interest. These nodes can communicate either directly with each other or

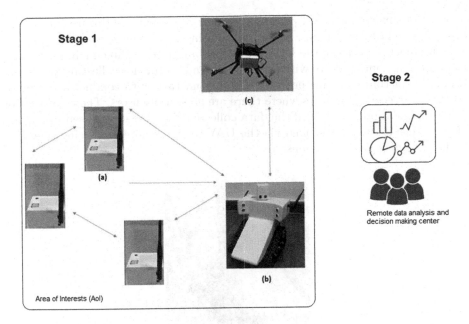

Fig. 1. Monitoring architecture: static sensor nodes (a), a UGV (b), and a UAV (c).

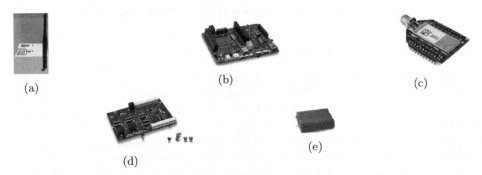

Fig. 2. A static node (a) and its components: a microcontroller (b), a wireless transceiver (c), sensors and related interface board (d), and battery (e).

through the mobile nodes (the UGV and the UAV). The static node consists of a microcontroller, sensor interface board, sensors and battery as shown in Fig. 2.

2.2   Unmanned Ground Vehicle (UGV)

The coverage and communication capabilities of our network are enhanced by using a mobile terrestrial device, namely the UGV shown in Fig. 3. The UGV is provided with ultrasonic sensors (marked in blue) to detect and avoid obstacles. It also has three antennas A1, A2, and A3, used to communicate with the UAV, static nodes, and the Global Position System (GPS), respectively. This robot is capable of autonomous path planning, namely it can explore the area and avoid obstacles and objects found along its path using ultrasonic sensors.

The functionalities of the UGV can be summarized in three main tasks. The first one is to communicate with the fixed ground sensors for collecting data from them thus acting as a cluster head. The second task is to conduct a survey of the area, especially for areas where there are no static sensors. The third task of these mobile robots is to send the data collected from the ground sensors to the UAV, which is then transferred via the UAV to the remote processing center to make the appropriate decisions.

Fig. 3. Unmanned ground vehicle (UGV). (Color figure online)

2.3   Unmanned Aerial Vehicle

The third fundamental component of our monitoring system is the Unmanned Aerial Vehicle shown in Fig. 4. The ground sensing system is complemented with an aerial sensing node onboard of a UAV which monitors the area from above, capturing features that could not be detected by ground devices only. In addition, this UAV is equipped with a wireless module that enables communications with mobile ground sensors, thus receiving the data gathered from the ground sensors and transferring it to the processing center for data analysis and decision making.

(a)

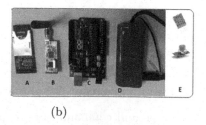

(b)

Fig. 4. A UAV with a sensor node on its base (a). Components of the UAV node (b) consisting of: an SD card for storing the data (A), a wireless transceiver (B), a microcontroller (C), a battery (D), and sensors (E).

3 Conclusion

In this paper, we presented the implementation of a heterogeneous wireless sensor network that consists of static, mobile and flying nodes, that can work collaboratively to cover an area of interest, and provide the sensed data for a remote center for data analysis and decision making, which not only saves people from investigating the area of interest personally thus saving time and effort, but also provides a convenient and safe monitoring process. As a future work, we are working on building an intelligent Human Computer Interaction (HCI) System that utilizes the developed data sensing and collection systems, which can make decisions and recommendations based on both the human and computer decision. Further, the energy consumption of the UGV and sensor nodes needs more optimization.

References

1. Bartolini, N., Calamoneri, T., La Porta, T., Petrioli, C., Silvestri, S.: Sensor activation and radius adaptation (SARA) in heterogeneous sensor networks. ACM Trans. Sen. Netw. **8**(3), 24:1–24:34 (2012)
2. Bartolini, N., Calamoneri, T., Massini, A., Silvestri, S.: On adaptive density deployment to mitigate the sink-hole problem in mobile sensor networks. Mob. Netw. Appl. **16**(1), 134–145 (2011)
3. Gu, D.L., Pei, G., Ly, H., Gerla, M., Zhang, B., Hong, X.: UAV aided intelligent routing for ad-hoc wireless network in single-area theater. In: 2000 IEEE Wireless Communications and Networking Conference, WCNC 2000, vol. 3, pp. 1220–1225. IEEE (2000)
4. Costa, F.G., Ueyama, J., Braun, T., Pessin, G., Osório, F.S., Vargas, P.A.: The use of unmanned aerial vehicles and wireless sensor network in agricultural applications. In: 2012 IEEE International Geoscience and Remote Sensing Symposium (IGARSS), pp. 5045–5048. IEEE (2012)
5. Al tahan, A.M., Watfa, M.K.: A position-based routing algorithm in 3D sensor networks. Wirel. Commun. Mob. Comput. **12**(1), 33–52 (2012)
6. Khalifeh, A.F., AlQudah, M., Tanash, R., Darabkh, K.A.: A simulation study for UAV- aided wireless sensor network utilizing ZigBee protocol. In: 2018 14th International Conference on Wireless and Mobile Computing, Networking and Communications (WiMob), pp. 181–184, October 2018
7. Khalifeh, A.F., Salah, H., Alouneh, S., Al-Assaf, A., Darabkh, K.A.: Performance evaluation of DigiMesh and ZigBee wireless mesh networks. In: 2018 International Conference on Wireless Communications, Signal Processing and Networking (WiSP-NET). IEEE, pp. 1–6 (2018)
8. Darabkh, K.A., Odetallah, S.M., Al-qudah, Z., Khalifeh, A., Shurman, M.M.: Energy-aware and density-based clustering and relaying protocol (EA-DB-CRP) for gathering data in wireless sensor networks. Appl. Soft Comput. **80**, 154–166 (2019)

Memories of Carvalhal's Palace: Haunted Encounters, a Museum Experience to Engage Teenagers

Vanessa Cesário[1,2]([⊠]), Rui Trindade[1]([⊠]), Sandra Olim[1]([⊠]), and Valentina Nisi[1,3]([⊠])

[1] ITI/LARSyS, 9020-105 Funchal, Portugal
{vanessa.cesario, rui.trindade, sandra.olim, valentina.nisi}@m-iti.org
[2] Faculty of Engineering, University of Porto, 4200-465 Porto, Portugal
[3] University of Madeira, 9000-208 Funchal, Portugal

Abstract. While museums are making great efforts in updating their communication and engagement strategies to include a wide variety of publics, teenagers (15–19) are still identified as an audience group that is often excluded from a museum's curatorial strategies. As consequence, this audience appears to be generally disinterested in what museums might offer. Our installation, deployed at the Natural History Museum of Funchal (NHMF), in Portugal, makes use of mobile interactive technologies and gaming strategies to promote more engaging museum experiences for teenage visitors. *Memories of Carvalhal's Palace: Haunted Encounters* is a location-based game that prompts teenagers to uncover the science in the museum, through investigating the site, which is presented as haunted. In order to complete the quest, the audience needs to find and collect scientific information about specific exhibits while interacting with their Augmented Reality (AR) three-dimensional (3D) models. The audience's interactions with the museum exhibits are rewarded with pieces of a map, which when completed, will guide them to the hidden scientific library where they can finally unlock the mysteries they have been trying to solve.

Keywords: Museums · Teenagers · Gaming · Augmented Reality · 3D models

1 Teenagers and Museums

Museums are slowly moving away from being places where exhibits are collected and displayed to a general public, by becoming centers where people can actively engage in active discoveries and personalized challenges [1]. Thanks to the huge uptake of interactive and mobile technologies, audiences are turning from passive to active participants. Museums adapt to this change by giving their public the opportunity to interact with the exhibits, although many remain behind glass shelves [2]. Augmented Reality (AR) three-dimensional (3D) representations of exhibits are promising technologies to be employed to expand the physical context of the exhibit and museum

Electronic supplementary material The online version of this chapter (https://doi.org/10.1007/978-3-030-29390-1_36) contains supplementary material, which is available to authorized users.

space by providing virtual and location-specific information [3]. Moreover, location-based AR games are valuable when applied to cultural heritage as a way to display historical content and context [4]. According to Falk [5], the so-called "one size fits all experiences" does not apply to the museum visitors. In particular, the "digital natives" generation's (15–19 years old) beliefs and behaviours are recognised as being quite different from previous generations [6]. While museums often offer guided tours tailored for children and/or adults, very little is designed for the "digital natives" and teens' generation in general [7].

2 Features on Enjoyable Museum Experiences for Teenagers

According to formal studies about teenage preferences regarding museum engagement, Cesário et al. [8, 9] identified that teenage audiences particularly appreciate mobile experiences that include (1) Gaming and storytelling aspects, (2) Interaction elements, (3) Social media connections, and (4) Museum and exhibits relevant information. To contribute in filling in the gap regarding teenage engagement in museums, we designed the *Memories of Carvalhal's Palace* dual experience, geared towards better understanding teenagers' preferences and needs in museum contexts. Based on the same museum premises and exhibits, the authors designed a storyfied game (*Haunted Encounters*) and gamified story (*Turning Point*), making use of the same characters and similar content, but different engagement strategies. The two experiences are currently being studied and compared in order to understand teenage preferences. The scope of this demonstration submission is to describe the *Haunted Encounters* game experience in detail.

Fig. 1. In this collage, from left to right, the image lists: (1) The opening splash screen of the game; (2) A screenshot of the two main characters and the call for action; (3) A screenshot of the shadows' interface of the game; (4) A Rune shaped marker used to unlock the 3D models; (5) A 3D model of the Blowfish displayed as Augmented Reality; (6) The ghost from Meara's storyline; (7) Details of the digital book reward.

3   Mobile Experience and Its Game Mechanics

The *Memories of Carvalhal's Palace: Haunted Encounters* is a location-specific non-linear game deployed at the Natural History Museum of Funchal (NHMF) in Madeira, Portugal. The museum was once the residence of a noble Madeiran family, and now, according to the game backstory, some obscure forces are at play, disturbing the museum spaces. In this section, we describe the gameplay and mechanics of *Haunted Encounters*.

Call for Action. Upon launching the app (Fig. 1), two fictional characters – Meara and Isabel – ask the user for help (Fig. 1). Depending on which character the players choose to help, two different museum tours and game endings are delivered. Meara leads the player to explore the marine species collection of the museum, while Isabel leads them to get to know the terrestrial fauna.

Game of Shadows. To uncover the truth about the haunting of the museum the players need to interact with the species in display on the glass shelves. The players engage in a game of shadows (Fig. 1), where they have to match museum exhibits with the silhouettes proposed by the application screen, one at the time.

Markers and Augmented Reality Exhibits. Since not all the species in display are part of the game, special markers, designed in the shape of Runes (ancient Nordic divining alphabet) contradistinguish the species that are part of the game. When the users find the animal that they recon corresponds to the shadow displayed on the app, they can capture the Rune shaped marker (Fig. 1).

AR 3D Models – Freeing Species from the Glass Shelves. By identifying the correct species from its shadow, the players unlock a corresponding AR 3D model (Fig. 1), which they can explore in detail by manipulating the 3D model on the mobile screen. They can rotate the model in all directions, complementing the knowledge and the experience gained from observing the exemplar in the glass shelves.

Quiz. After capturing the marker and the corresponding AR 3D model, the app requests the audience to answer a quiz related to the animal in the shelves. This is a question which requires the user to look closely at the exhibited species, as the question is related to an aspect of its physical details. After answering the question, correct or incorrectly, the audience is presented with a text reporting on several scientific facts about the animal.

The Puzzle and the Treasure Hunt Mechanism. For every completed interaction, from finding the silhouette corresponding animal, to receiving the scientific information, the audience is rewarded with a piece of a puzzle, representing a map. Once completed, the map will guide the players to a hidden location, the scientific library of the museum. In the library, the audience is asked to look for a small chest, containing the answer to their search for the truth. The chest can be found among the scientific publications of the library. Opening the chest reveals a final Rune (marker), which will present them with one of the two potentially different endings, depending which character they decided to help at the beginning. One character will lead the audience to discover a ghost (Fig. 1), who has been haunting the museum for almost a century while the other will menace the players herself with a malignant turn of events.

The Reward, a Token for Later Reflection. In the end, regardless of whom they have been helping, all players receive a reward for finishing their quest. They can take a selfie photograph with the specific ghost or malignant spirit they encountered, which will be emailed to them along with their game score. Moreover, they will receive a book (in a printable PDF format) containing pictures and scientific facts of the animals they engaged with during the tour (Fig. 1). The book also contains the Rune markers which can be recaptured at any time to release the AR 3D models of the species.

4 Conclusions

Through this teenage targeted mobile game deployed at the Natural History Museum of Funchal (Madeira, Portugal), the audience is called to solve a mystery by looking for and interacting with the museum exhibits, collecting Augmented Reality three-dimensional models of the species in display while gaining scientific knowledge about such species. The next phase of our work involves extensively testing this prototype inside the museum's premises in order to validate its game mechanics, and comparing results with its sister story-driven experience, *Turning Point*. The results from these studies will help us understand and facilitate the design of engaging interactive museum experiences for the understudied museum's teenage audiences.

Acknowledgments. ARDITI, project number M14-20-09-5369-FSE-000001.

References

1. Falk, J.H., Dierking, L.D.: Learning from Museums: Visitor Experiences and the Making of Meaning. AltaMira Press, Walnut Creek (2000)
2. Simon, N.: The Participatory Museum (2010). http://www.participatorymuseum.org/
3. Ardito, C., Buono, P., Desolda, G., Matera, M.: From smart objects to smart experiences: an end-user development approach. Int. J. Hum.-Comput. Stud. **114**, 51–68 (2018). https://doi.org/10.1016/j.ijhcs.2017.12.002
4. Haahr, M.: Creating location-based augmented-reality games for cultural heritage. In: Alcañiz, M., Göbel, S., Ma, M., Fradinho Oliveira, M., Baalsrud Hauge, J., Marsh, T. (eds.) JCSG 2017. LNCS, vol. 10622, pp. 313–318. Springer, Cham (2017). https://doi.org/10.1007/978-3-319-70111-0_29
5. Falk, J.H.: Identity and the Museum Visitor Experience. Routledge, Walnut Creek (2009)
6. Prensky, M.: Digital natives, digital immigrants part 1. Horizon **9**, 1–6 (2001). https://doi.org/10.1108/10748120110424816
7. Tzibazi, V.: Participatory action research with young people in museums. Mus. Manag. Curatorship **28**, 153–171 (2013). https://doi.org/10.1080/09647775.2013.776800
8. Cesário, V.: Analysing texts and drawings: the teenage perspective on enjoyable museum experiences. In: 32nd British Human Computer Interaction Conference, pp. 1–3 (2018). https://doi.org/10.14236/ewic/HCI2018.215
9. Cesário, V., Coelho, A., Nisi, V.: Design patterns to enhance teens' museum experiences. In: 32nd British Human Computer Interaction Conference, pp. 1–5 (2018). https://doi.org/10.14236/ewic/HCI2018.160

Multi-level Engagement in Augmented Reality Children's Picture Books

Nicholas Vanderschantz[✉], Annika Hinze, and Aysha AL-Hashami

Computer Science Department, University of Waikato, Hamilton, New Zealand
{vtwoz, hinze}@waikato.ac.nz,
asshal@students.waikato.ac.nz

Abstract. We demonstrate our AR enhanced picture book that provides multiple levels of interaction and engagement. Holding the camera at a range of heights facilitates reader exploration of layered book features and content. These multi-level enhancements extend the traditional learning possibilities of books while providing increased opportunities for both shared and individual reading.

Keywords: Augmented reality · Children's books · Reading · Shared reading

1 Introduction

The merging of augmented reality (AR) and picture book material has been explored for close to two decades, starting with Billinghurst et al.'s Magic Book [1]. Augmented reality adds virtual elements to a real scene, typically viewed through a headset or a phone's camera. In this way, AR interfaces enhance real-world experiences of books [2]. Inspiring examples of extending the experience of books through AR are the haunted book enhancing poetry by Scherrer [6], the AR colouring book [3], and the Vivid Encyclopedia, an AR book of insects [4]. A number of AR-enhanced picture books are available, few of which focus on providing extended engagement over time as a child grows in understanding. This demonstration showcases our picture book AR app that provides multiple levels for children at different learning stages.

Traditional book enhancements in the form of questions, answers, and content sequencing can prompt children to interact and engage with a book at a deeper level [7]. While 'touch and feel' books promote learning for very young readers, 'Search and Find' or 'Question and Answer' books are often considered useful to teach children how to solve problems, make connections and follow cues because they require critical inspection of a page [11]. Pop-up books are often considered to make the learning experience interactive, playful, and memorable. By promoting a hands-on approach to learning – both figuratively and literally – interactive books allow the depiction of a written concept in visual form. This concept can be translated into using AR enhancements for children books to encourage exploration and learning.

While the use of AR in formal learning environments (see e.g., [2, 3, 8]) and digital book use and design (see e.g., [5, 7, 9]) has been extensively explored our application

© IFIP International Federation for Information Processing 2019
Published by Springer Nature Switzerland AG 2019
D. Lamas et al. (Eds.): INTERACT 2019, LNCS 11749, pp. 558–562, 2019.
https://doi.org/10.1007/978-3-030-29390-1_37

focusses on playful learning during shared reading at home. Yuen et al. [10] observe that most likely AR-enhanced books will provide a stepping stone for the public to engage in the cross-over between digital and physical worlds. We agree with their observation that AR-enhanced books have the potential to provide many paths for learners. In our application, we provide these interaction and learning paths within the same page of a book, addressing young readers at different levels of comprehension through the layering of AR features.

2 Demonstration Application

Our AR-enhanced book prototype is based on the children's book 'Hannah's Favourite Place' by Fiona Mason, consisting of the printed book source and an AR companion app. The mobile app provides AR animations, audio, and additional textual elements to enhance the content of the printed book. Elements of the original book were removed from the printed page to allow these to be augmented within the AR app. The app delivers the animations based on recognition of visual marker location anchors which are extracted from the books original illustrations. No further changes were made to the printed book source to allow for the augmentation provided by the app.

Scenario. We propose a scenario where we first meet Maia as a 4-year-old pre-reader sat with her dad John. In front of them is the book Hannah's Favourite Place which is open to a middle spread. At first, Maia holds dads smart-phone in landscape mode with her two small hands holding the camera quite close to the book. She moves the phone around and explores the interactions that occur when individual characters in the book are viewed filling the camera's screen. John then helps Maia lift the phone a little further from the page. The two share the task of holding the phone and here the camera views more than one character or page feature at a time. Finally, Maia hands John the phone and he holds the camera farther from the page so that they can both see the entire spread through the phone.

A few years later we again meet Maia who as she grows older and more confident with books and reading and as her fine motor skills develop we find that she is able to read and interact with Hannah's Favourite Place on her own. Yet there are features of this book that have held her interest for longer than some other books in her collection. Interactive, animated, textual, and audio features of the book have engaged her at different learning phases in her life as if to say the book has grown with her. The features that gripped her during the first read with John are less amusing, yet the opportunities to practice spelling and pronunciation, as well as to read along with the story carry interest for Maia today.

Implementation. Exploration of multiple levels of interaction within a single page is achieved in our app through interactive features that become visible on the phone at three different camera heights, as shown on the left side of Fig. 1.

Fig. 1. Interacting with the book to encounter layered AR animations

At Level 1, the camera is held close to the page and playful interactions of individual image elements are provided. One of these is an animation and audio of a panda sleeping in the tree (see top of Fig. 1).

At Level 2, the camera is held slightly higher from the page and simple educational interactions with two or more objects at a time result. For example, in Fig. 1, middle we illustrate the identification of the two chimps; here they are pointed to by large playful arrows and the spelling of the animals' name is animated.

Level 3 requires the child or parent to hold the camera to view almost the entire page; the app provides both playful and educational interactions. In the example shown in Fig. 1, bottom, the story is narrated and animated bees fly across the page. These bees are objects that do not occur in the illustrated storybook, nor are they a part of the written text. However, the inclusion of such non-text illustration is common in children's books and enhances opportunities for discussion, emersion, and realistic building of a scene or environment.

Further details of design thinking for our AR-enhancement is discussed in [8]. An interaction of the app with the book spread (engaging with level 2) is shown in Fig. 2.

Fig. 2. User interacting with the enhanced book via AR app (Level 2 animation)

3 Summary

This paper discussed our mobile phone-based augmented reality picture book prototype that provides AR animations, audio, and additional textual elements to enhance the content of the printed book. We believe that enhanced picture books, be they with augmentation, physical interaction, or cognitive interaction will increase the learning possibilities and extend the useful lifespan of that book along with the child. The significant feature of our work is the investigation of the affordances of the 3-dimensional space between the camera and the book surface. At the time of our investigation, we are not aware of other children's books that presently exploit this multi-level enhancement in their implementation. Our future work will extend this prototype based on insights from parents about the role of books and technology in their homes.

References

1. Billinghurst, M., Duenser, A.: Augmented reality in the classroom. Computer **45**(7), 56–63 (2012)
2. Billinghurst, M., Kato, H., Poupyrev, I.: The magicbook-moving seamlessly between reality and virtuality. IEEE Comput. Graph. Appl. **21**(3), 6–8 (2001)
3. Clark, A., Dunser, A.: An interactive augmented reality coloring book. In: 2012 IEEE Symposium on 3D User Interfaces (3DUI), pp. 7–10. IEEE (2012)
4. Fumihisa, S., et al.: Vivid encyclopedia: MR pictorial book of insects. In: Proceedings of Virtual Reality Society of Japan Annual Conference (2004)
5. Kucirkova, N.: An integrative framework for studying, designing and conceptualising interactivity in children's digital books. Br. Educ. Res. J. **43**(6), 1168–1185 (2017)
6. Scherrer, C., Pilet, J., Fua, P., Lepetit, V.: The haunted book. In: Proceedings of the 7th IEEE/ACM International Symposium on Mixed and Augmented Reality (ISMAR 2008), pp. 163–164. IEEE (2008)

7. Timpany, C., Vanderschantz, N.: A categorisation structure for interactive children's books. Int. J. Book 9(4), 97–110 (2012)
8. Vanderschantz, N., Hinze, A., AL-Hashami, A.: Multiple level enhancement of children's picture books with augmented reality. In: Dobreva, M., Hinze, A., Žumer, M. (eds.) ICADL 2018. LNCS, vol. 11279, pp. 256–260. Springer, Cham (2018). https://doi.org/10.1007/978-3-030-04257-8_26
9. Vanderschantz, N., Timpany, C.: Analysing interaction in children's digital books. Int. J. Book 9(4), 31–47 (2012)
10. Yuen, S.C.Y., Yaoyuneyong, G., Johnson, E.: Augmented reality: an overview and five directions for AR in education. J. Educ. Technol. Dev. Exch. (JETDE) 4(1), 11 (2011)
11. Zeece, P.D.: Using current literature selections to nurture the development of kindness in young children. Early Child. Educ. J. 36(5), 447–452 (2009)

On-the-Fly Usability Evaluation
of Mobile Adaptive UIs Through
Instant User Feedback

Enes Yigitbas$^{(\boxtimes)}$, Ivan Jovanovikj, Klementina Josifovska, Stefan Sauer,
and Gregor Engels

Paderborn University, Fürstenallee 11, 33102 Paderborn, Germany
{enes.yigitbas,ivan.jovanovikj,klementina.josifovska,stefan.sauer,
gregor.engels}@upb.de

Abstract. Adaptive User Interfaces (AUIs) have been promoted as a
solution for context variability due to their ability to automatically adapt
to the context-of-use at runtime. For the acceptance of AUIs, usability
plays a crucial role. Classical usability evaluation methods like usability
tests, interviews or cognitive walkthroughs are not sufficient for evaluating end-user satisfaction of AUIs at runtime. The main reason is that
the UI and context-of-use are dynamically changing and acceptance of
UI adaptation features has to be evaluated in the moment and context-of-use when the adaptations occur. To address this challenge, we present
an on-the-fly usability evaluation solution that combines continuous context monitoring together with collection of instant user feedback to assess
end-user satisfaction of UI adaptation features. We demonstrate the usefulness and benefit of our solution based on a mobile Android mail app,
which served as basis for conducting a usability study.

Keywords: Adaptive User Interface · Usability evaluation

1 Introduction

Adaptive UIs (AUIs) have been promoted as a solution for plasticity [3] due
to their ability to automatically adapt to the context-of-use at runtime. With
regard to AUIs, usability evaluation of UI adaptations is still a challenging task,
especially in the ubiquitous domain of mobile UI platforms, where dynamically
changing context-of-use situations are usual. In the past, classical usability evaluation methods like usability tests, interviews or cognitive walkthroughs were
applied to evaluate the usability of AUIs [2]. However, these methods are not
sufficient for a proper evaluation of dynamically changing UI adaptation features
at runtime. The reason is that these methods mostly focus on *a posteriori* analysis techniques. However, the acceptance of each UI adaptation feature should
be evaluated at the very moment and in context-of-use when the adaptation
is triggered at runtime. To address this issue, we present an on-the-fly (OTF)

© IFIP International Federation for Information Processing 2019
Published by Springer Nature Switzerland AG 2019
D. Lamas et al. (Eds.): INTERACT 2019, LNCS 11749, pp. 563–567, 2019.
https://doi.org/10.1007/978-3-030-29390-1_38

usability evaluation solution that integrates UI adaptation features and a user feedback mechanism into a mobile app. The developed solution enables us to continuously track various context information data and collect user feedback, e.g. whether the users like or dislike the triggered UI adaptations.

The rest of the paper is structured as follows: In Sect. 2, we present the general solution idea for OTF usability evaluation of UI adaptations. Section 3 provides an overview of the concrete implementation of our adaptive mail app, which was used as a basis setup to perform an empirical experiment for evaluating AUIs. In Sect. 4, we describe the conducted usability study. Finally, Sect. 5 concludes our work with an outlook on future work.

2   Solution Idea

Our OTF usability evaluation solution targets rule-based UI adaptation approaches as introduced in our previous work [5]. We extended our existing rule-based UI adaptation approach with capabilities to support continuous context monitoring and collect context-driven instant user feedback.

Figure 1 illustrates the main idea of our OTF usability evaluation solution for UI adaptations. Based on IBM's MAPE-K loop [1], we have two main components *Adaptation Manager* and *Managed Element*. The *Adaptation Manager* is responsible for monitoring and adapting the *Managed Element*, which in our case is the user interface of a mobile platform. For supporting OTF usability evaluation of UI adaptation features, the existing monitoring and adaptation loop described in our previous work [5] needs to be extended. To this end, we integrated an instant

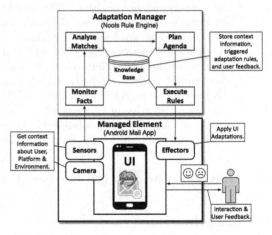

Fig. 1. On-the-fly usability evaluation of UI adaptation features

user feedback mechanism into the context monitoring and UI adaptation loop. The feedback mechanism allows users to explicitly rate the triggered UI adaptations. Users can give positive or negative feedback, but they can also ignore the feedback mechanism and concentrate on their main application task. As Fig. 1 shows, there is a *Knowledge Base* which is responsible for storing all context information, all triggered UI adaptation rules, and the corresponding instant user feedback. Based on the stored information, it is possible to analyze the acceptance of UI adaptations based on the current context of the user and the user's feedback.

3   Implementation

We implemented our on-the-fly usability evaluation solution based on an Android mail app using React Native[1]. We decided to use a mail app as email clients are one of the most frequently used apps on mobile platforms in various context-of-use situations. The implemented email app is based on Gmail and provides full email services. Beside the core mail application logic, inspired by [4], we implemented 28 UI adaptation features that cover different adaptation strategies like task-feature set-, layout-, navigation-, and modality-adaptation.

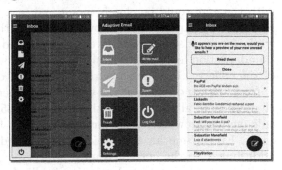

Figure 2 depicts three screenshots of the mail app showing the effect of exemplary UI adaptation features. The first screenshot in Fig. 2 shows a minimalistic UI where an icon-based representation is shown. In contrast to that, the second screenshot shows a grid layout that could be useful for novice users. The third screenshot shows an example for UI modality adaptation where a switch from the graphical UI

Fig. 2. UI Adaptations: minimalistic UI, "large" UI, and vocal UI (left to right)

(GUI) to the vocal UI (VUI) was made and mails are read out in the language of the mail. To realize the described UI adaptations, we integrated the Nools[2] rule engine into the mobile email app. It is fed with context information from various integrated sensors and cameras of the mobile platform. For example, we use different sensors like ambient light, accelerometer, gyroscope, battery or network sensor. Furthermore, we use timer, device information or existing recognition services such as *Amazon Rekognition*[3] to derive the user's emotion as well as estimated age or gender based on camera photos.

For realization of the feedback mechanism, we integrated a feedback prompt into the adaptive email app. The left screenshot in Fig. 3 shows how the feedback prompt was placed in the mail app. On the top of the screen the feedback prompt is shown whenever context changes were detected that lead to UI adaptations. The triggered UI adaptations are explained in the feedback prompt and the user is able to provide feedback by clicking the positive or negative smiley indi-

Fig. 3. Feedback prompts

[1] https://facebook.github.io/react-native/.

[2] http://noolsjs.com/.

[3] https://aws.amazon.com/de/rekognition/.

cating whether the user liked the UI adaptation or not. In some cases, for example, when the user is in a bad mood and the app detects this via camera, a feedback prompt in the form of a text field appears (see right screenshot in Fig. 3) that allows the users to provide more detailed feedback.

4 Usability Study

During the usability experiment, the developed app was used for one week by 23 participants. All users were made aware of the fact that their interaction with the app would be closely monitored (e.g. using facial recognition). During the usability experiment, various data about the users and their usage context, while feedback was given, have been collected to evaluate the usability of the UI adaptation features in detail. In the following, we will shortly describe some of the collected data to show the potential of our usability evaluation solution. During the conduction of the experiment, there were 104404 detected context changes from all devices. Of these, only 37465 triggered an adaptation by the rule engine. However, users gave feedback on the adaptation rules in only 663 cases. Every time an adaptation rule received feedback, the previous context additionally to the current context was saved. In total, the users gave positive feedback in 616 cases and negative feedback in 47 cases. With about 93% of the feedback provided by users being positive this means that most of the user interface adaptations were liked by the users.

5 Conclusion and Outlook

This paper presents a novel solution and demo for evaluating the usability of UI adaptations for mobile platforms with a special focus on end-user satisfaction. We introduce an on-the-fly usability evaluation solution that incorporates instant user feedback and the corresponding context-of-use. In this way, our solution enables us to continuously track various context information about the user, platform, and environmental characteristics and user feedback, e.g. if the users accept the triggered UI adaptations or not. For future work, we plan to extend our usability evaluation approach to cover further usability aspects like efficiency and effectiveness. In this regard, further long-term usability studies with a larger user group is planned.

References

1. An architectural blueprint for autonomic computing. Technical report, IBM, June 2005
2. van Velsen, L., et al.: User-centered evaluation of adaptive and adaptable systems: a literature review (2008)
3. Calvary, G., Coutaz, J., Thevenin, D.: A unifying reference framework for the development of plastic user interfaces. In: Little, M.R., Nigay, L. (eds.) EHCI 2001. LNCS, vol. 2254, pp. 173–192. Springer, Heidelberg (2001). https://doi.org/10.1007/3-540-45348-2_17

4. Paternò, F.: User interface design adaptation (Chap. 39). In: The Encyclopedia of Human-Computer Interaction, 2nd edn, Aarhus, Denmark (2013)
5. Yigitbas, E., Stahl, H., Sauer, S., Engels, G.: Self-adaptive UIs: integrated model-driven development of uis and their adaptations. In: Anjorin, A., Espinoza, H. (eds.) ECMFA 2017. LNCS, vol. 10376, pp. 126–141. Springer, Cham (2017). https://doi.org/10.1007/978-3-319-61482-3_8

SwipeBuddy

A Teleoperated Tablet and Ebook-Reader Holder for a Hands-Free Interaction

Max Pascher[1,2]([✉]) [iD], Stefan Schneegass[2], and Jens Gerken[1]

[1] Westphalian University of Applied Sciences, Human-Computer Interaction,
Gelsenkirchen, Germany
max.pascher@w-hs.de
[2] University of Duisburg-Essen, paluno, Essen, Germany

Abstract. Mobile devices are the core computing platform we use in our everyday life to communicate with friends, watch movies, or read books. For people with severe physical disabilities, such as tetraplegics, who cannot use their hands to operate such devices, these devices are barely usable. Tackling this challenge, we propose SwipeBuddy, a teleoperated robot allowing for touch interaction with a smartphone, tablet, or ebook-reader. The mobile device is mounted on top of the robot and can be teleoperated by a user through head motions and gestures controlling a stylus simulating touch input. Further, the user can control the position and orientation of the mobile device. We demonstrate the SwipeBuddy robot device and its different interaction capabilities.

Keywords: Self-determined Life · Head-based Interaction · Human-Robot Interaction

1 Introduction

Providing a hands-free interaction mode to interact with technology is an important feature which may in particular benefit people with severe physical disabilities, such as tetraplegics, who can not use their hands to interact with technology.

Interaction technologies such as gaze-based interaction and head movement have been explored to operate, e.g. a PC [2–4]. However, today's ubiquitous technology interaction scenarios are much more tightly integrated in everyday activities. Prime examples might be reading the news on a smartphone or tablet while eating breakfast, or surfing the web on such a device while at the same time watching TV on a shared big screen. Since people with tetraplegia are often relying on human assistants to interact with technology, this parallel interaction and seamless switching between tasks increases the burden on both assistants

Electronic supplementary material The online version of this chapter (https://doi.org/10.1007/978-3-030-29390-1_39) contains supplementary material, which is available to authorized users.

and users. From our experience and interviews with people with tetraplegia, we know that they may also be reluctant to have their human assistant constantly switch between such small tasks [1]. On the other hand, technological devices that may support e.g. reading, are also bound to certain locations and positions and do not offer the flexibility that people without such disabilities enjoy. In this demonstration paper, we present SwipeBuddy, a mobile robot with a hands-free Interface enables such flexibility and enhances a human's opportunities regarding task and attention switching.

2   The SwipeBuddy-System

SwipeBuddy is a physical robotic device that acts as a mobile ebook reader and photo browser and can be controlled by using head movements. Its main tasks are to (a) hold the digital device (e.g. Amazon Kindle) (b) provide an interaction mechanism with the device to swipe pages and (c) flexibly move around so that it does not interfere with parallel activities (e.g. eating). The SwipeBuddy acts as an r-c mobile ebook-reader that can be positioned using head movements.

2.1   Hardware Platform

The prototype of SwipeBuddy consists of a mobile robotic platform with a continuous track vehicle propulsion (caterpillar track) for high maneuverability, i.e. turning around its own axis. A mobile device (smartphone, Kindle etc.) is placed on a tilting platform that allows the user to easily manipulate the view-angle of the device. Furthermore, the robot has a mechanical swipe mechanism that helps flipping pages or pressing icons. The swiping mechanism consists of a tip of a stylus for capacitive touch displays and a motorized arm which provides contact pressure for swipe and scroll. Using a mechanical swipe mechanism enables a user to activate a swipe action with any application and with any device. A software controlled swipe would be device dependent and thus less flexible. A visual mock-up of the SwipeBuddy is depicted in Fig. 1.

Fig. 1. Draft concept of the SwipeBuddy. To increase mobility the robot is equipped with a continuous track vehicle propulsion. Furthermore, it features a tilting platform to change the tilt and therefore view-angle of the mobile device.

2.2   Interaction Design

The interaction concept consists of a **Magnetic-AngularRate-Gravity** (MARG) sensor that is mounted on a headband. This setup enables capturing of head motion data along the roll, pitch and yaw axis of the head when a user wears the headband in order to control the swipe arm to switch pages of the device and furthermore steer the robot itself.

Robustness of the measured orientation depends on the underlying method of sensor data fusion since various disturbances introduce errors. In this work, we use a robust quaternion based filter approach to estimate orientation from MARG-sensors that was introduced by Wöhle and Gebhard [5] and is implemented on a standalone micro-controller. Since the orientation is measured relative to the global quantities (gravity and magnetic field), there are no environmental restrictions that would limit usage to a local use-case. We are using a self-designed sensor system that enables wireless communication via WiFi UDP. The orientation data is mapped on the actuators of the system to achieve the defined tasks.

In our interaction design, the user can switch between different modes to steer the robotic platform, change the tilt angle of the electronic device, and perform a forward or backward swipe action. Additionally, an idle mode is available to block all interactions to put the sensor headband on or off. In particular, the user is switching modes by performing a movement along the yaw-axis, like it is shown in Fig. 2. Movements in roll and pitch axis are used n each mode different i.a. driving, steering, tilting, and swiping.

To provide a visual feedback to the user about which mode is selected and to help to orient, 25 RGB LEDs are installed and used in a way that supports intuitive insight. For Example in driving mode SwipeBuddy is following a car metaphor. White headlamp and red tail lamps are turned on and the continuous track is illuminated green (see Fig. 3). A slightly moving in the roll axis which is

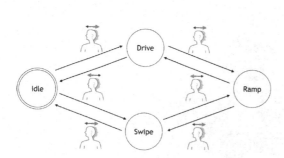

Fig. 2. The modes of SwipeBuddy are arranged in a circular queue and can be selected by movement along the yaw-axis of the head in both directions.

Fig. 3. The user is steering SwipeBuddy by his head movements. The white headlamps are turned on. (Color figure online)

used for steering is changing the green continuous track light to a yellow blinker to indicate a change of the steering direction on the respective side. Furthermore, all LEDs are mounted at special positions and on special parts of the robotic system where they could be recognized easily and show which parts are active.

3   Conclusion

With the SwipeBuddy we presented a software- and device independent robotic assistant system to people with severe physical disabilities. It does not aim to replace human assistants but support them for very specific tasks where users might not feel comfortable constantly asking for help. Our first informal tests with people with tetraplegia showed that the SwipeBuddy could potentially be a very welcome helper device with positive feedback regarding the use-case as well as the overall interaction design. While our scenario focuses on people who are physically limited in the usage of their hands, the SwipeBuddy could also assist people whose hands are currently tied to other activities, e.g. in an industrial context (industry 4.0) where an operator might need their hands to operate a machine interface and at the same time need to read a digital manual.

References

1. Baumeister, A., Pascher, M., Thietje, R., Gerken, J., Klein, B.: Anforderungen an die Interaktion eines Roboterarms zur Nahrungsaufnahme bei Tetraplegie – Eine ethnografische Analyse. In: Kongress und Ausstellung zu Alltagsunterstützenden Assistenzlösungen – Tagungsband, pp. 100–101. Karlsruher Messe- und Kongress GmbH (2018). https://hci.w-hs.de/wp-content/uploads/2018/11/pub_AAL_2018_Tagungsband_web.pdf
2. Duchowski, A.T.: Gaze-based interaction: a 30 year retrospective. Comput. Graph. **73**, 59–69 (2018). https://doi.org/10.1016/j.cag.2018.04.002. http://www.sciencedirect.com/science/article/pii/S0097849318300487
3. Plaumann, K., Ehlers, J., Geiselhart, F., Yuras, G., Huckauf, A., Rukzio, E.: Better than you think: head gestures for mid air input. In: Abascal, J., Barbosa, S., Fetter, M., Gross, T., Palanque, P., Winckler, M. (eds.) INTERACT 2015. LNCS, vol. 9298, pp. 526–533. Springer, Cham (2015). https://doi.org/10.1007/978-3-319-22698-9_36
4. Roig-Maimó, M.F., MacKenzie, I.S., Manresa-Yee, C., Varona, J.: Head-tracking interfaces on mobile devices: Evaluation using fitts' law and a new multi-directional corner task for small displays. Int. J. Hum.-Comput. Stud. **112**, 1–15 (2018). https://doi.org/10.1016/j.ijhcs.2017.12.003. http://www.sciencedirect.com/science/article/pii/S1071581917301647
5. Wöhle, L., Gebhard, M.: A robust quaternion based Kalman filter using a gradient descent algorithm for orientation measurement. In: 2018 IEEE International Instrumentation and Measurement Technology Conference (I2MTC), pp. 1–6, May 2018. https://doi.org/10.1109/I2MTC.2018.8409593

VibroSquare: Vibro-Tactile Display
for Body-Centric Implicit Interactions

Yulia Zhiglova(✉)(iD), David Lamas(✉)(iD), Ilja Smorgun(✉)(iD),
and Amir Zare Pashaei(✉)(iD)

Tallinn University, Tallinn, Estonia
{yzhigl,drl,ilja.smorgun,amirzp}@tlu.ee

Abstract. Importance of touch cannot be underestimated. Touch is the first sense that a human develops already in a womb and the last sense that one loses with age. Touch can serve as a powerful modality for developing novel human-computer interfaces. We present *VibroSquare* - our first vibro-tactile display we designed to enable first set of experiments to test our research assumptions. During the experiments we will explore how vibro-tactile feedback can be communicated on an unconscious (implicit) level of perception. The objective of the demonstration is to offer first hand experience of the interaction with *VibroSquare* and create conversations around designing technologies for supporting body-centric interactions using mediated touch.

Keywords: Peripheral interaction · Vibro-tactile · Body-centric

1 Introduction

The importance of touch for humans has been demonstrated in numerous studies. Sense of comfort and attachment through touch has been shown in humans. Other studies revealed that touch affects generosity level and increases oxytocin level - the hormone of "happiness" [4]. Knowing all the evident advantages of touch, why cannot we use haptic technology to mediate touch to make life of people more enriched and comfortable? A lot of research in HCI concerns the mediated-touch technology and understanding how various vibro-tactile stimuli may affect the perception [2]. We already know that specific combinations of parameters (frequency, intensity, location on a body) may simulate variety of touch types and are associated with qualitatively distinct affective states. Most of these studies work in the plane of conscious or explicit perception [3,5,7]. Very few however touch upon the implicit or unconscious [1,6]. *VibroSquare* is our first attempt to investigate how a vibro-tactile display can be designed to communicate information unconsciously.

© IFIP International Federation for Information Processing 2019
Published by Springer Nature Switzerland AG 2019
D. Lamas et al. (Eds.): INTERACT 2019, LNCS 11749, pp. 572–576, 2019.
https://doi.org/10.1007/978-3-030-29390-1_40

2   Application Scenarios

Unconscious perception, evoked by tactile stimulation, opens numerous opportunities for novel application scenarios in the contexts of remote communication, well-being, healthcare and many more.

We focus our research in the context of remote communication. We aim at recreating a sense of presence through mediated touch. Imagine a situation where a husband and a wife are remotely located from each other. The husband expresses his care by sending a caressing to his wife that she would feel on her skin via a wearable vibro-tactile display. Meanwhile, the wife who is fully engaged with her office tasks, perceives the virtual caressing. Since the stimuli is communicated on a periphery of her attention, she is not distracted from her main activity.

Thus, we are interested in recreating mediated touch for social support or simple notification but on an implicit (unconscious) level. In other words we aim at extending the ideas of 'calm technology' expressed by Weiser [8].

3   Design Rationale

By means of *VibroSquare* (Fig. 1), we plan to not only simulate various types of touch and test various interaction scenarios but most importantly investigate when and how the stimuli' parameters can be perceived unconsciously. The prototype is designed in a shape of a patch that can be attached to almost any location on a human body. The ability to program each actuator independently and place it in various body locations will provide greater flexibility for the experiments.

A well established classical apparatus of psychophysics [4] will constrain the vibration parameters and the intensity of the stimuli that will be programmed into the prototype. Humans can consciously detect the vibration from about 1 Hz to 1,000 Hz but they are not equally sensitive to frequencies over the whole range which is determined by the type of the mechanoreceptors. The vibrations below 15 Hz can often be not detected. We also know that slow stroking and low intensity touch is more pleasant than otherwise. The vibration at about 50 Hz are providing comfortable sensation, where the vibrations above 137 Hz create uncomfortable sensations on the skin [3,4,6]. This, and other aspects about human body are fundamental for configuring *VibroSquare*.

As the prototype is meant to be worn on a body, the materials chosen for constructing the display, were carefully selected. The goal was to choose the materials that would be perceived by skin in a most non-obtrusive, natural way. The coin-cell mini vibration motors are known for their ability to produce irritating sensation, so the materials had to serve as absorbents of the excessive stimulation. We tested several types of materials and selected the most appropriate one (highlighted in Fig. 1).

The dimension of the vibro-tactile matrix is 7 cm wide by 11 cm height, forming a matrix of 24 coin cell vibration actuators (4 by 6) with inter-actuator spacing of 1 cm. Such distribution of the actuators was constrained by the spatial

Fig. 1. Design process of *VibroSquare*: the selection of the face fabric, layout of the main hardware parts, prototype sketches, the latest version of the prototype (still in progress).

resolution mapping of cutaneous (tactile) receptors. Spatial resolution determines the sensitivity of the skin in various body parts and the ability to sense two closely related objects on the skin as two distinct stimuli. The discrimination ability is within 2.5 mm to 55 mm range [6]. This means that the prototype can be suitable for almost all body parts, except palmar surface of fingers and toes. Since we plan to work in the context of remote communication to simulate pleasant touch we will use an existing algorithm, "Tactile Brush" [3]. We chose this algorithm because it provides an optimum stimulus onset asynchrony (SOA) producing an illusion of a smooth tactile motion. Such illusion is essential for realistic perception of a pleasant touch.

4   Future Work and Limitations

Current prototype is limited by the current 'off the shelf' technology. It is bulky and the vibration motors are working in a very limited range of frequencies which makes it impossible to work with high (>200) and low frequencies (<80). In future we plan to develop a set of more comprehensive prototypes, integrated (or attached onto) into clothing seamlessly. For that we will need to build custom flexible PCBs to ensure the seamless integration. We will also use more powerful vibration motors that are cable of working in a wider range of frequencies.

5   Engaging with *VibroSquare*

VibroSquare will serve as a testbed for exploring how configured parameters of the prototype may affect the perception of the stimuli. Specifically, during the interaction a participant will experience several versions of pleasant touch. Each version will have a different frequency or intensity configuration or combination of both. The participants will be offered to wear a prototype on various parts of the body, adding another dimension to the interaction. So, we will be exploring three main parameters: frequency, intensity and location.

The infrastructure of interaction will consist of an input device and an output device. The input device will represent a tangible interface with several built-in pressure sensors corresponding to a specific predefined configuration of vibro-tactile parameters (frequency and intensity), resulting in a specific output (touch type). The output device is *VibroSquare*. Connection between the devices will be enabled through Bluetooth low energy protocol (MQTT).

At the conference, the visitors will be able to try *VibroSqure* in pairs or solo. We plan to gather feedback from the participants about their perception while wearing the prototype. We anticipate that participants will get the following insights by interacting with *VibroSquare*:

- Getting an awareness about the importance of psychophysics in designing technology for mediated touch;
- Getting an awareness about the key parameters that affect perception of tactile stimuli on a continuum of conscious and unconscious processing;
- The interaction with *VibroSquare* may spark curiosity in the topic, produce discussion and potentially result in future research cooperations.

To conclude, we presented design rationale of *VibroSquare*, with hope to probe our research ideas and gather valuable feedback during the demonstration.

Technical Details to Run the Demo

1. The connection between input and output devices will be enabled by the central processing unit (CPU) through Bluetooth low energy protocol (MQTT). The CPU gathers information from the input device and subscribes it to the output device by adapting publish-subscribe pattern.
2. Each device is powered by Lithium polymer battery. The input device needs a 5 V, 2500 mAh and the output device - a 3.7 V, 6000 mAh. The central processing unit requires a mobile battery bank to ensure it operates correctly. All will be supplied by our research team.
3. At the venue we will need a separate table and access to the electricity nearby in order to place laptop, prototype and be able to charge the devices.

References

1. Bakker, S., van den Hoven, E., Eggen, B.: Peripheral interaction: characteristics and considerations. Pers. Ubiquitous Comput. **19**(1), 239–254 (2015). https://doi.org/10.1007/s00779-014-0775-2
2. Eid, M.A., Al Osman, H.: Affective haptics: current research and future directions. IEEE Access **4**, 26–40 (2016). https://doi.org/10.1109/ACCESS.2015.2497316
3. Israr, A., Poupyrev, I.: Tactile brush: drawing on skin with a tactile grid display. In: Proceedings of the SIGCHI Conference on Human Factors in Computing Systems, pp. 2019–2028. CHI 2011. ACM, New York (2011). https://doi.org/10.1145/1978942.1979235
4. Montagu, A.: Touching: the Human Significance of the Skin. Perennial library, HarperCollins (1986). https://books.google.ee/books?id=XU7Z_aqCYggC

5. Niforatos, E., Fedosov, A., Elhart, I., Langheinrich, M.: Augmenting skiers' peripheral perception. In: Proceedings of the 2017 ACM International Symposium on Wearable Computers, ISWC 2017, pp. 114–121. ACM, New York (2017). https://doi.org/10.1145/3123021.3123052

6. Riener, A., Ferscha, A., Frech, P., Hackl, M., Kaltenberger, M.: Subliminal vibrotactile based notification of CO_2 economy while driving. In: AutomotiveUI (2010)

7. Tajadura-Jiménez, A., Basia, M., Deroy, O., Fairhurst, M., Marquardt, N., Bianchi-Berthouze, N.: As light as your footsteps: altering walking sounds to change perceived body weight, emotional state and gait. In: Proceedings of the 33rd Annual ACM Conference on Human Factors in Computing Systems, CHI 2015, pp. 2943–2952. ACM, New York (2015). https://doi.org/10.1145/2702123.2702374

8. Weiser, M., Brown, J.S.: The coming age of calm technology. In: Denning, P.J., Metcalfe, R.M. (eds.) Beyond Calculation, pp. 75–85. Springer, New York (1997). https://doi.org/10.1007/978-1-4612-0685-9_6

Industry Case Studies

A Human-Centred Business Scenario in SIoT – The Case of DANOS Framework

Daniel Defiebre$^{(\boxtimes)}$ and Panagiotis Germanakos

SAP SE, Dietmar-Hopp-Allee 16, 69190 Walldorf, Germany
{daniel.defiebre,panagiotis.germanakos}@sap.com

Abstract. The Social Internet of Things (SIoT) provides a landscape with a huge business potential, which affects both the producer and the consumer, and opens new business opportunities for delivering products and services with increased user experience. Such a potential is predominantly dependent on the quality of objects' relationships established over time, which might determine the value of the interactions and the information exchanged between them. Accordingly, in this paper we discuss a business case over a novel human-centered framework, namely DANOS, which employs human personality traits as the primal influential factor of the behaviors and interactions of things in a network of objects.

Keywords: SIoT · Personality · Framework · Human-centred model · Simulation

1 Introduction

Latest forecasts suggest that by the year 2021 there will be more or less 26 billion connected Internet of Things (IoT) units [3], portraying an intelligent network of things with a significant power, in terms of information availability, accessibility and shareability through its integrated nodes, and a highlighted potential for the business organizations [6]. A fundamental challenge towards that direction is for objects to be able to build strong and long-term relationships among themselves exchanging most apt information and services to the benefit of their users. Considering that such relationships could be established more effectively in a Social Internet of Things (SIoT) landscape [2], where things are able to create their own social networks, in this work we explore the potential of utilizing specific human characteristics in an objects' network for guiding their behaviours and actions as in the Human Social Networks (HSN) gaining e.g., on the navigability, scalability and trustworthiness. In this respect, we overview a real-life business consumer goods scenario using a novel framework in the area of SIoT, namely DANOS (Dynamic Anthropomorphic Network of Objects Simulator). It is based on a human-centered hierarchical model that maintains at its core human personality traits and drives the behavior and communication of objects while traveling autonomously in a space. Hereafter, we outline the main

© IFIP International Federation for Information Processing 2019
Published by Springer Nature Switzerland AG 2019
D. Lamas et al. (Eds.): INTERACT 2019, LNCS 11749, pp. 579–583, 2019.
https://doi.org/10.1007/978-3-030-29390-1_41

components of DANOS and present preliminary evaluation results showing more granular, stable and long-term relationships over time between the objects. As such, we expect higher accuracy on service requests, relevance on recommendations and enhanced user experience during information acquisition.

2   An Overview of the DANOS Framework

DANOS framework (see Fig. 1) enables SIoT objects to create autonomous context-aware relationships and to share best-fit recommendations among them and with their owners.

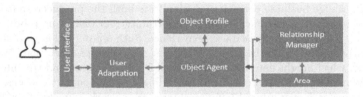

Fig. 1. Main components of the DANOS framework

The *user interface (UI)* (can be of any type, e.g., display on an object), maintains the communication with the user for collecting information and returning recommendations based on service requests. The *user adaptation (UA)* component is responsible for adapting the data to the user's preferences, e.g., adjusting recommendations on given user requirements. It includes various processes like locating specific information to create a service request, recording the interaction data between the user and his objects, extracting patterns (by applying, e.g., semantic reasoning) regarding his behavior, and ranking the collected information like recommendations proposed by other objects. The *object agent (OA)* component maintains the engine that facilitates the interaction with the DANOS network for requesting new friendships, gathering recommendations from friends, and registering its position in the *area*. It has an *object profile (OP)* which consists of all information that contribute to the creation of qualitative relationships between the objects, namely, *object specifics* (i.e., objects' specifications using various static attributes), *interaction specifics* (i.e., data that are generated through the objects' lifetime experience in the network, position in the area), and *user specifics* (i.e., characteristics, preferences, inherent human aspects (like personality traits) of the owners (users) of an object.) Once an object has inherited these characteristics during the initialization phase, it runs and interacts autonomously (through the OA detached from the user) in the network. Subsequently, the OA passes on the OP specifics to the *relationship manager (RM)* for calculating the similarity between two objects. The similarity calculation indicates if two objects will become friends while communicating in proximity in the area (we consider a *friendship* as an established relationship between two objects that share similar profile characteristics and can exchange information of common interest). In DANOS, one object may have a different opinion about another regarding the extent that they might fit based on their behavior. Hence, they might both want to become friends (full friendship), only one of them (partial friendship), or none of them (no friendship). Assuming that a friendship has been established, the OA receives various recommendations from similar objects to the targeted one, which is then prioritized, adapted and offered to the user (UA component).

3   A Real-Life Business Scenario

The proposed framework adheres to a decentralized workflow process which we highlight through the simple business scenario below. DANOS focuses on two main subsequent SIoT process activities, namely, *new friendship acquisition* and *recommendation discovery* (currently under development) [1]. Peter has recently bought a new IoT fridge, joining the DANOS network. During the initialization phase his fridge inherits some of his preferences (e.g., he drinks lactose-free milk in the morning) and human traits (e.g., he is strong in *neuroticism* and weak in *openness* with respect to the scale of personality traits [4]), adapting a human-centered behavior (HCB) during communication with the other objects. Accordingly, his fridge will exhibit a HCB of not taking excessive risks when interacting with other fridges (e.g., will not risk to make friendships with other fridges that their profiles might be related but are not fully matched), since the particular combination of those personality traits refer to behaviors that are risk-avoidant – avoiding to take more risks for gains in decision-making [5]. As a newcomer object, Peter's fridge has no friends as yet, but it has to **find new friends** to get relevant recommendations to the benefit of its owner. Therefore, it creates a service request (UA) to locate objects-friends that will provide the best matching milk for his preferences, defined as a service name with specifications (in this case as $MilkService_{[lactose-free,organic]}$). Carrying this information, the fridge travels (OA) into the virtual area of DANOS network autonomously to the position $MilkService_{[lactose-free,organic]}$ and requests the RM for creating new friendships with the surrounding objects. The RM forwards the friendship request to all fridges which have subscribed in the same vector space $[lactose-free, organic]$, and for each responding object it calculates the similarity with Peter's fridge, considering the OP specifics (e.g., personality traits, list of friends or runs, power supply status, energy class), as discussed earlier. If the similarity is above a dynamically calculated threshold, the objects become friends and share their information or recommendations irrespective of the time or space they travel. Next, Peter's fridge **asks its friends for related recommendations** to find the best-fit milk for him. Its friends provide a number of suggestions based on the interaction data and patterns generated between their owner and the (milk) product (e.g., the frequency of drinking milk during a specific time during the day, dietary preferences), which it has to rank by assigning weights. For this job, it considers its owner's preferences, semantic interaction patterns (e.g., between previous products (milk) and the object (fridges)), as well as previous experience regarding the received recommendations by its fridge's friends (e.g., how successful they have been in the past). Finally, the fridge presents Peter with the top milk recommendations (UA) through the UI and observes his satisfaction for future recommendations on incoming requests.

4   Preliminary Evaluation Results

To evaluate the quality of the recommendations provided by the objects, we first need to understand the quality of the relationships established between them while travelling in DANOS. Hence, we simulate the friendship generation process of 30000 requests from 2000 objects over time (average of 15 request per object). We are using a generic area to define the context vector as $Area_{x,y}$, where $\{x, y \in \mathbb{N} | 0 \leq x, y \leq 10000\}$. All objects travel randomly in this context area 25,5 times on average during the lifetime of the simulation. For the vector space, we divided the area into 10000 cells, where friendships can only be established in the same cell. In total, there were 3228 friendships established between the fridges (1135 full, 1173 partial and 892 no friendships – see Fig. 2). The threshold was calculated dynamically in time (the value was optimized across various training simulations) and stabilized around 0.63. In case of Peter's fridge, it travelled 25 times (searching for the specific kind of milk), with a total distance of $x = 1335, y = 1440$ and has visited 22 different cells in the area, establishing 3 full-friendships with an average similarity metric of 0.76, 4 partial-friendships with 0.52 and 2 no-friendships with 0.51.

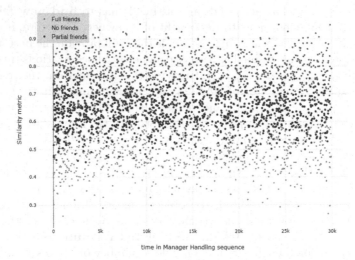

Fig. 2. The 3 types of friendships established between object pairs over time

5 Conclusion

In this paper we overviewed a business consumer goods case through a novel human-centred SIoT framework DANOS. We outlined its main components and decentralized workflow, and emphasized on the generation of relationships between the things over time while travelling autonomously in a virtual space. We found that the quality of the friendships established may generate best fit recommendations on given requests to the benefit if the owner-user.

References

1. Atzori, L., Iera, A., Morabito, G.: SIoT: giving a social structure to the Internet of Things. IEEE Commun. Lett. **15**(11), 1193–1195 (2011)
2. Atzori, L., Iera, A., Morabito, G., Nitti, M.: The Social Internet of Things (SIoT)-when social networks meet the internet of things: concept, architecture and network characterization. Comput. Netw. **56**(16), 3594–3608 (2012)
3. Gartner: Gartner Says the Internet of Things Installed Base Will Grow to 26 Billion Units By 2020 (2018). https://www.gartner.com/en/newsroom. Accessed 06 Nov 2018
4. Goldberg, L.R.: An alternative "description of personality": the big-five factor structure. J. Person. Soc. Psychol. **59**(6), 1216 (1990)
5. Lauriola, M., Levin, I.P.: Personality traits and risky decision-making in a controlled experimental task: an exploratory study. Pers. Individ. Differ. **31**(2), 215–226 (2001)
6. Manyika, J.: The Internet of Things: Mapping the Value Beyond the Hype. McKinsey Global Institute, New York City (2015)

A Method and Tool for Analyzing Usability Testing Data in the Business Sector

Panagiotis Germanakos[1(✉)] and Ludwig Fichte[2]

[1] SAP SE, Dietmar-Hopp-Allee 16, 69190 Walldorf, Germany
panagiotis.germanakos@sap.com
[2] Shopify Inc., 150 Elgin Street, Ottawa, ON K2P 1L4, Canada
ludwig.fichte@shopify.com

Abstract. Usability testing is a critical phase of the User-Centered Design and development process, where product teams can observe and measure the usability of their software solutions' functionality, interactions and user interfaces. The subsequent validation sessions may generate a large, overwhelming, volume of empirical and unstructured data that need to be analyzed to determine meaningful outcomes for informed decisions. In this paper, we overview a new method and tool, namely EUREKA, guiding a product team, through a real-life business scenario, to analyze its usability study qualitative data and to produce comparable and replicable results, improving the User Experience of its product.

Keywords: User Experience · User-Centred Design ·
Usability Testing · Data analysis · Framework

1 Introduction

The current business landscape could be characterized by a rapid digital transformation of products and services, where User Experience (UX) is in the center of attention. Business organizations invest a significant amount of resources on related activities for enhancing the quality and "look-and-feel" of their solutions [9], for gaining the competitive advantage in the market. Overarching goal is to offer more usable interactions with their business processes through the user interfaces that will increase the desirability, accessibility, usefulness, etc., of their functional systems. Such qualities can be evaluated through a series of usability tests during the validation phase of the User-Centred Design and software development process [7]. Main concern is to thoroughly analyze the collected information, behaviours, and observations and facilitate an inclusive understanding of the vague and unstructured data transformation into actionable items. Accordingly, the project teams will be able to make informed decisions, increasing the, e.g., effectiveness, efficiency and satisfaction [6,8] of their end-users during task

© IFIP International Federation for Information Processing 2019
Published by Springer Nature Switzerland AG 2019
D. Lamas et al. (Eds.): INTERACT 2019, LNCS 11749, pp. 584–588, 2019.
https://doi.org/10.1007/978-3-030-29390-1_42

execution. In this respect, we overview a new method and tool that guides the analysis of collected usability testing qualitative data, namely EUREKA (Engineering Usability Research Empirical Knowledge & Artifacts), providing a balanced and semantically enriched qualitative and quantitative perspective of the outcome to the benefit of the product teams and the end-users.

2 An Overview of the EUREKA Workflow Through a Real-Life Business Scenario

EUREKA is an end-to-end Workflow-as-a-Service methodology (see Fig. 1) and tool (currently in the form of an .xls prototype) for analyzing usability testing feedback (see also [2,3] for more details). It may be regarded as an improved approach that could provide guidance through a highly synergetic environment during the analysis of the empirical data captured from the validation sessions. It consists of 4 main goal-directed phases, i.e., Discover, Learn, Act, and Monitor, that may embody concepts (e.g., as interrelated layers) of a taxonomy that represents a comprehensive paradigm for supporting (either as a guide or as standalone categories and classifications) the extraction of insightful learning outcomes and meaningful action items through one or more refinement cycles during the qualitative data analysis process.

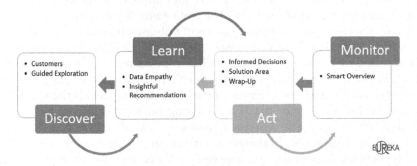

Fig. 1. Main process steps of EUREKA workflow

Next we briefly describe the main process steps of the EUREKA workflow through a real-life business scenario. A product team, composed of professionals with different roles (e.g., Product Owner, Business Expert, User Researcher, Interaction Designer, Architect, Developer), sharing different knowledge, experiences, expectations and data analysis skills, returned to their headquarters after executing a series of on-site usability testing sessions with their customers. Main scope was to validate their functional prototype of a newly launched mobile application. They tested the product with 3 end-users from 4 different customers that they visited in total. They now want to analyze and gain an inclusive insight on the empirical data and observations they collected (in total 320 feedback items) so to make viable decisions for their priorities and the backlog development items. However, they found themselves to be overwhelmed from the excessive amounts of unstructured usability test data (e.g., opinions, suggestions, sentiments, experiences, etc.) and for not knowing how to make a start; so to assign structure and meaning within a reasonable amount of time. Hence, they decided to use EUREKA, for guiding them through the data analysis process.

The team begins the analysis with the **Discover** phase, formulating a first understanding of the collected data, by capturing, consolidating, synthesizing and iterating on the content of the raw seeds of information. This stage consists of two subsequent process steps: The *Customers*, where the team records descriptive details about the end-users as well as the degree that they fit to the expected user profile and tasks. The role fit will be used throughout the analysis for weighting the responses of the end-users, assigning importance and treating data with fairness. During the *Guided Exploration* process step the team applies various iterative operations on the raw data for identifying inconsistencies, gaps or misconceptions, turning them into a coherent data set of feedback items. This activity will produce optimized clusters with the end-users' weighted references assigned to each one of them, specific aggregation calculations and the success with assistance for each end-user (degree of external influence for accomplishing a task). Moving to the next phase, **Learn**, the team can assign meaning to the derived clusters by identifying their type, polarity, association with other artefacts (e.g., use cases, designs), usability issues [4] or recommendations that they express, and their relevant importance and impact on the given application. Those actions are taking place during the *Data Empathy* subsequent process step that facilitates the objective observation and unbiased interpretation of the data by the team, as well as the precise association of the various units of information in an attempt to reveal holistic and inclusive meanings of a feedback item (or cluster). In parallel, the *Insightful Recommendations* process step generates suggestions (by considering the relevant importance and impact) if the team should take an immediate action or not. The following phase, **Act**, encompasses 3 subsequent process steps: The *Informed Decision*, that the team can discuss and assign possible high-level alternative solutions on one or more usability issues, and take actions as regards, i.e., proceed with one solution or not, and tracking their progress. The team may also deep dive to their solutions through the *Solution Area* process step, exploring alternative approaches and their viability for solving the discovered usability issues. They can determine the solutions' effectiveness and coverage across the usability issues, estimated effort, calculated risk, and likelihood of timely completion (based on the assigned effort and risk). Lastly, through the *Wrap-Up* process step, the team can similarly analyze all the information collected from post-questions (e.g., impressions, improvement points, or situation-specific comments), as well as usability or UX test tools' responses for cross-evaluation of the main tasks (e.g., SUS [1], or UEQ [5]). Finally, the product team can benefit from the **Monitor** phase, referring to the *Smart Overview* subsequent process step, that facilitates the continuous monitoring and exploration of the information that has been analyzed in the previous phases. The team can create visually enhanced cards containing various statistics for the feedback items' clusters, issues judgment, tasks assistance, usability issue types, etc., that may provide a quick overview of the empirical research outcome. It can also provide a structured documentation, fast reporting, and guide for prioritizing actions and decisions through an informed drill-down on the reformulated semantic data (e.g., by applying filters).

3   Preliminary Evaluation Results

During the year 2018 we evaluated EUREKA using 7 different data sets (approx. 1300 feedback items) from usability tests and 45 end-users, with different business roles and data analysis expertise. During the data analysis sessions, we observed the application of the method and tool, we conducted interviews and formulated focus groups gathering constructive feedback for its use and value.

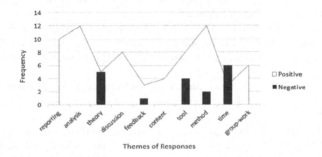

Fig. 2. Frequency of themes across the participants' responses (Color figure online)

For the analysis we applied: (a) frequency of themes for synthesizing the collected open-ended responses (referring to impressions, challenges, suggestions, etc.), and (b) sentiment analysis classifying them into two categories regarding their polarity, i.e., positive or negative. In Fig. 2, we highlight the main themes considering how often they semantically reappeared in each feedback statement across the participants. Indicatively, we observe that for the positive (orange line) the "analysis", "method", and "tool" appeared proportionally more frequently to the responses of the participants, while for the negative (grey bar) the "time" and "theory". For the former, example representative statements include: "None of the feedback items got lost during the analysis, and they are all relevant to the final assessment", "the method itself is of great help to UX professionals and development teams", or "I was amazed how I received numbers instead of only text as an outcome using the tool"; while for the latter: "We would need some time to familiarize ourselves with the prototype tool", or "the theory behind turns out to be a bit complex in cases".

4 Conclusion

EUREKA method and tool encapsulates a comprehensive and rather flexible approach that facilitates the analysis of qualitative data collected from usability tests. Its added value focuses on the collaborative transformation of vague feedback contents and behaviours into insightful and actionable items which can be tracked, followed-up and lead to informed decisions for business professionals that they want to enhance the UX and quality of their products.

References

1. Brooke, J., et al.: SUS-A quick and dirty usability scale. Usability Eval. Ind. **189**(194), 4–7 (1996)
2. Geramanakos, P., Fichte, L.: #EUREKA - Create Data Empathy Not Melancholy (2018). https://experience.sap.com/skillup/eureka-create-data-empathy-not-melancholy/. Accessed on 07 Apr 2019
3. Germanakos, P., Fichte, L.: EUREKA: engineering usability research empirical knowledge and artifacts. In: Zaphiris, P., Ioannou, A. (eds.) LCT 2018. LNCS, vol. 10924, pp. 85–103. Springer, Cham (2018). https://doi.org/10.1007/978-3-319-91743-6_6
4. Keenan, S.L., Hartson, H.R., Kafura, D.G., Schulman, R.S.: The usability problem taxonomy: a framework for classification and analysis. Empirical Softw. Eng. **4**, 71–104 (1999)
5. Laugwitz, B., Held, T., Schrepp, M.: Construction and evaluation of a user experience questionnaire. In: Holzinger, A. (ed.) USAB 2008. LNCS, vol. 5298, pp. 63–76. Springer, Heidelberg (2008). https://doi.org/10.1007/978-3-540-89350-9_6
6. Nielsen, J.: Usability Engineering. Elsevier, Amsterdam (1994)
7. Preece, J., Rogers, Y., Sharp, H.: Interaction Design: Beyond Human-Computer Interaction. Wiley, Hoboken (2015)
8. Shneiderman, B.: Designing the User Interface: Strategies for Effective Human-Computer Interaction. Pearson Education India (2010)
9. UserTesting: 2017 UX and User Research Industry Survey Report (2017). https://info.usertesting.com/ux-industry-survey-2017.html. Accessed 20 Nov 2018

Applying UCD for Designing Learning Experiences for Romanian Preschoolers. A Case Study

Guran Adriana-Mihaela[1](✉) [iD], Cojocar Grigoreta-Sofia[1] [iD],
and Moldovan Anamaria[2] [iD]

[1] Babeş-Bolyai University, Cluj-Napoca, Romania
{adriana,grigo}@cs.ubbcluj.ro
[2] Albinuţa Kindergarten, Cluj-Napoca, Romania
anabeekindergarten@gmail.com
http://www.cs.ubbcluj.ro

Abstract. Living in a world where almost every aspect of our life becomes digital requires attention on the digital skills development of young generations of citizens. Education is the driving force that can support equality of chances in digital skills acquirement. In this paper we describe our experience in developing, with the help of Computer Science Students, educational software for Romanian preschoolers (3–5/6 years) attending the public formal educational system. To be successful, the educational software should be both accepted by preschoolers and their teachers. We propose a two steps User (Child) Centered Design (UCD) approach focusing both on preschoolers and their teachers. The results obtained by applying the proposed method on a real case study are presented.

Keywords: UCD · Preschoolers · Education · Digital

1 Context

The world surrounding us becomes more and more digital, and the new children generations are considered *digital natives* [8]. This falsely suggest that the children posses the digital skills required by the future European Digital Market [3]. Romania, as part of the European Union, ranks on the last position (28th of 28 countries) on digital skills assessment [4]. Interventions need to be done for the future generations, and the public formal educational system should be the leading part of the process. ICT classes are thought starting from primary classes until the end of the mandatory studies program. In the public formal preschool educational system, no measures for fundamental digital skills development are considered. Although every class room from kindergartens has a computer connected to the Internet, it is used solely to play multimedia content (most of

© IFIP International Federation for Information Processing 2019
Published by Springer Nature Switzerland AG 2019
D. Lamas et al. (Eds.): INTERACT 2019, LNCS 11749, pp. 589–594, 2019.
https://doi.org/10.1007/978-3-030-29390-1_43

the time youtube videos). This approach is not appropriate, as the same studies [4] also show that Romanian citizens possess only the so-called *lifestyle digital skills*, but lack a vision of using technology to support work-related tasks. We consider that by appropriate interventions we can help the young generations embrace the technology as support in their knowledge gathering process and provide support on fundamental digital skills development. The form of intervention envisioned by us is the development of educational interactive products to support the classical teaching activities.

2 Method

Designing and developing educational applications for preschoolers brings two major challenges: designing for preschoolers and ensuring the educational nature of the products. The first challenge is determined by the lack of design guidelines for this particular age range. Although there is a large body of literature regarding designing for children, it focuses only on children aged 8 years or more [2,5–7]. Romanian preschoolers are 3 to 5–6/7 years old. The important differences between preschool children and school children are the following: preschoolers cannot read or write, they cannot complete adult stated tasks without being rewarded and their main activity is playing. The second challenge, referring to the educational characteristic of the interactive applications, needs focus on the content presented, on the engagement it determines, and on the fundamental digital skills that are required to interact with. In order to achieve the educational goal, we knew from the beginning that the participation of an expert in children education is mandatory. We have required the support of a kindergarten teacher to guide and support us through the design stages. Gaining children acceptance of the products was equally important as providing the right content and interaction. We decided to also involve children in the design process. Our intention was to apply UCD, although our final users lack some cognitive and physical skills that would empower them to actively participate in all steps of the design process. We considered that they can still be represented by the kindergarten teacher which will replace them (being a *surrogate*) when necessary. We have involved in the design process Computer Science students from the Faculty of Mathematics and Computer Science, Babeș-Bolyai University, attending the Human-Computer Interaction (HCI) elective course. The students have worked in 26 teams of 3 to 5 members. The final goal of the HCI classes is to make the students aware of the importance of user focus during the design of products. We considered that our project suits the goal of the HCI classes. The only doubt we had was if the final products will be accepted by the children and by other kindergarten teachers, their acceptance being the measure of our products success or failure. Thus, we have imagined a two steps process of creating successful products: the first one we have called *product design* and the second one we have called *product validation*.

The *product design* was organized as an adapted UCD, in the sense that in some design steps we have replaced our users (preschool children) with a kindergarten teacher with the role of representing their interests. Thus, in the requirements phase only the kindergarten teacher has participated by stating the curricula domains that will be targeted by the educational applications, the age range they address, the content (information) that should be presented and the tasks children should perform to gather the intended knowledge. Still, the children have been included in this step, as informants. The design teams have participated to observation sessions in the kindergarten to gather information about children knowledge about their project subject and their digital skills (verify if fundamental interaction skills are present: using the mouse, performing a click, drag and drop, key pressing: blank, enter). Each kindergarten class is composed of 26–30 preschoolers, such that members of each design team have observed and interacted with children groups. During the observation, we have allowed the members of at most three design teams to interact with the children, such that each design team has interacted with at least 5 children (of course, children were allowed to move between the students groups). At the same time, the design teams observed the children playing in the classroom. The kindergarten teacher required that all the phases in the teaching process (focus capturing, new knowledge presentation and fixation game) be covered by the applications. Also, she specified that the applications should be conceived as games or at least they should expose games-related characteristics in order to be suitable. After generating alternative design ideas, the kindergarten teacher has provided feedback on the designs and guided the design teams further in the process. Based on her feedback, the teams have built high fidelity executable prototypes. The prototypes have been evaluated twice: once by the surrogate user that gave feedback on the presented content, task order, task formulation, and second by the preschoolers. Individual play-testing sessions have been organized, followed by post-test interviews with the children. Each application has been evaluated by two children. The kindergarten teacher has been present during all user testing sessions to provide comfort and support to the little users. Peer tutoring has been used to replace think aloud protocols in order to assess how children have understood the applications. Satisfaction was also assessed by the use of smileyometers.

The *product validation* step was intended to check the opinion of other kindergarten teachers. We have considered that a positive evaluation would be a good predictor for the future intention of use. We considered that heuristic evaluation is the most cost and time-effective method. We have encountered the same problem as in the design phase: the lack of evaluation tools targeting preschool children educational applications. After researching the literature we have decided to adapt an existing heuristics set, namely Heuristic Evaluation of Child E-Learning (HECE) [1]. We considered it appropriate because it consists of three heuristics subsets referring to navigability, children skills and learnability. It was developed for children aged 10 or above. Twelve kindergarten teachers have participated in the heuristic evaluation. Each application has been assessed by two kindergarten teachers.

3   Results

During the play testing sessions the most frequent problem was that the children did not understand what is the goal of the application, because the applications lack an introductory part. This problem has been addressed by introducing characters that would welcome the children in the application's world, shortly presents the available functionality and how it is accessible, and guide them through the learning/interacting process. Another problem was related to task formulation. Initially, the tasks were stated using sentences like *select/find the object(s)*.... The children used to answer to these kind of tasks by pointing with their fingers on the screen. The solution was to explicitly state how the task is expected to be accomplished by saying *select with a click the object*.... Children were very engaged during the user testing sessions and they repeatedly played the proposed games. As the applications haven't been designed for multiple levels of difficulty, the children gave up using them when they became bored. Every child participating to the evaluation session has marked the happiest face on his/her smileyometer. The results of heuristic evaluation with the kindergarten teachers showed a large consensus on the children and learnability components of the heuristics set. All the participating evaluators agreed on these aspects, considering that the heuristics are successfully implemented. Regarding the navigation subset of heuristics, evaluators have identified problems about objects position consistency on the screens, lack of hints that would help children understand where they are in the application's space, interaction related terms that were considered too abstract.

4   Discussion

After having the experience of applying UCD for building educational software for preschoolers we can draw the conclusion that UCD is feasible even for such small age users. They can participate in every step of the design process, but the presence and support of an adult representing their interests is necessary in the requirements and alternative design evaluation steps. Although we did not involve the children in the alternative design evaluation phase, we consider that they could provide us new design ideas. Our decision was determined by the lack of time (the wireframes and sketches were too abstract to be understood by the children and too much time would have been spent to make the children understand and generate new ideas). The results of user testing show that children are eager to embrace technology during their learning activities as long as the learning experience takes the form of games or contain games-specific characteristics. The results of heuristic evaluation confirm the strength of participatory design: the kindergarten teacher participation during the entire design process has ensured a large agreement on the educational and children related aspects of the products. One drawback of our heuristic evaluation is that it was performed by colleagues of the kindergarten teacher participating in the design and a common organizational culture probably influenced the results. The presence of navigational problems may be explained by the fact that inexperienced developers have applied their first interaction design project to a category of special users (with supplementary interaction constraints). We must specify that during their studies, the Computer Science students have experience in building command-line systems or Graphical User Interfaces used only by (expert) adults. This project has challenged the students in multiple aspects: focusing on the user, understanding the cognitive and physical constraints and identifying proper solutions, evaluating the final product based on criteria they have never considered before (usability, acceptability). At the end of the semester, many students have mentioned that the participation on this project was the best experience during their studies. It makes them feel like having a contribution in the development of younger generations. Moreover, one of the kindergarten teacher participating in the evaluation step has expressed her availability and intention to be part of the design process in the future.

We consider that by providing access to the developed products to a large mass of children we create the context for equality of chances in acquiring digital skills. The kindergarten from the public educational system are the most appropriate choice, as most of the children are attending it. The kindergarten teachers will have multiple ways of teaching the curricula content and children will have the opportunity to see different approaches to introducing the new content and to interact with the computers in a learning context. We consider that this way children will build the basis of their fundamental digital skills in an appropriate and engaging manner. Starting to build their digital skills from an early age, they have the chance of becoming the digital citizens required by the Digital Market European strategy.

5   Conclusions and Further Work

In this paper we have presented our initiative of building educational software for public formal preschool educational system from Romania. We have applied a two steps approach: an adapted UCD approach in the design phase and an adapted heuristics set in the validation stage. The results of the first iteration show us that our approach was worth the effort, based on children and kindergarten teachers feedback. In the future we need to evaluate the learning outcomes of using the interactive products in the educational settings in terms of domain knowledge and fundamental computer skills acquisition/improvement.

References

1. Asmaa, A., Al-Osaimi, A.: Usability heuristics evaluation for child e-learning applications. In: Proceedings of the 11th International Conference on Information Integration and Web-based Applications & Services (iiWAS 2009), pp. 425–430. ACM, New York (2009)
2. Crescenzi, L., Grané, M.: An analysis of the interaction design of the best educational apps for children aged zero to eight. Comunicar **46**, 77–85 (2016). https://doi.org/10.3916/C46-2016-08

3. European Commission: Digital Single Market (2017). https://ec.europa.eu/digital-single-market/
4. Europe's Digital Progress Report (EDPR): How digital is your country? Europe needs digital single market to boost its digital performance (2018). https://ec.europa.eu/digital-single-market/en/news/how-digital-your-country-europe-needs-digital-single-market-boost-its-digital-performance
5. Fails, A., Guha, M.L., Druin, A.: Methods and Techniques for Involving Children in the Design of New Technology for Children. Now Publishers Inc., Hanover (2013)
6. Hourcade, J.P.: Interaction design and children found. Trends Hum. Comput. Interact. 1(4), 277–392 (2008)
7. Bekker, T., Markopoulos, P.: Interaction design and children. Interact. Comput. 15, 141–149 (2003)
8. Prensky, M.: Digital natives, digital immigrants. Horizon 9(5), 1–6 (2001). https://doi.org/10.1108/10748120110424816

Developing a User Interface for an Ultrasound Device Designed for Midwives and General Health Practitioners Situated in Low Resource Nations and Communities

Bassam Jabry[ID], Karin Aue[ID], John Chan[ID], and Jeffrey T. K. V. Koh[(✉)][ID]

Chemistry Form Pte. Ltd., Singapore 199149, Singapore
info@chemistryteam.com
http://www.chemistryteam.com

Abstract. As part of the United Nations-mandated Millennium Goals, GE Healthcare wanted to create a compact, robust, and easy-to-use ultrasound that would provide better access to healthcare for mothers in low-resource nations. Vscan Access is an ultrasound device designed for midwives and general practitioners to assess early pregnancy risks for mothers who need it most. Chemistry worked with the GE Healthcare team to conduct ethnographic research in Indonesia, facilitate cross-functional creative workshops with multi-stakeholder teams, as well as developed and executed a complete design and testing of the entire front-end user interface. Vscan Access won the President's Design Award in Singapore in 2016, and is now deployed across numerous developing nations in urban and rural communities around the world. This case study outlines the various challenges faced when developing a product intended for deployment in a mission-critical setting, employed by midwives and general health practitioners with varying degrees of expertise.

Keywords: UX · UI · Design research

1 Introduction

In response to the United Nations-mandated goal to reduce maternal mortality ratio by three quarters, GE Healthcare was motivated to develop an ultrasound medical device that was usable by the midwives in developing communities. Since 1990, the maternal mortality ratio has been cut nearly in half, and most of the reduction occurred since 2000. More than 71% of births were assisted by skilled health personnel globally in 2014, an increase from 59% in 1990. Globally, there were an estimated 289,000 maternal deaths in 2013[1].

---

[1] http://www.un.org/millenniumgoals/maternal.shtml.

© IFIP International Federation for Information Processing 2019
Published by Springer Nature Switzerland AG 2019
D. Lamas et al. (Eds.): INTERACT 2019, LNCS 11749, pp. 595–599, 2019.
https://doi.org/10.1007/978-3-030-29390-1_44

Chemistry, a Singapore-based service design consultancy, was appointed by GE Healthcare to conduct detailed research in the Indonesian market, particularly focusing on rural healthcare workers and midwives. Along with ethnographic and qualitative research, Chemistry was also appointed to execute iterative user experience and user interface design, informed by the research conducted in Indonesia. Finally, Chemistry also hosted and facilitated co-creation workshops, which brought together all stakeholders for the first time, in order to outline a development plan for Vscan Access.

The motivation for the development of Vscan Access is primarily articulated by its President's Design Award citation:

"Vscan Access is an innovative ultrasound device designed to help healthcare workers assess pregnancy risks early and expand quality care to mothers who need it most. With Vscan Access, midwives, paramedics, clinical officers and general practitioners can estimate gestational age and delivery date to help better plan and manage deliveries. They can conduct examinations that may result in early detection of potentially lifethreatening pregnancy complications, and guide critical decisions over the course of antenatal visits. The device wirelessly transfers data to patients, referral facilities or remote experts, ensuring accuracy and efficiency... Singapore-based creative design agency Chemistry was appointed by GE Healthcare to help with end-user research and to plan and facilitate creative workshops with multidisciplinary stakeholders. Through rigorous testing with midwives and general practitioners, Chemistry went on to deliver the complete design of the digital touchscreen user-interface. The depth of the initial field research and the rounds of testing helped the team refine the user experience to a level that made it naturally intuitive to the user. Aspects around consistency of icons, colour and placement of functions on the screen mean that a midwife could use the product almost immediately. The power of the touchscreen was leveraged to present contextually relevant information, thus helping to implicitly guide them through the steps they need to take."[2]

In this paper, we describe some of the challenges and learnings experienced, while developing the Vscan Access device.

1.1 Previous Work

Kimberly et al. found in Zambia that by empowering midwives with obstetric scan training, midwives became competent in conducting basic obstetric scans, and retained these skills for up to six months [1]. Specialised training is required for incumbent ultrasound devices, and this can be costly and time-consuming. The need for an easy-to-use, cost-effective and robust ultrasound device is apparent both from a user perspective, as well as a business opportunity due to the gap in the market.

Kimberly et al. go on to discuss how clinical decision-making and pregnancy management improved, when ultrasound was available to midwives in Zambia. The clinical management of 17% of obstetric cases was changed, particularly

---

[2] https://www.designsingapore.org/pda/award-recipients/2016/vscan-access.

patients with malpresentation and multiple gestations, once ultrasound devices were integrated into the healthcare process. This reiterates the need for ultrasound services for ANC in developing communities [1].

Ross et al. discovered that mobilised mothers would seek four or more antenatal care (ANC) visits. In Uganda, ultrasound implemented in a primary care facility led to both a 72% increase in total antenatal care visits, as well as a four-fold increase in women attending four or more ANC visits [2]. The increasing demand by mothers for ANC services is rising, and the need for competent ANC service providers grows with this need, demonstrates a further requirement for cost-effective and simple-to-use ultrasound devices.

Previous portable ultrasound devices have been developed and deployed in developing communities. Spenser tested one such device in Ghana and found that the challenge was incorporating the device into local medical practices [3].

Portable ultrasound devices have also been tested for pre-hospital emergencies. Busch discovered that pre–hospital ultrasound when applied by a proficient examiner using a goal–directed, time sensitive protocol was feasible, and did not delay patient management, providing diagnostic and therapeutic benefit [4].

2   Case Study

An ethnographic, qualitative research study was designed and administrated by Chemistry in Indonesia. This was conducted in order to better understand midwives and the mothers they serve in low-resource communities.

2.1   Study Design

The study was conducted in two phases with twelve midwives and six general medical practitioners (GPs) located in a suburb of Jakarta. Phase one included ethnographic, qualitative interviews to better understand the needs and challenges of both midwives and GPs when practicing ultrasound scans within their means, resources and capabilities on-site and also in hospitals.

Phase two of the study took the learnings from phase one, synthesised these insights into a seamless user experience journey for both patients and healthcare practitioners, and prototyped novel user interface and industrial design iterations in the form of click-though prototypes and product mockups, to better understand user acceptability from the point of view of both the medical practitioner and patient experience. Twenty GPs and midwives were subjects for phase two of the study.

2.2   Synthesis and Findings

Several key insights were derived from both phases of the study. From an industrial design perspective, the device could not be a handheld device, as both hands are needed for the interaction with the patient - one to hold the probe and the other to key in values as well as conduct measurements. The environment that the midwives and GPs worked in demanded a sturdy and durable device, with no flimsy or loose parts that could break or be lost, as often the medical practitioner would not have access to medical facilities and would need to conduct ultrasound testing in the field.

From a user interface perspective, the device interface had to be both intuitive and reassuring. Although most participants had been practising pre-natal medicine for years, they mostly were not used to handling ultrasound devices, or even touch screens, as of 2012/2013 most local Indonesians still used feature phones and Blackberry devices, and medical devices at the time did not use touch screens at all. In addition, the flat design trend promoted by the Google/Android interface language, which also debuted around that time, were not suitable for the target user base, and participants expressed that they preferred the three dimensional mockup of the user interface elements. With this in mind, the team used design language tropes such as drop-shadows and colour, in order to differentiate elements in the user interface.

Finally, the device needed to offer more than just simple ultrasound functionalities. To support their work and make the investment of the reduced but still substantial price tag of such a device worthwhile for participants, additional functionalities like patient records storage was very much desired. However the overall device needed to have a 'no fuss but professional' feel. Participants clearly stated a wish for a professional looking device and interface. Any attempts to give the design a more 'consumer product' look and feel, a more decorative look, or localised look via culturally-biased aesthetics, vibrant colour schemes, etc. were clearly rejected. It was important to strike a balance between an approachable yet professional look, for both the industrial design as well as the user interface.

3   Conclusion

To date, GE has shipped nearly 2000 units, with the product being used in Africa, Asia and Europe. Most of the devices have gone to countries like Nigeria, Ghana, and Ethiopia, where GE has Primary and Referral Care programs, which include training of midwives and healthcare workers to conduct basic obstetrics ultrasound testing using Vscan Access. This enabled task shifting and helped provide much needed antenatal care in rural and other local health centres.

In addition, the product is also being used in labour and delivery wards in Europe, where they use it to check for foetal presentation and position. This is particularly interesting as the original intent of the device was for low-resource and developing communities, however the success of the device has transcended this application into developed markets due to its usability and robustness.

Finally, the research and design implementation was recognised as a success beyond its market performance, by winning the President's Design Award in Singapore, in 2016. As the product continues to be used by medical practitioners around the world, incremental improvements are planned based on real-world usage and feedback.

References

1. Kimberly, H.H., et al.: Focused maternal ultrasound by midwives in rural Zambia. Ultrasound Med. Biol. **36**(8), 1267–1272 (2010)
2. Ross, A.B., et al.: A low-cost ultrasound program leads to increased antenatal clinic visits and attended deliveries at a health care clinic in rural Uganda. PLoS One **8**(10), e78450 (2013)
3. Spencer, J.K., Adler, R.S.: Utility of portable ultrasound in a community in Ghana. J. Ultrasound Med. **27**, 1735–1743 (2008)
4. Busch, M.: Portable ultrasound in pre-hospital emergencies: a feasibility study. Acta Anaesthesiologica Scandinavica **50**, 754–758 (2006)

It AIn't Nuttin' New – Interaction Design Practice After the AI Hype

Lassi A. Liikkanen[1,2(✉)]

[1] Qvik Ltd., Urho Kekkosenkatu 5c, 00100 Helsinki, Finland
lassi@qvik.com
[2] School of Engineering, Aalto University, AALTO, 00076 Espoo, Finland

Abstract. The year 2018 was the moment of increasing awareness of artificial intelligence (AI) in every imaginable domain. This article examines the question have AI technologies and their related hype already affects interaction design practice in the Western industry. It looks at the potential impact in tools, processes and products of interaction design. It highlights three potentially significant themes which stand out of the hype: 1) AI utilization as a technology push 2) generative AI, and 3) the ethics of AI. Each theme is analyzed to derive the claim that for now, AI has little specific impact on interaction design. On a closer observation, generative AI is one the themes that promises the biggest change in the longer run but is simultaneously an elusive hope, which may never lead to anything but AI-augmented creativity support tools, some of which already exist. The article describes the AI hype is partially positive, partially problematic for the advancement of design goals. The hype contributes positively by helping to surface healthy ethical debates that give more credence to designers' long-term attempts to be user-centered and ethical. This ethical discussion tends to neglect the fact that the ethical burden bestowed upon algorithms is not a new one but was going on long before the big data fuzz. It is evidently now more critical than ever. This articles' intention is to inform the academic researchers working on human-computer interaction and interaction design about the need to continue developing human-centered AI for both general audiences and specifically for interaction designers. There are already promising examples of HCI research that show potential to affect design practice. Common to all is that they do not attempt to roll out a full generative AI solution but rather support human designers in iterative and somewhat well-constrained tasks. Overall it seems that by 2020, interaction designers will be increasingly working on technology that involves AI elements, but those elements itself will not yet be core of how their work is carried out. Awareness of the ethical challenges and technical affordances related to AI technology and its utilization will become more important than the integration of AI into the interaction design process in the short term. By the end of 2020's, we maybe yet looking into a very different reality from now.

Keywords: Artificial intelligence · Interaction design · Technology push

© IFIP International Federation for Information Processing 2019
Published by Springer Nature Switzerland AG 2019
D. Lamas et al. (Eds.): INTERACT 2019, LNCS 11749, pp. 600–604, 2019.
https://doi.org/10.1007/978-3-030-29390-1_45

1 Background

The year 2018 was the moment of increasing awareness of artificial intelligence. One clear sign of that is found from Gartner's hype cycle [1]. Hype cycle is a tool that describes the lifecycle of technology phenomena from inception to deployment. In the past two years, tens of technological ideas related to *artificial intelligence* (called AI tech from now on) have quickly moved from expectation level towards production. These include machine learning, deep learning, autonomous vehicles, cognitive computing, natural language questions answering, and a few others. As the present generation of AI technology is quickly maturing towards commercial use, it feels warranted to ask does this already or in the immediate future show at large in professional interaction design practice? (Fig. 1).

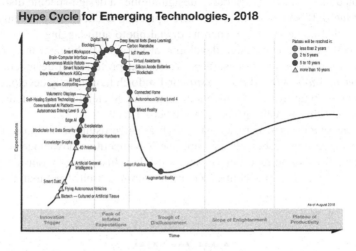

Fig. 1. Spot 10 directly AI related terms on Gartner's hype cycle. © Gartner, Inc. [1]

2 Expectations and Observations in 2019

As we want to examine the impact of AI tech on interaction design practice, we can lean on existing research on design practices [2] and set three questions that guide the exploration. These are: *What you design, how you design, and why you design*?

2.1 The Subject of Design Work

Observations concerning the subject of design, i.e. what you design, show little change. With few exceptions, AI tech is incorporated into existing products as new "AI features." The bulk of work goes around conventional systems and processes turning digital and "smart" with AI. As AI features are plugged into an existing technology stack, some changes will be visible and some invisible on the user interface. Designers need to adjust to the new technology choices, but can't affect them fundamentally as the adoption is technology driven. The biggest changes in design will be a result of new modalities such as voice interaction being incorporated into products.

At present the answer to the question of changing subject of design seems to be "not really." AI tech has hardly removed any particular domain of applications from the field and there are no *AI designers* compete with UX designers' jobs.

2.2   Design Methods

Second question is that does AI tech change how design-related tasks are carried out? A radical change in working practices could result from application of **generative design**. Algorithmic or generative design refers to a development in which AI tech is utilized to generate "creative" content traditionally considered to be a hallmark of human creativity. This can be music, imagery, text, or user interfaces (see, e.g. [3–5]).

On would first think that generative design implies a design-specific disruption, but that is not the only source of impact. Design practice is affected by all multi-purpose digital tools that come available, such as digital photo auto-tagging.

As of now, algorithmic design development has not yet brought into fruition any tool that could replace human designers. Tools that professional designers use daily, such as *Sketch, Adobe XD, InVision, Axure* and so forth have mostly developed towards management of complexity and collaboration, not AI. Sketch for one includes powerful automation, but that is nothing you could label AI tech.

There are specific and narrow tasks, such as advertising banner design [6, 7] in which generative approaches already provide a competitive advantage for machine. Robot journalists also do reporting on sports [8], but this is largely outside interaction designer's home turf, being content creation within a well-structured design space (Fig. 2).

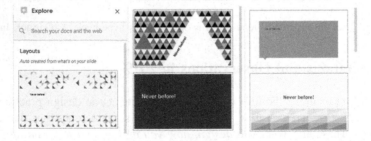

Fig. 2. Screenshot of Google Slides in Feb 2019 (vertical image has been split into two horizontal parts for layout reasons). This service has been one of first commercial services to deploy assistive, generative design functions for users, later followed by Microsoft Office. Their current usefulness is debatable, but their subtle integration subtle is suggests a support tool.

But design methods and tools change even without a strong, all-encompassing AI. With "narrow" AI [9] and in cooperative creativity, tedious and slow operations for a human will be handled by a machine, as well to a degree tasks of exploring the design space. This is the most promising development at the moment [10, 11]. It predicts a change in both what and how design practice operates: certain design tasks fall out of designer's table as they find better algorithmic solutions inside intelligent tools. But it will take time to discover them and currently designers are still mostly automating research with the tools of data-driven design [12]. The current development is gradual and results in what could be called intelligent/smart creativity support tools which by themselves don't design, but will improve as their own design matures [13].

2.3 Reasons for Design

A third, fundamental question regarding design practice is that will new technology somehow affect why we design and the ultimate motivations of the profession? Given the polarized treatment of AI in media, it seems warranted to ask if a new wave of ethical awareness is possibly arising among designers.

As we have learned from the recent past, ethical or societal issues generated by new technology are difficult to predict. For example, we are now observing that steadily increasing smartphone use, social media use, or mobile gaming can be akin to addictive substance abuse causing social, health, and economic issues. Several books have been published in just a few years to highlight these troubles. This is where we have ended up as an outcome of mostly continuous improvements to technology. Thus we should expect that the threat of AI should motivate the designers to further defend the humans, or particularly under-privileged users at risk, from being mistreated by biased AI algorithms or by any inherently non-user centered technology.

In preparation to deal with the emerging questions around AI, a public debate on AI ethics is emerging [14]. The discussion is once more neither specific nor driven by designers, but designers should also pay attention and also contribute actively to. Companies around the world are just figuring out how to demonstrate their social responsibility in this domain and should also lend an ear to what designers think.

3 Conclusion: Designer Be Aware

To wrap up these themes I make three claims of the current industry position on AI and design: AI technology is being implemented primarily through a technology push. Generative tools do not play a significant role in interaction design practice at the moment and they do not threaten the profession. Designers are curious about AI ethics and generative design, but don't see urgency to act upon in it.

The fact that designer profession is being most affected by AI tech features integrated into general purpose software does not mean that designers can just ignore what goes in the tech world. The quickly developing technology capabilities force designers to re-asses what can and what should be left to AI decision making. I strongly encourage designers to take an active role in choosing which AI tech to implement and utilize, or whether this technical feature takes place as all the other ones via technology push. I perceive that academic researchers working on HCI and interaction design maintain great opportunities and a need to discover ways how AI can be made an effective companion in professional interaction design practice. Acceptance can be good if ideas are compatible with existing processes and tools.

References

1. Panetta, K.: 5 Trends Emerge in the Gartner Hype Cycle for Emerging Technologies 2018. Gartner Inc. (2019). https://www.gartner.com/smarterwithgartner/5-trends-emerge-in-gartner-hype-cycle-for-emerging-technologies-2018/. Accessed 4 Feb 2019
2. Liikkanen, L.A., Laakso, M., Björklund, T.: Foundations for studying creative design practices. In: Procedings of the Second Conference on Creativity and Innovation in Design, pp. 309–315. ACM Press, New York (2011)
3. Todi, K., Weir, D., Oulasvirta, A.: Sketchplore: Sketch and Explore with a Layout Optimiser. 2016 ACM Conference on Designing Interactive Systems (DIS'16), pp. 543-555. ACM Press, Brisbane, QLD, Australia (2016)
4. Lomas, J.D., et al.: Interface design optimization as a multi-armed bandit problem. In: Proceedings of the 2016 CHI Conference on Human Factors in Computing Systems, pp. 4142–4153. ACM, Santa Clara (2016)
5. O'Donovan, P., Agarwala, A., Hertzmann, A.: DesignScape: design with interactive layout suggestions. In: 33rd Annual ACM Conference on Human Factors in Computing Systems (CHI 2015), pp. 1221–1224. ACM Press, Seoul (2015)
6. Xu, R.: AI visual design is already here—and it won't hesitate to take over your petty design job. Medium (2017). https://medium.com/@rexrothX/ai-visual-design-is-already-here-and-it-wont-hesitate-to-take-over-your-petty-design-job-934d756db82e. Accessed 4 Feb 2019
7. Low, A.: Alibaba's new AI can generate 20,000 lines of copy in a second. CNET (2018). https://www.cnet.com/news/alibabas-new-ai-can-generated-20000-lines-of-copy-in-a-second/. Accessed 4 Feb 2019
8. Moses, L.: The Washington Post's robot reporter has published 850 articles in the past year. Digiday UK. Digiday (2017). https://digiday.com/media/washington-posts-robot-reporter-published-500-articles-last-year/. Accessed 4 Feb 2019
9. Noessel, C.: Designing Agentive Technology. AI That Works for People. Rosenfeld, New York (2017)
10. Koch, J., Lucero, A., Hegemann, L., Oulasvirta, A.: May AI? Design ideation with cooperative contextual bandits. In: CHI 2019. ACM Press, New York (2019)
11. https://algorithms.design/
12. Liikkanen, L.A.: Era of data-driven design in professional web design. Interactions 24, 52–57 (2017)
13. Oulasvirta, A.: User interface design with combinatorial optimization. IEEE Comput. 50(1), 40–47 (2017)
14. European Commission: The Ethics Guidelines for Trustworthy Artificial Intelligence (AI). AI HLEG (2019). https://ec.europa.eu/futurium/en/ai-alliance-consultation/guidelines. Accessed 3 June 2019

R++, User-Friendly Statistical Software

Christophe Genolini[1]($\boxtimes$), Emmanuel Dubois[2], and David Furió[1]

[1] Zebrys, 5 place Jean Deschamps, 31100 Toulouse, France
cg@rplusplus.com
[2] IRIT-LIIHS, 188 route de Narbonne, 31062 Toulouse Cedex 4, France

Abstract. Statistical analysis is gradually entering all areas of society, be in academia or in the private sector. Statistical software is used by statisticians but also by non-experts (medical doctors, psychologists...). Unfortunately, this kind of software is integrated into obsolete interfaces that completely ignore the principles of HCI and are poorly adapted to non-expert users.

R++ project aims to develop a modern statistical analysis software program integrated into a user-friendly interface. In this paper, we present the methodology that led us to the design of R++. We also give two examples that this methodology allowed us to achieve.

Keywords: Statistical analysis · Video prototyping · R++

1 Introduction

Statistical analysis is gradually entering all areas of society [1]. In the academic world, it is becoming more and more difficult to publish an article without some tests or some model. In the private sector, insurers [2] use it to define their rates, bankers [3] to decide whether or not to grant a loan, the pharmaceutical industry [4,5] to validate its clinical trials, etc.

The users of statistical analysis are therefore very diverse. Some are experts like Data Scientists, but many are casual users like medical doctors, psychologists, educational scientists, pharmacists, etc. In order to publish international papers, they need high level statistics despite the fact that they are not statisticians.

From a software point of view, statistician software (SAS©, R, SPSS, Stata...) is complete in terms of methods available, but performs very poorly [7]. On the other hand, some languages (C, python) or software (Oracle) are very powerful but offer very few analytical tools and require serious programming skills. Furthermore, both types of software are integrated into obsolete interfaces that completely ignore the principles of HCI and are poorly adapted to non-expert users (Figure S1).

Electronic supplementary material The online version of this chapter (https://doi.org/10.1007/978-3-030-29390-1_46) contains supplementary material, which is available to authorized users.

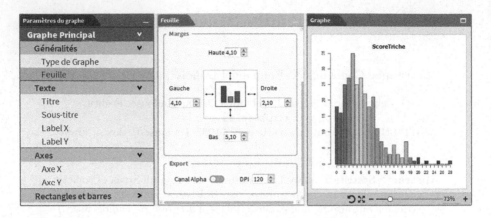

Fig. 1. The R++ project (graph modification interface).

The R++ project (Fig. 1) aims to develop modern statistical analysis software integrated into a user-friendly interface.

In this paper, we present the methodology that led us to the design of R++. Section 2 briefly recalls the concept of exploratory design and video prototyping. Sections 3 and 4 details elements that have been improved. Section 5 is the conclusion.

2   Methods

To conceive the user interface of R++, we used the exploratory design method and video prototyping: during 1 hour, statisticians and computer specialists brainstormed on: *What are the difficult, tedious, time-consuming or highly error-prone tasks with your current statistical software?* This round table meeting was done in an open mode: the participants intervened and a moderator took notes on the board. At the end of this first step, we selected two or three of the themes that were most frequently mentioned.

In the second step, we sought solutions for the previously selected themes: *Imagine the statistical analysis software of your dreams: how would it work?* For 10 min, participants were asked to write down three ideas, plus a "far-fetched" idea. The objective of this out-of-the-box idea was to avoid self-censorship: indeed, a participant may have a good idea but not say it for fear of being ridiculous. In doing so, it helped avoiding the said problem. When everyone had found their three plus one ideas, they were presented to the rest of the group and then debated, combined, and hopefully improved.

Finally, during the third hour, the participants created low-fidelity proto-types (Figure S2). With the help of paper, felt pens, post-its, and cut-outs, they created a scenario that they filmed using a telephone. These prototypes were then presented to the entire group. This provided the first feedback.

In total, we organized eight general sessions without specific instructions. We also organized thematic sessions where the agenda was announced in advance (e.g. "merging databases"). Only the statisticians directly concerned by the problem came to these sessions. The course of the session was then modified: (1) search for solutions (2) presentation of videos related to the theme discussed during the general sessions (3) creation of video prototypes.

During the "things to improve" phase, many ideas were suggested. They were then collectively grouped into frequently asked themes (see Table 1):

Table 1. Thematic grouping of the elements to be improved in statistical software.

Data-management (outlier detection, wrong type detection, merging databases,...)	33
Graphs (dynamic, interactive, automatic, exportable, DPI)	24
R Code (unified syntax, code folding, automatic generation, always visible)	17
Results layout (LaTeX or Word, table management)	16
Tables (interactives, with style)	16
Help (integrated, video, contextual, wiki)	14
Export (to Word, automatic reporting, document styling)	13
Timeline of the analysis	9
Interactive software (interactive graphs, interactive data)	7
Others	41

3   Focus on Data Management

Data management consists in preparing the data before analysis. Strictly speaking, this step is not really part of the statistical analysis but, unfortunately, it is essential. It consists of identifying inconsistencies in the data, such as a 350-year-old person, a binary variable encoded in three modalities: Female, Male and male[1], or an execution time of one hour for a task that should take a few seconds. This step does not require any special skills, and it is considered quite tedious by statisticians. This probably explains the large number of times it has been cited as an area for improvement.

Data management generally involves studying certain statistics (minimum, maximum, number of employees) and a graphical representation for each of the variables. A solution to simplify this process was to automate the calculation of the indices in question and the associated graphical representation. Thus, with a single mouse-click, it is possible to obtain a graphical representation of all the columns. The user can detect the problematic variables at a glance (Fig. 2 or S3). We also add a color in each column according to its type, e.g. the binary columns are in yellow. If a column that is supposed to be binary is not in yellow, then there is probably a problem in said column (Figure S4).

---

[1] Modalities are case sensitive by default, therefore, Male and male represent different modalities.

4 Focus on Graphs

The second highly problematic point concerns graphs. Traditional software produces graphs that are generally austere, fixed, and can only be manipulated by command lines. Statisticians are often forced to use additional software (Photoshop, Gimp) that they do not master well. In order to solve this, the following solutions have been chosen:

- Interactive graphs allow, when you click on a part of the graph (for example on an outlier) to select the corresponding data. This action also sorts the database so that the selected data is present at the top of the column. This makes it possible to access specific values very quickly.
- Some graphs are mandatory parts of an analysis. Their production has been automated: univariate analysis (Fig. 2 and S3) but also statistical test graphs (Fig. 3).
- An interface allows the user to easily modify the graph settings. A first window groups the parameters by theme. When a theme is selected, the details of the options are presented in a second window. The third shows the graph. For example, the publication of articles requires drawings with a resolution of 300 DPI and no alpha channel. Few statisticians know what these two terms mean. The interface simplifies the modification of these two parameters (Fig. 1 and S5).
- Finally, exporting a graph to other software can be done by a simple drag&drop (Figure S3).

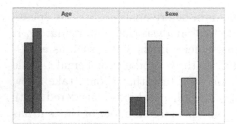   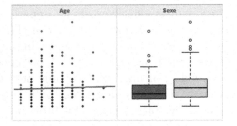

Fig. 2. Detection of problematic variables at a glance. There is an outlier in Age and Sex is incorrectly coded.

Fig. 3. Bivariate graphical representation. Age and Sexe relatively to another previously selected variable.

5 Conclusions

In this article, we have presented the methodology that led us to design R++, a statistical analysis software integrated into a user-friendly interface.

There are still many areas in which statistical analysis could benefit from HCI contributions. In Fig. 2, the appearance of the graphs limits the position of the displayed data. User feedback could allow us to determine if it is a blocking element. If so, could solutions such as *perspective wall* [8] help? Or could *Focus+Context* [9] be adapted to the statistical context? Similarly, the graph interface requires you to leave the data page. Would it be possible to use a more direct configuration solution, such as Magic Lenses? [10].

Another interesting field, one of the pillars of science is the possibility of being able to reproduce an analysis. All statistical software therefore produces code. But statisticians are not programmers. Similarly, unlike some computer codes, which no longer need to be modified when they are fully functional, statisticians' codes are intended to be read again by others (to verify the analyses). It would therefore be interesting to work on a script editor that would make programming accessible to the novice and facilitate code review.

Finally, statistical analysis requires the simultaneous display of a large amount of information. Statisticians almost always have two screens, although this is not always enough. Moving part of the interface (data control, 3D graph display control,...) to an external device could optimize the display of information on the screen.

References

1. Muenchen, R.A.: The Popularity of Data Science Software. http://r4stats.com/articles/popularity/. Accessed 19 Apr 2019
2. Grize, Y.L.: Applications of statistics in the field of general insurance: an overview. Int. Stat. Rev. **83**(1), 135–159 (2015)
3. Hand, D.: Statistics in Banking. Published online in Encyclopedia of Statistical Sciences. https://doi.org/10.1002/9781118445112.stat00179. Accessed 19 Apr 2019
4. Lewi, P.J.: The role of statistics in the success of a pharmaceutical research laboratory: a historical case description. J. Chemom. **19**(5–7), 282–287 (2005)
5. Peterson, J.J., Snee, R.D., McAllister, P.R., Schofield, T.L., Carella, A.J.: Statistics in pharmaceutical development and manufacturing. J. Qual. Technol. **41**(2), 111–134 (2009). https://doi.org/10.1080/00224065.2009.11917764
6. R Core Team: A language and environment for statistical computing. R Foundation for Statistical Computing, Vienna, Austria (2019). https://www.R-project.org/
7. Chai, A.: Accélération des méthodes statistiques sur GPU. Master 2 internship report. https://rplusplus.com/wp-content/uploads/2018/03/Rapport_Anchen03.pdf. Accessed 19 Apr 2019
8. Mackinlay, J.D., Robertson, G.G., Card, S.K.: The perspective wall: detail and context smoothly integrated. In: Proceedings of the SIGCHI Conference on Human Factors in Computing Systems (CHI 1991), pp. 173–176 (1991). https://doi.org/10.1145/108844.108870
9. Cockburn, A., Karlson, A., Bederson, Benjamin, B.: A review of overview+detail, zooming, and focus+context interfaces. ACM Comput. Surv. **41**(1), 31 p. (2009). Article no. 2. https://doi.org/10.1145/1456650.1456652
10. Bier, E.A., Stone, M.C., Pier, K., Buxton, W., DeRose, T.D.: Toolglass and magic lenses: the see-through interface. In: Proceedings of the 20th Annual Conference on Computer Graphics and Interactive Techniques (SIGGRAPH 1993), pp. 73–80 (1993). https://doi.org/10.1145/166117.166126

Towards a Framework for the Classification of Usability Issues

Martin Böckle[1]([envelope]) and Jens Rühmkorf[2]

[1] BCG Platinion, Design and Engineering, Berlin, Germany
boeckle.martin@bcgplatinion.com
[2] BCG Platinion, Cologne, Germany
ruehmkorf.jens@bcgplatinion.com

Abstract. This case study proposes a novel framework, which aims to support UX designers and practitioners in the classification of identified usability issues. Existing inspection methods often lack in providing further information and steps about the effort to fix those issues. Therefore, the developed framework provides four categories for classifying usability issues in order to generate a score, which represents the present level of UX maturity. Furthermore, the score enables the comparison of UX maturity levels between systems with similar customer journeys, based on the identified usability issues. Results support system designers in their decision-making process of replacing, maintaining or modernizing the system in question. First results reveal that the proposed framework could be used as a meaningful extension of existing usability methods within different application domains, for instance the heuristic evaluation.

Keywords: Usability issues · Classification · User experience · Usability method

1 Introduction

The rising level of end-user expectations for seamless user-experience (UX) including the development of novel user interfaces (UI), which aim to follow current usability standards, reveals the importance for the assessment of existing and probably outdated information technology applications. These type of systems (e.g., legacy systems) share common characteristics that certain usability issues have been identified, which conflict with some of the best practices of user-centered design (UCD) and therefore provide an overall negative user-experience (UX). Although, the present body of literature provides several metrics for measuring usability from different perspectives [1, 5], a classification for the identified issues, which aim to support the decision-making process about the overall the re-design or fixing a number of issues is currently missing. Therefore, this case study provides a framework, which clusters usability issues by their severity ratings [7] and the assumed effort to fix from a technological perspective.

We believe that the proposed framework provides a valuable contribution to UX researchers and practitioners, by highlighting the impact of usability issues on the user-journey and the relationship to the expected effort to fix those.

© IFIP International Federation for Information Processing 2019
Published by Springer Nature Switzerland AG 2019
D. Lamas et al. (Eds.): INTERACT 2019, LNCS 11749, pp. 610–614, 2019.
https://doi.org/10.1007/978-3-030-29390-1_47

2 Usability Metrics and Methods

The term usability has its roots in human computer interaction (HCI) and is defined as the *"capability to be used by humans easily and effectively"* [2, p. 340] or the *effectiveness, efficiency* and *satisfaction* with which specified users achieve defined goals in particular environments [3]. First approaches provided techniques (e.g., thinking aloud) for usability-testing, followed by guidelines and discussions on how to actually measure usability [4]. Further metrics are being discussed, for instance the system usability scale, which provides a rough indication about the systems overall usability, developed by [8] or how to summarize several metrics into one single score [5].

Moreover, the literature provides a range of methods, which can be used at different stages for the assessment of the usability, for instance a heuristic evaluation [6, 9] or the PURE methodology [10]. Although, after applying these methods, the following steps like how to deal with the identified issues has often been neglected. Specifically, for legacy systems, a decision for the overall redesign or how much effort is needed to solve each individual issue needs to be addressed as well and will be covered in this case study.

3 Framework Development

For the development of the proposed framework, two usability experts conducted a heuristic evaluation of two applications within the finance domain by following the guidelines of [9]. The evaluation was based on the fundamental customer-journey, which comprised of similar characteristics in their outcomes and goals. After the identification of several usability issues (first system = 10; second system = 24), the severity ratings [7], which indicate a rough estimation for usability problems, have been applied. Within this process, key concepts were uncovered including a cross-check between both raters. Furthermore, the identified usability-issues have been structured and clustered according to their characteristics and degree of conflict with the overall user journey. This iterative process has been performed with several software developers in order to come up with four generic categories, which represent the transition between the identified usability issues and the underlying system architecture, described in Table 1 and visualized in Fig. 1:

Table 1. Framework categories

(I) UI - Optimizations represent minor improvements on the UI level like: color codes, inconsistent buttons, menus, warnings and feedback. The effort to fix those issues is relatively low
(II) Weak System Support - The system does not support the end-users in their customer journey. For instance, the accomplishment of tasks (e.g., complete booking process) is connected with considerable effort
(III) Structural adjustments within the system architecture are connected to a higher effort to fix (e.g., changes in the business logic)
(IV) High usability conflict with intended customer journey - These issues prevent the end-user to accomplish their goals and need to be fixed immediately. While end-users will probably drop out of the process, the effort to fix as well as the severity rating is relatively high

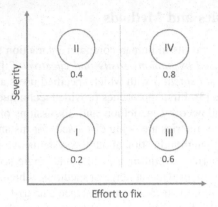

Fig. 1. Conceptual framework

The first quarter represents usability issues, which are easy to resolve. Generally, those issues don't touch the business logic of a system and only violate UI best practices, like consistency of colors or other elements like menus. In contrast to the second quarter, issues share a higher severity, but the effort to fix is still very low. Moreover, this classification summarizes issues which are connected to weak system support. Examples include the interaction with UI elements, like bad form design, weak error messages or bad general design of the customer journey, which lead to unknown end-user behaviors. The third quarter has a low severity rating but a relatively high effort to fix. For instance, if changes in the database design are necessary, like adding new fields to a form or migrations towards new technologies in order to improve usability aspects (e.g., loading times or adding personalization to an existing system). Furthermore, the redesign of complete processes, which require large changes in the frontend are part of this quarter as well. The fourth quarter represents the area with the highest severity and effort to fix. Those issues should be handled with care, because a high number informs the evaluators about serious usability problems, which are also connected to technological progress or accessibility. Generally, these issues prevent the user from the accomplishing of the intended user-journey like completing a buying process or a weak system architecture design, which makes the system unusable. Moreover, in order to compare similar applications and their effort to fix the identified usability issues, we came up with a simple formula, which aims to highlight the significance of each issue from a practical perspective. Firstly, we considered weights (e.g., $w1$) with a difference of 0.2 between each quarter to express an increasing relevance for the overall effort. Secondly, we added increasing exponents to the number of identified usability issues (x) in order to explicitly express the degree of severity and effort to fix, which will clearly lead to different scores. The overall score represents the maturity level of the assessed application:

$$y_u = w_1 * x^1 + w_2 * x^2 + w_3 * x^3 + w_4 * x^4$$

Finally, we calculated the proposed usability factor for both systems with following results, described in Table 2:

Table 2. Results usability inspection

Usability issues - system 1			Usability issues - system 2		
Quarter	Number of issues	Score	Quarter	Number of issues	Score
Q1	11	2.2	Q1	4	0,8
Q2	5	10	Q2	1	0,4
Q3	4	38,4	Q3	5	75
Q4	4	204	Q4	0	0
	24			10	
		254,6			76,2

First results reveal that system one contains a higher level of usability issues than system two. Especially, due the high exponent (4) in the last quarter, the four issues had a huge impact on these results. Thus, only through a high amount of usability problems in the third and specifically in the fourth quarter, the proposed factor will increase.

Generally, the framework represents an extension of the heuristic evaluation by classifying the ranked severity ratings into the proposed framework categories (Table 1) in order to generate an overview of the overall usability issues and their impact on the development process. The classification process should involve system designers, which are able to provide realistic effort assumptions about the identified issue and their relationship to the proposed categories in Table 1 (e.g., "Does the identified issue cover simple UI optimizations or structural adjustments as well?"). Furthermore, the proposed framework should also support the decision-making process of replacing, maintaining or modernizing the system in question (e.g., complete redesign or which issue should be solved first). Although the approach of comparing two systems on the basis of their usability and the effort to solve those issues seems promising, the technological perspective needs to be addressed as well. For instance, systems with different technology stacks cannot directly be compared. Thus, we analyzed the effort to fix from a practical perspective by considering technological dependencies, which may influence the evaluation process and need to be taken into consideration (Table 3):

Table 3. Technological dependencies

"Component based architectures foster reusable components and therefore aim to handle changes more quickly."
"UI libraries of modern web-based architectures can be updated much more flexible than older systems with less capabilities."
"Modern user interfaces solve problems in different ways and therefore a comparison of identified issues between two system could be unrealistic."
"Generally, current tech stacks have a higher focus on maintainability."
"Especially for legacy systems, the effort to fix evolves around the replacement, maintenance or the modernization of functionalities or the entire system. Consequently, this requires extensive expertise, preparation and planning as well. Therefore, the decision-making process is also more time consuming."

4   Conclusion

The presented framework aims to support the process of classifying identified usability issues regarding their effort to fix by coming up with a score, which highlights the present UX maturity level. The evaluation of two applications demonstrates the potential of this approach and reveals that the identified issues with a high severity rating and effort to fix should be considered as highly problematic. Furthermore, we discussed technological dependencies when comparing two similar applications within the same application domain. While this framework highlights a meaningful extension for a range of usability methods (e.g., heuristic evaluation, cognitive walkthrough etc.), we plan to further develop the scoring design and range of clusters to come up with more accurate results.

References

1. Hornbaek, K.: Current practice in measuring usability: challenges to usability studies and research. Int. J. Hum.-Comput. Stud. **64**, 79–102 (2005)
2. Shackel, B.: Usability - context, framework, definition, design and evaluation. Interact. Comput. **21**, 339–346 (2009)
3. ISO 9241: Ergonomics of human-system interaction – Part 11: usability: definitions and concepts (2018)
4. Nielsen, J., Levy, J.: Measuring usability: preference vs. performance. Commun. ACM **37** (4), 66–75 (1994)
5. Sauro, J., Kindlund, E.: A method to standardize usability metrics into a single score. In: Proceedings of the CHI 2005, Portland, USA (2005)
6. Nielsen, J., Molich, R.: Heuristic evaluation of user interfaces. In: Proceedings of ACM CHI 1990, Seattle, WA, pp. 249–256 (1990)
7. Nielsen, J.: Reliability of severity estimates for usability problems found by heuristic evaluation. In: Proceedings of CHI 1992, pp. 129–130 (1992)
8. Brooke, J.: SUS: a "quick and dirty" usability scale. In: Jordan, P.W., Thomas, B., Weerdmeester, B.A., McClelland, A.L. (eds.) Usability Evaluation in Industry. Taylor and Francis, London (1996)
9. Nielsen, J.: Heuristic Evaluation: How to conduct a heuristic evaluation? https://www.nngroup.com/articles/how-to-conduct-a-heuristic-evaluation/. Accessed 3 June 2019
10. Rohrer, C.P., Wendt, J., Sauro, J., Boyle, F., Cole, S.: Practical usability rating by experts (PURE): a pragmatic approach for scoring product usability. In: Proceedings CHI 2016, San Jose, USA, pp. 786–795 (2016)

Interactive Posters

A Mobile App for Illiterate and Semi-illiterate Pregnant Women- A User Centered Approach

Jane Katusiime[1,2(⊠)] and Niels Pinkwart[1]

[1] Humboldt Universität zu Berlin, Unter den Linden 6, 10099 Berlin, Germany
{jane.katusiime,pinkwart}@hu-berlin.de
[2] Mbarara University of Science and Technology,
P.O. Box 1410, Mbarara, Uganda
janek@must.ac.ug

Abstract. Mobile technology is utilized in health care to improve service delivery, but researchers and developers have mainly focused on developing applications that are usable by people who can read and write. While it is relatively easy for literate women to access maternal health information via mHealth apps and search engines like Google, it is almost impossible for their illiterate counterparts to enjoy such privileges. We present an android based mobile health application designed for illiterate and semi-illiterate women, that provides personalized maternal health information, a reminder functionality and a call functionality. To get user requirements for the application, we conducted a field study in form of semi-structured interviews and focused group discussions with illiterate and semi-illiterate pregnant women and health practitioners in maternal health care from Uganda, and designers/developers of applications for low resource settings. The design of the application follows a user centered iterative process. The application was tested for functionality and usability by the pregnant women.

Keywords: Maternal health · Mobile health · Illiteracy · User centered design

1 Introduction

Mobile technology continues to gain popularity globally. There were 4.57 billion mobile phone subscribers in 2018 which is estimated at 63.5% of the global population [1]. There is a high number of mobile phone subscribers observed in developing countries as well [1]. The popularity of mobile phones has created opportunities in health care. There have been mHealth interventions developed for maternal health. Some of these interventions have indeed been successful, for instance Mobile Moms and MomConnect [2] but despite these interventions, maternal mortality remains a big challenge especially in developing countries [3]. Maternal mortality is the death of women during pregnancy, childbirth or within 42 days after delivery due to pregnancy related complications. Maternal mortality is estimated at 216 deaths per 100,000 live births globally and the highest maternal mortality rates are in developing countries [4]. There are various indirect factors that contribute to high maternal mortality rates in developing countries such as scarcity of health workers, limited access to health information and high illiteracy levels [5, 6]. Illiteracy prohibits illiterate women from

© IFIP International Federation for Information Processing 2019
Published by Springer Nature Switzerland AG 2019
D. Lamas et al. (Eds.): INTERACT 2019, LNCS 11749, pp. 617–620, 2019.
https://doi.org/10.1007/978-3-030-29390-1_48

accessing available text-based interventions such as Mobile Moms and MomConnect, yet it is illiterate women that are prone to maternal mortality mostly.

Despite global reduction of illiteracy, gender-based illiteracy persists and this is evidenced by higher levels of illiteracy among women compared to men [7]. Some cultures are characterized by male dominance which puts females at a disadvantage in attaining education. Illiteracy contributes to maternal mortality by limiting illiterate women from accessing maternal health information and using the available text based digital artifacts that support maternal health care. Therefore, there is a need to empower illiterate and semi illiterate women with interventions that support maternal health care, are secure and usable by them.

We propose a multimedia (video, audio) based mobile app that provides personalized maternal health information to pregnant women based on the maturity of their pregnancy. It also has a reminder functionality for appointments and a call functionality for the pregnant women to contact their health practitioners.

2 Method

To gather user requirements, we conducted a field study in form of semi-structured interviews and focused group discussion (FGD) with 25 illiterate pregnant women, 10 health practitioners in maternal health care and 10 designers/developers of applications for low resource settings. The pregnant women and health practitioners were recruited from the department of Obstetrics and gynaecology of Mbarara Regional Referral Hospital in Southwestern Uganda while the designers/developers were recruited through referrals of those who already knew about the study. Areas discussed in the interviews and FGD included access to digital technologies and health information, and user requirements for the app. The user requirements were used to design the app which was tested for functionality and usability by 10 pregnant women following an iterative process. The women were given phones with the app pre-installed, trained on how to login in and access videos and audios. They were then allowed to use the app for not more than one hour. This was followed by an FGD about the app.

3 App Design

The android app is designed based on four core requirements, following a user centered design approach, which emphasizes involvement of users in all design phases. (1) Multimedia based: The app should enable users to retrieve multimedia (video and audio) maternal health content. (2) Have a reminder functionality to remind the women to go for their antenatal appointments. (3) Have a call functionality to enable women contact their health practitioners when they are away from the hospital. (4) Easy to use and secure: (4) The app should protect the information in the app from unauthorized access and should be easy to navigate.

3.1 App Functionalities and Challenges Faced

The login: The user taps a combination of four images (pictorial password) to login (Fig. 1). Provision of a wrong password triggers a vibration. Pictorial password was used because the illiterate users are unable to use the conventional text-based username and password. Biometric mechanisms such as face and voice recognition were also not possible because the users have low processing phones that are unable to process biometric information. It is important to note that the login was crucial because most of the users reported that they share the mobile phones.

Multimedia messages: During the first antenatal visit, the maturity of the woman's pregnancy and due date are determined. The pregnancy begin date is then set in the app calendar. The app counts down and pops up a video and/or audio tailored to the current maturity of her pregnancy every month. Tapping the watch button takes the user to the saved videos which are presented as scrollable thumbnails for easy accessibility (Fig. 1). Tapping the Listen button takes the user to the list of audio files which are saved with emojis to indicate the content of each file. Each video or audio is one to two minutes long. Messages were inbuilt in the app and pre-installed on the mobile phones because the users had no internet to dynamically download them.

Appointments and reminders: During the antenatal visit, the next appointment date is decided and input into the app by the health practitioner via the calendar module. The day before the appointment date, the app triggers an audio reminder reminding the woman to go for her appointment. This reminder is an audio voice in the local language stating, *"Your next antenatal appointment is tomorrow, please do not forget to go to the hospital."* The reminder was designed this way to enable illiterate women differentiate it from other reminders that may be set in the shared phone

The call functionality: The app has a call icon which the woman can tap, and her call is directed to the health care provider's pre-set phone number. If the call is not picked, the woman can leave an audio message for the health provider. The call button appears on all app screens for easy access because the illiterate women are unable to navigate to the contact list and choose the desired number or text-based contact.

3.2   App Workflow

After starting the app, the user is prompted to input a pictorial password. Upon successful login, the user has access to three options: watch video, listen to audio, or set pregnancy begin date and appointment date (Fig. 2). Choosing any of the options takes the user to the respective menu displays. The user can terminate the application by navigating away from it.

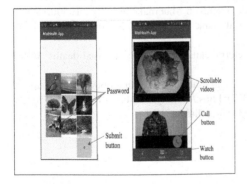

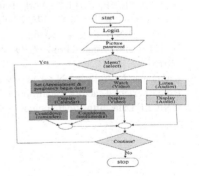

Fig. 1. Login and multimedia screen

Fig. 2. App workflow diagram

4 Discussion and Lessons Learnt

We found that designing for illiterate people follows the same design guidelines but presents a unique set of requirements such as exclusive use of multimedia. Artefacts for this category of users require constant user involvement. Participants in the design process of the app felt they owned the app and readily accepted it. However, engaging other stakeholders such as spouses and community leaders is also paramount.

Participants who were HIV positive or had sensitive conditions, and shared mobile phones were more concerned about privacy of the information and their communication with the health practitioners compared to those without.

There is a need to create a balance between the design trade-offs when designing for the illiterate. We faced two major trade-offs: (1) The conflict between allowing the illiterate users to be in control of the app and the need for prescriptive guidance/training on how to use the app. (2) The conflict between making the app easy to use versus keeping it secure. The more usable the application got, the less secure it became.

The strength of this intervention is that it is based on participants' contributions and needs, who are the end users, and this makes it acceptable to a similar category of users. Also, the requirements, design perspectives and procedures from this study are transferrable to other similar cases of designing for illiterate users.

In conclusion, Illiterate people can utilize mHealth systems, but they need to be involved in all the design phases if secure and usable systems are to be developed for them. Our next step is to roll out the intervention in real life settings and do more empirical studies to determine its impact on maternal healthcare. We also intend to add a sharing functionality to the app where the users can share their experiences.

References

1. Statista. https://www.statista.com/statistics/274774/forecast-of-mobile-phone-users-worldwide/
2. Peter, J.E., Barron, P., Pillay, Y.: Using mobile technology to improve maternal, child and youth health and treatment of HIV patients. South African Med J. (2016). https://doi.org/10.7196/samj.2016.v106i1.10209
3. Philbrick, W.C., Noordam, C., Kuepper, B.M., et al.: mHealth and MNCH: state of the evidence. BMC Public Health. (2013). https://doi.org/10.1111/j.1365-3156.2011.02747.x
4. WHO, UNICEF, UNFPA, World Bank, et.al.: Trends in Maternal Mortality : 1990 to 2015, Estimates by WHO, UNICEF, UNFPA, World Bank Group and UN Population Division (2015). ISBN 978 92 4 150363 1
5. World Health Organisation. WHO—Social determinants approach to maternal deaths. WHO (2015)
6. Katusiime, J., Pinkwart, N.: A review of privacy and usability issues in mobile health systems: Role of external factors. Health Inform. J. (2017). https://doi.org/10.1177/1460458217733121
7. UNICEF Data. https://data.unicef.org/topic/education/literacy/

Adding Images to Psychometric Questionnaires to Improve User Engagement

Mohammed Khwaja[1,2](✉) and Sarah Shepherd[1]

[1] Telefonica Alpha, Barcelona, Spain
{mohammed.khwaja,sarah.shepherd}@telefonica.com
[2] Imperial College, London, UK

Abstract. This paper presents an experiment to obtain personality traits using a psychometric questionnaire that is augmented with visual representations that support answer options. From the results, it is suggested that the use of visual media improves participants' perception of 'fun' or pleasure, while answering the questionnaire; thereby creating the potential to improve user engagement in commercial applications.

Keywords: Personality detection · Psychometric questionnaires · User engagement

1 Introduction

Most behaviour change applications in today's market are one-size-fits-all, and evidence suggests that personalisation is needed in order to bring about effective, engaging and long-lasting change [8]. Traditionally obtained using text questionnaires, personality traits have been used for personalising behaviour change applications [6]. However, completing questionnaires requires focused attention, as numerous cognitive processes are involved when answering questions about one's behaviours [3]. Past research has indicated that focused attention is an important component of user engagement [2], and when users have fun, there is increase in cognitive absorption of technology use [1]. Measuring and improving user engagement is important to the Human Computer Interaction (HCI) community, as is evidenced by past literature [4,9] that focused on this.

We present a study with a modified psychometric questionnaire using images and gifs (including pop culture references) to obtain the Big 5 personality traits. Inspired by the growth of communication through emojis, gifs, images and videos, over text, we test if the addition of a visual layer on top of psychometric questionnaires is as accurate in capturing personality as a gold-standard questionnaire; and makes the questionnaire more fun - potentially improving the engagement of commercial application that use these. Work has been done in the past to obtain personality scores by creating image based quizzes[1], and a

---

[1] http://you.visualdna.com/quiz/whoami?c=us#/quiz.

© IFIP International Federation for Information Processing 2019
Published by Springer Nature Switzerland AG 2019
D. Lamas et al. (Eds.): INTERACT 2019, LNCS 11749, pp. 621–625, 2019.
https://doi.org/10.1007/978-3-030-29390-1_49

patent [10] has been filed on this system. Our work does not create a new personality quiz for detecting personality traits, but rather augments visual imagery to a gold-standard personality questionnaire to improve its perception with users.

2   Study - Methodology

Our study required participants to complete two questionnaires: 1. the baseline questionnaire - the gold-standard that provides 'ground truth' data and 2. the visual questionnaire - our modified questionnaire. We do this to compare the scores and perception of our modified questionnaire with the gold-standard. The questionnaires were spaced one week apart so that participants don't rely on memory to provide answers. Half of the participants were asked to complete the baseline questionnaire first, while the other half were asked to complete the visual questionnaire first.

Before the first questionnaire, we provided an onboarding survey to collect demographics, including gender and age range. At the end of both questionnaires, we provided an exit survey with two questions: 1. 'Ease of Completion' to understand how easy the questionnaire was to complete and 2. 'Pleasure' to understand how fun the questionnaire was. We use a 5 point Likert scale for these. The questionnaire was anonymous and no personal data including names and email IDs were collected from participants. Users were given unique codes to answer both questionnaires, enabling us to match responses from the same user.

There are multiple questionnaires to obtain the Big 5 personality traits, including the mini-IPIP developed by Donnellan et al. [5]. In this work, the authors developed a 20 item questionnaire with a likert scale to obtain the Big 5 personality traits, namely Extroversion, Agreeableness, Conscientiousness, Neuroticism and Openness. The questionnaire can be broken down into 4 brackets, with each bracket containing 1 question related to each of the 5 personalities. The questionnaire is well regarded as the gold-standard in the Psychological community, for its length and accuracy. We use this questionnaire as the baseline, over which we build the visual questionnaire.

In the visual questionnaire, we used questions from the baseline in the same order with the same connotation, but modified it to suit images and gifs that we selected. The selection of images or gifs for answer options was based on mutual agreement between the researchers conducting the study, with subsequent validation from a subject expert. We provided three options for each question in a Likert scale, ranging from positive/agree/strong to negative/disagree/week. This was done to reduce the cognitive effort it takes for the user to select between strongly agree and agree (and the opposite), and to overcome the difficulty of obtaining images that clearly differentiate two consecutive options. While it would have been ideal to use a 5 point Likert scale, and most questionnaires and surveys use this, evidence has indicated that 3 point Likert scales are just as accurate to obtain user opinions and can be used for surveys that don't need a breadth of statistical tests [7].

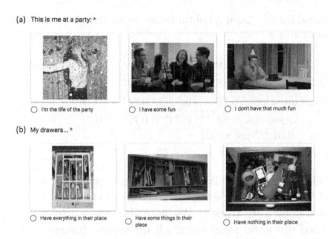

Fig. 1. Question to obtain a component of (a) Extroversion, (b) Conscientiousness

Two questions from the visual questionnaire are presented in Fig. 1. These are similar to the questions presented in the baseline questionnaire, albeit in a different form. To maintain consistency in the scores obtained from the baseline and visual questionnaires, the options for the baseline questionnaire were also presented in a 3 point Likert scale. The scores for each trait are calculated in the manner defined in [5] - positive questions were scored in the same order, and negative questions were reverse scored. Each trait has four questions that contribute to its score.

The study was performed by 26 participants, employed at a research institute in Barcelona, Spain. The call for participation was sent out to over 60 individuals using an internal mailing list, and participants registered to volunteer. The study was performed in late 2018. The number of females to males was 48% to 52%, and participants belonged to the age ranges of 18–24 (9%), 25–34 (56%), 35–44 (26%) and 45–54 (9%). Participants were citizens of countries including Spain, United Kingdom, United States, Germany and others, and included a mix of native and non-native English speakers.

3   Results

First we obtained the correlations ($r - values$) by regressing the trait scores obtained from both questionnaires. This is presented in Table 1. High correlation scores with significant $p - values$ indicate that the visual questionnaire is able to obtain the personality scores with a high similarity as the text based questionnaire. We also observed that no difference was observed between the two groups of participants, i.e., correlations obtained from participants who took the baseline questionnaire first were similar to those who took the visual questionnaire first.

Table 1. Correlations ($r - values$) obtained between the visual questionnaire and the baseline questionnaire

	Extr.	Agree.	Cons.	Neur.	Open.
All questions	0.88***	0.74**	0.77**	0.73***	0.88***
One question	0.75**	0.72**	0.68**	0.78***	0.82***
Two questions	0.84***	0.73**	0.77***	0.71**	0.84***

**$p < 0.01$, ***$p < 0.001$

Next we obtained the correlation between the answer from each question in a bracket and the personality score obtained from the baseline, and the highest correlations are shown in Table 1. We note that the correlations are not comparable to those obtained from using all questions. Subsequently, we selected the 2 questions from the visual questionnaire with the highest correlations to obtain a score with 2 questions and correlated this with the baseline scores. It is observed that the correlations obtained are similar to those obtained using all 4 questions, indicating that using 2 questions for each trait, or 10 questions overall can provide similar scores versus using 20.

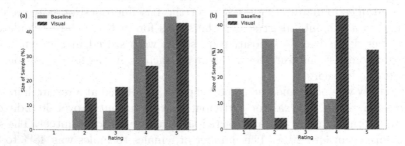

Fig. 2. Bar charts representing the rating distribution of (a) Ease of Completion, (b) Pleasure

The results obtained from the exit questionnaire are represented using bar graphs in Fig. 2. Results from the 'Ease of Completion' question indicate that both the baseline and visual questionnaires are easy to complete, with slight preference for the baseline as they maintain the same text answer options for all questions. However the 'Pleasure' question indicated that the visual questionnaire was perceived as significantly more fun than the baseline.

4   Conclusion and Future Work

This study indicates that the use of visual media to obtain personality traits from psychometric questionnaires is both accurate and fun to complete - providing the potential to improvement user engagement. Feedback from one of the participants: *"I loved this survey so much!! it was really engaging. I think all surveys should look like this."* further highlights its merit.

In the future, we plan to conduct a large scale study and explore if similar results hold with a larger population sample. We will incorporate this method in a commercial application for personalised interventions, explore improvements in user engagement and obtain further user feedback on this medium of answering questionnaires. This method also has the potential to be applied to other psychometric questionnaires, improving the application of psychology to HCI.

Acknowledgements. We would like to thank Dr Aleksandar Matic for his guidance. This work has been supported by the EU's Horizon 2020 research and innovation programme, under the Marie Sklodowska-Curie grant agreement no. 722561.

References

1. Agarwal, R., Karahanna, E.: Time flies when you're having fun: cognitive absorption and beliefs about information technology usage. MIS Q. **24**(4), 665–694 (2000)
2. Attfield, S., Kazai, G., Lalmas, M., Piwowarski, B.: Towards a science of user engagement (position paper). In: WSDM workshop on User Modelling for Web Applications, pp. 9–12 (2011)
3. Blair, E., Burton, S.: Cognitive processes used by survey respondents to answer behavioral frequency questions. J. Consum. Res. **14**(2), 280–288 (1987)
4. Doherty, K., Doherty, G.: Engagement in HCI: conception theory and measurement. ACM Comput. Surv. (CSUR) **51**(5), 99 (2018)
5. Donnellan, M.B., Oswald, F.L., Baird, B.M., Lucas, R.E.: The mini-IPIP scales: tiny-yet-effective measures of the big five factors of personality. Psychol. Assess. **18**(2), 192 (2006)
6. Halko, S., Kientz, J.A.: Personality and Persuasive technology: an exploratory study on health-promoting mobile applications. In: Ploug, T., Hasle, P., Oinas-Kukkonen, H. (eds.) PERSUASIVE 2010. LNCS, vol. 6137, pp. 150–161. Springer, Heidelberg (2010). https://doi.org/10.1007/978-3-642-13226-1_16
7. Jacoby, J., Matell, M.S.: Three-point likert scales are good enough (1971)
8. Noar, S.M., Benac, C.N., Harris, M.S.: Does tailoring matter? meta-analytic review of tailored print health behavior change interventions. Psychol. Bull. **133**(4), 673 (2007)
9. Peters, C., Castellano, G., de Freitas, S.: An exploration of user engagement in HCI. In: Proceedings of the International Workshop on Affective-Aware Virtual Agents and Social Robots, p. 9. ACM (2009)
10. Willcock, A.: System and method of segmenting and tagging entities based on profile matching using a multi-media survey, uS Patent 8,650,141, 11 February 2014

Applications for In-Situ Feedback on Social Network Notifications

Frederic Raber[✉] and Antonio Krüger[✉]

DFKI Saarland Informatics Campus, Saarbrücken, Germany
{frederic.raber,krueger}@dfki.de

Abstract. In social networks, it often arises that a post is shared with a broader audience than intended, which is often finally noticed when one of the unintentionally included friends likes or comments on the post. We present an approach for privacy setting adaptation based on in-situ feedback on such social network update notifications. We implemented a smartphone application that allows users to give positive or negative feedback using two buttons integrated into Facebook's update notifications. We collected qualitative feedback from focus groups to find out what impact of in-situ feedback on privacy settings is expected by users. Our findings indicate that there is no general rule of thumb on how the privacy settings should be adapted. Nevertheless, the discussion led to a new approach that allows users to manage and adapt her privacy settings, and which is also capable of performing content elicitation and filtering for social network sites.

Keywords: Feedback · Smartphone · Smartwatch · Social network · Privacy · User interface design

1 Introduction

Social network users usually underestimate the audience of their social network posts, which results in their posts being seen and commented on by friends and acquaintances that were not intended to do so, leading to privacy leaks which are often only discovered when comments or likes are posted by friends outside of the intended audience [1]. In fact, the perceived audience comprises on average only 27% [1] of its true size. There are solutions using machine learning to assist the user in doing his privacy settings [4,5], but those systems rely on inferred privacy setting suggestions rather than active user feedback. Another problem is the algorithmic curation to organize, select and present posts on a social network newswall that might be of interest for the user. Most of the users (62.5%) are not aware of the presence of such algorithms, and often feel anger when finding out about their existence [2]. A comparative study has shown that a user interface where users can see and influence the outcome of the curation algorithm led to a significantly more active engagement with Facebook and bolstered overall feelings of control on the site [2].

© IFIP International Federation for Information Processing 2019
Published by Springer Nature Switzerland AG 2019
D. Lamas et al. (Eds.): INTERACT 2019, LNCS 11749, pp. 626–629, 2019.
https://doi.org/10.1007/978-3-030-29390-1_50

We implemented a mockup smartphone application that adds feedback functionality to the update notification, so that the user can easily give feedback on his updates while he is on the go. Due to the limited space in a notification bar and to allow a fast feedback action, we used a binary feedback approach as a starting point for the discussion, where the user can either describe his feelings on the new comment or like as "positive" if he perceived it as a positive experience, e.g. if he liked that the post was seen and commented on, or as "negative" if the user would have preferred that the user had not seen and commented on the post. In a small-scale qualitative study with four focus groups, we found out that there is no direct implication of feedback on the privacy settings. Nevertheless, the input can be used to define privacy settings within an interactive privacy dashboard, as shown in the discussion.

2   Related Work

For systems that are embedded into the daily life of users, such as social networks or mobile phone apps, research has found in-situ feedback to be one of the most powerful approaches, due to its directness of feedback and the preservation of the feedback context [3]. A feedback method similar to ours has already been used for crowd contributions in short bursts of time, by taking advantage of the common habit of turning to the mobile phone in spare moments: Whenever the mobile phone is turned on, the user is asked to solve micro-tasks of one or two seconds, thereby lowering the threshold to participate in crowdsourcing activities [7]. In a study with 82 users, the participants made 11240 crowdsourcing contributions in total. The comparison between a conventional smartphone and one using the crowdsourcing application showed no statistical difference in either unlock speed or the users' cognitive load, leading to a high acceptance rate of the approach [7]. In-situ feedback for social network update notifications (like notifications or "likes" about new comments on the user's posts) has, to the best of our knowledge, not been part of a research study yet.

3   User Study

Although the app is not fully functional as the Facebook API does not allow the retrieval of a user's notification updates, we showed the participants the app for clarification on how such an app could look in later stages of the interview. The header of the notification shows the name of the person who liked/commented on the user's post, as well as the abbreviated text of the post. Below the header, two buttons labeled *"positive"* and *"negative"* can be found for giving positive feedback ("I liked that the person commented on the post/I liked that he saw the post") or negative feedback ("I did not like that the person commented on the post/I did not want him to see the post"). If the user does not want to give feedback on the update notification, or if he has neither a positive nor a negative feeling about the update, he can swipe away the notification as usual in Android.

In order to find out the desired effects of the provided feedback, we conducted focus groups at our institution. To be more precise, we conducted four focus groups, two with two participants, and two with three participants. All participants were required to be active social network users, and were recruited through postings at our university. Each participant was paid 8 EUR as compensation for their participation in the focus group. All participants were students of different disciplines, aged between 19 and 31 (mean 25.6). During the experiment, the participants should first state whether they already experienced an unwanted disclosement, and how they could imagine social network providers could help them in avoiding such scenarios. Afterwards, the particpants were shown the mock-up application, and asked to discuss possible implications of the feedback on their privacy settings as well as alternative ways of using the feedback.

4   Discussion and Outlook

Even within our small test set, there is no general opinion on which immediate effects the feedback should have, neither on the privacy settings for the commentator, nor for her close friends or friend groups. Some of the users just want to discuss with the commentator, some would put the commentator on a restricted list directly or after a certain amount of negative feedback, and others would block her instantly. The same holds for the closest friends of the commentator: Although most of the participants stated they should not be affected by negative feedback, four out of ten subjects also wanted the closest friends to be affected by the feedback and put onto some restricted list, either automatically based on tie strength, or after approval by the user. We therefore see little value for adapting the privacy settings, neither based on a rule-set derived within a large-scale user study, nor by using machine learning and a large data set. Although there is no rule of thumb for how a single feedback should directly affect the user's privacy settings, the participants of the study mentioned a different approach that could be used to adapt the privacy settings: Positive and negative feedback for the user's friends is collected to form a list of "positivity rankings" that can be used for defining the right audience for future social network posts. For this purpose, the ranking list is separated into three parts: The topmost part ("green list") receives the user's status updates directly on their wall. The next set of friends ("yellow list") can see the updates, but only when they visit the user's personal page. The last group of friends ("red list") does not receive any posts of the user. The user should have an interface to define the boundaries between the red, yellow and green lists and should be notified when a person is about to move to another list based on the user's feedback. Another application of the positivity ranking is content elicitation on social network sites: Facebook, for example, displays or hides content based on calculated tie strength. It is also possible for the user to give explicit feedback on some posts, so that "fewer posts like this" are displayed in the future. Nevertheless, studies have shown that the tie strength and friend lists do not completely fit the tie strength order that a user would expect [6]. Using the positivity ranking could therefore lead to better content elicitation than the current standard. Whether this is the case should be investigated in a future study. As space is very limited on smartphone devices, we concentrated on a minimalistic design for the update notification messages on our smartphone application, offering only a binary feedback choice (positive and negative). However, one focus group discussed a more fine-grained feedback option is needed, involving three, four or more buttons. Users often receive feedback that is on one hand negative, but that is useful for further improvement or that leads to a different, new point of view. Such *helpful feedback* might have a different impact on the positivity rating than destructive negative feedback. The same applies also for positive feedback that can be helpful, or not. We would like to investigate the optimal number of feedback options and the desired effects on the positivity score in future work. In the next step, we would like to publish the friendship dashboard as a Facebook application, to observe the acceptance level and effects in everyday social network usage. If the dashboard is accepted, we will extend the functionalities to allow content and notification elicitation based on the positivity scores, again in a two-step approach with a prototype in a lab study first, and an in-the-wild study later on.

Acknowledgements. This work was supported by the German Research Foundation (DFG) via the collaborative research center "Methods and Tools for Understanding and Controlling Privacy" (SFB 1223), project A7.

References

1. Bernstein, M.S., Bakshy, E., Burke, M., Karrer, B.: Quantifying the invisible audience in social networks, CHI 2013, pp. 21–30. ACM, New York (2013)
2. Eslami, M., et al.: "I always assumed that I wasn't really that close to [her]": reasoning about invisible algorithms in news feeds, CHI 2015, pp. 153–162. ACM, New York (2015)
3. Fields, B., Amaldi, P., Wong, B.L.W., Gill, S.: In use, in situ: Extending field research methods. Int. J. Hum. Comput. Interact. **22**(1&2), 1–6 (2007)
4. Raber, F., Kosmalla, F., Krueger, A.: Fine-grained privacy setting prediction using a privacy attitude questionnaire and machine learning. In: Bernhaupt, R., Dalvi, G., Joshi, A., Balkrishan, D.K., O'Neill, J., Winckler, M. (eds.) INTERACT 2017. LNCS, vol. 10516, pp. 445–449. Springer, Cham (2017). https://doi.org/10.1007/978-3-319-68059-0_48
5. Raber, F., Ziemann, D., Krüger, A.: The "Retailio" privacy wizard: assisting users with privacy settings for intelligent retail stores. In: Weir, C., Mazurek, M. (eds.) EuroUSEC 2018 : 3rd European Workshop on Usable Security. EuroUSEC European Workshop on Usable Security (EuroUSEC 2018), 23–23 April 2018, London, UCL, United Kingdom. Internet Society (2018)
6. Spiliotopoulos, T., Pereira, D., Oakley, I.: Predicting tie strength with the Facebook API. In: Proceedings of the 18th Panhellenic Conference on Informatics, pp. 9:1–9:5, PCI 2014. ACM, New York (2014)
7. Vaish, R., Wyngarden, K., Chen, J., Cheung, B., Bernstein, M.S.: Twitch crowdsourcing: crowd contributions in short bursts of time. In: Proceedings of the 32nd Annual ACM Conference on Human Factors in Computing Systems, CHI 2014, pp. 3645–3654. ACM, New York (2014)

Combating Misinformation Through Nudging

Loukas Konstantinou[1](✉), Ana Caraban[1,2](✉),
and Evangelos Karapanos[1](✉)

[1] Persuasive Tech Lab, Cyprus University of Technology, Limassol, Cyprus
lukekonsta@gmail.com, akc.caraban@hotmail.com,
evangelos.karapanos@cut.ac.cy
[2] Instituto Superior Tecnico, Universidade de Lisboa, Lisbon, Portugal

Abstract. Recent studies have shown that the spread and consumption of misinformation online can be attributed to errors in human decision making, facilitated by cognitive biases. The field of Behavioral Economics has contributed a repertoire of such cognitive biases that can be leveraged for the design of technological interventions. In particular, the concept of *nudging* refers to subtle changes in the 'choice architecture' that can alter people's behaviors in predictable ways. In this paper we present our ongoing work on the design of nudging interventions in the context of misinformation, including a systematic review of the use of nudging in HCI that has led to a design framework consisting of 23 mechanisms of nudging tapping to 15 different cognitive biases, the translation of this framework into a set of design cards, the *Nudge Deck*, and its use in a planned workshop that aims to explore the design space of misinformation in the context of nudging.

Keywords: Behavior change · Misinformation · Nudging

1 Introduction

In the era of "post-truth", the rise of falsehood content dissemination in the information environment has sparked significant public concern, since it has been posed as a threat to the very existence of democratic societies. Meinert et al. [1] define fake news and false information, in general, as purposeful publications of false, discrediting and deceitful content, motivated by various interests (e.g. political, financial, etc.) so as to manipulate and exploit its recipients.

A number of researchers have called for the examination of the factors that result in the dissemination and consumption of falsehood knowledge. As examined in the following sections, various cognitive and emotional biases facilitate the spread and consumption of misinformative content. For instance, Vosoughi et al. [2] found that increased speed and depth at which fake news diffuse can be attributed to mere novel effect, while Badke [3] discussed the role of the confirmation bias on the consumption and spread of misinformation.

Based on the concept of *nudging*, we suggest that knowledge about the different cognitive biases that we, as humans, are susceptible to, can be leveraged for the design of technological interventions that minimize the spread and consumption of

© IFIP International Federation for Information Processing 2019
Published by Springer Nature Switzerland AG 2019
D. Lamas et al. (Eds.): INTERACT 2019, LNCS 11749, pp. 630–634, 2019.
https://doi.org/10.1007/978-3-030-29390-1_51

misinformation. This paper presents a preliminary account of our ongoing work towards this goal.

2 The Role of Human Decision Making on the Spread and Consumption of Misinformation

Empirical studies have repeatedly highlighted that mis-informative content propagates faster, deeper, farther than truthful messages. Vosoughi et al. [2], for instance, used a data set of rumor cascades on Twitter from 2006 to 2017, and found that the top 1% of false news cascades diffused to between 1000 and 100,000 people, whereas the truth rarely diffused to more than 1000 people. They found that fake news was approximately 70% more likely to be retweeted than true ones. A key question raised is: what role does human decision-making play, and how can technology enable humans to make better decisions? Recent studies have highlighted that cognitive biases in decision making can facilitate the spread, or the consumption of misinformative content. For instance, Vosoughi et al. [2] found that, contrary to conventional wisdom, the spread of false news could not be attributed to the structure of social media outlets, website platforms and internet bots, but rather to a mere novelty effect. Novelty, as the authors claimed, "attracts human attention, contributes to productive decision-making, and encourages information sharing because novelty updates our understanding of the world". False news was found to be more novel than true news, suggesting that people were more likely to share novel information.

Badke [3] supports that humans see only what they expect or want to see, without inspecting news thoroughly. This, they argue, is a product of the confirmation bias, the internal tendency of people to seek out information that confirms and verifies what they already believe, instead of examining critically all the pieces of information. According to the theory of cognitive dissonance, whenever a presented piece of news includes information which conflicts with the currently held mental models of people, it immediately induces cognitive dissonance [4]. People are motivated to scale down this dissonance, thus they may avoid or even discount knowledge that contrasts their personal positions. Weeks [5] argues that emotional experience moderates the influence of partisanship on individuals' responses to misinformation. Specifically, when individuals experience anger, the influence of partisanship is boosted, making individuals more likely to believe claims that are associated with their political affiliation. On the contrary, anxiety reduces the influence of partisanship and increases the chance of making other political affiliations believable. Schwarz et al. [6] argue that whenever people come across a new piece of information, they tend to assess its truthfulness by focusing on five criteria. People usually ask themselves about the social consensus of the story, its supporting evidence, its consistency, coherence and credibility. However, instead of evaluating these questions analytically, individuals tend to use mental shortcuts in order to minimize the time and energy spent. This makes them susceptible to errors in decision making.

3 *Nudging* Away from Misinformation

Thaler and Sunstein [7] define a nudge as "any aspect of the choice architecture that has the capacity to change people's behavior in a predictable manner but without preventing any other alternatives or altering their economic incentives". Nudges leverage knowledge about systematic biases in decision making to support people in making optimal decisions. For instance, the status-quo bias reflects our tendency to resist change and to go along with the path of least resistance [8]. As such, we often chose the default option rather than taking the time to consider the alternatives, even when this is against our best interests. For example, several countries in Europe have changed their laws to make organ donation the default option. In such so called opt-out contexts, over 90% of the citizens donate their organs; while in opt-in contexts the rate falls down to 15%. Similarly, replacing cake with fruit in the impulse basket next to the cash register, has been found to lead people in buying more fruit and less cake, when both choices are still available [9]. As evident, nudges work on the assumption that people don't always make rational choices and they attempt to direct human behavior, yet without imposing a particular choice [9].

Our ongoing work seeks to explore the power of nudging in reducing the likelihood of spreading as well as consuming misinformation. Through a systematic review of the use of nudging in HCI research, we have identified 23 distinct mechanisms of nudging developed within HCI, clustered in 6 overall categories, and tapping to 15 different cognitive biases and heuristics [8]. One such mechanism is called *"reminding the consequences"*. Tapping on the *availability heuristic* which reflects our tendency to judge the probability of occurrence of an event based on the ease at which it can be recalled, thus making us susceptible to underestimate the probability of events when these are not readily available to our cognitive processing, such nudges prompt individuals to reflect on the consequences of their actions. One example is provided by Harbach et al. [10] who redesigned the permissions dialogue of the Google Play Store to incorporate personalized scenarios that disclosed potential risks from app permissions. If the app required access to one's storage, the system would randomly select images stored on the phone along with the message "this app can see and delete your photos".

We have translated this framework of the 23 mechanisms of nudging into a set of design cards, the *Nudge Deck* [11]. Each mechanism is described in a card (see Fig. 1 for an example card), where the front side includes a definition of the nudging mechanism, an image of a possible implementation and an explanation. The back side illustrates suggestions, directions, instructions to provoke motivation and inspiration during the design conception. Moreover, to distinguish the situations in which each nudge should be used, the 23 mechanisms are mapped into the three trigger types, as suggested by Fogg's Behavior Model: *sparks* (i.e., ones to increase motivation), *facilitators* (i.e., ones that increase ability) or *signals* (i.e., ones to remind of the behavior).

Using the Nudge Deck as a design support tool, we currently plan to conduct a workshop with the goal of ideating on nudging interventions to combat the spread, or consumption of misinformative content online. To provide an example, suppose we want to minimize the spread of fake news on Twitter through preventing unaware users from retweeting those fabricated stories. One nudge mechanism that can be exploited is called *"throttling mindless activity"* [8]. This mechanism taps into *regret aversion bias*, people's tendency to become more reflective and break their mindless activities whenever risk is identified. In this case, given that the user is about to post a tweet that contains bogus news, the tool could notify the user with a message like: "We estimate 90% chance of the article containing falsehood information. Are you sure you want to publish this tweet?". Through instilling doubt, this nudge encourages users to reconsider the tweet's content. A link to a fact-checking article may further provide an opportunity for learning. Our workshop will seek to explore how different nudging mechanisms can be applied in different platforms – from social media, to e-mail, and question and answer (Q&A) websites like WikiAnswers. We will engage students of interaction design in small design teams and seek to provide a first inquiry into the design space of technology-mediated nudging in the context of misinformation-resilience tools, through an analysis of the design ideas that come out of the workshop and the emerging design qualities of those ideas.

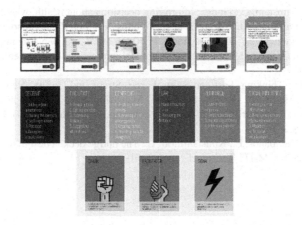

Fig. 1. The Nudge Decks consists of 23 *mechanism cards* (top), six *category cards* (middle), and three *trigger cards* (bottom)

4 Conclusion

This paper presented our ongoing work on the design of nudging mechanisms to combat the spread and consumption of misinformation online. Our future work will aim at exploring the design space of nudging interventions in the context of misinformation, as well as prototyping a set of intervention techniques with the goal of assessing their proximal effects on human behavior.

Acknowledgments. This research was supported by the European Union *Co-Inform* project (Horizon 2020 Research and Innovation Programme. Grant agreement 770302).

References

1. Meinert, J., Mirbabaie, M., Dungs, S., Aker, A.: Is it really fake? – Towards an understanding of fake news in social media communication. In: Meiselwitz, G. (ed.) Social Computing and Social Media. LNCS (Including Subseries Lecture Notes in Artificial Intelligence and Lecture Notes in Bioinformatics), vol. 10913, pp. 484–497. Springer, Cham (2018). https://doi.org/10.1007/978-3-319-91521-0_35
2. Vosoughi, S., Roy, D., Aral, S.: News Online 1151(March), 1146–1151 (2018). https://doi.org/10.1126/science.aap9559
3. Badke, W.: Fake news, confirmation bias, the search for truth, and the theology student. Theol. Libr. 11(2), 4–7 (2018). https://doi.org/10.31046/tl.v11i2.519
4. Festinger, L.: A Theory of Cognitive Dissonance. Palo Alto. Stanford University Press, California (1957)
5. Weeks, B.E.: Emotions, partisanship, and misperceptions: how anger and anxiety moderate the effect of partisan bias on susceptibility to political misinformation. J. Commun. 65(4), 699–719 (2015). https://doi.org/10.1111/jcom.12164
6. Schwarz, N., Newman, E., Leach, W.: Making the truth stick & the myths fade: lessons from cognitive psychology. Behav. Sci. Policy 2(1), 85–95 (2016). https://doi.org/10.1353/bsp.2016.0009
7. Thaler, R.H., Sunstein, C.: Nudge: improving decisions about health, wealth, and happiness. Choice Rev. Online 46(02), 46-0977 (2013). https://doi.org/10.5860/choice.46-0977
8. Caraban, A., Gonçalves, D., Karapanos, E., Campos, P.: 23 ways to nudge: a review of technology-mediated nudging in human-computer interaction. In: Proceedings of CHI 2019, pp. 1–15 (2019)
9. Kahneman, D.: Thinking, Fast and Slow. Farrar, Straus and Giroux, New York (2011)
10. Harbach, M., Hettig, M., Weber, S., Smith, M.: Using personal examples to improve risk communication for security & privacy decisions, pp. 2647–2656 (2014). https://doi.org/10.1145/2556288.2556978
11. Caraban, A., Karapanos, E., Konstantinou, L.: The nudge deck: a design tool for technology-mediated nudging, M-ITI Technical report (2019)

Exploring the Application of Social Robots in Understanding Bullying Perpetrators

Aiza Hasib[✉], Mehr-un-Nisa Arif Kitchlew, Saad Jamal, and Suleman Shahid

Lahore University of Management Sciences, Lahore, Pakistan
{19100255,19100141,18100153,suleman.shahid}@lums.edu.pk

Abstract. This paper examines a novel approach to the problem of bullying by employing Child-Robot Interaction to attempt to understand the causes of perpetrators behaviour. A comparative study was undertaken to understand the efficacy of such an approach. Children aged 9–10 years were first identified on the basis of their bullying perpetration record and characteristics. Half the children were made to interact individually with a social robot and the other half with a human agent over the span of 3 weeks. Our results exhibit that while children opened up to both kinds of agents, interaction with the human agent led to more insightful conversations that enhanced understanding of causes for the perpetrator's behaviour. As expected, the interactions varied from child to child and are to be considered on an individual basis. This is an ongoing study and shall be later extended to employ a hybrid of a within-subject and an in-between subject approach in order to examine the experience of each child individually and holistically.

1 Introduction

Bullying culture has been a persistently prevalent problem in schools across the world with interventions generally involving teachers and counsellors. However it is usually difficult for children to develop trust and open up to such agents given the power dynamic that generally exists between elders and children. A relatable agent with child-like disposition could be an effective alternative. However, children themselves should not be involved as agents of intervention due to unpredictability of their behaviour along with ethical considerations.

Substantial efforts are being made to study and address bullying behaviour. The most recent ones explore the use of social robots. Robots are perceived as social actors, with a recent trend towards building communication robots that participate in human daily life as a peer-type partner [1]. It is acknowledged that social robots have the potential to provide support in several practical domains such as learning and behaviour change [2,3]. Literature in Child-Robot Interaction shows the potential of using robots as intermediaries in conflict resolution as well as holding the capacity of being viewed as confidants and peers by children

© IFIP International Federation for Information Processing 2019
Published by Springer Nature Switzerland AG 2019
D. Lamas et al. (Eds.): INTERACT 2019, LNCS 11749, pp. 635–639, 2019.
https://doi.org/10.1007/978-3-030-29390-1_52

[8,10]. Work has also been done to measure the effects of dehumanization primes and anthropomorphic qualities of the robot on participants' bullying behaviour towards the robot [12]. Recent work in Child-Robot Interaction has aimed at eliciting experiences of bullying from victims [7]. However, there is an unexplored role robots could play in addressing bullying by attempting to understand and influence the bully's behaviour. Hence, while realizing the potential role of a bullying perpetrator as a victim of circumstances [13], this paper takes a novel approach to bullying by attempting to understand the causes of perpetrators behaviour via interaction with a social robot. Our research undertook a comparative study between a human and robotic agent to understand the efficacy of such an approach.

2 Methodology

2.1 Participants and Interaction Agents

The study spanned across 3 weeks and constituted of 3 sessions with 12 children aged 9–10 years. Children were selected by combining the results of (i) semi-structured interviews conducted with class teachers to gain insights regarding bullying behavior of students and (ii) Bullying Participant Behaviour Questionnaire (BPBQ), a preexisting self-report test that is used to classify people as bullies or victims [11].

Two groups of 6 children, each, were formed, where the first involved interaction with a robot (P1-P6) and the second involved interaction with a human agent (P7-P12). To avoid ambiguity, children identified as bullies by both teachers and the BPBQ were selected. To maintain homogeneity, they were equally divided into groups based on how they varied on the bullying spectrum with both groups containing some students that were identified as extreme bullies and some that only mildly exhibited the behaviour. To standardize the procedure for comparative analysis, the activity based content was kept similar while the conversations were semi-structured. A Lego Mindstorm robot (named 'Chotu', meaning 'little one') was presented as a social robot who is new to the school and wants to make friends. Chotu was given the ability to hold a conversation (implemented via Wizard of Oz techniques) along with limited movement. The human agent (one of the research team members) interacted with the second set and was presented as a friendly young individual who is eager to interact with children and make friends. The same member also controlled the robot to eliminate any differences that could arise owing to different personnel.

2.2 Session Design

A multimodal interaction technique was adapted to sustain a long term social interaction with the robot and followed a pattern of ice breaking, trust building and exploring possible causes for their bullying behaviour [2,5]. 3 sessions were held over the span of 3 weeks and were designed based on the findings of the literature review and further refined after a comprehensive interview with a professional psychologist. During the sessions, only the interacting agent was present in the room with the child.

Session 1 served as an icebreaker to initiate interaction between the child and the interacting agent. The interaction began with the agent greeting the child followed by an introduction. The agent told the child the apparent purpose of visit: to make friends and to interact with children. This was followed up by a conversation about how long the agent will be there, keeping in line with the ethical considerations of such psychological studies. The conversation then transitioned into a two-way exchange about friends and hobbies. This session lasted for 15 min on average.

Session 2 aimed at building trust and a rapport with the child while invoking the child's empathy towards the agent, making it more relatable [10]. The agent greeted the child by name and referred to things mentioned by the child in the previous session to exhibit memory retention. Next, the agent told the child that it had a fight with a friend and required help. The agent engaged in conversation with the child about the fight and possible solutions and then asked the child to write a letter addressed to the friend to help resolve the conflict.

Session 3 aimed at understanding the child's attitude towards and reasons for bullying, with an increased depth of conversation. Findings show that narratives can be a useful tool to explore children's past experiences with bullying behaviour [6]. In the beginning, the agent let the child know that it was the last session. While proceeding with filler small talk, it was noted whether the child brought up the letter from the previous session. If not, the agent brought the topic up and told the child that his/her help had been invaluable. The conversation then transitioned towards discussing cartoons in general after which the agent asked the child to watch a video cartoon clip showing a child being bullied. Simultaneously, the agent discussed with the child what was happening in the video. Following this, the agent steered the conversation towards their perception of why the child was being bullied in the video, following up with questions like 'have you ever seen this happen?.' Once the child appeared comfortable in the conversation, the agent asked the child if they had ever done something similar. The robot related its own example of bullying and creating mischief so that the child opened up and responded more freely.

3   Results and Discussion

Children expressed a novelty effect with the robot in the first two sessions and associated a whole slew of emotions with the robot. They wanted to help Chotu when it had a fight, which encouraged them to empathize with the robot and come up with a solution. When told the next day that their solution was helpful, they felt joyed and some believed that they could open up about their own issues. However, as we progressed with the sessions and started to shift towards longer conversations, the children started to become disinterested and tended to steer away from the conversation. Overall, we were able to get some interesting information from children. When children like P1 and P4 talked about their friends, we understood the type of social setting they were in. P5 showed he might have an underlying cause for his bullying since he mentioned that 'we all have problems at home' and that the victim had probably done something to deserve the beating. On the other hand, P6, P3 and P2 seem disinterested to connect emotionally and paid less attention to what Chotu was saying.

The sessions with the researcher were more successful in that nearly all of the kids opened up about themselves. Some narrated personal incidents that allowed for inferences regarding behavioural tendencies. The kids engaged in conversation with the researcher and most of them were quite expressive, listened with attention and responded well to all questions asked. When the kids were showed the video regarding bullying, they were initially reluctant to admit that they had engaged in such behaviour but after a little probing, admitted to the mischief they had committed. This opening up flowed into a conversation regarding their personal lives and provided very interesting insights. After seeing the video, P7 opened up about her tendency to get annoyed and bother those who refused to sit with her. She also talked about being irritated by her younger brother and the extra attention he received by their mother. P8 mentioned that when he gets upset with his parents, he does not speak to them till they get him something of his liking. He annoys the teachers he does not like and those that are strict. When showed the video, he spoke about how he often got involved in fights with his neighbourhood kids. P11 talked about how she and her friends enjoyed bothering new teachers and how it was a tradition to annoy new teachers before befriending them. P12 said that sometimes he and his friends threw water on each other and bothered the girls but stopped when someone got too annoyed. Inferring from the sessions, among the six kids, P7 and P8 could be categorized as troublemakers while P11 and P12 were infrequent mischief creators. P9 and P10 seemed relatively well mannered and seemed to have been misidentified.

While in both cases the children wanted to open up to the agent, conversations with the human agent were more meaningful as children expressed a lot more of their emotions and problems. Whereas with the robot, this process was a lot more damped. This could be attributed to the decreasing effect of novelty with passing sessions and lack of responsiveness of the robot [4,9]. The most substantial of them being the limited movement of the robot and the lack of facial and voice expressions. While conversing, the human agent can express a simple nod that expresses a sign of agreement and indicates to the child that the agent is listening and acknowledging and that he can continue talking. These interactions are absent in a robot as a child cannot properly gauge how the robot was responding to their conversations. This can be a reason for why interactions did not last very long with the robot.

Although limited by its number of participants, the study provides some interesting insights and observations regarding children's interaction with human and robotic agents alike and the nature of the relationship formed with both under a comparative framework. The work could be extended to further explore the potential use of robots in mediating classroom relations and bullying behaviour. Since the robot in this study was limited in its movement and expressions, it could be interesting to explore how varying such factors (e.g. by using other robots like NAO) could enhance their application for such a use case.

References

1. Fujita, M.: AIBO: towards the era of digital creatures. In: Hollerbach, J.M., Koditschek, D.E. (eds.) Robotics Research, pp. 315–320. Springer, London (2000). https://doi.org/10.1007/978-1-4471-0765-1_38
2. Coninx, A., Baxter, P., Oleari, E., et al.: Towards long-term social child-robot interaction: using multi-activity switching to engage young users. J. Hum. Robot Interact. **5**, 32 (2015). https://doi.org/10.5898/jhri.5.1.coninx
3. Cañamero, L., Lewis, M.: Making new "New AI" friends: designing a social robot for diabetic children from an embodied AI perspective. Int. J. Soc. Robot. **8**(4), 523-537 (2016). https://doi.org/10.1007/s12369-016-0364-9
4. Kanda, T., Hirano, T., Eaton, D., Ishiguro, H.: Interactive robots as social partners and peer tutors for children: a field trial. Hum. Comput. Interact. **19**, 61–84 (2004). https://doi.org/10.1207/s15327051hci1901|&2_4
5. Belpaeme, T., Baxter, P.E., Read, R., et al.: Multimodal child-robot interaction: building social bonds. J. Hum. Robot Interact. (2013). https://doi.org/10.5898/jhri.1.2.belpaeme
6. Woods, S., Davis, M., Dautenhahn, K., Schulz, J.: Can robots be used as a vehicle for the projection of socially sensitive issues? exploring childrens attitudes towards robots through stories. In: ROMAN 2005 IEEE International Workshop on Robot and Human Interactive Communication (2005). https://doi.org/10.1109/roman.2005.1513809
7. Bethel, C.L., Henkel, Z., Stives, K., et al.: Using robots to interview children about bullying: lessons learned from an exploratory study. In: 2016 25th IEEE International Symposium on Robot and Human Interactive Communication (RO-MAN) (2016). https://doi.org/10.1109/roman.2016.7745197
8. Bethel, C.L., Stevenson, M.R., Scassellati, B.: Secret-sharing: interactions between a child, robot, and adult. In: 2011 IEEE International Conference on Systems, Man, and Cybernetics (2011). https://doi.org/10.1109/icsmc.2011.6084051
9. Hoffman, G., Birnbaum, G.E., Vanunu, K., et al.: Robot responsiveness to human disclosure affects social impression and appeal. In: Proceedings of the 2014 ACM/IEEE International Conference on Human-Robot Interaction - HRI 14 (2014). https://doi.org/10.1145/2559636.2559660
10. Kwak, S.S., Kim, Y., Kim, E., et al.: What makes people empathize with an emotional robot?: the impact of agency and physical embodiment on human empathy for a robot. In: 2013 IEEE RO-MAN (2013). https://doi.org/10.1109/roman.2013.6628441
11. Demaray, M.K., Summers, K.H., Jenkins, L.N., Becker, L.D.: Bullying participant behaviors questionnaire (BPBQ): establishing a reliable and valid measure. J. Sch. Violence **15**, 158–188 (2014). https://doi.org/10.1080/15388220.2014.964801
12. Keijsers, M., Bartneck, C.: Mindless robots get bullied. In: Proceedings of the 2018 ACM/IEEE International Conference on Human-Robot Interaction - HRI 18 (2018). https://doi.org/10.1145/3171221.3171266
13. Why Do Kids Bully? In: STOMP Out Bullying. http://www.stompoutbullying.org/information-and-resources/about-bullying-and-cyberbullying/why-do-kids-bully. Accessed 9 Apr 2019

Initial Steps Towards Infrastructuring Body-Centric Computing

Amir Zare Pashaei[(✉)] [iD], Ilja Smorgun [iD], David Lamas [iD],
and Vladimir Tomberg [iD]

Tallinn University, Tallinn, Estonia
amirzp@tlu.ee

Abstract. Digital technologies are moving towards the human body. Designing for the body is commonly dubbed as body-centric computing (BCC) and includes two sides: (1) the neuro-science side; (2) the technical side mainly focuses on establishing and enabling the interactions. A conceptual framework enabling the systematic design and development of body-centric applications is introduced. Its novelty and importance are assessed within a set of application scenarios.

Keywords: Body-centric computing · Framework · Implementation · Scenarios

1 Introduction

Body-centric computing has proven to be quite difficult to implement. According to Mueller et al. [8], such difficulty was observed while they were doing the study around the topic of BCC. Additionally, some difficulties have affected the implementation of BCC because of technological barriers [11].

According to Svanaes et al. [10] it is a design challenge to understand how it would be possible to design such an artefact, which would make it easy for the body to learn to use it so that it becomes a natural part of the body and therefore can benefit from the user's *"bodily-kinesthetic intelligence"*.

Kistler proposes a generic framework *"FUBI"* [6] which recognises full-body gestures and postures in real-time from the data of a depth sensor integrated using OpenNI or the Kinect SDK. The Smart-Its project [2,3] proposes a generic layered architecture for sensor-based context computation, providing a programming abstraction that separates layers for raw sensor data, features extracted from sensors (cues), and abstract contexts derived from cues. However, previous work does not provide adequate support for organising contexts in a formal structured format.

Our work tries to establish a modular infrastructure for BCC, which has not been addressed before. This modular platform:

© IFIP International Federation for Information Processing 2019
Published by Springer Nature Switzerland AG 2019
D. Lamas et al. (Eds.): INTERACT 2019, LNCS 11749, pp. 640–643, 2019.
https://doi.org/10.1007/978-3-030-29390-1_53

- Would not require developers to perform additional programming
- Would support flexible interaction modalities
- Would have a structured format
- Would have a modular mechanism for querying and reasoning context and information
- Would offer the designers and researchers a foundation for the developments of their BCC applications.

2   Related Work

Kistler et al. [7] describe that people can interact with each other on several channels, such as speech, gestures or postures. For example, Microsoft has paved the way to controller-free user interaction by releasing Kinect [1]. Other vendors have since then adopted these interaction modalities in their own products, such as Animoji in Apple's iOS, which has been used as Realtime Performance-Based Facial Avatars [9] or BMW's HoloActive touch [4], which enables users to interact with their car's system in hands-free scenarios.

Digital technologies are moving towards having the human body at the centre of focus and all the computations should happen either on or around the body. The human body can be the core for in-body or on-body interactions, which as the result would enable novel interaction scenarios.

Mueller et al. [8] describe that the core application domains for BCC are entertainment, health, well-being and sport. It can be either improving one's bodily motions and interactions or enhancing resilience.

3   Conceptual Framework

Nowadays we know that a number of research is being done on smart environments, but we see that in the future the smart environment is going to go from the scale of the room to the scale of the body. The person's body is going to become the smart environment. This is what we call an on-body network of vibro-tactile interfaces (VTI).

To facilitate the connection between the interfaces in smart environments, e.g. smart homes, there are off-the-shelf products, such as smart home information hubs. These days, they are mostly provided in the form of a speaker, which controls the music at home and also controls all the other smart devices at home. We want to create a similar infrastructure, but for the body.

We are introducing a scalable, reliable and modular body-centric infrastructure. This infrastructure encapsulates underlying technologies with our integration of interaction modalities into well-established micro services that can be used as a foundation for building BCC applications. This infrastructure will have different characteristics, such as a set of predefined interaction patterns, which are going to be used for the purpose of communication in different scenarios, such as sense of presence in remote relationships, or behaviour change in environments such as classroom and others. On the other hand, the infrastructure includes interaction modalities such as vibration with specific pattern, which would be used in different interfaces such as VTIs.

The infrastructure has three layers. The first layer includes a set of VTIs that are going to be put on the person's body. These need to be designed in a way that they can communicate through a number of protocols. At the moment we are considering several communication protocols, such as WiFi, Bluetooth Low Energy, or USB. An individual VTI can be designed for:

- Input – collecting data from the user's body and the surrounding environment through a set of sensors
- Output – providing on-body feedback to the user through a set of actuators
- Both input and output, working as a combination of sensors and actuators.

The second layer is the central processing unit. The purpose of having this device is to facilitate the connection between the VTIs by having a ruling engine in its core. This device gathers information from the input devices and sends the correct values to the corresponding output devices, by adopting the "publish-subscribe" pattern. The central device would include software specifications on a number of levels. It is going to include a set of patterns for sending and receiving instructions and a repository for publishing vendor-specific modules. This way each VTI will be recognised by the central computing device. Otherwise the VTI will be registered and recognised as a generic device, supporting only a basic level of functionality. The third layer is the back-end cloud platform, which can be implemented on top of Microsoft Azure IoT Hub, or alternative configurations.

4   Application Scenarios

Body-centric wearable technology, enabled by the proposed BCC infrastructure will facilitate a variety of application scenarios in different contexts, such as social interactions in remote relationships, well-being, health care and entertainment. For instance, sense of presence in remote relationships can be enabled by a VTI placed on the body. The sense of presence, in this case, is achieved by perceiving mediated touch by skin receptors [5].

5   Current Status

So far, a number of initial prototypes have been developed. The current prototypes are of two types, input device and output device. The input device has built-in sensors (e.g. pressure sensors) and a processing unit, which supports Bluetooth Low Energy connection. The output device has built-in actuators (such as vibration motors/LED) and a similar processing unit for the input device. A central device has been set up to aid the sensor and actuator communication.

6   Future Work

The aim of this research is to enable BCC interaction scenarios by proposing an infrastructure, which would be used as the foundation for BCC developments. The purpose is to enable the BCC developments not only in controlled lab environments, but also to make it possible outside the lab so that everyone regardless of their location would be able to use it. In the future it would be possible to analyse how using this infrastructure would change people's behaviour and how people would use this infrastructure for different purposes. It is also important to understand how this infrastructure would affect people's lives and what would be the challenge for designers in their BCC solution.

7   Closing Remarks

An open infrastructure is being proposed to aid the design of BCC solutions. At the moment, the infrastructure is in its early stage and needs improvements. The infrastructure can be used in both lab and outside the lab.

References

1. Gabel, M., Gilad-Bachrach, R., Renshaw, E., Schuster, A.: Full body gait analysis with Kinect. In: 2012 Annual International Conference of the IEEE Engineering in Medicine and Biology Society (EMBC), pp. 1964–1967. IEEE (2012)
2. Gellersen, H., Kortuem, G., Schmidt, A., Beigl, M.: Physical prototyping with smart-its. IEEE Pervasive Comput. 3(3), 74–82 (2004)
3. Gellersen, H.W., Schmidt, A., Beigl, M.: Multi-sensor context-awareness in mobile devices and smart artifacts. Mob. Netw. Appl. 7(5), 341–351 (2002)
4. Hermann, D.S.: Automotive displays-trends, opportunities and challenges. In: 2018 25th International Workshop on Active-Matrix Flatpanel Displays and Devices (AM-FPD), pp. 1–6. IEEE (2018)
5. Israr, A., Abnousi, F.: Towards pleasant touch: vibrotactile grids for social touch interactions. In: Extended Abstracts of the 2018 CHI Conference on Human Factors in Computing Systems, p. LBW131. ACM (2018)
6. Kistler, F.: Full body interaction: design, implementation, and user support (2016)
7. Kistler, F., Endrass, B., Damian, I., Dang, C.T., André, E.: Natural interaction with culturally adaptive virtual characters. J. Multimodal User Interfaces 6(1–2), 39–47 (2012)
8. Mueller, F., et al.: Body-centric computing: results from a weeklong Dagstuhl seminar in a German castle. Interactions 25(4), 34–39 (2018)
9. Pauly, M.: Realtime performance-based facial avatars for immersive gameplay. In: Proceedings of Motion on Games, pp. 23–28. ACM (2013)
10. Svanaes, D., Solheim, M.: Wag your tail and flap your ears: the kinesthetic user experience of extending your body. In: Proceedings of the 2016 CHI Conference Extended Abstracts on Human Factors in Computing Systems, pp. 3778–3779. ACM (2016)
11. Yun, J., Ahn, I.Y., Choi, S.C., Kim, J.: TTEO (things talk to each other): programming smart spaces based on IoT systems. Sensors 16(4), 467 (2016)

Model-Driven Framework for Human Machine Interaction Design in Industry 4.0

Patrícia Leal[1,2], Rui Neves Madeira[1,2(✉)], and Teresa Romão[1]

[1] NOVA LINCS, DI, FCT, NOVA University of Lisboa, Lisbon, Portugal
p.leal@campus.fct.unl.pt, tir@fct.unl.pt
[2] Sustain.RD Center and ESTSetúbal, Polytechnic Institute of Setúbal,
Setúbal, Portugal
rui.madeira@estsetubal.ips.pt

Abstract. Industry 4.0 (I4.0) has brought many changes in the way workers operate on and interact with smarter industrial machinery and spaces. New Human-Machine Interaction (HMI) solutions are required as the workers' demands in the factory are still evolving. This paper introduces the development of a generic model-driven HMI solution that consists of a framework providing an API and widgets that can be (re)used to create the final interfaces for HMI across different I4.0 scenarios. The generic model takes into account the most important aspects of the shop floor context. As a first phase of evaluation, this solution is being tested in a prototype for a real use case, responding to the needs of an industrial partner. The paper ends by presenting this prototype to show the potential of the presented solution.

Keywords: Industry 4.0 · Human-Machine Interaction · Model-driven · OPC UA

1 Introduction

The fourth industrial revolution, known as Industry 4.0 (I4.0), marks the evolution to Cyber-Physical Systems (CPS), being strongly driven by the advent of the Internet of Things (IoT), towards a smarter automation and data exchange in manufacturing technologies. I4.0 has brought many changes in the way shop floor users should interact with smarter industrial machinery. HMI proposals need to allow a greater symbiosis between humans and machines, providing a smooth user interaction with a pervasive computing-based environment, leading to a safer, more productive and more engaging work-life [1, 2]. In general, new HMI solutions need to be tailored to specific scenarios, which can vary widely. It means designing, developing and testing HMI solutions from scratch make data reuse difficult due to the changes in data models and protocols used, which is costly and time-consuming [3]. The lack of a global framework serving as a common basis to guide in the HMI design for different scenarios may a key obstacle to the full realization of I4.0.

This paper introduces the development of a generic model-driven HMI solution (smartHMI4I4) that consists of a framework providing an API and widgets that can be (re)used to create the final HMI for different devices across many I4.0 scenarios. It aims

D. Lamas et al. (Eds.): INTERACT 2019, LNCS 11749, pp. 644–648, 2019.
https://doi.org/10.1007/978-3-030-29390-1_54

to make the process of mapping all the industry data more streamlined and agile, while trying to support a standard way of developing HMI solutions for I4.0. As a first phase of evaluation, this solution is being used in a prototype for a real use case to assess the potential of the developed solution, responding to the needs of an industrial partner.

2 Background and Related Work

It is common to find different types of users in a factory environment, such as, team leaders, machine operators, or even directors, who may interact with each other, directly with machines or with the shop floor as a whole, needing to access and manipulate different information that can still present overlaps [2, 4]. I4.0 aims to provide the relevant data and services in context of use to the shop floor's users, according to their needs and preferences. Appropriate HMI designs should present consistent, functional and easy-to-maintain interfaces with multi-platform and multi-device support toward a pervasive user experience that do not distract users from their primary functions. There are some interesting commercial solutions, such as iFix with their HMI/SCADA software [5] providing rapid application development for system integrators, and myHMI [6] an HMI architecture oriented towards the supervision of industrial plants, which comprises of a server that handles the communication with the field by using an OPC XML-DA based module to retrieve data. UX-FAB [7] seems to be an interesting project with points in common to our solution and focused on a Web-based platform for the development of interfaces oriented to industry, multi-platform and devices of different sizes. However, these solutions do not meet every necessity, or they are closed solutions that offer no possibilities for further customization by third party developers.

3 Generic HMI Solution for Industry 4.0

The architecture of smartHMI4I4 can be seen in Fig. 1, where the bottom layer represents a specific shop floor zone (can be a whole factory), feeding the Smart Object (SO) Model, which models the computing-augmented machines of the shop floor's CPS, and the HMI Model. This one uses the SO model and describes everything else in the smart factory scenario for HMI purposes. The API and widgets are based on the guiding HMI Model to provide a standard and agile development of applications (apps).

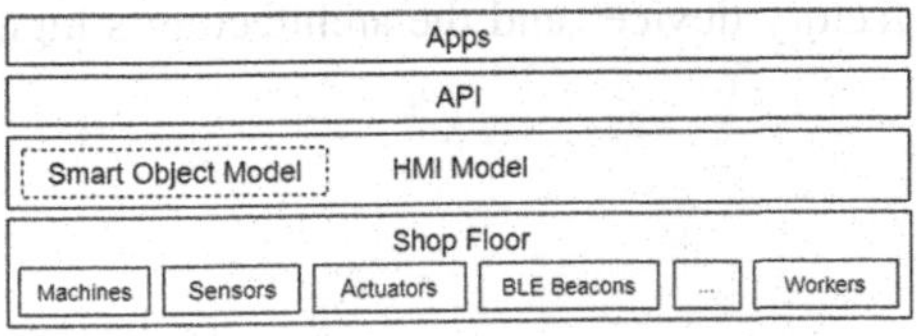

Fig. 1. Architecture of smartHMI4I4

3.1   The Generic HMI Model

The HMI Model characterizes the elements of the whole industry's scenario, considering important entities of the shop floor, such as the production numbers, the smart machines and their layout, the user profile, or the physical context (environment measures). Figure 2 shows the HMI model diagram, where the workers are represented by the User element, while the Scenario element represents the characteristics of the shop floor, such as noise, danger and temperature levels, which are important to define interaction features (e.g., screen type, mobile vs stationary, by voice). CPS is associated with the scenario and represents the smart objects (machines) composition (taken from the SO model). The ArrangedData element models the CPS data that have been transformed and structured to be shown in the HMI devices.

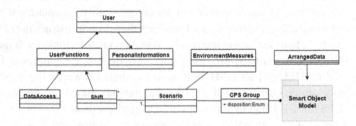

Fig. 2. A partial and simplified view of the HMI Model.

3.2   The SmartHMI4I4 Implementation

The implementation was divided into two components: HMI server; API/widgets for clients. The HMI Server Layer was created to support the HMI framework and it was implemented using Node.js. It manages the model and it is where data is stored, processed, aggregated and transformed, being prepared to be consumed. Figure 3a shows a diagram of the modules of the implemented server. The Data Retrieval module deals with data coming from the IIoT Platform that gathers data from the environment ("things" in the scenario) and transforms it in order to fit the HMI model. This component also contains both an OPC UA Client, which communicates with the Smart Objects (the machines with external sensors, actuators and OPC UA capabilities) of the shop floor, and an OPC UA Server, which connects to the HMI devices to track data coming from the Smart Objects. OPC UA is a platform-independent, scalable and high-performing communication protocol that provides a unified and standardized communication infrastructure for a greater degree of interoperability between different industrial machinery, factory devices and the architecture's higher-level tiers.

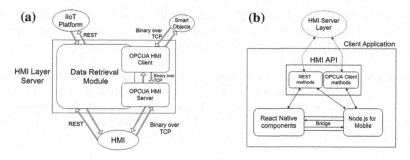

Fig. 3. (a) The HMI layer on server side; (b) the client side using the HMI API.

The client-side API was developed using JavaScript and Node.js. Figure 3b presents the diagram of the general implementation and illustrates the use of the API by an HMI app. The API's methods make requests to the server tier, which returns a Promise that can be used by the app to process the data that asynchronously arrives from the server. The API contains an OPC UA client module implemented in Node.js, offering methods that can be used to monitor and exchange data from the Smart Objects of the factory.

3.3 First SmartHMI4I4-Based Prototype - Preliminary Evaluation

As part of our evaluation plan, we created a first mobile prototype for a real scenario applying smartHMI4I4. MCG - Mind for Metal [8] presented us with the need to access information about a certain shop floor's area comprising three production machines (jigs) positioned in line. Three BLE (Bluetooth Low-Energy) beacons were placed near each jig and another one at the area's entrance, as it was required to differentiate the HMI according to the user profile (e.g. machine operator or team leader) and the user's proximity to machines. When a beacon is found (strongest signal → nearest) by the HMI mobile device of a user, it means s/he is facing the area/machine (a smart object) to which the beacon "belongs" and then the app automatically displays an adapted interface with data related to the object and tailored to the user profile.

The Node.js for Mobile module was used in order to integrate Node.js scripts with React Native (used in this app). As can be seen in Fig. 3(b), the information flow between the React Native components and the Node.js scripts in the application using the bridge built by the Node.js for Mobile module. This is the path used by the React Native client to transmit/receive information from the OPC UA client given by the API.

4 Conclusions and Future Work

Our solution is being developed to fulfil the need for a standard and agile solution that guides and supports the implementation of smart HMI across different I4.0 scenarios. smartHMI4I4 was created for application developers, being based on a generic, extendable and industry domain-independent model for HMI in I4.0.

We will develop new HMI applications applied to real case scenarios to test if smartHMI4I4-based applications work well in factory context. We also intend to conduct tests to study the usability of the framework from a developers point-of-view.

Acknowledgments. This research is supported by Polytechnic Inst. of Setúbal under the project "Smart Human Machine Interaction for Industry 4.0", FCT/MCTES NOVA LINCS PEst UID/CEC/04516/2019, and the European Regional Development Fund (FEDER) through a grant of the Operational Programme for Competitivity and Internationalization of Portugal 2020 Partnership Agreement (PRODUTECH-SIF, POCI-01-0247-FEDER-024541).

References

1. Cotteleer, M., Sniderman, B.: Forces of change: Industry 4.0. https://www2.deloitte.com/insights/us/en/focus/industry-4-0/overview.html. Accessed 28 Mar 2019
2. Johannsen, G.: Human-machine interaction. Control Syst. Robot. Autom. **21**, 132–162 (2009)
3. Fleischmann, H., Brossog, M., Beck, M., Franke, J.: Automated generation of human-machine interfaces in electric drives manufacturing. In: Proceedings of 7th International Electric Drives Production Conference (EDPC 2017), pp. 1–8. IEEE (2017)
4. Relatório Técnico-Científico Intercalar Consolidado: Programa Mobilizador PRODUTECH SIF - Soluções para a Indústria de Futuro. Technical report. PRODUTECH SIF (2018)
5. GE Digital: iFIX. https://www.ge.com/digital/applications/hmi-scada/ifix. Accessed 07 Apr 2019
6. Bozzon, A., Brambilla, M., Fraternali, P., Speroni, P.: Bringing internet architectures into the plant: the case of HMI. In: European Control Conference (ECC 2007), pp. 5530–5537. IEEE (2007)
7. Critical Manufacturing. UX-FAB: Universal Experience for advanced Fabs. http://www.criticalmanufacturing.com/en/r-d/ux-fab. Accessed 03 Apr 2019
8. MCG - Mind for Metal. http://www.mcg.pt/pt/. Accessed 03 June 2019

MyCompanion: A Digital Social Companion for Assisted Living

Fernando Loizides[1]([:envelope:])(iD), Kathryn E. Jones[1](iD), Daniel Abbasi[1],
Christopher Cardwell[1], Ieuan Jones[1], Liam D. Turner[1](iD),
Athanasios Hassoulas[1], Ashley Bale[2], and Scott Morgan[3]

[1] Cardiff University, Cardiff, UK
{floizides,jonesk90,abbasid,cardwellcj,jonesin,
turnerl19,hassoulasa2}@cardiff.ac.uk
[2] Innovate Trust, Cardiff, UK
ashley.bale@innovate-trust.org.uk
[3] Bridgend College, Bridgend, UK
smorgan@bridgend.ac.uk

Abstract. In this work, we present the initial progressive build of a prototype system, dubbed **MyCompanion**. MyCompanion to improve assisted living, ultimately targeting alleviating social exclusion and loneliness. The system, based on a Raspberry Pi, connects to a user's television set and tracks data from sensors placed around the house. An inbuilt artificial intelligence chat-bot then listens to, as well as instantiates, conversation with the user based on self-imposed triggers. Data from the sensors inform MyCompanion in real time user behaviour and records these readings. We also port MyCompanion software to an anthropomorphic version inside a humanoid robot for us to be able to give a physical dimension to the digital character.

Keywords: Digital companion · Robot · Loneliness ·
Digital exclusion

1 Introduction and Motivation

Depression is one of the prevalent chronic disease in ageing adults, with nearly half of the UK population (7.7 million) aged 55+ experiencing it at some point [1,2]. Loneliness has been shown to be a contributor towards depression [17], with a direct correlation between loneliness, and increasingly ageing population [3].

Technological intervention to provide aid, support and assist all stakeholders involved, including the elderly, carers, family, and friends has been of increasing research interest. In particular, we note that the emerging capability of AI and Robotics have been to shown to have positive effects on reducing the feeling of loneliness among the elderly. Robots for example, have been able to stimulate interaction between elderly people that are co-located [20]. Social robots are

D. Lamas et al. (Eds.): INTERACT 2019, LNCS 11749, pp. 649–653, 2019.
https://doi.org/10.1007/978-3-030-29390-1_55

"designed to interact with people in a socio-emotional way during interpersonal interaction" [15]. The timely fashion of this kind of research is paramount as there is an increased understanding of "the health care sector inability to provide qualitative care for older people" [15]. Other reasons include global ageing, shortage of health care professionals, to tackle the growing demands of patients and chronic diseases such as depression [12]. As research has shown, elderly now respond well to robots, even claiming emotions such as love for them [20]. Feelings of people with depression can also be improved by the use of robot intervention [25].

We hypothesise that with the appropriate use of anthropomorphic robots as companions in the home (instead of care homes) can strongly benefit the prevention or improvement of loneliness. We aim for the robots to have the attributes of 'companions' rather than helpers, since we are aware "that people who help others gain a sense of well-being compared to people who are only in need of help" [15]. In this paradigm the robot becomes something that needs to be governed. In fact, "the company of robots may be preferred to humans because we as human beings feel that we are in control in a human–robot relationship and that robots will not judge us like other people do" [23]. Furthermore, we are confident that the successful completion of a prototype for this project "reduce isolation and increase conversational opportunities with the robot itself as well as with other humans [22]; a robot or telecare-system might reduce certain risks and help the user to self-manage their health and well-being [13]. If technology is applied correctly, it can "enable and empower older people" [18]. This method of using a social robot, with all the characteristics we have included, has been shown to provide positive "feel well" results amongst elderly people [21] and therefore suitable for our goal of reducing mild depression through loneliness and social exclusion. In this work, we present the first working prototype system of **MyCompanion**, a digital assistant that provides company and enables individuals who are socially excluded to become more connected and healthier.

2 Artefact Creation and Description

The process of requirements gathering was performed by semi-structured interviews with stakeholders. Our participants ranged from health care workers to roboticists, carers and government medical advisers. Upon requirements elicitation, storyboards and use cases were created to guide the design and a structured dialogue design approach [14] was taken to collate the functional and non-functional components. Low fidelity prototypes were used as an initial point internally to the design and developer team. From these a round robin approach was used to produce the components that covered a minimum viable product in terms of stakeholder requirements.

The prototype system uses several components to create an interactive digital companion. It currently has four main functions. The first, is to 'be needy' and allow the user to take care of the companion, thus feeling useful and needed. Unlike digital assistants that are currently commercially available, MyCompanion will initiate a conversation and ask the user for help in some matters, such as for example asking what the weather is outside or for the user to tell it a joke or story. This invokes feelings of usefulness and of being needed by the users, a factor that has serious benefits to the health of an older adult [16]. The second, is to seamlessly present social media content from the users friends and family to them. The system will detect Twitter posts and ask the user whether they would like to see pictures of what their friends have posted or read out what they are saying. Thirdly, MyCompanion is also fitted with algorithms for Behavioural Activation for Depression [24] to ask the user at regular intervals how they are feeling and store the data for analysis, as well as respond with an appropriate suggestion to improve the situation. Finally, as a fourth main function, MyCompanion is connected to sensors around the home. These sensors include motion, temperature, door and light sensors currently implemented. The sensors take readings that are currently at an experimental phase. Using these readings, we are able to then apply machine learning techniques to detect normal routine over time and also deviations from this that may constitute a dangerous situation. As a predicted example, if one enters the kitchen at night time, and does not switch on the light for a few minutes then this would be flagged as abnormal behaviour, and MyCompanion would attempt to engage the user and establish that all is well. The full system technical architecture can be seen in Fig. 1.

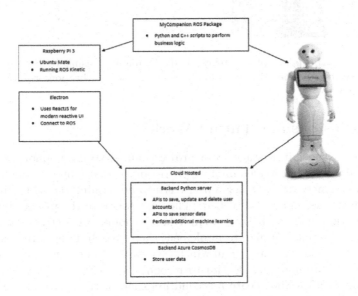

Fig. 1. MyCompanion system architecture

The system utilises Electron [4] to create a responsive front-end (See Fig. 2: Right). The artificial intelligence and conversational module of MyCompanion is built on the foundations of Mycroft [5] for the text to speech and vice versa and for natural language processing. This also allowed us to build a more robust system which can work as a basic version when an internet connection is made unavailable. Raspberry Pis (version 3 B+) [6] are used to control different sensors around a home. The sensors then transmit this data with timestamps to a cloud based Python server and uses Azure [7] to store a user's data. ROS [8] is used as the main SDK for communicating the concepts with the robot. The ability of this SDK to allow for messages (scripts) to communicate on different nodes makes is it ideal for communication between the robot body and the main server. For this prototype, we chose a Pepper type robot [9] to represent the anthropomorphic body (see Fig. 2: Left) of MyCompanion. Finally, a wireless omni-directional microphone is used in a generic area of the home as an input device for the user's speech.

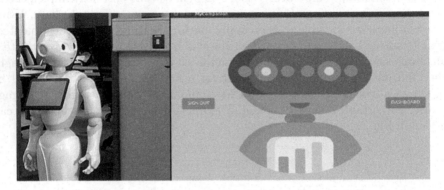

Fig. 2. Left: anthropomorphic version of MyCompanion, using ROS to connect the functionality to a Pepper Robot. Right: on screen (non-anthropomorphic) version of MyCompanion

3   Conclusions and Future Work

We presented the initial stages of a project names MyCompanion, which uses sensors and a chat bot loaded on a raspberry pi to create interactions with individuals We are now ready to begin user testing and refining the AI to understand user requirements and react to them. The next stages of the project involve the implementation of the technology to individuals' homes and extract data through in the field research. We plan to implement the research design process (slightly adapted) by Khakurel et al. [19] in which two stages, identifying and prioritising, is used. From the findings, we aim to recognise the effects of MyCompanion's need for interaction and create a second iteration of the system to build upon positive findings. We will then implement the installations on a larger scale and allow for larger data streams for behavioural analysis via machine learning which will be able to give us we are hoping will give us insight into changes of behaviour which are not clear with visual inspection.

Acknowledgements. We would like to thank Claire George & Carl Bickle (Bridgend College) [10] and Carl Clement (Emotion Robotics) [11] for their support.

References

1. https://tinyurl.com/y6bwo8yv. May 2019
2. https://tinyurl.com/y4syk49f. May 2019
3. http://www.monmouthshire.gov.uk/govtech-challenge. May 2019
4. https://electronjs.org/. May 2019
5. https://mycroft.ai/. May 2019
6. https://www.raspberrypi.org/. May 2019
7. https://azure.microsoft.com/en-gb/. May 2019
8. http://www.ros.org. May 2019
9. https://tinyurl.com/y5qtxqcf. May 2019
10. https://www1.bridgend.ac.uk/. May 2019
11. http://www.emotion-robotics.com. May 2019
12. Breazeal, C.L.: Designing Sociable Robots. MIT Press, Cambridge (2004)
13. Callén, B., Domènech, M., López, D., Tirado, F.: Telecare research: (Cosmo) politicizing methodology. ALTER-Eur. J. Disabil. Res./Rev. Européenne de Recherche sur le Handicap **3**(2), 110–122 (2009)
14. Christakis, A.N., Bausch, K.C.: CoLaboratories of Democracy: How People Harness Their Collective Wisdom to Create the Future. IAP (2006)
15. Frennert, S., Östlund, B.: Seven matters of concern of social robots and older people. Int. J. Soc. Robot. **6**(2), 299–310 (2014)
16. Gruenewald, T.L., Karlamangla, A.S., Greendale, G.A., Singer, B.H., Seeman, T.E.: Feelings of usefulness to others, disability, and mortality in older adults: the MacArthur study of successful aging. J. Gerontol. Ser. B: Psychol. Sci. Soc. Sci. **62**(1), P28–P37 (2007)
17. Hagerty, B.M., Williams, A.: The effects of sense of belonging, social support, conflict, and loneliness on depression. Nurs. Res. **48**(4), 215–219 (1999)
18. Joyce, K., Loe, M.: A sociological approach to ageing, technology and health. Sociol. Health Illn. **32**(2), 171–180 (2010)
19. Khakurel, J., Knutas, A., Melkas, H., Penzenstadler, B., Fu, B., Porras, J.: Categorization framework for usability issues of smartwatches and pedometers for the older adults. In: Antona, M., Stephanidis, C. (eds.) UAHCI 2018. LNCS, vol. 10907, pp. 91–106. Springer, Cham (2018). https://doi.org/10.1007/978-3-319-92049-8_7
20. Kidd, C.D., Taggart, W., Turkle, S.: A sociable robot to encourage social interaction among the elderly. In: Proceedings 2006 IEEE International Conference on Robotics and Automation, 2006. ICRA 2006, pp. 3972–3976. IEEE (2006)
21. Körtner, T., et al.: How social robots make older users really feel well – a method to assess users' concepts of a social robotic assistant. In: Ge, S.S., Khatib, O., Cabibihan, J.-J., Simmons, R., Williams, M.-A. (eds.) ICSR 2012. LNCS (LNAI), vol. 7621, pp. 138–147. Springer, Heidelberg (2012). https://doi.org/10.1007/978-3-642-34103-8_14
22. Sharkey, A., Sharkey, N.: Granny and the robots: ethical issues in robot care for the elderly. Ethics Inf. Technol. **14**(1), 27–40 (2012)
23. Turkle, S.: Alone Together: Why We Expect More from Technology and lEss from Each Other. Hachette, New York (2017)
24. Veale, D.: Behavioural activation for depression. Adv. Psychiatr. Treat. **14**(1), 29–36 (2008)
25. Wada, K., Shibata, T., Saito, T., Tanie, K.: Analysis of factors that bring mental effects to elderly people in robot assisted activity. In: IEEE/RSJ International Conference on Intelligent Robots and Systems, vol. 2, pp. 1152–1157. IEEE (2002)

OmniWedges: Improved Radar-Based Audience Selection for Social Networks

Frederic Raber$^{(\boxtimes)}$ and Antonio Krüger

DFKI Saarland Informatics Campus, Saarbrücken, Germany
{frederic.raber,krueger}@dfki.de

Abstract. Selecting the right audience for Facebook posts is a task that users often skip, resulting in unwanted post disclosure or avoidance of sharing sensitive posts. We present OmniWedges, a user interface designed to allow users of online social networks to make meaningful decisions on who to share their posts with. Our study results also show that with all Facebook friends, the error rate can be significantly reduced compared to the Facebook interface. In an interview, we were also able to spot a change in posting behavior and frequency with our interface.

1 Introduction

The current designs of the social network sites require users to scroll through their endless friend lists, or even to remember which of them they want to include or exclude from their post. Therefore most posts are shared with all of the user's friends, even though this is often not the best idea [3]. Radar interfaces have been shown to provide a better overview on the privacy settings [2] which furthermore engages users in adjusting their privacy settings more regularly [2]. Nevertheless, radar interfaces often suffer a space problem, in contrast to a list, which can be extended endlessly [6]. Especially when it comes to selecting the audience for social network posts, the number of potential recipients, which is the friend list of the user, can contain up to thousands of users. In our work, we took this use-case as an example to find out *How radar interfaces can be enhanced to be able to display a large amount of data items* and *Whether a radar interface is suitable to define the post audience for social networks*. Our interface *"OmniWedges"* uses a radar metaphor for aligning the users' friends around the user, based on their interpersonal distance and friend groups they belong to. OmniWedges is highly scalable and offers several functionalities to enable displaying *all* of a user's hundreds or thousands of friends while still providing an overview of who is selected and who is not. In a comparative user study with the Facebook custom privacy setting interface as a control condition, we found that OmniWedges is able to reduce the amount of errors made with *all* of the users' Facebook friends.

Electronic supplementary material The online version of this chapter (https://doi.org/10.1007/978-3-030-29390-1_56) contains supplementary material, which is available to authorized users.

© IFIP International Federation for Information Processing 2019
Published by Springer Nature Switzerland AG 2019
D. Lamas et al. (Eds.): INTERACT 2019, LNCS 11749, pp. 654–658, 2019.
https://doi.org/10.1007/978-3-030-29390-1_56

2   Related Work

Despite the existence of a privacy UI, social network users often do not use them at all [3]. The UIs are perceived as cumbersome and do not scale with respect to usual numbers of friends in a social network [3]. Social network providers therefore introduced lists or "circles" of friends, enabling users to create lists containing subsets of their online friends, and share posts only with those. Creating these lists manually comes at a significantly increased users burden [5]. Radar interfaces have been proven to be highly effective for such tasks, like getting an overview on data shared inside an intelligent retail store [7]. In our work, we try to adapt this metaphor on the domain of social network audience selection, which introduces one major obstacle, namely the high amount of data items (friends) to display in the limited space of the UI.

3   OmniWedges

OmniWedges offers a graphical user interface, which allows audience selection based on interpersonal distance, for different groups. The interface contains the profile picture for each social network friend, later denoted as "friend picture". Each of the user's friend groups is represented by a wedge in the UI. The friend pictures are aligned around the center according to the *tie strength* between the friend and the user. The current implementation of OmniWedges uses the tie strength calculation and friend groups offered by the Facebook website. To reduce side effects, we let the participants review and adapt the friend lists and tie strength ordering in the experiment. Initially, no friends are selected. The user clicks and drags from the center of a wedge to the outer rim to select a subset of friends as recipients for a post. The selected area is colored grayish. All friends which are inside the selected area of the wedge (from here on called the "wedge area") will receive the post. The number of selected friends and a list of the ten closest friends that are selected is displayed below the graph. In the bottom left corner, there are two buttons for selecting all friends and for resetting the selection. All selection possibilities of OmniWedges are shown in Fig. 1.

Radar interfaces often suffer from the limited space available in the radar UI, which limits the number of displayble friends in our case. **We therefore implemented several functionalities in order to reduce the problem of limited space within our UI**: Only a small subset of the Facebook friends are real friends that are of importance for recipient selection [1]. We therefore decrease the size of the friend images with decreasing tie strength, so that the closest friends gain the most importance (**"Incremental picture size"**). Using a double click, it is possible to zoom into and out of a certain area of the wedge to have a better overview, especially in crowded areas (**"Zooming"**). Based on the number of friends inside a wedge, OmniWedges selects some of the friend images (every second, third, fourth...) as lighthouse images that can be used as orientation points for the selection. All other friend images are shrunk to a small dot to avoid crowding (**"lighthouse design"**).

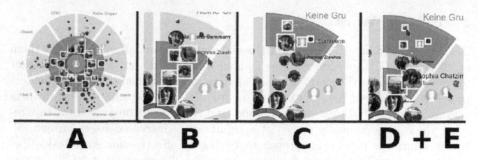

Fig. 1. Actions for the different use cases in OmniWedges: select all friends up to a given tie strength (A), select friends of one or more friend groups up to a given tie strength (B), exclude friends up to a given tie strength (C), select multiple areas inside a friend group (D) and Select/deselect single friends (E)

4   User Study

The study was performed with 20 participants using a within-subject design: Half of the subjects started with the Facebook interface and continued with OmniWedges, and vice versa for the other half of the subjects. At the day of the study, users had to organize the friends from their own Facebook profile into friend groups, and to sort them with ascending tie strength. **We gave no constraints on the number of friend groups, and used their Facebook friends an groups for the whole rest of the experiment.** The user was then given 12 tasks to solve for each interface: Six *explicit* tasks (for example *"select the 20 closest friends"*) and six implicit tasks, where the subjects were given sensitive posts like *"Please imagine you want to share pictures of a party that caused you to miss your family's Thanksgiving event"*. After each condition, the user was given a list of all friends with an indication whether the friend was selected or not. The user then had to identify friends that were included by mistake (false positive) or mistakenly not included as a recipient (false negative). The users had to fill in an AttrakDiff [4] usability questionnaire after each condition, and were given a five-minute break to rest and recover. The experiment closed with a semi-structured interview, where we tried to find out whether they would use OmniWedges on Facebook, and whether their posting behavior might change.

The number of Facebook friends of the participants ranged from 53 to 1260 (mean 437). As the amount is highly variable, we normalized the amount of false positives and negatives by dividing them by the number of friendlist entries. We performed a 2(condition) × 2(explicit or implicit task) × 2(false positive or false negative) ANOVA to compare the errors made throughout the study. Taking only the interface as an effect, the results indicate that significantly fewer errors are made using OmniWedges ($F = 5.57$, $p = 0.031$, $M_{Wedges} = 0.0076$, $M_{FB} = 0.020$). The type of task, explicit or implicit, did not have any significant effect on the error rate ($F = 0.677$, $p = 0.423$). OmniWedges outperforms its Facebook counterpart in terms of attractiveness

$(T = 6.115, p < 0.001, M_{Wedges} = 5.37, M_{FB} = 3.35)$ and hedonic quality $(T_{HQ-I} = 4.93, p_{HQ-I} < 0.001, M_{HQ-I-Wedges} = 5.09, M_{HQ-I-FB} = 3.66; T_{HQ-S} = 7.83, p_{HQ-S} < 0.001, M_{HQ-S-Wedges} = 5.26, M_{HQ-S-FB} = 3.17)$ with high significance, assuring a better user experience. There is also a tendency for a higher pragmatic quality using OmniWedges $(T = 1.83, p = 0.082, M_{Wedges} = 4.75, M_{FB} = 4.06)$. 50% of the users stated they preferred Omni-Wedges with an additional search field for finding specific friends, 33% preferred a combination of OmniWedges and the Facebook interface, and 8.3% wished to keep only OmniWedges or the Facebook interface, respectively. 85.7% stated they would change their posting behavior when using OmniWedges. Of those who would, 88.9% would do more narrowcasting, and the remaining 11.1% would post more sensitive posts.

5   Discussion and Outlook

In contrast to earlier work [6], we introduced several UI mechanisms that allow the display of all of a user's friends inside our radar interface. The results of the study show that, using these improvements, the a radar metaphor can also be used to display a large number of friends while still reducing the amount of errors. According to the interview results, a majority of users would replace the current Facebook UI with a version of OmniWedges. The interview answers also indicate a change in users' mental model: Most users tend to do more narrowcasting, or publish more sensitive posts. This may be caused by a different awareness of the post audience: Rather than always displaying only a small portion of all friends at once in a scrollable list, the radar interface displays *all* of a user's friends at once, allowing them to have an overview of the large number of friends that would receive the post, possibly resulting in a higher trust in the UI. Therefore, users begin to think about whether this large audience is really the desired audience for their post, resulting in a more rigorous limitation of the post audience with OmniWedges. As a first step in future work, we would like to integrate our approach into a social network website and evaluate the usage frequency of our tool against the standard audience selection functionality, especially when using the already existing friend groups (created either automatically or by the user) and the tie strength calculation offered by the social network provider.

Acknowledgments. This work was supported by the German Research Foundation (DFG) via the collaborative research center "Methods and Tools for Understanding and Controlling Privacy" (SFB 1223), project A7.

References

1. Christakis, N.A., Fowler, J.H.: Connected: The Surprising Power of Our Social Networks and How They Shape Our Lives. Back Bay Books, Boston (2011)
2. Christin, D., Reinhardt, A., Hollick, M., Trumpold, K.: Exploring user preferences for privacy interfaces in mobile sensing applications. In: MUM 2012. ACM, New York (2012)

3. Gross, R., Acquisti, A.: Information revelation and privacy in online social networks. In: WPES 2005, pp. 71–80. ACM, New York (2005)
4. Hassenzahl, M., Burmester, M., Koller, F.: AttrakDiff: Ein Fragebogen zur messung wahrgenommener hedonischer und pragmatischer Qualitaet. In: MuC 2003. B. G. Teubner (2013)
5. Paul, T., Puscher, D., Strufe, T.: Improving the usability of privacy settings in facebook. CoRR (2011)
6. Raber, F., Luca, A.D., Graus, M.: Privacy wedges: area-based audience selection for social network posts. In: SOUPS. Denver, CO (2016)
7. Raber, F., Vossebein, N.: URetail: privacy user interfaces for intelligent retail stores. In: Bernhaupt, R., Dalvi, G., Joshi, A., K. Balkrishan, D., O'Neill, J., Winckler, M. (eds.) INTERACT 2017. LNCS, vol. 10516, pp. 473–477. Springer, Cham (2017). https://doi.org/10.1007/978-3-319-68059-0_54

Reducing Anxiety for Dental Visits

Kathryn Elizabeth Jones[(✉)] [iD], Fernando Loizides[iD], Parisa Eslambolchilar[iD],
Ilona Johnson, Shannu Bhatia, Owen Crawford, McClaine Beirne, Raj Chand,
Laura Vuilleumier, and Idunah Araneta

Cardiff University, Cardiff, UK
{jonesk90,floizides,eslambolchilarp,johnsonig,bhatiask,crawford02,
beirnem,chandr,vuilleumierl,aranetaij}@cardiff.ac.uk

Abstract. This work addresses children's (under 6 years of age) fear and
apprehension to visit dental clinics. We present a bespoke interactive
Virtual Reality reproduction of the physical dental clinic, augmented
with virtual characters and enriched with gamification style information
for a richer user experience. The experience allows the user to navigate
and familiarise themselves with the location and the procedures they will
undertake before visiting the clinic. The experience is now being piloted
at the Dental Public Health at the University Hospital of Wales.

Keywords: Virtual Reality · Dental fear · Virtual tour · Children

1 Introduction and Motivation

Children and parents are often anxious about dental treatment. Children are
often reluctant to visit the dentist or a dental clinic due to dental fear. "Dental
fear is defined as a specific anxiety, which is the predisposition for a negative
experience in the dental surgery" [2,5]. There are many theories that give reasons
and measure the anxiety, and fear, of children in this setting, such as their
environment [4] and their perceptions of their dental staff [3].

Familiarisation with the dental setting, in advance of dental visits, can help
to reduce anxiety [1]. This is particularly useful for children who often find
the unfamiliar sights, sounds and equipment inside dental clinics unsettling.
Virtual tours [6] and gamification [7] have been shown to successfully improve
experiences for children undergoing operations under general anaesthetic.

In this paper, we present a fully functional prototype using Virtual Reality
to help children experience their visit in advance and attempt to make them
feel more at ease before a visit. The environment uses friendly digital characters and cues to make the experience more pleasant. Real 360° footage from the
dental clinic creates a reproduction of the actual environment that the children
can explore to demystify the visit and increase confidence levels. The prototype
system creates a Virtual Reality Environment which is interactive with a user.
It currently has two main functions: to reduce patient anxiety and to provide

© IFIP International Federation for Information Processing 2019
Published by Springer Nature Switzerland AG 2019
D. Lamas et al. (Eds.): INTERACT 2019, LNCS 11749, pp. 659–663, 2019.
https://doi.org/10.1007/978-3-030-29390-1_57

education on dental hygiene and prevention. Firstly, younger patients often miss their dentist appointments due to 'fear of the unknown' and lack of understanding of what they can expect from the environment and treatment when they get there. Therefore the prototype looks to simulate a dental appointment experience through a Virtual Reality tour. The dental patient will be able to navigate through the process at their own pace in order to familiarise themselves with the experience. Ultimately, this will significantly reduce their fear of the dentist as they gradually progress through their virtual appointment and become more familiar with what to expect when they arrive in the real world at the dental hospital. As a side effect it is hoped that reducing anxiety in young patients and making them more comfortable before coming to their appointment will reduce the DNA (Did Not Attend) rates at the hospital [8]. Secondly, within the Virtual Reality Environment there are opportunities to directly and passively communicate dental hygiene and prevention messages to patients through use of messages, games and quizzes.

2   Artefact Description

Using a user-centred design approach, we interviewed three dental practitioners to elicit requirements. We then created functional and non-functional requirements as well as personas. In order to begin phase one of the prototyping stages, we selected one of the three developed personas to focus on. The selected persona, a 6 year old girl called Evie, who had no disabilities, but her previous experience of dental appointments at her local dentistry practice meant she was already uncomfortable with the experience (creating a negative bias before visiting the dental hospital). Further to this Evie was generally uncomfortable with unfamiliar environments. Like most of the children her age, Evie is familiar with small screen display technologies, like mobile phones and tablets, and likes to play games using these devices.

Using the information relating to the identified stakeholders and requirements, Storyboards were created to help clarify the true goal of the application. Structured Dialogue Design (SDD) was used to for initial planning of the project because it gave the opportunity to hear the teams varying opinions without judgement. Following this a more detailed literature review was conducted, specifically looking at the user age and accessibility considerations, to support and enhance the design decisions being made. Based on the requirements Unified Modelling Language (UML) diagrams were made to consolidate ideas on what entities (Actors) would be interacting with the application and identify the core functionality that would be implemented.

Low-fidelity prototypes were developed as fully clickable mobile and desktop wire-frames in Axure. This allowed the whole team to brainstorm ideas of how the user would interact with the application. With regards to the web application wire-frames, the user's journey when using the application was the focus, including aspects such as how many clicks does it take to complete the journey, is it obvious to the user where to click next, is the text big and simple enough to read. Initially we created wire-frames for both mobile and desktop devices with the intention to make this tour optimised for mobile, either as a flat screen tour or as a Virtual Reality tour using Google Cardboard[1]. The web application would guide the parent through some simple questions in order to discern which type of tour to display.

Feedback from the stakeholders, as well as our own thoughts relating to design improvements were used to move from low-fidelity to high-fidelity prototype. Our bespoke high-fidelity prototype aims to reduce the anxiety by giving the child a way to view the exact route they will take, and by explaining objects and events that will happen during their visit, as well as being an educational tool for dental hygiene. This has been achieved in the form of a 360° Virtual Reality tour, which is designed to be viewed on desktop web browsers. Real 360° images were taken of the dental clinic and then stitched to produce the Virtual Reality Environment.

The high-fidelity fully functional prototype was built with Unity (version 2017.4.10)[2], making it easily customisable to a Head Mounted Display (HMD) or desktop experience. A web application was developed to host our tour involving a simple landing page with a brief description and guide, with links to a more in depth help page, and the tour itself. Built using React[3] and bootstrapped using create-react-app[4]. The use of WebGL library provides a method of hosting a unity project within a web page with Blender[5] being used to create 3D objects such as arrows and signs for use within the tour.

Care was also taken to produce appropriate interactions. Each interactive object can have an associated spoken element and some examples have been included in the prototype. This involved taking the full journey through the tour and deciding what a bunny would say at each point. This included interactions with a bunny (See Fig. 1), icons, menus and games (See Fig. 2). A fader was included to gently tele-port the user from one room to the other without being too abrupt, with the aim of maintaining a calm Virtual Reality Environment for the children.

Collaboration, co-production and inter-professional working provided a different view of the dental setting enabling the creation of Virtual Reality Environments designed to familiarise children and their parents with the dental setting. The prototype will be of use for developing a production ready application for children and parents visiting the dentist. It will also support dental student learning by providing an opportunity to view the dental environment from the point of view of a child, parent and someone unfamiliar with the dental environment and contribute information to the development of a final single application. An evaluation of prototype application is being undertaken to identify the most useful features to include in a single application for use by children and their parents.

---

[1] https://vr.google.com/cardboard/ - Accessed March 2019.

[2] https://unity.com/ - Accessed March 2019.

[3] https://reactjs.org/ - Accessed March 2019.

[4] https://developer.mozilla.org/en-US/docs/Web/API/WebGL_API - Accessed April 2019.

[5] https://www.blender.org/ - Accessed April 2019.

Fig. 1. The Virtual Reality Environment - exact replica of the dental clinic - with interactive characters to guide children.

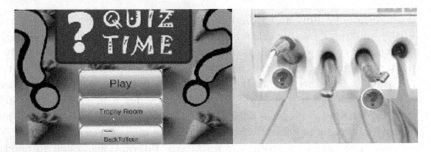

Fig. 2. Interactive scenes: left: quiz to learn about tooth hygiene, right: information on the tools the child will be seeing and will be used for treatment

References

1. Pharmacological behaviour management clinical guidelines (2019). https://www.rcseng.ac.uk/library-and-publications/rcs-publications/docs/non-pharmacological-behaviour-management
2. Aartman, I.H., Hoogstraten, J., Schuurs, A.H., et al.: Self-report measurements of dental anxiety and fear in children: a critical assessment. ASDC J. Dent. Child. **65**(4), 252–258 (1998)
3. Alsarheed, M.: Children's perception of their dentists. Eur. J. Dent. **5**(2), 186 (2011)
4. Koch, G., Poulsen, S., Espelid, I., Haubek, D.: Pediatric Dentistry: A Clinical Approach. Wiley, Hoboken (2017)
5. Raj, S., Agarwal, M., Aradhya, K., Konde, S., Nagakishore, V.: Evaluation of dental fear in children during dental visit using children's fear survey schedule-dental subscale. Int. J. Clin. Pediatr. Dent. **6**(1), 12 (2013)
6. Ryu, J.-H., Oh, A.-Y., Yoo, H.-J., Kim, J.-H., Park, J.-W., Han, S.-H.: The effect of an immersive virtual reality tour of the operating theater on emergence delirium in children undergoing general anesthesia: a randomized controlled trial. Pediatr. Anesth. **29**(1), 98–105 (2019)

7. Ryu, J.-H., et al.: The effect of gamification through a virtual reality on preoperative anxiety in pediatric patients undergoing general anesthesia: a prospective, randomized, and controlled trial. J. Clin. Med. **7**(9), 284 (2018)
8. Wogelius, P., Poulsen, S.: Associations between dental anxiety, dental treatment due to toothache, and missed dental appointments among six to eight-year-old danish children: a cross-sectional study. Acta Odontol. Scand. **63**(3), 179–182 (2005)

SCAH!RF: A Novel Wearable as a Subconscious Approach for Mitigating Anxiety Symptoms

Laís Lopes[1] and Pedro F. Campos[2(✉)]

[1] Madeira Interactive Technologies Institute, Funchal, Portugal
lais.lopes@m-iti.org
[2] ITI/Larsys, University of Madeira, Funchal, Portugal
pcampos@uma.pt

Abstract. Mobile and wearable interfaces have long been developed to improve mental health issues, including anxiety disorders, which represent a significant public health problem affecting more than 250 million people. However, most of the current approaches still operate in the so-called "reflective mind", which hampers results since reflecting on your own health data can induce even more stress and anxiety. In this poster we introduce an alternative approach towards mitigating anxiety symptoms through the use of "subtle" wearable interfaces. Capitalizing on the subconscious processes of the mind is particularly attractive for anxiety disorders. We present a smart wearable in the form of a scarf that implements a subconscious, less-invasive approach in the design of assistive technologies for mental health. Preliminary results bring important implications for interaction design: combining psychological conditioning therapy (via a mobile app) with our smart scarf provides a solution that can be worn anytime anywhere to fight anxiety symptoms. But this work also raises many privacy and ethical concerns which should be discussed by the HCI community: how can designers balance the opaqueness of subconscious approaches with the necessary ethical transparency? And how can mental health technologies be conceived in such a way they do not instigate societal stigma in users?

Keywords: Mental health · Anxiety disorders · Subconscious · Assistive technologies · Wearables · Haptic interfaces

1 Introduction and Background

Anxiety disorders, such as panic disorder and agoraphobia, are a group of mental disorders characterized by moderate to severe feelings of anxiety and fear, which can lead to behavioral change and situational avoidance. Recent studies have shown that more than 250 million people struggle with some form of anxiety disorder, near 15% of which are European [1]. This makes anxiety a public health concern of significant impact. In haptics, there is ample knowledge about the neuroscience aspects of touch [1, 3]. In this poster, we present a novel research direction for Wearables as subtle haptic interfaces aimed at improving mental health and mitigating the symptoms of anxiety disorders. We present the initial prototype for a new wearable (Scah!rf), under development, which

© IFIP International Federation for Information Processing 2019
Published by Springer Nature Switzerland AG 2019
D. Lamas et al. (Eds.): INTERACT 2019, LNCS 11749, pp. 664–667, 2019.
https://doi.org/10.1007/978-3-030-29390-1_58

exploits haptics and classical conditioning as a way to intervene when anxiety symptoms are experienced by the user. The innovation behind our contribution stems from the paired combination of a conditioning phase, when the user is repeatedly exposed to a mobile app user interface. This mobile app aims to shift the user's negative thoughts by replacing a pre-existent negative conditioned stimulus with a positive unconditional one, in the form of an audio clip. This same audio clip is triggered in a smart scarf when the user touches its fabric in a repetitive way, i.e. when anxiety symptoms occur. This approach goes against the dominant narrative of reflective-based approaches, such as cognitive-behavioral therapy, and leverages powerful processes of the neuroscience of touch in a subtle, unconscious way. This is particularly attractive for mental health issues, since the reflective mind - as defined by Kahneman [2] - does not bring solid results for anxiety. Reflecting on your own anxiety data can induce even more anxiety.

Touch is the paramount sense, and the first sensory system developed in animal species [3]. From an early age, touch is an important part of the development of immunological system in both animals and humans, and research suggests this type of stimulation help lower cortisol levels, which in turn can improve quality of life and mental health. In 1958, Harlow and Zimmermann [4] showed how the tactile sense can also impact affection, as their experiment made visible that infant monkeys were drawn to, and sought comfort in softer materials like cloths, opposed to cold, hard materials like wire. Such contact comfort is also a crucial part in the development of perception and emotion on human babies. As the largest, most sensitive sense organ humans have, the skin, when touched, sends information to the somatosensory cortex that allow us to perceive, process, and respond to information we interpret as texture, pressure, temperature, and vibration. This haptic perception is what puts us in direct contact with our surroundings and makes possible for us to explore and recognize attributes such as softness, thickness, and warmth. Although research has been done that proves touch can be a powerful and universal means of communicating emotion [5, 6] the majority of interfaces developed in this area still focus on haptics as a channel to deliver information - in an unobtrusive manner - to users, or to mediate social interactions, with much disregard on the potential of employing embodied cognition and incidental touch principles [7] into the design of haptic interfaces, making them a subtler, unconscious approach to help mitigate anxiety symptoms.

2 Wearables as Subtle Interfaces for Improving Mental Health

When discussing about mental health, the form-factor plays an important role in the success or failure of wearable devices. Several wearable interfaces have been developed that capitalize on the unobtrusiveness, familiarity, and social acceptance of designing garments embedded with technology. Lightwear [8], for example, takes advantage of this approach and presents an alternative to light boxes, the predominant yet outdated method of treatment for Seasonal Affective Disorder, which no longer constrains users to a sitting position nor requires them to learn new skills in order to operate and interact with such objects. However, we performed a systematic review of the literature ($N = 1108$ papers), outside the scope of this poster, and found there is still a lack of truly non-intrusive, wearable assistive technologies. Most wearables are just used for sensing purposes, and cannot be used in social settings, as they would draw unwanted attention to individuals who may already feel self-conscious.

Our approach combines a conditioning therapy phase during which the user is exposed explicitly and repeatedly (at the end of everyday) to a mobile app that invites the user to perform a 50-s deep breathing exercise, after which a positive reinforcement is provided, in the form of an audio clip. This same audio clip is triggered in a smart scarf when the user touches its fabric in a repetitive way, i.e. when anxiety symptoms occur. The exposure effect from the conditioning phase, coupled with the audio positive reinforcement signal, can then be reproduced via a mini-speaker embedded in the fabric of the scarf. Hence we present two separate interfaces that share the same affordances and help individuals cope with stressful situations by using a subliminal approach, where the physical manipulation of the wearable is unconsciously associated with a relaxed state of mind through a previous conditioning phase. Figure 1 illustrates both the wearable and the app's user interface.

Fig. 1. Scah!rf's prototype, embedded into a scarf using conductive ink and a mini-speaker (left). The mobile app used for conditioning through a 50-s breathing exercise (right).

The smart wearable prototype was developed using conductive ink and a touch board by Bare Conductive. The mobile app was designed to be platform-independent and works both in Android and iOS devices. A breathing exercise was selected, as it is currently one of the mainstream methods for dealing with anxiety available at Google Play and the App Store. The app also acts as a logging tool and surveys the users regarding their mental well-being, which will be used in an extensive, six-month long evaluation of the prototypes that is being performed with anxiety-suffering voluntary participants. We currently conducted informal observations, interviews (with patients and therapists) and qualitative analysis of the results.

As smart textile technologies evolve further, one can expect smaller and softer sensors and actuators to become mainstream. Future work includes further evaluation of wearable interfaces operating at a subconscious level, capable of improving mental well-being without the need for constant self-monitoring or overloading users with access to unnecessary health-related information.

3   Discussion and Conclusion

Anxiety disorders affect a significant part of today's society. Current wearable technologies hold the key to bringing more effective digital interventions. These will
always be limited and it is not our focus to replace therapists, psychologists or drug-
based approaches to mitigating the symptoms. Instead, we explore the design space of
wearable technology to address this problem and focus on discovering new approaches
based on the subconscious processes of the human mind. Our results are preliminary,
and are based on qualitative analysis, observation and interviews performed throughout
the iterations of the wearable, from its initial concept to its current form. They suggest
two main design implications: (i) subtle, non-intrusive approaches for mitigating
anxiety symptoms are much harder to conceive than the approaches based on the
reflective mind – to achieve solid results, the exposure period must be extensive (i.e.
more than just a few weeks); (ii) combining psychological conditioning therapy (via a
mobile app) with our smart scarf provides a solution that can be worn anytime anywhere to fight anxiety symptoms. The subtlety inherent to such solution reduces stigma
and brings convenience to users. This haptic-based approach, through a scarf form
factor, is less invasive and more portable than many other existing solutions. This is
extremely important for anxiety and mental health, since the symptoms can arise at any
moment in time and at any place (public or private). This work also raises many
privacy and ethical concerns which should be discussed by the HCI community: how
can designers balance the opaqueness of subconscious approaches with the necessary
ethical transparency? And how can mental health technologies be conceived in such a
way they do not instigate societal stigma in users?

References

1. Alonso, M.B., Keyson, D.V., Hummels, C.C.M.: Squeeze, rock, and roll; can tangible
   interaction with affective products support stress reduction? In: Proceedings of the 2nd
   International Conference on Tangible and Embedded Interaction (TEI 2008), pp. 105–108.
   ACM, New York (2008)
2. Kahneman, D.: Thinking, Fast and Slow. Penguin Books, London (2012)
3. Field, T.: Touch. The MIT Press, Cambridge (2001)
4. Harlow, H.F., Zimmermann, R.R.: The development of affectional responses in infant
   monkeys. Proc. Am. Philos. Soc. **102**(5), 501–509 (1958)
5. Hertenstein, M., Holmes, R., McCullough, M., Keltner, D.: The communication of emotion
   via touch. Emotion **9**, 566–573 (2009)
6. Wang, R., Quek, F.: Touch & talk: contextualizing remote touch for affective interaction. In:
   Proceedings of the Fourth International Conference on Tangible, Embedded, and Embodied
   Interaction – TEI 2010, pp. 13–20 (2010)
7. Ackerman, J.M., Nocera, C., Bargh, J.A.: Incidental haptic sensations influence social
   judgments and decisions. Science **328**, 1712–1715 (2010)
8. Profita, H., Roseway, A., Czerwinski, M.: Lightwear: an exploration in wearable light
   therapy. In: Proceedings of the Ninth International Conference on Tangible, Embedded, and
   Embodied Interaction – TEI 2015, pp. 321–328 (2015)

Search Results on Flight Booking Websites: Displaying Departure and Return Flights on a Single Page vs Two Consecutive Pages

Tatiana Zlokazova(iD), Irina Blinnikova(iD), Sergey Grigorovich(iD),
and Ivan Burmistrov(✉)(iD)

Lomonosov Moscow State University, Mokhovaya 11/9,
Moscow 125009, Russia
t.zlokazova@gmail.com, blinnikovamslu@hotmail.com,
grigorovich.sergey@gmail.com, ivan@interux.com

Abstract. Flight ticket booking engines on airline and online travel agency websites use two different designs to present roundtrip flight search results: some websites display outbound and return flights on a single page, while others show them on two consecutive pages. In our pilot experiment with 23 users we compared these two design options on a model flight booking website. Usability metrics like speed of performance and error rate were accompanied by eye-tracking and mouse-tracking indicators of cognitive load. The experiment produced mixed results: two-page design outperformed simultaneous presentation of outbound and inbound flights in terms of performance speed, but it also caused almost three times higher error rate and incurred a higher cognitive load compared to one-page design. Further research, with more users representing different age groups, different levels of task complexity, and analysis of users' subjective preferences, is necessary.

Keywords: Flight ticket booking · Usability · Eye movement ·
Mouse cursor movement · Experimental research

1 Introduction

The possibility of booking flights online first appeared on Alaska Airlines and British Midland Airways websites in 1995, and then rapidly spread to other airline websites. Soon thereafter air ticket booking engines were introduced to online travel agency (OTA) websites like Expedia and Travelocity [1]. The typical user flow on a booking engine is inherently linear and consists of five steps: (1) a search form where users enter departure and destination airports and dates of travel; (2) a flight search results page (FSRP) with lists of available flights and airfares; (3) a selected flight review and confirmation page; (4) a traveler details form; (5) a payment page. Research publications on the usability of airline and OTA websites started appearing in the late 90s; now this area is quite well researched (see for example [2–6]). In particular, a strong correlation between usability and the customer conversion rate on travel websites has been found, so websites that are easier to use, are more likely to convert [7]. However,

© IFIP International Federation for Information Processing 2019
Published by Springer Nature Switzerland AG 2019
D. Lamas et al. (Eds.): INTERACT 2019, LNCS 11749, pp. 668–671, 2019.
https://doi.org/10.1007/978-3-030-29390-1_59

almost no special attention has been paid to the design of a key aspect of the flight booking process – FSRP. This is where the supplier displays their core product, flights, and where travelers make their purchase decisions. Our 12-year longitudinal analysis of the evolution of FSRPs on major airline and OTA websites revealed that there are two popular design solutions for displaying roundtrip flights: some websites (e.g. Alitalia, Lufthansa) always showed outbound and return flights on a single webpage, while others (e.g. Air France, KLM, Delta) always used two consecutive pages. During the period analyzed, some websites (e.g. British Airways) changed their FSRP from single-page to two-page design, while some others (e.g. Expedia) went in the opposite direction.

From a theoretical point of view there may be arguments in favor of either design option, so this is a question that needs empirical research. In this article we present the results of pilot research into two competing FSRP designs: the presentation of out-bound and inbound flights on a single page and on two pages. In this work we analyzed not only traditional usability metrics like time on task and error rate, but also a number of eye-tracking and mouse-tracking indicators of cognitive load.

2 Method

The experiment modeled choosing flights on a simulated OTA-style FSRP (i.e. it displayed the airfares of multiple airlines). The task for participants was to search for air tickets within certain given time parameters, for example: *"outbound flight: first flight departing after 08:00 from Moscow to Rome; return flight: first possible return flight to Moscow not less than 4 h after arriving in Rome"*.

Within-subjects factor was webpage design with two levels: (1) combined display of outbound and return flights on a single webpage; (2) display of outbound and return flights on two consecutive webpages. The experiment consisted of 2 series, each of which was devoted to one type of design (see stimuli examples in Fig. 1) and consisted of 8 tasks.

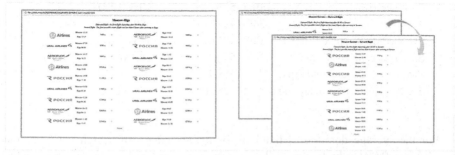

Fig. 1. Stimuli: one-page (combined) design (left), two-page (consecutive) design (right).

The order of the different series was counterbalanced. The position of the "correct" flight was randomly distributed between the 9 flight options in each list of the flights. Before each series the participants were given instructions and one training task.

Apparatus: 17″ LCD monitor with 1280 × 1024 screen resolution; eye-tracker EyeLink 1000 with a sampling rate of 500 Hz. Participants: 23 university students (12 female and 11 male), aged between 19 and 34 (mean: 22.6). As a result of the experiment 365 trials were recorded.

Three groups of dependent measures were analyzed: (1) search time and number of search errors; (2) oculomotor indicators of cognitive load (fixation duration and saccade amplitude) [8]; (3) parameters of cursor movements (number and amplitude of saccades), and gaze-cursor coordination that reflect user's search strategies [9].

3   Results

The results are given in Table 1. The effect of webpage design on search time was significant (1-way ANOVA, F = 4.8, p < 0.05). The mean time of completing one search task was 37.8 s with the single-page (combined) design and 34.3 s with the two-page (consequent) design – on average, two-page design allowed users to save nearly 10% of search time.

In addition, the error rate was analyzed. Each list of flights comprised only one correct pair of outbound and return flights satisfying the search criteria; any other answers were considered errors. As each search task consisted of two lists of flights, the subject could make a maximum of 2 errors. The results have shown that mean error rate was significantly (almost 3 times) higher with two-page (consecutive) design (F = 29.4, p < 0.001).

Table 1. Mean (σ) of the recorder parameters.

Design type	One-page (combined)	Two-page (consequent)
Search time (sec)	37.8 (21.4)	34.3 (14.2)
Error rate (%)	10.3 (5.5)	29.6 (19.3)
Eye fixation duration (ms)	349.7 (53.7)	368.7 (55.5)
Eye saccade amplitude (px)	149.8 (32.6)	125.9 (20.1)
Cursor saccade count (num)	14.9 (9.8)	14.1 (8.4)
Cursor saccade amplitude (px)	253.3 (88.9)	239.3 (89.1)
Eye and cursor time delay (ms)	417.7 (252.0)	377.6 (235.7)

For the average duration of fixations significant effects of design were obtained (F = 25, p < 0.001): the two-page design was associated with longer fixations, which indicates the higher cognitive complexity of the tasks performed. As for the saccade amplitude, they were significantly longer with one-page (F = 163, p < 0.001), which is not surprising since the subjects frequently had to move their gaze between outbound and return lists of flights on the webpage.

For the average cursor saccade count no significant differences in tasks with different webpage design were found. The amplitude of the cursor movements showed near-significant effect ($F = 3.3$, $p = 0.072$), which is also an expected result as it was in the case of eye saccade amplitude. Also near-significant effect of the webpage design was obtained for eye and mouse cursor time-delay parameter ($F = 2.9$, $p = 0.079$). With two-page design the discrepancy between the eye and the cursor was lower, which may indicate that the user tends to use mouse cursor as an auxiliary tool more intensively under these conditions.

4 Discussion and Future Work

The experiment produced mixed results: speed of search was significantly better for two-page design, but at the same time, the error rate and amount of cognitive load (as shown by eye and cursor movements) were higher compared with one-page design.

A possible way of thinking may be that although time on task is definitely an important usability factor, the higher error rate perhaps outweighs it, because errors are of primary concern when booking flights. Errors lead to logistical problems and serious financial losses for customers when flights are cancelled or rebooked.

However, at this stage in our research it may be premature to formulate concrete practical user interface design recommendations. Further research involving higher number of users representing different age groups, different levels of task complexity, and analysis of users' subjective preferences regarding two design options is still necessary to build on our results.

Acknowledgements. The research was supported by a grant from the Russian Foundation for Basic Research #17-06-00652.

References

1. Hanke, M.: Airline e-Commerce: Log on. Take off. Routledge, London (2016)
2. Selvidge, P.: Reservations about the usability of airline web sites. In: CHI 1999 Extended Abstracts, pp. 306–307. ACM, New York (1999). https://doi.org/10.1145/632716.632903
3. Carstens, D.S., Patterson, P.: Usability study of travel websites. J. Usability Stud. **1**, 47–61 (2005)
4. Webcredible: Flights Online: Ensuring Your Site Takes Off: Online Travel Usability Report. Webcredible, London (2011)
5. Ekşioğlu, M., Kırış, E., Çakır, T., Güvendik, M., Koyutürk, E.D., Yılmaz, M.: A user experience study of airline websites. In: Marcus, A. (ed.) DUXU 2013. LNCS, vol. 8015, pp. 173–182. Springer, Heidelberg (2013). https://doi.org/10.1007/978-3-642-39253-5_19
6. Linden, E., Bruschek, T., Wittmer, A.: Usability of airline websites in the ticket purchasing process: an eye-tracking study of air traffic passengers. In: Proceedings of 22nd ATRS World Conference. Air Transport Research Society, College Park (2018)
7. Change Sciences: Travel Web Site User Experience. Change Sciences, New York (2013)
8. Ehmke, C., Wilson, S.: Identifying web usability problems from eye-tracking data. In: Proceedings of HCI 2007, vol. 1, pp. 119–128. British Computer Society, Swindon (2007)
9. Cox, A.L., Silva, M.M.: The role of mouse movements in interactive search. In: Proceedings of CogSci/ICCS 2006, pp. 1156–1161. Lawrence Erlbaum Associates, Mahwah (2006)

Smart Objects for Speech Therapies at Home

Paolo Buono, Fabio Cassano, Antonio Piccinno$^{(\boxtimes)}$,
and Maria Francesca Costabile

Computer Science Department, University of Bari Aldo Moro, Bari, Italy
{paolo.buono, fabio.cassano, antonio.piccinno,
mariafrancesca.costabile}@uniba.it

Abstract. The pervasiveness of Internet of Things (IoT) devices is commonly used to create domestic ambient to support people daily life. In this paper we explore how IoT devices can be used in the smart home to administer the therapy to children with speech disorders. The speech therapist manages and controls patients' therapies by using End-User Development methods and tools.

Keywords: IoT · Smart home · Speech therapy · End-User Development

1 Introduction

The value of Internet of Things (IoT) technology is acknowledged in many scenarios of Ambient Assisted Living (AAL) [1, 2]. As several IoT devices are available today in a smart home, researchers are working a lot on smart home systems to be used by physicians and other therapists to remotely assist their patients living at home. Built-in IoT sensors can be exploited to monitor the health status of a person or to administer a therapy. As an example, a software and hardware prototype of a modular pill dispenser has been proposed in [3, 4]. It can be configured, according to the user's needs, with multiple pills, in which each pill is associated with a small smart box. The therapy, as well as the alerts are set using a mobile phone app.

This concept of "home hospitalization" both improves patients' life, who remain more comfortably at home and avoid hospitalization, and reduces healthcare costs. For this reason, smart home technologies are gaining a momentum in becoming assistive technology in home assistance.

IoT devices are also considered to support learning and to improving the quality of life for children with autism spectrum disorder. In [5], smart technologies are exploited for an IoT infrastructure for AAL scenarios where children with autism live in their homes with smart objects, communicating to the outside world in an intelligent and goal-orientated manner. Lack of space prevent us to report on several other proposals available in literature.

However, patients live in very different situations and have variable needs and behaviors. Our research aims at bringing innovation in AAL contexts by proposing new approaches to build spaces equipped with smart devices for monitoring patients' behavior, still fostering an independent lifestyle. We capitalize on years of experience on End-User Development (EUD), a research area whose goal is to support non-technical end users in the creation of products and services tailored to their needs and

D. Lamas et al. (Eds.): INTERACT 2019, LNCS 11749, pp. 672–675, 2019.
https://doi.org/10.1007/978-3-030-29390-1_60

desires [6–9]. Our current objective is to propose innovative AAL paradigms that empower end users to co-design, customize, evolve, and control the ecology of smart objects, which communicate with the outside world in an intelligent and goal-oriented manner. Providing such objects with new capabilities usually requires programming efforts.

Some approaches have been proposed in literature to support non-technical users to configure smart object behavior. However, most of them provide pre-packaged solutions for remotely controlling single smart objects without any possibility of adaptation to specific domains and contexts of use. Task-Automation (TA) tools overcome this limitation: users can specify object behavior by graphically sketching the interaction among the objects or defining event-condition-action (ECA) rules (see, e.g., [10–12]). However, the adoption of TA tools is still limited. Indeed, tools based on graph metaphors do not match the mental model of most users, while tools implementing ECA rules allow a trivial synchronization of smart-object behaviors, without the possibility to define powerful constraints on events activation and actions execution [13]. An example is IFTTT (If This Then That) [14]. The EFESTO platform offers a visual interaction paradigm to enable end users to easily express rules for smart object configuration that are more powerful than the rules created by a TA tool like IFTTT. EFESTO permits to build rules coupling multiple events and conditions exposed by smart objects and to define temporal and spatial constraints on rule activation and action execution.

This paper focus on the smart home as a medical setting for "speech therapy". Thanks to EFESTO, the therapist can easily create ECA rules to control the smart objects involved in administering the therapy, as it is described in the next section.

2 Speech Therapy Through Games and Smart Objects

Speech disorders or speech impediments are a type of communication disorder where "normal" speech is disrupted. They affect the vocal cords, muscles, nerves, and other structures within the throat, due for example to vocal cord damage, brain damage, muscle weakness or vocal cord paralysis. Some speech disorders improve with speech therapy: a professional therapist guides the patient through various exercises to strengthen the muscles of face and throat. Children have to exercise also at home, but they often find some exercises boring and either they do not perform them correctly or do not perform at all, and this is not verifiable by the therapist.

We describe in the following how we are using a gamified application to stimulate a child in performing the exercises of a speech therapy. The value of games in stimulating and engaging children to perform activities is well known and we have used them in various contexts (see e.g. [15, 16]).

A tablet app has been developed for children. Figure 1 presents screen shots of the game, which requires performing exercises to gain points. The player is represented by a small dragon that, moving on a pathway in a park, from left to right, pushes on a red button to perform the associated exercise (see Fig. 1 left). Figure 1 right shows an exercise in which the child has to guess a figure representing a whale. Below each button on the dragon path there are three stars that show the level of accomplishment of the specific exercise (an award for the obtained result). The button becomes green once the three awards are obtained, i.e., the exercise is completed. The child can also see its position in a "children ranking".

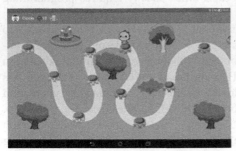

Fig. 1. The tablet app. Left: the game main page; right: a specific exercise (Color figure online)

A further app, called remote controller, has been implemented to be used by child's parents or caregivers to "certify" the real accomplishment of each exercise. Due to lack of space further details of this app and on how the children ranking is generated are not reported.

The speech therapist can create and modify speech exercises. S/He can adapt the therapy to the child (Fig. 2 left) and get feedback on the child progress (Fig. 2 right). By defining ECA rules in the EFESTO platform the therapist controls the IoT devices installed in the child home and orchestrates them to achieve a specific emotional response by the child, which favors exercise execution. For example, if the therapist knows that the child loves a TV cartoon, s/he can set a time for an exercise just before the beginning of the cartoon, which will be an award at the end of the exercise.

This is better presented by the following scenario. The speech therapy consists of one exercise a day of about 10 min. The child home is equipped with IoT devices: smart lamps and human body sensors in each room, smart speakers and a smart TV in the living room, where the therapy is supposed to be administered, because the TV will play the cartoon at the end of the exercise. The cartoon starts at 17:30, thus at 17:10 the smart home provides the child with two kinds of alerts: the tablet will send a notification, while smart light in the room the child is switch on and/or change color in green and start flashing. This indicates to the child that it is time to do the exercise. The lights on the way to the living room also switch on or become green to indicate the path to the living room, where the child starts the exercise.

Fig. 2. The therapist app allows to modify the therapy (left) and to get feedback about child progress (right)

So far, only some formative evaluations have been performed on the developed prototypes. More experimental studies are planned to validate our approach.

References

1. Ardito, C., et al.: Enabling end users to define the behavior of smart objects in AAL environments. In: Leone, A., et al. (eds.) ForItAAL 2018. LNEE, vol. 544, pp. 95–103. Springer, Cham (2019). https://doi.org/10.1007/978-3-030-05921-7_8
2. Atzori, L., Iera, A., Morabito, G.: The Internet of Things: a survey. Comput. Netw. **54**(15), 2787–2805 (2010)
3. Buono, P., Cassano, F., Legretto, A., Piccinno, A.: A homemade pill dispenser prototype supporting elderly. In: Garrigós, I., Wimmer, M. (eds.) ICWE 2017. LNCS, vol. 10544, pp. 120–124. Springer, Cham (2018). https://doi.org/10.1007/978-3-319-74433-9_10
4. Buono, P., Cassano, F., Legretto, A., Piccinno, A.: EUDroid: a formal language specifying the behaviour of IoT devices. IET Softw. **12**(5), 425–429 (2018)
5. Sula, A., Spaho, E., Matsuo, K., Barolli, L., Xhafa, F., Miho, R.: A new system for supporting children with autism spectrum disorder based on IoT and P2P technology. Int. J. Space-Based Situated Comput. **4**(1), 55–64 (2014)
6. Fischer, G., Fogli, D., Piccinno, A.: Revisiting and broadening the meta-design framework for end-user development. In: Paternò, F., Wulf, V. (eds.) New Perspectives in End-User Development, pp. 61–97. Springer, Cham (2017). https://doi.org/10.1007/978-3-319-60291-2_4
7. Barricelli, B.R., Cassano, F., Fogli, D., Piccinno, A.: End-user development, end-user programming and end-user software engineering: a systematic mapping study. JSS **149**, 101–137 (2019)
8. Ardito, C., Buono, P., Desolda, G., Matera, M.: From smart objects to smart experiences: an end-user development approach. IJHCS **114**, 51–68 (2018)
9. Desolda, G., Ardito, C., Jetter, H.-C., Lanzilotti, R.: Exploring spatially-aware cross-device interaction techniques for mobile collaborative sensemaking. IJHCS **122**, 1–20 (2019)
10. Pane, J.F., Ratanamahatana, C.A., Myers, B.A.: Studying the language and structure in non-programmers' solutions to programming problems. IJHCS **54**(2), 237–264 (2001)
11. Fogli, D., Lanzilotti, R., Piccinno, A.: End-User development tools for the smart home: a systematic literature review. In: Streitz, N., Markopoulos, P. (eds.) DAPI 2016. LNCS, vol. 9749, pp. 69–79. Springer, Cham (2016). https://doi.org/10.1007/978-3-319-39862-4_7
12. Caivano, D., Fogli, D., Lanzilotti, R., Piccinno, A., Cassano, F.: Supporting end users to control their smart home: design implications from a literature review and an empirical investigation. J. Syst. Softw. **144**, 295–313 (2018)
13. Namoun, A., Nestler, T., De Angeli, A.: Service composition for non-programmers: prospects, problems, and design recommendations. In: 2010 Eighth IEEE European Conference on Web Services, pp. 123–130 (2010)
14. IFTTT Inc.: AtomGraph, https://github.com/AtomGraph/Web-Client. Accessed 12 Feb 2018
15. Di Bitonto, P., Roselli, T., Rossano, V., Frezza, E., Piccinno, E.: An educational game to learn type 1 diabetes management. In: 18th International Conference on Distributed Multimedia Systems (DMS), pp. 139–143. KSI, Skokie (2012)
16. Benzi, F., Cabitza, F., Fogli, D., Lanzilotti, R., Piccinno, A.: Gamification techniques for rule management in ambient intelligence. In: De Ruyter, B., et al. (eds.) Ambient Intelligence, vol. 9425, pp. 353–356. Springer, Cham (2015)

Transparency Heuristic: Effect of Implicitness of Online Data Acquisition on Sensitivity Perception

Mariavittoria Masotina[1], Patrik Pluchino[1], Francesca Freuli[1],
Luciano Gamberini[1,2], and Anna Spagnolli[1,2(✉)]

[1] Human Inspired Technology Research Centre,
University of Padova, Padua, Italy
anna.spagnolli@unipd.it
[2] Department of General Psychology, University of Padova, Padua, Italy

Abstract. We present a study that investigates whether the transparency of the data acquisition technique can work as a heuristic when making evaluations about data protection and sensitivity. The study (N = 40) compares an explicit data acquisition technique (questionnaires) with an implicit one (eye-tracker) and varies also the actual sensitivity of the data collected (popularity evaluation vs. usability evaluation). The results suggest that, when judging general data sensitivity, the transparency of the data collection procedure might work as a heuristic; instead if more specific judgments or decisions are asked this effect is not observed. Implications are discussed.

Keywords: Sensitivity perception · Anonymity · Transparency

1 Introduction

Improving the transparency of a system or service collecting personal data is recommended as a way to increase users' ability to protect their identity (e.g. EU GDPR 2016/679). Paradoxically, however, transparency might backfire: users can interpret transparency as a cue to quickly decide that a system can be trusted [1, 2] and then disclose their personal data. Transparency would then work as a heuristic. In the present study we focus on the transparency of the data acquisition method, and check whether it would affect users' perception and decisions in the domain of data protection regardless of the actual sensitivity of the data acquired. To this goal, we had a sample of students participating in our study; their data were acquired either with a transparent technique (questionnaires), in which the act of providing data is a voluntary and conscious one in the users' side for each datum provided, or with an implicit one (eye-tracker), in which after the initial consent from the user the system takes care of the data collection and the user is unaware of each datum collected. The data collected could be either sensitive or non-sensitive, namely potentially damaging to the user or not; in the former case students had to rate their professors' popularity, in the latter case they had to rate the usability of the professors' institutional webpage. The effect of this

© IFIP International Federation for Information Processing 2019
Published by Springer Nature Switzerland AG 2019
D. Lamas et al. (Eds.): INTERACT 2019, LNCS 11749, pp. 676–679, 2019.
https://doi.org/10.1007/978-3-030-29390-1_61

manipulation on their judgment (perceived sensitivity of the collected data) and decisions (willingness to keep their anonymity) was then measured.

2   Method

The experiment followed a 2×2 between-participants design; the independent variables manipulated were the sensitivity of the data acquired (non-sensitive vs. sensitive) and the transparency of the data acquisition method (transparent vs. implicit). Our research questions were whether the two manipulated variables had any effect on participants' decision to keep anonymity and on the perceived sensitivity of the data.

The procedure was double-blind; neither the participants nor the member of the research team meeting the participants were aware of the goal of the study. Participants were randomly assigned to the different conditions. The whole procedure was automated via Atom software (https://atom.io/) so that there was no need for the researcher to provide instructions or intervene till the end of the session. A Tobii 1750 eye-tracker was used in the implicit conditions, while a tablet was used in the transparent conditions. Google Form was used to collect the participants' responses.

Before the beginning of the experimental session, every participant read and signed an informed consent to participate in the study. The study was described as one investigating professors' webpages usability or professors' popularity, depending on the sensitivity condition. In the implicit conditions the technique used to acquire their usability/popularity rates was described as based on the detection of fatigue/repulsion via pupillary response collected with an eyetracker. In the transparent condition the technique to acquire usability/popularity rates was a questionnaire. It was explained them that the acquired data would be used in aggregate form to preserve participants' anonymity. However, participants' e-mail address was asked in the questionnaire administered at the end of the experiment, justified by the need to contact them at the end of the study to obtain their permission to use the collected data.

The experimental session then began. Participants were sitting at a desk on which a computer was positioned. First they were asked to provide some demographic data and the name of their master or bachelor program. In the implicit conditions, the eye-tracker was activated and calibrated. Then, the researcher launched the application administering the experimental task and left the room. Participants saw displayed on the screen a list of all teachers in their master or bachelor program, and were asked to select the one they knew better. The webpage of the selected professor would then appear and be briefly inspected by the participant. In the implicit conditions, a message appeared on the screen notifying that the eye-tracker had successfully captured their reactions. In the transparent conditions participants were asked to rate the usability of the web page or the popularity of the professor in a short questionnaire. This task was repeated four times until the webpages of four professors (two men and two women) were visited. Afterwards, participants were automatically sent to a Google Form questionnaire asking on a 5-point Likert scale: (a) if they consented to waive the anonymity of their data ("Would you be willing to let us process your data renouncing anonymity, so we can associate your name and surname to the data and responses collected during the whole experiment?") and (b) to evaluate the perceived sensitivity of the data provided (Item 1 - Do you think that the data collected during this experiment is sensitive, namely that it could identify you in a counterproductive manner?; Item 2 - Do you think that the information derived from such data could be embarrassing for you?; Item 3 - Do you think that the data provided could offend the teachers?).

Sample. 40 university students enrolled in the Psychology School of the University of Padova participated in this study (mean age 23.61, SD = 1.71, men = 9, women = 31). They were all Italian native speakers. The webpage displayed in the study were the institutional webpage of each professor.

3   Results

The participants' willingness to waive anonymity and their perceived sensitivity of the collected data are reported in Fig. 1.

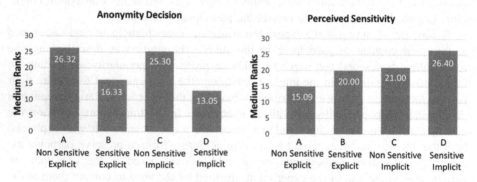

Fig. 1. Medium ranks of the willingness to waive anonymity (a, left) and of the perceived sensitivity of the data (b, right) broken down by condition.

To assess the effect of the two manipulated factors (type of data collected and transparency of the collection technique) on the dependent variables, a Mann-Whitney test was run (Table 1).

Table 1. Results of the Mann-Whitney test measuring the effects of the two factors, the type of data (usability vs. popularity) and the explicitness of the data collection technique.

	Data sensitivity		Transparency	
	W	p	W	p
Anonymity decision	311.5	0.002	226.5	0.47
Sensitivity item 1 (sensitive)	198	0.97	144	0.08
Sensitivity item 2 (embarrassing)	156	0.10	164	0.17
Sensitivity item 3 (offensive)	123	0.01	208	0.81
Consolidated score from items 1, 2, 3	145	0.12	136	0.07

The results show that the willingness to waive anonymity was affected only by the actual sensitivity of the data acquired and not by the transparency of the data collection method: frequency is significantly higher in the non-sensitive conditions (usability rates) than in the sensitive ones (popularity rates). Regarding the perceived sensitivity of the data collected, there seems to be an effect of the transparency of the data collection method in the consolidated scores of the three items and in Item n. 1 with a tendency to statistical significance. The other two items did not seem affected by the data collection method. There seem also to be a cumulative effect so that the highest difference in perceived sensitivity at a Mann Whitney test was between the two most extreme conditions in which the manipulated factors are both present or both absent, $W = 26.5$, p-value $= 0.037$.

4   Conclusions and Future Work

The results suggest that, when judging sensitivity in generic terms the transparency of the data collection procedure might be relied upon as a heuristic, decreasing the perceived sensitivity of the data regardless of its actual content. Transparency does not seem to be relied upon, instead, when specific sensitivity judgments are at stake. Likewise, the decision whether to waive the anonymity of the data is not affected by the data collection technique. What seems to make the difference across all these results is the clarity of the scenario in which the user is able to figure the possible risks. The more specific the question, the easier it is for them to estimate the actual risks and avoid recourse to heuristics. Studies seem to confirm that sensitivity is a contextual estimation (e.g.,[3]), connected to the possible detrimental uses of the data [4]. This hypothesis will be pursued in further studies by varying the specificity of the decision and of the judgment. To scholars in human-computer interaction, these initial results renew the challenge of finding a genuine way to implement transparency in a way that avoids backlashes. At the same time, it suggests to adopt compensatory measures when using implicit/background data techniques that per se might reduce trust in users.

References

1. Acquisti, A., Adjerid, I., Brandimarte, L.: Gone in 15 seconds: the limits of privacy transparency and control. IEEE Secur. Priv. **11**(4), 72–74 (2013)
2. Oulasvirta, A., Suomalainen, T., Hamari, J., Lampinen, A., Karvonen, K.: Transparency of intentions decreases privacy concerns in ubiquitous surveillance. Cyberpsychol. Behav. Soc. Netw. **17**(10), 633–638 (2014)
3. Sun, Y., Wang, N., Shen, X.L., Zhang, J.X.: Location information disclosure in location-based social network services: privacy calculus, benefit structure, and gender differences. Comput. Hum. Behav. **52**, 278–292 (2015)
4. Dinev, T., Hart, P.: Internet privacy concerns and their antecedents-measurement validity and a regression model. Behav. Inf. Technol. **23**(6), 413–422 (2004)

Using Virtual Reality to Enable Individuals with Severe Visual Disabilities to Read Books

Kurtis Weir[1]([✉])[iD], Fernando Loizides[2][iD], Vinita Nahar[1][iD],
and Amar Aggoun[1][iD]

[1] University of Wolverhampton, Wolverhampton, UK
{K.Weir,Vinita.Nahar,A.Aggoun}@wlv.ac.uk
[2] National Software Academy, Department of Computer Science and Informatics,
Cardiff University, Cardiff, UK
loizidesf@cardiff.ac.uk

Abstract. In this work, we present a bespoke assistive tool for people
with severe visual disabilities. We are able to download text from books
and present these books to our users in a virtual reality environment.
This gives them specific capabilities to manipulate the text and factors
such as brightness, size and contrast, in order for them to gain a comfortable reading experience.

Keywords: Reading · Virtual Reality · Visual disabilities

1 Introduction

The rise of Virtual Reality (VR) and Augmented Reality (AR) technologies has
bred a new competing market that is focused primarily on entertainment. This
technology advances rapidly with newer head mounted displays (HMD), featuring higher resolutions, improved ergonomics, and better portability. We are
concerned however, with a lack of attention to the needs of disabled users, and
specifically those with severe visual impairments. Exploration between current
available VR app marketplaces between different VR devices show that some
early attempts into digital eBooks already exist [4], yet they do not focus on
reasonable accessibility features that would make said applications usable for disabled persons. In previous research we investigated the potential for specialised
VR equipment for visually impaired users and conducted 24 case studies that
identified VR potential in improving their visual acuity(under review). The user
group tested were what we would consider legally blind, requiring daily assistance and having little to no reading ability without severe aids, many whom
were surprised at their increased acuity during testing over their current aids.
During that study, we also elicited requirements from the participants on assisted
living capabilities they wish to utilise VR/AR technology for. One dominant need

© IFIP International Federation for Information Processing 2019
Published by Springer Nature Switzerland AG 2019
D. Lamas et al. (Eds.): INTERACT 2019, LNCS 11749, pp. 680–684, 2019.
https://doi.org/10.1007/978-3-030-29390-1_62

was to improve (or in some cases restore) the ability to read. Currently, such software does not exist, and book readers that do exist are extremely limited in their accessibility. The aim of this paper is to present the development of specialised software that can accommodate the reading needs of severely visually impaired users and explain its features. The presented work will feed towards a full series of integrated disability software aimed to promote disability focus within VR systems.

2 Related Work

To highlight the potential and need for e-reading software on VR technology, we give a background foundation of similar electronic reading research and past findings. Low-vision aids are currently necessary for reading accessibility [5]. When looking at the history of electronic approaches to reading, extensive research on the comparative reading ability between physical paper and computer screen recreations already exist, with many authors mimicking results that computer screen reading has been slower between studies [2,3,6,9] Causes for these decreases in reading time via computer screens were credited to technical limitations such as display qualities, and even psychological aspects such as meta-cognitive regulation [1]. Although these findings surround typical computer screen readings (i.e. LCD monitors read at a distance), they serve to both demonstrate limitations with current technology as well as question the feasibility of newer alternatives to traditional reading. A recent study [7] looked at performing similar comparisons between both VR and AR reading speeds against digital screen reading. This research utilised the Oculus Rift CV1 (https://www.oculus.com/rift/ - Accessed April 2019) for VR, the Microsoft HoloLens (https://www.microsoft.com/en-CY/hololens - Accessed April 2019) for AR, and a LCD monitor to present a series of questions that required participants' responses via multiple choices. Results found that responses within both VR and AR devices were 10% slower than computer display, similar to results shown between computer screen and physical paper read speeds. Although results from this study suggest that time to perform tasks was diminished by 10% within VR and AR environments, it is important to note that many other factors could have attributed to this, such as unfamiliarity with new digital environments and interfaces, as well as device variables, such as distance to eyes, field of view, or backgrounds used. These studies discussed thus far have looked at standard reading ability between participants with normal vision, but what of those with severe visual disabilities, where the drawbacks of electronic reading are more than negated by the technology allowing for increased visual acuity over natural vision. Investigations into modern VR and AR systems have explored different visual enhancement techniques, such as the successful manipulation of magnification and contrast via ForeSee [10]. Specialist aid tools do exist that focus on providing reading capability, such as the OrCam device [8] which uses OCR (Optical Character Recognition) to read text via a camera mounted on one's glasses. This is limited by the need for voice feedback and lack of variable manipulation such as brightness and magnification. Finally, the human element of reading is also missing, both in the sense of a user being independently able to 'read' but also to make sense of OCR that may fail.

3   Artefact Description

This project utilises a Oculus Rift CV1 as the chosen VR HMD, and Unity (https://unity.com/ - Accessed April 2019) as the primary development platform for its strong VR documentation and compatibility, alongside the C# programming language. The goal was allowing the application to read standard UTF-8 formats and translate them onto a virtual reading panel for users to make their own reading adjustments. This common format allows greater compatibility with most text and books. For our testing we utilised Project Gutenberg (http://www.gutenberg.org/), a free to use eBook website offering over 58,000 royalty free books. Books were downloaded directly from their service and inserted into our application to be automatically translated. Once text is translated into our application, it is displayed in front of the user via a floating panel in a darkened environment. Graphical distractions are kept to a minimum to avoid accessibility issues, so only essentials are displayed to the user. Utilising the Oculus' touch controllers to simulate virtual hands, the user may freely grab a panel with lines of text (Fig. 1) by squeezing down the grip button to pick up and re-position the text, and releasing this grip freezes the new position in place. By default the first 5 lines of text from the chosen book are displayed to the user, which is adjustable. The user manipulates environmental variables via voice control, allowing them to change how the text and parts of the virtual world are displayed.

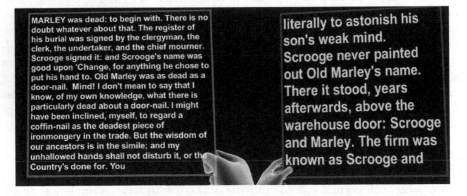

Fig. 1. Left: A user grabbing the book with their right hand. Right: Example of the book and font being enlarged, along with colour changes

Currently voice commands allow the user to manipulate these settings: Change the numbers of lines displayed ("more lines"), flip to next page ("next page"), change the font size ("bigger font"), change the size of the book display ("larger book"), change the font type ("font x")[1], change the lighting/light

---

[1] x represents number or colour (e.g. Background Black, Font 2).

sources ("brighter light", "darker light", "light x"), and multiple colour combinations. The panel or book itself is split between 3 different planes that can change colour, being the background of the book itself ("Panel x"), the border edges around the book ("Border x"), and the colour of the text itself ("Text x"). Additionally, the background virtual space can change colour from its default black if a voice command is used. The user may also move lights around the environment by utilising their virtual hands, as well as using voice commands to manipulate or enable/disable lighting variables, allowing them to use light sources from specific angles as virtual torches (Fig. 2), or simulate directional light sources for greater clarity depending on their conditions.

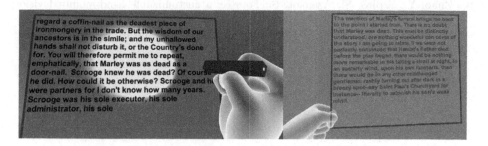

Fig. 2. Left: The torch tool being shined onto the text for clarity. Right: An example of further background colour combinations

This fully interactive functional prototype application serves as the foundation for developing a reader for severely visually disabled individuals. We aim to use the interactive elements of the technology as a stepping stone to also allow for further text interaction, such as subtitles in videos as augmented reality text reading through real time OCR. We now aim to test the application with patients suffering with macular degeneration, and also other similar limiting conditions to develop the interface to be as adaptive as possible.

Acknowledgements. This research is funded by Beacon Centre for the Blind (Registered Charity No. 216092) and the University of Wolverhampton.

References

1. Ackerman, R., Goldsmith, M.: Metacognitive regulation of text learning: on screen versus on paper. J. Exp. Psychol. Appl. **17**(1), 18 (2011)
2. Dillon, A.: Reading from paper versus screens: a critical review of the empirical literature. Ergonomics **35**(10), 1297–1326 (1992)
3. Gould, J.D., Grischkowsky, N.: Doing the same work with hard copy and with cathode-ray tube (CRT) computer terminals. Hum. Factors **26**(3), 323–337 (1984)
4. Hahn, J.F.: Virtual reality learning environments: development of multi-user reference support experiences. Inf. Learn. Sci. **119**(11), 652–661 (2018)

5. Latham, K.: Benefits of low vision aids to reading accessibility. Vis. Res. **153**, 47–52 (2018)
6. Mangen, A., Walgermo, B.R., Brønnick, K.: Reading linear texts on paper versus computer screen: effects on reading comprehension. Int. J. Educ. Res. **58**, 61–68 (2013)
7. Rau, P.L.P., Zheng, J., Guo, Z., Li, J.: Speed reading on virtual reality and augmented reality. Comput. Educ. **125**, 240–245 (2018)
8. Waisbourd, M., Ahmed, O., Siam, L., Moster, M.R., Hark, L.A., Katz, L.J.: The impact of a novel artificial vision device (OrCam) on the quality of life of patients with end-stage glaucoma. Invest. Ophthalmol. Vis. Sci. **56**(7), 519–519 (2015)
9. Wilkinson, R.T., Robinshaw, H.M.: Proof-reading: VDU and paper text compared for speed, accuracy and fatigue. BIT **6**(2), 125–133 (1987)
10. Zhao, Y., Szpiro, S., Azenkot, S.: Foresee: a customizable head-mounted vision enhancement system for people with low vision. In: Proceedings of the 17th International ACM SIGACCESS Conference on Computers and Accessibility, pp. 239–249. ACM (2015)

Vibro-Tactile Implicit Interactions: So What?

Yulia Zhiglova$^{(\boxtimes)}$ ⓘ, David Lamas$^{(\boxtimes)}$ ⓘ, Ilja Smorgun$^{(\boxtimes)}$ ⓘ,
and Paul Seitlinger$^{(\boxtimes)}$ ⓘ

Tallinn University, Tallinn, Estonia
{yzhigl,drl,ilja.smorgun,pseiti}@tlu.ee

Abstract. Tactile feedback is a powerful modality for designing human-computer interfaces. Here we explore new ways of communication through tactile senses that can be perceived implicitly. This paper outlines the preliminary phase of research the goal of which is to investigate to what extent a vibro-tactile stimulus can be meaningfully communicated on an unconscious/implicit level of perception. Ability to perceive information implicitly provides an alternative channel for communication and may therefore reduce our cognitive load. In this poster, we formulate our research problem, suggest a research framework and outline future experiments enabled by the prototype we have designed.

Keywords: Peripheral interaction · Vibro-tactile · Body-centric

1 Introduction

Touch is essential for humans. It elicits comfort and attachment and provides rich information about the world around us [5]. Tactile feedback can be a powerful modality for developing human-computer interfaces. A lot of HCI research concerns the mediated-touch technology and how various vibro-tactile stimuli may simulate sense of presence. Most of these studies work in the plane of conscious or explicit perception [2,3]. Very few touch upon the implicit or unconscious [1,6]. Unconscious perception can be defined as an automatic, effortless process which does not require bringing information into the attention focus [9]. Unconscious perception, evoked by tactile stimulation, may provide higher communication bandwidth. It can also reduce cognitive load that comes with using multiple devices simultaneously. Understanding the extent to which a mediated-touch technology may be used on a peripheral level can lay a foundation for numerous applications in healthcare, well-being and personal relationships. Further, the terms peripheral, implicit and unconscious will be used interchangeably.

2 Research Problem Formulation and Context

The traditional interaction with technology mostly happens through visual interfaces and keyboard. Such interactions require full attention from a person,

© IFIP International Federation for Information Processing 2019
Published by Springer Nature Switzerland AG 2019
D. Lamas et al. (Eds.): INTERACT 2019, LNCS 11749, pp. 685–688, 2019.
https://doi.org/10.1007/978-3-030-29390-1_63

increasing cognitive load. Therefore, HCI community sees a need in developing new ways of communication that would allow integrating technology seamlessly in everyday tasks. For instance, already in 1997 Weiser talked about 'calm technology' which 'engages both the center and the periphery of our attention', allowing to concentrate on the important task [8]. Haptic feedback can be a powerful tool in designing 'calm' technology. From previous studies we know that specific combinations of parameters of vibro-tactile displays may simulate not only a variety of touch types but potentially be perceived implicitly, given an appropriate configuration of parameters [3,6]. As there are few studies concerning unconscious perception of vibro-tactile stimuli, we see a need for further research. Our broader research goal is to explore how range of vibro-tactile displays can be designed to convey information on an unconscious level of perception in body-centric configurations. To achieve the goal we plan to answer the following question: What configurations of vibro-tactile parameters are more effective and efficient in communicating information on an unconscious level? The key parameters include frequency, intensity, and location on the body. The study will be based on controlled experiments, involving university students without tactile impairments as participants. We have designed a vibro-tactile prototype to enable first experiments. The purpose of the experiments is to investigate how parameters of the vibro-tactile display need to be configured. We assume that by changing one or a combination of the parameters the stimuli perception will vary with respect to the extent by which conscious vs. unconscious processes contribute to the person's somatosensory experience.

We focus our research in the context of remote relationships. Imagine a situation where a daughter and a mother are living in different cities. Daughter is about to have an exam at school and is busy preparing for it. Mother, knowing that, wants to support her daughter without distracting her by a phone call. Instead, she sends a caressing which daughter can feel on her skin through a wearable vibro-tactile display. The daughter perceives the virtual caressing, and since the stimuli is communicated on a periphery of her attention, she is not distracted from her main activity.

3   Related Work

Our overall research and methodology is greatly informed by the psychological studies of perception, specifically, by the dual process extension of the Signal Detection Theory [9]. We were inspired by research papers that applied these psychological theories in the domain of tactile and auditory perceptions. The focus of the papers was the ability to detect and identify physical changes evoked by the vibro-tactile device (e.g., [7]) and auditory stimuli (e.g., [4]). According to this prior work, two cognitive processes can be expected to be in play. In the event of a signal that enters the focus of attention, an explicit process takes effect that draws on working memory resources and leads to parsing the haptic (or auditory) scene and encoding the instances that have caused the change in perception. Consequently, the person will be able to not only detect a change but also identify the specific source of change. If, by contrast, the signal of change does not enter the attention focus, an implicit and effortless signal detection process can nevertheless become active that will not consume the individual's working memory resources. The stimuli will only operate on global qualities and low-level features. However, while being less resource consuming, this implicit process will also be more noisy and will only allow for sensing a global change but not for identifying the specific source of change. Thus, it is the latter, namely implicit process, that underlies the phenomenon that is typically referred to as peripheral perception in HCI research. Some HCI researchers already used dual-process and divided attention theories to inform their research [1].

4 Research Framework

Our research framework is based on the ongoing scoping study (not published yet) of the state of the art of the vibro-tactile body-centric displays, psychological studies of perception and principles of psychophysics. From the scoping study we identified existing vibro-tactile patterns that simulate various types of touch and the existing algorithms that enable these simulations [3]. We also identified key vibro-tactile parameters that influence the perception of the stimuli. In psychophysics domain we explored the principles of tactile senses and how they can be manipulated by vibro-tactile stimuli. We worked in close cooperation with a psychology expert to understand the complex interplay between physical stimuli and the psychological space. We formulated how the physical space (vibro-tactile stimulation) maps onto the psychological space (level of processing), and represented each of them as a multi-dimensional space. The dimensions of the physical space include frequency and intensity of vibration and the location on a human body. The physical dimension represents the design space for our vibro-tactile displays. The psychological space includes such dimensions as affective states (arousal and valence) and level of processing (implicit and explicit). Currently, we only focus on the latter dimension and examine the possibility to evoke and measure the perception both on a conscious and unconscious level of information processing. Summarizing, our goal is to define a psychophysical function g that maps states in the physical space $\mathbf{F}$ (vibrotactile) onto states in the psychological space $\mathbf{E}$. If there are three physical dimensions of frequency, intensity, and location, then a certain point in $\mathbf{F}$ represents a corresponding parameter configuration and can be notated as a vector f_t at some time t in the course of the experiment. f_t, in any case, will evoke a particular level of processing, and can be represented as the vector e_t. The research question is then where exactly this psychological point will be localized in $\mathbf{E}$. The goal will thus be to identify a function g in the form of an equation, by which we can quantitatively predict the level of processing of the physical event triggered by the device.

$$e_t = g(f_t)$$

5   Conclusion

The future work will entail controlled experiments based on the dual-process measurement model mentioned earlier [4]. The model will explore explicit and implicit change detection of vibro-tactile stimuli as a discrete and continuous process, respectively. The experimental design will be a change detection paradigm that has participants distinguish signal from noise (presence vs. non-presence of stimuli) and indicate their response confidence. This will result in a Receiver Operating Characteristic (ROC) curve, against which the dual-process measurement model [4] can be fitted to estimate contributions of both explicit and implicit processes of change detection. That way, we aim to address our main methodological challenge of measuring unconscious states without affecting them substantially. Also we plan to extend the psychophysical function by parameters representing additional modalities such as sound and temporal dynamics within the psychological space.

Thus far, we provided an overview of the initial stage of research with hope to probe our initial research ideas and gather feedback. We hope this work can spark curiosity for the topic and result in research collaborations.

References

1. Bakker, S., van den Hoven, E., Eggen, B.: Peripheral interaction: characteristics and considerations. Pers. Ubiquitous Comput. **19**(1), 239–254 (2015). https://doi.org/10.1007/s00779-014-0775-2
2. Eid, M.A., Al Osman, H.: Affective haptics: current research and future directions. IEEE Access **4**, 26–40 (2016). https://doi.org/10.1109/ACCESS.2015.2497316
3. Israr, A., Poupyrev, I.: Tactile brush: drawing on skin with a tactile grid display. In: Proceedings of the SIGCHI Conference on Human Factors in Computing Systems, CHI 2011, pp. 2019–2028. ACM, New York (2011). https://doi.org/10.1145/1978942.1979235
4. McAnally, K.I., Martin, R.L., Eramudugolla, R., Stuart, G.W., Irvine, D.R., Mattingley, J.B.: A dual-process account of auditory change detection. J. Exp. Psychol. Hum. Percept. Perform. **36**(4), 994–1004 (2010). https://doi.org/10.1037/a0016895
5. Montagu, A.: Touching: The Human Significance of the Skin. Perennial library/HarperCollins (1986). https://books.google.ee/books?id=XU7Z_aqCYggC
6. Riener, A., Ferscha, A., Frech, P., Hackl, M., Kaltenberger, M.: Subliminal vibro-tactile based notification of co2 economy while driving. In: AutomotiveUI (2010)
7. Spence, C., Gallace, A., Tan, H.Z.: The failure to detect tectile change: a tactile analogue of visual change blindness. Psychon. Bull. Rev. **13**(2), 300–303 (2006)
8. Weiser, M., Brown, J.S.: The coming age of calm technology. In: Weiser, M., Brown, J.S. (eds.) Beyond Calculation, pp. 75–85. Springer, New York (1997). https://doi.org/10.1007/978-1-4612-0685-9_6
9. Wixted, J.T.: Dual-process theory and signal-detection theory of recognition memory. Psychol. Rev. **114**(1), 152–176 (2007). https://doi.org/10.1037/0033-295X.114.1.152

Visualizations of User's Paths to Discover Usability Problems

Paolo Buono, Giuseppe Desolda$^{(\boxtimes)}$, Rosa Lanzilotti,
Maria Francesca Costabile, and Antonio Piccinno

Computer Science Department, University of Bari Aldo Moro, Bari, Italy
{paolo.buono, giuseppe.desolda, rosa.lanzilotti,
mariafrancesca.costabile, antonio.piccinno}@uniba.it

Abstract. This paper reports on an on-going work that investigates the use of visualization techniques to help evaluators discovering usability problems by visualizing data collected during usability tests of web sites. Two visualization techniques are described and some results of the evaluation study that compared the two techniques are provided.

Keywords: Usability test · Visualization techniques ·
Usability problems discovery · Web site evaluation

1 Introduction

Usability testing is performed by HCI experts to identify usability problems of interactive software systems. During a test, data like audio/video, PC logs, questionnaire results are gathered and analyzed to detect usability problems. This technique stands out positively from others (e.g. inspection techniques) since users are involved, critical tasks are executed, and a lot of qualitative and quantitative data can be collected and analyzed. It is considered expensive, especially due to the time needed to analyze data.

Some researchers propose the use of visualization techniques to help, in different ways, the evaluator discovering usability problems. For example, WebQuilt is a usability logging and visualization tool that presents logged data in an interactive graph, whose nodes are web pages visited by the users [1]. Each node details usability issues that occurred at that page. In [2], the user's actions during a task are shown on a timeline, and the optimal actions to perform a task are also represented; this should help the evaluator to detect deviations of the performed actions from the correct ones, speeding up the time to investigate something that occurred at a certain time.

In our research, we are primarily working on usability evaluation of web sites and we aim at supporting the evaluator on easily identifying the web pages presenting usability issues. Thus, we propose two techniques that visualize a graph whose nodes are web pages. The presented graphs also show the optimal path to perform a task, since the visual comparison with the optimal path provides useful indications of something that the user could not correctly perform (this was inspired by [2]). In the following, we describe the proposed interactive visualizations, and briefly report on an evaluation study that compared the two techniques.

© IFIP International Federation for Information Processing 2019
Published by Springer Nature Switzerland AG 2019
D. Lamas et al. (Eds.): INTERACT 2019, LNCS 11749, pp. 689–692, 2019.
https://doi.org/10.1007/978-3-030-29390-1_64

2   Two Visualization Techniques to Identify Usability Problems

In usability tests, the identification of sources of usability problems often needs the triangulation of different quantitative and qualitative methods. Quantitative data, like average task time and task success rate, provide indications on tasks that caused evident problems but not where the problem occurred. To get this information, evaluators should look at the videos, paying attention to which pages led participants to fail the tasks or too much longer routes to complete the task.

To support evaluators we propose two interactive visualization techniques that depict, for each task, the routes followed by participants, as well as the ideal path that participants would follow to successfully complete a task. The problematic web pages are the ones that mostly confused the participants, leading them to follow wrong paths.

The first visualization is based on the Arc Diagram [3], which places vertices along a horizontal line and arcs represent connections between nodes. Figure 1a, shows the adaptation of Arc Diagram to support the identification of web pages that caused problems during the execution of a task by all participants to the test. Nodes represent web pages visited by participants, their size is directly proportional to the number of visits. Blue node refers to the task starting page, *red* if participants wrongly terminated the task at that page, *green* node refers to the task ending page, *black* for the other pages. Arc thickness is proportional to the frequency of movement between connected pages. Green arc is the ideal path, otherwise it is *light grey*. *Violet* arcs represented below the node line indicate backward paths. The graph in Fig. 1a shows that 13 users correctly moved from the task starting page to the next one (the green arc with '13' label); then only 9 users correctly moved to the next page, and eventually all 15 users moved toward the page that completed the task. Only 1 user wrongly terminated the task, as shown by the red node. One of the most problematic web pages is the one where the arc with 13 users ends, since only 9 users were able to correctly move from this page to the next correct page.

The second visualization is called Page Tree because it shows a tree-like structure that better recalls the 'hierarchical' organization of a Website (see Fig. 1b). Nodes and arcs (branches) have the same meaning as other visualization, both in term of colors and dimensions/thickness. In this visualization, the backward paths are not explicitly shown. Here the 47% of participants correctly moved from the task starting page toward the final task page (percentage or absolute values can be switched), while the other participants followed wrong paths (in grey), sometimes wrongly terminating the task (to the red nodes) and sometimes correctly finishing the task (the other green nodes). Lack of space prevents us from detailing the motivation of the choice of these visualizations and reporting all their details and functionalities.

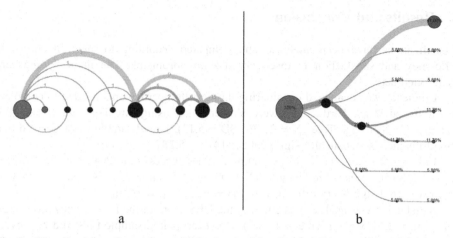

a   b

Fig. 1. Visualizations of participants paths inspired by the Arc Diagram (a) and Page Tree (b) (Color figure online)

3   Evaluation of the Proposed Visualizations

The design and development of the two visualizations followed the User-Centered Design methodology. Initial ideas were sketched and discussed among designers and evaluation experts. Prototypes of increasing complexity (starting from paper-based ones) were tested with few evaluators using the thinking aloud protocol. They allowed to detect various problems that were fixed in the next prototype. Figure 1a and b refer to the current interactive prototypes, implemented using D3 JavaScript library. These prototypes were used in an experimental study to understand to what extent the visualizations support HCI experts in identifying problematic Webpages. We recruited 15 participants (4 females, 11 males) among the students of the Computer Science and Digital Communication curriculum at our university, who completed a course on Human-Computer Interaction and had some basic experience about performing a usability test. Their average age was 26 years (min = 23, max = 29). The study was organized according to a within-subject design, with visualization as an independent variable and as within-subject factors the two visualizations. Each visualization showed data gathered in a study conducted with 15 employees of an Italian Administration, who used a Web platform for onsite and remote usability tests [4, 5]. With each system, the participants performed the following tasks: 1. Identify the page that caused most problems; 2. Identify the path(s) that led to the task's failure; 3. Identify the path that led to the task success following the ideal path, 4. Identify the paths that led to the task success following alternative paths; 5. Identify backward paths, if possible.

Visualizations and order of tasks were balanced according to a Latin-square design. At the end of all tasks with each visualization, participants filled the UES-short form questionnaire.

4 Results and Conclusion

Visualizations have been analyzed and compared according to their effectiveness, efficiency and satisfaction in discovery usability problems. The main findings are mentioned here.

Efficiency was evaluated considering the time that participants needed to complete the assigned tasks. Participants were slower when using Arc Diagram (x = 34.93, SD = 5.77) than Page Tree (X = 27.76, SD = 5.13). Paired sample t-test showed that this difference is statistically significant (t(14) = −5.287, p = .000).

Effectiveness was analyzed calculating the task success rate. Page Tree had a lower rate (x = 86,56%) than Arc Diagram (X = 93,00%). Even in this case, paired sample t-test revealed a significant difference (t(14) = −2.512, p = .025).

Satisfaction was analyzed calculating the UES score of the two visualizations (Arc Diagram = 4.61/5; Page Tree = 4.78/5). However, paired sample t-test did not reveal any significant difference (t(14) = −1.878, p = .081).

In conclusion, this on-going work proposes two interactive visualization techniques to support usability evaluators in identifying web pages that cause usability problems, speeding up data analysis and encouraging the adoption of usability test in software development lifecycle. Results have shown that both visualizations are adequate to identify web pages that cause usability errors. Page Tree resulted better in term of time to find errors and success rate, while no differences emerged in user engagement. Studies are in progress to investigate other visualization techniques to focus on other aspects of the user flow during task execution or to visualize user activities [6].

References

1. Waterson, S.J., Hong, J.I., Sohn, T., Landay, J.A., Heer, J., Matthews, T.: What did they do? Understanding clickstreams with the WebQuilt visualization system. In: Proceedings of Conference on Advanced Visual Interfaces (AVI 2002), pp. 94–102. ACM (2002). https://www.doi.org/10.1145/1556262.1556276
2. Paternò, F., Schiavone, A.G., Pitardi, P.: Timelines for mobile web usability evaluation. In: Proceedings of International Conference on Advanced Visual Interfaces (AVI 2014), pp. 88–91. ACM, New York (2016)
3. Wattenberg, M.: Arc diagrams: visualizing structure in strings. In: Proceedings of IEEE Symposium on Information Visualization (INFOVIS 2002), pp. 110–116 (2002)
4. Federici, S., et al.: UTAssistant: a new semi-automatic usability evaluation tool for Italian public administrations. In: Proceedings of International Conference on Advanced Visual Interfaces - ECONA Workshop (AVI 2018), pp. 1–3 (2018)
5. Federici, S., et al.: UX evaluation design of UTAssistant: a new usability testing support tool for Italian public administrations. In: Kurosu, M. (ed.) HCI 2018. LNCS, vol. 10901, pp. 55–67. Springer, Cham (2018). https://doi.org/10.1007/978-3-319-91238-7_5
6. Buono, P., Costabile, M.F., Lanzilotti, R.: A circular visualization of people's activities in distributed teams. J. Vis. Lang. Comput. 25(6), 903–911 (2014)

Word Association: Engagement of Teenagers in a Co-design Process

Vanessa Cesário[1,2](✉), António Coelho[2,3](✉),
and Valentina Nisi[1,4](✉)

[1] ITI/LARSyS, 9020-105 Funchal, Portugal
{vanessa.cesario,valentina.nisi}@m-iti.org
[2] Faculty of Engineering, University of Porto, 4200-465 Porto, Portugal
acoelho@fe.up.pt
[3] INESC TEC, 4200-465 Porto, Portugal
[4] University of Madeira, 9000-208 Funchal, Portugal

Abstract. This submission describes the analysis of an evaluation of 155 teenagers (15–19 years old) who took part in a co-design session centred around how mobile technology might enhance their own experiences in a natural history museum. At the end, participants were required to make a word association to evaluate the session. An analysis of how teen participants responded to the design session was conducted using thematic analysis to show the different categories of adjectives used by participants in their evaluations. The goal for the evaluation was mainly to pilot the design session process and if teens enjoyed participating in it. We believe this is of interest to designers and cultural heritage professionals.

Keywords: Co-design · Evaluation · Thematic analysis · Teenagers · Museums

1 Introduction

We follow the framework presented in our previous work [1] to engage teenage audiences in the design of interactive experiences for museums. We designed for a single session and engaged 155 participants in short bursts of co-design sessions [2–4] to gather ideas to be examined later for trends. We used the data from the sessions to gather feedback and reveal insights on how teens think mobile interactive technologies could enhance their overall experience at a museum. In total, 155 participants aged 15–19 took part in the studies. In each session, the students were divided into groups, and we ended up with a total of 46 groups with an average of 3–4 gender mixed students (49 females, 106 males). The sessions took place in their usual classrooms and took 90 min to complete, and the following topics were addressed: (1) introduction, (2) 45-min co-design session, (3) evaluation of the session by the participants (word association). At the end of the 45 min of co-design activity, the participants were invited to describe the co-design session in one word on a piece of paper, which would remain anonymous, in order to rapidly identify their feedback on the co-design session carried. Even though the participants were old enough to apply a questionnaire to gather their

© IFIP International Federation for Information Processing 2019
Published by Springer Nature Switzerland AG 2019
D. Lamas et al. (Eds.): INTERACT 2019, LNCS 11749, pp. 693–697, 2019.
https://doi.org/10.1007/978-3-030-29390-1_65

feedback on the session, we opted to use a word association to evaluate it, as Carl Jung [5] theorised that people connect thoughts, feelings, experiences and information by way of association. In the Association Test, a test used in psychology to study the organisation of mental life, the subject is instructed to state the first word that comes to mind in response to a word, concept, or other stimuli. In this study, the participants were told to report the first word that comes to mind in response to the co-design session carried. For this contribution, we are going to focus on the qualitative analysis of the word association made by the participants.

Table 1. Map of the thematic analysis conducted over the teens assessment of the session: the one-word evaluation by participants generated codes (column "count" shows us how many adjectives each code encompasses), then these codes generated subthemes, and finally themes. Column "total" indicates how many adjectives each theme comprises.

Code	Count	Subtheme	Theme	Total
coolness	51			
notable	34	Interesting		
fun	7			
interaction	12			
collaborative	9	Collaboration	POSITIVE	136
learnable	2			
creative	13	Innovation		
innovative	6			
easy	2	Simple		
tricky	6	Complex		
uninteresting	2	Unexciting		
not appealing	1		NEGATIVE	11
uncomfortable	1	Obtrusive		
repetitive	1			
different	6	Diverse		
indifferent	1	Somewhat	NEUTRAL	8
more or less	1			

2 Thematic Analysis

All words were brought together to identify the categories and themes about the engagement of teenagers in participating in a co-design session. We used thematic analysis to report the data gathered. This technique is used for identifying, analysing, and reporting patterns within data. It minimally organises and describes the data set in detail [6]. NVivo 11 was used to organise the analysis. A detailed analysis of the words was conducted to evaluate the teenagers' enjoyment in taking part on the sessions. We firstly started coding the words. All words were transcribed into NVivo 11 (we refer to them as adjectives) and then categorised into 17 preliminary codes that had the same meaning, highlighting patterns and trends emerging from participants' adjectives. Then, these codes were sorted into 9 subthemes, and finally, the codes were grouped into 3 overreaching <u>themes</u>. The relation between codes and themes was double checked by the research team to guarantee the same meaning. A thematic map with codes, subthemes and themes was generated from this step (Table 1). We organised the data into the 3 main themes shown in the Results section, where each of the three overarching themes, subthemes and codes are described.

3 Results

3.1 Positive Evaluation

Inside the *Positive Evaluation* theme (136 evaluations), we inserted all the subthemes which are related to positive experiences about the co-design sessions that teens took part in. We coded 4 subthemes for this theme: (1) interesting, (2) collaboration, (3) innovation, and (4) simple. For the subtheme "interesting" we coded (1) the adjectives that related to the "coolness" of the session, and aesthetic qualities of attitude, behavior, comportment, appearance and style which is generally admired, such as: *amazing* and *appealing*; (2) the adjectives that describe the co-design session as "notable", worthy of attention or notice, such as: *impressive* and *remarkable*; and (3) the adjectives related to having "fun", enjoyment, amusement, or light-hearted pleasure within the session, such as *hilarious*. For the subtheme "collaboration" we coded (1) the adjectives regarding "interaction", reciprocal action within the session and the other participants, such as: *dynamic* and *interactive*; (2) the adjectives regarding "collaborative" behaviours, where two or more parties work together, such as: *brainstorming* and *sociable*; (3) and the adjectives related to "learn", gain or acquire knowledge of something through experience, or being taught together with the other participants, such as *thoughtful* and *educational*. For the subtheme "innovation", we coded (1) the adjectives that defined the session as something "creative", relating to or involving the imagination or original ideas, especially in the production of an artistic work, such as *original* and *unique*; and (2) the adjectives concerning the session as "innovative", featuring new methods – advanced and original, such as *evolution* and *future*. For the subtheme "simple", we coded the adjectives which featured the experience as "easy" to take, presenting no difficulty, such as *approachable* and *easy*.

3.2 Negative Evaluation

Inside the *Negative Evaluation* theme (11 evaluations), we inserted all the subthemes which are related to negative experiences regarding the co-design sessions in which participants took part. We coded 3 subthemes for this theme: (1) complex, (2) unexciting, and (3) obtrusive. For the subtheme "complex" we coded the adjectives that described the session as "tricky", requiring care and skill because difficult or awkward, such as *complicated* and *complex*. For the subtheme "unexciting" we coded (1) the adjectives that referred to the session as "uninteresting", not arousing curiosity or interest; and (2) the ones concerning the session as "not appealing" such as *awful*. For the subtheme "obtrusive" we coded (1) the adjectives that described the session as "uncomfortable", causing or feeling slight discomfort, such as *annoying*; and (2) the ones that described the session as "repetitive", the action of repeating something that has already been said or written, such as *repetition*.

3.3 Neutral Evaluation

Inside the *Negative Evaluation* theme (8 evaluations), we inserted all the subthemes which refer to the co-design session as impartial, not helping or supporting either side – positive nor negative. We coded 2 subthemes for this theme: (1) diverse, and (2) somewhat. For the subtheme "diverse" we coded the adjectives that described the session as "different", not the same as another similar activity – unlike in nature, form, or quality that the participants are usually used, such as *different* and *fishes*. For the subtheme "somewhat" we coded (1) the adjectives that described the session as "in-different", having no particular interest or sympathy, such as *unconcerned*; and (2) the ones that described the session as "more or less", neither very good nor very bad, such as *so-so*.

4   Concluding Remarks

It is essential to have the perception of the participants on the co-design conducted to understand if teenagers are willing to jointly contribute with their thoughts for a common idea – in this case, for designing mobile technology to enhance their own experiences in a natural history museum. The good thing about applying a word association to gather feedback on the sessions from the participants it is because not only it is faster, but also it is a procedure for investigating which word meanings related to the session are stored in memory. Judging from the overall positive evaluation of the experience, participants enjoyed designing their ideal experiences in museums in a co-design session. However, as a limitation of this analysis, we cannot infer that all participants enjoyed the sessions because of its method or if they enjoyed it because it was conducted instead of a regular lecture.

Acknowledgments.   ARDITI, project number M14-20-09-5369-FSE-000001.

References

1. Cesário, V., Matos, S., Radeta, M., Nisi, V.: Designing interactive technologies for interpretive exhibitions: enabling teen participation through user-driven innovation. In: Bernhaupt, R., Dalvi, G., Joshi, A., Balkrishan, D., O'Neill, J., Winckler, M. (eds.) INTERACT 2017. LNCS, vol. 10513, pp. 232–241. Springer, Cham (2017). https://doi.org/10.1007/978-3-319-67744-6_16
2. Cesário, V., Coelho, A., Nisi, V.: Cultural heritage professionals developing digital experiences targeted at teenagers in museum settings: lessons learned. In: 32nd British Human Computer Interaction Conference, pp. 1–12 (2018). https://doi.org/10.14236/ewic/HCI2018.58
3. Cesário, V.: Analysing texts and drawings: the teenage perspective on enjoyable museum experiences. In: 32nd British Human Computer Interaction Conference, pp. 1–3 (2018). https://doi.org/10.14236/ewic/HCI2018.215

4. Cesário, V., Coelho, A., Nisi, V.: Design patterns to enhance teens' museum experiences. In: 32nd British Human Computer Interaction Conference, pp. 1–5 (2018). https://doi.org/10. 14236/ewic/HCI2018.160
5. Jung, C.G.: Studies in Word-Association. Routledge & K. Paul, London (1969)
6. Braun, V., Clarke, V.: Using thematic analysis in psychology. Qual. Res. Psychol. **3**, 77–101 (2006). https://doi.org/10.1191/1478088706qp063oa

Panels

Social Media and the Digital Enterprise

Wietske Van Osch[1]([✉]), Constantinos K. Coursaris[2], Dov Te'eni[3],
and George Giaglis[4]

[1] Michigan State University, East Lansing, MI 48824, USA
vanosch@msu.edu
[2] HEC Montreal, 3000 Chemin de La Côte-Sainte-Catherine, Montréal,
QC H3T 2A7, Canada
[3] Tel Aviv University, Tel Aviv-Yafo, Israel
[4] University of Nicosia, Nicosia, Cyprus

Abstract. Over the last decade, the role of social media in enabling the digital enterprise has been rapidly growing. In order for digital enterprises to embrace the opportunities afforded by social media technologies, including the use of social media for both inward- and external-facing communications and collaborations, several issues need to be addressed. The panelists will discuss contemporary issues and potential strategies to help establish a roadmap for social media research in the context of digital enterprises and digital transformation.

Keywords: Enterprise social media · Social media · Digital transformation · Business analytics · Knowledge Collaboration · Blockchain · Digital marketing

1 Social Media and the Digital Enterprise: A Research Agenda

The modern organization is a digital enterprise and part of a digital ecosystem, "a grouping of enterprises, competitors, customers, regulators and other stakeholders that exchange information and interact electronically" [1]. Although the digital enterprise is a topic of increasing focus for information systems and technology scholars, the practical relevance is also underscored by the tremendous growth in investments in digital transformation projects forecasted to increase 42% to $1.7 trillion by 2019 [2].

One of the main information and communication technologies (ICTs) at the heart of the digital enterprise is social media, a group of Internet-based applications that supports various actors in a multiplicity of communication activities for producing user-generated content, developing and maintaining connections and social relationships, or enabling other computer-mediated interactions and collaborations [3, 4].

Social media have reshaped almost every dimension of organizational communication and collaboration, both internally and externally. With social media spending estimated at $100 billion worldwide and 80% of companies currently using some form of enterprise social media (ESM), there is little scholarly guidance to identify ways in which today's organizations can make profitable, yet, safe and ethical usage of social media.

© IFIP International Federation for Information Processing 2019
Published by Springer Nature Switzerland AG 2019
D. Lamas et al. (Eds.): INTERACT 2019, LNCS 11749, pp. 701–705, 2019.
https://doi.org/10.1007/978-3-030-29390-1_66

Several areas appear to be in dire need for scholarly guidance, including:

- *Social Media and Intra-organizational Knowledge Collaborations:* Organizations have high hopes of social media to enhance knowledge transfer within and into the organization. Yet there is little evidence that social media, instead of extant knowledge management tools, successfully enhance knowledge transfer in organizations, while there is ample evidence that social media is an effective communication medium for social and professional communities. In fact, there is some evidence that social media may give an illusion of knowledge transfer with little actual learning. The panel will explore how knowledge transfer in organizations can be enabled through social media.

- *Social Media Marketing:* Investments in social media advertising continue to increase and social media ad revenue was estimated at $51.3 billion for 2018 [5]. Possibly the most researched topic pertaining to social media, the landscape of social media technologies and marketing tactics are constantly changing, requiring scholarly guidance. In this panel, we will focus on some of the latest industry trends, including omnichannel and influencer marketing, as well as topics pertaining to measuring the ROI of social media marketing.

- *Social Media Analytics:* Organizations are making growing investments in big data analytics [6]. A major source of data for such analytics is social media. Although the focus has hitherto been on using consumer data for marketing purposes, there is increasing awareness of how data from internal social media or ESM can be used by companies to build better work environments, improved collaboration, and foster greater innovation. This panel will showcase scholarly research on how to measure and visualize the digital traces from social media behaviors and content to provide managerial guidance for supporting evidence-based and increasingly automated decision-making in all strategic matters.

- *Blockchain and Social Media:* Social media platforms were initially hailed as the apotheosis of digital democracy, but were soon found to be plagued by a number of issues, not least the algorithmic decision making of which items to appear first in users' timelines. Blockchain can tackle this problem by allowing for decentralized applications, which actively encourage user participation by allowing voting on content trustworthiness and influencing the reputation of content generators and sharers. We will discuss how Blockchain-based platforms may combine information cascade verification with information trustworthiness scoring, benefitting from Blockchain technology to ensure transparency of the scoring process and that information has not been modified in a cascade.

Academic research is growing in these areas yet the relative volume of research publications has not reached a level that parallels the importance of these themes in industry. This panel will bring together a group of world-renowned experts that are at the forefront of research and practice on these and other topics related to social media and the digital enterprise.

2 Example Panel Questions

- *Unexplored research questions and agenda:* What may we recommend as a scholarly agenda for the research community in this context? Which questions regarding digital transformation can be investigated from a social media perspective? Questions framing the panelists discussion include the following:
    - What will be the main roles of social media in the digital enterprise of the future?
    - What is limiting social media in being an effective means of knowledge transfer?
    - How will Blockchain disrupt the social media landscape by allowing for trustful, user-oriented and secure decentralized social network platforms?
    - How can we use decentralized social media platforms to address the problem of trust (e.g. fake news spreading)?
- *Training digital transformation and social media practitioners:* How can we effectively train the current and next generation of practitioners using social media to enable digital transformation in enterprise settings?
- *Collaborations with social media researchers:* Where can we network with fellow social media scholars interested in interdisciplinary research? How can a mutually beneficial value proposition be generated?
- *Measurement on social media:* What is the role of data analytics, not only in facilitating better use of social media but also in enabling the most productive use of these tools in the context of digital transformation? What are the key analytics informing a digital enterprise strategy?

3 Panelist Biographies

Wietske Van Osch (vanosch@msu.edu) is an Associate Professor in the Department of Media and at Michigan State University. She received her Ph.D. in Economics (Information Systems) from the University of Amsterdam's Business School. Her research work has appeared in numerous high-impact, peer-reviewed journals including the *Journal of Management Information Systems*, *Journal of Information Technology*, *Information and Management*, and leading conferences, including the *International Conference on Information Systems*. Her current research interests focus on the role of enterprise social media (ESM) in team collaboration, knowledge management, boundary- spanning, and innovation. Wietske has received a total of $1,000,000 in funding from the National Science Foundation for her work on ESM. According to SCOPUS, Wietske is the most frequently published author in the domain of ESM. Her core research projects involve extensive industry collaborations for research on ESM, data science/artificial intelligence, and social media marketing with multinational companies including Steelcase and Leo Burnett.

Constantinos K. Coursaris (coursari@msu.edu) is Associate Professor in the Department of Information Technologies at HEC Montreal. Constantinos studies user motivations, expectations, and experiences with new media and the consequent design implications with a focus on social systems. His research is at the intersection of usability and mobile technologies for the purpose of health and/or commercial applications. Constantinos' research has been published in top peer-reviewed journals, such as *Information & Management, New Media & Society, Computers in Human Behavior, Transactions on Human-Computer Interaction,* and *Online Information Review*, among others. Working in interdisciplinary teams, he has received $4 million in external funding to support his research. He consults on social media for governance and/or marketing, and has trained organizations in North America, Europe, Middle East and North Africa, and ranks among the Top 50 Marketing Professors on Twitter.

Dov Te'eni is Research Associate Dean at the *School of Business, Tel Aviv University* and holds the *IS Mexico Chair*. Dov currently studies visualization and feedback, combining human and machine intelligence, and knowledge sharing. Dov has co-authored (with Zhang and Carey) a book published by Wiley- *Human-computer interaction for developing effective organizational systems* and co-edited (with Schwartz) the *Encyclopedia of Knowledge Management*, as well as other books on information systems and innovation. He has published articles in Management Science, MIS Quarterly, Organization Science, IEEE Transactions, JAIS, JASIST amongst other journals, and has served on the boards of *MIS Quarterly, AIS Transactions of HCI, JAIS, Information and Organizations,* and *Internet Research*. He is co-editor of *European Journal of IS*. Dov was awarded the *AIS Fellowship* (2008) and *LEO* award (2015).

Professor George M. Giaglis is General Director of the Institute for the Future at the University of Nicosia, as well as a leading expert on blockchain technology and applications and advisor to many blockchain projects and technology start-ups. Prior to joining UNIC, he was Professor at the Athens University of Economics and Business (2002–2017), where he also served as Vice Rector (2011–2015). George has been working on digital currencies and blockchain since 2012, with his main focus being on new forms of industrial organization (programmable smart contracts, decentralized applications and distributed autonomous organizations) and new forms of corporate financing (token economy, crypto-economics and ICOs). He has been one of the first academics to research and teach on blockchain, having: designed the curriculum of the world's first full academic degree on blockchain (MSc in Digital Currency at the University of Nicosia); led the development of blockchain credentialing technology that has resulted in the first ever publishing of academic certificates on the blockchain; taught on the disruptive innovation potential of blockchain, both at academic programs and in executive seminars worldwide; organized a number of prominent blockchain conferences and events, including Decentralized. Throughout his career, he has published more than 10 books and 150 articles in leading scientific journals and conferences, while he is frequently interviewed by media and invited as keynote speaker or trainer in events across the globe. He is the Chief Editor for Blockchain Technology at the Frontiers in Blockchain Journal and member of the Editorial Board at Ledger.

Acknowledgment. This material is based upon work supported by the National Science Foundation under Grant No. 1749018. Any opinions, findings, and conclusions or recommendations expressed in this material are those of the author(s) and do not necessarily reflect the views of the National Science Foundation.

References

1. Van Osch, W., Coursaris, C.K.: The duality of social media: enabling structuration and socialization through organizational communication. In: 11th Pre-International Conference on Information Systems Workshop on HCI Research in MIS, Orlando (2012)
2. Gartner: Gartner Survey of More Than 2,500 CIOs Charts the Rise of the Digital Ecosystem. http://www.gartner.com/newsroom/id/3481117. Accessed 8 Apr 2019
3. IDC: IDC FutureScape: Worldwide Digital Transformation Predictions (2018). https://www.idc.com/getdoc.jsp?containerId=US43154617. Accessed 8 Apr 2019
4. Kaplan, A.M., Haenlein, M.: Users of the world, unite! The challenges and opportunities of social media. Bus. Horiz. **53**(1), 59–68 (2010)
5. Cooper, P.: Social Media Advertising Stats that Matter to Marketers in (2018). https://blog.hootsuite.com/social-media-advertising-stats/. Accessed 8 Apr 2019
6. Columbus, L.: Data Analytics Dominates Enterprises' Spending Plans For (2015). https://www.forbes.com/sites/louiscolumbus/2015/03/15/data-analytics-dominates-enterprises-spending-plans-for-2015/#6ed5c4e18016. Accessed 8 Apr 2019

User Experience in an Automated World

Philippe Palanque[4(✉)], Pedro F. Campos[2], José Abdelnour Nocera[1,2],
Torkil Clemmensen[3], and Virpi Roto[5]

[1] University of West London, London, UK
jose.abdelnour-nocera@uwl.ac.uk
[2] Madeira-ITI, University of Madeira, Funchal, Portugal
pedro.campos@m-iti.org
[3] Department of Digitalization, Copenhagen Business School,
Frederiksberg, Denmark
tc.digi@cbs.dk
[4] ICS-IRIT, Université Paul Sabatier Toulouse 3, Toulouse, France
palanque@irit.fr
[5] School of Arts, Design and Architecture, Aalto University, Helsinki, Finland
virpi.roto@aalto.fi

Abstract. The aim of this panel is to raise awareness and to foster discussions around the notions of Automation and User Experience and their interplay in the design, development, evaluation and deployment of interactive systems. User Experience is taken in its broad meaning as defined in the white paper of https://www.allaboutux.org/ [11]. As for automation we consider here its wide perspective as proposed in [4] – The Seven Deadly Myths of "Autonomous Systems". In a time where there is strong push towards more and more automation in our daily life, the panel will question the impact of such trend on users' experiences in multiple contexts such as work, entertainment, learning, as well as question other important emerging issues such as ethics, engagement and automation rationale.

Keywords: Automation · User Experience · Engagement · Interaction design · Work

1 Introduction and Questions

Interaction design for work engagement has lately started to gather more attention, especially in designing interactive systems for employees at their workplace. As algorithms and machines take over parts of the work which were previously performed manually, a larger part of the work engagement is dependent on the employees' experience with (partly-) automated systems. Is automation making work less interesting or more engaging? How to improve work engagement through automation? How to optimally allocate work between humans and automation? How to maintain operators' vigilance in highly automated environments? How to support situation and/or automation awareness? How to evaluate the impact of automation on work engagement? How increased automation raises ethics issues? This panel aims to discuss these questions and to provide a forum for researchers, practitioners, and anyone engaged in

© IFIP International Federation for Information Processing 2019
Published by Springer Nature Switzerland AG 2019
D. Lamas et al. (Eds.): INTERACT 2019, LNCS 11749, pp. 706–710, 2019.
https://doi.org/10.1007/978-3-030-29390-1_67

work analysis and interaction design for the workplace. We will discuss tools, procedures, and professional competences needed for designing and evaluating engaging automation in workplace contexts.

2 Panel Topics and Objectives

The panel will bring diverse (potentially conflicting) perspectives on User Experience in a world that embeds increasing automation.

While early approaches in automation were focusing on allocating basic functions to the best player (e.g. Fitts' approach Machine Are Better At – Men Are Better At) [6], this panel focuses on the combined use of the concepts of automation within interactive systems development. The current push in automation is towards fully autonomous systems (such as google cars or robotic software agents in the case-handling processes of public service provision). This push raises critical issues such as: how to make it possible for users to foresee future states of the automation, how to disengage automation or how to make sure that users are able to take over when automation fails, and how to make sure that the highly qualified human does not completely loose interest in the automated processes.... When higher automation levels are considered [10], users' activity gets closer to supervision [7], which is a different interaction paradigm deeply impacting user experience. One question that the panel will address is **"how to keep employees motivated when automation pervades the workplace?"** However, recent studies [12] have demonstrated that very limited research work has been carried out on UX aspects in work environments, surprisingly leaving this aspect to practitioners. One question to consider is **"why is there limited research work at the intersection of automation, UX and work?"**.

When designing for User Experience, the focus is mostly put on users' emotions, aesthetics, users' stimulation, affinity towards a certain product or service as well as other aspect. Sometimes UX is performed overlooking usability concepts such as efficiency and effectiveness. In domains such as entertainment, UX is key and automation serves as a mean to improve UX. One question that the panel will consider is: **"is there a UX in automation that goes beyond games?"**

3 Panelists

The panel will be moderated by Pedro F. Campos who will be checking fairness and politeness in the arguments developed by the panelists. Beyond, he will also ensure that space is left for interaction with the audience.

Philippe Palanque (convener) – Automation and UX in Safety Critical Systems

In safety critical systems automation is a first class citizen with a very polymorphic nature. Autonomous systems can be there to protect the system (e.g. Traffic Collision Avoidance Systems), to increase comfort by migrating actions to an autonomous system (e.g. autopilot) but also to increase operations when conditions are not met (e.g. auto land system). UX is a second class citizen as major focus in design is on overall safety of operations.

Philippe is Professor in Computer Science at the University Toulouse 3. He is working on formal methods for engineering interactive systems and the application of such techniques to Higher Automation Levels in the field of Air Traffic Management, Interactive Cockpits of Large Civil Aircrafts [3] and Satellite Ground Segments. He was chair of (Application and Theories of Automation in Command and Control Systems) ATACCS 2015 conference and co-organized a workshop on Automation and autonomous vehicles [8]. Philippe has also co-organized several courses on automation (e.g. [9]) and has long been active in SIGCHI and other international societies such as IFIP.

Pedro F. Campos (moderator) – Automation and UX in Physical Artefacts
How can automation become embedded into the fabrics of everyday life in such a way that it *augments* human capabilities, as opposed to simply automate repetitive tasks or oversee human action in critical situations? One possible research approach is based on taking concepts from behavioral economics (e.g. nudging) and exploiting our innate cognitive biases to guide users' behavior towards the desired UX goals.

Pedro is Associate Professor with Habilitation at the University of Madeira, Portugal, and scientific director of the Madeira Interactive Technologies Institute. Pedro leads the Experience Augmentation group, bridging cognitive augmentation with experience design and exploring novel systems to augment human cognition and to design better user experiences. He has co-organized many workshops [15] and has also hosted conferences on work engagement and automation [2].

José Abdelnour Nocera – Automation, User Experience and Ethics
There a number of ethical considerations when choosing how and what to automate about work from a designer's perspective. These have to do with workers' and organizations' abilities to understand and experience the rationale for automating. In my short statement I will present these issues through ongoing case studies in a UK airport and an Indian fishing village.

José is Associate Professor in Sociotechnical Design and Head of the Sociotechnical Centre for Innovation and User Experience at the University of West London. He is the current Chair for IFIP TC 13.8 working group in Interaction Design for International Development as well as Chair for the British Computer Society Sociotechnical Specialist Group. His interests lie in the sociotechnical and cultural aspects of systems design, development and use. In pursuing these interests, he has been involved as researcher and consultant in several projects in the UK and overseas in the domains of mHealth, e-learning, social development, e-commerce, e-governance and enterprise resource planning systems. Dr. Abdelnour-Nocera gained an MSc in Social Psychology from Simon Bolivar University, Venezuela and a PhD in Computing from The Open University, UK.

Torkil Clemmensen – UX and Automation in SMEs
Automation is currently flooding SMEs (small and medium sized enterprises) to help develop their capacity to produce in a globalized world and ensure workers' wellbeing. One example of this is the use of collaborative robots' to extend and transform SME's manufacturing of specialized products, and to automate workers' repetitive work sequences. However, the collaborative robot requires specialized knowledge in

workers, thus reduces flexibility in its application, and it imposes its limitations and rhythm onto the workflow. Given that the human worker is supposed to collaborate with and not 'experience' the robot, should we as researchers continue to talk about workers' user experiences of automation?

Torkil Clemmensen, PhD, Professor at Department of IT Management, Copenhagen Business School, Denmark. His interest is in Human-Computer Interaction, in particular psychology as a science of design. As Danish representative in IFIP (International Federation of Information Processing) TC 13 (Technical committee on Human-Computer Interaction), and vice-chair of Working Group 13.6 on Human Work Interaction Design (HWID), he co-organizes a series of international working conferences on work analysis and usability/user experiences in organizational, human, social, cultural, and technological contexts. The long term aim is to develop a Human Work Interaction Design (HWID) framework as an easy-to-use development platform for a multitude of analytical tools for socio-technical interventions in various work domains [1, 5]. One recent example of this is a running project on using a HWID approach to empower workers to co-design their user experiences and collaboration with collaborative robots in a Danish glass processing SME.

Virpi Roto – UX and Automation in Remote Operations and Industry
Introducing AI systems in industry may look fancy from the technology perspective, but for me as a UX researcher, it looks like a jump back to 1970's: Suddenly, employees are the servants of the admirable computer systems again. As in the first wave of HCI, the focus is back on the human factors and ethical aspects of AI systems. I wish it will not take 30 years again to see that good user experience is in the core of computer systems, also in AI systems with high levels of automation.

Virpi Roto is a Professor of Practice in Experience Design in Aalto University, Finland. She has studied user experience of consumer products in Nokia Research Center for 15 years and UX of interactive products and services in heavy industry contexts for 8 years. One of the research projects study industrial automation, bringing the human perspectives such as UX, engagement, and ethics on the table.

4 Audience and Prerequisite

This panel is open to researchers, practitioners, educators and students of all experience levels. We especially welcome attendees who would like to debate the topics presented above. We also expect attendees to report on their experiences with design, development of use of automation within interactive technologies.

References

1. Abdelnour-Nocera, J., Clemmensen, T.: Theorizing about socio-technical approaches to HCI. In: Barricelli, B.R., et al. (eds.) HWID 2018. IAICT, vol. 544, pp. 242–262. Springer, Cham (2019). https://doi.org/10.1007/978-3-030-05297-3_17
2. Barricelli, B., et al.: Human-Work Interaction Design (HWID'18) – Designing Engaging Automation. IFIP Advances in Information and Communication Technology, vol. 544. Springer, Heidelberg (2019). https://doi.org/10.1007/978-3-030-05297-3

3. Bernhaupt, R., Cronel, M., Manciet, F., Martinie, C., Palanque, P.: Transparent automation for assessing and designing better interactions between operators and partly-autonomous interactive systems. In: ATACCS 2015, pp. 129–139. ACM DL (2015)
4. Bradshaw, J., Hoffman, R., Woods, D., Johnson, M.: The seven deadly myths of "autonomous systems". IEEE Intell. Syst. **28**(3), 54–61 (2013)
5. Clemmensen, T.: Designing a simple folder structure for a complex domain. Hum. Technol. Interdisc. J. Hum. ICT Environ. **7**(3), 216–249 (2011)
6. Fitts, P.M.: Human Engineering for an Effective Air Navigation and Traffic Control System. National Research Council, Washington (1951)
7. Mackworth, N.H.: The breakdown of vigilance during prolonged visual search. Q. J. Exp. Psychol. **1**, 6–21 (1948)
8. Meschtscherjakov, A., et al.: Interacting with autonomous vehicles: learning from other domains. In: CHI Conference (CHI EA 2018). ACM DL (2018)
9. Palanque, P., Martinie, C., Fayollas, C.: Automation: danger or opportunity? Designing and assessing automation for interactive systems. In: CHI Conference Extended Abstracts (CHI EA 2017). ACM DL (2017)
10. Parasuraman, R., Sheridan, T.B., Wickens, C.D.: A model for types and levels of human interaction with automation. IEEE Trans. Syst. Man Cybern. Part A Syst. Hum. **30**(3), 286–297 (2000)
11. Roto, V., Law, E., Vermeeren, A., Hoonhout, J. (eds).: User experience white paper – bringing clarity to the concept of user experience. In: Outcome of the Dagstuhl Seminar on Demarcating User Experience, Germany (2011). http://www.allaboutux.org/uxwhitepaper
12. Roto, V., Palanque, P., Karvonen, H.: Engaging automation at work – a literature review. In: Barricelli, B.R., et al. (eds.) HWID 2018. IAICT, vol. 544, pp. 158–172. Springer, Cham (2019). https://doi.org/10.1007/978-3-030-05297-3_11

Workshops

Challenging Misinformation: Exploring Limits and Approaches

Lara S. G. Piccolo[1]([✉]) [iD], Somya Joshi[2] [iD], Evangelos Karapanos[3] [iD], and Tracie Farrell[1] [iD]

[1] Knowledge Media Institute, The Open University, Milton Keynes MK7 8FE, UK
{lara.piccolo,tracie.farrell}@open.ac.uk
[2] eGovlab, Stockholm University, 16407 Stockholm, Sweden
somya@dsv.su.se
[3] Cyprus University of Technology, Limassol, Cyprus
evangelos.karapanos@cut.ac.cy

Abstract. The manipulation of information and the dissemination of *"fake news"* are practices that trace back to the early records of human history. Significant changes in the technological environment enabling ubiquity, immediacy and considerable anonymity, have facilitated the spreading of misinformation in unforeseen ways, raising concerns around people's (mis)perception of social issues worldwide. As a wicked problem, limiting the harm caused by misinformation goes beyond technical solutions, requiring also regulatory and behavioural changes. This workshop proposes to unpack the challenge at hand by bringing together diverse perspectives to the problem. Based on participatory design principles, it will challenge participants to critically reflect the limits of existing sociotechnical approaches and co-create scenarios in which digital platforms support misinformation resilience.

Keywords: Co-creation · Misinformation · Disinformation · Fake news

1 Context

The acknowledged influence of social media on the results of the UK's Brexit *referendum* and Donald Trump's election in the US, for example, are examples of the magnitude of the power granted to the online world to transform reality [3]. In such context, *misleading information*[1], be it deliberately false or not, is continuously harming individuals and societies by threatening democratic political processes and distorting values that shape public opinion in a variety of sectors,

---

[1] **Misinformation** refers to misleading information created without the intention to harm, while **disinformation** refers to deliberate fabricated information with the intention to impact social groups or societies. As a simplification, we refer to misinformation to represent the complexity of this information disorder.

© IFIP International Federation for Information Processing 2019
Published by Springer Nature Switzerland AG 2019
D. Lamas et al. (Eds.): INTERACT 2019, LNCS 11749, pp. 713–718, 2019.
https://doi.org/10.1007/978-3-030-29390-1_68

such as health and science (i.e. anti-vaccines movement [9]), foreign policy (i.e. Iraq war [10]), etc., and now in global scale [4].

Information disorder [2,8] has long been examined from multiple perspectives, including social science, journalism, psychology, and computer science [6]. As a *wicked problem*, there is not a single and comprehensive solution capable to stop misinformation. In Fig. 1, we graphically summarise some key aspects related to the spread of misinformation from a social (people's values, beliefs, motivations), regulatory and technical (social media, detection tools) perspectives, as well as some factors crossing boundaries, such as information literacy, with regulatory and social components, and social media regulations and fact-checking that concerns both regulatory and technical aspects.

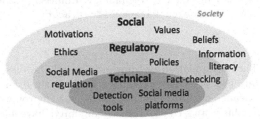

Fig. 1. Social, regulatory and technical aspects of misinformation as a social issue

In such a scenario, social media players, technology designers, policymakers, journalists, educators and citizens are all stakeholders with some responsibility in understanding the problem on its complexity and come up with pieces of solutions that will limit the spread and impact of misinformation worldwide.

Examining the limits of human cognition for dealing with and spreading misinformation [12,13], exploring approaches to nudge [11], 'vaccinating' social media users [1], fact-checking more effectively [5], automating detection and correction [7] are some of the approaches that have been currently explored in the literature. However, as pointed out in [6], existing approaches are all limited. With few exceptions, they tend to consider technology users as passive consumers rather than active co-creators, learners, and detectors of misinformation. We argue that more comprehensive solutions can only emerge when there is an articulation of diverse ideas and approaches, requiring the participation of different stakeholders, and including end users, social scientists, computer scientists, educators, and others, in the co-creation of their features, user interfaces, and delivery methods.

2   Objectives

The goal of this workshop is to propose an agenda for interdisciplinary research that critically analyses and aggregates socio-technical solutions that establish fundamental limits to misinformation. To this end, the workshop will engage the participants in:

- Discussing challenges and obstacles related to misinformation;
- Challenging existing approaches to tackle misinformation and identifying their limitations;
- Mapping stakeholders, and questioning the relationships between them;
- Co-creating future scenarios where digital platforms support misinformation resilience;
- Identifying criteria for assessing the potential of different solutions to make impact.

The workshop will be of interest to researchers and practitioners that hope to impact society through the design and development of socio-technical systems in the social media context, and it's current struggles between what is considered fact and fiction. As a longer-term goal, the workshop aims at building a multidisciplinary research community focusing on the design of misinformation resilient societies.

3   Workshop Rationale

The workshop is grounded on the principles of co-creation [14], focusing on where and what value is created with the digital solution [15]. The workshop agenda will engage participants in activities that challenge the status-quo and promote creative-thinking towards creating innovative solutions. Participants will be encouraged to ask questions, be critical, active, and bold in the idea-generation process.

3.1   Participation

Not only interaction designers researchers and practitioners will be invited to participate but also some journalists, educators, policymakers or other related stakeholders. The call for papers will be distributed via the network of a European project on misinformation, authors of related papers found at digital libraries, HCI-related mailing lists, and social media in general.

Participants will be encouraged to submit a 2 to 4 pages position paper describing their approach towards fighting misinformation, acknowledged limits of the approach, and how they envision a future in which the societies are more resilient to information disorder.

The number of participants should be between 12 to 20 in order to keep group activities feasible and interesting.

Topics of interest include, but are not limited to: socio-technical empirical studies, motivational and behavioral studies, human values, persuasive technology, games, gamification, information and media literacy, fact-checking, social media policies and regulation, automated tools for misinformation detection and notifications, legal and ethical aspects.

3.2   Overall Structure

The activities of this one-day workshop will be split into 2 main parts: during the morning, participants will debate and critically analyse existing approaches and solutions to tackle misinformation, while the afternoon activities will target future scenarios where digital innovations will support misinformation resilience. The core activities of the workshop have already been applied in different contexts and research scenarios. They are:

- **Ice-breaker (30")**: Everyone gets a cup of drink on which there is a label with a provocative 'fact' designed to spark a debate. Participants talk and validate/check these facts together, some reporting back to the entire group. After that, a quick round of introductions will happen.
- **Setting the stage (15")**: A short opening talk given by an inspirational speaker on a topic that undercuts the discussions of the day, either fact checking or social media and misinformation.
- **Mapping the Terrain (40")**: In groups, participants storyboard the present and map perceptions of stakeholders involved in the decision-making process of spreading or stopping misinformation, discussing their role and relations. The activity will involve some props, like the wooden dolls in Fig. 2, representing the stakeholders, their values and connections.

Fig. 2. Stakeholders mapping exercise using wooden dolls

- **Role Play (60")**: Group exercise to change perspectives, lenses and orientations. Validating the stakeholders map built previously, participants will swap perspectives by wearing different hats (fact-checker could take on the role of policymaker, for example) and identify positive and negative points in the relationship and communication between stakeholders. Each group present their sketches/maps to other groups.
- **Lightning Talks (60")**: The attendees will present a 3 min lightening talks on their area of research, providing inspirational content for the second part of the day, focusing on future research.
- **Future Making (120")**: The organisers first introduce the future-thinking part of the workshop by demonstrating a vision of future research communities, as a "food for thought". This can be done also by presenting iconic images and artifacts that reflect and provoke future imaginations. Then, the *Horns*

of the Dilemma co-creation exercise will engage participants with identifying criteria for assessing an innovation's potential for impact, such as tools to resolve the fact or diction' dichotomy, for example. The participants pinpoint the most promising points of intervention ('leverage points'), at each scale in the system, considering also particular concerns of other stakeholders along the journey. This process reveals the bottlenecks - the limits - and leverage points when describing futures.

- **Wrap up and Next Steps (45"):** The organisers summarise the discussions and insights and weave a red thread around the narrative. They will open up the discussion on next steps and future research, thereby paving the way for efforts that will take place collectively to publish and further research in this area.

More details on the workshop program and call for papers are available at the workshop website: http://events.kmi.open.ac.uk/misinformation/.

4   Organisers

The four organisers share the common challenge of co-designing interactive technology to foster critical thinking and digital literacy for a better-informed and resilient society.

Lara Piccolo investigates interaction design with a socio-technical and inclusive perspective, considering how technology can trigger a positive impact on people's lives. Community engagement, motivations and values are important drivers of her research. Her current research looks at voice-based systems to raise awareness of misinformation. Lara is also an Associated Lecturer on Interaction Design and User Experience.

Somya Joshi is an expert in the field of Sustainable Human-Computer Interaction (SHCI). Her specialisation falls within the applied context of technological innovation, particularly in how it translates into transparency in governance, environmental conservation and citizen engagement. She has experience working with a range of partners from academia, industry, NGOs, as well as international development organizations towards the common goal of facilitating inclusive development. Currently, Somya is Head of Research at *eGovernance-Lab*.

Evangelos Karapanos directs the *Persuasive Technologies Lab*. Evangelos' expertise is in experience-centered design of interaction with technology. His ongoing work explores technology-mediated nudging interventions for misinformation-resilient societies.

Tracie Farrell is a non-formal education specialist. Her research interests focus on technologies for awareness and reflection. In particular, she examines how technology can trigger metacognitive activity.

5   Expected Outcome

The accepted position papers will be published in the official adjunct conference proceedings. Furthermore, the main workshop results will be further disseminated to a wider audience via a poster presentation and a video reaching out the overall Interact community. The website will also be updated with the accepted papers and a summary of the workshop outcomes.

The possibility of a special journal issue will be discussed with the participants as a way to strengthen the community.

Acknowledgment. This workshop proposal has been supported by the EC within the Horizon 2020 programme under grant agreement 770302 - Co-Inform.

References

1. Van der Linden, S., et al.: Inoculating the public against misinformation about climate change. Glob. Challenges **1**(2) (2017). https://doi.org/10.1002/gch2.201600008
2. Claire, W., Hossein, D.: Information disorder: Toward an interdisciplinary framework for research and policymaking. Technical report, Council of Europe (2017). http://rm.coe.int/information-disorder-report-version-august-2018/16808c9c77
3. DiFranzo, D., Gloria-Garcia, K.: Filter bubbles and fake news. XRDS **23**(3), 32–35 (2017). https://doi.org/10.1145/3055153
4. European Commission - Directorate-General for Communications Networks, Content and Technology: A multi-dimensional approach to disinformation. Technical report, European Commission (2018). https://publications.europa.eu/s/iOLW
5. Facebook: Hard questions: How is facebook's fact-checking program working? June 2018. https://newsroom.fb.com/news/2018/06/hard-questions-fact-checking/. Accessed 12 Oct 2018
6. Fernandez, M., Alani, H.: Online misinformation: challenges and future directions. In: Companion Proceedings of the Web Conference 2018 (WWW 2018), pp. 595–602 (2018). https://doi.org/10.1145/3184558.3188730
7. Garrett, R.K., Weeks, B.E.: The promise and peril of real-time corrections to political misperceptions. In: Proceedings of the 2013 Conference on Computer supported cooperative work, pp. 1047–1058. ACM (2013)
8. Ireton, E.C., Posetti, J.: Journalism, 'Fake News' and Disinformation Handbook for Journalism Education and Training. United Nations Educational, Scientific and Cultural Organization - UNESCO Publishing, Paris (2018)
9. Kata, A.: A postmodern Pandora's box: anti-vaccination misinformation on the internet. Vaccine **28**(7), 1709–1716 (2010)
10. Kull, S., Ramsay, C., Lewis, E.: Misperceptions, the media, and the Iraq war. Polit. Sci. Q. **118**(4), 569–598 (2003)
11. Levy, N.: Nudges in a post-truth world. J. Med. Ethics **43**(8), 495–500 (2017)
12. Metaxas, P.: Technology, propaganda, and the limits of human intellect. arXiv preprint arXiv:1806.09541 (2018)
13. Pennycook, G., Rand, D.G.: Lazy, not biased: susceptibility to partisan fake news is better explained by lack of reasoning than by motivated reasoning. Cognition **188**, 39–50 (2018)
14. Prahalad, C.K., Ramaswamy, V.: The co-creation connection. Strategy and Business, pp. 50–61 (2002)
15. Voorberg, W.H., Bekkers, V.J., Tummers, L.G.: A systematic review of co-creation and co-production: embarking on the social innovation journey. Public Manag. Rev. **17**(9), 1333–1357 (2015)

Designing for Aging People

Masood Masoodian[1](✉) and Paula Alexandra Silva[2]

[1] School of Arts, Design and Architecture, Aalto University, Espoo, Finland
masood.masoodian@aalto.fi
[2] DigiMedia Research Center, University of Aveiro, Aveiro, Portugal
palexa@gmail.com

Abstract. Most existing design practices either do not specifically target the needs of aging people, or only consider their needs from a negative perspective, often as design "problems" that need to be "solved". However, with the ever-increasing aging world population, it is becoming even more important to better design for older people, taking their wants, needs, desires, and expectations into account as the underlying basis for design. Amongst other issues that need to be addressed, this also requires modifying current design practices, including commonly used design methodologies, to make them more effective for targeting aging user populations. Therefore, the aim of this workshop is to bring together researchers, designers, and developers interested in the design, development, evaluation, and deployment of digital products, technologies, tool, and services for aging people. The workshop will provide a venue for sharing experiences from different perspectives through presentations, discussions, and a hands-on design activity to provide innovative ideas for future directions in designing for aging people.

Keywords: Aging people · Older adults · Design for aging ·
Design without agism · Experience design for aging ·
Emotional design for aging

1 Introduction

It is a well-known fact that the world population is aging [8], with estimates predicting that, for instance, by 2040 over 21% of the population of the United States [10] will be over 65 years old. This is an increasing trend, with longer-term predictions putting the percentage of older population even higher. For example, it is estimated that by 2060, 25% of the population of the United States [9], and by 2070, 42% of the population of the European Union [4] will be over the age of 65 years.

As such, it is clearly important that the design of future products, tools, and services more directly take into consideration the needs, wants, requirements, and expectations of aging people. Furthermore, to make this more realistically possible and practically achievable, current design processes and practices also need to be modified and adapted to better accommodate designing for aging

© IFIP International Federation for Information Processing 2019
Published by Springer Nature Switzerland AG 2019
D. Lamas et al. (Eds.): INTERACT 2019, LNCS 11749, pp. 719–724, 2019.
https://doi.org/10.1007/978-3-030-29390-1_69

user populations. As Dankl [3] points out, the reason "design [for aging] has not yet succeeded [is] because it does not address the most fundamental topic: persisting images of ageing based on models of deficiency." These persistent negative images are perhaps the consequence of holding the attitude that "the person with a stigma is not quite human" [5], and as a result this is hindering serious changes being made in better designing for aging people.

This is particulary true for the design of digital technologies, tools and services, whose designers often have this misconception that older people are not, or have not been in the past, very technologically able. In reality, however, analysts not only point out that it is a misconception that "the 50+ are technologically challenged and unplugged", but in fact, "aging consumers are tech savvy and eager for more" [6]. Similarly, statistics show that, for instance in 2017, one in every three people over 65 years old owned a tablet [2], and that the people in this age group have the highest rates of technology adoption. For example, smartphone adoption by older adults nearly quadrupled in the five years between 2011 and 2016 [1].

While such misconceptions are slowly changing due to the adoption of more innovative, multi-disciplinary, collaborative, and user-led approaches to design, much more progress still needs to be made to change the current mainstream design culture and practices. Furthermore, "to re-design ageing and to change persistent negative images requires the multidimensional inclusion of foresight, insight and engagement", and must be promoted through the adaption of new design methodologies and methods, such as critical and speculative design, which "offer essential tools for creating the widespread momentum required for design age" or "design anthropological methods [which] are vital to contextualising insights on ageing practices" [3].

Despite the importance of this urgent need for change, there are not many opportunities for design researchers and practitioners to meet and discuss their interests and ideas. This workshop aims to provide such a forum, enabling researchers and practitioners to share learnings and experiences related to design, development, evaluation, and deployment of tools and services for aging people.

This workshop follows on from a successful DEAP 2018 workshop [7], which was held as part of the IFIP International Conference on Entertainment Computing (IFIP-ICEC 2018). We have now broadened the scope of this workshop to include all aspects of designing for aging people.

2 Objectives

The aim of this workshop is to promote better design for aging people by taking their wants, needs, desires, and well-being into account as the underlying basis for design, and thus combat ageism in design. To achieve this, the workshop will bring together researchers, designers, and developers interested in the design, development, evaluation, and deployment of digital products, technologies, tool, and services for aging people.

Further to this, the workshop will also provide a venue for sharing experiences from different perspectives, to encourage collaboration across disciplines and professional boundaries between the workshop participants.

3   Contributions

To achieve the above objectives, design researchers and practitioners from related backgrounds were invited to submit their papers reporting their contributions to the topics of the workshop. Proposed topics of interest covered the processes of ideation, design, prototyping, development, evaluation, and deployment of digital products, technologies, tool, and services. Following a peer-review process involving the workshop Program Committee, 5 papers were selected for presentation at the workshop. The abstracts of the selected papers are given below.

Keep on Using IT: Gracefully Adaptive User Interfaces for Digital Seniors. *by: Olof Torgersson and Alexandra Weilenmann*

"By studying how older adults who have been using ICT for a long time make use of technology today, i.e. digital seniors, we aim to contribute to knowledge regarding this growing user group. Over time, the digital senior will represent the typical older ICT user to design for. With a few exceptions, this topic has not been explored much earlier. In our ongoing studies, we examine what specific age-related problems that these digital seniors encounter, as their physical and cognitive capacities decline. In this workshop paper, we present the idea of a solution to designing for digital seniors: gracefully adaptive user interfaces. The idea of gracefully adaptive user interfaces presents a new approach to how one can design ICT that will enable older users to keep on doing what they are accustomed to as long as possible. A gracefully adaptive user interface can be seen as a form of reversed multi-layered design: the system starts out with a full set of features and adopts to the user's skills and abilities by simplifying presentation and features over time. What sets gracefully adaptive user interfaces apart from other approaches to adapting the user interface to the individual, is the strong focus on the specific question of how to create systems that adapts to age-related problems encountered by digital seniors in a disciplined and structured manner. By investigating the concept of gracefully adaptive user interfaces our research will go beyond state of the art in the areas of adaptive and adaptable user interfaces."

Breaking Interaction Barriers: Monitoring Elderly in Natural Settings Exploiting Everyday Objects. *by: Marina Buzzi*

"The European population is aging steadily. As a consequence neurodegenerative pathologies are becoming widespread, impacting heavily on social costs, so it is important to support independent living as long as possible, especially in the healthy elderly. This paper proposes an idea for advancing current monitoring technologies by breaking down the current paradigm and exploiting augmented everyday objects. Monitoring and behavior analysis can be exploited as triggers for motivating behavior changes in an elderly person. Thanks to progress in Internet of Things (IoT) and Artificial Intelligence (AI) one scenario is described to illustrate the proposed design concept. With a collaborative multidisciplinary effort, this view could be fast become a reality."

A Value-Sensitive Toolkit: Bringing Values into the Design Process When Designing for the Elderly. *by: Mert Oktay and Hanna-Liisa Pender*

"This paper gives an overview of developing a design toolkit for designers that would encourage them to keep the human values on the forefront, despite all the other constraints that need to be faced when designing new technologies. The toolkit was validated and refined in a series of workshops with designers and design students. The outcome of the work is a toolkit prototype that includes tools like design fiction, bootlegging and value review. It is intended to be used to compliment a human centred design process after user research to scaffold ideation and tackle design challenges related to aging in place and smart habitats for elderly."

A Storytelling-Based Approach to Designing for the Needs of Ageing People. *by: Elena Comincioli and Masood Masoodian*

"Identifying users' needs is the basis of many design methodologies centred around a problem-solution approach. Ageist views of designers and older adult users themselves, however, negatively affect the use of existing methods for identifying their needs. In this paper, we describe an alternative approach to designing for older adults' needs based on storytelling. We introduce a method which uses a set of visual cards to allow older adult participants to tell their stories in co-design workshops. These stories can then be used to identify their needs."

The Sailboat Exercise as a Method for User Understanding and Requirements Gathering. *by: Paula Alexandra Silva*

"To design digital products and services that truly empower end-users requires that design and development teams involve end-users early and throughout the design process. However, regardless of the wealth of methods available to Human-Computer Interaction designers, to identify tools that are both intuitive to use and allow for the active engagement of end-users, namely through co-design activities, is hardly ever easy. To identify a simple and straightforward method can be challenging especially when the end-user group are older adults. This paper proposes an adaptation of an exercise, traditionally used in agile retrospectives – the sailboat exercise – here modified and tailored to be used as a co-design generative tool for user understanding and requirements gathering. In short, the method leverages the analogy of a sailboat, and its surrounding factors, and combines it with a set of prompt questions, to create a shared understanding between the end-users and the members of the design team and to support identification of users' goals, desires, challenges and frustrations."

4   Workshop Structure

This workshop is structured to be engaging, practical, hands-on, and participatory in its approach. It will include plenty of time for interactions, discussions and exchanges of ideas – leading to concrete outcomes for its participants. The workshop will achieve this through the inclusion of:

- Short presentations of the accepted papers.
- A follow-up interactive session to allow further discussions.
- A collaborative design activity to trial novel approaches to design ideation.
- Creation of a short video for the INTERACT conference to showcase the experience of taking part in this collaborative design activity.
- Concluding discussions and planning of future directions and outcomes.

5   Expected Outcomes

The accepted workshop papers will be published in the adjunct conference proceedings of INTERACT 2019. In addition, through a planned discussion session at the workshop, we will investigate potential future outcomes. These may include a special issue of an international journal and/or a co-authored report for dissemination of the workshop findings. We will also use the workshop website[1] for publicizing its aims and objectives, as well as disseminating its outcomes.

6   Workshop Organizers

Prof. Masood Masoodian leads the Aalto Visual Communication Design (AVCD) research group at Aalto University, Finland. He has a Ph.D. from the University of Waikato, New Zealand. His research interests include visualization, interactive media, and interaction design, with particular interest in designing interactive visualizations to provide effective means of understating information by ordinary people in areas such as health, energy, and sustainability. He is also actively involved in research related to different aspect of designing for older adults, including emotional design for entertainment, health and well-being. Prof. Masoodian has served as the program chair, program committee member, and reviewer for many international conferences and journals. He has also been a co-organizer of several international conferences and workshops.

Dr. Paula Alexandra Silva is a Human-Computer Interaction (HCI) researcher and practitioner whose passion is to understand how to leverage technology to create a better future for us all. She has earned her Ph.D. in Computer Science from the University of Lancaster, United Kingdom. Since finishing her Ph.D. she focuses on designing applications for older adults with a view to improve their overall health and well-being and enable their active participation in society. She is also a passionate teacher who strives to create exceptional learning experiences for her students. She is currently a Research Fellow in the University of Aveiro. Before she held appointments as lecturer at a number of universities, as Postdoc Fellow at the University of Hawai'i and as Senior Scientist at Fraunhofer Portugal, where she managed the Human-Computer Interaction area and group.

---

[1] http://avcd.aalto.fi/deap2019/.

7   Program Committee

Sergi Bermúdez i Badia *(Universidade da Madeira, Portugal)*, Leah Burns *(Aalto University, Finland)*, Elena Comincioli *(Aalto University, Finland)*, Dohee Lee *(Aalto University, Finland)*, Eugène Loos *(University of Amsterdam, The Netherlands)*, Masood Masoodian *(Aalto University, Finland)*, Óscar Mealha *(Universidade de Aveiro, Portugal)*, Francisco Nunes *(Fraunhofer - AICOS, Portugal)*, Thomas Rist *(University of Applied Sciences Augsburg, Germany)*, Rita Santos *(Universidade de Aveiro, Portugal)*, Paula Alexandra Silva *(Universidade de Aveiro, Portugal)*, Telmo Silva *(Universidade de Aveiro, Portugal)*, Ana Vasconcelos *(Fraunhofer – AICOS, Portugal)*, Ana Veloso *Universidade de Aveiro, Portugal)*.

References

1. Anderson, M., Perrin, A.: Tech adoption climbs among older adults (2017). http://www.pewinternet.org/2017/05/17/tech-adoption-climbs-among-older-adults/. Accessed June 2019
2. Anderson, M., Perrin, A.: Technology use among seniors (2017). http://www.pewinternet.org/2017/05/17/technology-use-among-seniors/. Accessed June 2019
3. Dankl, K.: Design age: towards a participatory transformation of images of ageing. Des. Stud. **48**, 30–42 (2017). https://doi.org/10.1016/j.destud.2016.10.004
4. European Union: The 2018 ageing report (2017). https://ec.europa.eu/info/sites/info/files/economy-finance/ip065_en.pdf. Accessed June 2019
5. Goffman, E.: Stigma: Notes on the Management of Spoiled Identity, reissue edn. Touchstone, New York (1986)
6. Irving, P., Chatterjee, A.: The longevity economy: from the elderly, a new source of economic growth (2013). http://www.milkeninstitute.org/publications/view/687. Accessed June 2019
7. Silva, P.A., Masoodian, M.: Designing entertainment for the aging population. In: Clua, E., Roque, L., Lugmayr, A., Tuomi, P. (eds.) ICEC 2018. LNCS, vol. 11112, pp. 345–348. Springer, Cham (2018). https://doi.org/10.1007/978-3-319-99426-0_42
8. United Nations Department of Economic and Social Affairs Population Division: World population ageing (2015). http://www.un.org/en/development/desa/population/publications/pdf/ageing/WPA2015_Report.pdf. Accessed June 2019
9. United States Census Bureau: Facts for features: Older Americans month: May 2016 (2016). https://www.census.gov/newsroom/facts-for-features/2016/cb16-ff08.html. Accessed June 2019
10. United States Department of Health and Human Services: 2017 profile of older Americans (2018). https://www.acl.gov/aging-and-disability-in-america/data-and-research/profile-older-americans. Accessed June 2019

HCI Challenges in Human Movement Analysis

Lilian Genaro Motti Ader[1(✉)] [iD], Benoît Bossavit[2] [iD],
Brian Caulfield[1] [iD], Mathieu Raynal[3] [iD], Karine Lan Hing Ting[4],
Jean Vanderdonckt[5] [iD], and Nadine Vigouroux[3] [iD]

[1] School of Public Health, Physiotherapy and Sport Science,
University College Dublin, Dublin, Ireland
{lilian.mottiader,b.caulfield}@ucd.ie
[2] KDEG Group, Trinity College Dublin, Dublin, Ireland
bossavib@scss.tcd.ie
[3] IRIT, Université de Toulouse, Toulouse, France
{mathieu.raynal,vigourou}@irit.fr
[4] Living Lab ActivAgeing, Université de Technologie de Troyes, Troyes, France
karine.lan@utt.fr
[5] Louvain Interaction Lab, Université Catholique de Louvain,
Louvain-la-Neuve, Belgium
jean.vanderdonckt@uclouvain.be

Abstract. Assessing human bodies' postures and positions enables to design new interaction techniques, to understand users' performances and to evaluate ergonomics of devices. In addition to the applications for improving Human-Computer Interaction, human movement analysis is at the heart of other types of usages including sports, rehabilitation, gesture recognition, etc. This workshop aims at providing a platform for researchers and designers to discuss the challenges related to the processing (e.g., data collection, treatment, interpretation, recognition) of human movement (e.g., motor skills, amplitude of movements, limitations). We expect to identify the main challenges to be addressed and come up with a research agenda to give HCI new perspectives and suggest promising directions.

Keywords: Movement analysis · Human movement · Design evaluation ·
Biomechanics · Ergonomics · Accessibility

1 Introduction

The assessment of human movement, assisted by technologies, consists of identifying the user's body or body segments, capturing and tracking its position. Various technologies can be used for tracking movements, such as optical motion-capture systems, large scale trackers, sensors embedded in mobile devices and touchscreens. In Human-Computer Interaction (HCI), the possibility of assessing the movements of users generated new perspectives for understanding and enhancing interaction [1, 2], designing advanced interaction techniques [3, 4] and manipulating objects in 3D virtual environments [5]. Human movement analysis is also at the heart of several disciplines impacting HCI such as biomechanics, physical medicine, gesture recognition, and

© IFIP International Federation for Information Processing 2019
Published by Springer Nature Switzerland AG 2019
D. Lamas et al. (Eds.): INTERACT 2019, LNCS 11749, pp. 725–730, 2019.
https://doi.org/10.1007/978-3-030-29390-1_70

signal processing. However, across different applications, similar challenges remain: How to define the accuracy required for the execution or recognition of an interaction gesture? How to identify patterns of movements across individuals with different morphologies and motor skills? How to transfer observations in laboratory to less controlled environments and different settings?

To better present the scope of this workshop aiming at assessing HCI Challenges in Human Movement Analysis and defining goals to these challenges to be addressed, we present a short review of some current applications focusing on two aspects: human processing and machine processing.

1.1 Human Processing

To study the human motor system, it is necessary to consider the entire receptor-neural-effector system involved in the execution of a movement. For most applications, the human movement analysis falls into *Posture* (position of the body at one precise moment in time) and *Movement* (from an initial posture, the arrangements of the articulations involved in accomplishing a motor task evolve in time).

In HCI, this phenomenon created two main flows of research. The first one considers human movement as input for interaction. This flow aims to provide new experiences to users by detecting and tracking their movements to transform them into actions in the system. On the one hand, research focused on how the body actions can modify the instance of an interactive virtual environment. One example is full-body interaction, where a user can select different menu items associated to different parts of the body, such as user's head, shoulder or hips to interact with the system [6]. Another example is gesture-based interaction on touchscreen, where algorithms identify and recognize patterns of gestures and shapes designed by the user [4]. On the other hand, researchers assess how users move with and around devices and interfaces to study the gestures of interaction aiming at enhancing user's and system's performances. For instance, the identification of differences in postures of the wrist between younger and older adults during interaction with touchscreen was used to understand how the ergonomics of use of mobile devices can affect users' performances [1].

The second research stream focus on human movement as input for motor control and biofeedback. Current studies show a great potential for applications on health, rehabilitation and sports [7, 8]. In this flow, one of the main motivations is to obtain feedback from the system to help participants to increase the control of their own movements. For example, movement data obtained from Inertial Measurement Units (IMUs) can be used for mobility assessments, and after treatment, generate audio feedback to the users, allowing them to correct their postures and improve their balance [9, 10].

1.2 Machine Processing

The quantitative assessment of the movement is usually initiated by the detection of the body and its segments, then recording the variations in segment's positions or displacement of the user. Therefore, for the purposes of the current workshop, we consider machine processing the activities consisting of:

- Collecting data from sensors, instruments, markers, or other visual or non-visual indexes
- Treating the collected data for identifying segments and patterns, which may include several steps as filtering, sampling, resampling, extracting time and spatial parameters
- Extracting measures and defining indexes or parameters for evaluation
- Transforming these data into meaningful information using algorithms (e.g., Human Activity Recognition, Machine Learning, Biomechanical simulation)
- Providing feedback to the users, in real-time or after treatment. In some applications, data from movement analysis may be used as input for other algorithms and treatment would include multiple processing steps.

The machine processing of human movement face specific challenges related to human factors such as users' different morphologies, individuals motor skills, joints amplitudes and ranges of motion, etc. The accuracy requirements for collecting and treating data must be defined according to the application. Some examples of challenges in machine processing include: sources of errors (i.e., inaccuracy, noise, occlusion...), lack of feedback from instruments, poor usability, connectivity (i.e., synchronization between devices or systems, signal interferences, access cross platforms), and other technical problems (i.e., limitations on real time operations, systems' storage, processing capabilities...). However, challenging machine processing can have a positive outcome to facilitate and improve the accuracy of technologies and techniques used to assess human movement.

2 Objectives

This one-day workshop aims at providing a platform for researchers and designers to discuss about the challenges related to the machine processing (e.g., data collection, treatment, interpretation, recognition) of human movement (e.g., motor skills, amplitude of movements, limitations).

To explore all the potential applications of human movement analysis in HCI and advance the field, it is necessary to determine the needs to better capture, treat, present and interpret data related to the execution of human movements. The main purpose of this workshop is to define priority needs in terms of machine processing in benefit of users, across a large panel of applications. To that end, the main goals of this workshop are to:

- Identify needs in terms of machine processing to leverage potential limitations, whether technical or related to human factors, defining areas that should be developed
- Define a panel of applications, techniques and how users/participants/researchers/ designers are or could be getting benefits from movement analysis
- Discuss about the accuracy and refinement that are necessary for technology to embrace a larger panel of users, from experts to less skilled, with different motor-sensorial skills.

3 Call for Participation

Human movement analysis can provide enriching information for studying and enhancing Human-Computer Interaction (HCI) for a large panel of applications (e.g., rehabilitation, sports, entertainment, virtual reality). This workshop explores the potential of quantitative assessment of human movement as a new methodology for creating advanced interaction techniques, evaluating interaction performances, and providing insights to facilitate use of technologies for users with different skills. We also consider that addressing HCI challenges in human movement analysis will benefit users in a broader scope, reaching several domains as healthcare, biomechanics and ergonomics.

We invite researchers and designers applying or interested in assessing human movement to participate in this one-day workshop aiming at discussing limitations and perspectives for developing all the possible applications going forward. Participants should submit a position paper and engage with the workshop by considering the following main topics:

- Machine processing of human movement (e.g. data collection, treatment, recognition, interpretation, validation…)
- Human factors of human movement analysis and HCI (e.g. postures, movements, displacements, limitations, motor-skills…).

The position papers may present applications, case studies, design or evaluation methods specifying the following aspects:

- Which technologies or input device(s)
- What body part(s) are captured and how
- Which data
- Which processing
- Which outputs for which goals/tasks
- What original aspects and open challenges

The position papers should be up to 2 pages (approx. 1200 words), excluding references (self-references are also welcome). No specific format is required at this stage. More information about submissions, deadlines and planned agenda are available at the workshop website (https://hcihumanmovement.wordpress.com). Accepted position papers will be published in official adjunct conference proceedings during the conference.

Prior to the workshop, authors of accepted papers will be required to fill an "identity card" to be clustered according to criteria that would emerge from the workshop. These cards will be used to generate a comparative map, guiding the activities during the workshop.

4 Expected Outcomes

This workshop is intended to be the first of a series, to follow the evolution of challenges and applications of Movement Analysis in HCI. Authors of accepted workshop papers will be invited to submit an extended version of their work in a book covering this workshop theme, to appear in the HCI series of Springer[1]. Another possible outcome is a handbook defining techniques, solutions and best practices to appear as a SpringerBrief[2] in HCI for fast dissemination.

5 Organizers

From their current and previous projects, organizers have a strong background in assessing and analyzing human movement. For this workshop, we would like to outline their experience and expertise in the three themes of our proposal: biomechanics, machine processing and applications.

5.1 Biomechanics

Lilian Genaro Motti Ader is Post-doctoral Researcher at University College Dublin working on improving accuracy of gait analysis. Previously, she studied biomechanical evaluation of upper limbs for HCI applications.

Brian Caulfield is Full Professor of Physiotherapy at University College Dublin. His research is focused on the application of digital supports and data driven technologies for evaluating human behavior and performance in health and sport.

5.2 Machine Processing

Benoît Bossavit is Post-doctoral Researcher at Trinity College Dublin working on the design, development and evaluation of a system aiming at assessing gross-motor skills in children.

Jean Vanderdonckt is Full Professor in Information Systems at Louvain School of Management, Belgium. He conducts research and development in gesture recognition and gesture elicitation studies.

5.3 Diverse Panel of Applications

Karine Lan Hing Ting is Researcher at ActivAgeing Living Lab, Troyes University of Technology, France. She is currently applying human movement analysis to inform the design of multimodal Ambient Assisted Living (AAL) technologies.

---

[1] https://www.springer.com/series/6033.

[2] https://www.springer.com/series/15580.

Mathieu Raynal is Assistant Professor at University of Toulouse, France. His research focus on modelling, designing and evaluating advanced interaction techniques for text input and pointing tasks in different contexts (e.g. disabilities, mobility).

Nadine Vigouroux is Researcher at University of Toulouse, France. Her work focuses on development and evaluation of HCI for users with different motor and cognitive skills.

Acknowledgements. Lilian Genaro Motti Ader and Benoît Bossavit receive funding from the EU H2020 under the Marie Skłodowska-Curie Career-FIT fellowship (Co-fund grant No. 713654). Karine Lan Hing Ting's work is partially funded by EU ECHORD++ project (FP7-ICT-601116) and ANR project PRuDENCE (ANR-16-CE19-0015).

References

1. Motti Ader, L.G., Vigouroux, N., Gorce, P.: Biomechanical analysis of the user's movements during tactile interaction: postures of older aged users' wrists. In: Proceedings of the XVI Brazilian Symposium on Human Factors in Computing Systems (2017)
2. Jacquier-Bret, J., Gorce, P., Motti Lilian, G., Vigouroux, N.: Biomechanical analysis of upper limb during the use of touch screen: motion strategies identification. Ergonomics **60** (3), 358–365 (2017)
3. Perelman, G., Serrano, M., Raynal, M., Picard, C., Derras, M., Dubois, E.: The roly-poly mouse: designing a rolling input device unifying 2D and 3D interaction. In: Proceedings of ACM CHI 2015, Seoul, Korea, pp. 327–336 (2015)
4. Vanderdonckt, J., Roselli, P., Luis, J., Medina, P.: ! FTL, an articulation-invariant stroke gesture recognizer with controllable position, scale, and rotation invariances, pp. 125–134 (2018)
5. Bossavit, B., Marzo, A., Ardaiz, O., De Cerio, L.D., Pina, A.: Design choices and their implications for 3D mid-air manipulation techniques. Presence **23**, 377–392 (2014)
6. Bossavit, B., Marzo, A., Ardaiz, O., Pina, A.: Hierarchical menu selection with a body-centered remote interface. Interact. Comput. **26**, 389–402 (2014)
7. Zhou, H., Hu, H.: Human motion tracking for rehabilitation—a survey. Biomed. Signal Process. Control **3**, 1–18 (2008)
8. Doheny, E.P., et al.: Effects of a low-volume, vigorous intensity step exercise program on functional mobility in middle-aged adults. Ann. Biomed. Eng. **41**, 1748–1757 (2013)
9. Shahzad, A., Ko, S., Lee, S., Lee, J.A., Kim, K.: Quantitative assessment of balance impairment for fall-risk estimation using wearable triaxial accelerometer. IEEE Sens. J. **17**, 6743–6751 (2017)
10. Taylor, K., et al.: Context focused older adult mobility and gait assessment. In: 2015 37th Annual International Conference of the IEEE Engineering in Medicine and Biology Society EMBS, pp. 6943–6946 (2015)

The Human(s) in the Loop—Bringing AI and HCI Together

Tom Gross[1]([⊠]), Kori Inkpen[2], Brian Y. Lim[3], and Michael Veale[4]

[1] University of Bamberg, Bamberg, Germany
email@tomgross.net
[2] Microsoft Research, Redmond, WA, USA
kori@microsoft.com
[3] National University of Singapore, Singapore, Singapore
brianlim@compnus.edu.sg
[4] University College London, London, UK
m.veale@ucl.ac.uk

Abstract. This document presents the motivation, objectives and target audience, theme, submissions, structure as well as the expected outcome.

Keywords: HCI · Artificial Intelligence · AI · Human in the Loop

1 Motivation

As more and more artificial intelligent systems become incorporated into our everyday lives, it is critical that we understand the ways in which people will interact with these systems. Although some AI systems will be fully automated, a large number will be incorporated into a larger social ecosystem where people will be interacting with these systems. In some cases, advances in machine learning are enabling systems to make inferences on data that are more precise than human experts, however, there is also a growing body of literature that shows that these systems have inherent bias and can have a negative impact on human decision making [3]. It is imperative that researchers understand the smart interplay of AI systems and human experts such that the combination of the two can leverage the inherent strength and weaknesses of each to lead to optimal results. In this workshop, we seek to bring together researchers from both Artificial Intelligence and Human-Computer Interaction communities to discuss concepts, systems, designs, and empirical studies focusing on the communication and cooperation between individual users and teams of users with AI systems.

2 Objectives and Target Audience

The goal of this workshop is to bring together researchers from diverse communities such as Human-Computer Interaction, Machine Learning, Computer-Supported Cooperative Work, Interaction Design, Group Decision Support Systems, Visualisation, Philosophy and Ethics. It will build on the insights gained from a larger workshop

© IFIP International Federation for Information Processing 2019
Published by Springer Nature Switzerland AG 2019
D. Lamas et al. (Eds.): INTERACT 2019, LNCS 11749, pp. 731–734, 2019.
https://doi.org/10.1007/978-3-030-29390-1_71

we are organising at CHI 2019 (http://aka.ms/whereisthehuman), but focus in more specifically in issues related to Human+AI interaction.

The structure will focus on creating research partnerships and identifying collaborative projects. Although we will spend time discussing key trends, challenges, and opportunities, the overall goal is to have a focused workshop that will initiate projects that will extend beyond the workshop itself. The intimate nature of workshops at INTERACT is an ideal venue for this type of workshop.

3   Theme

This workshop will focus on three sub-themes related to Human + AI Collaboration:

1. **Integrating Artificial and Human Intelligence**: AI systems and humans both have unique abilities and are typically better at certain complementary tasks than others. For instance, while AI systems can summarize voluminous data to identify latent patterns, humans can extract meaningful, relatable, and theoretically grounded insights from such patterns. What kind of research designs are most amenable to and would benefit the most from combining artificial and human intelligence? What challenges might surface in attempting to do so? How do issues of trust and accountability impact results [5, 7]?
2. **Collaborative Decision Making**: How can we harness the best of humans and algorithms to make better decisions than either alone? How do we ensure that when there is a human-in-the-loop—such as in complex or life-changing decision-making —they remain critical and meaningful, while creating and maintaining an enjoyable user experience? Where is the line between decision support anticipating the needs of the user and it removing the user's ability to bring in novel, qualitative critical knowledge to enable the system's goals?
3. **Explainable and Explorable AI**: What does the human need to effectively utilize AI insights? How can users explore AI systems' results and logic to identify failure modes that might not be easy to spot? Examples might be undesirable impacts on latent groups not corresponding to categories in the dataset [6], difficult-to-spot changes ('concept drift'), or feedback loops in the socio-technical phenomena the AI system is modelling over time [2].

4   Submissions

Selection of participants and presentations will be based on refereed submissions. We invite authors to submit 4-page papers reporting their contributions in the field of the workshop or 2-page position statements motivating their interest in specific workshop topics. Papers should be formatted according to the INTERACT 2019 (Springer LNCS Series) format. An expert panel of 3–4 researchers will be recruited to review the submissions and participate in the conference.

Authors of accepted submissions as well as invited researchers will give short presentations. We will interweave presentation sessions with longer periods of discussions. Presentations will be grouped by key topics to foster spontaneous discussions. If participants are interested, archival publication opportunities will be discussed, in addition to follow-on workshops.

5 Proposed Workshop Structure

0900 - Welcome and Introduction
0915 - Lightning Talks by workshop participants
1015 - Mid-morning break
1030 - Full-group brainstorming of possibly project areas
1200 - Lunch break
1300 - Breakout Groups
1430 - Mid-afternoon break
1500 - Report back from Breakout Groups
1600 - Brainstorm next steps
1700 - Workshop concludes

6 Expected Outcomes

Three key outcomes are expected from this workshop. First, community building and networking among key researchers in the area of Human+AI collaboration, with the potential to lead to future collaborations on projects or larger grant proposals. Second, an outline of important research directions for this emerging area. Third, one or more research projects that will continue beyond the workshop, the results of which will be published in premiere research venues.

7 Organisers

All organisers have successfully organised workshops at various scientific events of HCI and CSCW individually and together.

Dr. Tom Gross is full professor and chair of Human-Computer Interaction at the University of Bamberg, Germany. His research interests are particularly in the fields of Computer-Supported Cooperative Work, Human-Computer Interaction, and Ubiquitous Computing. He has participated in and coordinated activities in various national and international research projects and is a member of the IFIP Technical Committee on 'Human Computer Interaction' (TC.13). He has been conference co-chair and organiser of many international conferences. Further information can be found at: http://www.tomgross.net.

Dr. Kori Inkpen is a Principal Researcher at Microsoft, where she is a member of the Microsoft Research AI team. Dr. Inkpen's research interests are focused on Human +AI Collaboration to enhance decision making, particularly in high-impact social contexts which inevitably delves into issues of Bias and Fairness. Kori has been a core member of the CHI community for over 20 years. Prior to joining Microsoft she was a

Professor of Computer Science at Dalhousie University and Simon Fraser University. Further information can be found at: http://research.microsoft.com/en-us/people/kori.

Dr. Brian Y. Lim is an assistant professor in the Department of Computer Science at the National University of Singapore. He is leading the NUS Ubicomp Lab, where he and his team design, develop, and evaluate needs-driven infocomm technologies to address new societal challenges, such as urban systems, sustainability and energy management, healthcare and well-being. He has conducted research in intelligent systems across multiple modalities (IoT sensors, mobile interfaces, web and dashboards) and multiple scales (smartphones, smart homes, and smart cities). This allows me to develop impactful technological solutions for multiple domains, and to translate these innovations from the lab to society. Further information can be found at: http://www.brianlim.net/.

Michael Veale is a doctoral researcher in responsible public sector machine learning at the Dept. of Science, Technology, Engineering & Public Policy at University College London. His work spans HCI, law and policy, looking at how societal and legal concerns around machine learning are understood and coped with on the ground. His work on the governance of data-driven technologies has been debated in Parliament; cited by regulators and utilised by a wide range of international civil society groups and think-tanks. He acts as a consultant to a range of national and international governments working to ensure that public values are reflected in public sector technologies. Michael sits on the Advisory Council of the Open Rights Group and is a technical advisor on machine learning to the Red Cross Red Crescent Climate Centre. Further information can be found at https://michae.lv/.

References

1. Amershi, S., et al.: Guidelines for human-AI interaction. In: Proceedings of the Conference on Human Factors in Computing Systems - CHI (2019)
2. Gama, J., Žliobaitė, I., Bifet, A., Pechenizkiy, M., Bouchachia, A.: A survey on concept drift adaptation. ACM Comput. Surv. 1, 1. https://doi.org/10.1145/2523813
3. Green, B., Chen, Y.: Disparate interactions: an algorithm-in-the-loop analysis of fairness in risk assessments. In: Proceedings of the ACM Conference on Fairness, Accountability, and Transparency - FAT* (2019)
4. Gross, T.: Supporting informed negotiation processes in group recommender systems. i-com - J. Interact. Media **14**(1), 53–61 (2015)
5. Saxena, N.A., Huang, K., DeFilippis, E., Radanovic, G., Parkes, D.C., Liu, Y.: How do fairness definitions fare? Examining public attitudes towards algorithmic definitions of fairness. In: Proceedings of Association for the Advancement of Artificial Intelligence – AAAI (2019)
6. Veale, M., Binns, R.: Fairer machine learning in the real world: mitigating discrimination without collecting sensitive data. Big Data Soc. 4(2). https://doi.org/10/gdcfnz
7. Yin, M., Wortman Vaughan, J., Wallach, H.: Understanding the effect of accuracy on trust in machine learning models. In: Proceedings of the Conference on Human Factors in Computing Systems - CHI (2019)

Visualizing Information Retrieved from (Large) WHAT Networks

Gerrit van der Veer[1], Achim Ebert[2], Nahum Gershon[3],
and Peter Dannenmann[4(✉)]

[1] Department of Computer Science, Vrije Universiteit Amsterdam,
Amsterdam, The Netherlands
`gerrit@acm.org`
[2] Computer Graphics and HCI Group, University of Kaiserslautern,
Kaiserslautern, Germany
`ebert@cs.uni-kl.de`
[3] The MITRE Corporation, McLean, USA
`schmooz@mac.com`
[4] Department of Engineering, RheinMain University of Applied Sciences,
Rüsselsheim, Germany
`peter.dannenmann@hs-rm.de`

Abstract. At INTERACT 2017 the organizers of this workshop had organized a very successful workshop called "Beyond Computers: Wearables, Humans, And Things – WHAT!" (The terms WHAT or WHAT! (Wearables, Humans, And Things) were coined by Nahum Gershon and Steve Mann [e.g., see "Wearables, Humans, And Things: The Veillance Games People Play", IEEE-GEM 2015, or "Wearables, Humans, and Things as a Single Ecosystem!", IEEE Internet of Things 2015].) Following that workshop, which focused on new and emerging WHAT technologies themselves, in this workshop, we want to address networks of WHATs as well as visualization- and interaction-technologies to deal with data emerging from these networks. Using WHATs as sensors, large networks of these provide large amounts of information. Such networks can range e.g. from smartwatches monitoring and transmitting the health status of participants in a fun run via smart tags monitoring and transmitting the storage conditions of perishable foods up to large networks of smart sensors monitoring environmental conditions in some urban or industrial environment. The large amounts of data generated from such networks need new paradigms for retrieving relevant information. In this workshop, we want to discuss such new paradigms for interacting with data generated from large networks of WHATs as well as new methods of information visualization to utilize these sensor data. Furthermore, utilizing WHATs themselves as means for interaction with and visualizing information contained in these large amounts of data will be a topic of this workshop.

Keywords: Wearable devices · Implantable devices · Internet of things · Interaction · Information visualization

© IFIP International Federation for Information Processing 2019
Published by Springer Nature Switzerland AG 2019
D. Lamas et al. (Eds.): INTERACT 2019, LNCS 11749, pp. 735–740, 2019.
https://doi.org/10.1007/978-3-030-29390-1_72

1 Introduction

In INTERACT 2017's workshop "Beyond Computers: Wearables, Humans, And Things – WHAT!" [1] the changing relationship between humans and computers was taken up. In the workshop, the participants discussed interaction techniques that arose from the fact that computer chips migrated from the computer internal organs to many other devices - to things, wearables, and even onto the skin (skinnables) and into the human body (implantables). Participants discussed the effects of this revolution on the way we look at the relationships between humans and among humans, human elements and computing devices and what should be done to improve these interactions and "entanglements" and to understand them better.

This workshop enhances the ideas developed in the previous workshop by discussing new interaction paradigms and mechanisms that arise from the large amounts of data that emerge from numerous WHATs that increasingly populate our environment, our skin, and even our bodies. These WHATs include smart textiles [2], smartwatches [3], smart implants [4], and of course the huge variety of items related to the Internet of Things.

With such WHATs becoming more and more popular as unobtrusive aides in our daily lives, these devices create huge amounts of data. In order to provide good support to our daily routines, information, which is relevant for these routines and that is contained in these data can be analyzed and visually presented to the users. The dealing with these large amounts of data, the retrieval and visualization of the information contained in these data and even the use of WHATs to interact with these data will be the topics in the focus of this workshop.

2 Objectives

This workshop is intended to act as a platform for discussions about

1. interacting with large amounts of data generated by wearable and implantable devices embedded into our environment. Typically, such devices are connected to some network and typically, such devices exchange data among each other. Wearable and implantable devices enhance the physiological and/or mental capabilities of their wearers and by interacting with other devices, they provide valuable information to them. However, this information typically is hidden in large amounts of data. Relevant information has to be retrieved from the data and subsequently has to be visualized in a suitable manner in order to be of use for the wearer of the wearable or implantable device. In this workshop, new paradigms for interacting with these large amounts of data generated by networked WHATs shall be discussed in conjunction with new paradigms for retrieving and visualizing the information contained in these data.
2. interacting with the same kind of data generated by elements of the Internet of Things. In addition to wearable of implantable devices, such objects provide various kinds of data (and information) about our environment. Although the objects generating the data and the type of information contained in them differ from

wearable and implantable devices, the methods to interact with the data and to retrieve and visualize information contained in the data is quite similar to the aforementioned methods.

3. using wearable and implantable devices as means of interaction and for visualizing information retrieved from the data generated by networks of wearable or implantable devices or data generated from devices connected to the Internet of Things. When using wearable or implantable devices, it is quite natural to use them also for interacting with or visualizing the information contained in the data generated by the large sensor networks made up of various connected devices.

Examples of such large sensor networks are connected smartwatches during e.g. some fun run, transmitting the health status of the run's participants. Giving medical personnel along the track relevant information about the health status of the runners, they can take quick action in case of emerging medical problems.

Another example can be smart tags on perishable food goods. Giving shoppers access to information provided by such smart tags can help them making informed decisions about which goods to buy. On the other hand, shop employees know which goods have not been stored in proper conditions and can prevent these goods from being sold.

As a third example, smart sensors in some environmental or industrial environment gather a lot of data about the status of the environment, may it be the amount of pollution or may it be the health status of the industrial process. Providing relevant information about the environment to decision makers can vastly improve the quality of their decisions.

Wearable or implantable devices can provide completely new paradigms of presenting relevant information about the above-mentioned situations to decision makers. Interacting with these data to filter out relevant information is greatly changed when using such devices as tools for quickly alerting personnel in case of any problems or just for plain information about current states of the system or situation under supervision.

In this workshop, we want to facilitate discussions among scholars, practitioners, and students to develop these needed new paradigms for interacting with such large amounts of sensor data created by networks of WHATs. These new paradigms include new methods for retrieving relevant information from the huge amounts of data made available by large networks of WHATs. We are especially interested in methods for defining which information is relevant and how new visualization and interaction paradigms can be tailored to fit this definition of "relevant".

We want to encourage the workshop's participants to think together about how to realize such the new interaction, engagement, and relationship between technology, humans, "modified" humans, the new reality and the data and information emerging from these elements.

We encourage researchers and practitioners to share their ideas and experience for these new realities of interaction, engagement, and interface mechanisms with the community. Researchers and practitioners from the areas of the Internet of things (IoT), wearables, implantables, skinnables, and embedded computing are in particular encouraged to participate.

3 Topics

In this workshop, we want to discuss topics related to interaction mechanisms suitable for large amounts of data emerging from networks of WHATs and the information contained therein. Additionally, we want to find new methods for an efficient information retrieval from these data as well as visualization methods suitable for such retrieved information. Especially we want to discuss, how WHATs themselves can help us to interact with these data and facilitate an easy search for and visualization of information in these data that is relevant for the user's task at hand. Therefore, topics to be discussed by the participants of this workshop include but are not limited to:

- What kinds of data generated by WHAT networks do we consider as sources of information that should be shared?
- Which different kinds of user groups should have access to and interact with data generated from WHAT networks?
- How can we define what information contained in data generated by WHATs is relevant to a user?
- Do we need an interactive process for information retrieval from WHAT-generated data or can such a process be automated?
- Is there a common interaction paradigm for shared WHAT network data or may there be several independent interaction paradigms? Especially: Is there a difference in interaction needs depending on the source of WHAT-generated data (i.e. is there a difference in interaction needs between data generated by wearables, implantables, or by elements of the Internet of Things)?
- How is the privacy of data ensured when a user takes part in a WHAT network?
- How can relationships among WHATs (e.g. mere interaction vs. symbiosis) be described?
- Could we define a scale from minimal interaction to full symbiosis?
- Holistic views: When does a group of WHATs become a team, group of organisms, or agents?
- What new interaction mechanisms are necessary to use wearable and implantable devices to interact with information retrieved from large networks of WHATs?
- How can users browse large amounts of data using WHATs?
- Which senses (e.g. touch and smell) can be used to interact with such information?
- What is the role of system thinking and practice in dealing and managing arrays of WHATs?

4 Target Audience

Interacting with WHATs is a truly interdisciplinary task. On the one hand, WHATs are applied in a variety of scientific disciplines and on the other, quite a number of disciplines use data generated by WHATs and the information retrieved from these. Moreover, various disciplines are involved in gathering the data, processing them and finally in the information retrieval.

This workshop should act as a platform for discussions among the different scientific disciplines that are involved in this kind of interaction. Therefore, we encourage researchers, scholars, and students interested in interdisciplinary discussions and unconventional solutions that cover several domains, to participate in this workshop. We especially expect that participants from the following domains might be interested in presenting and discussing their position papers in this workshop:

- Interaction Design
- Cognitive Science/Cognitive Psychology
- Visualization and Multimedia
- Artificial Intelligence and Robotics
- Developers and practitioners of wearables, implantables, skinnables and the Internet of Things
- Engineers applying networks of IoT-elements e.g. for SCADA purposes
- Common sense practitioners

5 Expected Outcome

Participants in the workshop will present their ideas in position papers that are made available to the workshop attendants prior to the workshop. During the workshop, the participants will present their ideas in brief workshop talks, followed by an immediate discussion with the other participants. Position papers and talks are grouped according to specific topics like "user modelling", "interaction among WHATs", or "interaction paradigms for large amounts of Data from WHAT networks". For every topic we expect several position papers or talks, respectively. In order to foster an extensive discussion of the presented topics, a specific discussion block will be held after the presentations related to one topic. In this discussion block, the workshop participants will reflect on all the presentations of the respective block. The position papers will be discussed openly. By taking this approach, we expect the workshop participants to develop new insights in interaction mechanisms among WHATS and with large amounts of data and information gathered from networks of WHATs. Specifically, by grouping the position papers by topics and discussing the papers of a whole block in general, we expect a more focused discussion where the single participants' ideas will complement each other providing a creative environment to develop new ideas for interaction mechanisms with WHATs.

We expect these insights to further the dissemination of WHATs by offering more intuitive interaction mechanisms with and among them. The results of the discussions will be noted down already during the workshop and edited in such a way that they can be presented to the main conference later during a session where all workshop results will be discussed.

In preparation of the workshop we encourage potential participants already to join discussions in advance in the Facebook page: Wearables, Humans And Things - WHAT (https://www.facebook.com/WHAT2016/).

After the Workshop, we will keep in touch with the participants in order to continue the discussions started at the workshop. For this purpose, again we want to use the

Facebook page and we will encourage the participants to send extended and revised versions of their position papers to the organizers for publishing e.g. in a Springer LNCS book or in a special issue of a suitable journal/magazine.

References

1. Gershon, N., Ebert, A., van der Veer, G., Dannenmann, P.: Beyond computers: wearables, humans, and things - WHAT! In: Bernhaupt, R., Dalvi, G., Joshi, A., Balkrishan, D., O'Neill, J., Winckler, M. (eds.) Human-Computer Interaction - INTERACT 2017, 16th IFIP TC 13 International Conference, Mumbai, India, September 25–29, 2017, Proceedings, Part IV, LNCS, vol. 10516, pp. 515–517. Springer, Heidelberg (2017)
2. Fraunhofer Institute for Reliability and Microintegration IZM: Smart textiles. https://www.izm.fraunhofer.de/en/abteilungen/system_integrationinterconnectiontechnologies/arbeitsgebiete/smart_textiles.html. Accessed 30 May 2019
3. Zhang, C., Yang, J., Southern, C., Starner, T., Abowd, G.: WatchOut: extending interactions on a smartwatch with inertial sensing. In: Beigl, M. (ed.) Proceedings of the 2016 ACM International Symposium on Wearable Computers. ACM Digital Library, New York (2016)
4. Ledet, E.H., Liddle, B., Kradinova, K., Harper, S.: Smart implants in orthopedic surgery, improving patient outcomes: a review. Innov. Entrepreneurship Health **5**, 41–51 (2018). Dovepress

#SociallyAcceptableHCI: Social Acceptability of Emerging Technologies and Novel Interaction Paradigms

Marion Koelle[1]($\boxtimes$), Ceenu George[2], Valentin Schwind[3], Daniel Perry[4], Yumiko Sakamoto[5], Khalad Hasan[6], Robb Mitchell[7], and Thomas Olsson[8]

[1] University of Oldenburg, Oldenburg, Germany
marion.koelle@uol.de
[2] Ludwig-Maximilians University, Munich, Germany
ceenu.george@ifi.lmu.de
[3] University of Regensburg, Regensburg, Germany
valentin.schwind@ur.de
[4] North Inc., Kitchener, ON, Canada
daniel.perry@bynorth.com
[5] University of Manitoba, Winnipeg, Canada
umsakamo@umanitoba.ca
[6] University of British Columbia, Okanagan, Canada
khalad.hasan@ubc.ca
[7] University of Southern Denmark, Kolding, Denmark
robb@sdu.dk
[8] Tampere University, Tampere, Finland
thomas.olsson@tuni.fi

Abstract. The spread of information and communication technologies (ICTs) in all aspects of our lives increases the range and scale of potential issues with social acceptance. In the HCI community there is a growing interest and recognition of social acceptability issues with emerging technologies and novel interaction paradigms. This workshop builds on the success of the CHI 2018 workshop on social acceptability by bringing together academics and practitioners to discuss what social acceptance and acceptability mean in the context of various emerging technologies and modern human-computer interaction. We aim to bring the concept of social acceptability in line with the current technology landscape, as well as to identify relevant research steps for making it more useful, actionable and researchable with well-operationalized metrics. The intended outcome of the workshop is two-fold: first, we will continue the efforts to provide an actionable conceptualization of social acceptability in HCI. Second, we will start a collection of best practices and practical examples to be brought together as a continuously updated "case book" of social acceptability in HCI.

Keywords: Social computing · Social acceptability ·
Social acceptance · Technology acceptance · Emerging technologies

© IFIP International Federation for Information Processing 2019
Published by Springer Nature Switzerland AG 2019
D. Lamas et al. (Eds.): INTERACT 2019, LNCS 11749, pp. 741–746, 2019.
https://doi.org/10.1007/978-3-030-29390-1_73

1   Introduction and Background

Technology-wise, we are living in exciting times: novel interactive technologies and applications enrich our lives and allow us to tackle challenges previously considered unsolvable. Examples include head-mounted-displays and smart personal devices for ubiquitous assistance, deep neural networks enabling the first true applications of artificial intelligence, or autonomous vehicles for increased comfort and safety. New interface technologies are the core of HCI and how they will be used in social situations is crucial to the field. Simultaneously, the very same technologies introduce new threats, raise new societal concerns, and can increase social tension between users and non-users. For example, unconventional interface technologies can face resistance from bystanders and can potentially cause embarrassment when used in public places. Increasing autonomy of agents can raise broader ethical and societal discussion on the roles and purposes of technology (c.f., [3,19]).

In light of this, we believe that HCI needs to account for how the social and cultural aspects of technology use are critical factors in successful innovation. The influence of ICTs upon not only the primary user but also their social networks and any surrounding public has opened up many new pitfalls to social acceptance – or non-acceptance, as it may be. As a consequence, research on social aspects of technology usage, particularly social acceptability (which had been named as part of system acceptability already in 1994 [13]) has drawn increasing interest from various areas of HCI and beyond. Nevertheless, research systematically studying "social acceptance" or "social acceptability" is rare. More often social acceptance considerations emerge as a by-product of studies or are discovered by accident, far too late in development processes, i.e., just before or even after a product is shipped. Only a few authors (e.g., Montero et al. [12]) have attempted to conceptualize social acceptability in HCI so far. In addition, there are no agreed upon best practices, or heuristics for designing socially acceptable interfaces, which has also been noted as a key research area during our CHI 2018 workshop on social acceptability [7,8].

Social acceptance is, however, a timely issue as everyday interfaces are becoming increasingly ubiquitous. For example, the acceptability of "performing" human-machine interactions in front of others has drawn HCI researchers' attention. Most prominent areas of interest include human-robot-interaction [18], mobile, gestural and on-body interfaces [1,12,16,17]. The advent of commercially available voice user interfaces (e.g., Amazon's Alexa or Google Home) also brought speech interfaces, their social acceptance [5,6], and their use in social context [14] to attention. The question of how to design for social acceptability has been taken up in the areas of wearable computing [10], drones [2,22], recording technologies [4,9], gaming [11], as well as accessibility [15,20].

This workshop will continue the efforts started at CHI 2018 and intends to foster critical re-thinking of social aspects in the adoption and creation of novel, interactive technologies. It will contribute to the conceptualization of social acceptability in HCI research; particularly how it is understood, encountered, evaluated and measured in the HCI community and beyond. In contrast to 2018, we aim for more tangible outcomes, namely a more mature conceptualization, and a collection of best practices. In light of this, we view INTERACT 2019 to be the ideal venue for this workshop.

2 Topics of Interests and Workshop Objectives

We aim for a highly interdisciplinary workshop, bringing together designers, researchers, and practitioners from different domains of HCI to generate a shared understanding of "social acceptance" and "social acceptability", and to discuss the implications of this for the HCI community. The first workshop of this series, at CHI 2018, attracted 11 submissions by 24 authors from different technology domains (AI, data science, wearables, extended reality) as well as from different epistemological standpoints (empirical reports, hypothesizing and argumentation papers, and preliminary theorizations). By bringing the workshop to INTERACT and Europe, we aim to broaden participation by reaching out to researchers and practitioners with different backgrounds, including various design disciplines, and social sciences. To help ensure strong participation from industry, we will also explicitly target practitioners through industry bodies and discussion groups and personalized invitations through our own networks.

During the workshop we will discuss which problems and challenges regarding social acceptance are being faced during research and design activities, along with solution strategies for mitigating risks of social non-acceptance of new HCI technologies and artifacts. In the interest of establishing a research community, we aim to maintain and extend the discourse about which methods and metrics are suitable to comprehensively measure the social acceptability of an interactive system. We believe INTERACT 2019 to be the ideal venue for this workshop as INTERACT invites an interdisciplinary dialogue and has a long tradition in critically discussing social and societal aspects of technology usage.

The workshop will provide a platform for presenting and discussing open issues and challenges as well as novel ideas on how to design for social acceptability. Its topics of interest include, but are not limited to (1) Design/system contributions, i.e., interactive systems that provide socially (more) acceptable qualities, provocative designs or breaching experiments. (2) User Studies about social aspects of technology acceptance, usage of human-machine interfaces in social context, or similar. (3) Experiences, case studies, and lessons learned from designing (not) socially acceptable interactive systems, and (4) Formal and theoretical approaches to social acceptability, e.g., conceptualizations, evaluation measures, design considerations, or heuristics.

The practical objectives of the proposed 2019 workshop are to distill what is already known in terms of best-practices and heuristics, and start a collection of design patterns for socially acceptable interfaces and interactions (to be included in a "case book", c.f. [21]). We furthermore aim to initiate a discourse about which methods and metrics are suitable to comprehensively measure the social acceptability of an interactive system. As reflected in the mixed background of workshop organizers, a priority is to bridge theoretical and practitioner perspectives. Thus we seek to produce a working definition and models that are both academically robust but also relevant and actionable for commercial development teams. Finally, we aim to put those theories in context through hands-on experiences (field trip in the second half of the workshop) and through design examples and the collection of best practices ("case book").

3   Target Audience and Expected Interest

Social acceptance is an element that often becomes apparent in user studies, whether it was purposefully studied or not. For this reason the workshop aims to include both those that are studying, tackling and working on social acceptability, and those that stumble across social acceptability issues when testing prototypes or deploying their products in the wild. We believe that the social acceptability of emerging technologies is of direct interest to all designers, researchers and practitioners who design, study or use (novel) interactive systems. The workshop has ties to various areas in HCI, including mobile, wearable and ubiquitous computing; interaction in public spaces; on-body interfaces; intelligent personal assistants and HRI; interactive and provocative design; and social software. The workshop is also intended to attract attendees having more socio-scientific interests, such as computer ethics, social computing, or any psycho-social dynamics of HCI.

4   Organizers

Marion Koelle is a research associate at the University of Oldenburg. She is currently pursuing her doctoral dissertation on designing body-worn cameras that intelligently adapt to social contexts. Her research on the social acceptability of emerging technologies and novel interaction paradigms was published at NordiCHI, MobileHCI, CHI, and TEI.

Ceenu George is a PhD student and research associate at LMU Munich. Her work focuses on interactions between HMD users and people not wearing HMD devices (bystanders). In the context of mixed presence collaboration, she is interested in the social acceptability of HMD devices for bystanders, usable security considerations between these two collaborators and in enabling a communication channel whilst maintaining presence in both realities.

Valentin Schwind is post-doctoral researcher at the University of Regensburg. His research is dedicated to improving extended reality systems that enabling immersive experiences. In his work, he also explores multimodal and social interaction with avatars in virtual reality, as well as social implications of using extended reality devices. He has experience as a committee member for international conferences and in organizing workshops.

Daniel Perry is research scientist at North Inc. where he conducts research on applications for wearable computing. He is interested in the social acceptability of wearable interfaces, games for work and learning, and visual analytics. He was previously a Data Science postdoctoral scholar at UC Berkeley. He has organized several workshops on STEM games at the University of Washington.

Yumiko Sakamoto is a psychologist and a research associate at the University of Manitoba, Canada. With her psychology background, she focuses on various types of HCI research involving human perception and behaviors.

Khalad Hasan is an assistant professor at the University of British Columbia (Okanagan), Canada. His research focus is on developing and studying novel interactions with mobile and wearable devices. More specifically, he is interested in exploring users' needs and making an impact in their lives when it concerns efficient and socially acceptable mobile interactivity. He was previously a post-doctoral fellow at the University of Waterloo, Canada. He also has experience serving in committees at international conferences.

Robb Mitchell is associate professor at University of Southern Denmark, and academic mentor for UX at Beijing Normal University. He is a graduate of Environmental Art at Glasgow School of Art and has a PhD in facilitation. He has led hands-on workshops at TEI, DRS, Participatory Innovation, and Service Design conferences. In addition, he organized many creative interdisciplinary gatherings for New Media Scotland, The Electron Club, and The Chateau, Glasgow.

Thomas Olsson is associate professor at Tampere University, focusing on the experiential and social implications of information technology and research through design. His research interests include designing socially aware and acceptable information technology, enhancing social interaction with the help of emerging ICT, Big Social Data analytics, and extended reality technologies. He has organized several interdisciplinary workshops in the field of HCI.

5   Expected Outcomes

In addition to the workshop contributions, which will be part of the adjunct proceedings, we will propose a discussion piece (e.g. Interactions magazine), where we intend to discuss the workshop outcomes along with recent research and future perspectives. On the practical side, we will start a collection of examples, case studies, and best practices for evaluating social acceptability, which will be brought together as a continuously updated "case book" of social acceptability in HCI (c.f. [21]), which we will publish online.

References

1. Alallah, F., et al.: Crowdsourcing vs laboratory-style social acceptability studies?: examining the social acceptability of spatial user interactions for head-worn displays. In: CHI 2018, pp. 310:1–310:7. ACM (2018). https://doi.org/10.1145/3173574.3173884
2. Avila Soto, M., Funk, M.: Look, a guidance drone! assessing the social acceptability of companion drones for blind travelers in public spaces. In: ASSETS 2018, pp. 417–419. ACM (2018). https://doi.org/10.1145/3234695.3241019
3. Courtland, R.: Bias detectives: the researchers striving to make algorithms fair. Nature **558**(7710), 357 (2018)
4. Denning, T., Dehlawi, Z., Kohno, T.: In situ with bystanders of augmented reality glasses: perspectives on recording and privacy-mediating technologies. In: CHI 2014, pp. 2377–2386. ACM (2014). https://doi.org/10.1145/2556288.2557352

5. Easwara Moorthy, A., Vu, K.P.L.: Privacy concerns for use of voice activated personal assistant in the public space. Int. J. Hum. Comput. Interact. **31**(4), 307–335 (2015)
6. Efthymiou, C., Halvey, M.: Evaluating the social acceptability of voice based smartwatch search. In: Ma, S., et al. (eds.) AIRS 2016. LNCS, vol. 9994, pp. 267–278. Springer, Cham (2016). https://doi.org/10.1007/978-3-319-48051-0_20
7. Koelle, M., Olsson, T., Mitchell, R., Williamson, J., Boll, S.: What is (un)acceptable?: thoughts on social acceptability in HCI research. Interactions **26**(3), 36–40 (2019). https://doi.org/10.1145/3319073
8. Koelle, M., et al.: (Un)acceptable!?!: re-thinking the social acceptability of emerging technologies. In: CHI EA 2018, pp. W03:1–W03:8. ACM (2018). https://doi.org/10.1145/3170427.3170620
9. Koelle, M., Wolf, K., Boll, S.: Beyond LED status lights - design requirements of privacy notices for body-worn cameras. In: TEI 2018, pp. 177–187. ACM (2018). https://doi.org/10.1145/3173225.3173234
10. Lee, D., Lee, Y., Shin, Y., Oakley, I.: Designing socially acceptable hand-to-face input. In: UIST 2018, pp. 711–723. ACM (2018). https://doi.org/10.1145/3242587.3242642
11. Linehan, C., Bull, N., Kirman, B.: BOLLOCKS!! designing pervasive games that play with the social rules of built environments. In: Reidsma, D., Katayose, H., Nijholt, A. (eds.) ACE 2013. LNCS, vol. 8253, pp. 123–137. Springer, Cham (2013). https://doi.org/10.1007/978-3-319-03161-3_9
12. Montero, C.S., Alexander, J., Marshall, M.T., Subramanian, S.: Would you do that?: understanding social acceptance of gestural interfaces. In: MobileHCI 2010, pp. 275–278. ACM (2010). https://doi.org/10.1145/1851600.1851647
13. Nielsen, J.: Usability Engineering. Elsevier, Amsterdam (1994)
14. Porcheron, M., Fischer, J.E., Reeves, S., Sharples, S.: Voice interfaces in everyday life. In: CHI 2018, pp. 640:1–640:12. ACM (2018). https://doi.org/10.1145/3173574.3174214
15. Profita, H., Albaghli, R., Findlater, L., Jaeger, P., Kane, S.K.: The AT effect: how disability affects the perceived social acceptability of head-mounted display use. In: CHI 2016, pp. 4884–4895. ACM (2016). https://doi.org/10.1145/2858036.2858130
16. Profita, H.P., et al.: Don't mind me touching my wrist: a case study of interacting with on-body technology in public. In: ISWC 2013, pp. 89–96. ACM (2013). https://doi.org/10.1145/2493988.2494331
17. Rico, J., Brewster, S.: Usable gestures for mobile interfaces: evaluating social acceptability. In: CHI 2010, pp. 887–896. ACM (2010). https://doi.org/10.1145/1753326.1753458
18. Savela, N., Turja, T., Oksanen, A.: Social acceptance of robots in different occupational fields: a systematic literature review. Int. J. Soc. Robot. **10**(4), 493–502 (2018)
19. Shilton, K.: Values and ethics in human-computer interaction. Found. Trends Hum.-Comput. Interact. **12**(2), 107–171 (2018)
20. Shinohara, K.: Design for social accessibility: incorporating social factors in the design of accessible technologies. Ph.D. thesis, University of Washington (2017)
21. Waycott, J., et al.: Ethical encounters in human-computer interaction. In: CHI EA 2016, pp. 3387–3394. ACM (2016). https://doi.org/10.1145/2851581.2856498
22. Yao, Y., Xia, H., Huang, Y., Wang, Y.: Privacy mechanisms for drones: perceptions of drone controllers and bystanders. In: CHI 2017, pp. 6777–6788. ACM (2017). https://doi.org/10.1145/3025453.3025907

Pushing the Boundaries of Participatory Design

Jessica Korte[1], Aurora Constantin[2]([✉]), Cristina Adriana Alexandru[2],
Jerry Alan Fails[3], Eva Eriksson[4,5], Judith Good[6], Helen Pain[2],
Juan Pablo Hourcade[7], Franca Garzotto[8], and Annalu Waller[9]

[1] The University of Queensland, Brisbane, Australia
j.korte@uq.edu.au
[2] The University of Edinburgh, Edinburgh, UK
{aurora.constantin,cristina.alexandru,helen.pain}@ed.ac.uk
[3] Boise State University, Boise, ID 83725, USA
jerryfails@boisestate.edu
[4] Aarhus University, Aarhus, Denmark
evae@cc.au.dk
[5] Chalmers University of Technology, Gothenburg, Sweden
[6] University of Sussex, Brighton, UK
j.good@sussex.ac.uk
[7] University of Iowa, Iowa City, IA 52242, USA
juanpablo-hourcade@uiowa.edu
[8] Politecnico di Milano, Milan, Italy
franca.garzotto@polimi.it
[9] University of Dundee, Dundee, UK
a.waller@dundee.ac.uk

Abstract. Participatory Design (PD) is a design approach which aims
to support users to contribute as partners throughout the entire design
process of a product or service intended for their use. PD researchers
are interested in employing and/or developing methods and techniques
that maximise users' contributions. By accommodating specific populations, PD proved to offer unique benefits when designing technology for
"fringe" groups. However, a lack of understanding of the appropriateness
of existing approaches across groups and contexts presents a challenge
for the PD community. This workshop will encourage discussion around
this challenge. The participants will have the opportunity to exchange
and reflect on their experiences with using PD with "fringe" groups.
Moreover, we aim to identify, synthesise and collate PD best practices
across contexts and participant groups.

Keywords: Participatory Design · PD · Co-design · Marginalised ·
Disempowered · Fringe · Methodology · Best practice · Reflection

© IFIP International Federation for Information Processing 2019
Published by Springer Nature Switzerland AG 2019
D. Lamas et al. (Eds.): INTERACT 2019, LNCS 11749, pp. 747–753, 2019.
https://doi.org/10.1007/978-3-030-29390-1_74

1 Background and Themes

Participatory design (PD) has expanded from workplace democratisation [9] to non-work settings [4] and to "fringe" groups who lack social power for a variety of reasons (e.g. age, disability, culture). This includes children [7,10], older adults [25], people with cognitive impairments such as dementia [26], neurodiverse people [21], people with motor impairments [16], people with visual impairments [32], Deaf[1] people [18], and people with communication difficulties [6].

PD can provide unique benefits in designing technology for "fringe" groups, including deeper understandings of users and contexts of use, leading to products which better fit their purpose [10,13], increased ownership [8,19] and adoption of technology [1,23], and higher user satisfaction [2,27]. Involvement in PD can create opportunities for some user groups (e.g. children) to develop increased self-esteem and confidence [15,17,20], and collaborative, communication and problem solving skills [15,17]. PD has been shown to enhance lives [5,31], and alter social attitudes [22].

PD with new user groups brings specific needs and challenges [12]. Some groups (e.g. children, minority cultures, people with a disability) require particular accommodations, or the creation or adaption of PD approaches to empower them to express their ideas [11,21,25,28] and maximise their contribution to design [3,14,24]; however the PD community faces a challenge in identifying the appropriateness of existing tools to new contexts and user groups [6,29,30].

2 Objectives, Target Audience and Expected Outcomes

This workshop aims to address two challenges identified by Vines et al. [30]:

- "Working as a community to identify the aspects of diverse participatory processes... that can support 'best practice' across multiple domains and contexts" and
- "Providing greater emphasis in literature to participant experience and researcher self-reflection...." (p. 5)

To this end, PD researchers will be engaged in a PD activity: adapting PD methods used with particular "fringe" groups to other contexts and user groups.

There are two target audiences for this workshop: (1) researchers who have created or adapted PD approaches for a specific "fringe" group, and (2) researchers who have undertaken PD with "fringe" groups. Prospective participants are invited to submit position papers describing their creation, adaptation and/or use of PD methods, techniques or tools with particular "fringe" groups, providing details of context of use, procedure, results, challenges and lessons learned. Within the workshop, a subset of novel or adapted PD approaches will be selected to be adapted once more to new contexts, based on reflection on

---

[1] Capitalised "Deaf" refers to people who identify as culturally Deaf, belonging to the Deaf community and usually using a sign language to communicate.

other participants' experiences working with different "fringe" groups. This will result in a series of newly adapted PD approaches, which will be reported at INTERACT.

The workshop organisers will contact an HCI journal (e.g. TOCHI or International Journal for Human-Computer Studies) to discuss the possibility of editing a special issue entitled *Pushing the Boundaries of Participatory Design*, which will publish extended versions of the participants' position papers, as well as summary reports of the newly adapted PD approaches.

3   Organisers

Jessica Korte (Co-chair) is a Postdoctoral Academic in The University of Queensland's Co-Innovation Group, Australia. She is passionate about PD's potential to empower "fringe" groups. She developed a PD approach for designing with young Deaf children. She hopes to work with Deaf and Indigenous communities to design language resources, language robots, and learning activities.

Aurora Constantin (Co-chair) is a University Teacher and postdoctoral researcher at the University of Edinburgh School of Informatics, UK. Her research focuses on designing technology for individuals with Autism Spectrum Disorder, PD, User-Centred Design, and Action Research with various stakeholders. Currently she is working on designing a tool to support children with ASD to express their creativity during PD. She leads the CISA HCI group.

Cristina Adriana Alexandru (Co-chair) is a Research Associate and University Teacher at the University of Edinburgh School of Informatics, UK. She specialises in UCD, development, and usability evaluation of healthcare systems and tools to cater for the needs of different healthcare practitioners. She has interests in PD and consideration of the viewpoints of very different user groups, and automating usability evaluation of user interfaces in healthcare.

Jerry Alan Fails is an Associate Professor in the Computer Science Department at Boise State University in Idaho, USA. He has designed technologies with and for children using PD methods for 15 years. His primary area of research is HCI, with a focus on technologies that engage children with one another, get them active, and encourage them to explore the world around them.

Judith Good is Professor of Interaction Design and Inclusion in the Department of Informatics, University of Sussex, UK. Her research interests focus on PD of new technologies for children, with and without disabilities, and developing new participatory methodologies for typically marginalised populations to have greater involvement in design and evaluation of new technologies.

Eva Eriksson is an Assistant professor at the School of Communication and Culture, Department of Information Studies at Aarhus University, Denmark, and a senior lecturer at Chalmers University of Technology, Sweden. Her research focus is interaction design in public knowledge institutions, specializing in PD with developmentally diverse children.

Helen Pain is Professor of Interactive Learning Environments at the University of Edinburgh School of Informatics/Design Informatics. Her research in

Interaction Design uses PD approaches to develop support for learning and communication (particularly social communication and affect) in children with special needs, using technology to support play and exploration.

Juan Pablo Hourcade is an Associate Professor at the University of Iowa's Department of Computer Science, USA. He has performed extensive research in the development of technologies for diverse user groups, including children, people with ASD and older adults. He is the author of the first comprehensive book on the topic of child-computer interaction, and is on the Editorial Board of the International Journal of Child-Computer Interaction.

Franca Garzotto is Professor of Information Engineering at Politecnico di Milano, Italy, where she leads the Innovative Interactive Interfaces Laboratory (i3lab). The lab focuses on advanced interactive technologies (Wearable Virtual and Augmented Reality, Social Robots, Smart Objects and Smart Spaces, Emotional Conversational Agents) for people with cognitive disability, particularly children, and works in strong collaboration with specialized therapeutic and educational institutions in Italy and Europe. Together with these persons and their caregivers, we co-design and create innovative tools and services that aim at providing new forms of interventions at school, home, and care centre.

Annalu Waller is a Personal Chair in Human Communication Technologies. She directs the Dundee Augmentative and Alternative Communication Research Group. Her primary research areas are HCI, natural language processing, personal narrative and assistive technology. In particular, she focuses on empowering end users, including disabled adults and children, by involving them in the design and use of technology.

4   Workshop Proposal

We propose a one-day workshop for 6–20 participants, in which PD researchers with experience working with a "fringe" group will reflect on the group's needs/abilities and any PD approaches they used. Created or adapted PD approaches for working with particular "fringe" groups will be shared and used as a starting point for adaptation to other, more or less similar, "fringe" groups.

4.1   Workshop Organisation

1. A subset of workshop participants who have created or adapted PD methods, tools or techniques to a particular "fringe" group ("creators") will pitch their approaches ("base approaches"), describing the context of use, procedures of use, results, challenges, lessons learned, and decisions made to support that "fringe" group.
2. Reflective brainstorming (whole group) will identify the needs/abilities of particular "fringe" groups, based on researchers' experiences of PD with them.
3. The organisers will run a "match-making" activity, to divide participants into subgroups based on similarities of their experiences working with "fringe" groups to the target groups of base approaches.

4. The organisers and creators of base approaches will facilitate group PD activities to:
   (a) Identify commonalities and differences between new "fringe" groups and those targeted by base approaches
   (b) Adapt base approaches to new "fringe" groups and new contexts
   (c) Document novel PD approaches for specific "fringe" groups
   (d) Present findings and discussion to the whole group
5. Subgroups will rotate to participants with experiences of "fringe" groups with greater differences from base approaches. PD activities will be repeated, with both base approaches and first novel approaches from which to adapt.
6. The whole group will reflect on motivations for creating/adapting approaches, and feasibility of "borrowing" from approaches intended for other groups.

It is expected that this process will take a full day, with coffee and lunch breaks after activities 2, 4 and 5.

4.2   Pre-workshop Plans

Multiple recruitment approaches will be used to attract academic participants who have experience with and insight into PD with "fringe" groups, including:

- organisers' professional networks via word-of-mouth, as all organisers have experience with PD and strong professional networks;
- research and professional email lists to which several organisers have access (e.g. University of Edinburgh's CISA HCI group, Center for Participatory IT (PIT) at Aarhus University, PDworld and NordiCHI);
- social media channels (e.g. Twitter, Academic Facebook groups)
- this workshop's website: www.pushing-boundaries-pd-fringe-groups.inf.ed.ac.uk

References

1. Albouys-Perrois, J., Laviole, J., Briant, C., Brock, A., Brock, A.M.: Towards a multisensory augmented reality map for blind and low vision people: a participatory design approach (2018). https://hal-enac.archives-ouvertes.fr/hal-01801116
2. Bano, M., Zowghi, D.: A systematic review on the relationship between user involvement and system success. Inf. Softw. Technol. **58**, 148–169 (2015)
3. Benton, L., Johnson, H., Ashwin, E., Brosnan, M., Grawemeyer, B.: Developing IDEAS: supporting children with autism within a participatory design team. In: Proceedings of the SIGCHI Conference on Human Factors in Computing Systems, pp. 2599–2608. CHI 2012. ACM, New York (2012). https://doi.org/10.1145/2207676.2208650
4. Björgvinsson, E., Ehn, P., Hillgren, P.A.: Participatory design and "democratizing innovation". In: Proceedings of the 11th Biennial Participatory Design Conference, pp. 41–50. PDC 2010. ACM, New York (2010). https://doi.org/10.1145/1900441.1900448

5. Carroll, J.M., Rosson, M.B.: Participatory design in community informatics. Des. Stud. **28**(3), 243–261 (2007). https://doi.org/10.1016/j.destud.2007.02.007. http://www.sciencedirect.com/science/article/pii/S0142694X07000191. participatory Design

6. Constantin, A., Johnson, H., Smith, E., Lengyel, D., Brosnan, M.: Designing computer-based rewards with and for children with autism spectrum disorder and/or intellectual disability. Comput. Hum. Behav. **75**, 404–414 (2017). https://doi.org/10.1016/j.chb.2017.05.030. http://www.sciencedirect.com/science/article/pii/S0747563217303515

7. Druin, A.: Cooperative inquiry: developing new technologies for children with children. In: Proceedings of ACM CHI 1999 Conference on Human Factors in Computing Systems. vol. 14, pp. 223–230. ACM, Pittsburgh (1999). http://dl.acm.org/citation.cfm?id=303166

8. Druin, A.: Inclusive ownership of participatory learning. Instr. Sci. **42**(1), 123–126 (2014)

9. Ehn, P.: Work-oriented design of computer artefacts. Ph.D. thesis, Stockholm (1988)

10. Fails, J.A., Guha, M.L., Druin, A.: Methods and techniques for involving children in the design of new technology for children. Found. Trends Hum.-Comput. Interact. **6**(2), 85–166 (2013). https://doi.org/10.1561/1100000018

11. Frauenberger, C., Good, J., Fitzpatrick, G., Iversen, O.S.: In pursuit of rigour and accountability in participatory design. Int. J. Hum.-Comput. Stud. **74**, 93–106 (2015)

12. Frauenberger, C., Good, J., Keay-Bright, W.: Designing technology for children with special needs: bridging perspectives through participatory design. CoDesign **7**(1), 1–28 (2011). https://doi.org/10.1080/15710882.2011.587013

13. Frauenberger, C., Good, J., Keay-Bright, W., Pain, H.: Interpreting input from children: a designerly approach. In: Proceedings of the SIGCHI Conference on Human Factors in Computing Systems, pp. 2377–2386. ACM (2012)

14. Guha, M.L., Druin, A., Fails, J.A.: Designing with and for children with special needs: an inclusionary model. In: Proceedings of the 7th International Conference on Interaction Design and Children, pp. 61–64. IDC 2008. ACM, New York (2008). https://doi.org/10.1145/1463689.1463719

15. Guha, M.L., Druin, A., Fails, J.A.: Investigating the impact of design processes on children. In: Proceedings of the 9th International Conference on Interaction Design and Children, pp. 198–201. ACM (2010)

16. Hornof, A.J.: Designing with children with severe motor impairments. In: Proceedings of the SIGCHI Conference on Human Factors in Computing Systems, pp. 2177–2180. CHI 2009. ACM, New York (2009). https://doi.org/10.1145/1518701.1519032

17. Korte, J., Potter, L.E., Nielsen, S.: How design involvement impacts Deaf children. In: 2017 International Conference on Research and Innovation in Information Systems (ICRIIS), pp. 1–6 (July 2017). https://doi.org/10.1109/ICRIIS.2017.8002527

18. Korte, J., Potter, L.E., Nielsen, S.: The impacts of Deaf culture on designing with Deaf children. In: Proceedings of the 29th Australian Conference on Computer-Human Interaction, pp. 135–142. OZCHI 2017. ACM, New York (2017). https://doi.org/10.1145/3152771.3152786

19. Light, A., Akama, Y.: Structuring future social relations: the politics of care in participatory practice. In: Proceedings of the 13th Participatory Design Conference: Research Papers-vol. 1, pp. 151–160. ACM (2014)

20. Macaulay, A.C., et al.: Participatory research maximises community and lay involvement. BMJ **319**(7212), 774–778 (1999). http://www.bmj.com/content/319/7212/774
21. Malinverni, L., Mora-Guiard, J., Padillo, V., Mairena, M., Hervás, A., Pares, N.: Participatory design strategies to enhance the creative contribution of children with special needs. In: Proceedings of the 2014 Conference on Interaction Design and Children, pp. 85–94. IDC 2014. ACM, New York (2014). https://doi.org/10.1145/2593968.2593981
22. Newell, A.F., Morgan, M.E., Gibson, L., Forbes, P.: Experiences with professional theatre for awareness raising. Interact. Comput. **23**(6), 594–603 (2011). https://doi.org/10.1016/j.intcom.2011.08.002
23. Östlund, B., Olander, E., Jonsson, O., Frennert, S.: STS-inspired design to meet the challenges of modern aging. Welfare technology as a tool to promote user driven innovations or another way to keep older users hostage? Technol. Forecast. Soc. Chang. **93**, 82–90 (2015)
24. Potter, L.E., Korte, J., Nielsen, S.: Design with the Deaf: do Deaf children need their own approach when designing technology? In: Proceedings of the 2014 Conference on Interaction Design and Children, pp. 249–252. IDC 2014. ACM, New York (2014). https://doi.org/10.1145/2593968.2610464
25. Richards, O.K.: Exploring the empowerment of older adult creative groups using maker technology. In: Proceedings of the 2017 CHI Conference Extended Abstracts on Human Factors in Computing Systems, pp. 166–171. CHI 2017. ACM (2017)
26. Rodgers, P.A.: Co-designing with people living with dementia. CoDesign **14**(3), 188–202 (2018). https://doi.org/10.1080/15710882.2017.1282527
27. Uzor, S., Baillie, L., Skelton, D.: Senior designers: empowering seniors to design enjoyable falls rehabilitation tools. In: Proceedings of the SIGCHI Conference on Human Factors in Computing Systems, pp. 1179–1188. CHI 2012. ACM, New York (2012). https://doi.org/10.1145/2207676.2208568
28. Van Dijk, J., et al.: Empowering people with impairments: how participatory methods can inform the design of empowering artifacts. In: Proceedings of the 14th Participatory Design Conference: Short Papers, Interactive Exhibitions, Workshops-vol. 2, pp. 121–122. ACM (2016)
29. Vines, J., et al.: Invited SIG - Participation and HCI: why involve people in design? In: CHI 2012 Extended Abstracts on Human Factors in Computing Systems, pp. 1217–1220. CHI EA 2012. ACM, New York (2012). https://doi.org/10.1145/2212776.2212427
30. Vines, J., et al.: Invited SIG: Participation and HCI: why involve people in design? In: Summary report on CHI 2012 Tech. rep, CHI (2012)
31. Vines, J., Clarke, R., Wright, P., McCarthy, J., Olivier, P.: Configuring participation: on how we involve people in design. In: Proceedings of the SIGCHI Conference on Human Factors in Computing Systems, pp. 429–438. ACM (2013)
32. Williams, M.A., Buehler, E., Hurst, A., Kane, S.K.: What not to wearable: using participatory workshops to explore wearable device form factors for blind users. In: Proceedings of the 12th Web for All Conference, pp. 31:1–31:4. W4A 2015. ACM, New York (2015). https://doi.org/10.1145/2745555.2746664

User Experiences and Wellbeing at Work

Ganesh Bhutkar[1](✉), Virpi Roto[2], Torkil Clemmensen[3],
Barbara Rita Barricelli[4], Jose Abdelnour-Nocera[5,8],
Alexander Meschtscherjakov[6], Arminda Guerra Lopes[7,8],
Pedro Campos[8], and Frederica Gonçalves[8]

[1] Vishwakarma Institute of Technology (VIT), Pune, India
ganesh.bhutkar@vit.edu
[2] School of Arts, Design and Architecture, Aalto University, Espoo, Finland
virpi.roto@aalto.fi
[3] Copenhagen Business School, Frederiksberg, Denmark
[4] Università degli Studi di Milano, Milan, Italy
[5] University of West London, London, UK
[6] Salzburg University, Salzburg, Austria
[7] Instituto Politécnico de Castelo Branco, Castelo Branco, Portugal
[8] ITI/Larsys, Funchal, Portugal

Abstract. As digitalization pervades diverse types of workplaces, an increasing part of employees' work is with interactive technologies. Therefore, user experience of the technologies at work has an important influence to the job satisfaction, work motivation, and employee wellbeing. However, previous research on these topics rarely considers the digitalized work processes and the tools used at work. This workshop invites experts studying work with digital technologies to discuss the impact of these kind of tools on employee wellbeing. The UX@Work workshop aims to build a research agenda for tackling a multitude of overlooked research topics in this area.

Keywords: UX at work · User experience · Employee wellbeing · Work analysis

1 Topic

Wellbeing of employees is an important challenge for today's organizations and companies. The mental and physical wellbeing of employees or staff can be assessed through a study of impact of user experiences at their workplaces [1, 3]. Work efficiency and personal health are affected if the employee wellbeing is not maintained in the organization. It can also lead to employee absenteeism as well as reduced productivity at workplaces such as IT companies, banks, factories, hospitals or even the municipalities and cities.

Use of digital technologies is an increasingly large part of the daily activities in most workplaces, thus an increasingly important part of wellbeing at work. User

© IFIP International Federation for Information Processing 2019
Published by Springer Nature Switzerland AG 2019
D. Lamas et al. (Eds.): INTERACT 2019, LNCS 11749, pp. 754–758, 2019.
https://doi.org/10.1007/978-3-030-29390-1_75

experiences[1] with the digital tools may influence job satisfaction either positively or negatively and thereby affect employee wellbeing and work engagement. While many employers understand the importance of user experience of work tools in the big picture of employee wellbeing, tools for work context are still often selected based on price, performance, and security criteria, forgetting their emotional impacts on employees. Perhaps because of the slow waking up of the industry, there is surprisingly little research on work tool user experiences. After the early works about a decade ago [2, 4, 6] only recently this topic has gained more momentum, e.g., a special issue on designing interactive systems for work engagement [5].

With the current set of still rather limited set of scientific literature, it is the right time to think about the topics that deserve more attention from scholars. UX@Work workshop aims to compile a research agenda for studying the role of interactive technologies at increasingly digitized workplaces as well as related Industry 4.0 scenarios.

2 Objectives

The UX@Work workshop has three main objectives:

1. To share the research needs on concepts, theories, practices and challenges related to user experiences and wellbeing in various work environments.
2. To compile a research agenda for future research in the area of user experiences and wellbeing at work.
3. To expand the IFIP TC13 WG6 Human Work Interaction Design community with researchers and practitioners from various disciplines and work environments.

3 Expected Outcomes

The workshop will produce a research agenda for studying design and impact of interactive technologies UX and employee wellbeing at work. A poster visualizing the research agenda will be compiled to be visible in the INTERACT posters session (if allowed by the Posters chairs). The extended versions of paper contributions at UX@Work workshop will be published as a Topical Collection of Quality and User Experience journal by Springer.

4 Target Audience

The ideal target audience for UX@Work workshop includes researchers, academicians and practitioners working on topics related to user experiences, work analysis, interaction design, work environments, and/or staff wellbeing at work. We pay special

---

[1]A person's perceptions and responses that result from the use and/or anticipated use of a product, system or service, ISO 9241-210:2010.

attention to attracting practitioners from various work environments to discuss real-life case studies featuring user experiences and wellbeing at work. Early-stage researchers and PhD students are also invited to submit posters on their work-in-progress research in this area.

5 Organizing Committee

The UX@Work workshop is organized by IFIP TC13 WG13.6 - Human Work Interaction Design (HWID).

Ganesh Bhutkar is a Coordinator, Centre of Excellence in HCI, Vishwakarma Institute of Technology (VIT) Pune, India. He is Assistant Head (Research) at Department of Computer Engineering at VIT, Pune. His research work is mainly focused on HCI, Assistive Technologies and Medical Usability. He has PhD in HCI from Indian Institute of Technology (IIT), Bombay. He is an active member of ACM as well as SIGCHI and is also member of IFIP TC 13, WG 13.6 since 2012. His centre has developed a utility Android app - Eye+ for visually impaired users, which was also nominated for National Award in 2018.

Virpi Roto is a Professor of Practice in Experience Design, Aalto University, Finland. She has worked both in industry (Nokia) and academia (Aalto) on user experiences, and is one of the most cited UX researchers. Lately, her research has focused on improving employee experiences during the digital transformation of metal and maritime industry. She is an experienced organizer of workshops at academic conferences, including INTERACT, CHI, and NordiCHI.

Torkil Clemmensen is a Professor at the Department of Digitalization, Copenhagen Business School, Denmark. His research interest is in psychology as a science of design. His research focus on cultural-psychological perspectives on usability, user experience, and digitalization of work. He contributes to Human-Computer Interaction, Design, and Information Systems. He is a co-founder of the HWID working group and has co-organized many workshops and working conferences in this area.

Barbara Rita Barricelli is an Assistant Professor at Department of Computer Science of Università degli Studi di Milano, Italy, where she obtained her PhD in Computer Science. Her research interests are Human-Computer Interaction, End-User Development, Computer Semiotics and Semiotic Engineering, Creative and Participatory Design. She has been involved in several International and Italian projects in collaboration with universities, research institutes, and private companies. She is Chair of IFIP TC13's Working Group on Human Work Interaction Design.

Jose Abdelnour-Nocera is Associate Professor in Human Centred Systems at the University of West London, UK. His interests lie in the role of cultural diversity in the design of people-centred systems and in software development teams. In pursuing these interests, he has been involved as researcher and consultant in several projects in the UK and overseas in the domains of international development, mhealth, enterprise resource planning systems, service design and higher education. Dr. Abdelnour-Nocera gained an MSc in Social Psychology from Simon Bolivar University, Venezuela and a PhD in Computing from The Open University, UK.

Alexander Meschtscherjakov Assistant Professor and deputy director of the Center for Human-Computer Interaction in Salzburg University, Austria. He leads the Car Interaction Lab and member of the senate of Salzburg University. His background is in Computer Sciences. He has co-organized many international workshops and hosted conferences on HCI-related topics. His research is focusing on persuasive interaction technologies for sports and older adults, interface design and evaluation for automotive user interfaces, as well as contextual user experience and challenges of work engagement in the area of automation.

Arminda Guerra Lopes is a professor at Polytechnic Institute of Castelo Branco, Portugal, for twenty five years. She is a research fellow at Madeira Interactive Technologies Institute (M-ITI) in Portugal and, recently, she was visitor professor at Carnegie Mellon University, USA. She teaches human computer interaction, interactive systems design and interactive environments courses. Her research interests are mainly: Human Computer Interaction, Information Systems and Technology for Organizational Agility. She has been working on Interaction Design, Human Work Interaction Design, Creativity and Innovation, and Quality of Life Technologies. She is a vice-chair of the HWID working group.

Pedro Campos is Associate Professor with Habilitation at the University of Madeira, Portugal. Pedro is interested in bridging cognitive augmentation with experience design and exploring novel systems to augment human cognition and to design better user experiences. He has co-organized many international workshops and has also hosted ACM conferences on CHI-related topics, work engagement and automation as well as CSCW.

Frederica Gonçalves, Ph.D., is an Assistant Professor at University of Madeira and Researcher at Madeira-ITI/LARSyS, Portugal. Designing news ways for people have an easier access to reading and writing with novel tools or user interfaces (Creativity Support Tools and HCI) is the main thread of her research. Recently she started investigating new ways to improve tourist experience and also look into novel systems to augment human cognition. Previously, she worked as a computer science teacher at higher school. She is member of IFIP TC 13, WG 13.6 since October 2014.

References

1. Demerouti, E., Derks, D., ten Brummelhuis, L.L., Bakker, A.B.: New ways of working: impact on working conditions, work–family balance, and well-being. In: Korunka, C., Hoonakker, P. (eds.) The Impact of ICT on Quality of Working Life, pp. 123–141. Springer, Dordrecht (2014). https://doi.org/10.1007/978-94-017-8854-0_8
2. Harbich, S., Hassenzahl, M.: Beyond task completion in the workplace: execute, engage, evolve, expand. In: Peter, C., Beale, R. (eds.) Affect and Emotion in Human-Computer Interaction. LNCS, vol. 4868, pp. 154–162. Springer, Heidelberg (2008). https://doi.org/10.1007/978-3-540-85099-1_13
3. Oades, L.G., Mossman, L.: The Science of Wellbeing and Positive Psychology. Wellbeing, Recovery and Mental Health, pp. 7–23. Cambridge University Press, Cambridge (2017)
4. Millard, N., Hole, L.: In the Moodie: using 'affective widgets' to help contact centre advisors fight stress. In: Peter, C., Beale, R. (eds.) Affect and Emotion in Human-Computer Interaction. LNCS, vol. 4868, pp. 186–193. Springer, Heidelberg (2008). https://doi.org/10.1007/978-3-540-85099-1_16

5. Roto, V., Clemmensen, T., Väätäjä, H., Law, E.: Designing interactive systems for work engagement. Spec. Issue Hum. Technol. **14**(2), 135–139 (2018)
6. Palviainen, J., Väänänen-Vainio-Mattila, K.: User experience in machinery automation: from concepts and context to design implications. In: Kurosu, M. (ed.) HCD 2009. LNCS, vol. 5619, pp. 1042–1051. Springer, Heidelberg (2009). https://doi.org/10.1007/978-3-642-02806-9_119

Handling Security, Usability, User Experience and Reliability in User-Centered Development Processes

IFIP WG 13.2 and WG 13.5 Workshop at INTERACT 2019

Carmelo Ardito[1(✉)], Regina Bernhaupt[2], Philippe Palanque[3], and Stefan Sauer[4]

[1] University of Bari Aldo Moro, Bari, Italy
carmelo.ardito@uniba.it
[2] Eindhoven University of Technology, Eindhoven, The Netherlands
r.bernhaupt@tue.nl
[3] Université Toulouse III – Paul Sabatier, Toulouse, France
palanque@irit.fr
[4] Paderborn University, Paderborn, Germany
sauer@uni-paderborn.de

Abstract. Human-Computer Interaction (HCI) research has been focusing on properties such as usability, accessibility, inclusive design, user experience. As new security risks are emerging with the continuous increase of Internet interconnections and the development of the Internet of Things, more recently security, trust and resilience have also become important for the development of interactive systems. Since users have been identified as one of the major security weaknesses in today's technologies, HCI becomes a fundamental pillar for designing more secure (but still usable) systems. However, interactive system properties might overlap and sometimes create conflicts in user-centered development processes. For example, security could reduce system usability by placing a burden on users when they have to deal with passwords. The HCI research has provided several tools and techniques that can support designers in making decisions, but there are no "cookbooks". This workshop promotes sharing of experiences in managing and resolving conflicts of multiple interactive system properties within the context of a user-centered design process. We are concerned by theories, methods and approaches for dealing with interactive system properties, managing potential conflicts and trade-offs. This workshop is organized by the IFIP WG 13.2 on Methodology for User-Centered System Design and the IFIP WG 13.5 on Human Error, Resilience, Reliability and Safety in System Development.

Keywords: User-centered design process · User interfaces properties · Usability · UX · Security · Privacy · Resilience · Reliability

© IFIP International Federation for Information Processing 2019
Published by Springer Nature Switzerland AG 2019
D. Lamas et al. (Eds.): INTERACT 2019, LNCS 11749, pp. 759–762, 2019.
https://doi.org/10.1007/978-3-030-29390-1_76

1 Overview and Goals

User-centered design has proven to be a key factor for leading towards the development of successful interactive systems [1]. Identifying user needs and requirements as well as desired system properties is a crucial phase, as poor or inadequate requirement specifications can lead to interaction difficulties and (more globally) usability problems. The requirements conflict-resolution process is essential in the user-centered development of interactive systems that, traditionally, has been focusing on properties such as *usability, accessibility* or *user experience (UX)*. A user property might complement or enlarge the scope of another. For example, whilst accessibility addresses the needs of impaired users to accomplish their tasks with the system [2], UX goes beyond the pragmatic aspect of usability by taking into account dimensions such as emotion, aesthetics or visual appearance, identification, stimulation, meaning/value or even fun, enjoyment, pleasure or flow [3]. In some situations, a user interface property might influence another one, positively or negatively. For example, an interactive software featuring poor *reliability* can jeopardize usability evaluation by showing unexpected or undesired behaviors [4]. On the opposite, increasing usability (for instance by providing undo mechanisms to users) will decrease reliability as the system will be more complex and more difficult to test. Moreover, there is evidence that properties can trade off against each other as it is the case for *usability* and *security* [5]. For example, requiring users to change their passwords periodically may improve security, but may reduce usability as it represents a burden for users to frequently create and remember passwords. It will also increase the likelihood of errors and decrease in performance. Therefore, users might be keen to setup workarounds such as taking hard notes of hard-to-remember passwords imposed by security administrators' policies.

The HCI research has provided several principles and guidelines that can drive the designers in taking their decisions. For example, conflicting user interface properties often appear in recommendations for user interface design [6], but there are no "cookbooks" for resolving them. The resolution of conflicts between user interface properties is a daunting and demanding task that might requires taking into account the trade-offs associated with alternative designs and rationalizing design decisions. It is interesting to notice that when the conflict between properties is understood, the effects of conflicts can be mitigated/reduced by innovative and appropriate designs. Examples of designs handling conflict resolution between *usability, privacy* and *security* can be, for instance, found at the SOUPS (Symposium on Usable Privacy and Security) conference (https://cups.cs.cmu.edu/soups/).

In this workshop, we aim to broaden the scope of this research domain and promote the study of the interplay of multiple user interface properties in a user-centered design process. Our aim is to cover a large set of user interface properties and try to reveal their inner dependencies. The long-term perspective of this workshop is to foster the development of theories, methods, tools and approaches for dealing with multiple properties that should be taken into account when developing interactive systems.

This workshop is a follow up of the successful workshop organized at INTERACT 2017 in Mumbai [7].

2 Target Audience and Expected Outcomes

This workshop is open to everyone who is interested in multiple user interface properties while designing and building interactive systems. We expect a high participation of IFIP working group 13.2 and 13.5 members. We invite participants to present position papers describing real-life case studies that illustrate the trade-offs between two or more properties of interactive systems. Any property related to user interface design is welcome, but two or more properties should be addressed in the same contribution. We are also interested in methods, theories and tools for managing multiple user interface properties. Position papers are published in INTERACT 2019 adjunct conference proceedings. We also expect to discuss at the workshop how to disseminate individual contributions to the community in a special issue in an HCI journal.

3 Structure of the Workshop

This proposal encompasses a full-day workshop organized around presentation of position papers and working activities in small groups. From the set of contributions, a subset of selected case studies is invited to be presented at the beginning of the workshop and is used to support the discussion that follows. The morning sessions are dedicated to welcoming participants and presenting case studies. Participants are invited to comment the case studies and to report similar experiences. The afternoon sessions are devoted to interactive sessions, where participants are engaged to work in small groups on and propose solutions to the problems of the case studies seen in the morning. Proposed solutions are compiled and compared. Based on the lessons learned, participants draft an agenda of future work that can be accomplished.

4 Workshop Organizers

Carmelo Ardito is Assistant Professor at the University of Bari Aldo Moro, Italy. His research interests are in Human-Computer Interaction. He is member of the Interaction, Visualization, Usability & UX (IVU) Lab, where he coordinates the research on "Novel Interaction Techniques and Pervasive Systems". Since 2001 he has been involved in various research projects sponsored by EU and Italian organizations. He has been visiting researcher/professor at several international research laboratories. He has been member of the scientific organization committee of several International Conferences. He is Expert Member of IFIP TC13 (International Federation for Information Processing Technical Committee on Human–Computer Interaction); member of the IFIP IoT Domain Committee; vice-chair of the IFIP TC13 Working Group 13.2; member of ACM SIGCHI Italy.

Regina Bernhaupt is a Full Professor at the Eindhoven University of Technology, Department of Industrial Design. Her research interest is on how to measure the impact of technology on large-scale real-life systems including changes on a societal level. Regina Bernhaupt is chair of the IFIP TC 13 Working Group 13.2, representative for TC 13 for the Netherlands and has been a long standing active member of WG 13.2. In her spare time, Regina is also the head of research for Austrian Remote Control Producer Ruwido.

Philippe Palanque is Professor in Computer Science at University of Toulouse 3, where he leads the Interactive Critical Systems research group. Since the late 1980s he has been working on the development and application of formal description techniques for interactive systems. He has worked on research projects at the Centre National d'Études Spatiales (CNES) for more than 10 years and on software architectures and user interface modeling for interactive cockpits in large civil aircraft (funded by Airbus). The main driver of Philippe's research over the last 20 years has been to address in an even way usability, safety and dependability in order to build trustable safety-critical interactive systems. As for conferences he was paper co-chair of INTERACT 2015 and is ACM CHI steering committee chair. He is a member of CHI academy, chair of the IFIP TC 13 committee on Human-Computer Interaction, and secretary of IFIP WG 13.5.

Stefan Sauer is Senior Researcher at Paderborn University, Germany and Managing Director of SICP – Software Innovation Campus Paderborn, a joint research and innovation initiative of the university and technology companies. He is furthermore manager of the center of competence for software engineering there. Stefan Sauer's main research areas are the integration of software engineering and usability engineering methods, model-based and model-driven software development, and situational method engineering. He has been involved in the organization of numerous conferences and workshops, for example as General Chair of HCSE 2014 and Technical Program Chair of HCSE+HESSD 2016. He is member and secretary of the IFIP TC13 Working Group 13.2.

References

1. ISO/IEC 9241-210: Ergonomics of human-system interaction – Part 210: human-centred design for interactive systems (2010). http://www.iso.org/iso/catalogue_detail.htm?csnu mber=52075
2. W3C: Accessibility, usability, and inclusion: related aspects of a web for all (2016). https://www.w3.org/WAI/intro/usable
3. Hassenzahl, M.: The interplay of beauty, goodness, and usability in interactive products. Hum.-Comput. Interact. **19**(4), 319–349 (2008)
4. Palanque, P., Basnyat, S., Bernhaupt, R., Boring, R., Johnson, C., Johnson, P.: Beyond usability for safety critical systems: how to be sure (safe, usable, reliable, and evolvable)? In: CHI 2007 Extended Abstracts on Human Factors in Computing Systems (CHI 2007 EA), pp. 2133–2136. ACM, New York (2007)
5. Sasse, M.A., Smith, M., Herley, C., Lipford, H., Vaniea, K.: Debunking security-usability tradeoff myths. IEEE Secur. Priv. **14**(5), 33–39 (2016)
6. Masip, L., Martinie, C., Winckler, M., Palanque, P., Granollers, T., Oliva, M.: A design process for exhibiting design choices and trade-offs in (potentially) conflicting user interface guidelines. In: Winckler, M., Forbrig, P., Bernhaupt, R. (eds.) HCSE 2012. LNCS, vol. 7623, pp. 53–71. Springer, Heidelberg (2012). https://doi.org/10.1007/978-3-642-34347-6_4
7. Winckler, M., Larusdottir, M., Kuusinen, K., Bogdan, C., Palanque, P.: Dealing with conflicting user interface properties in user-centered development processes. In: Bernhaupt, R., Dalvi, G., Joshi, A., Balkrishan, D.K., O'Neill, J., Winckler, M. (eds.). vol. LNCS 10516 - Part IV, pp. 521–523. Springer, Cham (2017)

Author Index